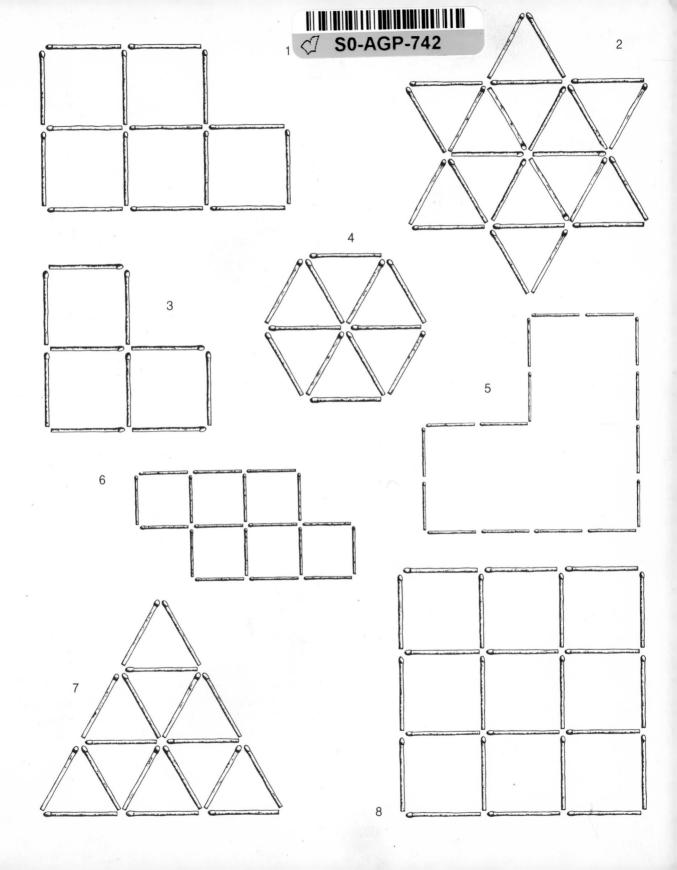

1

2

3

4

5

6

7

8

Third Edition

A PROBLEM SOLVING APPROACH TO

Mathematics for Elementary School Teachers

Rick Billstein
University of Montana
Missoula, Montana

Shlomo Libeskind
University of Oregon
Eugene, Oregon

Johnny W. Lott
University of Montana
Missoula, Montana

The Benjamin/Cummings Publishing Company, Inc.
Menlo Park, California • Reading, Massachusetts • Don Mills, Ontario
Wokingham, U.K. • Amsterdam • Sydney • Singapore • Tokyo
Madrid • Bogota • Santiago • San Juan

Sponsoring Editor: Craig S. Bartholomew
Production Coordinator: Greg Hubit
Copy Editor: Patricia Harris
Text Designer: Christy Butterfield

Library of Congress Cataloging in Publication Data
Billstein, Rick.
  A problem solving approach to mathematics for elementary school teachers.

  Includes bibliographies and index.
  1. Mathematics—Study and teaching (Elementary)
2. Mathematics—1961–   . 3. Problem solving.
I. Libeskind, Shlomo. II. Lott, Johnny W., 1944–
III. Title.
QA135.5.B49 1987   327.7   86-23219
ISBN 0-8053-0865-2

EFGHIJ-DO-898

The Benjamin/Cummings Publishing Company, Inc.
2727 Sand Hill Road
Menlo Park, California 94025

To Carrie and Hugo, happy 50th —R.B.

A Janek et Eugénie, leurs filles Brigette et Martine et leurs familles —S.L.

To Perry Warren Lott and Ouidamai Landreth Lott, the most courageous people I know —J.W.L.

Preface

The third edition of *A Problem Solving Approach to Mathematics for Elementary School Teachers* is our continuing response to suggestions for changes and revisions by the users of this text. In addition we again have considered the changes in curriculum suggested by the Committee on the Undergraduate Program in Mathematics (CUPM) of the Mathematical Association of America and other groups.

Our Goals

Our primary goals are:
- To survey appropriate mathematics in a way that is both intelligible and entertaining
- To present and use the heuristics of problem solving as an integral part of mathematics
- To encourage our students to extend their learning beyond the classroom by providing a diversity of problems (both elementary and challenging), discussion topics, and bibliographies for further investigation

Problem Solving in the Third Edition

The first recommendation of the National Council of Teachers of Mathematics (NCTM) in *An Agenda for Action: Recommendations for School Mathematics of the 1980's* was that problem solving be the focus of school mathematics in the 1980s. We have emphasized problem solving wherever possible. It has been a concern of ours that problem solving has become another fad phrase in the teaching of mathematics. Because of this, we have tried to focus attention on specific problems to showcase some of the methods of problem solving in the following ways:
- *Two chapters* (Chapters 1 and 14) are devoted to the problem-solving techniques used throughout the text. Chapter 1 develops a four-step problem-solving method, based upon Polya's work:

  Understanding the problem

  Devising a plan

Carrying out the plan

Looking back

This chapter presupposes only minimal mathematics skills from students. Chapter 14 reviews problem-solving strategies and presents challenging problems based upon topics covered in the preceding chapters.

- *A preliminary problem* begins Chapters 1 through 13. Each problem poses a question that students can answer after mastering the material in the chapter. We encourage our students to attempt to solve the preliminary problem before starting the chapter so that they might develop a sense of what is needed to solve the problem. The final section of each of these chapters gives a solution to the preliminary problem using the four-step method presented in Chapter 1.
- *New problems* have been introduced throughout the text. These problems are solved in detail using the four-step problem-solving format.

Features

Wherever possible, we have presented new topics in ways that could be used in an actual classroom. In addition, we have included a number of study aids and have incorporated end-of-section, end-of-chapter, and design features to make the book as useful and interesting as possible.

Study Aids

COMPUTER CORNER

BRAIN TEASERS

- *Sample textbook pages* from several elementary mathematics series are reproduced throughout the book. These pages show how various topics are introduced to students in kindergarten through eighth grade.
- *Computer Corners* included throughout the book illustrate content in the corresponding sections
- *Brain Teasers* are challenging and entertaining problems related to the subject matter of the sections in which they appear. Solutions to the Brain Teasers are in the *Instructor's Guide.*
- *Cartoons* are included throughout the book to add a lighter touch to the text and to illustrate the content in sections.
- Problems emphasizing *calculator usage* are indicated in problem sets by a calculator symbol ▦ .
- Problems emphasizing *computer usage* are indicated in problem sets by a computer symbol ▭ .
- *Historical notes* are included at strategic points throughout the text to emphasize the fact that mathematics was created by humans and to give some indication about the people who created the mathematics.

End-of-Section Features

- *Laboratory activities* are suggested at the end of many sections. These may be used to aid in the learning or in the eventual teaching of mathematics content.
- *Problem sets* at the end of each section include large numbers of problems generally arranged in order of increasing difficulty. Stars ★

indicate the most *challenging problems*. Asterisks (*) are used to indicate problems that are not necessarily harder than others but that are optional and may be omitted. (Many geometry proofs are denoted in this manner, as are questions on chapter tests from optional sections.)
- *Review problems* are included in problem sets. The review problems constitute a basic review of material from previous sections in the chapter.
- *Answers* to odd-numbered problems are included in the back of the book.

End-of-Chapter Features
- *Questions from the Classroom* sections appear at the end of each of Chapters 2–13. They are collections of questions students might ask their teachers about the material presented in that chapter. The questions can be discussed in class or assigned as research questions. Many questions have been added to these sections based upon our students' questions, and these should provide valuable preparation for future teaching. This feature is based upon *Mathematical Questions from the Classroom* by Richard Crouse and Clifford Sloyer (Prindle, Weber, Schmidt, 1977). Suggested answers to these questions are available in the *Instructor's Guide*.
- *Chapter Outlines* are included to help students review the chapter.
- *Chapter Tests* provide an opportunity for students to test themselves on important concepts developed in each chapter.
- A *Selected Bibliography* concludes each chapter except Chapter 14. The articles or books in these bibliographies can be assigned for outside reading or extra credit; they can be used as references for answering many of the Questions from the Classroom; or they can complement the text for those students who wish to read further on a particular topic.

Design Features
- *Key terms, definitions, theorems,* and other important concepts are highlighted in boldface type. Key terms are repeated in the margins to help students review the material.
- A functional *use of color* in the text material and illustrations helps to emphasize various concepts.
- *Graphs, charts, geometric drawings, cartoons,* and other kinds of illustrations reinforce the content presented.

Content
Because the mathematics preparations of students who take this course vary widely, we have written the book so that the material can be used by students with diverse backgrounds. We have built in flexibility for instructors: We have included enough topics to allow instructors to adapt the text to a variety of course lengths and organizations, including sections preceded by asterisks (*) that are optional and can be omitted without loss of continuity.

As we mentioned previously, Chapters 1 and 14 provide an explanation and review of problem solving.

In addition, the following topics are covered.

Calculator usage.   We present this topic (Chapter 1) as a problem-solving tool.

Sets, relations, functions, and logic.   We present these topics (Chapter 2) in a way that allows instructors to cover less than the complete chapter if they wish. Chapter 2 has been reorganized, with the work on functions expanded and logic presented in relation to sets and as a problem-solving tool.

Numeration systems, whole numbers, and integers.   The discussion of operations (Chapters 3 and 4) now emphasizes estimation and mental arithmetic.

Number theory.   Number theory concepts (Chapter 5) afford an excellent opportunity to develop the concept of proof. We have developed many of the properties in this chapter in a way that we believe is most meaningful to students at this level.

Rational and irrational numbers.   Chapter 6 deals with fractions, and Chapter 7 deals with decimals. Material on percents and an optional section on computing interest are included here.

Probability and statistics.   Probability and statistics have been separated into two chapters (Chapters 8 and 9). Topics in probability are presented through the use of tree diagrams. Simulations and formulas for combinations and permutations are also developed in this chapter. An introduction to statistics is presented with an emphasis on organizing, presenting, and interpreting data. Topics added include stem-and-leaf plots, misuses of statistics, and z-scores.

Geometry.   Chapters 10 through 13 cover informal geometry. Chapter 10 introduces basic concepts of geometry, including topological topics. Motion geometry, geometric constructions, and tessellations are taught in Chapter 11 by using compass and straightedge, paper folding, and Miras. Work with Miras can be omitted if they are not available. Chapter 12 deals with the Pythagorean Theorem and notions of measurement. Chapter 13 presents the fundamentals of coordinate geometry. Appendix III provides a summary of the basic compass-and-straightedge constructions. In each of these chapters, sections on Logo have been added, reflecting our notion that geometry may be better taught with this computer language.

Metric measurement.   We integrate metric measures with other geometric concepts and emphasize metric units throughout the text. Metric estimation exercises are included; conversions are metric to metric, rather than metric to English and vice versa.

Computers.   Two appendices on computers (Appendix I and Appendix II) appear in this edition, one of which covers BASIC and the other Logo. BASIC is and has for years been the computer language learned by college-bound students and college students. Logo, a language developed at The Massachusetts Institute of Technology, is rapidly being assimilated into the elementary school curriculum.

The Instructor's Guide

This supplement includes:
- Answers to odd- and even-numbered problems
- Complete solutions to the problems in Chapter 14 and Appendices I and II
- Two sample chapter tests that may be used as test questions or as make-up tests
- Suggested answers to Questions from the Classroom
- Solutions to Brain Teasers
- Solution to matchstick problems appearing on endpapers

Acknowledgments

We would like to thank the students we have taught over the past several years for their patience and suggestions as we class-tested and refined this text. The reviewers (listed below) who have contributed over the three editions of this book have offered us valuable guidance, and we are grateful to them for the care they took with their reviews. Finally, we would like to thank the staff at Benjamin/Cummings, especially Craig Bartholomew and Martine Westermann, who have worked extremely hard on this text and continue to share the excitement we have about this project.

Rick Billstein
Shlomo Libeskind
Johnny W. Lott

Reviewers

Leon J. Ablon
College of Staten Island (CUNY)

G. L. Alexanderson
University of Santa Clara

James R. Boone
Texas A and M University

Louis J. Chatterley
Brigham Young University

Donald J. Dessart
University of Tennessee, Knoxville

Marjorie Fitting
San Jose State University

Glenadine Gibb
University of Texas, Austin

Alice Guckin
University of Minnesota

Boyd Henry
College of Idaho

Allan Hoffer
Boston University

E. John Hornsby Jr.,
University of New Orleans

Wilburn C. Jones
Western Kentucky University

Robert Kalin
Florida State University

Herbert E. Kasube
Bradley University

Sarah Kennedy
Texas Tech University

Steven D. Kerr
Weber State College

Leland W. Knauf
Youngstown State University

Barbara Moses
Bowling Green State University

Glenn Nelson
University of Northern Iowa

Keith Peck
Northeast Missouri State University

Barbara Pence
San Jose State University

Glenn L. Pfeifer
University of New Mexico

Edward Rathnell
University of Northern Iowa

Helen R. Santiz
University of Michigan, Dearborn

M. Geralda Schaefer
Pan American University

Jane Schielack
Texas A and M University

Barbara Shabell,
California Polytechnic State University,
Pomona

Gwen Shufelt
University of Missouri, Kansas City

Joe K. Smith
Northern Kentucky University

Virginia Strawderman
Georgia State University

C. Ralph Verno
West Chester State College

John Wagner
Michigan State University

Mark F. Weiner
West Chester State College

Grayson Wheatley
Purdue University

Jerry L. Young
Boise State University

Brief Contents

Detailed Contents

BRAIN
TEASERS
106, 114

CHAPTER 4

The Integers 162

COMPUTER   BRAIN
CORNER   TEASERS
173   172, 180, 191

CHAPTER 5

Number Theory 196

COMPUTER   BRAIN
CORNER   TEASERS
214   206, 214,
221, 226

CHAPTER 6

Rational Numbers as Fractions 232

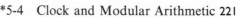

COMPUTER CORNER
250

BRAIN TEASERS
250, 258, 261, 268

CHAPTER 7   *Decimals* 285

COMPUTER CORNER
307, 320

BRAIN TEASERS
294, 314

CHAPTER 8   *Probability* 335

BRAIN TEASERS
346, 357, 384

BRAIN
TEASER
409

BRAIN
TEASERS
452, 470

BRAIN
TEASERS
505, 512
527, 551

CHAPTER 12

Concepts of Measurement 563

BRAIN
TEASERS
570, 583, 590

CHAPTER 13

Coordinate Geometry 620

BRAIN
TEASERS
644, 654

CHAPTER 1

Introduction to Problem Solving

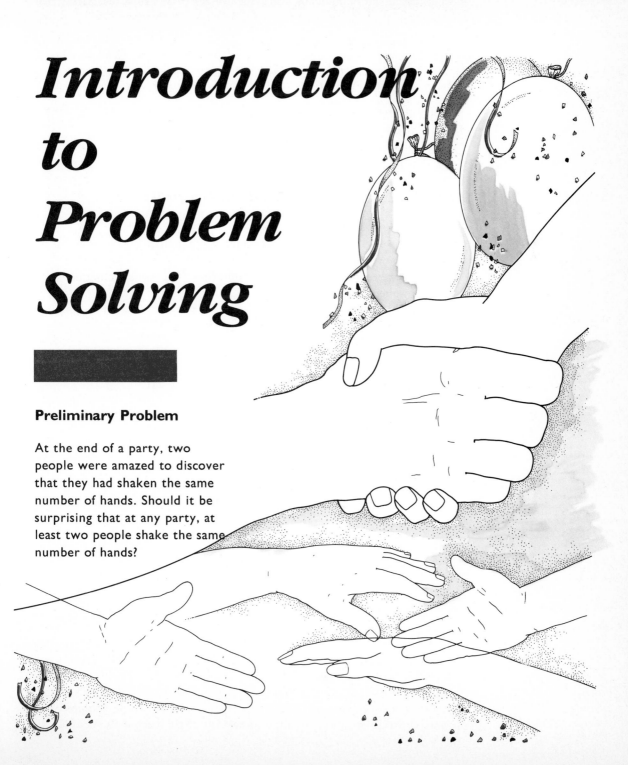

Preliminary Problem

At the end of a party, two people were amazed to discover that they had shaken the same number of hands. Should it be surprising that at any party, at least two people shake the same number of hands?

Introduction

A well-known mathematician and educator, George Polya, described the experience of problem solving in his book, *How To Solve It.*

> *A great discovery solves a great problem but there is a grain of discovery in the solution of any problem. Your problem may be modest; but if it challenges your curiosity and brings into play your inventive facilities, and if you solve it by your own means, you may experience the tension and enjoy the triumph of discovery.*

As part of his work in problem solving, Polya developed a four-step process for solving problems similar to the following:

1. Understanding the Problem
   (a) Can you state the problem in your own words?
   (b) What are the unknowns?
   (c) What information do you obtain from the problem?
   (d) What information, if any, is missing or not needed?
2. Devising a Plan
   The following list of strategies, although not exhaustive, is very useful.
   (a) Look for a pattern.
   (b) Examine related problems and determine if the same technique can be applied.
   (c) Examine a simpler or special case of the problem to gain insight into the solution of the original problem.
   (d) Make a table, diagram, or model.
   (e) Write an equation.
   (f) Use guess and check.
   (g) Work backwards.
   (h) Identify a subgoal.
3. Carrying Out the Plan
   (a) Perform the necessary computations, if any.
   (b) Check each step of the plan as you proceed. This may be an "intuitive" checking or a formal proof of each step.
4. Looking Back
   (a) Check the results in the original problem. (In some cases, this will require a proof.)
   (b) Interpret the solution in terms of the original problem.
   (c) Determine whether there is another solution, perhaps a more direct one.
   (d) Determine whether there is another method of finding the solution.
   (e) If possible, determine other related or more general problems for which the techniques will work.

We urge you to spend some time trying to analyze or solve the preliminary problem. If you do not see an immediate solution to the problem, do not give up convinced that the problem is beyond your capabilities. In many cases, problem solving does take time. If you try to solve the problem but are unable to do so, the solution is presented at the end of the chapter. If

HISTORICAL NOTE

George Polya (1887–1985) wrote *How To Solve It* in 1945. This book explores techniques of thought and methods of mathematical problem solving. It has sold more than a million copies and has been translated into 15 languages.

you have not solved the problem, read only enough of the solution to get a hint; then try to complete the solution on your own.

The problems you will encounter in this chapter and throughout the text usually are not just computational exercises. Doing exercises involves performing routine procedures for finding solutions, while solving problems involves applying previously acquired knowledge to new and unfamiliar situations. With this in mind, we can see that what is a problem for one person may be an exercise for another.

Paul Halmos, in "The Heart of Mathematics," wrote, "It is the duty of all teachers, and of teachers of mathematics in particular, to expose their students to problems much more than to facts." To this end, we present a variety of problems and use the four-step problem-solving process to solve many of them. It is not necessary to memorize these four steps, nor is it always necessary to use them. The four-step process does not assure a solution to a problem, but it gives valuable guidelines when there is no obvious way to proceed.

One of the strategies of problem solving, looking for a pattern, is used so often that it is discussed in a separate section. In addition, a separate section is devoted to choosing and using a calculator, an indispensable tool for saving time in performing routine computations and an invaluable aid in many problem-solving situations.

Section I-I

Exploration with Patterns

Discovering patterns is a very important strategy in problem solving. Police investigators study case files to find the modus operandi, or pattern of operation, when a series of crimes is committed. Their discovery of a pattern, sometimes using a computer, does not necessarily find the criminal, but may provide the necessary clues to do so. Similarly, in science and mathematics we try to find solutions to problems by studying patterns and searching for clues. The patterns may or may not provide solutions. Different people may see different patterns in the same data.

inductive reasoning

Reasoning based on examining a variety of cases or sets of data, discovering patterns, and forming conclusions is called **inductive reasoning.** Scientists use inductive reasoning when they perform experiments to discover various laws of nature. Statisticians use inductive reasoning when they form

conjecture

conclusions based on collected data. Inductive reasoning may lead to a **conjecture,** a statement thought to be true but not yet proven as either true or false. Inductive reasoning is an extremely helpful technique for making conjectures. However, it should be used cautiously because conjectures developed using inductive reasoning may be false. Example 1-1 shows that based on a given set of data, often more than one pattern is possible.

Example 1-1

Find the next three terms to complete a pattern.

1, 2, 4, ——— , ——— , ———

Solution

The difference between the first two terms is 1; the difference between the second two terms is 2; consequently, the difference between the next two terms might be 3, then 4, and so on. Thus, the completed sequence might appear as follows.

1, 2, 4, <u>7</u>, <u>11</u>, <u>16</u>

Another property that 1, 2, and 4 share is that each term is twice the preceding one; that is, $2 = 2 \cdot 1$ and $4 = 2 \cdot 2$. Thus, the next terms could be $2 \cdot 4$, or 8, $2 \cdot 8$, or 16, and $2 \cdot 16$, or 32. Hence, the completed sequence might appear as follows.

1, 2, 4, <u>8</u>, <u>16</u>, <u>32</u>

It is evident that more than one pattern is possible based on the given information.

Example 1-2

Find the next three terms to complete a pattern.

□, △, △, □, △, △, □, ——— , ——— , ———

Solution

Notice that between two squares there are two consecutive triangles. Based on this observation, the next three terms are two triangles followed by a square. Thus, the completed sequence might appear as follows.

□, △, △, □, △, △, □, <u>△</u>, <u>△</u>, <u>□</u>

Example 1-3

Find the pattern in the number of matchsticks required to continue the pattern shown below. Assume the matchsticks are arranged so that each figure has one more square than the preceding figure.

Solution

The numbers of matchsticks required to make the successive figures are 4, 7, 10, and 13. As seen below, each term is 3 units greater than the previous term.

Sequence   4 ⌣ 7 ⌣ 10 ⌣ 13

Difference   3   3   3

If this pattern continues, the next three terms will be 16, 19, and 22, and the numbers of matchsticks for each of the next three terms will be 16, 19, and 22, respectively.

Inductive reasoning is very useful in the real world to develop conjectures. However, even though inductive reasoning, based on many laboratory tests and case studies, is used to decide if a drug is safe, the pharmaceutical world has been shaken several times when a laboratory-tested drug (such as thalidomide) has later proved to be extremely harmful. Sometimes it is necessary to test a large number of cases to find that a conjectured pattern does not continue. In the following, a small number of cases is all that is required to disprove the conjecture.

Consider the drawings in Figure 1-1 in which points on the circumference of a circle are connected by segments to form distinct, nonoverlapping regions. Connecting 2 points determines 2 regions; 3 points give 4 regions; 4 points give 8 regions. Each time an additional point is used, it appears that the number of regions is doubled. However, this is not the case. No matter how the points are connected, the most regions that can be obtained with 6 points is 31.

Figure 1-1

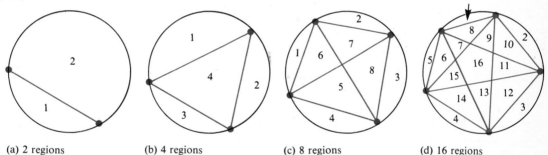

(a) 2 regions   (b) 4 regions   (c) 8 regions   (d) 16 regions

ARITHMETIC SEQUENCE

sequence

In each example above, the terms were given in an ordered arrangement. The word **sequence** is used to describe terms given in such a way that they can be thought of as being numbered; that is, there is a first, second, and so on. If each successive term in a sequence is obtained from the previous term by the addition of a fixed number, called the **difference,** then the sequence is called an **arithmetic sequence.** The sequence in Example 1-3 is an arithmetic sequence. The fixed number is 3. Neither pattern in Example 1-1 illustrates an arithmetic sequence because no fixed number has been added.

difference
arithmetic sequence

It is often useful to predict the terms in a sequence. Tables are helpful problem-solving aids for finding such values. Table 1-1 shows the sequence in Example 1-3. The column headed "Number of Term" refers to the order of the term in the sequence. The column headed "Term" lists the accompanying terms of the sequence. We use an **ellipsis,** denoted by three dots, to indicate that the sequence continues in the same manner.

ellipsis

Table I-1

Number of Term	Term
1	4
2	$7 = 4 + 3 = 4 + 1 \cdot 3$
3	$10 = 4 + 3 + 3 = 4 + 2 \cdot 3$
4	$13 = 4 + 3 + 3 + 3 = 4 + 3 \cdot 3$
⋮	⋮

Notice that the number of 3s in each term is one less than the number of the term. Assuming this pattern continues, the 10th term is $4 + 9 \cdot 3$, or 31, and the 100th term is $4 + 99 \cdot 3$, or 301. The general term of a sequence *n*th term is called the **nth term.** Knowing the general term enables us to find any term given the number of the term. In the above sequence, the *n*th term is $4 + (n - 1) \cdot 3$. Thus, for example, the 200th term can be obtained by substituting 200 for *n*. The 200th term is $4 + (200 - 1) \cdot 3$, or $4 + 199 \cdot 3$, or 601.

In the sequence in Table 1-1, we saw that the *n*th term is $4 + (n - 1) \cdot 3$. We could use this expression to find the number of a term if given the value of the term. For example, suppose we have the term 1798. Whatever *n*, the number of the term is, we know that $4 + (n - 1) \cdot 3 = 1798$. This tells us that $(n - 1) \cdot 3 = 1794$, or that $n - 1 = 598$. Thus, $n = 599$.

It is possible to generalize our work with arithmetic sequences. Suppose the first term is *a* and the difference is *d*. Table 1-2 can be used to investigate the general term for the sequence $a, a + d, a + 2d, a + 3d, \ldots$. Thus, we see that *the nth term of any sequence with the first term a and difference d is given by* $a + (n - 1)d$.

Table I-2

Number of Term	Term
1	a
2	$a + d$
3	$a + 2 \cdot d$
4	$a + 3 \cdot d$
5	$a + 4 \cdot d$
⋮	⋮
n	$a + (n - 1) \cdot d$

GEOMETRIC SEQUENCE

A different type of sequence is investigated in the following discussion. A child in a family has 2 parents, 4 grandparents, 8 great-grandparents, 16 great-great-grandparents, and so on. Assuming that none of the ancestors in the family married a relative, we see that the numbers of ancestors from previous generations form the sequence $2, 4, 8, 16, 32, \ldots$. This type of sequence is called a **geometric sequence.** Each successive term of a geometric sequence is obtained from its predecessor by multiplying by a fixed number called the **ratio.** In this example, the ratio is 2. To find the *n*th term, examine Table 1-3.

geometric sequence

ratio

Table 1-3

Number of Term	Term
1	$2 = 2^1$
2	$4 = 2 \cdot 2 = 2^2$
3	$8 = 2 \cdot (2 \cdot 2) = 2^3$
4	$16 = 2 \cdot (2 \cdot 2 \cdot 2) = 2^4$
5	$32 = 2 \cdot (2 \cdot 2 \cdot 2 \cdot 2) = 2^5$
⋮	⋮

The table reveals a pattern: When the given term is written as a power of 2, the number of the term is the exponent of 2. Following this pattern, the 10th term is 2^{10}, or 1024, the 100th term is 2^{100}, and the nth term is 2^n. Thus, the number of ancestors in the nth previous generation is 2^n.

Just as we could determine a formula for finding the nth term of an arithmetic sequence, we can also find the nth term of a geometric sequence. Consider Table 1-4, where a is the first term and r is the ratio.

Table 1-4

Number of Term	Term
1	a
2	$a \cdot r$
3	$a \cdot r^2$
4	$a \cdot r^3$
5	$a \cdot r^4$
⋮	⋮
n	$a \cdot r^{n-1}$

We see that the nth term of any geometric sequence where the first term is a and the ratio is r is given by the formula $a \cdot r^{n-1}$. Notice that for $n = 1$ we have $a \cdot r^{1-1} = a \cdot r^0$. If $r \neq 0$, then $r^0 = 1$. (This is discussed in Chapter 6.) Thus, when $n = 1$, we have a.

OTHER SEQUENCES

Some sequences are neither arithmetic nor geometric. One such sequence was studied by the ancient Greeks, who believed there was a close relationship between numbers and geometric figures. The numbers they used are now called **figurate numbers** because they could be pictured as geometric figures. The number 1 was the beginning of most patterns of these numbers because it was felt that 1 was the beginning of all numbers. Consider the arrays in Figure 1-2, which represent the first four terms of a sequence of numbers known as the **square numbers**. Observe that each successive figure has one more row of dots on each of two sides.

figurate numbers

square numbers

Figure 1-2

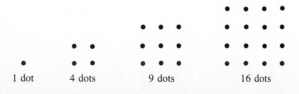

1 dot   4 dots   9 dots   16 dots

The square numbers pictured may be written as 1^2, 2^2, 3^2, and 4^2. If each array of dots in the pattern continues in the form of a square, the number of dots in the 10th array is 10^2, the number of dots in the 100th array is 100^2, and the number of dots in the nth array is n^2.

Figure 1-3

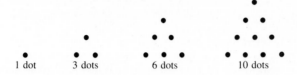

1 dot   3 dots   6 dots   10 dots

Example 1-4

The arrays shown in Figure 1-3 represent the first four terms of a sequence of numbers called triangular numbers. What is the 10th term? What is the 100th term? What is the nth term?

Solution

Table 1-5 suggests the sequence of numbers and a pattern for finding the desired terms.

Table 1-5

Number of Term	Term
1	1
2	$3 = 1 + 2$
3	$6 = 1 + 2 + 3$
4	$10 = 1 + 2 + 3 + 4$
5	$15 = 1 + 2 + 3 + 4 + 5$
$\vdots$	$\vdots$
10	$55 = 1 + 2 + 3 + 4 + 5 + 6 + 7 + 8 + 9 + 10$

From Table 1-5 we see that each successive term can be obtained from the previous term by adding the number of the term. Following this pattern, the 10th term is $1 + 2 + 3 + 4 + 5 + 6 + 7 + 8 + 9 + 10$, or 55, the 100th term is $1 + 2 + 3 + 4 + 5 + \cdots + 99 + 100$, and the nth term is $1 + 2 + 3 + 4 + 5 + \cdots + (n - 1) + n$.

Example 1-4 suggests another interesting problem, that is, developing a technique for finding sums of the form $1 + 2 + 3 + \cdots + (n - 1) + n$. This problem is discussed in the next section.

The next examples involve sequences for which it is helpful to take more than one successive difference to find a pattern.

Example 1-5

Find the seventh term in the following sequence.

5, 6, 14, 29, 51, 80, . . .

Solution

The pattern for the differences between successive terms is not easily recognizable.

Sequence   5   6   14   29   51   80

Difference   1   8   15   22   29

To discover a pattern for the original sequence, we try to find a pattern for the sequence of differences 1, 8, 15, 22, 29, ... This sequence is an arithmetic sequence with fixed difference 7, as shown below.

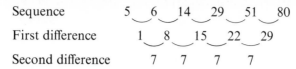

Sequence   5   6   14   29   51   80

First difference   1   8   15   22   29

Second difference   7   7   7   7

Thus, the sixth term in the first-difference row is 29 + 7, or 36, and hence the seventh term in the original sequence is 80 + 36, or 116. What number follows 116?

Remark   The general term for this sequence can be found algebraically to be $(\frac{7}{2})n^2 - (\frac{19}{2})n + 11$. However, justifying the general term for this particular sequence is beyond the scope of this text. Both Examples 1-5 and 1-6 are given to show that with some sequences, a pattern can be discovered by taking successive differences.

Example 1-6   Find the seventh term in the following sequence.

2, 3, 9, 23, 48, 87, . . .

Solution   As in the previous example, we find the first and second differences. Since the second difference is not a fixed number, we go on to the third difference, as shown.

Sequence   2   3   9   23   48   87

First difference   1   6   14   25   39

Second difference   5   8   11   14

Third difference   3   3   3

Since the third difference is a fixed number, the second difference is an arithmetic sequence. The fifth term in the second-difference sequence is 14 + 3, or 17, the sixth term in the first-difference sequence is 39 + 17, or 56, and the seventh term in the original sequence is 87 + 56, or 143.

When asked to find a pattern for a given sequence, first look for some easily recognizable pattern. If none exists, determine whether the sequence is either arithmetic or geometric. If a pattern is still unclear, taking successive differences may help. *It is possible that none of the methods described will reveal a pattern.*

In the previous examples, we were given sequences and were asked to find succeeding terms. In some of those sequences we were able to find the *n*th terms. A related problem is to generate the sequence if given the *n*th term.

Example I-7

Find the first four terms of a sequence whose nth term is given by:
(a) $4 \cdot n + 3$; (b) $n^2 - 1$.

Solution

(a) To find the first term, we substitute $n = 1$ in the formula $4 \cdot n + 3$ to obtain $4 \cdot 1 + 3$, or 7. Similarly, substituting $n = 2, 3, 4$, we obtain $4 \cdot 2 + 3$, or 11, $4 \cdot 3 + 3$, or 15, and $4 \cdot 4 + 3$, or 19, respectively. Hence, the first four terms of the sequence are 7, 11, 15, 19.

(b) Substituting $n = 1, 2, 3, 4$ in the formula $n^2 - 1$, we obtain $1^2 - 1$, or 0, $2^2 - 1$, or 3, $3^2 - 1$, or 8, $4^2 - 1$, or 15, respectively. Thus, the first four terms of the sequence are 0, 3, 8, 15.

PROBLEM SET I-I

1. List the terms that complete a possible pattern. Then describe the pattern.
   (a) 1×2, 2×3, 3×4, 4×5, _____, _____, _____,
   (b) □, 00, □□□, 0000, □□□□□, _____, _____,
   (c) 61, 57, 53, 49, _____, _____, _____
   (d) 5, 6, 8, 11, _____, _____, _____
   (e) 2, 5, 10, 17, _____, _____, _____
   (f) X, Y, X, X, Y, X, X, _____, _____, _____
   (g) 1, 3, 1, 8, 1, 13, _____, _____, _____
   (h) 1, 1, 2, 3, 5, 8, 13, 21, _____, _____, _____
   (i) 1, 11, 111, 1111, 11111, _____, _____,
   (j) 1, 12, 123, 1234, 12345, _____, _____,
   (k) 1×2, 2×2^2, 3×2^3, 4×2^4, 5×2^5, _____,
   (l) $2, 2^2, 2^4, 2^8, 2^{16}$, _____, _____, _____

   (m)  , ____ , ____ , ____

2. In each case, list terms that complete a possible pattern. Which of the following sequences are arithmetic, which are geometric, and which are neither?
   (a) 1, 3, 5, 7, 9, _____, _____, _____
   (b) 0, 50, 100, 150, 200, _____, _____, _____
   (c) 3, 6, 12, 24, 48, _____, _____, _____
   (d) 10, 100, 1000, 10000, 100000, _____, _____,
   (e) $5^2, 5^3, 5^4, 5^5, 5^6$, _____, _____, _____
   (f) 11, 22, 33, 44, 55, _____, _____, _____
   (g) $2^1, 2^3, 2^5, 2^7, 2^9$, _____, _____, _____
   (h) 9, 13, 17, 21, 25, 29, _____, _____, _____
   (i) 1, 8, 27, 64, 125, _____, _____, _____
   (j) 2, 6, 18, 54, 162, _____, _____, _____

3. The following geometric arrays suggest a sequence of numbers.

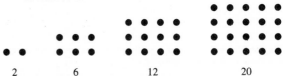

2   6   12   20

   (a) Find the next three terms.
   (b) Find the 100th term.
   ★(c) Find the nth term.

4. (a) Consider the following geometric arrays of pentagonal numbers. The numbers are formed by counting the dots. Find the first six numbers suggested by this sequence.

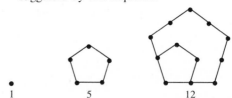

   1   5   12

   ★(b) What is the 100th pentagonal number?

5. The first difference of a sequence is a sequence of consecutive even numbers, 2, 4, 6, 8, ... Find the first six terms of the original sequence in each of the following cases.
   (a) The first term of the original sequence is 3.
   (b) The sum of the first two terms of the original sequence is 10.
   (c) The fifth term of the original sequence is 35.

6. List the next three terms to complete a pattern in each of the following. (Finding differences may be helpful.)
   (a) 5, 6, 14, 32, 64, 115, 191, _____, _____,
   (b) 0, 2, 6, 12, 20, 30, 42, _____, _____, _____
   ★(c) 10, 8, 3, 0, 4, 20, 53, _____, _____, _____

7. How many terms are there in the following sequences?
   (a) 1, 2, 3, 4, ... , 100
   (b) 51, 52, 53, 54, ... , 151
   (c) 2, 4, 6, 8, ... , 200
   (d) $1, 2, 2^2, 2^3, ... , 2^{60}$
   (e) 10, 20, 30, 40, ... , 2000

8. The following is an example of term-by-term addition of two arithmetic sequences.

$$\begin{array}{r} 1, 3, \quad 5, \quad 7, \quad 9, 11, ... \\ + 2, 4, \quad 6, \quad 8, 10, 12, ... \\ \hline 3, 7, 11, 15, 19, 23, ... \end{array}$$

   Notice that the resulting sequence is also arithmetic. Investigate whether this happens again by trying two other examples.

9. Find the first five terms of the sequence with the nth term given as follows.
   (a) $n^2 + 2$ (b) $5n - 1$ (c) $10^n - 1$

10. Find the 100th term and the nth term in each of the sequences of Problem 2.

11. The sequence 1, 1, 2, 3, 5, 8, 13, 21, ... , in which each term starting with the third one is the sum of the two preceding terms, is called a *Fibonacci sequence*. This sequence is named after the great Italian mathematician Leonardo Fibonacci, who lived in the twelfth and thirteenth centuries.
    (a) Write the first 12 terms of the sequence.
    (b) Notice that the sum of the first 3 terms in the sequence is one less than the fifth term of the sequence. Does a similar relationship hold for the sum of the first 4 terms, 5 terms, and 6 terms?
    (c) Guess the sum of the first 10 terms of the sequence.
    ★(d) Make a conjecture concerning the sum of the first n terms of the sequence.

12. The school population for a certain school was predicted to increase by 50 students a year for the next 10 years. If the current enrollment is 700 students, what will the enrollment be after 10 years?

13. A tank contains 15,360 L of water. At the end of each day one half of the water is removed and not replaced. How much water is left in the tank after 10 days?

14. A well driller charges $10 a foot for the first 10 feet, $10.50 a foot for the next 10 feet, $11 a foot for the next 10 feet, and so on, increasing the price by 50¢ for each 10 feet. What is the cost of drilling a 100-foot well?

15. An employee is paid $1200 at the end of the first month on the job. Each month after that, the worker is paid $20 more than in the preceding month.
    (a) What is the employee's monthly salary at the end of the second year on the job?
    (b) How much will the employee have earned after 6 months?
    (c) After how many months will the employee's monthly salary be $3240?

16. A commuter train picks up passengers at 7:30 A.M. If 1 person gets on at the first stop, 3 at the second stop, 5 at the third stop, and so on, how many people get on at the tenth stop?

17. (a) If a fixed number is added to each term of an arithmetic sequence, is the resulting sequence an arithmetic sequence? Justify your answer.
    (b) If each term of an arithmetic sequence is multiplied by a fixed number, will the resulting sequence always be an arithmetic sequence? Justify your answer.

18. Answer the questions in Problem 17 for a geometric sequence.

★19. A student claims that the first difference of every geometric sequence is itself a geometric sequence. Is the student correct? Justify your answer.

BRAIN TEASER

Find the next three terms of the following sequence.

O, T, T, F, F, S, S, E, _____ , _____ , _____

Section 1-2   Using the Problem-Solving Process

If you follow only certain patterns in attacking problems, there is a danger that you may form a *mind set*. A mind set occurs when you draw a faulty conclusion by assuming that you know the answer to a problem without really examining the problem. For example, consider the following children's nursery rhyme.

As I was going to St. Ives
I met a man with seven wives.
Every wife had seven sacks,
Every sack had seven cats,
Every cat had seven kits,
Kits, cats, sacks, and wives,
How many were going to St. Ives?

Without carefully reading the rhyme, you may start counting the number of wives, sacks, cats, and kits. If you do, you have a mind set. Reread the rhyme. There is only one person going to St. Ives. Could you solve the problem if the question were "How many were coming from St. Ives?"

Other common mind sets follow: Spell the word "spot" three times aloud. "S-P-O-T! S-P-O-T! S-P-O-T!" Now answer the question: "What do you do when you come to a green light?" Write your answer. If you answered "Stop," you may be guilty of forming a mind set. You do not stop at a *green* light.

Consider the following problem: "A man had 36 sheep. All but 10 died. How many lived?"

Did you answer "10"? If you did, you are catching on and are ready to try some problems. If you did not answer "10," then you should reread the problem and make sure you really understand the question. As pointed out in the introduction, one could benefit by examining the four-step problem-solving process. We now discuss the four-step process in more detail.

COMPREHENDING "UNDERSTANDING THE PROBLEM"

As discussed earlier, Understanding the Problem involves being able to state the problem in your own words, determine what is to be found, and determine what information is given in the problem, what is needed, and what is not needed. Consider the following.

Bo and Jojo went to a football game. The tickets cost $4.00 each. Bo gave the cashier $10.00 and received $2.00 in change. At the concession stand, Jojo bought two pops at $1.25 each and two candy bars at $0.80 each. At three minutes before halftime, Bo bought a hot dog for $0.75 and a pop. They left the game with 4 minutes and 13 seconds left to play. How much did they spend on pop?

In this problem, the question is clear. However, there are many extraneous numbers to delete. All that is important is that three pops were bought and each one cost $1.25 for a total of $3.75.
Another example follows.

Thanksgiving was on November 24, 1983. Memorial Day was on May 28, 1984. How many days were there between the two holidays?

In this problem there is no extraneous information, but there is information needed. We have to know how many days there are in the months of November, December, January, February, March, and April. In addition, we have to recognize that 1984 is a leap year and that February has an additional day in a leap year. Finally, we have to know what "between" means. In mathematics, "between" is not inclusive, meaning that we do not count November 24 and May 28.

COMPREHENDING "DEVISING A PLAN"

Devising a Plan involves finding a strategy to aid in finding a solution to the problem. We consider some strategies in detail later in this section. Students often ask which strategy to use for a specific problem. There is no definite answer to this question. However, being aware of general strategies for problem solving and practicing using various strategies should be helpful in determining an appropriate strategy for a particular problem. A specific strategy is learned by practicing it. Once learned, strategies are simply tools to aid in the problem-solving process. The notion here is similar to the following ancient proverb.

> *If you give a person a loaf of bread, you feed the person for a day;*
> *If you teach the person to bake, you feed the person for a lifetime.*

COMPREHENDING "CARRYING OUT THE PLAN"

Carrying Out the Plan involves performing any necessary computations. One very important tool for doing this is a calculator. We feel that the use of a calculator is so important for elementary school teachers that we include a separate section on this topic later in the chapter. Accurate computations are important because it can be very frustrating to understand a problem, devise a plan, and attempt to carry it out only to make a mistake in computing.

COMPREHENDING "LOOKING BACK"

The Looking Back step is frequently one of the most interesting. It is here that we should check the solution. However, there is much more than that to this step; it is here that we should consider extensions to the completed problem and other ways to solve the problem. In the problems in this text, you should try the extensions mentioned. In many cases the extension is more interesting than the original problem.

STRATEGIES FOR PROBLEM SOLVING

For each of the strategies described, a problem is given that can be solved using that strategy. Read each problem and try to solve it before reading the solution. If you need a hint, read only enough of the solution to help you get started. After you have solved the problem, compare your solution with the one in the text.

STRATEGY—LOOK FOR A PATTERN

The strategy of looking for a pattern was examined in the previous section, where we concentrated on sequences of numbers. We continue that investigation here. Now study the following problems exemplifying the four-step process and different strategies.

PROBLEM I

When the famous German mathematician Karl Gauss (1777–1855), shown on the stamp in Figure 1-4, was a child, his teacher required the students to find the sum of the first 100 natural numbers. The teacher expected this problem to keep the class occupied for a considerable amount of time. Gauss gave the answer almost immediately. Can you?

Figure 1-4

natural numbers

UNDERSTANDING THE PROBLEM The **natural numbers** are 1, 2, 3, 4, ... Thus, the problem is to find the sum $1 + 2 + 3 + 4 + \cdots + 100$.

DEVISING A PLAN Gauss may have used the strategy of *looking for a pattern*. By considering $1 + 100$, $2 + 99$, $3 + 98$, ..., $50 + 51$, it is evident that there are 50 pairs of numbers, each with a sum of 101, as shown in Figure 1-5.

Figure 1-5

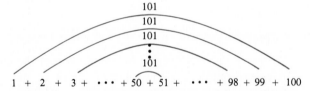

$$1 + 2 + 3 + \cdots + 50 + 51 + \cdots + 98 + 99 + 100$$

CARRYING OUT THE PLAN There are 50 pairs, each with the sum 101. Thus, the total sum is 50(101), or 5050.

LOOKING BACK It is easy to check the computation involved. It is also easy to see that the method is mathematically correct because addition can be performed in any order, and multiplication is repeated addition. A more general problem is to find the sum of the first n numbers, $1 + 2 + 3 + 4 + 5 + \cdots + n$, where n is any natural number. We use the same plan as before and notice the relationship in Figure 1-6. If n is an even natural number, there are $n/2$ pairs of numbers. The sum of each pair is $n + 1$. Therefore, the sum $1 + 2 + 3 + \cdots + n$ is given by $(n/2)(n + 1)$. Does the same formula work if n is odd?

Figure 1-6

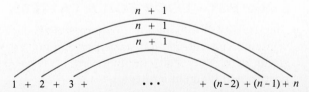

$$1 + 2 + 3 + \cdots + (n-2) + (n-1) + n$$

A different approach to finding the sum $1 + 2 + 3 + \cdots + n$ is to think of the sum geometrically as a stack of blocks, as pictured in Figure 1-7(a). To find the sum, we might consider the stack in Figure 1-7(a) and a stack of the same size placed differently, as in Figure 1-7(b). The total number of blocks in the stack in Figure 1-7(b) is $n(n + 1)$ and it is twice the desired sum. Thus, the desired sum is $n(n + 1)/2$.

Figure 1-7

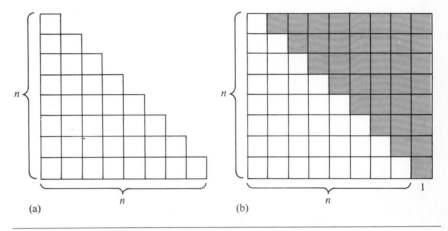

(a) n (b) n 1

STRATEGY—MAKE A TABLE

The next strategy that we consider is making a table. A table can be used to summarize data or to help us see a pattern. It may be especially helpful if there are large amounts of data to be summarized, as seen in Chapter 9.

PROBLEM 2

How many ways are there to make change for a quarter using only dimes, nickels, and pennies?

UNDERSTANDING THE PROBLEM There are no limits on the number of coins to be used to make change for a quarter. Nickels, dimes, and pennies need not all be used; that is, 25 pennies is an acceptable answer, as is 2 dimes and 1 nickel.

HISTORICAL NOTE

Karl Gauss (1777–1855) is regarded as the greatest mathematician of the nineteenth century and one of the greatest mathematicians of all time. He was born to humble parents in Brunswick, Germany. He was an infant prodigy who, it is said, at age 3 corrected an arithmetic error in his father's bookkeeping. Gauss used to claim that he could figure before he could talk.

Gauss made contributions in the areas of astronomy, geodesy, and electricity. After his death, the King of Hanover ordered a commemorative medal prepared in his honor. On the medal was an inscription referring to Gauss as the "Prince of Mathematics," a title that has stayed with his name.

DEVISING A PLAN In this problem the strategy of *making a table* is used to keep a record of all possibilities as they are examined. First, consider the possibilities when the number of nickels and dimes is zero and the number of pennies is 25. Continue the chart by trading nickels for pennies, as shown in Table 1-6. Are there other combinations? What about dimes? To finish the problem, consider all possibilities using dimes.

Table 1-6

D	N	P
0	0	25
0	1	20
0	2	15
0	3	10
0	4	5
0	5	0

CARRYING OUT THE PLAN Start with combinations using one dime. With one dime, the greatest number of pennies possible is 15. Next, trade nickels for pennies, as shown in Table 1-7.

Table 1-7

D	N	P
1	0	15
1	1	10
1	2	5
1	3	0

The last case to consider is possibilities with 2 dimes. Proceeding as before, we obtain Table 1-8.

Table 1-8

D	N	P
2	0	5
2	1	0

All three cases are shown in Table 1-9.

Table 1-9

D	N	P
0	0	25
0	1	20
0	2	15
0	3	10
0	4	5
0	5	0
1	0	15
1	1	10
1	2	5
1	3	0
2	0	5
2	1	0

Thus, there are 12 ways to make change for a quarter using only dimes, nickels, and pennies.

LOOKING BACK Check each row of Table 1-9 to see that it shows change for a quarter. The systematic listing used in the table shows that all cases have been considered. The problem can be extended easily by starting with an initial amount other than one quarter.

Another interesting, related problem is as follows. Given the number of coins it takes to make change for a quarter, is it possible to determine exactly which coins they are? (*Hint:* Look at Table 1-9 listing the 12 different combinations. Is the number of coins in each combination different?) If you think you know the answer, try it with a friend to see if it works.

STRATEGY—LOOK FOR SIMPLER CASES

In many problems, because of the complexity, it is often easier to consider a simpler case of the problem and build to the original problem.

PROBLEM 3

Using the existing lines in Figure 1-8, how many different squares are there?

Figure 1-8

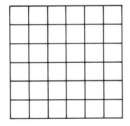

UNDERSTANDING THE PROBLEM Before proceeding, it is important to know what is meant by square and also what is meant by "different squares." A square is a four-sided figure whose sides are line segments of equal length and whose adjacent sides meet at right angles. Two squares are different if they have either different dimensions or different locations. For example, the colored lines in Figure 1-9 show four different squares.

Figure 1-9

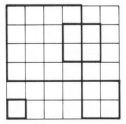

DEVISING A PLAN The strategy of *looking at simpler cases* is one of the most important strategies in problem solving and will be used repeatedly in this text. This strategy appears to be appropriate here. The simplest case to consider is given in Figure 1-10(a). How many different squares are there in a 1 × 1 grid? This is very easy—only one. Now consider the 2 × 2 grid in Figure 1-10(b). There are four 1 × 1 squares and one 2 × 2 square, for a total of five squares. How many squares are in a 3 × 3 grid? As can be determined from Figure 1-10(c), there are nine 1 × 1 squares, four 2 × 2 squares, and one 3 × 3 square for a total of 14 squares. How many squares are in Figure 1-10(d)?

Figure I-10

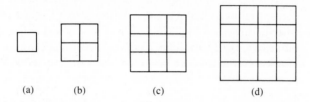

(a)   (b)   (c)   (d)

The problem now becomes more involved. Table 1-10 records information obtained from Figure 1-10.

Table I-10

Grid Size	1 × 1 Squares	2 × 2 Squares	3 × 3 Squares	4 × 4 Squares	Total Squares
1 × 1	1, or 1^2				1
2 × 2	4, or 2^2	1, or 1^2			5
3 × 3	9, or 3^2	4, or 2^2	1, or 1^2		14
4 × 4	16, or 4^2	9, or 3^2	4, or 2^2	1, or 1^2	30

Notice that each total is a sum of perfect squares and that the total of 30 is obtained by finding $1^2 + 2^2 + 3^2 + 4^2$. The table reveals a pattern that is very helpful for counting squares with larger grids. Thus, in a 5 × 5 grid, the total is given by $1^2 + 2^2 + 3^2 + 4^2 + 5^2$; in a 6 × 6 grid, the total is $1^2 + 2^2 + 3^2 + 4^2 + 5^2 + 6^2$.

CARRYING OUT THE PLAN The only computation involved is finding $1^2 + 2^2 + 3^2 + 4^2 + 5^2 + 6^2$, which equals 91.

LOOKING BACK The more general problem is to find the number of squares in an $n \times n$ grid. Following the preceding pattern, it seems that the number of squares in such a grid is $1^2 + 2^2 + 3^2 + \cdots + n^2$. However, we cannot be absolutely certain of this answer since the observation of a pattern from a few cases does not assure that the pattern always holds. As problem solvers learn more mathematics, they will be able to complete proofs. *Observing a pattern from a few cases does not constitute a proof.* This problem, with a proof of the result, is discussed in detail in the article "Checkerboard Mathematics" by Billstein.

In the preceding problem, two strategies were used: *looking at a simpler case* and *looking for a pattern*. This is often the case in problem solving. The following student page from *Invitation to Mathematics, Grade 6* (Scott, Foresman, 1985) also discusses a problem in which more than one strategy is used. Can you identify the strategies?

Problem Solving: Find a Pattern

Read   In a round-robin tournament, each team plays against each of the other teams once. If there are 5 teams, how many games will there be?

Plan   Try solving easier, related problems. Put the results in a table to help you find a pattern.

Solve   If there were 2 teams, A and B, there would be just 1 game (A vs. B).

2 teams
1 game

If there were 3 teams, A, B, and C, there would be 3 games (A vs. B, A vs. C, and B vs. C). A would play 2 games.

3 teams
3 games

If there were 4 teams, A, B, C, and D, there would be 6 games. A would play 3 games.

4 teams
6 games

Put the results in a table and continue the pattern.

Answer   A round-robin tournament with 5 teams has 10 games.

How many teams?	How many games for team A?	How many other games?	Total
2	1	0	1
3	2	1	3
4	3	2 + 1	6
5	4	3 + 2 + 1	10

Look Back   Look for another way to count all the games. There are 5 teams and each team plays 4 games. There should be 5 × 4, or 20 games, then, but that counts each game twice. 2 × 10 = 20, so the answer is correct.

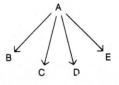

STRATEGY—LOOK FOR A SUBGOAL

In an attempt to devise a plan for solving some problems, it may become apparent that the problem could be solved if the solution to a somewhat easier or more familiar problem could be found. In such a case, the solution to the easier problem may become a subgoal to reaching our goal of solving the original problem. An example of this is seen in Problem 4.

PROBLEM 4

Kasey Kassion, a disk jockey for a 24-hour radio station, announces and plays each week's top forty rock songs on the radio all week. Suppose he decides to play the top song 40 times, the number two song 39 times, the number three song 38 times, and so on. If each song takes 4 minutes to play, how much time is left for other songs, commercials, news breaks, and other activities?

UNDERSTANDING THE PROBLEM We know how many times each top forty song is to be played, and we know that each of these songs takes 4 minutes to play. Furthermore, we know that each of the 7 days of the week has 24 hours and that there are 60 minutes in an hour. We are to find how much time is left once the top forty songs are played.

DEVISING A PLAN To find the amount of time left after the top forty songs are played, we could first find the amount of time it takes to play the songs and then subtract that amount from the total number of minutes in a week. To find the amount of time devoted to the top forty songs, we need to multiply the number of songs by 4 to determine how many minutes it takes to play those songs. Thus, we need to find the number of songs played. This becomes our *subgoal*. Because the top song is played 40 times, the number two song is played 39 times, the number three song is played 38 times, and so on, the fortieth song is played only once. The number of times the songs are played is $40 + 39 + 38 + \cdots + 1$. If we solve the number-of-songs subproblem, then we can solve the original problem.

CARRYING OUT THE PLAN We find the sum $40 + 39 + 38 + \cdots + 1$ to be $(41 \cdot 40)/2$, or 820. Then, because there are 820 songs played for 4 minutes each, it takes $820 \cdot 4$, or 3280, minutes for the songs to play. Furthermore, we know that 7 days of 24 hours with 60 minutes in each hour is $7 \cdot 24 \cdot 60$, or 10,080, minutes. Hence, there are $10,080 - 3280$, or 6800, minutes left after these songs are played.

LOOKING BACK At the end of the year, Kasey tries to play the top 100 songs of the year in the pattern given above. How many days will it take?

STRATEGY—LOOK FOR A RELATED PROBLEM

Sometimes in attempting to solve a problem, you will discover that it is very similar to a problem you have previously considered. In such a case, you may solve the new problem in a manner almost identical to the previous one. An example of this is seen in Problem 5.

PROBLEM 5

Find the following sum.

$$1 + 4 + 7 + 10 + 13 + \cdots + 3004$$

UNDERSTANDING THE PROBLEM From our experience with patterns in Section 1-1, we recognize the sequence $1, 4, 7, 10, 13, \ldots, 3004$ as an arithmetic sequence whose fixed difference is 3. We are asked to find the sum of the numbers in this sequence.

DEVISING A PLAN A *related problem* is Gauss' problem of finding the sum $1 + 2 + 3 + 4 + \cdots + 100$. In that problem, we paired 1 with 100, 2 with 99, 3 with 98, and so on and observed that there were 50 pairs of numbers, each with a sum of 101. A similar approach in the present problem yields a sum of 3005, as shown in Figure 1-11. To find the total, we need to know the number of pairs in Figure 1-11 that have a sum of 3005. We could find the number of pairs if we knew the number of terms in the sequence. Thus we have identified a *subgoal,* which is to find the number of terms in the sequence. In previous related problems, we used tables to find a given term or *n*th term. We try a similar approach and make Table 1-11.

Figure 1-11

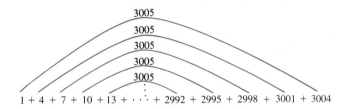

$$1 + 4 + 7 + 10 + 13 + \cdots + 2992 + 2995 + 2998 + 3001 + 3004$$

Table 1-11

Number of Term	Term
1	1
2	$4 = 1 + 3$
3	$7 = 1 + 3 + 3 = 1 + 2 \cdot 3$
4	$10 = 1 + 3 + 3 + 3 = 1 + 3 \cdot 3$
5	$13 = 1 + 3 + 3 + 3 + 3 = 1 + 4 \cdot 3$
$\vdots$	$\vdots$
?	3004

From Table 1-11 we see that the number of 3s in a term is one less than the number of the term, or the number of each term is one more than the number of 3s in the term. Thus, if we can write 3004 as 1 plus some number of 3s, we can find the number of the term. We see that $3004 = 1 + 3003 = 1 + 1001 \cdot 3$. Thus, the number of terms is 1002, and there are 1002 terms in the given sequence.

CARRYING OUT THE PLAN Because the number of terms is 1002, there are 501 pairs whose sum is 3005. Therefore, the total is $501 \cdot 3005$, or $1{,}505{,}505$.

LOOKING BACK Using the outlined procedure, we should be able to find the sum of any arithmetic sequence in which we know the first two terms and the last term. Can you find the sum of the first n terms of the arithmetic sequence whose first term is a and whose fixed difference is d?

STRATEGY—WORK BACKWARDS

In some problems, it is easier to start with what might be considered the final result and to work backwards. This is seen in Problem 6.

PROBLEM 6

Charles and Cynthia play a game called NIM. Each has a box of matchsticks. They take turns putting 1, 2, or 3 matchsticks in a common pile. The person who is able to add a number of matchsticks to the pile to make a total of 24 wins the game. What should be Charles' strategy to be sure he wins the game?

UNDERSTANDING THE PROBLEM Each of the players chooses 1, 2, or 3 matchsticks to place in the pile. If Charles puts 3 matchsticks in the pile, Cynthia may put 1, 2, or 3 matchsticks in the pile, which makes a total of 4, 5, or 6. It is now Charles' turn. Whoever makes a total of 24 wins the game.

DEVISING A PLAN Here the strategy of *working backwards* can be used. If there are 21, 22, or 23 matchsticks in the pile, Charles would like it to be his turn because he can win by adding 3, 2, or 1 matchsticks, respectively. However, if there are 20 matchsticks in the pile, Charles would like for it to be Cynthia's turn because she must add 1, 2, or 3, which would give a total of 21, 22, or 23. A *subgoal* for Charles is to reach 20 matchsticks, which forces Cynthia's total to be 21, 22, or 23. The subgoal of 20 matchsticks can be reached if there are 17, 18, or 19 matchsticks in the pile when Cynthia has completed her turn. For this to happen, there should be 16 matchsticks in the pile when Charles has completed his turn. Hence, a new subgoal for Charles is to reach 16 matchsticks. By similar reasoning, we see that Charles' additional subgoals are to reach 12, 8, and 4 matchsticks.

CARRYING OUT THE PLAN Using the reasoning developed in Devising a Plan, we see that the winning strategy for Charles is to be the person who creates a total of 4 matchsticks and then makes the totals of 8, 12, 16, 20, and 24 on successive turns. To do this, Charles should play second; if Cynthia puts 1, 2, or 3 matchsticks in the pile, Charles should add 3, 2, or 1, respectively, to make a total of 4. The totals 8, 12, 16, 20, and 24 can be achieved in a similar fashion.

LOOKING BACK A related problem is to solve the game in which the person who reaches 24 or more matchsticks loses. Now what is the winning strategy? Other related games can be examined in which different numbers are used as goals or different numbers of matchsticks are allowed to be added. For example, suppose the goal is 21 and 1, 3, or 5 matchsticks can be added each time.

STRATEGY—WRITE AN EQUATION

A problem-solving strategy commonly used in algebra is to write an equation. We discuss how to write equations and solve them in Chapter 4. Here we discuss the strategy for problems in which the solutions to the corresponding equations require little or no algebra.

PROBLEM 7

As he grew older, Abraham De Moivre (1667–1754), a mathematician who helped in the development of probability, discovered one day that he had begun to require 15 minutes more sleep each day. Based on the assumption that he required 8 hours of sleep on date A and that from date A he had begun to require an additional 15 minutes of sleep each day, he predicted when he would die. The predicted date of death was the day when he would require 24 hours of sleep. If this indeed happened, how many days did he live from date A?

UNDERSTANDING THE PROBLEM De Moivre found that if he needed 8 hours of sleep on Monday, for example, then he needed 8 hours and 15 minutes of sleep on Tuesday, 8 hours and 30 minutes on Wednesday, and so on. If we assume his prediction to be correct, we are to determine how many days he lived until he required 24 hours of sleep. The only other needed information is that there are 60 minutes in an hour.

DEVISING A PLAN Various strategies can be used to solve this problem. One of them is to write an equation involving the number of hours of sleep required. We recognize that the problem entails looking at an arithmetic sequence. The difference in this case is 15 minutes, or $\frac{15}{60}$ or $\frac{1}{4}$ of an hour. The first term in the sequence is $8 + \frac{1}{4}$, and we need to know the number of the term which has value 24. From our work in Problem 5, we discovered that we could find the number of a term in an arithmetic sequence if we knew the first two terms and the last term considered. We summarize what we know in Table 1-12.

Table 1-12

Number of Term	Term
1	$8 + \frac{1}{4}$
2	$8 + \frac{1}{4} + \frac{1}{4} = 8 + 2(\frac{1}{4})$
3	$8 + \frac{1}{4} + \frac{1}{4} + \frac{1}{4} = 8 + 3(\frac{1}{4})$
$\vdots$	$\vdots$
n	$8 + n \cdot (\frac{1}{4}) = 24$

Hence, all we need to do is solve the equation:

$$24 = 8 + n \cdot \tfrac{1}{4}$$

CARRYING OUT THE PLAN In solving the equation, we see that 8 plus some number is 24. That number must be 16. Now, $n \cdot \frac{1}{4} = 16$. Since $\frac{1}{4}$ of some number is 16, that number must be 64. Finally, n must be 64. We summarize this as follows.

$$24 = 8 + n \cdot \tfrac{1}{4}$$

$$16 = n \cdot \tfrac{1}{4}$$

$$4 \cdot 16 = n$$

$$64 = n$$

LOOKING BACK Now we need to interpret the answer, 64. Our equation revealed that if De Moivre was correct in his prediction, he had 64 days to live after date A. This is a reasonable answer because after that day, if he required an extra 15 minutes of sleep each day, then for the 64 days he needed $64 \cdot 15$ minutes, or 16 hours, of extra sleep. With 8 hours of regular sleep and 16 hours of extra sleep, the entire 24 hours in a day were required for sleep.

STRATEGY—DRAW A DIAGRAM

It has often been said that a picture is worth a thousand words. This is particularly true in problem solving. In geometry, drawing a picture often gives the insight necessary to solve a problem. A nongeometric problem that can be solved by using a picture is seen in Problem 8.

PROBLEM 8

It is the first day of class for the course in mathematics for elementary school teachers, and there are 20 people present in the room. To become acquainted with one another, each person shakes hands just once with everyone else. How many handshakes take place?

UNDERSTANDING THE PROBLEM There are 20 people in the room, and each person shakes hands with each other person only once. It takes 2 people for one handshake; that is, if Maria shakes hands with John and John shakes hands with Maria, this counts as one handshake, not two. The problem is to find the number of handshakes that take place.

DEVISING A PLAN One plan that would certainly work is to take 20 people and actually count the handshakes. Although this plan provides a solution, it would be nice to find a less elaborate one. One way of investigating this problem is to use the strategy of *drawing diagrams*. A diagram showing a handshake between persons A and B can be indicated by a line segment connecting A and B as shown.

Diagrams showing handshakes for 3, 4, and 5 people are given in Figure 1-12. From the diagrams, we see that the problem becomes one of counting

Figure 1-12

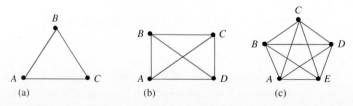

(a)   (b)   (c)

the different line segments needed to connect various numbers of points. In looking at the problem for 5 people [Figure 1-12(c)], we see that *A* shakes hands with persons *B*, *C*, *D*, and *E* (4 handshakes). Also, *B* shakes hands with *A*, *C*, *D*, and *E* (4 handshakes). In fact, each person shakes hands with 4 other people. Therefore, it appears that there are $5 \cdot 4$, or 20, handshakes. However, notice that the handshake between *A* and *B* is counted twice. This dual counting occurs for all 5 people. Consequently, each handshake was counted twice; thus, to obtain the answer, we must divide by 2. The answer is $\frac{(5 \cdot 4)}{2}$, or 10. This approach can be generalized for any number of people.

CARRYING OUT THE PLAN Using the outlined strategy, we see that with 20 people there are $(20 \cdot 19)/2$, or 190, handshakes.

LOOKING BACK Our answer can be checked by solving the problem by a different strategy. We try the strategy of *looking at a simpler problem*. With one person in the room, there are no handshakes. If a second person enters the room, there is 1 handshake (remember, 2 persons shaking hands counts as 1 handshake). If a third person enters the room, he or she shakes hands with each of the other persons present, so there are 2 additional handshakes for a total of $1 + 2$. If a fourth person enters the room, he or she shakes hands with each of the other three members present, so there is an addition of 3 shakes for a total of $1 + 2 + 3$. If a fifth person enters the room, an additional 4 shakes take place.

In Table 1-13, we record the number of handshakes.

Table 1-13

Number of People	Number of Handshakes
1	0
2	1
3	$1 + 2 = 3$
4	$1 + 2 + 3 = 6$
5	$1 + 2 + 3 + 4 = 10$

Notice that the last number in the expression $1 + 2 + 3 + 4$ is one less than the number of people shaking hands. Following this pattern, the answer for 20 people is given by $1 + 2 + 3 + 4 + \cdots + 19$. The technique used by Gauss (Problem 1) to find sums of consecutive natural numbers is very useful in completing the problem. Applying this technique, we have the following.

$$1 + 2 + 3 + \cdots + 19 = \frac{19(20)}{2} = 190$$

STRATEGY—GUESS AND CHECK

In the strategy of guess and check, we first attempt to guess at a solution using as reasonable a guess as possible. Once the guess is made, we check to see if the guess is the actual solution. If the guess is not a solution, the next step is to learn as much as possible about the solution based on the guess before we make the next guess. This strategy is somewhat akin to trial and error but, unlike trial and error, this strategy assumes that we are not using random guesses. The guess and check strategy is seen in Problem 9.

PROBLEM 9

Marques, a fourth grader, said to Mr. Treacher, "I'm thinking of a number less than or equal to 1000. Can you guess my number?"

Mr. Treacher replied, "Not only can I guess your number, but I can guess it in no more than ten questions, provided that your answers to my questions are yes or no and are truthful."

How could Mr. Treacher have been so positive about the maximum number of questions he would have to ask?

UNDERSTANDING THE PROBLEM To guarantee that Mr. Treacher could make good his statement, we need to know that Marques is thinking of a natural number. There are 1000 possibilities for the number. What types of questions could Mr. Treacher ask? Suppose he asked "Is the number 47?" With this type of question, it seems impossible to determine Marques' number in ten or fewer guesses. He needs to ask questions of a form such that he learns information about more than one number each time he receives Marques' answer to that question. For example, if he asked if the number is even, then no matter what Marques answered, Mr. Treacher would have only 500 numbers left to worry about with his next question. In other words, he would reduce the number of possibilities for his next question.

DEVISING A PLAN As discussed above, the primary concern is what type of questions Mr. Treacher should ask. A strategy that he should use here is guess and check, where each successive guess is based on the information learned from Marques' previous answer. In his questions, Mr. Treacher should try not only to narrow the number of numbers left to choose from but also to determine how far apart they are, that is, to find the range of the numbers. For example, if Mr. Treacher's first question is, "Is the number less than 500?" and Marques answers affirmatively, his number is in the range from 1 to 499. If he answers negatively, then his number is in the range from 500 to 1000. An equally good question is, "Is the number greater than 500?" Questions like this are better than, "Is it an even number?" because if the answer to "Is it even?" is yes, then there are 500 numbers left, but the range is from 2 to 1000. By successively asking questions such as, "Is the number less than 500?", where each question determines the range for the next question, Mr. Treacher successively halves both the field of numbers and the range in which the number lies.

CARRYING OUT THE PLAN Suppose Marques chose 38 for his number. Mr. Treacher's questions and Marques' answers might be as follows.

Is the number less than 500?	Yes
Is the number less than 250?	Yes
Is the number less than 125?	Yes
Is the number less than 62?	Yes
Is the number less than 31?	No

At this point, the number is in the range from 31 to 61. Halfway between these numbers is 46.

Is the number less than 46?   Yes

Continuing in this manner, we have

Is the number less than 38?   No
Is the number less than 42?   Yes
Is the number less than 40?   Yes
Is the number less than 39?   Yes

Consequently, Marques' number is 38.

LOOKING BACK Using the guess and check strategy, in which we utilize the information gleaned from a guess to determine the next guess, appears to be the most efficient way to attack the problem. We could change the range for Marques' number in order to change the problem. We could also use a calculator to find the values to ask about in the questions. If Marques' number were between 1 and 1,000,000, what would be the maximum number of questions that Mr. Treacher would have to ask to determine the number? If Mr. Treacher were allowed to ask 30 questions, what would be the largest range for Marques' number to enable Mr. Treacher to determine the chosen number?

TIME OUT

Before attempting the problems in the problem set, we suggest that you try the puzzles below. These puzzles have been around in one form or another for many years. They should help you begin to think and to understand what is really being asked in a problem.

1. How much dirt is in a hole 2 feet long, 3 feet wide, and 2 feet deep?
2. Two U.S. coins have a total value of 55¢. One coin is not a nickel. What are the two coins?
3. Walter had a dozen apples in his office. He ate all but 4. How many were left?
4. Sal owns 20 blue and 20 brown socks, which he keeps in a drawer in complete disorder. What is the minimum number of socks that he must pull out of the drawer on a dark morning to be sure he has a matching pair?
5. A heavy smoker wakes up in the middle of the night and finds herself out of cigarettes. The stores are closed, so she looks through all the ashtrays for butts. She figures that with 5 butts she can make one new cigarette. She finds 25 butts and decides they will last her till morning if she smokes only 1 cigarette every hour. How long does her supply last?

6. You have 8 sticks. Four of them are exactly half the length of the other 4. Enclose 3 squares of equal size with them.

7. Suppose you have only one 5-L (liter) container and one 3-L container. How can you measure exactly 4 L of water if neither container is marked for measuring?

8. It takes 1 hour and 20 minutes to drive to the airport, yet the return trip takes only 80 minutes using the same route and driving at what seems to be the same speed. How can this be?

9. What is the minimum number of pitches possible for a pitcher to make in a major league baseball game, assuming he plays the entire game and it is not called prior to completion?

10. Consider the following banking transaction. Deposit $50 and withdraw it as follows.

withdraw $20	leaving $30
withdraw 15	leaving 15
withdraw 9	leaving 6
withdraw 6	leaving 0
$50	$51

Where did the extra dollar come from? To whom does it belong?

11. A businessman bought four pieces of solid-gold chain, each consisting of three links.

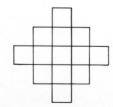

He wanted to keep them as an investment, but his wife felt that, joined together, the pieces would make a lovely necklace. A jeweler charges $10.50 to break a link and $10.50 to melt it together again. What is the minimum charge possible to form a necklace using all the pieces?

PROBLEM SET 1-2

1. An alternate version of the story of Gauss computing $1 + 2 + 3 + \cdots + 100$ reports that he simply listed the numbers in the following way to discover the sum.

$$
\begin{array}{r}
1 + \quad 2 + \quad 3 + \quad 4 + \quad 5 + \cdots + \quad 98 + \quad 99 + 100 \\
100 + \quad 99 + \quad 98 + \quad 97 + \quad 96 + \cdots + \quad 3 + \quad 2 + \quad 1 \\
\hline
101 + 101 + 101 + 101 + 101 + \cdots + 101 + 101 + 101
\end{array}
$$

Does this method give the same answer? Discuss the advantages of this method over the one described in the text.

2. How many different squares are in the following figure?

3. What is the largest sum of money—all in coins and no silver dollars—that I could have in my pocket without being able to give change for a dollar, a half-dollar, a quarter, a dime, or a nickel?

4. Arrange the numbers 1 through 9 into a square arranged like the one shown so that the sums of every row, column, and diagonal are the same. (The result is called a *magic square*.)

5. Molly is building a staircase out of blocks in the pattern shown. How many blocks will it take to build a staircase that is 25 blocks high?

6. How can you cook an egg for exactly 15 minutes if all you have are a 7-minute and an 11-minute timer?

7. How many different ways can you make change for a $50 bill using $5, $10, and $20 bills?

8. How many four-digit numbers have the same digits as 1984?

9. There are four volumes of Shakespeare's collected works on a shelf. The volumes are in order from left to right. The pages of each volume are exactly 2 inches thick. The covers are each $\frac{1}{6}$ inch thick. A bookworm started eating at page 1 of Volume I and ate through to the last page of Volume IV. What is the distance the bookworm traveled?

10. Looking out in the backyard one day, I saw an assortment of boys and dogs. Counting heads, I got 22. Counting feet, I got 68. How many boys and how many dogs were in the yard?

11. A compass and a ruler together cost $4. The compass costs 90¢ more than the ruler. How much does the compass cost?

12. A cat is at the bottom of an 18-foot well. Each day it climbs up 3 feet, and each night it slides back 2 feet. How long will it take the cat to get out of the well?

13. A pioneer moving west had a goose, a bag of corn, and a fox. He came to a river. The ferry was large enough to carry him and one of his possessions. If he were to leave the fox and the goose alone, the fox would eat the goose. If he were to leave the goose and corn alone, the goose would eat the corn. How did he get himself and his possessions across the river?

14. In a horse race:
    (a) Fast Jack finished a length ahead of Lookout.
    (b) Lookout did not finish in last place.
    (c) Null Set finished 7 lengths ahead of Bent Leg.
    (d) Fast Jack finished 7 lengths behind Applejack.
    (e) Bent Leg finished 3 lengths behind Fast Jack.
    What was the finishing position of each horse?

15. Eight marbles all look alike, but one is slightly heavier than the others. By using a balance scale, how can you determine the heavier one in exactly:
    (a) 3 weighings? (b) 2 weighings?

16. Marc went to the store with $1.00 in change. He had at least one of each coin less than a half-dollar, but he did not have a half-dollar coin.
    (a) What is the least number of coins he could have?
    (b) What is the greatest number of coins he could have?

17. A farmer needs to fence a rectangular piece of land. She wants the length of the field to be 80 feet longer than the width. If she has 1080 feet of fencing material, what should the length and the width of the field be?

18. You are given a checkerboard with the two squares on opposite corners removed and a set of dominoes such that each domino can cover two squares on the board. Can the dominoes be arranged in such a way that all of the 62 remaining squares on the board can be covered? If not, why not?

19. How many terms are there in the following sequences?
    (a) 1, 3, 5, 7, 9, ..., 2001
    (b) 2, 5, 8, 11, 14, ..., 899
    (c) 5, 9, 13, 17, 21, ..., 601

20. Find the following sums.
    (a) 2 + 4 + 6 + 8 + 10 + ··· + 1020
    (b) 1 + 6 + 11 + 16 + 21 + ··· + 1001
    (c) 3 + 7 + 11 + 15 + 19 + ··· + 403

21. There were 20 people at a round table for dinner who shook hands with the people on their immediate right and left. At the end of the dinner, each person got up and shook hands with everybody except with the people who sat to the immediate

right or left at dinner. Find the number of handshakes that took place after dinner.

22. A student has a sheet of $8\frac{1}{2}$ by 11 inch paper. She needs to measure exactly 6 inches. Can she do it using the sheet of paper?

23. At Dunkirk, 20 boats were supposed to carry 120 soldiers across the English Channel. Some of the boats did not make it to the shore to pick up the soldiers. Instead of the 20 boats that were to carry only 6 people each, some of the boats that did make it to shore carried 6, some carried 7, and some carried 8. How many boats might have carried 7 people?

24. Russian Babushka dolls are wooden nested dolls made so that each doll fits inside the next largest one. If, in an entire collection of eight dolls, the largest weighs 32 ounces, and each weighs 2 ounces more than the one immediately preceding it in size, what does the entire set weigh?

25. Arrange the four aces, four kings, four queens, and four jacks of an ordinary bridge deck so that there is exactly one ace, king, queen, and jack in each row, column, and diagonal of a 4×4 square and so that there is exactly one spade, heart, diamond, and club in each row, column, and diagonal of the square. (For help, read "Behold! A Magic Square" by J. Lott.)

26. In the game of Life, Jose had to pay $1500 when he was married; then he lost half of the money that he had left. Next, he paid half of the money that he had for a house. When the game was stopped, he had $3000 left. With how much money did he start?

*27. Ten women are fishing all in a row in a boat. One seat in the center of the boat is empty. The five women in the front of the boat want to change seats with the five women in the back of the boat. A person can move from her seat to the next empty seat or she can step over one person without capsizing the boat. What is the minimum number of moves needed for the five women in front to change places with the five in back?

Review Problems

28. List the terms to complete a possible pattern.
    (a) 3, 6, 9, 12, 15, 18, _____, _____, _____
    (b) 1, 2, 3, 2, 9, 2, 27, 2, 81, 2, ____, ____, ____
29. Find the nth term for the sequence 22, 32, 42, 52, ...
30. How many terms are in the following sequence? 3, 7, 11, 15, 19, . . . , 83
31. Find the sums of the terms in the sequence in Problem 30.

LABORATORY ACTIVITY

Place a half-dollar, a quarter, and a nickel in position A as shown in the figure. Try to move these coins, one at a time, to position C. At no time may a larger coin be placed on a smaller coin. Coins may be placed in position B. How many moves does it take? Now, add a penny to the pile and see how many moves it takes. This is a simple case of the famous Tower of Hanoi problem, in which ancient Brahman priests were required to move a pile of 64 disks of decreasing size, after which the world would end. How long would this take at a rate of one move per second?

Section 1-3

Using a Calculator as a Problem-Solving Tool

Calculators depend on the user knowing how and when to perform desired computations. Different calculators work in different ways, and there are many features that we must know to obtain maximum usage from the calculator. In this section, we discuss features of calculators and give some examples and problems appropriate for calculators. Calculator problems are marked with a calculator symbol in the problem sets throughout the text. Since there are vast differences in the calculator models available, the following discussion lists some of the features to be considered before purchasing a calculator.

Physically, the calculator should have an easily accessible off–on switch. The position of the keys on the keyboard may vary, but they should be adequately spaced and large enough that fingers hit no more than one key at a time. Separate $\boxed{\text{CLEAR}}$ and $\boxed{\text{CLEAR ENTRY}}$ keys are desirable. The display should have at least an eight-digit readout. The user must decide whether the light-emitting diode (LED) or the liquid crystal display (LCD) is best for a given purpose. Consideration should be given to solar-powered calculators or calculators with long-life batteries.

If you have a calculator and are unfamiliar with its features, we suggest that you use it as you read the remainder of this section.

TYPE OF LOGIC

The type of logic built into a calculator determines how a computation is entered into the calculator. For example, the most natural way to compute $2 + 4 \cdot 5 - 4 \div 2$ is to enter the computation on a calculator exactly as it is written. With different types of logic, this may or may not produce the correct result. The order in which operations are done in mathematics is very important, and you must be familiar with how your calculator works if you are to compute correctly.

Algebraic Logic On some calculators with algebraic logic, the calculator processes the operations in the order in which they are entered. For example,

$$\boxed{2}\,\boxed{+}\,\boxed{4}\,\boxed{\times}\,\boxed{5}\,\boxed{-}\,\boxed{4}\,\boxed{\div}\,\boxed{2}\,\boxed{=}$$

would be evaluated as

$6 \cdot 5 - 4 \div 2$

then as

$30 - 4 \div 2$

and finally as

$26 \div 2 = 13$

However, multiplications and divisions should be done in order from left to right before additions and subtractions, and thus the correct solution to the problem $2 + 4 \cdot 5 - 4 \div 2$ is $2 + 20 - 2 = 22 - 2 = 20$. Algebraic logic is especially disturbing when we try a computation like $\frac{1}{2} + \frac{1}{4}$ by pressing the keys in the order given—that is, $\boxed{1}\,\boxed{\div}\,\boxed{2}\,\boxed{+}\,\boxed{1}\,\boxed{\div}\,\boxed{4}\,\boxed{=}$. A calculator with this type of logic will evaluate $\frac{1}{2} + \frac{1}{4}$ as 0.375 rather than 0.75. (Do you see why?) Algebraic logic is used in many models and is adequate if users are aware of the order in which operations must be performed.

algebraic operating
system

Many calculators with algebraic logic also include a feature called an **algebraic operating system.** It evaluates expressions inside parentheses first, then multiplications and divisions, and then additions and subtractions. For example, in the problem $2 + 4 \cdot 5 - 4 \div 2$, if $\boxed{2}\ \boxed{+}\ \boxed{4}$ is entered, the calculator will not perform the addition. If $\boxed{2}\ \boxed{+}\ \boxed{4}\ \boxed{\times}$ is entered, no calculations will be completed. After $\boxed{2}\ \boxed{+}\ \boxed{4}\ \boxed{\times}\ \boxed{5}\ \boxed{-}$ is entered, the display will show 22. In other words, the calculator performs 4×5 before adding 2. A calculator with the algebraic operating system feature will complete the original problem $2 + 4 \cdot 5 - 4 \div 2$ and give the desired answer of 20 if the computation is entered in the order it is written and the $\boxed{=}$ key is pressed.

Reverse Polish Notation On a calculator that uses Reverse Polish Notation (RPN), all operations are entered after the numbers have been entered. For example, to find $2 + 4$ on a machine that uses RPN, both 2 and 4 must be entered before the operation of addition. There is an $\boxed{\text{ENTER}}$ key on a calculator with RPN. To compute $2 + 4$, the keys are pressed as follows.

$$\boxed{2}\ \boxed{\text{ENTER}}\ \boxed{4}\ \boxed{+}$$

The display shows 6. No $\boxed{=}$ key is necessary since the computation is completed when the operation key is pressed. The absence of an $\boxed{=}$ key is the easiest way to identify a calculator with Reverse Polish Notation. Some of the most advanced scientific calculators utilize RPN, but their use is not recommended for elementary schools.

DECIMAL NOTATION

The calculator should have a floating decimal point. For example, when $\boxed{1}\ \boxed{\div}\ \boxed{3}\ \boxed{=}$ is entered, the display should show 0.3333333, rather than 0.33 as some displays do on fixed-point machines. Be aware of how a calculator rounds decimals, if it does. For example, in $\boxed{2}\ \boxed{\div}\ \boxed{3}\ \boxed{=}$, the display with a floating decimal may show 0.6666666 or 0.6666667. If the display shows 0.6666667, the round-off is apparent. If it shows 0.6666666, then we can multiply by 3 and observe the result, which may be either 1.9999998, 1.9999999, or 2. If 1.9999998 appears, there is no round-off by the calculator. If 1.9999999 or 2 appears, there is an internal round-off.

Also, when considering decimal notation, we should determine if the calculator uses scientific notation and, if so, how it works. In scientific notation, a number like 238,000 is written as a product of a number, greater than or equal to 1 but less than 10, times a power of 10. Thus, $238,000 = 2.38 \times 10^5$. The owner's manual should be consulted to see how scientific notation is displayed.

ERROR INDICATOR

There should be some signal on the calculator to indicate when an "illegal" operation is entered. For example, $\boxed{1}\ \boxed{\div}\ \boxed{0}\ \boxed{=}$ should cause the display to show an error. This indicator should also show when the computing limit of the calculator is exceeded.

SPECIAL KEYS

There are several special keys that are convenient. The first of these is the constant key, $\boxed{\text{K}}$, which allows an operation to be repeated without pressing all the keys each time. For example, the calculator might be designed so that if $\boxed{7}$ $\boxed{+}$ $\boxed{\text{K}}$ is entered, then 7 is added to whatever appears on the display each time $\boxed{=}$ is pressed. Some machines have constants built into them rather than a separate constant key. In such cases, the owner's manual should be consulted.

The second of the convenient special keys is the change-of-sign key, $\boxed{+/-}$. This allows for the entry of negative numbers. Normally, each number entered into a calculator is positive. Pressing $\boxed{3}$ $\boxed{+/-}$ changes 3 to $^-3$. It is desirable that the negative sign immediately precede a number to denote a negative number rather than leaving a space between the sign and the number, as is done on some calculators.

The third and fourth special keys are the parentheses keys, $\boxed{(}$ and $\boxed{)}$. With parentheses keys, operations may be ordered as desired. A calculator with parentheses keys will perform operations inside the parentheses before any others. For example, there is no confusion in the computation $2 + 4 \cdot 5 - 4 \div 2$ if parentheses are added as shown: $2 + (4 \cdot 5) - (4 \div 2)$.

The fifth special key is the percent key, $\boxed{\%}$. This key may operate in a variety of ways, depending on the calculator. It may change a percent to a decimal. For example, pressing $\boxed{6}$ $\boxed{\%}$ may give 0.06 on the display. On other machines, the $\boxed{\%}$ key may be a function key. For example, pressing $\boxed{2}$ $\boxed{\times}$ $\boxed{3}$ $\boxed{\%}$ may yield 0.06 without using the $\boxed{=}$ key. If the $\boxed{=}$ key is used, the display might show 2.06, which is $2 + 2(3\%)$. You should carefully check how the $\boxed{\%}$ key operates.

For work in this text, the y-to-the-x-power key, $\boxed{y^x}$, is very important. It raises y to the power of x. For example, pressing $\boxed{2}$ $\boxed{y^x}$ $\boxed{1}$ $\boxed{0}$ $\boxed{=}$ yields 1024, which is 2^{10}.

Other keys that may be convenient are $\boxed{\sqrt{}}$, the square-root key, and $\boxed{x^2}$, the squaring key. Numerous other keys are available for very little cost and may be useful, depending on individual needs.

MEMORY

The memory feature is particularly important in using the calculator. Many calculators use a two-key memory system—$\boxed{\text{STO}}$ for storing a displayed number in the memory and $\boxed{\text{RCL}}$ for recalling a number from the memory. This arrangement is adequate for most uses. Other machines have four-key memories. These are usually memory-plus, $\boxed{\text{M}+}$, which allows addition to be performed on the content of a memory register, memory-minus, $\boxed{\text{M}--}$, which does subtraction from the content of a memory register, memory recall, $\boxed{\text{MR}}$, and memory clear, $\boxed{\text{MC}}$.

OTHER CONSIDERATIONS

There are many other considerations involved in choosing calculators. Among these are size, shape, and weight of the machine; power source, cost, durability, and warranty; and reliability of the vender and/or manufacturer. These are individual items on which the user must decide.

Calculators can be invaluable in problem solving and can be used to reinforce mathematical learning. One problem-solving strategy that lends itself well to a calculator is guess and check. In spite of the implication in the Hi & Lois cartoon, guessing can play an important role in mathematics.

HI & LOIS

PROBLEM 10

Sara and David were reading the same novel. When Sara asked David what page he was reading, he replied that the product of the page number he was reading and the next page number was 98,282. On what page was David reading?

UNDERSTANDING THE PROBLEM We know that the product of the page number on which David was reading and the next page number is 98,282. We are asked to find the number of the page on which David was reading.

DEVISING A PLAN Adjacent pages must have consecutive numbers. If we denote the page number David was on by x, then the next page number is $x + 1$. The product of these page numbers is 98,282, so we write the equation as $x \cdot (x + 1) = 98{,}282$. The solution to this equation is not easily recognizable. To solve the equation, we use the *guess and check* strategy. A calculator is used as a tool to multiply various consecutive numbers, trying to obtain the product 98,282. Each new guess should be based on the information obtained from previous trials.

CARRYING OUT THE PLAN Table 1-14 shows a series of guesses.

Table 1-14

x	$x + 1$	$x \cdot (x + 1)$
100	101	$100 \cdot 101$, or 10,100
200	201	$200 \cdot 201$, or 40,200
300	301	$300 \cdot 301$, or 90,300
400	401	$400 \cdot 401$, or 160,400

From Table 1-14, we see that the desired page number must be closer to 300 than 400. Checking $x = 310$ yields $310 \cdot 311 = 96{,}410$, which shows that 310 is too small for the solution. Successive trials reveal that $313 \cdot 314 = 98{,}282$, so David was reading page 313.

LOOKING BACK An alternate solution is possible using the concept of square root. Consequently, the desired page number is close to the number that, when multiplied by itself, yields the product 98,282. This number is called the *square root* of 98,282. Using a calculator, we press the keys ⑨⑧②⑧②√. This yields 313.4996. Thus, a good guess for the desired page number is 313.

PROBLEM 11

Would you rather work for a month (31 days) and get $1,000,000 or be paid 1¢ the first day, 2¢ the second day, 4¢ the third day, and so on, but be allowed to keep only the amount that would be paid on the 31st day?

UNDERSTANDING THE PROBLEM Because we know that the wages are $1,000,000 for 31 days' work under the first option, we must compute the amount of pay under the second option. If 1¢ is paid for the first day, 2¢ for the second day, 4¢ for the third day, and so on, we need to find the amount paid on the 31st day. Then we can determine the better plan.

DEVISING A PLAN One strategy may be to build a table and look for a pattern for the amount of pay for each day. Table 1-15 shows a pattern for the second pay plan.

Table 1-15

Day	Amount of Pay in Cents
1	1
2	$2 = 2^1$
3	$4 = 2^2$
4	$8 = 2^3$
5	$16 = 2^4$
6	$32 = 2^5$
⋮	⋮
31	?

From Table 1-15, we see that the pay for consecutive days generates a geometric sequence with ratio 2. The exponent in each case is one less than the number of the day. Thus, the amount of money for the 31st day is 2^{30} cents. To see how great a number 2^{30} is, a calculator could be used. This number could then be converted to dollars and compared with $1,000,000 to determine which is greater.

CARRYING OUT THE PLAN Determining the value of 2^{30} can be done in various ways using a calculator. If the calculator has a $\boxed{y^x}$ key, which allows the user to raise numbers to powers, then 2^{30} could be determined by pressing ②$\boxed{y^x}$③⓪=. If the $\boxed{y^x}$ key is not present and the calculator has a constant feature, then that feature could be used. Another way is to use the calculator to compute $2^{10} = 1024$ and then compute $2^{30} = 2^{10} \cdot 2^{10} \cdot 2^{10} = 1024 \cdot 1024 \cdot 1024 = 1,073,741,824$. Depending on the calculator, this result may be displayed in scientific notation; for example, the calculator might read 1.0737 09, which means $1.0737 \cdot 10^9$, or 1,073,700,000. Notice that numbers in scientific notation are rounded. To convert this number of cents to dollars, we divide by 100 and see that the rounded amount received on the 31st day is much greater than $1,000,000; hence, the second option is better.

LOOKING BACK An alternate problem might be to consider which option is better if we keep only the money on the 25th day. How many days are needed before the second option is more attractive than $1,000,000? What if we are allowed to keep all the money from each day? How do the above answers change?

PROBLEM SET 1-3

1. (a) Place the digits 1, 2, 4, 5, and 7 in the boxes so that in (i) the greatest product is obtained and in (ii) the greatest quotient is obtained.

   (i) ☐ ☐ ☐   (ii) ☐ ☐) ☐ ☐ ☐
       × ☐ ☐

   (b) Use the same digits as in (a) to obtain (i) the least product and (ii) the least quotient.
2. Determine the best savings plans of those listed below.
   (a) $10 a day for a year
   (b) $120 a week for a year
   (c) 25¢ an hour for a year
   (d) 1¢ a minute for a year
3. Vera spent $16.33 for three of the items listed below. Which three did she buy?

   $5.77, $3.99, $4.33, $5.87, $6.47

4. Pick your favorite single-digit number greater than zero. Multiply it by 259. Now multiply your result by 429. What is your answer? Try it with other numbers. Why does it work?
5. Use your calculator's constant feature, if it has one, to count the number of terms in the following sequence.

   1, 8, 15, 22, . . . , 113

6. If 0.2 ounce of catsup is used on each of 22 billion hamburgers, how many 16-ounce bottles are needed?
7. How many natural numbers that are evenly divisible by 5,230,010 can be displayed on your calculator without using scientific notation?
8. Suppose the ⑦, ⑧, ⑨, and ÷ keys on your calculator do not work. Devise ways to perform the following computations on your calculator.
   (a) 756 + 183   (b) 155 ÷ 31
9. Suppose your ⑦, ⑧, and + keys are broken; how could you make your calculator display 73?
10. Suppose you could spend $10 every minute, night and day. How much could you spend in a year? (Assume 365 days in a year.)

11. How many times does your heart beat in each of the following?
    (a) One minute   (b) One hour
    (c) One day   (d) One week
    (e) One year ($365\frac{1}{4}$ days)
12. Suppose a number is entered on the calculator. Then it is divided by 25, 18 is subtracted from it, and it is multiplied by 37. If the answer is 259, what is the original number?
13. The number 5! (read "five factorial") is defined to be $5 \cdot 4 \cdot 3 \cdot 2 \cdot 1$, and $4! = 4 \cdot 3 \cdot 2 \cdot 1$. Evaluate 10!. If your calculator has a factorial key, $\boxed{x!}$, work the exercise with and without using the key.
14. Find 21 numbers that divide into 108 with zero remainder.
15. If your calculator displays .33333333 when 1 is divided by 3, what other division could be performed to display .03333333?
16. The distance around the world is approximately 40,000 kilometers. Approximately how many people holding hands would it take to stretch around the world?
17. The following is one version of a game called NIM. Two players and one calculator are needed. Player 1 presses ① or ② and +. Player 2 presses ① or ② and +. The players take turns until the target number of 21 is reached. The first player to make the display read 21 is the winner. Determine a strategy for deciding who always wins.
18. Try a game of NIM (see Problem 17) using the digits 1, 2, 3, and 4, with a target number of 104. The first player to reach 104 wins. What is the winning strategy?
19. Try a game of NIM using the digits 3, 5, and 7, with target number 73. The first player to exceed 73 loses. What is the winning strategy?
20. In the game of NIM in Problem 17, two players and one calculator are needed. Player 1 presses ① or ② and +. Player 2 presses ① or ② and +, and both try to reach the target number of 21. Now play Reverse NIM. Instead of +, use −. Put 21 on the display. Let the new target number be 0. Determine a strategy for winning Reverse NIM.

21. Try Reverse NIM using the digits 1, 2, and 3, and starting with 24 on the display. (See Problem 20.) The target number is 0. What is the winning strategy?

22. Try Reverse NIM using the digits 3, 5, and 7, and starting with 73 on the display. The first player to display a negative number loses. What is the winning strategy?

Review Problems

23. List the terms to complete a possible pattern.
(a) 7, 14, 21, 28, _____, _____, _____
(b) 4, 1, 8, 1, 12, _____, _____, _____

24. Find the nth term for the sequence

12, 32, 52, 72, ...

25. How many terms are in the following sequence?

6, 10, 14, 18, . . . , 86

26. Find the sums of the terms in the sequences in Problem 23.

27. If someone on the diet given in the Blondie cartoon below weighed 110 pounds at the end of 4 months, how much did the person weigh at the beginning of the diet? Assume that the pattern given in the cartoon continues.

BLONDIE

Reprinted with special permission of King Features Syndicate, Inc.

CALCULATOR TIME OUT

Many words can be formed when the calculator display is turned upside down. For example, to become better acquainted with your calculator, press 0.7734 and turn the calculator upside down. The digits and the letters they represent are given below.

$0 \rightarrow$ O	$3 \rightarrow$ E	$7 \rightarrow$ L
$1 \rightarrow$ I	$4 \rightarrow$ H	$8 \rightarrow$ B
$2 \rightarrow$ Z	$5 \rightarrow$ S	$9 \rightarrow$ G

An example of a small vocabulary list is given below.

338 → BEE	35007 → LOOSE
37818 → BIBLE	35380 → OBESE
379908 → BOGGLE	0.140 → OHIO
37819173 → ELIGIBLE	372215 → SIZZLE
35339 → GEESE	491375 → SLEIGH
5379919 → GIGGLES	45075 → SLOSH
378809 → GOBBLE	0.02 → ZOO
3781937 → LEGIBLE	

BRAIN TEASER

What holiday is suggested
by the following array?

A	B	C	D	E
F	G	H	I	J
K	M	N	O	P
Q	R	S	T	U
V	W	X	Y	Z

It is possible to make up word problems to make your calculator talk. Four examples are given. Make up four new words and four new word problems.

1. There is a set of children's stories known as Mother _____ Rhymes. To find the answer, complete the following, turn the calculator upside down, and read the display.

    $$67845 - 32839 =$$

2. Is 13632 greater than or less than 19169? Work the following problem, turn the calculator upside down, and read the display.

    $$19169 - 13632 =$$

3. In the Winter Olympics, one of the most dangerous events is the _____ race. Complete the following problem, turn the calculator upside down, and read the display.

    $$144 \times 349{,}832 =$$

4. The fire in the burning building reached 418 degrees; 128 firemen showed up to battle the blaze but were not successful because they forgot their _____. Multiply these numbers and turn your calculator upside down to find out what they forgot.

SOLUTION TO THE PRELIMINARY PROBLEM

UNDERSTANDING THE PROBLEM Two people were surprised to learn that they had shaken the same number of hands at a party. The problem is to help them figure out if this result is unusual. We assume that some people shake hands at a party, no people shake their own hands, and no people shake the same person's hand twice.

DEVISING A PLAN To aid in solving the problem, we look at simpler, special cases in which we know the number of people at the party. The problem is not meaningful if a "party" consists of only one person. In the event that there are two people at a party, they either do or do not shake hands with each other. Therefore, each shakes either one hand or no hands.

Next, consider a party with three people. Is it possible that no two of these people shake the same number of hands? If one person shakes no hands, then the other two people must shake hands with each other. (Why?) This can be shown as in Figure 1-13(a), where dots A, B, and C represent people and a segment connecting dots represents a handshake between two people.

In Figure 1-13(a), A and B shake 1 hand each and, hence, the same number of hands. Another possibility is that C shakes hands with one of A or B, as shown in Figure 1-13(b). In this case, A and C each shake 1 hand. The other

Figure 1-13

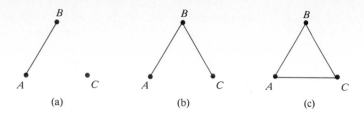

possibility is that *A*, *B*, and *C* shake each person's hand as shown in Figure 1-13(c). That is, each person shakes 2 hands.

This approach becomes more and more complicated when the number of people at a party increases. Thus, we try an alternate approach. Is it possible that in a party of 3 people, everybody shakes a different number of hands? The least number of hands that one could shake is 0, and the most is 2. If everybody shook a different number of hands, the number of handshakes corresponding to each of the three people would have to be 0, 1, and 2. However, that would mean that some person shook 2 hands; that is, the person shook hands with everybody else at the party. This is impossible because one of the people shook no one's hand. Therefore, it is impossible that everyone shakes a different number of hands. A similar approach should work for a party of four people, or, in general, for a party of *n* people.

CARRYING OUT THE PLAN Consider a party of *n* people. Since no people shake their own hands, we know that the most number of hands anyone can shake is $n - 1$. The least number of hands that anyone can shake is 0. If each person shook a different number of hands, then the number of handshakes corresponding to the people in the party would have to be *n* different numbers: $0, 1, 2, \ldots, n - 1$. This means that someone shook $n - 1$ hands, which could only happen if that person shook everybody else's hand. However, this is impossible because there is a person who shakes no one's hand. Therefore, it is not surprising that at a party, two people should have shaken hands with the same number of people. Some two people had to shake the same number of hands.

LOOKING BACK As an extension of this problem, we could consider a party attended only by couples. If, in addition to the rules above for handshakes, we suppose that no partners in a couple shake hands, is it possible that every two people at the party shake a different number of hands?

CHAPTER OUTLINE

I. Mathematical patterns
   A. Patterns are an important part of problem solving.
   B. Patterns are used in **inductive reasoning** to form conjectures. A **conjecture** is a statement that is thought to be true but has not yet been proven.
   C. A **sequence** is a group of terms in a definite order.

1. **Arithmetic sequence:** Each successive term is obtained from the previous one by the addition of a fixed number called the **difference.**
2. **Geometric sequence:** Each successive term is obtained from its predecessor by multiplying it by a fixed number called the **ratio.**
3. Finding differences for a sequence is one technique for finding the next terms.

II. Problem solving
   A. Problem solving should be guided by the following four-step process:
      1. Understanding the Problem
      2. Devising a Plan
      3. Carrying Out the Plan
      4. Looking Back
   B. Important problem-solving strategies include:
      1. Look for a pattern.
      2. Examine related problems and determine if the same technique can be applied.
      3. Examine a simpler or special case of the problem to gain insight to the solution of the original problem.
      4. Make a table, diagram, or model.
      5. Write an equation.
      6. Use guess and check.
      7. Work backwards.
      8. Identify a subgoal.
   C. Beware of mind sets!

III. Features of calculators
   A. Types of logic
      1. Algebraic logic
         a. Without algebraic operating system
         b. With algebraic operating system
      2. Reverse Polish Notation
   B. Special keys
      1. Constant key
      2. Change-of-sign key
      3. Parentheses keys
      4. Percent key
      5. y-to-the-x-power key
      6. Square-root key
      7. Memory keys

CHAPTER TEST

1. List the terms that complete a possible pattern in each of the following.
   (a) 0, 1, 3, 6, 10, ——, ——, ——
   (b) 52, 47, 42, 37, ——, ——, ——
   (c) 6400, 3200, 1600, 800, ——, ——, ——
   (d) 1, 2, 3, 5, 8, 13, ——, ——, ——
   (e) 2, 5, 8, 11, 14, ——, ——, ——
   (f) 1, 4, 16, 64, ——, ——, ——
   (g) 1, ——, ——, 125
   (h) 0, 4, 8, 12, ——, ——, ——
   (i) 1, 8, 27, 64, ——, ——, ——

2. Classify each of the sequences in Problem 1 as arithmetic, geometric, or neither.

3. Find the nth term in each of the following.
   (a) 5, 8, 11, 14, . . .   (b) 1, 8, 27, 64, . . .
   (c) 3, 9, 27, 81, 243, . . .

4. Find the first five terms of the sequences with nth term given as follows.
   (a) $3n + 2$ (b) $n^2 + n$ (c) $4n - 1$

5. Find the following sums.
   (a) $2 + 4 + 6 + 8 + 10 + \cdots + 200$
   (b) $51 + 52 + 53 + 54 + \cdots + 151$

6. Complete the following magic square; that is, complete the square so that the sum in each row, column, and diagonal is the same.

16	3	2	13
	10		
9		7	12
4		14	

7. How many years are there between the fifth day of the year 45 B.C. and the fifth day of the year A.D. 45?

8. A worm is at the bottom of a glass that is 20 cm deep. Each day the worm crawls up 3 cm and each night it slides back 1 cm. How long will it take the worm to climb out of the glass?

9. How many people can be seated at 12 square tables lined up end to end if each table used individually holds four persons?

10. A shirt and a tie sell for $9.50. The shirt costs $5.50 more than the tie. What is the cost of the tie?

11. If fence posts are to be placed 5 m apart, how many posts are needed for 100 m of fence?

12. One hundred twenty-nine players entered a single-elimination handball tournament. In the first round

of play, the top-seeded player received a bye, and the remaining 128 players played in 64 matches so that 65 players entered the second round of play. How many matches must be played to determine the tournament champion?

13. Given the six numbers 3, 5, 7, 9, 11, and 13, pick five of these which, when multiplied, give 19,305.

14. If a complete turn of a car tire moves a car forward 6 feet, how many turns of a tire occur before a tire goes off its 50,000-mile warranty?

SELECTED BIBLIOGRAPHY

Selected references are given. An excellent bibliography is available in *Problem Solving in School Mathematics,* 1980 Yearbook, published by the National Council of Teachers of Mathematics.

Bartalo, D. "Calculators and Problem-Solving Instruction: They Were Made for Each Other." *Arithmetic Teacher* 30 (January 1983):18–21.

Bernard, J. "Creating Problem-Solving Experiences with Ordinary Arithmetic Processes." *Arithmetic Teacher* 30 (September 1982):52–53.

Billstein, R. "Checkerboard Mathematics." *The Mathematics Teacher* 86 (December 1975):640–646.

Bruni, J. "Problem Solving for the Primary Grades." *Arithmetic Teacher* 29 (February 1982):10–15.

Burns, M. "How to Teach Problem Solving." *Arithmetic Teacher* 29 (February 1982):46–49.

Butts, T. "In Praise of Trial and Error." *The Mathematics Teacher* 78 (March 1985):167–173.

Dolan, D., and J. Williamson. *Teaching Problem-Solving Strategies.* Menlo Park, Calif.: Addison-Wesley, 1983.

Easterday, K., and C. Clothiaux. "Problem-Solving Opportunities." *Arithmetic Teacher* 32 (January 1985):18–20.

Gathany, T. "Involving Students in Problem Solving." *The Mathematics Teacher* 72 (November 1979):617–621.

Green, D. "Ant, Aardvark and Fudge Brownies." *Arithmetic Teacher* 27 (March 1979):38–39.

Greenes, C., J. Gregory, and D. Seymour. *Successful Problem-Solving Techniques.* Palo Alto, Calif.: Creative Publications, 1977.

Greenes, C., and L. Schulman. "Developing Problem-Solving Ability with Multiple-Condition Problems." *Arithmetic Teacher* 30 (October 1982):18–21.

Greenes, C., R. Spungin, and J. Dombrowski. *Problemmathics.* Palo Alto, Calif.: Creative Publications, 1977.

Greenes, C., et al. *Techniques of Problem Solving (TOPS) Problem Card Decks.* Palo Alto, Calif.: Seymour, 1980.

Halmos, P. "The Heart of Mathematics." *American Mathematical Monthly* 87 (July 1980):519–524.

Hecht, A. "Environmental Problem Solving." *Arithmetic Teacher* 27 (December 1979):42–43.

Kantowski, M. "The Microcomputer and Problem Solving." *Arithmetic Teacher* 30 (February 1983):20–21, 58–59.

Kenney, M., and S. Bezuszka. "A Square Share: Problem Solving with Squares." *The Mathematics Teacher* 77 (September 1984):414–420.

Krulik, S. "Problem Solving: Some Considerations." *Arithmetic Teacher* 25 (December 1977):51–52.

Krulik, S., and R. Reys, eds. *Problem Solving in School Mathematics,* 1980 Yearbook of the National Council of Teachers of Mathematics. Reston, Va.: National Council of Teachers of Mathematics, 1980.

Krulik, S., and J. Rudnick. *Problem Solving: A Handbook for Teachers.* Boston: Allyn and Bacon, 1980.

Krulik, S., and J. Rudnick. "Strategy Gaming and Problem Solving—An Instructional Pair Whose Time Has Come." *Arithmetic Teacher* 31 (December 1983):26–29.

Krulik, S., and J. Rudnick. "Suggestions for Teaching Problem Solving—A Baker's Dozen." *School Science and Mathematics* 81 (January 1981):37–42.

Laing, R. "Extending Problem-Solving Skills." *The Mathematics Teacher* 78 (January 1985):36–44.

Lappan, G., et al. "Powers and Patterns: Problem Solving with Calculators." *Arithmetic Teacher* 30 (October 1982):42–44.

LeBlanc. J. "Teaching Textbook Story Problems." *Arithmetic Teacher* 29 (February 1982):52–54.

Lee, K. "Guiding Young Children in Successful Problem Solving." *Arithmetic Teacher* 29 (January 1982): 15–17.

Liedtke, W. "The Young Child as a Problem Solver." *The Arithmetic Teacher* 25 (April 1977):333–338.

Linquist, M. "Problem Solving with Five Easy Pieces." *Arithmetic Teacher* 25 (November 1977):7–10.

Lott, J. "Behold! A Magic Square." *The Arithmetic Teacher* 24 (March 1977):228–229.

Lyon, B. "Using Magic Borders to Generate Magic Squares." *The Mathematics Teacher* 77 (March 1984):223–226.

Meyer, C., and T. Sallee. *Make It Simpler: A Practical Guide to Problem Solving in Mathematics.* Menlo Park, Calif.: Addison-Wesley, 1983.

Polya, G. *How To Solve It.* Princeton, N.J.: Princeton University Press, 1957.

Schaaf, O. "Teaching Problem-Solving Skills." *The Mathematics Teacher* 77 (December 1984):694–699.

Slesnick, T. "Problem Solving: Some Thoughts and Activities." *Arithmetic Teacher* 31 (March 1984):41–43.

Spencer, J., and F. Lester. "Second Graders Can Be Problem Solvers." *Arithmetic Teacher* 29 (September 1981):15–17.

Suydam, M. "Untangling Clues from Research on Problem Solving." In *Problem Solving in School Mathematics,* 1980 Yearbook of the National Council of Teachers of Mathematics. S. Krulik and R. Reys, eds. Reston, Va.: National Council of Teachers of Mathematics, 1980.

Thompson, A. "On Patterns, Conjectures, and Proof: Developing Students' Mathematical Thinking." *Arithmetic Teacher* 33 (September 1985):20–23.

Wheatley, C., and G. Wheatley. "Problem Solving in the Primary Grades." *Arithmetic Teacher* 31 (April 1984):22–25.

Whitin, D. "Patterns with Square Numbers." *Arithmetic Teacher* 27 (December 1979):38–39.

Wickelgren, W. *How to Solve Problems.* San Francisco: Freeman, 1974.

Worth, J. "Problem Solving in the Intermediate Grades: Helping Your Students Learn to Solve Problems." *Arithmetic Teacher* 29 (February 1982):16–19.

Zalewski, D. "Magic Triangles—More Discoveries!" *Arithmetic Teacher* 27 (September 1979):46–47.

Zur, M., and F. Silverman. "Problem Solving for Teachers." *Arithmetic Teacher* 28 (October 1980):48–50.

Zweng, M. "The Problem of Solving Story Problems." *Arithmetic Teacher* 27 (September 1979):2–3.

CHAPTER 2

Sets, Functions, and Logic

Preliminary Problem

Mike Angelo's art class was examining colors obtained by mixing the primary colors of pigment, that is, red, blue, and yellow. According to the pigments mixed (or left alone), the entire class was separated into seven smaller groups: red, blue, yellow, purple, green, orange, and brown. When Mike asked his students how they mixed their colors, he obtained the following information: 20 used red pigment, 11 used red but no blue pigment, 27 used blue or yellow pigments, 6 made an orange color using red and yellow but no blue pigments, 3 made a brown color using red, blue, and yellow pigments, and 2 made a green color using blue and yellow but no red pigments. How many students were in the class?

Introduction

It was Georg Cantor, in the years 1871–1884, who created a new and special area of mathematics called set theory. His theories have had a profound effect on mathematical research and on the teaching of mathematics.

The language of set theory was introduced into elementary schools in the 1960s in the post-Sputnik era. It contained words such as *set, subset, union,* and *intersection.* In the 1970s, numerous people felt that the new language and symbolism caused confusion for children, as well as for teachers and other adults. The cartoon illustrates the feelings of many of these people.

© 1965 United Feature Syndicate, Inc.

However, the basic set concepts clarify many mathematical ideas and are used in elementary school texts.

Section 2-1

set / elements / members

Describing Sets

In mathematics, a **set** is any collection or group of objects. The individual objects in a set are called **elements,** or **members,** of the set. If we consider the set of letters in the English alphabet, each letter is an element of that set. We use braces to enclose the elements of the set. The set of letters of the English alphabet can be written as

$\{a, b, c, d, e, f, g, h, i, j, k, l, m, n, o, p, q, r, s, t, u, v, w, x, y, z\}$

The order in which the elements are written makes no difference, and each element is listed only once. For example, the set of letters in the word "book" could be written as $\{b, o, k\}$, $\{o, b, k\}$, or $\{k, o, b\}$.

well defined   For a given set to be useful in mathematics, it must be **well defined.** This means that if we are given a set and some particular object, the object does

HISTORICAL NOTE

Georg Cantor, 1845–1918, was born in Russia and educated in Germany. Much of his professional life was spent at the University of Halle, now in East Germany. His later years were spent in controversy over his work on set theory.

or does not belong to the set. For example, the set of all citizens of Hong Kong who ate rice on January 1, 1987, is well defined. We may not know if a particular resident of Hong Kong ate rice or not, but we do know that person either did or did not.

It is often convenient to name a set using capital letters. For example, the set of letters of the English alphabet can be named as A (or any other capital letter). The set A of letters of the English alphabet is well defined. We know that m is an element of set A. This can be written in symbols as $m \in A$. The number 12 is not an element of A. This is written as $12 \notin A$.

natural numbers
counting numbers

We may use sets to define mathematical terms. For example, the set of **natural,** or **counting, numbers** is defined by the following.

$$N = \{1, 2, 3, 4, \ldots\}$$

set-builder notation

Sometimes the individual elements of a set are not known or they are too numerous to list. In these cases, the elements are indicated using **set-builder notation.** The set of animals in the San Diego Zoo can be written as

$$Z = \{x \mid x \text{ is an animal in the San Diego Zoo}\}$$

This is read, "Z is the set of all elements x such that x is an animal in the San Diego Zoo." The vertical line is read, "such that."

Example 2-1

Write the following sets using set-builder notation.

(a) $\{51, 52, 53, 54, \ldots, 498, 499\}$
(b) $\{2, 4, 6, 8, 10, \ldots\}$

Solution

(a) $\{x \mid x \text{ is a natural number greater than 50 and less than 500}\}$
(b) $\{x \mid x \text{ is an even natural number}\}$

equal sets

Two sets are **equal** if and only if they contain exactly the same elements. (An alternate definition of set equality is introduced later in this section.) The order in which the elements are listed does not matter. If A and B are equal, written $A = B$, then every element of A is an element of B, *and* every element of B is an element of A. If A does not equal B, we write $A \neq B$. Consider sets $D = \{1, 2, 3\}$, $E = \{2, 5, 1\}$, and $F = \{1, 2, 5\}$. Sets D and E are not equal. Sets E and F are equal.

ONE-TO-ONE CORRESPONDENCE

Even though sets D and E are not equal, the elements of the sets can be matched. As another example of sets that can be matched, consider the set of people $P = \{\text{Tomas, Dick, Mari}\}$ and the set of numbers $S = \{1, 2, 3\}$. Suppose that each person in P is to receive a number from S so that no two people receive the same number. One possible way to show that each person receives a number is to pair the elements of the two sets. Such a

one-to-one
correspondence

pairing is called a **one-to-one correspondence.** One way to exhibit a one-to-one correspondence is: Tomas ↔ 1, Dick ↔ 2, Mari ↔ 3. Another way is shown in Figure 2-1.

Figure 2-1

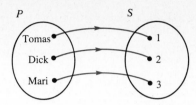

DEFINITION

> If the elements of sets A and B can be paired so that for each element of A there is exactly one element of B, and for each element of B there is exactly one element of A, then the two sets A and B are said to be in **one-to-one correspondence** (or matched).

Other possible one-to-one correspondences exist between the sets P and S given earlier. There are several schemes for exhibiting them. For example, all six possible one-to-one correspondences for sets P and S can be listed as follows.

(1) Tomas ↔ 1   (3) Tomas ↔ 2   (5) Tomas ↔ 3
    Dick ↔ 2   Dick ↔ 1   Dick ↔ 1
    Mari ↔ 3   Mari ↔ 3   Mari ↔ 2

(2) Tomas ↔ 1   (4) Tomas ↔ 2   (6) Tomas ↔ 3
    Dick ↔ 3   Dick ↔ 3   Dick ↔ 2
    Mari ↔ 2   Mari ↔ 1   Mari ↔ 1

It is not always possible to set up a one-to-one correspondence between two sets. For example, let $Q = \{$Tomas, Dick, Mari, Harry$\}$ and $S = \{1, 2, 3\}$. In any attempted one-to-one correspondence between Q and S, one person will be without a number. This is true regardless of how the elements are paired. One example of a pairing is

$Q = \{$Tomas, Dick, Mari, Harry$\}$
$\quad\quad\quad\updownarrow\quad\quad\updownarrow\quad\quad\updownarrow$
$S = \{\quad 1,\quad\quad 2,\quad\quad 3\quad\}$

In this case, we say that S has *fewer* elements than Q.

Suppose a room contains 20 chairs and one student is sitting in each chair with no one standing. There is a one-to-one correspondence between the set of chairs and the set of students in the room. In this case, the set of chairs and the set of students are **equivalent sets.**

equivalent sets

DEFINITION

> Two sets A and B are said to be **equivalent,** written $A \sim B$, if and only if there exists a one-to-one correspondence between the sets.

The term *equivalent* should not be confused with *equal*. The difference should be made clear by the following example.

Example 2-2

Let

$A = \{1, 2, 3, 4, 5\}$

$B = \{a, b, c\}$

$C = \{x, y, z\}$

$D = \{b, a, c\}$

Compare the sets using the terms *equal* and *equivalent*.

Solution

Sets A and B are not equivalent ($A \nsim B$) and not equal ($A \neq B$).
Sets A and C are not equivalent ($A \nsim C$) and not equal ($A \neq C$).
Sets A and D are not equivalent ($A \nsim D$) and not equal ($A \neq D$).
Sets B and C are equivalent ($B \sim C$), but not equal ($B \neq C$).
Sets B and D are equivalent ($B \sim D$) and equal ($B = D$).
Sets C and D are equivalent ($C \sim D$), but not equal ($C \neq D$).

Remark Observe that if two sets are equal, they are equivalent; however, if two sets are equivalent, they are not necessarily equal.

Consider the five sets $\{a, b\}$, $\{1, 2\}$, $\{x, y\}$, $\{b, a\}$, and $\{*, \#\}$. How are these sets related? They are equivalent to one another. In fact, they are equivalent in a special way; they share the property of "twoness." In mathematics, we say that these sets have the same cardinal number, namely, 2. The **cardinal number** of a set X, denoted by $n(X)$, indicates the number of elements in the set X. If $D = \{a, b, c\}$, we say that the cardinal number of D is 3 and write $n(D) = 3$.

cardinal number

Note that if A is equivalent to B, then A and B have the same cardinal number; that is, $n(A) = n(B)$. Also, if $n(A) = n(B)$, the two sets are equivalent, but not necessarily equal. Furthermore, if $A = B$, then $A \sim B$ and $n(A) = n(B)$.

finite set

A set is called a **finite set** if the number of elements in the set is zero or a natural number. For example, the set of letters in the English alphabet is a finite set because it contains exactly 26 elements. Another way to think of this is to say that the set of letters in the English alphabet can be put into a one-to-one correspondence with the set $\{1, 2, 3, \ldots, 26\}$. The entire set of natural numbers N is an example of an infinite set. An **infinite set** is a set that is not finite. A more formal definition of an infinite set is given in Problem 22 of Problem Set 2-1.

infinite set

ORDINAL NUMBERS

ordinal number

Cardinal numbers answer the question "How many?" **Ordinal numbers** are used to describe the relative position an element can occupy in an ordered set rather than the number of elements in the set. For example, we might say that Carla sits in the *fourth* row and she is reading page 87 of this book. These are examples of ordinal numbers, rather than cardinal numbers, because they refer to position or order. Ordinal numbers answer the question "Which one?"

MORE ABOUT SETS

empty set
null set

A set that contains no elements has cardinal number 0 and is called an **empty set,** or **null set.** The empty set is designated by the symbols $\varnothing$ or $\{\ \ \}$. The empty set is often incorrectly recorded as $\{\varnothing\}$. This set is not empty. It contains one element, namely, $\varnothing$. Likewise, $\{0\}$ does not represent the empty set.

Two examples of sets with no elements are the following.

$C = \{x \mid x$ was a female president of the United States before 1900$\}$

$D = \{x \mid x$ is a natural number less than 1$\}$

universal set / universe

The **universal set,** or the **universe,** is the set that contains all elements being considered in a given discussion. The universal set is denoted by U. While the empty set never changes, the universal set may vary from one discussion to another. For this reason, you should be aware of what the universal set is in any given problem. Suppose $U = \{x \mid x$ is a person living in California$\}$ and $F = \{x \mid x$ is a female living in California$\}$. The universal set and set F can be represented by a diagram. The universal set is usually indicated by a large rectangle, and particular sets are indicated by geometric figures inside

Venn diagram

the rectangle, as shown in Figure 2.2. This figure is an example of a **Venn diagram,** named after the Englishman John Venn, who used such diagrams to illustrate ideas in logic. The set of elements in the universe that are not in

complement

F is the set of males living in California and is called the **complement** of F.

Figure 2-2

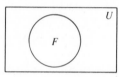

DEFINITION

> The **complement** of a set F, written $\bar{F}$, is the set of all elements in the universal set U that are not in F. $\bar{F} = \{x \mid x \in U$ and $x \notin F\}$.

Venn diagrams can also be used to represent complements. The shaded region in Figure 2-3 represents $\bar{F}$.

Figure 2-3

Example 2-3

(a) If $U = \{a, b, c, d\}$ and $B = \{c, d\}$, find: (i) $\bar{B}$; (ii) $\bar{U}$; (iii) $\bar{\varnothing}$.
(b) If $U = \{x \mid x$ is an animal in the zoo$\}$ and $S = \{x \mid x$ is a snake in the zoo$\}$, find $\bar{S}$.

Solution

(a) (i) $\bar{B} = \{a, b\}$ (ii) $\bar{U} = \varnothing$ (iii) $\bar{\varnothing} = U$
(b) Because the individual animals in the zoo are not known, $\bar{S}$ must be described using set-builder notation.

$\bar{S} = \{x \mid x$ is an animal in the zoo that is not a snake$\}$

SUBSETS

subset

Consider the sets $U = \{1, 2, 3, 4, 5, 6, 7, 8, 9, 10\}$, $A = \{1, 2, 3, 4, 5, 6\}$, and $B = \{2, 4, 6\}$. Notice that all the elements of B are contained in A. We say that B is a **subset** of A and write $B \subseteq A$. In general, we have the following definition.

DEFINITION

> B is a **subset** of A, written $B \subseteq A$, if and only if every element of B is also an element of A.

proper subset

This definition allows B to be equal to A. The definition is written with the phrase "if and only if," which means "if B is a subset of A, then every element of B is also an element of A, and if every element of B is also an element of A, then B is a subset of A." If both $A \subseteq B$ and $B \subseteq A$, then $A = B$.

If B is a subset of A and B is not equal to A, then B is called a **proper subset** of A, written $B \subset A$. This means that every element of B is contained in A and there exists at least one element of A that is not in B.

Example 2-4

Given that $U = \{1, 2, 3, 4, 5\}$, $D = \{1, 3, 5\}$, and $E = \{1, 3\}$:

(a) Which sets are subsets of each other?
(b) Which sets are proper subsets of each other?

Solution

(a) $D \subseteq U$, $E \subseteq U$, $E \subseteq D$, $D \subseteq D$, $E \subseteq E$, and $U \subseteq U$.
(b) $D \subset U$, $E \subset U$, and $E \subset D$.

When a set A is not a subset of another set B, we write $A \nsubseteq B$. To show that $A \nsubseteq B$, we must find at least one element of A that is not in B. If $A = \{1, 3, 5\}$ and $B = \{1, 2, 3\}$, then A is not a subset of B because there is an element—namely, 5—belonging to A but not to B. Likewise, $B \nsubseteq A$ because there exists an element—namely, 2—belonging to B but not to A. (Note that $\{2\} \subseteq \{1, 2\}$ and $2 \in \{1, 2\}$, but $\{2\} \notin \{1, 2\}$ and $2 \nsubseteq \{1, 2\}$.)

PROBLEM 1

Of which sets, if any, is the empty set a subset?

UNDERSTANDING THE PROBLEM It is not clear how the empty set fits the definition of a subset because there are no elements in the empty set that are elements of another set. The next question then might be, does the empty set being a subset of a set violate the definition of a subset?

DEVISING A PLAN To investigate this problem, we use the strategy of *looking at a special case*. For example, is it true that $\varnothing \subseteq \{1, 2\}$? Suppose $\varnothing \nsubseteq \{1, 2\}$. Then there must be some element in $\varnothing$ that is not in $\{1, 2\}$. Because the empty set has no elements, there cannot be an element in the empty set that is not in $\{1, 2\}$. Consequently, $\varnothing \nsubseteq \{1, 2\}$ is false, and therefore $\varnothing \subseteq \{1, 2\}$ is true. The same reasoning can be applied in the case of the empty set and any other set.

CARRYING OUT THE PLAN Suppose A is any set. To show that $\varnothing \not\subseteq A$, we must produce an element of $\varnothing$ that does not belong to A. Because the empty set has no elements, there can be no element in the empty set that is not in A. Therefore, it is false that $\varnothing \not\subseteq A$ and hence, the empty set is a subset of any set A.

LOOKING BACK In particular, we note that the empty set is a subset of itself. Investigate to see if the empty set is a proper subset of any set.

PROBLEM 2

A committee of senators consists of Abel, Baro, Carni, and Davis. Suppose each member of the committee has exactly one vote, and a simple majority is needed either to pass any measure or to reject any measure. If a measure is neither passed nor rejected, it is considered to be blocked and will be voted on again. Determine the number of ways that a measure could be passed or rejected and the number of ways that a measure could be blocked.

UNDERSTANDING THE PROBLEM A committee of the Senate consisting of four members—Abel, Baro, Carni, and Davis—requires a simple majority of votes either to pass or reject a measure. We are asked to determine how many ways the committee could pass or reject a proposal and how many ways the committee could block a proposal. To pass or reject a proposal, there must be a winning coalition of senators, that is, a group of people that can pass or reject the proposal, regardless of what the others, if any, do. To block a proposal, there must be a blocking coalition, that is, a group that can prevent any proposal from passing but at the same time does not have enough votes to reject the measure.

DEVISING A PLAN What is needed to solve the problem is a list of subsets of the set of senators. Any subset of the set of senators with three or four members will form a winning coalition. Any subset of the set of senators that contains exactly two members will form a blocking coalition.

CARRYING OUT THE PLAN To solve the problem, we must find all subsets of the set $S = \{$Abel, Baro, Carni, Davis$\}$ that have at least three elements and all subsets that have exactly two elements. For ease, we identify the members as follows: A—Abel, B—Baro, C—Carni, D—Davis. All the subsets are given below.

$\varnothing$	$\{A, B\}$	$\{A, B, C\}$	$\{A, B, C, D\}$
$\{A\}$	$\{A, C\}$	$\{A, B, D\}$	
$\{B\}$	$\{A, D\}$	$\{A, C, D\}$	
$\{C\}$	$\{B, C\}$	$\{B, C, D\}$	
$\{D\}$	$\{B, D\}$		
	$\{C, D\}$		

Thus, we see that there are five subsets with at least three members that can form a winning coalition and pass or reject a measure, and six subsets with exactly two members that can block a measure.

LOOKING BACK From the above, we know that there are five winning coalitions and six blocking coalitions. Other questions that might be considered include the following.

1. How many minimal winning coalitions are there; that is, how many subsets are there of which no proper subset could pass a measure?
2. Devise a method to solve this problem without listing all subsets.
3. Solve the problem if the committee had six members.

Problem 2 suggests a more general problem, that is, finding the number of subsets that a set containing n elements has. To obtain a general formula, we try some simple cases first.

1. If $B = \{a\}$, then B has 2 subsets, $\varnothing$ and $\{a\}$.
2. If $C = \{a, b\}$, then C has 4 subsets, $\varnothing$, $\{a\}$, $\{b\}$, and $\{a, b\}$.
3. If $D = \{a, b, c\}$, then D has 8 subsets, $\varnothing$, $\{a\}$, $\{b\}$, $\{c\}$, $\{a, b\}$, $\{a, c\}$, $\{b, c\}$, and $\{a, b, c\}$.

Using the information from these cases, we make a table and search for a pattern.

Table 2-1

Number of Elements	Number of Subsets
1	2, or 2^1
2	4, or 2^2
3	8, or 2^3
⋮	⋮

Table 2-1 suggests that for 4 elements, there are 2^4, or 16, subsets. Is this guess correct? If $E = \{a, b, c, d\}$, then all the subsets of $D = \{a, b, c\}$ are also subsets of E. Eight new subsets are also formed by adjoining the element d to each of the 8 subsets of D. The 8 new subsets are $\{d\}$, $\{a, d\}$, $\{b, d\}$, $\{c, d\}$, $\{a, b, d\}$, $\{a, c, d\}$, $\{b, c, d\}$, and $\{a, b, c, d\}$. Thus, there are twice as many subsets of set E (with 4 elements) as there are of set D (with 3 elements). There are indeed 16, or 2^4, subsets of a set with 4 elements. Extending the pattern, there are 2^5, or 32, subsets of a set with 5 elements, and 2^6, or 64, subsets of a set with 6 elements. Notice that in each case the number of elements and the power of 2, which is used to obtain the number of subsets, match exactly. Thus, *if there are n elements in a set, there are 2^n subsets that can be formed.*

The formula 2^n for the number of subsets of a set with n elements is based on the observation that adding one more element to a set doubles the number of possible subsets of the new set. If we apply this formula to the empty set, that is, when $n = 0$, then we have $2^0 = 1$ because the empty set has only one subset, itself. The fact that $a^0 = 1$, where a is a natural number, is investigated in Chapter 6.

The brain teaser is a version of Russell's paradox, named after Bertrand Russell. Russell's paradox was one of the causes of controversy over Cantor's set theory.

BRAIN TEASER

A soldier, Joe, was ordered to shave those soldiers, and only those soldiers, of his platoon who did not shave themselves. Let $A = \{x \mid x$ is a soldier who shaves himself$\}$ and $B = \{x \mid x$ is a soldier who does not shave himself$\}$. Notice that every soldier must belong to one set or the other. To which set does Joe belong?

PROBLEM SET 2-I

1. Which of the following sets are well defined?
   (a) The set of wealthy school teachers.
   (b) The set of great books.
   (c) The set of natural numbers greater than 100.
2. Write the following sets by listing the members or using set-builder notation.
   (a) The set of letters in the word *mathematics*.
   (b) The set of pink elephants taking this class.
   (c) The set of months whose names begin with J.
   (d) The set of natural numbers greater than 20.
   (e) The set of states in the United States.
3. Rewrite the following statements using mathematical symbols.
   (a) B is equal to the set whose elements are x, y, z, and w.
   (b) 3 is not an element of set B.
   (c) The set consisting of the elements 1 and 2 is a proper subset of the set consisting of the elements 1, 2, 3, and 4.
   (d) The set D is not a subset of set E.
   (e) The set A is not a proper subset of set B.
4. Describe three sets of which you are a member.
5. If U is the set of all college students and A is the set of all college students with a straight-A average, describe $\bar{A}$.
6. Describe three sets that have no members.
7. Find the set of all subsets of $\{x, y, z\}$.
8. (a) If $A = \{a, b, c, d, e, f\}$, how many subsets does A have? How many proper subsets does A have?
   (b) If a set B has n elements where n is some natural number, how many proper subsets does B have?
9. Which of the following represent equal sets?
   $A = \{a, b, c, d\}$

   $B = \{x, y, z, w\}$

   $C = \{c, d, a, b\}$

   $D = \{x \mid x$ is one of the first four letters of the English alphabet$\}$

   $E = \varnothing$

   $F = \{\varnothing\}$

   $G = \{0\}$

   $H = \{\ \}$

10. If $B \subset C$, what is the least possible number of elements in C? Why?
11. If $C \subseteq D$ and $D \subseteq C$, what other relationship exists between C and D?
12. Is $\varnothing$ a proper subset of every set? Why?
13. Indicate which symbol, $\in$ or $\notin$, makes each of the following statements true.
    (a) $3 \underline{\hspace{1cm}} \{1, 2, 3\}$ (b) $2 \underline{\hspace{1cm}} \{2\}$
    (c) $0 \underline{\hspace{1cm}} \varnothing$ (d) $a \underline{\hspace{1cm}} \varnothing$
    (e) $\{1\} \underline{\hspace{1cm}} \{1, 2\}$ (f) $\varnothing \underline{\hspace{1cm}} 1$
    (g) $\varnothing \underline{\hspace{1cm}} \varnothing$ (h) $\{1, 2\} \underline{\hspace{1cm}} \{1, 2\}$
    (i) $\{1\} \underline{\hspace{1cm}} \{\{1\}, \varnothing\}$ (j) $\{1, 2\} \underline{\hspace{1cm}} \{1\}$
14. Indicate which symbol, $\subseteq$ or $\nsubseteq$, makes each part of Problem 13 true.
15. Is it always true that $A \nsubseteq B$ implies $B \subseteq A$? Why?
16. Classify each of the following as true or false. If you answer "false," tell why.
    (a) If $A = B$, then $A \subseteq B$.
    (b) If $A \subseteq B$, then $A \subset B$.
    (c) If $A \subset B$, then $A \subseteq B$.
    (d) If $A \subseteq B$, then $A = B$.
17. Which of the following pairs of sets can be placed in one-to-one correspondence?
    (a) $\{1, 2, 3, 4, 5\}$ and $\{m, n, o, p, q\}$
    (b) $\{m, a, t, h\}$ and $\{f, u, n\}$
    (c) $\{a, b, c, d, e, f, \ldots, m\}$ and $\{1, 2, 3, 4, 5, 6, \ldots, 13\}$
    (d) $\{x \mid x$ is a letter in the word "mathematics"$\}$ and $\{1, 2, 3, 4, \ldots, 11\}$
    (e) $\{\bigcirc, \triangle\}$ and $\{2\}$
18. Show all possible one-to-one correspondences between the sets A and B if $A = \{1, 2\}$ and $B = \{a, b\}$.
19. How many different one-to-one correspondences are there in each case?
    (a) Between two sets with four elements each
    (b) Between two sets with five elements each
    (c) Between two sets with n elements each
20. Indicate whether a cardinal number or an ordinal number is used in each of the following cases.
    (a) The book has 562 pages.
    (b) Christmas falls on December 25.
    (c) Turn to page 125.
    (d) She paid $15 for the book.
★21. On a certain Senate committee there are seven senators: Abel, Brooke, Cox, Dean, Eggers, Funk, and Gage. Three of these members are to be appointed

to a subcommittee. How many possible subcommittees are there?

⋆**22.** A set A can be defined to be **infinite** if and only if it can be put into a one-to-one correspondence with a proper subset of itself. For example, the one-to-one correspondence below shows that N is an infinite set.

$$N = \{1, 2, 3, 4, \quad 5, \ldots, \quad n, \ldots\}$$
$$\updownarrow \updownarrow \updownarrow \updownarrow \updownarrow \qquad \updownarrow$$
$$E = \{2, 4, 6, 8, 10, \ldots, 2n, \ldots\}$$

Use this definition to show that the following sets are infinite.
(a) $\{1, 3, 5, 7, 9, \ldots\}$
(b) $\{100, 101, 102, 103, \ldots\}$

Section 2-2   Other Set Operations and Their Properties

In the previous section, we considered set complements. Finding the complement of a set is an operation that acts on only one set at a time. In this section, we consider operations on two sets.

SET INTERSECTION

Suppose that during the fall quarter, one college wants to mail a survey to all students who are enrolled in both art and biology classes. To do this, the school officials must identify these students. If A is the set of students taking art courses during the fall quarter and B is the set of students taking biology courses during the fall quarter, then the desired set of students for the survey is called the **intersection** of A and B.

intersection

DEFINITION

> The **intersection** of two sets A and B, written $A \cap B$, is the set of all elements common to both A and B. $A \cap B = \{x \mid x \in A \text{ and } x \in B\}$.

The key word in the definition of intersection is the word *and*. In everyday language, as in mathematics, *and* implies that both conditions must be met. For example, if the registrar wanted to survey those students majoring in both art and biology, then the desired set of students could be designated as the set $A \cap B$, where A is the set of art majors and B is the set of biology majors. In other words, the desired set of students was those with double majors in art and biology.

disjoint sets   If sets such as A and B have no elements in common, we call them **disjoint sets.** In other words, two sets A and B are disjoint if and only if $A \cap B = \varnothing$.

SET UNION

union   We can also form a new set from two given sets using an operation called **union.** For example, if A is the set of students taking art courses during the fall quarter and B is the set of students taking biology courses during the fall quarter, then the set of students taking either art or biology or both is the union of sets A and B.

DEFINITION

> The **union** of two sets A and B, written $A \cup B$, is the set of all elements in A or in B or in both A and B. $A \cup B = \{x \mid x \in A \text{ or } x \in B\}$.

The key word in the definition of union is *or*. In everyday language, *or* usually means one thing or another but not both, as in "I am going to the ball game or to the play." Such usage is referred to as the *exclusive or*. In mathematics, *or* usually means "one or the other or both." This usage is known as the *inclusive or*.

Venn diagrams showing the intersection and union of sets *A* and *B* are given in Figure 2-4(a) and (b), respectively.

Figure 2-4

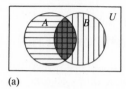   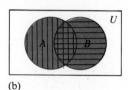

(a)   (b)

SET DIFFERENCE

complement of *A*
relative to *B*
set difference

If *A* is the set of students taking art classes during the fall quarter and *B* is the set of students taking biology classes, then the set of all students taking biology classes but not art classes is called the **complement of *A* relative to *B*** or the **set difference** of *B* and *A*.

DEFINITION

> The **complement of *A* relative to *B*,** written $B - A$, is the set of all elements in *B* that are not in *A*. $B - A = \{x \mid x \in B \text{ and } x \notin A\}$.

A Venn diagram representing $B - A$ is shown in Figure 2-5(a). A Venn diagram for $B \cap \bar{A}$ is given in Figure 2-5(b). These diagrams imply $B - A = B \cap \bar{A}$. Observe that Venn diagrams can be used to demonstrate set equality.

Figure 2-5

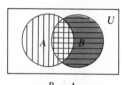   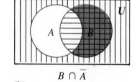

$B - A$ $B \cap \bar{A}$
(a)   (b)

Example 2-5

If $U = \{a, b, c, d, e, f, g\}$, $A = \{d, e, f\}$, and $B = \{a, b, c, d, e\}$, find each of the following.

(a) $A \cup B$ (b) $A \cap B$ (c) $A - B$
(d) $B - A$ (e) $B \cup A$ (f) $B \cap A$

HISTORICAL NOTE

John Venn, 1834–1923, was an English logician who used "Venn diagrams" in his book *Symbolic Logic* in 1894.

Solution

(a) $A \cup B = \{a, b, c, d, e, f\}$
(b) $A \cap B = \{d, e\}$
(c) $A - B = \{f\}$
(d) $B - A = \{a, b, c\}$
(e) $B \cup A = \{a, b, c, d, e, f\}$
(f) $B \cap A = \{d, e\}$

PROPERTIES OF SET OPERATIONS

From Example 2-5(a) and (e), we see that $A \cup B$ is equal to $B \cup A$. This is an example of the commutative property of set union. Also, from Example 2-5(b) and (f), we see that $A \cap B = B \cap A$. This is an example of the commutative property of set intersection. Both of these properties are true for any two sets.

Other properties of set operations can be discovered by considering special cases and then trying to generalize. From Example 2-5(c) and (d), we see that set difference is not a commutative operation. That is, it matters whether we write $A - B$ or $B - A$.

When more than one operation is given, does it matter in which order the operations are done? For example, do we evaluate $A \cup B \cup C$ by first finding $B \cup C$ and then finding the union of set A and the set $B \cup C$, or by first finding the set $A \cup B$ and then finding the union of that set and C? We leave it as an exercise for you to verify that it does not matter which operation is done first. This and other set properties are summarized below.

Properties   **Commutative Properties**   For all sets A and B:

(a) $A \cup B = B \cup A$ Commutative property of set union.
(b) $A \cap B = B \cap A$ Commutative property of set intersection.

Associative Properties   For all sets A, B, and C:

(a) $(A \cap B) \cap C = A \cap (B \cap C)$ Associative property of set intersection.
(b) $(A \cup B) \cup C = A \cup (B \cup C)$ Associative property of set union.

Identity Properties   For every set A and universe U:

(a) $A \cap U = U \cap A = A$ U is the identity for set intersection.
(b) $A \cup \varnothing = \varnothing \cup A = A$ $\varnothing$ is the identity for set union.

Complement Properties   For every set A and universe U:

(a) $\bar{U} = \varnothing$ (b) $\bar{\varnothing} = U$ (c) $A \cap \bar{A} = \varnothing$
(d) $A \cup \bar{A} = U$ (e) $\bar{\bar{A}} = A$

Is grouping important when two different set operations are involved? For example, is it true that $A \cap (B \cup C) = (A \cap B) \cup C$? To investigate this, let $A = \{a, b, c, d\}$, $B = \{c, d, e\}$, and $C = \{d, e, f, g\}$.

$$A \cap (B \cup C) = \{a, b, c, d\} \cap (\{c, d, e\} \cup \{d, e, f, g\})$$
$$= \{a, b, c, d\} \cap \{c, d, e, f, g\}$$
$$= \{c, d\}$$

$$(A \cap B) \cup C = (\{a, b, c, d\} \cap \{c, d, e\}) \cup \{d, e, f, g\}$$
$$= \{c, d\} \cup \{d, e, f, g\}$$
$$= \{c, d, e, f, g\}$$

counterexample

In this case, $A \cap (B \cup C) \neq (A \cap B) \cup C$. We have found what is called a **counterexample** in mathematics, that is, an example that illustrates that a general statement is not always true. One counterexample is enough to make a conjecture false. Thus, in general, $A \cap (B \cup C) \neq (A \cap B) \cup C$. (Drawing Venn diagrams to show that $A \cap (B \cup C) \neq (A \cap B) \cup C$ and $A \cup (B \cap C) \neq (A \cup B) \cap C$ is left as an exercise.)

To discover an expression that is equal to $A \cap (B \cup C)$, consider the Venn diagram for $A \cap (B \cup C)$ shown by the shaded region in Figure 2-6. According to the figure, two regions, $A \cap C$ and $A \cap B$, are parts (subsets) of the shaded region. The union of these two regions is the entire shaded region of the figure. Thus, this shaded region can be identified as $(A \cap C) \cup (A \cap B)$. Consequently, $A \cap (B \cup C) = (A \cap B) \cup (A \cap C)$. A similar approach illustrates that $A \cup (B \cap C) = (A \cup B) \cap (A \cup C)$. These properties that relate intersection and union are called **distributive properties.**

distributive properties

Figure 2-6

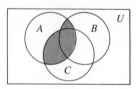

Properties   For all sets A, B, and C:

1. **Distributive property of set intersection over union.**
   $$A \cap (B \cup C) = (A \cap B) \cup (A \cap C)$$

2. **Distributive property of set union over intersection.**
   $$A \cup (B \cap C) = (A \cup B) \cap (A \cup C)$$

Example 2-6

If $A = \{a, b, c\}$, $B = \{b, c, d\}$, and $C = \{d, e, f, g\}$, verify the distributive property of intersection over union for these sets.

Solution

$$A \cap (B \cup C) = \{a, b, c\} \cap (\{b, c, d\} \cup \{d, e, f, g\})$$
$$= \{a, b, c\} \cap \{b, c, d, e, f, g\}$$
$$= \{b, c\}$$

$$(A \cap B) \cup (A \cap C) = (\{a, b, c\} \cap \{b, c, d\}) \cup (\{a, b, c\} \cap \{d, e, f, g\})$$
$$= \{b, c\} \cup \varnothing$$
$$= \{b, c\}$$

Thus, $A \cap (B \cup C) = (A \cap B) \cup (A \cap C)$.

USING VENN DIAGRAMS AS A PROBLEM-SOLVING TOOL

Venn diagrams can be used as a problem-solving tool for modeling information, as seen in this section.

Example 2-7

Use set notation to describe the shaded portions of the Venn diagrams in Figure 2-7(a) and (b).

Figure 2-7

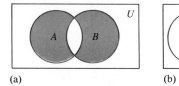

(a)   (b)

Solution

The solutions can be described in many different, but equivalent, forms.

(a) $(A \cup B) \cap (\overline{A \cap B})$, or $(A \cup B) - (A \cap B)$
(b) $(A \cap B) \cup (B \cap C)$, or $B \cap (A \cup C)$

Example 2-8

Suppose M is the set of all students taking mathematics and E is the set of all students taking English. Identify the students described by each region in Figure 2-8.

Figure 2-8

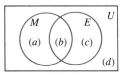

Solution

Region (a) contains all students taking mathematics but not English.
Region (b) contains all students taking both mathematics and English.
Region (c) contains all students taking English but not mathematics.
Region (d) contains all students taking neither mathematics nor English.

Example 2-9

Suppose a survey was taken of college freshmen to determine something about their high school backgrounds. The following information was gathered from interviews with 110 students:

25 took physics
45 took biology
48 took mathematics
10 took physics and mathematics
 8 took biology and mathematics
 6 took physics and biology
 5 took all three subjects

How many students took biology, but neither physics nor mathematics? How many did not take any of the three subjects?

Solution

To solve this problem, we build a model using sets. Because there are three distinct subjects, three circles should be used. The maximum number of regions of a Venn diagram using three circles is 8. In Figure 2-9, P is the

Figure 2-9

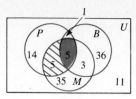

set of students taking physics, B is the set taking biology, and M is the set taking mathematics. The shaded region represents the 5 students who took all three subjects. The lined region represents the students who took physics and mathematics, but who did not take biology.

One mind set to beware of in this problem is thinking that the 25 who took physics, for example, took only physics. That is not necessarily the case. If those students had been taking physics only, then we should have been told so.

Because a total of 10 students took physics and mathematics, and because 5 of those also took biology, $10 - 5$, or 5, students took physics and math, but not biology. The other numbers in the diagram were derived using similar reasoning. After completing the diagram, we interpret the results. Of all the students, 36 took biology, but neither physics nor mathematics; 11 did not take any of the three subjects.

CARTESIAN PRODUCTS

Cartesian product

Two ways that a third set can be created from two given sets are by forming the union of the two sets or by forming the intersection of the two sets. Another way to produce a set from two given sets is by forming the **Cartesian product.** Forming the Cartesian product involves pairing the elements of one set with the elements of another set. For example, suppose a person has three pairs of pants, $P = \{$blue, white, green$\}$, and two shirts, $S = \{$blue, red$\}$. How many different pant-and-shirt pairs does the person have? The possible pairs follow, with the color of pants listed first and the color of shirt listed second.

blue—blue   white—blue   green—blue
blue—red   white—red   green—red

Six pairs are possible. The pairs of pants and shirts form a set of all possible pairs in which the first member of the pair is an element of set P and the second member is an element of set S. The set of all possible pairs is

$\{$(blue, blue), (blue, red), (white, blue), (white, red), (green, blue), (green, red)$\}$

ordered pairs

components

Because the first component in each pair represents pants and the second component in each pair represents shirts, *the order in which the components are written is important.* Thus, (green, blue) represents green pants and a blue shirt, whereas (blue, green) represents blue pants and a green shirt. Therefore, the two pairs represent different outfits. Because the order in each pair is important, the pairs are called **ordered pairs.** The positions that the ordered pairs occupy within the set of outfits is immaterial. Only the order of the **components** within each pair is significant.

An ordered pair (x, y) is formed by choosing x from one set and y from another set in such a way that x is designated as the first component and y is designated as the second component. By definition, $(x, y) = (m, n)$ if and only if $x = m$ and $y = n$. Thus, (green, blue) $\neq$ (blue, green), although {green, blue} = {blue, green}.

A set consisting of ordered pairs such as the ones in the pants-and-shirt example is the Cartesian product of the set of pants and the set of shirts.

DEFINITION

> For any sets A and B, the **Cartesian product** of A and B, written $A \times B$, is the set of all ordered pairs such that the first element of each pair is an element of A and the second element of each pair is an element of B.
>
> $A \times B = \{(x, y)\,|\,x \in A \text{ and } y \in B\}$

Remark $A \times B$ is commonly read as "A cross B." Be careful not to say "A times B." We multiply numbers, but we take Cartesian products of sets.

Example 2-10

If $A = \{a, b, c\}$ and $B = \{1, 2, 3\}$, find each of the following.

(a) $A \times B$ (b) $B \times A$ (c) $A \times A$

Solution

(a) $A \times B = \{(a, 1), (a, 2), (a, 3), (b, 1), (b, 2), (b, 3), (c, 1), (c, 2), (c, 3)\}$
(b) $B \times A = \{(1, a), (1, b), (1, c), (2, a), (2, b), (2, c), (3, a), (3, b), (3, c)\}$
(c) $A \times A = \{(a, a), (a, b), (a, c), (b, a), (b, b), (b, c), (c, a), (c, b), (c, c)\}$

It is possible to form a Cartesian product involving the null set. Suppose $A = \{1, 2\}$. Because there are no elements in $\emptyset$, no ordered pairs (x, y) with $x \in A$ and $y \in \emptyset$ are possible, so $A \times \emptyset = \emptyset$. This is true for all sets A. Similarly, $\emptyset \times A = \emptyset$ for all sets A.

PROBLEM SET 2-2

1. Suppose $U = \{e, q, u, a, l, i, t, y\}$, $A = \{l, i, t, e\}$, $B = \{t, i, e\}$, and $C = \{q, u, e\}$. Decide whether the following pairs of sets are equal.
   (a) $A \cap B$ and $B \cap A$
   (b) $A \cup B$ and $B \cup A$
   (c) $A \cup (B \cup C)$ and $(A \cup B) \cup C$
   (d) $A \cup \emptyset$ and A
   (e) $(A \cap A)$ and $(A \cap \emptyset)$
   (f) $\bar{\bar{C}}$ and C

2. Tell whether each of the following is true or false. If false, give a counterexample.
   (a) For all sets A, $A \cup \emptyset = A$.
   (b) For all sets A and B, $A - B = B - A$.
   (c) For all sets A, $A \cup A = A$.
   (d) For all sets A and B, $\overline{A \cap B} = \bar{A} \cap \bar{B}$.
   (e) For all sets A and B, $A \cap B = B \cap A$.
   (f) For all sets A, B, and C, $(A \cup B) \cup C = A \cup (B \cup C)$.
   (g) For all sets A, $A - \emptyset = A$.

3. If $B \subseteq A$, find a simpler expression for each.
   (a) $A \cap B$ (b) $A \cup B$

4. For each of the following, indicate the portion of the Venn diagram that illustrates the set.
   (a) $A \cup B$ (b) $\bar{A} \cap B$
   (c) $A \cap \bar{B}$ (d) $(A \cup B) \cap \bar{C}$
   (e) $\overline{A \cap B}$ (f) $(A \cap B) \cup C$
   (g) $(A \cap B) \cup (A \cap C)$ (h) $(\bar{A} \cap B) \cup C$

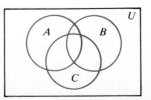

5. Use set notation to identify each of the following shaded regions.

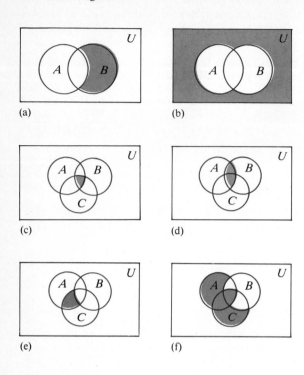

(a) (b)

(c) (d)

(e) (f)

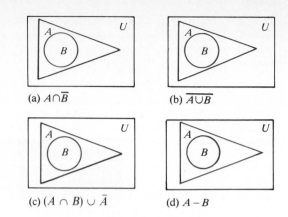

(a) $A \cap \bar{B}$ (b) $\overline{A \cup B}$

(c) $(A \cap B) \cup \bar{A}$ (d) $A - B$

6. Given that the universe is the set of all humans, $B = \{x \mid x$ is a college basketball player$\}$, and $S = \{x \mid x$ is a college student more than 200 cm tall$\}$, describe each of the following in words.
   (a) $B \cap S$ (b) $\bar{S}$ (c) $B \cup S$
   (d) $\overline{B \cup S}$ (e) $\bar{B} \cap S$ (f) $B \cap \bar{S}$
7. If S is a subset of the universe U, find each of the following.
   (a) $S \cup \bar{S}$ (b) $S \cup U$ (c) $\varnothing \cup S$
   (d) $\bar{U}$ (e) $S \cap U$ (f) $\bar{\varnothing}$
   (g) $S \cap \bar{S}$ (h) $S - \bar{S}$ (i) $U \cap \bar{S}$
   (j) $\bar{\bar{S}}$
8. Answer each of the following and justify your answer.
   (a) If $a \in A \cap B$, is it true that $a \in A \cup B$?
   (b) If $a \in A \cup B$, is it true that $a \in A \cap B$?
9. For each of the following conditions, find $A - B$.
   (a) $A \cap B = \varnothing$ (b) $B = U$
   (c) $A = B$ (d) $A \subseteq B$
10. For each of the following, draw a Venn diagram so that sets A, B, and C satisfy the given conditions.
    (a) $A \cap B \neq \varnothing$, $C \subset (A \cap B)$
    (b) $A \cap C \neq \varnothing$, $B \cap C \neq \varnothing$, $A \cap B = \varnothing$
    (c) $A \subset B$, $C \cap B \neq \varnothing$, $A \cap C = \varnothing$
11. Shade the portion of the diagram that represents the given sets.

12. (a) If A has 3 elements and B has 2 elements, what is the greatest number of elements possible in (i) $A \cup B$; (ii) $A \cap B$?
    (b) If A has n elements and B has m elements, what is the greatest number of elements in (i) $A \cup B$; (ii) $A \cap B$?
13. Try examples or use Venn diagrams to determine if each of the following is true.
    (a) $A \cup (B \cap C) = (A \cup B) \cap C$
    (b) $A \cap (B \cup C) = (A \cap B) \cup C$
14. Use Venn diagrams to verify the associative property of union; that is, show $A \cup (B \cup C) = (A \cup B) \cup C$.
15. Investigate the following properties of the set difference operation.
    (a) Is it commutative; that is, does $A - B = B - A$?
    (b) Is it associative; that is, does $A - (B - C) = (A - B) - C$?
    (c) Does the distributive property of set difference over union hold; that is, does $A - (B \cup C) = (A - B) \cup (A - C)$?
16. The equations $\overline{A \cup B} = \bar{A} \cap \bar{B}$ and $\overline{A \cap B} = \bar{A} \cup \bar{B}$ are referred to as *DeMorgan's Laws* in honor of the famous British mathematician who first discovered them. Use Venn diagrams to show each of the following.
    (a) $\overline{A \cup B} = \bar{A} \cap \bar{B}$ (b) $\overline{A \cap B} = \bar{A} \cup \bar{B}$
    (c) Verify (a) and (b) for specific sets A and B.
17. If $A \cap B = A \cup B$, how are A and B related?
18. Suppose P is the set of all eighth-grade students at the Paxson school, with B the set of all students in the band and C the set of all students in the choir. Identify in words the students described by each region of the diagram.

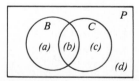

19. Of the eighth graders at the Paxson school, there were 7 who played basketball, 9 who played volleyball, 10 who played soccer, 1 who played basketball and volleyball only, 1 who played basketball and soccer only, 2 who played volleyball and soccer only, and 2 who played volleyball, basketball, and soccer. How many played one or more of the three sports?

20. In a fraternity with 30 members, 18 take mathematics, 5 take both mathematics and biology, and 8 take neither mathematics nor biology. How many take biology but not mathematics?

21. At the end of a tour of the Grand Canyon, several guides were talking about the people on the latest British-American tour. The guides could not remember the total number in the group; however, together they compiled the following statistics about the group. It contained 26 British females, 17 American women, 17 American males, 29 girls, 44 British citizens, 29 women, and 24 British adults. Find the total number of people in the group.

22. Three types of antigens are looked for in blood tests; they are A, B, and Rh. Whenever the antigen A or B is present, it is listed, but if both these antigens are absent, the blood is said to be type O. If the Rh antigen is present, the blood is said to be positive; otherwise it is negative. Thus, the main blood types are as follows.

$$\{A^+, A^-, B^+, B^-, AB^+, AB^-, O^+, O^-\}$$

A Venn diagram for blood types is shown.

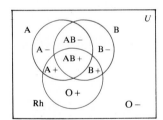

(a) Indicate the area representing the people who react positively to the A antigen but not the B antigen nor the Rh antigen.

(b) Suppose a laboratory technician reports the following results after testing the blood samples of 100 people. How many of the 100 people were classified as O negative?

Number of Samples	Antigens in Blood
40	A
18	B
82	Rh
5	A and B
31	A and Rh
11	B and Rh
4	A, B, and Rh

23. Classify the following as true or false. If false, give a counterexample.
    (a) If $n(A) = n(B)$, then $A = B$.
    (b) If $A \sim B$, then $A \cup B$ is not equivalent to B.
    (c) If $A - B = \varnothing$, then $A = B$.
    (d) If $B - A = \varnothing$, then $B \subseteq A$.
    (e) If $A \subset B$, then $n(A) < n(B)$.
    (f) If $n(A) < n(B)$, then $A \subset B$.

24. Howie, O. J., and Frank each tried to predict the winners of Sunday's professional football games. The only team not picked that is playing Sunday was the Giants. The choices for each person were as follows.

    Howie: Cowboys, Steelers, Vikings, Bills
    O. J.: Steelers, Packers, Cowboys, Redskins
    Frank: Redskins, Vikings, Jets, Cowboys

    If the only teams playing Sunday are those just mentioned, which teams will play which other teams?

25. Let $A = \{x, y\}$, $B = \{a, b, c\}$, and $C = \{0\}$. Find each of the following.
    (a) $A \times B$ (b) $C \times B$
    (c) $B \times A$ (d) $B \times \varnothing$
    (e) $C \times C$ (f) $\varnothing \times C$
    (g) $(A \times C) \cup (B \times C)$ (h) $(A \cup B) \times C$
    (i) $A \times (B \cap C)$ (j) $(A \times B) \cap (A \times C)$

26. For each of the following, the Cartesian product $C \times D$ is given by the following sets. Find C and D.
    (a) $\{(a, b), (a, c), (a, d), (a, e)\}$
    (b) $\{(1, 1), (1, 2), (1, 3), (2, 1), (2, 2), (2, 3)\}$
    (c) $\{(0, 1), (0, 0), (1, 1), (1, 0)\}$

27. Answer each of the following.
    (a) If A has 3 elements and B has 1 element, how many elements are in $A \times B$?
    (b) If A has 3 elements and B has 2 elements, how many elements are in $A \times B$?
    (c) If A has 3 elements and B has 3 elements, how many elements are in $A \times B$?
    (d) If A has 5 elements and B has 4 elements, how many elements are in $A \times B$?
    (e) If A has m elements and B has n elements, how many elements are in $A \times B$?
    (f) If A has m elements, B has n elements, and C has p elements, how many elements are in $(A \times B) \times C$?

28. If $A = \{1, 2, 3\}$, $B = \{0\}$, and $C = \varnothing$, find the number of elements in each of the following.
    (a) $A \times B$
    (b) $A \times C$
    (c) $B \times C$

29. If the number of elements in set B is 3 and the number of elements in $(A \cup B) \times B$ is 24, what is the number of elements in A if $A \cap B = \varnothing$?

30. If A and B are nonempty sets such that $A \times B = B \times A$, does $A = B$?

31. Suppose you can choose one piece of fruit from the set {apple, orange, banana} and one piece of candy from the set {sucker, jawbreaker, candy kiss, licorice}. How many different combinations could you choose?

32. If there are 6 teams in the Alpha league and 5 teams in the Beta league, and if each team from one league plays each team from the other league exactly once, how many games are played?

33. José has 4 pairs of slacks, 5 shirts, and 3 sweaters. From how many different combinations can he choose if he chooses a pair of slacks, a shirt, and a sweater each time?

34. (a) Is the operation of forming Cartesian products commutative?
    (b) Is the operation of forming Cartesian products associative?

★35. A paper carrier delivers 31 copies of the Town Gazette and 37 copies of the Daily Flyer each day to 60 houses. If no house received 2 copies of the same paper, answer the following.
    (a) What is the least number of houses to which 2 papers could have been delivered?
    (b) What is the greatest number of houses to which 2 papers could have been delivered?

★36. Two families each having three children are assembled for a birthday party. Each of the six children has either blue or brown eyes and brown or blond hair. Children in one family may differ by at most one characteristic. The following are descriptions of the six children.

Tom: blue eyes, brown hair
Dick: brown eyes, blond hair
Mary: brown eyes, brown hair
Harry: blue eyes, blond hair
Jane: blue eyes, brown hair
Abby: blue eyes, blond hair

Separate the children into two families.

★37. Using set notation, describe the shaded region shown.

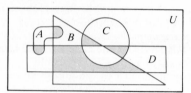

Review Problems

38. List all the subsets of $A = \{a, b, c\}$.

39. Are the following two sets equal?

$$\{2, 4, 6, 8, 10, \dots\}$$

$$\{x \mid x = 2n, n \in N\}$$

40. Given $B = \{p, q, r, s\}$, list the nonempty, proper subsets of B.

41. Write the set of states of the United States that begin with the letter M by:
    (a) listing them
    (b) using set-builder notation

LABORATORY ACTIVITY

A set of attribute blocks consists of 32 blocks. Each block is identified by its own shape, size, and color. The four shapes in a set are square, triangle, rhombus, and circle; the four colors are red, yellow, blue, and green; the two sizes are large and small. In addition to the blocks, each set contains a group of 20 cards. Ten of the cards specify one of the attributes of the blocks, for example, red, large, square. The other 10 cards are negation cards and specify the lack of an attribute, for example, not green, not circle. There are many set-type problems that can be studied with these blocks. For example, let $A = \{$all green blocks$\}$ and $B = \{$all large blocks$\}$. Using the set of all blocks as the universal set, verify that the following properties are true.

1. $(A \cup B) = (B \cup A)$
2. $\overline{(A \cup B)} = \overline{A} \cap \overline{B}$
3. $\overline{(A \cap B)} = \overline{A} \cup \overline{B}$
4. $A - B = A \cap \overline{B}$

BRAIN TEASER

Every doodad is a doohickey. Half of all thingamajigs are doohickeys. Half of all doohickeys are doodads. There are 30 thingamajigs and 20 doodads. No thingamajig is a doodad. How many doohickeys are neither doodads nor thingamajigs?

Section 2-3   Relations and Functions

RELATIONS

relation   A subset of a Cartesian product is called a **relation.** Before formally examining this mathematical concept, let us examine nonmathematical relations. The word "relations" brings to mind members of a family—parents, brothers, sisters, grandfathers, aunts, and so on. If we say Billy is the brother of Jimmy, "is the brother of" expresses the relation between Billy and Jimmy.

Other familiar relations occur in everyday life. For example, 543-8975 is the telephone number of Rick. "Is the telephone number of" expresses the relation between the number and Rick. Other examples of relations include the following.

"Is the daughter of"   "Is the hometown of"
"Is the same color as"   "Is the author of"
"Sits in the same row as"   "Is the social security number of"

Examples of relations in mathematics are

"Is less than"   "Is three more than"
"Is parallel to"   "Is the area of"

To illustrate relations, a diagram like Figure 2-10 is useful.

Figure 2-10

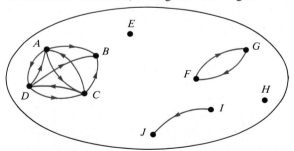

Suppose that each point in Figure 2-10 represents a child on a playground, the letters represent their names, and an arrow going from *I* to *J* means that *I* "is the sister of" *J*.

If all sister relationships are indicated in Figure 2-10, can you tell which of the children are boys and which are girls? Try to answer this question before reading further.

The information in Figure 2-10 indicates that A, C, D, F, G, and I are definitely girls and that B and J are definitely boys. Why? It also indicates that H and E have no sisters on the playground, but it does not indicate the gender of H and E.

Another way to exhibit the relation "is a sister of" is by using the same set twice, with arrows, as in Figure 2-11.

Figure 2-11

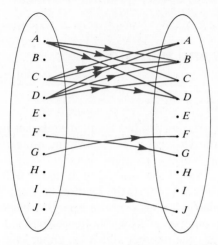

Still another way to show the relation "is a sister of" is to write the relation "A is a sister of B" as an ordered pair (A, B). Notice that (B, A) means that B is a sister of A. Using this method, the relation "is a sister of" can be described for the children on the playground as the set

$\{(A, B), (A, C), (A, D), (C, A), (C, B), (C, D), (D, A), (D, B), (D, C), (F, G),$ $(G, F), (I, J)\}$

Observe that this set is a subset of $\{A, B, C, D, E, F, G, H, I, J\} \times \{A, B, C,$ $D, E, F, G, H, I, J\}$.

Next, we illustrate relations in Figure 2-12, letting the arrows represent "is less than" on the set $\{1, 3, 6, 7\}$. The relation can be shown by using one set, as in Figure 2-12(a), or by using two sets, as in Figure 2-12(b).

Figure 2-12

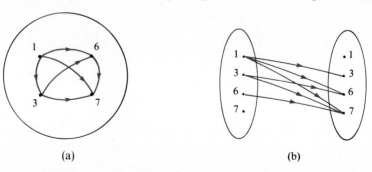

(a)   (b)

Ordered pairs can also be used to describe the relation pictured in Figure 2-12(a) and (b). The relation "is less than" of Figure 2-12 would appear as

$\{(1, 3), (1, 6), (1, 7), (3, 6), (3, 7), (6, 7)\}$

Example 2-11

The pairs (Helena, Montana), (Denver, Colorado), (Springfield, Illinois), and (Juneau, Alaska) are included in some relation. Give a rule that describes the relation.

Solution

One possible rule is that the ordered pair (x, y) indicates that x is the capital of y.

A relation is a pairing of elements of two sets according to some criterion. In Example 2-11, the first components of the ordered pairs are state capitals; the second components are states of the United States. Each ordered pair in the example is an element of the Cartesian product $A \times B$, where A is the set of state capitals and B is the set of states in the United States. Notice that not all the possible ordered pairs in $A \times B$ are in the relation in Example 2-11.

DEFINITION

> Given any two sets A and B, a **relation** from A to B is a subset of $A \times B$; that is, if R is a relation, then $R \subseteq A \times B$.

relation on A

In the definition, the phrase "from A to B" means that the first components in the ordered pairs are elements of A and the second components are elements of B. If $A = B$, we say that the **relation is on A.**

PROPERTIES OF RELATIONS

Figure 2-13 represents a set of children in a small group. They have drawn all possible arrows representing the relation "has the same first letter in his or her name as." Notice that the children were very careful to observe that each child in the group has the same first initial as himself or herself. Three properties of relations are illustrated in Figure 2.13.

Figure 2-13

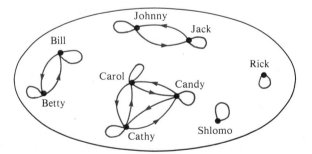

Property **The Reflexive Property**   A relation R on a set X is reflexive if and only if, for every element $a \in X$, a is related to a. That is, for every $a \in X$, $(a, a) \in R$.

In terms of the diagram, there is a loop at every point. For example, Rick has the same first initial as himself, namely R. A relation such as "is taller than" is not reflexive because people cannot be taller than themselves.

Property The Symmetric Property A relation R on a set X is symmetric if and only if, for all elements a and b in X, whenever a is related to b, then b also is related to a. That is, if $(a, b) \in R$, then $(b, a) \in R$.

In terms of the diagram, every pair of points that has an arrow headed in one direction also has a return arrow.

For example, if Bill has the same first initial as Betty, then Betty has the same first initial as Bill. A relation such as "is a brother of" is not symmetric since Dick can be a brother of Jane, but Jane cannot be a brother of Dick.

Property The Transitive Property A relation R on a set X is transitive if and only if, for all elements a, b, and c of X, whenever a is related to b and b is related to c, then a is related to c. That is, if $(a, b) \in R$ and $(b, c) \in R$, then $(a, c) \in R$.

Remark a, b, and c do not have to be different. Three symbols are used to allow for difference.

In terms of the diagram in Figure 2-13, every connected portion satisfies the transitive property. For example, if Carol has the same first initial as Candy, and Candy has the same first initial as Cathy, then Carol has the same first initial as Cathy. A relation such as "is the father of" is not transitive since, if Tom Jones is the father of Tom Jones, Jr. and Tom Jones, Jr. is the father of Joe Jones, then Tom Jones is not the father of Joe Jones. He is instead the grandfather.

The relation "is the same color as" is reflexive, symmetric, and transitive. The common relation "is equal to" also satisfies all three properties. In general, relations that satisfy all three properties are called **equivalence relations.**

equivalence relations

DEFINITION

> An **equivalence relation** is any relation R that satisfies the reflexive, symmetric, and transitive properties.

The most natural equivalence relation encountered in elementary school is "is equal to" on the set of all numbers.

Example 2-12

If $X = \{\{1\}, \{1, 2\}, \{1, 2, 3\}, \{2, 4\}, \{2, 4, 5\}, \{6\}\}$, draw a diagram in which the points represent subsets, illustrating the relation "is a subset of" on the set X, and indicate which properties are satisfied.

Solution

The diagram might be like Figure 2-14. This relation is reflexive, since every element of X is a subset of itself. (Notice that there is a loop at every point.) The relation is not symmetric since $\{2, 4\} \subseteq \{2, 4, 5\}$ but $\{2, 4, 5\} \nsubseteq \{2, 4\}$. (Notice that there is an arrow connecting the two sets, but no return arrow.) Since this relation is not symmetric on the set X, it is not an equivalence relation. However, it is transitive.

Figure 2-14

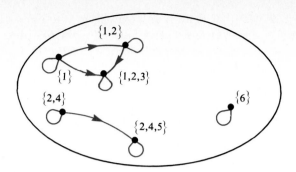

Example 2-13

Tell whether or not the following relations are reflexive, symmetric, or transitive on the set of all people.

(a) "Is older than"
(b) "Sits in the same row as"
(c) "Is heavier than"

Solution

The solution is given in the form of a table.

Relation	Reflexive	Symmetric	Transitive
(a) "Is older than"	No	No	Yes
(b) "Sits in the same row as"	Yes	Yes	Yes
(c) "Is heavier than"	No	No	Yes

Note that "sits in the same row as" is an equivalence relation.

Example 2-14

Are the following relations equivalence relations?

(a) $R = \{(1, 1)(1, 2)(2, 2), (2, 1)\}$
(b) $R = \{(a, a)(a, c), (c, b), (a, b), (b, a), (b, c), (b, b)(c, c)\}$

Solution

(a) It is reflexive, symmetric, and transitive; hence, it is an equivalence relation.
(b) A diagram for this relation follows.

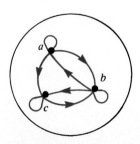

Notice that there is an arrow from a to c but not from c to a. Thus, the symmetric property fails. In terms of ordered pairs, $(a, c) \in R$ but $(c, a) \notin R$. Since the symmetric property does not hold, R is not an equivalence relation.

Suppose P is the set consisting of all persons attending Mu University and consider the relation "is the same sex as." This relation is an equivalence relation. The relation partitions the persons at Mu University into two classes, females and males. Any equivalence relation defined on a set has the effect of partitioning the set into disjoint subsets, called **equivalence classes.** In this example, the class of females can be described as the set of all students who are the same sex as Jane, a student at M.U., and the set can be called Jane's equivalence class. This class also can be called Mary's equivalence class as long as Mary is a student at M.U. An equivalence class can be named after any of its members.

equivalence classes

When elementary school childern sort objects, putting all the red objects in one pile, the blue objects in another pile, and the white in another pile, they are forming equivalence classes using the relation "is the same color as." A principal in an elementary school with grades one through six uses the relation "is in the same grade as" to sort the children into six equivalence classes—the six grades in the school.

FUNCTIONS

function

The following is an example of a game called "guess my rule." The game is one way a special kind of relation, called a **function,** is often introduced in elementary school.

When Tom said 2, Noah said 5. When Dick said 4, Noah said 7. When Mary said 10, Noah said 13. When Liz said 6, what did Noah say? What is Noah's rule?

The answer to the first question may be 9, and the rule could be "Take the original number and add 3"; that is, for any number n, Noah's answer is $n + 3$.

HISTORICAL NOTE

The Babylonians (ca. 2000 B.C.) probably had a working idea of what a function was. To them, it was a table or a correspondence. René Descartes (1637), Gottfried Wilhelm von Leibnitz (1692), Johann Bernoulli (1718), Leonhard Euler (1750), Joseph Louis Lagrange (1800), and Jean Joseph Fourier (1822) were among the mathematicians contributing to the notion of function. The modern definition began to be used in the late 1800s by Georg Cantor and others.

Example 2-15

Guess the teacher's rule for the following responses.

(a) You	Teacher	(b) You	Teacher	(c) You	Teacher
1	3	2	5	2	0
0	0	3	7	4	0
4	12	5	11	7	1
10	30	10	21	21	1

Solution

(a) The teacher's rule could be "Multiply the given number n by 3," that is, $n \cdot 3$.

(b) The teacher's rule could be "Double the original number n and add 1," that is, $2n + 1$.

(c) The teacher's rule could be "If the number n is even, answer 0; if the number is odd, answer 1."

Another way to prepare students for the concept of a function is by using common, everyday items. For example, consider Table 2-2, which shows the results of a game in which the students name an animal and the teacher responds with a number.

Table 2-2

Animal	Teacher's Response
Snake	0
Dog	4
Cat	4
Horse	4
Chicken	2
Human	2

A rule for the pairing in Table 2-2 might be "State the number of legs that the animal has." As we can see, for any animal named, exactly one number is assigned (if the animal has a normal number of legs).

Yet another way to prepare students for the formal idea of a function is by using a "function machine," consisting of an input set, called the **domain,** a processing unit (normally a rule), and an output set, called the **range.** The function machine is sometimes pictured as in Figure 2-15. The processing unit normally consists of some rule to assign a value from the domain to a value of the range.

domain

range

Figure 2-15

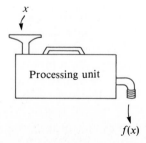

Function machine

In a function machine, for any input element x there is an output element denoted by $f(x)$, read "f of x." A function machine is a machine that associates *exactly one output with each input* according to some rule. That is, if you enter some number x as input and obtain some number $f(x)$ as output, then *every* time you enter that same x as input, you will obtain that same $f(x)$ as output.

Example 2-16

Consider the function machine shown.

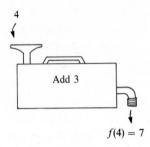

What will happen if the numbers 0, 1, 3, and 6 are entered?

Solution

Each time a number is entered as input, the machine adds 3 to it. The numbers corresponding to the inputs 0, 1, 3, and 6 are 3, 4, 6, and 9. Using the notation above, we see that $f(0) = 3$, $f(1) = 4$, $f(3) = 6$, and $f(6) = 9$.

If the numbers output in Example 2-16 are denoted by $f(x)$, the corresponding values can be described using Table 2-3.

Table 2-3

x	$f(x)$
0	3
1	4
3	6
6	9

Normally, if no domain is given to describe a function, then the domain is assumed to be the largest set for which the rule is meaningful. For example, if the domain were not pictured, it would be assumed to be the entire set of natural numbers. (If students know about rational, real, or complex numbers, then any of those sets could be considered as acceptable domains.)

We can write an equation to depict the rule in Example 2-16 as follows. If the input is x, the output is $x + 3$; that is, $f(x) = x + 3$. Note that the output values can be obtained by substituting the values 0, 1, 3, 4, and 6 for x in $f(x) = x + 3$, as shown.

$$f(0) = 0 + 3 = 3$$
$$f(1) = 1 + 3 = 4$$
$$f(3) = 3 + 3 = 6$$
$$f(4) = 4 + 3 = 7$$
$$f(6) = 6 + 3 = 9$$

The idea of a function machine associating exactly one output with each input according to some rule leads us to the following definition.

DEFINITION

A **function** from A to B is a relation from A to B in which each element of A is paired with one *and only one* element of B.

The set of all first components, all the elements of A, is called the domain. The set of the second components, a subset of B, is called the range. In terms of a function machine, the domain is the set of all possible input values. The range is the set of all possible output values.

Example 2-17

Suppose a given machine is a doubling machine; that is, for any given input, it will produce its double as output. If the domain is the set of natural numbers, describe the range.

Solution

The range is the set of all even natural numbers (all multiples of two).

A calculator can be used as a function machine. For example, a student can make up a rule such as "times 9." The student then enters $\boxed{9}\,\boxed{\times}\,\boxed{\text{K}}$ on the calculator using the constant key, $\boxed{\text{K}}$. The student then presses $\boxed{0}$ and hands the calculator to another student. The other student is to determine the rule by entering various numbers followed by the $\boxed{=}$ key. Machines with an automatic constant feature can also be used.

Are all input-output machines function machines? Consider the machine in Figure 2-16. For any natural-number input x, the machine outputs a number that is less than x.

Figure 2-16

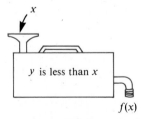

If, for example, you input the number 10, the machine may output 9 since 9 is less than 10. If you input 10 again, the machine may output 3, since 3 is less than 10. This clearly violates the definition of a function, since 10 can be paired with more than one element. The machine is not a function machine.

Consider the relations described in Figure 2-17. Do they illustrate functions?

Figure 2-17

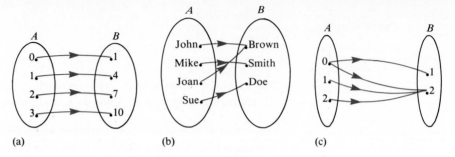

(a)   (b)   (c)

In Figure 2-17(a), for every element belonging to the domain A, there is one and only one element belonging to B. Thus, this relation is a function from A to B. A diagram, then, shows a function from A to B if there is one and only one arrow leaving each element of the domain pointing to an element of B. Figure 2-17(b) illustrates a function since there is only one arrow leaving each element in A. It does not matter that an element of set B, Brown, has two arrows pointing to it. Figure 2-17(c) does not define a function because 0 is paired with more than one element.

Example 2-18

Which, if any, of the following three diagrams exhibits a function from A to B?

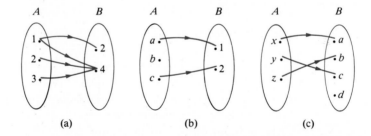

(a)   (b)   (c)

Solution

(a) This diagram does not define a function from A to B since the element 1 is paired with both 2 and 4.

(b) This diagram does not define a function from A to B since the element b is not paired with any element of B. (It is a function from a subset of A to B.)

(c) This diagram does define a function from A to B since there is one and only one arrow leaving each element of A. The fact that d, an element of B, is not paired with any element in the domain does not violate the definition.

Consider the relation $\{(a, b), (b, c), (c, d), (d, e)\}$. Since each first component of the ordered pairs is associated with one and only one second component, this relation is a function from the set $\{a, b, c, d\}$ of the first components to the set $\{b, c, d, e\}$ of the second components.

Example 2-19

Determine whether the following relations are functions from the set of first components to the set of second components.

(a) {(1, 2), (2, 5), (3, 7), (1, 4), (4, 8)}
(b) {(1, 2), (2, 2), (3, 2), (4, 2)}

Solution

(a) This is not a function since the first component, 1, is associated with two different second components, namely, 2 and 4.
(b) This is a function from {1, 2, 3, 4} to {2}, since each first component is associated with exactly one second component. The fact that the second component, 2, is associated with more than one first component does not matter.

OPERATIONS ON FUNCTIONS

composition of two functions

Consider the two function machines in Figure 2-18. If 2 is entered in the top machine, then $f(2) = 2 + 4 = 6$. Six is then entered in the second machine and $g(6) = 2 \cdot 6 = 12$. The functions in Figure 2-18 illustrate the **composition of two functions.** In the composition of two functions, the range of the first function becomes the domain of the second function.

Figure 2-18

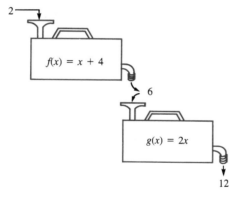

If the first function f is followed by a second function g, then we symbolize the composition of the functions as $g \circ f$. If we input 3 in the function machines of Figure 2-18, then the output is $(g \circ f)(3)$, or $g(3 + 4)$, or $g(7) = 2 \cdot 7 = 14$.

Remark With the notation $g \circ f$, f is the first function to act on the input. Contrast this with $f \circ g$ and note that composition of functions is not commutative.

Example 2-20

Find the range of $g \circ f$ for each of the following where the domain of $g \circ f$ is the set {1, 2, 3}.

(a) $f(x) = 2x$; $g(x) = 3x$
(b) $f(x) = x + 2$; $g(x) = x - 2$

Solution

(a) The composition may be pictured as follows.

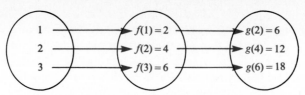

Thus, the range of $g \circ f$ is the set $\{6, 12, 18\}$.
(b) The composition may be pictured as follows.

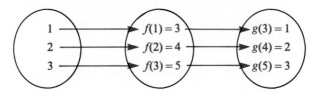

Thus, the range of $g \circ f$ is the set $\{1, 2, 3\}$.

INVERSE FUNCTIONS

inverse function

Example 2-20(b) showed two functions, f and g, that are considered to be **inverses** of each other. That is, g "undoes" what f does. Observe that for any value of the domain that is acted on by function f and then by g, the original value of the domain is returned. To find the inverse of a function like $f(x) = 2x - 3$, consider how $f(5)$ would be found. We would first multiply 2 times 5 and then subtract 3. To find the inverse of the function f, we try to undo what has been done. That is, we add 3 and then take half of the result obtained at that stage.

Example 2-21

Describe the inverses of each of the following functions.

(a) $f(x) = \dfrac{x}{2} + 5$

(b) $f(x) = 3x - 7$

Solution

(a) To find the inverse of f, we first subtract 5 and then multiply by 2. The inverse function might be written as $g(x) = (x - 5) \cdot 2$.
(b) To find the inverse of f, we add 7 and then divide by 3. It might be written as $g(x) = \dfrac{x + 7}{3}$.

Example 2-22

If $f(x) = 2x + 3$ and $g(x) = \dfrac{x - 3}{2}$, find the following:

(a) $(f \circ g)(3)$
(b) $(g \circ f)(3)$

Solution

(a) $(f \circ g)(3) = f(\frac{0}{2}) = f(0) = 2 \cdot 0 + 3 = 3$

(b) $(g \circ f)(3) = g(9) = \dfrac{9 - 3}{2} = 3$

APPLICATIONS OF FUNCTIONS

The concept of a function appears in many real-life applications. For example, on direct-dial, long-distance calls, you pay only for the minutes you talk. The initial rate period is 1 minute. Suppose the weekday rate for a long-distance phone called from Missoula, Montana, to Butte, Montana, is 50¢ for the first minute and 30¢ for each additional minute or part of a minute. We have seen that one way to describe a function is by writing an equation. The equation in this case is $C = 50 + 30(t - 1)$, where C is the cost of the call in cents and t is the length of the call in minutes. This could also be written as $f(t) = 50 + 30(t - 1)$, where $f(t)$ is the cost of the call.

We restrict the time in minutes to the first five natural numbers. The function can be described as shown in Table 2-4 or as the set of ordered pairs $\{(1, 50), (2, 80), (3, 110), (4, 140), (5, 170)\}$.

Table 2-4

Number of Minutes Talked	Total Cost
1	50¢
2	80¢
3	110¢
4	140¢
5	170¢

The information in Table 2-4 might also be shown on a lattice graph as in Figure 2-19. The *lattice graph* is formed by taking the Cartesian product of the sets $\{1, 2, 3, 4, 5\}$ and $\{50, 80, 110, 140, 170\}$ and plotting points corresponding to the ordered pairs. If (a, b) is in the Cartesian product, then the corresponding point in the lattice is found by starting at the lower left corner and moving horizontally a units, then moving vertically b units.

Figure 2-19

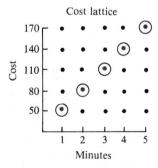

Elementary school math texts sometimes introduce functions as simple formulas, as seen on page 76 from *Addison-Wesley Mathematics,* 1987, Grade 7.

PROBLEM SOLVING: Using a Formula

QUESTION
DATA
PLAN
ANSWER
CHECK

Ronald typed 285 words in 5 minutes. He made 6 errors. For each error made, 10 words are subtracted from the total. What is his typing speed?

The formula for finding typing speed is

$$S = \frac{W - (10 \cdot e)}{n}$$

Each letter represents a number.

S = typing speed e = number of errors
W = number of words n = number of minutes

Step 1: List the value for each letter in the formula.

$W = 285$ $e = 6$ $n = 5$

Step 2: Substitute the numbers for the letters in the formula.

$$S = \frac{285 - (10 \cdot 6)}{5}$$

Remember, this bar means divide.

Step 3: Perform the operations in the formula.

$$S = \frac{285 - 60}{5} = \frac{225}{5} = 45$$

Ronald's typing speed is 45 words per minute.

Use the formula to find these typing speeds.

1. Dave typed 380 words in 5 minutes with 7 errors.

2. Lamar typed 886 words in 9 minutes. He made 13 errors.

3. A legal secretary typed 2,450 words in 20 minutes with 17 errors.

4. Vicky typed 554 words in 12 minutes and made 11 errors.

5. **DATA HUNT** What is your typing speed? Have another person watch the time while you type for 5 minutes. Use the formula to find your speed.

6. **Strategy Practice** Ann typed 5 more words per minute than Jeff. Together they typed 73 words in one minute. How many words did each person type in one minute?

PROBLEM SET 2-3

1. Each of the following gives pairs that are included in some relation. Give a rule or phrase that could describe each relation and list two more pairs that could be included in the relation.
   (a) (1, 1), (2, 4), (3, 9), (4, 16)
   (b) (Blondie, Dagwood), (Martha, George), (Rosalyn, Jimmy), (Flo, Andy), (Scarlett, Rhett), (Nancy, Ronald)
   (c) (a, A), (b, B), (c, C), (d, D)
   (d) (3 candies, 10¢), (6 candies, 20¢)

2. Let $X = \{a, b, c\}$ and $Y = \{m, n\}$, and suppose X and Y represent two sets of students. The students in X point to the shorter students in Y. The following diagrams list two possibilities. Tell as much as you can about the students in each diagram.

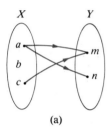 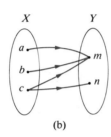

   (a)   (b)

3. Write three ordered pairs that satisfy the relation "is owned by."

4. The following are the ages of the children in a family: Bill, 17; Becky, 14; John, 9; Abby, 3; Karly, 1. Draw an arrow diagram showing the names of the children and the relation "is younger than."

5. Tell whether each of the following is reflexive, symmetric, or transitive on the set of all people. Which are equivalence relations?
   (a) "Is a parent of"
   (b) "Is the same age as"
   (c) "Has the same last name as"
   (d) "Is a brother or sister of"
   (e) "Is the same height as"
   (f) "Is married to"

6. Tell whether each of the following is reflexive, symmetric, or transitive on the set of subsets of a nonempty set. Which are equivalence relations?
   (a) "Is equal to"   (b) "Is a proper subset of"
   (c) "Is not equal to"

7. Tell whether or not each of the following relations is reflexive, symmetric, or transitive.
   (a) $\{(a, a), (a, b), (a, c), (b, b), (b, c), (c, c)\}$
   (b) $\{(1, 1), (1, 2), (2, 1)\}$
   (c) $\{(1, 1), (1, 2), (2, 1), (2, 2)\}$

8. If $S = \{5, 7, 10, 13, 14, 30\}$ and a relation on S is defined by the following diagram, what properties does this relation have?

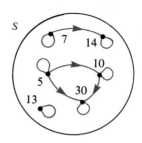

9. Consider the set S such that $S = \{$Abe, George, Laura, Ben, Sue, Betty, Dax, Zachary, Doug, Mike, Mary, Carolyn, Aza$\}$. Identify the equivalence classes formed by each of the following relations.
   (a) "Has the same first letter in his or her name as"
   (b) "Has the same last letter in his or her name as"
   (c) "Has the same number of letters in his or her name as"

10. For each of the following, guess the teacher's rule.

(a) You	Teacher
3	8
4	11
5	14
10	29

(b) You	Teacher
0	1
3	10
5	26
8	65

(c) You	Teacher
6	42
0	0
8	72
2	6

11. The following sets of ordered pairs are functions. Give a rule that describes each function. For example, in $\{(1, 3), (3, 9), (5, 15), (7, 21)\}$, the rule is $f(x) = 3x$, where $x \in \{1, 3, 5, 7\}$.
   (a) $\{(2, 4), (3, 6), (9, 18), (12, 24)\}$
   (b) $\{(5, 3), (7, 5), (11, 9), (14, 12)\}$
   (c) $\{(2, 8), (5, 11), (7, 13), (4, 10)\}$
   (d) $\{(2, 5), (3, 10), (4, 17), (5, 26)\}$

12. Following are five relations from the set $\{1, 2, 3\}$ to the set $\{a, b, c, d\}$. Which are functions? (A diagram may help.) If the relation is not a function, tell why it is not.
   (a) $\{(1, a), (2, b), (3, c), (1, d)\}$
   (b) $\{(1, c), (3, d)\}$
   (c) $\{(1, a), (2, b), (3, a)\}$
   (d) $\{(1, a), (1, b), (1, c)\}$

13. Does the diagram define a function from A to B? Why or why not?

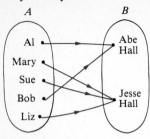

14. If $g(x) = 3x + 5$, find each value.
(a) $g(0)$ (b) $g(2)$ (c) $g(10)$ (d) $g(a)$

15. Draw a diagram of a function with domain $\{1, 2, 3, 4, 5\}$ and range $\{a, b\}$. (There are many possibilities.)

16. Tell which of the relations shown are functions and why.

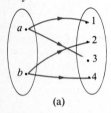
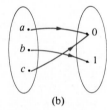

(a)   (b)

17. Suppose $f(x) = 2x + 1$ and the domain is $\{0, 1, 2, 3, 4\}$. Describe the function in the following ways.
(a) Draw an arrow diagram involving two sets.
(b) Use ordered pairs.
(c) Make a table.
(d) Draw a lattice graph to depict the function.

18. Consider two function machines that are placed as shown.

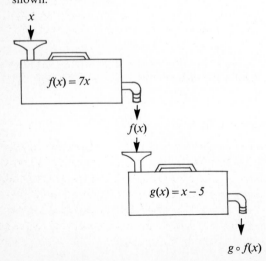

Find the final output for each of the following inputs.
(a) 0   (b) 3   (c) 10

19. (a) Find the inverse of the function f in Problem 18.
(b) Find the inverse of the function g in Problem 18.

20. The rule for computing the cost of a first-class letter is a function of its weight. Suppose the rule is that the first ounce costs 20¢ and each additional ounce up to 13 ounces costs 15¢.
(a) What is the cost of an 11-ounce letter?
(b) Find the equation relating the cost C of the letter to its weight W.

21. According to wildlife experts, the rate at which crickets chirp is a function of the temperature; that is, $C = T - 40$, where C is the number of chirps every 15 seconds and T is the temperature in degrees Fahrenheit.
(a) How many chirps does the cricket make per second if the temperature is 70°F?
(b) What is the temperature if the cricket chirps 40 times in 1 minute?

22. If taxi fares are 95¢ for the first half mile and 40¢ for each additional quarter mile, what is the fare for a 2-mile trip?

23. Find the nth term for each of the following sequences, whose domains are the natural numbers.
(a) $\{3, 8, 13, 18, 23, \ldots\}$
(b) $\{3, 9, 27, 81, 243, \ldots\}$
(c) $\{2, 4, 6, 8, 10, \ldots\}$

24. Is the rule "has as mother" a function whose domain is the set of all people?

25. Is the relation "has as brother" a function on the set of all boys?

Review Problems

26. Draw Venn diagrams to verify the following.
(a) $A - (B \cup C) = (A - B) \cap (A - C)$
(b) If $A \subseteq B$, then $A \cup B = B$.

27. Is the set of all rich men well defined? Why or why not?

28. Suppose U is the set of natural numbers, $\{1, 2, 3, 4, \ldots\}$. Write each of the following using set-builder notation.
(a) The set of even numbers greater than 12.
(b) The set of numbers less than 14.

29. If $U = \{a, b, c, d\}$, $A = \{a, b, c\}$, $B = \{b, c\}$, and $C = \{d\}$, find each of the following.
(a) $A \cup \overline{B}$ (b) $\overline{A \cap B}$ (c) $A \cap \varnothing$
(d) $B \cap C$ (e) $B - A$

30. Write two sets with three elements each and establish a one-to-one correspondence between them.

31. Write a set that is equivalent to, but not equal to, the set $\{5, 6, 7, 8\}$.

32. How many different one-to-one correspondences are possible between $A = \{a, b, c\}$ and $B = \{1, 2, 3\}$?

33. Illustrate the associative property of set union with the sets $U = \{h, e, l, p, m, e, n, o, w\}$, $A = \{h, e, l, p\}$, $B = \{m, e\}$, and $C = \{n, o, w\}$.

BRAIN TEASER

Only 10 rooms were vacant in the Village Hotel. Eleven men went into the hotel at the same time, each wanting a separate room. The clerk, settling the argument, said, "I'll tell you what I'll do. I'll put two men in Room 1 with the understanding that I will come back and get one of them a few minutes later." The men agreed to this. The clerk continued, "I will put the rest of you men in rooms as follows: the 3rd man in Room 2, the 4th man in Room 3, the 5th man in Room 4, the 6th man in Room 5, the 7th man in Room 6, the 8th man in Room 7, the 9th man in Room 8, and the 10th man in Room 9." Then the clerk went back and got the extra man he had left in Room 1 and put him in Room 10. Everybody was happy. What is wrong with this plan?

*Section 2-4   Logic: An Introduction

Logic deals with reasoning and is a tool used in mathematical thinking. In this section, we deal with the basics of logic necessary for problem solving. In logic, a **statement** is a sentence that is either true or false, but not both.

statement

Expressions such as "2 + 3," "Close the door," or "How tall are you?" are not statements since they cannot be classified as true or false. The following expressions also are not statements since their truth value cannot be determined without more information.

1. She has blue eyes.
2. $x + 7 = 18$
3. $2y + 7 > 1$

Each of the preceding expressions becomes a statement if, for (1), "she" is identified, and for (2) and (3), values are assigned to x and y, respectively. However, an expression involving *he* or *she* or x or y may already be a statement. For example, "If he is over 210 cm tall, then he is over 2 m tall," and "$2(x + y) = 2x + 2y$" are both statements since they are true no matter who *he* is or what the values of x and y are.

negation

From a given statement, it is possible to create a new statement by forming a **negation.** The negation of a statement is a statement with the opposite truth value of the given statement; that is, if the statement is true, its negation is false, and if the statement is false, its negation is true. Consider the statement "It is snowing." The negation of this statement is "It is not true that it is snowing." Stated in a simpler form, the negation is "It is not snowing."

Example 2-23

Negate each of the following statements.

(a) $2 + 3 = 5$
(b) A hexagon has six sides.
(c) Today is not Monday.

Solution

(a) $2 + 3 \neq 5$
(b) A hexagon does not have six sides.
(c) Today is Monday.

Are the statements "The shirt is blue" and "The shirt is green" negations of each other? To check, we recall that a statement and its negation must have opposite truth values. If the shirt is actually red, then both of the statements are false and, hence, cannot be negations of each other. However, the statements "The shirt is blue" and "The shirt is not blue" are negations of each other, since they have opposite truth values no matter what color the shirt really is.

quantifiers

Some statements involve **quantifiers** and are more complicated to negate. Quantifiers include words such as *all, some, every,* and *there exists.*

universal quantifiers

The quantifiers *all, every,* and *no* refer to each and every element in a set and are called **universal quantifiers.** The quantifiers *some* and *there exists at least one* refer to one or more, or possibly all, of the elements in a set. *Some* and *there exists* are called **existential quantifiers.** Examples with universal and existential quantifiers follow.

existential quantifiers

1. All roses are red. (universal)
2. Every student is important. (universal)
3. For each counting number x, $x + 0 = x$. (universal)
4. Some roses are red. (existential)
5. There exists at least one even counting number less than 3. (existential)
6. There exist women who are taller than 200 cm. (existential)

Venn diagrams can be used to picture statements involving quantifiers. For example, Figure 2-20(a) and (b) picture statements (1) and (4) above. The x in Figure 2-20(b) can be used to show that there must be at least one element of the set of roses that is also red.

Figure 2-20

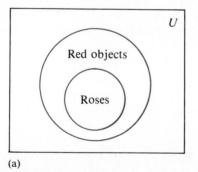
(a)

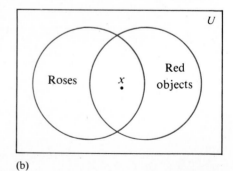
(b)

Consider the following statement involving the existential quantifier *some.* "Some professors at Paxson University have blue eyes." This means that at least one professor at Paxson University has blue eyes. It does not rule out the possibilities that all the Paxson professors have blue eyes or that some of the Paxson professors do not have blue eyes. Since the negation of a true statement is false, neither "Some professors at Paxson University do not have blue eyes" nor "All professors at Paxson have blue eyes" are negations of the original statement. One possible negation of the original statement is "No professors at Paxson University have blue eyes."

To discover if one statement is a negation of another, we use arguments similar to the above to determine if they have opposite truth values in all possible cases. Some general forms of quantified statements with their negations follow.

Statement	*Negation*
Some a are b.	No a is b.
Some a are not b.	All a are b.
All a are b.	Some a are not b.
No a is b.	Some a are b.

Example 2-24

Negate each of the following statements.

(a) All students like hamburgers.
(b) Some people like mathematics.
(c) There exists a counting number x such that $3x = 6$.
(d) For all counting numbers, $3x = 3x$.

Solution

(a) Some students do not like hamburgers.
(b) No people like mathematics.
(c) There does not exist a counting number x such that $3x = 6$.
(d) There exists a counting number x such that $3x \neq 3x$.

truth table

There is a symbolic system defined to help in the study of logic. If p represents a statement, the negation of the statement p is denoted by $\sim p$. **Truth tables** are often used to show all possible true-false patterns for statements. Table 2-5 summarizes the truth tables for p and $\sim p$.

Table 2-5

Statement p	Negation $\sim p$
T	F
F	T

Observe that p and $\sim p$ are analogous to sets P and $\bar{P}$. If x is an element of P, then x is not an element of $\bar{P}$.

COMPOUND STATEMENTS

compound statement

From two given statements it is possible to create a new, **compound statement** by using a connective such as *and*. For example, "It is snowing" and "The ski run is open" together with *and* give "It is snowing and the ski run is open." Other compound statements can be obtained by using the connective *or.* For example, "It is snowing or the ski run is open."

The symbols ∧ and ∨ are used to represent the connectives *and* and *or,* respectively. For example, if *p* represents "It is snowing," and if *q* represents "The ski run is open," then "It is snowing and the ski run is open" is denoted by $p \wedge q$. Similarly, "It is snowing or the ski run is open" is denoted by $p \vee q$.

The truth value of any compound statement, such as $p \wedge q$, is defined using the truth table of each of the simple statements. Since each of the statements *p* and *q* may be either true or false, there are four distinct possibilities, as

conjunction

shown in Table 2-6. The compound statement $p \wedge q$ is called the **conjunction** of *p* and *q* and is defined to be true if and only if both *p* and *q* are true. Otherwise, it is false.

Table 2-6

p	q	Conjunction $p \wedge q$
T	T	T
T	F	F
F	T	F
F	F	F

We can find similarities between conjunction and set intersection. Consider Table 2-7, which shows all possibilities of whether or not an element is a member of sets *P*, *Q*, and $P \cap Q$.

Table 2-7

P	Q	$P \cap Q$
∈	∈	∈
∈	∉	∉
∉	∈	∉
∉	∉	∉

If we consider ∈ analogous to T and ∉ analogous to F, we see that Tables 2-6 and 2-7 are equivalent. The language involving set intersection and the language involving *and* in logic should be equivalent. Thus, for every property involving set intersection, there should be an equivalent property involving *and.* For example, *and* should be commutative and associative.

disjunction

The compound statement *p* or *q* is called the **disjunction** of *p* and *q*. In everyday language, *or* is not always interpreted in the same way, as we mentioned in the discussion of set union in Section 2-2. For example, "I will go to a movie or I will read a book" usually means that I will either go to a movie or read, but not do both. Recall that in this statement, the *or* is an *exclusive or.* However, in logic, we use an *inclusive or.* With the above sentence, an inclusive *or* would mean that the person would either go to a movie, or read a book, or do both. Hence, in logic, *p* or *q*, symbolized as $p \vee q$, is defined to be false if both *p* and *q* are false, and true in all other cases. This is summarized in Table 2-8.

Table 2-8

p	q	Disjunction $p \vee q$
T	T	T
T	F	T
F	T	T
F	F	F

Just as set intersection and *and* are analogous, so are set union and *or*. And in a similar way, for all properties involving set union, there are corresponding properties involving *or*, such as the commutative and associative properties. Expressions involving statements inside parentheses are treated similarly to expressions involving set unions and intersections.

Example 2-25

Given the following statements, classify each of the conjunctions and disjunctions as true or false.

p: $2 + 3 = 5$ r: $5 + 3 = 9$

q: $2 \cdot 3 = 6$ s: $2 \cdot 4 = 9$

(a) $p \wedge q$ (b) $p \wedge r$ (c) $s \wedge q$ (d) $r \wedge s$
(e) $\sim p \wedge q$ (f) $\sim (p \wedge q)$ (g) $p \vee q$ (h) $p \vee r$
(i) $s \vee q$ (j) $r \vee s$ (k) $\sim p \vee q$ (l) $\sim (p \vee q)$

Solution

(a) p is true and q is true, so $p \wedge q$ is true.
(b) p is true and r is false, so $p \wedge r$ is false.
(c) s is false and q is true, so $s \wedge q$ is false.
(d) r is false and s is false, so $r \wedge s$ is false.
(e) $\sim p$ is false and q is true, so $\sim p \wedge q$ is false.
(f) $p \wedge q$ is true [part (a)], so $\sim (p \wedge q)$ is false.
(g) p is true and q is true, so $p \vee q$ is true.
(h) p is true and r is false, so $p \vee r$ is true.
(i) s is false and q is true, so $s \vee q$ is true.
(j) r is false and s is false, so $r \vee s$ is false.
(k) $\sim p$ is false and q is true, so $\sim p \vee q$ is true.
(l) $p \vee q$ is true [part (g)], so $\sim (p \vee q)$ is false.

Not only are truth tables used to summarize the truth values of compound statements, they are also used to determine if two statements are logically equivalent. Two statements are **logically equivalent** if and only if they have the same truth values. For example, we could show that $p \wedge q$ is logically equivalent to $q \wedge p$ using truth tables as in Table 2-9.

logically equivalent

Table 2-9

p	q	$p \wedge q$	$q \wedge p$
T	T	T	T
T	F	F	F
F	T	F	F
F	F	F	F

Table 2-9 shows that *and* is commutative. A summary of properties of *and* and *or* is given below.

Properties

1. **Commutative properties**
   (a) $p \wedge q$ is logically equivalent to $q \wedge p$.
   (b) $p \vee q$ is logically equivalent to $q \vee p$.
2. **Associative properties**
   (a) $(p \wedge q) \wedge r$ is logically equivalent to $p \wedge (q \wedge r)$.
   (b) $(p \vee q) \vee r$ is logically equivalent to $p \vee (q \vee r)$.
3. **Distributive properties**
   (a) $p \wedge (q \vee r)$ is logically equivalent to $(p \wedge q) \vee (p \wedge r)$.
   (b) $p \vee (q \wedge r)$ is logically equivalent to $(p \vee q) \wedge (p \vee r)$.

As another example, consider $\sim p \vee \sim q$ and $\sim(p \wedge q)$. Table 2-10 shows headings and the four distinct possibilities for p and q. In the column headed $\sim p$, we write the negations of the p column. In the $\sim q$ column, we write the negation of the q column. Next, we use the values in the $\sim p$ and the $\sim q$ columns to construct the $\sim p \vee \sim q$ column. To find the truth values for $\sim(p \wedge q)$, we use the p and q columns to find the truth value for $p \wedge q$ and then negate $p \wedge q$.

Table 2-10

p	q	$\sim p$	$\sim q$	$\sim p \vee \sim q$	$p \wedge q$	$\sim(p \wedge q)$
T	T	F	F	F	T	F
T	F	F	T	T	F	T
F	T	T	F	T	F	T
F	F	T	T	T	F	T

Note that $\sim p \vee \sim q$ has the same truth values as $\sim(p \wedge q)$. Thus, the statements are logically equivalent. The equivalence between $\sim p \vee \sim q$ and $\sim(p \wedge q)$, along with the equivalence between $\sim(p \vee q)$ and $\sim p \wedge \sim q$, are

DeMorgan's Laws   referred to as **DeMorgan's Laws.** An analogue to this logical equivalence was encountered in Problem 16 of Problem Set 2-2.

PROBLEM SET 2-4

1. Determine which of the following are statements and then classify each statement as true or false.
   (a) $2 + 4 = 8$ (b) Shut the window.
   (c) Los Angeles is a state.   (d) He is in town.
   (e) What time is it?   (f) $5x = 15$
   (g) $3 \cdot 2 = 6$ (h) $2x^2 > x$
2. Use quantifiers to make each of the following true where x is a natural number.
   (a) $x + 8 = 11$ (b) $x + 0 = x$
   (c) $x^2 = 4$ (d) $x + 1 = x + 2$
3. Use quantifiers to make each equation in Problem 2 false.

4. Write the negation for each of the following statements.
   (a) The book has 500 pages.
   (b) Six is less than eight.
   (c) Johnny is not thin.
   (d) $3 \cdot 5 = 15$
   (e) Some people have blond hair.
   (f) All dogs have four legs.
   (g) Some cats do not have nine lives.
   (h) No dogs can fly.
   (i) All squares are rectangles.
   (j) Not all rectangles are squares.

(k) For all natural numbers x, $x + 3 = 3 + x$.

(l) There exists a natural number x such that $3 \cdot (x + 2) = 12$.

(m) Every counting number is divisible by itself and 1.

(n) Not all natural numbers are divisible by 2.

(o) For all natural numbers x, $5x + 4x = 9x$.

5. Complete each of the following truth tables.

(a)

p	$\sim p$	$\sim(\sim p)$
T		
F		

(b)

p	$\sim p$	$p \vee \sim p$	$p \wedge \sim p$
T			
F			

(c) Based on part (a), is p logically equivalent to $\sim(\sim p)$?

(d) Based on part (b), is $p \vee \sim p$ logically equivalent to $p \wedge \sim p$?

6. If q stands for "This course is easy" and r stands for "Lazy students do not study," write each of the following in symbolic form.

(a) This course is easy and lazy students do not study.

(b) Lazy students do not study or this course is not easy.

(c) It is false that both this course is easy and lazy students do not study.

(d) This course is not easy.

7. If p is false and q is true, find the truth values for each of the following.

(a) $p \wedge q$ (b) $p \vee q$

(c) $\sim p$ (d) $\sim q$

(e) $\sim(\sim p)$ (f) $\sim p \vee q$

(g) $p \wedge \sim q$ (h) $\sim(p \vee q)$

(i) $\sim(\sim p \wedge q)$ (j) $\sim q \wedge \sim p$

8. Find the truth value for each statement in Problem 7 if p is false and q is false.

9. For each of the following, is the pair of statements logically equivalent?

(a) $\sim(p \vee q)$ and $\sim p \vee \sim q$

(b) $\sim(p \vee q)$ and $\sim p \wedge \sim q$

(c) $\sim(p \wedge q)$ and $\sim p \wedge \sim q$

(d) $\sim(p \wedge q)$ and $\sim p \vee \sim q$

10. Complete the following truth table.

p	q	$\sim p$	$\sim q$	$\sim p \vee q$
T	T			
T	F			
F	T			
F	F			

11. Apply DeMorgan's Laws to restate the following in a logically equivalent form.

(a) It is not true that both today is Wednesday and the month is June.

(b) It is not true that yesterday I both ate breakfast and watched television.

(c) It is not raining or it is not July.

Review Problems

12. Use set-builder notation to write a set that is well defined.

13. Given $U = \{1, 2, 3, 4, 5, 6, 7, 8\}$, $A = \{1, 2, 3\}$, $B = \{2, 3\}$, and $C = \{5\}$, find each of the following.

(a) $A \cap B$ (b) $B \cup C$ (c) $A \cup \bar{B}$

(d) $\overline{A \cup B}$ (e) $A - B$

14. Draw a Venn diagram to show $(\overline{A \cup B}) \cup C$.

15. Illustrate the commutative property of set intersection using sets $A = \{a, b, c, d\}$ and $B = \{b, c, d\}$.

16. The given Venn diagram contains the cardinal numbers (not elements) of the different regions. For example, the cardinal number of $A \cap B \cap C$ is 3; that is, $n(A \cap B \cap C) = 3$. Complete the following.

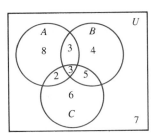

(a) $n(A) = $ _____

(b) $n(B) = $ _____

(c) $n(B \cup C) = $ _____

(d) $n(B \cap C) = $ _____

(e) $n((A \cup B) \cap \bar{C}) = $ _____

(f) $n(\overline{A \cup B \cup C}) = $ _____

(g) $n(A - B) = $ _____

17. A fraternity is planning a bus trip, which will include the math club, the English club, and the computer club. Eighteen students belong to both the math club and the English club, 12 belong to both the math club and the computer club, 14 belong to both the English club and the computer club, and 5 belong to all three clubs. If there are 30 students in the math club, 40 students in the English club, and 50 students in the computer club, how many bus seats are needed?

BRAIN TEASER

An explorer landed on an island inhabited by two tribes, the Abes and the Babes. Abes always tell the truth and Babes always lie. The explorer met three natives on the shore. He asked the first native to name his tribe and the native responded in his native tongue, which the explorer did not understand. The second native stated that the first native said that he was an Abe. The third native then stated that the first native had said he was a Babe. To what tribes do the second and third natives belong?

*Section 2-5

conditionals
implications / hypothesis
conclusion

Conditionals and Biconditionals

Statements expressed in the form "if p, then q" are called **conditionals,** or **implications,** and are denoted by $p \rightarrow q$. Such statements can also be read "p implies q." The "if" part of a conditional is called the **hypothesis** of the implication and the "then" part is called the **conclusion.**

Many types of statements can be put in "if-then" form. Examples follow.

Statement: All first-graders are 6 years old.
If-then form: If a child is a first-grader, then the child is 6 years old.

Statement: All gardenias are flowers.
If-then form: If a plant is a gardenia, then it is a flower.

An implication may also be thought of as a promise. Suppose Betty makes the promise, "If I get a raise, then I will take you to dinner." If Betty keeps her promise, the implication is true; if Betty breaks her promise, the implication is false. Consider the following four possiblities.

	p	q	
(1)	T	T	Betty gets the raise; she takes you to dinner.
(2)	T	F	Betty gets the raise; she does not take you to dinner.
(3)	F	T	Betty does not get the raise; she takes you to dinner.
(4)	F	F	Betty does not get the raise; she does not take you to dinner.

The only case in which Betty breaks her promise is when she gets her raise and fails to take you to dinner, case (2). If she does not get the raise, she can either take you to dinner or not without breaking her promise. The definition of implication is summarized in Table 2-11. Observe that the only case for which the implication is false is when p is true and q is false.

Table 2-11

p	q	Implication $p \rightarrow q$
T	T	T
T	F	F
F	T	T
F	F	T

Implications may be worded in several ways.

1. If the sun shines, then the swimming pool is open. (If p, then q.)
2. If the sun shines, the swimming pool is open. (If p, q.)
3. The swimming pool is open if the sun shines. (q if p.)
4. The sun shines implies the swimming pool is open. (p implies q.)
5. The sun is shining only if the pool is open. (p only if q.)
6. The sun shining is a sufficient condition for the swimming pool to be open. (p is a sufficient condition for q.)
7. The swimming pool open is a necessary condition for the sun to be shining. (q is a necessary condition for p.)

Any implication $p \rightarrow q$ has three related implication statements.

Statement: If p, then q. $p \rightarrow q$
Converse: If q, then p. $q \rightarrow p$
Inverse: If not p, then not q. $\sim p \rightarrow \sim q$
Contrapositive: If not q, then not p. $\sim q \rightarrow \sim p$

Example 2-26

Write the converse, the inverse, and the contrapositive for each of the following statements.

(a) If $2x = 6$, then $x = 3$.
(b) If I am in San Francisco, then I am in California.

Solution

(a) Converse: If $x = 3$, then $2x = 6$.
Inverse: If $2x \neq 6$, then $x \neq 3$.
Contrapositive: If $x \neq 3$, then $2x \neq 6$.
(b) Converse: If I am in California, then I am in San Francisco.
Inverse: If I am not in San Francisco, then I am not in California.
Contrapositive: If I am not in California, then I am not in San Francisco.

As Example 2-26(b) shows, a statement and its converse do not necessarily have the same truth value. On the other hand, an implication and its contrapositive do have the same truth value. Table 2-12 shows that, in general, a conditional statement and its contrapositive are logically equivalent and the converse and inverse of a conditional statement are logically equivalent. (Note that the converse and the inverse are contrapositives of each other.)

Table 2-12

p	q	$\sim p$	$\sim q$	Implication $p \rightarrow q$	Converse $q \rightarrow p$	Inverse $\sim p \rightarrow \sim q$	Contrapositive $\sim q \rightarrow \sim p$
T	T	F	F	T	T	T	T
T	F	F	T	F	T	T	F
F	T	T	F	T	F	F	T
F	F	T	T	T	T	T	T

Connecting a statement and its converse with the connective *and* gives $(p \rightarrow q) \wedge (q \rightarrow p)$. This compound statement can be written as $p \leftrightarrow q$ and

biconditional

usually is read "p if and only if q." The statement "p if and only if q" is called a **biconditional.** A truth table for $p \leftrightarrow q$ is given in Table 2-13. Observe that $p \leftrightarrow q$ is true if and only if p and q have the same truth values—that is, if and only if both statements are true or both are false. Observe that p is a necessary and sufficient condition for q, and vice versa.

Table 2-13

p	q	$p \rightarrow q$	$q \rightarrow p$	Biconditional $(p \rightarrow q) \wedge (q \rightarrow p)$ or $p \leftrightarrow q$
T	T	T	T	T
T	F	F	T	F
F	T	T	F	F
F	F	T	T	T

Example 2-27

Given the following statements, classify each of the biconditionals as true or false.

p: $2 = 2$ r: $2 = 1$
q: $2 \neq 1$ s: $2 + 3 = 1 + 3$

(a) $p \leftrightarrow q$ (b) $p \leftrightarrow r$ (c) $s \leftrightarrow q$ (d) $r \leftrightarrow s$

Solution

(a) $p \rightarrow q$ is true and $q \rightarrow p$ is true, so $p \leftrightarrow q$ is true.
(b) $p \rightarrow r$ is false and $r \rightarrow p$ is true, so $p \leftrightarrow r$ is false.
(c) $s \rightarrow q$ is true and $q \rightarrow s$ is false, so $s \leftrightarrow q$ is false.
(d) $r \rightarrow s$ is true and $s \rightarrow r$ is true, so $r \leftrightarrow s$ is true.

Now consider a statement such as the following.

It is raining or it is not raining.

The above statement can be modeled as $p \vee (\sim p)$ and has the truth table shown in Table 2-14.

Table 2-14

p	$\sim p$	$p \vee (\sim p)$
T	F	T
F	T	T

tautology

Observe that $p \vee (\sim p)$ is always true. A statement that is always true is called a **tautology.** One way to make a tautology is to take two logically equivalent statements such as $p \rightarrow q$ and $\sim q \rightarrow \sim p$ (from Table 2-12) and form them into a biconditional as follows.

$$(p \rightarrow q) \leftrightarrow (\sim q \rightarrow \sim p)$$

Since both $p \rightarrow q$ and $\sim q \rightarrow \sim p$ have the same truth values, then $(p \rightarrow q) \leftrightarrow (\sim q \rightarrow \sim p)$ is a tautology.

As another example of a tautology, consider Table 2-15.

Table 2-15

p	q	$p \to q$	$\sim(p \to q)$	$\sim q$	$p \wedge \sim q$	$\sim(p \to q) \leftrightarrow (p \wedge \sim q)$
T	T	T	F	F	F	T
T	F	F	T	T	T	T
F	T	T	F	F	F	T
F	F	T	F	T	F	T

In Table 2-15, we see that the negation of $p \to q$ is logically equivalent to $p \wedge \sim q$; that is, $\sim(p \to q) \leftrightarrow (p \wedge \sim q)$ is a tautology.

VALID REASONING

valid reasoning In problem solving, the reasoning used is said to be **valid** if the conclusion follows unavoidably from the hypotheses. Consider the following example.

Hypotheses: All roses are red.
　　　　　　　This flower is a rose.
Conclusion: Therefore, this flower is red.

The statement "All roses are red" can be written as the implication "If a flower is a rose, then it is red" and pictured with the Venn diagram in Figure 2-21(a).

Figure 2-21

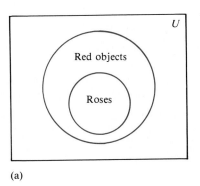 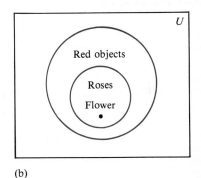

(a)　　　　　　　　　　　　　　　　(b)

The information "This flower is a rose" implies that this flower must belong to the circle containing roses, as pictured in Figure 2-21. This flower must also belong to the circle containing red objects. Thus, the reasoning is valid because it is impossible to draw a picture satisfying the hypotheses and contradicting the conclusion.

Consider the following argument.

Hypotheses: All elementary school teachers are rich.
　　　　　　　Some rich people are not thin.
Conclusion: Therefore, no elementary school teacher is thin.

Let E be the set of elementary school teachers, R be the set of rich people, and T be the set of thin people. Then the statement "All elementary school teachers are rich" can be pictured as in Figure 2-22(a). The statement "Some

(a)

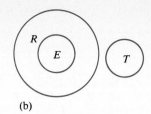
(b)

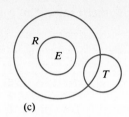
(c)

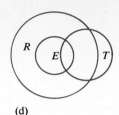
(d)

Figure 2-22

rich people are not thin" can be pictured in several ways. Three of these are illustrated in Figure 2-22(b)–(d).

According to Figure 2-22(d), it is possible that some elementary school teachers are thin, and yet the given statements are satisfied. Therefore, the conclusion that "No elementary school teacher is thin" does not follow from the given hypotheses. Hence, the reasoning is not valid.

If a single picture can be drawn to satisfy the hypotheses of an argument and contradict the conclusion, the argument is not valid. However, to show that an argument is valid, *all* possible pictures must be considered to show that there are no contradictions, that is, that there is no way to satisfy the hypotheses and contradict the conclusion. (Note that a valid argument can also be presented verbally.)

Example 2-28

Determine if the following argument is valid.

Hypotheses: All wasps are unfriendly.
No puppy is unfriendly.
Conclusion: Puppies are not wasps.

Solution

The first hypothesis is pictured as shown in Figure 2-23(a). The second hypothesis is pictured along with the first in Figure 2-23(b). Because puppies are outside the circle representing unfriendly creatures and wasps are inside the circle representing unfriendly creatures, the conclusion is valid and no puppy can be a wasp.

Figure 2-23

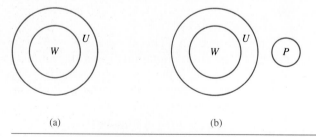
(a)   (b)

direct reasoning

A different method for determining if an argument is valid uses **direct reasoning** and a form of argument called the Law of Detachment (or **Modus**

Modus Ponens
Ponens). For example, consider the following true statements.

If the sun is shining, then we shall take a trip.
The sun is shining.

Law of Detachment

Using these two statements, we can conclude that we shall take a trip. In general, the **Law of Detachment** is stated as follows:

If a statement is in the form "if p, then q," and p is true, then q must also be true.

Example 2-29

Determine if each of the following arguments is valid.

(a) Hypotheses: If you eat spinach, then you will be strong.
You eat spinach.
Conclusion: Therefore, you will be strong.
(b) Hypotheses: If Claude goes skiing, he will break his leg.
If Claude breaks his leg, he cannot enter the dance contest. Claude goes skiing.
Conclusion: Therefore, Claude cannot enter the dance contest.

Solution

(a) Using the Law of Detachment, we see that the conclusion is valid.
(b) By using the Law of Detachment twice, the conclusion is shown to be valid.

indirect reasoning
Modus Tollens

A different type of reasoning, **indirect reasoning,** uses a form of argument called **Modus Tollens.** For example, consider the following true statements.

If Chicken Little had been hit by a jumping frog, he would have thought the earth was rising.
Chicken Little did not think the earth was rising.

What is the conclusion? The conclusion is that Chicken Little did not get hit by a jumping frog. This leads us to the generalized form of Modus Tollens:

If we have a conditional accepted as true, and we know the conclusion is false, then the hypothesis must be false.

Example 2-30

Determine conclusions for each of the following sets of true statements.

(a) If an old woman lives in a shoe, then she does not know what to do.
Mrs. Pumpkin Eater, an old woman, knows what to do.
(b) If Jack is nimble, he will not get burned.
Jack was burned.

Solution

(a) Mrs. Pumpkin Eater does not live in a shoe.
(b) Jack was not nimble.

Chain Rule

The final reasoning argument to be considered here involves the **Chain Rule.** Consider the following statements.

If my wife works, I can retire early.
If I retire early, I will become lazy.

What is the conclusion? The conclusion is that if my wife works, I will become lazy. In general, the Chain Rule can be stated as follows:

If "if a, then b" and "if b, then c" are true, then "if a, then c" is true.

Example 2-31   Determine conclusions for each of the following sets of true statements.

(a) If Alice follows the White Rabbit, she falls into a hole. If she falls into a hole, she goes to a tea party.

(b) If Chicken Little is hit by an acorn, we think the sky is falling. If we think the sky is falling, we will go to a fallout shelter. If we go to a fallout shelter, we will stay there a month.

Solution   (a) If Alice follows the White Rabbit, she goes to a tea party.

(b) If Chicken Little is hit by an acorn, we will stay in a fallout shelter for a month.

Remark   Note that in Example 2-31(b), the Chain Rule can be extended to contain several implications.

PROBLEM SET 2-5

1. Write each of the following in symbolic form if p is the statement "It is raining" and q is the statement "The grass is wet."
   (a) If it is raining, then the grass is wet.
   (b) If it is not raining, then the grass is wet.
   (c) If it is raining, then the grass is not wet.
   (d) The grass is wet if it is raining.
   (e) The grass is not wet implies that it is not raining.
   (f) The grass is wet if and only if it is raining.

2. For each of the following implications, state the converse, inverse, and contrapositive.
   (a) If you eat Meaties, then you are good in sports.
   (b) If you do not like this book, then you do not like mathematics.
   (c) If you do not use Ultra Brush toothpaste, then you have cavities.
   (d) If you are good at logic, then your grades are high.

3. Construct a truth table for each of the following.
   (a) $p \rightarrow (p \lor q)$ (b) $(p \land q) \rightarrow q$
   (c) $p \leftrightarrow \sim(\sim p)$ (d) $\sim(p \rightarrow q)$

4. If p is true and q is false, find the truth values for each of the following.
   (a) $\sim p \rightarrow \sim q$ (b) $\sim(p \rightarrow q)$
   (c) $(p \lor q) \rightarrow (p \land q)$ (d) $p \rightarrow \sim p$
   (e) $(p \lor \sim p) \rightarrow p$ (f) $(p \lor q) \leftrightarrow (p \land q)$

5. If p is false and q is false, find the truth values for each of the statements in Problem 4.

6. Can an implication and its converse both be false? Explain your answer.

7. Tom makes the true statement, "If it rains, then I am going to the movies." Does it follow logically that if it does not rain, then Tom does not go to the movies?

8. Consider the statement "If every digit of a number is 6, then the number is divisible by 3." Which of the following is logically equivalent to the statement?
   (a) If every digit of a number is not 6, then the number is not divisible by 3.
   (b) If a number is not divisible by 3, then every digit of the number is not 6.
   (c) If a number is divisible by 3, then every digit of the number is 6.

9. Write a statement logically equivalent to the statement "If a number is a multiple of 8, then it is a multiple of 4."

10. Use truth tables to prove that the following are tautologies.
    (a) $(p \rightarrow q) \rightarrow [(p \land r) \rightarrow q]$ Law of Added Hypothesis
    (b) $[(p \rightarrow q) \land p] \rightarrow q$ Law of Detachment
    (c) $[(p \rightarrow q) \land (\sim q)] \rightarrow \sim p$ Modus Tollens
    (d) $[(p \rightarrow q) \land (q \rightarrow r)] \rightarrow (p \rightarrow r)$ Chain Rule

11. Translate the following statements into symbolic form. Give the meanings of the symbols that you use.
    (a) If Mary's little lamb follows her to school, then it will break the rules and Mary will be sent home.
    (b) If it is not the case that Jack is nimble and quick, then Jack will not make it over the candlestick.
    (c) If the apple had not hit Isaac Newton on the head, then the laws of gravity would not have been discovered.

12. Investigate the validity of each of the following arguments.
    (a) All men are mortal.
        Socrates was a man.
        Therefore, Socrates was mortal.

(b) All squares are quadrilaterals.
All quadrilaterals are polygons.
Therefore, all squares are polygons.

(c) All teachers are intelligent.
Some teachers are rich.
Therefore, some intelligent people are rich.

(d) All xs are ys.
Some zs are xs.
Therefore, all zs are ys.

(e) If a student is a freshman, then she takes mathematics.
Jane is a sophomore.
Therefore, Jane does not take mathematics.

(f) If A, then not B.
If not B, then C.
Therefore, if A, then C.

(g) All fat people are jolly.
Some thin people are intelligent.
Therefore, no fat people are intelligent.

13. For each of the following, form a conclusion that follows logically from the given statements.
(a) All college students are poor.
Helen is a college student.

(b) Some freshmen like mathematics.
All people who like mathematics are intelligent.

(c) If I study for the final, then I will pass the final.
If I pass the final, then I will pass the course.
If I pass the course, then I will look for a teaching job.

(d) Every eagle can fly.
Some pigs cannot fly.

(e) Every equilateral triangle is isosceles.
There exist triangles that are isosceles.

14. Write the following in if-then form.
(a) Every figure that is a square is a rectangle.
(b) All integers are rational numbers.
(c) Figures with exactly three sides may be triangles.
(d) It only rains if it is cloudy.

★15. C. L. Dodgson, whose pseudonym was Lewis Carroll, wrote many books, including *Alice in Wonderland, Through the Looking-Glass,* and *Symbolic Logic.* In *Symbolic Logic,* he developed a series of puzzles in which the object is to use all the in-formation to reach some valid conclusion. In each of the following, reach a valid conclusion.

(a) No ducks waltz.
No officers ever decline to waltz.
All my poultry are ducks.

(b) Babies are illogical.
Nobody is despised who can manage a crocodile.
Illogical persons are despised.

(c) No kitten, that loves fish, is unteachable.
No kitten without a tail will play with a gorilla.
Kittens with whiskers always love fish.
No teachable kitten has green eyes.
No kittens have tails unless they have whiskers.

(d) Everyone who is sane can do logic.
No lunatics are fit to serve on a jury.
None of your sons can do logic.

Review Problems

16. Let $U = \{l, u, c, y, i, s, a, d, o, g\}$, $A = \{l, u, c, y\}$, $B = \{d, o, g\}$, $C = \{l, o, g\}$, and $D = \{g, l, a, d\}$, and find the following.
(a) $\overline{A}$ (b) $\overline{A \cup D}$
(c) $\overline{B \cap C}$ (d) $(B \cup C) \cap D$

17. In a recent township election, there were 340 registered voters. On election day 83 did not vote; those who did vote were registered as Republicans, Democrats, or Libertarians. Republicans always vote a straight Republican ticket, Democrats always vote a straight Democratic ticket, and Libertarians vote either a straight Libertarian ticket, a straight Republican ticket, or a straight Democratic ticket. If there were 84 Republican tickets, 127 Democratic tickets, and 57 Libertarian tickets, how many Libertarians voted for non-Libertarian tickets?

18. If A is the set of Americans, B is the set of basketball players, and O is the set of Olympic basketball players, describe a member of each of the following sets.
(a) $B - A$ (b) $A \cap O$
(c) $B - O$ (d) $A \cap B \cap O$

SOLUTION TO THE PRELIMINARY PROBLEM

UNDERSTANDING THE PROBLEM The problem is to determine the number of students in an art class, using information involving the types of pigment the students were working with. We know that the students were using three primary colors: red, blue, and yellow. We also know that the other colors obtained (orange, brown, and green) are a mixture of the primary colors. In addition, we have the following information about numbers of students using various pigments: 20 use red, 11 use red but no blue, 27 use blue or yellow, 6 use orange made from red and yellow but no blue, 3 use brown made from red, blue, and yellow, and 2 use green made from blue and yellow but no red. We also know that all students were using some type of pigment.

DEVISING A PLAN The Venn diagram, introduced in this chapter, can be used as a tool for classifying and sorting information. If we can use the three primary colors as the circles with which to sort the information, then we can use the strategy of drawing a diagram to answer the question.

CARRYING OUT THE PLAN With the Venn diagram in Figure 2-24, we can identify the various regions determined by the types of pigment used.

Figure 2-24

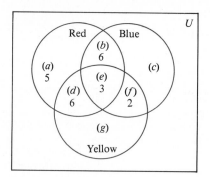

From the information given, we see that there are 3 students in region (e) and 2 students in region (f) because 3 students used all three pigments and 2 used blue and yellow but no red. In addition, we see that there are 6 students in region (d) who used red and yellow but no blue. Now, because there were 11 students using red but no blue, there are $11 - 6$, or 5, students in region (a). Knowing that there are 20 who are using red and $11 + 3$, or 14, for whom we have accounted, then there must be $20 - 14$, or 6, students represented in region (b). At this point, we know the numbers of students in all regions except (c) and (g). We also have used all the given information except that there are 27 students using blue or yellow. We have no way of separating out the number of students in regions (c) and (g), but we can still determine the total number of students in the class. The numbers of students using blue or yellow and the number of students using only red comprise the total number of students. Thus, we need only add 27 and 5 to determine that there are 32 students in all.

LOOKING BACK Another way to approach the problem is to add the number of students using red to the number of students using blue or yellow and subtract the number of students who are counted twice in that group. We could also vary the problem by changing the numbers of students in each group.

QUESTIONS FROM THE CLASSROOM

1. A student argues that $\{\varnothing\}$ is the proper notation for the empty set. What is your response?
2. A student does not believe that the empty set is a subset of every set. What is your response?
3. A student asks, "If $A = \{a, b, c\}$ and $B = \{b, c, d\}$, why isn't it true that $A \cup B = \{a, b, c, b, c, d\}$?" What is your response?
4. A student asks, "How can I tell if a set is infinite?" What is your response?
5. A student asks, "Are any two infinite sets equivalent? What is your response?
6. A student claims that a finite set of numbers is any set that has a largest element. Do you agree?
7. A student claims that the complement bar can be broken over the operation of intersection; that is, $\overline{A \cap B} = \bar{A} \cap \bar{B}$. What is your response?
8. A student claims that $\bar{A} \cap B$ includes all elements

that are not in A. What is your response?
9. A student asks whether a formula and a function are the same. What is your response?
10. A student asks whether all functions are relations. What is your reply?
11. A student states that either $A \subseteq B$ or $B \subseteq A$. Is the student correct?
12. A student is asked to find all one-to-one correspondences between two given sets. He finds the Cartesian product of the sets and claims that his answer is correct because it includes all possible pairings between the elements of the sets. How do you respond?
13. A student claims that the study of sets is worthwhile because it helps in understanding the mathematical concepts studied in elementary school. Do you agree? Why?

CHAPTER OUTLINE

I. Set definitions and notation
   A. A **set** can be described as any collection of objects.
   B. Sets should be **well defined;** that is, it must be true that an object either does or does not belong to the set.
   C. An **element** is any **member** of a set; for example, $a \in \{a, b\}$.
   D. Sets can be specified by either listing all the elements or using **set-builder notation.**
   E. The **empty set,** written $\varnothing$, contains no elements.
   F. The **universal set** contains all the elements being discussed.
II. Relationships and operations on sets
   A. Two sets are **equal** if and only if they have exactly the same elements.
   B. Two sets A and B are in **one-to-one correspondence** if and only if each element of A can be paired with exactly one element of B and each element of B can be paired with exactly one element of A.
   C. Two sets are **equivalent** if and only if their elements can be placed into one-to-one correspondence (written $A \sim B$).
   D. Set A is a **subset** of set B if and only if every element of A is an element of B (written $A \subseteq B$).
   E. Set A is a **proper subset** of set B if and only if every element of A is an element of B and there is at least one element of B that is not in A (written $A \subset B$).
   F. The **union** of two sets A and B is the set of all elements in A, in B, or in both A and B (written $A \cup B$).
   G. The **intersection** of two sets A and B is the set of all elements belonging to both A and B (written $A \cap B$).
   H. The **cardinal number** of a set indicates the number of elements in the set.
   I. **Ordinal numbers** are used to describe the relative position an element can occupy in an ordered set.
   J. A set is **finite** if the number of elements in the set is zero or a natural number.
   K. A set is **infinite** if it is not finite.
   L. Two sets A and B are **disjoint** if they have no elements in common.
   M. The **complement** of a set A is the set consisting of the elements of the universal set not in A (written $\bar{A}$).
   N. The **complement of set A relative to set B** (set difference) is the set of all elements in B that are not in A (written $B - A$).
   O. The **Cartesian product** of sets A and B is the set of all ordered pairs such that the

first element of each pair is an element of A and the second element of each pair is an element of B (written $A \times B$).

P. **Venn diagrams** are useful in determining relationships between sets.

III. Properties of set operations

For all sets A, B, C, and universal set U, the following properties hold:

A. $A \cap B = B \cap A$; **commutative property of set intersection**

B. $A \cup B = B \cup A$; **commutative property of set union**

C. $(A \cap B) \cap C = A \cap (B \cap C)$; **associative property of set intersection**

D. $(A \cup B) \cup C = A \cup (B \cup C)$; **associative property of set union**

E. $A \cap (B \cup C) = (A \cap B) \cup (A \cap C)$; **distributive property of set intersection over union**

F. $A \cup (B \cap C) = (A \cup B) \cap (A \cup C)$; **distributive property of set union over intersection**

G. $A \cap U = U \cap A = A$; U is the **identity for set intersection**

H. $A \cup \varnothing = \varnothing \cup A = A$; $\varnothing$ is the **identity for set union**

I. $\bar{U} = \varnothing$; $\bar{\varnothing} = U$; $A \cap \bar{A} = \varnothing$; $A \cup \bar{A} = U$; $A = \bar{\bar{A}}$; **complement properties**

IV. Relations and functions

A. A **relation** R from set A to set B is a subset of $A \times B$; that is, if R is a relation, then $R \subseteq A \times B$.

B. Properties of relations

1. A relation R on a set X is **reflexive** if and only if for every element a of X, a is related to a.

2. A relation R on a set X is **symmetric** if and only if for all elements a and b of X, whenever a is related to b, then b is related to a.

3. A relation R on a set X is **transitive** if and only if, for all elements a, b, and c of X, whenever a is related to b and b is related to c, then a is related to c.

C. An **equivalence relation** is any relation R

that satisfies the reflexive, symmetric, and transitive properties.

D. A **function** from set A to set B is a relation from A to B in which each element of A is paired with one and only one element of B.

1. The set of all first components of a function, all the elements of A, is called the **domain** of the function.

2. The set of all second components of a function, a subset of B, is called the **range** of the function.

*V. Logic

A. A **statement** is a sentence that is either true or false, but not both.

B. The **negation** of a statement is a statement with the opposite truth value of the given statement.

C. **Universal quantifiers** refer to each and every element in a set.

D. **Existential quantifiers** refer to one or more, or possibly all, of the elements in a set.

E. The **compound statement** $p \wedge q$ is called the **conjunction** of p and q and is defined to be true if and only if both p and q are true.

F. The compound statement $p \vee q$ is called the **disjunction** of p and q and is true if either p or q or both are true.

G. Given a statement in the form $p \rightarrow q$, the following can be found:

1. **Converse:** $q \rightarrow p$

2. **Inverse:** $\sim p \rightarrow \sim q$

3. **Contrapositive:** $\sim q \rightarrow \sim p$

H. Two statements are **logically equivalent** if and only if they have the same truth value.

I. Statements of the form "if p, then q" are called **conditionals** or **implications** and are false only if p is true and q is false.

J. The statement "p if and only if q" is called a **biconditional.** It is true only if p and q have the same truth values.

K. A **tautology** is a statement that is always true.

L. Laws to determine validity of arguments include the **Law of Detachment, Modus Tollens,** and the **Chain Rule.**

CHAPTER TEST

1. Write the set of letters of the English alphabet using set-builder notation.

2. List all the subsets of $\{m, a, t, h\}$.

3. Let

$U = \{x \mid x$ is a person living in Montana$\}$

$A = \{x \mid x$ is a person 30 years or older$\}$

$B = \{x \mid x$ is a person less than 30 years old$\}$

$C = \{x \mid x$ is a person who owns a gun$\}$

Describe in words a member of each of the following sets.
(a) $\bar{A}$ (b) $A \cap C$ (c) $A \cup B$
(d) $\bar{C}$ (e) $\overline{A \cap C}$ (f) $A - C$

4. Let

$U = \{u, n, i, v, e, r, s, a, l\}$

$A = \{r, a, v, e\}$ $C\{l, i, n, e\}$

$B = \{a, r, e\}$ $D = \{s, a, l, e\}$

Find each of the following.
(a) $A \cup B$ (b) $C \cap D$
(c) $\bar{D}$ (d) $A \cap \bar{D}$
(e) $\overline{B \cup C}$ (f) $(B \cup C) \cap D$
(g) $(\bar{A} \cup B) \cap (C \cap \bar{D})$ (h) $(C \cap D) \cap A$
(i) $n(\bar{C})$ (j) $n(C \times D)$

5. Indicate the following sets by shading.

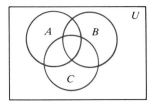

(a) $A \cap (B \cup C)$

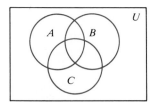

(b) $\overline{A \cup B} \cap C$

6. Let $A = \{s, e, t\}$ and $B = \{i, d, e, a\}$. Find each of the following.
(a) $B \times A$ (b) $A \times A$
(c) $n(A \times \varnothing)$ (d) $n(B - A)$

7. If $C = \{e, q, u, a, l, s\}$, how many proper subsets does C have?

8. Show one possible one-to-one correspondence between sets D and E if $D = \{t, h, e\}$ and $E = \{e, n, d\}$. How many different one-to-one correspondences between sets D and E are possible?

9. Use a Venn diagram to determine whether $A \cap (B \cup C) = (A \cap B) \cup C$ for all sets A, B, and C.

10. Describe, using symbols, the shaded portion in each of the following.

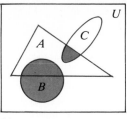

(a)

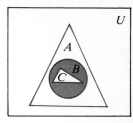

(b)

11. If $A = \{1, 2, 3\}$, $B = \{2, 3, 4, 5\}$, and $C = \{3, 4, 5, 6, 7\}$, illustrate the associative property of intersection of sets. Using sets A and B, illustrate the commutative property of union of sets.

12. Classify each of the following as true or false. If false, tell why.
(a) For all sets A and B, either $A \subseteq B$ or $B \subseteq A$.
(b) The empty set is a proper subset of every set.
(c) For all sets A and B, if $A \sim B$, then $A = B$.
(d) The set $\{5, 10, 15, 20, \ldots\}$ is a finite set.
(e) No set is equivalent to a proper subset of itself.
(f) If A is an infinite set and $B \subseteq A$, then B also is an infinite set.
(g) For all finite sets A and B, if $A \cap B \neq \varnothing$, then $n(A \cup B) \neq n(A) + n(B)$.
(h) If A and B are sets such that $A \cap B = \varnothing$, then $A = \varnothing$ or $B = \varnothing$.
(i) $\varnothing \in \varnothing$

13. In a student survey, it was found that 16 students liked history, 19 liked English, 18 liked mathematics, 8 liked mathematics and English, 5 liked history and English, 7 liked history and mathematics, 3 liked all three subjects, and every student liked at least one of the subjects. Draw a Venn diagram describing this information and answer the following questions.
(a) How many students were in the survey?
(b) How many students liked only mathematics?
(c) How many students liked English and mathematics but not history?

14. Which of the following relations are functions from the set of first components to the set of second components?
(a) $\{(a, b), (c, d), (e, a), (f, g)\}$
(b) $\{(a, b), (a, c), (b, b), (b, c)\}$
(c) $\{(a, b), (b, a)\}$

15. If $f(x) = 3x + 7$, find each of the following.
(a) $f(0)$ (b) $f(8)$ (c) $f(10)$

16. Given the following function rules and the domains, find the associated ranges.
(a) $f(x) = x + 3$ domain $= \{0, 1, 2, 3\}$
(b) $f(x) = 3x - 1$ domain $= \{5, 10, 15, 20\}$
(c) $f(x) = x^2$ domain $= \{0, 1, 2, 3, 4\}$
(d) $f(x) = x^2 + 3x + 5$ domain $= \{0, 1, 2\}$

17. What properties do each of the following relations, defined on the set of all people, have?
    (a) Belongs to the same book club as.
    (b) Is thinner than.
    (c) Is married to.
    (d) Is the father of.
*18. Which of the following are statements?
    (a) The moon is inhabited.
    (b) $3 + 5 = 8$
    (c) $x + 7 = 15$
    (d) Some women smoke.
    (e) How much is that doggie in the window?
*19. Negate each of the following.
    (a) Some women smoke.
    (b) $3 + 5 = 8$
    (c) All acid rock is loud.
    (d) Beethoven wrote only classical music.
*20. Write truth tables for each of the following.
    (a) $[p \vee (\sim q)] \wedge p$
    (b) $[p \rightarrow (\sim q)] \vee q$
    (c) $[p \rightarrow (\sim q)] \wedge [(\sim q) \rightarrow p]$
    (d) $[(\sim p) \vee (\sim q)] \rightarrow (q \wedge p)$
*21. Decide whether or not the following are equivalent.
    (a) $p \wedge (q \vee r);\ (p \wedge q) \vee (p \wedge r)$
    (b) $p \rightarrow q;\ q \rightarrow p$
*22. Write the converse, inverse, and contrapositive of the following: If we have a rock concert, someone will faint.
*23. Find valid conclusions for the following arguments.
    (a) All Americans love Mom and apple pie.
        Joe Czernyu is an American.

    (b) Steel eventually rusts.
        The Statue of Liberty has a steel structure.
    (c) Albertina will pass Math 100 or be a dropout.
        Albertina is not a dropout.
*24. Write the following argument symbolically and then determine its validity.
    If you are fair-skinned, you will sunburn.
    If you sunburn, you will not go to the dance.
    If you do not go to the dance, your parents will want to know why you didn't go to the dance.
    Your parents do not want to know why you didn't go to the dance.
    Therefore, you are not fair-skinned.
*25. Determine whether each of the following arguments is valid.
    (a) All diets are ridiculous.
        All diets are degrading.
        Therefore, all ridiculous diets are degrading.
    (b) No professors are stupid.
        All stupid people are rich.
        Therefore, no professors are rich.
    (c) Blondes have more fun.
        Some blondes are really brunettes.
        Therefore, some brunettes have more fun.
    (d) If Gloria goes fishing, she does not use flies.
        If Gloria does not use flies, then she is not a real fisherwoman.
        Gloria goes fishing.
        Therefore, Gloria is not a real fisherwoman.

SELECTED BIBLIOGRAPHY

Blomgrem, G. "What's in the Box—Subsets!" *The Arithmetic Teacher* 17 (March 1970):242.

Brieske, T. "Functions, Mappings, and Mapping Diagrams." *The Mathematics Teacher* 66 (May 1973): 463–468.

Bruni, J., and H. Silverman. "Using Classification to Interpret Consumer Information." *The Arithmetic Teacher* 24 (January 1977):4–12.

Cetorelli, N. "Teaching Function Notation." *The Mathematics Teacher* 72 (November 1979):590–591.

Coltharp, F. "Mathematical Aspects of the Attribute Games." *The Arithmetic Teacher* 21 (March 1974): 246–251.

Cruikshank, D. "Sorting, Classifying and Logic." *The Arithmetic Teacher* 21 (November 1974):588–598.

Geddes, D., and S. Lipsey, "The Hazards of Sets." *The Mathematics Teacher* 62 (October 1969): 454.

Gilbert, R. "Hey Mister! It's Upside Down!" *Arithmetic Teacher* 25 (December 1977):18–19.

Horak, V., and W. Horak. "Let's Do It: 'Button Bag' Mathematics." *Arithmetic Teacher* 30 (March 1983): 10–16.

Lettieri, F. "Meet the Zorkies: A New Attribute Material." *Arithmetic Teacher* 26 (September 1978):36–39.

Liedtke, W. "Experiences with Blocks in Kindergarten." *The Arithmetic Teacher* 22 (May 1975):406–412.

Liedtke, W. "Rational Counting." *Arithmetic Teacher* 26 (October 1978):20–26.

McGinty, R., and J. Van Beynen. "Deductive and Analytical Thinking." *Mathematics Teacher* 78 (March 1985):188–194.

National Council of Teachers of Mathematics. *Topics in Mathematics for Elementary School Teachers*. Booklet Number 1. Sets. 1964.

Papy, F. *Graphs and The Child*. New Rochelle, N.Y.: Cuisenaire Company of America, Inc., 1970.

Papy, F. *Mathematics and The Child*. New Rochelle, N.Y.: Cuisenaire Company of America, Inc., 1971.

Pereira-Mendoza, L. "Graphing and Prediction in the Elementary School." *The Arithmetic Teacher* 24 (February 1977):112–113.

Peterson, J., and G. Dolson. "Property Games." *The Arithmetic Teacher* 24 (January 1977):36–38.

Schoen, H. "Some Difficulty in the Language of Sets." *The Arithmetic Teacher* 21 (March 1974):236–237.

Scott, T. "A Different Attribute Game." *Arithmetic Teacher* 28 (March 1981): 47–48.

Silverman, H. "Teacher Made Materials for Teaching Numbers and Counting." *The Arithmetic Teacher* 19 (October 1972):431–433.

Vance, J. "The Large-Blue-Triangle: A Matter of Logic." *The Arithmetic Teacher* 22 (March 1975): 237–240.

Vilenkin, N. *Stories about Sets.* New York and London: Academic Press, 1969.

Warman, M. "Fun with Logical Reasoning." *Arithmetic Teacher* 29 (May 1982): 26–30.

Woodward, E., and L. Schroeder. "Detective Stories." *Arithmetic Teacher* 29 (December 1982):26–27.

CHAPTER 3

Numeration Systems and Whole Numbers

Preliminary Problem

Oscar developed a code in which letters were substituted for digits. Each letter in the addition given below represents one of the digits 0 through 9. What digit does each letter represent if different letters represent different digits? Is there more than one solution?

```
   MA
   MA
 + MA
 ----
  EEL
```

Introduction

Early people needed only a few numbers for their daily activities. With the coming of civilization, however, people invented a system to handle greater numbers. Such a system did not come readily, but developed over centuries. In this chapter, we examine different numeration systems that appeared during the development of our present system. After investigating early systems, we examine the Hindu-Arabic system, the base-ten system we use today. Algorithms for the operations of addition, subtraction, multiplication, and division of whole numbers are considered. Finally, properties and algorithms in number bases other than ten are discussed as another mechanism for developing a more generalized understanding of our present system.

Section 3-1

Numeration Systems

Early methods of "writing down" numbers included making notches or strokes on stone or wood and tying knots in a cord. The recorded symbols usually represented numbers of animals. Since that time, numerals have changed extensively. Figure 3-1 shows some changes leading to our present-day Hindu-Arabic system. Even today, there are variations in the Hindu-Arabic symbols used around the world. For example, Arabs use 0 for 5 and . for 0.

Figure 3-1

(Hindu 300 B.C.)

(Hindu 876 A.D.)

(Hindu 11th century)

(West Arabic 11th century)

(East Arabic 1575)

(European 15th century)

(European 16th century)

numeral   Different symbols can be used to represent the same quantity. For example, 3 and III both represent the quantity we call three. The symbols 3 and III are called numerals. Strictly speaking, a **numeral** is a written symbol used

HISTORICAL NOTE

Multiplications and divisions were performed using Egyptian numerals by using successive additions and subtractions. The Egyptians recorded unit fractions, that is, fractions in the form $1/n$, by placing the symbol $\bigcirc$ over the numeral that represented the denominator. For example,

Fractions other than unit fractions were expressed as sums of unit fractions. For example, $\frac{3}{5}$ would be expressed as $\frac{1}{2} + \frac{1}{10}$. Addition was indicated by a pair of legs walking to the left and subtraction by a pair of legs walking to the right.

$$\underset{|\,|\,|}{\bigcirc} = \frac{1}{3}; \qquad \underset{|\,|\,|\,|}{\bigcirc} = \frac{1}{4}; \qquad \underset{\cap\,|}{\bigcirc} = \frac{1}{11}$$

number
to represent a quantity or number. A **number** is an abstract concept used to describe quantity. You can see a numeral but not a number. In this text, we distinguish between number and numeral only if the distinction clarifies a concept.

EGYPTIAN NUMERATION SYSTEM

numeration systems
Many civilizations developed **numeration systems,** that is, logically structured methods of denoting numbers. Some early systems—such as the Egyptian system, which dates back to about 3400 B.C.—were based on tally marks. Tally marks are scratches or marks that represent the items being counted. One tally mark is used for each object being counted, so that a one-to-one correspondence exists between tally marks and the objects. The Egyptian system was a very simple, but inefficient system for recording large numbers. Later improvements on the tally-mark system led to new numerals for certain groupings. This use of symbols to stand for groupings was a major development. The Egyptians drew on their environment for their symbols. For example, the Egyptians used a heel bone symbol, $\cap$, to stand for a grouping of ten tally marks.

$$|\,|\,|\,|\,|\,|\,|\,|\,|\,| \longrightarrow \cap$$

Other numerals that the Egyptians used in their system are given in Table 3-1.

Table 3-1

Egyptian Numeral	Description	Hindu-Arabic Face Value
|	Vertical staff	1
∩	Heel bone	10
9	Scroll	100
₤	Lotus flower	1000
⌀	Pointing finger	10,000
☾	Polliwog or burbot	100,000
☥	Astonished man	1,000,000

additive property   The Egyptian system involved an **additive property;** that is, the value of a number was the sum of the values of the numerals. An example is given below.

⌒	represents	100,000	
999	represents	300	(100 + 100 + 100)
∩∩	represents	20	(10 + 10)
||	represents	2	(1 + 1)
⌒999∩∩||	represents	100,322	

In the Egyptian system, the order of the numerals made no difference. However, the Egyptians customarily wrote the numerals in decreasing order from left to right.

BABYLONIAN NUMERATION SYSTEM

The Babylonian system was developed at about the same time as the Egyptian system. Records of the Babylonian system have been preserved for centuries on clay tablets that the Babylonians indented with a wedge-shaped stylus and baked in the sun. The symbols shown in Table 3-2 were made by using the stylus either vertically or horizontally.

Table 3-2

Babylonian Numeral	Hindu-Arabic Face Value
▼	1
◄	10

The Babylonian numerals 1 through 59 were similar to the Egyptian numerals, but the staff and the heel bone were replaced by the symbols in Table 3-2. For example, ◄◄ ▼▼ represented 22. For numbers greater than 59, the Babylonians used **place value.** The value of a digit in a given numeral depends on the placement of the digit with respect to other digits in the numeral. Numbers greater than 59 were represented by repeated groupings of sixty, much as we use groupings of ten today. For example, ▼▼   ◄◄▼▼ represents $2 \cdot 60 + 22$, or 142. The space indicates that ▼▼ represents $2 \cdot 60$ rather than 2. Numerals to the left of a second space have a value $60 \cdot 60$ times their face value, and so on.

place value

◄◄   ▼   represents $20 \cdot 60 + 1$, or 1201

◄▼ ◄▼   ▼   represents $11 \cdot 60 \cdot 60 + 11 \cdot 60 + 1$, or 40,261

▼ ◄▼ ◄▼   ▼   represents $1 \cdot 60 \cdot 60 \cdot 60 + 11 \cdot 60 \cdot 60 + 11 \cdot 60 + 1$, or 256,261

The initial Babylonian system contained inadequacies. For example, the symbol ▼▼ could have represented 2 or $2 \cdot 60$ because the Babylonian system lacked a symbol for zero until after 300 B.C.

ROMAN NUMERATION SYSTEM

Another system without a symbol for zero was the Roman numeration system, which remains in use today, as seen on cornerstones, on the opening pages of books, and on the faces of clocks. The basic Roman numerals are pictured in Table 3-3.

Table 3-3

Roman Numeral	Hindu-Arabic Face Value
I	1
V	5
X	10
L	50
C	100
D	500
M	1000

Roman numerals can be combined using an additive property. For example, MDCLXVI represents $1000 + 500 + 100 + 50 + 10 + 5 + 1 = 1666$, CCCXXVIII represents 328, and VI represents 6. A symbol may be repeated at most three times; that is, IV is used rather than IIII. With some Roman

subtractive property

numerals, a **subtractive property** applies. For example, I is less than V, so if it is to the left of V, it is subtracted. Thus, IV has a value of $5 - 1$, or 4, and XC represents $100 - 10$, or 90. The only allowed pairings of symbols based on the subtractive property are given in Table 3-4.

Table 3-4

Roman Numeral	Hindu-Arabic Face Value
IV	$5 - 1$, or 4
IX	$10 - 1$, or 9
XL	$50 - 10$, or 40
XC	$100 - 10$, or 90
CD	$500 - 100$, or 400
CM	$1000 - 100$, or 900

Some extensions of the subtractive property could lead to ambiguous results. For example, IXC could be 91 or 89. By custom, 91 is written XCI, and 89 is written LXXXIX. In general, only one smaller symbol can be to the left of a larger symbol, and the pair must be one of those listed in Table 3-4.

multiplicative property

The Romans adopted the use of bars to write large numbers. The use of bars is based on a **multiplicative property.** A bar over a symbol or symbols indicates that the value is multiplied by 1000. For example, $\overline{V}$ represents $5 \cdot 1000$, or 5000, and $\overline{CDX}$ represents $410 \cdot 1000$, or 410,000. To indicate even greater numbers, more bars appear. For example, $\overline{\overline{V}}$ represents $5 \cdot 1000 \cdot 1000$, or 5,000,000; $\overline{\overline{\overline{CXI}}}$ represents $111 \cdot 1000 \cdot 1000 \cdot 1000$, or 111,000,000,000; and $\overline{CX}I$ represents $110 \cdot 1000 + 1$, or 110,001.

HINDU-ARABIC NUMERATION SYSTEM

The properties of numeration systems illustrated in this section are not definitive, but several of them are used in the Hindu-Arabic system. The Hindu-

digits

decimal system

Arabic numeration system we use today has ten basic symbols, called **digits:** 0, 1, 2, 3, 4, 5, 6, 7, 8, 9. Each place in a Hindu-Arabic numeral represents a power of 10. Thus, the system is called a **decimal system,** after the Latin word *decem* for ten.

The Hindu-Arabic system has the following important characteristics:

1. All numerals are constructed from the ten basic digits.
2. The system uses place value.
3. There is a symbol for zero.

In the base-ten system, we can write a numeral to represent any number of objects using only ten digits, 0 through 9. Numbers in the system are based on groupings of ten; ten groups of tens, or hundreds; ten groups of hundreds, or thousands; and so on.

Each digit in a numeral has two functions:

1. Its position in the numeral names its *place value.*
2. The digit itself names its *face value;* that is, it tells how many groupings of ten are indicated.

For example, in the numeral 5984, the 5 has place value "thousands," the 9 has place value "hundreds," the 8 has place value "tens," and the 4 has place value "units," as shown in Figure 3-2.

Figure 3-2

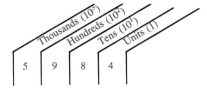

expanded form

factor

Hence, $5984 = 5 \cdot 1000 + 9 \cdot 100 + 8 \cdot 10 + 4 \cdot 1$. This representation is called the **expanded form** of the number. The expanded form consists of the sum of the products resulting from multiplying face values by place values. Using exponents, products such as $10 \cdot 10 \cdot 10$ and $10 \cdot 10$ can be written as 10^3 and 10^2, respectively; in each case, 10 is called a **factor** of the products. Thus, 5984 can be written using exponents as $5 \cdot 10^3 + 9 \cdot 10^2 + 8 \cdot 10 + 4$, which is another way of writing the expanded form of 5984. The notion of exponents can be generalized as shown below.

DEFINITION

If a is any number and n is any natural number, then a^n is defined by the following equation.

$$a^n = \underbrace{a \cdot a \cdot a \cdot \ldots \cdot a}_{n \text{ factors}}$$

*n*th power of *a*

exponent   base

a^n is called the **nth power of a;** n is called the **exponent;** a is called the **base.**

In Chapter 6 the definitions and properties of exponents are discussed in detail. It is shown there why it is useful to define a^0 as 1 if $a \neq 0$.

Computations involving exponents can be made using a calculator. If the calculator has a constant key, the following steps will compute $5^4 = 625$.

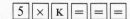

Some calculators have an exponential key such as $\boxed{y^x}$. This function computes some number y raised to the x power. For example, to compute 5^4, we press $\boxed{5}$ $\boxed{y^x}$ $\boxed{4}$ $\boxed{=}$.

PROBLEM SET 3-1

1. For each of the following, tell which numeral represents the greater number and why.
   (a) $\overline{\text{MCDXXIV}}$ and $\overline{\overline{\text{MCDXXIV}}}$
   (b) 4632 and 46,032
   (c) ⟨▼▼ and ⟨ ▼▼
   (d) 999∩∩|| and ⟨̊∩|

2. For each of the following, name both the succeeding and preceding numerals (one more and one less).
   (a) MCMXLIX   (b) $\overline{\text{MI}}$ (c) CMXCIX
   (d) ⟨⟨ ⟨▼   (e) ⟨̊99

3. For each of the following systems, discuss how you might add 245 and 989.
   (a) Babylonian   (b) Egyptian   (c) Roman

4. Write each of the following in Roman symbols.
   (a) 121   (b) 42   (c) 89   (d) 5282

5. Write each of the following using Egyptian symbols.
   (a) 52   (b) 103   (c) 100,003   (d) 38

6. How might you perform the following subtraction problem using Egyptian numerals?

   9 ∩∩|||
   −∩∩∩∩|||||

7. Complete the following table, which compares symbols for numbers in different numeration systems.

Hindu-Arabic	Babylonian	Egyptian	Roman
72			
	⟨ ▼▼		
		⟨̊99∩∩|||	
			DCLXVII

8. (a) Create a numeration system of your own with unique symbols and write a paragraph explaining the properties of your system.
   (b) Complete the table using your system.

Hindu-Arabic Numeral	Your System Numeral	Hindu-Arabic Numeral	Your System Numeral
1		100	
5		5,000	
10		10,000	
50		15,280	

9. For each of the following decimal numerals, give the place value of the underlined numeral.
   (a) 827,367   (b) 8,421,000
   (c) 97,998   (d) 810,485

10. Rewrite each of the following as a base-ten numeral.
    (a) $3 \cdot 10^6 + 4 \cdot 10^3 + 5$
    (b) $2 \cdot 10^4 + 1$
    (c) $3 \cdot 10^3 + 5 \cdot 10^2 + 6 \cdot 10$
    (d) $9 \cdot 10^6 + 9 \cdot 10 + 9$

11. Use the constant feature on a calculator to determine the value of $9 \cdot 9 \cdot 9 \cdot 9 \cdot 9 \cdot 9 \cdot 9$, or 9^7.

12. Use only the keys $\boxed{1}$, $\boxed{2}$, $\boxed{3}$, $\boxed{4}$, $\boxed{5}$, $\boxed{6}$, $\boxed{7}$, $\boxed{8}$, and $\boxed{9}$ for each of the following.
    (a) Fill the display to show the greatest number possible; each key may be used only once.
    (b) Fill the display to show the least number possible; each key may be used only once.
    (c) Fill the display to show the greatest number possible if a key may be used more than once.
    (d) Fill the display to show the smallest number possible if a key may be used more than once.

BRAIN TEASER

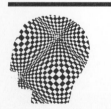

There are 3 nickels and 3 dimes concealed inside three boxes. Two coins are placed in each of the boxes, which are labeled 10¢, 15¢, and 20¢. The coins are placed in such a way that no box contains the amount of money showing on its label; for example, the box labeled 10¢ does not really have a total of 10¢ in it. What is the minimum number of coins that you would have to remove from a box, and from which box or boxes, to determine which coins are in which boxes?

Section 3-2

Whole Numbers and the Operations of Addition and Subtraction

Place value has been very important in the evolution of numeration systems, and the use of zero is essential. When zero is joined with the set of natural numbers, $N = \{1, 2, 3, 4, 5, \ldots\}$, we have the set of numbers called **whole numbers,** denoted by $W = \{0, 1, 2, 3, 4, 5, \ldots\}$. An alternate way of defining a whole number is to define it as the cardinal number of a finite set.

whole numbers

ADDITION OF WHOLE NUMBERS

The concept of addition of whole numbers is normally introduced to children using the notion of "combining." Suppose Jane has 4 pencils in one pile and 3 pencils in another. If she combines the two groups of pencils into one pile, how many pencils are in the combined pile? Figure 3-3 shows the solution as it might appear in an elementary school text.

Figure 3-3

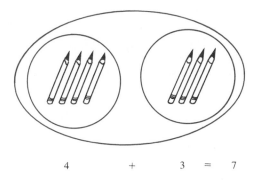

4   +   3   =   7

As shown, addition of whole numbers can be used to describe the situation in Figure 3-3. The combined set of pencils is the union of the set of 4 pencils and the set of 3 pencils. This leads to the following definition.

DEFINITION

> Let A and B be two disjoint finite sets. If $n(A) = a$ and $n(B) = b$, then $a + b = n(A \cup B)$.

Note that a and b are whole numbers and A and B are sets. The importance of A and B being disjoint in this definition is explored in the problem set.

addends / sum

The numbers a and b in this definition are the **addends;** $(a + b)$ is the **sum.** Addition is a *binary operation,* that is, a function that involves using two numbers at a time. (The domain of the function in this case is the set $W \times W$ and the range is W.)

In elementary school classrooms, a number line is one way to model whole numbers. Any line marked with two fundamental points, one representing 0 and the other representing 1, can be turned into a number line. On a horizontal line, choose an arbitrary point and label the point 0. Then choose any other point on the line to the right of the point labeled 0, and label this point 1. The points representing 0 and 1 mark the ends of a **unit segment.**

unit segment

Other points are marked and labeled as shown in Figure 3-4. Any two consecutive points in Figure 3-4 mark the ends of a segment that has the same length as the unit segment.

Figure 3-4

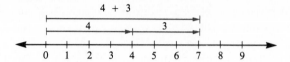

Using directed arrows on the number line, it is possible to model addition problems. For example, the sum of $4 + 3$ is shown in Figure 3-4. Arrows representing the addends, 4 and 3, are combined into one arrow representing the sum.

GREATER-THAN AND LESS-THAN RELATIONS

greater-than
less-than

A number line can also be used to describe **greater-than** and **less-than** relations on the set of whole numbers. For example, in Figure 3-4, notice that 7 is to the right of 4 on the number line. We say, "seven is greater than four," and we write $7 > 4$. Since 7 is to the right of 4, there is a natural number that can be added to 4 to get 7, namely, 3. Thus, $7 > 4$ since $7 = 4 + 3$. We can generalize this discussion to form a definition for "greater than."

DEFINITION

> For any whole numbers a and b, a is **greater than** b, written $a > b$, if and only if there exists a natural number k such that $a = b + k$.

The expression $a > b$ can also be read from right to left. From right to left, it reads "b is less than a," and this can be written as $b < a$. Thus, $b < a$ if and only if $a > b$. For example, 7 is greater than 3 implies that 3 is less than 7. Sometimes equality is combined with the inequalities greater than and less than to give the relations **greater than or equal to** and **less than or equal**

greater than or equal to
less than or equal to

to, denoted by $\geq$ and $\leq$. Note that $5 \geq 3$ and $3 \geq 3$ are both true statements.

WHOLE-NUMBER ADDITION PROPERTIES

We now examine properties of whole-number addition. These properties will be used to develop algorithms for more complicated addition. The first property says that when two whole numbers are added, the result is a unique whole number. This property is called the *closure property for addition of whole numbers,* and we say, "The set of whole numbers is closed under addition."

Property Closure Property for Addition of Whole Numbers If a and b are any whole numbers, then $a + b$ is a unique whole number.

Note that this property guarantees both the existence and the uniqueness of the sum. With some sets, the addition of two numbers from the set results in a number that does not belong to the set. In this case, we say the set is *not closed* under addition. For example, the set $\{0, 1, 2, 3\}$ is not closed under addition because a sum such as $2 + 3$ is not an element of the set.

Example 3-1

Which of these sets are closed under addition?

(a) $\{0, 1\}$ (b) $\{x \mid x$ is an even whole number$\}$
(c) $\{x \mid x$ is an odd whole number$\}$

Solution

(a) This set is not closed under addition. Although the sum of two different numbers such as 0 and 1 belongs to the set $\{0, 1\}$, it is not true for all sums involving numbers from the set. For example, $1 + 1 \notin \{0, 1\}$.
(b) This set is closed under addition because the sum of any two even whole numbers is always an even whole number. For example, $8 + 10 = 18$.
(c) This set is not closed under addition because the sum of two odd numbers is an even number. For example, the sum of $5 + 3$ is not odd.

The closure property for addition can be extended to any finite sum of whole numbers. If $a \in W$ and $b \in W$, then by the closure property of addition, $a + b \in W$. If $c \in W$, it follows that $(a + b) + c \in W$. This reasoning can be extended to more than three whole numbers.

Figure 3-5 shows two additions. Pictured above the number line is $3 + 5$, and below the number line is $5 + 3$. The sums are exactly the same. This demonstrates that $3 + 5 = 5 + 3$. This idea that two whole numbers can be added in either order is true for any two whole numbers a and b. (This can be easily proved using the definition of addition of whole numbers and the fact that $A \cup B = B \cup A$.) This property is called the *commutative property for addition of whole numbers* and we say, "Addition of whole numbers is commutative."

Figure 3-5

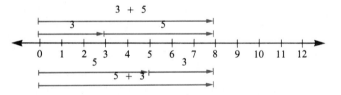

Property   **Commutative Property for Addition of Whole Numbers**   If a and b are any whole numbers, then $a + b = b + a$.

Remark   The commutative property can be justified using the definition of addition and the set properties developed in Chapter 2.

The commutative property for addition of whole numbers is not obvious to many children. They may be able to find the sum $9 + 2$ and not be able to find the sum $2 + 9$. (Why?)

When adding three or more numbers, it is necessary to select the order in which to add the numbers. For example, consider $4 + 8 + 2$. One person might group the 4 and the 8 together and do the computation as $4 + 8 + 2 = (4 + 8) + 2 = 12 + 2 = 14$. The parentheses indicate that the first two numbers are grouped together. Another person might recognize that it is easy to add any number to 10 and work the problem as $4 + 8 + 2 = 4 + (8 + 2) = 4 + 10 = 14$. Thus, we see that $4 + 8 + 2 = (4 + 8) + 2 = 4 + (8 + 2)$. This example illustrates the *associative property for addition of whole numbers* and we say, "Addition of whole numbers is associative."

Property   **Associative Property for Addition of Whole Numbers**   If a, b, and c are any whole numbers, then $(a + b) + c = a + (b + c)$.

Remark   In many elementary school texts in the lower grades this property is referred to as the *grouping property for addition*. This property is useful to elementary school students in exercises such as $15 + 6 + 4$. Using the associative property, they can group as follows: $15 + 6 + 4 = 15 + (6 + 4) = 15 + 10 = 25$.

When several numbers are being added, the parentheses are usually omitted because the grouping does not alter the result. The commutative and associative properties for addition are often used together. For example, to find the sum $20 + 5 + 60 + 4$, we group the addends as $(20 + 60) + (5 + 4)$ to obtain $80 + 9$, or 89.

Another property of addition of whole numbers is seen when one addend is 0. In Figure 3-6, set A has 5 blocks and set B has 0 blocks. The union of sets A and B has only 5 blocks.

Figure 3-6

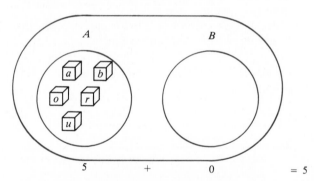

$$5 \quad\quad + \quad\quad 0 \quad\quad = 5$$

This example illustrates the following property of whole numbers.

Property   **Identity Property of Addition of Whole Numbers**   There is a unique whole number 0 such that for any whole number a, $a + 0 = a = 0 + a$.

additive identity   **Remark**   The number 0 is called the **additive identity** for whole numbers.

Example 3-2

Which of the properties for whole-number addition are used in each of the following?

(a) $5 + 7 = 7 + 5$
(b) $1001 + 733$ is a whole number.
(c) $(3 + 5) + 7 = (5 + 3) + 7$
(d) $(8 + 5) + 2 = 8 + (5 + 2)$
(e) $(10 + 5) + (10 + 3) = (10 + 10) + (5 + 3)$

Solution

(a) Commutative property for addition.
(b) Closure property for addition.
(c) Commutative property for addition.
(d) Associative property for addition.
(e) Commutative and associative properties for addition.

SUBTRACTION OF WHOLE NUMBERS

Subtraction is another operation on the set of whole numbers. Subtraction can be modeled in several ways. In this section, we discuss four models for subtraction: the take-away model, the comparison model, the missing-addend model, and the number-line model.

One way to think about subtraction is this: Instead of a second set of objects being joined to a first set, as in addition, the second set is being "*taken away*" from a first set. For example, suppose we have 8 blocks and we take away 3 of them, as shown in Figure 3-7.

Figure 3-7

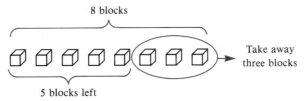

We record this process as $8 - 3$. Because 5 blocks remain, we write $8 - 3 = 5$.

A second way to consider subtraction is by using a *comparison* model. Suppose we have 8 blocks and 3 balls and we would like to know how many more blocks we have than balls. We can pair the blocks and balls, as shown in Figure 3-8, take away the paired objects, and determine that there are 5 more blocks than balls. We also write this as $8 - 3 = 5$.

Figure 3-8

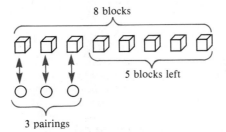

A third model for subtraction, the *missing-addend* model, relates subtraction and addition. Recall that in Figure 3-7, $8 - 3$ is pictured with blocks as 8 blocks "take away" 3 blocks. The number of blocks left is the number $8 - 3$, or 5. This can also be thought of as the number of blocks that could be added to 3 blocks in order to get 8 blocks; that is,

$$\boxed{8 - 3} + 3 = 8$$

missing addend

Thus, $8 - 3$ can be thought of as the number that can be added to 3 to obtain 8. The number $8 - 3$, or 5, is called the **missing addend** in the equation

$\square$ + 3 = 8. This idea can be generalized for whole numbers a and b as shown below.

DEFINITION

> For any whole numbers a and b, $a - b$ is the unique whole number c such that $a = b + c$.

minuend / subtrahend
difference

Remark   The notation $a - b$ is read "a minus b." The number a is called the **minuend**; b is called the **subtrahend**; c is called the **difference**.

Subtraction can also be defined in terms of set theory. This will be investigated in Problem 15 of Problem Set 3-2.

The above discussion shows how addition and subtraction are related. Many elementary school texts refer to this relationship in terms of "fact families." Notice the fact families on the student page below from *Addison-Wesley Mathematics,* 1987, Grade 4. Also notice that at the fourth-grade level, the commutative property of addition is referred to as the *order property for addition.*

We can also model subtraction using a number line. For example, $5 - 3$ is shown using a number line in Figure 3-9. Observe that an arrow extends

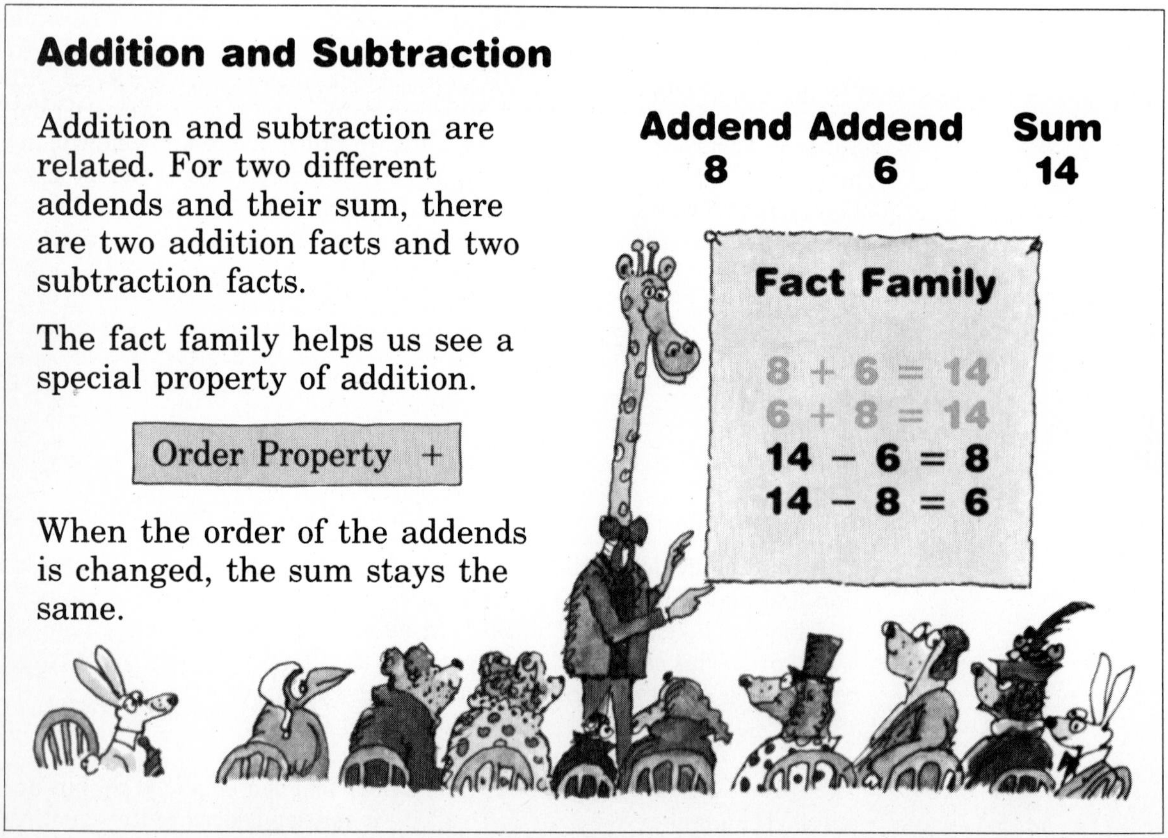

Addition and Subtraction

Addition and subtraction are related. For two different addends and their sum, there are two addition facts and two subtraction facts.

The fact family helps us see a special property of addition.

| Order Property + |

When the order of the addends is changed, the sum stays the same.

Addend   Addend   Sum
8   6   14

Fact Family

$8 + 6 = 14$
$6 + 8 = 14$
$14 - 6 = 8$
$14 - 8 = 6$

5 units to the right from 0. Because the operation is subtraction, the second arrow extends 3 units to the left from the end of the first arrow. Thus, we see that $5 - 3 = 2$.

Figure 3-9

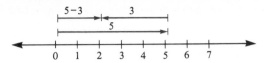

An alternate way to find $5 - 3$ using a number line is to determine the missing number that must be added to 3 to obtain the sum of 5. In Figure 3-10, the missing number is 2, and we have $5 - 3 = 2$.

Figure 3-10

Consider the difference $3 - 5$. Using the definition of subtraction, $3 - 5 = c$ means $c + 5 = 3$. Since there is no whole number c that satisfies the equation, the solution for $3 - 5$ cannot be found in the set of whole numbers. This means that the set of whole numbers is *not* closed under subtraction. We also see that for whole numbers a and b, $a - b$ is meaningful if and only if $a - b$ is a whole number, that is, if a is greater than or equal to b. Later, we consider the set of integers, which is closed under subtraction. Showing that subtraction of whole numbers is not commutative, not associative, and has no identity property is left as an exercise.

PROBLEM SET 3-2

1. Explain why $5 < 7$ and why $6 > 3$ by finding natural numbers k such that each is true.
   (a) $5 + k = 7$ (b) $6 = 3 + k$
2. In the definition of "greater than," can the natural number k be replaced by the whole number k? Why or why not?
3. Give an example to show why, in the definition of addition, sets A and B must be disjoint.
4. Use the number-line model to illustrate $6 + 3 = 9$.
5. For each of the following, find whole numbers to make the statements true, if possible.
   (a) $2 + \square = 7$ (b) $\square + 4 = 6$
   (c) $3 + \square \leq 5$ (d) $\square + 6 \geq 9$
6. Tell whether or not the following sets are closed under addition. If not, give a counterexample.
   (a) $B = \{0\}$
   (b) $T = \{0, 3, 6, 9, 12, \ldots\}$
   (c) $N = \{1, 2, 3, 4, 5, \ldots\}$
   (d) $V = \{3, 5, 7\}$
7. Each of the following is an example of one of the properties for addition of whole numbers. Identify the property illustrated.
   (a) $6 + 3 = 3 + 6$
   (b) $(6 + 3) + 5 = 6 + (3 + 5)$
   (c) $(6 + 3) + 5 = (3 + 6) + 5$

   (d) If $a \in W$ and $b \in W$, then $a + b \in W$.
   (e) If $q, r, s \in W$, $(q + r) + s = q + (r + s)$.
8. (a) For each of the following, use the underlined expressions to illustrate that English expressions are not always commutative.
      (i) Siamese <u>cat</u> <u>show</u>
      (ii) <u>Going to school</u> <u>I saw the birds</u>.
   (b) For each of the following, use the three words to illustrate that English expressions are not always associative.
      (i) dog house broken
      (ii) short story writer
9. For each of the following, find whole numbers to make the statements true, if possible. $a \in W$.
   (a) $8 - 5 = \square$ (b) $8 - \square = 5$
   (c) $\square - 4 = 9$ (d) $a - 0 = \square$
   (e) $a - \square = a$ (f) $\square - 3 \leq 6$
   (g) $\square - 3 > 6$
10. Rewrite each of the following subtraction problems as an addition problem.
   (a) $x - 119 = 213$
   (b) $213 - x = 119$
   (c) $213 - 119 = x$

11. Angelo read 6 pages of *Black Beauty* on Monday. He had read a total of 15 pages before Wednesday. How many pages did he read on Tuesday?

12. Find the next three terms in each of the following sequences.
(a) 8, 13, 18, 23, 28, _____, _____, _____
(b) 98, 91, 84, 77, 70, 63, _____, _____, _____

13. Use a number line to illustrate each of the following subtractions.
(a) $11 - 3$
(b) $8 - 4$

14. Illustrate $9 - 2$ using each of the models listed below.
(a) Take-away model.
(b) Comparison model.
(c) Missing-addend model.

15. Suppose $A \subseteq B$. If $n(A) = a$ and $n(B) = b$, then $b - a$ could be defined as $n(B - A)$. Choose two sets A and B and illustrate this definition.

16. Give a counterexample to show that each of the following is false in the set of whole numbers.
(a) $a - b = b - a$
(b) $(a - b) - c = a - (b - c)$
(c) $a - 0 = 0 - a = a$

17. For each of the following, determine possible whole numbers a, b, and c for which the statement is true.
(a) $a - b = b - a$
(b) $(a - b) - c = a - (b - c)$
(c) $a - 0 = 0 - a = a$
(d) $a(b - c) = ab - ac$

18. A palindrome is any number that reads the same backward and forward—for example, 121 and 2332. Try the following. Begin with any number. Is it a palindrome? If not, reverse the digits and add this new number to the original number. Is this a palindrome? If not, repeat the above procedure until a palindrome is obtained. For example, start with 78. Because 78 is not a palindrome, we add: $78 + 87 = 165$. Because 165 is not a palindrome, we add: $165 + 561 = 726$. Again, 726 is not a palindrome, so we add $726 + 627$ to obtain 1353. Finally, $1353 + 3531$ yields 4884, which is a palindrome.

(a) Try the above method with the following numbers.
(i) 93   (ii) 588   (iii) 2003
(b) Find a number for which the procedure described takes more than five steps to form a palindrome.

19. A magic square is an array of numbers in which the sum of every row, column, and diagonal is the same. Make each of the following a magic square.

(a)
	1	6
	5	7
4		2

(b)
17	10	
		14
13	18	

20. Make a calculator display numbers that have the following values.
(a) Seven tens
(b) Nine thousands
(c) Eleven hundreds
(d) Fifty-six tens
(e) Three hundred forty-seven tens

21. Make a calculator count to 100. (Use a constant operation if available.)
(a) By ones   (b) By twos   (c) By fives

22. Make a calculator count backwards to 0 from 27. (Use a constant operation if possible.)
(a) By ones   (b) By threes   (c) By nines

23. If a calculator is made to count by twos starting at 2, what is the thirteenth number in the sequence?

Review Problems

24. Write the number that precedes each of the following.
(a) CMLX   (b) XXXIX

25. What are the advantages of the Babylonian system over the Egyptian system?

BRAIN TEASER   Place the numbers 1 through 11 in the circles shown so that the sums are the same in each direction.

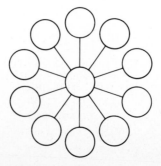

Section 3-3 — Multiplication and Division of Whole Numbers

MULTIPLICATION OF WHOLE NUMBERS

In this section, we discuss multiplication using three models: the repeated-addition model, the array model, and the Cartesian-product model. The *repeated-addition model* is introduced in Example 3-3.

Example 3-3

Looking at her empty classroom before the first bell, a mathematics teacher noticed that there were 6 rows of chairs with 4 chairs in each row. When the bell rang, each chair was occupied by a student. How many students were present?

Solution

A strategy here is to reduce the problem to one that we know how to solve. In this case, the problem can be rewritten as an addition problem. Since each chair is occupied, there are 6 rows of students with 4 students in each row for a total of

$$\underbrace{4 + 4 + 4 + 4 + 4 + 4}_{\text{six 4s}} = 24$$

We use the notation 6×4, or $6 \cdot 4$, to mean six 4s are added. Thus, multiplication of whole numbers can be interpreted as repeated addition. In general, for any whole numbers n and a,

$$n \cdot a = \underbrace{a + a + \cdots + a}_{n \text{ terms}}$$

Remark   In terms of set theory, $n \cdot a$ can be thought of as the union of n equivalent, disjoint sets, each with a elements.

Note that if $n = 0$, then $0 \cdot a$ means there are 0 terms. This is interpreted to mean $0 \cdot a = 0$.

A calculator can be used to show that multiplication and repeated addition yield the same result. For example, we may use the constant key to compute $6 \cdot 9$, as follows.

$$\boxed{9}\;\boxed{+}\;\boxed{\text{K}}\;\boxed{6}\;\boxed{=}\;\boxed{=}\;\boxed{=}\;\boxed{=}\;\boxed{=}\;\boxed{=}$$

(Remember, different calculators have different constant features.) If we press $\boxed{6}\;\boxed{\times}\;\boxed{9}\;\boxed{=}$, we obtain the same result.

HISTORICAL NOTE

William Oughtred (1575–1660), an English mathematician, placed emphasis on mathematical symbols. He first introduced the use of "St. Andrew's cross" as the symbol for multiplication. This symbol was not readily adopted because, as Gottfried Wilhelm von Leibnitz (1646–1716) objected, it was too easily confused with the letter x. Leibnitz adopted the use of the dot ($\cdot$) for multiplication, which then became prominently used.

Repeated addition can be modeled on a number line. For example, the number line for $5 \cdot 4$ is shown in Figure 3-11.

Figure 3-11

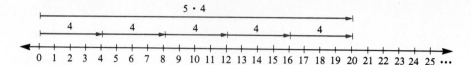

Another model that is useful in exploring multiplication of whole numbers is the *array model.* We introduce this model by crossing sticks (toothpicks) to create intersection points, which form an array. For example, to show $2 \cdot 3$, we place three toothpicks side by side and then cross them with two toothpicks, as shown in Figure 3-12(a). The product of $2 \cdot 3$ is the number of intersection points. The product of $4 \cdot 3$ is modeled in Figure 3-12(b). In Figure 3-12(c), we see that the product of $2 \cdot 0$ is 0 because there are no intersection points.

Figure 3-12

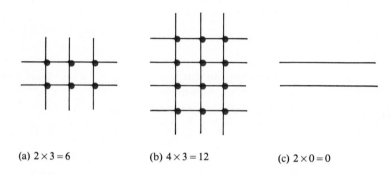

(a) $2 \times 3 = 6$ (b) $4 \times 3 = 12$ (c) $2 \times 0 = 0$

The following problem suggests the *Cartesian-product* model for multiplication of whole numbers.

PROBLEM I

At a health-food bar, you can order a soyburger on dark or light bread with any one of the following: mustard, mayonnaise, or horseradish. How many different soyburgers can a waiter call out to the cook?

UNDERSTANDING THE PROBLEM The problem asks for the number of combinations of bread and condiments, where the bread is chosen from a set $B = \{$light, dark$\}$ and the condiment is chosen from a set $C = \{$mustard, mayonnaise, horseradish$\}$.

DEVISING A PLAN One strategy is to list all possibilities in an organized manner. A model called a *tree diagram* can be used to accomplish this, as shown in Figure 3-13. To solve the problem, simply count the items under "What the cook hears."

CARRYING OUT THE PLAN All the possible ways of ordering the soyburgers are listed in Figure 3-13, so we see there are six orders that can be called out by the waiter.

Figure 3-13

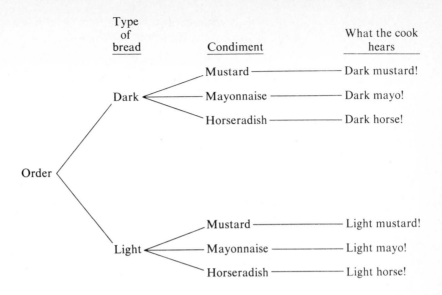

Type
of
bread   Condiment   What the cook
                                                      hears

Order
Dark
Mustard ——————— Dark mustard!
Mayonnaise ——————— Dark mayo!
Horseradish ——————— Dark horse!

Light
Mustard ——————— Light mustard!
Mayonnaise ——————— Light mayo!
Horseradish ——————— Light horse!

LOOKING BACK We could investigate problems involving different numbers of available breads and condiments at this point in order to find out if there is a general formula for finding the number of different orders the cook hears. What the cook hears could be written as ordered pairs—for example, (dark, mustard). The entire set of ordered pairs formed is the Cartesian product, $B \times C$, of sets $B = \{$light, dark$\}$ and $C = \{$mustard, mayonnaise, horseradish$\}$. The number of ordered pairs in $B \times C$ is the answer to the problem. Because the answer is $2 \cdot 3$, we see that $2 \cdot 3 = n(B) \cdot n(C) = n(B \times C)$.

Problem 1 demonstrates how multiplication can be defined in terms of Cartesian products. The definition is given below.

DEFINITION

> For finite sets A and B, if $n(A) = a$ and $n(B) = b$, then $a \cdot b = n(A \times B)$.

Remark   Note that in this definition, sets A and B do not have to be disjoint.

product   The expression $a \cdot b$ is called the **product** of a and b, and a and b are called
factors   **factors.** Also, note that $A \times B$ indicates the Cartesian product, not multiplication. We multiply numbers, not sets.

As with addition, multiplication on the set of whole numbers has the closure, commutative, associative, and identity properties.

Properties   **Closure Property for Multiplication of Whole Numbers**   For any whole numbers a and b, $a \cdot b$ is a unique whole number.

Commutative Property for Multiplication of Whole Numbers
For any whole numbers a and b, $a \cdot b = b \cdot a$.

Associative Property for Multiplication of Whole Numbers
For any whole numbers a, b, and c, $(a \cdot b) \cdot c = a \cdot (b \cdot c)$.

Identity Property for Multiplication of Whole Numbers   There is a unique whole number 1 such that for any whole number a, $a \cdot 1 = a = 1 \cdot a$.

The commutative property for multiplication of whole numbers is easily illustrated by building a 3×5 grid and then turning it sideways, as shown in Figure 3-14. We see that the number of 1×1 squares present in either case is 15—that is, $3 \cdot 5 = 15 = 5 \cdot 3$. Arrays using crossed sticks could also be used to demonstrate $3 \cdot 5 = 5 \cdot 3$. In general, the commutative property can be verified by recalling that $n(A \times B) = n(B \times A)$.

Figure 3-14

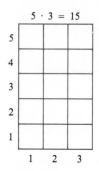

The associative property for multiplication of whole numbers can be illustrated as follows. Suppose $a = 3$, $b = 5$, and $c = 4$. Compare $3 \cdot (5 \cdot 4)$ and $(3 \cdot 5) \cdot 4$. First, $5 \cdot 4$ is illustrated with blocks, as shown in Figure 3-15(a). Then, 3 stacks of $(5 \cdot 4)$ blocks are pictured in Figure 3-15(b). Finally, we see $3 \cdot (5 \cdot 4)$ blocks in Figure 3-15(c).

Figure 3-15

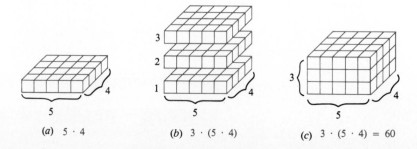

(a) $5 \cdot 4$ (b) $3 \cdot (5 \cdot 4)$ (c) $3 \cdot (5 \cdot 4) = 60$

In Figure 3-16, the blocks are combined in a different way to show $(3 \cdot 5) \cdot 4$. In Figures 3-15(c) and 3-16(c), the same set of blocks is used. Hence, $3 \cdot (5 \cdot 4) = (3 \cdot 5) \cdot 4$.

Figure 3-16

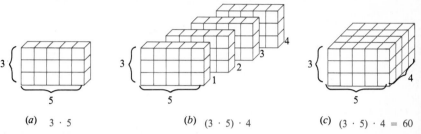

(*a*) $3 \cdot 5$ (*b*) $(3 \cdot 5) \cdot 4$ (*c*) $(3 \cdot 5) \cdot 4 = 60$

Students find the associative property useful in working exercises like the following.

$$3 \cdot 40 = 3 \cdot (4 \cdot 10) = (3 \cdot 4) \cdot 10 = 12 \cdot 10 = 120$$

multiplicative identity

The **multiplicative identity** for whole numbers is 1. For example, $3 \cdot 1 = 1 + 1 + 1 = 3$. In general, for any whole number a,

$$a \cdot 1 = \underbrace{1 + 1 + 1 + \cdots + 1}_{a \text{ terms}} = a$$

Thus, $a \cdot 1 = a$, which—along with the commutative property for multiplication—implies that $a \cdot 1 = a = 1 \cdot a$. Cartesian products can also be used to show that $a \cdot 1 = a = 1 \cdot a$.

Next, consider multiplication involving 0. For example, $6 \cdot 0 = 0 + 0 + 0 + 0 + 0 + 0 = 0$. Thus, we see that multiplying 6 by 0 yields a product of 0 and, by commutativity, $0 \cdot 6 = 0$. This is true in general and can be stated as follows.

Property   Zero Multiplication Property of Whole Numbers   For any whole number a, $a \cdot 0 = 0 = 0 \cdot a$.

The zero multiplication property of whole numbers can also be verified using the definition of multiplication in terms of Cartesian products. Let A be any set such that $n(A) = a$. Then, $a \cdot 0 = n(A \times \varnothing) = n(\varnothing) = 0$. Similarly, we can show that $0 \cdot a = 0$.

The next property that we investigate involves the use of both addition and multiplication. For example, in Figure 3-17, $5 \cdot (3 + 4) = (5 \cdot 3) + (5 \cdot 4)$.

Figure 3-17

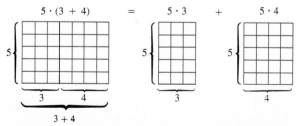

The properties of addition and multiplication also can be used to justify this result.

$$5 \cdot (3 + 4) = \underbrace{(3 + 4) + (3 + 4) + (3 + 4) + (3 + 4) + (3 + 4)}_{5 \text{ terms}}$$

Multiplication is repeated addition.

$$= (3 + 3 + 3 + 3 + 3) + (4 + 4 + 4 + 4 + 4)$$

Commutative and associative properties of addition

$$= 5 \cdot 3 + 5 \cdot 4$$

Multiplication is repeated addition.

This example illustrates the *distributive property of multiplication over addition* for whole numbers, which is stated in general as follows.

Property   **Distributive Property for Multiplication over Addition of Whole Numbers**   For any whole numbers a, b, and c,

$$a \cdot (b + c) = a \cdot b + a \cdot c$$

Students find the distributive property of multiplication over addition useful when doing mental arithmetic. For example,

$$11 \cdot 17 = (10 + 1) \cdot 17 = 10 \cdot 17 + 1 \cdot 17 = 170 + 17 = 187$$

Because the commutative property for multiplication of whole numbers holds, the distributive property for multiplication over addition can be rewritten as $(b + c) \cdot a = b \cdot a + c \cdot a$. The distributive property can be generalized to any finite number of terms. For example, $a \cdot (b + c + d) = a \cdot b + a \cdot c + a \cdot d$.

Example 3-4

Rename each of the following using the distributive property.

(a) $3 \cdot (x + y)$ (b) $(x + 1) \cdot x$
(c) $3 \cdot (2x + y + 3)$ (d) $a \cdot x + a \cdot y$
(e) $a \cdot x + a$ (f) $(x + 2) \cdot 5 + (x + 2) \cdot a$

Solution

(a) $3 \cdot (x + y) = 3 \cdot x + 3 \cdot y = 3x + 3y$
(b) $(x + 1) \cdot x = x \cdot x + 1 \cdot x = x^2 + x$
(c) $3 \cdot (2x + y + 3) = 3 \cdot (2x) + 3 \cdot y + 3 \cdot 3 = (3 \cdot 2) \cdot x + 3 \cdot y + 9$
$$= 6x + 3y + 9$$
(d) $a \cdot x + a \cdot y = a \cdot (x + y) = a(x + y)$
(e) $a \cdot x + a = a \cdot x + a \cdot 1 = a \cdot (x + 1) = a(x + 1)$
(f) $(x + 2) \cdot 5 + (x + 2) \cdot a = (x + 2) \cdot (5 + a) = (x + 2)(5 + a)$

Remark   Where there is no ambiguity, we omit the multiplication dot and, for example, write $3x$ rather than $3 \cdot x$. Furthermore, an expression such as $2 \cdot (a \cdot b)$ can be written as $2ab$.

Example 3-5

If $a \in W$ and $b \in W$, use the distributive property to simplify $(a + b)^2$.

Solution

By the definition of exponents, $(a + b)^2 = (a + b)(a + b)$. We consider the first term, $(a + b)$, as a single whole number and apply the distributive property. Then, applying the commutative and associative properties, we obtain the following.

$$(a + b)(a + b) = (a + b)a + (a + b)b$$
$$= (aa + ba) + (ab + bb)$$
$$= (a^2 + ba) + (ab + b^2)$$
$$= a^2 + (ba + ab) + b^2$$
$$= a^2 + (ab + ab) + b^2$$
$$= a^2 + 2ab + b^2$$

Remark By the closure property for addition, $ab \in W$, and since multiplication of whole numbers can be considered as repeated addition, $ab + ab = 2ab$.

The result in Example 3-5 can be demonstrated geometrically using the fact that the area A of a rectangle is given by $A = l \cdot w$, where l is the length of the rectangle and w is the width. If we build a square of length $(a + b)$ units as shown in Figure 3-18, then it has area $(a + b)^2$. Notice that this figure is divided into four disjoint regions that make up the large square. From the figure we see that $(a + b)^2 = a^2 + ab + ab + b^2 = a^2 + 2ab + b^2$. Students often mistakenly think that $(a + b)^2 = a^2 + b^2$. From Figure 3-18, we see that this is not the case.

Figure 3-18

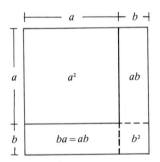

Difficulties involving the order of operations sometimes arise. For example, many students will treat $2 + 3 \cdot 6$ as $(2 + 3) \cdot 6$, while others will treat it as $2 + (3 \cdot 6)$. In the first case, the value is 30. In the second case, the value is 20. In order to avoid confusion, mathematicians agree that when no parentheses are present, multiplications are performed *before* additions. Thus, $2 + 3 \cdot 6 = 2 + 18 = 20$. This order of operations is not built into calculators that display the incorrect answer of 30.

DIVISION OF WHOLE NUMBERS

We have seen that one way to define subtraction is in terms of addition. Similarly, multiplication can be used to define a new operation called *division*. One approach to division is illustrated in Example 3-6.

Example 3-6

Benny Crocker baked 18 cookies. He decided to give an equal number of cookies to each of his three best friends, Bob, Charlie, and Dean. How many did each friend receive?

Solution

If we use the strategy of drawing a picture, we see that we can divide (or partition) the 18 cookies into three sets, with an equal number of cookies in each set. Figure 3-19 shows that each friend received 6 cookies.

Figure 3-19

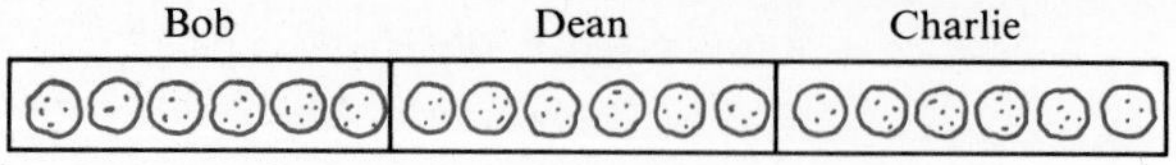

Bob   Dean   Charlie

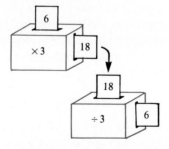

The solution to Example 3-6 can be designated using the division symbol, $\div$; that is, $18 \div 3 = 6$. Thus, $18 \div 3$ in Example 3-6 is the number of cookies in each of three disjoint sets whose union is 18 cookies. In this approach to division, we partition a set into a number of equivalent subsets.

Another strategy for solving Example 3-6 is to write an equation. Suppose that each friend receives c cookies. Then the three friends receive $3 \cdot c$ cookies, or 18 cookies. Hence, $3 \cdot c = 18$. Since $3 \cdot c = 18$, then $c = 6$. We have solved the division problem using multiplication. This leads us to the following definition of division of whole numbers.

DEFINITION

> For any whole numbers a and b with $b \neq 0$, $a \div b$ is the *unique* whole number c, if it exists, such that $b \cdot c = a$.

dividend / divisor
quotient

Remark   If the whole number c in the definition does not exist or is not unique, then $a \div b$ is not defined in the set of whole numbers. The notation $a \div b = c$ is read "a divided by b is equal to c." The number a is called the **dividend,** b is called the **divisor,** and c is called the **quotient.** Note that $a \div b$ can also be written as $\dfrac{a}{b}$ or $b\,\overline{)\,a}$.

The relationship between division and multiplication is shown using function machines in Figure 3-20. Multiplication and division are inverses of each other; that is, one operation "undoes" the other, as long as division by 0 is not involved.

Figure 3-20

Just as subtraction of whole numbers is not always meaningful, division of whole numbers is not always meaningful. For example, to find $383 \div 57$, we look for a whole number c such that

$57 \cdot c = 383$

There is no whole number c that satisfies this equation, so $383 \div 57$ has no meaning in the set of whole numbers. Thus, the set of whole numbers is not closed under division. (Other properties of division on the set of whole numbers are investigated in Problem 16 of Problem Set 3-3.)

It is not always easy to tell by looking whether a division is meaningful on the set of whole numbers. Consider $383 \div 57$. To find a solution to this division, we need to find a number c such that $57 \cdot c = 383$. Table 3-5 shows several products of whole numbers times 57. Since 383 is between 342 and 399, there is no whole number c such that $57 \cdot c = 383$.

Table 3-5

$57 \cdot 1$	$57 \cdot 2$	$57 \cdot 3$	$57 \cdot 4$	$57 \cdot 5$	$57 \cdot 6$	$57 \cdot 7$
57	114	171	228	285	342	399

remainder

division algorithm

In the real world, if 383 apples were to be divided among 57 students, then the division would have a solution; each student would receive 6 apples, and 41 apples would remain. The number 41 is called the **remainder.** Thus, 383 contains six 57s with a remainder of 41. Observe that the remainder is a whole number less than 57. The concept illustrated is called the **division algorithm.**

DIVISION ALGORITHM

Given any whole numbers a and b with $b \neq 0$, there exist unique whole numbers q (quotient) and r (remainder) such that

$$a = b \cdot q + r \quad \text{with} \quad 0 \leq r < b$$

Remark   The quotient q is the greatest whole number of bs in a.

Example 3-7

Solution

Find whole numbers q and r such that $16 = 3q + r$ with $0 \leq r < 3$.

$16 = 15 + 1 = 3 \cdot 5 + 1$. Thus, $q = 5$ and $r = 1$.

Remark   Note that $16 = 3 \cdot 4 + 4$ is not the correct form of the division algorithm because the remainder must be less than 3.

The whole numbers 0 and 1 deserve special attention with respect to division of whole numbers. Before reading on, try finding the values of the following three expressions:

1. $3 \div 0$
2. $0 \div 3$
3. $0 \div 0$

Consider the following explanations:

1. By definition, $3 \div 0 = c$ if there is a unique number c such that $0 \cdot c = 3$. Since the zero property of multiplication states that $0 \cdot c = 0$ for any whole number c, there is no whole number c such that $0 \cdot c = 3$. Thus, $3 \div 0$ is undefined.

2. By definition, $0 \div 3 = c$ if there exists a unique number c such that $3 \cdot c = 0$. The zero property of multiplication states that any number times 0 is 0. Since $3 \cdot 0 = 0$, then $c = 0$ and $0 \div 3 = 0$. Note that $c = 0$ is the only number that satisfies $3 \cdot c = 0$.
3. By definition, $0 \div 0 = c$ if there is a unique whole number c such that $0 \cdot c = 0$. Notice that for *any* c, $0 \cdot c = 0$. According to the definition of division, c must be unique. Since there is no *unique* number c such that $0 \cdot c = 0$, it follows that $0 \div 0$ is indeterminate, or undefined.

Division involving 0 may be summarized as follows.
Let n be any natural number. Then:

1. $n \div 0$ is undefined;
2. $0 \div n = 0$;
3. $0 \div 0$ is indeterminate, or undefined.

Recall that $n \cdot 1 = n$ for any whole number n. Thus, by the definition of division, $n \div 1 = n$. For example, $3 \div 1 = 3$, $1 \div 1 = 1$, and $0 \div 1 = 0$.

PROBLEM SET 3-3

1. Use the number-line model to illustrate why $3 \cdot 5 = 15$.
2. For each of the following, find the whole numbers that make the equations true.
   (a) $2 \cdot \square = 10$ (b) $\square \cdot 3 = 21$
   (c) $3 \cdot \square = 15$ (d) $\square \cdot 4 = 12$
3. Each ticket to the band concert costs \$2.00. Each ticket to the football game costs \$5.00. Jim bought 5 tickets to each event. What was his total bill?
4. Tell whether or not the following sets are closed under multiplication. If not, give a counterexample.
   (a) $\{0, 1\}$ (b) $\{0\}$
   (c) $\{2, 4, 6, 8, 10, \ldots\}$ (d) $\{1, 3, 5, 7, 9, \ldots\}$
   (e) $\{1, 4, 7, 10, 13, 16, \ldots\}$
   (f) $\{0, 1, 2\}$
5. Use the distributive property to describe how you might find the product $8 \cdot 3$ if you know only the addition table and the two and six multiplication facts.
6. Identify the property being illustrated in each of the following.
   (a) $3 \cdot 2 = 2 \cdot 3$ (b) $3(2 \cdot 4) = (3 \cdot 2)4$
   (c) $3(2 + 3) = 3(3 + 2)$ (d) $8 \cdot 0 = 0 = 0 \cdot 8$
   (e) $1 \cdot 8 = 8 = 8 \cdot 1$ (f) $6(3 + 5) = (3 + 5)6$
   (g) $6(3 + 5) = 6 \cdot 3 + 6 \cdot 5$
   (h) $(3 + 5)6 = 3 \cdot 6 + 5 \cdot 6$
7. Rename each of the following using the distributive property for multiplication over addition so that there are no parentheses in the final answer.
   (a) $(a + b)(c + d)$ (b) $3(x + y + 5)$
   (c) $\square(\triangle + \bigcirc)$ (d) $(x + y)(x + y + z)$
8. For each of the following, find—if possible—the whole numbers that make the equations true.

(a) $3 \cdot \square = 15$ (b) $18 = 6 + 3 \cdot \square$
(c) $\square \cdot \square = 25$ (d) $\square \cdot (5 + 6) = \square \cdot 5 + \square \cdot 6$
9. Rename each of the following using the distributive property for multiplication over addition and whole-number addition, if appropriate.
   (a) $2x + 3x$ (b) $x + 5x + 8x$
   (c) $2(x + 1) + 3(x + 1)$ (d) $2(x + 3) + x(x + 3)$
10. Perform each of the following computations.
    (a) $2 \cdot 3 + 5$ (b) $2(3 + 5)$
    (c) $2 \cdot 3 + 2 \cdot 5$ (d) $3 + 2 \cdot 5$
11. The generalized distributive property for three terms states that for any whole numbers a, b, c, and d, $a(b + c + d) = ab + ac + ad$. Justify this property using the distributive property for two terms.
12. The FOIL method is often used as a shortcut to multiply expressions like $(m + n)(x + y)$.

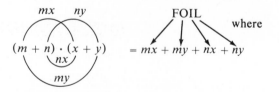

where F stands for product of the *f*irst terms, mx
      O stands for product of the *o*uter terms, my
      I stands for product of the *i*nner terms, nx
      L stands for product of the *l*ast terms, ny
   (a) Use the FOIL method on each of the following.
      (i) $(a + b)(a + b)$ (ii) $(50 + 8)(20 + 6)$
   (b) Use the distributive property to show why the FOIL method works.

13. Illustrate geometrically each of the following, using the concept of area.
  (a) $a \cdot (b + c) = ab + ac$
  (b) $(a + b) \cdot (c + d) = ac + ad + bc + bd$
14. For each of the following, find whole numbers to make the statement true, if possible.
  (a) $18 \div 3 = \square$
  (b) $\square \div 76 = 0$
  (c) $28 \div \square = 7$
15. Rewrite each of the following division problems as a multiplication problem.
  (a) $40 \div 8 = 5$ (b) $326 \div 2 = x$
  (c) $48 \div x = 16$ (d) $x \div 5 = 17$
  (e) $a \div b = c$ (f) $(48 - 36) \div 6 = x$
16. Show that, in general, each of the following is false if a, b, and c are whole numbers.
  (a) $a \div b = b \div a$
  (b) $(a \div b) \div c = a \div (b \div c)$
  (c) $a \div (b + c) = (a \div b) + (a \div c)$
  (d) $a \div b$ is a whole number.
17. Use the definition of division to justify that for any whole numbers a and b, where $b \neq 0$, $(ab) \div b = a$.
18. Because the Jones' water meter was stuck, they were billed the same amount for water each month for 5 months. If they paid $160, what was the monthly bill?
19. There were 17 sandwiches for 7 people on a picnic. How many whole sandwiches were there for each person if they were divided equally? How many were left over?
20. If it takes 1 minute per cut, how long will it take to cut a 10-foot log into 10 equal pieces?
21. For each of the following, name all the possible pairs of replacements for $\square$ and $\triangle$.
  (a) $34 = \square \cdot 8 + \triangle$
  (b) $\triangle = 4 \cdot 16 + 2$
  (c) $28 = \square \cdot \triangle + 3$
22. Find all the pairs of whole numbers whose product is 36.

23. A new model of a car is available in 4 different exterior colors and 3 different interior colors. How many different color schemes are possible for the car?
24. Tony has 5 ways to get from his home to the park. He has 6 ways to get from the park to the school. How many ways can Tony get from his home to school by way of the park?
25. To find $7 \div 5$ on the calculator, press $\boxed{7}\boxed{\div}\boxed{5}\boxed{=}$, which yields 1.4. To find the whole-number remainder, ignore the decimal portion of 1.4, multiply $5 \cdot 1$, and subtract this product from 7. The result is the remainder. Use a calculator to find the whole-number remainder for each of the following divisions.
  (a) $28 \div 5$ (b) $32 \div 10$ (c) $29 \div 3$
  (d) $41 \div 7$ (e) $49,382 \div 14$
26. In the problems below, use only the designated number keys. Use any function keys on the calculator.
  (a) Use the keys $\boxed{1}$, $\boxed{9}$, and $\boxed{7}$ exactly once each in any order and use any operations available to write as many of the whole numbers as possible from 1 to 20. For example, $9 - 7 - 1 = 1$ and $1 \cdot 9 - 7 = 2$.
  (b) Use the $\boxed{4}$ key as many times as desired with any operations to display 13.
  (c) Use the $\boxed{2}$ key three times with any operations to display 24.
  (d) Use the $\boxed{1}$ key five times with any operations to display 100.

Review Problems

27. Write 75 using Egyptian, Roman, and Babylonian numerals.
28. Write 35,206 in expanded form.
29. Give a set that is not closed under addition.
30. Are the whole numbers commutative under subtraction? If not, give a counterexample.
31. Illustrate $11 - 3$ using a number-line model.

LABORATORY ACTIVITY

Enter a number less than 20 on the calculator. If the number is even, divide it by 2; if it is odd, multiply it by 3 and add 1. Next, use the number on the display. Follow the given directions. Repeat the process again:
1. Will the display eventually reach 1?
2. Which number less than 20 takes the most steps in order to reach 1?
3. Do even or odd numbers reach 1 more quickly?
4. Investigate what happens with numbers greater than 20.

Section 3-4

Algorithms for Whole-Number Addition and Subtraction

algorithm

An **algorithm** (named for the ninth-century Arabian mathematician Mohammed al-Khowârizmî) is a step-by-step procedure used to accomplish a mathematical operation. It is valuable for every prospective elementary school teacher to know more than one algorithm to do operations. Not all students learn in the same manner, and the shortest, most efficient algorithms may not be the best for every individual. Single-digit addition and subtraction facts, the properties of addition, and the meaning of place value are prerequisites for understanding the algorithms in this section.

ADDITION ALGORITHMS

The use of concrete teaching aids—such as chips, bean sticks, an abacus, or base-ten blocks—helps provide insight into the creation of algorithms for addition. A set of base-ten blocks, shown in Figure 3-21, consists of *units, longs, flats,* and *blocks,* representing 1, 10, 100, and 1000, respectively.

Figure 3-21

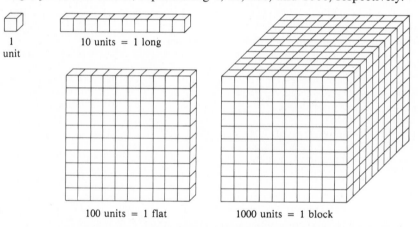

1 unit   10 units = 1 long

100 units = 1 flat   1000 units = 1 block

Students trade blocks by regrouping; that is, they take a set of base-ten blocks representing a number and trade them until they have the fewest possible pieces representing the same number. For example, suppose you have 58 units and want to trade them. What is the smallest number of pieces you can receive in exchange? The units can be grouped into tens to form longs. Five sets of 10 units each can be traded for 5 longs. Thus, 58 units can be traded for 5 longs and 8 units. In terms of numbers, this is analogous to rewriting 58 as $5 \cdot 10 + 8$. In this case, you cannot receive flats or blocks. The smallest number of pieces you can receive is 13.

Example 3-8

Suppose you have 11 flats, 17 longs, and 16 units. What is the smallest number of pieces you can receive in exchange?

Solution

The 16 units can be traded for 1 long and 6 units.

11 flats	17 longs	16 units	(16 units = 1 long and 6 units)
	1 long	6 units	(Trade)
11 flats	18 longs	6 units	(After the first trade)

The 18 longs can be traded for 1 flat and 8 longs.

11 flats	18 ~~longs~~	6 units ⎫	(18 longs = 1 flat and 8 longs)
1 flat	8 longs	⎬	(Trade)
12 flats	8 longs	6 units ⎭	(After the second trade)

The 12 flats can be traded for 1 block and 2 flats.

	~~12 flats~~	8 longs	6 units ⎫	(12 flats = 1 block and 2 flats)
1 block	2 flats		⎬	(Trade)
1 block	2 flats	8 longs	6 units ⎭	(After the third trade)

The smallest number of pieces is $1 + 2 + 8 + 6$ or 17, that is, 1 block, 2 flats, 8 longs, and 6 units. In terms of numbers, this is analogous to rewriting $11 \cdot 10^2 + 17 \cdot 10 + 16$ as $1 \cdot 10^3 + 2 \cdot 10^2 + 8 \cdot 10 + 6$, which implies that there are 1286 units.

We now use base-ten blocks to help develop an algorithm for whole-number addition. Suppose we wish to add $14 + 23$. We show this computation using a concrete model in Figure 3-22(a), an introductory algorithm in Figure 3-22(b), and the familiar algorithm in Figure 3-22(c).

Figure 3-22

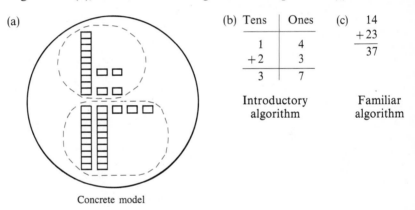

(a)

(b)

Tens	Ones
1	4
+2	3
3	7

Introductory algorithm

(c)
```
  14
 +23
 ───
  37
```
Familiar algorithm

Concrete model

A mathematical justification for this addition is the following.

$14 + 23 = (1 \cdot 10 + 4) + (2 \cdot 10 + 3)$	Expanded form
$= (1 \cdot 10 + 2 \cdot 10) + (4 + 3)$	Commutative and associative properties of addition
$= (1 + 2) \cdot 10 + (4 + 3)$	Distributive property of multiplication over addition
$= 3 \cdot 10 + 7$	Single-digit addition facts
$= 37$	Place value

Although this mathematical justification is not usually presented in the elementary school, the ideas and properties shown are necessary to understand why the algorithm works. Some problems are more involved than this one because they involve "regrouping," or "carrying," in which students trade by regrouping. This is described in terms of the base-ten blocks on the student page on page 128 from *Addison-Wesley Mathematics*, 1987, Grade 4.

Adding: Two or More Trades

Nina and Bert are circus elephants.
One night Nina ate 196 kg of hay and Bert ate 227 kg.
How many kilograms of hay did they eat together?

Since we want the total amount, we add.

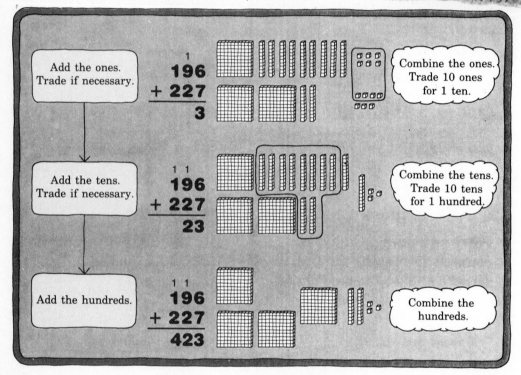

Nina and Bert ate 423 kg of hay that night.

After using concrete aids, children are ready to complete a computation such as 28 + 34 as shown in Figure 3-23(a); after some practice, they can complete the computation as shown in Figure 3-23(b).

Figure 3-23

(a)

Tens	Ones	
2	8	
+ 3	4	
5	12	(Add)
+ 1	2	(Regroup)
6	2	

(b)
$$\begin{array}{r} \overset{1}{2}8 \\ +34 \\ \hline 62 \end{array}$$

The following is a mathematical justification for this addition.

$$28 + 34 = (2 \cdot 10 + 8) + (3 \cdot 10 + 4) \qquad \text{Expanded form}$$

$$= (2 \cdot 10 + 3 \cdot 10) + (8 + 4) \qquad \text{Commutative and associative properties of addition}$$

$$= (2 \cdot 10 + 3 \cdot 10) + 12 \qquad \text{Single-digit addition fact}$$

$$= (2 \cdot 10 + 3 \cdot 10) + (1 \cdot 10 + 2) \qquad \text{Expanded form}$$

$$= (2 \cdot 10 + 3 \cdot 10 + 1 \cdot 10) + 2 \qquad \text{Associative property of addition}$$

$$= (2 + 3 + 1) \cdot 10 + 2 \qquad \text{Distributive property of multiplication over addition}$$

$$= 6 \cdot 10 + 2 \qquad \text{Associative property and single-digit addition facts}$$

$$= 62 \qquad \text{Expanded form}$$

scratch addition

An algorithm for addition called **scratch addition** is shown for $87 + 65 + 49$. This algorithm allows students to do complicated additions by doing a series of additions involving only two single digits.

1. Add the numbers in the units place starting at the top. When the sum is 10 or more, record this sum by scratching a line through the last number added and writing the number of units next to the scratched number. For example, since $7 + 5 = 12$, the "scratch" represents 10 and the 2 written down represents the units.

2. Continue adding the units. When the addition again results in a sum of 10 or more, repeat the process described in (1); $2 + 9 = 11$.

3. When the first column of additions is completed, write the number of units, 1, below the addition line. Count the number of scratches, 2, and add this number to the second column.

4. Repeat the procedure for each successive column.

Example 3-9

Compute the following additions using the scratch algorithm.

(a)   296
       840
     + 27

(b)   1369
       4813
       5879
     + 6183

Solution

(a)
$$
\begin{array}{r}
\overset{1}{}\;\overset{1}{}\; \\
2\;\;\overset{\diagup}{9}_{0}\;\;6 \\
8_{1}\;\;4\;\;0 \\
+\;\;\;\;2\;\;7_{3} \\
\hline
1\;\;1\;\;6\;\;3
\end{array}
$$

(b)
$$
\begin{array}{r}
\overset{2}{}\;\overset{2}{}\;\overset{2}{}\; \\
1\;\;3\;\;6\;\;9 \\
4\;\;\overset{\diagup}{8}_{3}\;\;1\;\;\overset{\diagup}{3}_{2} \\
\overset{\diagup}{5}_{2}\;\;\overset{\diagup}{8}_{1}\;\;\overset{\diagup}{7}_{6}\;\;\overset{\diagup}{9}_{1} \\
+\;\;6\;\;1\;\;8_{4}\;\;3^{1} \\
\hline
1\;\;8\;\;2\;\;4\;\;4
\end{array}
$$

MENTAL ADDITION

Many addition problems can be performed using mental arithmetic. Several examples for addition are given below. Work through these examples and try to explain why they work.

1. $67 + 36$
   (a) Add the tens. $60 + 30 = 90$
   (b) Add the units. $7 + 6 = 13$
   (c) Add the two sums. $90 + 13 = 103$

2. $67 + 36$
   (a) Add the first whole number to the tens in the second number. $67 + 30 = 97$
   (b) Add the units in the second number to the sum in (a). $97 + 6 = 103$

                $+3$ -3
3. $67 + 36$
   (a) Add a number to one addend to make it a multiple of 10. $67 + 3 = 70$
   (b) Subtract the same number from the other addend. $36 - 3 = 33$
   (c) Add the two results. $70 + 33 = 103$

4. $67 + 29$
   (a) Add 30 to the first number (30 is the next higher multiple of 10 after 29). $67 + 30 = 97$
   (b) Subtract 1 from the sum. $97 - 1 = 96$

5. $35 + 29 + 65$
   (a) Add the first addend to the tens of the second addend. $35 + 20 = 55$
   (b) Add the sum in (a) to the units of the second addend. $55 + 9 = 64$
   (c) Add the sum in (b) to the tens of the third addend. $64 + 60 = 124$
   (d) Add the sum in (c) to the units of the third addend. $124 + 5 = 129$

SUBTRACTION ALGORITHMS

As with addition, the use of base-ten blocks can provide a concrete model for subtraction. Consider $36 - 24$. We do this computation in Figure 3-24(a) using base-ten blocks, in Figure 3-24(b) using an introductory algorithm based on the blocks, and finally in Figure 3-24(c) using the familiar algorithm. The slashes through the blocks in the concrete model indicate that these blocks are taken away.

Figure 3-24

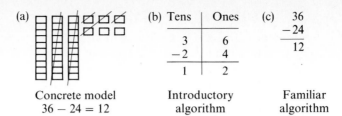

(a) Concrete model	(b) Introductory algorithm	(c) Familiar algorithm

(b)

Tens	Ones
3	6
−2	4
1	2

(c)

$$\begin{array}{r} 36 \\ -24 \\ \hline 12 \end{array}$$

Concrete model
36 − 24 = 12

Introductory algorithm

Familiar algorithm

Notice that this subtraction problem can be checked using the definition of subtraction: 36 − 24 = 12 because 12 + 24 = 36.

Subtractions become more involved when renaming is necessary, as in 56 − 29. The three stages for working this problem are shown in Figure 3-25.

Figure 3-25

(a)

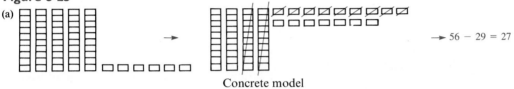

→ 56 − 29 = 27

Concrete model

(b)

Tens	Ones
5	6
−2	9

⟶

Tens	Ones
4	16
−2	9
2	7

(c)

$$\begin{array}{r} \overset{4\,1}{56} \\ -29 \\ \hline 27 \end{array}$$

Introductory algorithm

Familiar algorithm

The "cashier's algorithm" for subtraction is closely related to the formal definition of subtraction; that is, $a - b = c$ if and only if $b + c = a$. An example of the cashier's algorithm follows.

Example 3-10

Noah owed $11 for his groceries. He used a $50 check to pay the bill. While handing Noah the change, the cashier said, "$11, $12, $13, $14, $15, $20, $30, $50. Thank you. Have a good day." How much change did Noah receive?

Solution

Table 3-6 shows what the cashier said and how much money Noah received each time. Since $11 plus $1 is $12, Noah must have received $1 when the cashier said $12. The same reasoning follows for $13, $14, and so on. Thus, the total amount of change that Noah received is given by $1 + $1 + $1 + $1 + $5 + $10 + $20 = $39. In other words, $50 − $11 = $39 because $39 + $11 = $50.

Table 3-6

What the cashier said	$11	$12	$13	$14	$15	$20	$30	$50
Amount of money Noah received each time	0	$1	$1	$1	$1	$5	$10	$20

MENTAL SUBTRACTION

Mental arithmetic procedures can also be used to perform subtractions. For example, consider the following.

1. $67 - 36$
   (a) Subtract the tens in the second number from the first number. $67 - 30 = 37$
   (b) Subtract the units in the second number from the difference in (a). $37 - 6 = 31$
2. $71 - 39$
   (a) Add 1 to both numbers to make the second number a multiple of 10. $72 - 40$
   (b) Perform the new subtraction, which is an easier problem. $72 - 40 = 32$

Explore why these algorithms work.

ESTIMATIONS

Estimations are useful in determining whether answers to computations are reasonable. For example, the following computations can be estimated as follows.

	Exercise		Estimate
1.	4724 +3192	$\longrightarrow$	5000 +3000 ——— 8000
2.	1267 − 510	$\longrightarrow$	1300 − 500 ——— 800

Performing estimations, as seen above, requires a knowledge of place value and rounding skills. We illustrate a rounding procedure that can be generalized to all rounding situations. For example, suppose we wish to round 4724 to the nearest thousand. We may proceed as shown below:

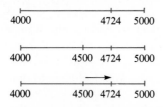

1. Determine between which two consecutive thousands the number lies.
2. Determine the midpoint between the thousands.
3. Determine which thousand the number is closer to by observing whether it is greater than or less than the midpoint.

4. If the number we wish to round is greater than or equal to the midpoint, we round the given number to the greater thousand. Otherwise, we round to the lesser thousand. In this case, we round 4724 to 5000.

Remark   Not all texts use the same rule for rounding when a number falls at a midpoint.

Estimations are very useful when working with calculators. They can be used to determine if the answer obtained on the calculator is reasonable or not. For example, consider how estimations are used on the student page below from *Addison-Wesley Mathematics,* 1987, Grade 7.

Estimating Sums and Differences

Tim Griffin manages a large record store. On Friday the store sold 376 records. On Saturday, 519 records were sold. Tim uses a calculator to add the two numbers.

First try

Second try

Which sum seems more reasonable? We can make an **estimate** of the sum by rounding each addend to the nearest hundred.

376 + 519 $\left(400 + 500 = 900 \atop \textbf{estimate} \right)$

The estimate 900 is close to 895, so 895 seems more reasonable.

Estimates may vary because of the way the numbers are rounded.

Estimate the difference. 2,261 − 914

Round to the nearest thousand.

2,261 − 914 $\left(2,000 - 1,000 = 1,000 \atop \textbf{estimate} \right)$

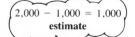

Round to the nearest hundred.

2,261 − 914 $\left(2,300 - 900 = 1,400 \atop \textbf{estimate} \right)$

PROBLEM SET 3-4

1. Perform the following additions using both the scratch and conventional algorithms. Use estimations to determine if your answers are reasonable.
   (a) 3789   (b) 3004   (c) 524
       9296   + 987   328
      +6843   567
                                  +135

2. Explain why the scratch addition algorithm works.

3. An addition algorithm from an elementary school text follows. Explain why it works.

2	7
+6	8
1	5
8	
9	5

4. Find the missing numbers in each of the following.
   (a)   _ _ 1   (b)   _ 0 2 5
        + 4 2 _   1 1 _ 6
        _ 4 0 2   +3 1 4 8
                               6 _ 6 _

   (c)   1 _ 6 9   (d)   2 _ 1
         2 _ 9 4   4 5 _
         9 5 4 6   + _ 8 4
         9 _ _ 3   1 3 2 6
       + 7 _ 6 4
        2 8 7 7 6

5. Perform the following subtractions. Verify your answers by using the definition of subtraction.
   (a) 436   (b) 1001   (c) 3003
     − 79   − 99   − 129

6. Find the missing numbers in each of the following.
   (a) 8 7 6 9 3   (b)   8 1 3 5
      − _ _ _ _ _   −4 6 8 2
        4 1 2 7 9   _ _ _ _

   (c) 3 _ _   (d) 1 _ _ _ 6
      −1 5 9   − 8 3 0 9
       _ 2 4   4 9 8 7

7. Place the digits 7, 6, 8, 3, 5, and 2 in the boxes to obtain: (a) the greatest sum; (b) the least sum.

   ☐ ☐ ☐
   + ☐ ☐ ☐
   ─────

8. Place the digits 7, 6, 8, 3, 5, and 2 in the boxes to obtain: (a) the greatest difference; (b) the least difference.

   ☐ ☐ ☐
   − ☐ ☐ ☐
   ─────

9. Paul went to the basketball game. There were 8767 people who purchased tickets for the game. The field house holds 9200 people. How many seats were not sold?

10. At the beginning of the year, the library had 15,282 books. During fall quarter, 125 books were added; during winter quarter, 137 were added; and during spring quarter, 238 were added. How many books did the library have at the end of the school year?

11. Find the next three numbers in each of the sequences given below.
    (a) 9, 14, 19, 24, 29, _____, _____, _____
    (b) 97, 94, 91, 88, 85, _____, _____, _____

12. Maria goes into a store with 87¢. If she buys a candy bar for 25¢, a balloon for 15¢, and a comb for 17¢, how much money does she have left?

13. Tom's diet allows only 1500 calories per day. For breakfast, Tom had skim milk (90 calories), a waffle with no syrup (120 calories), and a banana (119 calories). For lunch, he had $\frac{1}{2}$ cup of salad (185 calories) with mayonnaise (110 calories), tea (0 calories), and then he "blew it" with pecan pie (570 calories). Can he have dinner consisting of steak (250 calories), a salad with no mayonnaise, and tea?

14. The temperature is ⁻5°C. The weatherman predicts that the temperature will rise 3°C an hour for the next 10 hours. If the weatherman is correct, what will the temperature be after 10 hours?

15. Given the following addition problem, replace nine digits with 0s so that the sum of the numbers is 1111.

    999
    777
    555
    333
    111

16. Arrange eight 8s so that the sum is 1000.

17. (a) Use a calculator to place the whole numbers 24, 25, 26, 27, 28, 29, 30, 31 and 32 in the empty circles so that the sum of the values of the num-

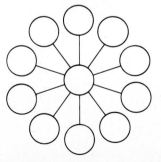

bers in the circles connected by each line is the same. Each number may be used exactly once.

(b) How many different numbers can be placed in the middle to obtain a solution?

18. The following is a supermagic square taken from an engraving called *Melancholia* by Dürer (1514).

16	3	2	13
5	10	11	8
9	6	7	12
4	15	14	1

(a) Find the sum of each row, the sum of each column, and the sum of each diagonal.

(b) Find the sum of the four numbers in the center.

(c) Find the sum of the four numbers in each corner.

(d) Add 11 to each number in the square. Is the square still a magic square? Explain your answer.

(e) Subtract 11 from each number in the square. Is the square still a magic square?

Review Problems

19. Write 5280 in expanded form.

20. Give an example of the associative property of addition for whole numbers.

21. Illustrate $11 + 8$ using a number-line model.

22. What is the value of $\overline{\text{MCDX}}$ in Hindu-Arabic numerals?

23. Rename the following using the distributive property of multiplication over addition.
(a) $ax + a$ (b) $3(x + y) + a(x + y)$

24. Jim has 5 new shirts and 3 new pairs of pants. How many combinations of new shirts and pants does he have?

LABORATORY ACTIVITY

1. For each of the following, subtract the numbers in each row and column, as shown in Figure 3-26. Investigate why this works.

(a)
16	3	
8	1	

(b)
28	7	
15	12	

Figure 3-26

12	7	5
5	4	1
7	3	4

2. The Chinese abacus, *suan pan* (see Figure 3-27), is still in use today. A bar separates two sets of bead counters. Each counter above the

Figure 3-27

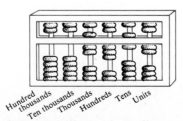

Hundred thousands   Ten thousands   Thousands   Hundreds   Tens   Units

> bar represents five times the counter below the bar. Numbers are illustrated by moving the counter toward the bar. The number 7362 is pictured. Practice demonstrating numbers and adding on the *suan pan*.

Section 3-5

Algorithms for Whole-Number Multiplication and Division

MULTIPLICATION ALGORITHMS

To aid in developing algorithms for multiplying multidigit whole numbers, we use the strategy of examining simpler computations first. Consider $4 \cdot 12$. Because we have seen that multiplication can be thought of as repeated addition, this computation could be pictured as in Figure 3-28—that is, as 4 rows of 12 dots, or 48 dots.

Figure 3-28

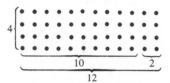

The dots in Figure 3-28 can also be partitioned to show that $4 \cdot 12 = 4 \cdot (10 + 2) = 4 \cdot 10 + 4 \cdot 2$. The numbers $4 \cdot 10$ and $4 \cdot 2$ are called *partial products*. We know that $4 \cdot 2 = 8$ from previous work with single-digit multiplication facts. Also, using the additive identity and place value, $4 \cdot 10 = 4 \cdot 10 + 0 \cdot 1 = 40$. Thus, $4 \cdot 12 = 4 \cdot (10 + 2) = 4 \cdot 10 + 4 \cdot 2 = 40 + 8 = 48$.

Figure 3-28 illustrates the distributive property of multiplication over addition on the set of whole numbers, a property essential to the development and understanding of multiplication algorithms. The process leading to an algorithm for multiplying $4 \cdot 12$ is as follows.

Tens	Ones
1	2
×	4

$$
\begin{array}{r} 10 + 2 \\ \times \quad\quad 4 \\ \hline 40 + 8 \end{array}
\longrightarrow
\begin{array}{r} 12 \\ \times \ 4 \\ \hline 8 \\ 40 \\ \hline 48 \end{array}
\longrightarrow
\begin{array}{r} 12 \\ \times \ 4 \\ \hline 48 \end{array}
$$

To compute products involving powers of 10, such as $3 \cdot 200$ or $3 \cdot (2 \cdot 10^2)$, we proceed as follows.

$$3 \cdot 200 = 3 \cdot (2 \cdot 10^2)$$

$$= (3 \cdot 2) \cdot 10^2$$

$$= 6 \cdot 10^2$$

$$= 6 \cdot 10^2 + 0 \cdot 10^1 + 0 \cdot 1$$

$$= 600$$

In the exercise above, we see that $6 \cdot 10^2 = 600$; that is, multiplication of 6 by 10^2 resulted in annexing two zeros to 6. This idea can be generalized to the statement that *multiplication of any natural number by 10^n, where n is a natural number, results in annexing n zeros to the number.*

When multiplying powers of 10, an extension of the definition of exponents is used. For example, $10^2 \cdot 10^1 = (10 \cdot 10) \cdot 10 = 10^3$. Observe that $10^3 = 10^{2+1}$. In general, where a is a natural number and m and n are whole numbers, $a^m \cdot a^n$ is given by the following.

$$a^m \cdot a^n = \underbrace{(a \cdot a \cdot a \cdot \ldots \cdot a)}_{m \text{ factors}}\underbrace{(a \cdot a \cdot a \cdot \ldots \cdot a)}_{n \text{ factors}}$$

$$= \underbrace{a \cdot a \cdot a \cdot \ldots \cdot a}_{m + n \text{ factors}} = a^{m+n}$$

Consequently, $a^m \cdot a^n = a^{m+n}$.

Example 3-11

Multiply:

(a) $10^5 \cdot 36$ (b) $10^3 \cdot 279$ (c) $10^{13} \cdot 10^8$ (d) $7 \cdot 200$

Solution

(a) $10^5 \cdot 36 = 3,600,000$
(b) $10^3 \cdot 279 = 279,000$
(c) $10^{13} \cdot 10^8 = 10^{13+8} = 10^{21}$
(d) $7 \cdot 200 = 7 \cdot (2 \cdot 10^2) = (7 \cdot 2) \cdot 10^2 = 1400$

Next, we consider computations with two-digit factors, such as $14 \cdot 23$. We know how to multiply by powers of 10 and by a single-digit number, so we write 14 as $10 + 4$ and use the distributive property of multiplication over addition.

$$14 \cdot 23 = (10 + 4) \cdot 23$$

$$= 10 \cdot 23 + 4 \cdot 23$$

$$= 230 + 92$$

This leads to an algorithm for multiplication.

```
  23                           23
× 14     10 + 4              × 14
────     ──────      or     ────
  92     (4 · 23)             92
 230     (10 · 23)            23
────                        ────
 322                         322
```

We are accustomed to seeing the partial product 230 written without the zero as 23. When children first learn multiplication algorithms, they should be encouraged to include the zero in order to avoid errors and promote better understanding. Children should also be encouraged to check whether their answers are reasonable. In this exercise, we know that the answer must be between $10 \cdot 20 = 200$ and $20 \cdot 30 = 600$ because $10 < 14 < 20$ and $20 < 23 < 30$. Because 322 is between 200 and 600, the answer is reasonable.

lattice multiplication   An algorithm called **lattice multiplication** for multiplying 14 and 23 follows. (Determining the reasons why lattice multiplication works is left as an exercise.)

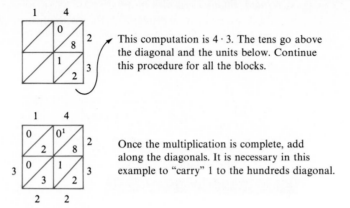

This computation is $4 \cdot 3$. The tens go above the diagonal and the units below. Continue this procedure for all the blocks.

Once the multiplication is complete, add along the diagonals. It is necessary in this example to "carry" 1 to the hundreds diagonal.

MENTAL MULTIPLICATION

Two procedures for performing mental multiplication are given below. Investigate each procedure to see why it works. The key to these procedures is being able to multiply by multiples of 10.

1. $5 \cdot 64$
   (a) Multiply the number of tens in the second factor by the first factor. $5 \cdot 60 = 300$
   (b) Multiply the number of units in the second factor by the first factor. $5 \cdot 4 = 20$
   (c) Add the two products. $300 + 20 = 320$
2. $5 \cdot 64$
   (a) Round the second factor to the next higher number of tens. $64 \rightarrow 70$
   (b) Multiply this number of tens by the first factor. $5 \cdot 70 = 350$
   (c) Multiply the difference of the rounded number and the second factor by the first factor. $70 - 64 = 6; 6 \cdot 5 = 30$
   (d) Subtract the product in (c) from the product in (b). $350 - 30 = 320$

DIVISION ALGORITHMS

Algorithms for division can be developed by using repeated subtraction or by using partitions. Consider the following:

> *A shopkeeper is packaging soda pop in cartons that hold 6 bottles each. She has 726 bottles. How many cartons does she need?*

We might reason that if 1 carton holds 6 bottles, then 10 cartons hold 60 bottles and 100 cartons hold 600 bottles. If 100 cartons are filled, there are

$726 - 100 \cdot 6$, or 126, bottles remaining. If 10 more cartons are filled, then $126 - 10 \cdot 6$, or 66, bottles remain. Similarly, if 10 more cartons are filled, $66 - 10 \cdot 6$, or 6, bottles remain. Finally, 1 carton will hold the remaining 6 bottles. The total number of cartons necessary is $100 + 10 + 10 + 1$, or 121. This procedure is summarized in Figure 3-29(a). A more efficient way to determine the number of cartons is shown in Figure 3-29(b).

Figure 3-29

(a)
```
  6 ) 726
    -600        100 sixes
    ────
     126
     -60        10 sixes
    ────
      66
     -60        10 sixes
    ────
       6
      -6         1 six
    ────
       0        121 sixes
```

(b)
```
  6 ) 726
    -600        100 sixes
    ────
     126
    -120         20 sixes
    ────
       6
      -6          1 six
    ────
       0        121 sixes
```

Divisions such as the one in Figure 3-29 are usually shown in elementary school texts as in Figure 3-30(a), or in the most efficient form, as in Figure 3-30(b), in which the numbers in color are omitted.

Figure 3-30

(a)
```
      1 ⎫
     20 ⎬ 121
    100 ⎭
  6 ) 726
    -600
    ────
     126
    -120
    ────
       6
      -6
    ────
       0
```

(b)
```
      121
  6 ) 726
    -6
    ──
     12
    -12
    ──
      6
     -6
    ──
      0
```

Base-ten blocks can also be used to model division. This is done by *partitioning* the number of blocks in the dividend into groups. Consider the operation $46 \div 2$ as demonstrated on the student page on page 140 from *Heath Mathematics, 1987*, Grade 6.

An example of division by a divisor of more than one digit is given below.

1. Estimate the quotient in $32\,)\,\overline{2618}$. Because $1 \cdot 32 = 32$, $10 \cdot 32 = 320$, $100 \cdot 32 = 3200$, we see that the quotient is between 10 and 100.

2. Find the number of tens in the quotient. Because $26 \div 3$ is approximately 8, then 26 hundreds divided by 3 tens is approximately 8 tens. We then write the 8 in the tens place, as shown.

```
         8
  32 ) 2618
     -2560      (32 · 80)
     ────
        58
```

3. Find the number of units in the quotient. Because $5 \div 3$ is approximately 1, then 5 tens divided by 3 tens is approximately 1. We then write 1 in the ones place, as shown.

$$
\begin{array}{r}
81 \\
32\overline{)\,2618} \\
-2560 \\
\hline
58 \\
-32 \qquad (32 \cdot 1) \\
\hline
26
\end{array}
$$

4. Write the remainder with the quotient.

$$
\begin{array}{r}
81 \text{ R } 26 \\
32\overline{)\,2618}
\end{array}
$$

5. Check: $32 \cdot 81 + 26 = 2618.$

Dividing by a 1-digit number

Remember that you divide from left to right one
place at a time.

EXAMPLE 1.
Step 1.   Divide tens.

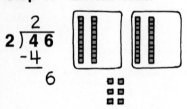

$$
\begin{array}{r}
2 \\
2\overline{)\,4\,6} \\
-4 \\
\hline
6
\end{array}
$$

Step 2.   Divide ones.

$$
\begin{array}{r}
23 \\
2\overline{)\,4\,6} \\
-4 \\
\hline
6 \\
-6 \\
\hline
0
\end{array}
$$

EXAMPLE 2.
Step 1.   Divide tens. Subtract.

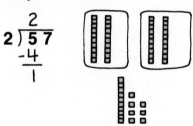

$$
\begin{array}{r}
2 \\
2\overline{)\,5\,7} \\
-4 \\
\hline
1
\end{array}
$$

Step 2.   Regroup 1 ten for 10 ones.

$$
\begin{array}{r}
2 \\
2\overline{)\,5\,7} \\
-4 \\
\hline
17
\end{array}
$$

Step 3.   Divide ones. Subtract.

$$
\begin{array}{r}
28 \text{ R }1 \\
2\overline{)\,5\,7} \\
-4 \\
\hline
17 \\
-16 \\
\hline
1
\end{array}
$$

Because of the advent of calculators, many mathematics educators are suggesting that long division by divisors of more than two digits should not be taught. What do you think?

The process just described is usually referred to as "long" division. Another technique, called "short" division, can be used when the divisor is a one-digit number and most of the work is done mentally. An example of short division is given on the student page below from *Addison-Wesley Mathematics,* 1987, Grade 6.

Calculators can be used to show that division of whole numbers can be thought of as repeated subtraction. For example, consider 135 ÷ 15. If the

Short Division

A company paid \$2,850 for 6 minutes of prime time advertising on radio. How much did the company pay per minute?

Since we want to separate the total into equal amounts, we divide.

Decide where to start.	→	Divide the hundreds. Write the remainder by the tens.	→	Divide the tens. Write the remainder by the ones.	→	Divide the ones.

$$\overset{4}{6)\overline{2,8\,5\,0}}$$

Not enough thousands 6 < 28 Divide the hundreds.

$$\overset{4}{6)\overline{2,8^45\,0}}$$

28 ÷ 6 = 4, R4

$$\overset{4\ 7}{6)\overline{2,8^45^30}}$$

45 ÷ 6 = 7, R3

$$\overset{4\ 7\ 5}{6)\overline{2,8^45^30}}$$

30 ÷ 6 = 5, R0

The company paid \$475 per minute for the advertising.

calculator has a constant key, press $\boxed{1}\,\boxed{5}\,\boxed{-}\,\boxed{\text{K}}\,\boxed{1}\,\boxed{3}\,\boxed{5}\,\boxed{=}\ldots$, and then count how many times you must press the $\boxed{=}$ key in order to make the display read 0. (Calculators with a different constant feature may require a different sequence of entries.) Compare your answer with the one achieved by pressing this sequence of keys.

$$\boxed{1}\,\boxed{3}\,\boxed{5}\,\boxed{\div}\,\boxed{1}\,\boxed{5}\,\boxed{=}$$

PROBLEM SET 3-5

1. Perform the following multiplications, using both the conventional and lattice multiplication algorithms.

   (a) 728
        × 94

   (b) 306
        × 24

2. Explain why the lattice multiplication algorithm works.

3. Use the distributive property to explain why $386 \cdot 10{,}000 = 3{,}860{,}000$.

4. Fill in the missing numbers in each of the following.

   (a)   4_6
         × 783
         ─────
         1_78
         3408
        _982
        ──────
        3335_8

   (b)   327
         × 9_1
         ─────
          327
         1_08
        _9_3
        ──────
        30__07

5. Simplify each of the following, using properties of exponents.

   (a) $5^7 \cdot 5^{12}$ (b) $6^{10} \cdot 6^2 \cdot 6^3$
   (c) $10^{296} \cdot 10^{17}$ (d) $2^7 \cdot 10^5 \cdot 5^7$

6. The following chart gives average water usage for one person for one day.

Use	Average Amount
Taking bath	110 L (liters)
Taking shower	75 L
Flushing toilet	22 L
Washing hands, face	7 L
Getting a drink	1 L
Brushing teeth	1 L
Doing dishes (one meal)	30 L
Cooking (one meal)	18 L

   (a) Use the chart to calculate how much water you use each day.
   (b) The average American uses approximately 200 L of water per day. Are you average?
   (c) If there are 215,000,000 people in the United States, approximately how much water is used in the United States per day?

7. How many seconds are in a day? A week? A year?

8. The given model illustrates $23 \cdot 14$.

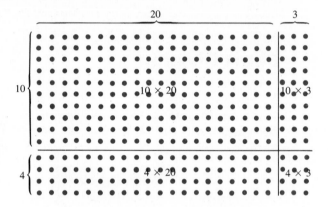

```
  23
× 14
────
  12   (4 × 3)
  80   (4 × 20)
  30   (10 × 3)
 200   (10 × 20)
────
 322
```

Draw similar models illustrating each of the following.

   (a) $6 \cdot 23$ (b) $18 \cdot 25$

9. Consider the following.

```
   476
 × 293
 ─────
   952  │ (2 · 476)
  4284  │ (9 · 476)
  1428  │ (3 · 476)
 ──────
 139468
```

   (a) Show that by using the conventional algorithm, the answer is correct.
   (b) Explain why the algorithm works.
   (c) Try the method to multiply 84 × 363.

10. The Russian peasant algorithm for multiplying 27 × 68 follows. (Disregard remainders when halving.)

Halves	Doubles	
	27 × ⑥⑧	
Halve 27 → 13	⑬⑥	Double 68.
Halve 13 → 6	272	Double 136.
Halve 6 → 3	⑤④④	Double 272.
Halve 3 → 1	⑩⑧⑧	Double 544.

In the "Halves" column, choose the odd numbers. In the "Doubles" column, circle the numbers paired with the odds from the "Halves" column. Add the circled numbers.

$$68$$
$$136$$
$$544$$
$$1088$$
$$\overline{1836} \quad \text{This is the product } 27 \cdot 68.$$

Try this algorithm for $17 \cdot 63$ and other numbers.

11. Find the two-digit number that, when added to its reverse, is closest to each of the following (for example, $12 + 21 = 33$).
(a) 50   (b) 100

12. Find the largest possible whole-number value of n such that
(a) $14n < 300$ (b) $21n \leq 7459$
(c) $7n \leq 2134$ (d) $483n < 79485$

13. Find the smallest possible whole number such that
(a) $14n > 300$ (b) $23n \geq 4369$
(c) $123n > 782$ (d) $222n > 8654$

14. Compute $6 \cdot 411$, showing the mathematical justification for each step.

15. Perform each division using both the repeated-subtraction and familiar algorithms.
(a) $8\overline{)623}$ (b) $36\overline{)298}$ (c) $391\overline{)4001}$

16. Place the digits 7, 6, 8, and 3 in the boxes to obtain: (a) the greatest quotient; (b) the least quotient.

☐)☐ ☐ ☐

17. If the astronauts from Apollo-Saturn 10 traveled 720 km in 1 minute at reentry, how far did they travel in 1 second?

18. Rudy is buying a new car that costs $8600. The car salesman said that Rudy could pay cash or pay $1500 down and $450 a month for 2 years.
(a) Which option is more expensive?
(b) How much more expensive?

19. Jill's book is 668 pages long. She has read 324 pages. If she reads 32 pages a day, how long will it take her to finish the book?

20. A 1K computer memory chip can store 1024 bits of information. How many bits of information can be stored in a 64K chip?

21. Using a calculator, Ralph multiplied by 10 when he should have divided by 10. The display read 300. What should the correct answer be?

22. In a certain book, 2981 digits were used to print the page numbers. How many pages are in the book?

23. Place the digits 7, 6, 8, and 3 in the boxes to obtain: (a) the greatest product; (b) the least product.

☐ ☐ ☐
× ☐

24. Place the digits 7, 6, 8, 3, and 2 in the boxes to obtain: (a) the greatest product; (b) the least product.

☐ ☐ ☐
× ☐ ☐

25. If a cow produces 700 pounds of hamburger, and there are 4 Quarter Pounders to a pound, how many cows would it take to produce 21 billion hamburgers?

26. Use a calculator to find the missing numbers.

(a)   3 7
       × 4 3
      ─────
      ─ ─ ─
      ─ ─ ─ ─
      ─ 5 9 1

(b)   9 ？
       × 3 6
      ─────
        5 5 8
      2 7 9 0
      ─ ─ ─ ─

27. Given the following problems, find all the possible whole-number divisors.

(a))123
      −9
      ───
      33
      −27
      ───
      6

(b))147
      −10
      ───
      47
      −45
      ───
      2

(c))146
      ───
      3

(d))335
      ───
      2

28. Find the products of the following and describe the pattern that emerges. Through how many steps does this pattern continue?

1×1
11×11
111×111
1111×1111

29. How many sevens are in 98?
(a) Use the constant feature to count backwards from 98 to 0 by sevens, and count the number of sevens subtracted.
(b) Count forward from 0 to 98 by sevens.
(c) Use a calculator to find $98 \div 7$.

30. Estimate which of the following division problems have quotients between 20 and 50. Use a calculator to verify the answers.
(a) $436 \div 13$ (b) $4368 \div 131$
(c) $4368 \div 13$ (d) $436 \div 131$

31. Suppose a person can spend $1 per second. How much can that person spend in a minute? An hour? A day? A week? A month? A year? Twenty years?

32. Compare $2^{12} + 2^{12}$ and 2^{24}. Which is greater?

33. Suppose a friend chooses a number between 250,000 and 1,000,000. What is the fewest number of questions you must ask in order to guess the number if the friend answers only "yes" or "no" to the questions?

Review Problems

34. Write the number succeeding 673 in Egyptian numerals.

35. Write $3 \cdot 10^5 + 2 \cdot 10^2 + 6 \cdot 10$ as a Hindu-Arabic numeral.

36. Illustrate the identity property of addition for whole numbers.

37. Rename each of the following using the distributive property of multiplication over addition.
(a) $ax + bx + 2x$
(b) $3(a + b) + x(a + b)$

38. At the beginning of a trip, the odometer registered 52,281. At the end of the trip, the odometer registered 59,260. How many miles were traveled on this trip?

39. The registration for the computer conference was 192 people on Thursday, 215 on Friday, and 317 on Saturday. What was the total registration?

BRAIN TEASER

For each of the following, replace the letters with digits in such a way that the computation is correct. Each letter may represent only one digit.

$$\begin{array}{r} \text{LYNDON} \\ \times\, \text{B} \\ \hline \text{JOHNSON} \end{array}$$

LABORATORY ACTIVITY

Finger multiplication has long been popular in many parts of the world. Multiplication of single digits by 9 is very simple using the following steps.

1. Place your hands next to each other as shown.

Second finger bent

2. To multiply 2 by 9, bend down the second finger from the left. The remaining fingers show the product.

3. Similarly, to multiply 3 by 9, bend down the third finger from the left. The remaining fingers will show the product $3 \times 9 = 27$. Try this procedure with other multiplications by 9.

*Section 3-6   Other Number Bases

The Babylonian numeration system was based on 60 and the digital computer is based on 2, while the Hindu-Arabic system is based on 10. Mathematical historians believe that one reason the majority of the world uses the base-ten system, with the ten digits 0 through 9, is that most people have ten fingers. When you count with two hands and reach the last finger, you begin using two-digit numbers. Suppose you can use only one hand and the digits available for counting are 0, 1, 2, 3, and 4. In the "one-hand system," you count 1, 2, 3, 4, 10, where 10 represents one hand and no fingers. The one-hand system is a base-five system. (Recall that in base ten, 10 represents 1 ten and 0 units.)

In the one-hand, or base-five, system, counting is in groups of five rather than in groups of ten. In Figure 3-31(a), xs are grouped into tens, and in Figure 3-31(b), they are grouped into fives. In Figure 3-31(a), the grouping shows 1 set of ten xs and 9 other xs. This is written as 19_{ten}, or just 19. *When the number base is not indicated, it is understood to be base ten.*

Figure 3-31

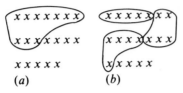

(a)   (b)

Figure 3-31(b) shows 3 groups of five xs and 4 other xs. This is written as 34_{five}. Thus, $19_{ten} = 34_{five}$. We write the small "five" below the numeral as a reminder that the number is written in base five. Counting in base five proceeds as shown in Figure 3-32.

Figure 3-32

Base-Five Symbol	Base-Five Grouping	One-Hand System
0_{five}		0 fingers
1_{five}	x	1 finger
2_{five}	xx	2 fingers
3_{five}	xxx	3 fingers
4_{five}	xxxx	4 fingers
10_{five}	(xxxxx)	1 hand and 0 fingers
11_{five}	(xxxxx) x	1 hand and 1 finger
12_{five}	(xxxxx) xx	1 hand and 2 fingers
13_{five}	(xxxxx) xxx	1 hand and 3 fingers
14_{five}	(xxxxx) xxxx	1 hand and 4 fingers
20_{five}	(xxxxx) (xxxxx)	2 hands and 0 fingers
21_{five}	(xxxxx) (xxxxx) x	2 hands and 1 finger

What number follows 44_{five}? There are no more two-digit numbers in the system after 44_{five}. In base ten, the same situation occurs at 99. We use 100 to represent ten tens or one hundred. In the base-five system, we need a symbol to represent five fives. To continue the analogy with base ten, we use 100_{five} to represent 1 group of five fives, 0 groups of five, and 0 units. To distinguish from "one hundred" in base ten, the name for 100_{five} is "one-zero-zero base five." The number 100_{ten} means $(1 \cdot 10^2 + 0 \cdot 10^1 + 0)_{ten}$, whereas the number 100_{five} means $(1 \cdot 10^2 + 0 \cdot 10^1 + 0)_{five}$, or $(1 \cdot 5^2 + 0 \cdot 5^1 + 0)_{ten}$ or 25.

Example 3-12

Solution

Convert 11244_{five} to base ten.

$$11244_{\text{five}} = 1 \cdot 5^4 + 1 \cdot 5^3 + 2 \cdot 5^2 + 4 \cdot 5 + 4 \cdot 1$$
$$= 1 \cdot 625 + 1 \cdot 125 + 2 \cdot 25 + 4 \cdot 5 + 4 \cdot 1$$
$$= 625 + 125 + 50 + 20 + 4$$
$$= 824$$

Example 3-12 also suggests a method for changing a base-ten number to a base-five number. Notice that the conversion involves powers of five. To convert 824 to base five, we divide by the successive powers of five: 5^1, or 5; 5^2, or 25; 5^3, or 125; 5^4, or 625; 5^5, or 3125; and so on. For example, the greatest power of 5 contained in 824 is 5^4, or 625. There is $1 \cdot 5^4$, with 199 left over. Thus,

$$824 = 1 \cdot 5^4 + 199$$

The greatest power of 5 contained in 199 is 5^3. There is $1 \cdot 5^3$, with 74 left over, in 199. Thus,

$$824 = 1 \cdot 5^4 + 1 \cdot 5^3 + 74$$

The greatest power of 5 contained in 74 is 5^2. There are $2 \cdot 5^2$, with 24 left over, in 74.

$$824 = 1 \cdot 5^4 + 1 \cdot 5^3 + 2 \cdot 5^2 + 24$$

Finally, the greatest power of 5 in 24 is 5^1. There are $4 \cdot 5^1$, with 4 left, in 24, and there are 4 ones in 4. Thus,

$$824 = 1 \cdot 5^4 + 1 \cdot 5^3 + 2 \cdot 5^2 + 4 \cdot 5 + 4 = 11244_{\text{five}}$$

Thus, changing from base ten to base five can be accomplished by dividing by successive powers of five. A shorthand method for illustrating this conversion follows.

$$
\begin{array}{r|r|l}
625 & 824 & 1 \quad \text{How many groups of 625 in 824?} \\
     & -625 & \\
\hline
125 & 199 & 1 \quad \text{How many groups of 125 in 199?} \\
    & -125 & \\
\hline
25 & 74 & 2 \quad \text{How many groups of 25 in 74?} \\
   & -50 & \\
\hline
5 & 24 & 4 \quad \text{How many groups of 5 in 24?} \\
  & -20 & \\
\hline
1 & 4 & 4 \quad \text{How many 1s in 4?} \\
  & -4 & \\
\hline
  & 0 & \\
\end{array}
$$

Thus, $824 = 11244_{\text{five}}$.

Historians tell of early tribes that used base two. Some Australian tribes still count "one, two, two and one, two twos, two twos and one, ..." Be-

binary system

cause base two has only two digits, it is called the **binary system.** Base two is especially important because of its use in computers. One of the two digits may be represented by the presence of an electrical signal and the other by the absence of an electrical signal. Although base two works well for computers, it is inefficient for everyday use because multidigit numbers are reached very rapidly in counting in this system.

Conversions from base two to base ten, and vice versa, may be accomplished in a manner similar to base-five conversions.

Example 3-13

(a) Convert 10111_{two} to base ten.
(b) Convert 27 to base two.

Solution

(a) $10111_{two} = 1 \cdot 2^4 + 0 \cdot 2^3 + 1 \cdot 2^2 + 1 \cdot 2^1 + 1$

$= 16 + 0 + 4 + 2 + 1$

$= 23$

(b)

16	27	1	How many groups of 16 in 27?
	−16		
8	11	1	How many groups of 8 in 11?
	−8		
4	3	0	How many groups of 4 in 3?
	−0		
2	3	1	How many groups of 2 in 3?
	−2		
1	1	1	How many 1s in 1?
	−1		
	0		

Thus, 27 is equivalent to 11011_{two}.

Another commonly used number base system is the base-twelve, or duodecimal, system, known popularly as the "dozens" system. Eggs are bought by the dozens, and pencils are bought by the gross (a dozen dozens). In base twelve, there are twelve digits, just as there are ten digits in base ten, five digits in base five, and two digits in base two. In base twelve, new symbols are needed to represent the following groups of xs.

$$\overbrace{x\,x\,x\,x\,x\,x\,x\,x\,x\,x}^{10 \; xs} \quad \text{and} \quad \overbrace{x\,x\,x\,x\,x\,x\,x\,x\,x\,x\,x}^{11 \; xs}$$

The new symbols chosen are T and E, respectively, so that the base-twelve digits are 0, 1, 2, 3, 4, 5, 6, 7, 8, 9, T, E. Thus, in base twelve you count "1, 2, 3, 4, 5, 6, 7, 8, 9, T, E, 10, 11, 12, . . . , 17, 18, 19, $1T$, $1E$, 20, 21, 22, . . . , 28, 29, $2T$, $2E$, 30, ..." Notice that T_{twelve} is another way of writing 10_{ten} and E_{twelve} is another way of writing 11_{ten}. Also, $10_{twelve} = 12_{ten}$.

Example 3-14

(a) Convert $E2T_{\text{twelve}}$ to base ten.   (b) Convert 1277 to base twelve.

Solution

(a) $E2T_{\text{twelve}} = 11 \cdot 12^2 + 2 \cdot 12^1 + 10$

$= 11 \cdot 144 + 24 + 10$

$= 1584 + 24 + 10$

$= 1618$

(b)

$$
\begin{array}{r|r|l}
144 & 1277 & 8 \\
& -1152 &
\end{array}
$$
How many groups of 144 in 1277?

$$
\begin{array}{r|r|l}
12 & 125 & T \\
& -120 &
\end{array}
$$
How many groups of 12 in 125?

$$
\begin{array}{r|r|l}
1 & 5 & 5 \\
& -5 & \\
& 0 &
\end{array}
$$
How many 1s in 5?

Thus, $1277 = 8T5_{\text{twelve}}$.

PROBLEM 2

In a small rural community, the elementary school had no refrigerators. Through a federally financed program, the school provided 1 cup of milk per day for each student. Milk for the day was purchased at the local store each morning and the school bought the exact amount necessary. The milk was available in gallons, half-gallons, quarts, pints, or cups, and the larger containers were better buys. If 1 gallon, 1 quart, and 1 pint of milk were purchased on Tuesday, how many students were at school that day? On Wednesday, 31 students were at school. How much milk was purchased on Wednesday to make the best buy?

UNDERSTANDING THE PROBLEM A school provided 1 cup of milk for each student each day. Milk was cheaper when purchased in large quantities, but the exact amount had to be purchased each day. Milk could be bought in gallons, half-gallons, quarts, pints, and cups. If 1 gallon, 1 quart, and 1 pint were bought on Tuesday, we are to find the number of students that were present on Tuesday. In addition, we are to find out how much milk was purchased if there were 31 students present on Wednesday.

DEVISING A PLAN To answer the first question, we must determine how many cups are in 1 gallon, 1 quart, and 1 pint. Thus, we need the following information.

$$1 \text{ pint} = 2 \text{ cups}$$
$$1 \text{ quart} = 2 \text{ pints} = 2 \cdot (2 \text{ cups}) = 4 \text{ cups}$$
$$1 \text{ half-gallon} = 2 \text{ quarts} = 2 \cdot (4 \text{ cups}) = 8 \text{ cups}$$
$$1 \text{ gallon} = 2 \text{ half-gallons} = 2 \cdot (8 \text{ cups}) = 16 \text{ cups}$$

A table is helpful in answering the first question. To answer the second question, we determine what combinations of containers of milk must be bought for 31 students. To do this, we use the number of cups in each quantity. Thirty-one students require 31 cups of milk.

CARRYING OUT THE PLAN To determine the number of students present on Tuesday, we record in Table 3-7 the fact that 1 gallon, 1 quart, and 1 pint were bought, along with the equivalent number of cups.

Table 3-7

Amount bought	1 gallon	0 half-gallons	1 quart	1 pint	0 cups
No. of cups in quantity	$1 \cdot (16 \text{ cups})$	$0 \cdot (8 \text{ cups})$	$1 \cdot (4 \text{ cups})$	$1 \cdot (2 \text{ cups})$	$0 \cdot (1 \text{ cup})$

The total number of cups bought on Tuesday is $16 + 0 + 4 + 2 + 0 = 22$. Since each student received 1 cup, there were 22 students present.

To determine how much milk was purchased for 31 students on Wednesday, we use the number of cups in each quantity. Since 1 gallon = 16 cups, then 31 cups = 1 gallon + 15 cups. Since 1 half-gallon = 8 cups, then 31 cups = 1 gallon + 1 half-gallon + 7 cups. Since 1 quart equals 4 cups, 31 cups = 1 gallon + 1 half-gallon + 1 quart + 3 cups. Since 1 pint equals 2 cups, 31 cups = 1 gallon + 1 half-gallon + 1 quart + 1 pint + 1 cup. Therefore, 31 cups is equivalent to 1 gallon, 1 half-gallon, 1 quart, 1 pint, and 1 cup.

LOOKING BACK Questions like those in this problem can be modeled in the base-two number system. To understand the problem, we looked back at powers of 2 to determine the number of cups in each of the quantities that could be purchased. In the base-two setting, the first question of converting 1 gallon, 0 half-gallons, 1 quart, 1 pint, and 0 cups to cups becomes a question of converting 10110_{two} to base ten. The second question becomes one of converting 31 to base two.

ADDITION AND SUBTRACTION IN DIFFERENT BASES

One reason for studying computations in different number bases is to enhance our understanding of base-ten computations. Another reason is to put you in essentially the same role as a child studying arithmetic. We hope that by studying bases other than ten, you will better understand the problems that the children encounter in learning place value and computational skills.

Recall that before studying algorithms in base ten, you had to assume a knowledge of the basic addition and multiplication facts. The same is true for other bases.

A table of basic addition facts for base five can be developed using the number line or other models similar to the models used for base-ten numbers. A number line for base five illustrating $4_{\text{five}} + 3_{\text{five}} = 12_{\text{five}}$ is shown in Figure 3-33.

Using a number line such as the one pictured in Figure 3-33, we could construct the base-five addition table shown in Table 3-8.

Figure 3-33

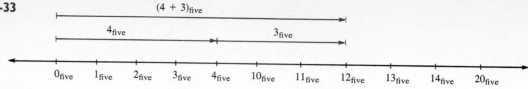

Table 3-8
Addition Table
(Base Five)

+	0	1	2	3	4
0	0	1	2	3	4
1	1	2	3	4	10
2	2	3	4	10	11
3	3	4	10	11	12
4	4	10	11	12	13

Using the addition facts in Table 3-8, we can begin to develop algorithms for base-five addition similar to those for base-ten addition. Concrete teaching aids, such as multibase blocks, chip trading, and bean sticks, can be used to develop these algorithms.

Suppose we wish to add $12_{five} + 31_{five}$. We show the problem using a concrete model in Figure 3-34(a), an introductory algorithm in Figure 3-34(b), and the familiar algorithm in Figure 3-34(c).

Figure 3-34

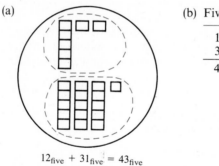

(a)

$12_{five} + 31_{five} = 43_{five}$

(b)

Fives	Ones
1	2
3	1
4	3

(c)
$$\begin{array}{r} 12_{five} \\ +31_{five} \\ \hline 43_{five} \end{array}$$

Additions in other number bases can be handled similarly.

Subtractions such as $12_{five} - 4_{five}$ can be modeled using a number line, as shown in Figure 3-35.

Figure 3-35

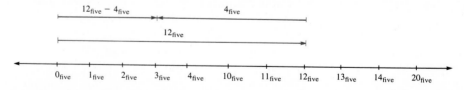

Thus, we see that $12_{five} - 4_{five} = 3_{five}$. The subtraction facts for base five can also be derived from the addition-facts table by using the definition of subtraction. For example, to find $(12 - 4)_{five}$, recall that $(12 - 4)_{five} = c_{five}$ if and only if $(c + 4)_{five} = 12_{five}$. From Table 3-8, $c = 3_{five}$. More involved subtraction problems can be performed using the same ideas developed for base ten.

An example of subtraction involving regrouping, $32_{five} - 14_{five}$, is developed in Figure 3-36.

Figure 3-36

(a)

$32_{five} - 14_{five} = 13_{five}$

(b)

Fives	Ones		Fives	Ones
3	2		2	12
−1	4	→	−1	4
			1	3

(c)
$$\overset{2\ 1}{3\!\!\!/\,2}_{five}$$
$$-\,14_{five}$$
$$\overline{13_{five}}$$

Addition and subtraction in other number bases can be handled similarly, as shown in Example 3-15.

Example 3-15

(a) Add: (b) Subtract:

$\quad 101_{two}$ $\quad 1010_{two}$

$\quad 111_{two}$ $-\ \ 111_{two}$

$+\,110_{two}$

Solution

(a)
$$\overset{11}{101_{two}}$$
$$111_{two}$$
$$+\ \ 110_{two}$$
$$\overline{10010_{two}}$$

(b)
$$1010_{two}$$
$$-\ 111_{two}$$
$$\overline{11_{two}}$$

MULTIPLICATION AND DIVISION IN DIFFERENT BASES

As with addition and subtraction, the basic facts of multiplication must be learned before algorithms can be used. The multiplication facts for base five are given in Table 3-9. These facts can be derived by using repeated addition.

Table 3-9
Multiplication Table (Base Five)

×	0	1	2	3	4
0	0	0	0	0	0
1	0	1	2	3	4
2	0	2	4	11	13
3	0	3	11	14	22
4	0	4	13	22	31

There are various ways to do the multiplication $21_{five} \cdot 3_{five}$.

Fives	Ones
2	1
×	3

$$\begin{array}{r} (20+1)_{five} \\ \times \qquad 3_{five} \\ \hline (110+3)_{five} \end{array}$$

$$\begin{array}{r} 21_{five} \\ \times\ 3_{five} \\ \hline 3 \\ 110 \end{array}$$

$$\begin{array}{r} 21_{five} \\ \times\ 3_{five} \\ \hline 113_{five} \end{array}$$

$$113_{five}$$

The multiplication of a two-digit number by a two-digit number is developed next.

$$
\begin{array}{r}
23_{\text{five}} \\
\times\, 14_{\text{five}} \\
\hline
22 \\
130 \\
30 \\
200 \\
\hline
432_{\text{five}}
\end{array}
\qquad
\begin{array}{l}
\overbrace{10 + 4}^{}{}_{\text{five}} \\
(4 \cdot 3)_{\text{five}} \\
(4 \cdot 20)_{\text{five}} \\
(10 \cdot 3)_{\text{five}} \\
(10 \cdot 20)_{\text{five}}
\end{array}
\qquad
\begin{array}{r}
23_{\text{five}} \\
\times\, 14_{\text{five}} \\
\hline
\rightarrow 202 \\
\rightarrow 230 \\
\hline
432_{\text{five}}
\end{array}
$$

Lattice multiplication can also be used to multiply numbers in various number bases. This will be explored in Problem 29 of Problem Set 3-6.

Division in different bases can be performed using the multiplication facts and the definition of division. For example, $22_{\text{five}} \div 3_{\text{five}} = c$ if and only if $c \cdot 3_{\text{five}} = 22_{\text{five}}$. From Table 3-9, we see that $c = 4_{\text{five}}$. As with base ten, computing multidigit divisions efficiently in different bases requires practice. The ideas behind the algorithms for division can be developed using repeated subtraction, just as they were for base ten. For example, $3241_{\text{five}} \div 43_{\text{five}}$ is shown using the repeated-subtraction technique in Figure 3-37(a) and the conventional algorithm in Figure 3-37(b).

Figure 3-37

$$
\text{(a)} \quad
\begin{array}{r}
43_{\text{five}}\,\overline{)\,3241_{\text{five}}} \\
-\ 430 \\
\hline
2311 \\
-\ 430 \\
\hline
1331 \\
-\ 430 \\
\hline
401 \\
-\,141 \\
\hline
210 \\
-\,141 \\
\hline
14
\end{array}
\quad
\begin{array}{l}
\\
(10 \cdot 43)_{\text{five}} \\
\\
(10 \cdot 43)_{\text{five}} \\
\\
(10 \cdot 43)_{\text{five}} \\
\\
(2 \cdot 43)_{\text{five}} \\
\\
(2 \cdot 43)_{\text{five}} \\
(34 \cdot 43)_{\text{five}}
\end{array}
\qquad
\text{(b)} \quad
\begin{array}{r}
34_{\text{five}} \\
43_{\text{five}}\,\overline{)\,3241_{\text{five}}} \\
-\,234 \\
\hline
401 \\
-\,332 \\
\hline
14
\end{array}
$$

Thus, $3241_{\text{five}} \div 43_{\text{five}} = 34_{\text{five}}$ with remainder 14_{five}.

Multiplication and division involving base two is demonstrated in Example 3-16.

Example 3-16

Multiply: Divide:

(a) $\begin{array}{r} 101_{\text{two}} \\ \times\ 11_{\text{two}} \end{array}$ (b) $101_{\text{two}}\,\overline{)\,110110_{\text{two}}}$

Solution

(a) $\begin{array}{r} 101_{\text{two}} \\ \times\ 11_{\text{two}} \\ \hline 101 \\ 101 \\ \hline 1111_{\text{two}} \end{array}$ (b) $\begin{array}{r} 1010_{\text{two}} \\ 101_{\text{two}}\,\overline{)\,110110_{\text{two}}} \\ -\,101 \\ \hline 111 \\ -\,101 \\ \hline 100 \end{array}$

PROBLEM SET 3-6

1. Write the first 15 counting numbers for each of the following bases.
   (a) base two   (b) base three
   (c) base four   (d) base eight
2. How many different digits are needed for base twenty?
3. Write 2032_{four} in expanded base-four notation.
4. What is the greatest three-digit number in each base?
   (a) base two   (b) base six
   (c) base ten   (d) base twelve
5. What, if anything, is wrong with the numerals below?
   (a) 204_{four} (b) 607_{five} (c) $T12_{three}$
6. Find the numbers preceding and succeeding each of the following.
   (a) $EE0_{twelve}$ (b) 100000_{two} (c) 555_{six}
   (d) 100_{seven} (e) 1000_{five} (f) 110_{two}
7. Convert each of the following base-ten numbers to numbers in the indicated bases.
   (a) 432 to base five   (b) 1963 to base twelve
   (c) 404 to base four   (d) 37 to base two
   (e) $3 \cdot 10^4 + 2 \cdot 10^2 + 4$ to base five
   (f) $4 \cdot 10^4 + 3 \cdot 10^2$ to base twelve
   (g) $9 \cdot 12^5 + 11 \cdot 12$ to base twelve
8. Write each of the following numbers in base ten.
   (a) 432_{five} (b) 101101_{two} (c) $92E_{twelve}$
   (d) $T0E_{twelve}$ (e) 111_{twelve} (f) 346_{seven}
   (g) 551_{six} (h) 3002_{four}
9. Change 42_{eight} to base two.
10. Suppose you have two quarters, four nickels, and two pennies. What is the value of your money in cents? Write a base-five representation to indicate the value of your fortune.
11. You are asked to distribute $900 in prize money. The dollar amounts for the prizes are $625, $125, $25, $5, and $1. How should this $900 be distributed in order to give the fewest number of prizes?
12. What is the minimum number of quarters, nickels, and pennies necessary to make 97¢?
13. Convert each of the following.
    (a) 58 days to weeks and days
    (b) 54 months to years and months
    (c) 29 hours to days and hours
    (d) 68 inches to feet and inches
14. For each of the following, find b.
    (a) $b2_{seven} = 44_{ten}$ (b) $5b2_{twelve} = 734_{ten}$
    (c) $23_{ten} = 25_b$
15. A bookstore ordered 11 gross, 6 dozen, and 6 pencils. Express the number of pencils in base twelve and in base ten.
16. George was cooking an elaborate meal for Thanksgiving. He could only cook one thing at a time in his microwave oven. His turkey takes 75 minutes; the pumpkin pie takes 18 minutes; rolls take 45 seconds; and a cup of coffee takes 30 seconds to heat. How much time did he need to cook the meal?
17. An inspector of weights and measures has a special set of weights used to check the accuracy of scales. Various weights are placed on a scale to check accuracy of any amount from 1 ounce through 15 ounces. What is the least number of weights that the inspector needs? What weights are needed to check the accuracy of scales from 1 ounce through 15 ounces? From 1 through 31 ounces?
18. Anna's bank contains only pennies, nickels, and quarters. What is the minimum number of coins she could trade for 117 pennies? If she trades 2 quarters, 4 nickels, and 3 pennies for pennies, how many pennies will she have?
19. Perform each of the following operations using the bases shown.
    (a) $43_{five} + 23_{five}$ (b) $43_{five} - 23_{five}$
    (c) $432_{five} + 23_{five}$ (d) $42_{five} - 23_{five}$
    (e) $110_{two} + 11_{two}$ (f) $10001_{two} - 111_{two}$
20. Construct addition and multiplication tables for base eight.
21. Perform each of the following operations.
    (a)   3 hours 36 minutes 58 seconds
        $+$ 5 hours 56 minutes 27 seconds

    (b)   5 hours 36 minutes 38 seconds
        $-$ 3 hours 56 minutes 58 seconds

22. Perform each of the following operations (2 cups = 1 pint, 2 pints = 1 quart, 4 quarts = 1 gallon).
    (a)   1 quart 1 pint 1 cup   (b)   1 quart 1 cup
        $+$ 1 pint 1 cup $-$ 1 pint 1 cup

    (c)   1 gallon 3 quarts 1 cup
        $-$ 4 quarts 2 cups

23. Use scratch addition to perform the following.

    32_{five}
    13_{five}
    22_{five}
    43_{five}
    23_{five}
    $+ 12_{five}$

24. Perform each of the following operations.
    (a)   4 gross 4 dozen 6 ones
        $-$ 5 dozen 9 ones

    (b)   2 gross 9 dozen 7 ones
        $+$ 3 gross 5 dozen 9 ones

25. What is wrong with the following?

$$\begin{array}{r} 22_{\text{five}} \\ + 33_{\text{five}} \\ \hline 55_{\text{five}} \end{array}$$

26. Fill in the missing numbers in each of the following.

(a)
$$\begin{array}{r} 2\_\_\,_{\text{five}} \\ + \;\;2\,2_{\text{five}} \\ \hline \_\,0\;3_{\text{five}} \end{array}$$

(b)
$$\begin{array}{r} 2\,0\,0\,1\,0_{\text{three}} \\ - \;\;2\,\_\,2\,\_\,_{\text{three}} \\ \hline 1\,\_\,2\,\_\,1_{\text{three}} \end{array}$$

27. Perform each of the following operations using the bases shown.

(a) $(32_{\text{five}}) \cdot (4_{\text{five}})$
(b) $32_{\text{five}} \div 4_{\text{five}}$
(c) $(43_{\text{five}}) \cdot (23_{\text{five}})$
(d) $143_{\text{five}} \div 3_{\text{five}}$
(e) $(13_{\text{eight}}) \cdot (5_{\text{eight}})$
(f) $67_{\text{eight}} \div 4_{\text{eight}}$
(g) $10010_{\text{two}} \div 11_{\text{two}}$
(h) $(10110_{\text{two}}) \cdot (101_{\text{two}})$

28. For what possible bases are each of the following computations correct?

(a)
$$\begin{array}{r} 213 \\ + 308 \\ \hline 522 \end{array}$$

(b)
$$\begin{array}{r} 322 \\ - 233 \\ \hline 23 \end{array}$$

(c)
$$\begin{array}{r} 213 \\ \times \;\;32 \\ \hline 430 \\ 1043 \;\;\; \\ \hline 11300 \end{array}$$

(d)
$$\begin{array}{r} 101 \\ 11\overline{)1111} \\ -11\;\;\;\;\; \\ \hline 11 \\ -11 \\ \hline 0 \end{array}$$

29. Use lattice multiplication to compute $(323_{\text{five}}) \cdot (42_{\text{five}})$.

30. (a) Write $12^6 + 4 \cdot 12^3 + 120$ in base twelve.
(b) Write $12^5 \cdot (8 \cdot 12 + 4)$ in base twelve.

LABORATORY ACTIVITY

1. Messages can be coded on paper tape using base two. A hole in the tape represents 1, while a space represents 0. The value of each hole depends on its position; from left to right, 16, 8, 4, 2, 1 (all powers of 2). Using base two, letters of the alphabet may be coded according to their position in the alphabet. For example, G is the seventh letter. Since $7 = 1 \cdot 4 + 1 \cdot 2 + 1$, the holes appear as they do in the figure below.

(a) Decode the message below.
(b) Write your name on a tape using base two.

2. The following number game uses base-two arithmetic.

Card A		Card B		Card C		Card D		Card E	
16	24	8	24	4	20	2	18	1	17
17	25	9	25	5	21	3	19	3	19
18	26	10	26	6	22	6	22	5	21
19	27	11	27	7	23	7	23	7	23
20	28	12	28	12	28	10	26	9	25
21	29	13	29	13	29	11	27	11	27
22	30	14	30	14	30	14	30	13	29
23	31	15	31	15	31	15	31	15	31

Suppose a person's age appears on cards A, C, and D. Then, the person is 22. Can you discover how this works and why?

SOLUTION TO THE PRELIMINARY PROBLEM

UNDERSTANDING THE PROBLEM Each letter in the addition below represents one of the digits 0 through 9. Based on our experience with whole-number addition and place value, we are to determine which digit each letter represents. We are also to determine if there is more than one solution.

$$\begin{array}{r} MA \\ MA \\ + MA \\ \hline EEL \end{array}$$

DEVISING A PLAN We know that the greatest possible value of $A + A + A$, or $3A$, is $3 \cdot 9$, or 27, so if there is a carry from the units column to the tens column, it must be either 1 or 2. Because $M + M + M$, or $3M$, plus the carry from the units column, if any, must be a two-digit number, then M cannot equal 0, 1, or 2. (Why?) These conditions imply that there are only three possibilities that must be considered to determine values for M. These possibilities are given below.

Case 1: $3M = EE$ (no carry)

Case 2: $3M + 1 = EE$ (carry of 1)

Case 3: $3M + 2 = EE$ (carry of 2)

Because M must equal one of the numbers 3, 4, 5, 6, 7, 8, or 9, we consider the following possibilities for 3M.

$3 \cdot 3 = 9$ $3 \cdot 7 = 21$

$3 \cdot 4 = 12$ $3 \cdot 8 = 24$

$3 \cdot 5 = 15$ $3 \cdot 9 = 27$

$3 \cdot 6 = 18$

Because none of these products is in the form of a two-digit number with identical digits, case 1 cannot yield a solution. Thus, if a solution exists, then M and E must satisfy the equations in case 2 or case 3. If we analyze these cases in a manner similar to that used above, we should be able to determine a solution.

CARRYING OUT THE PLAN We now consider case 2. Because M must be one of the numbers 3, 4, 5, 6, 7, 8, or 9, we consider the possibilities below.

$3 \cdot 3 + 1 = 10$

$3 \cdot 4 + 1 = 13$

$3 \cdot 5 + 1 = 16$

$3 \cdot 6 + 1 = 19$

$3 \cdot 7 + 1 = 22$

$3 \cdot 8 + 1 = 25$

$3 \cdot 9 + 1 = 28$

Hence, $3 \cdot 7 + 1$ yields the desired form, and a possibility for M is 7, in which case E must be equal to 2. At this point we have the following.

$$\begin{array}{r} 7A \\ 7A \\ +\,7A \\ \hline 22L \end{array}$$

Because there is a carry of 1 to the tens column, it follows that

$$A + A + A = 1 \cdot 10 + L$$

Because 3A is a two-digit number, A cannot be equal to 0, 1, 2, or 3. If A = 4, then 3A = $3 \cdot 4$ = 12 and L = 2, which cannot happen because E = 2, and each letter represents a different numeral. If A = 5, then 3A = $3 \cdot 5$ = 15 and L = 5, which cannot happen because A = 5. If A = 6, then 3A = $3 \cdot 6$ = 18 and L = 8. This causes no contradiction, and we have the following.

$$\begin{array}{r} MA \\ MA \\ +\,MA \\ \hline EEL \end{array} \longrightarrow \begin{array}{r} 76 \\ 76 \\ +\,76 \\ \hline 228 \end{array}$$

To determine if this is the only solution for case 2, we continue with the remaining possibilities. We know that A ≠ 7 because M = 7. Also, A ≠ 8 and A ≠ 9 because $3 \cdot 8$ = 24 and $3 \cdot 9$ = 27, which would result in a carry of 2.

The only remaining possibility of other solutions is from case 3, that is, $3M + 2 = EE$. We consider the possibilities below.

$3 \cdot 3 + 2 = 11$

$3 \cdot 4 + 2 = 14$

$$3 \cdot 5 + 2 = 17$$
$$3 \cdot 6 + 2 = 20$$
$$3 \cdot 7 + 2 = 23$$
$$3 \cdot 8 + 2 = 26$$
$$3 \cdot 9 + 2 = 29$$

Thus, $3 \cdot 3 + 2$ yields the desired form, and a possibility for M is 3, in which case E must equal 1. Because there is a carry of 2 to the tens column, it follows that

$$3A = 2 \cdot 10 + L$$

Because 3A is a two-digit number, A cannot be 0, 1, 2, or 3. Because there must be a carry of 2, A cannot be equal to 4, 5, or 6. If A = 7, then 3A = $3 \cdot 7 = 21$ and L = 1, which cannot happen because E = 1. If A = 8, then 3A = $3 \cdot 8 = 24$ and L = 4. If A = 9, then 3A = $3 \cdot 9 = 27$ and L = 7. Thus, there are two more solutions, as shown below.

```
   38        39
   38        39
 +38       +39
 ----      ----
  114       117
```

LOOKING BACK We have checked that our solutions are correct by performing the required additions. We have also checked all possible cases to determine all possible solutions. Related problems such as those given below could also be considered.

(1)	HE	(2)	WRONG	(3)	HOCUS
	+ EE		+ WRONG		+ POCUS
	BOO		R I GHT		PRESTO

Other Looking Back activities might include making up your own problems and trying them with a friend or trying some problems involving an operation other than addition.

QUESTIONS FROM THE CLASSROOM

1. A student asks, "Does $2 \cdot (3 \cdot 4)$ equal $(2 \cdot 3) \cdot (2 \cdot 4)$?" Is there a distributive property of multiplication over multiplication?
2. Since $39 + 41 = 40 + 40$, is it true that $39 \cdot 41 = 40 \cdot 40$?
3. The division algorithm, $a = bq + r$, holds for $a > b$; $a, b, q, r \in W$. Is this true when $a < b$?
4. A student asks if 5 times 4 is the same as 5 multiplied by 4. How do you respond?

5. Can we define $0 \div 0$ as 1? Why or why not?
6. A student divides as follows. How do you help?

```
      15
  6 ) 36
       6
      --
      30
      30
      --
```

7. When using Roman numerals, a student asks whether or not it is correct to write $\overline{\text{II}}$, as well as MI, for 1001. How do you respond?

8. A student says that $(x + 7) \div 7 = x + 1$. What is that student doing wrong?

9. A student says $x \div x$ is always 1. Is the student correct?

10. A student claims that the expressions $(2^3)^2$ and $2^{(3^2)}$ are equal. How do you respond?

11. A student asks if division on the set of whole numbers is distributive over subtraction. How do you respond?

12. A student says that 0 is the identity for subtraction. How do you respond?

13. A student asks if zero is the same as nothing. What is your answer?

CHAPTER OUTLINE

I. Numeration systems
  A. Properties of numeration systems give basic structure to the systems.
    1. Additive property
    2. Place-value property
    3. Subtractive property
    4. Multiplicative property

II. Exponents
  A. For any whole number a and any natural number n,

$$a^n = \underbrace{a \cdot a \cdot a \cdot \ldots \cdot a}_{n \text{ factors}}$$

  where a is the **base** and n is the **exponent.**
  B. For any natural number a with whole numbers m and n, $a^m \cdot a^n = a^{m+n}$.

III. Whole numbers
  A. The set of **whole numbers** W is $\{0, 1, 2, 3, \ldots\}$.
  B. The basic operations for whole numbers are addition, subtraction, multiplication, and division.
    1. Addition: If $n(A) = a$ and $n(B) = b$, where $A \cap B = \varnothing$, then $a + b = n(A \cup B)$. The numbers a and b are **addends** and $a + b$ is the **sum.**
    2. Subtraction: If a and b are any whole numbers, then $a - b$ is the unique whole number c such that $a = b + c$. The number a is the **minuend,** b is the **subtrahend,** and c is the **difference.**
    3. Multiplication: If a and b are any whole numbers,

$$a \cdot b = \underbrace{b + b + b + \cdots + b}_{a \text{ terms}}$$

a and b are called **factors** and $a \cdot b$ is the **product.**
    4. Multiplication: If A and B are sets such that $n(A) = a$ and $n(B) = b$, then $a \cdot b = n(A \times B)$.
    5. Division: If a and b are any whole numbers with $b \neq 0$, $a \div b$ is the unique whole number c such that $b \cdot c = a$. The number a is the **dividend,** b is the **divisor,** and c is the **quotient.**
    6. **Division algorithm:** Given any whole numbers a and b with $b \neq 0$, there exist unique whole numbers q and r such that $a = b \cdot q + r$ with $0 \leq r < b$.
  C. Properties of addition and multiplication of whole numbers
    1. Closure: If $a, b \in W$, then $a + b \in W$ and $a \cdot b \in W$.
    2. Commutative: If $a, b \in W$, then $a + b = b + a$ and $a \cdot b = b \cdot a$.
    3. Associative: If $a, b, c \in W$, then $(a + b) + c = a + (b + c)$ and $a \cdot (b \cdot c) = (a \cdot b) \cdot c$.
    4. Identity: 0 is the unique identity element for addition of whole numbers; 1 is the unique identity element for multiplication.
    5. Distributive property of multiplication over addition: If $a, b, c \in W$, then $a \cdot (b + c) = a \cdot b + a \cdot c$.
  D. Relations on whole numbers
    1. $a < b$ if and only if there is a natural number c such that $a + c = b$.
    2. $a > b$ if and only if there is a natural number c such that $a = b + c$.

CHAPTER TEST

1. Convert each of the following to base ten.
   (a) $\overline{\text{CDXLIV}}$ *(b) 432_{five} *(c) $ET0_{\text{twelve}}$
   *(d) 1011_{two} *(e) 4136_{seven}

2. Convert each of the following base-ten numbers to numbers in the indicated system.
   (a) 999 to Roman
   *(b) 346_{ten} to base five
   *(c) 1728_{ten} to base twelve
   *(d) 27_{ten} to base two
   *(e) 928_{ten} to base nine
   *(f) 13_{eight} to base two

3. Simplify each of the following, if possible. Write your answers in exponential form, a^b.
   (a) $3^4 \cdot 3^7 \cdot 3^6$ (b) $2^{10} \cdot 2^{11}$
   (c) $3^4 + 2 \cdot 3^4$

4. For each of the following, identify the properties of the operation(s) for whole numbers illustrated.
   (a) $3 \cdot (a + b) = 3 \cdot a + 3 \cdot b$
   (b) $2 + a = a + 2$
   (c) $16 \cdot 1 = 1 \cdot 16 = 16$
   (d) $6 \cdot (12 + 3) = 6 \cdot 12 + 6 \cdot 3$
   (e) $3 \cdot (a \cdot 2) = 3 \cdot (2 \cdot a)$
   (f) $3 \cdot (2 \cdot a) = (3 \cdot 2) \cdot a$

5. Using the definitions of less than or greater than, prove that each of the following inequalities is true.
   (a) $3 < 13$ (b) $12 > 9$

6. Explain why the product of $1000 \cdot 483$, namely, $483,000$, has 0 for the hundreds, tens, and units digits.

7. Use both the scratch and traditional algorithms to perform each of the following.

   (a) $\begin{array}{r} 316 \\ 712 \\ +\ 91 \\ \hline \end{array}$ *(b) $\begin{array}{r} 316_{\text{twelve}} \\ 712_{\text{twelve}} \\ +913_{\text{twelve}} \\ \hline \end{array}$

8. Use both the traditional and lattice multiplication algorithms to perform each of the following.

   (a) $\begin{array}{r} 613 \\ \times\ 98 \\ \hline \end{array}$ *(b) $\begin{array}{r} 216_{\text{eight}} \\ \times\ 54_{\text{eight}} \\ \hline \end{array}$

9. Use both the repeated-subtraction and the conventional algorithms to perform each of the following.
   (a) $912 \overline{)\,4803}$ (b) $11 \overline{)\,1011}$
   *(c) $23_{\text{five}} \overline{)\,3312_{\text{five}}}$

10. Use the division algorithm to check your answers in Problem 9.

11. For each of the following base-ten numbers, tell the place value for each of the circled digits.
    (a) $4\circled{3}2$ (b) $\circled{3}432$ (c) $19\circled{3}24$

12. For each of the following, find all possible whole-number replacements that make the following statements true.

    (a) $4 \cdot \square - 36 < 27$ (b) $398 = \square \cdot 37 + 28$
    (c) $\square \cdot (3 + 4) = \square \cdot 3 + \square \cdot 4$
    (d) $42 - \square \geq 16$

13. Use a number line to perform each of the following operations.
    (a) $27 - 15$ (b) $17 + 2$
    *(c) $3_{\text{five}} + 11_{\text{five}}$ *(d) $12_{\text{three}} + 2_{\text{three}}$

14. Use the distributive property of multiplication and addition facts, if possible, to rename each of the following.
    (a) $3a + 7a + 5a$ (b) $3x^2 + 7x^2 - 5x^2$
    (c) $x(a + b + y)$ (d) $(x + 5)3 + (x + 5)y$

15. For each of the following, decide which operations apply and then solve the problems.
    (a) Mary had 5 apples, 14 oranges, and 6 raisins. How many fruits did she have?
    (b) Carlos had 32 apricots and 4 friends. If he wished to give each friend an equal number of apricots, how many did each receive?
    (c) Joe had 6 books, each with 12 chapters. How many chapters were there in all?
    (d) Jerry paid $24 for a shirt with a $50 bill. How much change did he receive?

16. You had a balance in your checking account of $720 before writing checks for $162, $158, and $33 and making a deposit of $28. What is your new balance?

17. Jim was paid $320 a month for 6 months and $410 a month for 6 months. What were his total earnings for the year?

18. A soft drink manufacturer produces 15,600 cans of his product each hour. Cans are packed 24 to a case. How many cases are produced in 4 hours?

19. A limited partnership of 120 investors sold a piece of land for $461,040. How much did each investor receive?

20. Use each of the digits 1 through 9 to obtain a correct sum. Is only one answer possible?

$$\begin{array}{r} \square\square\square \\ +\ \square\square\square \\ \hline \square\square\square \end{array}$$

21. Merle took a 2040-mile trip, which took 10 days. Each day he drove 30 miles more than the day before. How many miles did he cover on the first day?

22. How many 12-ounce cans of juice would it take to give 60 people an 8-ounce serving?

23. Heidi has a brown and a gray pair of slacks; a brown, a yellow, and a white blouse; and a blue and a white sweater. How many different outfits does she have?

24. Complete the following addition table.

+			9
8		15	
	16		
	26		30

*25. Write $9 \cdot 12^7 + 11 \cdot 12^4 + 10$ as a base-twelve numeral.

SELECTED BIBLIOGRAPHY

Balin, F. "Finger Multiplication," *Arithmetic Teacher* 26 (March 1979):34–37.

Baroidy, A. "Children's Difficulties in Subtraction: Some Causes and Cures." *Arithmetic Teacher* 32 (November 1984):14–19.

Beard, E., and R. Polis. "Subtraction Facts with Pattern Explorations." *Arithmetic Teacher* 29 (December 1981):6–9.

Bernard, J. "Creating Problem-Solving Experiences with Ordinary Arithmetic Process." *Arithmetic Teacher* 30 (September 1982):52–53.

Boykin, W. "The Russian-Peasant Algorithm: Rediscovery and Extension." *The Arithmetic Teacher* 20 (January 1973):29–32.

Bradford, J., "Methods and Materials for Learning Subtraction." *Arithmetic Teacher* 25 (February 1978):19–21.

Brown, R. "A 'No Borrow' Subtraction Algorithm." *Mathematics Teacher* 75 (September 1982):467–468.

Brulle, A., and C. Brulle. "Basic Computational Facts: A Problem and a Procedure." *Arithmetic Teacher* 29 (March 1982):34–36.

Burton, G. "Teaching the Most Basic Basic." *Arithmetic Teacher* 32 (September 1984):20–25.

Colton, B. "Subtraction Without Borrowing." *Mathematics Teacher* 73 (March 1980):196.

Dunkels, A. "More Popsicle-Stick Multiplication." *Arithmetic Teacher* 29 (March 1982):20–21.

Engelhardt, J. "Using Computational Errors in Diagnostic Teaching." *Arithmetic Teacher* 29 (April 1982):16–19.

Ewbank, W. "Subtraction Drill with a Difference," *Arithmetic Teacher* 31 (January 1984):49–51.

Ferguson, A. "The Stored-Ten Method of Subtraction." *Arithmetic Teacher* 29 (December 1981):15–18.

Folsom, M. "Operations on Whole Numbers." *Mathematics Learning in Early Childhood, 1975 Yearbook.* Reston, Va.: National Council of Teachers of Mathematics, 1975.

Hall, W. "Using Arrays for Teaching Multiplication." *Arithmetic Teacher* 29 (November 1981):20–21.

Kolb, J. "When Does a Subtraction Algorithm Involve Borrowing?" *Mathematics Teacher* 75 (December 1982):771–775.

Kulm, G. "Multiplication and Division Algorithms in German Schools." *Arithmetic Teacher* 27 (May 1980):26–27.

Laing, R., and R. Meyer. "Transitional Division Algorithms."*Arithmetic Teacher* 29 (May 1982):10–12.

Lazerick, B. "Mastering Basic Facts of Addition: An Alternate Strategy." *Arithmetic Teacher* 28 (March 1981):20–24.

Lessen, E., and C. Cumblad. "Alternatives for Teaching Multiplication Facts." *Arithmetic Teacher* 31 (January 1984):46–48.

McKillip, W. "Computational Skill in Division: Results and Implications from National Assessment." *Arithmetic Teacher* 28 (March 1981):34–35.

Musser, G. "Let's Teach Mental Algorithms for Addition and Subtraction." *Arithmetic Teacher* 29 (April 1982):40–42.

O'Neil, D., and R. Jenson. "Some Aids for Teaching Place Value." *Arithmetic Teacher* 29 (December 1981):6–9.

O'Neil, D., and R. Jenson. "Strategies for Learning the Basic Facts." *Arithmetic Teacher* 29 (December 1981):6–9.

Patrick, S. "Expanded Division." *Arithmetic Teacher* 30 (November 1982):44–45.

Rathmell, E. "Using Thinking Strategies to Teach the Basic Facts." *Developing Computational Skills, 1978 Yearbook.* Reston, Va.: National Council of Teachers of Mathematics, 1978.

Reardin, C., Jr. "Understanding the Russian Peasant." *The Arithmetic Teacher* 20 (January 1973):33–35.

Reys, B. "Mental Computation." *Arithmetic Teacher* 32 (February 1985):43–46.

Robitaille, D. "An Investigation of Some Numerical Properties." *Arithmetic Teacher* 29 (May 1982):13–15.

Robold, A. "Grid Arrays for Multiplication." *Arithmetic Teacher* 30 (January 1983):14–17.

Sawada, D. "Mathematical Symbols: Insight through Invention." *Arithmetic Teacher* 32 (February 1985): 20–22.

Schultz, J. "Using a Calculator to Do Arithmetic in Bases Other than Ten." *Arithmetic Teacher* 26 (September 1978):25–27.

Seymour, D., M. Laycock, B. Larsen, R. Heller, and V. Holmberg. *Aftermath, Volumes 1–4.* Palo Alto, Calif.: Creative Publications, 1971. (Creative Publications, Inc., P. O. Box 10328, Palo Alto, CA 94303.)

Shaw, J., and M. Cliatt. "Number Walks." *Arithmetic Teacher* 28 (May 1981):9–12.

Shaw, R., and P. Pelosi. "In Search of Computational Errors." *Arithmetic Teacher* 30 (March 1983):50–51.

Shokoohi, G-H. "Manipulative Devices for Teaching Place Value." *Arithmetic Teacher* 25 (March 1978): 49–51.

Spitler, G. "Painless Division with Doc. Spitler's Magic Division Estimator." *Arithmetic Teacher* 28 (March 1981):34–35.

Stuart, M., and B. Bestgen. "Productive Pieces: Exploring Multiplication on the Overhead." *Arithmetic Teacher* 29 (January 1982):22–23.

Suydam, M. "Improving Multiplication Skills." *Arithmetic Teacher* 32 (March 1985):52.

Thompson, C., and J. Babcock. "A Successful Strategy for Teaching Missing Addends." *Arithmetic Teacher* 26 (December 1978):38–41.

Thompson, C., and J. Van de Walle. "Modeling Subtraction Situations." *Arithmetic Teacher* 32 (October 1984):8–12.

Thompson, C., and J. Van de Walle. "The Power of 10." *Arithmetic Teacher* 32 (November 1984):6–11.

Thompson, C., and J. Van de Walle. "Transition Boards: Moving from Materials to Symbols in Subtraction." *Arithmetic Teacher* 28 (January 1981):4–7.

Tierney, C. "Patterns in the Multiplication Table." *Arithmetic Teacher* 32 (March 1985):36.

Trafton, P. "Estimation and Mental Arithmetic: Important Components of Computation." *Developing Computational Skills, 1978 Yearbook.* Reston, Va.: National Council of Teachers of Mathematics, 1978.

Tucker, B. "Give and Take: Getting Ready to Regroup." *Arithmetic Teacher* 28 (April 1981):24–26.

Unenge, J. "Introducing the Binary System in Grades Four to Six." *The Arithmetic Teacher* 20 (March 1973):182–183.

Vance, I. "More on Subtraction Without Borrowing." *Mathematics Teacher* 75 (February 1982): 128–129.

Van de Walle, J., and C. Thompson. "Estimate How Much." *Arithmetic Teacher* 32 (May 1985):4–8.

Wheatley, C., and G. Wheatley. "How Shall We Teach Column Addition? Some Evidence." *Arithmetic Teacher* 25 (January 1978):18–19.

Woodward, E. "Calculators with a Constant Arithmetic Feature." *Arithmetic Teacher* 29 (October 1981):40–41.

Young, J. "Uncovering the Algorithms." *Arithmetic Teacher* 32 (November 1984):20.

CHAPTER 4

The Integers

Preliminary Problem

Professor Noah Little designed a 24-question true-false test on which he hoped to discourage guessing. When the test was graded, a student received 5 points for each correct answer and lost 7 points for each incorrect answer. Stu took the test, answered every question, and scored 0. How many problems did he answer correctly?

Introduction

Negative numbers serve useful purposes in everyday life. For example, they are used to report losses on the stock market, to record below-zero temperatures, and to report lost yardage in a football game. In mathematics, the need for negative numbers arises because subtractions cannot always be performed using only whole numbers. The cartoon depicts Linus attempting a subtraction using only whole numbers.

© 1957 United Feature Syndicate, Inc.

To compute $4 - 6$ using the definition of subtraction for whole numbers, a whole number a must be found such that $6 + a = 4$. Because there is no whole number a such that $6 + a = 4$, Linus' subtraction is not possible using only whole numbers. In order to perform the computation in the cartoon, a new number must be invented. This new number is called a negative integer. This chapter deals with the creation of negative integers, operations involving integers, and properties of integers.

Section 4-1

Integers and the Operations of Addition and Subtraction

If we attempt the subtraction $4 - 6$ on a horizontal number line, as we did with whole numbers, we see that it is necessary to draw intervals to the left of 0. On the extended number line in Figure 4-1, $4 - 6$ is pictured as an arrow that starts at 0 and ends 2 units to the left of 0.

GIROLAMO CARDANO

HISTORICAL NOTE

The Chinese used red rods for positive numbers and black rods for negative numbers in calculations possibly as early as 500 B.C. Brahmagupta, a seventh-century Hindu mathematician, wrote, "Positive divided by positive, or negative by negative, is affirmative." The Italian mathematician

Girolamo Cardano (1501–1576) provided the first significant treatment of negative numbers (which he called "false numbers"). However, as late as the eighteenth century, some mathematicians worried whether two negative numbers could be multiplied.

Figure 4-1

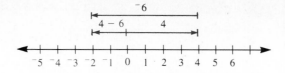

The name that we give to the new number that corresponds to a point 2 units to the left of 0 is *negative two,* which is symbolized by ⁻2. Other numbers to the left of 0 are created similarly. The new set of numbers, {⁻1, ⁻2, ⁻3, ⁻4, ⁻5, ...} is called the set of **negative integers.** Unfortunately, the symbol "−" is used to indicate both a subtraction and a negative sign. To reduce confusion between the uses of this symbol, it is customary initially to use a raised "−" sign for negative numbers, as in ⁻2, in contrast to the ordinary minus sign for subtraction. To emphasize that an integer is positive, some people use a raised plus sign, as in ⁺3. In this text, we use the plus sign for addition only and write ⁺3 simply as 3. The union of the set {⁻1, ⁻2, ⁻3, ⁻4, ⁻5, ...} and the set of whole numbers, {0, 1, 2, 3, ...}, is called the set of **integers.** The set of integers is denoted by *I*:

negative integers

integers

$$I = \{..., ^-5, ^-4, ^-3, ^-2, ^-1, 0, 1, 2, 3, 4, 5, ...\}$$

Frequently, it is convenient to partition the set of integers into the three subsets {1, 2, 3, 4, ...}, {0}, and {⁻1, ⁻2, ⁻3, ⁻4, ...}. The three subsets are called the *positive integers, zero,* and the *negative integers,* respectively. *Zero is neither positive nor negative.*

In Figure 4-1, the negative integers can be described as mirror images of the positive integers (assuming the mirror is placed at 0, perpendicular to the number line). For example, the mirror image of 5 is ⁻5, and the mirror image of 0 is 0. Similarly, the positive integers can be described as mirror images of the negative integers. For example, 4 is the mirror image of ⁻4. Another term for "mirror image of" is **opposite of.** Thus, the opposite of 4 is denoted by ⁻4, and the opposite of ⁻4 can be denoted as ⁻(⁻4), or 4. In general, we have the following definition.

opposite

DEFINITION

> If *n* is an integer, then the unique integer ⁻*n* is called the opposite of *n* if *n* + (⁻*n*) = 0 = (⁻*n*) + *n*.

HISTORICAL NOTE

The dash has not always been used for both the subtraction operation and the negative sign. Other notations were developed but never adopted. One such notation was used by Mohammed al-Khowârizmî (ca. 825), who indicated a negative number by placing a small circle over it. For example, ⁻4 was recorded as 4̊. The Hindus denoted a negative number by enclosing it in a circle; for example, ⁻4 was recorded as ④. The symbols + and − first appeared in print in European mathematics in the late fifteenth century. The symbols referred not to addition or subtraction or to positive or negative numbers, but to surpluses and deficits in business problems.

Remark   The "opposite" sign, as in $^-2$, is often confused with the subtraction sign. The difference between the two can be seen by thinking of "opposite" and subtraction as functions. "Opposite," as in $^-9$, is a function requiring a single number as input; subtraction, as in $4 - 6$, is a function requiring a pair of numbers as input.

Example 4-1

For each of the following, find the opposite of x.

(a) $x = 3$ (b) $x = ^-5$ (c) $x = 0$

Solution

(a) $^-x = ^-3$ (b) $^-x = ^-(^-5) = 5$ (c) $^-x = ^-0 = 0$

Remark   *Notice that ^-x does not necessarily represent a negative integer. For example, the value of ^-x in Example 4-1(b) is 5.*

ABSOLUTE VALUE

As we mentioned, 4 and $^-4$ are opposites of each other. As such, they are on opposite sides of 0 on the number line and are the same distance—4 units—from 0, as shown in Figure 4-2.

Figure 4-2

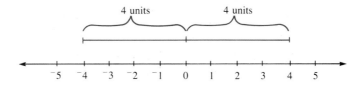

absolute value

Distance is always a positive number or zero. The distance between the points corresponding to an integer and 0 is called the **absolute value** of the integer. Thus, the absolute value of both 4 and $^-4$ is 4, written as $|4| = 4$ and $|^-4| = 4$, respectively. (A more formal definition of absolute value as a function is given in Problem 20 of Problem Set 4-1.)

Example 4-2

Evaluate each of the following.

(a) $|20|$ (b) $|^-5|$ (c) $|0|$ (d) $^-|^-3|$

Solution

(a) $|20| = 20$ (b) $|^-5| = 5$ (c) $|0| = 0$ (d) $^-|^-3| = ^-3$

INTEGER ADDITION

Absolute value can be used to define addition of integers, but we consider more informal approaches first. The following model from the stock market illustrates integer addition using gains and losses:

1. A stock gains 7 points on Monday and 6 points on Tuesday. Interpreting both gains as positive numbers, the net gain can be written as $7 + 6 = 13$.
2. A stock drops 10 points on Monday and then drops an additional 15 points on Tuesday. We think about the total loss in points as $^-10 + ^-15$. Because the total loss is 25 points, we record this as $^-10 + ^-15 = ^-25$.

3. A stock drops 10 points on Monday and then gains 10 points on Tuesday. The net gain is 0. Thus, $^-10 + 10 = 0$.

4. A stock gains 8 points on Monday and drops 5 points on Tuesday. The net gain is $8 - 5 = 3$. We interpret a gain of 8 points as (positive) 8 and a loss of 5 points as $^-5$, so the net gain can be written as $8 + \ ^-5$. Thus, $8 + \ ^-5 = 8 - 5 = 3$.

5. A stock gains 10 points on Monday and then drops 25 points on Tuesday. We think of the total loss in points as $10 + \ ^-25$. Because the total loss is 15 points, we record this as $10 + \ ^-25 = \ ^-15$. Because $25 - 10 = 15$, we see that $10 + \ ^-25 = \ ^-(25 - 10)$.

Another model for addition of integers involves a number line. Consider Example 4-3, which involves a thermometer with a scale in the form of a vertical number line.

Example 4-3

The temperature was $^-4°C$. In an hour, it rose $10°C$. What is the new temperature?

Solution

Figure 4-3 shows that the new temperature is $6°C$ and that $^-4 + 10 = 6$.

Figure 4-3

On a horizontal number line, we can picture a positive integer as an arrow pointing to the right and a negative integer as an arrow pointing to the left. For example, $^-5 + \ ^-3$ can be pictured as shown in Figure 4-4.

Figure 4-4

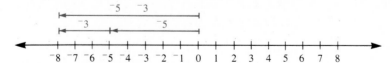

Figure 4-5 shows how to find $8 + \ ^-5$ on a number line. Place the starting end of the arrow representing the second number, $^-5$, at the point of the arrow representing the first number, 8. An arrow from 0 to the tip of the second arrow represents the sum of the two integers. Notice that the representation of $8 + \ ^-5$ is the same as that of $8 - 5$.

From the gain-loss model, we saw that $8 + \ ^-5$ is $8 - 5$, or 3. From the number-line model of Figure 4-5, we see that $8 + \ ^-5$ is represented by an

Figure 4-5

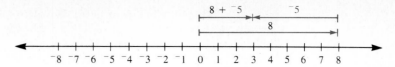

arrow of length 3 to the right. Thus, $8 + {}^-5 = 8 - 5$, or 3. In both models, a difference involving the whole numbers 8 and 5 is found. Because 8 and 5 are the absolute values of 8 and ${}^-5$, respectively, the pattern appears to be one of finding the difference of the absolute values of these integers. In fact, this pattern is true and is summarized in general as follows:

> *To add integers with unlike signs, subtract the lesser of the two absolute values of the integers from the greater. The sum has the same sign as the integer with the greater absolute value. If the two integers with unlike signs have equal absolute values, their sum is 0.*

The pattern for addition of integers with like signs can also be summarized using absolute values:

> *To add integers with like signs, add the absolute values of the integers. The sum has the same sign as the integers.*

Addition of integers can be defined in general without using absolute value as follows.

DEFINITION

For any whole numbers a and b:
1. $a + b = n(A \cup B)$ where $n(A) = a, n(B) = b$, and $A \cap B = \varnothing$ for sets A and B.
2. ${}^-a + {}^-b = {}^-(a + b)$
3. $a + {}^-b = {}^-b + a = a - b$ if $a > b$
4. $a + {}^-b = {}^-b + a = 0$ if $a = b$
5. $a + {}^-b = {}^-b + a = {}^-(b - a)$ if $a < b$

Example 4-4

Find each of the following sums.

(a) $9 + {}^-4$ (b) ${}^-5 + {}^-8$ (c) ${}^-5 + 5$ (d) $3 + {}^-10$

Solution

(a) $9 + {}^-4 = 5$ (b) ${}^-5 + {}^-8 = {}^-13$
(c) ${}^-5 + 5 = 0$ (d) $3 + {}^-10 = {}^-7$

Integer addition has all the properties of whole-number addition. These properties are summarized below.

Properties   Given any two integers a and b:

Closure Property for Addition of Integers $a + b$ is a unique integer.

Commutative Property for Addition of Integers $a + b = b + a$

Associative Property for Addition of Integers $(a + b) + c = a + (b + c)$

Identity Element for Addition of Integers   0 is the unique integer such that for all integers a, $0 + a = a = a + 0$.

An additional property that we acquire when we expand from the set of whole numbers to the set of integers is that each member of the set of integers has an opposite. This opposite is also called the **additive inverse.** The fact that the set of integers has an additive inverse for each element in the set is recorded in the following property.

additive inverse

Property Additive Inverse Property For every integer a, there exists a unique integer ^-a, called the additive inverse of a, such that $a + {}^-a = 0 = {}^-a + a.$

Observe that the additive inverse of ^-a can be written as $^-(^-a)$, or a. Because the additive inverse of ^-a must be unique, we have $^-(^-a) = a$.

Example 4-5

Find the additive inverse of each of the following.

(a) $^-(3 + x)$ (b) $(a + {}^-4)$ (c) $^-3 + (^-x)$

Solution

(a) $3 + x$
(b) $^-(a + {}^-4)$, which can be written as $^-(a) + {}^-(^-4)$, or $^-a + 4$.
(c) $^-[^-3 + (^-x)]$, which can be written as $^-(^-3) + {}^-(^-x)$, or $3 + x$.

INTEGER SUBTRACTION

Subtraction of integers, as with whole numbers, can be defined in terms of addition. Recall that $5 - 3$ can be computed by finding a whole number n as follows.

$5 - 3 = n$ if and only if $5 = 3 + n$

Because $3 + 2 = 5$, then $n = 2$.
    Similarly, we compute $3 - 5$ as follows.

$3 - 5 = n$ if and only if $3 = 5 + n$

To find n, we use a number line as shown in Figure 4-6.

Figure 4-6

Hence, $3 - 5 = {}^-2$. In general, for integers a and b, we have the following definition of subtraction.

DEFINITION

For integers a and b, $a - b$ is the unique integer n such that $a = b + n$.

From our previous work with addition of integers, we know that $3 + {}^-5 = {}^-2$. Hence, $3 - 5 = 3 + {}^-5$. In general, the following is true.

Property Subtraction Property   For all integers a and b, $a - b = a + (^-b)$

Example 4-6

Use the definition of subtraction to compute the following.

(a) $3 - 10$ (b) $^-2 - 10$

Solution

(a) Let $3 - 10 = n$. Then $10 + n = 3$, so $n = {}^-7$. Therefore, $3 - 10 = {}^-7$.
(b) Let $^-2 - 10 = n$. Then $10 + n = {}^-2$, so $n = {}^-12$. Therefore, $^-2 - 10 = {}^-12$.

Example 4-7

Compute each of the following using the fact that $a - b = a + (^-b)$.

(a) $2 - 8$ (b) $2 - (^-8)$ (c) $^-12 - (^-5)$ (d) $^-12 - 5$

Solution

(a) $2 - 8 = 2 + {}^-8 = {}^-6$
(b) $2 - (^-8) = 2 + {}^-(^-8) = 2 + 8 = 10$
(c) $^-12 - (^-5) = {}^-12 + {}^-(^-5) = {}^-12 + 5 = {}^-7$
(d) $^-12 - 5 = {}^-12 + {}^-5 = {}^-17$

Many calculators have a change-of-sign key, either $\boxed{\text{CHS}}$ or $\boxed{+/-}$, that allows for computation with integers. For example, to compute $8 - (^-3)$, we would press $\boxed{8}\ \boxed{-}\ \boxed{3}\ \boxed{+/-}\ \boxed{=}$.

Subtraction of integers is developed on page 170, which is from *Addison-Wesley Mathematics,* 1987, Grade 7. This student page uses the missing-addend approach as well as the addition-of-the-opposite approach.

Subtraction on the set of integers is neither commutative nor associative, as illustrated in these counterexamples.

$$5 - 3 \neq 3 - 5 \quad \text{because} \quad 2 \neq {}^-2$$

$$(3 - 15) - 8 \neq 3 - (15 - 8) \quad \text{because} \quad {}^-20 \neq {}^-4$$

Remember, if parentheses are present in an arithmetic expression, any computations within parentheses must be completed before other computations.

An expression such as $3 - 15 - 8$ is ambiguous unless there is agreement about the order in which subtractions are performed. Mathematicians agree that $3 - 15 - 8$ means $(3 - 15) - 8$; that is, the subtractions in $3 - 15 - 8$ are performed in the order of their appearance from left to right. Similarly, $3 - 4 + 5$ means $(3 - 4) + 5$ and not $3 - (4 + 5)$. Thus, $(a - b) - c$ may be written without parentheses as $a - b - c$.

Example 4-8

Compute each of the following.

(a) $2 - 5 - 5$ (b) $3 - 7 + 3$ (c) $3 - (7 - 3)$

Solution

(a) $2 - 5 - 5 = {}^-3 - 5 = {}^-8$
(b) $3 - 7 + 3 = {}^-4 + 3 = {}^-1$
(c) $3 - (7 - 3) = 3 - 4 = {}^-1$

From Example 4-8(b) and (c), we see that $3 - (7 - 3) = 3 - 7 + 3$.

In general, for integers a, b, and c,

$$a - (b - c) = a - b + c$$

Substituting $a = 0$, we obtain

$$^-(b - c) = {}^-b + c$$

Subtracting Integers

The air temperature outside a plane was ⁻10°C at an altitude of 1,500 m. The temperature at ground level was 2°C. What is the difference between the ground level temperature and the temperature at 1,500 m?

To find the difference, we subtract.

2 − ⁻10 (What number added to ⁻10 equals 2?)

Since **12 + ⁻10 = 2**, then **2 − ⁻10 = 12**.

The difference in the temperature is 12°C.

To *subtract* any integer, we *add* its *opposite*.

2 − ⁻10 = 2 + 10 = 12

opposites

3 − 8 = 3 + ⁻8 = ⁻5

opposites

Other Examples

0 − ⁻6 = 0 + 6 = 6

opposites

3 − 5 = 3 + ⁻5 = ⁻2

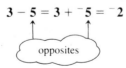

opposites

⁻1 − ⁻3 = ⁻1 + 3 = 2

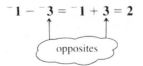

opposites

Example 4-9

Simplify each of the following.

(a) $2-(5-x)$ (b) $5-(x-3)$ (c) $^-(x-y)-y$

Solution

(a) $2-(5-x)=2-5+x={}^-3+x$
(b) $5-(x-3)=5-x+3=8-x$
(c) $^-(x-y)-y=(^-x+y)-y={}^-x+(y-y)={}^-x$

PROBLEM SET 4-1

1. Find the opposite of each of the following integers. Write your answer in the simplest possible form.
   (a) 2   (b) $^-5$ (c) m
   (d) 0   (e) ^-m (f) $a + b$

2. Simplify each of the following.
   (a) $^-(^-2)$ (b) $^-(^-m)$ (c) $^-0$

3. Evaluate each of the following.
   (a) $|^-5|$ (b) $|10|$ (c) $|2 + ^-5|$
   (d) $|^-3 + ^-4|$ (e) $^-|^-5|$ (f) $^-|5|$

4. Add each of the following.
   (a) $10 + ^-3$ (b) $10 + ^-12$
   (c) $10 + ^-10$ (d) $^-10 + 10$
   (e) $^-2 + ^-8$ (f) $(^-2 + ^-3) + 7$
   (g) $^-2 + (^-3 + 7)$

5. Demonstrate each addition on a number line.
   (a) $5 + ^-3$ (b) $^-2 + 3$ (c) $^-3 + 2$
   (d) $^-3 + ^-2$ (e) $(2 + ^-4) + ^-3$

6. Write an addition fact corresponding to each of the following sentences, and then answer the question.
   (a) A certain stock dropped 17 points and the following day gained 10 points. What was the net change in the stock's worth?
   (b) The temperature was $^-10°C$ and then it rose $8°C$. What is the new temperature?
   (c) The plane was at 5000 feet and dropped 100 feet. What is the new altitude of the plane?
   (d) A visitor in a Las Vegas casino lost $200, won $100, and then lost $50. What was the change in the gambler's net worth?
   (e) In four downs, the football team lost 2 yards, gained 7 yards, gained 0 yards, and lost 8 yards. What was the total gain or loss?

7. On January 1, Jane's bank balance was $300. During the month, she wrote checks for $45, $55, $165, $35, and $100 and made deposits of $75, $25, and $400.
   (a) If a check is represented by a negative integer and a deposit by a positive integer, express Jane's transactions as a sum of positive and negative integers.
   (b) What was the balance in Jane's account at the end of the month?

8. Evaluate each of the following using the definition of subtraction.
   (a) $2 - 11$ (b) $^-3 - 7$
   (c) $5 - (^-8)$ (d) $0 - 4$

9. Perform each of the following.
   (a) $^-2 + (3 - 10)$ (b) $[8 - (^-5)] - 10$
   (c) $(^-2 - 7) + 10$ (d) $^-2 - (7 + 10)$
   (e) $8 - 11 - 10$ (f) $^-2 - 7 + 3$

10. A model for subtraction of integers involves charged particles. Examples of this model are given in the figures. A plus sign and a negative sign neutralize each other. A subtraction can be thought of as "take away." Investigate the three examples given and try some problems on your own.

   (a) $^+3 - ^-2 = ^+5$

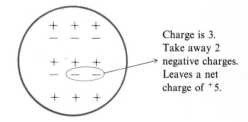

Charge is 3.
Take away 2 negative charges.
Leaves a net charge of $^+5$.

   (b) $^-3 - ^+2 = ^-5$

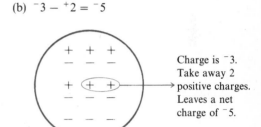

Charge is $^-3$.
Take away 2 positive charges.
Leaves a net charge of $^-5$.

   (c) $^-3 - ^-2 = ^-1$

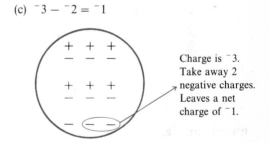

Charge is $^-3$.
Take away 2 negative charges.
Leaves a net charge of $^-1$.

11. Consider the expressions $(x + y) - (z + w)$ and $(x - z) + (y - w)$.
   (a) Are the expressions equal if $x = 30$, $y = 4$, $z = 10$, and $w = 7$?
   (b) Are the expressions equal if $x = ^-4$, $y = 5$, $z = ^-9$, and $w = 7$?

12. Let W stand for the set of whole numbers, I the set of integers, I^+ the set of positive integers, and I^- the set of negative integers. Find each of the following.
   (a) $W \cup I$ (b) $W \cap I$ (c) $I^+ \cup I^-$
   (d) $I^+ \cap I^-$ (e) $W - I$ (f) $I - W$
   (g) $W - I^+$ (h) $W - I^-$ (i) $I \cap I$

13. Complete the magic square using the following integers: ⁻13, ⁻10, ⁻7, ⁻4, 2, 5, 8, 11.

	⁻1	

14. Answer each of the following.
    (a) In a game of Triominoes, Jack's scores in five successive turns were 17, ⁻8, ⁻9, 14, and 45. What was his total at the end of five turns?
    (b) The largest bubble chamber in the world is 15 feet in diameter and contains 7259 gallons of liquid hydrogen at a temperature of ⁻247°C. If the temperature is dropped 11°C per hour for 2 consecutive hours, what is the new temperature?
    (c) The greatest recorded temperature ranges in the world are around the Siberian "cold pole" in the USSR. Temperatures in Verkhoyansk have varied from ⁻94°F to 98°F. What is the difference between the high and low temperatures in Verkhoyansk?
    (d) A turnpike driver had car trouble. He knew that he had driven 12 miles from milepost 68 before the trouble. If he is confused and disoriented when he calls on his CB for help, what are his possible locations?

15. Donna picked the Knicks basketball team to win by 12 points. Instead, they lost by 21. By how many points did Donna misjudge the score?

16. Place the integers 1 through 8 in the boxes so that no two consecutive integers are in boxes that share a common side or vertex (corner).

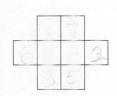

17. Distribute the integers 1 through 8 in two columns so that no number in a column is the sum of any other two numbers in that column.

18. Find the opposites for each of the following using the ⊡ key on a calculator.
    (a) 14   (b) 24   (c) ⁻2   (d) ⁻5

19. Complete each of the following integer arithmetic problems on the calculator making use of the ⊡ key. For example, to find ⁻5 + ⁻4, press ⑤ ⊡ ⊞ ④ ⊡ ⊟.
    (a) ⁻12 + ⁻6   (b) ⁻7 + (⁻99)
    (c) ⁻12 + 6   (d) 27 + (⁻5)
    (e) 3 + (⁻14)   (f) ⁻7 − (⁻9)
    (g) ⁻12 − 6   (h) 16 − (⁻7)

20. The following is the definition for the absolute value function where the domain is the set of integers.

    If x is a positive integer or 0, then $|x| = x$.

    If x is a negative integer, then $|x| = {}^-x$.

    (a) What is the range of this function?
    (b) Use the definition to evaluate each of the following.
        (i) $|5|$ (ii) $|{}^-5|$
        (iii) $|0|$ (iv) ${}^-|{}^-7|$

★21. Classify each of the following as true or false. If false, give a counterexample.
    (a) $|{}^-x| = |x|$
    (b) $|x - y| = |y - x|$
    (c) $|{}^-x + {}^-y| = |x + y|$
    (d) $|x^2| = x^2$
    (e) $|x^3| = x^3$
    (f) $|x^3| = x^2|x|$

BRAIN TEASER

If the digits 1 through 9 are written in order, it is possible to place plus and minus signs between the numbers or to use no operation symbol at all to obtain a total of 100. For example,

$$1 + 2 + 3 + {}^-4 + 5 + 6 + 78 + 9 = 100$$

Can you obtain a total of 100 using fewer plus or minus signs than in the given example? Notice that digits, such as 7 and 8, may be combined.

COMPUTER CORNER

1. Type the BASIC program below on your computer.

```
10 PRINT "THIS PROGRAM FINDS THE ABSOLUTE VALUE ";
20 PRINT "OF A NUMBER."
30 PRINT "AFTER THE QUESTION MARK, TYPE ";
40 PRINT "YOUR NUMBER."
50 INPUT N
60 IF N < 0 GOTO 90
70 PRINT "THE ABSOLUTE VALUE OF "; N;" IS "; N
80 GOTO 100
90 PRINT "THE ABSOLUTE VALUE OF "; N;" IS ";-N
100 PRINT "IF YOU WANT TO FIND ANOTHER ABSOLUTE VALUE, "
110 PRINT "TYPE 1 AFTER THE QUESTION MARK. IF NOT, TYPE 0."
120 INPUT V
130 IF V = 1 GOTO 30
140 END
```

Run this program and input the following values.
(a) ⁻7   (b) 0   (c) 140   (d) ⁻21

2. Type the given Logo program on your computer.

```
TO ABS :X
IF :X < 0 THEN OUTPUT (-:X)
OUTPUT :X
END
```

Run this program and input the following values.
(a) ⁻7   (b) 0   (c) 140   (d) ⁻21

Section 4-2   Multiplication and Division of Integers

INTEGER MULTIPLICATION

Multiplication of integers can be approached through a variety of models. One model is to imagine a person walking along a number line. The rules for walking along the number line are as follows.

1. Traveling to the left (west) means moving in the negative direction and traveling to the right (east) means moving in the positive direction.
2. Time in the future is denoted by a positive value and time in the past is denoted by a negative value.

Consider the number line shown in Figure 4-7. Various cases using this number line are given on the following page.

Figure 4-7

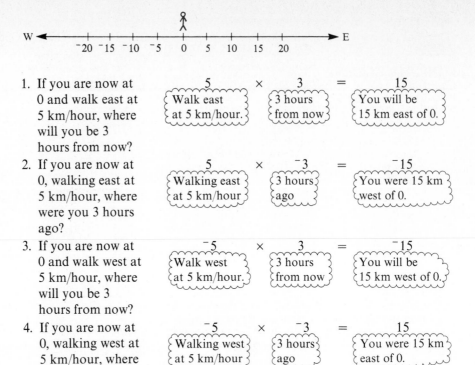

1. If you are now at 0 and walk east at 5 km/hour, where will you be 3 hours from now?

    5 (Walk east at 5 km/hour.) × 3 (3 hours from now) = 15 (You will be 15 km east of 0.)

2. If you are now at 0, walking east at 5 km/hour, where were you 3 hours ago?

    5 (Walking east at 5 km/hour) × ⁻3 (3 hours ago) = ⁻15 (You were 15 km west of 0.)

3. If you are now at 0 and walk west at 5 km/hour, where will you be 3 hours from now?

    ⁻5 (Walk west at 5 km/hour.) × 3 (3 hours from now) = ⁻15 (You will be 15 km west of 0.)

4. If you are now at 0, walking west at 5 km/hour, where were you 3 hours ago?

    ⁻5 (Walking west at 5 km/hour) × ⁻3 (3 hours ago) = 15 (You were 15 km east of 0.)

Next, we approach multiplication of integers using patterns. For example, if E. T. Simpson lost 2 yards on each of three carries in a football game, then he had a net loss of $^-2 + {}^-2 + {}^-2$, or $^-6$, yards. Since $^-2 + {}^-2 + {}^-2$ can be written as $3 \cdot (^-2)$ using repeated addition, we have $3 \cdot (^-2) = {}^-6$.

Next, consider a product like $(^-2) \cdot 3$. It is meaningless to say that there are $^-2$ threes in a sum. To develop a feeling for what $(^-2) \cdot 3$ should be, consider this pattern.

$$4 \cdot 3 = 12$$
$$3 \cdot 3 = 9$$
$$2 \cdot 3 = 6$$
$$1 \cdot 3 = 3$$
$$0 \cdot 3 = 0$$
$$^-1 \cdot 3 = ?$$
$$^-2 \cdot 3 = ?$$

The first five products, 12, 9, 6, 3, and 0, are terms of an arithmetic sequence with fixed difference $^-3$. If the pattern continues, the next two terms in the sequence are $^-3$ and $^-6$. Thus, it appears that $(^-2) \cdot 3 = {}^-6$. Recall that $3 \cdot (^-2)$ also equals $^-6$. Hence, if $(^-2) \cdot 3 = {}^-6$, we have $(^-2) \cdot 3 = 3 \cdot (^-2)$.

This result is consistent with the commutative property of multiplication developed for whole numbers.

Next, consider the product $(^-2) \cdot (^-3)$. Using the previous results, the following pattern can be developed.

$$(^-2) \cdot 3 = {^-6}$$

$$(^-2) \cdot 2 = {^-4}$$

$$(-2) \cdot 1 = {^-2}$$

$$(^-2) \cdot 0 = 0$$

$$(^-2) \cdot (^-1) = \ ?$$

$$(^-2) \cdot (^-2) = \ ?$$

$$(^-2) \cdot (^-3) = \ ?$$

The first four products, $^-6$, $^-4$, $^-2$, and 0, are terms in an arithmetic sequence with fixed difference 2. If the pattern continues, the next three terms in the sequence are 2, 4, and 6. Thus, it appears that $(^-2) \cdot (^-3) = 6$.

The patterns above, along with the number-line model, illustrate the following definition of multiplication of integers.

DEFINITION

For any whole numbers a and b:
1. $a \cdot b = n(A \times B)$, where $a = n(A)$ and $b = n(B)$, for sets A and B.
2. $(^-a) \cdot (^-b) = ab$
3. $(^-a) \cdot b = b \cdot (^-a) = {^-(ab)}$

The set of integers has properties under multiplication analogous to those of the set of whole numbers under multiplication. These properties are summarized below.

Properties The set of integers I satisfies the following properties of multiplication for all integers $a, b, c \in I$.

Closure Property for Multiplication of Integers $a \cdot b$ is a unique integer.

HISTORICAL NOTE

Euler, in his book *Anleitung zur Algebra* (1770), was one of the first mathematicians to attempt to prove that $(^-1) \cdot (^-1) = 1$. He reasoned that the product must be either 1 or $^-1$. It was already known that $(1) \cdot (^-1) = {^-1}$, so he reasoned that $(^-1) \cdot (^-1) = 1$. Do you agree with this reasoning?

Commutative Property for Multiplication of Integers $a \cdot b = b \cdot a$.

Associative Property for Multiplication of Integers $(a \cdot b) \cdot c = a \cdot (b \cdot c)$

Identity Element for Multiplication of Integers   1 is the unique integer such that for all integers a, $1 \cdot a = a = a \cdot 1$.

Distributive Properties of Multiplication over Addition for Integers $a \cdot (b + c) = a \cdot b + a \cdot c$ and $(b + c) \cdot a = b \cdot a + c \cdot a$

Zero Multiplication Property of Integers   0 is the unique integer such that for all integers a, $a \cdot 0 = 0 = 0 \cdot a$

A mathematical approach for showing that $(^-2) \cdot 3 = {}^-(2 \cdot 3)$ uses the uniqueness property of additive inverses. If we can show that $(^-2) \cdot 3$ and $^-(2 \cdot 3)$ are additive inverses of the same number, then they must be equal. By definition, the additive inverse of $(2 \cdot 3)$ is $^-(2 \cdot 3)$. That $(^-2) \cdot 3$ is also the additive inverse of $2 \cdot 3$ can be proved by showing $(^-2) \cdot 3 + 2 \cdot 3 = 0$. The proof follows.

$(^-2) \cdot 3 + 2 \cdot 3 = (^-2 + 2) \cdot 3$ Distributive property of multiplication over addition

$\qquad\qquad\qquad = 0 \cdot 3$ Additive inverse

$\qquad\qquad\qquad = 0$ Zero multiplication

Because $(^-2) \cdot 3$ and $^-(2 \cdot 3)$ are both additive inverses of $(2 \cdot 3)$ and the additive inverse must be unique, $(^-2) \cdot 3 = {}^-(2 \cdot 3)$.

The above proof holds for any integers a and b.

Property For any integers a and b, $(^-a) \cdot b = {}^-(a \cdot b)$.

Similarly, we can prove the following.

Property For any integers a and b, $(^-a) \cdot (^-b) = a \cdot b$.

Note that there is no restriction that a must be positive or that ^-a must be negative.

Example 4-10

Find each of the following products.

(a) $(^-3) \cdot (^-15)$ (b) $(^-5) \cdot 7$ (c) $0 \cdot (^-3)$
(d) $0 \cdot (^-n), n \in W$ (e) $(^-5)^4$ (f) $^-5^4$

Solution

(a) $(^-3) \cdot (^-15) = 45$ (b) $(^-5) \cdot 7 = {}^-35$
(c) $0 \cdot (^-3) = 0$ (d) $0 \cdot (^-n) = 0$
(e) $(^-5)^4 = (^-5) \cdot (^-5) \cdot (^-5) \cdot (^-5) = 625$ (f) $^-5^4 = {}^-(5^4) = {}^-625$

Remark   Notice that from Example 4-10(e) and (f), we have $(^-5)^4 \neq {}^-5^4$.

Another property that can be developed using the distributive property of multiplication over addition is the distributive property of multiplication over subtraction. Consider the following.

$$a(b - c) = a(b + {}^-c)$$
$$= ab + a({}^-c)$$
$$= ab + {}^-(ac)$$
$$= ab - ac$$

Consequently, $a(b - c) = ab - ac$. Similarly, it can be shown that $(b - c)a = ba - ca$.

> **Property** **Distributive Property of Multiplication over Subtraction for Integers**   For any integers a, b, and c,
>
> $$a(b - c) = ab - ac$$
> $$(b - c)a = ba - ca$$

Example 4-11

Simplify each of the following so that there are no parentheses in the final answer.

(a) $({}^-3)(x - 2)$ (b) $(a + b)(a - b)$

Solution

(a) $({}^-3)(x - 2) = ({}^-3)x - ({}^-3)(2) = {}^-3x - ({}^-6) = {}^-3x + 6$
(b) $(a + b)(a - b) = (a + b)a - (a + b)b$
$$= (a^2 + ba) - (ab + b^2)$$
$$= a^2 + ab - ab - b^2$$
$$= a^2 - b^2$$

Thus, $(a + b)(a - b) = a^2 - b^2$.

The result $(a + b)(a - b) = a^2 - b^2$ in Example 4-11(b) generally is called the **difference-of-squares** formula.

difference of squares

Example 4-12

Use the difference-of-squares formula to aid in simplifying the following.

(a) $22 \cdot 18$ (b) $(4 + b)(4 - b)$ (c) $({}^-4 + b)({}^-4 - b)$

Solution

(a) $22 \cdot 18 = (20 + 2)(20 - 2) = 20^2 - 2^2 = 400 - 4 = 396$
(b) $(4 + b)(4 - b) = 4^2 - b^2 = 16 - b^2$
(c) $({}^-4 + b)({}^-4 - b) = ({}^-4)^2 - b^2 = 16 - b^2$

Both the difference-of-squares formula and the distributive properties of multiplication over addition and subtraction can be used for factoring.

Example 4-13

Factor each of the following completely.

(a) $x^2 - 9$ (b) $(x + y)^2 - z^2$ (c) ${}^-3x + 5xy$ (d) $3x - 6$

Solution

(a) $x^2 - 9 = x^2 - 3^2 = (x + 3)(x - 3)$
(b) $(x + y)^2 - z^2 = (x + y + z)(x + y - z)$
(c) ${}^-3x + 5xy = x({}^-3 + 5y)$
(d) $3x - 6 = 3(x - 2)$

INTEGER DIVISION

Division is the last operation on integers to be considered. Recall that on the set of whole numbers, $a \div b$, where $b \neq 0$, is defined to be the unique whole number c such that $a = bc$. If such a whole number c does not exist, then $a \div b$ is undefined. Division in the set of integers is defined analogously.

DEFINITION

> If a and b are any integers with $b \neq 0$, then $a \div b$ is the unique integer c, if it exists, such that $a = bc$.

Example 4-14

Use the definition of division to evaluate each of the following.

(a) $12 \div (^-4)$ (b) $^-12 \div 4$ (c) $^-12 \div (^-4)$ (d) $^-12 \div 5$

Solution

(a) Let $12 \div (^-4) = c$. Then, $12 = ^-4c$, and consequently, $c = ^-3$. Thus, $12 \div (^-4) = ^-3$.

(b) Let $^-12 \div 4 = c$. Then, $^-12 = 4c$, and therefore, $c = ^-3$. Thus, $^-12 \div 4 = ^-3$.

(c) Let $^-12 \div (^-4) = c$. Then, $^-12 = ^-4c$, and consequently, $c = 3$. Thus, $^-12 \div (^-4) = 3$.

(d) Let $^-12 \div 5 = c$. Then, $^-12 = 5c$. Because no integer c exists to satisfy this equation, $^-12 \div 5$ is undefined.

Example 4-14 suggests that, if it exists, the quotient of two negative integers is a positive integer and, if it exists, the quotient of a positive and a negative integer or a negative and a positive integer is negative.

ORDER OF OPERATIONS ON INTEGERS

The following rules apply to the order in which arithmetic operations are performed. Recall that when addition and multiplication appear in a problem without parentheses, multiplication is done first.

> *When addition, subtraction, multiplication, and division appear without parentheses, multiplications and divisions are done first in the order of their appearance from left to right and then additions and subtractions in the order of their appearance from left to right. Any arithmetic operation appearing inside parentheses must be done first.*

Example 4-15

Evaluate each of the following.

(a) $2 - 5 \cdot 4 + 1$ (b) $(2 - 5) \cdot 4 + 1$
(c) $2 - 3 \cdot 4 + 5 \cdot 2 - 1 + 5$ (d) $2 + 16 \div 4 \cdot 2 + 8$

Solution

(a) $2 - 5 \cdot 4 + 1 = 2 - 20 + 1 = ^-18 + 1 = ^-17$
(b) $(2 - 5) \cdot 4 + 1 = ^-3 \cdot 4 + 1 = ^-12 + 1 = ^-11$
(c) $2 - 3 \cdot 4 + 5 \cdot 2 - 1 + 5 = 2 - 12 + 10 - 1 + 5 = 4$
(d) $2 + 16 \div 4 \cdot 2 + 8 = 2 + 4 \cdot 2 + 8 = 2 + 8 + 8 = 10 + 8 = 18$

BRAIN TEASER

Express each of the numbers from 1 through 10 using four 4s and any operations. For example,

$$1 = 44 \div 44 \quad \text{or}$$

$$1 = (4 \div 4)^{44} \quad \text{or}$$

$$1 = {}^-4 + 4 + (4 \div 4)$$

PROBLEM SET 4-2

1. Evaluate each of the following.
   (a) $^-3(^-4)$ (b) $3(^-5)$
   (c) $(^-5) \cdot 3$ (d) $^-5 \cdot 0$
   (e) $^-2(^-3 \cdot 5)$ (f) $[^-2(^-5)](^-3)$
   (g) $(^-4 + 4)(^-3)$ (h) $(^-5 - {}^-3)(^-5 - 3)$

2. Use the definition of division to find each quotient (if possible). If a quotient is not defined, explain why.
   (a) $^-40 \div {}^-8$ (b) $143 \div (^-11)$
   (c) $^-143 \div 13$ (d) $0 \div (^-5)$
   (e) $^-5 \div 0$ (f) $0 \div 0$

3. Evaluate each of the following (if possible).
   (a) $(^-10 \div {}^-2)(^-2)$ (b) $(^-40 \div 8)8$
   (c) $(a \div b)b$ (d) $(^-10 \cdot 5) \div 5$
   (e) $(ab) \div b$ (f) $(^-8 \div {}^-2)(^-8)$
   (g) $(^-6 + {}^-14) \div 4$ (h) $(^-8 + 8) \div 8$
   (i) $^-8 \div (^-8 + 8)$ (j) $(^-23 - {}^-7) \div 4$
   (k) $(^-6 + 6) \div (^-2 + 2)$ (l) $^-13 \div (^-1)$
   (m) $(^-36 \div 12) \div 3$ (n) $|^-24| \div (3 - 15)$

4. Compute each of the following.
   (a) $(^-2)^3$ (b) $(^-2)^4$
   (c) $(^-10)^5 \div (^-10)^2$ (d) $(^-3)^5 \div (^-3)$
   (e) $(^-1)^{10}$ (f) $(^-1)^{15}$
   (g) $(^-1)^{50}$ (h) $(^-1)^{151}$

5. Consider the distributive property of multiplication over addition, $a(b + c) = ab + ac$. Show that this property is true for each of the following values of a, b, and c.
   (a) $a = {}^-1, b = {}^-5, c = {}^-2$
   (b) $a = {}^-3, b = {}^-3, c = 2$
   (c) $a = {}^-5, b = 2, c = {}^-6$

6. Show that $a \div (b + c) \neq (a \div b) + (a \div c)$ for each of the following values of a, b, and c.
   (a) $a = 12, b = {}^-2, c = 4$
   (b) $a = {}^-20, b = 4, c = {}^-5$
   (c) $a = {}^-10, b = 1, c = 1$

7. Consider the statement $(a + b) \div c = (a \div c) + (b \div c)$. Is this statement true for each of the following values of a, b, and c?
   (a) $a = {}^-9, b = 21, c = 3$
   (b) $a = {}^-9, b = {}^-21, c = {}^-3$
   (c) $a = 9, b = {}^-21, c = {}^-3$
   (d) $a = {}^-50, b = 25, c = {}^-25$

8. (a) On each of four consecutive plays in a football game, Foo University lost 11 yards. If lost yardage is interpreted as a negative integer, write the information as a product of integers and determine the total number of yards lost.
   (b) If Jack Jones lost a total of 66 yards in 11 plays, how many yards, on the average, did he lose on each play?

9. The temperature has been rising $6°C$ each hour. If the temperature is $9°C$ now, what was it 4 hours ago?

10. In 1979, it was predicted that the farmland acreage lost to family dwellings over the next 9 years would be 12,000 acres per year. If this prediction were true, and if this pattern were to continue, how much acreage would be lost to homes by the end of 1988?

11. Find a pattern for each of the following and write the next three terms.
    (a) $7, 3, {}^-1, {}^-5, {}^-9,$ _____, _____, _____
    (b) $^-2, {}^-4, {}^-6, {}^-8, {}^-10,$ _____, _____, _____
    (c) $2187, {}^-729, 243, {}^-81, 27,$ _____, _____, _____
    (d) $^-20, {}^-17, {}^-14, {}^-11, {}^-8,$ _____, _____, _____

12. For each of the following, find all integers x (if possible) that make the given equation true.
    (a) $^-3x = 6$ (b) $^-3x = {}^-6$
    (c) $^-2x = 0$ (d) $5x = {}^-30$
    (e) $x \div 3 = {}^-12$ (f) $x \div (^-3) = {}^-2$
    (g) $x \div (^-x) = {}^-1$ (h) $0 \div x = 0$
    (i) $x \div 0 = 1$ (j) $x^2 = 9$
    (k) $x^2 = {}^-9$ (l) $^-x \div {}^-x = 1$

13. Use patterns to show that $(^-1)(^-1) = 1$.

14. Compute each of the following.
    (a) $^-2 + 3 \cdot 5 - 1$
    (b) $10 - 3 \cdot 7 - 4(^-2) + 3$
    (c) $10 - 3 - 12$ (d) $10 - (3 - 12)$
    (e) $(^-3)^2$ (f) $^-3^2$
    (g) $^-5^2 + 3(^-2)^2$ (h) $^-2^3$
    (i) $(^-2)^5$ (j) $^-2^4$

15. If x is an integer and $x \neq 0$, which of the following are always positive and which are always negative?
    (a) $^-x^2$ (b) x^2 (c) $(^-x)^2$ (d) $^-x^3$
    (e) $(^-x)^3$ (f) $^-x^4$ (g) $(^-x)^4$ (h) x^4
    (i) x (j) ^-x

16. Which of the expressions in Problem 15 are equal to each other for all values of x except 0?

17. Simplify each of the following expressions by removing parentheses to write an equivalent expression.
   - (a) $(^-x)(^-y)$
   - (b) $^-2x(^-y)$
   - (c) $^-(x + y) + x + y$
   - (d) $^-1 \cdot x$
   - (e) $x - 2(^-y)$
   - (f) $a - (a - b)$
   - (g) $y - (y - x)$
   - (h) $^-(x - y) + x$

18. Multiply each of the following.
   - (a) $^-2(x - 1)$
   - (b) $^-2(x - y)$
   - (c) $x(x - y)$
   - (d) $^-x(x - y)$
   - (e) $^-2(x + y - z)$
   - (f) $^-x(x - y - 3)$
   - (g) $(^-5 - x)(5 + x)$
   - (h) $(x - y - 1)(x + y + 1)$
   - (i) $(^-x^2 + 2)(x^2 - 1)$

19. Use the difference-of-squares formula to simplify each of the following, if possible.
   - (a) $52 \cdot 48$
   - (b) $(5 - 100)(5 + 100)$
   - (c) $(^-x - y)(^-x + y)$
   - (d) $(2 + 3x)(2 - 3x)$
   - (e) $(x - 1)(1 + x)$
   - (f) $213^2 - 13^2$

20. Can $(^-x - y)(x + y)$ be multiplied by using the difference-of-squares formula? Explain why or why not.

21. Factor each of the following expressions completely and then simplify, if possible.
   - (a) $3x + 5x$
   - (b) $ax + 2x$
   - (c) $xy + x$
   - (d) $ax - 2x$
   - (e) $x^2 + xy$
   - (f) $3x - 4x + 7x$
   - (g) $3xy + 2x - xz$
   - (h) $3x^2 + xy - x$
   - (i) $abc + ab - a$
   - (j) $(a + b)(c + 1) - (a + b)$
   - (k) $16 - a^2$
   - (l) $x^2 - 9y^2$
   - (m) $4x^2 - 25y^2$
   - (n) $(x^2 - y^2) + x + y$

22. Identify the property of integers being illustrated in each of the following.
   - (a) $(^-3) \cdot (4 + 5) = (4 + 5) \cdot (^-3)$
   - (b) $^-4 + ^-7 \in I$
   - (c) $5 \cdot [4 \cdot (^-3)] = (5 \cdot 4) \cdot (^-3)$
   - (d) $(^-9) \cdot [5 + (^-8)] = (^-9) \cdot 5 + (^-9) \cdot (^-8)$

23. A population of bacteria doubles every day. On the 30th day, the population is 20 million. On what day was it 5 million?

24. (a) Given a calendar for any month of the year such as the one shown, pick several 3×3 groups of numbers and find the sum of these numbers. How are the obtained sums related to the middle number?

JULY						
S	M	T	W	T	F	S
		1	2	3	4	5
6	7	8	9	10	11	12
13	14	15	16	17	18	19
20	21	22	23	24	25	26
27	28	29	30	31		

   - ★(b) Prove that the sum of any 9 digits in any 3×3 set of numbers selected from a monthly calendar will always be equal to 9 times the middle number.

★25 Use the properties of integers to justify each of the following.
   - (a) $(^-a)b = ^-(ab)$
   - (b) $(^-a)(^-b) = ab$
   - (c) $^-(a + b) = ^-a + ^-b$

26. Use the $\boxed{+/-}$ key on the calculator to compute each of the following.
   - (a) $^-27 \times 3$
   - (b) $^-46 \times ^-4$
   - (c) $^-26 \div 13$
   - (d) $^-26 \div ^-13$

Review Problems

27. Compute each of the following.
   - (a) $3 - 6$
   - (b) $8 + ^-7$
   - (c) $5 - ^-8$
   - (d) $^-5 - ^-8$
   - (e) $^-8 + 5$
   - (f) $^-8 + ^-5$

28. Illustrate $^-8 + ^-5$ on a number line.

29. Find the opposite of each of the following.
   - (a) $^-5$
   - (b) 7
   - (c) 0

30. Compute each of the following.
   - (a) $|^-14|$
   - (b) $|^-14| + 7$
   - (c) $8 - |^-12|$
   - (d) $|11| + |^-11|$

BRAIN TEASER

If $a, \ldots, z$ are integers, find the product

$$(x - a)(x - b)(x - c) \cdots (x - z)$$

Section 4-3

Solving Equations and Inequalities

The topic of this section is solving equations and inequalities. Equations can be simple or earth shattering, as demonstrated in the cartoon.

B.C.   **BY JOHNNY HART**

$$2 + 2 = 4$$
SIMPLE

$$(x^2 - Zxy + y^2)$$
MIND BOGGLING

$$E = MC^2$$
EARTH SHATTERING

By permission of Johnny Hart and News America Syndicate.

PROPERTIES OF EQUATIONS

Before we start solving equations, we need several properties. The following properties of equality hold for integers.

Properties   **The Addition Property of Equality**   For any integers a, b, and c, if $a = b$, then $a + c = b + c$.

The Multiplication Property of Equality   For any integers a, b, and c, if $a = b$, then $ac = bc$.

According to the addition property of equality, it is possible to add the same integer to both sides of an equation without affecting the equality. According to the multiplication property of equality, it is possible to multiply both sides of an equation by the same integer without affecting the equality. Multiplication of both sides by zero is rarely used.

In mathematical equations, it is valid to substitute a number for its equal. This property is referred to as the **substitution property.** Examples of substitution follow:

substitution property

1. If $a + b = c + d$ and $d = 5$, then $a + b = c + 5$.
2. If $a + b = c + d$, if $b = e$, and if $d = f$, then $a + e = c + f$.

The addition property of equality was formulated as follows. For any integers a, b, and c, if $a = b$, then $a + c = b + c$. A new statement results from reversing the order of the *if* and *then* parts of this addition property. This new statement is called the converse of the original statement. In the case of the addition property, the converse is a true statement. The converse of the multiplication property of equality is also true when $c \neq 0$. These properties, called the *cancellation properties of equality,* are given below.

Property   **The Cancellation Properties of Equality for Addition and Multiplication:**
1. For any integers a, b, and c, if $a + c = b + c$, then $a = b$.
2. For any integers a, b, and c, with $c \neq 0$, if $ac = bc$, then $a = b$.

PROPERTIES OF INEQUALITIES

Before we consider solving equations and inequalities, we have to develop additional properties of inequalities for integers. As with whole numbers, "greater-than" and "less-than" relations can be defined for integers.

DEFINITION

> For any integers a and b, a is **greater than** b, written $a > b$, if and only if there exists a positive integer k such that $a = b + k$. Also, b is less than a, written $b < a$, if and only if $a > b$.

By the definition of "greater than," $a > b$ if and only if there exists a positive integer k such that $a = b + k$. By the definition of subtraction, $a = b + k$ if and only if $a - b = k$. Thus, because k is positive, $a - b > 0$. We summarize this discussion as follows.

For any two integers a and b, $a > b$ if and only if $a - b > 0$, that is, $a - b$ is positive.

Table 4-1 compares the properties of the inequality relations with the properties of the equality relation. Assume that a, b, and c represent integers.

Table 4-1

Property	Equality	Inequality
Addition	$a = b$ implies $a + c = b + c$	$a > b$ implies $a + c > b + c$ $a < b$ implies $a + c < b + c$
Multiplication	$a = b$ implies $ac = bc$	$a > b$ and $c > 0$ implies $ac > bc$ $a > b$ and $c < 0$ implies $ac < bc$ $a < b$ and $c > 0$ implies $ac < bc$ $a < b$ and $c < 0$ implies $ac > bc$

Remark   It is possible to combine properties of equality and inequality using the $\geq$ or $\leq$ symbols.

Examples of the addition property of "greater than" follow.

$5 > 2$	implies	$5 + 10 > 2 + 10$
$^-2 > {}^-5$	implies	$^-2 + 2 > {}^-5 + 2$
$x > 3$	implies	$x + 2 > 3 + 2$
$x - 3 > 5$	implies	$x - 3 + 3 > 5 + 3$

Consider the following examples involving the multiplication property.

$$5 > 3 \quad \text{implies} \quad 5 \cdot 2 > 3 \cdot 2, \text{ but } 5 \cdot (^-2) < 3 \cdot (^-2)$$

$$^-3 > ^-5 \quad \text{implies} \quad (^-3)2 > (^-5)2, \text{ but } (^-3)(^-2) < (^-5)(^-2)$$

$$x > 3 \quad \text{implies} \quad 2x > 2 \cdot 3, \text{ but } ^-2x < ^-2 \cdot 3$$

When both sides of an inequality are multiplied by a positive integer, the direction of inequality is preserved, but if both sides of an inequality are multiplied by a negative integer, the direction of inequality is reversed.

Properties for subtraction and division of inequalities follow from the addition and multiplication properties of inequality.

Property   If a, b, and c are any integers, then:
1. $a > b$ implies $a - c > b - c$;
2. $a > b$ and $c > 0$ implies $a \div c > b \div c$, provided that the divisions are defined;
3. $a > b$ and $c < 0$ implies $a \div c < b \div c$, provided that the divisions are defined.

Example 4-16

Justify each of the following.

(a) $^-2 > ^-5$ implies $^-7 > ^-10$
(b) $10 > 6$ implies $5 > 3$
(c) $10 > 6$ implies $^-5 < ^-3$

Solution

(a) By the subtraction property of inequality, $^-2 > ^-5$ implies $^-2 - 5 > ^-5 - 5$; that is, $^-7 > ^-10$.
(b) By the division property of inequality, $10 > 6$ implies $10 \div 2 > 6 \div 2$; that is, $5 > 3$.
(c) By the division property of inequality, $10 > 6$ implies $10 \div ^-2 < 6 \div ^-2$; that is, $^-5 < ^-3$.

SOLVING EQUATIONS

Part of the study of algebra concerns operations on numbers and other elements represented by symbols. Finding solutions to equations and inequalities is one part of algebra.

HISTORICAL NOTE

The word "algebra" comes from the Arabic book *Al-jabr wa'l muqabalah* written by Mohammed al-Khowârizmî (ca. 825). *Al-jabr* means restoring the balance in an equation by putting on one side of an equation a term that has been removed from the other side. Algebra was introduced in Europe in the thirteenth and fourteenth centuries by Leonardo of Pisa (also called Fibonacci). Algebra was occasionally referred to as *Ars Magna*, "the great art."

Example 4-17

Solve each of the following for x, where x is an integer.

(a) $x + 4 = {}^-6$ (b) $x + 4 > {}^-6$
(c) ${}^-x - 5 = 8$ (d) ${}^-x - 5 \geq 8$
(e) ${}^-2x + 3 = {}^-11$ (f) ${}^-2x + 3 > {}^-11$

Solution

(a)
$$x + 4 = {}^-6$$
$$(x + 4) + {}^-4 = {}^-6 + {}^-4$$
$$x + (4 + {}^-4) = {}^-6 + {}^-4$$
$$x + 0 = {}^-10$$
$$x = {}^-10$$

(b)
$$x + 4 > {}^-6$$
$$(x + 4) + {}^-4 > {}^-6 + {}^-4$$
$$x + (4 + {}^-4) > {}^-6 + {}^-4$$
$$x + 0 > {}^-10$$
$$x > {}^-10, \quad x \in I$$

(c)
$$^-x - 5 = 8$$
$$({}^-x - 5) + 5 = 8 + 5$$
$$^-x = 13$$
$$({}^-x)({}^-1) = 13({}^-1)$$
$$x = {}^-13$$

(d)
$$^-x - 5 \geq 8$$
$$({}^-x - 5) + 5 \geq 8 + 5$$
$$^-x \geq 13$$
$$({}^-x)({}^-1) \leq 13({}^-1)$$
$$x \leq {}^-13, \quad x \in I$$

(e)
$$^-2x + 3 = {}^-11$$
$$({}^-2x + 3) + {}^-3 = {}^-11 + {}^-3$$
$$^-2x = {}^-14$$
$$({}^-2x) \div {}^-2 = {}^-14 \div {}^-2$$
$$x = 7$$

(f)
$$^-2x + 3 > {}^-11$$
$$({}^-2x + 3) + {}^-3 > {}^-11 + {}^-3$$
$$^-2x > {}^-14$$
$$({}^-2x) \div {}^-2 < ({}^-14) \div {}^-2$$
$$x < 7, \quad x \in I$$

Algebra can be used to solve many types of problems. Naturally, the types of problems we attempt in the elementary school are not the complex problems involved with topics such as world economics or space travel, but they can help develop competence in problem solving. Students need to practice problem solving at a low level before they can attempt higher-order problems. The following simple model demonstrates a method for solving word problems: Formulate the word problem as a mathematical problem, solve the mathematical problem, and then interpret the solution in terms of the original problem.

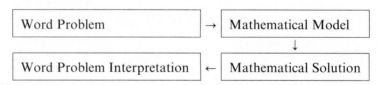

At the third-grade level, an example of this model appears as follows.

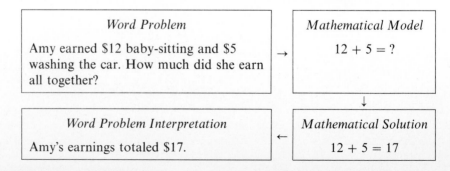

Polya's four-step problem-solving process can be carried over into the solution of word problems in which the use of algebra is appropriate. In Understanding the Problem, we identify what is given and what is to be found. In Devising a Plan, we assign letters to the unknown quantities and translate the information in the problem into a model involving equations or inequalities. In Carrying Out the Plan, we solve the equations or inequalities. In Looking Back, we interpret the solution in terms of the original problem and check the solution to be sure the original problem is answered. This process is demonstrated on page 186, which is from *Addison-Wesley Mathematics,* 1987, Grade 8, and in the following problems. Work through the problems at the bottom of the student page.

PROBLEM 1

David is thinking of a number. If he multiplies that number by $^-3$ and then adds 6, he has $^-4$ times his original number. What is David's original number?

UNDERSTANDING THE PROBLEM The problem asks us to find David's number. We are given that the number times $^-3$, plus 6, equals $^-4$ times the number.

DEVISING A PLAN Let n represent David's number. Now, we translate the information from the problem into mathematical symbols and solve the resulting equation.

Information	*Mathematical Translation*
David is thinking of a number.	n
He multiplies that number by $^-3$.	^-3n
He adds 6.	$^-3n + 6$
He has $(^-4)$ times his original number.	$^-3n + 6 = (^-4)n$

CARRYING OUT THE PLAN Solve the equation.

$$^-3n + 6 = {}^-4n$$
$$4n + {}^-3n + 6 = 4n + {}^-4n$$
$$n + 6 = 0$$
$$n = {}^-6$$

Thus, the number David is thinking about is $^-6$.

LOOKING BACK To check that $^-6$ is the correct solution, follow the written information using $^-6$ as David's number. The number, $^-6$, times $^-3$, is 18. Next, 18 plus 6 is 24. Also, $^-4$ times the number, $^-6$, is 24. So the answer is correct.

PROBLEM SOLVING: Writing and Solving Equations

QUESTION
DATA
PLAN
ANSWER
CHECK

Ken and May Yamamoto bought living room furniture. The total cost with tax and interest was $2,250. They made a down payment of $450. The balance was to be paid in 8 equal payments. How much was each payment?

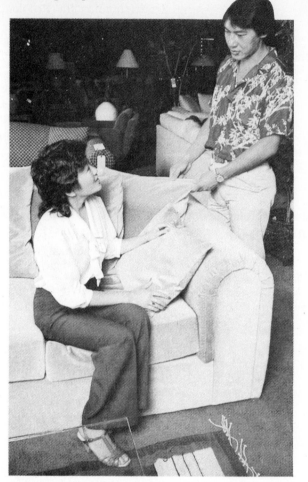

To solve the problem, you can write and solve a two-step equation.

Let p = the amount of each payment.

$8p$ = amount for 8 payments

$8p + 450$ = total cost

Equation: $8p + 450 = 2{,}250$

$$8p + 450 - 450 = 2{,}250 - 450$$

$$8p = 1{,}800$$

$$\frac{8p}{8} = \frac{1{,}800}{8}$$

$$p = 225$$

Check: $8 \times 225 + 450 = 1{,}800 + 450 = 2{,}250$

Each payment was $225.

Write and solve an equation for each problem.

1. A certain number is divided by 6 and 17 is added to the quotient. The result is 21. What is the number?

   Let n = the number.

2. If 15 is subtracted from 8 times a certain number, the difference is 57. What is the number?

   Let n = the number.

3. A number is multiplied by 7 and then 36 is added to the product. The sum is 106. What is the number?

4. A number is divided by 4 and then 19 is subtracted from the quotient. The difference is 2. What is the number?

PROBLEM 2   Beans that cost 75¢ per pound are mixed with beans that cost 95¢ per pound to produce a 20-pound mixture that costs 80¢ per pound. How many pounds of the beans costing 75¢ per pound are used?

UNDERSTANDING THE PROBLEM The problem asks how many pounds of beans costing 75¢ per pound are necessary to make 20 pounds of a mixture costing 80¢ per pound. To make the 20-pound mixture, beans costing 95¢ per pound are mixed with beans costing 75¢ per pound. Thus, the number of pounds of beans costing 95¢ per pound is 20 minus the number of pounds of beans costing 75¢ per pound. Also, the total cost of the beans costing 75¢ per pound and the beans costing 95¢ per pound must be the cost of 20 pounds of beans costing 80¢ per pound.

DEVISING A PLAN Let x stand for the number of pounds of beans costing 75¢ per pound. Using this symbolism, we know that the number of pounds of beans costing 95¢ per pound is $20 - x$ pounds. Since the rest of the given information involves cost, we need the cost of each type of beans. The cost of x pounds of beans costing 75¢ per pound is $75x$ (in cents). Similarly, the cost of $20 - x$ pounds of beans costing 95¢ per pound is $95(20 - x)$ (in cents). The total mixture, 20 pounds, costs 80¢ per pound or $80 \cdot 20$ cents. We use this information to write the following equation.

$$75x + 95(20 - x) = 80 \cdot 20$$

We must solve the equation for x. This will give the number of pounds of beans costing 75¢ per pound.

CARRYING OUT THE PLAN

$$75x + 95(20 - x) = 80 \cdot 20$$
$$75x + 1900 - 95x = 1600$$
$$^{-}20x + 1900 = 1600$$
$$^{-}20x = {}^{-}300$$
$$x = 15$$

Thus, 15 pounds of beans costing 75¢ per pound are required. Because there are 20 pounds of the final mixture, of which 15 pounds are of beans costing 75¢ per pound, $20 - 15$, or 5, pounds of beans costing 95¢ per pound are used.

LOOKING BACK The solution should be checked in the original problem. The cost of 15 pounds of beans costing 75¢ per pound is $15 \cdot 75¢$, or \$11.25. The cost of 5 pounds of beans costing 95¢ per pound is $5¢ \cdot 95¢$, or \$4.75. The cost of 20 pounds of the final mixture at 80¢ per pound is $20 \cdot 80¢$, or \$16.00. The conditions of the problem are satisfied because \$11.25 + \$4.75 = \$16.00.

A different method of solving the problem involves using two unknowns. We let x stand for the number of pounds of 75¢ beans and y stand for the number of pounds of 95¢ beans. Next, we translate the information from the problem into mathematical statements. There are 20 pounds in the blend, so we have $x + y = 20$. The remaining information tells us about the cost per pound of each type of bean. To produce an equation using this information, notice that the value of beans costing 75¢ per pound plus the value of beans costing 95¢ per pound equals the value of the 20-pound mixture of beans.

Cost of 75¢ per pound beans plus cost of 95¢ per pound beans = cost of mixture

$$75x \qquad\qquad + \qquad\qquad 95y \qquad\qquad = \qquad 80 \cdot 20$$

The two equations obtained are as follows.

$$x + \quad y = 20$$

$$75x + 95y = 80 \cdot 20$$

We know how to solve equations with one unknown, so we try to combine these two equations into one equation with one unknown. This can be achieved by solving one of the equations for y and then substituting the expression for y in the other equation. Because $x + y = 20$ implies $y = 20 - x$, we substitute $20 - x$ for y in the second equation and solve for x. We then use the value of x obtained to find the value of y.

PROBLEM 3

In a certain factory, machine A produces three times as many bolts as machine B. Machine C produces 13 more bolts than machine A. If the total production is 4997 bolts per day, how many bolts does each machine produce in a day?

UNDERSTANDING THE PROBLEM The problem asks for the number of bolts that each of machine A, machine B, and machine C produce in 1 day. The problem gives information that compares the production of A to B and of C to A.

DEVISING A PLAN Let a, b, and c be the number of bolts produced by machines A, B, and C, respectively. We translate the given problem into equations as follows.

Machine A produces 3 times as many bolts as B: $a = 3b$

Machine C produces 13 more bolts than A: $c = a + 13$

Total production is 4997: $a + b + c = 4997$

In order to reduce the number of variables, we substitute $3b$ for a in the second and third equations.

$$c = a + 13 \quad \text{becomes} \qquad\qquad c = 3b + 13$$

$$a + b + c = 4997 \quad \text{becomes} \quad 3b + b + c = 4997$$

Next, we make an equation in one variable, b, by substituting $3b + 13$ for c in the equation $3b + b + c = 4997$, solve for b, and then find a and c.

CARRYING OUT THE PLAN

$$3b + b + 3b + 13 = 4997$$

$$7b + 13 = 4997$$

$$7b = 4984$$

$$b = 712$$

Thus, $a = 3b = 3 \cdot 712 = 2136$. Also, $c = a + 13 = 2136 + 13 = 2149$. Machine A produces 2136 bolts, machine B produces 712 bolts, and machine C produces 2149 bolts.

LOOKING BACK To check the answers, we follow the original information, using $a = 2136$, $b = 712$, and $c = 2149$. The information in the first sentence, "Machine A produces 3 times as many bolts as machine B," checks, since $2136 = 3 \cdot 712$. The second sentence, "Machine C produces 13 more bolts than machine A," is true because $2149 = 13 + 2136$. The information in the last sentence, "The total production was 4997 bolts," checks, since $2136 + 712 + 2149 = 4997$.

An alternate solution to Problem 3 is as follows. Let x be the number of bolts produced by machine B. Then, we express the number of bolts that machines A and C produce in terms of x.

Information	*Mathematical Translation*
The number of items that machine B produces.	x
Machine A produces three times as many items as machine B.	$3x$
Machine C produces 13 more items than machine A.	$3x + 13$
The total production is 4997.	$x + 3x + (3x + 13) = 4997$

Solve the equation.

$$x + 3x + (3x + 13) = 4997$$
$$7x + 13 = 4997$$
$$7x = 4984$$
$$x = 712$$

Hence, machine B produces 712 bolts. Because $3x = 3 \cdot 712 = 2136$, machine A produces 2136 bolts; $3x + 13 = 2136 + 13 = 2149$, so machine C produces 2149 bolts.

If we had let x be the number of bolts that machine A produces, the problem would have been more complicated to solve because machine B then produces $x \div 3$ bolts.

PROBLEM 4

Mary, a 10-year-old calculator genius, announced a discovery to her classmates one day. She said, "I have found a special five-digit number I call *abcde*. If I enter 1 and then the number on my calculator and then multiply by 3, the result is the number with 1 on the end!" Can you find her number?

UNDERSTANDING THE PROBLEM Mary found a five-digit number called *abcde*, so that three times the display 1*abcde* gives the display *abcde*1 on the calculator. It will help us to understand the problem if we guess any five-digit number and see if our guess is correct. Suppose we guess 34,578. With 1 after it, it becomes 345,781. With 1 before it, it becomes 134,578. Since $3 \cdot 134,578 \neq 345,781$, our guess is incorrect.

DEVISING A PLAN We know that three times $1abcde$ is $abcde1$. This can be translated to an equation by letting the unknown number on the display $abcde$ be n and using place value. Note that $1abcde$ equals $1 \cdot 10^5 + n$, or $100,000 + n$, and $abcde1$ equals $n \cdot 10 + 1$, or $10n + 1$. Thus, Mary's computation tells us that

$$3(100,000 + n) = 10n + 1$$

Now all that is necessary to solve the problem is to solve this equation for n.

CARRYING OUT THE PLAN We use properties of equality to solve the equation for n.

$$3(100,000 + n) = 10n + 1$$
$$300,000 + 3n = 10n + 1$$
$$299,999 = 7n$$
$$42,857 = n$$

Consequently, the five-digit number is 42,857.

LOOKING BACK To check the answer, we compute $3 \cdot 142,857 = 428,571$ and see that the solution is correct. Similar problems can be investigated by asking analogous questions for six-, seven-, or eight-digit numbers. Another generalization is to find a five-digit number n such that $k(100,000 + n) = 10n + 1$, where k is different from 3.

An alternate solution to this problem can be found by considering the multiplication one digit at a time. For example, in Figure 4-8(a), we see that $3 \cdot e$ has a 1 in the units digit of the product. Because e is a single digit and 7 is the only single digit that can be multiplied by 3 to yield a product with units digit 1, then e must be 7.

Figure 4-8

$$
\begin{array}{r}
1abcde \\
\times \quad 3 \\
\hline
abcde1
\end{array}
\qquad
\begin{array}{r}
2 \\
1abcd7 \\
\times \quad 3 \\
\hline
abcd71
\end{array}
$$

(a)   (b)

If we substitute 7 for e, as shown in Figure 4-8(b), we see that $3 \cdot d + 2$ has 7 as a units digit, or—equivalently—that $3 \cdot d$ has 5 as units digit. Because d is a single digit and 5 is the only single digit that can be multiplied by 5 to yield a product with a units digit 5, then $d = 5$. Similarly, each of the digits a, b, and c can also be found.

BRAIN TEASER

The following is an argument showing that an ant weighs as much as an elephant. What is wrong?

Let e be the weight of the elephant and a the weight of the ant. Let $e - a = d$. Consequently, $e = a + d$. Multiply each side of $e = a + d$ by $e - a$. Then simplify.

$$e(e - a) = (a + d)(e - a)$$
$$e^2 - ea = ae + de - a^2 - da$$
$$e^2 - ea - de = ae - a^2 - da$$
$$e(e - a - d) = a(e - a - d)$$
$$e = a$$

Thus, the weight of the elephant equals the weight of the ant.

PROBLEM SET 4-3

1. Write each of the following lists of numbers in increasing order.
   (a) $^-13, \ ^-20, \ ^-5, 0, 4, \ ^-3$
   (b) $^-5, \ ^-6, 5, 6, 0$
   (c) $^-20, \ ^-15, \ ^-100, 0, \ ^-13$
   (d) $13, \ ^-2, \ ^-3, 5$

2. Show that each of the following is true.
   (a) $^-3 > \ ^-5$ (b) $^-6 < 0$
   (c) $^-8 > \ ^-10$ (d) $^-5 < 4$

3. Solve each of the following if x is an integer.
   (a) $x + 3 = \ ^-15$ (b) $x + 3 > \ ^-15$
   (c) $3 - x = \ ^-15$ (d) $^-x + 3 > \ ^-15$
   (e) $^-x - 3 = 15$ (f) $^-x - 3 \geq 15$
   (g) $3x + 5 = \ ^-16$ (h) $3x + 5 < \ ^-16$
   (i) $^-3x + 5 = 11$ (j) $^-3x + 5 \leq 11$
   (k) $5x - 3 = 7x - 1$ (l) $5x - 3 > 7x - 1$
   (m) $3(x + 5) = \ ^-4(x + 5) + 21$
   (n) $^-5(x + 3) > 0$

4. Give a counterexample to show that the symmetric property does not hold for the "less than" relation on the set of integers.

5. Which of the following are true for all possible integer values of x?
   (a) $3(x + 1) = 3x + 3$ (b) $x - 3 = 3 - x$
   (c) $x + 3 = 3 + x$
   (d) $2(x - 1) + 2 = 3x - x$
   (e) $x^2 + 1 > 0$
   (f) $3x > 4x - x$

6. For each of the following, which elements of the given set, if any, satisfy the equation or inequality?
   (a) $x^3 + x^2 = 2x, \ \{1, \ ^-1, \ ^-2, 0\}$
   (b) $3x - 3 = 24, \ \{^-9, 9\}$
   (c) $^-x \geq 5, \ \{6, \ ^-6, 7, \ ^-7, 2\}$
   (d) $x^2 < 16, \ \{^-4, \ ^-3, \ ^-2, \ ^-1, 0, 1, 2, 3, 4\}$

7. Solve each of the following equations. Check your answers by substituting in the given equation. Assume x, y, and z represent integers.
   (a) $^-2x + \ ^-11 = 3x + 4$ (b) $5(^-x + 1) = 5$
   (c) $^-3y + 4 = y$ (d) $^-3(z - 1) = 8z + 3$

8. If you multiply Tom's age by 3 and add 4, the result is more than 37. What can you tell about Tom's age?

9. If you multiply a number by $^-6$ and then add 20 to the product, the result is 50. What is the number?

10. David has three times as much money as Rick. Together, they have $400. How much does each have?

11. Ran is 4 years older than Nureet. Six years ago Ran was twice as old as Nureet was then. How old are they now?

12. Factory A produces twice as many cars per day as factory B. Factory C produces 300 cars more per day than factory A. If the total production in the three factories is 7300 cars per day, how many cars per day are produced in each factory?

13. Tea that costs 60¢ per pound is mixed with tea that costs 45¢ per pound to produce a 100-pound blend that costs 51¢ per pound. How much of each kind of tea is used?

14. For a certain event, 812 tickets were sold, totaling $1912. If students paid $2 per ticket and nonstudents paid $3 per ticket, how many student tickets were sold?

15. The sum of three consecutive integers is 237. Find the three integers.

16. The sum of three consecutive even integers is 240. Find the three integers.

17. The sum of two integers is 21. The first number is twice the second number. Find the integers.

18. A man left an estate of $64,000 to three children. The eldest child received three times as much as the youngest. The middle child received $14,000 more than the youngest. How much did each child receive?

★19. (a) Is it always true that for any integers x and y, $x^2 + y^2 \geq 2xy$? Prove your answer.
   (b) For which integers x and y is $x^2 + y^2 = 2xy$?

★20. If $0 < a < b$ where a and b are integers, prove that $a^2 < b^2$.

⋆**21.** If $a < b$ where a and b are integers, is it always true that $a^2 < b^2$?

⋆**22.** If $a < b$ where a and b are integers, prove that $c - b < c - a$, if c is an integer.

⋆**23.** For each of the following, find all integers x such that the statement is true.
   (a) $x + 1 < 3$ and $^-x + 1 < 5$
   (b) $2x < \,^-6$ or $1 + x < 0$

Review Problems

24. Find the additive inverse of each of the following.
   (a) $^-7$ (b) 5
   (c) $^-(^-3)$ (d) $3 - (^-7)$

25. Compute each of the following.
   (a) $^-3 + \,^-7$ (b) $^-3 - \,^-7$
   (c) $3 + \,^-7$ (d) $3 - \,^-7$
   (e) $^-3 \cdot 7$ (f) $^-3 \cdot \,^-7$
   (g) $3 - 7$ (h) $^-21 \div 7$
   (i) $^-21 \div \,^-7$ (j) $7 - 3 - 8$
   (k) $8 + 2 \cdot 3 - 7$ (l) $^-8 - 7 - 2 \cdot 3$
   (m) $|^-7| \cdot |^-3|$ (n) $|^-7| \cdot |^-8|$
   (o) $|^-7| + 8$ (p) $|^-7| - |^-8|$

26. Compute $^-7 + (^-3)$ using a number line.

___

SOLUTION TO THE PRELIMINARY PROBLEM

UNDERSTANDING THE PROBLEM Stu took the 24-question true-false test and answered every question. For each correct answer, he received 5 points, and for each incorrect answer, he lost 7 points. His final score was 0. We are to determine the number of problems he answered correctly.

DEVISING A PLAN The strategy of guess and check may be useful. Guess the number of questions he answered correctly. Because there were only 24 questions, our guess must be 24 or fewer. Because he received a zero, the number he answered correctly should be slightly greater than the number that he missed. Next, we make a guess, say 13, and check to see if the guess is correct. If it is not, we see what we can learn from our guess and try again.

CARRYING OUT THE PLAN Suppose we guess that Stu answered 13 problems correctly. To check our guess, we reason as follows. If he answered 13 correctly, then he missed 11 problems. Thus, his score would be $13 \cdot 5 - 11 \cdot 7 = -12$. This implies that the number he answered correctly must be greater than 13. If we choose 15 as a guess, then we would have $15 \cdot 5 - 9 \cdot 7 = 75 - 63 = 12$, and we know that this guess is too large. The only answer between 13 and 15 is 14, which checks because $14 \cdot 5 - 10 \cdot 7 = 0$. Thus, the solution to our problem is that Stu answered 14 problems correctly.

LOOKING BACK An alternate strategy for this problem might be writing an equation. If we let R be the number of correct answers, then $24 - R$ is the number of wrong answers. Thus, we would have the following.

$$5 \cdot R - 7 \cdot (24 - R) = 0$$
$$5R - 168 + 7R = 0$$
$$12R - 168 = 0$$
$$12R = 168$$
$$R = 14$$

If the same scoring scheme had been used on a 25-question test, could Stu have scored 0?

___

QUESTIONS FROM THE CLASSROOM

1. A student argues that $(^-1)(^-1) = 1$ since $^-(^-1) = 1$. What is your response?

2. A fourth-grade student devised the following subtraction algorithm for subtracting $84 - 27$.
   Four minus seven equals negative three.

   $$\begin{array}{r} 84 \\ -27 \\ \hline ^-3 \end{array}$$

   Eighty minus twenty equals sixty.

   $$\begin{array}{r} 84 \\ -27 \\ \hline ^-3 \\ 60 \end{array}$$

   Sixty plus negative three equals fifty-seven.

   $$\begin{array}{r} 84 \\ -27 \\ \hline ^-3 \\ +60 \\ \hline 57 \end{array}$$

   Thus, the answer is 57. What is your response as a teacher?

3. A seventh-grade student does not believe that $^-5 < {}^-2$. The student argues that a debt of $5 is greater than a debt of $2. How do you respond?

4. An eighth-grade student claims she can prove that subtraction of integers is commutative. She points out that if a and b are integers, then $a - b = a + {}^-b$. Since addition is commutative, so is subtraction. What is your response?

5. A student claims that if $x \neq 0$, then $|x| = {}^-x$ is never true since absolute value is always positive. What is your response?

6. A student claims that since $(a \cdot b)^2 = a^2 \cdot b^2$, it must also be true that $(a + b)^2 = a^2 + b^2$. How do you respond?

7. A student solves $1 - 2x > x - 5$, where x is an integer, and reports the solution as $x < 2$. The student asks if it is possible to check the answer in a way similar to the method of substitution for equations. What is your response?

8. A student computes $^-8 - 2(^-3)$ by writing $^-10(^-3) = 30$. How would you help this student?

9. A student says that his father showed him a very simple method for dealing with expressions like $^-(a - b + 1)$ and $x - (2x - 3)$. The rule is: If there is a negative sign before the parentheses, change the signs of the expressions inside the parentheses. Thus, $^-(a - b + 1) = {}^-a + b - 1$ and $x - (2x - 3) = x - 2x + 3$. What is your response?

10. A student solving word problems always checks her solutions by substituting in equations rather than following the written information. Is this an accurate check for the word problem?

11. A student shows you the following proof that $(^-1)(^-1) = 1$: There are two possibilities, either $(^-1)(^-1) = 1$ or $(^-1)(^-1) = {}^-1$. Suppose $(^-1)(^-1) = {}^-1$. Since $^-1 = (^-1) \cdot 1$, then $(^-1)(^-1) = {}^-1$ can be written as $(^-1)(^-1) = (^-1) \cdot 1$. By the cancellation property of multiplication, it follows that $^-1 = 1$, which is impossible. Hence, $(^-1)(^-1)$ cannot equal $^-1$ and must, therefore, equal 1. What is your reaction?

CHAPTER OUTLINE

I. Basic concepts of integers
   A. The set of **integers**, I, is $\{\ldots, {}^-3, {}^-2, {}^-1, 0, 1, 2, 3, \ldots\}$.
   B. The distance from any integer to 0 is called the **absolute value** of the integer. The absolute value of an integer x is denoted $|x|$.
   C. Operations with integers
      1. **Addition:** For any whole numbers a and b:
         (a) $a + b = n(A \cup B)$ where $n(A) = a$, $n(B) = b$, and $A \cap B = \emptyset$ for sets A and B.
         (b) $^-a + {}^-b = {}^-(a + b)$
         (c) $a + {}^-b = {}^-b + a = a - b \qquad$ if $a > b$
         (d) $a + {}^-b = {}^-b + a = 0 \qquad$ if $a = b$
         (e) $a + {}^-b = {}^-b + a = {}^-(b - a) \qquad$ if $a < b$
      2. **Subtraction:**
         (a) If a and b are any integers, then $a - b = n$ if and only if $a = b + n$
         (b) For all integers a and b, $a - b = a + {}^-b$
      3. **Multiplication:** For any whole numbers a and b:
         (a) $a \cdot b = n(A \times B)$, where $a = n(A)$ and $b = n(B)$, for sets A and B.
         (b) $(^-a) \cdot (^-b) = ab$
         (c) $(^-a) \cdot b = b \cdot (^-a) = {}^-(ab)$

4. **Division:** If a and b are any integers with $b \neq 0$, then $a \div b$ is the unique integer c, if it exists, such that $a = bc$.

5. **Order of operations:** When addition, subtraction, multiplication, and division appear without parentheses, multiplications and divisions are done first in the order of their appearance from left to right and then additions and subtractions in the order of their appearance from left to right. Any arithmetic in parentheses is done first.

II. The system of integers

A. The set of integers, $I = \{\ldots, {}^-3, {}^-2, {}^-1, 0, 1, 2, 3, \ldots\}$, along with the operations of addition and multiplication, satisfy the following properties.

Property	+	×
Closure	Yes	Yes
Commutative	Yes	Yes
Associative	Yes	Yes
Identity	Yes, 0	Yes, 1
Inverse	Yes	No

Distributive property of multiplication over addition

B. **Zero multiplication property of integers**

$a \cdot 0 = 0 = 0 \cdot a$

C. **Addition property of equality:** For any integers a, b, and c, if $a = b$, then $a + c = b + c$.

D. **Multiplication property of equality:** For any integers a, b and c, if $a = b$, then $ac = bc$.

E. **Substitution property:** Any number may be substituted for its equal.

F. **Cancellation properties for addition and multiplication:**
(a) For any integers $a, b,$ and c, if $a + c = b + c$, then $a = b$.
(b) For any integers $a, b,$ and c, if $c \neq 0$ and $ac = bc$, then $a = b$.

G. For all integers $a, b,$ and c:
1. ${}^-({}^-a) = a$
2. $a - (b - c) = a - b + c$
3. $(a + b)(a - b) = a^2 - b^2$ (**Difference-of-squares formula**)

III. Inequalities

A. $a > b$ if and only if there exists a positive integer k such that $a = b + k$. $b < a$ if and only if $a > b$.

B. Let a and b be any two integers. Then, $a > b$ if and only if $a - b > 0$.

C. Properties of inequalities:
1. **Addition property:** If $a > b$ and c is any integer, then $a + c > b + c$.
2. **Multiplication properties:**
(a) If $a > b$ and $c > 0$, then $ac > bc$.
(b) If $a > b$ and $c < 0$, then $ac < bc$.

IV. Solving word problems

A. Solving word problems involves each of the following.
1. **Understanding the Problem:** Identify what is given and what is to be found.
2. **Devising a Plan:** Assign letters to the unknown quantities and translate the data into equations or inequalities.
3. **Carrying Out the Plan:** Solve the equations or inequalities.
4. **Looking Back:** Check and interpret the solution in terms of the situation given in the problem.

CHAPTER TEST

1. Find the additive inverse of each of the following.
   (a) 3   (b) ${}^-a$ (c) 0
   (d) $x + y$ (e) ${}^-x + y$

2. Perform each of the following operations.
   (a) $({}^-2 + {}^-8) + 3$ (b) ${}^-2 - ({}^-5) + 5$
   (c) ${}^-3({}^-2) + 2$ (d) ${}^-3({}^-5 + 5)$
   (e) ${}^-40 \div ({}^-5)$ (f) $({}^-25 \div 5)({}^-3)$

3. For each of the following, find all integer values of x (if there are any) that make the given equation true.
   (a) ${}^-x + 3 = 0$ (b) ${}^-2x = 10$
   (c) $0 \div ({}^-x) = 0$ (d) ${}^-x \div 0 = {}^-1$
   (e) $3x - 1 = {}^-124$ (f) ${}^-2x + 3x = x$

4. Use a pattern approach to show that $({}^-2)({}^-3) = 6$.

5. (a) Show that $(x - y)(x + y) = x^2 - y^2$.
   (b) Use the result in (a) to compute $({}^-2 - x)({}^-2 + x)$.

6. Simplify each of the following expressions.
   (a) ${}^-1x$ (b) $({}^-1)(x - y)$
   (c) $2x - (1 - x)$ (d) $({}^-x)^2 + x^2$
   (e) $({}^-x)^3 + x^3$ (f) $({}^-3 - x)(3 + x)$

7. Factor each of the following expressions and then simplify, if possible.
   (a) $x - 3x$
   (b) $x^2 + x$

   (c) $5 + 5x$

   (d) $(x - y)(x + 1) - (x - y)$

8. Solve each of the following for x, if x is an integer.

   (a) $^-3x + 7 = ^-x + 11$

   (b) $|x| = 5$

   (c) $^-2x + 1 < 0$

   (d) $^-2(^-3x + 7) < ^-2(^-x + 11)$

9. A certain college has 5715 undergraduates. There are 115 more seniors than juniors. The number of sophomores is twice the number of seniors, and the number of freshmen is twice the number of juniors. How many freshmen, sophomores, juniors, and seniors attend the college?

10. Classify each of the following as true or false (all letters represent integers).

   (a) $|x|$ always is positive.

   (b) For all x and y, $|x + y| = |x| + |y|$.

   (c) If $a < ^-b$, then $a < 0$.

   (d) For all x and y, $(x - y)^2 = (y - x)^2$.

   (e) $(^-a)(^-b)$ is the additive inverse of ab.

11. If the temperature was $^-16°C$ and it rose by $9°C$, what is the new temperature?

12. Find a counterexample to disprove each of the properties on the set of integers.

   (a) Commutative property of division

   (b) Associative property of subtraction

   (c) Closure property for division

   (d) Distributive property of division over subtraction

13. Twice Molly's weight added to 50 pounds is equal to 78 pounds. Find Molly's weight.

14. A truck contains 150 small packages, some weighing 1 kg each and some weighing 2 kg each. How many packages of each weight are in the truck if the total weight of the packages is 265 kg?

15. John has a collection of nickels and dimes. He has three more dimes than twice the number of nickels. If he has $2.05, how many of each type of coin does he have?

SELECTED BIBLIOGRAPHY

Battista, M. "A Complete Model for Operations on Integers." *Arithmetic Teacher* 30 (May 1983):26–31.

Brumfiel, C. "Teaching the Absolute Value Function." *The Mathematics Teacher* 73 (January 1980):24–30.

Charles, R. "Get the Most Out of Word Problems." *Arithmetic Teacher* 29 (November 1981):39–40.

Crowley, M., and K. Dunn. "On Multiplying Negative Numbers." *The Mathematics Teacher* 78 (April 1985):252–256.

DiDomenico, A. "Discovery of a Property of Consecutive Integers." *The Mathematics Teacher* 72 (April 1979):285–286.

Grady, M. "A Manipulative Aid for Adding and Subtracting Integers." *Arithmetic Teacher* 26 (November 1978):40.

Jacobs, H. *Algebra*. San Francisco: Freeman, 1979.

Jencks, S., and D. Peck. "Hot and Cold Cubes." *The Arithmetic Teacher* 24 (January 1977):70–71.

Johnson, J. "Working With Integers." *The Mathematics Teacher* 71 (January 1978):31.

Kilhefner, D. "Equation Hangman." *Arithmetic Teacher* 27 (January 1979):46–47.

Kindle, G. "Droopy, The Number Line, and Multiplication of Integers." *The Arithmetic Teacher* 23 (December 1976):647–650.

Kohn, J. "A Physical Model for Operations with Integers." *The Mathematics Teacher* 71 (December 1978):734–736.

Morrow, L. "Flow Charts for Equation Solving and Maintenance of Skills." *The Mathematics Teacher* 66 (October 1973):499–506.

National Council of Teachers of Mathematics. *More Topics in Mathematics for Elementary School Teachers*. Thirtieth Yearbook. Reston, Va.: NCTM, 1968.

National Council of Teachers of Mathematics. "The System of Integers." Booklet number 9. *Topics in Mathematics for Elementary School Teachers*. Reston, Va.: NCTM, 1968.

Peterson, J. "Fourteen Different Strategies for Multiplication of Integers, or Why $(^-1)(^-1) = ^+1$." *The Arithmetic Teacher* 19 (May 1972):396–403.

Pratt, E. "A Teaching Aid for Signed Numbers." *The Arithmetic Teacher* 13 (November 1966):589–590.

Rheins, J., and G. Rheins. "The Additive Inverse in Elementary Algebra." *The Mathematics Teacher* 54 (November 1961):538–539.

Richardson, L. "The Role of Strategies for Teaching Pupils to Solve Verbal Problems." *The Arithmetic Teacher* 22 (May 1975):414–421.

Sconyers, J. "Something New on Number Lines." *The Mathematics Teacher* 67 (March 1974):253–254.

Shoemaker, R. "Please, My Dear Aunt Sally." *Arithmetic Teacher* 27 (May 1980):34–35.

Zlot, W., and R. Roberts. "The Multiplication of Signed Numbers." *The Mathematics Teacher* 75 (April 1982):302–304.

Zweng, M. "One Point of View: The Problem of Solving Story Problems." *Arithmetic Teacher* 27 (September 1979):2.

CHAPTER 5

Number Theory

Preliminary Problem

In the central prison of Ilusia, there were 1000 cells numbered from 1 to 1000. Each cell was occupied by a single prisoner, and each had a separate guard. After a revolution, the new queen ordered the guards to free certain prisoners based on the following scheme. The guards walk through the prison one at a time. The first guard opens all 1000 cells. The second guard follows immediately and closes all the cells with even numbers. The third guard follows and changes every third cell starting with cell 3, that is, closing the open cells and opening the closed cells. Similarly, the fourth guard starts at cell 4 and changes every fourth cell. This process continues until the 1000th guard passes through the prison, at which point the prisoners whose cells are open are freed. How many prisoners are freed?

Introduction

Number theory is concerned primarily with relationships among integers. These relationships have fascinated mathematicians for centuries. Number theory is associated with names like Pythagoras (500 B.C.), Euclid (300 B.C.), and Diophantus (A.D. 300). As a field of study, number theory began to flourish in the seventeenth century with the work of the lawyer Pierre de Fermat, the father of number theory. Topics from number theory include multiples, factors, divisibility tests, prime numbers, prime factorizations, greatest common divisors, and least common multiples. A major use of topics in number theory arises in work with fractions, specifically rational numbers.

Section 5-1

Divisibility

In a division such as $12 \div 3 = 4$, we can make any of the statements given in the column on the left below. In general, if $a \div b = c$, where a, b, and c are integers, then the statements in the column on the right are true.

Example	*General Statement*
12 is divisible by 3.	a is divisible by b.
3 is a divisor of 12.	b is a divisor of a.
12 is a multiple of 3.	a is a multiple of b.
3 is a factor of 12.	b is a factor of a.
3 divides 12.	b divides a.

Each statement in the left column can be written as $3 \mid 12$ and each statement in the right column can be written as $b \mid a$. The expression $b \mid a$ is usually read

divides

"b **divides** a." Note that $b \neq 0$ because division by 0 is undefined.

DEFINITION

> If a and b are any integers with $b \neq 0$, then b divides a, written $b \mid a$, if and only if there is a unique integer c such that $a = cb$.

Remark Do not confuse $b \mid a$ with b/a, which is interpreted as $b \div a$. The former, a relation, is either true or false. The latter, an operation, has a numerical value, as shown in Chapter 6.

HISTORICAL NOTE

Pierre de Fermat (1601–1665) conjectured that there are no positive-integer solutions to the equation $x^n + y^n = z^n$, where n is greater than 2, and wrote in the margin of one of his books, "I have found an admirable proof of this, but the margin is too narrow to contain it." No one else has ever been able to prove it.

To symbolize that 12 is not divisible by 5, or 5 does not divide 12, we write $5 \nmid 12$. The notation $5 \nmid 12$ also is used to show that 12 is not a multiple of 5 and 5 is not a factor of 12.

Example 5-1

Classify each of the following as true or false. Explain your answer.

(a) $^-3 \mid 12$ (b) $0 \mid 3$ (c) $3 \mid 0$ (d) $8 \nmid 2$
(e) For all integers a, $1 \mid a$ (f) For all integers a, $^-1 \mid a$
(g) $0 \mid 0$

Solution

(a) $^-3 \mid 12$ is true because $12 = {}^-4({}^-3)$.
(b) $0 \mid 3$ is false because there is no integer c such that $3 = c \cdot 0$.
(c) $3 \mid 0$ is true because $0 = 0 \cdot 3$.
(d) $8 \nmid 2$ is true because there is no integer c such that $2 = c \cdot 8$.
(e) $1 \mid a$ is true for all integers a because $a = a \cdot 1$.
(f) $^-1 \mid a$ is true for all integers a because $a = ({}^-a)({}^-1)$.
(g) $0 \mid 0$ is false because there is no unique integer c such that $0 = c \cdot 0$.

To obtain multiples of any integer, we need only to multiply the integer by other integers. We now use multiples of 3 to investigate some properties of divisibility. Consider two bags of apples. Suppose the number of apples in each bag can be equally divided among three students; that is, the number of apples in each bag is a multiple of 3. If all the apples are put in one large bag, it is still possible to divide the apples equally among the three students. Consequently, if the number of apples in the first bag is a and the number of apples in the second bag is b, then we can record the preceding discussion as follows: If $3 \mid a$ and $3 \mid b$, then $3 \mid (a + b)$. If the number of apples in one bag cannot be divided among three students, then the total number of apples cannot be equally divided among three students. That is, if $3 \mid a$ and $3 \nmid b$, then $3 \nmid (a + b)$. These ideas may be generalized in the following theorem.

THEOREM 5-1

For any integers a, b, and d with $d \neq 0$:
(a) If $d \mid a$ and $d \mid b$, then $d \mid (a + b)$.
(b) If $d \mid a$ and $d \nmid b$, then $d \nmid (a + b)$.

Since subtraction is defined in terms of addition, a similar theorem holds for subtraction.

THEOREM 5-2

For any integers a, b, and d with $d \neq 0$.
(a) If $d \mid a$ and $d \mid b$, then $d \mid (a - b)$.
(b) If $d \mid a$ and $d \nmid b$, then $d \nmid (a - b)$.

The proofs of most theorems in this section are left as exercises, but the proof of Theorem 5-2(a) is given as an illustration.

Proof   To show that $d|(a - b)$, we must show that $(a - b) = d \cdot p$, for some $p \in I$. To do this, we proceed as follows.

$$d|a \quad \text{implies} \quad a = m \cdot d, \quad m \in I$$

$$d|b \quad \text{implies} \quad b = n \cdot d, \quad n \in I$$

Substituting, we obtain

$$a - b = md - nd \quad \text{Substitution property}$$
$$\qquad = (m - n)d \quad \text{Distributive property of multiplication} $$
$$\qquad\qquad\qquad\quad \text{over subtraction}$$

Thus, $a - b = (m - n)d$.

Because $m \in I$ and $n \in I$ and the set of integers is closed under subtraction, $(m - n) \in I$. Therefore, $d|(a - b)$, and the proof is complete.

Theorems 5-1 and 5-2 can be used to deduce another theorem. Substituting a for b in Theorem 5-1(a), we have: If $d|a$ and $d|a$, then $d|(a + a)$, or $d|2a$. Now, $d|a$ and $d|2a$ imply that $d|(a + 2a)$, or $d|3a$. Continuing in this way, it is possible to show that if d divides a, then d divides any positive multiple of a. That is, $d|a$ implies $d|ka$, where k is a positive integer. Similarly, using Theorem 5-2(a), it can be shown that this statement is also true when k is a negative integer. The result for all integers k is stated in Theorem 5-3.

THEOREM 5-3

> For any integers a and d with $d \neq 0$, if $d|a$ and k is any integer, then $d|ka$.

Remark   Theorem 5-3 can be proved directly from the definition of "divides."

Example 5-2

Classify each of the following as true or false where x, y, and z are integers. If a statement is true, prove it. If a statement is false, exhibit a counterexample.

(a) If $3|x$ and $3|y$, then $3|xy$.
(b) If $3|(x + y)$, then $3|x$ and $3|y$.
(c) If $9 \nmid a$, then $3 \nmid a$.

Solution

(a) True. By Theorem 5-3, if $3|x$, then for any integer k, $3|kx$. If $k = y$, then $3|yx$ or $3|xy$. (Notice that $3|xy$ regardless of whether $3|y$ or $3 \nmid y$.)
(b) False. For example, $3|(7 + 2)$ but $3 \nmid 7$ and $3 \nmid 2$. [How does this compare with Theorem 5-1(a)?]
(c) False. For example, $9 \nmid 21$, but $3|21$.

Example 5-3

Five students found a padlocked money box, which had a deposit slip attached to it. The deposit slip was water-spotted, so the currency total appeared as shown in Figure 5-1. One student remarked that if the

Figure 5-1

money listed on the deposit slip was in the box, it could easily be divided equally among the five students without using coins. How did the student know this?

Solution

Because the units digit of the amount of the currency is zero, the solution to the problem becomes one of determining whether any natural number whose units digit is 0 is divisible by 5. One method for attacking this problem is to look for a pattern. Natural numbers whose units digit is zero form a pattern, that is, 10, 20, 30, 40, 50, ... These numbers are multiples of 10. We are to determine whether 5 divides all multiples of 10.

We know that the amount of money in the box is a multiple of 10. Since $5 \mid 10$, by Theorem 5-3, 5 divides any multiple of 10. Hence, 5 divides the amount of money in the box, and the student is correct.

DIVISIBILITY RULES

Procedures similar to those used in Example 5-3 can be used to investigate divisibility by 2. Consider the number 358, whose expanded form is $3 \cdot 10^2 + 5 \cdot 10 + 8$. Since $2 \mid 10$, then $2 \mid 10^2$ and $2 \mid (5 \cdot 10)$. Likewise, $2 \mid 10^2$ implies that $2 \mid (3 \cdot 10^2)$. Hence, $2 \mid (3 \cdot 10^2 + 5 \cdot 10)$. Now, since $358 = (3 \cdot 10^2 + 5 \cdot 10) + 8$ and $2 \mid 8$, it follows that 2 divides the sum $[(3 \cdot 10^2 + 5 \cdot 10) + 8]$; that is, $2 \mid 358$. The same argument holds if the units digit is any even number. A similar argument shows that 2 does not divide a number whose units digit is odd. For example, consider 357, or $3 \cdot 10^2 + 5 \cdot 10 + 7$. Since $2 \mid (3 \cdot 10^2 + 5 \cdot 10)$ and $2 \nmid 7$, it follows that $2 \nmid (3 \cdot 10^2 + 5 \cdot 10 + 7)$; that is, $2 \nmid 357$. In general, the following divisibility test holds.

Divisibility Test for 2

An integer is divisible by 2 if and only if its units digit is divisible by 2.

There are similar tests for divisibility by 5 and 10. The tests follow from the fact that the only positive integers other than 1 and 2 that divide 10 are 5 and 10.

Divisibility Test for 5

An integer is divisible by 5 if and only if its units digit is divisible by 5, that is, the units digit is 0 or 5.

Divisibility Test for 10

An integer is divisible by 10 if and only if its units digit is divisible by 10, that is, the units digit is 0.

Because both 4 and 8 divide certain powers of 10, there exist divisibility rules for 4 and 8. We first develop a divisibility rule for 4. Consider any four-digit number n such that $n = a \cdot 10^3 + b \cdot 10^2 + c \cdot 10 + d$. The first step is to write the given number as a sum of two numbers, one of which is as great as possible and divisible by 4. Since $10 = 2 \cdot 5$, $4 \nmid 10$, but $4 \mid 10^2$ because $10^2 = 2^2 \cdot 5^2$. Consequently, $4 \mid 10 \cdot 10^2$; that is, $4 \mid 10^3$. Now, $4 \mid 10^2$ implies $4 \mid b \cdot 10^2$, and $4 \mid 10^3$ implies $4 \mid a \cdot 10^3$. Finally, $4 \mid a \cdot 10^3$ and $4 \mid b \cdot 10^2$ imply $4 \mid (a \cdot 10^3 + b \cdot 10^2)$. Since $4 \mid (a \cdot 10^3 + b \cdot 10^2)$, the divisibility of $a \cdot 10^3 + b \cdot 10^2 + c \cdot 10 + d$ by 4 depends on the divisibility of $(c \cdot 10 + d)$ by 4. If $4 \mid (c \cdot 10 + d)$, then 4 divides the given number n. If $4 \nmid (c \cdot 10 + d)$, then 4 does not divide the given number n. Notice that $c \cdot 10 + d$ is the number represented by the last two digits in the given number n. We summarize this in the following.

Divisibility Test for 4

An integer is divisible by 4 if and only if the last two digits of the integer represent a number divisible by 4.

To investigate divisibility by 8, we note that the least positive power of 10 divisible by 8 is 10^3 since $10^3 = 2^3 \cdot 5^3$. Consequently, all integral powers of 10 greater than 10^3 also are divisible by 8. Hence, the following is a divisibility test for 8.

Divisibility Test for 8

An integer is divisible by 8 if and only if the last three digits of the integer represent a number divisible by 8.

Example 5-4

(a) Determine whether 97,128 is divisible by 2, 4, and 8.
(b) Determine whether 83,026 is divisible by 2, 4, and 8.

Solution

(a) $2 \mid 97,128$ because $2 \mid 8$.
$4 \mid 97,128$ because $4 \mid 28$.
$8 \mid 97,128$ because $8 \mid 128$.

(b) $2 \mid 83,026$ because $2 \mid 6$.
$4 \nmid 83,026$ because $4 \nmid 26$.
$8 \nmid 83,026$ because $8 \nmid 026$.

Next, we consider a divisibility test for 3. We illustrate the procedure on the number 5721, that is, $5 \cdot 10^3 + 7 \cdot 10^2 + 2 \cdot 10 + 1$. No power of 10 is divisible by 3, but there are numbers close to powers of 10 that are divisible by 3. The numbers 9, 99, 999, and so on are such numbers. To determine whether 5721, or $5 \cdot 10^3 + 7 \cdot 10^2 + 2 \cdot 10 + 1$, is divisible by 3, we see that the number $5 \cdot 999 + 7 \cdot 99 + 2 \cdot 9$ is close to 5721 and is divisible by 3. (Why?) Next, look for a number x to make the following equation true.

$$5721 = 5 \cdot 10^3 + 7 \cdot 10^2 + 2 \cdot 10 + 1 = (5 \cdot 999 + 7 \cdot 99 + 2 \cdot 9) + x$$

What must be added to $5 \cdot 999$ to obtain $5 \cdot 10^3$? Because $5 \cdot 10^3 = 5 \cdot 1000 = 5(999 + 1) = 5 \cdot 999 + 5 \cdot 1$, the answer is 5. Similarly, $7 \cdot 10^2 = 7 \cdot 100 = 7(99 + 1) = 7 \cdot 99 + 7 \cdot 1$, and $2 \cdot 10 = 2 \cdot (9 + 1) = 2 \cdot 9 + 2 \cdot 1$. Thus, the number x is $5 \cdot 1 + 7 \cdot 1 + 2 \cdot 1 + 1$, or $5 + 7 + 2 + 1$. Consequently,

$$5721 = 5 \cdot 10^3 + 7 \cdot 10^2 + 2 \cdot 10 + 1$$
$$= (5 \cdot 999 + 7 \cdot 99 + 2 \cdot 9) + (5 + 7 + 2 + 1)$$

The sum in the first set of parentheses is divisible by 3, so the divisibility of 5721 by 3 depends on the sum in the second set of parentheses. In this case,

$5 + 7 + 2 + 1 = 15$ and $3 | 15$, so $3 | 5721$. Hence, to test 5721 for divisibility by 3, simply test $5 + 7 + 2 + 1$ for divisibility by 3. Notice that $5 + 7 + 2 + 1$ is the sum of the digits of 5721. The example suggests the following test for divisibility by 3.

Divisibility Test for 3

An integer is divisible by 3 if and only if the sum of its digits is divisible by 3.

An argument similar to the one used to demonstrate that $3 | 5721$ can be used to prove the test for divisibility by 3 on an integer with any number of digits and in particular for any four-digit number $n = a \cdot 10^3 + b \cdot 10^2 + c \cdot 10 + d$. Even though $a \cdot 10^3 + b \cdot 10^2 + c \cdot 10 + d$ is not necessarily divisible by 3, the number $a \cdot 999 + b \cdot 99 + c \cdot 9$ is close to n and *is* divisible by 3. We have

$$a \cdot 10^3 = a \cdot 1000 = a(999 + 1) = a \cdot 999 + a \cdot 1$$

$$b \cdot 10^2 = b \cdot 100 = b(99 + 1) = b \cdot 99 + b \cdot 1$$

$$c \cdot 10^1 = c \cdot 10 = c(9 + 1) = c \cdot 9 + c \cdot 1$$

Thus, $n = a \cdot 10^3 + b \cdot 10^2 + c \cdot 10 + d = (a \cdot 999 + b \cdot 99 + c \cdot 9) + (a + b + c + d)$. Because $3 | 9$, $3 | 99$, and $3 | 999$, it follows that $3 | (a \cdot 999 + b \cdot 99 + c \cdot 9)$. If $3 | (a + b + c + d)$, then $3 | [(a \cdot 999 + b \cdot 99 + c \cdot 9) + (a + b + c + d)]$; that is, $3 | n$. If, on the other hand, $3 \nmid (a + b + c + d)$, it follows from Theorem 5-2(b) that $3 \nmid n$.

Since $9 | 9$, $9 | 99$, $9 | 999$, and so on, a test similar to that for divisibility by 3 applies to divisibility by 9.

Divisibility Test for 9

An integer is divisible by 9 if and only if the sum of the digits of the integer is divisible by 9.

Example 5-5

Use divisibility tests to determine whether each of the following numbers is divisible by 3 and divisible by 9.

(a) 1002　　(b) 14,238

Solution

(a) Because $1 + 0 + 0 + 2 = 3$ and $3 | 3$, it follows that $3 | 1002$. Because $9 \nmid 3$, $9 \nmid 1002$.
(b) Because $1 + 4 + 2 + 3 + 8 = 18$ and $3 | 18$, it follows that $3 | 14,238$. Because $9 | 18$, it follows that $9 | 14,238$.

Divisibility tests can be devised for 7 and 11. We state such tests, but omit the proofs.

Divisibility Test for 7

An integer is divisible by 7 if and only if the integer represented without its units digit, minus twice the units digit of the original integer, is divisible by 7.

Divisibility Test for 11   An integer is divisible by 11 if and only if the sum of the digits in the places that are even powers of 10, minus the sum of the digits in the places that are odd powers of 10, is divisible by 11.

At this point, the only number less than 11 for which we have no divisibility test is 6. The divisibility test for 6 depends on the divisibility tests for 2 and 3, as investigated in Problem 8 of Problem Set 5-1.

Divisibility Test for 6   An integer is divisible by 6 if and only if the integer is divisible by both 2 and 3.

Example 5-6   Test each of the following numbers for divisibility by: (i) 7; (ii) 11; (iii) 6.

(a) 462   (b) 964,194

Solution   (a) (i) $7 \mid (46 - 2 \cdot 2)$, so $7 \mid 462$.

(ii) $11 \mid (2 + 4 - 6)$, so $11 \mid 462$.

(iii) $2 \mid 462$ and $3 \mid 462$, so $6 \mid 462$.

(b) (i)   To determine whether or not 7 divides 964,194, we use the process several times.

$7 \mid 964{,}194$ if and only if $7 \mid (96{,}419 - 2 \cdot 4)$, or $7 \mid 96{,}411$

$7 \mid 96{,}411$ if and only if $7 \mid (9641 - 2 \cdot 1)$, or $7 \mid 9639$

$7 \mid 9639$ if and only if $7 \mid (963 - 2 \cdot 9)$ or $7 \mid 945$

$7 \mid 945$ if and only if $7 \mid (94 - 2 \cdot 5)$, or $7 \mid 84$

Because $7 \mid 84$ is true, then $7 \mid 964{,}194$.

(ii) $11 \mid [(4 + 1 + 6) - (9 + 4 + 9)]$, so $11 \mid 964{,}194$.

(iii) $2 \mid 964{,}194$ and $3 \mid 964{,}194$, so $6 \mid 964{,}194$.

PROBLEM 1   A class from Washington School visited a neighborhood cannery warehouse. The warehouse manager told the class that there were 11,368 cans of juice in the inventory and that the cans were packed in boxes of 6 or 24, depending on the size of the can. One of the students, Sam, thought for a moment and announced that there was a mistake in the inventory. Is Sam's announcement correct? Why or why not?

UNDERSTANDING THE PROBLEM The problem is to determine whether Sam is correct in his announcement that the manager's inventory of 11,368 cans was not correct. To solve the problem, we must assume that there are no partial boxes of cans; that is, a box must contain exactly 6 or exactly 24 cans of juice.

DEVISING A PLAN We know that the boxes contain either 6 cans or 24 cans, but we do not know how many boxes of each type there are. One strategy for solving this problem is to find an equation that involves the total number of cans in all the boxes.

The total number of cans, 11,368, equals the number of cans in all the 6-can boxes plus the number of cans in all the 24-can boxes. If there are n boxes containing 6 cans each, there are $6n$ cans altogether in those boxes. Similarly, if there are m boxes with 24 cans each, these boxes contain a total of $24m$ cans. Because the total was reported to be 11,368 cans, we have the equation $6n + 24m = 11{,}368$. Sam claimed that $6n + 24m \neq 11{,}368$.

One way to show that $6n + 24m \neq 11{,}368$ is to show that $6n + 24m$ and 11,368 do not have the same divisors. Both $6n$ and $24m$ are divisible by 6, which implies that $6n + 24m$ must be divisible by 6. If 11,368 is not divisible by 6, then Sam is correct.

CARRYING OUT THE PLAN The divisibility test for 6 states that a number is divisible by 6 if and only if the number is divisible by both 2 and 3. Because 11,368 is an even number, it is divisible by 2. Is it divisible by 3?

The divisibility test for 3 states that a number is divisible by 3 if and only if the sum of the digits in the number is divisible by three. We see that $1 + 1 + 3 + 6 + 8 = 19$, which is not divisible by 3, so 11,368 is not divisible by 3. Hence, Sam is correct.

LOOKING BACK Suppose 11,368 had been divisible by 6. Would that have implied that the manager was correct? The answer is no; it would have implied only that we would have to change our approach to the problem.

As a further Looking Back activity, suppose the manager is correct. Can we determine values for m and n? This, in fact, can be done, and if a computer is available, a program can be written to determine all possible natural-number values of m and n.

PROBLEM SET 5-1

1. Classify each of the following as true or false.
   (a) 6 is a factor of 30.
   (b) 6 is a divisor of 30.
   (c) $6 \mid 30$
   (d) 30 is divisible by 6.
   (e) 30 is a multiple of 6.
   (f) 6 is a multiple of 30.
2. Use Theorem 5-1(a) to complete each of the following sentences. Assume a, b, and d are integers with $d \neq 0$. Simplify your answers, if possible.
   (a) If $7 \mid 14$ and $7 \mid 21$, then _____.
   (b) If $d \mid (213 - 57)$ and $d \mid 57$, then _____.
   (c) If $d \mid (a - b)$ and $d \mid b$, then _____.
3. There are 1379 children signed up to play Little League baseball. If exactly 9 players are assigned to each team, will any teams be short of players?
4. A forester has 43,682 seedlings to be planted. Can these be planted in an equal number of rows with 11 seedlings in each row?
5. For each of the following, state the theorems that justify the given statements, assuming a, b, and c

are integers. If a statement cannot be justified by one of the theorems in this section, answer "none."
   (a) $4 \mid 20$ implies $4 \mid 113 \cdot 20$.
   (b) $4 \mid 100$ and $4 \nmid 13$ imply $4 \nmid (100 + 13)$.
   (c) $4 \mid 100$ and $4 \nmid 13$ imply $4 \nmid 1300$.
   (d) $3 \mid (a + b)$ and $3 \nmid c$ imply $3 \nmid (a + b + c)$.
   (e) $3 \mid a$ implies $3 \mid a^2$.
6. Classify each of the following as true or false, assuming a, b, c and d are integers with $d \neq 0$. If a statement is false, give a counterexample.
   (a) If $d \mid (a + b)$, then $d \mid a$ and $d \mid b$.
   (b) If $d \mid (a + b)$, then $d \mid a$ or $d \mid b$.
   (c) If $d \mid a$ and $d \mid b$, then $d \mid ab$.
   (d) If $d \mid ab$, then $d \mid a$ or $d \mid b$.
   (e) If $ab \mid c$, $a \neq 0$, and $b \neq 0$, then $a \mid c$ and $b \mid c$.
   (f) $1 \mid a$.
   (g) $d \mid 0$

7. (a) If we multiply any odd number by 5, what is the units digit of the product?

(b) If we multiply any even whole number by 5, what is the units digit of the product?

8. Classify each of the following as true or false.

(a) If every digit of a number is divisible by 3, the number itself is divisible by 3.

(b) If a number is divisible by 3, then every digit of the number is divisible by 3.

(c) A number is divisible by 3 if and only if every digit of the number is divisible by 3.

(d) If a number is divisible by 6, then it is divisible by 2 and by 3.

(e) If a number is divisible by 2 and 3, then it is divisible by 6.

(f) If a number is divisible by 2 and 4, then it is divisible by 8.

(g) If a number is divisible by 8, then it is divisible by 2 and 4.

9. Devise a test for divisibility by each given number.

(a) 16   (b) 25

10. Devise divisibility tests for 12 and 15.

11. Jack owes $7812 on a new car. Can this be paid in 12 equal monthly installments?

12. A group of people ordered No-Cal candy bars. The bill was $2.09. If the original price of each was 12¢ but the price has been inflated, how much does each cost?

13. When the two missing digits in the given number are replaced, the number is divisible by 99. What is the number?

85__1

14. Test each of the following numbers for divisibility by 2, 3, 4, 5, 6, 7, 8, 9, 10, 11, 12, and 15.

(a) 746,988   (b) 81,342   (c) 15,810

(d) 183,324   (e) 901,815   (f) 4,201,012

(g) 1001   (h) 10,001   (i) 30,860

15. Answer each of the following and justify your answer.

(a) If a number is not divisible by 5, can it be divisible by 10?

(b) If a number is not divisible by 10, can it be divisible by 5?

16. Fill each blank with the greatest digit that makes the statement true.

(a) $3|74\_$ (b) $9|83\_45$ (c) $11|6\_55$

17. A number in which each digit except 0 appears exactly three times is divisible by 3. For example, 777,555,222 and 414,143,313 are divisible by 3. Explain why this statement is true.

★**18.** Prove the following theorem: For any integers a, b, and c with $a \neq 0$ and $b \neq 0$, if $a|b$ and $b|c$, then $a|c$.

19. Leap years occur in years that are divisible by 4. However, if the year ends in two zeros, for the year to be a leap year, it must be divisible by 400. Determine which of the following are leap years.

(a) 1776   (b) 1986   (c) 2000   (d) 2024

20. A palindrome is a number that reads the same forward and backwards.

(a) Check the following four-digit palindromes for divisibility by 11.

(i) 4554   (ii) 9339   (iii) 2002

(iv) 2222

★(b) Prove that any four-digit palindrome is divisible by 11.

(c) Is every five-digit palindrome divisible by 11? Why or why not?

(d) Is every six-digit palindrome divisible by 11? Why or why not?

21. (a) Choose a two-digit number such that the number in the tens place is one greater than the number in the units place. Reverse the digits in your number and subtract this number from your original number; for example, $87 - 78 = 9$. Make a conjecture concerning the results of performing these kinds of operations.

(b) Choose any two-digit number such that the number in the tens place is two greater than the number in the units place. Reverse the digits in your number and subtract this number from your original number; for example, $31 - 13 = 18$. Make a conjecture concerning the results of performing these kinds of operations.

★(c) Prove that for any two-digit number, if the digits are reversed and the numbers subtracted, the difference is a multiple of 9.

(d) Investigate what happens whenever two-digit numbers with equal digit sums are subtracted; for example, $62 - 35 = 27$.

★**22.** Prove each of the following.

(a) Theorem 5-1   (b) Theorem 5-2(b)

★**23.** Prove the test for divisibility by 9 for any five-digit number.

★**24.** Prove the test for divisibility by 2 for any number n, such that

$$n = a_k 10^k + a_{k-1} 10^{k-1} + \cdots + a_3 10^3$$
$$+ a_2 10^2 + a_1 10 + a_0$$

25. Enter any three-digit number on the calculator; for example, enter 243. Repeat it: 243,243. Divide by 7. Divide by 11. Divide by 13. What is the answer? Try it again with any other three-digit number. Will this always work? Why?

26. The calculator may be used to test for divisibility of one number by another. Test the divisibility of the first number by the second in each of the following.

(a) 490 by 2   (b) 575 by 5

(c) 353 by 3   (d) 4907 by 7

(e) 4074 by 4   (f) 123,123 by 11

BRAIN TEASER

Dee finds that she has an extraordinary social security number. Its nine digits contain all the numbers from 1 through 9. They also form a number such that, when read from left to right, its first two digits form a number divisible by 2, its first three digits form a number divisible by 3, its first four digits form a number divisible by 4, and so on, until the complete number is divisible by 9. What is Dee's social security number?

Section 5-2

Prime and Composite Numbers

In Section 5-1, we discussed divisors of numbers. For example, the number 12 has six divisors, 1, 2, 3, 4, 6, and 12. The number 7 has only two divisors, 1 and 7. To introduce the next concept, we construct Table 5-1, which shows the number of divisors for various numbers. For example, 12 is in the 6 column because it has six divisors and 7 is in the 2 column because it has only two divisors.

Table 5-1

0	1	2	3	4	5	6	7	8	More than 8
	1	2	4	6	16	12		24	36
		3	9	8		18		30	
		5	25	10		20			
		7		14		28			
		11		15		32			
		13		21					
		17		22					
		19		26					
		23		27					
		29		33					
		31		34					
		37		35					

Do you see any patterns forming in the table? Will the 0 column stay empty? Do you see why there will be no other entries in the 1 column? What is the next number in the 3 column? The numbers in the 2 column are of particular importance. Notice that they have exactly two divisors, namely, 1 and themselves. Any positive integer with exactly two distinct, positive divisors is called a *prime number,* or a **prime.** Any number that has a postive factor other than 1 and itself is called a *composite number,* or a **composite.** For example, 4, 6, and 16 are composites because they have factors other than 1 and themselves. The number 1 has only one positive factor, so it is neither prime nor composite.

prime

composite

From the 2 column in Table 5-1, we see that the first eleven primes are 2, 3, 5, 7, 11, 13, 17, 19, 23, 29, and 31. Other patterns in the table are explored in the problem set.

Example 5-7

Show that the following numbers are composite.

(a) 1564   (b) 2781   (c) 1001

Solution

(a) Since $2|4$, 1564 is divisible by 2.

(b) Since $3|(2 + 7 + 8 + 1)$, 2781 is divisible by 3.

(c) Since $11|[(1 + 0) - (0 + 1)]$, 1001 is divisible by 11.

Composite numbers can be expressed as products of two or more whole numbers greater than 1. For example, $18 = 2 \cdot 9$, $18 = 3 \cdot 6$, or $18 = 2 \cdot 3 \cdot 3$. Each expression of 18 as a product of factors is called a **factorization.** A factorization containing only prime numbers is called a **prime factorization.** To find a prime factorization of a given composite number, first rewrite the number as a product of two smaller numbers. Continue the process, factoring the lesser numbers until all factors are primes. For example, consider 260.

factorization
prime factorization

$$260 = 26 \cdot 10 = 2 \cdot 13 \cdot 2 \cdot 5 = 2 \cdot 2 \cdot 5 \cdot 13 = 2^2 \cdot 5 \cdot 13$$

factor tree

The procedure for finding a prime factorization of a number can be organized using a model called a **factor tree.** A factor tree is demonstrated in Figure 5-2(a). Notice that the last branches of the trees display the prime factors of 260.

Figure 5-2

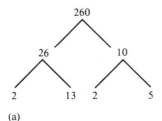

(a)

(b)

The factorization of 260, or other composite numbers, can be started in different ways. A second way for factoring 260 is shown in Figure 5-2(b). The two trees produce the same prime factorization, except for the order in which the primes appear in the products.

In general, if order is disregarded, the prime factorization of a number is unique. The *Fundamental Theorem of Arithmetic,* sometimes called the *Unique Factorization Theorem,* states this fact.

THEOREM 5-4

> **Fundamental Theorem of Arithmetic**   Each composite number has one and only one prime factorization.

The Fundamental Theorem of Arithmetic has many uses, some of which we will see in the discussion of terminating decimals and rational numbers in Chapters 6 and 7.

The Fundamental Theorem of Arithmetic is a basis for a more algorithmic approach to finding the prime factorization of a number. We start with the smallest prime and check to see if it divides the number. If not, we try the next greater prime and check for divisibility by this prime. Once we find a prime that divides the number in question, then we must find the quotient of the number divided by the prime. Now, we check to see if the prime divides the quotient. If so, we repeat the process. If not, we try the next greater prime and check to see if it divides the quotient. We continue the procedure, using greater primes, until a quotient of 1 is reached. The original number is the product of all the primes used. The prime factorization of 260 using this method is shown in Figure 5-3. Hence, $260 = 2^2 \cdot 5 \cdot 13$.

Figure 5-3

$$\begin{array}{r|r} 2 & 260 \\ \hline 2 & 130 \\ \hline 5 & 65 \\ \hline 13 & 13 \\ \hline & 1 \end{array}$$

Normally, the primes in the prime factorization of a number are listed in increasing order from left to right. If a prime appears in a product more than once, exponential notation is used. Thus, $13 \cdot 2 \cdot 2 \cdot 2 \cdot 5 \cdot 5 \cdot 5 \cdot 7$ is customarily written as $2^3 \cdot 5^3 \cdot 7 \cdot 13$.

In determining the factorization of a number such as 8127, observe that $9 | 8127$ or $8127 = 9k$, where k is an integer. Because $8127 = 9k$, then k is a factor of 8127 and $k = \frac{8127}{9}$. Theorem 5-5 states the general case.

THEOREM 5-5

> If d is a factor of n, where $n \neq 0$ and $d \neq 0$, then $\frac{n}{d}$ is a factor of n.

Remark Sometimes we do not obtain a different factor when using this process. This occurs when $\frac{n}{d} = d$. For example, 7 is a factor of 49 and so is $\frac{49}{7}$, or 7.

Suppose p is the *least* prime factor of the number n. If n is prime, then $p = n$, but if n is composite, we have $p \leq \frac{n}{p}$ because $\frac{n}{p}$ is also a factor of n and p is the least factor of n. Thus, $p^2 \leq n$. This idea is summarized in the following theorem.

THEOREM 5-6

> If n is composite, then n has a prime factor p such that $p^2 \leq n$.

Theorem 5-6 can be used to help determine whether a given number is prime or composite. Consider, for example, the number 109. If 109 is composite, it must have a prime divisor p such that $p^2 \leq 109$. The primes whose squares do not exceed 109 are 2, 3, 5, and 7. Checking for divisibility by these primes reveals that $2 \nmid 109$, $3 \nmid 109$, $5 \nmid 109$, and $7 \nmid 109$. Hence, 109 is prime. The argument used leads to the following theorem.

THEOREM 5-7

> If n is an integer greater than 1 such that n is not divisible by any prime p, where $p^2 \leq n$, then n is prime.

Example 5-8

Is 397 composite or prime?

Solution

The possible primes p such that $p^2 \leq 397$ are 2, 3, 5, 7, 11, 13, 17, and 19. Because $2 \nmid 397$, $3 \nmid 397$, $5 \nmid 397$, $7 \nmid 397$, $11 \nmid 397$, $13 \nmid 397$, $17 \nmid 397$, and $19 \nmid 397$, the number 397 is prime.

MORE ABOUT PRIMES

Another way to find all the primes less than a given number is to use the Sieve of Eratosthenes, named after the Greek mathematician Eratosthenes. If all the natural numbers greater than 1 are considered (or placed in the sieve), the numbers that are not prime are methodically crossed out (or drop through the holes of the sieve). The remaining numbers are prime. The following procedure illustrates this process.

1. In Figure 5-4, we cross out 1 because 1 is not prime.
2. Circle 2 because 2 is prime.
3. Cross out other multiples of 2; they are not prime.
4. Circle 3 because 3 is prime.
5. Cross out other multiples of 3.
6. Circle 5 and 7 because they are primes; cross out their multiples.
7. The numbers left are primes.

Figure 5-4

1	2	3	4	5	6	7	8	9	10
11	12	13	14	15	16	17	18	19	20
21	22	23	24	25	26	27	28	29	30
31	32	33	34	35	36	37	38	39	40
41	42	43	44	45	46	47	48	49	50
51	52	53	54	55	56	57	58	59	60
61	62	63	64	65	66	67	68	69	70
71	72	73	74	75	76	77	78	79	80
81	82	83	84	85	86	87	88	89	90
91	92	93	94	95	96	97	98	99	100

HISTORICAL NOTE

Eratosthenes (ca. 270–190 B.C.) was a Greek mathematician who devised a pattern to identify prime numbers by writing the sequence of counting numbers on parchment and punching out the composite numbers. The remaining numbers were prime. The parchment with holes resembled a sieve and hence the process became known as the Sieve of Eratosthenes. Eratosthenes also knew that the earth was spherical and computed its diameter to within 50 miles of the actual length.

We leave it as an exercise to explain why, after crossing out all the multiples of 2, 3, 5, and 7, the remaining numbers in the sieve are prime.

There are infinitely many whole numbers, infinitely many odd numbers, and infinitely many even numbers. Are there infinitely many primes? Because prime numbers do not appear in any known pattern, the answer to this question is not obvious. Euclid was the first to prove that there are infinitely many primes (see Problem Set 5-2, Problem 23).

PROBLEM 2

Although Euclid proved that there are infinitely many primes, it has been shown that there are strings of as many consecutive composite numbers as desired. Find 1000 consecutive natural numbers that are composite.

UNDERSTANDING THE PROBLEM The goal is to find 1000 consecutive natural numbers that are not prime. Because the numbers must be consecutive, they can be written in the form $n, n + 1, n + 2, n + 3, \ldots, n + 999$ or in a similar ordering, where n is some natural number. Also, since each of the numbers is to be composite, each must have at least one divisor other than 1 and itself.

DEVISING A PLAN To find a set of 1000 consecutive composite natural numbers using the Sieve of Eratosthenes would seem to require a large list of numbers. In the sieve in Figure 5-4, we can find no more than seven consecutive composites, namely, 90, 91, 92, 93, 94, 95 and 96. Constructing a large sieve and counting the number of composites would be very time-consuming, so we try other alternatives.

A possible strategy is to look at a simpler problem. For example, we might consider finding a string of ten consecutive composites, which we can label

HISTORICAL NOTE

Euclid (ca. 300 B.C.) is renowned for his book *The Elements* and is known as the father of geometry, but, in fact, *The Elements* contains chapters on algebra, ratio, proportion and number theory.

$n, n + 1, n + 2, \ldots, n + 9$. We want to choose n so that these ten numbers are composite. The greatest number in the list, $n + 9$, will be composite if n is a multiple of 9. Similarly, $n + 8$ will be composite if n is a multiple of 8. Continuing in this way, the numbers, $n + 7, n + 6, \ldots, n + 2$ will be composite if n is a multiple of 7, 6, $\ldots$, 2, respectively. This process reveals little about $n + 1$, but the process can be used to create the number n. Because n is to be a multiple of 9, 8, 7, 6, $\ldots$, 2, perhaps the simplest value for n is $9 \cdot 8 \cdot 7 \cdot 6 \cdot \ldots \cdot 3 \cdot 2$.

With $n = 9 \cdot 8 \cdot 7 \cdot 6 \cdot \ldots \cdot 3 \cdot 2$, we have $n + 9, n + 8, n + 7, \ldots, n + 2$ as composite numbers. Notice that this process yields eight consecutive composite numbers, rather than ten, Also, observe that to obtain eight consecutive composites, we used $n + 9$ as the greatest number. Similarly, to obtain ten consecutive composites, we choose $n + 11$ as the greatest composite, with $n = 11 \cdot 10 \cdot 9 \cdot 8 \cdot \ldots \cdot 3 \cdot 2$; to obtain 1000 consecutive composites, we use $n + 1001$, with $n = 1001 \cdot 1000 \cdot 999 \cdot \ldots \cdot 3 \cdot 2$.

CARRYING OUT THE PLAN Using the process developed above, we consider the 1000 consecutive natural numbers $n + 2, n + 3, \ldots, n + 1000$, $n + 1001$. We choose $n = 2 \cdot 3 \cdot 4 \cdot \ldots \cdot 1001$. With this choice of n, the 1000 consecutive natural numbers we have just described are composite.

LOOKING BACK In a similar manner, we can find as many consecutive composite numbers as desired. Though there are infinitely many primes, we can find a million, a billion, or a trillion consecutive composite numbers and, in general, as many as we want.

For centuries, mathematicians have looked for a formula that produces only primes, but no one has ever found one. One such attempt resulted in the expression $n^2 - n + 41$, where n is a whole number. Substituting 0, 1, 2, 3, $\ldots$, 40 for n in the expression always results in a prime number. However, substituting 41 for n gives $41^2 - 41 + 41$, or 41^2, a composite number.

Mersenne primes   Prime numbers of the form $2^p - 1$, where p is a prime, are called **Mersenne primes,** after the French mathematician Marin Mersenne (1588–1648). One of the greatest known primes, which is a Mersenne prime, was discovered at the University of Illinois. It has 3376 digits and can be written in the form $2^{11,213} - 1$. To realize just how great this number is, note that 2^{64} grains of wheat is more wheat than has ever been produced in the history of the world. The University of Illinois advertised the discovery on its postal meter, as shown in Figure 5-5.

Figure 5-5

In 1971, the largest known prime was $2^{19,937} - 1$, found by Bryant Tuckerman of IBM. In 1978, two high school students—Laura Nickel and Curt Noll, from Hayward, California—found a larger prime, $2^{23,209} - 1$, using a computer. Other larger primes have since been discovered, one of the latest being $2^{132,049} - 1$. It too was discovered by a computer, in 1983.

There are many interesting problems concerning primes. For example, Christian Goldbach (1690–1764) asserted that every even integer greater than 2 is the sum of two primes. This statement is known as **Goldbach's conjecture.** For example, $4 = 2 + 2$, $6 = 3 + 3$, $8 = 3 + 5$, $10 = 3 + 7$, $12 = 5 + 7$, and $14 = 3 + 11$. In spite of the simplicity of the statement, no one knows for sure whether or not the statement is true.

Goldbach's conjecture

PROBLEM 3

A woman with a basket of eggs finds that if she removes the eggs from the basket either 2, 3, 4, 5, or 6 at a time, there is always 1 egg left. However, if she removes the eggs 7 at a time, there are no eggs left. If the basket holds up to 500 eggs, how many eggs does the woman have?

UNDERSTANDING THE PROBLEM When a woman removes eggs from the basket 2, 3, 4, 5, or 6 at a time, there is always 1 egg left. That means that if the number of eggs is divided by 2, 3, 4, 5, or 6, the remainder is always 1. We also know that when she removes the eggs 7 at a time, there are no eggs left; that is, the number of eggs is a multiple of 7. Finally, we know that the basket holds up to 500 eggs. We have to find the number of eggs in the basket.

DEVISING A PLAN One way to solve the problem is to write all the multiples of 7 between 7 and 500 and check which ones have a remainder of 1 when divided by 2, 3, 4, 5, or 6. Since this method is tedious, we look for a different approach. Let the number of eggs be n. Then, if n is divided by 2, the remainder is 1. Consequently, $n - 1$ will be divisible by 2. Similarly, 3, 4, 5, and 6 divide $n - 1$.

Since 2 and 3 divide $n - 1$, the primes 2 and 3 appear in the prime factorization of $n - 1$. Note that $4 | (n - 1)$ implies that $2 | (n - 1)$, and hence, from the information $2 | (n - 1)$ and $4 | (n - 1)$, we can conclude only that 2^2 appears in the prime factorization of $n - 1$. Since $5 | (n - 1)$, 5 appears in the prime factorization of $n - 1$. The fact that $6 | (n - 1)$ does not provide any new information, since it only implies that 2 and 3 are prime factors of $n - 1$, which we already know. Now, $n - 1$ may also have other prime factors. Denoting the product of these other prime factors by k, we have $n - 1 = 2^2 \cdot 3 \cdot 5 \cdot k = 60k$, where k is some natural number, and so $n = 60k + 1$. We now find all possible values for n in the form $60k + 1$ less than 500 and determine which ones are divisible by 7.

CARRYING OUT THE PLAN Because $n = 60k + 1$ and k is any natural number, we substitute $k = 1, 2, 3, \ldots$ to obtain the following possible values for n that are less than 500:

61, 121, 181, 241, 301, 361, 421, 481

Among these values, only 301 is divisible by 7; hence, 301 is the only possible answer to the problem.

LOOKING BACK In the preceding situation, we still had to test eight numbers for divisibility by 7. Is it possible to further reduce the computations? We know that $n = 60k + 1$ and that the possible values for k are $k =$

1, 2, 3, 4, 5, 6, 7, 8. We also know that $7|n$; that is, $7|(60k + 1)$. The problem is to find for which of the above values of k, $7|(60k + 1)$. The question would have been easier to answer if instead of $60k + 1$, we had a smaller number. We know that the multiple of k closest to $60k$ that is divisible by 7 is $56k$. Since $7|(60k + 1)$ and $7|56k$, we conclude that $7|(60k + 1 - 56k)$; that is, $7|(4k + 1)$. We now see that $7|(60k + 1)$, if and only if $7|(4k + 1)$. The only value of k between 1 and 8 that makes $4k + 1$ divisible by 7 is 5. Consequently, $7|(60 \cdot 5 + 1)$, and 301 is the solution to the problem.

PROBLEM SET 5-2

1. Use a factor tree to find the prime factorization for each of the following.
   (a) 504   (b) 2475   (c) 11,250
2. Which of the following numbers are primes?
   (a) 149   (b) 923   (c) 433
3. What is the greatest prime you must consider to test whether or not 5669 is prime?
4. Explain why, in the Sieve of Eratosthenes in Figure 5-4, after crossing out all the multiples of 2, 3, 5, and 7, the remaining numbers are primes.
5. Extend the Sieve of Eratosthenes to find all primes less than 200.
6. Factors of a locker number are 2, 5, and 9. If there are exactly nine other factors, what is the locker number?
7. (a) When the United States flag had 48 stars, the stars were arranged in a 6 × 8 rectangular array. In what other rectangular arrays could they have been arranged?
   (b) How many different rectangular arrays of stars could there be if there were only 47 states?
8. If the Spanish Armada had 177 galleons, could it have gone to sea in an equal number of small flotillas? If so, how many ships would have been in each?
9. Suppose the 435 members of the House of Representatives are placed on committees with more than 2 members but less than 30 members. Each committee is to have an equal number of members and each member is on only one committee.
   (a) What size committees are possible?
   (b) How many committees are there of each size?
10. Mr. Arboreta wants to set out fruit trees in a rectangular array. For each of the following numbers of trees, find all possible numbers of rows if each row is to have the same number of trees.
    (a) 36   (b) 28   (c) 17   (d) 144
11. What is the smallest number that has exactly seven positive factors?
12. (a) Find a composite number different from 41^2 that is of the form $n^2 - n + 41$.
    ★(b) Prove that there are infinitely many composite numbers of the form $n^2 - n + 41$.

13. Find the least number divisible by each natural number less than or equal to 12.
14. The primes 2 and 3 are consecutive integers. Is there another pair of consecutive integers both of which are prime? Justify your answer.
15. The prime numbers 11 and 13 are called **twin primes** because they differ by 2. Find all the twin primes less than 200. (The existence of infinitely many twin primes has not been proved.)
16. (a) Use the Fundamental Theorem of Arithmetic to justify that if $2|n$ and $3|n$, then $6|n$.
    (b) Is it always true that if $a|n$ and $b|n$, then $ab|n^2$? Either prove the statement or give a counterexample.
17. In order to test for divisibility by 12, one student checked to determine divisibility by 3 and 4, while another checked for divisibility by 2 and 6. Are both students using a correct approach to divisibility by 12? Why or why not?
18. (a) Is it always true that if $3|ab$, then $3|a$ or $3|b$?
    (b) Is is always true that if $4|ab$, then $4|a$ or $4|b$?
19. Show that if 1 were considered a prime, every number would have more than one prime factorization.
20. (a) Find all the positive divisors of 2^8.
    (b) Find all the positive divisors of 3^5.
    (c) How many positive divisors does $2^8 \cdot 3^5$ have?
    ★(d) If p and q are primes, how many divisors does $p^k q^m$ have?
21. Use Table 5-1 for each of the following.
    (a) Guess the next three numbers in the 3 column. Describe a pattern for forming the numbers.
    (b) Guess the next three numbers in the 5 column. Describe a pattern for forming the numbers.
    ★(c) Guess the next three numbers in the 4 column. Describe a pattern for forming the numbers.
22. Find the greatest four-digit number that has exactly three factors.
★23. Complete the details for the following proof, which shows that there are infinitely many prime numbers.
    If the number of primes is finite, then there is a greatest prime denoted by p. Consider the product

of all the primes, $2 \cdot 3 \cdot 5 \cdot \ldots \cdot p$, and let $N = (2 \cdot 3 \cdot 5 \cdot \ldots \cdot p) + 1$. Because $N > p$, where p is the greatest prime, N is composite, Because N is composite, there is a prime q among the primes $2, 3, 5, \ldots, p$ such that $q \mid N$. However, none of the primes $2, 3, 5, \ldots, p$ divides N. (Why?)

Consequently, $q \nmid N$, which is a contradiction. Thus, the assumption that there are finitely many primes is false and the set of primes must be infinite.

24. One formula yielding several primes is $n^2 + n + 17$. Substitute $n = 1, 2, 3, \ldots, 17$ in the formula and find which of the resulting numbers are primes and which are composites.

Review Problems

25. Classify each of the following as true or false.
   (a) 11 is a factor of 189.
   (b) 1001 is a multiple of 13.
   (c) $7 \mid 1001$ and $7 \nmid 12$ imply $7 \nmid (1001 - 12)$.
   (d) If a number is divisible by both 7 and 11, then its prime factorization contains 7 and 11.

26. Test each of the following for divisibility by 2, 3, 4, 5, 6, 7, 8, 9, 10, and 11.
   (a) 438, 162   (b) 2,345,678,910

27. Prove that if a number is divisible by 12, then it is divisible by 3.

28. Could \$3376 be divided exactly among either 7 or 8 people?

BRAIN TEASER

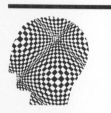

Consider the factorization of numbers in the set E of even counting numbers, $\{2, 4, 6, 8, 10, \ldots\}$. In this set, there are numbers that cannot be written as products of other numbers in the set. For example, 6 is not a product of two other elements of the set ($6 = 2 \cdot 3$, but 3 is not in E). A number in E that cannot be written as a product of other numbers in E is called an E-prime. A number in E that can be written as a product of numbers in E is called an E-composite.

(a) List the first 10 E-primes.
(b) Find an even number whose E-prime factorization is not unique, that is, an even number that can be factored into a product of E-primes in more than one way.
(c) Find a test for determining whether or not an even number is an E-prime.

COMPUTER CORNER

The following BASIC program will determine if a positive integer N is prime. Type it into your computer.

```
10 PRINT "THIS PROGRAM DETERMINES IF A POSITIVE INTEGER IS "
15 PRINT "PRIME."
20 PRINT "AFTER THE QUESTION MARK, TYPE A POSITIVE INTEGER."
30 INPUT N
40 IF N = 1 GOTO 90
50 IF N = 2 GOTO 120
60 FOR K = 2 TO SQR(N)
70 IF N/K = INT(N/K) THEN 90
80 GOTO 110
90 PRINT N; "IS NOT PRIME."
100 GOTO 130
110 NEXT K
120 PRINT N; "IS PRIME."
130 PRINT "IF YOU WANT TO CHECK ANOTHER NUMBER, TYPE 1. IF "
135 PRINT "NOT, TYPE 0."
140 INPUT V
150 IF V = 1 GOTO 20
160 END
```

Run this program using different values for N.

Section 5-3

Greatest Common Divisor and Least Common Multiple

greatest common divisor (GCD)

The **greatest common divisor (GCD)** of two whole numbers is the greatest divisor or factor that the two numbers have in common. The concept of GCD is used in Chapter 6 to reduce fractions to lowest terms.

There are several ways to find the GCD of two or more numbers. One way is to list all members of the set of positive divisors of the two numbers, then find the set of all common divisors, and, finally, pick the greatest element in that set. For example, to find the GCD of 20 and 32, denote the sets of divisors of 20 and 32 by D_{20} and D_{32}, respectively.

$$D_{20} = \{1, 2, 4, 5, 10, 20\}$$

$$D_{32} = \{1, 2, 4, 8, 16, 32\}$$

The set of all common positive divisors of 20 and 32 is

$$D_{20} \cap D_{32} = \{1, 2, 4\}$$

Because the greatest number in the set of common positive divisors is 4, the GCD of 20 and 32 is 4, written GCD(20, 32) = 4.

The method for finding the GCD of two numbers just described, called the *intersection-of-sets method*, is rather time-consuming and tedious if the numbers have many divisors. Another, more efficient, method involves finding the prime factorization of each number. To find GCD(180, 168), first notice that $180 = 2 \cdot 2 \cdot 3 \cdot 3 \cdot 5$ and $168 = 2 \cdot 2 \cdot 2 \cdot 3 \cdot 7$. Prime factorization shows that 180 and 168 have two factors of 2 and one of 3 in common. These common primes divide both 180 and 168. In fact, the only numbers other than 1 that divide both 180 and 168 must have no more than two 2s and one 3 and no other prime factors in their prime factorizations. The possible common divisors are 1, 2, 2^2, 3, $2 \cdot 3$, and $2^2 \cdot 3$. Hence, the greatest common divisor of 180 and 168 is $2^2 \cdot 3$. This procedure works in general.

> To find the GCD of two or more numbers, first find the prime factorizations of the given numbers, then take each common prime factor of the given numbers; the GCD is the product of these common factors, each raised to the lowest power of that prime that occurs in either of the prime factorizations.

Example 5-9

Find each of the following.

(a) GCD(108, 72)
(b) GCD(x, y) if $x = 2^3 \cdot 7^2 \cdot 11 \cdot 13$ and $y = 2 \cdot 7^3 \cdot 13 \cdot 17$
(c) GCD(x, y, z) if $z = 2^2 \cdot 7$, using x and y from part (b)

Solution

(a) Since $108 = 2^2 \cdot 3^3$, and $72 = 2^3 \cdot 3^2$, it follows that GCD(108, 72) = $2^2 \cdot 3^2 = 36$.
(b) GCD(x, y) = $2 \cdot 7^2 \cdot 13 = 1274$.
(c) Because $x = 2^3 \cdot 7^2 \cdot 11 \cdot 13$, $y = 2 \cdot 7^3 \cdot 13 \cdot 17$, and $z = 2^2 \cdot 7$, then GCD(x, y, z) = $2 \cdot 7 = 14$. Notice that GCD(x, y, z) can also be obtained by finding the GCD of z and 1274, the answer from part (b).

If we apply the prime factorization technique to finding GCD(4, 9), we see that 4 and 9 have no common prime factors. Consequently, 1 is the

relatively prime

only common divisor, so GCD(4, 9) = 1. Numbers such as 4 and 9, whose GCD is 1, are called **relatively prime.**

Some numbers are hard to factor. For these numbers, another method is more efficient for finding the GCD. For example, suppose we want to find GCD(676, 221). If we could find two smaller numbers whose GCD is the same as GCD(676, 221), our task would be easier. Observe that GCD(15, 10) = 5 and GCD(15 − 10, 10) = 5. Also, GCD(15, 6) = 3 and GCD(15 − 6, 6) = 3. Similarly, GCD(676, 221) = GCD(676 − 221, 221). From Theorem 5-2(a), every divisor of 676 and 221 is also a divisor of 676 − 221 and 221. Conversely, every divisor of 676 − 221 and 221 is also a divisor of 676 and 221. Thus, the set of all the common divisors of 676 and 221 is the same as the set of all common divisors of 676 − 221 and 221. Consequently, GCD(676, 221) = GCD(676 − 221, 221). This argument holds in general, and we have the following theorem.

THEOREM 5-8

> If a and b are any whole numbers and $a \geq b$, then
>
> $$GCD(a, b) = GCD(a - b, b)$$

Using Theorem 5-8 repeatedly, we can find the GCD of any two numbers; for example, consider GCD(676, 221). By using Theorem 5-8 several times, we have

GCD(676, 221) = GCD(676 − 221, 221)

= GCD(455, 221)	Because 676 − 221 = 455
= GCD(234, 221)	Because 455 − 221 = 234
= GCD(13, 221)	Because 234 − 221 = 13

Notice that we have actually subtracted 3 · 221 from 676, and the difference is 676 − 3 · 221 = 13. Because division can be thought of as repeated subtraction, the three subtractions could have been achieved by dividing 676 by 221 and recording the remainder, as follows.

```
        3
221 ) 676
      663
      ---
       13
```

It follows that GCD(676, 221) = GCD(13, 221). Since the only divisors of 13 are 1 and 13, the only possible values for GCD(13, 221) are 1 and 13. Because 221 = 17 · 13, we know that 13|221, and we have GCD(13, 221) = 13. This implies that GCD(676, 221) = 13. We could continue to use Theorem 5-8 to calculate GCD(13, 221). Because GCD(13, 221) = GCD(221, 13), we can subtract 13 from 221 as many times as needed. If 13 is subtracted from 221 seventeen times, we conclude that GCD(221, 13) = GCD(0, 13). Every integer except 0 divides 0, so GCD(0, 13) = 13. Thus, GCD(221, 13) = 13. Notice that GCD(221, 13) could also have been found using division rather than repeated subtraction:

$$
\begin{array}{r}
17 \\
13 \overline{)\ 221} \\
13 \\
\hline
91 \\
91 \\
\hline
0
\end{array}
$$

Because the remainder in the division is 0, $GCD(221, 13) = GCD(0, 13) = 13$. The process of repeated division ends when we obtain a zero remainder in some division. Because each remainder is smaller than the remainder in a preceding division, we must eventually obtain a remainder of 0.

Based on this development, Theorem 5-8 can be generalized as follows.

THEOREM 5-9

> If a and b are any whole numbers and $a \geq b$, then $GCD(a, b) = GCD(r, b)$, where r is the remainder when a is divided by b.

Euclidean algorithm

Finding the GCD of two numbers by the repeated use of Theorem 5-9 until the remainder 0 is reached is referred to as the **Euclidean algorithm.**

Example 5-10   Use the Euclidean algorithm to find $GCD(10{,}764, 2300)$.

Solution

$$
\begin{array}{r}
4 \\
2300 \overline{)\ 10{,}764} \\
9\ 200 \\
\hline
1\ 564
\end{array}
$$
Thus, $GCD(10{,}764, 2300) = GCD(2300, 1564)$.

$$
\begin{array}{r}
1 \\
1564 \overline{)\ 2300} \\
1564 \\
\hline
736
\end{array}
$$
Thus, $GCD(2300, 1564) = GCD(1564, 736)$.

$$
\begin{array}{r}
2 \\
736 \overline{)\ 1564} \\
1472 \\
\hline
92
\end{array}
$$
Thus, $GCD(1564, 736) = GCD(736, 92)$.

$$
\begin{array}{r}
8 \\
92 \overline{)\ 736} \\
736 \\
\hline
0
\end{array}
$$
Thus, $GCD(736, 92) = GCD(92, 0)$.

Because $GCD(92, 0) = 92$, it follows that $GCD(10{,}764, 2300) = 92$.

Remark   The procedure for finding the GCD using the Euclidean algorithm can be stopped at any step at which the GCD is obvious.

LEAST COMMON MULTIPLE

least common multiple
(LCM)

Another useful concept in number theory is least common multiple. This concept is useful for determining the least common denominator of two fractions. The **least common multiple (LCM)** of two natural numbers is the least positive multiple that the two numbers have in common. To find the LCM of two given natural numbers, we can use the intersection-of-sets method. First, find the set of all positive multiples of both the first and second numbers, then find the set of all common multiples of both numbers, and, finally, pick the least element in that set. For example, to find the LCM of 8 and 12, denote the sets of positive multiples of 8 and 12 by M_8 and M_{12}, respectively.

$$M_8 = \{8, 16, 24, 32, 40, 48, 56, 64, 72, \ldots\}$$
$$M_{12} = \{12, 24, 36, 48, 60, 72, 84, 96, 108, \ldots\}$$

The set of common multiples is

$$M_8 \cap M_{12} = \{24, 48, 72, \ldots\}$$

Because the least number in $M_8 \cap M_{12}$ is 24, the LCM of 8 and 12 is 24, written LCM(8, 12) = 24.

The method described above for finding the LCM is often lengthy, especially when finding the LCM of three or more natural numbers. Another, more efficient method for finding the LCM of several numbers involves prime factorization. For example, to find LCM(40, 12), first find the prime factorizations of 40 and 12, namely, $2^3 \cdot 5$ and $2^2 \cdot 3$, respectively.

Next, let $m = $ LCM(40, 12). Because m is a multiple of 40, it must contain both 2^3 and 5 as factors. Also, m is a multiple of 12, so it must contain 2^2 and 3 as factors. Since 2^3 is a multiple of 2^2, then $m = 2^3 \cdot 5 \cdot 3 = 120$. In general, we have the following.

To find the LCM of two natural numbers, first find the prime factorization of each number. Then take each of the primes that are factors of either of the given numbers. The LCM is the product of these primes, each raised to the greatest power of the prime that occurs in either of the prime factorizations.

Example 5-11

Solution

Find the LCM of 2520 and 10,530.

$$2520 = 2^3 \cdot 3^2 \cdot 5 \cdot 7$$
$$10,530 = 2 \cdot 3^4 \cdot 5 \cdot 13$$
$$\text{LCM}(2520, 10,530) = 2^3 \cdot 3^4 \cdot 5 \cdot 7 \cdot 13$$

The similarity between the prime factorization algorithms for GCD and LCM suggests a connection. Consider the GCD and LCM of 6 and 9. Because $6 = 2 \cdot 3$ and $9 = 3^2$, it follows that GCD(6, 9) = 3 and LCM(6, 9) = 18. Notice that GCD(6, 9) $\cdot$ LCM(6, 9) = $3 \cdot 18 = 54$. Observe that 54 is also the product of the original numbers 6 and 9. In general, for any two natural numbers a and b, the connection between their GCD and LCM is given by Theorem 5-10.

THEOREM 5-10

For any two natural numbers a and b,

$GCD(a, b) \cdot LCM(a, b) = ab$

This result is useful for finding the LCM of two numbers a and b when their prime factorizations are not easy to find. $GCD(a, b)$ can be found by the Euclidean algorithm, the product ab can be found by simple multiplication, and $LCM(a, b)$ can be found by division.

Example 5-12

Find $LCM(731, 952)$.

Solution

By the Euclidean algorithm, $GCD(731, 952) = 17$. By Theorem 5-10, $17 \cdot LCM(731, 952) = 731 \cdot 952$. Consequently,

$$LCM(731, 952) = \frac{731 \cdot 952}{17} = 40{,}936$$

Although Theorem 5-10 cannot be used to find the LCM of more than two numbers, it is possible to find the LCM for three or more numbers. For example, to find $LCM(12, 108, 120)$, we can use a method similar to the one for two numbers.

$12 = 2^2 \cdot 3$

$108 = 2^2 \cdot 3^3$

$120 = 2^3 \cdot 3 \cdot 5$

Then, $LCM(12, 108, 120) = 2^3 \cdot 3^3 \cdot 5 = 1080$.

Another procedure for finding the LCM of several natural numbers involves division by primes. For example, to find $LCM(12, 75, 120)$, we start with the least prime that divides at least one of the given numbers and divide as follows.

$$2 \mid \underline{12, 75, 120}$$
$$6, 75, \ 60$$

Because 2 does not divide 75, simply bring down the 75. In order to obtain the LCM using this procedure, continue the division process until the row of answers consists of relatively prime numbers.

$$2 \mid \underline{12, 75, 120}$$
$$2 \mid \underline{\ 6, 75, \ 60}$$
$$2 \mid \underline{\ 3, 75, \ 30}$$
$$3 \mid \underline{\ 3, 75, \ 15}$$
$$5 \mid \underline{\ 1, 25, \ \ 5}$$
$$1, \ 5, \ \ 1$$

Thus, $LCM(12, 75, 120) = 2 \cdot 2 \cdot 2 \cdot 3 \cdot 5 \cdot 1 \cdot 5 \cdot 1 = 2^3 \cdot 3 \cdot 5^2 = 600$.

PROBLEM SET 5-3

1. Find the GCD and the LCM for each of the following using the intersection-of-sets method.
   (a) 18 and 10   (b) 24 and 36
   (c) 8, 24, and 52

2. Find the GCD and the LCM for each of the following using the prime factorization method.
   (a) 132 and 504   (b) 65 and 1690
   (c) 900, 96, and 630

3. Find the GCD for each of the following using the Euclidean algorithm.
   (a) 220 and 2924   (b) 14,595 and 10,856
   (c) 122,368 and 123,152

4. Find the LCM for each of the following using any method.
   (a) 24 and 36   (b) 72 and 90 and 96
   (c) 90 and 105 and 315

5. Find the LCM for each of the following pairs of numbers using Theorem 5-10 and the answers from Problem 3.
   (a) 220 and 2924
   (b) 14,595 and 10,856
   (c) 122,368 and 123,152

6. Find each of the following by using any method.
   (a) GCD(56, 72)   (b) GCD(84, 92)
   (c) GCD(1804, 328)   (d) LCM(56, 72)
   (e) LCM(24, 82)   (f) LCM(963, 657)

7. Bill and Sue both work at night. Bill has every sixth night off and Sue has every eighth night off. If they are both off tonight, how many nights will it be before they are both off again?

8. Midas has 120 gold coins and 144 silver coins. He wants to place his gold coins and his silver coins in stacks so that there are the same number of coins in each stack. What is the greatest number of coins that he can place in each stack?

9. By selling cookies at 24¢ each, José made enough money to buy several cans of pop costing 45¢ per can. If he had no money left over after buying the pop, what is the least number of cookies he could have sold?

10. Bijous I and II start their movies at 7:00 P.M. The movie at Bijou I takes 75 minutes, while the movie at Bijou II takes 90 minutes. If the shows run continuously, when will they start at the same time again?

11. Assume a and b are any natural numbers, and answer each of the following.
    (a) If GCD$(a, b) = 1$, find LCM(a, b).
    (b) Find GCD(a, a) and LCM(a, a).
    (c) Find GCD(a^2, a) and LCM(a^2, a).
    (d) If $a|b$, find GCD(a, b) and LCM(a, b).
    (e) If a and b are two different primes, find GCD(a, b) and LCM(a, b).

(f) What is the relationship between a and b if GCD$(a, b) = a$?
(g) What is the relationship between a and b if LCM$(a, b) = a$?

12. Classify each of the following as true or false. Justify your answers.
    (a) If GCD$(a, b) = 1$, then a and b cannot both be even.
    (b) If GCD$(a, b) = 2$, then both a and b are even.
    (c) If a and b are even, then GCD$(a, b) = 2$.
    (d) For all natural numbers a and b, LCM$(a, b)|$GCD(a, b).
    (e) For all natural numbers a and b, LCM$(a, b)|ab$.
    (f) GCD$(a, b) \leq a$
    (g) LCM$(a, b) \geq a$

13. To find GCD(24, 20, 12), it is possible to find GCD(24, 20), which is 4, and then find GCD(4, 12), which is 4. Use this approach and the Euclidean algorithm to find GCD(120, 75, 105).

14. Is it true that GCD$(a, b, c) \cdot$ LCM$(a, b, c) = abc$? Justify your answer.

15. Two bike riders ride around in a circular path. The first rider completes one round in 12 minutes and the second rider completes it in 18 minutes. If they both start at the same place and the same time and go in the same direction, after how many minutes will they meet again at the starting place?

16. (a) Show that 97,219,988,751 and 4 are relatively prime.
    (b) Show that 181,345,913 and 11 are relatively prime.
    (c) Show that 181,345,913 and 33 are relatively prime.

17. Find all natural numbers x such that GCD$(25, x) = 1$ and $1 \leq x \leq 25$.

18. If GCD$(a, b) = 1$, what can be said about GCD(a^2, b^2)? Justify your answer.

19. One use of GCD is to reduce fractions to lowest terms (see Chapter 6). For example, $\frac{12}{54}$ can be reduced to $\frac{2}{9}$ by dividing both 12 and 54 by GCD(12, 54), or 6. Use the GCD to reduce each of the following.
    (a) $\frac{28}{48}$ (b) $\frac{63}{99}$ (c) $\frac{117}{288}$ (d) $\frac{65}{260}$

20. (a) A number is called *perfect* if it is equal to the sum of its proper divisors, that is, all its divisors except the number itself. For example, because $6 = 1 + 2 + 3$, it is perfect. Find another perfect number less than 30.
    (b) Two numbers are said to be *amicable* if each is the sum of the proper divisors of the other. Show that 220 and 284 are amicable.

21. Is it always true that if $d|$GCD(a, b), then $d|a$ and $d|b$? Why or why not?

22. Find two integers x and y such that $x \cdot y = 1{,}000{,}000$ and neither x nor y contains any zeros as digits.

Review Problems

23. Is 3111 a prime? Prove your answer.
24. Find a number with exactly six prime factors.

25. Produce the least positive number that is divisible by 2, 3, 4, 5, 6, 7, 8, 9, 10, and 11.
26. What is the greatest prime that must be used to determine if 2089 is prime?

BRAIN TEASER

Figure 5-6

For any $n \times m$ rectangle such that $\text{GCD}(n, m) = 1$, find a rule for determining the number of unit squares (1×1) that a diagonal passes through. For example, in Figure 5-6(a) and (b), the diagonal passes through 8 and 6 squares, respectively.

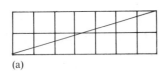
(a)

(b)

---

*Section 5-4   # Clock and Modular Arithmetic

CLOCK ARITHMETIC

The book *Disquisitiones Arithmeticae* is among Karl Friedrich Gauss' great mathematical works. Many problems that had been attacked without success by other mathematicians were solved by Gauss for the first time in this book. In his book, Gauss introduced a new topic, the theory of congruences, which very rapidly gained general acceptance and has since become a foundation for number theory. The basics of the theory of congruences can be understood in elementary school and can provide enrichment for students.

One type of enrichment activity involving congruences uses the arithmetic of a 12-hour clock. For example, if it is 9 o'clock, what time will it be 8 hours later? It is possible to use the clock in Figure 5-7 to determine that 8 hours after 9 o'clock is 5 o'clock. We record this as $9 \oplus 8 = 5$, where $\oplus$ denotes clock addition.

Figure 5-7

The answer, $9 \oplus 8 = 5$, can also be obtained by performing the regular addition $9 + 8 = 17$ and then subtracting 12 (or by dividing 17 by 12 and taking the remainder). Thus, whenever the sum of two digits on a 12-hour clock under regular addition exceeds 12, add the numbers in the regular way and then subtract 12 to obtain the answer for clock addition.

It is possible to perform other operations on the clock. For example, $2 \ominus 9$ on the clock, where $\ominus$ denotes clock subtraction, could be interpreted as the time 9 hours before 2 o'clock. Counting backwards (counterclockwise) 9 units from 2 reveals that $2 \ominus 9 = 5$. If subtraction on the clock is defined in terms of addition, we have $2 \ominus 9 = x$, if and only if $2 = 9 \oplus x$. Consequently, $x = 5$.

Example 5-13

Perform each of the following computations on a 12-hour clock.

(a) $8 \oplus 8$ (b) $4 \ominus 12$ (c) $4 \ominus 4$

Solution

(a) $8 + 8 - 12 = 4$. Hence, $8 \oplus 8 = 4$.
(b) $4 \ominus 12 = 4$, since by counting forward or backwards 12 hours, you arrive at the original position.
(c) $4 \ominus 4 = 12$. This should be clear by looking at the clock, but it can also be found using the definition of subtraction in terms of addition.

As with whole numbers, clock multiplication can be defined using repeated addition. For example, $2 \otimes 8 = 8 \oplus 8 = 4$, where $\otimes$ denotes clock multiplication. Similarly, $3 \otimes 5 = (5 \oplus 5) \oplus 5 = 10 \oplus 5 = 3$. As with whole numbers, clock division can be defined in terms of multiplication. For example, $8 \oslash 5 = x$, where $\oslash$ denotes clock division, if and only if $8 = 5 \otimes x$, for a unique x in the set $\{1, 2, 3, \ldots, 12\}$. Because $5 \otimes 4 = 8$, then $8 \oslash 5 = 4$.

Example 5-14

Perform the following operations on a 12-hour clock, if possible.

(a) $3 \otimes 11$ (b) $2 \oslash 7$ (c) $3 \oslash 2$ (d) $5 \oslash 12$

Solution

(a) $3 \otimes 11 = (11 \oplus 11) \oplus 11 = 10 \oplus 11 = 9$
(b) $2 \oslash 7 = x$ if and only if $2 = 7 \otimes x$. Consequently, $x = 2$.
(c) $3 \oslash 2 = x$ if and only if $3 = 2 \otimes x$. Multiplying each of the numbers $1, 2, 3, 4, \ldots, 12$ by 2 shows that none of the multiplications yield 3. Thus, the equation $3 = 2 \otimes x$ has no solution, and consequently, $3 \oslash 2$ is undefined.
(d) $5 \oslash 12 = x$ if and only if $5 = 12 \otimes x$. However, $12 \otimes x = 12$ for every x in the set $\{1, 3, 4, \ldots, 12\}$. Thus, $5 = 12 \otimes x$ has no solution on the clock, and therefore, $5 \oslash 12$ is undefined.

On a 12-hour clock, addition, subtraction, and multiplication can be performed for any two numbers but, as shown in Example 5-14, not all divisions can be performed. Division by 12, the additive identity, on a 12-hour clock either can never be performed or is not meaningful, since it does not yield a unique answer. However, there are clocks on which all divisions can be performed, except by the corresponding additive identities. One such clock is a 5-hour clock, shown in Figure 5-8.

On this clock, $3 \oplus 4 = 2$, $2 \ominus 3 = 4$, $2 \otimes 4 = 3$, and $3 \oslash 4 = 2$. Since adding 5 to any number yields the original number, 5 is the additive identity

Figure 5-8

for this 5-hour clock, as seen in Table 5-2(a). Consequently, you might suspect that division by 5 is not possible on a 5-hour clock. To determine which divisions are possible, consider Table 5-2(b), a multiplication table for 5-hour clock arithmetic.

Table 5-2

(a)

$\oplus$	1	2	3	4	5
1	2	3	4	5	1
2	3	4	5	1	2
3	4	5	1	2	3
4	5	1	2	3	4
5	1	2	3	4	5

(b)

$\otimes$	1	2	3	4	5
1	1	2	3	4	5
2	2	4	1	3	5
3	3	1	4	2	5
4	4	3	2	1	5
5	5	5	5	5	5

To find $1 \oplus 2$, we write $1 \oplus 2 = x$, which is equivalent to $1 = 2 \otimes x$. The second row of part (b) of the table shows that $2 \otimes 1 = 2, 2 \otimes 2 = 4, 2 \otimes 3 = 1$, $2 \otimes 4 = 3$, and $2 \otimes 5 = 5$. The solution of $1 = 2 \otimes x$ is $x = 3$, so $1 \oplus 2 = 3$. The information given in the second row of the table can be used to determine the following divisions.

$2 \oplus 2 = 1$ because $2 = 2 \otimes 1$

$3 \oplus 2 = 4$ because $3 = 2 \otimes 4$

$4 \oplus 2 = 2$ because $4 = 2 \otimes 2$

$5 \oplus 2 = 5$ because $5 = 2 \otimes 5$

According to the table, division by 2 is always possible because every element occurs in the second row. Similarly, division by all other numbers, except 5, is always possible. In the problem set, you are asked to perform arithmetic on different clocks and investigate for which clocks all computations, except division by the additive identity, can be performed.

MODULAR ARITHMETIC

Many of the concepts for clock arithmetic can be used to work problems involving a calendar. On the calendar in Figure 5-9, notice that the five Sundays have dates 1, 8, 15, 22, and 29. Any two of these dates for Sunday

Figure 5-9

April

S	M	T	W	T	F	S
1	2	3	4	5	6	7
8	9	10	11	12	13	14
15	16	17	18	19	20	21
22	23	24	25	26	27	28
29	30					

differ by a multiple of 7. The same property is true for any other day of the week. If the second day of the month falls on Monday, then 7 days later the day will be Monday again. In fact, it will be Monday after any multiple of 7 days. For example, the second and thirtieth days fall on the same day since $30 - 2 = 28$ and 28 is a multiple of 7. We say that 30 is congruent to 2, modulo 7, and write $30 \equiv 2$ (mod 7). Similarly, because 18 and 6 differ by a multiple of 12, we write $18 \equiv 6$ (mod 12). This leads to the following definition.

DEFINITION

> For integers a and b, *a* **is congruent to** *b* **modulo** *m,* written $a \equiv b$ (mod m), if and only if $a - b$ is a multiple of m, where m is a positive integer greater than 1.

Example 5-15

Tell why each of the following is true.

(a) $23 \equiv 3$ (mod 10)
(b) $23 \equiv 3$ (mod 4)
(c) $23 \not\equiv 3$ (mod 7)
(d) $10 \equiv {}^-1$ (mod 11)
(e) $25 \equiv 5$ (mod 5)

Solution

(a) $23 \equiv 3$ (mod 10), because $23 - 3$ is a multiple of 10.
(b) $23 \equiv 3$ (mod 4), because $23 - 3$ is a multiple of 4.
(c) $23 \not\equiv 3$ (mod 7), because $23 - 3$ is not a multiple of 7.
(d) $10 \equiv {}^-1$ (mod 11), because $10 - ({}^-1) = 11$ is a multiple of 11.
(e) $25 \equiv 5$ (mod 5), because $25 - 5 = 20$ is a multiple of 5.

Example 5-16

Find all integers x such that $x \equiv 1$ (mod 10).

Solution

$x \equiv 1$ (mod 10) if and only if $x - 1 = 10k$, where k is any integer. Consequently, $x = 10k + 1$. Letting $k = 0, 1, 2, 3, \ldots$ yields the sequence $1, 11, 21, 31, 41, \ldots$. Also, letting $k = {}^-1, {}^-2, {}^-3, {}^-4, \ldots$ yields the negative integers ${}^-9, {}^-19, {}^-29, {}^-39, \ldots$. The two sequences can be combined to give the solution set

$$\{\ldots, {}^-39, {}^-29, {}^-19, {}^-9, 1, 11, 21, 31, 41, 51, \ldots\}$$

In Example 5-16, the positive integers obtained, $1, 11, 21, 31, 41, 51, \ldots$, all differ from each other by a multiple of 10 and, hence, are congruent to each other modulo 10. Notice that each of the numbers $1, 11, 21, 31, 41, 51, \ldots$ has a remainder of 1 when divided by 10. In general, *two whole numbers are congruent modulo m if and only if their remainders, on division by m, are the same.*

Many properties of congruence are similar to properties for equality. Several of these are listed below.

Properties For all integers a, b, and c:
1. $a \equiv a \pmod{m}$.
2. If $a \equiv b \pmod{m}$, then $b \equiv a \pmod{m}$.
3. If $a \equiv b \pmod{m}$ and $b \equiv c \pmod{m}$, then $a \equiv c \pmod{m}$.
4. If $a \equiv b \pmod{m}$, then $a + c \equiv b + c \pmod{m}$.
5. If $a \equiv b \pmod{m}$, then $ac \equiv bc \pmod{m}$.
6. If $a \equiv b \pmod{m}$ and $c \equiv d \pmod{m}$, then $ac \equiv bd \pmod{m}$.
7. If $a \equiv b \pmod{m}$ and k is a natural number, then $a^k \equiv b^k \pmod{m}$.

With these properties, it is possible to solve a variety of problems such as the following.

PROBLEM 4

Find the remainder when 3^{100} is divided by 5.

UNDERSTANDING THE PROBLEM No calculator will accurately find 3^{100}, and thus we cannot actually divide 3^{100} by 5 to find the remainder. We do know that the remainder when a number is divided by 5 should be 0, 1, 2, 3, or 4.

DEVISING A PLAN Since use of a calculator will not work, we have to look for an alternate plan. The use of modular arithmetic may help. If we can find small integers that are equivalent to powers of 3, then we can use properties (5) and (7) to build up 3^{100} and find the mod 5 equivalent.

CARRYING OUT THE PLAN We know that $3^2 \equiv 4 \pmod{5}$
Thus, $3^3 \equiv 3 \cdot 4 \equiv 2 \pmod{5}$
$3^4 \equiv 3 \cdot 2 \equiv 1 \pmod{5}$
Using property (7), then $(3^4)^{25} \equiv 1^{25} \pmod{5}$ or $3^{100} \equiv 1 \pmod{5}$. It follows that 3^{100} and 1 have the same remainder when divided by 5. Thus, 3^{100} has remainder 1 when divided by 5.

LOOKING BACK This type of problem can be changed to find the remainders when dividing by different numbers or to find the units digit of numbers such as 2^{96}.

Example 5-17

(a) If it is now Monday, October 14, on what day of the week will October 14 fall next year, if next year is not a leap year?
(b) If Christmas falls on Thursday this year, on what day of the week will Christmas fall next year, if next year is a leap year?

Solution

(a) Because next year is not a leap year, we have 365 days in the year. Because $365 = 52 \cdot 7 + 1$, we have $365 \equiv 1 \pmod{7}$. Thus, 365 days after October 14 will be 52 weeks and one day later. Thus, October 14 will be on a Tuesday.
(b) Because there are 366 days in a leap year, we have $366 \equiv 2 \pmod{7}$. Thus, Christmas will be two days after Thursday, or Saturday.

PROBLEM SET 5-4

1. Perform each of the following operations on a 12-hour clock, if possible.
   (a) $7 \oplus 8$ (b) $4 \oplus 10$ (c) $3 \ominus 9$
   (d) $4 \ominus 8$ (e) $3 \otimes 9$ (f) $4 \otimes 4$
   (g) $1 \ominus 3$ (h) $2 \ominus 5$

2. Perform each of the following operations on a 5-hour clock.
   (a) $3 \oplus 4$ (b) $3 \oplus 3$ (c) $3 \otimes 4$
   (d) $1 \otimes 4$ (e) $3 \otimes 4$ (f) $2 \otimes 3$
   (g) $3 \ominus 4$ (h) $1 \ominus 4$

3. (a) Construct an addition table for a 7-hour clock.
   (b) Using the addition table in (a), find $5 \ominus 6$ and $2 \ominus 5$.
   (c) Using the addition table in (a), show that subtraction can always be performed on a 7-hour clock.

4. (a) Construct a multiplication table for a 7-hour clock.
   (b) Use the multiplication table in (a) to find $3 \oslash 5$ and $4 \oslash 6$.
   (c) Use the multiplication table to find whether division by numbers different from 7 is always possible.

5. (a) Construct the multiplication tables for 3-, 4-, 6-, and 11-hour clocks.
   (b) On which of the clocks in part (a) can divisions by numbers other than the additive identity always be performed?
   (c) How do the multiplication tables of clocks for which division can always be performed (except by an additive identity) differ from the multiplication tables of clocks for which division is not always meaningful?

6. On a 12-hour clock, the additive inverse of m is a number x such that $m \oplus x = 12$. Denote the additive inverse of m by ^-m and find each of the following.
   (a) additive inverse of 2 (b) additive inverse of 3
   (c) $(^-2) \oplus (^-3)$ (d) $^-(2 \oplus 3)$
   (e) $(^-2) \ominus (^-3)$ (f) $(^-2) \otimes (^-3)$

7. If September 3 falls on Monday, on what day of the week will it fall next year, if next year is a leap year?

8. Show that each of the following statements is true.
   (a) $81 \equiv 1 \pmod 8$
   (b) $81 \equiv 1 \pmod{10}$
   (c) $1000 \equiv {}^-1 \pmod{13}$
   (d) $10^{84} \equiv 1 \pmod 9$
   (e) $10^{100} \equiv 1 \pmod{11}$
   (f) $937 \equiv 37 \pmod{100}$

9. Fill in each blank so that the answer is nonnegative and the least possible number.
   (a) $29 \equiv$ _____ $\pmod 5$
   (b) $3498 \equiv$ _____ $\pmod 3$
   (c) $3498 \equiv$ _____ $\pmod{11}$
   (d) $^-23 \equiv$ _____ $\pmod{10}$

10. Show that $a \equiv 0 \pmod m$, if and only if $m \mid a$.

11. Translate each of the following statements into the language of congruences.
    (a) $8 \mid 24$ (b) $3 \mid {}^-90$
    (c) Any nonzero integer n divides itself.

12. (a) Find all x such that $x \equiv 0 \pmod 2$.
    (b) Find all x such that $x \equiv 1 \pmod 2$.
    (c) Find all x such that $x \equiv 3 \pmod 5$.

13. Find the remainder for each of the following.
    (a) 5^{100} is divided by 6. (b) 5^{101} is divided by 6.
    (c) 10^{99} is divided by 11.

★14. (a) Find a negative integer value for x such that $10^3 \equiv x \pmod{13}$ and $|x|$ is the least possible.
    (b) Find the remainder when 10^{99} is divided by 13.

★15. Use the fact that $100 \equiv 0 \pmod 4$ to find and prove a test for divisibility by 4.

★16. (a) Show that, in general, the cancellation property for multiplication does not hold for congruences; that is, show that $ac \equiv bc \pmod m$ does not always imply $a \equiv b \pmod m$.
    (b) Show that, in general, $a^k \equiv b^k \pmod m$ does not imply $a \equiv b \pmod m$.

★17. Prove each of the properties of congruences mentioned in this section.

BRAIN TEASER

How many primes are in the following sequence?

9, 98, 987, 9876, . . . , 987654321, 9876543219, 98765432198, . . .

SOLUTION TO THE PRELIMINARY PROBLEM

UNDERSTANDING THE PROBLEM A certain prison has 1000 cells numbered 1 through 1000. Each cell contains a single prisoner. The queen designs a plan in which her guards walk through the prison opening and closing cell doors. The prisoners whose doors are left open after 1000 guards have walked through are to be freed. Guard 1 opens every cell starting at cell 1. Guard 2 follows and closes every second cell starting at cell 2. Guard 3 follows and changes the state of every third cell starting with cell 3; that is, if the cell is open, he closes it, and if it is closed, he opens it. The remaining guards pass through in a similar manner. We are to determine how many prisoners are to be freed.

DEVISING A PLAN We use the strategy of examining a simpler problem in order to gain insight into the solution of the original problem. Suppose there are only 20 cells. In the queen's scheme, no guard after the 20th touches the first 20 cells. If we denote an open cell by o and a closed cell by c, we can record the state of each cell changed by the guards as shown in Table 5-3. For example, the fourth guard opens cell 4, opens cell 8, closes cell 12, opens cell 16, and closes cell 20.

Table 5-3

Cell Number

Guard Number	1	2	3	4	5	6	7	8	9	10	11	12	13	14	15	16	17	18	19	20
1	o	o	o	o	o	o	o	o	o	o	o	o	o	o	o	o	o	o	o	o
2		c		c		c		c		c		c		c		c		c		c
3			c			o			c			o			c			o		
4				o				o				c				o				o
5					c					o					o					c
6						c						o						c		
7							c							o						
8								c								c				
9									o									o		
10										c										o
11											c									
12												c								
13													c							
14														c						
15															c					
16																o				
17																	c			
18																		c		
19																			c	
20																				c

The table shows that after 20 guards pass through, the only open cells are 1, 4, 9, and 16. Each of these numbers is a perfect square. We must determine if this pattern will continue for 1000 cells and 1000 guards. If it does, we must count the number of perfect squares less than 1000.

CARRYING OUT THE PLAN To determine if the pattern determined above continues, consider cell 25. The cell is opened by guard 1, closed by guard 5, and opened by guard 25. This suggests that the pattern is correct. (Note that 1, 5, and 25 are the only positive divisors of 25.) What happens with a cell number such as 26, which is not a square? Cell 26 is opened by guard 1, closed by guard 2, opened by guard 13, and closed by guard 26, and, hence, remains closed. In general, we observe that a cell is changed only by guards whose numbers divide the cell number.

For the final state of a cell to be open, it must be opened one more time than it is closed; that is, the state must be changed an odd number of times. For this to happen, the number of the cell must have an odd number of divisors. We can show that the open cells have numbers that are prefect squares by showing that only perfect squares have an odd number of divisors.

Recall that the divisors of a number appear in pairs. For example, the pairs of divisors of 80 and 81 are given by the following.

$$80 = 1 \cdot 80 = 2 \cdot 40 = 4 \cdot 20 = 5 \cdot 16 = 10 \cdot 8$$

$$81 = 1 \cdot 81 = 3 \cdot 27 = 9 \cdot 9$$

Thus, 80 has ten distinct divisors, or five pairs. On the other hand, the perfect square 81 has five distinct divisors—the pairs 1 and 81 and 3 and 27, and a single divisor, 9, which is paired with itself. In this chapter, we have seen that if d is a divisor of n, then n/d is a divisor of n. Consequently, for all divisors d of n, if $d \neq n/d$, then each divisor can be paired with a different divisor and n must have an even number of positive divisors. If for some divisor d, $d = n/d$, then $n = d^2$, and all the divisors of n, except d, are paired with a different divisor. Hence, the number of divisors of n is odd. Because $d = n/d$ occurs only when $n = d^2$, it follows that n has an odd number of divisors if and only if n is a perfect square. As a result, the freed prisoners leave the cells with numbers that are perfect squares less than 1000, namely, 1^2, 2^2, 3^2, 4^2, 5^2, 6^2, . . . , 31^2. Thus, 31 prisoners are freed.

LOOKING BACK This problem suggests the following questions.

1. Which guards will open or close only one cell?
2. How many times will a cell with a prime number be opened or closed?
3. Determine a method of finding the number of factors a number has without actually listing all the factors. (*Hint*: Consider prime factorizations.)

QUESTIONS FROM THE CLASSROOM

1. A student claims that $a|a$ and $a|a$ implies $a|(a-a)$, and hence, $a|0$. Is the student correct?
2. A student argues that $0|0$, since $0 = k \cdot 0$ for any integer k. How do you respond?
3. A student writes, "If $d \nmid a$ and $d \nmid b$, then $d \nmid (a+b)$." How do you respond?
4. Your seventh-grade class just completed a unit on divisibility rules. One of the better students asks why divisibility by numbers other than 3 and 9 cannot be tested by dividing the sum of the digits by the tested number. How should you respond?
5. A student claims that a number with an even number of digits is divisible by 7 if and only if each of the numbers formed by pairing the digits into groups of two is divisible by 7. For example, 49,562,107 is divisible by 7, since each of the numbers 49, 56, 21, and 07 is divisible by 7. Is this true?
6. A sixth-grade student argues that there are infinitely many primes because "there is no end to numbers." How do you respond?
7. A student claims that a number is divisible by 21 if and only if it is divisible by 3 and by 7, and, in general, a number is divisible by $a \cdot b$ if and only if it is divisible by a and by b. What is your response?
8. A student claims that there are no integers x and y that make the equation $12x - 9y = 7$ true. How do you respond?
9. A student claims that for any two integers a and b, GCD(a, b) divides LCM(a, b) and, hence, GCD$(a, b) <$ LCM(a, b). Is the student correct? Why or why not?

CHAPTER OUTLINE

I. Divisibility
  A. If a and b are any integers with $b \neq 0$, then b **divides** a, denoted $b|a$, if and only if there is a unique integer c such that $a = cb$.
  B. The following are basic divisibility theorems for integers a, b, and d with $d \neq 0$.
    1. If $d|a$ and $d|b$, then $d|(a+b)$.
    2. If $d|a$ and $d \nmid b$, then $d \nmid (a+b)$.
    3. If $d|a$ and $d|b$, then $d|(a-b)$.
    4. If $d|a$ and $d \nmid b$, then $d \nmid (a-b)$.
    5. If $d|a$ and k is any integer, then $d|ka$.
  C. Divisibility tests
    1. An integer is divisible by 2, 5, or 10 if and only if its units digit is divisible by 2, 5, or 10, respectively.
    2. An integer is divisible by 4 if and only if the last two digits of the integer represent a number divisible by 4.
    3. An integer is divisible by 8 if and only if the last three digits of the integer represent a number divisible by 8.
    4. An integer is divisible by 3 or by 9 if and only if the sum of its digits is divisible by 3 or 9, respectively.
    5. An integer is divisible by 7 if and only if the integer represented without its units digit minus twice the units digit of the original number is divisible by 7.
    6. An integer is divisible by 11 if and only if the sum of the digits in the places that are even powers of 10 minus the sum of the digits in the places that are odd powers of 10 is divisible by 11.
    7. An integer is divisible by 6 if and only if the integer is divisible by both 2 and 3.
II. Prime and composite numbers
  A. Positive integers that have exactly two positive divisors—namely, 1 and themselves—are called **primes.** Integers greater than 1 that are not primes are called **composites.**
  B. **Fundamental Theorem of Arithmetic:** Every composite number has one and only one prime factorization.
  C. Criterion for determining if a given number n is prime: *If n is not divisible by any prime p such that $p^2 \leq n$, then n is prime.*

III. Greatest common divisor and least common multiple
  A. The **greatest common divisor (GCD)** of two or more natural numbers is the greatest divisor, or factor, that the numbers have in common.
  B. The **least common multiple (LCM)** of two or more natural numbers is the least positive multiple that the numbers have in common.
  C. **Euclidean algorithm:** If a and b are whole numbers and $a \geq b$, then GCD(a, b) = GCD(b, r), where r is the remainder when a is divided by b. The procedure of finding the GCD of two numbers a and b by using the above result repeatedly is called the *Euclidean algorithm.*
  D. GCD(a, b) $\cdot$ LCM(a, b) = ab.
*IV. Clock and modular arithmetic
  A. For any integers a and b, **a is congruent to b modulo m** if and only if $a - b$ is a multiple of m, where m is a positive integer greater than 1.
  B. Two integers are congruent modulo m if and only if their remainders upon division by m are the same.

CHAPTER TEST

1. Classify each of the following as true or false.
   (a) $8|4$ (b) $0|4$ (c) $4|0$
   (d) If a number is divisible by 4 and by 6, then it is divisible by 24.
   (e) If a number is not divisible by 12, then it is not divisible by 3.
2. Classify each of the following as true or false. If false, show a counterexample.
   (a) If $7|x$ and $7 \nmid y$, then $7 \nmid xy$.
   (b) If $d \nmid (a + b)$, then $d \nmid a$ and $d \nmid b$.
   (c) If $16|10^4$, then $16|10^6$.
   (d) If $d|(a + b)$ and $d \nmid a$, then $d \nmid b$.
   (e) If $d|(x + y)$ and $d|x$, then $d|y$.
   (f) If $4 \nmid x$ and $4 \nmid y$, then $4 \nmid xy$.
3. Test each of the following numbers for divisibility by 2, 3, 4, 5, 6, 7, 8, 9, and 11.
   (a) 83,160   (b) 83,193
4. Assume that 10,007 is prime. Without actually dividing 10,024 by 17, prove that 10,024 is not divisible by 17.
*5. Prove the test for divisibility by 9 using a three-digit number n such that $n = a \cdot 10^2 + b \cdot 10 + c$.
6. Determine whether each of the following numbers is prime or composite.
   (a) 143   (b) 223
7. How can you tell if a number is divisible by 24? Check 4152 for divisibility by 24.

8. Find the GCD for each of the following.
   (a) 24 and 52   (b) 5767 and 4453
9. Find the LCM for each of the following.
   (a) $2^3 \cdot 5^2 \cdot 7^3$, $2 \cdot 5^3 \cdot 7^2 \cdot 13$, and $2^4 \cdot 5 \cdot 7^4 \cdot 29$
   (b) 278 and 279
10. Construct a number with exactly five divisors.
11. Find all divisors of 144.
12. Find the prime factorization of each of the following.
   (a) 172   (b) 288   (c) 260   (d) 111
13. Jane and Ramon are running laps on a track. If they start at the same time and place and go in the same direction with Jane running a lap in 5 minutes and Ramon running a lap in 3 minutes, how long will it take for them to be at this place if they continue to run at the same pace?
14. Candy bars priced at 50¢ each were not selling, so the price was reduced. Then they all sold in one day for a total of $31.93. What was the reduced price for each candy bar?
15. Two bells ring at 8:00 A.M. For the remainder of the day, one bell rings every half hour and the other bell rings every 45 minutes. What time will it be when the bells ring together again?
*16. Find the remainder when 2^{96} is divided by 7.

SELECTED BIBLIOGRAPHY

Adams, V. "A Variation on the Algorithm for GCD and LCM." *Arithmetic Teacher* 30 (November 1982): 46.

Avital, S. "The Plight and Might of Number Seven." *Arithmetic Teacher* 25 (February 1978):22–24.

Beard, E., and R. Polis. "Subtraction Facts with Pattern Explorations." *Arithmetic Teacher* 29 (December 1981): 13–14.

Bezuszka, S. "Even Perfect Numbers—An Update." *Mathematics Teacher* 74 (September 1981):460–461.

Bezuszka, S. "A Test for Divisibility by Primes." *Arithmetic Teacher* 33 (October 1985):36–38.

Bezuszka, S., and M. Kenney. "Challenges For Enriching the Curriculum: Arithmetic and Number Theory." *Mathematics Teacher* 76 (April 1983):250–252.

Brown, G. "Searching for Patterns of Divisors." *Arithmetic Teacher* 32 (December 1984):32–34.

Brown, S. *Some Prime Comparisons*. Reston, Va.: National Council of Teachers of Mathematics, 1978.

Burton, G., and J. Knifong. "Definitions for Prime Numbers." *Arithmetic Teacher* 27 (February 1980): 44–47.

Cassidy, C., and B. Hodgson. "Because a Door Has to Be Open or Closed. . ." *The Mathematics Teacher* 75 (February 1982):155–158.

Cavanaugh, W. "The Spirograph and the Greatest Common Factor." *The Mathematics Teacher* 68 (February 1975):162–163.

Duncan, D., and B. Litwiller. "A Pattern in Number Theory: Example Generalization Proof." *The Mathematics Teacher* 64 (November 1971):661–664.

Eggan, L. "Number Theory." *Enrichment Mathematics for High School, 1963 Yearbook*. Reston, Va.: National Council of Teachers of Mathematics, 1963.

Engle, J. "A Rediscovered Test for Divisibility by Eleven." *The Mathematics Teacher* 69 (December 1976):669.

Gullen, G., III. "The Smallest Prime Factor of a Natural Number." *The Mathematics Teacher* 67 (April 1974):329–332.

Hadar, N. "Odd and Even Numbers—Magician's Approach." *The Mathematics Teacher* 75 (May 1982): 408–412.

Henry, B. "Modulo 7 Arithmetic—A Perfect Example of Field Properties." *The Mathematics Teacher* 65 (October 1972): 525–528.

Henry, L. "Another Look at Least Common Multiple and Greatest Common Factor." *Arithmetic Teacher* 25 (March 1978):52–53.

Hoffer, A. "What You Always Wanted to Know about Six But Have Been Afraid to Ask." *The Arithmetic Teacher* 20 (March 1973):173–180.

Hohfold, J. "An Inductive Approach to Prime Factors." *Arithmetic Teacher* 29 (December 1981):28–29.

Horak, V., and W. Horak. "The Versatile Handset Board." *Arithmetic Teacher* 30 (October 1982):10–16.

Johnson, P. "Understanding the Check of Nines." *Arithmetic Teacher* 26 (November 1978):54–55.

Kennedy, R. "Divisibility for Integers Ending in 1, 3, 7, or 9." *The Mathematics Teacher* 64 (February 1971): 137–138.

Lamb, C., and L. Hutcherson. "Greatest Common Factor and Least Common Multiple." *Arithmetic Teacher* 31 (April 1984):43–44.

Lappan, G., and M. Winter. "Prime Factorizations." *Arithmetic Teacher* 27 (March 1980):24–27.

Litwiller, B., and D. Duncan. "Pentagonal Patterns in the Addition Table." *Arithmetic Teacher* 32 (April 1985):36–38.

Long, C. "A Simpler '7' Divisibility Rule," *The Mathematics Teacher* 64 (May 1971):473–475.

Mann, N., III. "Modulo Systems: One More Step." *The Mathematics Teacher* 65 (March 1972):207–209.

Ore, O. *Invitation to Number Theory*. New York: Random House, The L. W. Singer Company New Mathematical Library, 1967.

Pagni, D. "Number Theory for Secondary Schools?" *Mathematics Teacher* 72 (January 1979):20–22.

Parkerson, E. "Patterns in Divisibility." *Arithmetic Teacher* 25 (January 1978):58.

Prielipp, R. "Perfect Numbers, Abundant Numbers, and Deficient Numbers." *The Mathematics Teacher* 63 (December 1970):692–696.

Robold, A. "Patterns in Multiples." *Arithmetic Teacher* 29 (April 1982):21–23.

Rockwell, C. "Another 'Sieve' for Prime Numbers." *The Arithmetic Teacher* 20 (November 1973):603–605.

Roy, S. "LCM and GCF in the Hundred Chart." *Arithmetic Teacher* 26 (December 1978):53

Scheuer, D., Jr. "All-Star GCF." *Arithmetic Teacher* 26 (November 1978):34–35.

Sconyers, J. "Prime Numbers—A Locust's View." *The Mathematics Teacher* 74 (February 1981):105–108.

Shaw, J. "A-Plus for Counters." *Arithmetic Teacher* 31 (September 1983):10–14.

Sherzer, L. "A Simplified Presentation for Finding the LCM and the GCF." *The Arithmetic Teacher* 21 (May 1974):415–416.

Singer, R. "Modular Arithmetic and Divisibility Criteria." *The Mathematics Teacher* 63 (December 1970):653–656.

Smith, L. "A General Test of Divisibility." *The Mathematics Teacher* 71 (November 1978):668–669.

Snover, S., and M. Spikell. "Problem Solving and Programming: The License Plate Curiosity." *The Mathematics Teacher* 74 (November 1981):616–617.

Stern, P. "GCF and LCM, Korean Style!" *Arithmetic Teacher* 32 (December 1984):3.

Stock, M. "On What Day Were You Born?" *The Mathematics Teacher* 65 (January 1972):73–75.

Szetela, W. "A General Divisibility Test for Whole Numbers." *The Mathematics Teacher* 73 (March 1980):223–225.

Tucker, B. "The Division Algorithm." *The Arithmetic Teacher* 20 (December 1973):639–646.

White, P. "An Application of Clock Arithmetic." *The Mathematics Teacher* 66 (November 1973):645–647.

Yazbak, N. "Some Unusual Tests of Divisibility." *The Mathematics Teacher* 69 (December 1976):669.

CHAPTER 6

Rational Numbers as Fractions

Preliminary Problem

Madame Castafiore, a famous opera singer, had a large collection of jewels. One day all her precious stones disappeared. The investigating detectives wanted to know how many emeralds she owned and how many jewels she had altogether. She did not remember either number, but she did know that one fourth of her jewels were diamonds, three tenths were pieces of jade, one fifth were rubies, and one tenth were sapphires. She also remembered that she had six fewer emeralds than diamonds. If Ms. Castafiore's entire jewel collection consisted of diamonds, jade, rubies, sapphires, and emeralds, how large was her jewel collection and how many emeralds did she own?

Introduction

The word *fraction* is derived from the French word *frangere,* which means "to break." Fractions were first needed for measurements that represented less than a whole unit.

Table 6-1 shows several different ways in which fractions are used.

Table 6-1

Use	Example
Division problem or solution to a multiplication problem	The solution to $2x = 3$ is $\frac{3}{2}$.
Partition, or part, of a whole	Joe received one half of Mary's salary each month for alimony.
Ratio	The ratio of Republicans to Democrats in the Senate is three to five.

Figure 6-1 illustrates the use of fractions as part of a whole and as part of a given set. For example, in Figure 6-1(a), one part out of three congruent parts, or $\frac{1}{3}$ of the rectangle, is shaded. In Figure 6-1(b), two parts out of three parts, or $\frac{2}{3}$ of the unit segment, are shaded. In Figure 6-1(c), three circles out of five circles, or $\frac{3}{5}$ of the circles, are shaded.

Figure 6-1

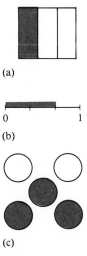

(a)

(b)

(c)

HISTORICAL NOTE

The early Egyptian numeration system had symbols for fractions with numerators of 1. Most fractions with numerators other than 1 were expressed as a sum of different fractions with numerators of 1; for example, $\frac{7}{12} = \frac{1}{3} + \frac{1}{4}$.

Section 6-1   The Set of Rational Numbers

Children often encounter fractions before they are exposed to them in school. This early exposure usually takes the form of oral descriptions rather than mathematical notations. A child hears phrases such as "one half of a pizza," "one third of a cake," or "three fourths of a pie." In schools, fractions are introduced as parts of a whole and the bar notation is used, as in $\frac{2}{3}$ or 2/3 for two thirds. Children also encounter such division problems as "If two identical fruit bars are equally divided among three friends, how much does each get?" The answer is that each child receives $\frac{2}{3}$ of a fruit bar. Numbers represented by fractions such as $\frac{1}{3}$, $\frac{3}{5}$, and $\frac{2}{3}$ belong to the set of rational numbers. Any number that can be represented by $\frac{a}{b}$, where a and b are

rational number   integers and $b \neq 0$, is called a **rational number.**

> **Remark**   In elementary school, children are first exposed to rational num-
> bers $\frac{a}{b}$ such that a and b are nonnegative integers ($b \neq 0$). In this
> text, we do not restrict the values of a and b to nonnegative in-
> tegers. Mathematically, a development using all integers gives a
> fuller picture of rational numbers.

Rational numbers can be developed in a way similar to the way that integers were developed. Recall that because the equation $x + 3 = 0$ had no solution in the set of whole numbers, we made up a new number, denoted by $^-3$, that is the unique solution of the equation. In general, the unique solution of the equation $x + a = 0$ is denoted by ^-a, and hence $^-a + a = 0$. Similarly, the need for rational numbers arises from the need to have a unique solution to an equation like $6x = 5$. We can make up a number denoted by $\frac{5}{6}$ that is the unique solution of the equation. Thus, $\frac{5}{6}$ can be thought of as a number such that $6 \cdot \frac{5}{6} = 5$. In general, the unique solution for x in the equation $b \cdot x = a$, where $b \neq 0$, is denoted by $\frac{a}{b}$. Thus, $\frac{a}{b}$ can be thought of as a num-

ber such that $b \cdot \frac{a}{b} = a$.

numerator   In the rational number $\frac{a}{b}$, a is called the **numerator** and b is called the

denominator   **denominator.** The rational number $\frac{a}{b}$ may also be represented as a/b or as

$a \div b$. The set of rational numbers, denoted by Q, can be written as follows.

$$Q = \left\{ \frac{a}{b} \,\middle|\, a \text{ and } b \text{ are integers and } b \neq 0 \right\}$$

If we use the division representation of a rational number, then $a \div 1 = \frac{a}{1}$.

Since $a \div 1 = a$, every integer a can be represented by $\frac{a}{1}$. This and the fact that not every rational number is an integer show that the set of integers is a proper subset of the set of rational numbers; that is, $I \subset Q$.

fraction   Rational numbers are often referred to as fractions. A **fraction** is a number of the form $\frac{a}{b}$ where a and b are any numbers and not necessarily integers ($b \neq 0$). In Chapter 7, we will see numbers of the form $\frac{a}{b}$ that are not rational $\left(\text{for example, } \frac{\sqrt{2}}{2}\right)$. Hence, it will follow that the set of rational numbers is a proper subset of the set of fractions. Because every rational number is a fraction, it is correct to refer to a rational number as a fraction. All the properties of rational numbers developed in this chapter also hold for fractions in general.

In Figure 6-2(a), one of three congruent parts, or $\frac{1}{3}$, is shaded. Also, in Figure 6-2(a), two of six congruent parts, or $\frac{2}{6}$, are shaded. Thus, both $\frac{1}{3}$ and $\frac{2}{6}$ represent exactly the same shaded portion. Although the symbols $\frac{1}{3}$ and $\frac{2}{6}$ do not look alike, they represent the same rational number. Strictly speaking, $\frac{1}{3}$ and $\frac{2}{6}$ are **equivalent** fractions. However, because they represent equal amounts, we write $\frac{1}{3} = \frac{2}{6}$ and say that $\frac{1}{3}$ equals $\frac{2}{6}$.

Figure 6-2

(a)

(b)

Figure 6-2(b) shows the rectangle subdivided into twelve parts, with four parts shaded. Thus, $\frac{1}{3}$ is equal to $\frac{4}{12}$ because the same portion of the model is covered. Similarly, we could illustrate that $\frac{1}{3}, \frac{2}{6}, \frac{3}{9}, \frac{4}{12}, \frac{5}{15}, \ldots$ are equal. In other words, there are infinitely many ways of naming the rational number $\frac{1}{3}$. Similarly, there are infinitely many ways of naming any rational number.

This process of generating fractions equal to $\frac{1}{3}$ can be thought of as follows: If each of 3 equal-sized parts of a whole are halved, there must be twice as many of the smaller pieces. Hence, $\frac{1}{3} = \frac{2}{6}$. Similarly, $\frac{1}{3} = \frac{4}{12}$ because if each of three equal-sized parts of a whole are divided into four equal-sized parts, then there must be four times as many of the smaller pieces. In general, we have the following property of fractions, called the *Fundamental Law of Fractions.*

Property **Fundamental Law of Fractions** For any rational number $\frac{a}{b}$ and any integer $c \neq 0$,

$$\frac{a}{b} = \frac{ac}{bc}$$

The Fundamental Law of Fractions may be stated in words as follows: *The value of a fraction does not change if its numerator and denominator are multiplied by the same nonzero number.* However, the Fundamental Law of Fractions does not imply that adding the same nonzero number to the numerator and the denominator results in an equivalent fraction. For example,

$$\frac{1}{2} \neq \frac{1+2}{2+2}, \quad \text{or} \quad \frac{3}{4}$$

The Fundamental Law of Fractions and equivalent fractions are illustrated on page 237, which is from *Heath Mathematics,* 1986, Grade 5.

Remark In higher mathematics, rational numbers are often introduced as a collection of disjoint sets called equivalence classes. For example, the fractions in the set

$$\left\{ \cdots, \frac{^-3}{^-6}, \frac{^-2}{^-4}, \frac{^-1}{^-2}, \frac{1}{2}, \frac{2}{4}, \frac{3}{6}, \cdots \right\}$$

are called *equivalent fractions* and the set is called an *equivalence class of fractions.*

Example 6-1

Find a value for x so that $\frac{x}{210} = \frac{12}{42}$.

Solution

By the Fundamental Law of Fractions, $\frac{12}{42} = \frac{12 \cdot 5}{42 \cdot 5} = \frac{60}{210}$. Hence,

$$\frac{x}{210} = \frac{60}{210} \text{ and } x = 60.$$

SIMPLIFYING FRACTIONS

simplifying fractions

The Fundamental Law of Fractions justifies a process called **simplifying fractions.** Consider the following.

$$\frac{60}{210} = \frac{6 \cdot 10}{21 \cdot 10} = \frac{6}{21}$$

Also,

$$\frac{6}{21} = \frac{2 \cdot 3}{7 \cdot 3} = \frac{2}{7}$$

We can simplify $\frac{60}{210}$ because the numerator and denominator have a common factor of 10. Also, we can simplify $\frac{6}{21}$ because 6 and 21 have a common factor

Equivalent fractions

When you multiply both the numerator and the denominator of a fraction by the same number (not zero), you get an equivalent fraction.

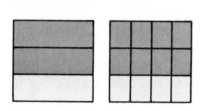

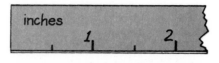

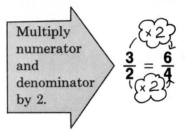

Multiply numerator and denominator by 4.

$$\frac{2}{3} = \frac{8}{12}$$

(×4) (×4)

Multiply numerator and denominator by 2.

$$\frac{3}{2} = \frac{6}{4}$$

(×2) (×2)

EXERCISES
Complete.

1. $\frac{1}{2} = ?$

2. $\frac{1}{3} = ?$

3. $\frac{1}{4} = ?$

4. $\frac{1}{2} = ?$

5. $\frac{2}{3} = ?$

6. $\frac{3}{4} = ?$

7. 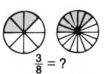 $\frac{3}{8} = ?$

8. 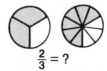 $\frac{2}{3} = ?$

9. 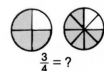 $\frac{3}{4} = ?$

of 3. However, we cannot simplify $\frac{2}{7}$ because 2 and 7 have no common factors other than 1. The fraction $\frac{2}{7}$ is called the **simplest form** of $\frac{60}{210}$ and it is said to be written in **lowest terms**. In general, *a fraction* $\dfrac{a}{b}$ *is in* **simplest form** *if a and b have no common factor other than 1, that is, if a and b are relatively prime.* Finding the simplest form of $\frac{60}{210}$ can be achieved with fewer steps by writing

$$\frac{60}{210} = \frac{2 \cdot 30}{7 \cdot 30} = \frac{2}{7}$$

The number 30 is the GCD of 60 and 210. This process amounts to dividing 60 and 210 by their greatest common divisor, 30. *In general, a fraction* $\dfrac{a}{b}$ *can be written in simplest form by dividing a and b by GCD(a, b).*

simplest form

lowest terms

Example 6-2

Write each of the following in simplest form.

(a) $\dfrac{45}{60}$ (b) $\dfrac{35}{17}$

Solution

(a) GCD(45, 60) = 15, so $\dfrac{45}{60} = \dfrac{3 \cdot 15}{4 \cdot 15} = \dfrac{3}{4}$.

Another method for writing the fraction in simplest form is to find the prime factorization of the numerator and denominator and then divide both numerator and denominator by common primes.

$$\frac{45}{60} = \frac{3 \cdot 3 \cdot 5}{2 \cdot 2 \cdot 3 \cdot 5} = \frac{3 \cdot 3}{2 \cdot 2 \cdot 3} = \frac{3}{2 \cdot 2} = \frac{3}{4}$$

(b) GCD(35, 17) = 1, so $\frac{35}{17}$ is in simplest form.

It is often possible to simplify an algebraic fraction—that is, a fraction involving variables—to its simplest form. For example,

$$\frac{a^2 b}{ab^2} = \frac{a \cdot (ab)}{b \cdot (ab)} = \frac{a}{b}$$

Example 6-3

Write each of the following in simplest form.

(a) $\dfrac{28ab^2}{42a^2b^2}$ (b) $\dfrac{(a+b)^2}{3a+3b}$ (c) $\dfrac{x^2+x}{x+1}$ (d) $\dfrac{3+x^2}{3x}$ (e) $\dfrac{3+3x^2}{3x}$

Solution

(a) $\dfrac{28ab^2}{42a^2b^2} = \dfrac{2 \cdot (14ab^2)}{3a \cdot (14ab^2)} = \dfrac{2}{3a}$

(b) $\dfrac{(a+b)^2}{3a+3b} = \dfrac{(a+b) \cdot (a+b)}{3 \cdot (a+b)} = \dfrac{a+b}{3}$

(c) $\dfrac{x^2+x}{x+1} = \dfrac{x(x+1)}{x+1} = \dfrac{x \cdot (x+1)}{1 \cdot (x+1)} = \dfrac{x}{1} = x$

(d) $\dfrac{3 + x^2}{3x}$ cannot be further reduced because $3 + x^2$ and $3x$ have no factors in common except 1.

(e) $\dfrac{3 + 3x^2}{3x} = \dfrac{3 \cdot (1 + x^2)}{3 \cdot x} = \dfrac{1 + x^2}{x}$

Two fractions such as $\frac{12}{42}$ and $\frac{10}{35}$ can be shown to be equal by several methods.

1. Reduce both fractions to the same simplest form.

$$\frac{12}{42} = \frac{2^2 \cdot 3}{2 \cdot 3 \cdot 7} = \frac{2}{7} \quad \text{and} \quad \frac{10}{35} = \frac{5 \cdot 2}{5 \cdot 7} = \frac{2}{7}$$

Thus,

$$\frac{12}{42} = \frac{10}{35}$$

2. Rewrite both fractions with a common denominator (not necessarily the least). A common multiple of 42 and 35 may be found by finding the product $42 \cdot 35$ or 1470. Now,

$$\frac{12}{42} = \frac{420}{1470} \quad \text{and} \quad \frac{10}{35} = \frac{420}{1470}$$

Hence,

$$\frac{12}{42} = \frac{10}{35}$$

3. Rewrite both fractions with the same least common denominator. Since LCM(42, 35) = 210, then

$$\frac{12}{42} = \frac{60}{210} \quad \text{and} \quad \frac{10}{35} = \frac{60}{210}$$

Thus,

$$\frac{12}{42} = \frac{10}{35}$$

The second method suggests a general algorithm for determining if two fractions $\dfrac{a}{b}$ and $\dfrac{c}{d}$ are equal. Rewrite both fractions with common denominator bd. That is,

$$\frac{a}{b} = \frac{ad}{bd} \quad \text{and} \quad \frac{c}{d} = \frac{bc}{bd}$$

Because the denominators are the same, $\dfrac{ad}{bd} = \dfrac{bc}{bd}$ if and only if $ad = bc$. For example, $\frac{24}{36} = \frac{6}{9}$ because $24 \cdot 9 = 216 = 36 \cdot 6$. In general, the following property results.

Property Two fractions $\dfrac{a}{b}$ and $\dfrac{c}{d}$ are equal if and only if $ad = bc$.

Remark It is important to keep in mind that this property compares the numerators of the fractions when each is rewritten with the common denominator bd. The process is often referred to as *cross multiplication*.

Using a calculator, we can determine if two fractions are equal by using the property that $\dfrac{a}{b} = \dfrac{c}{d}$ if and only if $ad = bc$. We see that $\dfrac{2}{4} = \dfrac{1098}{2196}$ since both $\boxed{2}\boxed{\times}\boxed{2}\boxed{1}\boxed{9}\boxed{6}\boxed{=}$ and $\boxed{4}\boxed{\times}\boxed{1}\boxed{0}\boxed{9}\boxed{8}\boxed{=}$ yield a display of 4392.

PROBLEM SET 6-1

1. Write a sentence illustrating $\frac{7}{8}$ used in each of the following ways.
   (a) As a division problem
   (b) As a part of a whole
   (c) As a ratio

2. For each of the following, write a fraction to represent the shaded portion.

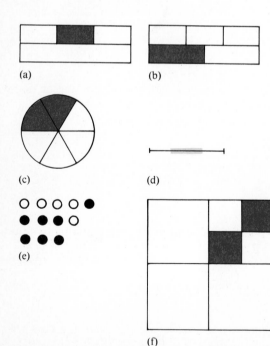

(a)   (b)

(c)   (d)

(e)

(f)

3. For each of the four squares below, write a fraction to represent the shaded portion. What property of fractions does the diagram illustrate?

(a)   (b)   (c)   (d)

4. For each of the following, write three fractions equal to the given fraction.

   (a) $\dfrac{2}{9}$ (b) $\dfrac{^-2}{5}$ (c) $\dfrac{0}{3}$ (d) $\dfrac{a}{2}$

5. Find the simplest form for each of the following fractions.

   (a) $\dfrac{156}{93}$ (b) $\dfrac{27}{45}$ (c) $\dfrac{^-65}{91}$

   (d) $\dfrac{0}{68}$ (e) $\dfrac{84^2}{91^2}$ (f) $\dfrac{6629}{70{,}395}$

6. Determine if the following pairs are equal by writing each in simplest form.

   (a) $\dfrac{3}{8}$ and $\dfrac{375}{1000}$ (b) $\dfrac{18}{54}$ and $\dfrac{23}{69}$

   (c) $\dfrac{6}{10}$ and $\dfrac{600}{1000}$ (d) $\dfrac{17}{27}$ and $\dfrac{25}{45}$

   (e) $\dfrac{24}{36}$ and $\dfrac{6}{9}$ (f) $\dfrac{^-7}{49}$ and $\dfrac{^-14}{98}$

7. Determine if the following pairs are equal by changing both to the same denominator.

   (a) $\dfrac{10}{16}$ and $\dfrac{12}{18}$ (b) $\dfrac{3}{12}$ and $\dfrac{41}{154}$

(c) $\dfrac{3}{^-12}$ and $\dfrac{^-36}{144}$ (d) $\dfrac{^-21}{86}$ and $\dfrac{^-51}{215}$

(e) $\dfrac{6}{10}$ and $\dfrac{6000}{10,000}$ (f) $\dfrac{^-a}{b}$ and $\dfrac{a}{^-b}$

8. (a) If $\dfrac{a}{c} = \dfrac{b}{c}$, what must be true?

   (b) If $\dfrac{a}{b} = \dfrac{a}{c}$, what must be true?

9. Solve for x in each of the following.

   (a) $\dfrac{2}{3} = \dfrac{x}{16}$ (b) $\dfrac{3}{4} = \dfrac{^-27}{x}$ (c) $\dfrac{3}{x} = \dfrac{3x}{x^2}$

10. Represent each of the following as a fraction.
   (a) The dots inside the circle as a part of all the dots in the figure
   (b) The dots inside the rectangle as a part of all the dots in the figure
   (c) The dots in the intersection of the rectangle and the circle as a part of all the dots in the figure
   (d) The dots outside the circle but inside the rectangle as a part of all the dots in the figure

11. Mr. Gonzales and Ms. Price gave the same test to their fifth-grade classes. In Mr. Gonzales' class, 20 out of 25 students passed the test, and in Ms. Price's class, 24 out of 30 students passed the test. One of Ms. Price's students heard about the results of the tests and claimed that the classes did equally well. Is the student right? Explain.

12. Choose the expression in parentheses that equals or best describes the given fraction.

   (a) $\dfrac{0}{0}$ (1, undefined, 0)

   (b) $\dfrac{5}{0}$ (undefined, 5, 0)

   (c) $\dfrac{0}{5}$ (0, undefined, 5)

   (d) $\dfrac{2 + a}{a}$ (2, 3, cannot be simplified)

   (e) $\dfrac{15 + x}{3x}$ $\left(\dfrac{5 + x}{x}, 5, \text{cannot be simplified}\right)$

   (f) $\dfrac{2^6 + 2^5}{2^4 + 2^7}$ $\left(1, \dfrac{2}{3}, \text{cannot be simplified}\right)$

   (g) $\dfrac{2^{100} + 2^{98}}{2^{100} - 2^{98}}$ $\left(2^{196}, \dfrac{5}{3}, \text{too large to simplify}\right)$

13. Find the simplest form for each of the following fractions.

   (a) $\dfrac{x}{x}$ (b) $\dfrac{14x^2y}{63xy^2}$ (c) $\dfrac{a^2 + ab}{a + b}$

   (d) $\dfrac{a^3 + 1}{a^3b}$ (e) $\dfrac{a}{3a + ab}$ (f) $\dfrac{a}{3a + b}$

14. Let W be the set of whole numbers, I be the set of integers, and Q be the set of rational numbers. Classify each of the following as true or false.
   (a) $W \subseteq Q$
   (b) $(I \cup W) \subset Q$
   (c) If Q is the universal set, $\bar{I} = W$.
   (d) $Q \cap I = W$
   (e) $Q \cap W = W$

15. Use a calculator to check whether each of the following pairs of fractions are equal.

   (a) $\dfrac{24}{31}$ and $\dfrac{23}{30}$ (b) $\dfrac{86}{75}$ and $\dfrac{85}{74}$

   (c) $\dfrac{1513}{1691}$ and $\dfrac{1581}{1767}$

Section 6-2   Addition and Subtraction of Rational Numbers

ADDITION OF RATIONAL NUMBERS WITH LIKE DENOMINATORS

To be able to describe mathematically the amount of liquid in a cup when $\frac{1}{3}$ cup of water is added to $\frac{1}{2}$ cup of water, it is necessary to add $\frac{1}{2} + \frac{1}{3}$. Before adding rational numbers with unlike denominators, we try the simpler problem of adding rational numbers with like denominators. For example, suppose a pizza is divided into five parts of equal size. If one person ate one piece of the pizza and another person ate two pieces of the pizza, then they ate $\frac{1}{5}$ and $\frac{2}{5}$ of the pizza, respectively, as shown in Figure 6-3.

Figure 6-3

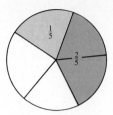

We see from the figure that $\frac{3}{5}$ of the pizza was eaten. That is, $\frac{1}{5} + \frac{2}{5} = \frac{3}{5}$, or

$$\frac{1}{5} + \frac{2}{5} = \frac{1+2}{5}$$

In general, we have the following definition for addition of rational numbers with like denominators.

DEFINITION

> If $\dfrac{a}{b}$ and $\dfrac{c}{b}$ are rational numbers, then $\dfrac{a}{b} + \dfrac{c}{b} = \dfrac{a+c}{b}$.

Remark   All properties of rational numbers in this section hold for any fractions.

The sum of two rational numbers can also be found using a number line. For example, to compute $\frac{1}{5} + \frac{2}{5}$, we use a number line with one unit divided into fifths, as shown in Figure 6-4.

Figure 6-4

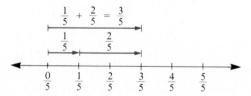

ADDITION OF RATIONAL NUMBERS WITH UNLIKE DENOMINATORS

To determine how to add fractions with unequal denominators—for example, $\frac{3}{8} + \frac{1}{6}$—we use the strategy of changing the problem into an equivalent problem that we already know how to do. We know how to add fractions with the same denominators, so we rewrite $\frac{3}{8}$ and $\frac{1}{6}$ with the same denominators and add.

$$\frac{3}{8} = \frac{3 \cdot 6}{8 \cdot 6} \quad \text{and} \quad \frac{1}{6} = \frac{8 \cdot 1}{8 \cdot 6}$$

Hence,

$$\frac{3}{8} + \frac{1}{6} = \frac{3 \cdot 6}{8 \cdot 6} + \frac{8 \cdot 1}{8 \cdot 6} = \frac{3 \cdot 6 + 8 \cdot 1}{8 \cdot 6} = \frac{18 + 8}{48} = \frac{26}{48}$$

In general, given two rational numbers $\frac{a}{b}$ and $\frac{c}{d}$, we may add the fractions as follows.

$$\frac{a}{b} + \frac{c}{d} = \frac{a \cdot d}{b \cdot d} + \frac{b \cdot c}{b \cdot d} = \frac{ad + bc}{bd}$$

This leads to a general definition for addition of rational numbers with unlike denominators.

DEFINITION

> If $\frac{a}{b}$ and $\frac{c}{d}$ are any two rational numbers, then $\frac{a}{b} + \frac{c}{d} = \frac{ad + bc}{bd}$.

Remark   It can be shown that the above definition also holds for addition of rational numbers with like denominators.

Example 6-4

Find each of the following sums.

(a) $\dfrac{2}{15} + \dfrac{4}{21}$ (b) $\dfrac{2}{^-3} + \dfrac{1}{5}$ (c) $\left(\dfrac{3}{4} + \dfrac{1}{5}\right) + \dfrac{1}{6}$

Solution

(a) $\dfrac{2}{15} + \dfrac{4}{21} = \dfrac{2 \cdot 21 + 15 \cdot 4}{15 \cdot 21} = \dfrac{102}{315}$, or $\dfrac{34}{105}$

(b) $\dfrac{2}{^-3} + \dfrac{1}{5} = \dfrac{(2)(5) + (^-3)(1)}{(^-3)(5)} = \dfrac{10 + {}^-3}{^-15} = \dfrac{7}{^-15}$

(c) $\dfrac{3}{4} + \dfrac{1}{5} = \dfrac{3 \cdot 5 + 4 \cdot 1}{4 \cdot 5} = \dfrac{19}{20}$. Hence, $\left(\dfrac{3}{4} + \dfrac{1}{5}\right) + \dfrac{1}{6} = \dfrac{19}{20} + \dfrac{1}{6} =$
$\dfrac{19 \cdot 6 + 20 \cdot 1}{20 \cdot 6} = \dfrac{134}{120}$ or $\dfrac{67}{60}$.

Remark   In Example 6-4(b), because $\dfrac{7}{^-15} = \dfrac{7(^-1)}{^-15(^-1)} = \dfrac{^-7}{15}$, then $\dfrac{7}{^-15} = \dfrac{^-7}{15}$.

Although $\dfrac{7}{^-15}$ is an acceptable answer, $\dfrac{^-7}{15}$ is the preferred form for the answer because it is customary to write fractions with positive denominators. $\left(\text{We later show that } \dfrac{^-7}{15} = -\dfrac{7}{15}.\right)$

In Example 6-4(a), we used the product of the denominators as a common denominator to add the fractions $\frac{2}{15}$ and $\frac{4}{21}$. We also could find LCM(15, 21), which is the *least common denominator* for these two fractions. Because LCM(15, 21) = 105, we have the following.

$$\frac{2}{15} + \frac{4}{21} = \frac{14}{105} + \frac{20}{105} = \frac{34}{105}$$

MIXED NUMBERS

mixed number   The sum of an integer and a rational number is often written as a **mixed number.** For example, $1 + \frac{3}{4}$ can be written as $1\frac{3}{4}$. Children sometimes infer that $1\frac{3}{4}$ means 1 times $\frac{3}{4}$, since yx means $y \cdot x$. This is not the case; $1\frac{3}{4}$ means $1 + \frac{3}{4}$. Also, the number $^-4\frac{3}{4}$ means $^-(4 + \frac{3}{4})$, not $^-4 + \frac{3}{4}$.

A mixed number is a rational number, and therefore it can always be written in the form $\frac{a}{b}$. For example,

$$1\frac{3}{4} = 1 + \frac{3}{4} = \frac{1}{1} + \frac{3}{4} = \frac{1 \cdot 4 + 1 \cdot 3}{1 \cdot 4} = \frac{4 + 3}{4} = \frac{7}{4}$$

proper fraction   A fraction $\frac{a}{b}$, where $0 \le |a| < |b|$, is called a **proper fraction.** For example, $\frac{4}{7}$ is a proper fraction, but $\frac{7}{4}$ and $\frac{4}{4}$ are not proper fractions.

Example 6-5

Change each of the following mixed numbers to the form $\frac{a}{b}$, where a and b are integers.

(a) $4\frac{1}{3}$ (b) $^-3\frac{2}{5}$

Solution

(a) $4\frac{1}{3} = 4 + \frac{1}{3} = \frac{4}{1} + \frac{1}{3} = \frac{4 \cdot 3 + 1 \cdot 1}{1 \cdot 3} = \frac{12 + 1}{3} = \frac{13}{3}$

(b) $^-3\frac{2}{5} = ^-\left(3 + \frac{2}{5}\right) = ^-\left(\frac{3}{1} + \frac{2}{5}\right) = ^-\left(\frac{3 \cdot 5 + 1 \cdot 2}{1 \cdot 5}\right) = \frac{^-17}{5}$

Example 6-6

Change $\frac{29}{5}$ to a mixed number.

Solution

By the division algorithm, $29 = 5 \cdot 5 + 4$. Thus,

$$\frac{29}{5} = \frac{5 \cdot 5 + 4}{5} = \frac{5 \cdot 5}{5} + \frac{4}{5} = 5 + \frac{4}{5} = 5\frac{4}{5}$$

In elementary schools, problems like Example 6-6 are usually solved using division.

$$
\begin{array}{r}
5 \\
5\overline{)29} \\
\underline{25} \\
4
\end{array}
$$

Hence, $\frac{29}{5} = 5 + \frac{4}{5} = 5\frac{4}{5}$.

Example 6-7

Find $2\frac{4}{5} + 3\frac{5}{6}$.

Solution

The problem is solved in two ways for comparison.

Add the fractional parts and the integers of the mixed numbers separately.

$$2\frac{4}{5} = \quad 2\frac{24}{30}$$

$$+3\frac{5}{6} = +3\frac{25}{30}$$

$$\overline{\phantom{+3\frac{5}{6}}\quad 5\frac{49}{30}}$$

But,

$$\frac{49}{30} = 1\frac{19}{30}$$

so

$$5\frac{49}{30} = 5 + \frac{49}{30} = 5 + 1\frac{19}{30} = 6\frac{19}{30}$$

Change each mixed number into a rational number in the form $\frac{a}{b}$ and then add.

$$2\frac{4}{5} + 3\frac{5}{6} = \frac{14}{5} + \frac{23}{6}$$

$$= \frac{14 \cdot 6 + 5 \cdot 23}{5 \cdot 6}$$

$$= \frac{84 + 115}{30}$$

$$= \frac{199}{30}$$

$$= 6\frac{19}{30}$$

Remark   The first method of adding mixed numbers is more efficient when the fractional parts add up to a fraction less than 1. For example, $178\frac{2}{13} + 22\frac{5}{13} = (178 + 22) + (\frac{2}{13} + \frac{5}{13}) = 200 + \frac{7}{13} = 200\frac{7}{13}$

PROPERTIES OF ADDITION FOR RATIONAL NUMBERS

As with integers, rational numbers have the following properties for addition: closure property, commutative property, associative property, additive identity property, and additive inverse property. To emphasize the additive inverse property of rational numbers, we state it explicitly.

Property   **Additive Inverse Property of Rational Numbers**   For any rational number $\frac{a}{b}$, there exists a unique rational number $-\frac{a}{b}$, called the additive inverse of $\frac{a}{b}$, such that $\frac{a}{b} + \left(-\frac{a}{b}\right) = 0 = \left(-\frac{a}{b}\right) + \frac{a}{b}$.

Another form of $-\frac{a}{b}$ can be found by considering the sum $\frac{a}{b} + \frac{^-a}{b}$. Because

$$\frac{a}{b} + \frac{^-a}{b} = \frac{a + \,^-a}{b} = \frac{0}{b} = 0$$

$-\dfrac{a}{b}$ and $\dfrac{^-a}{b}$ are both additive inverses of $\dfrac{a}{b}$, so $-\dfrac{a}{b} = \dfrac{^-a}{b}$. Also, since $\dfrac{^-a}{b} = \dfrac{a}{^-b}$,

then $-\dfrac{a}{b} = \dfrac{a}{^-b}$.

Example 6-8

Find the additive inverses for each of the following.

(a) $\dfrac{3}{5}$ (b) $\dfrac{^-5}{11}$ (c) $4\dfrac{1}{2}$

Solution

(a) $\dfrac{^-3}{5}$ or $-\dfrac{3}{5}$ (b) $-\left(\dfrac{^-5}{11}\right)$ or $\dfrac{5}{11}$ (c) $^-4\dfrac{1}{2}$

Properties of the additive inverse for rational numbers are analogous to those of the additive inverse for integers, as shown in Table 6-2.

Table 6-2

Properties of Additive Inverse

Integers	Rational Numbers
1. $^-(^-a) = a$	1. $-\left(-\dfrac{a}{b}\right) = \dfrac{a}{b}$
2. $^-(a + b) = {}^-a + {}^-b$	2. $-\left(\dfrac{a}{b} + \dfrac{c}{d}\right) = \dfrac{^-a}{b} + \dfrac{^-c}{d}$

As with the set of integers, the set of rational numbers also has the addition property of equality.

Property Addition Property of Equality If $\dfrac{a}{b}$ and $\dfrac{c}{d}$ are any rational numbers such that $\dfrac{a}{b} = \dfrac{c}{d}$, and if $\dfrac{e}{f}$ is any rational number, then

$$\dfrac{a}{b} + \dfrac{e}{f} = \dfrac{c}{d} + \dfrac{e}{f}.$$

SUBTRACTION OF RATIONAL NUMBERS

Subtraction of rational numbers, like subtraction of integers, is defined in terms of addition.

DEFINITION

Subtraction of Rational Numbers If $\dfrac{a}{b}$ and $\dfrac{c}{d}$ are any rational numbers, then

$$\dfrac{a}{b} - \dfrac{c}{d} = \dfrac{e}{f} \text{ if and only if } \dfrac{a}{b} = \dfrac{c}{d} + \dfrac{e}{f}.$$

As with integers, it can be shown that subtraction of rational numbers can be performed by adding the additive inverses. This is stated in the following theorem.

THEOREM 6-1

> If $\dfrac{a}{b}$ and $\dfrac{c}{d}$ are any rational numbers, then $\dfrac{a}{b} - \dfrac{c}{d} = \dfrac{a}{b} + \dfrac{^{-}c}{d}$.

Now, using the definition of addition of rational numbers, we obtain the following.

$$\frac{a}{b} - \frac{c}{d} = \frac{a}{b} + \frac{^{-}c}{d}$$

$$= \frac{ad + b(^{-}c)}{bd}$$

$$= \frac{ad - bc}{bd}$$

We summarize this result in the following theorem.

THEOREM 6-2

> If $\dfrac{a}{b}$ and $\dfrac{c}{d}$ are any rational numbers, then $\dfrac{a}{b} - \dfrac{c}{d} = \dfrac{ad - bc}{bd}$.

Example 6-9

Find each difference.

(a) $\dfrac{5}{8} - \dfrac{1}{4}$ (b) $5\dfrac{1}{3} - 2\dfrac{3}{4}$

Solution

(a) $\dfrac{5}{8} - \dfrac{1}{4} = \dfrac{5 \cdot 4 - 8 \cdot 1}{8 \cdot 4} = \dfrac{5 \cdot 4 - 8 \cdot 1}{32} = \dfrac{12}{32}$ or $\dfrac{3}{8}$

An alternative and often more efficient approach is to first find the least common denominator for the fractions. Because LCM(8, 4) = 8, we have

$$\frac{5}{8} - \frac{1}{4} = \frac{5}{8} - \frac{2}{8} = \frac{3}{8}$$

(b) Two methods of solution are given.

$$
\begin{array}{l}
5\dfrac{1}{3} = \quad 5\dfrac{4}{12} = \quad 4 + 1\dfrac{4}{12} = \quad 4\dfrac{16}{12} \\[2mm]
-2\dfrac{3}{4} = -2\dfrac{9}{12} = \qquad\quad -2\dfrac{9}{12} \quad = -2\dfrac{9}{12} \\[2mm]
\hline
\qquad\qquad\qquad\qquad\qquad\qquad\qquad\qquad\quad 2\dfrac{7}{12}
\end{array}
$$

$$
\begin{aligned}
5\dfrac{1}{3} - 2\dfrac{3}{4} &= \dfrac{16}{3} - \dfrac{11}{4} \\[2mm]
&= \dfrac{16 \cdot 4 - 3 \cdot 11}{3 \cdot 4} \\[2mm]
&= \dfrac{64 - 33}{12} \\[2mm]
&= \dfrac{31}{12} \text{ or } 2\dfrac{7}{12}
\end{aligned}
$$

PROBLEM SET 6-2

1. Use a number line to find $\frac{1}{5} + \frac{2}{3}$.
2. In each case, perform the computation using the least common denominator.

   (a) $\dfrac{3}{16} + \dfrac{7}{-8}$ (b) $\dfrac{4}{12} - \dfrac{2}{3}$

   (c) $\dfrac{5}{6} + \dfrac{-4}{9} + \dfrac{2}{3}$ (d) $\dfrac{2}{21} - \dfrac{3}{14}$

3. Use the definition of addition of rational numbers to find each of the following.

   (a) $\dfrac{6}{5} + \dfrac{-11}{4}$ (b) $\dfrac{4}{5} + \dfrac{6}{7}$

   (c) $\dfrac{-7}{8} + \dfrac{2}{5}$ (d) $\dfrac{5}{x} + \dfrac{-3}{y}$

4. Add the following rational numbers. Write your answers in simplest form.

   (a) $\dfrac{6}{7} + \dfrac{3}{14}$ (b) $\dfrac{-2}{3} + \dfrac{-4}{7} + \dfrac{3}{21}$

   (c) $\dfrac{-3}{2x} + \dfrac{3}{2y} + \dfrac{-1}{4xy}$ (d) $\dfrac{-3}{2x^2y} + \dfrac{5}{6xy^2} + \dfrac{7}{x^2}$

5. Change each of the following fractions to mixed numbers.

   (a) $\dfrac{56}{3}$ (b) $\dfrac{14}{5}$

   (c) $-\dfrac{293}{100}$ (d) $-\dfrac{47}{8}$

6. Change each of the following mixed numbers to fractions in the form $\dfrac{a}{b}$ where a and b are integers.

   (a) $6\dfrac{3}{4}$ (b) $7\dfrac{1}{2}$

   (c) $^-3\dfrac{5}{8}$ (b) $^-4\dfrac{2}{3}$

7. Compute the following.

   (a) $2\dfrac{1}{3} - 1\dfrac{3}{4}$ (b) $2\dfrac{1}{3} + 1\dfrac{3}{4}$ (c) $3\dfrac{5}{6} - 2\dfrac{1}{8}$

   (d) $\dfrac{5}{6} + 2\dfrac{1}{8}$ (e) $^-4\dfrac{1}{2} - 3\dfrac{1}{6}$ (f) $^-4\dfrac{3}{4} + 2\dfrac{5}{6}$

   (g) $\dfrac{5}{2^4 \cdot 3^2} - \dfrac{1}{2^3 \cdot 3^4}$ (h) $\dfrac{11}{2^3 \cdot 5^4 \cdot 7^5} + \dfrac{3}{2^4 \cdot 5^3 \cdot 7}$

   (i) $11 - \left(\dfrac{3}{5} + \dfrac{-4}{45}\right)$ (j) $\dfrac{3}{4} - \left(2\dfrac{3}{4} - 1\dfrac{1}{2}\right)$

   (k) $134\dfrac{13}{16} - 131\dfrac{1}{4}$

8. Perform the indicated operations and write your answers in simplest form.

   (a) $\dfrac{d}{bc} - \dfrac{a}{bc}$ (b) $\dfrac{d}{b} + \dfrac{a}{bc}$

   (c) $\dfrac{7}{a-b} + \dfrac{5}{a+b}$ (d) $\dfrac{a^2b}{c} - \dfrac{bc}{ad}$

   (e) $\dfrac{a}{a-b} + \dfrac{b}{a+b}$ (f) $\dfrac{a}{a^2-b^2} - \dfrac{b}{a-b}$

9. What, if anything, is wrong with each of the following?

   (a) $2 = \dfrac{6}{3} = \dfrac{3+3}{3} = \dfrac{3}{3} + 3 = 1 + 3 = 4$

   (b) $1 = \dfrac{4}{2+2} = \dfrac{4}{2} + \dfrac{4}{2} = 2 + 2 = 4$

   (c) $\dfrac{ab + c}{a} = \dfrac{\cancel{a}b + c}{\cancel{a}} = b + c$

   (d) $\dfrac{a^2 - b^2}{a - b} = \dfrac{a \cdot \cancel{a} - b \cdot \cancel{b}}{\cancel{a} - \cancel{b}} = a - b$

   (e) $\dfrac{a+c}{b+c} = \dfrac{a + \cancel{c}}{b + \cancel{c}} = \dfrac{a}{b}$

10. Joe lives $\frac{4}{10}$ mile from the university, and Mary lives $\frac{1}{6}$ mile away from it. How much further from the university does Joe live than Mary?
11. A clerk sold three pieces of ribbon. One piece was $\frac{1}{3}$ yard long, another piece was $2\frac{3}{4}$ yards long, and the third was $3\frac{1}{2}$ yards long. What was the total length of ribbon sold?
12. In a certain Swiss city, each resident speaks only one language: $\frac{3}{4}$ speak German, $\frac{1}{8}$ speak French, and $\frac{1}{16}$ speak Italian. What fraction of the residents speak neither German, French, nor Italian?
13. A recipe requires $3\frac{1}{4}$ cups of flour. Dan has $1\frac{3}{8}$ cups of flour. How much more flour does he need?
14. A recipe requires $3\frac{1}{2}$ cups of milk. Ran put in $\frac{3}{4}$ cup and then another cup. How much more milk does he need to put in?
15. Joel worked $9\frac{1}{2}$ hours one week grading math assignments and $11\frac{2}{3}$ hours the next week. How many more hours did he work the second week than the first?

16. Martine bought $8\frac{3}{4}$ yards of fabric. If she wants to make a skirt using $1\frac{7}{8}$ yards, pants using $2\frac{3}{8}$ yards, and a vest using $1\frac{2}{3}$ yards, how much fabric will be left over?

17. A plywood board $15\frac{3}{4}$ inches long is cut from a $38\frac{1}{4}$-inch board. The saw cut takes $\frac{3}{8}$ inch. How long is the piece of board left after cutting?

18. Make up a word problem that can be solved by finding each of the following.

(a) $10\frac{3}{4} - 6\frac{7}{8}$ (b) $\left(2\frac{1}{2} + 3\frac{1}{4}\right) - 5$

(c) $12\frac{1}{4} - \left(\frac{3}{8} + \frac{5}{12}\right)$ (d) $\frac{5}{12} + \frac{7}{8} - \left(\frac{1}{4} + \frac{3}{12}\right)$

19. Demonstrate by example that each of the following properties of rational numbers holds.
(a) Closure property of addition
(b) Commutative property of addition
(c) Addition property of equality
(d) Associative property of addition

20. Does each of the following properties hold for subtraction of rational numbers? Justify your answer.
(a) Closure   (b) Commutative
(c) Associative   (d) Identity
(e) Inverse
(f) Subtraction property of equality

21. For each of the following sequences, discover a pattern and write three more terms of the sequence if the pattern continues. Which of the sequences are arithmetic and which are not? Justify your answers.

(a) $\dfrac{1}{4}, \dfrac{1}{2}, \dfrac{3}{4}, 1, \dfrac{5}{4}, \ldots$

(b) $\dfrac{1}{2}, \dfrac{2}{3}, \dfrac{3}{4}, \dfrac{4}{5}, \dfrac{5}{6}, \ldots$

(c) $\dfrac{2}{3}, \dfrac{5}{3}, \dfrac{8}{3}, \dfrac{11}{3}, \dfrac{14}{3}, \ldots$

(d) $\dfrac{1}{2}, \dfrac{1}{3}, \dfrac{1}{4}, \dfrac{1}{5}, \dfrac{1}{6}, \ldots$

(e) $\dfrac{5}{4}, \dfrac{3}{4}, \dfrac{1}{4}, \dfrac{^-1}{4}, \dfrac{^-3}{4}, \ldots$

22. Find the nth term in each of the sequences in Problem 21.

23. Insert five fractions between the numbers 1 and 2 so that the seven numbers (including 1 and 2) constitute an arithmetic sequence.

24. Let $f(x) = x + \frac{3}{4}$.
(a) Find the outputs if the inputs are:

(i) 0   (ii) $\dfrac{4}{3}$ (iii) $\dfrac{^-3}{4}$

(b) For which inputs will the outputs be:

(i) 1   (ii) -1 (iii) $\dfrac{1}{2}$

25. Let $f(x) = \dfrac{x+2}{x-1}$ and let the domain of the function be the set of all integers except 1. Find the following:
(a) $f(0)$ (b) $f(^-2)$ (c) $f(^-5)$ (d) $f(5)$

26. (a) Check that each of the following is true.

$$\frac{1}{3} = \frac{1}{4} + \frac{1}{3\cdot4} \qquad \frac{1}{4} = \frac{1}{5} + \frac{1}{4\cdot5}$$

$$\frac{1}{5} = \frac{1}{6} + \frac{1}{5\cdot6}$$

(b) Based on the examples in (a), write $\dfrac{1}{n}$ as a sum of two unit fractions, that is, fractions with numerator 1.

★(c) Prove your answer in (b).

27. (a) Check that each of the first five fractions in the following sequence is in simplest form.

$$\frac{2}{3}, \frac{3}{5}, \frac{5}{7}, \frac{7}{9}, \frac{9}{11}, \cdots$$

★(b) Create a new, infinite sequence whose terms are fractions in simplest form.

★(c) Prove that all the fractions in the original sequence and the sequence you created in (b) are in simplest form.

Review Problems

28. Write each of the following fractions in simplest form.

(a) $\dfrac{14}{21}$ (b) $\dfrac{117}{153}$ (c) $\dfrac{5^2}{7^2}$

(d) $\dfrac{a^2+a}{1+a}$ (e) $\dfrac{a^2+1}{a+1}$

29. Determine if each of the following pairs of fractions is equal.

(a) $\dfrac{3}{17}$ and $\dfrac{69}{391}$ (b) $\dfrac{^-145}{261}$ and $\dfrac{^-155}{279}$

(c) $\dfrac{a^2}{b}$ and $\dfrac{a^2b^2}{b^3}$ (d) $\dfrac{377}{400}$ and $\dfrac{378}{401}$

(e) $\dfrac{0}{10}$ and $\dfrac{0}{^-10}$ (f) $\dfrac{a}{b}$ and $\dfrac{a+1}{b+1}$, where $a \neq b$

COMPUTER CORNER

The following is a **BASIC** program for adding two rational numbers and obtaining the result in the simplest form. The program may be used as a drill for addition of fractions. Type this program into your computer and run it to add the following:

(a) $\dfrac{2}{5} + \dfrac{8}{10}$ (b) $\dfrac{3}{4} + \dfrac{1}{3}$

```
 10 REM ADDITION OF FRACTIONS
 15 PRINT "THIS PROGRAM IS AN ADDITION OF FRACTIONS DRILL."
 20 PRINT "ENTER THE NUMERATOR AND DENOMINATOR OF"
 30 PRINT "THE FIRST FRACTION SEPARATED BY A COMMA."
 40 INPUT A, B
 50 PRINT "ENTER THE NUMERATOR AND DENOMINATOR OF"
 60 PRINT "THE SECOND FRACTION SEPARATED BY A COMMA."
 70 INPUT C, D
 80 LET N = D * A + B * C
 90 LET E = B * D
100 REM REDUCE THE FRACTION N/E
110 IF N < E THEN M = N
115 IF N > = E THEN M = E
120 FOR I = M TO 1 STEP -1
130 IF N/I = INT (N/I) AND E/I = INT (E/I) THEN 150
140 NEXT I
150 REM GCD = I
160 LET N = N/I
170 LET E = E/I
180 PRINT
190 PRINT "ENTER NUMERATOR AND DENOMINATOR OF THE"
200 PRINT "SUM IN LOWEST TERMS"
210 INPUT X, Y
220 IF X = N AND Y = E THEN PRINT "CORRECT" GOTO 240
230 PRINT "NO, THAT IS WRONG."
240 PRINT "DO YOU WANT TO ADD OTHER FRACTIONS (YES OR NO)"
250 INPUT Q$
260 IF Q$ = "YES" THEN 15
270 END
```

BRAIN TEASER

When Professor Sum was asked by Mr. Little how many students were in his classes, he answered, "All of them study either languages, physics, or not at all. One half of them study languages only, one fourth of them study French, one seventh of them study physics only, and there are 20 who do not study at all." How many students does Professor Sum have?

Section 6-3

Multiplication and Division of Rational Numbers

MULTIPLICATION OF RATIONAL NUMBERS

To approach the definition of multiplication of rational numbers, we first consider multiplication by 1. As with integers, we would like 1 to be the multiplicative identity for rationals; that is, we want $\frac{a}{b} \cdot 1 = 1 \cdot \frac{a}{b} = \frac{a}{b}$. Because $\frac{2}{3}$ can be interpreted as 2 of 3 equal parts of a whole, $\frac{2}{3} \cdot 1$ can be thought of as 2 of 3 equal parts of 1, that is, $\frac{2}{3}$ of 1. Similarly, we interpret $\frac{2}{3} \cdot \frac{2}{5}$ as 2 of 3 equal parts of $\frac{2}{5}$. Using this interpretation, we will show how to write $\frac{2}{3} \cdot \frac{2}{5}$ as a rational number in the form $\frac{a}{b}$.

Figure 6-5(a) shows a one-unit rectangle separated into fifths, with $\frac{2}{5}$ shaded. Figure 6-5(b) shows the rectangle further separated into thirds, with $\frac{2}{3}$ shaded. The crosshatched portion represents $\frac{2}{3}$ of $\frac{2}{5}$. In order to find $\frac{2}{3}$ of $\frac{2}{5}$, we could divide just the shaded portion of the rectangle in Figure 6-5(a) into 3 equal parts and take 2 of those parts. The result would be the crosshatched portion of 6-5(b). However, the crosshatched portion represents 4 parts out of 15, or $\frac{4}{15}$, of the one-unit rectangle. Thus,

$$\frac{2}{3} \cdot \frac{2}{5} = \frac{4}{15} = \frac{2 \cdot 2}{3 \cdot 5}$$

Figure 6-5

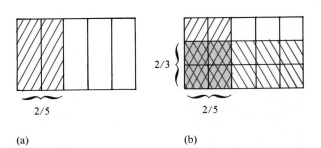

2/3

2/5   2/5

(a)   (b)

This discussion leads to the following definition of multiplication for rational numbers.

DEFINITION

If $\frac{a}{b}$ and $\frac{c}{d}$ are any rational numbers, then $\frac{a}{b} \cdot \frac{c}{d} = \frac{a \cdot c}{b \cdot d}$.

Another approach for motivating the definition of multiplication of rational numbers involves the interpretation of multiplication as repeated addition. Using repeated addition, $8 \cdot \frac{1}{4}$ can be interpreted as follows.

$$8 \cdot \frac{1}{4} = \frac{1}{4} + \frac{1}{4} + \frac{1}{4} + \frac{1}{4} + \frac{1}{4} + \frac{1}{4} + \frac{1}{4} + \frac{1}{4} = \frac{8}{4} = 2$$

If the commutative property of multiplication for rational numbers is to be true, then $8 \cdot \frac{1}{4} = \frac{1}{4} \cdot 8 = 2$. The product $\frac{1}{4} \cdot 8$ may be thought of as $\frac{1}{4}$ of 8, because if 8 is divided into four equal parts, the result is also 2. Similarly, we can interpret $\frac{1}{4} \cdot \frac{1}{3}$ as $\frac{1}{4}$ of $\frac{1}{3}$—that is, one part when $\frac{1}{3}$ is divided into four equal parts.

Example 6-10

Find each of the following products.

(a) $\frac{5}{6} \cdot \frac{7}{11}$ (b) $6 \cdot \frac{1}{5}$ (c) $2\frac{1}{3} \cdot 3\frac{1}{5}$

Solution

(a) $\frac{5}{6} \cdot \frac{7}{11} = \frac{5 \cdot 7}{6 \cdot 11} = \frac{35}{66}$

(b) $6 \cdot \frac{1}{5} = \frac{6}{1} \cdot \frac{1}{5} = \frac{6 \cdot 1}{1 \cdot 5} = \frac{6}{5}$

(c) $2\frac{1}{3} \cdot 3\frac{1}{5} = \frac{7}{3} \cdot \frac{16}{5} = \frac{7 \cdot 16}{3 \cdot 5} = \frac{112}{15} = 7\frac{7}{15}$

PROPERTIES OF MULTIPLICATION FOR RATIONAL NUMBERS

Multiplication of rational numbers has properties analogous to the properties of addition of rational numbers. These include the following properties for multiplication: closure property, commutative property, associative property, multiplicative identity, and multiplicative inverse. For emphasis, we list the last two properties.

Properties   **Multiplicative Identity of Rational Numbers**   The number 1 is the unique number such that for every rational number $\frac{a}{b}$,

$$1 \cdot \left(\frac{a}{b}\right) = \frac{a}{b} = \left(\frac{a}{b}\right) \cdot 1$$

Multiplicative Inverse of Rational Numbers   For any nonzero rational number $\frac{a}{b}$, $\frac{b}{a}$ is the unique rational number such that $\frac{a}{b} \cdot \frac{b}{a} = 1 = \frac{b}{a} \cdot \frac{a}{b}$. The multiplicative inverse of $\frac{a}{b}$ is also called the **reciprocal** of $\frac{a}{b}$.

reciprocal

As with integers, multiplication and addition are connected through the distributive property for multiplication over addition, as shown on next page.

Property Distributive Property for Multiplication over Addition of Rational Numbers   If $\frac{a}{b}, \frac{c}{d}$, and $\frac{e}{f}$ are any rational numbers, then

$$\frac{a}{b}\left(\frac{c}{d}+\frac{e}{f}\right)=\left(\frac{a}{b}\cdot\frac{c}{d}\right)+\left(\frac{a}{b}\cdot\frac{e}{f}\right)$$

Example 6-11

Find the multiplicative inverse of each of the following rational numbers.

(a) $\frac{2}{3}$ (b) $\frac{^-2}{5}$ (c) 4   (d) 0   (e) $6\frac{1}{2}$

Solution

(a) $\frac{3}{2}$

(b) $\frac{5}{-2}$, which can be written as $\frac{^-5}{2}$

(c) Because $4=\frac{4}{1}$, the multiplicative inverse of 4 is $\frac{1}{4}$.

(d) Even though $0=\frac{0}{1},\frac{1}{0}$ is undefined, so there is no multiplicative inverse of 0.

(e) Because $6\frac{1}{2}=\frac{13}{2}$, the multiplicative inverse of $6\frac{1}{2}$ is $\frac{2}{13}$.

The following are additional properties for multiplication on the set of rational numbers.

Properties Multiplication Property of Equality for Rational Numbers   If $\frac{a}{b}$ and $\frac{c}{d}$ are any rational numbers such that $\frac{a}{b}=\frac{c}{d}$, and $\frac{e}{f}$ is any rational number, then $\frac{a}{b}\cdot\frac{e}{f}=\frac{c}{d}\cdot\frac{e}{f}$.

Multiplication Property of Zero for Rational Numbers   If $\frac{a}{b}$ is any rational number, then $\frac{a}{b}\cdot 0=0=0\cdot\frac{a}{b}$.

Example 6-12

Solve for x.

(a) $\frac{3}{2}x=\frac{3}{4}$ (b) $\frac{2}{3}x-\frac{1}{5}=\frac{3}{4}$

Solution

(a) The reciprocal of a fraction times the fraction yields 1, so we multiply both sides of the equation by $\frac{2}{3}$, the reciprocal of $\frac{3}{2}$.

$$\frac{3}{2}x = \frac{3}{4}$$

$$\frac{2}{3} \cdot \frac{3}{2}x = \frac{2}{3} \cdot \frac{3}{4}$$

$$1 \cdot x = \frac{2 \cdot 3}{3 \cdot 4} \qquad x = \frac{1}{2}$$

(b) We would like to "eliminate" $-\frac{1}{5}$ from the left side of the equation. To achieve this goal, we add $\frac{1}{5}$ to both sides of the equation and proceed using the technique of part (a).

$$\frac{2}{3}x - \frac{1}{5} = \frac{3}{4}$$

$$\frac{2}{3}x - \frac{1}{5} + \frac{1}{5} = \frac{3}{4} + \frac{1}{5}$$

$$\frac{2}{3}x = \frac{19}{20}$$

$$\frac{3}{2} \cdot \frac{2}{3}x = \frac{3}{2} \cdot \frac{19}{20}$$

$$x = \frac{57}{40}$$

Remark In part (a) of Example 6-12, $\frac{3}{2}x$ can be treated as $\frac{3}{2} \cdot \frac{x}{1}$, or $\frac{3 \cdot x}{2 \cdot 1} = \frac{3x}{2}$. Hence, $\frac{3}{2}x = \frac{3x}{2}$.

DIVISION OF RATIONAL NUMBERS

Children should have many concrete experiences with problems involving division of rational numbers before being introduced to the formal definition and algorithm. Consider the following examples.

Example 6-13

The fraction $2\frac{1}{4}$ is modeled in Figure 6-6(a). How many of the pieces shown in Figure 6-6(b) are there in the $2\frac{1}{4}$ piece?

Figure 6-6

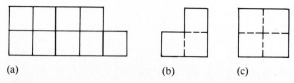

(a)   (b)   (c)

Solution

Figure 6-6(b) represents $\frac{3}{4}$ of a larger square pictured in Figure 6-6(c). To determine $2\frac{1}{4} \div \frac{3}{4}$, we may find how many $\frac{3}{4}$ pieces, shown in Figure 6-6(b), would fit in the $2\frac{1}{4}$ piece in Figure 6-6(a). In Figure 6-7, we see that exactly three of the $\frac{3}{4}$ pieces fit in the $2\frac{1}{4}$ piece.

Figure 6-7

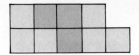

Example 6-14

An empty swimming pool is to be filled until it is $\frac{9}{10}$ full. If it takes half an hour to fill $\frac{3}{10}$ of the pool, how long will it take to fill $\frac{9}{10}$ of the pool?

Solution

We need to find how many $\frac{3}{10}$s there are in $\frac{9}{10}$, that is, solve the division problem $\frac{9}{10} \div \frac{3}{10}$. Because $3 \cdot \frac{3}{10} = \frac{9}{10}$, the answer is 3. Thus, it would take 3 half hours, or $1\frac{1}{2}$ hours, to fill the pool.

Formally, we define division for rational numbers in terms of multiplication in the same way as we define division for integers.

DEFINITION

> If $\frac{a}{b}$ and $\frac{c}{d}$ are any rational numbers and $\frac{c}{d}$ is not zero, then $\frac{a}{b} \div \frac{c}{d} = \frac{e}{f}$ if and only if $\frac{e}{f}$ is the unique rational number such that $\frac{c}{d} \cdot \frac{e}{f} = \frac{a}{b}$.

Remark   In the definition of division, $\frac{c}{d}$ is not zero because division by zero is impossible. Also, $\frac{c}{d} \neq 0$ implies that $c \neq 0$.

ALGORITHM FOR DIVISION OF RATIONAL NUMBERS

Recall that the set of integers is not closed under division. However, the set of rational numbers is closed under division as long as we do not divide by 0. To find an algorithm for rational-number division, examine the following examples.

Example 6-15

Find $1 \div \frac{2}{3}$.

Solution

By definition, $1 \div \frac{2}{3} = x$ if and only if $\frac{2}{3} \cdot x = 1$. Since $\frac{2}{3}$ and x must be multiplicative inverses of each other, $x = \frac{3}{2}$. Thus, $1 \div \frac{2}{3} = \frac{3}{2}$.

Example 6-15

Find $\frac{2}{3} \div \frac{5}{7}$.

Solution

Let $\frac{2}{3} \div \frac{5}{7} = x$. Then, $\frac{5}{7} \cdot x = \frac{2}{3}$. To solve for x, multiply both sides of the equation by the reciprocal of $\frac{5}{7}$, namely, $\frac{7}{5}$. Thus,

$$\frac{7}{5}\left(\frac{5}{7} x\right) = \frac{7}{5} \cdot \frac{2}{3}$$

Hence,

$$x = \frac{7}{5} \cdot \frac{2}{3} = \frac{14}{15}$$

The procedures in Examples 6-15 and 6-16 suggest using an extension of the Fundamental Law of Fractions, $\frac{a}{b} = \frac{ac}{bc}$, where a, b, and c are all fractions.

$$\frac{2}{3} \div \frac{5}{7} = \frac{\frac{2}{3}}{\frac{5}{7}} = \frac{\frac{2}{3} \cdot \frac{7}{5}}{\frac{5}{7} \cdot \frac{7}{5}} = \frac{\frac{2}{3} \cdot \frac{7}{5}}{1} = \frac{2}{3} \cdot \frac{7}{5} = \frac{2}{3} \cdot \frac{7}{5}$$

Thus,

$$\frac{2}{3} \div \frac{5}{7} = \frac{2}{3} \cdot \frac{7}{5}$$

The preceding equations illustrate the standard algorithm "invert and multiply" that is taught in elementary school.

ALGORITHM FOR DIVISION OF FRACTIONS

$$\frac{a}{b} \div \frac{c}{d} = \frac{a}{b} \cdot \frac{d}{c}, \text{ where } \frac{c}{d} \neq 0.$$

Examples of this algorithm are seen on page 257, which is from *Addison-Wesley Mathematics*, 1987, Grade 6.

Remark An alternative approach for developing an algorithm for division of fractions can be found by first dividing fractions with equal denominators. For example, $\frac{9}{10} \div \frac{3}{10} = 9 \div 3$ and $\frac{15}{23} \div \frac{5}{23} = 15 \div 5$. These examples suggest that when two fractions with the same denominators are divided, the result can be obtained by dividing the numerator of the first fraction by the numerator of the second. To divide fractions with different denominators, we rename the fractions so that the denominators are equal. Thus,

$$\frac{a}{b} \div \frac{c}{d} = \frac{ad}{bd} \div \frac{bc}{bd} = ad \div bc = \frac{ad}{bc}.$$

Example 6-17

Perform each of the following divisions and write your answers in simplest form.

(a) $\dfrac{^-5}{6} \div \dfrac{^-3}{8}$ (b) $5\dfrac{1}{6} \div 4\dfrac{2}{3}$ (c) $\dfrac{\frac{1}{4} + \frac{^-3}{2}}{\frac{5}{6} + \frac{7}{8}}$

Solution

(a) $\dfrac{^-5}{6} \div \dfrac{^-3}{8} = \dfrac{^-5}{6} \cdot \dfrac{8}{^-3} = \dfrac{^-40}{^-18} = \dfrac{20}{9}$

(b) $5\dfrac{1}{6} \div 4\dfrac{2}{3} = \dfrac{31}{6} \div \dfrac{14}{3} = \dfrac{31}{6} \cdot \dfrac{3}{14} = \dfrac{93}{84} = \dfrac{31}{28}$, or $1\dfrac{3}{28}$

(c) We first perform the additions and then do the division.

$$\frac{1}{4} + \frac{^-3}{2} = \frac{1}{4} + \frac{^-6}{4} = \frac{^-5}{4}$$

$$\frac{5}{6} + \frac{7}{8} = \frac{20}{24} + \frac{21}{24} = \frac{41}{24}$$

Hence,

$$\frac{\frac{1}{4} + \frac{-3}{2}}{\frac{5}{6} + \frac{7}{8}} = \frac{\frac{-5}{4}}{\frac{41}{24}} = \frac{-5}{4} \cdot \frac{24}{41} = \frac{-30}{41}$$

Dividing Fractions

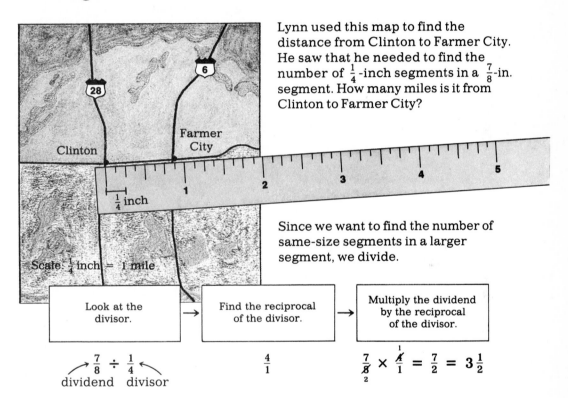

Lynn used this map to find the distance from Clinton to Farmer City. He saw that he needed to find the number of $\frac{1}{4}$-inch segments in a $\frac{7}{8}$-in. segment. How many miles is it from Clinton to Farmer City?

Since we want to find the number of same-size segments in a larger segment, we divide.

Look at the divisor.	→	Find the reciprocal of the divisor.	→	Multiply the dividend by the reciprocal of the divisor.

$$\frac{7}{8} \div \frac{1}{4}$$
dividend   divisor

$$\frac{4}{1}$$

$$\frac{7}{8} \times \frac{4}{1} = \frac{7}{2} = 3\frac{1}{2}$$

The distance from Clinton to Farmer City is $3\frac{1}{2}$ mi.

Other Examples

$$\frac{3}{5} \div \frac{2}{3} = \frac{3}{5} \times \frac{3}{2} = \frac{9}{10} \qquad 6 \div \frac{3}{4} = \frac{6}{1} \times \frac{4}{3} = 8 \qquad 6 \div 9 = \frac{6}{1} \times \frac{1}{9} = \frac{2}{3}$$

Check: $\frac{9}{10} \times \frac{2}{3} = \frac{3}{5}$

Remark   Another method for dividing the two fractions in Example 6-17(c) is based on multiplying each fraction by the LCM of their denominators. Thus,

$$\frac{\frac{-5}{4}}{\frac{41}{24}} = \frac{\frac{-5}{4} \cdot 24}{\frac{41}{24} \cdot 24} = \frac{^-5 \cdot 6}{41} = \frac{^-30}{41}$$

BRAIN TEASER

A castle in the faraway land of Aluossim was surrounded by four moats. One day, the castle was besieged by a fierce tribe from the north. Guards were stationed at each bridge. Prince Juanaricmo was allowed to take a number of bags of gold from the castle as he went into exile. However, the guard at the first bridge demanded half the bags of gold plus one more bag. Prince Juanaricmo met this demand and proceeded to the next bridge. The guards at the second, third, and fourth bridges made identical demands, all of which the prince met. When the prince finally crossed all the bridges, he had a single bag of gold left. With how many bags did he start?

PROBLEM SET 6-3

1. In the following figures, a unit rectangle is used to illustrate the product of two fractions. Name the fractions and their product.

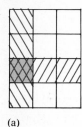
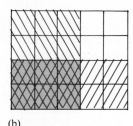

   (a)   (b)

2. Use a rectangular region to illustrate each of the following products.

   (a) $\frac{3}{4} \cdot \frac{1}{3}$ (b) $\frac{1}{5} \cdot \frac{2}{3}$

3. Find each product. Write your answers in simplest form.

   (a) $\frac{10}{9} \cdot \frac{27}{40}$ (b) $\frac{^-3}{5} \cdot \frac{^-15}{24}$ (c) $\frac{49}{65} \cdot \frac{26}{98}$

   (d) $\frac{a}{b} \cdot \frac{b^2}{a^2}$ (e) $\frac{2a}{3b} \cdot \frac{^-5ab}{2ab}$ (f) $\frac{xy}{z} \cdot \frac{z^2 a}{x^3 y^2}$

   (g) $2\frac{1}{3} \cdot 3\frac{3}{4}$ (h) $^-5\frac{1}{6} \cdot 4\frac{1}{2}$

   (i) $\frac{22}{7} \cdot 4\frac{2}{3}$ (j) $\frac{^-5}{2} \cdot 2\frac{1}{2}$

4. Use the distributive property to find each product.

   (a) $4\frac{1}{2} \cdot 2\frac{1}{3}$ $\left[Hint: \left(4 + \frac{1}{2}\right) \cdot \left(2 + \frac{1}{3}\right). \right]$

   (b) $3\frac{1}{3} \cdot 2\frac{1}{2}$ (c) $248\frac{2}{5} \cdot 100\frac{1}{8}$

5. Find the multiplicative inverse for each of the following.

   (a) $\frac{^-1}{3}$ (b) $\frac{3}{5}$

   (c) $\frac{14}{7}$ (d) $3\frac{1}{3}$

   (e) $\frac{x}{y}$, if $x \neq 0$ and $y \neq 0$ (f) $^-7$

6. Perform each of the following divisions and write your answers in simplest form.

   (a) $3 \div \frac{1}{9}$ (b) $\frac{2}{3} \div \frac{7}{12}$ (c) $\frac{^-3}{4} \div \frac{7}{8}$

   (d) $\frac{x}{y} \div \frac{x^2}{y^2}$, where $x, y \neq 0$

   (e) $\frac{\frac{3}{16}}{\frac{4}{9}}$ (f) $\frac{\frac{3}{16}}{\frac{9}{4}}$ (g) $\frac{\frac{8}{7}}{\frac{3}{4}}$

   (h) $\frac{\frac{^-3}{5}}{\frac{^-6}{7}}$ (i) $\frac{^-3}{1\frac{1}{14}}$

7. Express each of the following in simplest form.

(a) $\dfrac{2\frac{3}{4}}{1\frac{1}{4}}$

(b) $2\dfrac{3}{4}\cdot 1\dfrac{4}{3}$

(c) $\left(3\dfrac{2}{5}+1\right)\left(4\dfrac{1}{3}-2\dfrac{2}{3}\right)$

(d) $1\dfrac{1}{2}\cdot 1\dfrac{1}{3}\cdot 1\dfrac{1}{4}$

(e) $\dfrac{\frac{1}{2}+\frac{1}{3}}{\frac{1}{2}-\frac{1}{3}}$

(f) $\dfrac{\frac{1}{4}+\frac{3}{2}}{\frac{5}{6}+\frac{-7}{8}}$

(g) $\dfrac{1\frac{1}{2}-2\frac{3}{4}}{\frac{1}{4}+\frac{-7}{8}}$

(h) $\dfrac{x}{y}\div\dfrac{x}{z}$

(i) $\dfrac{x}{y}\cdot\dfrac{yz}{x}$

(j) $x\cdot\dfrac{5}{xy}\cdot\dfrac{y}{x}$

(k) $\dfrac{x^2y^3}{z^3}\cdot\dfrac{z^2}{xy^2}$

8. Solve each of the following for x and write your answers in simplest form.

(a) $\dfrac{1}{3}x=\dfrac{7}{8}$

(b) $\dfrac{2}{5}\cdot\dfrac{3}{6}=x$

(c) $\dfrac{1}{5}=\dfrac{7}{3}\cdot x$

(d) $x\div\dfrac{3}{4}=\dfrac{5}{8}$

(e) $\dfrac{1}{2}x-7=\dfrac{3}{4}x$

(f) $2\dfrac{1}{3}x+7=3\dfrac{1}{4}$

(g) $\dfrac{2}{3}\left(\dfrac{1}{2}x-7\right)=\dfrac{3}{4}x$

(h) $\dfrac{-2}{5}(10x+1)=1-x$

(i) $\dfrac{1}{x}+\dfrac{1}{3}=\dfrac{1}{5}$

9. Create a problem that has the same structure as each of the following, using whole numbers if possible (if not, use simpler fractions such as $\frac{1}{2}$ or $\frac{1}{4}$) so that the answer will be a whole number. Solve your problem and then solve the original problem.
(a) Four students share three pizzas equally. How much pizza does each student get?
(b) If a pizza has $\frac{5}{8}$ pound of cheese uniformly distributed on it, and John ate $\frac{2}{3}$ of the pizza, how much cheese did John eat?
(c) John ate $\frac{3}{8}$ pound of sausage while eating $\frac{2}{3}$ of a pizza. If the sausage was uniformly distributed over the pizza, how much sausage was on the whole pizza?
(d) Michael can paint $\frac{2}{5}$ of a house in one day. If he continues working at this rate, how many days will it take him to paint the whole house?
(e) If Nora spent $\frac{3}{10}$ of her salary on presents for friends and $\frac{2}{5}$ of her salary on presents for family this month, what part of her salary did she spend on presents?

(f) On a scale drawing of a house, the caption read, "$\frac{7}{16}$ inch represents 1 foot." How long is the living room in reality if it is $10\frac{1}{2}$ inches long on the drawing?
(g) Joanna is entitled to $\frac{2}{5}$ of her parents' estate, which is valued at $\frac{3}{4}$ million dollars. How much should Joanna receive?

10. Find two consecutive integers, x and $x+1$, such that one half of the greater integer exceeds one third of the lesser integer by 9.

11. Di Paloma University had a faculty reduction and lost one fifth of its faculty. If there were 320 faculty members left after the reduction, how many members were there originally?

12. Ten minutes is what part of an hour? Of a week?

13. Alberto owns five ninths of the stock in the North West Tofu company. His sister, Renatta, owns half as much stock as Alberto. What part of the stock is owned by neither Alberto nor Renatta?

14. A person has $29\frac{1}{2}$ yards of material available to make uniforms. Each uniform requires $\frac{3}{4}$ yard of material.
(a) How many uniforms can be made?
(b) How much material will be left over?

15. Show that the following properties do *not* hold for division of rational numbers.
(a) Commutative   (b) Associative
(c) Identity   (d) Inverse

16. Peppermint Patty is frustrated with a problem. Help her solve it.

© 1979 United Feature Syndicate, Inc.

17. For each of the following sequences, find a pattern and write two more terms of the sequence, assuming that the pattern continues. Which of the sequences

are geometric and which are not? Justify your answers.

(a) $1, \frac{1}{2}, \frac{1}{4}, \frac{1}{8}, \frac{1}{16}, \cdots$

(b) $1, \frac{-1}{2}, \frac{1}{4}, \frac{-1}{8}, \frac{1}{16}, \cdots$

(c) $\frac{4}{3}, 1, \frac{3}{4}, \frac{9}{16}, \frac{27}{64}, \cdots$

(d) $\frac{1}{3}, \frac{2}{3^2}, \frac{3}{3^3}, \frac{4}{3^4}, \cdots$

18. Let $f(x) = (\frac{3}{4})x + \frac{1}{2}$, where the domain is all rational numbers.

(a) Find the outputs if the inputs are:

   (i) 0   (ii) $\frac{2}{5}$ (iii) $\frac{-2}{5}$

(b) For which inputs will the outputs be:

   (i) 0   (ii) 1   (iii) $\frac{-1}{2}$

19. Let $f(x) = \dfrac{3x + 4}{4x - 5}$, where the domain is all rational numbers for which the function has a value.

(a) Find the outputs if the inputs are:

   (i) 0   (ii) $\frac{2}{5}$ (iii) $\frac{-2}{5}$

(b) For which inputs will the outputs be:

   (i) 0   (ii) $\frac{2}{5}$ (iii) $\frac{-1}{2}$

(c) What value for x is not in the domain of the function?

★**20.** If Sherwin can paint the house in 2 days working by himself and William can paint the house in 4 days working by himself, how many days would it take Sherwin and William working together?

★**21.** If Mary and Carter can paint a house in 5 hours and Mary alone can do the same job in 8 hours, how long would it take Carter working alone?

★**22.** Prove that if x, y, and z are rational numbers and $z \neq 0$, then $(x \cdot y) \div z = x \cdot (y \div z)$.

★**23.** Investigate under what conditions, if any,

$$\frac{a}{b} = \frac{a + c}{b + c}.$$

24. Consider these products.

   First product: $\left(1 + \frac{1}{1}\right)\left(1 + \frac{1}{2}\right)$

Second product: $\left(1 + \frac{1}{1}\right)\left(1 + \frac{1}{2}\right)\left(1 + \frac{1}{3}\right)$

Third product: $\left(1 + \frac{1}{1}\right)\left(1 + \frac{1}{2}\right)\left(1 + \frac{1}{3}\right)\left(1 + \frac{1}{4}\right)$

(a) Calculate the value of each product. Based on the pattern in your answers, guess the value of the fourth product; then check to determine if your guess is correct.

(b) Guess the value of the 100th product.

(c) Find as simple an expression as possible for the nth product.

★**25.** Let $S = \dfrac{1}{2} + \dfrac{1}{2^2} + \dfrac{1}{2^3} + \cdots + \dfrac{1}{2^{64}}$.

(a) Use the distributive property of multiplication over addition to find an expression for $2S$.

(b) Show that $2S - S = S = 1 - (\frac{1}{2})^{64}$.

(c) Find a simple expression for the sum

$$\frac{1}{2} + \frac{1}{2^2} + \frac{1}{2^3} + \cdots + \frac{1}{2^n}$$

★**26.** Find the sum of the first 100 terms of the arithmetic sequence

$$\frac{1}{4}, 1, \frac{7}{4}, \frac{5}{2}, \frac{13}{4}, \cdots$$

★**27.** In an arithmetic sequence, the first term is 1 and the 100th term is 2. Find the following.

(a) The 50th term

(b) The sum of the first 50 terms

Review Problems

28. Perform each of the following computations. Leave your answers in the simplest form.

(a) $\dfrac{-3}{16} + \dfrac{7}{4}$ (b) $\dfrac{1}{6} + \dfrac{-4}{9} + \dfrac{5}{3}$

(c) $\dfrac{-5}{2^3 \cdot 3^2} - \dfrac{-5}{2 \cdot 3^3}$ (d) $3\dfrac{4}{5} + 4\dfrac{5}{6}$

(e) $5\dfrac{1}{6} - 3\dfrac{5}{8}$ (f) $-4\dfrac{1}{3} - 5\dfrac{5}{12}$

29. Each student at Sussex Elementary School takes one foreign language. Two thirds of the students take Spanish, $\frac{1}{9}$ take French, $\frac{1}{18}$ take German, and the rest take some other foreign language. If there are 720 students in the school, how many do not take Spanish, French, or German?

30. Perform the indicated operations and write your answers in simplest form.

(a) $\dfrac{-3}{5x} + \dfrac{1}{x} - \dfrac{-2}{3x}$ (b) $\dfrac{-2}{2xy^2} + \dfrac{3}{x^2y} - \dfrac{1}{xy}$

BRAIN TEASER

A woman's will decreed that her cats be shared among her three daughters as follows: $\frac{1}{2}$ of the cats to the eldest daughter, $\frac{1}{3}$ of the cats to the middle daughter, and $\frac{1}{9}$ of the cats to the youngest daughter. Since the woman had 17 cats, the daughters decided that they could not carry out their mother's wishes. The judge who held the will agreed to lend the daughters a cat so they could share the cats as their mother wished. Now, $\frac{1}{2}$ of 18 is 9; $\frac{1}{3}$ of 18 is 6; and $\frac{1}{9}$ of 18 is 2. Since $9 + 6 + 2 = 17$, the daughters were able to divide the 17 cats and return the borrowed cat. They obviously did not need the extra cat to carry out the mother's will, but they could not divide 17 into halves, thirds, and ninths. Has the woman's will really been followed?

Section 6-4

Some Properties of Rational Numbers

ORDERING OF RATIONAL NUMBERS

What does it mean for one rational number to be greater than (or less than) another rational number? Children know that $\frac{7}{8} > \frac{5}{8}$ because if a pizza is divided into 8 parts, then 7 parts of a pizza is more than 5 of those parts. Similarly, $\frac{3}{7} < \frac{4}{7}$. Thus, given two fractions with common positive denominators, the one with the greater numerator is the greater fraction. This can be written as follows.

THEOREM 6-3

> If a, b, and c are integers and $b > 0$, then $\dfrac{a}{b} > \dfrac{c}{b}$ if and only if $a > c$.

Remark The condition $b > 0$ is essential in the property. Check to see that if $b < 0$, the theorem is not necessarily true.

Theorem 6-3 can be proved using a formal definition of "greater-than" and "less-than" relations. The greater-than and less-than relations for rational numbers are defined in such a way that the definitions of these relations for integers are still true. Thus, we have the following definition.

DEFINITION

> If $\dfrac{a}{b}$ and $\dfrac{c}{d}$ are rational numbers, then $\dfrac{a}{b} > \dfrac{c}{d}$ if and only if there is a positive rational number k such that $\dfrac{c}{d} + k = \dfrac{a}{b}$, or, equivalently, if and only if $\dfrac{a}{b} - \dfrac{c}{d}$ is positive.

How do we determine the greater of two fractions that do not have common denominators? For example, consider $\frac{6}{7}$ and $\frac{8}{11}$. Suppose we have two pizzas of equal size, one cut into 11 pieces and the other cut into 7 pieces. Is there more pizza in 8 slices of the first than there is in 6 slices of the second? To answer this, we need to divide a whole into equal parts in such a way that $\frac{6}{7}$ and $\frac{8}{11}$ will be easily comparable. This can be accomplished by finding fractions equal to $\frac{6}{7}$ and $\frac{8}{11}$ with common denominators. We have $\frac{6}{7} = \frac{6 \cdot 11}{7 \cdot 11} = \frac{66}{77}$ and $\frac{8}{11} = \frac{7 \cdot 8}{7 \cdot 11} = \frac{56}{77}$. Because $66 > 56$, it follows that $\frac{66}{77} > \frac{56}{77}$, so $\frac{6}{7} > \frac{8}{11}$. Similarly, to compare $\frac{-5}{12}$ and $\frac{1}{-2}$, we first write them with common denominators as follows.

$$\frac{1}{-2} = \frac{1 \cdot (-6)}{-2 \cdot (-6)} = \frac{-6}{12}$$

Because $-5 > -6$, $\frac{-5}{12} > \frac{-6}{12}$; therefore, $\frac{-5}{12} > \frac{1}{-2}$.

A general criterion for the greater-than relation on rational numbers can be developed for the case when the denominators are positive. Using the common denominator bd, the fractions $\frac{a}{b}$ and $\frac{c}{d}$ can be written as $\frac{ad}{bd}$ and $\frac{bc}{bd}$.

Because $b > 0$ and $d > 0$, $bd > 0$ and $\frac{ad}{bd} > \frac{bc}{bd}$ if and only if $ad > bc$. Thus, we have the following theorem.

THEOREM 6-4

> For any rational numbers $\frac{a}{b}$ and $\frac{c}{d}$, with b and d positive integers, $\frac{a}{b} > \frac{c}{d}$ if and only if $ad > bc$. Similarly, $\frac{a}{b} < \frac{c}{d}$ if and only if $ad < bc$.

Example 6-18

Prove that the following order relations are true.

(a) $\frac{8}{9} > \frac{16}{19}$ (b) $\frac{-7}{8} < \frac{14}{15}$ (c) $\frac{1}{-4} < \frac{2}{11}$

Solution

(a) $\frac{8}{9} > \frac{16}{19}$ because $8 \cdot 19 > 9 \cdot 16$, or $152 > 144$.

(b) $\frac{-7}{8} < \frac{14}{15}$ because $-7 \cdot 15 < 8 \cdot 14$, or $-105 < 112$.

(c) $\frac{1}{-4} < \frac{2}{11}$ because a negative number is less than a positive number.

Remark   Theorem 6-4 cannot be applied directly to $\frac{1}{-4}$ and $\frac{2}{11}$ because the denominator in the first fraction is negative.

Often we can compare the size of fractions by inspection and common sense. Such approaches should be strongly encouraged, as they strengthen children's intuitive understanding of fractions. Consider, for example, finding which is greater, $\frac{3}{4}$ or $\frac{4}{5}$. Three fourths of a pizza is a whole pizza with $\frac{1}{4}$ cut out, while $\frac{4}{5}$ of a pizza is a whole pizza with $\frac{1}{5}$ cut out. Can you find a similar way to determine which of the fractions $\frac{6}{5}$ and $\frac{7}{6}$ is greater? How about $\frac{134}{137}$ and $\frac{131}{130}$?

The proofs of the following theorems of the greater-than relation on rational numbers are similar to those involving integers and are left as exercises. Similar properties hold for $<$, $\leq$, and $\geq$.

THEOREM 6-5

> **Transitive Property of Greater Than**   For any rational numbers $\frac{a}{b}, \frac{c}{d}$, and $\frac{e}{f}$,
>
> if $\frac{a}{b} > \frac{c}{d}$ and $\frac{c}{d} > \frac{e}{f}$, then $\frac{a}{b} > \frac{e}{f}$.

THEOREM 6-6

> **Addition Property of Greater Than**   For any rational numbers $\frac{a}{b}, \frac{c}{d}$, and $\frac{e}{f}$,
>
> if $\frac{a}{b} > \frac{c}{d}$, then $\frac{a}{b} + \frac{e}{f} > \frac{c}{d} + \frac{e}{f}$.

THEOREM 6-7

> **Multiplication Property of Greater Than**   For any rational numbers $\frac{a}{b}, \frac{c}{d}$, and $\frac{e}{f}$:
>
> 1. If $\frac{a}{b} > \frac{c}{d}$ and $\frac{e}{f} > 0$, then $\frac{a}{b} \cdot \frac{e}{f} > \frac{c}{d} \cdot \frac{e}{f}$.
>
> 2. If $\frac{a}{b} > \frac{c}{d}$ and $\frac{e}{f} < 0$, then $\frac{a}{b} \cdot \frac{e}{f} < \frac{c}{d} \cdot \frac{e}{f}$.

SOLUTIONS TO ALGEBRAIC INEQUALITIES

The preceding theorems can be used to aid in solving algebraic inequalities, as shown in the following example.

Example 6-19

Solve for x, where x is a rational number.

(a) $\dfrac{3}{2}x < \dfrac{3}{4}$

(b) $\dfrac{1}{4}x + \dfrac{1}{5} \geq \dfrac{2}{3}x - \dfrac{1}{7}$

Solution

(a)
$$\frac{3}{2}x < \frac{3}{4}$$

$$\left(\frac{2}{3}\right)\left(\frac{3}{2}x\right) < \left(\frac{2}{3}\right)\left(\frac{3}{4}\right)$$

$$x < \frac{6}{12}, \quad \text{or } x < \frac{1}{2}$$

(b)
$$\frac{1}{4}x + \frac{1}{5} \geq \frac{2}{3}x - \frac{1}{7}$$

$$\frac{1}{4}x + \frac{1}{5} + \frac{^-1}{5} \geq \frac{2}{3}x - \frac{1}{7} + \frac{^-1}{5}$$

$$\frac{1}{4}x \geq \frac{2}{3}x - \frac{12}{35}$$

$$\frac{^-2}{3}x + \frac{1}{4}x \geq \frac{^-2}{3}x + \frac{2}{3}x - \frac{12}{35}$$

$$\left(\frac{^-2}{3} + \frac{1}{4}\right)x \geq \frac{^-12}{35}$$

$$\frac{^-5}{12}x \geq \frac{^-12}{35}$$

$$\left(\frac{^-12}{5}\right)\left(\frac{^-5}{12}x\right) \leq \left(\frac{^-12}{5}\right)\left(\frac{^-12}{35}\right)$$

$$x \leq \frac{144}{175}$$

Often there is more than one way to solve an inequality. Two alternate methods for solving Example 6-19(b) follow.

1. First, add the fractions on each side of the inequality. Then, solve the resulting inequality.

$$\frac{1}{4}x + \frac{1}{5} \geq \frac{2}{3}x - \frac{1}{7}$$

$$\frac{5x + 4}{20} \geq \frac{14x - 3}{21}$$

$$21(5x + 4) \geq 20(14x - 3)$$

$$105x + 84 \geq 280x - 60$$

$$^-175x \geq ^-144$$

$$\left(\frac{^-1}{175}\right)(^-175x) \leq \left(\frac{^-1}{175}\right)(^-144)$$

$$x \leq \frac{144}{175}$$

2. First, multiply both sides of the inequality by the LCM of all the denominators. (This gives an inequality that does not involve fractions.) Then, solve the resulting inequality.

$$\frac{1}{4}x + \frac{1}{5} \geq \frac{2}{3}x - \frac{1}{7}$$

Since LCM(4, 5, 3, 7) = 420,

$$420\left(\frac{1}{4}x + \frac{1}{5}\right) \geq 420\left(\frac{2}{3}x - \frac{1}{7}\right)$$

$$105x + 84 \geq 280x - 60$$

$$^-175x \geq {}^-144$$

$$x \leq \frac{144}{175}$$

Properties of greater-than or less-than relations sometimes can be used to estimate the answers to problems. For example, to find the number of curtains requiring $5\frac{3}{8}$ yards of cloth that can be prepared from a bolt that contains $19\frac{3}{4}$ yards, we could compute $\frac{19\frac{3}{4}}{5\frac{3}{8}}$. However, because $19\frac{3}{4}$ is approximately 20, and $5\frac{3}{8}$ is close to 5, we estimate that the answer should be approximately $\frac{20}{5}$, or 4. Is the actual answer greater than or less than 4? To answer that question, notice that if two positive fractions have equal denominators, the one with the greater numerator is greater, and if two positive fractions have equal numerators, the one with the greater denominator is smaller. (Do you see intuitively why this is so?) Hence, $\frac{19\frac{3}{4}}{5\frac{3}{8}} < \frac{20}{5\frac{3}{8}} < \frac{20}{5}$. Thus (by Theorem 6-5), $\frac{19\frac{3}{4}}{5\frac{3}{8}} < \frac{20}{5}$. Similarly, it is possible to show that $\frac{19\frac{3}{4}}{5\frac{3}{8}} > \frac{18}{5\frac{3}{8}} > \frac{18}{6}$. Because $\frac{19\frac{3}{4}}{5\frac{3}{8}}$ is between 3 and 4, we can conclude that only 3 curtains can be prepared.

Example 6-20

In each of the following, estimate the answer by finding two integers, one smaller than the answer and one greater than the answer.

(a) $9\frac{3}{4} \cdot 14\frac{5}{9}$ (b) $35\frac{1}{3} \div 6\frac{3}{5}$

Solution

(a) $9 \cdot 14 < 9\frac{3}{4} \cdot 14\frac{5}{9} < 10 \cdot 15$

Hence,

$$126 < 9\frac{3}{4} \cdot 14\frac{5}{4} < 150$$

(b) $\dfrac{35\frac{1}{3}}{6\frac{3}{5}} < \dfrac{36}{6\frac{3}{5}} < \dfrac{36}{6}$

Hence,

$\dfrac{35\frac{1}{3}}{6\frac{3}{5}} < 6$

Similarly,

$\dfrac{35\frac{1}{3}}{6\frac{3}{5}} > 5$

Thus,

$5 < \dfrac{35\frac{1}{3}}{6\frac{3}{5}} < 6$

PROBLEM 1

Two cyclists, David and Sara, started riding their bikes at 9:00 A.M. at City Hall. They followed the local bike trail and returned to City Hall at the same time. However, David rode three times as long as Sara rested on her trip and Sara rode four times as long as David rested on his trip. Assuming that each cyclist rode at a constant speed, who rode faster?

UNDERSTANDING THE PROBLEM David and Sara started riding their bikes at 9:00 A.M. at City Hall. They followed the local bike trail and returned to City Hall at the same time. David rode three times as long as Sara rested and Sara rode four times as long as David rested. We know that each rode at a constant speed and we want to find who rode faster.

DEVISING A PLAN Since we are not asked how fast each cyclist rode, we do not need to find their exact speeds. Both cyclists covered the same distance, so it follows that the one who rode longer is the slower one. If we denote David's riding time in hours (or any other unit of time) by d and Sara's riding time, also in hours, by s, it would be sufficient to determine if $d < s$. For that purpose, we use the strategy of *writing an equation*. We translate the given information in terms of s and d and try to find an equation involving s and d. If we can express d in terms of s, or vice versa, we should be able to deduce which is greater.

CARRYING OUT THE PLAN Because David rode three times as long as Sara rested, we can deduce that Sara rested one third as long as David rode, that is, $\dfrac{d}{3}$ hours. Similarly, because Sara rode four times as long as David rested, we can deduce that David rested one fourth as long as Sara rode, that is, $\dfrac{s}{4}$. Using the expressions $\dfrac{d}{3}$ and $\dfrac{s}{4}$, we can write expressions for the total time of the trip, as shown in Table 6-3.

Table 6-3

	Riding Time	Resting Time	Total Time of Trip
David	d	$\dfrac{s}{4}$	$d + \dfrac{s}{4}$
Sara	s	$\dfrac{d}{3}$	$s + \dfrac{d}{3}$

Both cyclists started and returned at the same time, so their total trip times are the same. As shown in Table 6-3, David's total trip time is $d + \dfrac{s}{4}$ and Sara's total trip time is $s + \dfrac{d}{3}$. Consequently, we have the following equation and solution in terms of s.

$$d + \frac{s}{4} = s + \frac{d}{3}$$

$$d - \frac{d}{3} = s - \frac{s}{4}$$

$$\frac{2}{3}d = \frac{3}{4}s$$

$$d = \frac{3}{2} \cdot \frac{3}{4}s$$

$$d = \frac{9}{8}s$$

Because $\frac{9}{8} > 1$, it follows that $\frac{9}{8}s > s$, or that $d > s$. Thus, it took David longer to travel the same distance that Sara traveled, so Sara rode faster than David.

LOOKING BACK The problem also could have been solved by using all four variables mentioned in the question—that is, each cyclist's riding and resting times. By proper substitutions, we should obtain the same relation between d and s.

DENSENESS PROPERTY

denseness property

The set of rational numbers has a very special property called the **denseness property.** Neither the set of whole numbers nor the set of integers has this property. *Given any two rational numbers $\dfrac{a}{b}$ and $\dfrac{c}{d}$, there is another rational number between these two.* Also, between $\dfrac{a}{b}$ and the new rational number, there is another rational number. Continuing this process shows that between any two rational numbers $\dfrac{a}{b}$ and $\dfrac{c}{d}$ there are infinitely many other rational

BRAIN TEASER

Find the exact time between 2 o'clock and 3 o'clock when the hands of a clock coincide.

numbers. For example, consider $\frac{1}{2}$ and $\frac{2}{3}$. To find a rational number between $\frac{1}{2}$ and $\frac{2}{3}$, we first rewrite the fractions with a common denominator, as $\frac{3}{6}$ and $\frac{4}{6}$. Because there is no whole number between the numerators 3 and 4, we next find two fractions equivalent to $\frac{1}{2}$ and $\frac{2}{3}$ with greater denominators. For example, $\frac{1}{2} = \frac{6}{12}$ and $\frac{2}{3} = \frac{8}{12}$, and $\frac{7}{12}$ is between the two fractions $\frac{6}{12}$ and $\frac{8}{12}$. So, $\frac{7}{12}$ is between $\frac{1}{2}$ and $\frac{2}{3}$.

Another way to find a rational number between two given rationals $\frac{a}{b}$ and $\frac{c}{d}$ is to find the arithmetic mean of the two numbers. For example, the arithmetic mean of $\frac{1}{2}$ and $\frac{2}{3}$ is $\frac{1}{2}(\frac{1}{2} + \frac{2}{3})$, or $\frac{7}{12}$. The proof that the arithmetic mean of two given rational numbers always is between them is left as an exercise.

PROBLEM SET 6-4

1. For each of the following pairs of fractions, replace the comma with the correct symbol ($<$, $=$, $>$) to make a true statement.

   (a) $\frac{7}{8}, \frac{5}{6}$ (b) $2\frac{4}{5}, 2\frac{3}{6}$ (c) $\frac{-7}{8}, \frac{-4}{5}$

   (d) $\frac{1}{-7}, \frac{1}{-8}$ (e) $\frac{2}{5}, \frac{4}{10}$ (f) $\frac{0}{7}, \frac{0}{17}$

2. Arrange each of the following in decreasing order.

   (a) $\frac{11}{22}, \frac{11}{16}, \frac{11}{13}$ (b) $\frac{33}{16}, \frac{23}{16}, 3$

   (c) $\frac{-1}{5}, \frac{-19}{36}, \frac{-17}{30}$

3. Solve for x in each of the following.

   (a) $\frac{2}{3}x - \frac{7}{8} \le \frac{1}{4}$ (b) $\frac{1}{5}x - 7 \ge \frac{2}{3}$

   (c) $x - \frac{1}{3} < \frac{2}{3}x + \frac{4}{5}$ (d) $5 - \frac{2}{3}x \le \frac{1}{4}x - \frac{7}{8}$

4. (a) If $b < 0$ and $d > 0$, is it true that $\frac{a}{b} > \frac{c}{d}$ if and only if $ad > bc$? Explain your answer.

   (b) If $b < 0$ and $d < 0$, is it true that $\frac{a}{b} > \frac{c}{d}$ if and only if $ad > bc$? Explain your answer.

5. Estimate each of the following, then perform the multiplications to see how good your estimates are.

   (a) $19\frac{8}{9} \cdot 20\frac{1}{9}$ (b) $19\frac{8}{9} \cdot 9\frac{1}{10}$ (c) $3\frac{9}{10} \cdot \frac{81}{82}$

6. In each of the following, estimate the answer by finding two integers such that the answer is between them.

   (a) $19\frac{8}{9} \cdot 9\frac{1}{10}$ (b) $80\frac{3}{4} \cdot 9\frac{1}{8}$ (c) $77\frac{3}{5} \cdot 6\frac{1}{4}$

   (d) $\frac{48\frac{2}{3}}{8\frac{4}{9}}$ (e) $\frac{5\frac{2}{3}}{2\frac{1}{17}}$

7. Estimate the number of $11\frac{3}{4}$-ounce bird seed packages that can be produced from a supply of 21 pounds of bird seed.

8. (a) Choose several proper fractions. Square each of the fractions and compare the size of the original fraction and its square. Make a conjecture concerning a fraction and its square.

   ★(b) Justify your conjecture in (a).

   (c) If a fraction is greater than 1, make a conjecture concerning which is greater, the fraction or its square.

   ★(d) Justify your conjecture in (c).

9. If $\frac{a}{b} < 1$ and $\frac{c}{d} > 0$, compare $\frac{c}{d}$ with $\frac{a}{b} \cdot \frac{c}{d}$.

10. If x and y are two rational numbers such that $x > 1$ and $y > 0$, which is greater, xy or y? Justify your answer.

11. Show that the sequence $\frac{1}{2}, \frac{2}{3}, \frac{3}{4}, \frac{4}{5}, \frac{5}{6}, \frac{6}{7}, \ldots$ is an increasing sequence, that is, that each term in the sequence is greater than the preceding one.

12. Find an infinite, decreasing sequence (each term is smaller than the preceding one) of positive, rational numbers such that all the terms are greater than 1.

13. The sequence $\frac{0}{1}, \frac{1}{4}, \frac{1}{3}, \frac{1}{2}, \frac{2}{3}, \frac{3}{4}, \frac{1}{1}$, called the *Farey sequence* of order 4, consists of all rational numbers in simplest form between 0 and 1 in increasing order whose denominators do not exceed 4. In general,

the Farey sequence of order n consists of all rational numbers in simplest form between 0 and 1 in increasing order whose denominators do not exceed n. Answer the following questions about Farey sequences.

(a) Write the Farey sequences of order 5 and of order 6.

(b) Check several special cases and make a conjecture concerning the fraction obtained by finding the difference between any term and the preceding term in a given Farey sequence.

★(c) Notice that in the Farey sequence of order 4, we have $\frac{0}{1} + \frac{1}{1} = 1$, $\frac{1}{4} + \frac{3}{4} = 1$, and $\frac{1}{3} + \frac{2}{3} = 1$. Check that a similar relation occurs in the Farey sequence of order 5. Is such a relation true in all Farey sequences? Why?

(d) If $\frac{a}{b}$ and $\frac{c}{d}$ are any two consecutive fractions in some Farey sequence, check for several cases in which the fractions $\frac{a}{b}, \frac{a+c}{b+d}$, and $\frac{c}{d}$ are consecutive terms in some Farey sequence.

14. (a) Explain why the system of whole numbers does not have the denseness property.

(b) Explain why the system of integers does not have the denseness property.

15. For each of the following, find two rational numbers between the given fractions.

(a) $\frac{3}{7}$ and $\frac{4}{7}$ (b) $\frac{-7}{9}$ and $\frac{-8}{9}$

(c) $\frac{5}{6}$ and $\frac{83}{100}$ (d) $\frac{-1}{3}$ and $\frac{3}{4}$

★16. Show that the arithmetic mean of two rational numbers is between the two numbers; that is, for $0 < \frac{a}{b} < \frac{c}{d}$, prove that $0 < \frac{a}{b} < \frac{1}{2}\left(\frac{a}{b} + \frac{c}{d}\right) < \frac{c}{d}$.

★17. If the same positive number is added to the numerator and denominator of a positive proper fraction, is the new fraction greater than, less than, or equal to the original fraction? Justify your answer.

Review Problems

18. Write each of the following in simplest form.

(a) $3\frac{5}{8}$ (b) $3\frac{5}{8} \div 2\frac{5}{6}$

(c) $\frac{-5}{12} \div \frac{-12}{5}$ (d) $\frac{(x-y)^2}{x^2-y^2} \cdot \frac{x+y}{x-y}$

19. The distance from Albertson to Florance is $28\frac{3}{4}$ miles. Roberto walks at the rate of $4\frac{1}{2}$ miles per hour. How long will it take him to walk from Albertson to Florance?

20. Solve each of the following for x and write your answer in simplest form.

(a) $\frac{-3}{4}x = 1$ (b) $^-x - \frac{3}{4} = \frac{5}{8}$

(c) $\frac{3}{4}x = \frac{-2}{3}x + 2$ (d) $\frac{3}{4}\left(1 - \frac{2}{3}x\right) = \frac{-3}{4}x$

Section 6-5

Ratio and Proportion

One of the common uses of fractions is as ratios. For example, there may be a two-to-three ratio of Democrats to Republicans on a certain legislative committee, a friend may be given a speeding ticket for driving 63 miles per

ratio

hour, or eggs are 98¢ per dozen. Each of these illustrates a **ratio,** or a quotient. A 1-to-2 ratio of males to females means that the number of males is $\frac{1}{2}$ the number of females, or that there is 1 male for every 2 females. The ratio 1 to 2 can be written as $\frac{1}{2}$ or 1:2. In general, a ratio is denoted by $\frac{a}{b}$ or $a:b$, where $b \neq 0$. Thus, a ratio is just another name for a quotient of two numbers.

Example 6-21

There were 7 males and 12 females in the Dew Drop Inn on Monday evening. In the Game Room, next door, there were 14 males and 24 females.

(a) Express the number of males to females in the Inn as a ratio.

(b) Express the number of males to females in the Game Room as a ratio.

Solution

(a) The ratio is $\frac{7}{12}$. (b) The ratio is $\frac{14}{24}$.

The ratios $\frac{7}{12}$ and $\frac{14}{24}$ in Example 6-21 are said to be proportional to each other. In general, two ratios are **proportional** if and only if the fractions representing them are equal. Two equal ratios are said to form a **proportion.**

proportional
proportion

We know that for rational numbers, $\frac{a}{b} = \frac{c}{d}$ if and only if $ad = bc$. Thus, $\frac{a}{b} = \frac{c}{d}$ is a proportion if and only if $ad = bc$. For example, $\frac{14}{24} = \frac{7}{12}$ is a proportion, because $14 \cdot 12 = 24 \cdot 7$.

Frequently, one term in a proportion is missing, as in

$$\frac{3}{8} = \frac{x}{16}$$

Finding x requires solving an equation. The definition of equality of rational numbers can be used to solve such an equation.

$$\frac{3}{8} = \frac{x}{16}$$

$$3 \cdot 16 = 8 \cdot x$$

$$48 = 8 \cdot x$$

$$6 = x$$

Another way to solve the equation is to multiply both sides by 16 as follows.

$$\frac{3}{8} \cdot 16 = \frac{x}{16} \cdot 16$$

$$3 \cdot 2 = x$$

$$x = 6$$

It is important to remember that in the ratio $a \div b$, a and b do not have to be integers. For example, if the owner of a grocery store makes 75¢ for each $2 sale of pistachio nuts, then the ratio of profit to sale price is $\frac{3}{4} \div 2$. This ratio can be expressed using only integers as follows.

$$\frac{\frac{3}{4}}{2} = \frac{\frac{3}{4} \cdot 4}{2 \cdot 4} = \frac{3}{8}$$

Thus, the owner of the store makes $3 for every $8 sale. Similarly, we can have a ratio between two fractions. For example, if in Eugene, Oregon, $\frac{7}{10}$ of the population exercises regularly, then $\frac{3}{10}$ of the population does not exercise regularly, and the ratio of those that do exercise regularly to those that do not is $\frac{7}{10} \div \frac{3}{10}$, or $\frac{7}{3}$.

The following are examples of problems utilizing ratio and proportion.

Example 6-22

If there should be 3 calculators for every 4 students in an elementary school class, how many calculators are needed for 44 students?

Solution

Set up a table (Table 6-4). The ratio of calculators to students should always be the same.

Table 6-4

Number of Calculators	3	x
Number of Students	4	44

$$\frac{3}{4} = \frac{x}{44}$$

$$3 \cdot 44 = 4 \cdot x$$

$$132 = 4x$$

$$33 = x$$

Thus, 33 calculators are needed.

Example 6-23

Suppose a car travels 50 km per hour.

(a) How far will it travel in $3\frac{1}{2}$ hours?
(b) How long will it take the car to travel 1300 km?

Solution

(a) Again, set up a table (Table 6-5).

Table 6-5

Distance (km)	50	x
Number of Hours	1	$3\frac{1}{2}$

We assume that the car travels at a constant speed. Because the speed of the car is the ratio between distance and time that the distance is traveled, the ratios form a proportion. Hence,

$$\frac{50}{1} = \frac{x}{3\frac{1}{2}}$$

$$50(3\tfrac{1}{2}) = 1 \cdot x$$

$$175 = x$$

Therefore, the distance traveled in $3\frac{1}{2}$ hours is 175 km.

(b) Because the question asks about the time corresponding to the 1300-km distance, we set up Table 6-6 comparing distance and corresponding times.

Table 6-6

Distance (km)	50	1300
Number of Hours	1	x

The ratio between a distance and the corresponding number of hours is the speed of the car. Because the speed does not change, the ratio remains the same. Hence,

$$\frac{50}{1} = \frac{1300}{x}$$

$$50x = 1300$$

$$x = 26$$

Thus, to travel 1300 km requires 26 hours.

Consider the proportion $\frac{15}{30} = \frac{3}{6}$. Because the ratios in the proportion are equal fractions and equal nonzero fractions have equal reciprocals, then $\frac{30}{15} = \frac{6}{3}$.

THEOREM 6-8

> For any rational numbers $\frac{a}{b}$ and $\frac{c}{d}$ with $a \neq 0$ and $c \neq 0$, $\frac{a}{b} = \frac{c}{d}$ if and only if $\frac{b}{a} = \frac{d}{c}$.

Suppose that Jaffa oranges sell at 7 for $1 in one store and 21 for $3 in another. Which store has a better buy? We see that the price of one orange is $1/7 in the first store and $3/21 in the second. Because $\frac{1}{7} = \frac{3}{21}$, each store charges the same price per orange. Another way to see this is to observe that if 7 oranges cost $1, then 3 times that many oranges should cost 3 times that much. Using ratios, we see that the ratio of the numbers of oranges is the same as the ratio of the prices; that is, $\frac{7}{21} = \frac{1}{3}$. This is true in general and is summarized in the following theorem, whose proof is left as an exercise.

THEOREM 6-9

> For any rational numbers $\frac{a}{b}$ and $\frac{c}{d}$ with $c \neq 0$, $\frac{a}{b} = \frac{c}{d}$ if and only if $\frac{a}{c} = \frac{b}{d}$.

Remark In the preceding theorem, it was not necessary to stipulate that $b \neq 0$ and $d \neq 0$ since these are inherent in the definition of rational numbers.

It is important to notice units of measure when working with proportions. For example, if a turtle travels 5 inches every 10 seconds, how many feet does it travel in 50 seconds? If units of measure are ignored, the following proportion might be set up.

$$\frac{5 \text{ inches}}{10 \text{ seconds}} = \frac{x \text{ feet}}{50 \text{ seconds}}$$

This statement is incorrect. A correct statement must involve the same units in each ratio. We may write the following:

$$\frac{5 \text{ inches}}{10 \text{ seconds}} = \frac{x \text{ inches}}{50 \text{ seconds}}$$

This implies that $x = 25$ inches. Consequently, since 12 in. = 1 ft the turtle travels $\frac{25}{12}$ feet, or $2\frac{1}{12}$ feet.

Sometimes a proportion is not immediately apparent, as can be seen in the following two problems.

PROBLEM 2

Tom can beat Dick by $\frac{1}{10}$ of a mile in a 5-mile race. Dick can beat Harry by $\frac{1}{5}$ of a mile in a 5-mile race. By how far can Tom beat Harry in a 5-mile race?

UNDERSTANDING THE PROBLEM In a 5-mile race. Tom can beat Dick by $\frac{1}{10}$ of a mile and Dick can beat Harry by $\frac{1}{5}$ of a mile. We are to determine the distance by which Tom can beat Harry in a 5-mile race.

DEVISING A PLAN If we let x be the distance run by Harry when Tom completes the 5-mile race, we can construct Table 6-7 for the distances run when Tom and Dick each complete their 5-mile run.

Table 6-7

Tom	Dick	Harry
5	$\frac{49}{10}$ 5	x $\frac{24}{5}$

Using the table, we construct a proportion, solve for x, and subtract x from 5 miles to obtain the desired distance.

CARRYING OUT THE PLAN We solve for x in the following proportion.

$$\frac{\frac{49}{10}}{5} = \frac{x}{\frac{24}{5}}$$

Thus, $5x = \left(\frac{49}{10}\right) \cdot \left(\frac{24}{5}\right)$, and $x = \frac{588}{125}$. Therefore, the distance by which Tom could beat Harry is $5 - \frac{588}{125}$, or $\frac{37}{125}$, of a mile.

LOOKING BACK The problem can be varied by changing the length of the race or the distances by which the runners can beat one another. Also, notice that it would have been easier to work with decimals. (Decimals will be introduced in the next chapter.)

An important question to ask is why the ratios are equal. This may be intuitively clear to some people, but it can be explained as follows. Let D and H be Dick's and Harry's speeds, respectively. The time that it takes Dick to cover $\frac{49}{10}$ of a mile is the same as the time it takes Harry to cover x miles, because each equals the time it takes Tom to complete 5 miles. Assuming that each runs at a constant speed, time is given by the ratio between distance covered and speed. Hence, $\dfrac{\frac{49}{10}}{D} = \dfrac{x}{H}$. Similarly, $\dfrac{5}{D} = \dfrac{\frac{24}{5}}{H}$. (Why?) Thus, $\dfrac{\frac{49}{10}}{D} \div \dfrac{5}{D} =$ $\dfrac{x}{H} \div \dfrac{\frac{24}{5}}{H}$. This can be simplified to give the proportion $\dfrac{\frac{49}{10}}{5} = \dfrac{x}{\frac{24}{5}}$, which is the one used in Carrying Out the Plan.

PROBLEM 3

In the Klysler Auto Factory, robots assemble cars. If 3 robots can assemble 17 cars in 10 minutes, how many cars can 14 robots assemble in 45 minutes if all robots work at the same rate all the time?

UNDERSTANDING THE PROBLEM Knowing that the robots work at the same rate, we are to determine the number of cars that 14 robots can assemble in 45 minutes given that 3 robots can assemble 17 cars in 10 minutes. If we knew how many cars one robot could assemble in 45 minutes, or how many cars one robot could assemble in 1 minute, we could solve the problem.

DEVISING A PLAN Let x be the number of cars that 14 robots assemble in 45 minutes. Because the robots work at the same rate, we can express this rate by taking the information that 3 robots assemble 17 cars in 10 minutes and equating it with the information that 14 robots assemble x cars in 45 minutes. The rate would be the number of cars (or parts of a car) that 1 robot can assemble in 1 minute. Thus, we first need to find the number of cars that 1 robot can assemble in 1 minute. Then, we need to write and solve the desired equation to solve the problem.

CARRYING OUT THE PLAN If 3 robots assemble 17 cars in 10 minutes, then the 3 robots assemble $\frac{17}{10}$ cars in 1 minute. Consequently, 1 robot assembles $\frac{1}{3} \cdot \frac{17}{10}$, or $\frac{17}{30}$, of a car in 1 minute. Similarly, if 14 robots assemble x cars in 45 minutes, then the 14 robots assemble $\dfrac{x}{45}$ cars in 1 minute. Thus, 1 robot assembles $\dfrac{1}{14} \cdot \dfrac{x}{45}$, or $\dfrac{x}{14 \cdot 45}$, of a car in 1 minute. Because the rates are equal, we have the proportion $\dfrac{x}{14 \cdot 45} = \dfrac{17}{30}$. Solving this equation, we obtain $x = 357$, or 357 cars.

LOOKING BACK The problem can be solved without writing any equations as follows. Because 1 robot assembles $\frac{17}{30}$ of a car in 1 minute, 14 robots assemble $14 \cdot \frac{17}{30}$ cars in 1 minute. Thus, in 45 minutes, 14 robots assemble $45 \cdot 14 \cdot \frac{17}{30}$, or 357, cars.

The problem can be varied by changing the data or by considering two kinds of robots, each kind working at a different rate. Similar problems can be constructed concerning other jobs such as painting houses or washing cars.

PROBLEM SET 6-5

1. If there are 18 poodles and 12 cocker spaniels in a dog show, what is the ratio of poodles to cockers?
2. If a 4-ounce can of pepper costs 98¢, what is the cost per ounce?
3. If a new car is 8 feet long and $4\frac{1}{2}$ feet high, what is the ratio of length to height?
4. Solve for x in each proportion.

   (a) $\dfrac{12}{x} = \dfrac{18}{45}$ (b) $\dfrac{x}{7} = \dfrac{-10}{21}$

   (c) $\dfrac{5}{7} = \dfrac{3x}{98}$ (d) $3\frac{1}{2}$ is to 5 as x is to 15.

5. There are five adult drivers for each teenage driver in Aluossim. If there are 12,345 adult drivers in Aluossim, how many teenage drivers are there?
6. If 3 grapefruits sell for 79¢, how much do 18 grapefruits cost?
7. On a map, $\frac{1}{3}$ inch represents 5 miles. If New York and Aluossim are 18 inches apart on the map, what is the actual distance between them?
8. David read 40 pages of a book in 50 minutes. How many pages should he be able to read in 80 minutes if he reads at a constant rate?
9. A candle is 30 inches long. After burning for 12 minutes, the candle is 25 inches long. How long would the whole candle burn?
10. Three painters can paint 4 houses in 5 days. How long would it take 7 painters to paint 18 houses if all work was done at the same rate all the time?
★11. Prove: For any rational numbers $\dfrac{a}{b}$ and $\dfrac{c}{d}$, if $\dfrac{a}{b} = \dfrac{c}{d}$ where $a \neq 0$ and $c \neq 0$, then $\dfrac{b}{a} = \dfrac{d}{c}$.
★12. Prove that the product of two proper fractions greater than 0 is less than either of the fractions.
13. (a) In Room A of the University Center there are one man and two women; in Room B there are two men and four women; and in Room C there are five men and ten women. If all the people in Rooms B and C go to Room A, what will be the ratio of men to women in Room A?

   ★(b) Prove the following generalization of the proportions used in (a).

   If $\dfrac{a}{b} = \dfrac{c}{d} = \dfrac{e}{f}$, then $\dfrac{a}{b} = \dfrac{c}{d} = \dfrac{e}{f} = \dfrac{a+c+e}{b+d+f}$

14. (a) Prove that if

   $$\dfrac{a}{b} = \dfrac{c}{d}, \quad \text{then} \quad \dfrac{a+b}{b} = \dfrac{c+d}{d}$$

   $\left(\text{Hint: } \dfrac{a}{b} + 1 = \dfrac{c}{d} + 1. \right)$

   ★(b) Prove that if

   $$\dfrac{a}{b} = \dfrac{c}{d}, \quad \text{then} \quad \dfrac{a-b}{a+b} = \dfrac{c-d}{c+d}$$

Review Problems

15. Arrange each of the following in increasing order.

   (a) $\dfrac{-2}{5}, \dfrac{-3}{5}, 0, \dfrac{1}{5}, \dfrac{2}{5}$ (b) $\dfrac{7}{12}, \dfrac{13}{18}, \dfrac{13}{24}$

16. Find the solution sets for each of the following.

   (a) $\dfrac{3}{4}x - \dfrac{5}{8} \geq \dfrac{1}{2}$ (b) $\dfrac{-x}{5} + \dfrac{1}{10} < \dfrac{-1}{2}$

   (c) $\dfrac{-2}{5}(10x+1) < 1 - x$

   (d) $\dfrac{2}{3}\left(\dfrac{1}{2}x - 7\right) \geq \dfrac{3}{4}x$

17. For each of the following, find three rational numbers between the given fractions.

   (a) $\dfrac{1}{3}$ and $\dfrac{2}{3}$ (b) $\dfrac{-5}{12}$ and $\dfrac{-1}{18}$

Section 6-6   Exponents Revisited

Recall that for whole numbers a, m, and n, with $a \neq 0$, the following properties hold:

1. $a^m = \underbrace{a \cdot a \cdot a \cdot \ldots \cdot a}_{m \text{ factors}}$

2. $a^m \cdot a^n = a^{m+n}$

3. $a^0 = 1$ where $a \neq 0$

Property (3) is consistent with property (2). If $m = 0$, then $a^m \cdot a^n = a^{m+n}$ becomes $a^0 \cdot a^n = a^{0+n} = a^n$ and 1 is the only number that, on multiplying by a^n, gives a^n. The above notions can be extended for rational-number values of a. For example, consider the following.

$$\left(\frac{2}{3}\right)^4 = \frac{2}{3} \cdot \frac{2}{3} \cdot \frac{2}{3} \cdot \frac{2}{3}$$

$$\left(\frac{2}{3}\right)^2 \cdot \left(\frac{2}{3}\right)^3 = \left(\frac{2}{3} \cdot \frac{2}{3}\right) \cdot \left(\frac{2}{3} \cdot \frac{2}{3} \cdot \frac{2}{3}\right) = \left(\frac{2}{3}\right)^{2+3} = \left(\frac{2}{3}\right)^5$$

$$\left(\frac{2}{3}\right)^0 = 1$$

Exponents can also be extended to negative integers as follows:

$10^3 = 10 \cdot 10 \cdot 10$

$10^2 = 10 \cdot 10$

$10^1 = 10$

$10^0 = 1$

Notice that as the exponents decrease by 1, the numbers on the right are divided by 10. Thus, the pattern might be continued as

$$10^{-1} = \frac{1}{10} = \frac{1}{10^1}$$

$$10^{-2} = \frac{1}{10} \cdot \frac{1}{10} = \frac{1}{10^2}$$

$$10^{-3} = \frac{1}{10^2} \cdot \frac{1}{10} = \frac{1}{10^3}$$

If the pattern is extended, then we would predict that $10^{-n} = \frac{1}{10^n}$. This is true, and—in general—for any nonzero number a, $a^{-n} = \frac{1}{a^n}$.

Remark   Another explanation for the definition of a^{-n} is as follows. If the property $a^m \cdot a^n = a^{m+n}$ is to hold for all integer exponents, then $a^{-n} \cdot a^n = a^{-n+n} = a^0 = 1$. Thus, a^{-n} is the multiplicative inverse of a^n, and, consequently, $a^{-n} = \frac{1}{a^n}$.

Consider whether the property $a^m \cdot a^n = a^{m+n}$ can be extended to include all powers of a, where the exponents are integers. For example, is it true that $2^4 \cdot 2^{-3} = 2^{4+-3} = 2^1$? The definitions of 2^{-3} and the properties of non-negative exponents assure that this is true.

$$2^4 \cdot 2^{-3} = 2^4 \cdot \frac{1}{2^3} = \frac{2^4}{2^3} = \frac{2^1 \cdot 2^3}{2^3} = 2^1$$

Also, $2^{-4} \cdot 2^{-3} = 2^{-4+-3} = 2^{-7}$ is true because

$$2^{-4} \cdot 2^{-3} = \frac{1}{2^4} \cdot \frac{1}{2^3} = \frac{1 \cdot 1}{2^4 \cdot 2^3} = \frac{1}{2^{4+3}} = \frac{1}{2^7} = 2^{-7}$$

In general, with integer exponents the following property holds.

Property For any nonzero rational number a and any integers m and n, $a^m \cdot a^n = a^{m+n}$.

Other properties of exponents can be developed using the notions of rational numbers.

$$\frac{2^5}{2^3} = \frac{2^3 \cdot 2^2}{2^3} = 2^2 = 2^{5-3} \qquad \frac{2^5}{2^8} = \frac{2^5}{2^5 \cdot 2^3} = \frac{1}{2^3} = 2^{-3}$$

Thus, for any rational number a such that $a \neq 0$ and for integers m and n such that $m > n$, $\frac{a^m}{a^n} = a^{m-n}$. Now, consider the case when $m < n$, such as $\frac{2^5}{2^8}$.

If the property $\frac{a^m}{a^n} = a^{m-n}$ is to hold, then $\frac{2^5}{2^8} = 2^{5-8} = 2^{-3}$. This is true as above. Since a similar argument holds if $m = n$, we have the following property.

Property For any rational number a such that $a \neq 0$ and any integers m and n, $\frac{a^m}{a^n} = a^{m-n}$.

Suppose a is a nonzero rational number and m and n are positive integers.

$$(a^m)^n = \underbrace{a^m \cdot a^m \cdot a^m \cdot \ldots \cdot a^m}_{n \text{ factors}} = \overbrace{a^{m+m+\cdots+m}}^{n \text{ terms}} = a^{nm} = a^{mn}$$

Thus, $(a^m)^n = a^{mn}$. For example, $(2^3)^4 = 2^{3\cdot4} = 2^{12}$.

Does this property hold for negative-integer exponents? For example, does $(2^3)^{-4} = 2^{(3)(-4)} = 2^{-12}$? The answer is yes, because $(2^3)^{-4} = \frac{1}{(2^3)^4} = \frac{1}{2^{12}} = 2^{-12}$. Also, $(2^{-3})^4 = \left(\frac{1}{2^3}\right)^4 = \frac{1}{2^3} \cdot \frac{1}{2^3} \cdot \frac{1}{2^3} \cdot \frac{1}{2^3} = \frac{1^4}{(2^3)^4} = \frac{1}{2^{12}} = 2^{-12}$.

Property For any rational number $a \neq 0$ and any integers m and n, $(a^m)^n = a^{mn}$.

Using the definitions and properties developed, additional properties can be derived. Notice, for example, that

$$\left(\frac{2}{3}\right)^4 = \frac{2}{3} \cdot \frac{2}{3} \cdot \frac{2}{3} \cdot \frac{2}{3} = \frac{2 \cdot 2 \cdot 2 \cdot 2}{3 \cdot 3 \cdot 3 \cdot 3} = \frac{2^4}{3^4}$$

This can be generalized as follows.

Property For any nonzero rational number $\dfrac{a}{b}$ and any integer m,

$$\left(\frac{a}{b}\right)^m = \frac{a^m}{b^m}$$

Note that from the definition of negative exponents, the above property, and division of fractions, we have

$$\left(\frac{a}{b}\right)^{-m} = \frac{1}{\left(\dfrac{a}{b}\right)^m} = \frac{1}{\dfrac{a^m}{b^m}} = \frac{b^m}{a^m} = \left(\frac{b}{a}\right)^m$$

Consequently, $\left(\dfrac{a}{b}\right)^{-m} = \left(\dfrac{b}{a}\right)^m$.

A property similar to this holds for multiplication. For example,

$$(2 \cdot 3)^{-3} = \frac{1}{(2 \cdot 3)^3} = \frac{1}{2^3 \cdot 3^3} = \left(\frac{1}{2^3}\right) \cdot \left(\frac{1}{3^3}\right) = 2^{-3} \cdot 3^{-3}$$

and in general, it is true that $(a \cdot b)^m = a^m \cdot b^m$ if a and b are rational numbers and m is an integer.

The definitions and properties of exponents are summarized in the following list.

Properties   **Properties of Exponents**

1. $a^m = \underbrace{a \cdot a \cdot a \cdot \ldots \cdot a}_{m \text{ factors}}$, where m is a positive integer

2. $a^0 = 1$, where $a \neq 0$

3. $a^{-m} = \dfrac{1}{a^m}$, where $a \neq 0$

4. $a^m \cdot a^n = a^{m+n}$

5. $\dfrac{a^m}{a^n} = a^{m-n}$, where $a \neq 0$

6. $(a^m)^n = a^{mn}$

7. $\left(\dfrac{a}{b}\right)^m = \dfrac{a^m}{b^m}$, where $b \neq 0$

8. $(ab)^m = a^m \cdot b^m$

Observe that all the properties of exponents refer to powers with either the same base or the same exponent. Hence, to evaluate expressions using exponents where different bases or powers are used, perform all the computations or rewrite the expressions using either the same base or exponent if possible. For example, $\dfrac{27^4}{81^3}$ can be rewritten as $\dfrac{27^4}{81^3} = \dfrac{(3^3)^4}{(3^4)^3} = \dfrac{3^{12}}{3^{12}} = 1$.

Example 6-24

Write each of the following in simplest form, using positive exponents in the final answer.

(a) $16^2 \cdot 8^{-3}$
(b) $20^2 \div 2^4$
(c) $(3x)^3 + 2y^2x^0 + 5y^2 + x^2 \cdot x$, where $x \neq 0$
(d) $(a^{-3} + b^{-3})^{-1}$

Solution

(a) $16^2 \cdot 8^{-3} = (2^4)^2 \cdot (2^3)^{-3} = 2^8 \cdot 2^{-9} = 2^{8+-9} = 2^{-1} = \dfrac{1}{2}$

(b) $\dfrac{20^2}{2^4} = \dfrac{(2^2 \cdot 5)^2}{2^4} = \dfrac{2^4 \cdot 5^2}{2^4} = 5^2$

(c) $(3x)^3 + 2y^2x^0 + 5y^2 + x^2 \cdot x = 27x^3 + 2y^2 \cdot 1 + 5y^2 + x^3$
$\qquad = (27x^3 + x^3) + (2y^2 + 5y^2) = 28x^3 + 7y^2$

(d) $(a^{-3} + b^{-3})^{-1} = \left(\dfrac{1}{a^3} + \dfrac{1}{b^3}\right)^{-1} = \left(\dfrac{b^3 + a^3}{a^3b^3}\right)^{-1} = \dfrac{1}{\frac{a^3+b^3}{a^3b^3}} = \dfrac{a^3b^3}{a^3+b^3}$

PROBLEM SET 6-6

1. Write each of the following in simplest form with positive exponents in the final answer.
(a) $3^{-7} \cdot 3^{-6}$ (b) $3^7 \cdot 3^6$
(c) $5^{15} \div 5^4$ (d) $5^{15} \div 5^{-4}$
(e) $(^-5)^{-2}$ (f) $\dfrac{a^2}{a^{-3}}$, where $a \neq 0$
(g) $\dfrac{a}{a^{-1}}$, where $a \neq 0$

2. Write each of the following in simplest form, using positive exponents in the final answer.
(a) $\left(\dfrac{1}{2}\right)^3 \cdot \left(\dfrac{1}{2}\right)^7$ (b) $\left(\dfrac{1}{2}\right)^9 \div \left(\dfrac{1}{2}\right)^6$
(c) $\left(\dfrac{2}{3}\right)^5 \cdot \left(\dfrac{4}{9}\right)^2$ (d) $\left(\dfrac{3}{5}\right)^7 \div \left(\dfrac{3}{5}\right)^7$
(e) $\left(\dfrac{3}{5}\right)^{-7} \div \left(\dfrac{5}{3}\right)^4$ (f) $\left[\left(\dfrac{5}{6}\right)^7\right]^3$

3. If a and b are rational numbers with $a \neq 0$ and $b \neq 0$ and m and n are integers, which of the following are true and which are false? Justify your answer.
(a) $a^m \cdot b^n = (ab)^{m+n}$ (b) $a^m \cdot b^n = (ab)^{mn}$
(c) $a^m \cdot b^m = (ab)^{2m}$ (d) $a^0 = 0$
(e) $(a + b)^m = a^m + b^m$
(f) $(a + b)^{-m} = \dfrac{1}{a^m} + \dfrac{1}{b^m}$ (g) $a^{mn} = a^m \cdot a^n$
(h) $\left(\dfrac{a}{b}\right)^{-1} = \dfrac{b}{a}$

4. Solve for the integer n in each of the following.
(a) $2^n = 32$ (b) $n^2 = 36$
(c) $2^n \cdot 2^7 = 2^5$ (d) $2^n \cdot 2^7 = 8$
(e) $(2 + n)^2 = 2^2 + n^2$ (f) $3^n = 27^5$

5. A human has approximately 25 trillion ($25 \cdot 10^{12}$) red blood cells, each with an average radius of $4 \cdot 10^{-3}$ mm (millimeters). If these cells were placed end to end in a line, how long would the line be in millimeters? If 1 km is 10^6 mm, how long would the line be in kilometers?

6. Solve each of the following inequalities for x, where x is an integer.
(a) $3^x \leq 81$ (b) $4^x < 8$
(c) $3^{2x} > 27$ (d) $2^x > 1$

7. Rewrite the following expressions using positive exponents and expressing all fractions in simplest form.
(a) $x^{-1} - x$ (b) $x^2 - y^{-2}$
(c) $y^{-3} + y^3$ (d) $2x^2 + (2x)^2 + 2^2x$
(e) $\dfrac{3a - b}{(3a - b)^{-1}}$

(f) $(2x^2) + (4a)^3 + a^2 \cdot 3a + 4x^2$
(g) $(x^{-2} + 3y^{-1})^{-1}$

8. Which of the fractions in each pair is greater?

(a) $\left(\dfrac{1}{2}\right)^3$ or $\left(\dfrac{1}{2}\right)^4$ (b) $\left(\dfrac{3}{4}\right)^{10}$ or $\left(\dfrac{3}{4}\right)^8$

(c) $\left(\dfrac{4}{3}\right)^{10}$ or $\left(\dfrac{4}{3}\right)^8$ (d) $\left(\dfrac{3}{4}\right)^{10}$ or $\left(\dfrac{4}{5}\right)^{10}$

(e) $\left(\dfrac{4}{3}\right)^{10}$ or $\left(\dfrac{5}{4}\right)^{10}$ (f) $\left(\dfrac{3}{4}\right)^{100}$ or $\left(\dfrac{3}{4} \cdot \dfrac{9}{10}\right)^{100}$

(d) $\dfrac{13 \cdot 4}{40 \cdot 130}$ (e) $\dfrac{4}{3} \cdot \dfrac{27}{16}$ (f) $\dfrac{10^4 \cdot 7^8}{10^6 \cdot 7^6}$

(g) $\dfrac{3}{4} \div \dfrac{4}{3}$ (h) $\dfrac{x^3}{x^3 + x^2 y}$

12. Solve for x in each of the following.

(a) $\dfrac{-3}{4} x = 1$ (b) $\dfrac{2}{3} x = \dfrac{-3}{5}$

(c) $\dfrac{1}{3} x - 5 = \dfrac{-3}{4} x$ (d) $\dfrac{x}{3} = \dfrac{-3}{4}$

(e) $\dfrac{x}{3} = \dfrac{27}{x}$ (f) $\dfrac{x+1}{3} = \dfrac{3}{4} x$

Review Problems

9. If a machine produces 6 items every 5 seconds, how many items can the machine produce in 3 minutes?

10. If 3 out of every 80 items are defective, how many defective items are there among 720 items?

11. Find the simplest form for each of the following:

(a) $\dfrac{24}{84}$ (b) $\dfrac{12 \cdot 180}{18 \cdot 9}$ (c) $\dfrac{8^4}{24^4}$

13. If Rachel can paint $\frac{5}{6}$ of a house in 1 day, how long will it take her to paint the whole house?

14. If the ratio of boys to girls in a class is 3 to 8, will the ratio of boys to girls change, become greater, or become smaller if 2 new boys and 2 new girls join the class? Justify your answer.

15. Arrange the following in increasing order: $\frac{-2}{3}, \frac{-3}{4}, \frac{-6}{7}, \frac{-1}{2}, 0, \frac{4}{5}, \frac{6}{7}, \frac{7}{9}, \frac{9}{7}.$

SOLUTION TO THE PRELIMINARY PROBLEM

UNDERSTANDING THE PROBLEM To understand the problem, suppose the collection consisted of 40 precious stones. (We try 40 because $\frac{1}{4}$ of 40, $\frac{3}{10}$ of 40, and $\frac{1}{5}$ of 40 are all integers. Twenty also would have been a good number to try.) In this case, the number of diamonds is $\frac{1}{4} \cdot 40$, or 10; the number of pieces of jade is $\frac{3}{10} \cdot 40$, or 12; the number of rubies is $\frac{1}{5} \cdot 40$, or 8; and the number of sapphires is $\frac{1}{10} \cdot 40$, or 4. The number of emeralds could be found by subtracting the total number of all the other precious stones from 40, that is, $40 - (10 + 12 + 8 + 4)$, or 6. Could 40 be the correct answer to the original problem? To see whether this is the case, we must determine if the condition that Ms. Castafiore had 6 fewer emeralds than diamonds is satisfied. Because 6 is 4 less than 10, not 6 less, 40 is an incorrect solution.

DEVISING A PLAN Because the total number of jewels is not known, we designate it by x and set up an equation involving x. An equation can be formed from the information in the last sentence of Understanding the Problem. We know that the number of emeralds is 6 less than the number of diamonds. We record this as follows.

Number of emeralds = (Number of diamonds) − 6

From the given information, we try to find expressions for the number of diamonds and the number of emeralds in terms of x. Substituting the expressions into the equation, we obtain an equation in terms of x. The solution of the equation will give the value of x. The number of emeralds can be found by finding the total of the other precious stones and subtracting that number from x.

CARRYING OUT THE PLAN Let x be the number of jewels. The number of diamonds is $\frac{1}{4}x$. We may find what fraction the number of emeralds is of the stone collection. The fraction of the total collection that constitutes the diamonds, jade, rubies, and sapphires is $\frac{1}{4} + \frac{3}{10} + \frac{1}{5} + \frac{1}{10}$, which equals $\frac{5}{20} + \frac{6}{20} + \frac{4}{20} + \frac{2}{20} = \frac{17}{20}$. Hence, the fraction that is emeralds is $1 - \frac{17}{20}$, or $\frac{3}{20}$. Consequently, the number of emeralds is $\frac{3}{20}x$. Thus, we have

Number of emeralds = (Number of diamonds) − 6

or

$$\frac{3}{20}x = \frac{1}{4}x - 6$$

We may solve the equation as follows.

$$20 \cdot \frac{3}{20}x = 20\left(\frac{1}{4}x - 6\right)$$

$$3x = 20 \cdot \frac{1}{4}x - 20 \cdot 6$$

$$3x = 5x - 120$$

$$120 = 5x - 3x$$

$$120 = 2x$$

$$60 = x$$

Thus, there are 60 precious stones altogether. Because the emeralds are $\frac{3}{20}$ of the collection, the number of emeralds was $\frac{3}{20} \cdot 60$, or 9.

LOOKING BACK We can check that 60 is the correct answer to the first part of the question by reasoning as we did in Understanding the Problem. Another way to find the solution is by the "guess and check" strategy. Realizing that 40 was too small a guess (why?), we try a greater number. Notice that the total number of jewels must be divisible by 4 and by 5. Hence, it must be a multiple of 20, that is, one of the numbers $20, 2 \cdot 20, 3 \cdot 20, \ldots$. Thus, our next guess should be 60.

QUESTIONS FROM THE CLASSROOM

1. A student wrote the solution set to the equation $\frac{x}{7} - 2 < {}^-3$ as $\{{}^-8, {}^-9, {}^-10, {}^-11, \ldots\}$. Is the student correct?

2. A student simplified the fraction $\frac{(m+n)}{(p+n)}$ to $\frac{m}{p}$. Is that student correct?

3. Without thinking, one student argued that a pizza cut into 12 pieces was more than a pizza cut into 6 pieces. How would you respond?

4. When working on the problem of simplifying $\frac{3}{4} \cdot \frac{1}{2} \cdot \frac{2}{3}$, a student did the following.

$$\frac{3}{4} \cdot \frac{1}{2} \cdot \frac{2}{3} = \left(\frac{3 \cdot 1}{4 \cdot 2}\right)\left(\frac{3 \cdot 2}{4 \cdot 3}\right) = \frac{3}{8} \cdot \frac{6}{12} = \frac{18}{96}$$

What was the error?

5. A student asks, "If the ratio of boys to girls in the class is $\frac{2}{3}$, and 4 boys and 6 girls join the class, then the new ratio is $\frac{2+4}{3+6}$, or $\frac{6}{9}$. Since $\frac{2}{3}+\frac{4}{6}=\frac{2+4}{3+6}$, can all fractions be added in the same way?

6. Is $\frac{0}{6}$ in simplest form? Why or why not?

7. A student says that taking one half of a number is the same as dividing the number by one half. Is this correct?

8. A student writes $\frac{15}{53}<\frac{1}{3}$ because $3\cdot15<53\cdot1$. Another student writes $\frac{15}{53}=\frac{1}{3}$. Where is the fallacy?

9. On a test, a student wrote the following.

$$\frac{x}{7}-2<{}^-3$$

$$\frac{x}{7}<{}^-1$$

$$x>{}^-7$$

What is the error?

10. A student claims that each of the following is an arithmetic sequence. Is the student right?

(a) $\frac{1}{2},\frac{2}{3},\frac{3}{4},\frac{4}{5},\frac{5}{6},\frac{6}{7},\frac{7}{8},\cdots$

(b) $\frac{1}{2},\left(\frac{1}{2}\right)^{-2},\left(\frac{1}{2}\right)^{-5},\left(\frac{1}{2}\right)^{-8},\left(\frac{1}{2}\right)^{-11},\cdots$

11. A student claims that she found a new way to obtain a fraction between two positive fractions: If $\frac{a}{b}$ and $\frac{c}{d}$ are two positive fractions, then $\frac{a+c}{b+d}$ is between these fractions. Is she right?

12. A student claims that if $\frac{a}{b}=\frac{c}{d}$, then $\frac{a+c}{b+d}=\frac{a}{b}=\frac{c}{d}$. Is he right?

13. A student claims that $\frac{1}{x}<\frac{1}{y}$ if and only if $x>y$. Assuming that $x\neq0$ and $y\neq0$, is this right?

14. A student claims that if x is positive, then $\frac{1}{x}<x$. What is your response?

CHAPTER OUTLINE

I. Rational numbers

A. Numbers of the form $\frac{a}{b}$, where a and b are integers and $b\neq0$, are called **rational numbers.**

B. A rational number can be used as:
   1. A division problem or the solution to a multiplication problem.
   2. A partition, or part, of a whole.
   3. A ratio.

C. **Fundamental Law of Fractions:** For any rational number $\frac{a}{b}$ and any integer $c\neq0$, $\frac{a}{b}=\frac{ac}{bc}$.

D. Two rational numbers $\frac{a}{b}$ and $\frac{c}{d}$ are **equal** if and only if $ad=bc$.

E. If GCD$(a,b)=1$, then $\frac{a}{b}$ is said to be in **simplest form.**

F. If $0<a<b$, then $\frac{a}{b}$ is called a **proper fraction.**

II. Operations on rational numbers

A. $\frac{a}{b}+\frac{c}{b}=\frac{a+c}{b}$

B. $\frac{a}{b}+\frac{c}{d}=\frac{ad+bc}{bd}$

C. $\frac{a}{b}-\frac{c}{d}=\frac{ad-bc}{bd}$

D. $\frac{a}{b}\cdot\frac{c}{d}=\frac{ac}{bd}$

E. $\frac{a}{b}\div\frac{c}{d}=\frac{a}{b}\cdot\frac{d}{c}=\frac{ad}{bc}$, where $c\neq0$

III. Properties of rational numbers
A.

	Addition	Subtraction	Multiplication	Division
Closure	Yes	Yes	Yes	Yes, except for division by 0
Commutative	Yes	No	Yes	No
Associative	Yes	No	Yes	No
Identity	Yes	No	Yes	No
Inverse	Yes	No	Yes, except 0	No

B. **Distributive property for multiplication over addition** of rational numbers x, y, and z: $x(y+z)=xy+xz$

C. **Denseness property:** Between any two rational numbers, there is another rational number.

IV. Ratio and proportion

A. A quotient $a \div b$ is a **ratio.**

B. A **proportion** is an equation of two ratios.

C. Properties of proportions

1. If $\dfrac{a}{b} = \dfrac{c}{d}$, then $\dfrac{b}{a} = \dfrac{d}{c}$, where $a \neq 0$ and $c \neq 0$.

2. If $\dfrac{a}{b} = \dfrac{c}{d}$, then $\dfrac{a}{c} = \dfrac{b}{d}$, where $c \neq 0$.

V. Exponents

A. $a^m = \underbrace{a \cdot a \cdot a \cdot \ldots \cdot a}_{m \text{ factors}}$, where m is a positive integer and a is a rational number.

B. Properties of exponents involving rational numbers

1. $a^0 = 1$, where $a \neq 0$

2. $a^{-n} = \dfrac{1}{a^n}$, where $a \neq 0$ and n is any rational number

3. $a^m \cdot a^n = a^{m+n}$

4. $(a^m)^n = a^{mn}$

5. $(ab)^m = a^m b^m$

6. $\left(\dfrac{a}{b}\right)^m = \dfrac{a^m}{b^m}, \quad b \neq 0$

7. $\dfrac{a^m}{a^n} = a^{m-n}, \quad a \neq 0$

CHAPTER TEST

1. For each of the following, draw a diagram illustrating the fraction.

 (a) $\dfrac{3}{4}$ (b) $\dfrac{2}{3}$

2. Write three rational numbers equal to $\frac{5}{6}$.

3. Reduce each of the following rational numbers to simplest form.

 (a) $\dfrac{24}{28}$ (b) $\dfrac{ax^2}{bx}$ (c) $\dfrac{0}{17}$

 (d) $\dfrac{45}{81}$ (e) $\dfrac{b^2 + bx}{b + x}$ (f) $\dfrac{16}{216}$

4. Replace the comma with $>$, $<$, or $=$ in each of the following pairs to make a true statement.

 (a) $\dfrac{6}{10}, \dfrac{120}{200}$ (b) $\dfrac{^-3}{4}, \dfrac{^-5}{6}$

 (c) $\left(\dfrac{4}{5}\right)^{10}, \left(\dfrac{4}{5}\right)^{20}$ (d) $\left(1 + \dfrac{1}{3}\right)^2, \left(1 + \dfrac{1}{3}\right)^3$

5. Perform each of the following computations.

 (a) $\dfrac{5}{6} + \dfrac{4}{15}$ (b) $\dfrac{4}{25} - \dfrac{3}{35}$

 (c) $\dfrac{5}{6} \cdot \dfrac{12}{13}$ (d) $\dfrac{5}{6} \div \dfrac{12}{15}$

 (e) $\left(5\dfrac{1}{6} + 7\dfrac{1}{3}\right) \div 2\dfrac{1}{4}$ (f) $\left(-5\dfrac{1}{6} + 7\dfrac{1}{3}\right) \div \dfrac{^-9}{4}$

6. Find the additive and multiplicative inverses for each of the following.

 (a) 3 (b) $3\dfrac{1}{7}$ (c) $\dfrac{5}{6}$ (d) $-\dfrac{3}{4}$

7. Simplify each of the following. Write your answer in the form $\dfrac{a}{b}$, where a and b are integers and $b \neq 0$.

 (a) $\dfrac{\frac{1}{2} - \frac{3}{4}}{\frac{5}{6} - \frac{7}{8}}$ (b) $\dfrac{\frac{3}{4} \cdot \frac{5}{6}}{\frac{1}{2}}$ (c) $\dfrac{(\frac{1}{2})^2 - (\frac{3}{4})^2}{\frac{1}{2} + \frac{3}{4}}$

8. Solve each of the following for x, where x is a rational number.

 (a) $\dfrac{1}{4}x - \dfrac{3}{5} \leq \dfrac{1}{2}(3 - 2x)$

 (b) $\dfrac{x}{3} - \dfrac{x}{2} \geq \dfrac{^-1}{4}$

 (c) $\dfrac{2}{3}\left(\dfrac{3}{4}x - 1\right) = \dfrac{2}{3} - x$

 (d) $\dfrac{5}{6} = \dfrac{4 - x}{3}$

9. Justify the invert-and-multiply algorithm for division of rational numbers.

10. If the ratio of boys to girls in Mr. Good's class is 3 to 5, the ratio of boys to girls in Ms. Garcia's is the same, and you know that there are 15 girls in Ms. Garcia's class, how many boys are in her class?

11. Write each of the following in simplest form with nonnegative exponents in the final answer.

(a) $\left(\frac{1}{2}\right)^4\left(\frac{1}{2}\right)^7$ (b) $5^{-16} \div 5^4$

(c) $\left[\left(\frac{2}{3}\right)^7\right]^{-4}$ (d) $3^{16} \cdot 3^2$

12. John has $54\frac{1}{4}$ yards of material. If he needs to cut the cloth into pieces that are $3\frac{1}{12}$ yards long, how many pieces can be cut? How much material will be left over?

13. Without actually performing the given operations, choose the most appropriate estimation (among the numbers in parentheses) for the given expression.

(a) $\frac{30\frac{3}{8}}{4\frac{1}{9}} \cdot \frac{8\frac{1}{3}}{3\frac{8}{9}}$ (15, 20, 8)

(b) $\left(\frac{3}{800} + \frac{4}{5000} + \frac{15}{6}\right) \cdot 6$ (15, 0, 132)

(c) $\frac{1}{407} \div \frac{1}{1609}$ $(\frac{1}{4}, 4, 0)$

SELECTED BIBLIOGRAPHY

Bennett, A., Jr., and P. Davidson. *Fraction Bars.* Palo Alto, Calif.: Creative Publications.

Brown, C. "Fractions on Grid Paper." *Arithmetic Teacher* 27 (January 1979):8–10.

Carlisle, E. "Fractions and Popsicle Sticks," *Arithmetic Teacher* 27 (February 1980):50–51.

Chiosi, L. "Fractions Revisited." *Arithmetic Teacher* 31 (April 1984):46–47.

Coxford, A., and L. Ellerbruch. "Fractional Numbers." In *Mathematics Learning in Early Childhood,* 37th Yearbook of the National Council of Teachers of Mathematics. Reston, Va.: National Council of Teachers of Mathematics, 1975.

Ellerbruch, L., and J. Payne. "A Teaching Sequence from Initial Concepts Through the Addition of Unlike Fractions." In *Developing Computational Skills,* 1978 Yearbook of the National Council of Teachers of Mathematics. Reston, Va.: National Council of Teachers of Mathematics, 1978.

Ettline, J. "A Uniform Approach to Fractions." *Arithmetic Teacher* 32 (March 1985):42–43.

Feinberg, M. "Is It Necessary to Invert?" *Arithmetic Teacher* 27 (January 1980):50–52.

From the File. "Fractions." *Arithmetic Teacher* 32 (January 1985):43.

From the File. "Fractions Made Easy." *Arithmetic Teacher* 32 (September 1985):39.

Hollis, L. "Teaching Rational Numbers—Primary Grades." *Arithmetic Teacher* 31 (February 1984):36–39.

Jacobson, M. "Teaching Rational Numbers—Intermediate Grades." *Arithmetic Teacher* 31 (February 1984):40–42.

Jencks, S., D. Peck, and L. Chatterley. "Why Blame the Kids? We Teach Mistakes." *Arithmetic Teacher* 28 (October 1980):38–42.

Kalman, D. "Up Fractions! Up *n/m*!" *Arithmetic Teacher* 32 (April 1985):42–43.

Kiernen, T. "One Point of View: Helping Children Understand Rational Numbers." *Arithmetic Teacher* 31 (February 1984):3.

Lester, F. "Teacher Education: Preparing Teachers to Teach Rational Numbers." *Arithmetic Teacher* 31 (February 1984):54–56.

Leutzinger, L., and G. Nelson. "Let's Do It—Fractions With Models." *Arithmetic Teacher* 27 (May 1980): 6–11.

Payne, J. "Curricular Issues: Teaching Rational Numbers." *Arithmetic Teacher* 31 (February 1984):14–17.

Payne, J. "One Point of View: Sense and Nonsense about Fractions and Decimals." *Arithmetic Teacher* 27 (January 1980):4–7.

Post, T. "Fractions: Results and Implications from National Assessment." *Arithmetic Teacher* 28 (May 1981):26–31.

Prevost, F. "Teaching Rational Numbers—Junior High School." *Arithmetic Teacher* 31 (February 1984):43–46.

Sanok, G. "Mathematics and Saltine Crackers." *Arithmetic Teacher* 28 (December 1980):36.

Scott, W. "Fractions Taught by Folding Paper Strips." *Arithmetic Teacher* 28 (January 1981):18–21.

Shookoohi, G-H. "Readiness of Eight-Year-Old Children to Understand the Division of Fractions." *Arithmetic Teacher* 27 (March 1980):40–43.

Skypek, D. "Special Characteristics of Rational Numbers." *Arithmetic Teacher* 31 (February 1984):10–12.

Sweetland, R. "Understanding Multiplication of Fractions." *Arithmetic Teacher* 32 (September 1984):48–52.

Thiessen, D. "David's Algorithm for the L.C.D." *Arithmetic Teacher* 28 (March 1981):18.

Trafton, P., and Zawojewski, J.S. "Teaching Rational Number Division: A Special Problem." *Arithmetic Teacher* 31 (February 1984):20–22.

Van de Walle, J., and Thompson, C. "Fractions with Fraction Strips." *Arithmetic Teacher* 32 (December 1984):48–52.

CHAPTER 7

Decimals

Preliminary Problem

Big Save Airlines allows each passenger to carry x pounds of luggage free of charge, with an additional charge for each extra pound. The combined weight of luggage for Mr. and Mrs. Byrd was 105 pounds. Mr. Byrd and Mrs. Byrd had to pay $1.00 and $1.50, respectively, for extra weight. They then noticed that a third passenger also had 105 pounds of luggage and was charged $6.50 for the number of pounds over the x-pound limit. How many pounds are allowed for each passenger without a charge?

Introduction

Although the Hindu-Arabic numeration system discussed in Chapter 3 was perfected around the sixth century, the extension of the system to decimals did not take place until about a thousand years later. Suggestions for decimals were recorded long before the Dutch scientist Simon Stevin was credited as being responsible for their invention. The only significant improvement in the system since Stevin's time has been in notation. Even today there is no universally accepted form of writing a decimal point. For example, in the United States we write 6.75; in England this number is written as 6 · 75; and in Germany and France it is written 6,75.

Today, the increased use of the metric system, which uses decimals, and the emergence of calculators and computers make a knowledge of decimals even more important in schools and in homes. The full impact of these developments on the teaching of decimals is not yet known.

Section 7-1   Decimals and Decimal Operations

The word *decimal* comes from the Latin *decem*, which means ten. Most people first see decimals when dealing with our notation for money. For example, a sign that says that a doll costs $9.95 means that the cost is nine whole dollars and some part of a dollar. The dot in $9.95 is called the **decimal point.** The digits to the left of the dot form the integer part of the decimal. The digits to the right represent the sum of the elements of a set of rational numbers whose numerators are the given digits and whose denominators are successive natural-number powers of 10 starting with 10^1. For example, 12.61843 represents

decimal point

$$12 + \frac{6}{10^1} + \frac{1}{10^2} + \frac{8}{10^3} + \frac{4}{10^4} + \frac{3}{10^5} \quad \text{or} \quad 12\frac{61,843}{100,000}$$

The decimal 12.61843 is read "twelve and sixty-one thousand eight hundred forty-three hundred-thousandths." The decimal point is read as "and." Each place to the right of a decimal point may be named by its power of 10. For example, the places of 12.61843 can be named as shown in Table 7-1.

HISTORICAL NOTE

In 1584, Simon Stevin (1548–1620) wrote *La Disme,* a work that gave rules for computing with decimals. He recognized the need to shorten work with fractions. He not only stated the rules for decimal computations, but also suggested practical applications for decimals. He recommended that his government adopt the decimal system.

Stevin's other achievements include being a quartermaster general for the Dutch army; his contributions in physics to statics and hydrostatics; his work with military engineering; and his invention of a carriage that carried 28 people and that was propelled by sails and ran along the seashore.

Table 7-1

Tens	Units	And	Tenths	Hundredths	Thousandths	Ten-thousandths	Hundred-thousandths
1	2	.	6	1	8	4	3

Table 7-2 shows other examples of decimals, their meanings, and their fractional forms.

Table 7-2

Decimal	Meaning	Fraction
5.3	$5 + \dfrac{3}{10}$	$5\dfrac{3}{10}$, or $\dfrac{53}{10}$
0.02	$0 + \dfrac{0}{10} + \dfrac{2}{100}$	$\dfrac{2}{100}$
2.0103	$2 + \dfrac{0}{10} + \dfrac{1}{100} + \dfrac{0}{1000} + \dfrac{3}{10,000}$	$2\dfrac{103}{10,000}$, or $\dfrac{20,1}{10,0}$
⁻3.6	$^{-}\left(3 + \dfrac{6}{10}\right)$	$^{-}3\dfrac{6}{10}$, or $-\dfrac{36}{10}$

Every decimal can be written in expanded form using place value and negative exponents. Thus, 12.61843 also may be written as $1 \cdot 10^1 + 2 \cdot 10^0 + 6 \cdot 10^{-1} + 1 \cdot 10^{-2} + 8 \cdot 10^{-3} + 4 \cdot 10^{-4} + 3 \cdot 10^{-5}$. However, to avoid negative exponents, most elementary school texts use fractional notation as in Table 7-2. The decimal 12.61843 also could be written as

$$12.61843 = 1 \cdot 10^1 + 2 \cdot 10^0 + 6\left(\frac{1}{10}\right) + 1\left(\frac{1}{100}\right) + 8\left(\frac{1}{1000}\right)$$

$$+ 4\left(\frac{1}{10,000}\right) + 3\left(\frac{1}{100,000}\right)$$

Example 7-1 shows how to convert rational numbers, whose denominators are powers of 10, to decimals.

Example 7-1

Convert each of the following to decimals.

(a) $\dfrac{56}{100}$ (b) $\dfrac{205}{10,000}$

Solution

(a) $\dfrac{56}{100} = \dfrac{5 \cdot 10 + 6}{10^2} = \dfrac{5 \cdot 10}{10^2} + \dfrac{6}{10^2} = \dfrac{5}{10} + \dfrac{6}{10^2} = 0.56$

(b) $\dfrac{205}{10,000} = \dfrac{2 \cdot 10^2 + 0 \cdot 10 + 5}{10^4} = \dfrac{2 \cdot 10^2}{10^4} + \dfrac{0 \cdot 10}{10^4} + \dfrac{5}{10^4}$

$= \dfrac{2}{10^2} + \dfrac{0}{10^3} + \dfrac{5}{10^4} = 0.0205$

The ideas in Example 7-1 can be reinforced using a calculator. For example, in part (a), press $\boxed{5}\ \boxed{6}\ \boxed{\div}\ \boxed{1}\ \boxed{0}\ \boxed{0}\ \boxed{=}$ and watch the display. Divide by 10 again and look at the new placement of the decimal point. Once more, divide by 10 (which amounts to dividing the original number, 56, by 10,000), and note the placement of the decimal point. This leads to the following general rule for dividing an integer by a power of 10.

To divide an integer by 10^n, count n digits from right to left, annexing zeros if necessary, and insert the decimal point to the left of the nth digit.

The fractions in Example 7-1 are easy to convert to decimals because the denominators are powers of 10. If the denominator of a fraction is not a power of 10, then the conversion to a decimal requires more work. For example, to write $\frac{3}{5}$ as a decimal, we use the problem-solving strategy of converting the problem to one we already know how to do. We know how to convert fractions in which the denominators are powers of 10 to decimals. Hence, we first change $\frac{3}{5}$ to a fraction in which the denominator is a power of 10, and then we convert it to a decimal.

$$\frac{3}{5} = \frac{3 \cdot 2}{5 \cdot 2} = \frac{6}{10} = 0.6$$

The reason for multiplying the numerator and denominator by 2 is apparent when we observe that in the denominator, $10 = 2 \cdot 5$. Because $10^n = (2 \cdot 5)^n = 2^n \cdot 5^n$, the prime factorization of the denominator must be $2^n \cdot 5^n$, in order for the denominator of a rational number to be 10^n. We use these ideas to write each fraction in Example 7-2 as a decimal.

Example 7-2

Express each of the following as decimals.

(a) $\dfrac{7}{2^6}$ (b) $\dfrac{1}{2^3 \cdot 5^4}$ (c) $\dfrac{1}{125}$ (d) $\dfrac{7}{250}$

Solution

(a) $\dfrac{7}{2^6} = \dfrac{7 \cdot 5^6}{2^6 \cdot 5^6} = \dfrac{7 \cdot 15,625}{(2 \cdot 5)^6} = \dfrac{109,375}{10^6} = 0.109375$

(b) $\dfrac{1}{2^3 \cdot 5^4} = \dfrac{1 \cdot 2^1}{2^3 \cdot 5^4 \cdot 2^1} = \dfrac{2}{2^4 \cdot 5^4} = \dfrac{2}{(2 \cdot 5)^4} = \dfrac{2}{10^4} = 0.0002$

(c) $\dfrac{1}{125} = \dfrac{1}{5^3} = \dfrac{1 \cdot 2^3}{5^3 \cdot 2^3} = \dfrac{8}{(5 \cdot 2)^3} = \dfrac{8}{10^3} = 0.008$

(d) $\dfrac{7}{250} = \dfrac{7}{2 \cdot 5^3} = \dfrac{7 \cdot 2^2}{(2 \cdot 5^3)2^2} = \dfrac{28}{(2 \cdot 5)^3} = \dfrac{28}{10^3} = 0.028$

terminating decimals   The answers in Example 7-2 are illustrations of **terminating decimals,** decimals that can be written with only a finite number of places to the right of the decimal point. If we attempt to rewrite $\frac{2}{11}$ as a terminating decimal using the method just developed, we first try to find a natural number b such that the following holds.

$$\frac{2}{11} = \frac{2b}{11b}, \qquad \text{where } 11b \text{ is a power of } 10$$

By the Fundamental Theorem of Arithmetic (discussed in Chapter 5), the only prime factors of a power of 10 are 2 and 5. Because $11b$ has 11 as a factor, we cannot write $11b$ as a power of 10, and therefore $\frac{2}{11}$ cannot be written as a terminating decimal. A similar argument using the Fundamental Theorem of Arithmetic holds in general, so we have the following result.

> A rational number $\frac{a}{b}$ in simplest form can be written as a terminating decimal
> if and only if the prime factorization of the denominator contains no primes other
> than 2 or 5.

Example 7-3

Which of the following fractions can be written as terminating decimals?

(a) $\frac{7}{8}$ (b) $\frac{6}{125}$ (c) $\frac{21}{28}$ (d) $\frac{37}{768}$

Solution

(a) $\frac{7}{8} = \frac{7}{2^3}$. Because the denominator is 2^3, $\frac{7}{8}$ can be written as a terminating decimal.

(b) $\frac{6}{125} = \frac{6}{5^3}$. The denominator is 5^3, so $\frac{6}{125}$ can be written as a terminating decimal.

(c) $\frac{21}{28} = \frac{21}{(2^2 \cdot 7)} = \frac{3}{2^2}$. The denominator of the fraction in simplest form is 2^2, so $\frac{21}{28}$ can be written as a terminating decimal.

(d) $\frac{37}{768} = \frac{37}{(2^8 \cdot 3)}$. This fraction is in simplest form and the denominator contains a factor of 3, so $\frac{37}{768}$ cannot be written as a terminating decimal.

Remark   As seen in Example 7-3(c), to determine whether a rational number $\frac{a}{b}$ can be represented as a terminating decimal, we consider the prime factorization of the denominator *only* if the fraction is in simplest form.

ADDING AND SUBTRACTING DECIMALS

To develop an algorithm for decimal addition, consider the sum $3.26 + 14.7$. We can compute the sum by changing it to a problem we already know how to solve, that is, a sum involving fractions. We then use the commutative and associative properties of addition to complete the computation.

$$3.26 + 14.7 = \left(3 + \frac{2}{10} + \frac{6}{100}\right) + \left(14 + \frac{7}{10}\right)$$

$$= (3 + 14) + \left(\frac{2}{10} + \frac{7}{10}\right) + \left(\frac{6}{100}\right)$$

$$= 17 + \frac{9}{10} + \frac{6}{100}$$

$$= 17.96$$

This addition, using fractions, was accomplished by grouping the integers, the tenths, and the hundredths, and adding. Because $14.7 = 14 + \frac{7}{10} = 14 + \frac{7}{10} + \frac{0}{100} = 14.70$, the addition $3.26 + 14.7$ can be accomplished by lining up the decimal points and adding as with whole numbers.

$$\begin{array}{r} 3.26 \\ + 14.70 \\ \hline 17.96 \end{array}$$

The algorithm for adding terminating decimals is a three-step process:

1. *List the numbers vertically, lining up the decimal points. (Append zeros if necessary.)*
2. *Add the numbers as though they were whole numbers.*
3. *Insert the decimal point in the sum directly below the decimal points in the numbers being added.*

Subtraction of terminating decimals also can be accomplished by lining up the decimal points and subtracting as with whole numbers. The justification of the method is left as an exercise.

Example 7-4

Compute each of the following.

(a) $14.36 + 5.2 + 0.036$ (b) $17.013 - 2.98$
(c) $17.01 - 2.938$

Solution

(a)
$$\begin{array}{r} 14.360 \\ 5.200 \\ + 0.036 \\ \hline 19.596 \end{array}$$

(b)
$$\begin{array}{r} 17.013 \\ - 2.980 \\ \hline 14.033 \end{array}$$

(c)
$$\begin{array}{r} 17.010 \\ - 2.938 \\ \hline 14.072 \end{array}$$

MULTIPLYING DECIMALS

Algorithms for multiplication of terminating decimals can be found by multiplying the corresponding fractions, each in the form $\frac{a}{b}$, where a and b are integers. Consider the product $(4.62)(2.4)$.

$$(4.62)(2.4) = \frac{462}{100} \cdot \frac{24}{10} = \frac{462}{10^2} \cdot \frac{24}{10^1} = \frac{462 \cdot 24}{10^2 \cdot 10^1} = \frac{11{,}088}{10^3} = 11.088$$

Notice that the answer to this computation was obtained by multiplying the whole numbers 462 and 24 and then dividing the result by 10^3.

The algorithm for multiplying decimals can be stated as follows.

If there are n digits to the right of the decimal point in one number and m digits to the right of the decimal point in a second number, multiply the two numbers, ignoring the decimals, and then place the decimal point so that there are n + m digits to the right of the decimal point in the product.

There are $n + m$ digits to the right of the decimal point in the product because $10^n \cdot 10^m = 10^{n+m}$.

Example 7-5

Compute each of the following.

(a) (6.2)(1.43)   (b) (0.02)(0.013)   (c) (1000)(3.6)

Solution

(a)
```
      1.4 3      (2 digits after the decimal point)
   ×    6.2      (1 digit after the decimal point)
      ─────
      2 8 6
    8 5 8
    ───────
    8.8 6 6      (3 digits after the decimal point)
```

(b)
```
       0.0 1 3
    ×    0.0 2
    ──────────
    0.0 0 0 2 6
```

(c)
```
         3.6
    ×  1 0 0 0
    ─────────
    3 6 0 0.0
```

Remark   Example 7-5(c) suggests that multiplication by 10^n, where n is a positive integer, results in moving the decimal point in the multiplicand n places to the right.

DIVIDING DECIMALS

To develop an algorithm for dividing decimals, we first consider the case of dividing a terminating decimal by a whole number. Consider $0.96 \div 3$. This division can be approached by rewriting the decimal as a fraction and then dividing.

$$0.96 \div 3 = \frac{96}{100} \div \frac{3}{1} = \frac{96}{100} \cdot \frac{1}{3} = \frac{96 \cdot 1}{100 \cdot 3} = \frac{1}{100} \cdot \frac{96}{3} = \frac{32}{100} = 0.32$$

The computation can also be accomplished using the following procedure.

```
     0.32
3 ) 0.96
     9
    ──
     6
     6
    ──
     0
```

When the divisor is a whole number, we see that the division can be handled as with whole numbers and the decimal point placed directly over the decimal point in the dividend. When the divisor is not a whole number, we use the strategy of changing the division problem to an equivalent division where the divisor is a whole number. For example, consider $1.2032 \div 0.32$. To obtain a whole-number divisor in the problem, we express the quotient as a fraction, then multiply the numerator and denominator of the fraction by 100.

$$\frac{1.2032}{0.32} = \frac{1.2032 \cdot 100}{0.32 \cdot 100} = \frac{120.32}{32}$$

This corresponds to rewriting the division problem in form (a) to an equivalent problem in form (b).

(a) $0.32\overline{)1.2032}$ (b) $32\overline{)120.32}$

In elementary school texts, this process is usually described as "moving" the decimal point two places to the right in both the dividend and the divisor. This process is usually indicated with arrows as shown below.

```
              3.7 6
   0.3 2)1.2 0,3 2      Multiply divisor and
          9 6           dividend by 100.
          2 4 3
          2 2 4
            1 9 2
            1 9 2
                0
```

Example 7-6

Compute each of the following.

(a) $13.169 \div 0.13$ (b) $9 \div 0.75$

Solution

(a)
```
           1 0 1.3
   0.1 3)1 3.1 6 9
         1 3
           1 6
           1 3
             3 9
             3 9
               0
```

(b)
```
            1 2
   0.75)9.0 0
        7 5
        1 5 0
        1 5 0
            0
```

Notice that in Example 7-6(b), we annexed two zeros in the dividend because $9/(0.75) = (9 \cdot 100)/(0.75 \cdot 100) = \frac{900}{75}$.

Example 7-7

An owner of a gasoline station must collect a gasoline tax of $0.11 on each gallon of gasoline sold. One week the owner paid $1595 in gasoline taxes. The pump price of a gallon of gas that week was $1.35.

(a) How many gallons of gas were sold during the week?

(b) What was the revenue after taxes for the week?

Solution

(a) To find the number of gallons of gas sold during the week, we must divide the total gas tax bill by the amount of the tax per gallon.

$$\frac{1595}{0.11} = 14,500$$

Thus, 14,500 gallons were sold.

(b) To obtain the revenue after taxes, we must first determine the revenue before taxes by multiplying the number of gallons sold times the cost per gallon.

$$(14,500)(\$1.35) = \$19,575$$

We then subtract the cost remitted in gasoline taxes.

$$\$19,575 - \$1595 = \$17,980$$

Thus, the revenue after gasoline taxes is $17,980.

PROBLEM SET 7-1

1. Write each of the following in expanded form.
   (a) 0.023   (b) 206.06
   (c) 312.0103   (d) 0.000132

2. Rewrite each of the following as decimals.
   (a) $4 \cdot 10^3 + 3 \cdot 10^2 + 5 \cdot 10 + 6 + 7 \cdot 10^{-1} + 8 \cdot 10^{-2}$
   (b) $4 \cdot 10^3 + 6 \cdot 10^{-1} + 8 \cdot 10^{-3}$

3. Write each of the following as numerals.
   (a) Five hundred thirty-six and seventy-six ten-thousandths
   (b) Three and eight thousandths
   (c) Four hundred thirty-six millionths
   (d) Five million and two tenths

4. Write each of the following terminating decimals as fractions.
   (a) 0.436   (b) 25.16   (c) $^-$316.027
   (d) 28.1902   (e) $^-$4.3   (f) $^-$62.01

5. Without performing the actual divisions, determine which of the following represent terminating decimals.

   (a) $\dfrac{4}{5}$ (b) $\dfrac{61}{2^2 \cdot 5}$ (c) $\dfrac{3}{6}$

   (d) $\dfrac{1}{2^5}$ (e) $\dfrac{36}{5^5}$ (f) $\dfrac{133}{625}$

   (g) $\dfrac{1}{3}$ (h) $\dfrac{2}{35}$ (i) $\dfrac{1}{13}$

6. Where possible, write each of the numbers in Problem 5 as terminating decimals.

7. Compute each of the following.
   (a) $36.812 + 0.43 + 1.96$
   (b) $200.01 - 32.007$ (c) $^-4.612 - 386.0193$
   (d) $(3.61)(0.413)$ (e) $(^-2.6)(4)$
   (f) $10.7663 \div 2.3$

8. Calculate the following by converting each decimal to a fraction, performing the computation, and then converting the fraction answer to a decimal.
   (a) $13.62 + 4.082$ (b) $12.62 - 4.082$
   (c) $(1.36)(0.02)$ (d) $(1.36) \div (0.02)$

9. Multiply each of the following by 10^8.
   (a) 4.63   (b) 0.04   (c) 46.3
   (d) 463.0   (e) 0.00463   (f) 0.0000000463

10. Which of the following divisions are equivalent to $18 \div 2$?
    (a) $20 \overline{)\, 180}$ (b) $0.2 \overline{)\, 0.18}$
    (c) $0.002 \overline{)\, 0.018}$ (d) $20 \overline{)\, 1800}$
    (e) $0.0002 \overline{)\, 0.00018}$ (f) $0.2 \overline{)\, 1.8}$

11. Continue the decimal patterns shown below. (Assume each sequence is either arithmetic or geometric.)
    (a) 0.9, 1.8, 2.7, 3.6, 4.5, _____, _____, _____
    (b) 0.3, 0.5, 0.7, 0.9, 0.11, _____, _____, _____
    (c) 1, 0.5, 0.25, 0.125, _____, _____, _____
    (d) 0.2, 1.5, 2.8, 4.1, 5.4, _____, _____, _____

12. The following are answers to various types of computations. Write an exercise for each answer.
    (a) 86.04 as an addition of two numbers
    (b) 353.76 as an addition of four numbers
    (c) 96.72 as a subtraction of two numbers

(d) 0.0138 as a multiplication of two numbers
(e) 0.12 as a subtraction of two numbers
(f) 2.03 as a division of two numbers

13. Explain why subtraction of terminating decimals can be accomplished by lining up the decimal points, subtracting as if the numbers were whole numbers, and then placing the decimal point in the difference.

14. If 0.896 inch of rain fell during 7 hours, what was the average amount of rain per hour?

13. If the average for common stocks rose 8.395 points during 5 days of trading, what was the average gain per day?

16. If Moose went to the store and bought a chair for $17.95, a lawn rake for $13.59, a spade for $14.86, a lawn mower for $179.98, and two six-packs for $2.43 each, what was the bill?

17. If the rainfall was 1.9 inches in March and 2.7 inches in April, how much more rain was there in April than in March?

18. At 60°F, 1 quart of water weighs 2.082 pounds. One cubic foot of water is 29.922 quarts. What is the weight of a cubic foot of water to the nearest thousandth of a pound?

19. Complete the following magic square; that is, make the sum of every row, column, and diagonal the same.

8.2		
3.7	5.5	
	9.1	2.8

20. Keith bought 30 pounds of nuts at $3.00 per pound and 20 pounds of nuts at $5.00 per pound. If he wanted to buy 10 more pounds of a different kind of nut to make the average price per pound equal to $4.50, what price should he pay for the additional 10 pounds?

21. (a) Find the product of 0.22 and 0.35 on the calculator. How does the placement of the decimal point in the answer on the calculator compare with the placement of the decimal point using the rule in this chapter? Explain.

(b) In a similar manner, investigate placement of the decimal point in the quotient obtained by performing the division 0.2436 ÷ 0.0006.

22. At a local bank, two different systems are available for charging for checking accounts. System A is a "dime-a-time" plan, as there is no monthly service charge and the charge is 10¢ per check written. System B is a plan with a service charge of 75¢ per month plus 7¢ per check written during that month.
(a) Which plan is the most economical if an average of 12 checks per month is written?
(b) Which system is the most economical if an average of 52 checks per month is written?
(c) What is the "break-even point" for the number of checks written (that is, the number of checks for which the costs of the two plans are as close as possible)?

23. A bank statement from a local bank shows that a checking account has a balance of $83.62. The balance recorded in the checkbook shows only $21.69. After checking the canceled checks against the record of these checks, the customer finds that the bank has not yet recorded six checks in the amounts of $3.21, $14.56, $12.44, $6.98, $9.51, $7.49. Is the bank record correct? (Assume the person's checkbook records *are* correct.)

24. The winner of the big sweepstakes has 15 minutes to decide whether to receive $1,000,000 cash immediately or to receive 1¢ on the first day of the month, 2¢ on the second day, 4¢ on the third, and so on, each day receiving double the previous day's amount, until the end of a 30-day month. However, only the amount received on that last day may be kept and all the rest of the month's "allowance" must be returned. Use a calculator to find which of these two options is more profitable, and determine how much more profitable one way is than the other.

★25. Given any reduced rational $\frac{a}{b}$ with $0 < a < b$, where b is of the form $2^m \cdot 5^n$ (m and n are whole numbers), determine a relationship between m and/or n and the number of digits in the terminating decimal.

BRAIN TEASER

Arrange four 7s using any operations and decimal points needed to obtain a value of 100.

Section 7-2

More About Decimals and Their Properties

The division processes described in Section 7-1 can be used to develop a procedure for converting any rational number to a decimal. (Recall that $\frac{7}{8}$ can be written as a terminating decimal because it is in simplest form and the denominator contains only factors of 2.)

```
        0.875
   8 ) 7.000
       6 4
       ̶ ̶ ̶ ̶
         60
         56
         ̶ ̶ ̶
           40
           40
           ̶ ̶ ̶
```

In a similar way, nonterminating decimals can be obtained for other rational numbers. For example, to find a decimal representation for $\frac{2}{11}$, consider the following division.

```
        0.18
  11 ) 2.00
       1 1
       ̶ ̶ ̶
         90
         88
         ̶ ̶ ̶
          2
```

repeating decimal

repetend

At this point, if the division is continued, then the division pattern repeats. Thus, the quotient is $0.181818\ldots$. A decimal of this type is called a **repeating decimal,** and the repeating block of digits is called the **repetend.** The repeating decimal is written as $0.\overline{18}$, where the bar indicates that the block of digits underneath is repeated infinitely.

Example 7-8

Convert $\frac{1}{7}$ to a decimal.

Solution

```
        0.142857
   7 ) 1.000000
       7
       ̶ ̶
       30
       28
       ̶ ̶
        20
        14
        ̶ ̶
         60
         56
         ̶ ̶
          40
          35
          ̶ ̶
           50
           49
           ̶ ̶
            1
```

If the division process is continued at this point, the division pattern repeats; thus, $\frac{1}{7} = 0.\overline{142857}$.

In Example 7-8, the remainders obtained in the division are 3, 2, 6, 4, 5, and 1. These are all the possible nonzero remainders that can be obtained when dividing by 7. (If the remainder of 0 had been obtained, the decimal would terminate.) If $\frac{a}{b}$ is any rational number in simplest form with $b > a$ and it does not represent a terminating decimal, then the possible remainders on division by b are 1, 2, 3, 4, ..., $b - 1$. Thus, after b or fewer divisions, at least one remainder appears twice. When this happens, a block of at most $b - 1$ digits in the quotient repeats. Therefore, *a rational number may always be represented either as a terminating decimal or as a repeating decimal.*

We have already considered how to write terminating decimals in the form $\frac{a}{b}$, where $a, b \in I$, $b \neq 0$. For example,

$$0.55 = \frac{55}{10^2} = \frac{55}{100}$$

To write $0.\overline{5}$ in a similar way, we may try the same method. We see that because the repeating decimal has infinitely many digits, there is no single power of 10 that can be placed in the denominator. To overcome this difficulty, we must somehow eliminate the infinitely repeating part of the decimal. Suppose $n = 0.\overline{5}$. It can be shown that $10(0.555\ldots) = 5.555\ldots = 5.\overline{5}$. Hence, $10n = 5.\overline{5}$. Using this information, we subtract to obtain an equation whose solution is a fraction.

$$
\begin{aligned}
10n &= 5.\overline{5} \\
-n &= -0.\overline{5} \\
\hline
9n &= 5
\end{aligned}
$$

$$n = \frac{5}{9}$$

Thus, $0.\overline{5} = \frac{5}{9}$. This result can be checked by performing the division $5 \div 9$. Notice that performing the subtraction above gives an equation containing only integers. (The repeating blocks "cancel" each other.)

Suppose a decimal has a repetend of more than one digit, such as $0.\overline{235}$. In order to write it in the form $\frac{a}{b}$, it is reasonable to multiply by 10^3, since there is a three-digit repetend. Let $n = 0.\overline{235}$. Then,

$$
\begin{aligned}
1000n &= 235.\overline{235} \\
-n &= -0.\overline{235} \\
\hline
999n &= 235
\end{aligned}
$$

$$n = \frac{235}{999}$$

Hence, $0.\overline{235} = \frac{235}{999}$.

Notice that $0.\overline{5}$ repeats in blocks of one digit, and to write it in the form $\frac{a}{b}$, we first multiply by 10^1; $0.\overline{235}$ repeats in blocks of three digits, and we first multiply by 10^3. In general, if the repetend is immediately to the right of the decimal point, first multiply by 10^n, where n is the number of digits in the repetend, and continue as above.

Now, suppose the repeating block does *not* occur immediately after the decimal point. For example, let $n = 2.3\overline{45}$. A strategy for solving this problem is to change it to a problem we already know how to do, that is, change it to a problem where the repeating block immediately follows the decimal point. To do this, we multiply both sides by 10.

$$10n = 23.\overline{45}$$

We now proceed as with previous problems. Since $10n = 23.\overline{45}$, then $100(10n) = 2345.\overline{45}$. Thus,

$$1000n = 2345.\overline{45}$$
$$-10n = -23.\overline{45}$$
$$\overline{990n = 2322}$$

$$n = \frac{2322}{990}, \text{ or } \frac{387}{165}$$

Hence, $2.3\overline{45} = \frac{2322}{990}$, or $\frac{387}{165}$.

Since rational numbers can be written as either terminating or repeating decimals and vice versa, decimals of this type have all the properties of rational numbers. The properties of rational numbers that hold for all operations are summarized in Table 7-3. Because the denseness property holds for the set of rational numbers, it also holds for the set of all repeating or terminating decimals.

Table 7-3
Properties of Operations of Rational Numbers

Property	+	×	−	÷
Closure	Yes	Yes	Yes	Yes (except for division by 0)
Commutative	Yes	Yes	No	No
Associative	Yes	Yes	No	No
Identity	Yes	Yes	No	No
Inverse	Yes	Yes (except for 0)	No	No

The distributive properties of multiplication over addition and subtraction hold.

ORDERING DECIMALS

Some students have trouble ordering decimals. They incorrectly reason that $0.36 > 0.9$ because $36 > 9$. One way to see that this is not true is to convert both decimals to fractions and then compare the fractions. For example, because $0.36 = \frac{36}{100}$ and $0.9 = \frac{9}{10} = \frac{90}{100}$ and $\frac{36}{100} < \frac{90}{100}$, then $0.36 < 0.9$.

Decimals can also be ordered without conversion to fractions. For example, because $0.9 = 0.90$, we can line up the decimal points as follows.

0.36
0.90

The digit in the tenths place of 0.36 is less than the tenths digit in 0.90, so $0.36 < 0.90$. A similar procedure works for repeating decimals.

For example, to compare repeating decimals, such as $1.\overline{3478}$ and $1.34\overline{7821}$, we write the decimals one under the other in their equivalent forms without the bars and line up the decimal points.

1.34783478 . . .
1.34782178 . . .

The digits to the left of the decimal points and the first four digits after the decimal points are the same in each of the numbers. Since the digit in the hundred-thousandths place of the top number, which is 3, is greater than the digit 2 in the hundred-thousandths place of the bottom number, $1.\overline{3478}$ is greater than $1.34\overline{7821}$.

It is easy to compare two fractions, such as $\frac{21}{43}$ and $\frac{37}{75}$, using a calculator. We convert each to a decimal and then compare the decimals.

$\boxed{2}\,\boxed{1}\,\boxed{\div}\,\boxed{4}\,\boxed{3}\,\boxed{=} \longrightarrow 0.4883721$

$\boxed{3}\,\boxed{7}\,\boxed{\div}\,\boxed{7}\,\boxed{5}\,\boxed{=} \longrightarrow 0.4933333$

Examining the digits in the hundredths place, we see that $\frac{37}{75} > \frac{21}{43}$.

Example 7-9

Find a rational number in decimal form between $0.\overline{35}$ and $0.\overline{351}$.

Solution

First, line up the decimals.

0.353535 . . .
0.351351 . . .

To find a decimal between these two, observe that starting from the left, the first place that the two numbers differ is the thousandths place. Clearly, one decimal between these two is 0.352. Some others are 0.3514, $0.35\overline{15}$, and 0.35136. In fact, there are infinitely many others.

ROUNDING

Frequently, it is not necessary to know the exact numerical answer to a question. For example, if we ask a person's age, we usually are not interested in an exact answer. Also, we do not know exactly how far it is to the moon or how many people live in New York City. However, we do know approximately how old we are, and we can find that it is approximately 239,000 miles to the moon and that there are approximately 7,772,000 people who live in New York City.

In order to approximate numbers, we adopt rules for rounding. The rounding rules given in the flowchart below are those used in most elementary schools and are thus the ones used in this text. As an example, 0.867 is rounded to the nearest tenth directly below the flowchart.

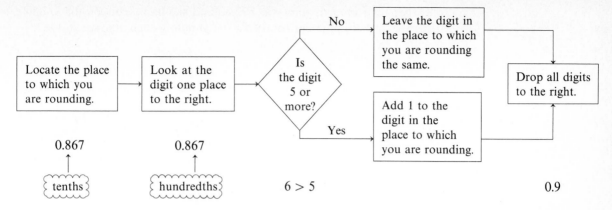

0.867
↑

{ tenths }

0.867
↑

{ hundredths }   6 > 5   0.9

Therefore, 0.867 rounded to the nearest tenth is 0.9, and we write $0.867 \doteq 0.9$ to symbolize the approximation. Rounding rules often vary at the high school and college levels when the digit to the right of the last digit to be retained is 5. The following rules, although *not* used in this text, are frequently used elsewhere. If the digit to the right of the last digit to be retained is 5, then increase by 1 the last digit to be retained when there is at least one nonzero digit to the right of the 5; when there is no nonzero digit to the right of the 5, increase by 1 the last digit to be retained only if the last digit is odd.

Example 7-10

Round each of the following numbers.

(a) 7.456 to the nearest hundredth
(b) 7.456 to the nearest tenth
(c) 7.456 to the nearest unit
(d) 7456 to the nearest thousand
(e) 745 to the nearest ten
(f) 74.56 to the nearest ten

Solution

(a) $7.456 \doteq 7.46$ (b) $7.456 \doteq 7.5$ (c) $7.456 \doteq 7$
(d) $7456 \doteq 7000$ (e) $745 \doteq 750$ (f) $74.56 \doteq 70$

Rounded numbers can be useful for estimating answers to computations. For example, consider each of the following.

1. Karly goes to the grocery store to buy items that cost the following amounts. She can estimate the total cost by rounding each amount to the nearest dollar and adding the rounded numbers.

$$
\begin{array}{rcr}
\$2.39 & \longrightarrow & \$2 \\
0.89 & \longrightarrow & 1 \\
6.13 & \longrightarrow & 6 \\
4.75 & \longrightarrow & 5 \\
+\ 5.05 & \longrightarrow & +\ 5 \\
\hline
& & \$19
\end{array}
$$

Thus, Karly's estimate for her grocery bill is $19.

2. Karly's bill for car repairs was $72.80 and she had a coupon for $17.50 off. She can estimate her total cost by rounding each amount to the nearest ten dollars and subtracting.

$$
\begin{array}{rr}
\$72.80 & \$70 \\
-\ 17.50 & -\ 20 \\
\hline
 & \$50
\end{array}
$$

Thus, an estimate for the repair bill is $50.

3. Karly sees a flash of lightning and hears the thunder 3.2 seconds later. She knows that sound travels at 0.33 km per second. She may estimate the distance she is from the lightning by rounding the time to the nearest unit and the speed to the nearest tenth and multiplying.

$$
\begin{array}{rcr}
0.33 & \longrightarrow & 0.3 \\
\times\ 3.2 & \longrightarrow & \times\ 3 \\
\hline
 & & 0.9
\end{array}
$$

Thus, Karly is approximately 0.9 km from the lightning.

An alternate approach is to recognize that $0.33 \doteq \frac{1}{3}$ and 3.2 is close to 3.3, so an approximation using "nice numbers" is $(\frac{1}{3}) \cdot 3.3$, or 1.1, km.

4. Karly wants to estimate the cost per kilogram of a frozen turkey that sells for $17.94 and weighs 6.42 kg. She rounds and divides as follows.

$$
6.42 \overline{)\ 17.94} \longrightarrow 6 \overline{)\ 18.00}^{\ \ \ 3.00}
$$

Thus, the turkey sells for approximately $3.00 per kilogram.

An example of estimating sums and differences using rounding and also *front-end estimation* is shown on the student page on page 301, from *Addison-Wesley Mathematics,* 1987, Grade 8.

SCIENTIFIC NOTATION

scientific notation

In disciplines such as chemistry, microbiology, and physics, where either very large or very small numbers are used, a special notation called scientific notation is used to help handle such numbers. In **scientific notation,** *a positive number is written as the product of a number greater than or equal to 1 and less than 10, and a power of 10.* For example, "the sun is 93,000,000 miles from Earth" is expressed as "the sun is $9.3 \cdot 10^7$ miles from Earth." A micrometer, a metric unit of measure that is 0.000001 m (meter), is written as $1 \cdot 10^{-6}$ m.

Example 7-11

Write each of the following in scientific notation.

(a) 413,682,000 (b) 0.0000231
(c) 83.7 (d) 10,000,000

Solution

(a) $413,682,000 = 4.13682 \cdot 10^8$ (b) $0.0000231 = 2.31 \cdot 10^{-5}$
(c) $8.37 \cdot 10^1$ (d) $1 \cdot 10^7$

Estimating Sums and Differences with Decimals

Jon Stein needed some supplies for his home computer system. He made this list of prices from a catalog. Then he made an estimate of the total cost. What is his estimate of the total?

Floppy disc	$ 3.15
Printer ribbon	6.95
Print wheel	9.67
Printer paper	8.09

To estimate the total we can **round** the numbers or we can use **front-end** estimation.

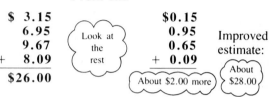

<table>
<tr><td colspan="2" align="center">Rounding</td><td colspan="3" align="center">Front-end</td></tr>
<tr><td>$3.15 ⟶</td><td>$3.00</td><td>$ 3.15</td><td></td><td>$0.15</td></tr>
<tr><td>6.95 ⟶</td><td>7.00</td><td>6.95</td><td>Look at</td><td>0.95</td></tr>
<tr><td>9.67 ⟶</td><td>10.00</td><td>9.67</td><td>the</td><td>0.65</td></tr>
<tr><td>+ 8.09 ⟶</td><td>+ 8.00</td><td>+ 8.09</td><td>rest</td><td>+ 0.09</td></tr>
<tr><td>Estimate ⟶</td><td>$28.00</td><td>$26.00</td><td></td><td></td></tr>
</table>

Improved estimate: About $28.00

About $2.00 more

His estimate is $28.00.

Other Examples

0.0813 ⟶	0.08
−0.0324 ⟶	−0.03
Estimate ⟶	0.05

0.718 ⟶	0.7
0.893 ⟶	0.9
+0.415 ⟶	+0.4
Estimate ⟶	2.0

Practice Estimate the sum or difference by rounding.

1. 0.937
   −0.329

2. 61.37
   38.44
   + 23.81

3. 0.52
   0.277
   + 0.3954

4. $87.19
   − 28.75

5. $0.59
   0.79
   0.42
   + 0.39

6. 31.87 + 18.75 + 22.05   7. 0.23 + 0.40 + 0.883   8. $20.66 − $14.95

Estimate. Use the front-end method.

9. 0.613
   0.184
   +0.511

10. 0.892
    −0.257

11. $2.69
    3.57
    + 5.98

12. 0.072
    0.0309
    +0.05941

13. 29.804
    −14.766

14. 838.06 − 337.45   15. $82.46 + $75.98 + $19.95   16. 0.0848 − 0.0559

Mixed Applications

17. Estimate how much more the printer paper costs than the floppy disc.

18. Estimate the total cost of 6 printer ribbons.

Example 7-12

Convert each of the following to standard numerals.

(a) $6.84 \cdot 10^{-5}$ (b) $3.12 \cdot 10^{7}$

Solution

(a) $6.84 \cdot 10^{-5} = 6.84 \cdot \left(\dfrac{1}{10^{5}}\right) = 0.0000684$

(b) $3.12 \cdot 10^{7} = 31{,}200{,}000$

It is possible to perform computations involving numbers in scientific notation, using the laws of exponents. For example, $(5.6 \cdot 10^5) \cdot (6 \cdot 10^4)$ can be rewritten as $[(5.6) \cdot 6] \cdot (10^5 \cdot 10^4) = 33.6 \cdot 10^9$, which is $3.36 \cdot 10^{10}$ in scientific notation. Also,

$$(2.35 \cdot 10^{-15}) \cdot (2 \cdot 10^8) = (2.35 \cdot 2) \cdot (10^{-15} \cdot 10^8) = 4.7 \cdot 10^{-7}.$$

To investigate how your calculator handles scientific notation, consider the computation $41,368,200 \times 1000$. The answer is $41,368,200,000$, or $4.13682 \cdot 10^{10}$. On a calculator, perform the computation below.

$$\boxed{4}\,\boxed{1}\,\boxed{3}\,\boxed{6}\,\boxed{8}\,\boxed{2}\,\boxed{0}\,\boxed{0}\,\boxed{\times}\,\boxed{1}\,\boxed{0}\,\boxed{0}\,\boxed{0}\,\boxed{=}$$

On many calculators, the display will read

$$\boxed{4.1368 \quad 10}$$

The number to the right of the space is the power to which 10 is raised when the number is written in scientific notation.

Calculators with an $\boxed{\text{EE}}$ key can be used to represent numbers in scientific notation. For example, to represent $5.2 \cdot 10^{16}$, we press

$$\boxed{5}\,\boxed{.}\,\boxed{2}\,\boxed{\text{EE}}\,\boxed{1}\,\boxed{6}.$$

LARGE NUMBERS

We are frequently exposed to the use of very large numbers. For example, we read that a certain restaurant chain has served over 60 billion hamburgers. In ancient systems of numeration, there was little need for large numbers. The word *billion* first appeared in the fifteenth century as the name for 10^{12}. The French later defined a billion as 10^9, and this probably led to the American adoption of 10^9 as the value for one billion. However, the British system still uses 10^{12} for one billion. In the twentieth century, larger numbers are needed, not only in connection with the number of hamburgers sold, but also with respect to items such as federal budgets. The names for numbers greater than one trillion (10^{12}) are typically not learned, but we give them in Table 7-4 for your information.

Table 7-4

Name	Value	Name	Value
thousand	10^3	septillion	10^{24}
million	10^6	octillion	10^{27}
billion	10^9	nonillion	10^{30}
trillion	10^{12}	decillion	10^{33}
quadrillion	10^{15}	undecillion	10^{36}
quintillion	10^{18}	duodecillion	10^{39}
sextillion	10^{21}		

Names for even greater numbers exist. Two interesting names that represent very large numbers are *googol,* which is the name for 10^{100}, and *googolplex,* which is 10^{googol}, or $10^{10^{100}}$. The googolplex is such a large number that it has been estimated that if a person could write out the number on a single line, it would reach the moon.

It is much easier to learn the names of these large numbers than it is to develop a feeling for their magnitude. For example, could you walk one million inches in one day? One million inches turns out to be over 16 miles. Consider how long it would take to count to one million. If we could count one number per second without stopping, it would take over eleven days. How long would it take to count to one billion at the same rate? It turns out that it would take over 30 years to count to one billion and over 30,000 years to count to a trillion, which is a number that is becoming better known as the national debt becomes larger.

HISTORICAL NOTE

The words "googol" and "googolplex" grew out of a discussion between Edward Kasner of Columbia University and some kindergarten children concerning numerals needed to describe the number of raindrops falling on New York City during a spring rainfall. The terms "googol" and "googolplex" were invented by Kasner's nine-year-old nephew.

PROBLEM 1

The story is told of the wise man who performed a great service for a wealthy king. As a reward, the king announced that he would grant the wise man any wish that sounded reasonable. The wise man simply requested the amount of wheat that would be required to cover a checkerboard beginning by placing one grain on the first square, two grains on the second square, four grains on the third square, eight grains on the fourth square, and so on, always doubling the number of grains. The king quickly agreed to such a modest-sounding request. How many grains of wheat did the wise man request?

UNDERSTANDING THE PROBLEM We are to determine the number of grains of wheat obtained by placing 1 grain on the first square of a checkerboard, 2 grains on the second square, 4 grains on the third square, and so on until all 64 squares on the checkerboard have been accounted for.

DEVISING A PLAN Rather than attempt the more difficult problem, we reduce the problem to some simpler cases of boards with 4 and 9 squares, as shown in Figure 7-1. From these simpler cases, we hope to gain insight on how to solve the more difficult problem.

Figure 7-1

1	2
4	8

1	2	4
8	16	32
64	128	256

The 2 × 2 board holds $1 + 2 + 2^2 + 2^3 = 15$ grains, and the 3 × 3 board holds $1 + 2 + 2^2 + 2^3 + 2^4 + 2^5 + 2^6 + 2^7 + 2^8 = 511$ grains. We notice that 15 is one less than 16 (or 2^4) and 511 is one less than 512 (or 2^9). Thus, we conjecture that the number of grains on the 8×8 checkerboard is $1 + 2 + 2^2 + 2^3 + 2^4 + \cdots + 2^{63} = 2^{64} - 1$.

CARRYING OUT THE PLAN The number of grains of wheat to be calculated is $1 + 2 + 2^2 + 2^3 + 2^4 + \cdots + 2^{63}$. It has been conjectured that this sum is given by $2^{64} - 1$. A justification for this conjecture is the following. Let

$$S = 1 + 2 + 2^2 + 2^3 + \cdots + 2^{62} + 2^{63}$$

Multiply both sides of this equation by 2 to obtain

$$2S = 2 + 2^2 + 2^3 + 2^4 + \cdots + 2^{63} + 2^{64}$$

Subtracting S from $2S$, we obtain the following.

$$2S - S = (2 + 2^2 + 2^3 + \cdots + 2^{64}) - (1 + 2 + 2^2 + \cdots + 2^{63})$$
$$= (2 - 2) + (2^2 - 2^2) + (2^3 - 2^3) + \cdots + (2^{63} - 2^{63}) + 2^{64} - 1$$
$$= 2^{64} - 1$$

Do you have a feeling for how large a number this is? For estimating purposes, a useful fact is that $2^{10} = 1024$, or approximately 1000. Therefore, $2^{64} = 2^4 \cdot 2^{60} = 2^4 \cdot (2^{10})^6$, which is approximately $2^4 \cdot (10^3)^6$, or $16 \cdot 10^{18}$, which is 16 billion billion, or 16 quintillion. On a calculator, if we find 2^{64} using the $\boxed{y^x}$ key, the value $\boxed{1.8447 \quad 19}$ is displayed. Remember, this number is in scientific notation and represents $1.8447 \cdot 10^{19}$ or 18,447,000,000,000,000,000. The exact value of 2^{64} is 18,446,744,073,709,551,616. Notice that we are obtaining only an approximation on the calculator. It has been estimated that it would take the United States approximately 14,000 years to produce the amount of wheat necessary to place on the last square. Consider how small the number 2^{64} is compared with a googol or a googolplex.

LOOKING BACK An alternate proof showing that $1 + 2 + 2^2 + 2^3 + 2^4 + \cdots + 2^{63} = 2^{64} - 1$ makes use of base two. Recall that $11111_{two} = 1 \cdot 2^4 + 1 \cdot 2^3 + 1 \cdot 2^2 + 1 \cdot 2 + 1$, and notice the following pattern.

$$1_{two} + 1_{two} = 10_{two} = 2^1 = 2$$
$$11_{two} + 1_{two} = 100_{two} = 2^2 = 4$$
$$111_{two} + 1_{two} = 1000_{two} = 2^3 = 8$$
$$1111_{two} + 1_{two} = 10000_{two} = 2^4 = 16$$

Therefore,

$$1 + 2 + 2^2 + 2^3 = 1111_{two} = 10000_{two} - 1_{two} = 2^4 - 1$$

and

$$1 + 2 + 2^2 + 2^3 + 2^4 + 2^5 + 2^6 + 2^7 + 2^8$$
$$= 111111111_{two} = 1000000000_{two} - 1_{two} = 2^9 - 1$$

If we proceed in this manner, we see that

$$1 + 2 + 2^2 + 2^3 + 2^4 + \cdots + 2^{63} = 2^{64} - 1$$

The size of the checkerboard could be varied to introduce more problems. Questions concerning the length of time required to count the grains or the amount of storage space required to store the grain could also be asked. We might also compute the number of grains if each square contains three times as many grains as the previous square or, in general, n times as many as the previous square, where n is a positive integer.

PROBLEM SET 7-2

1. Find the decimal representation for each of the following.

   (a) $\dfrac{4}{9}$ (b) $\dfrac{2}{7}$ (c) $\dfrac{3}{11}$ (d) $\dfrac{1}{15}$

   (e) $\dfrac{2}{75}$ (f) $\dfrac{1}{99}$ (g) $\dfrac{5}{6}$ (h) $\dfrac{1}{13}$

2. Convert each of the following repeating decimals to fractions.
   (a) $2.4\overline{5}$ (b) $2.\overline{45}$ (c) $2.4\overline{54}$
   (d) $0.2\overline{45}$ (e) $0.02\overline{45}$ (f) $24.\overline{54}$
   (g) $0.\overline{4}$ (h) $0.\overline{6}$ (i) $0.\overline{55}$
   (j) $0.\overline{34}$ (k) $^-2.3\overline{4}$ (l) $^-0.0\overline{2}$

3. Order each of the following sets of decimals from greatest to least.
   (a) $\{3.2, 3.\overline{22}, 3.\overline{23}, 3.2\overline{3}, 3.\overline{23}\}$
   (b) $\{^-1.454, ^-1.45\overline{4}, ^-1.45, ^-1.4\overline{54}, ^-1.\overline{454}\}$

4. Find a decimal between each of the following pairs of decimals.
   (a) 3.2 and 3.3   (b) 462.24 and 462.25
   (c) $462.2\overline{4}$ and $462.\overline{24}$ (d) 0.003 and 0.03

5. (a) Find a rational number in the form a/b for $0.\overline{9}$.
   (b) $0.\overline{9}$ is either less than 1, greater than 1, or equal to 1. Argue that $0.\overline{9} < 1$ is false and $0.\overline{9} > 1$ is false; so $0.\overline{9} = 1$.
   (c) Use the fact that $\frac{1}{3} = 0.\overline{3}$ and multiply both sides of the equation by 3 to show that $1 = 0.\overline{9}$.

6. Suppose $a = 0.\overline{32}$ and $b = 0.\overline{123}$.
   (a) Find $a + b$ by adding from left to right. How many digits are in the repetend of the sum?
   (b) Find $a + b$ if $a = 1.2\overline{34}$ and $b = 0.\overline{1234}$. Is the answer a rational number? How many digits are in the repetend?

7. Find the decimal halfway between the two given decimals.
   (a) 3.2 and 3.3   (b) 462.24 and 462.25
   (c) 0.0003 and 0.03   ★(d) $462.2\overline{4}$ and $462.\overline{24}$

8. Round each of the following numbers as specified.
   (a) 203.651 to the nearest hundred *200*
   (b) 203.651 to the nearest ten *200*
   (c) 203.651 to the nearest unit *204*
   (d) 203.651 to the nearest tenth *203.7*
   (e) 203.651 to the nearest hundredth *203.65*

9. Express each of the following numbers in scientific notation.
   (a) 3325   (b) 46.32
   (c) 0.00013   (d) 930,146

10. Convert each of the following numbers to standard numerals.
    (a) $3.2 \cdot 10^{-9}$ (b) $3.2 \cdot 10^9$
    (c) $4.2 \cdot 10^{-1}$ (d) $6.2 \cdot 10^5$

11. Write the numerals in each of the following sentences in scientific notation.
    (a) The diameter of the earth is about 12,700,000 m.
    (b) The distance from Pluto to the sun is 5,797,000 km.
    (c) Each year, about 50,000,000 cans are discarded in the United States.

12. Write the numerals in each sentence in decimal form.
    (a) A computer requires $4.4 \cdot 10^{-6}$ seconds to do an addition problem.
    (b) There are about $1.99 \cdot 10^4$ km of coastline in the United States.
    (c) The earth has existed approximately $3 \cdot 10^9$ years.

13. Audrey wants to buy some camera equipment to take pictures on her daughter's birthday. To estimate the total cost, she rounded each price to the nearest dollar and added the rounded prices. What is her estimate for the items listed below?

    Camera $24.95
    Film $3.50
    Case $7.85

14. Estimate the sum or difference in each of the following by using (i) rounding and (ii) front-end estimation. (Front-end estimation is demonstrated on the student page in this section.) Perform the computations to see how close your estimates were to the actual answers.
    (a)   65.84   (b)   89.47
          24.29 -32.16
          12.18   ——————
        $+19.75$
        ——————

(c)   5.85   (d)   223.75
       6.13   − 87.60
       9.10   _____
     + 4.32
     _____

15. Continue the decimal patterns shown below.
    (a) $0, 0.\overline{3}, 0.\overline{6}, 1, 1.\overline{3},$ _____, _____, _____
    (b) $0. 0.5, 0.\overline{6}. 0.75, 0.8, 0.8\overline{3},$ _____, _____, _____

16. Some digits in the number shown below have been covered by squares. If each of the digits 1 through 9 is used exactly once in the number, what is the number in each of the following cases?

    4 ☐ ☐ 3 ☐ . ☐ ☐ 8 ☐

    (a) The number is as great as possible.
    (b) The number is as small as possible.

17. Write the results of each of the following in scientific notation.
    (a) $(8 \cdot 10^{12}) \cdot (6 \cdot 10^{15})$
    (b) $(16 \cdot 10^{12}) \div (4 \cdot 10^5)$
    (c) $(5 \cdot 10^8) \cdot (6 \cdot 10^9) \div (15 \cdot 10^{15})$

18. Which of the following numbers is the greatest?
    $10{,}000^3$; 1000^5; $100{,}000^2$

19. Write a googol squared as a power of 10.

20. Jane's car travels 224 miles on 12 gallons of gas. How many miles to the gallon does her car get, rounded to the nearest mile?

21. In Problem 1 in this section, it was estimated that it would take the United States approximately 14,000 years to produce the amount of wheat placed on the last square of a checkerboard if one grain was placed on the first square, two grains were placed on the second square, and so on, doubling the amount of wheat each time. At this rate, approximately how many years would it take the United States to produce the amount of wheat to cover all the squares?

★22. Find a simpler expression for

    $$1 + 3 + 3^2 + 3^3 + \cdots + 3^{63}$$

★23. Prove that the sum of n terms of a geometric sequence whose first term is a and whose ratio is r is given by $a \cdot (r^n - 1)/(r - 1)$.

24. Sooner or later, most people are faced with the task of buying a number of items at the store, knowing that they have just barely enough money to cover the needed items. In order to avoid the embarrassment of coming up short and having to put some of the items back, they must use their estimating or rounding skills. For each of the following sets of items, estimate the cost. If you are short of funds, tell what must be returned to come just under the allotted amount to be spent. Use your calculator to check your answers.

(a) Amount on hand—$2.98

    2 packs of gum at 24¢ each
    3 suckers at 10¢ each
    1 licorice at 4 for 20¢
    1 soft drink at 35¢
    1 pack dental floss at 99¢

(b) Amount on hand—$20.00

    7 gallons of gas at $1.089 per gallon
    2 quarts of oil at $1.05 per quart
    a car wash at $1.99
    flashlight batteries at $3.39
    air in a tire at 0¢ per pound
    air freshener at 99¢
    starter fluid at 99¢
    parking ticket at $1.00
    windshield wiper at $1.59
    soft drink for your date at 35¢

25. This group of exercises concentrates on finding repeating decimals.
    (a) Use a calculator to find decimals for each of the following.

        (i) $\dfrac{1}{7}$ Do this by pressing ☐1☐ ☐÷☐ ☐7☐ ☐=☐.

        (ii) $\dfrac{2}{7}$

        (iii) $\dfrac{3}{7}$

        (iv) $\dfrac{4}{7}$

        (v) $\dfrac{5}{7}$

        (vi) $\dfrac{6}{7}$

    (b) How many places were used before each decimal repeated?
    (c) Do you see any relationship among your answers in (i)–(vi) of (a)?

26. Use a calculator to find $\frac{26}{99}$ and $\frac{78}{99}$. Can you predict a decimal value for $\frac{51}{99}$? Will the technique used in your prediction always work? Why or why not?

Review Problems

27. (a) Human bones make up 0.18 of a person's total body weight. How much do the bones of a 120-pound person weigh?
    (b) Muscles make up about 0.4 of a person's body weight. How much do the muscles of a 120-pound person weigh?

28. John is a payroll clerk for a small company. Last month, the employees' gross earnings (earnings before deductions) totaled $27,849.50. He then deducted $1520.63 for social security, $723.30 for unemployment insurance, and $2843.62 for federal income tax. What was the employees' net pay (their earnings after deductions)?

29. How can you tell whether a fraction will represent a terminating decimal without performing the actual division?

30. Write each of the following decimals as fractions.
(a) 16.72   (b) 0.003
(c) ⁻5.07   (d) 0.123

COMPUTER CORNER

The following BASIC program rounds decimals to a given number of places. See if it gives the same results as the rules given in this chapter.

```
10 PRINT "THIS PROGRAM ROUNDS DECIMALS."
20 PRINT
30 PRINT "ENTER YOUR DECIMAL AND PRESS RETURN."
40 INPUT D
50 PRINT "HOW MANY DIGITS WOULD YOU LIKE TO THE "
55 PRINT "RIGHT OF THE DECIMAL POINT?"
60 INPUT N
70 LET S = INT (D * 10 ^ N + .5)
80 LET R = S / (10 ^ N)
90 PRINT
100 PRINT D ; " ROUNDS TO "; R
110 PRINT
120 PRINT "TO ENTER ANOTHER DECIMAL: TYPE RUN."
130 END
```

Section 7-3

Percents

Percents are very useful in conveying information. Many children become acquainted with percents before they study them in school. They hear that there is a 60 percent chance of rain or that their savings accounts are drawing 6 percent interest. Many become familiar with the sales tax when they make a purchase. The word **percent** comes from the Latin phrase *per centum,* which can be translated as *per hundred.* For example, a bank that pays 6 percent simple interest on a savings account pays $6 for each $100 in the account for one year; that is, it pays $\frac{6}{100}$ of whatever amount is in the account for one year. We use the symbol % to indicate percent and, for example, write 6% for $\frac{6}{100}$.

percent

In general, we have the following definition.

DEFINITION

$$n\% = \frac{n}{100}.$$

Percents can be illustrated using a hundreds grid. For example, what percent of the squares are shaded in Figure 7-2? Because 30 out of the 100, or $\frac{30}{100}$, of the squares are shaded, we say that 30% of the grid is shaded.

Figure 7-2

We can convert any number to a percent by first writing the number as a fraction with denominator 100. For instance, consider the example in the cartoon that follows. Obviously, the adult is incorrect.

THE BORN LOSER by Art Sansom

© 1981 Newspaper Enterprise Association.

The child in the cartoon missed 6 questions out of 10 and hence had 4 correct answers, or $\frac{4}{10}$ of the answers were correct. Because $\frac{4}{10} = \frac{40}{100}$, the child had 40%, not 90%, correct answers.

From the definition of percent, $n\% = n/100$, it follows that $n = 100 \cdot n\%$. Using this equality, we can convert a number to a percent by multiplying it by 100. For example,

$$0.0002 = 100 \cdot 0.0002\% = 0.02\%$$

$$\frac{3}{4} = 100 \cdot \frac{3}{4}\% = \frac{300}{4}\% = 75\%$$

Example 7-13

Write each of the following as a percent.

(a) 0.03   (b) $0.\overline{3}$ (c) 1.2   (d) 0.00042

(e) 1   (f) $\frac{3}{5}$ (g) $\frac{2}{3}$ (h) $2\frac{1}{7}$

Solution

(a) $0.03 = 100 \cdot 0.03\% = 3\%$
(b) $0.\overline{3} = 100 \cdot 0.\overline{3}\% = 33.\overline{3}\%$
(c) $1.2 = 100 \cdot 1.2\% = 120\%$
(d) $0.00042 = 100 \cdot 0.00042\% = 0.042\%$
(e) $1 = 100 \cdot 1\% = 100\%$

(f) $\dfrac{3}{5} = 100 \cdot \dfrac{3}{5}\% = \dfrac{300}{5}\% = 60\%$

(g) $\dfrac{2}{3} = 100 \cdot \dfrac{2}{3}\% = \dfrac{200}{3}\% = 66.\overline{6}\%$

(h) $2\dfrac{1}{7} = 100 \cdot 2\dfrac{1}{7}\% = \dfrac{1500}{7}\% = 214\dfrac{1}{7}\%$

A number can also be converted to a percent by using a proportion. For example, to write $\frac{3}{5}$ as a percent, we need only find the value of n in the following proportion.

$$\dfrac{3}{5} = \dfrac{n}{100}$$

Solving the proportion, we obtain $(\frac{3}{5}) \cdot 100 = n$, or $n = 60$. Hence, the answer is 60%.

Estimations are also helpful when working with percents. They can be used to determine whether answers are reasonable or not. For example, $\frac{11}{40}$ is a little more than $\frac{10}{40}$, or $\frac{1}{4}$, or 25%, so $\frac{11}{40}$ should be a little more than 25%. Also, $9\frac{2}{3}\%$ of 200 is a little less than 10% of 200, or 20, so $9\frac{2}{3}\%$ of 200 should be a little less than 20.

In doing computations, it is sometimes useful to convert percents to decimals. This can be done by writing the percent as a fraction and then converting the fraction to a decimal.

Example 7-14

Write each percent as a decimal.

(a) 5%   (b) 6.3%   (c) 100%
(d) 250%   (e) $\frac{1}{3}\%$ (f) $33\frac{1}{3}\%$

Solution

(a) $5\% = \dfrac{5}{100} = 0.05$

(b) $6.3\% = \dfrac{6.3}{100} = 0.063$

(c) $100\% = \dfrac{100}{100} = 1$

(d) $250\% = \dfrac{250}{100} = 2.50$

(e) $\dfrac{1}{3}\% = \dfrac{\frac{1}{3}}{100} = \dfrac{0.\overline{3}}{100} = 0.00\overline{3}$

(f) $33\dfrac{1}{3}\% = \dfrac{33\frac{1}{3}}{100} = \dfrac{33.\overline{3}}{100} = 0.\overline{3}$

Example 7-14 may be used to discover an algorithm for converting percents to decimals: *To change a percent to a decimal, drop the percent sign and divide by* 100. A percent key on a calculator may perform this algorithm. For example, if the keys $\boxed{3}\boxed{4}\boxed{.}\boxed{5}\boxed{\%}$ are pressed in the order given, many calculators will display 0.345. You should investigate how your calculator handles percents.

Application problems involving percents are usually in one of the following forms:

1. Finding a percent of a number.
2. Finding what percent one number is of another.
3. Finding a number when a percent of that number is known.

Before doing examples illustrating these forms, recall what it means to find a fraction "of" a number. For example, $\frac{2}{3}$ of 70 means $\frac{2}{3} \cdot 70$. Similarly, to find 40% of 70, we have $\frac{40}{100}$ of 70, which means $\frac{40}{100} \cdot 70$, or $0.40 \cdot 70 = 28$.

Example 7-15

A house that sells for $72,000 requires a 20% down payment. What is the amount of the down payment?

Solution

The down payment is 20% of $72,000, or $0.20 \cdot \$72,000 = \$14,400$. Hence, the amount of the down payment is $14,400.

Example 7-16

If Alberto has 45 correct answers on an 80-question test, what percent of his answers are correct?

Solution

Alberto has $\frac{45}{80}$ of the answers correct. To find the percent of correct answers, we need to convert $\frac{45}{80}$ to a percent. This can be done by writing an equation as follows.

$$\frac{45}{80} = 100 \cdot \frac{45}{80}\% = \frac{4500}{80}\% = 56.25\%$$

Thus, 56.25% of the answers are correct.

An alternate solution can be found by using a proportion. Let n be the percent of correct answers. Hence, we have the following.

$$\frac{45}{80} = \frac{n}{100}$$

$$\frac{45}{80} \cdot 100 = n$$

$$n = \frac{4500}{80} = 56.25$$

Example 7-17

Forty-two percent of the parents of the school children in the Paxson School District are employed at Di Paloma University. If the number of parents employed by D.P.U. is 168, how many parents are in the school district?

Solution

If we let n be the number of parents in the school district, then we know that 42% of n is 168. We translate this information into an equation and solve for n.

$$42\% \text{ of } n = 168$$

$$\frac{42}{100} \cdot n = 168$$

$$0.42 \cdot n = 168$$

$$n = \frac{168}{0.42} = 400$$

Hence, there are 400 parents in the school district.

The problem can also be solved using a proportion. We know that 42%, or $\frac{42}{100}$, of the parents are employed at D.P.U. If n is the total number of parents, then $168/n$ also represents the fraction of parents employed at D.P.U. Thus,

$$\frac{42}{100} = \frac{168}{n}$$

$$42n = 100 \cdot 168$$

$$n = \frac{16,800}{42} = 400$$

Example 7-18

Mike bought a bicycle and then sold it for 20% more than he paid for it. If he sold the bike for $144, what did he pay for it?

Solution

We are looking for the original price P that Mike paid for the bike. We know that he sold the bike for $144 and that this included a 20% profit. Thus, we can write the following equation.

$$\$144 = P + \text{Mike's profit}$$

Since Mike's profit is 20% of P, we proceed as follows.

$$144 = P + 20\% \cdot P$$

$$144 = P + 0.20 \cdot P$$

$$144 = (1 + 0.20) \cdot P$$

$$144 = 1.20P$$

$$\frac{144}{1.20} = P$$

$$120 = P$$

Thus, Mike originally paid $120 for the bike.

Example 7-19

Westerner's Clothing Store advertised a suit for 10% off, for a savings of $15. Later, they marked the suit at 30% off the original price. What is the amount of the current discount?

Solution

A 10% discount amounts to a $15 savings. This information can be used to find the original price P. Since 10% of P is $15, we have the following.

$$10\% \cdot P = \$15$$

$$0.10 \cdot P = \$15$$

$$P = \$150$$

We must now calculate 30% of $150 to find the current discount. Because $0.30 \cdot \$150 = \$45$, the amount of the 30% discount is $45.

In the Looking Back stage of problem solving, we check the answer and look for other ways to solve the problem. A different approach leads to a more efficient solution. If 10% of the price is $15, then 30% of the price is 3 times $15, or $45.

PROBLEM 2

A watermelon weighing 100 pounds was found to be 99% water. After sitting in the sunlight all day, some of the water evaporated, leaving the melon 98% water. How much did the melon weigh after the evaporation occurred?

UNDERSTANDING THE PROBLEM A watermelon weighing 100 pounds was 99% water. After some evaporation occurred, the melon was only 98% water. We are to determine the weight of the melon when it was 98% water.

DEVISING A PLAN A common strategy in solving word problems is *writing an equation*. Because we have information about the amount of water that evaporated, it seems convenient to designate the amount of water that evaporated as the unknown. After finding the amount of water that evaporated, we can subtract that amount from 100 to find the new weight of the watermelon. If we let w be the weight of the water that the melon lost due to evaporation, then the new weight of the melon after evaporation is $(100 - w)$ pounds and the new weight of the water content is 98% of $(100 - w)$ pounds. The new weight of the water content can also be computed by subtracting the number of pounds of water lost from the original weight of the water, which is 99 pounds. Thus, the new weight of the water content is $(99 - w)$ pounds. An equation can be written using this information as follows.

$$\left(\begin{array}{c}\text{New weight of}\\\text{water content}\end{array}\right) = 98\% \text{ of weight of melon after evaporation}$$

$$99 - w = 0.98 \times (100 - w)$$

To complete this problem, we solve the equation for w.

CARRYING OUT THE PLAN The equation given above is solved for w as follows.

$$99 - w = 0.98(100 - w)$$

$$99 - w = 98 - 0.98w$$

$$1 = 0.02w$$

$$50 = w$$

Thus, the weight of the water that was lost due to evaporation is 50 pounds, and hence the melon weighs (100 − 50), or 50, pounds after evaporation.

LOOKING BACK An alternate solution can be found using the fact that the amount of material other than water does not change after evaporation. Let x be the weight of the watermelon after evaporation. We know that in the original 100 pounds of watermelon, there was 99% water and hence 1%, or 1 pound, was not water. After evaporation, the watermelon's weight was x pounds and 98% of the weight was water; hence, 2% of it was not water. Because the amount of material that was not water did not change, we know that 2% of x equals 1, which implies that $x = 50$ pounds.

Another way to solve the problem is think of the question as, "2% of how much weight is equal to 1% of 100?" Because 2% of 50 is the same as 1% of 100, the answer is 50 pounds.

PROBLEM SET 7-3

1. Express each of the following as percents.
   (a) 7.89   (b) 0.032   (c) 193.1
   (d) 0.2   (e) $\frac{5}{6}$ (f) $\frac{3}{20}$
   (g) $\frac{1}{75}$ (h) $\frac{40}{7}$

2. Convert each of the following percents to decimals.
   (a) 16%   (b) $4\frac{1}{2}\%$
   (c) $\frac{1}{5}\%$ (d) $\frac{2}{7}\%$

3. Answer each of the following.
   (a) Find 6% of 34.
   (b) 17 is what percent of 34?
   (c) 18 is 30% of what number?
4. Marc had 84 boxes of candy to sell. He sold 75% of the boxes. How many did he sell?
5. Gail made $16,000 last year and received a 6% raise. How much does she make now?
6. Gail received a 7% raise last year. If her salary is now $15,515, what was her salary last year?
7. Joe sold 180 newspapers out of 200. Bill sold 85% of his 260 newspapers. Ron sold 212 newspapers, 80% of those he had.
   (a) Who sold the most newspapers? How many?
   (b) Who sold the greatest percent of his newspapers? What percent?
   (c) Who started with the greatest number of newspapers? How many?
8. If a dress that normally sells for $35 is on sale for $28, what is the "percent off"? (This could be called a *percent of decrease,* or a discount.)

9. Mort bought his house in 1975 for $29,000. It was recently appraised at $55,000. What is the *percent of increase* in value?
10. Sally bought a dress marked at 20% off. If the regular price was $28.00, what was the sale price?
11. What is the sale price of a softball if the regular price is $6.80 and there is a 25% discount?
12. Xuan weighed 9 pounds when he was born. At 6 months, he weighed 18 pounds. What was the percent of increase in Xuan's weight?
13. In 1965, 728 eagles were counted in Glacier Park. Five years later, 594 were counted. What is the percent of decrease in the number of eagles counted?
14. A car originally cost $8000. One year later, it was worth $6800. What is the percent of depreciation?
15. Fill in the blanks to find other expressions for 4%.
    (a) _____ for every 100
    (b) _____ for every 50
    (c) 1 for every _____
    (d) 8 for every _____
    (e) 0.5 for every _____
16. If a $\frac{1}{4}$-cup serving of Crunchies breakfast food has 0.5% of the minimum daily requirement of Vitamin C, how many cups would you have to eat in order to obtain the minimum daily requirement of Vitamin C?
17. An airline ticket cost $320 without the tax. If the tax rate is 5%, what is the total bill for the airline ticket?
18. Bill got 52 correct answers on an 80-question test. What percent of the questions did he not answer correctly?
19. A real estate broker receives 4% of an $80,000 sale. How much does the broker receive?
20. A survey reported that $66\frac{2}{3}\%$ of 1800 employees favored a new insurance program. How many employees favored the new program?

21. A family has a monthly income of $2400 and makes a monthly house payment of $400. What percent of the income is the house payment?

22. A company bought a used typewriter for $350, which was 80% of the original cost. What was the original cost of the typewriter?

23. A plumber's wage one year was $19.80 an hour. This was a 110% increase over last year's hourly wage. What was the increase in the hourly wage over last year?

24. Ms. Price has received a 10% raise in salary in each of the last 2 years. If her annual salary this year is $100,000, what was her salary 2 years ago rounded to the nearest penny?

25. Mental mathematics is useful when working with percents. For example, to find 15% of $84, we could proceed as follows.

10% of $84 = $8.40

5% of \$84 $= \dfrac{1}{2}$ of \$8.40 $=$ \$4.20

So,

15% of $84 = $8.40 + $4.20 = $12.60

Solve each of the following using mental mathematics.
(a) 15% of $22   (b) 20% of $120
(c) 5% of $38   (d) 25% of $98

26. Soda is advertised at 45¢ a can or $2.40 for a six-pack. If 6 cans are to be purchased, what percent is saved by purchasing the six-pack?

27. John paid $330 for a new mountain bicycle to sell in his shop. He wants to price it so that he can offer a 10% discount and still make 20% of the price he paid for it. At what price should the bike be marked?

28. The price of a suit that sold for $100 was reduced by 25%. By what percent must the price of the suit be increased to bring the price back to $100?

29. If we build a 10 × 10 model with blocks, as shown in the figure, and paint the entire model, what percent of the cubes will have each of the following?

(a) Four faces painted   (b) Three faces painted
(c) Two faces painted

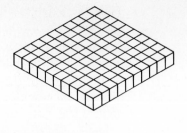

30. Answer the questions in Problem 29 for models of the following sizes.
(a) 9 × 9   (b) 8 × 8   (c) 7 × 7
(d) 12 × 12   (e) $n \times n$

31. Howard entered a store and said to the owner, "Give me as much money as I have with me and I will spend 80% of the total." After this was done, Howard repeated the operation at a second store and at a third store and was finally left with $12. With how much money did he start?

32. Different calculators compute percents in various ways. To investigate this, consider $5 \cdot 6\%$.
(a) If the following sequence of keys is pressed, is the correct answer of 0.3 displayed on your calculator?

$$\boxed{5}\ \boxed{\times}\ \boxed{6}\ \boxed{\%}\ \boxed{=}$$

(b) Press $\boxed{6}\ \boxed{\%}\ \boxed{\times}\ \boxed{5}\ \boxed{=}$. Is the answer 0.3?

33. The car Elsie bought 1 year ago has depreciated $1116.88, which is 12.13% of the price she paid for it. How much did she pay for the car to the nearest cent?

Review Problems

34. A state charged a company $63.27 per day for overdue taxes. The total bill for the overdue taxes was $6137.19. How many days were the taxes overdue?

35. Write 33.21 as a fraction in simplest form.

36. Write $\frac{2}{9}$ as a decimal.

37. Write $31.0\overline{5}$ as a fraction in simplest form.

38. Write each of the following in scientific notation.
(a) 3,250,000   (b) 0.00012

39. Round 32.015 to the indicated place.
(a) The nearest tenth   (b) The nearest ten

BRAIN TEASER

The crust of a certain pumpkin pie is 25% of the pie. By what percent should the amount of crust be reduced in order to make it constitute 20% of the pie?

*Section 7-4

principal
interest rate

simple interest

Computing Interest

When a bank advertises a $5\frac{1}{2}\%$ interest rate on a savings account, this means that the bank is willing to pay for the privilege of using that money. The amount of money the bank will pay is called interest. If we borrow money from a bank, we must pay interest to the bank for using that money. The original amount deposited or borrowed is called the **principal.** The percent used to determine the interest is called the **interest rate.** Interest rates are given for specific periods of time, such as years, months, or days. Interest computed on the original principal is called **simple interest.** For example, suppose we borrow $5000 from a company at a simple interest rate of 12% for 1 year. The interest we owe on the loan for 1 year is 12% of $5000, or $12\% \cdot 5000$. (This is usually computed as $5000 \cdot 0.12$.) In general, if a principal P is invested at an annual interest rate of r, then the simple interest after 1 year is $P \cdot r \cdot 1$; after t years it is $P \cdot r \cdot t$, or Prt. If I represents simple interest, we have

$$I = Prt$$

The amount needed to pay off a $5000 loan at 12% simple interest is the $5000 borrowed plus the interest on the $5000, that is, $5000 + 5000 \cdot 0.12$, or $5600. In general, an amount (or balance) A is equal to the principal P plus the interest I; that is, $A = P + I$, or $A = P + Prt$. This formula can also be written as

$$A = P(1 + rt)$$

Example 7-20

Vera opens a savings account that pays simple interest at the rate of $5\frac{1}{4}\%$ per year. If she deposits $2000 and makes no other deposits, find the interest and the final amount for the following periods of time.

(a) 1 year   (b) 90 days

Solution

(a) To find the interest for 1 year, we proceed as follows.

$$I = \$2000 \cdot 5\tfrac{1}{4}\% \cdot 1 = \$2000 \cdot 0.0525 = \$105$$

Thus, her amount at the end of 1 year is

$2000 + 105 = 2105$

(b) When the interest rate is annual and the interest period is less than 1 year, we represent the time as a fractional part of a year by dividing the number of days by 365. Thus, to find the interest and the final amount, we perform the following computations.

$$I = \$2000 \cdot 5\tfrac{1}{4}\% \cdot \frac{90}{365}$$

$$= \$2000 \cdot 0.0525 \cdot \frac{90}{365} \doteq \$25.89$$

Hence, $A = \$2000 + \$25.89 = \$2025.89$.

Example 7-21

Find the annual interest rate if a principal of $10,000 increased to $10,900 at the end of 1 year.

Solution

We use the strategy of writing an equation based on the relationship $I = Prt$. We need to solve for r, so we divide both sides of the equation by Pt, obtaining

$$r = \frac{I}{Pt}$$

To find the interest, we compute the difference between the balance and the principal. Thus, $I = \$10,900 - \$10,000 = \$900$. Substituting the values of I, P, and t in the above equation, we obtain

$$r = \frac{900}{(10,000) \cdot 1} = 0.09, \text{ or } 9\%$$

Thus, the interest rate is 9%.

COMPOUND INTEREST

In all our discussions thus far, we have computed simple interest, which is based only on the original principal. This principal stayed fixed for the entire interest period. A second method of computing interest involves compound interest. **Compound interest** is different from simple interest because after the first interest calculation, the interest is added to the principal, so interest is earned on previous interest in addition to the principal. Compound interest rates are usually given as annual rates no matter how many times the interest is compounded per year. The most common compounding periods are annual (1 time a year), semiannual (2 times a year), quarterly (4 times a year), monthly (12 times a year), and daily (365 times a year). A formula can be developed for problems involving compound interest. The amount A at the end of each period is equal to the principal P at the beginning of the period plus the interest I for the period. If the interest rate per period is i, then we have the following.

compound interest

$$A = P + I = P + P \cdot i = P(1 + i)$$

For example, suppose we have $100 invested at 8% compounded quarterly. Since the interest rate is 8% per year, it is $\frac{1}{4}$ of 8%, or 2% per quarter. Thus, at the end of one quarter, we have

$$A = P + I = 100 + 100 \cdot \frac{0.08}{4} = \$102$$

To compute the amount we have at the end of the second quarter, we treat $102 as the principal and we have

$$A = P + I = 102 + 102 \cdot \frac{0.08}{4} = \$104.04$$

To compute the amount at the end of the third quarter, we treat $104.04 as the principal and we have

$$A = P + I = 104.04 + 104.04 \cdot \frac{0.08}{4} \doteq \$106.12$$

Similarly, at the end of one year, we have

$$A = P + I = 106.12 + 106.12 \cdot \left(\frac{0.08}{4}\right) \doteq \$108.24$$

This process is rather easy to understand, but rather hard to apply because increasing the number of compounding periods increases the number of computations required to find the balance. A formula generalizing the above discussion is given in Table 7-5.

Table 7-5

Period	Initial Amount	Final Amount
1	P	$P(1 + i)$
2	$P(1 + i)$	$[P(1 + i)](1 + i)$, or $P(1 + i)^2$
3	$P(1 + i)^2$	$[P(1 + i)^2](1 + i)$, or $P(1 + i)^3$
4	$P(1 + i)^3$	$[P(1 + i)^3](1 + i)$, or $P(1 + i)^4$
$\vdots$	$\vdots$	$\vdots$
n	$P(1 + i)^{n-1}$	$[P(1 + i)^{n-1}](1 + i)$, or $P(1 + i)^n$

Therefore, the amount at the end of the nth period is $P(1 + i)^n$. If the formula $A = P(1 + i)^n$ is applied to the example of finding the amount at the end of one year when $100 earns 8% compounded quarterly, we have the following.

$$A = P(1 + i)^n = \$100\left(1 + \frac{0.08}{4}\right)^4 \doteq \$108.24$$

Notice that this answer agrees with our previous result.

Example 7-22

Suppose we deposit $1000 in a savings account that pays 6% interest compounded quarterly.

(a) What is the balance at the end of 1 year?
(b) What is the effective annual yield on this investment, that is, the rate that would have been paid if the amount had been invested using simple interest?

Solution

(a) An annual interest rate of 6% earns $\frac{1}{4}$ of 6%, or an interest rate of $\frac{0.06}{4}$, in one quarter. Since there are four periods, we have the following.

$$A = 1000\left(1 + \frac{0.06}{4}\right)^4 \doteq \$1061.36$$

Thus, the balance at the end of one year is $1061.36.
(b) Because the interest earned is $1061.36 − $1000.00 = $61.36, the effective annual yield can be computed using the simple interest formula, $I = Prt$.

$$61.36 = 1000 \cdot r \cdot 1$$

$$\frac{61.36}{1000} = r$$

$$0.06136 = r$$

$$6.136\% = r$$

Hence, the effective annual yield is 6.136%.

Compound Interest

If $500 is invested at 8% interest compounded annually, the interest is computed on the principal plus previously-earned interest. The table shows that the total amount after 3 years will be about $629.86.

Period	Principal	Interest: $I = P \times R \times T$	Total: $A = P + (P \times R \times T)$
First year	500	$(500)(0.08)(1) = 40$	$500 + 40 = 540$
Second year	540	$(540)(0.08)(1) = 43.20$	$540 + 43.20 = 583.20$
Third year	583.20	$(583.20)(0.08)(1) \approx 46.66$	$583.20 + 46.66 = 629.86$

You can also use the compound-interest formula to find the answer.

Total   Principal   Rate per interest period

$A = P(1 + R)^n$ ← Number of interest periods

$A = 500(1 + 0.08)^3$ The interest is compounded annually, so the number of interest periods is 3. The interest rate per period is 8%.

$A = 500(1.08)^3$ $(1.08)^3 = (1.08)(1.08)(1.08) \approx 1.26$

$A \approx 500(1.26) \approx 630$

Suppose the interest on the $500 is computed semiannually (twice a year). Then the total amount after 3 years will be about $635.

$A = P(1 + R)^n$

$A = 500(1 + 0.04)^6$ The interest is compounded twice a year, so the number of interest periods is 3×2, or 6. The interest rate per period is 8% ÷ 2, or 4%.

$A = 500(1.04)^6$

$A \approx 500(1.27) \approx 635$

Finding compound interest is demonstrated on the student page on page 318, which is from Scott, Foresman's *Invitation to Mathematics*, 1985, Grade 7.

Example 7-23

To save for their child's college education, a couple deposits $3000 into an account that pays 11% annual interest compounded daily. Find the amount in this account after 12 years.

Solution

The principal in the problem is $3000, the daily rate i is 0.11/365, and the number of compounding periods is 12 · 365, or 4380. Thus, we have

$$A = \$3000\left(1 + \frac{0.11}{365}\right)^{4380} \doteq \$11,228$$

PROBLEM SET 7-4

A calculator is needed in most of these problems.

1. Complete the following compound-interest chart.

	Compounding Period	Principal	Annual Rate	Length of Time (Years)	Interest Rate Per Period	Number of Periods	Amount of Interest Paid
(a)	Semiannual	$1000	6%	2			
(b)	Quarterly	$1000	8%	3			
(c)	Monthly	$1000	10%	5			
(d)	Daily	$1000	12%	4			

2. Ms. Jackson borrowed $42,000 at 13% annual simple interest to buy her house. If she won the Irish Sweepstakes exactly 1 year later and was able to repay the loan without penalty, how much interest did she owe?

3. Carolyn went on a shopping spree with her Bank-amount card and made purchases totaling $125. If the interest rate is 1.5% per month on the unpaid balance and she does not pay this debt for 1 year, how much interest will she owe at the end of the year?

4. A man collected $28,500 on a loan of $25,000 he made 4 years ago. If he charged simple interest, what was the rate he charged?

5. Burger Queen will need $50,000 in 5 years for a new addition. To meet this goal, money is deposited today in an account that pays 9% annual interest compounded quarterly. Find the amount that should be invested to total $50,000 in 5 years.

6. A company is expanding its line to include more products. To do so, it borrows $320,000 at 13.5% annual simple interest for a period of 18 months. How much interest must the company pay?

7. An amount of $3000 was deposited in a bank at a rate of 5% compounded quarterly for 3 years; the rate then increased to 8% and was compounded quarterly for the next 3 years. If no money was withdrawn, what was the balance at the end of this time period?

8. To save for their retirement, a couple deposits $4000 in an account that pays 9% interest compounded quarterly. What will be the value of their investment after 20 years?

9. A money-market fund pays 14% annual interest compounded daily. What is the value of $10,000 invested in this fund after 15 years?

10. A car company is offering car loans at a simple-interest rate of 9%. Find the interest charged to a customer who finances a car loan of $7200 for 3 years.

11. Linda deposits $200 at the end of the month in an account that pays 9% compounded monthly. If she does this each month, what will be the value of her account at the end of 6 months?

12. The New Age Savings Bank advertises 9% interest rates compounded daily, while the Pay More Bank pays 10.5% interest compounded annually. Which bank offers a better rate for a customer if she plans to leave her money in for exactly 1 year?

13. Johnny and Carolyn have three different savings plans, which accumulated the following amounts of interest for 1 year:
    (a) A passbook savings account that accumulated $53.90 on a principal of $980.
    (b) A certificate of deposit that accumulated $55.20 on a principal of $600.
    (c) A money market certificate that accumulated $158.40 on a principal of $1200.
    Which of these accounts paid the best interest rate for the year?

14. If a hamburger costs $1.35 and if the price continues to rise at a rate of 11% a year for the next 6 years, what will the price of a hamburger be at the end of 6 years?

15. If college tuition is $2500 this year, what will it be 10 years from now if we assume a constant inflation rate of 9% a year?

16. Sara invested money at a bank that paid 6.5% compounded quarterly. If she received $4650 at the end of 4 years, what was her initial investment?

17. A car is purchased for $15,000. If each year the car depreciates 10% of its value the preceding year, what will its value be at the end of 3 years?

★ 18. Determine the number of years to the nearest tenth that it would take for any amount of money deposited at a 10% interest rate compounded annually to double.

COMPUTER CORNER

The following BASIC program will compute compound interest. Type it into the computer and compare the results with those obtained in this chapter.

```
10 PRINT "COMPOUND INTEREST PROGRAM"
20 PRINT
30 PRINT "TYPE IN THE PRINCIPAL AND PRESS RETURN."
40 INPUT P
50 PRINT "TYPE IN THE RATE AS A DECIMAL AND PRESS RETURN."
60 INPUT R
70 PRINT "TYPE IN THE NUMBER OF YEARS AND PRESS RETURN."
80 INPUT T
90 PRINT "TYPE IN THE COMPOUNDING PERIOD AND PRESS RETURN."
100 PRINT "ENTER 2 FOR SEMIANNUALLY, 4 FOR QUARTERLY, "
110 PRINT "12 FOR MONTHLY, OR 365 FOR DAILY."
120 INPUT C
130 LET N = T * C
140 LET I = R/C
150 LET A = P * ((1 + I) ∧ N)
160 PRINT
170 PRINT "PRINCIPAL"; TAB(11); "RATE"; TAB(16) ;
180 PRINT "TIME"; TAB(21); "COMPOUNDED"; TAB(32) ; "AMOUNT"
190 PRINT P; TAB(11) ; R; TAB(16) ; T; TAB(21) ; C; TAB(32) ; A
200 PRINT
210 PRINT "TO ENTER ANOTHER PROBLEM TYPE RUN."
220 END
```

Section 7-5   Real Numbers

As we have seen, every rational number can be expressed as a repeating or terminating decimal. The ancient Greeks discovered numbers that are not rational. Such numbers must have a decimal representation that neither terminates nor repeats. To find such decimals, we focus on the characteristics they must have:

1. There must be an infinite number of nonzero digits to the right of the decimal point.
2. There cannot be a repeating block of digits (a repetend).

Does a decimal like 0.1432865 . . . have these characteristics? Because the decimal is infinite, the first characteristic is satisfied. However, without more information, there is no way to tell whether there is a repeating block of digits in the decimal.

There are several ways to construct a nonterminating, nonrepeating decimal. Perhaps the simplest is to devise a pattern of infinite digits in such a way that there will definitely be no repeated block. Consider the number 0.1010010001 . . . . If the pattern shown continues, the next groups of digits are four zeros followed by 1, five zeros followed by 1, and so on. It is possible to describe a pattern for this decimal, but there is no repeating block of digits. Because this decimal is nonterminating and nonrepeating, it cannot represent a rational number. Numbers that are not rational numbers are called **irrational numbers.**

irrational numbers

In the mid-eighteenth century, it was proved that the number that is the ratio of the circumference of a circle to its diameter, symbolized by π**(pi),** is an irrational number. In schools, we traditionally use $\frac{22}{7}$, 3.14, or 3.14159 for π. These are only rational-number approximations of π. The value of π has been computed to thousands of decimal places with no apparent pattern.

π(pi)

Other irrational numbers occur in the study of area. For example, to find the area of a square, we use the formula $A = s^2$, where A is the area and s is the length of a side of the square. If a side of a square is 3 cm long, then the area of the square is 9 cm^2 (square centimeters). Conversely, we can use the formula to find the length of a side of a square, given its area. If the area of a square is 25 cm^2, then $s^2 = 25$, so $s = 5$ or $^-5$. Each of these solutions is called a **square root** of 25. However, because lengths are always nonnegative, 5 is the only possible solution. The positive solution of $s^2 = 25$—namely, 5—is called the **principal square root** of 25 and is denoted by $\sqrt{25}$. Similarly, the principal square root of 2 is denoted by $\sqrt{2}$. Note that $\sqrt{16} \neq {}^-4$, because $^-4$ is not the principal square root of 16.

square root

principal square root

HISTORICAL NOTE

The discovery of irrational numbers by members of the Pythagorean Society (founded by Pythagoras) is one of the greatest events in the history of mathematics. This discovery was very disturbing to the Pythagoreans, who believed that everything depended on whole numbers, and so they decided to keep the matter secret. One legend has it that Hippasus, a society member, was drowned because he relayed the secret to persons outside the society.

DEFINITION

> If a is any whole number, the **principal square root** of a is the nonnegative number b such that $b^2 = a$.

radical sign / radicand

Remark   The principal square root of a is denoted by $\sqrt{a}$, where the symbol $\sqrt{}$ is called a **radical sign** and a is called the **radicand.**

Example 7-24

Find: (a) the square roots of 144;
(b) the principal square root of 144.

Solution

(a) The square roots of 144 are 12 and $^-12$.
(b) The principal square root of 144 is 12.

Some square roots are rational numbers. For example, $\sqrt{25}$ is 5, a rational number. Other square roots, like $\sqrt{2}$, are irrational numbers. To see why this is so, note that since $1^2 = 1$ and $2^2 = 4$, there is no whole number s such that $s^2 = 2$. Is there a rational number $\dfrac{a}{b}$ such that $\left(\dfrac{a}{b}\right)^2 = 2$? If we assume there is such a rational number, then the following must be true.

$$\left(\frac{a}{b}\right)^2 = 2$$

$$\frac{a^2}{b^2} = 2$$

$$a^2 = 2b^2$$

Since $a^2 = 2b^2$, the Fundamental Theorem of Arithmetic says that the prime factorizations of a^2 and $2b^2$ are the same. In particular, the prime 2 appears the same number of times in the prime factorization of a^2 as it does in the factorization of $2b^2$. Since $b^2 = b \cdot b$, then no matter how many times 2 appears in the prime factorization of b, it appears twice as many times in $b \cdot b$. Also, a^2 has an even number of 2s for the same reason that b^2 does. In $2b^2$, another factor of 2 is introduced, resulting in an odd number of 2s in the prime factorization of $2b^2$ and hence of a^2. But 2 cannot appear both an odd number of times and an even number of times in the same prime factorization of a^2. We have a contradiction. This contradiction could have been caused only by the assumption that $\sqrt{2}$ is a rational number. Consequently, $\sqrt{2}$ must be an irrational number. A similar argument can be used to show that $\sqrt{3}$ is irrational or $\sqrt{n}$ is irrational, where n is a whole number but not the square of another whole number.

Example 7-25

Prove that $2 + \sqrt{2}$ is an irrational number.

Solution

Suppose $2 + \sqrt{2} = \dfrac{a}{b}$, where $\dfrac{a}{b}$ is a rational number. Then,

$$\sqrt{2} = \frac{a}{b} - 2$$

$$\sqrt{2} = \frac{a - 2b}{b}$$

But $\dfrac{(a-2b)}{b}$ is a rational number (why?), and this is a contradiction because $\sqrt{2}$ is an irrational number. Thus, $2+\sqrt{2}$ is an irrational number.

Remark   In a similar manner, we could prove $m+n\sqrt{2}$ is an irrational number for all rational numbers m and n except $n=0$.

Many irrational numbers can be interpreted geometrically. For example, a point on a number line can be found to represent $\sqrt{2}$ by using the **Pythagorean Theorem** (see Chapter 12). That is, if a and b are the lengths of the shorter sides (legs) of a right triangle and c is the length of the longer side (hypotenuse), then $a^2+b^2=c^2$, as shown in Figure 7-3.

Pythagorean Theorem

Figure 7-3

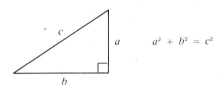

Figure 7-4 shows a segment one unit long constructed perpendicular to a number line at point P. Thus, two sides of the triangle shown are one unit long. By the Pythagorean Theorem, $1^2+1^2=c^2$. Thus, $c^2=2$, and $c=\sqrt{2}$.

Figure 7-4

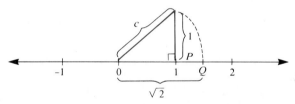

Because $\sqrt{2}$ is the length of the hypotenuse, there must be some point Q on the number line such that the distance from zero to Q is $\sqrt{2}$. Similarly, other square roots can be constructed, as shown in Figure 7-5.

Figure 7-5

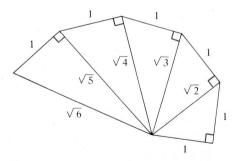

From Figure 7-4, we see that $\sqrt{2}$ must have a value between 1 and 2—that is, $1<\sqrt{2}<2$. To obtain a closer approximation of $\sqrt{2}$, we attempt to "squeeze" $\sqrt{2}$ between two numbers that are between 1 and 2. Because $(1.5)^2=2.25$ and $(1.4)^2=1.96$, it follows that $1.4<\sqrt{2}<1.5$, or $\sqrt{2}\doteq1.4$. Because a^2 can be interpreted as the area of a square with side of length a, this discussion can be pictured geometrically, as in Figure 7-6.

Figure 7-6

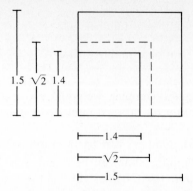

If a more accurate approximation for $\sqrt{2}$ is desired, then this squeezing process can be continued. We see that $(1.4)^2$, or 1.96, is closer to 2 than $(1.5)^2$, or 2.25, so we choose numbers closer to 1.4 in order to find the next approximation. We find the following.

$$(1.42)^2 = 2.0164$$

$$(1.41)^2 = 1.9981$$

Thus, $1.41 < \sqrt{2} < 1.42$, or $\sqrt{2} \doteq 1.41$. We can continue this process until we obtain the desired approximation. Note that if the calculator has a square-root key, the approximation can be obtained directly.

Another algorithm for approximating square roots is called the *divide-and-average method,* or *Newton's method.* It is demonstrated on page 325, which is from *Addison-Wesley Mathematics,* 1987, Grade 8.

THE SYSTEM OF REAL NUMBERS

real numbers   The set of **real numbers** R is the union of the set of rational numbers and the set of irrational numbers. Real numbers represented as decimals can be terminating; repeating; or nonterminating, nonrepeating. The concept of fractions can now be extended to include all numbers of the form $\dfrac{a}{b}$, where a and b are real numbers with $b \neq 0$, such as $\dfrac{\sqrt{3}}{5}$. Addition, subtraction, multiplication, and division are defined on the set of real numbers in such a way that all the properties of these operations on rationals still hold. The properties are summarized below.

Properties   **Closure Properties**   For real numbers a and b, $a + b$ and $a \cdot b$ are unique real numbers.

Commutative Properties   For real numbers a and b, $a + b = b + a$ and $a \cdot b = b \cdot a$.

Associative Properties   For real numbers a, b, and c, $a + (b + c) = (a + b) + c$ and $a \cdot (b \cdot c) = (a \cdot b) \cdot c$.

Identity Properties   The number 0 is the unique additive identity and 1 is the unique multiplicative identity such that for any real number a, $0 + a = a = a + 0$ and $1 \cdot a = a = a \cdot 1$.

Inverse Properties   (1) For every real number a, ^-a is its unique additive inverse; that is, $a + {}^-a = 0 = {}^-a + a$.

(2) For every nonzero real number a, $\dfrac{1}{a}$ is its unique multiplicative inverse; that is, $a \cdot \left(\dfrac{1}{a}\right) = 1 = \left(\dfrac{1}{a}\right) \cdot a$.

Distributive Property of Multiplication over Addition   For real numbers a, b, and c, $a \cdot (b + c) = a \cdot b + a \cdot c$.

Denseness Property   For real numbers a and b, there exists a real number c such that $a < c < b$.

Finding Square Roots Without a Table

The directions below show the steps for finding the square root of a number using a method called **divide and average**.

Find $\sqrt{937}$ to the nearest tenth.

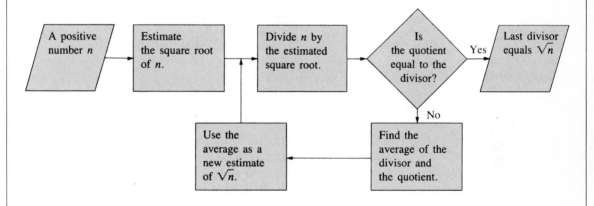

Estimate

$$\sqrt{937} \approx 30$$

Divide

$$
\begin{array}{r}
3\,1.2 \\
3\,0\overline{)9\,3\,7.0} \\
9\,0 \\
\hline
3\,7 \\
3\,0 \\
\hline
7\,0 \\
6\,0 \\
\hline
1\,0
\end{array}
$$

Average

$$\frac{30 + 31.2}{2} = 30.6$$

Divide

$$
\begin{array}{r}
3\,0.6 \\
3\,0.6\overline{)9\,3\,7.0\,0} \\
9\,1\,8 \\
\hline
1\,9\,0\,0 \\
1\,8\,3\,6 \\
\hline
6\,4
\end{array}
$$

Divisor and quotient are equal, to the nearest tenth.

$\sqrt{937} \approx 30.6$, to the nearest tenth.

Properties of equality and inequality similar to those for rational numbers hold for real numbers. Using these properties, real-number equations and inequalities can be solved. The number line can be used to picture real numbers because every point on a number line corresponds to a real number and every real number corresponds to a point on the number line. Because such a one-to-one correspondence is possible, solution sets of real-number equations and inequalities can be graphed on a number line.

Example 7-26

Solve each of the following and show the solution on a number line.

(a) $x - 3 \leq \sqrt{2} + {}^-2$ (b) $\dfrac{3x^2}{2} - 4 = 5$ (c) $|x| \geq 2$

Solution

(a) $x - 3 \leq \sqrt{2} + {}^-2$

$x \leq \sqrt{2} + 1$

Thus, the solution is $x \leq \sqrt{2} + 1$, where x is a real number, and it is shown in Figure 7-7.

Figure 7-7

(b) $\dfrac{3x^2}{2} - 4 = 5$

$\dfrac{3x^2}{2} = 9$

$3x^2 = 18$

$x^2 = 6$

$x = \sqrt{6}, \text{ or } x = {}^-\sqrt{6}$

The solution is shown on the number line in Figure 7-8.

Figure 7-8

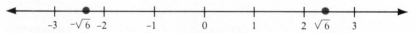

(c) To solve $|x| \geq 2$, we look for all the points on the number line whose distance from the origin is greater than or equal to 2. All such points are shown on the number line in Figure 7-9. The answer can be written as $x \leq {}^-2$ or $x \geq 2$. Note that the answer could not be written as $2 \leq x \leq {}^-2$. Why not?

Figure 7-9

PROBLEM SET 7-5

1. Without using a radical sign, write an irrational number all of whose digits are 2s and 3s.
2. Arrange the following real numbers in order from least to greatest.

   $0.78, 0.\overline{7}, 0.\overline{78}, 0.788, 0.7\overline{8}, 0.7\overline{88}, 0.77, 0.787787778\ldots$

3. Which of the following represent irrational numbers?
   (a) $\sqrt{51}$ (b) $\sqrt{64}$ (c) $\sqrt{324}$
   (d) $\sqrt{325}$ (e) $2 + 3\sqrt{2}$ (f) $\sqrt{2} \div 5$
4. Find the square roots, correct to tenths, for each of the following, if possible.

(a) 225   (b) 251   (c) 169
(d) 512   (e) $^-81$ (f) 625

5. Find the approximate square roots for each of the following, rounded to hundredths, by the squeezing method.
   (a) 17   (b) 7   (c) 21
   (d) 0.0120   (e) 20.3   (f) 1.64

6. Classify each of the following as true or false. If false, give a counterexample.
   (a) The sum of any rational number and any irrational number is a rational number.
   (b) The sum of any two irrational numbers is an irrational number.
   (c) The product of any two irrational numbers is an irrational number.
   (d) The difference of any two irrational numbers is an irrational number.

7. Is it true that $\sqrt{a+b} = \sqrt{a} + \sqrt{b}$? Either prove the statement or give a counterexample.

8. Solve each of the following for real numbers and graph the solution.
   (a) $5x - 1 \leq \frac{7}{2}x + 3$ (b) $4 + 3x \geq \sqrt{5} - 7x$
   (c) $\frac{2}{3}x + \sqrt{3} \leq {}^-5x$ (d) $(2x - 1)^2 = 4$
   (e) $|x| \geq 7$ (f) $|x| \leq 3$

9. Find three irrational numbers between 1 and 3.

10. Find an irrational number between $0.\overline{53}$ and $0.\overline{54}$.

11. Pi (π) is an irrational number. Could $\pi = \frac{22}{7}$? Why or why not?

12. Is it true that $\sqrt{13} = 3.60\overline{5}$? Why or why not?

13. For what real values of x is each statement true?
    (a) $\sqrt{x} = 8$ (b) $\sqrt{x} = {}^-8$
    (c) $\sqrt{{}^-x} = 8$ (d) $\sqrt{{}^-x} = {}^-8$
    (e) $\sqrt{x} > 0$ (f) $\sqrt{x} < 0$

14. If R is the set of real numbers, Q is the set of rational numbers, I is the set of integers, W is the set of whole numbers, and S is the set of irrational numbers, find each of the following.
    (a) $Q \cup S$ (b) $Q \cap S$ (c) $Q \cap R$
    (d) $S \cap W$ (e) $W \cup R$ (f) $Q \cup R$

15. If the letters below correspond to the sets listed in Problem 14, put a check mark under each set of numbers for which a solution to the problem exists. (N is the set of natural numbers.)

	N	I	Q	R
(a) $x^2 + 1 = 5$				
(b) $2x - 1 = 32$				
(c) $x^2 = 3$				
(d) $x^2 = 4$				
(e) $\sqrt{x} = {}^-1$				
(f) $\sqrt[3]{x} = 4$				

16. A diagonal brace is placed in a 4-foot by 5-foot rectangular gate. What is the length of the brace to the nearest tenth of a foot? (*Hint:* Use the Pythagorean Theorem.)

17. For a simple pendulum of length l, given in centimeters (cm), the time of the period T in seconds is given by $T = 2\pi \sqrt{\dfrac{l}{g}}$, where $g = 9.8$ cm/sec^2. Find the time T rounded to hundredths if:
    (a) $l = 20$ cm   (b) $l = 100$ cm

★18. Prove: $\sqrt{3}$ is irrational.

★19. Prove: If p is a prime number, then $\sqrt{p}$ is an irrational number.

★20. (a) For what whole numbers m is $\sqrt{m}$ a rational number?
    ★(b) Prove your answer in (a).

21. (a) Show that $0.5 + \dfrac{1}{0.5} \geq 2$.
    ★(b) Prove that any positive real number x plus its reciprocal $\dfrac{1}{x}$ is greater than or equal to 2.

Review Problems

22. Write 0.00024 as a fraction in simplest form.

23. Arrange the following from least to greatest.
    4.09, 4.099, $4.0\overline{9}$, $4.09\overline{1}$

24. Write $0.\overline{24}$ as a fraction in simplest form.

25. Write each of the following as a standard numeral.
    (a) $2.03 \cdot 10^5$ (b) $3.8 \cdot 10^{-4}$

26. Joan's salary this year is $18,600. If she receives a 9% raise, what is her salary next year?

27. If 800 of the 2000 students at the university are males, what percent of the university students are females?

---

*Section 7-6   Radicals and Rational Exponents

nth root   index

The positive solution to $x^2 = 5$ is $\sqrt{5}$. Similarly, the positive solution to $x^4 = 5$ can be denoted as $\sqrt[4]{5}$. In general, the positive solution to $x^n = 5$ is $\sqrt[n]{5}$ and is called the **nth root** of 5. The numeral n is called the **index.** Note that in the expression $\sqrt{5}$, the index 2 is understood and is not expressed.

In general, the positive solution to $x^n = b$, where b is *nonnegative*, is $\sqrt[n]{b}$. Substituting $\sqrt[n]{b}$ for x in the equation $x^n = b$ gives the following.

$(\sqrt[n]{b})^n = b$

If b is negative, $\sqrt[n]{b}$ cannot always be defined. For example, consider $\sqrt[4]{-16}$. If $\sqrt[4]{-16} = x$, then $x^4 = {}^-16$. Since any nonzero real number raised to the fourth power is positive, there is no real-number solution to $x^4 = {}^-16$ and, therefore, $\sqrt[4]{-16}$ cannot be a real number. Similarly, it is not possible to find *any* even root of a negative number. However, the value $^-2$ satisfies the equation $x^3 = {}^-8$. Hence, $\sqrt[3]{-8} = {}^-2$. *In general, the odd root of a negative number is a negative number.*

Because $\sqrt{a}$, if it exists, is positive by definition, $\sqrt{(-3)^2} = \sqrt{9} = 3$ and not $^-3$. Many students think that $\sqrt{a^2}$ always equals a. This is true if $a \geq 0$, but false if $a < 0$. *In general, $\sqrt{a^2} = |a|$.*

Now, consider an expression like $4^{1/2}$. What does it mean? By extending the properties of exponents previously developed for integer exponents, it must be that $4^{1/2} \cdot 4^{1/2} = 4^{1/2+1/2} = 4^1$. This implies that $(4^{1/2})^2 = 4$, or $4^{1/2}$ is a square root of 4. The number $4^{1/2}$ is assumed to be the principal square root of 4; that is, $4^{1/2} = \sqrt{4}$. In general, if x is a nonnegative real number, then $x^{1/2} = \sqrt{x}$. Similarly, $(x^{1/3})^3 = x^{(1/3)\cdot 3} = x^1$, and $x^{1/3} = \sqrt[3]{x}$. This discussion leads to the following definition.

DEFINITION

For any real number x and any positive integer n, $x^{1/n} = \sqrt[n]{x}$, where $\sqrt[n]{x}$ is meaningful.

Also, since $(x^m)^{1/n} = \sqrt[n]{x^m}$, and if $(x^m)^{1/n} = x^{m/n}$, it follows that $x^{m/n} = \sqrt[n]{x^m}$.

Example 7-27

Write each of the following in radical form.

(a) $16^{1/4}$ (b) $32^{1/6}$
(c) $({}^-8)^{1/3}$ (d) $64^{3/2}$

Solution

(a) $16^{1/4} = \sqrt[4]{16}$ (b) $32^{1/6} = \sqrt[6]{32}$
(c) $({}^-8)^{1/3} = \sqrt[3]{-8}$ (d) $64^{3/2} = \sqrt{64^3}$ or $(\sqrt{64})^3$

The properties of integer exponents also hold for rational exponents. These properties are equivalent to the corresponding properties of radicals if the expressions involving radicals are meaningful.

Properties   Let r and s be any rational numbers, x and y be any real numbers, and n be any nonzero integer.

(a) $(xy)^r = x^r \cdot y^r$ implies $(xy)^{1/n} = x^{1/n}y^{1/n}$ and $\sqrt[n]{xy} = \sqrt[n]{x}\sqrt[n]{y}$.

(b) $\left(\dfrac{x}{y}\right)^r = \dfrac{x^r}{y^r}$ implies $\left(\dfrac{x}{y}\right)^{1/n} = \dfrac{x^{1/n}}{y^{1/n}}$ and $\sqrt[n]{\dfrac{x}{y}} = \dfrac{\sqrt[n]{x}}{\sqrt[n]{y}}$.

(c) $(x^r)^s = x^{rs}$ implies $(x^{1/n})^s = x^{s/n}$ and, hence, $(\sqrt[n]{x})^s = \sqrt[n]{x^s}$.

The preceding properties can be used to simplify the square roots of many numbers. For example, $\sqrt{96} = \sqrt{16 \cdot 6} = \sqrt{16}\sqrt{6} = 4\sqrt{6}$. When $\sqrt{96}$ is written as $4\sqrt{6}$, it is said to be in *simplest form*. In general, *to write an nth root in simplest form, factor out as many nth powers as possible.* Note that $\sqrt{32} = \sqrt{4 \cdot 8} = 2\sqrt{8}$. Hence, $2\sqrt{8}$ is a simplified form, but not the simplest form. The simplest form of $\sqrt{32}$ is $\sqrt{16 \cdot 2} = \sqrt{16} \cdot \sqrt{2} = 4\sqrt{2}$.

Example 7-28

Write each of the following in simplest form.

(a) $\sqrt{200}$ (b) $\sqrt{75}$ (c) $\sqrt[3]{240}$
(d) $\sqrt{3} \cdot \sqrt{15}$ (e) $\sqrt[3]{81} \cdot \sqrt[3]{32}$

Solution

(a) $\sqrt{200} = \sqrt{100 \cdot 2} = \sqrt{100}\sqrt{2} = 10\sqrt{2}$
(b) $\sqrt{75} = \sqrt{25 \cdot 3} = \sqrt{25}\sqrt{3} = 5\sqrt{3}$
(c) $\sqrt[3]{240} = \sqrt[3]{8 \cdot 30} = \sqrt[3]{8}\sqrt[3]{30} = 2\sqrt[3]{30}$
(d) $\sqrt{3} \cdot \sqrt{15} = \sqrt{3 \cdot 15} = \sqrt{45} = \sqrt{9 \cdot 5} = \sqrt{9} \cdot \sqrt{5} = 3\sqrt{5}$
(e) $\sqrt[3]{81} \cdot \sqrt[3]{32} = \sqrt[3]{81 \cdot 32} = \sqrt[3]{3^4 \cdot 2^5} = \sqrt[3]{3^3 \cdot 2^3 \cdot 3 \cdot 2^2}$
    $= \sqrt[3]{3^3 \cdot 2^3} \cdot \sqrt[3]{3 \cdot 2^2} = 6\sqrt[3]{12}$

Some expressions in the form $\sqrt{x} + \sqrt{y}$ can be simplified. For example.

$$\sqrt{24} + \sqrt{54} = \sqrt{4 \cdot 6} + \sqrt{9 \cdot 6}$$
$$= \sqrt{4}\sqrt{6} + \sqrt{9}\sqrt{6}$$
$$= 2\sqrt{6} + 3\sqrt{6}$$
$$= (2 + 3)\sqrt{6}$$
$$= 5\sqrt{6}$$

Be careful! Notice that $\sqrt{9} + \sqrt{4} = 3 + 2 = 5$, but $\sqrt{9 + 4} = \sqrt{13}$. Thus, $\sqrt{9} + \sqrt{4} \neq \sqrt{9 + 4}$ and, in general, $\sqrt{x} + \sqrt{y} \neq \sqrt{x + y}$.

Example 7-29

Write each expression in simplest form.

(a) $\sqrt{20} + \sqrt{45} - \sqrt{80}$ (b) $\sqrt{12} + \sqrt{13}$
(c) $\sqrt{49x} + \sqrt{4x}$

Solution

(a) $\sqrt{20} + \sqrt{45} - \sqrt{80} = 2\sqrt{5} + 3\sqrt{5} - 4\sqrt{5} = \sqrt{5}$
(b) $\sqrt{12} + \sqrt{13} = 2\sqrt{3} + \sqrt{13}$
(c) $\sqrt{49x} + \sqrt{4x} = 7\sqrt{x} + 2\sqrt{x} = 9\sqrt{x}$

PROBLEM SET 7-6

1. Write each of the following square roots in simplest form.

   (a) $\sqrt{180}$ (b) $\sqrt{529}$ (c) $\sqrt{363}$

   (d) $\sqrt{252}$ (e) $\sqrt{\dfrac{169}{196}}$ (f) $\sqrt{\dfrac{49}{196}}$

2. Write each of the following in simplest form.

   (a) $\sqrt[3]{-27}$ (b) $\sqrt[5]{96}$ (c) $\sqrt[5]{32}$
   (d) $\sqrt[3]{250}$ (e) $\sqrt[5]{-243}$ (f) $\sqrt[4]{64}$

3. Write each of the following expressions in simplest form.

(a) $2\sqrt{3} + 3\sqrt{2} + \sqrt{180}$

(b) $\sqrt[3]{4} \cdot \sqrt[3]{10}$

(c) $(2\sqrt{3} + 3\sqrt{2})^2$

(d) $\sqrt{6} \div \sqrt{12}$

(e) $5\sqrt{72} + 2\sqrt{50} - \sqrt{288} - \sqrt{242}$

(f) $\sqrt{\dfrac{8}{7}} \div \sqrt{\dfrac{4}{21}}$

4. Rewrite each of the following in simplest form.

(a) $16^{1/2}$ (b) $16^{-1/2}$

(c) $27^{2/3}$ (d) $27^{-2/3}$

(e) $64^{5/6}$ (f) $32^{2/5}$

(g) $3^{1/2} \cdot 3^{3/2}$ (h) $8^{3/2} \cdot 4^{1/4}$

(i) $\dfrac{(32)^{-2/5}}{(\frac{1}{16})^{-3/2}}$ (j) $(10^{1/3} \cdot 10^{-1/6})^6$

(k) $9^{2/3} \cdot 27^{2/9}$

5. Is $\sqrt{x^2 + y^2} = x + y$ for all values of x and y?

6. The following exponential function approximates the number of bacteria after t hours: $E(t) = 2^{10} \cdot 16^t$.

(a) What is the initial number of bacteria, that is, when $t = 0$?

(b) After $\frac{1}{4}$ hour, how many bacteria are there?

(c) After $\frac{1}{2}$ hour, how many bacteria are there?

7. Solve for x, where x is a rational number.

(a) $3^x = 81$ (b) $4^x = 8$

(c) $128^{-x} = 16$ (d) $\left(\dfrac{4}{9}\right)^{3x} = \dfrac{32}{243}$

8. Write $\sqrt{2\sqrt{2\sqrt{2}}}$ in the form $\sqrt[n]{2^m}$, where n and m are positive integers.

★9. In the cartoon, Woodstock illustrates the technique for rationalizing fractions (removing the radical symbol from the denominator of a fraction). Use the technique demonstrated in the cartoon to rationalize the denominators for each of the following.

(a) $\dfrac{2}{\sqrt{3}}$ (b) $\dfrac{7\sqrt{2}}{\sqrt{5}}$ (c) $\dfrac{5\sqrt{5}}{\sqrt{18}}$

(d) $\dfrac{1}{\sqrt{3}}$ (e) $\dfrac{2}{\sqrt{2}}$ (f) $\dfrac{3}{\sqrt{8}}$

SOLUTION TO THE PRELIMINARY PROBLEM

UNDERSTANDING THE PROBLEM The airline charges an additional amount for each passenger with luggage weight over x pounds. Mr. and Mrs. Byrd had a combined luggage weight of 105 pounds and were charged $1.00 and $1.50, respectively. A third passenger also had 105 pounds of luggage and was charged $6.50 for the number of pounds over the x-pound limit. We are to determine the number of pounds that are allowed free of charge for each passenger.

DEVISING A PLAN Because Mr. and Mrs. Byrd are each allowed x pounds of luggage free, they must pay for $(105 - 2x)$ pounds of luggage while the third passenger must pay for $(105 - x)$ pounds. Assuming that the airline charges the same rate for each pound over the allowed limit for each person, we can express the rate per pound for Mr. and Mrs. Byrd and for the third passenger, equate the rates, and obtain an equation in terms of x. If we solve the equation for x, then we obtain the number of pounds allowed for each passenger free of charge.

CARRYING OUT THE PLAN Because Mr. and Mrs. Byrd paid $2.50 on their overweight $(105 - 2x)$ pounds of luggage, the price per pound on their excess luggage was $2.50/(105 - 2x)$. Because the third passenger paid $6.50 for his $(105 - x)$ pounds of excess luggage, the airline charged him $6.50/(105 - x)$ dollars per pound. Equating the rates per pound, we obtain the following proportion.

$$\frac{2.50}{105 - 2x} = \frac{6.50}{105 - x}$$

We solve the equation for x as follows.

$$2.50(105 - x) = 6.50(105 - 2x)$$
$$262.5 - 2.5x = 682.5 - 13x$$
$$10.5x = 420$$
$$x = 40$$

This shows that the number of pounds allowed for each passenger free of charge is 40 pounds.

LOOKING BACK Checking the value for $x = 40$, we find that Mr. and Mrs. Byrd's luggage is $(105 - 2 \cdot 40)$, or 25, pounds overweight. Because they were charged $2.50, we see that the charge is 10¢ per pound for each pound over 40 pounds. Checking that this ratio applies to the third passenger, we see that his luggage is $(105 - 40)$, or 65, pounds overweight. At 10¢ per pound, this agrees with the airline charge of $6.50. Luggage weights and/or charges can also be varied to create new problems.

QUESTIONS FROM THE CLASSROOM

1. A student argues that $0.\overline{9} \neq 1$. How do you respond?

2. A student says that $3\frac{1}{4}\% = 0.03 + 0.25 = 0.28$. What is the error, if any?

3. Why is $\sqrt{25} \neq {}^-5$?

4. A student says, "I know another way to express $\sqrt{n^2}$. It is $|n|$." Is the student correct?

5. A student claims that $\sqrt{({}^-5)^2} = {}^-5$ because $\sqrt{a^2} = a$. Is this correct?

6. Another student says that $\sqrt{({}^-5)^2} = [({}^-5)^2]^{1/2} = ({}^-5)^{2/2} = ({}^-5)^1 = {}^-5$. Is this correct?

7. A student claims that the equation $\sqrt{{}^-x} = 3$ has no solution since the square root of a negative number does not exist. Why is this argument wrong?

8. A student multiplies $(6.5)(8.5)$ to obtain the following.

$$\begin{array}{r} 8.5 \\ \times\ 6.5 \\ \hline 4\,2\,5 \\ 5\,1\,0 \\ \hline 5\,5.2\,5 \end{array}$$

However, when the student multiplies $8\frac{1}{2} \cdot 6\frac{1}{2}$, the following is obtained.

$$8\frac{1}{2}$$

$$\times\ 6\frac{1}{2}$$

$$\begin{array}{ll} 4\frac{1}{4} & \left(\frac{1}{2} \cdot 8\frac{1}{2}\right) \\ \underline{48} & (6 \cdot 8) \\ 52\frac{1}{4} & \end{array}$$

How is this possible?

9. On a test, a student wrote the following.

$$\frac{x^2}{7} - 2 \geq {}^{-}3$$

$$\frac{x^2}{7} \geq {}^{-}1$$

$$x^2 \geq {}^{-}7$$

Hence, there is no solution. What is the error?

10. A student reports that it is impossible to mark a product up 150% because 100% of something is all there is. What is your response?

11. A student reports that $^{-}438{,}340{,}000$ cannot be written in scientific notation. How do you respond?

CHAPTER OUTLINE

I. Decimals
   A. Every rational number can be represented as a terminating or repeating decimal.
   B. A rational number $\frac{a}{b}$, whose denominator is of the form $2^m \cdot 5^n$, where m and n are whole numbers, can be expressed as a **terminating decimal.**
   C. A **repeating decimal** is a decimal with a block of digits, called the **repetend,** repeated infinitely many times.
   D. A number is in **scientific notation** if it is written as the product of a number greater than or equal to 1 and less than 10, and a power of 10.
   E. An **irrational number** is represented by a nonterminating, nonrepeating decimal.
   F. **Percent** means *per hundred.* Percent is written using the % symbol; $x\% = \dfrac{x}{100}$.

*II. Interest
   A. **Simple interest** is computed using the formula $I = Prt$, where I is the interest, P is the principal, r is the annual interest rate, and t is the time in years.

   B. When **compound interest** is involved we use the formula $A = P(1 + i)^n$, where A is the balance, P is the principal, i is the interest rate per period, and n is the number of periods.

III. Real numbers
   A. The set of **real numbers** is the set of all decimals, namely, the union of the set of rational numbers and the set of irrational numbers.
   B. If a is any whole number, then the **principal square root** of a, denoted by $\sqrt{a}$, is the nonnegative number b such that $b \cdot b = b^2 = a$.
   C. Square roots can be found using the **squeezing method.**

*IV. Radicals and rational exponents
   A. $\sqrt[n]{x}$, or $x^{1/n}$, is called **nth root** of x and n is called the **index.**
   B. The following properties hold for radicals if the expressions involving radicals are meaningful.
      (a) $\sqrt[n]{xy} = \sqrt[n]{x} \cdot \sqrt[n]{y}$
      (b) $\sqrt[n]{\dfrac{x}{y}} = \dfrac{\sqrt[n]{x}}{\sqrt[n]{y}}$
      (c) $(\sqrt[n]{x})^m = \sqrt[n]{x^m}$

CHAPTER TEST

1. Perform the following operations.
   (a) $3.6 + 2.007 - 6.3$ (b) $(5.2) \cdot (6.07)$
   (c) $(5.1 + 6.32) \cdot 0.02$ (d) $0.12032 \div 3.76$
   (e) $0.012 - 0.109$ (f) $(0.02)^4$

2. Write each of the following in expanded form.
   (a) 32.012 (b) 0.00103

3. Give a test to determine if a fraction can be written

as a terminating decimal without actually performing the division.

4. A board is 442.4 cm long. How many shelves can be cut from it if each shelf is 55.3 cm long? (Disregard the width of the cuts.)

5. Write each of the following as a decimal.

(a) $\dfrac{4}{7}$ (b) $\dfrac{1}{8}$ (c) $\dfrac{2}{3}$ (d) $\dfrac{5}{8}$

6. Write each of the following as a fraction in simplest form.

(a) 0.28 (b) $0.\overline{3}$ (c) $2.0\overline{8}$

7. Round each of the following numbers as specified.
(a) 307.625 to the nearest hundredth
(b) 307.625 to the nearest tenth
(c) 307.625 to the nearest unit
(d) 307.625 to the nearest hundred

8. Solve each of the following for x, where x is a real number.
(a) $0.2x - 0.75 \geq \frac{1}{2}(x - 3.5)$
(b) $0.\overline{9} + x = 1$
(c) $23\%(x) = 4600$
(d) 10 is x percent of 50
(e) 17 is 50% of x
(f) $0.\overline{3} + x = 1$

9. Answer each of the following.
(a) 6 is what percent of 24?
(b) What is 320% of 60?
(c) 17 is 30% of what number?
(d) 0.2 is what percent of 1?

10. Change each of the following to percents.

(a) $\dfrac{1}{8}$ (b) $\dfrac{3}{40}$ (c) 6.27

(d) 0.0123 (e) $\dfrac{3}{2}$

11. Change each of the following percents to decimals.

(a) 60% (b) $\left(\dfrac{2}{3}\right)\%$ (c) 100%

12. Answer each of the following and explain your answers.
(a) Is the set of irrational numbers closed under addition?
(b) Is the set of irrational numbers closed under subtraction?
(c) Is the set of irrational numbers closed under multiplication?
(d) Is the set of irrational numbers closed under division?

13. Find an approximation for $\sqrt{23}$ correct to three decimal places.

14. Rewrite each of the following in scientific notation.
(a) 426,000 (b) 0.00000237
(c) 32 (d) 0.325

15. Classify each of the following as rational or irrational. (Assume the patterns shown continue.)
(a) 2.19119911999119999119 . . .

(b) $\dfrac{1}{\sqrt{2}}$ (c) $\dfrac{4}{9}$

(d) 0.0011001100110011 . . .
(e) 0.001100011000011 . . .

16. Sandy received a dividend that equals 11% of the value of her investment. If her dividend was \$1020.80, how much was her investment?

17. Five computers in a shipment of 150 were found to be defective. What percent of the computers were defective?

18. On a mathematics examination, a student missed 8 of 70 questions. What percent of the questions, rounded to the nearest tenth, did the student do correctly?

19. A microcomputer system costs \$3450 at present. This is 60% of the cost 4 years ago. What was the cost of the system 4 years ago?

20. If, on a purchase of one new suit, you are offered successive discounts of 5%, 10%, or 20% in any order you wish, what order should you choose?

21. Jane bought a bicycle and sold it for 30% more than she paid for it. She sold it for \$104; how much did she pay for it?

*22. A company was offered a \$30,000 loan at a 12.5% annual interest rate for 4 years. Find the simple interest due on the loan at the end of 4 years.

*23. A money-market fund pays 14% annual interest compounded quarterly. What is the value of a \$10,000 investment after 3 years?

*24. Find the simplest form for each of the following.
(a) $\sqrt{242}$ (b) $\sqrt{288}$
(c) $\sqrt{360}$ (d) $\sqrt[3]{162}$

*25. Write each of the following in simplest form with nonnegative exponents in the final answer.

(a) $\left(\dfrac{1}{2}\right)^4 \left(\dfrac{1}{2}\right)^7$ (b) $5^{-16} \div 5^4$

(c) $\left[\left(\dfrac{2}{3}\right)^7\right]^{-4}$ (d) $3^{16} \cdot 3^2$

SELECTED BIBLIOGRAPHY

Boling, B. "A Different Method for Solving Percentage Problems." *The Mathematics Teacher* 78 (October 1985):523–524.

Carpenter, T., et al. "Decimals: Results and Implications from National Assessment." *Arithmetic Teacher* 28 (April 1981):34–37.

Chow, P., and T. Lin. "Extracting Square Root Made Easy." *Arithmetic Teacher* 29 (November 1981): 48–50.

Cole, B., and H. Weissenfluh. "An Analysis of Teaching Percentages." *The Arithmetic Teacher* 21 (March 1974):226–228.

Dana, M., and M. Lindquist. "Let's Do It: From Halves to Hundredths." *Arithmetic Teacher* 26 (November 1978):4–8.

deP. Soler, F., and R. Schuster. "Compound Growth and Related Situations: A Problem-Solving Approach." *The Mathematics Teacher* 75 (November 1982):640–643.

Dewar, J. "Another Look at the Teaching of Percent." *Arithmetic Teacher* 31 (March 1984):48–49.

Firl, D. "Fractions, Decimals and Their Futures." *The Arithmetic Teacher* 24 (March 1977):238–240.

Glatzer, D. "Teaching Percentage: Ideas and Suggestions." *Arithmetic Teacher* 31 (February 1984): 24–26.

Grossman, A. "Decimal Notation: An Important Research Finding." *Arithmetic Teacher* 30 (May 1983): 32–33.

Hilferty, M. "Some Convenient Fractions for Work with Repeating Decimals." *The Mathematics Teacher* 65 (March 1972):240–241.

Hutchinson, M. "Investigating the Nature of Periodic Decimals." *The Mathematics Teacher* 65 (April 1972):325–327.

Jacobs, J., and E. Herbert. "Making $\sqrt{2}$ Seem 'Real'." *The Arithmetic Teacher* 21 (February 1974):133–136.

Kidder, F. "Ditton's Dilemma, or What To Do About Decimals." *Arithmetic Teacher* 28 (October 1980): 44–46.

Manchester, M. "Decimal Expansions of Rational Numbers." *The Mathematics Teacher* 65 (December 1972):698–702.

McGinty, R., and W. Mutch. "Repeating Decimals, Geometric Patterns, and Open-Ended Questions." *The Mathematics Teacher* 75 (October 1982): 600–602.

Mielke, P. "Rational Points on the Number Line." *The Mathematics Teacher* 63 (October 1970): 475–479.

Payne, J. "Curricular Issues: Teaching Rational Numbers." *Arithmetic Teacher* 31 (February 1984):14–17.

Payne, J. "One Point of View: Sense and Nonsense about Fractions and Decimals." *Arithmetic Teacher* 27 (January 1980):4–7.

Prielipp, R. "Decimals." *The Arithmetic Teacher* 23 (April 1976):285–288.

Robidoux, D., and N. Montefusco. "An Easy Way to Change Repeating Decimals to Fractions–Nick's Method." *The Arithmetic Teacher* 24 (January 1977): 81–82.

Schmalz, R. "A Visual Approach to Decimals." *Arithmetic Teacher* 25 (May 1978):22–25.

Shoemaker, R. "Please, My Dear Aunt Sally." *Arithmetic Teacher* 27 (May 1980):34–35.

Skypek, D. "Special Characteristics of Rational Numbers." *Arithmetic Teacher* 31 (February 1984):10–12.

Sullivan, K. "Money—A Key to Mathematical Success." *Arithmetic Teacher* 29 (November 1981):34–35.

Teahan, T. "How I Learned to Do Percents." *Arithmetic Teacher* 27 (January 1979):16–17.

Usiskin, Z. "The Future of Fractions." *Arithmetic Teacher* 27 (January 1979):18–20.

Wagner, S. "Fun with Repeating Decimals." *The Mathematics Teacher* 26 (March 1979):209–212.

Writt, E. "Mr. Manning's Money." *Arithmetic Teacher* 29 (September 1981):47.

Zawojewski, J. "Initial Decimal Concepts: Are They Really So Easy?" *Arithmetic Teacher* 30 (March 1983):52–56.

CHAPTER 8

Probability

Preliminary Problem

A publishing company hires two proofreaders, Al and Betsy, to read a manuscript. Al finds 48 errors and Betsy finds 42 errors. The editor finds that 30 common errors were found by the proofreaders; that is, 30 errors were found by both Al and Betsy. What is your estimate of the number of errors not yet found?

tes. La

res (56 k

ts size, The

l is only 15 fe

s the lake ove

rglades. This

source of fresh

Everglades.

lake Georg

String of lakes t

t. Johns Riv

l the

l dirt

blown

Vow,

collect

Introduction

Concepts of probability appear frequently in daily life. For example, uses of probability are found in ordinary conversations such as these.

"What is the *probability* the Braves will win the World Series?"
"The *odds* are 2 to 1 that Flea Bag will win the dog show."
"There is no *chance* I would marry you."

In this chapter, we use tree diagrams to determine probabilities and to analyze games involving spinners, cards, and dice. Counting techniques are also introduced to aid in the solution of certain probability problems. The role of simulations in probability is also discussed. Many of the ideas in this chapter are adapted from the materials available from the Comprehensive School Mathematics Project (CSMP).

Section 8-1

How Probabilities Are Determined

Probabilities are ratios that may be expressed as fractions, decimals, or percents. The ratios are determined by considering results or outcomes of *experiment* experiments. An **experiment** is an activity under consideration such as tossing a coin. In this chapter, we consider experiments with two or more distinct *outcomes* possible **outcomes.** If we toss a coin and if we assume that the coin cannot land on its edge, then there are two distinct possible outcomes: heads (*H*) and tails (*T*).

sample space A set of possible outcomes for an experiment is called a **sample space,** or
outcome set **outcome set,** if every possible result of the experiment corresponds to one and only one outcome in the sample space. In the case of a single coin toss, a sample space *S* is given by $S = \{H, T\}$. Determining a sample space for an experiment is an important step in solving a probability problem. The sample
tree diagram space for the coin-tossing experiment can be modeled using a **tree diagram** as shown in Figure 8-1. Each outcome of the experiment is designated by a separate branch in the tree diagram.

Figure 8-1

Example 8-1

(a) Write the sample space *S* for rolling a standard die.
(b) Use a tree diagram to develop the sample space for tossing a fair coin twice.
(c) Use a tree diagram to develop the sample space for an experiment consisting of tossing a fair coin and then rolling a die.

Solution

(a) The sample space is $S = \{1, 2, 3, 4, 5, 6\}$.
(b) The tree diagram is given in Figure 8-2.
    The sample space is $S = \{HH, HT, TH, TT\}$.
(c) The sample space for this experiment is taken from the tree diagram in Figure 8-3. The sample space is

$$S = \{H1, H2, H3, H4, H5, H6, T1, T2, T3, T4, T5, T6\}$$

Figure 8-2

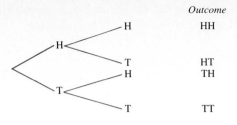

Figure 8-3

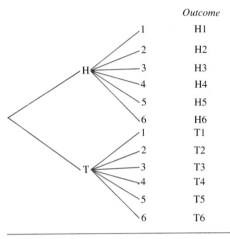

event   Any subset of a sample space is called an **event.** For example, the set of all even-numbered rolls of a die is a subset of all possible rolls of a die. The set of all even-numbered rolls is an event.

Example 8-2

Suppose an experiment consists of drawing one slip of paper from a jar containing 12 slips of paper, each with a different month of the year written on it. Find each of the following.

(a) The sample space S for the experiment.
(b) The event A consisting of outcomes from drawing a slip having a month beginning with J.
(c) The event B consisting of outcomes from drawing a slip having the name of a month that has exactly four letters.
(d) The event C consisting of outcomes from drawing a slip having a month that begins with M or N.

Solution

(a) $S = \{$January, February, March, April, May, June, July, August, September, October, November, December$\}$
(b) $A = \{$January, June, July$\}$
(c) $B = \{$June, July$\}$
(d) $C = \{$March, May, November$\}$

Example 8-3

Two spinners are shown in Figure 8-4. Suppose an experiment is to spin X and then spin Y. Find each of the following.

Figure 8-4

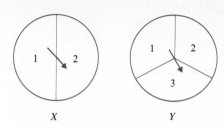

X   Y

(a) The sample space S for the experiment.
(b) The event A consisting of outcomes from spinning an even number followed by an even number.
(c) The event B consisting of outcomes from spinning at least one 2.
(d) The event C consisting of outcomes from spinning exactly one 2.

Solution

(a) The sample space for this experiment can be described using ordered pairs. The first component in each pair is the result of the first spin, and the second component is the result of the second spin.

$$S = \{(1, 1), (1, 2), (1, 3), (2, 1), (2, 2), (2, 3)\}$$

(b) $A = \{(2, 2)\}$
(c) $B = \{(1, 2), (2, 1), (2, 2), (2, 3)\}$
(d) $C = \{(1, 2), (2, 1), (2, 3)\}$

Suppose a fair coin is tossed 40 times with the following result.

HTTHT HHHHH TTTHH HTTTH TTHTH TTHHT THTHT TTHTT

Observe the following.

$$\frac{\text{Number of heads}}{\text{Number of trials}} = \frac{18}{40}$$

HISTORICAL NOTE

Girolamo Cardano (1501–1576), a mathematician, physician, and astrologer, wrote one of the first books concerning probability and gambling. However, the founders of probability theory, Blaise Pascal (1623–1662) and Pierre de Fermat (1601–1665), became involved in probability as a result of questions asked of them by Chevalier de Meré, a professional gambler. He wanted to know how to divide the stakes if two players start, but fail to complete, a game in which the winner is the one who wins three matches out of five. The correspondence between Fermat and Pascal led to what is considered to be the beginning of probability theory.

Based on this experience, we might guess that the probability of tossing heads is $\frac{18}{40}$. When a probability is determined by observing outcomes of experiments, it is called an **experimental probability.** Insurance companies use probabilities based on experiences in order to set their premiums. When the coin was tossed 40 times, we observed that heads occurred in approximately $\frac{1}{2}$ of the tosses. The exact number of heads that occur when a fair coin is tossed a few times cannot be accurately predicted. However, when the fair coin is tossed many times, the fraction (or proportion) of heads is near $\frac{1}{2}$. For this reason, we say that the probability of heads occurring is $\frac{1}{2}$ and write $P(H) = \frac{1}{2}$. We also say that the two outcomes, H and T, are **equally likely;** that is, one outcome is just as likely to occur as the other.

experimental probability

equally likely

Because a fair coin is symmetric and has two sides, we could argue that each side should appear roughly one half of the time in long strings of tosses, and hence again conclude that

$$P(H) = P(T) = \frac{1}{2}$$

If a fair die (one that is just as likely to land on any of the numerals 1 through 6) is rolled many times, each outcome will appear about $\frac{1}{6}$ of the time. Hence, we assign to each outcome a probability of $\frac{1}{6}$ and write, for example, $P(4) = \frac{1}{6}$ for the probability of tossing a 4. Notice that saying that $P(4) = \frac{1}{6}$ means that we expect the fraction of 4s that occur in many tosses of the die to be near $\frac{1}{6}$. Since there are six faces on a die and because the die is symmetric, we can also argue that $P(4) = \frac{1}{6}$ and that any other face should also be assigned probability $\frac{1}{6}$.

For a fair coin, the sample space is given by $S = \{H, T\}$ and $P(H) = P(T) = \frac{1}{2}$, while for the fair die, $S = \{1, 2, 3, 4, 5, 6\}$ and $P(1) = P(2) = P(3) = P(4) = P(5) = P(6) = \frac{1}{6}$. Notice that in each case, the probability for each outcome is a number between 0 and 1 and the sum of the probabilities for the distinct outcomes in the sample space is equal to 1. Each of the preceding experiments has a sample space with equally likely outcomes. Not all experiments have equally likely outcomes; for example, a bent coin might yield $P(H) = 0.4$ and $P(T) = 0.6$.

For a sample space with equally likely outcomes, the probability of an event A can be defined as follows.

DEFINITION

> For an experiment with sample space S and equally likely outcomes, the probability of an event A is given by
>
> $$P(A) = \frac{n(A)}{n(S)}$$

Remark   Recall that $n(A)$ means "the number of elements in A." Also, if A is an event, then $A \subseteq S$.

Example 8-4

One number is selected at random from the numbers in the set S given by $S = \{1, 2, 3, 4, \ldots, 24, 25\}$. List the elements in each event given below and calculate each probability.

(a) The event A that an even number is drawn
(b) The event B that a number less than 10 and greater than 20 is drawn
(c) The event C that a prime number is drawn
(d) The event E that a number both even and prime is drawn

Solution

In this experiment, $n(S) = 25$ and all outcomes are equally likely since the numbers are drawn at random. The phrase **at random** means that each number has an equal chance of being drawn.

at random

(a) $A = \{2, 4, 6, 8, 10, 12, 14, 16, 18, 20, 22, 24\}$, so $n(A) = 12$. Thus,

$$P(A) = \frac{n(A)}{n(S)} = \frac{12}{25}$$

(b) $B = \varnothing$, so $n(B) = 0$. Thus, $P(B) = \frac{0}{25} = 0$.

(c) $C = \{2, 3, 5, 7, 11, 13, 17, 19, 23\}$, so $n(C) = 9$. Thus,

$$P(C) = \frac{n(C)}{n(S)} = \frac{9}{25}$$

(d) $E = \{2\}$, so $n(E) = 1$. Thus,

$$P(E) = \frac{n(E)}{n(S)} = \frac{1}{25}$$

In Example 8-4(b) event B is the empty set. An event such as B that has no outcomes in it is called an **impossible event**. An impossible event always has probability 0. Note that if the word "and" was replaced by "or" in Example 8-4(b), then event B would no longer be the empty set.

impossible event

Consider event A consisting of rolling a number less than 7 on a single roll of a die. Since every face of the die has fewer than 7 spots, $A = \{1, 2, 3, 4, 5, 6\}$ and $P(\text{number less than } 7) = P(A) = \frac{6}{6} = 1$. *An event that has probability 1 is called a **certain event**.*

certain event

No event has a probability greater than 1 because the number of outcomes in an event cannot be greater than the total number of outcomes in the sample space. Likewise, no event has a probability less than 0. Consequently, if A is any event, then the following inequality holds.

$$0 \le P(A) \le 1$$

MUTUALLY EXCLUSIVE EVENTS

Consider one spin of the wheel shown in Figure 8-5. For this experiment, we have $S = \{0, 1, 2, 3, 4, 5, 6, 7, 8, 9\}$. If $A = \{0, 1, 2, 3, 4\}$ and $B = \{5, 7\}$, then $A \cap B = \varnothing$. Two such events are called **mutually exclusive** events. If event A occurs, then event B cannot, and we have the following definition.

mutually exclusive

DEFINITION

Events A and B are mutually exclusive if $A \cap B = \varnothing$.

Figure 8-5

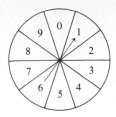

Each outcome in S above is equally likely, with probability $\frac{1}{10}$. Thus, the probability of event A or B occurring is

$$P(A \cup B) = \frac{n(A \cup B)}{n(S)} = \frac{7}{10} = \frac{5 + 2}{10} = \frac{5}{10} + \frac{2}{10}$$

$$= \frac{n(A)}{n(S)} + \frac{n(B)}{n(S)} = P(A) + P(B)$$

The result developed in this example is true in general for mutually exclusive events. In general, we have the following.

Property If events A and B are mutually exclusive, then $P(A \cup B) = P(A) + P(B)$.

Remark This follows immediately from the fact that $n(A \cup B) = n(A) + n(B)$, if $A \cap B = \varnothing$.

event
complementary to A

If A is an event, we can also discuss the case where event A fails to happen. The case where A fails to happen is also an event, which we call the **event complementary to A,** written $\bar{A}$. For example, if we spin the spinner in Figure 8-5 once and if event A is the event that the number obtained is greater than 0, then $\bar{A} = \{0\}$. Because events are sets, $A \cup \bar{A} = S$ and $A \cap \bar{A} = \varnothing$. Because A and $\bar{A}$ are mutually exclusive, then $P(A \cup \bar{A}) = P(A) + P(\bar{A})$. Since $A \cup \bar{A} = S$, then $P(A \cup \bar{A}) = 1$. Therefore,

$$P(A) + P(\bar{A}) = 1 \quad \text{or} \quad P(A) = 1 - P(\bar{A})$$

Thus, the probability that we spin a number greater than 0 is given by

$$P(A) = 1 - P(\bar{A}) = 1 - \frac{1}{10} = \frac{9}{10}$$

Example 8-5

A golf bag contains 2 red tees, 4 blue tees, and 5 white tees.

(a) What is the probability of the event A that a tee drawn at random is red?
(b) What is the probability of the event "not A," that is, that a tee drawn at random is not red?
(c) What is the probability of the event that a tee drawn at random is either red or blue?

Solution

(a) Because the bag contains a total of $2 + 4 + 5$, or 11, tees and 2 tees are red, $P(A) = \frac{2}{11}$.
(b) The bag contains 11 tees and 9 are not red, so the probability of "not A" is $\frac{9}{11}$. Also, notice that $P(\bar{A}) = 1 - P(A) = 1 - \frac{2}{11} = \frac{9}{11}$.

(c) The bag contains 2 red tees and 4 blue tees and $R \cap B = \varnothing$, so
$P(R \cup B) = \frac{2}{11} + \frac{4}{11}$, or $\frac{6}{11}$.

PROBABILITIES OF EVENTS WITHOUT EQUALLY LIKELY OUTCOMES

It is important to remember that the definition of probability introduced earlier applies *only to a sample space with equally likely outcomes*. Applying the definition to outcomes that are not equally likely leads to incorrect conclusions. For example, the sample space for spinning the spinner in Figure 8-6 is given by $S = \{$Red, Blue$\}$. However, the outcome Blue is more likely to occur than the outcome Red, and hence P(Red) is not equal to $\frac{1}{2}$. If the spinner were spun 100 times, it would seem reasonable to expect that about $\frac{1}{4}$, or 25, of the outcomes would be Red, while about $\frac{3}{4}$, or 75, of the outcomes would be Blue.

Figure 8-6

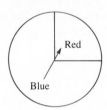

Next, consider tossing a loaded die in which $P(1) = P(2) = \frac{3}{10}$ and $P(3) = P(4) = P(5) = P(6) = \frac{1}{10}$. If event A is tossing a 2 and event B is tossing a 4, then events A and B are mutually exclusive events and the probability of tossing a 2 *or* a 4 is given by the following.

$$P(A \cup B) = P(A) + P(B) = P(2) + P(4) = \frac{3}{10} + \frac{1}{10} = \frac{4}{10}$$

We see that the probability of tossing a 2 or a 4 is found by adding the probabilities of events A and B. Likewise, the probability of an event C of tossing an even number, $\{2, 4, 6\}$, is given by finding the sum of $P(A \cup B)$ and $P(6)$; that is,

$$P(C) = [P(A) + P(B)] + P(6) = \left(\frac{3}{10} + \frac{1}{10}\right) + \frac{1}{10} = \frac{5}{10}$$

This leads to the following definition.

DEFINITION

> The probability of an event A is equal to the sum of the probabilities of all the outcomes in set A.

Example 8-6

If a card is drawn at random from an ordinary deck of playing cards, what is the probability that it is an ace?

Solution

Because the card is drawn at random, we have a sample space with equally likely outcomes and $n(S) = 52$. If event A is drawing an ace, then we can use the definition of probability involving equally likely outcomes to compute the following.

$$P(A) = \frac{n(A)}{n(S)} = \frac{4}{52}$$

A different approach is to notice that, because the probability of drawing any of the four aces on a single draw is $\frac{1}{52}$, then

$$P(A) = \frac{1}{52} + \frac{1}{52} + \frac{1}{52} + \frac{1}{52} = \frac{4}{52}$$

PROBLEM I

A butcher wrapped three 1-pound packages of meat in butcher paper while having a conversation with a customer. The packages contained round steak, ground beef, and sausage and were to be labeled R, G, and S, respectively. During the conversation, the butcher forgot which package was which, but labeled them anyway. What is the probability that each of the packages is labeled correctly?

UNDERSTANDING THE PROBLEM The packages of round steak, ground beef, and sausage were labeled R, G, and S. The problem of determining the probability that each of the three packages of meat is labeled correctly depends on determining the sample space, or at least how many elements are in the sample space.

DEVISING A PLAN To aid in the solution, we represent the contents—round steak, ground beef, and sausage—as r, g, and s, respectively. To construct the sample space, we use the strategy of *making a table*. The table should show all the possibilities of what could be in each package; that is, the table should show all the one-to-one correspondences between the set of labels $\{R, G, S\}$ and the set of contents $\{r, g, s\}$. Once the table is completed, the probability that each package is labeled correctly can be determined.

CARRYING OUT THE PLAN Table 8-1 is constructed using the package labels R, G, and S as headings and listing all equally likely possibilities of contents r, g, and s underneath the headings.

Table 8-I

Labels

Cases		R	G	S
	1	r	g	s
	2	r	s	g
	3	g	r	s
	4	g	s	r
	5	s	r	g
	6	s	g	r

Case 1 is the only case out of six in which each of the packages is labeled correctly, so the probability that each package is labeled correctly is $\frac{1}{6}$.

LOOKING BACK Another question to consider is whether the probability of having each package labeled incorrectly is the same as the probability of having each package labeled correctly. A first guess might be that the probabilities are the same, but that is not true. Can you determine why?

PROBLEM SET 8-I

1. Write the sample space for each of the following experiments.
   (a) Spin spinner 1 once.
   (b) Spin spinner 2 once.
   (c) Spin spinner 1 once and then spin spinner 2 once.
   (d) Spin spinner 2 once and then roll a die.
   (e) Spin spinner 1 twice.
   (f) Spin spinner 2 twice.

Spinner 1   Spinner 2

2. An experiment consists of selecting the last digit of a telephone number. Assume that each of the ten digits is equally likely to appear as a last digit. List each of the following.
   (a) The sample space.
   (b) The event consisting of outcomes that the digit is less than 5.
   (c) The event consisting of outcomes that the digit is odd.
   (d) The event consisting of outcomes that the digit is not 2.
3. Find the probability of each of the events (b)–(d) in Problem 2.
4. A card is selected from an ordinary bridge deck consisting of 52 cards. Find the probabilities for each of the following.
   (a) A red card   (b) A face card
   (c) A red card or a ten   (d) A queen
   (e) Not a queen
   (f) A face card or a club
   (g) A face card and a club
   (h) Not a face card and not a club

5. A drawer contains six black socks, four brown socks, and two green socks. Suppose one sock is drawn from the drawer, and it is equally likely that any one of the socks is drawn. Find the probabilities for each of the following.
   (a) The sock is brown.
   (b) The sock is either black or green.
   (c) The sock is red.
   (d) The sock is not black.
6. What, if anything, is wrong with each of the following statements?
   (a) The probability that the Steelers will win the Super Bowl is $\frac{3}{4}$ and the probability that they will lose is $\frac{1}{5}$.
   (b) Since there are 50 states, the probability of being born in Montana is $\frac{1}{50}$.
7. If each letter of the alphabet is written on a separate piece of paper and placed in a box and then one piece of paper is drawn at random, what is the probability that the paper has a vowel written on it? What is the probability that the paper has a consonant written on it?
8. The questions below refer to a very popular dice game, craps, in which a player rolls two dice.
   (a) Rolling a sum of 7 or 11 on the first roll of the dice is a win. What is the probability of winning on the first roll?
   (b) Rolling a sum of 2, 3, or 12 on the first roll of the dice is a loss. What is the probability of losing on the first roll?
   (c) Rolling a sum of 4, 5, 6, 8, 9, or 10 on the first roll is neither a win nor a loss. What is the probability of neither winning nor losing on the first roll?
   (d) After rolling a sum of 4, 5, 6, 8, 9, or 10, a player must roll the same sum again before rolling a sum of 7. Which sum, 4, 5, 6, 8, 9, or 10, has the highest probability of occurring again?
   (e) What is the probability of rolling a sum of 1 on any roll of the dice?
   (f) What is the probability of rolling a sum less than 13 on any roll of the dice?

(g) If the two dice are rolled 60 times, how many times should you expect a sum of 7?

9. A roulette wheel has 38 slots around the rim. The first 36 slots are numbered from 1 to 36. Half of these 36 slots are red and the other half are black. The remaining 2 slots are numbered 0 and 00 and are colored green. As the roulette wheel is spun in one direction, a small ivory ball is rolled along the rim in the opposite direction. The ball has an equally likely chance of falling into any one of the 38 slots. Find each of the following.
   (a) The probability the ball lands in a black slot.
   (b) The probability the ball lands on 0 or 00.
   (c) The probability the ball does not land on a number from 1 through 12.
   (d) The probability the ball lands on an odd number or a green slot.

10. If the roulette wheel in Problem 9 is spun 190 times, how many times should we expect the ball to land on 0 or 00?

11. According to a weather report, there is a 30% chance that it will rain tomorrow. What is the probability that it will not rain tomorrow?

12. Determine if each player has an equal probability of winning each of the following games.
   (a) Toss a fair coin. If heads appears, I win; if a tail appears, you lose.
   (b) Toss a fair coin. If heads appears, I win; otherwise, you win.
   (c) Toss a fair die numbered 1 through 6. If 1 appears, I win; if 6 appears, you win.
   (d) Toss a fair die numbered 1 through 6. If an even number appears, I win; if an odd number appears, you win.
   (e) Toss a fair die numbered 1 through 6. If a number greater than or equal to 3 appears, I win; otherwise, you win.
   (f) Toss two fair dice numbered 1 through 6. If a 1 appears on each die, I win; if a 6 appears on each die, you win.
   (g) Toss two fair dice numbered 1 through 6. If the sum is 3, I win; if the sum is 2, you win.
   (h) Toss two dice numbered 1 through 6; one die is red and one die is white. If the number on the red die is greater than the number on the white die, I win; otherwise, you win.

LABORATORY ACTIVITY

1. Suppose a paper cup is tossed in the air. The different ways it can land are shown below.

Top   Bottom   Side

Toss a cup 100 times and record each result. From this information, calculate the experimental probability of each outcome. Do the outcomes appear to be equally likely? Based on experimental probabilities, how many times would you predict the cup will land on its side if tossed 200 times?

2. Toss a coin 100 times and record the results. From this information, calculate the experimental probability of tossing a head. Does the experimental result agree with the expected theoretical probability of $\frac{1}{2}$?

A game called WIN is played with a set of nonstandard dice whose faces are shown flattened out. The game is played with two players. Each player chooses one die and the players roll the dice at the same time. The player with the greater number showing on his die wins the game. If you were to play WIN, would you choose your die first or second? Why? Can you find a strategy for maximizing your chances of winning the game?

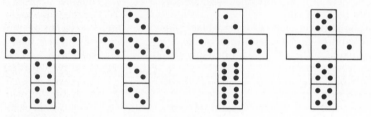

(The game of WIN was suggested by Joseph Smyth of Santa Rosa Junior College.)

Section 8-2

Multistage Experiments

In Section 8-1, we considered one-stage experiments—that is, experiments that are over after one step. For example, the box in Figure 8-7 has one black ball and three white balls. Suppose one ball is drawn at random from the box. Thus, the probability of any one particular ball being drawn is $\frac{1}{4}$. Since there are three indistinguishable white balls and one black ball, the probability of drawing a white ball is $\frac{3}{4}$, and the probability of drawing a black ball is $\frac{1}{4}$.

Figure 8-7

A tree diagram for this experiment is given in Figure 8-8. Notice that the sum of the probabilities of the branches coming from a single point equals one.

Figure 8-8

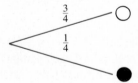

Next, we consider several multistage experiments. The box in Figure 8-9 contains one black and two white balls. A ball is drawn at random and its color is recorded. The ball is then *replaced* and a second ball is drawn and its color is recorded. Figure 8-10 shows a tree diagram for this two-stage experiment.

Figure 8-9

Figure 8-10

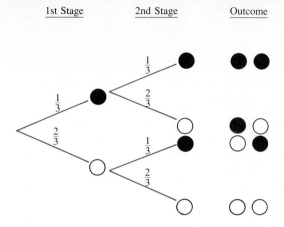

What probability should be assigned to each pictured outcome? Consider the path for the outcome ●○. In the first stage, the probability of obtaining a black ball is $\frac{1}{3}$. Then, the probability of obtaining a white ball in the second stage (second draw) is $\frac{2}{3}$. Thus, we expect to obtain a black ball on the first draw $\frac{1}{3}$ of the time and then to draw a white ball $\frac{2}{3}$ of those times that we obtained a black ball, that is, $\frac{2}{3}$ of $\frac{1}{3}$, or $\frac{2}{3} \cdot \frac{1}{3}$. Observe that this product may be obtained by multiplying the probabilities along the branches used for the path leading to ●○, that is, $\frac{1}{3} \cdot \frac{2}{3}$, or $\frac{2}{9}$. The probabilities shown in Table 8-2 are obtained by following the paths leading to each of the four outcomes and by multiplying the probabilities along the paths.

Table 8-2

Outcome	● ●	● ○	○ ●	○ ○
Probability	$\frac{1}{3} \cdot \frac{1}{3}$, or $\frac{1}{9}$	$\frac{1}{3} \cdot \frac{2}{3}$, or $\frac{2}{9}$	$\frac{2}{3} \cdot \frac{1}{3}$, or $\frac{2}{9}$	$\frac{2}{3} \cdot \frac{2}{3}$, or $\frac{4}{9}$

For all multistage experiments, the probability of the outcome along any path is equal to the product of all the probabilities along the branches of the path. The sum of the probabilities on branches from any point always equals 1, and the sum of the probabilities for the possible outcomes must also be 1.

Look at the box pictured in Figure 8-9 again. This time, suppose two balls are drawn one by one without replacement. A tree diagram for this experiment, along with the set of possible outcomes, is shown in Figure 8-11. Notice that the denominators of the fractions along the second branch are all two. Since the draws are made without replacement, there are only two balls remaining for the second draw. The probabilities for the second stage are conditional probabilities because their values depend on what happens at the first stage. Conditional probabilities are discussed further in Section 8-3. Table 8-3 gives a probability model for this example.

Figure 8-11

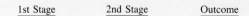

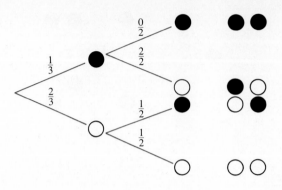

Table 8-3

Outcome	●●	●○	○●	○○
Probability	$\frac{1}{3}\cdot\frac{0}{2}$, or 0	$\frac{1}{3}\cdot\frac{2}{2}$, or $\frac{2}{6}$	$\frac{2}{3}\cdot\frac{1}{2}$, or $\frac{2}{6}$	$\frac{2}{3}\cdot\frac{1}{2}$, or $\frac{2}{6}$

    Table 8-3 can be used to find the probabilities of various events. Consider the event A consisting of the outcomes for drawing exactly one black ball in the two draws without replacement. This event is given by $A = \{●○, ○●\}$. Since the outcome ●○ appears $\frac{2}{6}$ of the time, and the outcome ○● appears $\frac{2}{6}$ of the time, then either ●○ or ○● will appear $\frac{4}{6}$ of the time. Thus, $P(A) = \frac{2}{6} + \frac{2}{6} = \frac{4}{6}$.

    The event B, consisting of outcomes for drawing *at least* one black ball, could be recorded as $B = \{●○, ○●, ●●\}$. Because $P(●○) = \frac{2}{6}$, $P(○●) = \frac{2}{6}$, and $P(●●) = 0$, then $P(B) = \frac{2}{6} + \frac{2}{6} + 0 = \frac{4}{6}$. Since $\bar{B} = \{○○\}$ and $P(\bar{B}) = \frac{2}{6}$, the probability of B could have been computed as follows: $P(B) = 1 - P(\bar{B}) = 1 - \frac{2}{6} = \frac{4}{6}$.

    Figure 8-12 shows a box with 11 letters. An example of a four-stage experiment is to draw four letters at random from the box one by one *without replacement*. The probability of the outcome BABY may be found by using just one branch of a much larger tree diagram. Because the entire tree is not needed to find this probability, only the portion required to complete the problem is pictured in Figure 8-13. Notice that, because the experiment is performed without replacement, each successive denominator decreases by one. Also note that the probability of the first B is $\frac{2}{11}$ because there are 2 Bs out of 11 letters. The probability of the second B is $\frac{1}{9}$ because there are 9 letters left after one B and an A have been chosen.

Figure 8-12

PROBABILITY

Figure 8-13

$$\xrightarrow{\frac{2}{11}} B \xrightarrow{\frac{1}{10}} A \xrightarrow{\frac{1}{9}} B \xrightarrow{\frac{1}{8}} Y$$

Thus, $P(BABY) = (\frac{2}{11}) \cdot (\frac{1}{10}) \cdot (\frac{1}{9}) \cdot (\frac{1}{8})$, or $\frac{2}{7920}$.

Suppose four letters are drawn one by one from the box in Figure 8-13 and the letters are replaced after each drawing. In this case, the branch needed to find $P(BABY)$ is pictured in Figure 8-14.

Figure 8-14

$$\xrightarrow{\frac{2}{11}} B \xrightarrow{\frac{1}{11}} A \xrightarrow{\frac{2}{11}} B \xrightarrow{\frac{1}{11}} Y$$

Thus, $P(BABY) = (\frac{2}{11}) \cdot (\frac{1}{11}) \cdot (\frac{2}{11}) \cdot (\frac{1}{11})$, or 4/14,641.

Example 8-7

Consider the three boxes in Figure 8-15.

Figure 8-15

AAB	AB	ABBB
1	2	3

A letter is drawn from box 1 and placed in box 2. Then, a letter is drawn from box 2 and placed in box 3. Finally, a letter is drawn from box 3. What is the probability that the letter drawn from box 3 is B?

Solution

A tree diagram for this experiment is given in Figure 8-16.

Figure 8-16

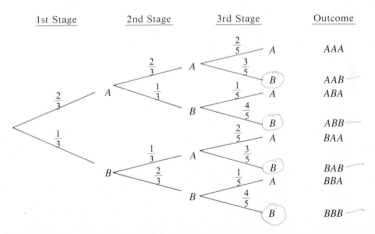

To find the probability that a B is drawn from box 3, add the probabilities for the outcomes AAB, ABB, BAB, and BBB that make up this event.

$$P(AAB) = \frac{2}{3} \cdot \frac{2}{3} \cdot \frac{3}{5} = \frac{12}{45}$$

$$P(ABB) = \frac{2}{3} \cdot \frac{1}{3} \cdot \frac{4}{5} = \frac{8}{45}$$

$$P(BAB) = \frac{1}{3} \cdot \frac{1}{3} \cdot \frac{3}{5} = \frac{3}{45}$$

$$P(BBB) = \frac{1}{3} \cdot \frac{2}{3} \cdot \frac{4}{5} = \frac{8}{45}$$

Thus, the probability of obtaining a B on the draw from box 3 in this experiment is $\frac{12}{45} + \frac{8}{45} + \frac{3}{45} + \frac{8}{45} = \frac{31}{45}$.

PROBLEM 2

A woman in a small foreign town applies for a marriage permit when she is 18. To obtain the permit, she is handed six strings that she must hold in her hand so that the ends of the strings are exposed. On one side, the ends (top or bottom) are picked randomly, two at a time, and tied, forming three separate knots. The same procedure is then repeated for the other set of string ends, forming three more knots. If the tied strings form one closed ring, the woman obtains the permit. If not, she must wait until her next birthday to reapply for a permit. What is the probability that she will obtain a marriage permit on her first try?

UNDERSTANDING THE PROBLEM The problem is to determine the probability that one closed ring will be formed. One closed ring means that all six pieces are joined end to end to form one and only one ring.

DEVISING A PLAN Figure 8-17(a) shows what happens when the ends of the strings of one set are tied in pairs. Notice that no matter in what order those ends are tied, the result appears as in Figure 8-17(a).

Figure 8-17

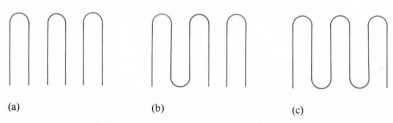

(a)   (b)   (c)

Then, the other ends are tied in a three-stage experiment. If we pick any string in the first stage, then there are five choices for its mate. Four of these choices are favorable choices for forming a ring. Thus, the probability of forming a favorable first tie is $\frac{4}{5}$. Figure 8-17(b) shows a favorable tie at the first stage.

For any one of the remaining four strings, there are three choices for its mate. Two of these choices are favorable ones. Thus, the probability of forming a favorable second tie is $\frac{2}{3}$. Figure 8-17(c) shows a favorable tie at the second stage.

Now, two ends remain. Since nothing can go wrong at the third stage, the probability of making a favorable tie is 1. If we use the probabilities completed at each stage and a single branch of a tree diagram, we can calculate the probability for performing three successful ties in a row and hence the probability of forming one closed ring.

CARRYING OUT THE PLAN If we let S represent a successful tie at each stage, then the branch of the tree with which we are concerned is shown in Figure 8-18.

Figure 8-18

Thus, the probability of forming one ring is $P(\text{ring}) = \frac{4}{5} \cdot \frac{2}{3} \cdot \frac{1}{1} = \frac{8}{15} = 0.5\overline{3}$.

LOOKING BACK The probability of a woman obtaining a marriage permit in any given year is $\frac{8}{15}$. The fact that this result is greater than $\frac{1}{2}$ is surprising to most people. A class might simulate this problem several times with strings to see how the fraction of successes compares with the theoretical probability of $\frac{8}{15}$.

Related problems that could be attempted are the following:

1. If a woman fails to get a ring 10 years in a row, she must remain single. What is the probability of such a streak of bad (good) luck?
2. If the number of strings were reduced to three and the rule was that an upper end must be tied to a lower end, what is the probability of a single ring?
3. If the number of strings were three, but an upper end could be tied to either an upper or lower end, what is the probability of a single ring?
4. What is the probability of forming three rings in the original problem?
5. What is the probability of forming two rings in the original problem?

PROBLEM 3

Leah, a princess, fell in love with Ronald, a peasant. Her father, the king, found out and ordered Ronald thrown to the lions. In response to Leah's pleas, the king proposed the following compromise. He designed a maze that opened into two rooms, as shown in Figure 8-19. Leah could choose one of the rooms in which to wait, and lions would be placed in the other room. Ronald was to walk through the maze until one of the rooms was entered. If Leah was in the room, they could be married; otherwise, the lions would take care of Ronald's fate. If Ronald makes each decision in the maze at random, in which room should Leah choose to wait?

Figure 8-19

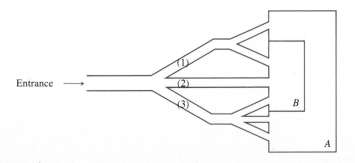

UNDERSTANDING THE PROBLEM Leah is to choose one of the rooms marked *A* or *B* in Figure 8-19. Lions are to be placed in the other room. Ronald enters the maze and makes each choice of paths at random. We are to determine in which room Leah should wait, that is, determine which room has the greater probability of being entered by Ronald after he walks through the maze.

DEVISING A PLAN One way to determine which choice Leah should make is to calculate the probability of Ronald's reaching each room and choose the one with the greater probability. A tree diagram can be used to determine these probabilities.

CARRYING OUT THE PLAN A tree diagram for the maze in Figure 8-19 along with the possible outcomes is shown in Figure 8-20.

Figure 8-20

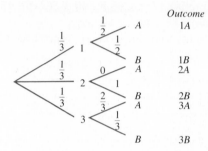

From Figure 8-20, we compute the following.

$$P(A) = \frac{1}{6} + 0 + \frac{2}{9} = \frac{7}{18} \qquad P(B) = \frac{1}{6} + \frac{1}{3} + \frac{1}{9} = \frac{11}{18}$$

Thus, room *B* has the greater probability of being chosen, and this is the room in which Leah should wait.

LOOKING BACK An alternate model for this problem and for many probability problems is an area model. The rectangle in Figure 8-21 represents the first three choices that Ronald can make. Because each choice is equally likely, each is represented by an equal area.

Figure 8-21

If the upper path is chosen, then rooms *A* and *B* have an equal chance of being chosen. If the middle path is chosen, then only room *B* can be entered. If the lower path is chosen, then room *A* is entered $\frac{2}{3}$ of the time. This can be shown in terms of the area model as in Figure 8-22.

Figure 8-22

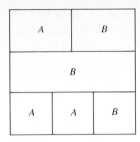

Dividing the rectangle into pieces of equal area, we obtain the model in Figure 8-23 in which the area representing room B is shaded. Because the area representing room B is greater than the area representing room A, room B has the greater probability of being chosen. If desired, Figure 8-23 enables us to find the probability of choosing room B. Because the shaded area consists of 11 squares out of a total of 18 squares, the probability of choosing room B is $\frac{11}{18}$. The problem can be varied by changing the maze or by changing the locations of the rooms.

Figure 8-23

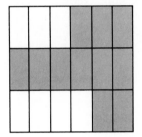

MODELING GAMES

Al and Betsy play the following game. There are two black marbles and one white marble in a box. Betsy mixes the marbles and Al draws two marbles at random without replacement. If they match, Al wins. If they don't match, Betsy wins. Does each player have an equal chance of winning? How can we tell? We could play it many times and see if each player wins about the same number of times. Another way is to develop a model for analyzing the game. One possible model is a tree diagram as shown in Figure 8-24.

Figure 8-24

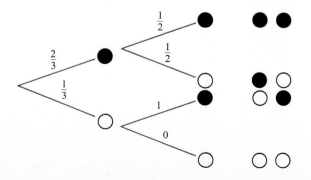

The probability that the marbles are the same color is $\frac{2}{3} \cdot \frac{1}{2} + \frac{1}{3} \cdot 0$, or $\frac{2}{6}$, and the probability that they are not the same color is $\frac{2}{3} \cdot \frac{1}{2} + \frac{1}{3} \cdot 1$, or $\frac{4}{6}$. Because $\frac{2}{6} \neq \frac{4}{6}$, the players do not have the same chance of winning.

An alternate model for analyzing this game is given in Figure 8-25, where the black and white marbles are shown along with the possible ways of drawing two marbles; S indicates the same color, and D represents different colors.

Figure 8-25

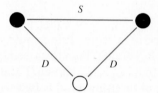

Because there are two Ds in the set $\{S, D, D\}$, we see that the probability of drawing two different-colored marbles is $\frac{2}{3}$. Likewise, the probability of drawing two marbles of the same color is $\frac{1}{3}$. Because $\frac{2}{3} \neq \frac{1}{3}$, the players do not have an equal chance of winning. Will adding another white marble give each player an equal chance of winning? With two white and two black marbles, we have the model in Figure 8-26. Therefore, $P(D) = \frac{4}{6}$, or $\frac{2}{3}$, and $P(S) = \frac{2}{6}$, or $\frac{1}{3}$. We see that adding another white marble did not change the probabilities.

Figure 8-26

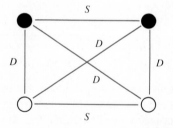

Next, consider a game with the same rules using three black marbles and one white marble. A model for this situation is shown in Figure 8-27.

Figure 8-27

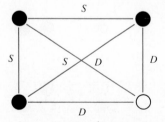

Thus, the probability of drawing two marbles of the same color is $\frac{3}{6}$, and the probability of drawing two marbles with different colors is $\frac{3}{6}$; finally, we have a game in which each player has an equal chance of winning.

Does each player have an equal chance of winning if only one white marble and one black marble are used and the ball is replaced after the first draw? Can you find additional fair games involving different numbers of marbles? Can you find a pattern for the numbers of black and white marbles that allow each player to have an equal chance of winning?

PROBLEM SET 8-2

1. A box contains six letters as shown. What is the probability of the outcome DAN if three letters are drawn one by one (a) with replacement and (b) without replacement?

RANDOM

2. Three boxes containing letters are shown.

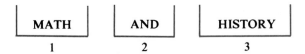

MATH	AND	HISTORY
1	2	3

Answer each of the following questions about the boxes.

(a) From box 1, three letters are drawn one by one without replacement and recorded in order. What is the probability that the outcome is HAT?

(b) From box 1, three letters are drawn one by one with replacement and recorded in order. What is the probability that the outcome is HAT?

(c) One letter is drawn at random from box 1, then box 2, and then box 3, with the results recorded in order. What is the probability that the outcome is HAT?

(d) If a box is chosen at random and then a letter is drawn at random from the box, what is the probability that the outcome is A?

3. An executive committee consisted of ten members—four women and six men. Three members were selected at random to be sent to a meeting in Hawaii. A blindfolded woman drew three of the ten names from a hat. All three names drawn were women. If the woman who drew the names was honest, what was the probability of such luck?

4. Two boxes with letters follow. Choose a box and draw three letters at random, one by one, without replacement. If the outcome is SOS, you win a prize.

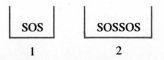

SOS	SOSSOS
1	2

(a) Which box should you choose?

(b) Which box would you choose if the letters are drawn with replacement?

5. Three boxes containing balls are shown. Draw a ball from box 1 and place it in box 2. Then draw a ball from box 2 and place it in box 3. Finally, draw a ball from box 3.

(a) What is the probability that the last ball, drawn from box 3, is white?

(b) What is the probability that the last ball drawn is black?

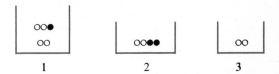

1	2	3

6. Carolyn will win a large prize if she wins two tennis games in a row out of three games. She is to play alternately against Billie and Bobby. She may choose to play Billie-Bobby-Billie or Bobby-Billie-Bobby. She wins against Billie 50% of the time and against Bobby 80% of the time. Which alternative should she choose and why?

7. Two boxes with black and white balls are shown below. A ball is drawn at random from box 1, then a ball is drawn at random from box 2, and the colors are recorded in order.

1	2

Find each of the following.

(a) The probability of two white balls

(b) The probability of at least one black ball

(c) The probability of at most one black ball

(d) The probability of ●○ or ○●

8. A penny, nickel, dime, and quarter are tossed. What is the probability of at least three heads?

9. Assume the probability that a child born is a boy is $\frac{1}{2}$. What is the probability that if a family is going to have four children that they will all be boys?

10. The numbers of symbols on each of the three dials of a standard slot machine are shown in the table.

Symbol	Dial 1	Dial 2	Dial 3
Bar	1	3	1
Bell	1	3	3
Plum	5	1	5
Orange	3	6	7
Cherry	7	7	0
Lemon	3	0	4
Total	20	20	20

Find the probability for each of the following.
(a) Three plums   (b) Three oranges
(c) Three lemons   (d) No plums

11. If a person takes a five-question true-false test, what is the probability that the score is 100% if the person guesses on every question?

12. In a drawer, there are 10 blue socks and 12 black socks. Suppose it is dark and you choose 3 socks. What is the probability that you will choose a matching pair?

13. Rattlesnake and Paxson Colleges play four games against each other in a chess tournament. Rob Fisher, the chess whiz from Paxson, withdrew from the tournament, so the probabilities of Rattlesnake and Paxson winning each game are $\frac{2}{3}$ and $\frac{1}{3}$, respectively. What are the following probabilities?
(a) Paxson loses all four games.
(b) The match is a draw with each school winning two games.

14. The combinations on the lockers at the high school consist of three numbers, each ranging from 0 to 39. If a combination is chosen at random, what is the probability that the first two numbers are multiples of nine and the third number is a multiple of four?

15. A box contains the 11 letters shown. The letters are drawn one by one without replacement and the results are recorded in order. Find the probability of the outcome MISSISSIPPI.

$$\boxed{\text{MIIIIPPSSSS}}$$

*16. Abe proposes the following game. He lets you choose one of the four equally likely outcomes obtained by tossing a coin twice: {HH, HT, TH, TT}. Abe then chooses one of the other outcomes. A coin is flipped until either your choice or Abe's choice appears. For example, suppose you choose TT and Abe chooses HT. If the first two flips yield TH, then no one wins and the game continues. If, after five flips, the string THH<u>HT</u> appears, then Abe is the

winner because the sequence HT finally appeared. Is this game fair? Why?

*17. Consider the three spinners A, B, and C shown in the figure. The probabilities for the various outcomes are given below each spinner.

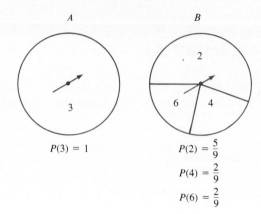

$P(3) = 1$

$P(2) = \dfrac{5}{9}$

$P(4) = \dfrac{2}{9}$

$P(6) = \dfrac{2}{9}$

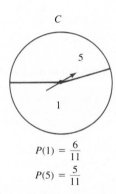

$P(1) = \dfrac{6}{11}$

$P(5) = \dfrac{5}{11}$

(a) Suppose you choose a spinner and then a friend chooses a spinner, and each person spins the chosen spinner. If the person spinning the highest number wins, which spinner should you choose?
(b) This time you are to play the same game as in (a), but two friends play. If each player chooses a spinner, would you make the same choice that you did in (a)? Why?

Review Problems

18. Match the phrase to the probability that describes it.
(a) A certain event
(b) An impossible event
(c) A very likely event
(d) An unlikely event
(e) A 50% chance

(i) $\frac{1}{1000}$
(ii) $\frac{999}{1000}$
(iii) 0
(iv) $\frac{1}{2}$
(v) 1

19. A date in the month of April is chosen at random. Find the probabilities of the date being each of the following.

(a) April 7
(b) April 31
(c) Before April 20

BRAIN TEASER

Suppose n people are in a room. Two people bet on whether at least two of the people in the room have a birthday on the same date during the year (for example, October 14). Assume that a person is as likely to be born on one day as another and ignore leap years. How many people must be in the room before the bet is even? (If $n = 366$, it is a sure bet.) Poll your class to see if two people have the same birthday. Use this information to find an experimental answer. Then find a theoretical solution. A calculator is very helpful for the computations.

*Section 8-3

Conditional Probability, Independent Events, and Simulations

Assume that the probabilities that a child born a boy (B) or girl (G) are equal. Then, the sample space for the sexes of the children in a two-child family is $S = \{BB, BG, GB, GG\}$, where the first element represents the elder child and the second element represents the younger child and the probability of having two girls in a two-child family is $\frac{1}{4}$. A tree diagram could also be used to determine this probability.

Sometimes in considering probabilities, we obtain additional information. Suppose we know that a selected family has two children and that the elder child is a girl. What is the probability that both children are girls? In this case, the sample space is altered to $\{GB, GG\}$, and $P(GG) = \frac{1}{2}$. What is the probability that the family has two girls if it is known that at least one child is a girl? In this case, the sample space is $S = \{BG, GB, GG\}$, and $P(GG) = \frac{1}{3}$.

conditional probability   These are examples of conditional probability. In **conditional probability,** we talk about the probability of an event A happening, given that event B has happened. We denote this as $P(A|B)$ and read this as "the probability of A, given B." In our example, we might ask, "What is the probability of a two-child family having two girls, given that the elder child is a girl?"

Example 8-8

There are two mice in a cage, one black mouse and one white one. Suppose it is known that one of the mice is a male.

(a) What is the probability that they are both males?
(b) If it is known that the black mouse is a male, what is the probability that both mice are males?

Solution

(a) Given two mice, four possibilities can occur, where the first entry represents the sex of the black mouse and the second entry represents the sex of the white mouse. For example, MF represents a male black mouse and a female white mouse.

$$\{MM, MF, FM, FF\}$$

Because we are told that one of the mice is a male, the only possibility that has been eliminated is FF. Hence, the sample space is $\{MM, MF, FM\}$, and $P(MM) = \frac{1}{3}$.

(b) Because the black mouse is a male, the only possibilities are $\{MM, MF\}$, and $P(MM) = \frac{1}{2}$.

To develop a formula for computing conditional probability, consider the following example. At a certain hospital, it is known that 40 patients have lung cancer (C), 30 patients smoke (S), and 25 have lung cancer and smoke. Suppose that there are 200 patients. A Venn diagram for this information is given in Figure 8-28. If $P(C)$ is the probability that a patient selected at

Figure 8-28

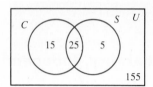

random from the 200 patients has lung cancer, then $P(C) = \frac{40}{200}$. Similarly, $P(S) = \frac{30}{200}$, and $P(C \cap S) = \frac{25}{200}$. If a patient chosen at random is known to smoke, what is the probability that the patient has lung cancer? We would like to know the probability that a patient has lung cancer, given that the patient smokes, that is, $P(C \mid S)$. From the Venn diagram, we see that of the 30 smokers, there are 25 who have lung cancer. Thus, $P(C \mid S) = \frac{25}{30} = n(C \cap S)/n(S)$. In this case, $P(C \mid S) = \frac{25}{30} = (\frac{25}{200})/(\frac{30}{200})$, and we have $P(C \mid S) = P(C \cap S)/P(S)$. This idea can be generalized in the following definition.

DEFINITION

If A and B are events in a sample space, and $P(B) \neq 0$, the **conditional probability** of A, given B, denoted by $P(A \mid B)$, is defined as $P(A \mid B) = \dfrac{P(A \cap B)}{P(B)}$.

If A and B are events in a sample space with $P(B) \neq 0$, then multiplying both sides of the equation $P(A \mid B) = \dfrac{P(A \cap B)}{P(B)}$ by $P(B)$, we obtain $P(A \cap B) =$

Multiplication Rule for Probabilities

$P(B) \cdot P(A \mid B)$. This is called the **Multiplication Rule for Probabilities.**

The Multiplication Rule for Probabilities justifies multiplying probabilities on tree diagrams as we did in Section 8-2. For example, suppose a container has three black marbles and two white marbles and two marbles are drawn at random without replacement. What is the probability that both marbles are white? If we let W_2 represent drawing a white ball on the second draw and W_1 represent drawing a white ball on the first draw, then applying the Multiplication Rule for Probabilities we have

$$P(W_2 \cap W_1) = P(W_1) \cdot P(W_2 \mid W_1) = \frac{2}{5} \cdot \frac{1}{4} = \frac{2}{20}$$

Therefore, the probability of obtaining two white balls is $\frac{2}{20}$.

A tree diagram for this problem is given in Figure 8-29.

Figure 8-29

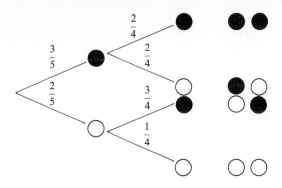

We see that the Multiplication Rule for Probabilities in the example above is represented by the bottom branch of the tree diagram.

Example 8-9

There are 40 employees in a certain firm, and it is known that 28 of these employees are males (M), 2 of these males are secretaries (S), and there are 10 secretaries employed with the firm. What is the probability that an employee chosen at random is a secretary, given that the person is a male?

Solution

We would like to compute the probability of an employee being a secretary, given that the employee is a male, that is, $P(S|M)$. From the formula given above, we have the following.

$$P(S|M) = \frac{P(S \cap M)}{P(M)} = \frac{\frac{2}{40}}{\frac{28}{40}} = \frac{2}{28}, \text{ or } \frac{1}{14}$$

The Venn diagram given in Figure 8-30 could also be used to find this probability.

Figure 8-30

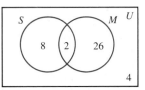

INDEPENDENT EVENTS

Consider an experiment consisting of tossing a fair coin three times. What is the probability that the second and third tosses are heads? The sample space for the experiment is given below.

$S = \{$HHH, HHT, HTH, HTT, THH, THT, TTH, TTT$\}$

If A is the event that the second and third tosses are heads, then $A = \{$HHH, THH$\}$. Hence, $P(A) = \frac{2}{8}$, or $\frac{1}{4}$.

Next, consider finding the probability that the second and third tosses are heads, given that the first toss is a tail. If B represents the event that the first toss is a tail, then we are to find $P(A|B)$. To use the formula for conditional probability, we need to find $P(B)$ and $P(A \cap B)$. Because $B = \{THH, THT, TTT, TTH\}$, $P(B) = \frac{4}{8}$. Because $A \cap B = \{THH\}$, then $P(A \cap B) = \frac{1}{8}$. Hence,

$$P(A|B) = \frac{P(A \cap B)}{P(B)} = \frac{\frac{1}{8}}{\frac{4}{8}} = \frac{1}{4}$$

In this example, we see that the probability of event A is not affected by the occurrence or nonoccurrence of event B; that is,

$$P(A|B) = P(A)$$

In other words, what happens on the second and third tosses is not at all influenced by what occurred on the first toss.

independent events   In these types of cases, we say that events A and B are **independent events.** This leads to the following definition.

DEFINITION

independent

Two events A and B are **independent** if $P(A|B) = P(A)$.

dependent events   If $P(A|B) \neq P(A)$, then the events are called **dependent.**

In the case of independent events A and B, we may use the equation for conditional probability to obtain the following equivalent statements.

$$\frac{P(A \cap B)}{P(B)} = P(A|B) \qquad \text{[Definition of conditional probability]}$$

$$\frac{P(A \cap B)}{P(B)} = P(A) \qquad \text{[Substitute $P(A)$ for $P(A|B)$.]}$$

$$P(A \cap B) = P(A) \cdot P(B) \qquad \text{[Multiply both sides by $P(B)$.]}$$

Thus, if A and B are independent events, we have $P(A \cap B) = P(A) \cdot P(B)$.

Example 8-10

A box contains five black balls, two red balls, and five white balls. One ball is drawn at random, its color is recorded, and it is replaced in the box. A second ball is then drawn at random. Find the probability that the first ball is red and the second is black.

Solution

If R is the event of drawing a red ball on the first draw and B is the event of drawing a black ball on the second draw, then the events R and B are independent because the first ball is replaced, and so the probability of drawing a black ball on the second draw is not influenced by the first draw. Since $P(R) = \frac{2}{12}$ and $P(B|R) = P(B) = \frac{5}{12}$, we have

$$P(R \cap B) = P(R) \cdot P(B) = \left(\frac{2}{12}\right)\left(\frac{5}{12}\right) = \frac{10}{144}, \text{ or } \frac{5}{72}$$

If a tree diagram were used for computing this probability, the branch used in obtaining the answer would appear as shown in Figure 8-31.

Figure 8-31

Outcome Probability

$$\frac{2}{12} \qquad \frac{5}{12}$$
$$\rule{2cm}{0.4pt} R \rule{2cm}{0.4pt} B \qquad RB \qquad \frac{10}{144}$$

Remark   The preceding independent events are different from the dependent events that would occur if the ball drawn on the first draw was not replaced.

USING SIMULATIONS IN PROBABILITY

Because many elementary school students have studied little or no probability, many problems are beyond their capabilities. Simulations can be used by students to study phenomena that are too complex to analyze by other means. If a problem is simulated many times, the results can be used to estimate probabilities rather than determining them analytically. Consider how we might simulate the problem of determining if a couple will have two girls. One way is to use a fair coin and let a toss of heads represent the birth of a girl and a toss of tails represent the birth of a boy. In this example, a success would be tossing two heads in two throws of the coin. An estimate for the probability that a two-child family has two girls is given by dividing the number of successes by the number of trials. The more trials that are conducted, the more accurate the estimate will become. Table 8-4 represents 50 tosses of two coins.

Table 8-4

Outcome of 50 Pairs of Coin Tosses

HH	HT	HT	TT	HT
HT	TH	HT	HT	TT
TT	TT	TT	HT	TH
HH	TH	HT	HT	TT
TH	TH	TH	HH	TT
TH	HT	TT	HH	HT
HH	HH	TT	HT	TT
TT	HH	TH	TH	HT
HT	TT	TH	TH	HH
HT	TT	HH	HH	HH

In this simulation, we have 11 sets of two girls out of 50 trials, so we estimate that the probability of having two girls in a two-child family is $\frac{11}{50}$. Compare this with the theoretical probability of having two girls in a two-child family. Other devices, such as dice or spinners, could also be used to perform this simulation.

Random-digit tables are also used in simulations. Random-digit tables are tables of digits selected at random, often by a computer. A portion of a random-digit table is given in Table 8-5. A starting place on this table could be picked at random, and we could start reading across, letting an even digit represent the birth of a girl and an odd digit represent the birth of a boy. Use the random-digit table to simulate the probability of births in a two-child family for 50 cases by reading pairs of numbers and comparing the results with the coin-tossing simulation given above.

Table 8-5

Random Digits

36422	93239	76046	81114	77412	86557	19549	98473	15221	87856
78496	47197	37961	67568	14861	61077	85210	51264	49975	71785
95384	59596	05081	39968	80495	00192	94679	18307	16265	48888
37957	89199	10816	24260	52302	69592	55019	94127	71721	70673
31422	27529	95051	83157	96377	33723	52902	51302	86370	50452
07443	15346	40653	84238	24430	88834	77318	07486	33950	61598
41348	86255	92715	96656	49693	99286	83447	20215	16040	41085
12398	95111	45663	55020	57159	58010	43162	98878	73337	35571
77229	92095	44305	09285	73256	02968	31129	66588	48126	52700
61175	53014	60304	13976	96312	42442	96713	43940	92516	81421
16825	27482	97858	05642	88047	68960	52991	67703	29805	42701
84656	03089	05166	67571	25545	26603	40243	55482	38341	97782
03872	31767	23729	89523	73654	24626	78393	77172	41328	95633
40488	70426	04034	46618	55102	93408	10965	69744	80766	14889
98322	25528	43808	05935	78338	77881	90139	72375	50624	91385
13366	52764	02407	14202	74172	58770	65348	24115	44277	96735
86711	27764	86789	43800	87582	09298	17880	75507	35217	08352
53886	50358	62738	91783	71944	90221	79403	75139	09102	77826
99348	21186	42266	01531	44325	61042	13453	61917	90426	12437
49985	08787	59448	82680	52929	19077	98518	06251	58451	91140
49807	32863	69984	20102	09523	47827	08374	79849	19352	62726
46569	00365	23591	44317	55054	99835	20633	66215	46668	53587
09988	44203	43532	54538	16619	45444	11957	69184	98398	96508
32916	00567	82881	59753	54761	39404	90756	91760	18698	42852
93285	32297	27254	27198	99093	97821	46277	10439	30389	45372
03222	39951	12738	50303	25017	84207	52123	88637	19369	58289
87002	61789	96250	99337	14144	00027	43542	87030	14773	73087
68840	94259	01961	42552	91843	33855	00824	48733	81297	80411
88323	28828	64765	08244	53077	50897	91937	08871	91517	19668
55170	71062	64159	79364	53088	21536	39451	95649	65256	23950

The Peanuts cartoon suggests a simulation problem concerning chocolate chip cookies.

CARTOON

© 1981 United Feature Syndicate, Inc.

Example 8-11

Suppose Lucy makes enough batter for exactly 100 chocolate chip cookies and mixes 100 chocolate chips into the batter. If the chips are distributed at random and Charlie chooses a cookie at random from the 100 cookies, estimate the probability that it will contain exactly one chocolate chip.

Solution

A simulation can be used to estimate the probability of choosing a cookie with exactly one chocolate chip. We can construct a 10 × 10 grid as shown in Figure 8-32. This grid represents the 100 cookies made by Lucy. Each square (cookie) can be associated with some ordered pair, where the first component is for the horizontal scale and the second component is for the vertical scale. For example, the squares (0, 2) and (5, 3) are pictured in Figure 8-32.

Figure 8-32

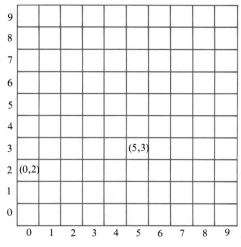

Using the table of random digits, close your eyes, take a pencil, and point to one number to start. Look at the number and the number immediately following it. Consider these numbers as an ordered pair and continue on until 100 ordered pairs are obtained. For example, suppose we start at a 3 and the numbers following 3 that are as shown.

39968   80495   00192 . . .

Then the ordered pairs would be given as (3, 9), (9, 6), (8, 8), (0, 4), and so on. Use each pair of numbers as the coordinates for the square (cookie) and place a tally on the grid to represent each chip as shown in Figure 8-33. (Note that there are other schemes for using the random-digit

Figure 8-33

	0	1	2	3	4	5	6	7	8	9
9		I	I	II				I	III	I
8				I		IIII	I	II		
7	II	III	II	I	II	II		I	II	I
6	I	I		III		I	I	I		III
5		I			I	III	I	I		
4	I	I			I		II		I	
3	I	I	I	III	II		I	IIII		I
2		I	II		I		II		I	
1	II	I	I		II	II				II
0		II	II	I	I	II	II			II

table to select the 100 ordered pairs.) We estimate the probability that a cookie has exactly one chip by counting the number of squares with exactly one tally and dividing by 100. Table 8-6 shows the results of one simulation.

Table 8-6

Number of Chips	Number of Cookies
0	38
1	34
2	20
3	6
≥ 4	2

Thus, the estimate for the probability of Charlie's receiving a cookie with exactly one chip is $\frac{34}{100}$.

Try a simulation on your own and compare the results with those shown above and with the results given in Table 8-7, which we obtained by theoretical methods.

Table 8-7

Number of Chips	Number of Cookies
0	36.8
1	36.8
2	18.4
3	6.1
≥ 4	1.9

Example 8-12

A baseball player, Reggie, has a batting average of 0.400; that is, his probability of getting a hit on any particular time at bat is 0.400. Estimate the probability that he will get at least one hit in his next 3 times at bat.

Solution

We use a random-digit table to simulate this example. We choose a starting point, and place the random digits in groups of three. Because Reggie's probability of getting a hit on any particular time at bat is 0.400, or 0.4, we could use the occurrence of four particular numbers from 0 through 9 in the table to represent a hit. Suppose a hit is represented by the digits 0, 1, 2, and 3. At least one hit is obtained in three times at bat if, in any sequence of three digits, a 0, 1, 2, or 3 appears. Data for 50 trials are given below.

780	862	760	580	783	720	590	506	021	366
848	118	073	077	042	254	063	667	374	153
377	883	573	683	780	115	662	591	685	274
279	652	754	909	754	892	310	673	964	351
803	034	799	915	059	006	774	640	298	961

We see that a 0, 1, 2, or 3 appears in 42 out of the 50 trials; thus, an estimate for the probability of at least one hit in Reggie's next 3 times at bat is $\frac{42}{50}$. Try to determine the theoretical probability for this experiment.

How might we use the random-digit table to pick 5 states at random from the 50 states? One possibility is to number the states 00, 01, 02, 03, . . . , 49. We now go to the table of random digits and select blocks of two digits, for example,

74   19   30   44   00   52   42   99   21   85   53 . . .

If we ignore blocks of two that have values greater than or equal to 50, we obtain the following state numbers to be selected.

19, 30, 44, 00, 42

This is a random sample of 5 states chosen from the 50 states.

From a random sample, we can deduce information about the population from which the sample was taken. To see how this can be done, consider Example 8-13.

Example 8-13

We wish to determine the number of fish in a certain pond. Suppose we capture 300 fish, mark them, and throw them back into the pond. Suppose that the next day, 200 fish are caught and 20 of these are already marked. Then these 200 fish are thrown back into the pond. Estimate how many fish are in the pond.

Solution

Because 20 of the 200 fish are marked, we assume that $\frac{20}{200}$, or $\frac{1}{10}$, of the fish are marked. Thus, $\frac{1}{10}$ of the population is marked. If n represents the population, then $\frac{1}{10}n = 300$, and $n = 300 \cdot 10 = 3000$. Hence, an estimate for the fish population of the pond is 3000 fish.

PROBLEM 4

Assume that Magic Smith, a basketball player, makes free throws with 80% probability of success and is placed in a one-and-one situation. This means that Magic is given a second foul shot only if the first shot goes through the basket. Thus, in a one-and-one situation, Magic can score 0, 1, or 2 points. How can we simulate 25 attempts from the foul line in one-and-one situations to determine how many times we would expect Magic to score 0 points, 1 point, and 2 points?

UNDERSTANDING THE PROBLEM The probability that Magic Smith makes any given free throw is 80%. He is shooting in a one-and-one situation: If he misses the first shot, he receives 0 points; if he makes the first shot, he receives 1 point and is allowed to shoot *one* more time. Each basket made counts as 1 point. Thus, Magic has the opportunity to score 0, 1, or 2 points. We are to determine by simulation how many times Magic can be expected to score 0 points, 1 point, or 2 points in 25 attempts at one-and-one situations.

DEVISING A PLAN One way to simulate the number of times that Magic could be expected to score 0, 1, or 2 points in 25 one-and-one situations is to use a random-digit table. Because his probability of making any basket is 80%, we could use the occurrence of a 0, 1, 2, 3, 4, 5, 6, or 7 to simulate making the basket and the occurrence of an 8 or a 9 to simulate missing the basket. Another way to simulate the problem would be to construct a spinner with 80% of the spinner devoted to making a basket and 20% of the spinner devoted to missing the basket. This could be done by constructing the spinner with 80% of the 360 degrees, or 288 degrees, devoted to making the basket and 72 degrees devoted to missing the basket. A spinner for this simulation is shown in Figure 8-34.

Figure 8-34

CARRYING OUT THE PLAN We use a spinner similar to the one in Figure 8-34. We spin the spinner to simulate 25 sets of one-and-one situations. If the spinner lands on "miss," 0 points are recorded for the set. If the spinner lands on "make," a second spin is taken. If the spinner shows another "make," then 2 points are recorded; otherwise, 1 point is recorded. This is repeated for 25 sets and the results are recorded. Four simulations of 25 sets are given in Table 8-8.

Table 8-8

Number of Points	Trial 1	Trial 2	Trial 3	Trial 4	Total	Estimated Probability
0	4	6	5	5	20	$\frac{20}{100}$
1	2	4	5	4	15	$\frac{15}{100}$
2	19	15	15	16	65	$\frac{65}{100}$

We used four trials to obtain a better estimate than we would get from only a single trial. To solve the problem, we use the estimated probability and multiply by 25 to obtain the results in Table 8-9.

Table 8-9

Number of Points	Expected Number of Times Points Are Scored in 25 Attempts
0	5
1	3.75
2	16.25

LOOKING BACK Similar problems could be attempted using different models for the simulation. The shooting percentage for Magic could also be raised or lowered, and the effects on the number of points scored could be compared. Could you write a computer program to perform these simulations?

It is possible to compute the theoretical probability for this experiment by using a tree diagram as shown in Figure 8-35.

Figure 8-35

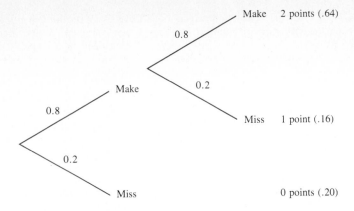

Thus, theoretical estimates for the number of points scored in 25 attempts can be computed. These estimates are given in Table 8-10. Compare these results with the experimental probability obtained above.

Table 8-10

Number of Points	Expected Number of Times Points Are Scored in 25 Attempts
0	5
1	4
2	16

PROBLEM SET 8-3

1. Two standard dice are thrown.
   (a) What is the probability of a sum of 7 showing, given that the sum is an odd number?
   (b) What is the probability of a sum of 7 showing, given that one die shows a 1?
2. A penny, a nickel, and a quarter are tossed. What is the probability of obtaining three heads if it is known that the penny landed on heads?
3. A family is known to have three children. What is the probability that the family has all boys if it is known that the eldest child is a boy?
4. Al and Betsy are drawing cards to determine who has to clean the house. Al draws an ace and does not replace it in the deck. Now it is Betsy's turn. What is the probability that Betsy will also draw an ace?
5. A single card is drawn from a standard deck of cards. What is the probability that it is a king, given that it is a face card?
6. An assembly line has two inspectors. The probability that the first inspector will miss a defective item is 0.05. If the defective item passes the first inspec-

tor, the probability that the second inspector will miss it is 0.01. What is the probability that a defective item will pass by both inspectors?

7. A die is rolled and a coin is tossed. Find the probability of tossing a prime number on the die and a tail on the coin.
8. If 75% of a store's customers are female and 60% of the female customers have charge accounts at the store, what is the probability that a customer chosen at random is female and has a charge account?
9. A box contains three red balls, four white balls, and five blue balls. Balls are drawn at random from the box without replacement until a red ball is drawn. Find the probability that the first time that a red ball is drawn is on:
   (a) The first draw.   (b) The second draw.
   (c) The third draw.   (d) The fourth draw.
10. In a certain population of caribou, the probability of an animal being sickly is $\frac{1}{20}$. If a caribou is sickly, the probability of it being eaten by wolves is $\frac{1}{3}$. If a caribou is not sickly, the probability of it being

eaten by wolves is $\frac{1}{150}$. If a caribou is chosen at random from the herd, what is the probability that it will be eaten by wolves?

11. In a survey of 100 students, it was determined that 15 students were taking algebra, biology, and chemistry; 25 were taking algebra and biology; 30 were taking algebra and chemistry; 22 were taking biology and chemistry; 5 were taking only algebra; 4 were taking only biology; and 6 were taking only chemistry. If a student is chosen at random from the 100 students, what is the probability of each of the following?
   (a) The student is not taking any of the three subjects.
   (b) The student is taking algebra and biology, but not chemistry.
   (c) The student is taking algebra, given that he or she is taking biology.

12. How might you use a table of random digits to simulate each of the following?
   (a) Tossing a single die
   (b) Choosing 3 persons at random from a group of 20 people
   (c) Spinning the spinner, where the probability of each color is as shown.

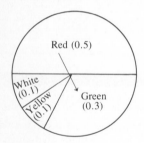

13. To estimate the fish population of a certain pond, 200 fish were caught, marked, and returned to the pond. The next day, 300 fish were caught, of which 50 had been marked the previous day. Estimate the fish population of the pond.

14. Pick a block of two digits from the random-digit table. What is the probability that the number picked is less than 30?

15. A cereal company places coupons with a number 1 through 9 in each box of cereal. If the numbers are distributed at random in the boxes of cereal, estimate the number of boxes of cereal on the average that would have to be purchased in order to obtain all nine numbers. Explain how the table of random digits could be used to estimate the number of coupons.

16. A school has 500 students. The principal is to pick 30 students at random from the school to go to the Rose Bowl. How can this be done by using a random-digit table?

17. In a certain city, the probability that it will rain on a certain day is 0.8 if it rained the day before. The probability that it will be dry on a certain day is 0.3 if it was dry the day before. It is now Sunday and it is raining. Use the table of random digits to simulate the weather for the rest of the week.

*18. Montana duck hunters are all perfect shots. Ten Montana hunters are in a duck blind when ten ducks fly over. All ten hunters pick a duck at random to shoot at, and all ten hunters fire at the same time. How many ducks could be expected to escape, on the average, if this experiment were repeated a large number of times? How could this problem be simulated?

---

*Section 8-4   Odds and Mathematical Expectation

COMPUTING ODDS

odds

People often speak about the *odds in favor of* or the *odds against* a particular team in an athletic contest. For example, when we say that the **odds** in favor of the Falcons' winning a particular football game are 4 to 1, we are speaking of how likely the Falcons are to win relative to how likely they are to lose. In other words, in this example, the probability of their winning is four times the probability of their losing. Thus, if W represents the event Falcons win and L represents the event Falcons lose, then $P(W) = 4P(L)$; as a proportion, we have

$$\frac{P(W)}{P(L)} = \frac{4}{1}$$

Furthermore, because W and L are complements of each other, we have

$$\frac{P(W)}{P(\overline{W})} = \frac{P(W)}{1 - P(W)} = \frac{4}{1}$$

Formally, odds are defined as follows.

DEFINITION

odds in favor

> The **odds in favor** of an event A, where $P(A)$ is the probability that A occurs and $P(\overline{A})$ is the probability that A does not occur, are given by the following.
>
> $$\frac{P(A)}{P(\overline{A})} \quad \text{or} \quad \frac{P(A)}{1 - P(A)}$$

odds against

> The **odds against** an event A are given by the following.
>
> $$\frac{P(\overline{A})}{P(A)} \quad \text{or} \quad \frac{1 - P(A)}{P(A)}$$

Thus, the odds against tossing a 4 on one throw of a die are $(\frac{5}{6})/(\frac{1}{6}) = \frac{5}{1}$, or 5 to 1.

Notice that in calculating odds, the denominators of the probabilities divide out. Thus, alternate definitions for odds in case of equally likely outcomes are as follows.

$$\text{Odds in favor} = \frac{\text{Number of favorable outcomes}}{\text{Number of unfavorable outcomes}}$$

$$\text{Odds against} = \frac{\text{Number of unfavorable outcomes}}{\text{Number of favorable outcomes}}$$

When rolling a die, the number of favorable ways of rolling a four in one throw of a die is 1, and the number of unfavorable ways is 5. Thus, the odds in favor of rolling a four are 1 to 5.

This technique is demonstrated on the student page on page 370 taken from *Addison-Wesley Mathematics*, 1987, Grade 8.

Example 8-14

For each of the following, find the odds in favor of the event occurring.

(a) Rolling a number less than 5 on a die
(b) Tossing heads on a fair coin
(c) Drawing an ace from an ordinary 52-card deck
(d) Drawing a heart from an ordinary 52-card deck

Solution

(a) Because the probability of rolling a number less than 5 is $\frac{4}{6}$ and the probability of rolling a number not less than 5 is $\frac{2}{6}$, the odds in favor of rolling a number less than 5 are $(\frac{4}{6}) \div (\frac{2}{6})$, or 4 to 2, or 2 to 1.
(b) Because $P(H) = \frac{1}{2}$ and $P(\overline{H}) = \frac{1}{2}$, the odds in favor of getting heads are $(\frac{1}{2}) \div (\frac{1}{2})$, or 1 to 1.
(c) Because the probability of drawing an ace is $\frac{4}{52}$ and the probability of not drawing an ace is $\frac{48}{52}$, the odds in favor of drawing an ace are $(\frac{4}{52}) \div (\frac{48}{52})$, or 4 to 48. The odds 4 to 48 are the same as the odds 1 to 12.

Odds

Nina is trying to draw a blue marble from the box without looking into the box.

There are **2** ways she can succeed.

There are **3** ways she can fail.

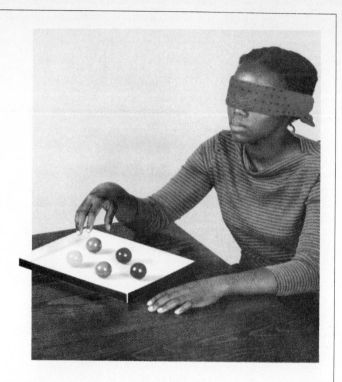

The **odds in favor** of drawing a blue marble are 2 to 3.

$$\frac{2}{3} \quad \begin{array}{l} \leftarrow \text{Successes} \\ \leftarrow \text{Failures} \end{array}$$

The **odds against** drawing a blue marble are 3 to 2.

$$\frac{3}{2} \quad \begin{array}{l} \leftarrow \text{Failures} \\ \leftarrow \text{Successes} \end{array}$$

Find the odds for each event.

1. Spin the spinner.

Event: Get a 2
Odds in favor = ▦
Odds against = ▦

2. Draw a marble from the box without looking.

Event: Draw a red marble
Odds in favor = ▦
Odds against = ▦

3. Toss a coin.

Event: Comes up heads
Odds in favor = ▦
Odds against = ▦

4. Spin the spinners.

Event: Sum of 6
Odds in favor = ▦
Odds against = ▦

5. Toss both coins.

Event: The coins match
Odds in favor = ▦
Odds against = ▦

6. Toss the dice.

Event: Sum of 2
Odds in favor = ▦
Odds against = ▦

(d) Because the probability of drawing a heart is $\frac{13}{52}$, or $\frac{1}{4}$, and the probability of not drawing a heart is $\frac{39}{52}$, or $\frac{3}{4}$, the odds in favor of drawing a heart are $(\frac{13}{52}) \div (\frac{39}{52}) = \frac{13}{39}$, or 13 to 39. This can be expressed as 1 to 3.

Given the probability of an event, it is possible to find the odds in favor of (or against) the event. Conversely, given the odds in favor of (or against) an event, it is possible to find the probability of the event. For example, if the odds in favor of an event A are 5 to 1, then the following proportion holds.

$$\frac{P(A)}{1 - P(A)} = \frac{5}{1}$$

$$P(A) = 5[1 - P(A)]$$

$$6P(A) = 5$$

$$P(A) = \frac{5}{6}$$

Remark   Note that the probability $\frac{5}{6}$ is a ratio. The exact number of favorable outcomes and the exact total of all outcomes is not necessarily known.

Example 8-15

In the cartoon, Snoopy is told that the odds are 1000 to 1 that he will end up with a broken arm if he touches Linus' blanket. What is the probability of this event E?

© 1974 United Feature Syndicate, Inc.

Solution

$$\frac{P(E)}{1 - P(E)} = \frac{1000}{1}, \text{ which implies } P(E) = \frac{1000}{1001}$$

MATHEMATICAL EXPECTATION

An important concept related to probability is *mathematical expectation*. Suppose Jane has won an $800 oven on a television game show. She has a choice of keeping the oven or trading it for a prize behind one of three doors. Behind one of the doors is a $2400 vacation prize, behind another is a $1200 living room set, and behind the third is $90 worth of peanuts. Should she trade her $800 for what is behind one of the doors? If each door has a probability of $\frac{1}{3}$ of being chosen, then to determine how much Jane could expect to win if the experiment were repeated a large number of times, we multiply the probability of choosing a door by the payoff behind the door, as shown in Table 8-11, and then find the sum of these products.

Table 8-11

Probability	Payoff	Product
$\frac{1}{3}$	$2400	$800
$\frac{1}{3}$	$1200	$400
$\frac{1}{3}$	$90	$30
		$1230

mathematical expectation
expected value

The total value of the products, $1230, is called the **mathematical expectation,** or **expected value,** of the experiment. The expected value is a kind of average of winnings for the long run. If Jane were allowed to repeat the game a large number of times, she could expect to win an average of $1230 per game. However, Jane has only one try, so she may lose. Mathematical expectation can be used to predict the average result of an experiment when it is repeated many times, but expectation cannot be used to determine the outcome of any single experiment.

DEFINITION

> If, in an experiment, the possible outcomes are numbers $a_1, a_2, \ldots, a_n$, occurring with probabilities $p_1, p_2, \ldots, p_n$, respectively, then the **mathematical expectation** (expected value) E is given by the equation
>
> $$E = a_1 \cdot p_1 + a_2 \cdot p_2 + a_3 \cdot p_3 + \cdots + a_n \cdot p_n$$

Suppose Mega-Mouth Toothpaste Company is giving away $20,000 in a contest. To win the contest, a person must send in a postcard with his or her name on it (no purchase of toothpaste is necessary). Suppose the company expects to receive 1 million postcards. Is this contest fair? *A game is considered fair if the net winnings are* $0; that is, the expected value of the game equals the price of playing the game. The expected value is one millionth of $20,000; that is, $E = (1/1,000,000) \cdot (20,000/1) = \frac{2}{100} = 0.02$. Because the cost of the postcard and postage exceeds $0.02, the contest is not fair.

Example 8-16

Consider the spinner in Figure 8-36 with the payoff for each region written on the spinner. Should the owner of this spinner expect to make money over an extended period of time if the charge is $2.00 per spin?

Figure 8-36

Solution

If the spinner is fair, then the following probabilities can be assigned to each region.

$$P(\$1.00) = \frac{1}{2} \qquad P(\$2.00) = \frac{1}{4} \qquad P(\$3.00) = \frac{1}{8} \qquad P(\$4.00) = \frac{1}{8}$$

The expected value is given by $E = (\frac{1}{2})1 + (\frac{1}{4})2 + (\frac{1}{8})3 + (\frac{1}{8})4 = 1.875$, or about 1.88. The owner can expect to pay out about $1.88 per spin, and $1.88 is less than the $2.00 charge, so the owner should make a profit on the spinner if it is used many times. The game in this example is not fair.

Example 8-17

Lori spends $1.00 for 1 ticket in a raffle with a $100 prize. If 200 tickets are sold, is $1.00 a fair price to pay for the ticket?

Solution

The probability of winning $100 is $\frac{1}{200}$. Thus, $E = (\frac{1}{200})100$, or 0.50. Because $1.00 is greater than $0.50, $1.00 is not a fair price. If the raffle is repeated many times, Lori can expect to lose $0.50 per raffle ticket on the average.

PROBLEM 5

Al and Betsy were playing a coin-tossing game in which a fair coin was to be tossed until a total of either three heads or three tails occurred. Al was to win when a total of three heads were tossed and Betsy was to win when a total of three tails were tossed. Each bet $50 on the game. The coin was lost when Al had two heads and Betsy had one tail. How should the stakes be fairly split if the game is not continued?

UNDERSTANDING THE PROBLEM Al and Betsy each bet $50 on a coin-tossing game in which a fair coin was to be tossed five times. Al was to win when a total of three heads was obtained; Betsy was to win when a total of three tails was obtained. When Al had two heads and Betsy had one tail, the coin was lost. The problem is how to split the stakes fairly.

If the stakes of the game are to be split fairly, then we should agree on what this means. There could be many interpretations, but possibly the best is to agree that the pot will be split in proportion to the probabilities of each player's winning the game when play was halted; that is, we must calculate the expected value for each player and split the pot accordingly.

DEVISING A PLAN A third head would have made Al the winner, whereas Betsy would have needed two more tails to win. A tree diagram that simulates the completion of the game allows us to find the probability of each player winning the game. Once the probabilities are found, all that is necessary is to multiply the probabilities by the amount of the pot, $100, to determine each player's fair share.

CARRYING OUT THE PLAN The tree diagram in Figure 8-37 shows the possibilities for game winners if the game is completed.

Figure 8-37

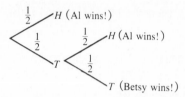

We can find the probabilities of each player's winning as follows:

$$P \text{ (Betsy wins)} = \frac{1}{2} \cdot \frac{1}{2} = \frac{1}{4}$$

$$P \text{ (Al wins)} = 1 - \frac{1}{4} = \frac{3}{4}$$

Hence, the fair way to split the stakes is for Al to receive $\frac{3}{4}$ of $100, or $75, while Betsy should receive $\frac{1}{4}$ of $100, or $25.

LOOKING BACK The problem could be made even more interesting by assuming that the coin is not fair so that the probability is not $\frac{1}{2}$ for each branch in the tree diagram. Other possibilities arise if the players have unequal amounts of money in the pot or more tosses are required to win.

PROBLEM SET 8-4

1. What are the odds in favor of drawing a face card from an ordinary deck of playing cards? What are the odds against drawing a face card?
2. On a single roll of a pair of dice, what are the odds against rolling a sum of 7?
3. Assume that the probability of a boy being born is $\frac{1}{2}$. If a family plans to have four children, what are the odds against having all boys?
4. Diane tossed a coin nine times and got nine tails. Assume Diane's coin is fair and answer each of the following questions.
   (a) What is the probability of tossing a tail on the tenth toss?
   (b) What is the probability of tossing ten more tails in a row?
   (c) What are the odds against tossing ten more tails in a row?

5. If the odds against Sam winning his first prize fight are 3 to 5, what is the probability he will win the fight?
6. What are the odds in favor of tossing at least two heads if a fair coin is tossed three times?
7. A game involves tossing two coins. A player wins $1.00 if both tosses result in heads. What should you pay to play this game in order to make it a fair game?
8. Suppose a player rolls a fair die and receives the number of dollars equal to the number of spots showing on the die. What is the expected value?
9. A punch-out card contains 500 spaces. One particular space pays $1000, five other spaces each pay $100, and the other spaces pay nothing. If a player chooses one space, what is the expected value of the game?

10. The following chart shows the probabilities assigned by Stu to the number of hours spent on homework on a given night.

Hours	Probability
1	0.15
2	0.20
3	0.40
4	0.10
5	0.05
6	0.10

If Stu's friend Stella calls and asks how long his homework will take, what would you expect his answer to be based on this table?

11. Suppose five quarters, five dimes, five nickels, and ten pennies are in a box. One coin is selected at random. What is the expected value of this experiment?

12. If the odds in favor of Fast Leg winning a horse race are 5 to 2 and the first prize is $14,000, what is the expected value of Fast Leg winning?

13. Al and Betsy are playing a coin-tossing game in which a fair coin is tossed. Al wins when a total of ten heads are tossed, and Betsy wins when a total of ten tails are tossed.
(a) If nine heads and eight tails have been tossed and the game is stopped, how should a pot of $100 be fairly divided?
(b) What are the odds against Betsy winning at the time the game was stopped in (a)?
(c) Suppose eight heads and five tails have been tossed when the game is stopped. How should a pot of $100 be fairly divided?
(d) What are the odds in favor of Al winning at the time the game was stopped in (c)?

Section 8-5

Methods of Counting

Tree diagrams can be used to list possible outcomes of experiments. For example, the tree diagram in Figure 8-38 lists the different ways three different flavors of ice cream, chocolate (c), vanilla (v), and strawberry (s), can be arranged on a cone, with no flavor used more than once.

Figure 8-38

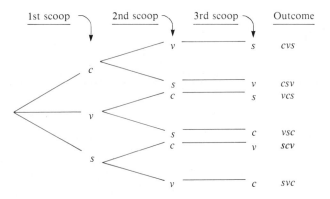

The tree starts out with three branches in the first stage, representing the three possibilities for the first scoop. For each outcome at the first stage, there are two possibilities at the second stage. Hence, there are 3 · 2 possibilities at the second stage. Then, for each outcome in the second stage, there is only one possibility at the third stage. Consequently, there are 3 · 2 · 1, or 6, different arrangements.

Now, consider a double-dip ice cream cone for which there are ten flavors of ice cream and six flavors of sherbet. How many different double-dip cones can be made with ice cream on the bottom and sherbet on the top? Since for each of the ten ice cream flavors there are six flavors of sherbet, the number of all possible double-dip cones is

$$\underbrace{6 + 6 + 6 + \cdots + 6}_{10 \text{ terms}} \quad \text{or} \quad 10 \cdot 6 = 60$$

A tree diagram can be used to verify the result. The counting argument used to find the number of possible double-dip cones is an example of the Fundamental Counting Principle.

Property   **Fundamental Counting Principle**   If event M can occur in m ways and, after it has occurred, event N can occur in n ways, then event M followed by event N can occur in $m \cdot n$ ways.

Remark   The Fundamental Counting Principle can be extended to any number of events.

Example 8-18   Solve each of the following.

(a) If a man owns seven shirts and six pairs of pants, how many different shirt-pant combinations are possible?
(b) Sally is taking a five-item true-false test. If she guesses at every item, how many different patterns of answers are possible?
(c) Suppose eight horses are entered in a race. In how many different ways can the first three horses finish?
(d) If automobile license plates consist of two letters followed by four digits, what is the total number of different license plates possible if numbers and letters may be repeated?

Solution

(a) Because a shirt can be chosen in seven ways and a pair of pants can be chosen in six ways, there are $7 \cdot 6$, or 42, shirt-pant combinations.
(b) Because there are two ways to answer question 1 on the test, two ways to answer question 2, and so on, there are $2 \cdot 2 \cdot 2 \cdot 2 \cdot 2$, or 32, different possible patterns of answers.
(c) There are eight possible winners, leaving seven possible second places and six possible third places. Thus, there are $8 \cdot 7 \cdot 6$, or 336, ways in which the first three horses can finish the race.
(d) There are $26 \cdot 26 \cdot 10 \cdot 10 \cdot 10 \cdot 10$, or 6,760,000, different license plates possible.

Now consider how many ways the owner of an ice cream parlor can display ten ice cream flavors in a row along the front of the display case. The first position can be filled in ten ways, the second position in nine ways, the third position in eight ways, and so on. Thus, by the Fundamental Counting Principle, there are $10 \cdot 9 \cdot 8 \cdot 7 \cdot 6 \cdot 5 \cdot 4 \cdot 3 \cdot 2 \cdot 1$, or 3,628,800, ways to display the flavors. If there were 16 flavors, there would be $16 \cdot 15 \cdot 14 \cdot 13 \cdot \ldots \cdot 3 \cdot 2 \cdot 1$ ways to arrange them. In general, *if there are n objects, then the number of ways to arrange the objects in a row is the product of all the natural numbers from 1 to n inclusive.* This expression is called **n factorial** and is denoted by **n!,** as shown below.

n factorial

n!

$$n! = n \cdot (n-1) \cdot (n-2) \cdot \ldots \cdot 3 \cdot 2 \cdot 1$$

For example, $5! = 5 \cdot 4 \cdot 3 \cdot 2 \cdot 1$, $3! = 3 \cdot 2 \cdot 1$, and $1! = 1$. Using factorial notation is helpful in counting and probability problems. A calculator is also very useful for finding the products in such problems. Practice problems with factorials are included in the exercises.

PERMUTATIONS

permutation

The ice cream cone arrangements discussed previously were in a definite order and no flavor could be chosen twice. A scoop of chocolate ice cream on top of a scoop of vanilla is a different arrangement from a scoop of vanilla on top of a scoop of chocolate. An arrangement of things in a definite order with no repetitions is called a **permutation.** For example, RAT, RTA, TAR, TRA, ART, and ATR are all different arrangements of the letters R, A, and T.

Consider the set of people in a small club, {Al, Betty, Carl, Dan}. In how many ways can they elect a president and a secretary? Order is important and no repetitions are possible. Thus, this is a permutation problem. Since there are four ways of choosing a president and then three ways of choosing a secretary, by the Fundamental Counting Principle, there are $4 \cdot 3$, or 12, ways of choosing a president and secretary. Note that an Al-Betty choice is different from a Betty-Al choice. Choosing two officers from a club of four is a permutation of four people chosen two at a time. The number of possible permutations of four objects taken two at a time is denoted by $_4P_2$. Hence, $_4P_2 = 4 \cdot 3$, or 12. In general, *if n objects are chosen r at a time, then the number of possible permutations is denoted by $_nP_r$.* Because there are n choices for the first object, $n - 1$ choices for the second object, $n - 2$ choices for the third object, and so on, then by the Fundamental Counting Principle, we have

$$_nP_r = n \cdot (n - 1) \cdot (n - 2) \cdot \ldots \cdot [n - (r - 1)]$$

or

$$_nP_r = n \cdot (n - 1) \cdot (n - 2) \cdot \ldots \cdot (n - r + 1)$$

The formula for permutations can be written in terms of factorials. This can be done by noticing the following.

$$n! = n \cdot (n - 1) \cdot (n - 2) \cdot \ldots \cdot (n - r + 1) \cdot (n - r) \cdot (n - r - 1) \cdot \ldots \cdot 3 \cdot 2 \cdot 1$$

Also, since

$$_nP_r = n \cdot (n - 1) \cdot (n - 2) \cdot \ldots \cdot (n - r + 1)$$

we have

$$_nP_r = n \cdot (n - 1) \cdot (n - 2) \cdot \ldots \cdot (n - r + 1) \cdot \frac{[(n - r) \cdot (n - r - 1) \cdot \ldots \cdot 3 \cdot 2 \cdot 1]}{[(n - r) \cdot (n - r - 1) \cdot \ldots \cdot 3 \cdot 2 \cdot 1]}$$

$$_nP_r = \frac{n!}{(n - r)!}$$

Notice that $_nP_n$ is the number of permutations of n objects chosen n at a time, that is, the number of ways of rearranging n objects in a row. We have seen that this number is $n!$. If we use the formula for $_nP_r$ to compute $_nP_n$, we obtain

$$_nP_n = \frac{n!}{(n-n)!} = \frac{n!}{0!}$$

Consequently, $n! = n!/0!$. For this equation to be true, *we must define* 0! *as* 1.

Example 8-19

(a) A baseball team has nine players. Find the number of ways a baseball coach can arrange the batting order.
(b) Find the number of ways of choosing three initials from the alphabet if none of the letters can be repeated.

Solution

(a) Here order is important, and this is a permutation problem. Because there are nine ways to choose the first batter, eight ways to choose the second batter, and so on, there are $9 \cdot 8 \cdot 7 \cdot \ldots \cdot 2 \cdot 1 = 9!$, or 362,880, ways of arranging the batting order. Hence, $_9P_9 = 9! = 362,880$.
(b) Because order is important, this is a permutation problem. There are 26 ways of choosing the first letter, 25 ways of choosing the second letter, and 24 ways of choosing the third letter; hence, there are $26 \cdot 25 \cdot 24$, or 15,600, ways of choosing the three letters. Hence, $_{26}P_3 = 26 \cdot 25 \cdot 24 = 15,600$.

COMBINATIONS

Reconsider the club {Al, Betty, Carl, Dan}. Suppose a two-person committee is selected with no chair. In this case, order is not important. In other words, an Al-Betty choice is the same as a Betty-Al choice. An arrangement of objects in which the order does not make any difference is called a **combination.** A comparison of the results of electing a president and secretary for the club and the results of simply selecting a two-person committee are shown in Figure 8-39. From Figure 8-39, we see that the number of permutations divided

combination

Figure 8-39

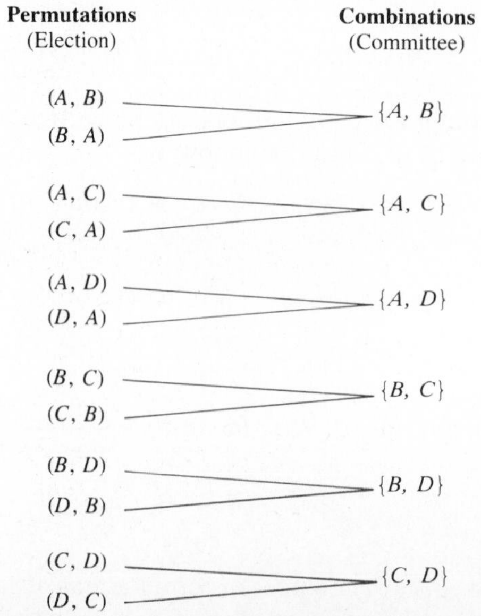

Permutations
(Election)

Combinations
(Committee)

(A, B) ——————
(B, A) —————— $\{A, B\}$

(A, C) ——————
(C, A) —————— $\{A, C\}$

(A, D) ——————
(D, A) —————— $\{A, D\}$

(B, C) ——————
(C, B) —————— $\{B, C\}$

(B, D) ——————
(D, B) —————— $\{B, D\}$

(C, D) ——————
(D, C) —————— $\{C, D\}$

by 2 is the number of combinations, $\dfrac{(4 \cdot 3)}{2}$, or 6. We divide the number of permutations by 2 because each two-person choice can be arranged in 2!, or 2, ways.

In how many ways can a committee of three people be selected from the club {A1, Betty, Carl, Dan}? To solve this problem, we first solve the simpler problem of finding the number of three-person committees, assuming that a president, vice president and secretary are chosen. A partial list of possibilities for both problems is shown in Figure 8-40.

Figure 8-40

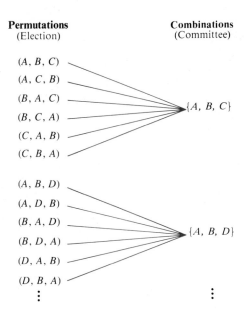

By the Fundamental Counting Principle, the number of permutations is $4 \cdot 3 \cdot 2$, or 24. There are 3!, or 6, times as many permutations as there are combinations. Hence the number of combinations is

$$\frac{(4 \cdot 3 \cdot 2)}{3!} = 4$$

The number of permutations is divided by 3! since each committee choice can be arranged in 3! ways. In general, we use the following rule to count combinations: *To find the number of combinations possible in a counting problem, first use the Fundamental Counting Principle to find the number of permutations and then divide by the number of ways in which each choice can be arranged.*

Symbolically, the number of combinations of n objects taken r at a time is denoted by $_nC_r$. Based on the above rule, we develop the following formula.

$$_nC_r = \frac{_nP_r}{_rP_r} = \frac{\dfrac{n!}{(n-r)!}}{r!} = \frac{n!}{r!(n-r)!}$$

Note that this formula could also be written as

$$_nC_r = \frac{n \cdot (n-1) \cdot \ldots \cdot (n-r+1)}{r!}$$

Remark In many texts, the notation $_nC_r$ is written as $\binom{n}{r}$.

An example of combinations is shown on the page below, which is taken from *Addison-Wesley Mathematics*, 1987, Grade 8.

Counting Selections: Combinations

How many selections of 2 topics from the 4 topics are possible?

First we find the number of permutations of 2 topics from 4 topics.

Permutations = **4 × 3 = 12**

The **order** of the topics is not important. Choosing A, then B, is the same as choosing B, then A. We need to divide by the number of permutations of 2 topics from 2 topics.

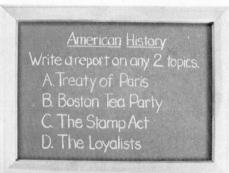

American History
Write a report on any 2 topics.
A. Treaty of Paris
B. Boston Tea Party
C. The Stamp Act
D. The Loyalists

Permutations of
2 topics from 4 topics → $\dfrac{4 \times 3}{2 \times 1} = \dfrac{12}{2} = 6$
Permutations of   →
2 topics from 2 topics

There are 6 possible selections.

A selection of a number of objects from a set of objects, *without regard to order*, is called a **combination** of the objects.

List of Permutations

A,B	A,C	A,D	B,C	B,D	C,D
B,A	C,A	D,A	C,B	D,B	D,C

Selections

A and B	A and D	B and D
A and C	B and C	C and D

Other Examples

How many combinations or selections of 3 topics from 5 topics are possible?

Combinations $= \dfrac{5 \times 4 \times 3}{3 \times 2 \times 1} = \dfrac{60}{6} = 10$

	Combinations of	
Topics	**3 topics from 5 topics**	
A	ABC	ADE
B	ABD	BCD
C	ABE	BCE
D	ACD	BDE
E	ACE	CDE

Example 8-20

A book-of-the-month club offers 3 free books from a list of 42 books. How many combinations are possible?

Solution

By the Fundamental Counting Principle, there are $42 \cdot 41 \cdot 40$ ways to choose the 3 free books in order. The number of ways the 3 choices of books can be arranged is 3!, or 6. Therefore, the number of combinations possible for 3 books is

$$\frac{42 \cdot 41 \cdot 40}{3!} = 11{,}480$$

Example 8-21

At the beginning of the second quarter of a mathematics class for elementary school teachers, each of the 25 students shook hands with each of the other students exactly once. How many handshakes took place?

Solution

Since the handshake between persons A and B is the same as that between persons B and A, order is not important in this problem. This is a problem of choosing combinations of 25 people two at a time. Thus, there are

$$\frac{25 \cdot 24}{2!} = 300$$

different handshakes.

PROBLEM 6

In the cartoon, Peppermint Patty took a ten-question true-false test. If she answered each question true or false at random, what is the probability that she answered 50% of the questions correctly?

© 1980 United Feature Syndicate, Inc.

UNDERSTANDING THE PROBLEM A score of 50% indicates that Peppermint Patty got $\frac{1}{2}$ of the ten questions, or five questions, correct. Also, if she answered questions true or false at random, then this means that the probability that she answers a given question correctly is $\frac{1}{2}$. We are asked to determine the probability that Patty answered exactly five of the questions correctly.

DEVISING A PLAN We do not know which five questions Patty missed. She could have missed any five questions out of ten on the test. Suppose she answered questions 2, 4, 5, 6, and 8 incorrectly. In this case, she would have answered questions 1, 3, 7, 9, and 10 correctly. We can compute the probability of this set of answers by using Figure 8-41, where C represents a correct answer and I represents an incorrect answer.

Figure 8-41

Question: 1   2   3   4   5   6   7   8   9   10

$\xrightarrow{\frac{1}{2}}C\xrightarrow{\frac{1}{2}}I\xrightarrow{\frac{1}{2}}C\xrightarrow{\frac{1}{2}}I\xrightarrow{\frac{1}{2}}I\xrightarrow{\frac{1}{2}}I\xrightarrow{\frac{1}{2}}C\xrightarrow{\frac{1}{2}}I\xrightarrow{\frac{1}{2}}C\xrightarrow{\frac{1}{2}}C$

To find the probability for the set of answers in Figure 8-41, we multiply the probabilities along the branches. Hence, $(\frac{1}{2})^{10}$ is the probability of answering questions 1–10 in the following way: C I C I I I C I C C. However, there are other ways to answer exactly five questions correctly: for example, C C C C C I I I I I. The probability of answering questions 1–10 in this way is also $(\frac{1}{2})^{10}$. How many such ways are possible to answer the questions? The number of such ways is simply the number of ways of arranging five Cs and 5 Is in a row, which is also the number of ways of choosing five correct questions out of ten, that is, $_{10}C_5$. Because all these arrangements give Patty a score of 50%, then the desired probability is the sum of the probabilities for each arrangement.

CARRYING OUT THE PLAN There are $_{10}C_5$, or 252, ways that the Cs and Is can be arranged. Hence, there are 252 sets of answers similar to the one in Figure 8-41 with five correct and five incorrect answers. The product of the probabilities for each of these sets of answers is $(\frac{1}{2})^{10}$, so the sum of the probabilities for all 252 sets is $252 \cdot (\frac{1}{2})^{10}$, or approximately 0.246. Thus, Peppermint Patty has a probability of 0.246 of obtaining a score of exactly 50% on the test.

LOOKING BACK It seems paradoxical to learn that the probability of obtaining a score of 50% on a ten-question true-false test is not close to $\frac{1}{2}$. As an extension of the problem, suppose that a passing score is a score of at least 70%. Now what is the probability that Peppermint Patty will pass? What is the probability of obtaining a score of at least 50% on the test?

PROBLEM SET 8-5

1. The eighth-grade class at a grade school has 16 girls and 14 boys. How many different possible boy-girl dates can be arranged?
2. How many different three-digit numbers can be formed from the digits 1, 2, 3, 4, 5, 6, and 7? Each digit can be used only once.
3. If a coin is tossed five times, in how many different ways can the sequence of heads and tails appear?
4. The telephone prefix for a university is 243. The prefix is followed by four digits. How many telephones are possible before a new prefix is needed?
5. Radio stations in the United States have call letters that begin with either K or W. Some have a total of three letters, while others have four letters. How many sets of three-letter call letters are possible? How many sets of four-letter call letters are possible?
6. Carlin's Pizza House offers 3 kinds of salads, 15 kinds of pizza, and 4 kinds of desserts. How many different three-course meals can be ordered?
7. Decide whether each of the following is true or false.
   (a) $6! = 6 \cdot 5!$ (b) $3! + 3! = 6!$

(c) $\dfrac{6!}{3!} = 2!$ (d) $\dfrac{6!}{3} = 2!$

(e) $\dfrac{6!}{5!} = 6$ (f) $\dfrac{6!}{4!2!} = 15$

(g) $n!(n + 1) = (n + 1)!$

8. In how many ways can the letters in the word SCRAMBLE be rearranged?

9. How many two-person committees can be formed from a group of six people?

10. Explain the difference between a permutation and a combination.

11. Assume a class has 30 members.
   (a) In how many ways can a president, vice president, and secretary be selected?
   (b) How many committees of three persons can be chosen?

12. A basketball coach was criticized in the newspaper for not trying out every combination of players. If the team roster has 12 players, how many 5-player combinations are possible?

13. Solve the problem posed by the following cartoon. (AAUGHH! is not an acceptable answer.)

© 1979 United Feature Syndicate, Inc.

14. A five-volume numbered set of books is placed randomly on a shelf. What is the probability that the books will be numbered in the correct order from left to right?

15. Take ten points in a plane, no three on a line. How many straight lines can be drawn if each line is drawn through a pair of points?

16. A committee of three people is selected at random from a set consisting of seven Americans, five French people, and three English people.
   (a) What is the probability that the committee consists of all Americans?
   (b) What is the probability that the committee has no Americans?

17. The triangular array of numbers pictured is called **Pascal's triangle.** Notice that the first and last number in each row is 1. Every other number is the sum of the two numbers immediately above it. The rows are counted starting at 0.

								Row
			1					(0)
		1		1				(1)
	1		2		1			(2)
1		3		3		1		(3)
1		4	6	4		1		(4)
1	5	10	10	5	1			(5)
1	6	15	20	15	6	1		(6)

It can be shown that the entries in Pascal's triangle are the numbers of combinations of n objects taken r at a time where n is the number of the row and r is the number of the item in the row. (Note that r could be 0.) For example, the number of combinations of six objects taken three at a time is 20, the fourth number in the sixth row. Use the triangle to determine the following.
   (a) $_5C_3$ (b) $_5C_5$ (c) $_6C_0$ (d) $_3C_2$

18. The probability of a basketball player making a successful free throw at any time in a game is $\frac{2}{3}$. If the player attempts ten free throws in a game, what is the probability that exactly six free throws are made?

★19. In a word such as LOOP, the Os are indistinguishable. To determine how many ways the letters of the word LOOP can be arranged, consider four empty slots. Where can the Os be placed in these four slots? The choice of slots is a combination of four slots taken two at a time. Thus, there are $_4C_2$, or 6, ways the Os can fit in the slots. Once the Os are placed, there are two slots left to place the L and then one slot left for the P. Thus there are $6 \cdot 2 \cdot 1$, or 12, arrangements altogether. Find the number of ways to rearrange the letters in the following words.
   (a) OHIO   (b) ALABAMA
   (c) ILLINOIS   (d) MISSISSIPPI
   (e) TENNESSEE

★20. In how many ways can five couples be seated in a row of ten chairs if no couple is separated?

★21. From a group of six girls and nine boys, how many five-member committees can be formed involving three boys and two girls?

22. Which is greater, $10!$ or 2^{10}?

★**23.** Solve the problem for Peppermint Patty.

© 1974 United Feature Syndicate, Inc.

Review Problems

24. A single card is drawn from an ordinary bridge deck. What is the probability of obtaining each of the following?
  (a) A club   (b) A queen and a spade
  (c) Not a queen   (d) Not a heart
  (e) A spade or a heart   (f) The six of diamonds
  (g) A queen or a spade   (h) Either red or black

25. From a sack containing seven red marbles, eight blue marbles, and four white marbles, marbles are drawn at random for several experiments. What is the probability of each of the following events?
  (a) One marble drawn at random is either red or blue.
  (b) The first draw is red and the second is blue if one marble is drawn at random, the color is recorded, the marble is replaced, and another marble is drawn.
  (c) The event in (b) if the first marble is not replaced.

BRAIN TEASER

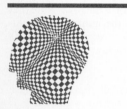

Jane has two tennis serves, a hard serve and a soft serve. Her hard serve has a 50% chance of being good. If her hard serve is good, then she has an 80% chance of winning the point. Her soft serve has a 90% chance of being good. If her soft serve is good, she has a 50% chance of winning the point.
(a) What is the probability that Jane wins the point if she serves hard and then, if necessary, soft?
(b) What is the probability that Jane wins the point if she serves hard and then, if necessary, hard?

SOLUTION TO THE PRELIMINARY PROBLEM

UNDERSTANDING THE PROBLEM Al and Betsy were hired as proofreaders for a manuscript. Al found 48 errors and Betsy found 42 errors; 30 of the errors were listed by both of them. From this information, we are to estimate the number of errors not yet detected in the manuscript.

DEVISING A PLAN If we could estimate how efficient either Al or Betsy was at finding errors, then we could estimate the fraction of errors that he or she could be expected to find and thus be able to estimate the number of errors not yet found. This amounts to finding the probability that either Al or Betsy will find a given error. To accomplish this, we draw a Venn diagram for the given information. From Figure 8-42, we see that the total number of errors found is $18 + 30 + 12$, or 60.

Figure 8-42

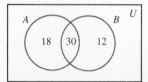

Next, we compute the probability that Al will find a given error. To accomplish this, we use the set of errors found by Betsy as a sample space. Thus, Al found $\frac{30}{42}$ of the errors in the set of 42 errors. From this information, we can estimate the number of errors in the manuscript.

CARRYING OUT THE PLAN We have estimated that Al finds $\frac{30}{42}$ of the errors in a given sample. If we let n be the total number of errors in the manuscript, then we know that $(\frac{30}{42})n = 48$. Thus, $n = (\frac{42}{30}) \cdot (48) \doteq 67$. Because 60 errors were found, the estimate is that $67 - 60$, or 7, errors remain undetected.

LOOKING BACK We might wonder what result is obtained if we use Betsy's probability of finding an error instead of Al's probability. If we use Al's 48 errors as a sample space, then Betsy found $\frac{30}{48}$ of these errors. Solving as before, we have $(\frac{30}{48}) \cdot n = 42$, and $n \doteq 67$. The estimate for the number of undetected errors is $67 - 60$, or 7. We see that it makes no difference which proofreader is chosen to make the estimates. Do you think it would be worthwhile to hire a third proofreader? Investigate this probability by trying various inputs for a third proofreader.

Another approach is to realize that this problem is a version of Example 8-13. Let n be the population of errors. Imagine that Al draws a sample of 48 errors, marks them, and returns them to the population. Betsy then draws 42 errors, of which 30 are marked. The total number of errors in the population is given by $(\frac{30}{42}) \cdot n = 48$, and $n \doteq 67$.

QUESTIONS FROM THE CLASSROOM

1. A student claims that if a fair coin is tossed and a head appears five times in a row, then, according to the law of averages, the probability of a tail on the next toss is greater than the probability of a head. What is your reply?

2. A student observes the spinner and claims that the color red has the highest probability of appearing since there are two red areas on the spinner. What is your reply?

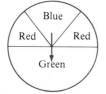

3. A student tosses a coin three times and tails appears each time. The student concludes that the coin is not fair. What is your response?

4. An experiment consists of tossing a coin twice. The student reasons that there are three possible outcomes; two heads, one head and one tail, or two tails. Thus, $P(HH) = \frac{1}{3}$. What is your reply?

5. A student says that there is really no need to learn the formulas for combinations and permutations. How do you reply?

6. Conditional probabilities can be determined by using tree diagrams. Why is the Multiplication Rule for Probabilities necessary?

7. In response to the question "If a fair die is rolled twice, what is the probability of rolling a pair of 5s?" a student replies, "One third, because $\frac{1}{6} + \frac{1}{6} = \frac{1}{3}$." How do you respond?

CHAPTER OUTLINE

I. Probability
   A. A **sample space** is the set of all possible **outcomes** of an **experiment.**
   B. Sample spaces can be modeled using **tree diagrams.**
   C. An **event** is a subset of a sample space.

D. Outcomes are **equally likely** if each outcome is as likely to occur as another.

E. If all outcomes of an experiment are equally likely, the **probability** of an event A from sample space S is given by

$$P(A) = \frac{n(A)}{n(S)}$$

F. An **impossible event** is an event with a probability of zero. An impossible event can never occur.

G. A **certain event** is an event with a probability of one. A certain event is sure to happen.

H. Two events are **mutually exclusive** if and only if exactly one of the events can occur at any given time, that is, the events are disjoint.

I. The probability of the **complement of an event** is given by $P(\bar{A}) = 1 - P(A)$, where A is the event and $\bar{A}$ is its complement.

*II. Conditional probability, independent events, and simulations

A. If A and B are events in a sample space, and $P(B) \neq 0$, the **conditional probability of A, given B,** denoted by $P(A|B)$, is defined as $P(A|B) = P(A \cap B)/P(B)$.

B. **Multiplication Rule for Probabilities**

$$P(A \cap B) = P(B) \cdot P(A|B)$$

C. Two events A and B are **independent** if $P(A|B) = P(A)$. If $P(A|B) \neq P(A)$, then events A and B are **dependent.**

D. **Simulations** can play an important part in probability. Fair coins, dice, spinners, and random-digit tables are useful in performing simulations.

*III. Odds and expectation

A. The **odds in favor** of an event A are given by

$$\frac{P(A)}{1 - P(A)}$$

B. The **odds against** an event A are given by

$$\frac{1 - P(A)}{P(A)}$$

C. If, in an experiment, the possible outcomes are numbers $a_1, a_2, \ldots, a_n$, occurring with probabilities $p_1, p_2, \ldots, p_n$, respectively, then the **mathematical expectation** E is defined as

$$E = a_1 \cdot p_1 + a_2 \cdot p_2 + a_3 \cdot p_3 + \cdots + a_n \cdot p_n$$

IV. Counting principles

A. **Fundamental Counting Principle** If an event M can occur in m ways and, after it has occurred, event N can occur in n ways, then event M followed by event N can occur in $m \cdot n$ ways.

B. **Permutations** are arrangements in which order is important. The formula for a permutation of n objects taken r at a time is

$$_nP_r = \frac{n!}{(n-r)!}$$

C. **Combinations** are arrangements in which order is *not* important. To find the number of combinations possible, first use the Fundamental Counting Principle to find the number of permutations and then divide by the number of ways in which each choice can be arranged.

$$_nC_r = \frac{n!}{r!(n-r)!}$$

D. The expression **$n!$,** called **n factorial,** represents the product of all the natural numbers less than or equal to n. $0!$ is defined as 1.

CHAPTER TEST

1. Suppose the names of the days of the week are placed in a box and one name is drawn at random.
   (a) List the sample space for this experiment.
   (b) List the event consisting of outcomes that the day drawn starts with the letter T.
   (c) What is the probability of drawing a day that starts with T?

2. Complete each of the following.
   (a) If A is an impossible event, then $P(A) = $ _____.
   (b) If A is a certain event, then $P(A) = $ _____.
   (c) If A is any event, then _____ $\leq P(A) \leq$ _____.
   (d) If A is any event, then $P(\bar{A}) = $ _____.

3. A box contains three red balls, five black balls, and four white balls. Suppose one ball is drawn at

random. Find the probability for each of the following events.

(a) A black ball is drawn.

(b) A black or a white ball is drawn.

(c) Neither a red nor a white ball is drawn.

(d) A red ball is not drawn.

(e) A black ball and a white ball are drawn.

(f) A black or white or red ball is drawn.

4. One card is selected at random from an ordinary set of 52 cards. Find the probability for each of the following events.

(a) A club is drawn.

(b) A spade and a 5 are drawn.

(c) A heart or a face card is drawn.

(d) A jack is not drawn.

5. A box contains five black balls and four white balls. If three balls are drawn one by one, find the probability that they are all white if the draws are made as follows.

(a) With replacement

(b) Without replacement

6. Suppose a three-stage rocket is launched into orbit. The probability for failure at stage one is $\frac{1}{10}$, at stage two is $\frac{1}{5}$, and at stage three is $\frac{1}{3}$. What is the probability for a successful flight?

7. Consider the two boxes in the figure. If a letter is drawn from box 1 and placed into box 2, and then a letter is drawn from box 2, what is the probability that the letter is an L?

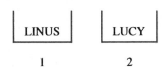

8. Use the following boxes for a two-stage experiment. First, select a box at random and then select a letter at random from the box. What is the probability of drawing an A?

9. Consider the boxes shown. Draw a ball from box 1 and put it into box 2. Then draw a ball from box 2 and put it into box 3. Finally, draw a ball from box 3. Construct a tree diagram for this experiment and calculate the probability that the last ball chosen is black.

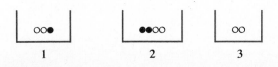

*10. What are the odds in favor of drawing a jack when one card is drawn from an ordinary deck of playing cards?

*11. A die is rolled once. What are the odds against rolling a prime number?

*12. If the odds in favor of a certain event are 3 to 5, what is the probability that the event will occur?

*13. A game consists of rolling two dice. Rolling double 1s pays $7.20. Rolling double 6s pays $3.60. Any other roll pays nothing. What is the expected value for this game?

*14. A total of 3000 tickets have been sold for a drawing. If one ticket is drawn for a single prize of $1000, what is a fair price for a ticket?

15. How many four-digit numbers can be formed if the first digit cannot be zero and the last digit must be two?

16. A club consists of ten members. In how many different ways can a group of three people be selected to go on a European trip?

17. In how many ways can the names of four candidates be listed on a ballot for an election?

18. Compute 100!/98!. (Look for shortcuts!)

19. Find the number of different ways that four flags can be displayed on a flagpole, one above the other, if ten different flags are available.

20. Five women live together in an apartment. Two of the women have blue eyes. If two of the women are chosen at random, what is the probability that they both have blue eyes?

21. Five horses—Deadbeat, Applefarm, Bandy, Cash, and Egglegs—run in a race.

(a) In how many ways can the first-, second-, and third-place horses be determined?

(b) Find the probability that Deadbeat finished first and Bandy finished second in the race.

(c) Find the probability that the first-, second-, and third-place horses are Deadbeat, Egglegs, and Cash, in that order.

22. Charles and Rudy each roll an ordinary die once. What is the probability that the number of Rudy's roll is greater than the number of Charles' roll?

23. Amy has a quiz on which she is to answer any three of the five questions. If she is equally versed on all questions and chooses three questions at random, what is the probability that question 1 is not chosen?

24. On a certain street there are three traffic lights. At any given time, the probability that a light is green is 0.3. What is the probability that a person will hit all three lights green?

25. Simplify each of the following.

(a) $(n-1)! \cdot n$ (b) $\dfrac{n!}{(n-1)!}$

*26. A three-stage rocket has the following probabilities for failure. The probability for failure at stage one is $\frac{1}{6}$; at stage two it is $\frac{1}{8}$; and at stage three it is $\frac{1}{10}$.

What is the probability of a successful flight, given that the first stage was successful?

*27. Two standard dice are rolled. What is the probability that a sum of 7 is rolled, given that at least one die shows an even number?

*28. How could each of the following be simulated by using a random-digit table?
   (a) Tossing a fair die
   (b) Picking 3 months at random from the 12 months of the year

(c) Spinning the spinner shown.

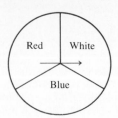

SELECTED BIBLIOGRAPHY

Armstrong, R., and P. Pederson, eds. *Probability and Statistics*. St. Louis, Mo.: Comprehensive School Mathematics Project, 1982.

Billstein, R. "A Fun Way to Introduce Probability." *The Arithmetic Teacher* 24 (January 1977):39–42.

Boas, R. "Snowfalls and Elephants, Pop Bottles and π." *The Mathematics Teacher* 74 (January 1981): 49–55.

Burns, M. "Put Some Probability in Your Classroom." *Arithmetic Teacher* 30 (March 1983):21–22.

Carpenter, T., M. Corbitt, H. Kepner, Jr., M. Lindquist, and R. Reys. "What Are the Chances of Your Students Knowing Probability?" *The Mathematics Teacher* 74 (May 1981):342–344.

Choate, S. "Activities in Applying Probability Ideas." *Arithmetic Teacher* 26 (February 1979):40–42.

Curlette, W. "The Randomized Response Technique: Using Probability to Ask Sensitive Questions." *The Mathematics Teacher* 73 (November 1980):618–621, 627.

Dahlke, R. "Geometrical Probability—A Source of Interesting and Significant Applications of High School Mathematics." *The Mathematics Teacher* 75 (December 1982):736–745.

Engel, A. *A Short Course in Probability*. St. Louis, Mo.: Comprehensive School Mathematics Project, 1970.

Enman, V. "Probability in the Intermediate Grades." *Arithmetic Teacher* 26 (February 1979):38–39.

Ernest, P. "Introducing the Concept of Probability." *The Mathematics Teacher* 77 (October 1977): 524–525.

Heiny, R. "Gambling, Casinos and Game Simulation." *The Mathematics Teacher* 74 (February 1981): 139–143.

Hinders, D. "Monte Carlo, Probability, Algebra, and Pi." *The Mathematics Teacher* 74 (May 1981): 335–339.

Horak, V., and W. Horak. "Take a Chance." *Arithmetic Teacher* 30 (May 1983):8–15.

Houser, L. "Baseball Monte Carlo Style." *The Mathematics Teacher* 74 (May 1981):340–341.

Jones, G. "A Case For Probability." *Arithmetic Teacher* 26 (February 1979):37, 57.

Lappan, G., and M. Winter. "Probability Simulation in Middle School." *The Mathematics Teacher* 73 (September 1980):446–449.

Milton, S., and J. Corbet. "Strategies in Yahtzee: An Exercise in Elementary Probability." *The Mathematics Teacher* 75 (December 1982):746–750.

Mullet, G. "Watch the Red, Not the Black." *The Mathematics Teacher* 73 (May 1980):349–353.

Reeves, C. "Volleyball and Probability." *The Mathematics Teacher* 71 (October 1978):595–596.

Richbart, L. "Probability and Statistics for Grades 9–11." *The Mathematics Teacher* 74 (May 1981): 346–348.

Rudd, D. "A Problem in Probability." *The Mathematics Teacher* 67 (February 1974):180–181.

Travers, K., and K. Gray. "The Monte Carlo Method: A Fresh Approach to Teaching Probabilistic Concepts." *The Mathematics Teacher* 74 (May 1981): 327–334.

Shaw, J. "Roll 'n' Spin." *Arithmetic Teacher* 31 (February 1984):6–9.

Shulte, A., ed. *The Teaching of Statistics and Probability*, 1981 Yearbook of the National Council of Teachers of Mathematics. Reston, Va.: National Council of Teachers of Mathematics, 1981.

Shulte, A., and S. Choate. *What Are My Chances?* Book A. Palo Alto, Ca.: Creative Publications, 1977.

Sterba, D. "Probability and Basketball." *The Mathematics Teacher* 74 (November 1981):624–627, 656.

Stone, J. "Place Value and Probability (with Promptings from Pascal)," *Arithmetic Teacher* 27 (March 1980): 47–49.

Woodward, E. "An Interesting Probability Problem." *The Mathematics Teacher* 75 (December 1982): 765–768.

Woodward, E. "A Second-Grade Probability and Graphing Lesson." *Arithmetic Teacher* 30 (March 1983):23–24.

CHAPTER 9

Statistics: An Introduction

Preliminary Problem

On a recent test, Professor Norma L. Kurf reported that in her two classes, composed of graduate and undergraduate students, the following results were obtained.

Class A
Graduate mean: 84
Undergraduate mean: 72

Class B
Graduate mean: 80
Undergraduate mean: 60

However, she startled the 24 students in each class by reporting that the overall means for classes A and B were 73 and 75, respectively. Several students thought this was impossible. Determine whether this situation could occur.

Introduction

For a long time, the word *statistics* referred to numerical information about state or political territories. The word itself comes from the Latin *statisticus,* meaning "of the state." Statistics as we know it today took several centuries and many great minds to develop. John Graunt was one of the first people to record his work in the area of statistics.

descriptive statistics   **Descriptive statistics** is the science of organizing and summarizing numerical data. Newspapers, magazines, radio, and television all use descriptive statistics to inform and persuade us on certain courses of action. Governments and organizations use statistics to make decisions that directly affect our lives. Statistics are both used and abused. Sometimes the abuse is of little consequence and entirely unintentional. This may or may not be true in Sally's case, below.

PEANUTS

© 1979 United Feature Syndicate, Inc.

Section 9-1   Statistical Graphs

Visual illustrations are an important part of statistics. Such illustrations take many forms—stem and leaf plots, frequency tables, histograms, bar graphs, frequency polygons or line graphs, pictographs, and circle graphs or pie charts.

STEM AND LEAF PLOTS

Consider the data in Table 9-1 containing the names of some of the presidents of the United States and the ages at which they died.

HISTORICAL NOTE

John Graunt (1620–1674) was an English haberdasher who studied birth and death records and discovered that more boys were born than girls. He also found that because men were more subject to death from occupational accidents, diseases, and war, the number of men and women at the age of marriage was about equal. This work led to the development of actuarial science, which is used by life insurance companies today.

Table 9-1

President	Age at Death
George Washington	67
John Adams	90
Thomas Jefferson	83
James Madison	85
James Monroe	73
John Q. Adams	80
Andrew Jackson	78
Martin Van Buren	79
William H. Harrison	68
John Tyler	71
James K. Polk	53
Zachary Taylor	65
Millard Fillmore	74
Franklin Pierce	64
James Buchanan	77
Abraham Lincoln	56
Andrew Johnson	66
Ulysses Grant	63
Rutherford Hayes	70
James Garfield	49
Chester Arthur	57
Grover Cleveland	71
Benjamin Harrison	67
William McKinley	58
Theodore Roosevelt	60
William Taft	72
Woodrow Wilson	67
Warren Harding	57
Calvin Coolidge	60
Herbert Hoover	90
Franklin Roosevelt	63
Harry Truman	88
Dwight Eisenhower	78
John Kennedy	46
Lyndon Johnson	64

raw data

stem and leaf plot

The ages of the presidents at their deaths might be referred to as **raw data.** The raw data may become more meaningful when it is summarized in a different way than it is in Table 9-1. For example, we might organize the ages in a **stem and leaf plot.** In Table 9-1, we see that the presidents died in their forties, fifties, sixties, seventies, eighties, or nineties. Thus, in this set of data, we are to concentrate on numbers from 40 to 99, or, explicitly, from 46 to 90. For our display of the data, we choose the stems as the tens digits of the numbers in the raw data. The leaves are the units digits of the numbers in the raw data. The plot itself is formed by placing the stems in rows from least to greatest on the left side of a vertical line as shown in Figure 9-1(a). We write only the tens digits as stems because the leaves, which represent the units digits of the ages, are to be given on the right side of the vertical line and on the row containing their stem, as in Figure 9-1(b). For example, the top row has 4 as a stem with 9 and 6 as leaves. These numbers represent the ages 49 and 46, the death ages of James Garfield and John Kennedy, from Table 9-1.

Figure 9-1

Stem	Leaf		Stem	Leaf
4			4	96
5			5	36787
6			6	785463707034
7			7	38914701128
8			8	3508
9			9	00
	(a)			(b)

In some sense, the data in Figure 9-1(b) are still unordered because the leaves are not in order from least to greatest on a given row. To make an ordered stem and leaf plot, we arrange the leaves on their given rows from least to greatest starting at the left, as in Figure 9-2.

Figure 9-2

Stem	Leaf
4	69
5	36778
6	003344567778
7	01112347889
8	0358
9	00

We summarize the construction of a stem and leaf plot as follows:

1. Find the high and low values of the data.
2. Decide on the stems.
3. List the stems in a column from least to greatest.
4. Use each piece of data to list the leaves to the right of the stems on the appropriate rows.
5. If the plot is to be ordered, list the leaves in order from least to greatest.

Table 9-2

TV Program	Percent of Households Watching
60 Minutes	28.1
Dallas	25.6
M*A*S*H	25.1
Dynasty	23.5
Three's Company	22.7
Newhart	22.6
Magnum, P.I.	21.8
Gloria	21.0
9 to 5	20.9
Archie Bunker's Place	20.8
Laverne and Shirley	20.5
Love Boat	20.4
Happy Days	20.2
Fall Guy	20.2
Falcon Crest	20.0

Source: *The World Almanac and Book of Facts, 1984*. New York: Newspaper Enterprise Association, 1983.

Example 9-1 shows another stem and leaf plot in which the stems are not just the tens digits of the raw data.

Example 9-1

Table 9-2 shows the Nielsen average-audience estimates of percents of households watching various television programs in November, 1982. Construct a stem and leaf plot depicting the data in Table 9-2.

Solution

To construct a stem and leaf plot for the data, we first note that the lowest estimate is 20.0 and the highest is 28.1. Hence, we could list the stems from 20 to 28 in intervals of 1. The leaves would then represent the tenths in the data. The unordered plot is shown in Figure 9-3.

Figure 9-3

Stem	Leaf
20	9854220
21	80
22	76
23	5
24	
25	61
26	
27	
28	1

A stem and leaf plot shows how wide the range of values is that the data cover; where the values are concentrated; the symmetry, if any, of the data; where gaps in the data are; and whether any data points are decidedly different from the rest of the data.

FREQUENCY TABLES

frequency table

A slightly different way to display data is to use a frequency table. A **frequency table** shows how many times a certain piece of data occurs. A frequency table may be constructed with or without the use of a stem and leaf plot. For example, suppose that Dan offers the following deal. He rolls a die. If any number other than 6 appears, he pays $5. If a 6 appears, you pay him $5. With a fair die, the probability of Dan's winning is $\frac{1}{6}$. Thus, it is not likely that Dan will win unless the die is loaded, or 6 appears more often than normally expected. The data in Table 9-3 show the results of 60 rolls with Dan's die.

Table 9-3

			Results of Dan's Die Tosses						
1	6	6	2	6	3	6	6	4	6
6	2	6	6	4	5	6	6	1	6
1	6	6	5	6	6	4	6	5	6
6	5	6	2	4	2	5	6	3	4
3	6	1	6	3	6	6	1	6	6
6	4	6	3	6	3	6	4	6	5

The raw data of Table 9-3 may be summarized as shown in the frequency table in Table 9-4.

Table 9-4

Number	Tally	Frequency
1	ⅢⅢ	5
2	‖‖	4
3	ⅢⅢ‖	6
4	ⅢⅢ‖‖	7
5	ⅢⅢ‖	6
6	ⅢⅢ ⅢⅢ ⅢⅢ ⅢⅢ ⅢⅢ ⅢⅢ ‖‖	32
	Total	60

According to the frequency table, 6 appears many more times than could be expected from a fair die. (If the die were fair, the number of 6s should be close to $\frac{1}{6} \cdot 60$, or 10.)

BAR GRAPHS

histogram

The data from Table 9-4 may be pictured graphically as well as in a table. Figure 9-4 shows a **histogram** that gives a good picture of the results from throwing Dan's die. A histogram is made up of adjoining vertical rectangles, or bars, comparing various frequencies. The numbers on the die are shown on the horizontal axis. The numbers along the vertical axis give the scale for the frequency. The frequencies of the numbers on the die are shown by the bars, which are all the same width. The higher the bar, the greater the frequency. The scale on the vertical axis must also be of uniform interval size. In addition, all histograms should have the axes labeled and should include a title telling what the graph contains.

Figure 9-4

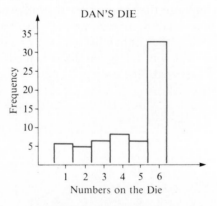

bar graph

A histogram is a particular kind of **bar graph.** A typical bar graph showing the heights in centimeters of five students is given in Figure 9-5. This bar graph is not a histogram because of the spaces between the bars.

Figure 9-5

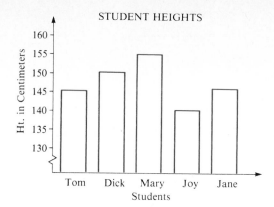

The break in the vertical axis, denoted by a squiggle, indicates that part of the scale has been omitted. Therefore, the scale is not accurate from 0 to 130. The height of each bar represents the height in centimeters of each student named on the horizontal axis. Each space between the bars is usually one half the width of the bars.

FREQUENCY POLYGONS AND LINE GRAPHS

frequency polygon
line graph

Another graphic form for presenting the data from a frequency table is a **frequency polygon,** or **line graph.** A frequency polygon can be plotted from a frequency table, or it can be constructed from a histogram by using line segments to connect the midpoints of the tops of each of the rectangular bars. Figure 9-6(a) shows the frequency polygon (line graph) for the data from Table 9-4. Figure 9-6(b) shows how to obtain the same frequency polygon from the histogram of Figure 9-4.

Figure 9-6

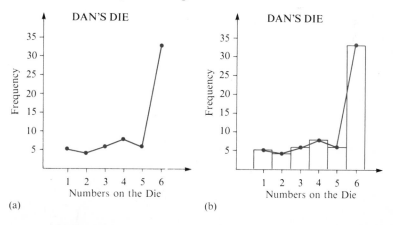

PICTOGRAPHS

pictograph

A **pictograph** is a graph in which pictures or symbols are used. A pictograph uses one or more rows of identical symbols, has a key explaining the meaning of the symbol, and is frequently used to compare output. Examples are shown in Figure 9-7.

Figure 9-7

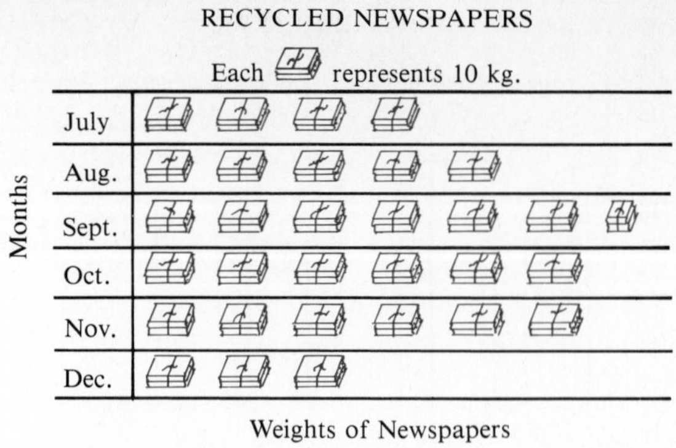

RECYCLED NEWSPAPERS

Each 📰 represents 10 kg.

(a)

HILLVIEW FIFTH-GRADE
STUDENT DISTRIBUTION

Each 🧍 represents 5 students

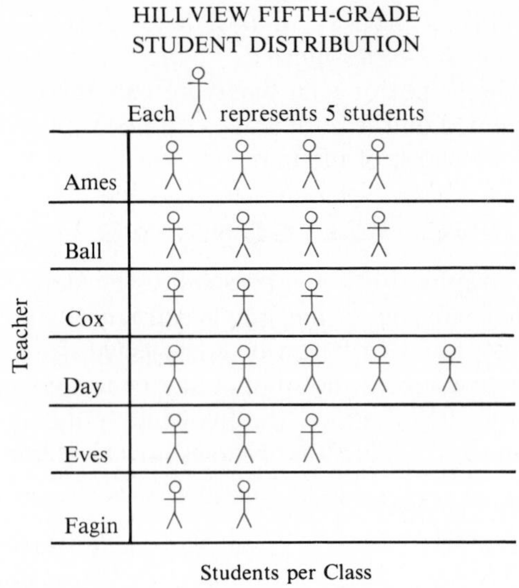

(b)

A major disadvantage of pictographs is seen in Figure 9-7(a). The month of September contains a partial bundle of newspapers. It is impossible to accurately tell the weight of that bundle. Other examples of graphs in student texts are seen on page 397, which is from *Heath Mathematics,* 1987, Grade 7.

GROUPED DATA

The greater the amount of data, the more difficult it becomes to construct a frequency table for individual items. In such cases, the data may be grouped. For example, consider the scores in Table 9-5.

Table 9-5

50 Student Scores									
52	56	25	56	68	73	66	64	56	100
20	39	9	50	98	54	54	40	50	96
36	44	18	97	109	65	21	60	44	54
92	49	37	94	72	88	89	35	59	34
48	32	15	53	84	72	88	16	52	60

Peter Fairbrother kept track of his work time by making this broken-line graph.

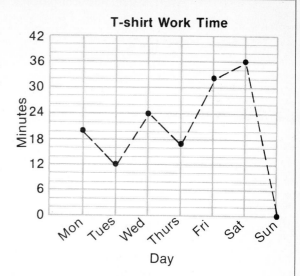

T-shirt Work Time

8. <u>Estimate</u> the number of minutes Peter worked on Thursday. On Friday.

9. On how many days did he work more than 20 minutes?

10. About how many minutes did he work during the week?

11. How many minutes did he average per day?

Brooke made this pictograph to show how much money they took in each week.

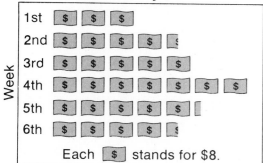

T-shirt Weekly Sales

Each $ stands for $8.

12. What were the sales during the first week? The fourth week? The fifth week?

13. How many weeks were sales more than $30? Less than $50?

14. What was the sales total for the 6 weeks? What was the weekly average?

Brooke made a circle graph of the expenses.

15. What item represented the greatest expense?

16. How much money was spent for stencils?

★ 17. What was the profit (sales less expenses) for the sale? (See exercise 14.)

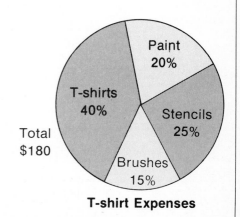

T-shirt Expenses

A stem and leaf plot for the data in Table 9-5 is shown in Figure 9-8.

Figure 9-8

Stem	Leaf
0	9
1	856
2	051
3	692754
4	84904
5	266034460924
6	856400
7	232
8	4898
9	27486
10	09

classes

grouped frequency table

The construction of the stem and leaf plot leads in a natural way to a grouping of scores in intervals. The intervals are called **classes;** for the data in Figure 9-8, the classes are the following: 0–9, 10–19, 20–29, 30–39, 40–49, 50–59, 60–69, 70–79, 80–89, 90–99, 100–109. Each class has an interval size of 10; that is, ten different scores can fall within the interval 0 through 9. (Students often incorrectly report the interval size as 9 because $9 - 0 = 9$). The **grouped frequency table** for the data in Table 9-5 with intervals of length 10 is given in Table 9-6.

Table 9-6

Classes	Tally	Frequency
0–9	|	1
10–19	|||	3
20–29	|||	3
30–39	ᚎᚎ |	6
40–49	ᚎᚎ	5
50–59	ᚎᚎ ᚎᚎ ||	12
60–69	ᚎᚎ |	6
70–79	|||	3
80–89	||||	4
90–99	ᚎᚎ	5
100–109	||	2

Figure 9-8 contains more information than Table 9-6 because the raw scores themselves are not available in Table 9-6. Although Table 9-6 shows that 12 scores fall in the interval 50–59, it does not show the particular scores in the interval. The greater the size of the interval, the greater the amount of information lost (possibly beyond the usable point). The choice of the interval size may vary. Classes should be chosen to accommodate *all* the data, and each item should fit into only one class; that is, the classes should not overlap.

A bar graph can be used to display the data from a grouped frequency table. A bar graph for the data in Table 9-6 is shown in Figure 9-9(a). To construct a histogram for the data in Table 9-6, we find the midpoint of each class to mark the horizontal axis as follows: $(0 + 9)/2 = 4.5, (10 + 19)/2 = 14.5$, and so on. The completed histogram is given in Figure 9-9(b).

Figure 9-9

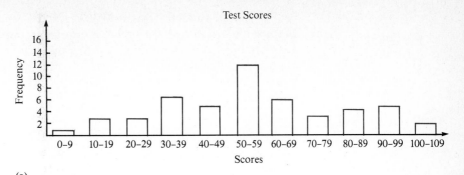

(a)

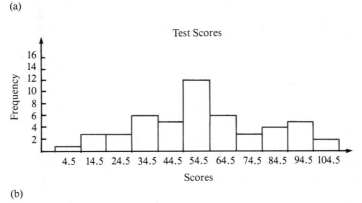

(b)

CIRCLE GRAPHS

circle graph / pie chart

Another type of graph used to represent data is the circle graph. **A circle graph,** or **pie chart,** consists of a circular region partitioned into disjoint sections, with each section representing a part or percentage of the whole. A circle graph shows how parts are related to the whole. This type of picture usually is used when money is involved and various distributions of dollars are to be displayed.

Suppose two college roommates, Larry and Moe, kept a record of their expenses and at the end of the quarter made Table 9-7 based on their records. Figure 9-10 shows a circle graph with the data. A circle has a total of 360 degrees, written 360°. Thus, 360° represents the total expenses for the month, or 100% of the expenses. Since food is 30% of the total expenses, 30% of

Figure 9-10

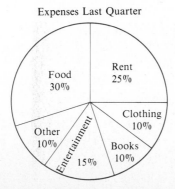

Expenses Last Quarter

360° is devoted to food. Thus, 0.30(360°), or 108°, is devoted to food expense. In the same way, 0.25(360°), or 90°, is devoted to rent. The remaining sections are computed in a similar manner. A protractor is used to construct circle graphs, and a calculator is useful in determining the percentages. The circle graph is usually marked with section identification and the percent of the circle represented by the section.

Table 9-7

Item	Percent of Total
Food	30
Rent	25
Clothing	10
Books	10
Entertainment	15
Other	10

Example 9-2

Construct a circle graph for the following data obtained by tossing Dan's loaded die 60 times.

Number	Frequency
1	5
2	4
3	6
4	7
5	6
6	32
	$\overline{60}$

Solution

Two computation steps are necessary to prepare the data for a circle graph. We need to determine the number of degrees in each section in order to draw the graph, and we need to determine what percent of the circle is pictured in each section. Table 9-8 shows this information. A circle graph depicting the information is given in Figure 9-11.

Table 9-8

Item	Degrees	Percent
1	$\frac{5}{60} \cdot 360°$, or 30°	$\frac{5}{60} \doteq 8.3\%$
2	$\frac{4}{60} \cdot 360°$, or 24°	$\frac{4}{60} \doteq 6.7\%$
3	$\frac{6}{60} \cdot 360°$, or 36°	$\frac{6}{60} = 10\%$
4	$\frac{7}{60} \cdot 360°$, or 42°	$\frac{7}{60} \doteq 11.7\%$
5	$\frac{6}{60} \cdot 360°$, or 36°	$\frac{6}{60} = 10\%$
6	$\frac{32}{60} \cdot 360°$, or 192°	$\frac{32}{60} \doteq 53.3\%$

Figure 9-11

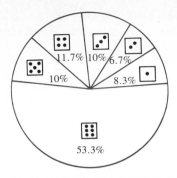

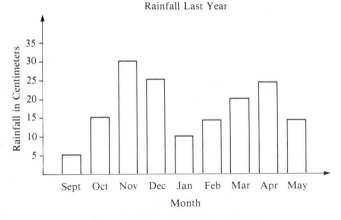

PROBLEM SET 9-1

1. The figure shows a bar graph for the rainfall in centimeters during the last school year. Answer each of the following questions.
   (a) Which month had the greatest rainfall and how much did it have?
   (b) What were the amounts of rainfall in October, December, and January?

Rainfall Last Year

2. A list of presidents with the number of children for each follows.
   1. Washington, 0
   3. Jefferson, 6
   5. Monroe, 2
   7. Jackson, 0
   9. W. H. Harrison, 10
   11. Polk, 0
   2. J. Adams, 5
   4. Madison, 0
   6. J. Q. Adams, 4
   8. Van Buren, 4
   10. Tyler, 14
   12. Taylor, 6
   13. Fillmore, 2
   15. Buchanan, 0
   17. A. Johnson, 5
   19. Hayes, 8
   21. Arthur, 3
   23. B. Harrison, 3
   25. T. Roosevelt, 6
   27. Wilson, 3
   29. Coolidge, 2
   31. F. D. Roosevelt, 6
   33. Eisenhower, 2
   35. L. B. Johnson, 2
   37. Ford, 4
   39. Reagan, 4
   14. Pierce, 3
   16. Lincoln, 4
   18. Grant, 4
   20. Garfield, 7
   22. Cleveland, 5
   24. McKinley, 2
   26. Taft, 3
   28. Harding, 0
   30. Hoover, 2
   32. Truman, 1
   34. Kennedy, 3
   36. Nixon, 2
   38. Carter, 3
   (a) Make a frequency table for these data.
   (b) What is the most frequent number of children?

3. The given data represent total car sales for Johnson's car lot from January through June. Draw a bar graph for the data.

Month	Jan.	Feb.	Mar.	Apr.	May	June
Number of Cars Sold	90	86	92	96	90	100

4. Five coins are tossed 64 times. A distribution for the number of heads obtained is shown.

Number of Heads	0	1	2	3	4	5
Frequency		2	10	20	20	10	2

   (a) Draw a histogram for the data.
   (b) Draw a frequency polygon for the data.

5. The grade distribution for the final examination for the mathematics course for elementary teachers is shown.

Grade	Frequency
A	4
B	10
C	37
D	8
F	1

(a) Draw a bar graph for the data.
(b) Draw a circle graph for the data.

6. The following are the amounts (rounded to the nearest dollar) paid by 25 students for textbooks during the fall term.

35	37	53
42	37	62
33	16	30
48	23	50
45	49	39
42	62	51
50	60	40
39	58	23
41		

(a) Draw a stem and leaf plot to illustrate the data.
(b) Construct a grouped frequency table for the data, starting the first class at $15.00 with intervals of $5.00 each.
(c) Draw a histogram for the data.
(d) Draw a frequency polygon for the data.

7. Make a pictograph to represent the data, using 🥛 to represent 10 glasses of lemonade sold.

GLASSES OF LEMONADE SOLD

	Tally	Frequency
Monday	卌 卌 卌	15
Tuesday	卌 卌 卌 卌	20
Wednesday	卌 卌 卌 卌 卌 卌	30
Thursday	卌	5
Friday	卌 卌	10

8. Give an example of a situation in which a circle graph would be preferable to a bar graph or line graph.

9. Give an example of a situation in which a line graph would be preferable to a bar graph.

10. The following graphs give the temperatures for a certain day. Which graph is more helpful for guessing the actual temperature at 10:00 A.M.? Why?

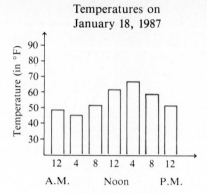

Temperatures on
January 18, 1987

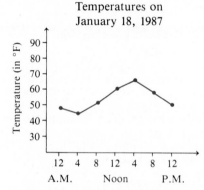

Temperatures on
January 18, 1987

11. Give an example of a set of data in which a stem and leaf plot is more informative than a histogram.

12. The circle graph shown is from *Economic Road Maps*, Nos. 1898–1899, March 1981. Use it to answer the following.
(a) Find the number of degrees in the sections representing Italy and Japan.
(b) Which country had the most investments?

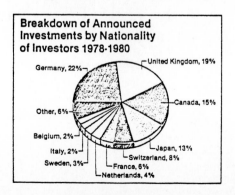

Breakdown of Announced
Investments by Nationality
of Investors 1978-1980

Germany, 22%
United Kingdom, 19%
Other, 6%
Canada, 15%
Belgium, 2%
Italy, 2%
Japan, 13%
Sweden, 3%
Switzerland, 8%
France, 6%
Netherlands, 4%

Section 9-2

Measures of Central Tendency and Variation

In the previous section, we examined data by looking at graphs and tables involving the data. It often is convenient to describe a set of data by choosing a single number that indicates where the data in the set are centered or concentrated.

Examine the following set of data for three teachers, each of whom claims that his or her class scored better than the other two classes.

Mr. Smith: 62, 94, 95, 98, 98

Mr. Jones: 62, 62, 98, 99, 100

Ms. Leed: 40, 62, 85, 99, 99

All these teachers are correct in their assertions. Each one has used a different number to characterize the scores in his or her particular class. In general, there are three different ways to compute a number to characterize where data are centered: the arithmetic mean, the median, and the mode. As we study these numbers, *a calculator is a definite aid.*

COMPUTING MEANS

arithmetic mean

average / mean

The number most commonly used to characterize a set of data is the **arithmetic mean,** frequently called the **average,** or the **mean.** For example, suppose that three office mates make $20,000, $21,000, and $25,000 annually. The mean salary is the salary that each worker would make if the total earnings in the office were divided equally among the three people, that is, (20,000 + 21,000 + 25,000)/3, or $22,000.

To find the mean of scores for each of the teachers given above, we find the sum of the scores in each case and divide by 5, the number of scores.

Mean (Smith): $\dfrac{62 + 94 + 95 + 98 + 98}{5} = \dfrac{447}{5} = 89.4$

Mean (Jones): $\dfrac{62 + 62 + 98 + 99 + 100}{5} = \dfrac{421}{5} = 84.2$

Mean (Leed): $\dfrac{40 + 62 + 85 + 99 + 99}{5} = \dfrac{385}{5} = 77$

Thus, using the mean, Mr. Smith's class scored better than the other two classes. In general, we calculate the mean as follows.

DEFINITION

The **mean** of the numbers $x_1, x_2, \ldots, x_n$, denoted by $\bar{x}$ and read "x bar," is given by

$$\bar{x} = \frac{x_1 + x_2 + x_3 + \cdots + x_n}{n}$$

COMPUTING MEDIANS

median   The value exactly in the middle of an ordered set of numbers is called the **median.** To find the median for the teachers' scores, arrange each of their scores in increasing order and pick the middle score. Intuitively, half the scores are greater than the median and half are less.

Median (Smith):   62, 94, ⑨⑤, 98, 98   median = 95

Median (Jones):   62, 62, ⑨⑧, 99, 100   median = 98

Median (Leed):   40, 62, ⑧⑤, 99, 99   median = 85

Thus, using the median, Mr. Jones' class scored better than the other two classes.

With an odd number of scores, as in the preceding case, the median is the middle score. With an even number of scores, the median is defined as the mean of the middle two scores; that is, to find the median, add the middle two scores and divide by 2. For example, the median of the scores 64, 68, 70, 74, 82, 90 is

$$\frac{(70 + 74)}{2}, \text{ or } 72$$

In general, to find the median for a set of n numbers, proceed as follows.

1. Arrange the numbers in order from least to greatest.
2. (a) If n is odd, the median is the middle number.
      (b) If n is even, the median is the mean of the two middle numbers.

FINDING MODES

mode   The **mode** of a set of data is the number that appears most frequently, if there is one. In some distributions, no number appears more than once, and other distributions may have more than one mode. For example, the set of scores 64, 79, 80, 82, 90 has no mode (or five modes). The set of scores 64, 75, bimodal   75, 82, 90, 90, 98 is **bimodal** (two modes), because both 75 and 90 are modes. It is possible for a set of data to have too many modes for this type of average to be useful.

For the three classes listed earlier, if the mode is used as a criterion, then Ms. Leed's class scored better than the other two classes.

Mode (Smith):   62, 94, 95, 98, 98   mode = 98

Mode (Jones):   62, 62, 98, 99, 100   mode = 62

Mode (Leed):   40, 62, 85, 99, 99   mode = 99

Example 9-3

Find the (a) mean, (b) median, and (c) mode for the following collection of data.

60, 60, 70, 95, 95, 100

Solution

(a) $\bar{x} = \dfrac{60 + 60 + 70 + 95 + 95 + 100}{6} = \dfrac{480}{6} = 80$

(b) The median is $\dfrac{(70 + 95)}{6}$, or 82.5.

(c) The set of data is bimodal and has both 60 and 95 as modes.

Although the mean is the number most commonly used to describe a set of data, it may not always be the best number to use. Suppose, for example, a company employs twenty people. The president of the company earns $200,000, the vice president earns $75,000, and eighteen employees earn $10,000 each. The mean salary for this company is

$$\frac{\$200{,}000 + \$75{,}000 + 18(\$10{,}000)}{20} = \frac{\$455{,}000}{20} = \$22{,}750$$

In this case, the mean salary of $22,750 is not representative, and either the median or mode, which are both $10,000, would better describe the typical salary. Notice that *the mean is affected by extreme values.*

In most cases, the median is not affected by extreme values. The median, however, can be misleading. For example, suppose nine students make the following scores on a test: 30, 35, 40, 40, 92, 92, 93, 98, 99. From the median score of 92, one might possibly infer that the individuals all scored very well, yet 92 is certainly not a typical score.

The mode can be misleading in describing a set of data with very few items or many frequently occurring items. For example, the scores 40, 42, 50, 62, 63, 65, 98, 98 have a mode of 98, which is not a typical value.

PROBLEM I

Lacking time to record his students' homework grades, Dr. Van Gruff asked them to keep track of their own grades. A few days later, Dr. Van Gruff asked the students to report their grades. One of the students, Eddy, had lost his papers but remembered the grades on four of six assignments—100, 82, 74, and 60. Also, according to Eddy, the mean of all six papers was 69, and the other two papers had identical grades. What were the grades on Eddy's other two homework papers?

UNDERSTANDING THE PROBLEM Eddy reported that he had scores of 100, 82, 74, and 60 on four of his six papers, that the mean of all six papers was 69, and that he had identical scores on the missing two grades. The problem is to determine the two missing grades from this information.

DEVISING A PLAN Because the mean is obtained by finding the sum of the scores and then dividing by the number of scores, which is six, if we let x stand for each of the two missing grades, we have

$$69 = \frac{100 + 82 + 74 + 60 + x + x}{6}$$

To find the missing grades, we solve this equation for x.

CARRYING OUT THE PLAN We now solve the equation as follows.

$$69 = \frac{100 + 82 + 74 + 60 + x + x}{6}$$

$$69 = \frac{316 + 2x}{6}$$

$$49 = x$$

Since the solution to the equation is $x = 49$, we conclude that each of the two missing scores was 49.

LOOKING BACK The answer of 49 seems reasonable since the mean of 69 is below three of the four given scores. This can be easily checked by computing the mean of the scores 100, 82, 74, 60, 49, 49 and showing that it is indeed 69.

MEASURES OF DISPERSION

The choice of which number to use to represent a particular set of data is not always easy. In the example involving the three teachers, each teacher chose the number that best suited his or her needs. For clarity and honesty, the number that is used should always be specified. However, in many cases, no single number gives adequate information about a set of data. The need for other numbers to describe data will be apparent in the following discussion.

Suppose Professors Abel and Babel each taught a section of a statistics course and each professor had six students. Both professors gave the same final exam. The results, along with the means for each group of scores, are given in Table 9-9 with stem and leaf plots in Figure 9-12(a) and (b), respectively.

Table 9-9

Abel	Babel
100	70
80	70
70	60
50	60
50	60
10	40
$\bar{x} = \dfrac{360}{6} = 60$	$\bar{x} = \dfrac{360}{6} = 60$

As seen in the stem and leaf plots, the sets of data are very different. The first set of scores is more spread out, or varies more, than the second. However, each set of scores has 60 as the mean. Each median also equals 60. Although the mean and median for these two groups are the same, the two distributions of scores are very different.

There are several ways to measure the spread (variation) of data. The simplest way is to subtract the least number from the greatest number. This

Figure 9-12

Stem	Leaf
1	0
2	
3	
4	
5	00
6	
7	0
8	0
9	
10	0

Stem	Leaf
4	0
5	
6	000
7	00

(a)   (b)

range

difference is called the **range.** The range for Professor Abel's class is $100 - 10$, or 90. The range for Professor Babel's class is $70 - 40$, or 30. Although the range is easy to calculate, it has the disadvantage of being determined by two scores. For example, the sets of scores 10, 20, 25, 30, 100 and 10, 80, 85, 90, 90, 100 both have a range of 90.

There are several ways to measure the spread of data that are more useful than the range. We consider the two most commonly used measures of variation: variance and standard deviation. The two measures are essentially

standard deviation

equivalent, but the **standard deviation** has the same units as the original data and is particularly useful in making precise statements about the spread of data.

variance

The steps for calculating the **variance** v and standard deviation s of n numbers are as follows.

1. Find the mean of the numbers.
2. Subtract the mean from each number.
3. Square each difference found in step 2.
4. Find the sum of the squares in step 3.
5. Divide by n to obtain the variance.
6. Find the square root of v to obtain the standard deviation.

These six steps can be summarized for the numbers $x_1, x_2, x_3, \ldots, x_n$ as follows, where $\bar{x}$ is the mean of these numbers.

$$s = \sqrt{v} = \sqrt{\frac{(x_1 - \bar{x})^2 + (x_2 - \bar{x})^2 + (x_3 - \bar{x})^2 + \cdots + (x_n - \bar{x})^2}{n}}$$

Remark   In some textbooks, the formula just given involves division by $n - 1$ instead of n. Division by $n - 1$ is more useful for advanced work in statistics.

The variances and standard deviations for the final exam data for the classes of Professors Abel and Babel are calculated by using Tables 9-10 and 9-11, respectively.

The standard deviation is a large number when the values from a set of data are widely spread. The standard deviation is a small number (close to 0) when the data values are close together. This is further illustrated in Example 9-4.

Table 9-10

Abel's Scores

x	$x - \bar{x}$	$(x - \bar{x})^2$
100	40	1600
80	20	400
70	10	100
50	$^-10$	100
50	$^-10$	100
10	$^-50$	2500
Totals 360	0	4800

$$\bar{x} = \frac{360}{6} = 60$$

$$v = \frac{4800}{6} = 800$$

$$s = \sqrt{800} \doteq 28.3$$

Table 9-11

Babel's Scores

x	$x - \bar{x}$	$(x - \bar{x})^2$
70	10	100
70	10	100
60	0	0
60	0	0
60	0	0
40	$^-20$	400
Totals 360	0	600

$$\bar{x} = \frac{360}{6} = 60$$

$$v = \frac{600}{6} = 100$$

$$s = \sqrt{100} = 10$$

Example 9-4

Professor Boone gave two exams. Exam A had grades of 0, 0, 0, 100, 100, and 100, and exam B had grades of 50, 50, 50, 50, 50, and 50.
Find the following for each exam.
(a) The mean   (b) The median   (c) The standard deviation

Solution

(a) The means for exams A and B are each 50.
(b) The medians for the exams are each 50.
(c) The standard deviations for exams A and B are given below.

$$s_A = \sqrt{\frac{3(0 - 50)^2 + 3(100 - 50)^2}{6}} = 50$$

$$s_B = \sqrt{\frac{6(50 - 50)^2}{6}} = 0$$

Example 9-5

Given the data 32, 41, 47, 53, 57, find each of the following.

(a) The range   (b) The variance
(c) The standard deviation

Solution

(a) The range is $57 - 32$, or 25.
(b) The variance v is computed by using the information in the table.

x	$x - \bar{x}$	$(x - \bar{x})^2$
32	⁻14	196
41	⁻5	25
47	1	1
53	7	49
57	11	121
Totals 230	0	392

$$\bar{x} = \frac{230}{5} = 46$$

$$v = \frac{392}{5} = 78.4$$

(c) $s = \sqrt{78.4} \doteq 8.9$

BRAIN TEASER

The speeds of racing cars were timed after 3 miles, $4\frac{1}{2}$ miles, and 6 miles. Freddy averaged 140 miles per hour (mph) for the first 3 miles, 168 mph for the next $1\frac{1}{2}$ miles, and 210 mph for the last $1\frac{1}{2}$ miles. What was his mean speed for the total 6-mile run?

PROBLEM SET 9-2

1. Calculate the mean, median, and mode for each of the following collections of data.
   (a) 2, 8, 7, 8, 5, 8, 10, 5
   (b) 10, 12, 12, 14, 20, 16, 12, 14, 11
   (c) 18, 22, 22, 17, 30, 18, 12
   (d) 82, 80, 63, 75, 92, 80, 92, 90, 80, 80
   (e) 5, 5, 5, 5, 5, 10
2. Suppose each of ten students scored 50 on a test. Find the mean, median, and mode of the test scores.
3. The mean score on a set of 20 tests is 75. What is the sum of the 20 test scores?
4. The tram at a ski area has a capacity of 50 people with a load limit of 7500 pounds. What is the mean weight of the passengers if the tram is loaded to capacity?
5. The mean for a set of 28 scores is 80. Suppose 2 more students take the test and score 60 and 50. What is the new mean?
6. The names and ages for each person in a family of five follow.

Name	Age
Dick	40
Jane	36
Kirk	8
Jean	6
Scott	2

(a) What is the mean age?
(b) Find the mean of the ages 5 years from now.
(c) Find the mean 10 years from now.
(d) Describe the relationships between the means found in (a), (b), and (c).

7. Ten alumni of a state college are chosen at random and asked their annual incomes, which are $15,000, $20,000, $18,000, $28,000, $12,000, $30,000, $20,000, $14,000, $20,000, and $50,000. Find the mean, median, and mode for these incomes.

8. Suppose you own a hat shop and decide to order hats in only *one* size for the coming season. To decide which size to order, you look at last year's sales figures, which are itemized according to size. Should you find the mean, median, or mode for the data?

9. The results of Jon's fall quarter grades follow. Find his grade point average for the term (A = 4, B = 3, C = 2, D = 1, F = 0).

Course	Credits	Grades
Math	5	B
English	3	A
Physics	5	C
German	3	D
Handball	1	A

10. If the mean weight of seven linemen on a football team is 230 pounds and the mean weight of the four backfield members is 190 pounds, what is the mean weight of the eleven-man team?

11. A total of 210 people stayed at the Rancho Costa Plenty over the weekend for a total cost of $67,200. What was the mean cost per person?

12. If 99 people had a mean income of $12,000, how much is the mean income increased by the addition of a single income of $200,000?

13. The following table gives the annual salaries for the 40 players of a certain professional football team.
    (a) Find the mean annual salary for the team.
    (b) Find the standard deviation of the salaries.

Salary	Number of Players
$18,000	2
22,000	4
26,000	4
35,000	3
38,000	12
44,000	8
50,000	4
80,000	2
150,000	1

14. For each of the following sets of data, find the range, the variance, and the standard deviation.
    (a) 5, 7, 8, 9, 1
    (b) 18, 32, 17, 43, 63, 10, 35, 90, 80, 72

15. What is the standard deviation of the heights of seven trapeze artists if their heights are 175 cm, 182 cm, 190 cm, 180 cm, 192 cm, 172 cm, and 190 cm?

16. What happens to the mean and standard deviation of a set of data when the same number is added to each value in the data?

17. (a) If all the numbers in a set are equal, what is the standard deviation?

(b) If the standard deviation of a set of numbers is zero, must all the numbers in the set be equal?

18. In a Math 131 class at DiPaloma University, the grades on the first exam were as follows.

```
96  71  43  77  75  76  61
83  71  58  97  76  74  91
74  71  77  83  87  93  79
```

(a) Find the mean average.
(b) Find the median score.
(c) Find the mode.
(d) Find the variance of the scores.
(e) Find the standard deviation of the scores.

★19. Show that the following formula for variance is equivalent to the one given in the text.

$$v = \frac{x_1^2 + x_2^2 + \cdots + x_n^2}{n} - \bar{x}^2$$

Review Problems

20. Raw test scores from a history test are as follows.

```
86  85  87  96  55
90  94  82  68  77
88  89  85  74  90
72  80  76  88  73
64  79  73  85  93
```

(a) Construct a stem and leaf plot for the given data.
(b) Construct a grouped frequency table for these scores with intervals of 5, starting the first class at 55.
(c) Draw a histogram for the data.
(d) Draw a frequency polygon for the data.
(e) If a circle graph were drawn for the grouped data in (b), how many degrees would be in the section representing the 85–89 interval?

HISTORICAL NOTE

Abraham De Moivre (1667–1754), a French Huguenot, was the first to develop and study the normal curve. Along with this, he was one of the first to study actuarial information and did work in trigonometry with complex numbers.

*Section 9-3

Normal Distributions

A histogram drawn to depict the frequencies of many sets of data may resemble the one shown in Figure 9-13.

Figure 9-13

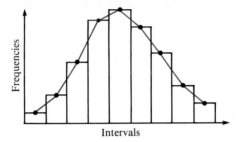

If the frequency polygon is sketched on the histogram as in Figure 9-13, we see a mound-shaped curve. In statistics, the Empirical Rule relates mound-shaped distributions and standard deviations to the measurements being depicted.

DEFINITION

empirical rule

> The **Empirical Rule** applies to sets of data with frequency polygons that are mound-shaped.
> (a) Approximately 68% of the data will fall within one standard deviation of the mean.
> (b) Approximately 95% of the data will fall within two standard deviations of the mean.
> (c) Almost all the data will fall within three standard deviations of the mean.

normal curve

The Empirical Rule was taken from the study of a normal curve and developed as a rule of thumb. A **normal curve** is a smooth, bell-shaped curve that depicts frequency values distributed symmetrically about the mean. (Also, the mean, median, and mode all have the same value.) On a normal curve, 68% of the values lie within one standard deviation of the mean, 95% lie within two standard deviations, and 99% are within three standard deviations. The percentages represent approximations of the total percent of area under the curve. The curve and the percentages are illustrated in Figure 9-14.

Figure 9-14

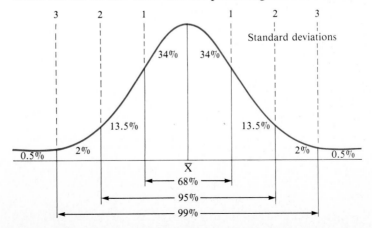

Example 9-6

A standardized test was scored, and there was a mean of 500 and a standard deviation of 100. Suppose 10,000 students took the test and their scores had a mound-shaped distribution, making it possible to use a normal curve to approximate the distribution.

(a) How many scored between 400 and 600?
(b) How many scored between 300 and 700?
(c) How many scored between 200 and 800?

Solution

(a) Since one standard deviation on either side of the mean is from 400 to 600, about 68% of the scores fall in this interval. Thus, 0.68(10,000), or 6800, students scored between 400 and 600.
(b) About 95% of 10,000, or 9500, students scored between 300 and 700.
(c) About 99% of 10,000, or 9900, students scored between 200 and 800.

Remark About 1%, or 100, students' scores in Example 9-6 fall outside three standard deviations. About 50 of these students did very well on the test and about 50 students did very poorly.

Suppose a group of students asked their teacher to grade "on a curve." If the teacher gave a test to 200 students and the mean on the test was 71 with a standard deviation of 7, the graph in Figure 9-15 shows how the grades could be assigned. In Figure 9-15, the teacher has used the normal curve in grading. (The use of the normal curve presupposes that the teacher had a mound-shaped distribution of scores and also that the teacher arbitrarily decided to use the lines marking standard deviations to determine the boundaries of the As, Bs, Cs, Ds, and Fs.

Figure 9-15

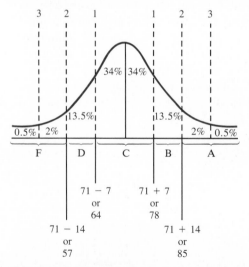

Thus, compiling the grades from the normal curve in Table 9-12, we see the range of grades that the teacher might use if he or she uses the rounding rules given in Chapter 7.

Table 9-12

Test Score	Grade	Number of People per Grade	Percentage Receiving Grade
85 and Above	A	5	2.5%
78–84	B	27	13.5%
64–77	C	136	68%
57–63	D	27	13.5%
Below 77	F	5	2.5%

COMPARING SCORES FROM DIFFERENT TESTS

All normal curves have the same basic shape. However, they can differ in means and standard deviations. As a result, it is not easy to compare scores from two different curves or tests. One way to deal with this is to translate all scores into standard scores. One such standard score is the z-score. A **z-score** gives the position of a score in relation to the remainder of the distribution, using the standard deviation as the unit of measure. Specifically, a z-score gives the number of standard deviations by which the score differs from the mean. It can be found by using the following formula, where x is the score, $\bar{x}$ is the mean, and s is the standard deviation.

z-score

$$z = \frac{x - \bar{x}}{s}$$

For example, consider three student scores on a test with a mean of 71 and a standard deviation of 7. If the student scores are 71, 64, and 85, then the respective z-scores are as follows.

$$z = \frac{71 - 71}{7} = 0$$

$$z = \frac{64 - 71}{7} = {}^{-}1$$

$$z = \frac{85 - 71}{7} = 2$$

Figure 9-16 can be used to interpret the z-scores.

Figure 9-16

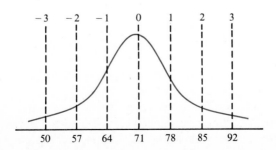

A z-score of 0 indicates that the score of 71 is the mean. A z-score of $^{-}1$ indicates that the score of 64 is one standard deviation to the left of the mean. Similarly, a z-score of 2 indicates that the score of 85 is two standard deviations to the right of the mean.

   z-scores are useful when comparing results on various tests taken by the same reference group. Suppose a group of students took both an English test and a mathematics test; then a comparison of the z-scores would be reasonable. For example, if George scored 10 on the English test when the mean is 9 and standard deviation is 2, and scored 8 on the mathematics test with mean of 7 and standard deviation of 1.55, then his z-scores follow.

$$z = \frac{10 - 9}{2} = 0.5 \qquad z = \frac{8 - 7}{1.55} = 0.65$$

Thus, George did slightly better in mathematics than in English on these tests. Use of z-scores allows us to compare the different test scores.

   If a college class and a fourth-grade class took a mathematics test, then a comparison of z-scores is not reasonable because the reference groups are different.

Example 9-7

For a certain group of people, the mean height is 182 cm, with a standard deviation of 11 cm. Juanita's height has a z-score of 1.4. What is her height?

Solution

We use the formula for z-scores, $z = \dfrac{x - \bar{x}}{s}$. We know that $z = 1.4$, $\bar{x} = 182$, and $s = 11$.

$$1.4 = \frac{x - 182}{11}$$

$$15.4 = x - 182$$

$$x = 197.4$$

Therefore, Juanita's height is 197.4 cm.

   In a large group of scores, such as on various standardized tests, we generally expect the scores to approximate a normal curve. Each test may determine a different normal curve; that is, the mean and the standard deviation may be different. However, the shapes are the same. If all scores are translated to z-scores, then with any given z-score, we should be able to determine the approximate percentage of people who scored either above or below this z-score. For example, suppose a z-score on a test is 1.5. To determine the percentage of people who scored below this, we know from the graph of Figure 9-14 that the percentage is more than 84% and less than 97.5%. Table 9-13 can be used to find that percentage.

   Column 1 of Table 9-13 contains the z-score; column 2 contains the percent of the population between the mean and the positive-value z-score; column 3 gives the fraction of the population to the right of the z-score. In our example, the z-score of 1.5 has approximately 43.32% of the population between

Table 9-13

z	Area Between Mean and z	Area Beyond z
1.45	0.4265	0.0735
1.46	.4279	.0721
1.47	.4292	.0708
1.48	.4306	.0694
1.49	.4319	.0681
1.50	.4332	.0668
1.51	.4345	.0655
1.52	.4357	.0643
1.53	.4370	.0630
1.54	.4382	.0618

the mean and the z-score and 50% of the population below the mean, so that approximately 93.32% of the population had z-scores below 1.5.

Figure 9-17 shows visually the type of information that is presented in Table 9-13.

Figure 9-17

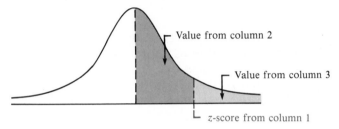

Value from column 2

Value from column 3

z-score from column 1

A table such as Table 9-13 does not have to be constructed to contain negative z-scores. Because of the symmetry of the normal curve, the percentages should be the same. For example, if a z-score was $^-$1.5, then approximately 93.32% of the population scored above that score. Accordingly, $100\% - 93.32\%$, or 6.68%, scored below $^-$1.5.

Example 9-8

Use Table 9-13 to find the percentage of population below each of the following z-scores.

(a) 1.54   (b) $^-$1.45

Solution

(a) If $z = 1.54$, then from Table 9-13 the percentage between the mean and 1.54 is approximately 43.82. With the 50% below the mean, we have $(50 + 43.82)\%$, or 93.82%, below the given z-score.

(b) The z-score of 1.45 has 7.35% of the population above it. Hence, there is 7.35% of the population below the score of $^-$1.45.

PERCENTILES

Scores on tests can also be reported by giving a person's percentage relative to others taking the test. For example, if Tomas reported that he scored at the 50th percentile (the median) on the SAT, then he is saying that he scored better than 50% of the people taking the test. In general, the **rth percentile,**

rth percentile

denoted by P_r, is a score such that r percent of the scores are less than P_r. In a case in which the distribution is normal, as in Figure 9-18, we see several percentages and a relationship between percentiles and standard deviations.

Figure 9-18

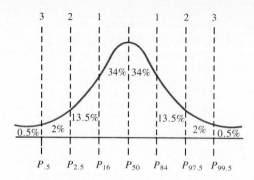

Typically, percentiles are reported only to whole-number percents such as $P_1, P_2, P_3, \ldots, P_{97}, P_{98}, P_{99}$. However, as seen in Figure 9-18, $P_{.5}, P_{2.5}, P_{97.5}$, and $P_{99.5}$ correspond to specific whole numbers of standard deviations and are easy to recognize and find in a set of data.

The discussion of percentiles thus far has centered on distributions that can be represented by a normal curve. Percentiles can also be found from distributions that are not mound-shaped. This can be done by constructing a frequency table, determining the number of scores less than the score for which we are trying to determine a percentile, and then dividing that number by the total number of scores in the set of data. This is investigated further in the problem set.

deciles   **Deciles** are points that divide a distribution into ten equally spaced sections. There are nine deciles, denoted $D_1, D_2, \ldots, D_9$, and $D_1 = P_{10}, D_2 = $
quartiles $P_{20}, \ldots, D_9 = P_{90}$. **Quartiles** are points that divide a distribution into quarters. There are three quartiles:

$$Q_1 = P_{25} \qquad Q_2 = P_{50} \qquad Q_3 = P_{75}$$

Remark   It should be noted that in any finite set of test scores, a particular percentile may not be represented. This does not stop their being used with small sets of data but does inhibit their usefulness.

Example 9-9

The standardized test of Example 9-6 had a mean of 500 and a standard deviation of 100. The 16th percentile, P_{16}, is 400 since 400 is one standard deviation from the mean, or better than 16% of the scores. Find each of the following.

(a) P_{50} (b) P_{84}

Solution

(a) Since 500 is the mean, 50% of the distribution is less than 500. Thus, $P_{50} = 500$.
(b) Since 600 is one standard deviation to the right of the mean, 84% of the distribution is less than 600. Thus, $P_{84} = 600$.

PROBLEM SET 9-3

1. The mean IQ score for 1500 students is 100, with a standard deviation of 15. Assuming the scores have a normal curve,
   (a) how many have an IQ between 85 and 115?
   (b) how many have an IQ between 70 and 130?
   (c) how many have an IQ under 55 or over 145?
   (d) how many have an IQ over 145?

2. Sugar Plops boxes say they hold 16 ounces. To make sure, the manufacturer fills the box to a mean weight of 16.1 ounces with a standard deviation of 0.05 ounce. If the weights have a normal curve, what percent of the boxes actually contain 16 ounces or more?

3. For certain workers, the mean wage is $5.00 per hour with standard deviation of $0.50. If a worker is chosen at random, what is the probability that the worker's wage is between $4.50 and $5.50? Assume a normal distribution of wages.

4. In a job-applicant test, there were three parts: verbal, quantitative, and logical reasoning. The means and standard deviations for each part are given below.

	Verbal	Quantitative	Logical Reasoning
$\bar{x}$	84	118	14
s	10	18	4

   (a) Holly's scores were 90 on verbal, 133 on quantitative, and 18 on logical reasoning. Determine her z-score for each part.
   (b) Use the answers in (a) to determine each of the following.
      (i) On which part did she perform the relative highest?
      (ii) On which part did she perform the relative lowest?
      (iii) To determine an overall composite score, we find the mean of the z-scores. What is Holly's composite score?

5. If a standardized test has a mean of 65 and a standard deviation of 12, find
   (a) Q_2 (b) P_{16} (c) P_{84}

6. In a normal distribution, how are the mean and median related?

7. Listed in the table is a set of children's weights and the cumulative total of children.
   (a) Find the percentiles for each weight by dividing the cumulative total in each case by the total number of children.
   (b) Sketch the "cumulative" curve, in which weights

are marked on a horizontal axis and percentiles are marked on a vertical axis.
   (c) Should "cumulative" curves, or percentile curves, always have the shape you found in (b)? Why or why not?

Cumulative Totals and Percentiles of Children's Weights			
Weights	F	Cum	$(\text{Cum}/n)\cdot 100$
90	0	0	
91	1	1	
92	0	1	
93	3	4	
94	2	6	
95	6	12	
96	5	17	
97	7	24	
98	5	29	
99	8	37	
100	2	39	

Total $39 = n$
F = Frequency
Cum = Cumulative total

8. Use Table 9-13 to find the percentages of scores below each of the following z-scores.
   (a) $^{-}1.47$ (b) 1.51 (c) $^{-}1.53$

9. Use Table 9-13 to find the percentage of scores between z-scores of 1.46 and 1.53.

Review Problems

10. On the English 100 exam, the scores were as follows.

43	91	73	65
56	77	84	91
82	65	98	65

   (a) Find the mean.
   (b) Find the median.
   (c) Find the mode.
   (d) Find the variance.
   (e) Find the standard deviation.
   (f) Make a frequency table for the data.
   (g) Draw a line graph depicting the data.

11. If the mean of a set of 36 scores is 27, and two additional scores of 40 and 42 are added, what is the new mean?

*Section 9-4   Abuses of Statistics

Not only are statistics frequently used, they are also frequently abused. Benjamin Disraeli (1804–1881), an English prime minister, once remarked, "There are three kinds of lies: lies, damned lies, and statistics." People sometimes use statistics to deliberately mislead others. In the past, this has been seen in advertising. More often, the misuse of statistics is the result of misinterpreting what the statistics actually mean. For example, if we were told that the average depth of water in a lily pond was 2 feet, most of us would presume that a flamingo could stand up in any part of the pond. That this is not necessarily the case is seen in the following Far Side cartoon.

THE FAR SIDE

© 1985 Universal Press Syndicate. Reprinted with Permission. All Rights Reserved.

Now, consider an advertisement in which it is reported that of the people responding to a recent survey, 98% reported that Buffepain is the most effective pain reliever of headaches and arthritis of all those tested. To make sure that the statistics are not being misused, the following information also should have been reported:

1. The number of people surveyed
2. The number of people responding
3. How the people participating in the survey were chosen
4. The number and type of pain relievers tested

Without the information listed, the following situations are possible, all of which could cause the advertisement to be misleading:

1. Suppose 1,000,000 people nationwide were sent the survey, and only 50 responded. This would mean that there was only a 0.005% response, which would certainly cause someone to mistrust the ad.

2. Of the 50 responding in (1), suppose 49 responses were affirmative. The 98% claim is true, but there were 999,950 people not responding at all.
3. Suppose all the people sent the survey were chosen from a town in which the major industry was the manufacture of Buffepain. It is very doubtful that the survey would represent an unbiased sample.
4. Suppose only two pain relievers were tested: Buffepain, which is 100% aspirin, and a placebo containing only powdered sugar.

This is not to say that advertisements of this type are all misleading or dishonest but simply that statistics are only as honest as their users. The next time you hear an advertisement that "After using Ultraguard toothpaste, Joseph has 40% fewer cavities," you might ask whether or not Joseph has 40% fewer teeth than the normal person.

A different type of misuse of statistics involves the use of graphs. Among the things to look for in a graph are the following. If they are not there, then the graph may be misleading.

1. Title
2. Labels
3. Source of the data
4. Key in a pictograph
5. Uniform size of symbols in a pictograph
6. Scale—does it start with zero? If not, is there a break shown?
7. Scale—are the numbers evenly spaced?

As an example of misleading use of graphs, consider how they can be used to distort data or exaggerate certain pieces of information. A frequency polygon, histogram, or bar graph can be altered by changing the scale of the graph. For example, consider the data in Table 9-14 for the number of graduates from a community college for the years 1982 to 1986.

Table 9-14

Year	1982	1983	1984	1985	1986
Number of graduates	140	180	200	210	160

The two graphs in Figure 9-19(a) and (b) represent the same data, but different scales are used in each. The statistics presented are the same, but these two graphs do not convey the same psychological message. Notice that in Figure 9-19(b), the years on the horizontal axis of the graph are spread out and the numbers on the vertical axis are condensed. Both of these changes minimize the variability of the data. A college administrator probably would use the graph in Figure 9-19(b) to convince people that the college was not in serious enrollment trouble.

Bar graphs can also be misleading. Suppose, for example, the number of boxes of cereal sold by Sugar Plops last year was 2 million and the number of boxes of cereal sold by Korn Krisp was 8 million. The Korn Krisp executives prepared the bar graph in Figure 9-20 to demonstrate the data. The Sugar Plops people objected. Do you see why?

Figure 9-19

No. of Graduates of Community College

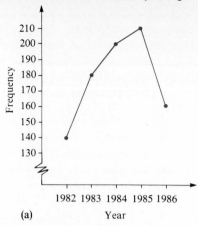

(a)

No. of Graduates of Community College

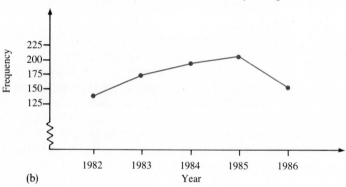

(b)

Figure 9-20

Cereal Sales

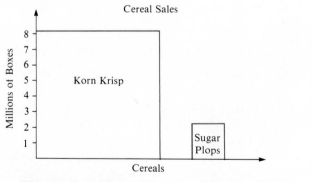

The graph in Figure 9-20 clearly distorts the data, since the bar for Korn Krisps is both 4 times as high and 4 times as wide as the bar for Sugar Plops. Thus, the area representing Korn Krisp is 16 times the area representing Sugar Plops, rather than 4 times the area, as indicated by the original data.

There are other ways to distort bar graphs that are less subtle. These may include omitting the scales, as in Figure 9-21(a). The scale is given in Figure 9-21(b).

Figure 9-21

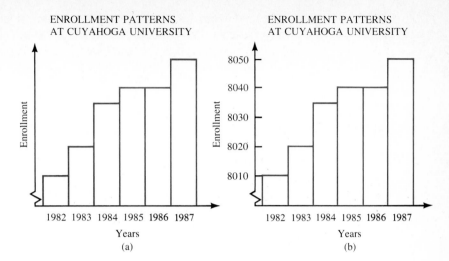

ENROLLMENT PATTERNS
AT CUYAHOGA UNIVERSITY

ENROLLMENT PATTERNS
AT CUYAHOGA UNIVERSITY

1982 1983 1984 1985 1986 1987
Years
(a)

1982 1983 1984 1985 1986 1987
Years
(b)

Figure 9-22

USE OF FORESTS

Circle graphs lend themselves to distortion when attempts are made to make them three-dimensional. Many graphs of this type do not take into account either the thickness or the distortion due to perspective. Observe that the 27% sector pictured in Figure 9-22 looks far greater than the 23% sector though they should be very nearly the same size.

Figure 9-23 shows how the comparison of Sugar Plops and Korn Krisp cereals from Figure 9-20 might look if the bars were made three-dimensional. Now the figure for Korn Krisp has a volume 64 times the volume of Sugar Plops.

Figure 9-23

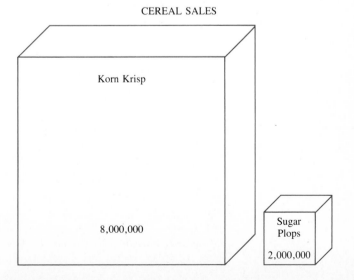

CEREAL SALES

Korn Krisp

8,000,000

Sugar
Plops

2,000,000

The final examples we discuss of the misuses of statistics involve the uses of mean, median, and mode. All these are "averages" and may be used to suit a person's purposes. As discussed in Section 9-2 in the example concerning the teachers Smith, Jones, and Leed, each had reported that his or her particular class had done better. Each of the teachers was using a different number to represent the test scores.

The use of statistics in this way is often misleading. For example, college administrators wishing to portray to prospective employees a rosy salary picture may find the mean of $38,000 for ranked professors along with deans, vice-presidents, and presidents in the schedule of salaries. At the same time, a faculty union or teachers' group, who is bargaining for faculty salaries, may include part-time employees and instructors along with ranked professors and may exclude all administration personnel to present a mean salary of $29,000 at the bargaining table. The important thing to note when a mean is reported is disparate cases in the reference group. If the sample is small, then a few extremely high or low scores have a great influence on the mean.

If the median is being used as the average, then suppose Figure 9-24 shows the salaries of both administrators and faculty members at the college. The median in this case might be $33,500, which is representative of neither major group of employees. The bimodal distribution allows the median to be nonrepresentative of the distribution.

Figure 9-24

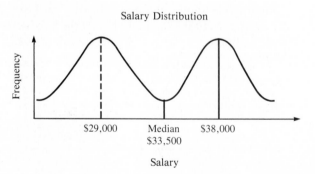

Salary Distribution

Frequency

$29,000   Median $38,000
            $33,500

Salary

To conclude the comments on the misuse of statistics, consider the quote by Darrell Huff from his book *How to Lie with Statistics* (p. 8):

> *So it is with much that you read and hear. Averages and relationships and trends and graphs are not always what they seem. There may be more in them than meets the eye, and there may be a great deal less.*
>
> *The secret language of statistics, so appealing in a fact-minded culture, is employed to sensationalize, inflate, confuse, and oversimplify. Statistical methods and statistical terms are necessary in reporting the mass data of social and economic trends, business conditions, "opinion" polls, census. But without writers who use the words with honesty and understanding and readers who know what they mean, the result can be semantic "nonsense."*

PROBLEM SET 9-4

1. Write a list of scores for which the mean and median are not representative of the list.

2. Discuss problems with a rectangular pie chart, such as the one shown.

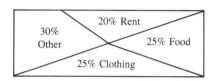

3. The city of Podunk advertised that its temperature was the ideal temperature in the country because its mean temperature was 25°C. What are possible misconceptions that people could draw from this advertisement?

4. Jenny averaged 70 on her quizzes during the first part of the quarter and 80 on her quizzes the second part of the quarter. When she found out that her final average for the quarter was not 75, she went to argue with her teacher. Give a possible explanation for Jenny's misunderstanding.

5. Suppose the following circle graphs are used to illustrate the fact that the number of elementary teaching majors at teachers' colleges has doubled from 1977 to 1987, while the percentage of male elementary teaching majors has stayed the same. What is misleading about the way the graphs are constructed?

400 Elementary Teaching Majors

15% Males

85% Females

1977

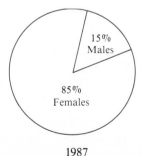

800 Elementary Teaching Majors

15% Males

85% Females

1987

6. What is wrong with the line graph shown?

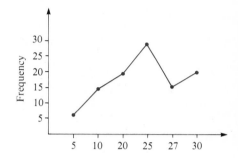

7. Make up three distributions, in each of which one of the following is not representative of the group, but the other two are.
(a) Mean   (b) Median   (c) Mode

8. Can you draw any valid conclusions about a set of data in which the mean is less than the median?

9. A student read that nine out of ten pickup trucks sold in the last 10 years are still on the road. She concluded that the average life of a pickup is around 10 years. Is she correct?

10. General Cooster once asked a person by the side of a river if it was too deep to ride his horse across. The person responded that the average depth was 2 feet. If General Cooster rides out across the river, what assumptions is he making, based on the person's information?

11. What is misleading in the graph of Problem 12 in Problem Set 9-1?

Review Problems

12. Use the following scores to make a frequency distribution:

96 71 95 74 96
83 83 74 83 71 74

13. Find the mode of the data in Problem 12.

*14. If the mean of a group of scores is 76 and the standard deviation is 5, what is the z-score of a person scoring 87?

15. What size angle should be used in a circle graph to represent 17% of the graph for taxes?

SOLUTION TO THE PRELIMINARY PROBLEM

UNDERSTANDING THE PROBLEM In each of two classes of 24 students, Professor Norma L. Kurf reported the following means.

Class A	*Class B*
Graduate mean: 84	Graduate mean: 80
Undergraduate mean: 72	Undergraduate mean: 60

In addition, Professor Kurf reported that the overall means for classes A and B were 73 and 75, respectively. Students questioned Professor Kurf's results; we are to determine if it is possible that both the means of class A are higher than the respective means of class B, but the overall mean for class A is lower. Intuitively, we may sense that class A must have many more undergraduates, while class B must have more graduate students.

DEVISING A PLAN Since we do not have a list of Professor Kurf's scores for the classes, we do not have at our disposal the most convincing argument—the actual grades. The next best argument is to produce a set of scores that has comparable means. To do this, consider what must be true. Both individual means of class A are higher than the corresponding ones of class B, but the overall mean of 75 of class B is higher; this tells us that more scores of class B must be closer to 80 than to 60. Why? Similarly, there must be more scores of class A close to 72 to achieve a mean of 73. We use this information to carry out the plan.

CARRYING OUT THE PLAN Consider what we know about class A. There are 24 students: undergraduates and graduates. If we let u be the number of undergraduates and g be the number of graduate students, then we have $u + g = 24$. In addition, we know the means, 84 and 72, of each group. Recall how a mean is found. We add all scores and divide by the number in the group. If the undergraduate mean is 72, then the total of all undergraduate scores must be 72 times the number of students in this group, or $72u$. Similarly, the total of all graduate scores must be $84g$. Because the class average is 73, we must have the following.

$$\frac{72u + 84g}{u + g} = 73$$

However, $u + g = 24$, or $u = 24 - g$. If we make these substitutions in the above equation, we find the following.

$$\frac{72(24 - g) + 84g}{24} = 73$$

$$1728 - 72g + 84g = 1752$$

$$12g = 24$$

$$g = 2$$

If there were 2 graduates in class A, each scoring 84, then there may be 22 undergraduates, each scoring 72, to achieve the given means.

Similarly, for class B, we have the following.

$$u + g = 24 \quad \text{or} \quad u = 24 - g$$

$$\frac{60u + 80g}{u + g} = 75$$

$$\frac{60(24 - g) + 80g}{24} = 75$$

$$1440 - 60g + 80g = 1800$$

$$20g = 360$$

$$g = 18$$

If there were 18 graduate students in class B, each scoring 80, then there may be 6 undergraduate students scoring 60 to achieve the given means.

LOOKING BACK The solution should be checked to determine that the means are accurate to the nearest tenth as required. Readers should do this.

What was obtained is not necessarily the scores of the classes at all. They are used only to show that the means reported could be accurate. This type of problem is an example of what was called Simpson's Paradox in *Teaching Statistics and Probability,* the 1981 Yearbook of the National Council of Teachers of Mathematics.

QUESTIONS FROM THE CLASSROOM

1. A student asks, "If the average income of each of ten people is $10,000 and one person gets a raise of $10,000, is the median, the mean, or the mode changed and, if so, by how much?"
2. A student asks for an example of when the mode is the best average. What is your response?
3. A student says that a stem and leaf plot is always the best way to present data. How do you respond?
4. Suppose the class takes a test and the following averages are obtained: mean, 80; median, 90; mode, 70. Tom, who scored 80, would like to know if he did better than half the class. What is your response?
5. A student asks for the advantages of presenting data in graphic form rather than in tabular form. What is your response? What are the disadvantages?
6. A student asks if it is possible to find the mode for data in a grouped frequency table. What is your response?
7. A student asks if she can make any conclusions about a set of data knowing that the mean for the data is less than the median. How do you answer?
8. A student asks if it is possible to have a standard deviation of $^-5$. How do you respond?
9. A student asks if it is possible to score at the 0th percentile on a test. How do you answer?

CHAPTER OUTLINE

I. Descriptive statistics
   A. **Descriptive statistics** is the science of organizing and summarizing numerical data.
   B. Information can be summarized in **stem and leaf plots** and **frequency tables.**

C. Data can be pictured on different graphs:
1. **Histograms** or **bar graphs**
2. **Frequency polygons** or **line graphs**
3. **Pictographs**
4. **Circle graphs** or **pie charts**
II. Numbers Used to Describe Data
A. The **mean** of n given numbers is the sum of the numbers divided by n.
B. The **median** of a set of numbers is the middle number if the numbers are arranged in numerical order or, if there is no middle number, it is the mean of the two middle numbers.
C. The **mode** of a set of numbers is the number or numbers that occur most frequently in the set.
III. Measures of variation
A. The **range** is the difference between the greatest and least numbers in the set.
B. The **variance** is found by subtracting the mean from each value, squaring each of these differences, finding the sum of these squares, and dividing by n, when n is the number of observations.

C. The **standard deviation** is equal to the square root of the variance.
*D. In a **normal curve**, 68% of the values are within one standard deviation of the mean, 95% are within two standard deviations of the mean, and 99% are within three standard deviations of the mean.
*E. A **z-score** gives the position of a score in relation to the remainder of the distribution, using the standard deviation as the unit of measure.

$$z = \frac{x - \bar{x}}{s}$$

*F. The **rth percentile**, denoted by P_r, is a score such that r percent of the scores are less than P_r.
*G. **Deciles** are points that divide a distribution into ten equally spaced sections. $D_1 = P_{10}$, $D_2 = P_{20}, \ldots, D_9 = P_{90}$.
*H. **Quartiles** are points that divide a distribution into quarters. $Q_1 = P_{25}$, $Q_2 = P_{50}$, and $Q_3 = P_{75}$.

CHAPTER TEST

1. Suppose you read that "the average family in Rattlesnake Gulch has 2.41 children." What average is being used to describe the data? Explain your answer. Suppose the sentence said 2.5. Then what are the possibilities?
2. At Bug's Bar-B-Q restaurant, the average weekly wage for full-time workers is $150. If there are ten part-time employees whose average weekly salary is $50 and the total weekly payroll is $3950, how many full-time employees are there?
3. Find the mean, median, and mode for each of the following groups of data.
(a) 10, 50, 30, 40, 10, 60, 10
(b) 5, 8, 6, 3, 5, 4, 3, 6, 1, 9
4. Find the range, variance, and standard deviation for each set of scores in Problem 3.
5. The masses, in kilograms, of children in a certain class follow.

40	49	43	48
42	41	42	39
46	42	49	39
47	49	44	42
41	40	45	43

(a) Make a stem and leaf plot for the data.
(b) Make a frequency table for the data.
(c) Draw a bar graph for the data.
6. The grades on a test for 30 students follow.

96	73	61	76	77	84
78	98	98	80	67	82
61	75	79	90	73	80
85	63	86	100	94	77
86	84	91	62	77	64

(a) Make a grouped frequency table for these scores, using four classes and starting the first class at 61.
(b) Draw a histogram for the grouped data.
(c) Draw a line graph for the data.
7. The budget for the Wegetem Crime Company is $2,000,000. If $600,000 is spent on bribes, $400,000 is spent for legal fees, $300,000 for bail money, $300,000 for contracts, and $400,000 for public relations, draw a circle graph to indicate how the company spends its money.

8. What, if anything, is wrong with the following bar graph?

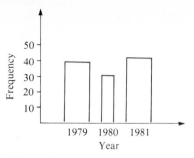

9. The mean salary of 24 people is $9000. How much will one additional salary of $80,000 increase the mean salary?

*10. A standardized test has a mean of 600 and a standard deviation of 75. If 1000 students took the test and their scores approximated a normal curve, how many scored between 600 and 750?

*11. Use the information in Problem 10 to find:
(a) P_{16} (b) D_5 (c) P_{84}

*12. If a student scored 725 on the test in Problem 10, what is his z-score?

*13. Find the percentile for a score of 79 in the data of Problem 6.

*14. The Nielsen Television Index rating of 30 means that an estimated 30% of American televisions are tuned to the show with that rating. The ratings are based on preferences of a scientifically selected sample of 1200 homes.
(a) Discuss possible ways in which viewers could bias this sample.
(b) How could networks attempt to bias the results?

*15. List and give examples of several ways to misuse statistics graphically.

SELECTED BIBLIOGRAPHY

Bestgen, B. "Making and Interpreting Graphs and Tables: Results and Implications from National Assessment." *Arithmetic Teacher* 28 (December 1980):26–29.

Bruni, J., and H. Silverman. "Graphing as a Communication Skill." *The Arithmetic Teacher* 22 (May 1975):354–366.

Buzitis, B., and J. Kella. *The New Math.* Seattle: The Seattle Times, 1974.

Christopher, L. "Graphs Can Jazz Up the Mathematics Curriculum." *Arithmetic Teacher* 30 (September 1982):28–30.

Collis, B. "Teaching Descriptive and Inferential Statistics Using a Classroom Microcomputer." *The Mathematics Teacher* 76 (May 1983):318–322.

Duncan, D., and B. Litwiller. "Randomness, Normality, and Hypothesis Testing: Experiences for the Statistics Class." *The Mathematics Teacher* 74 (May 1981):368–374.

Ewbank, W. "The Summer Olympic Games: A Mathematical Opportunity." *The Mathematics Teacher* 77 (May 1984):344–348.

Fennell, F. "Ya Gotta Play to Win: A Probability and Statistics Unit for the Middle Grades." *Arithmetic Teacher* 31 (March 1983):26–30.

Ferber, R., et al. *What Is a Survey?* Washington, D.C.: American Statistical Association, 1980.

Fielker, D. *Topics from Mathematics, Statistics.* New York: Cambridge University Press, 1967.

Haylock, D. "A Simplified Approach to Correlation." *The Mathematics Teacher* 76 (May 1983):332–336.

Henningsen, J. "An Activity for Predicting Performances in the 1984 Summer Olympics." *The Mathematics Teacher* 77 (May 1984):338–341.

Horak, V., and W. Horak. "Collecting and Displaying the Data Around Us." *Arithmetic Teacher* 30 (September 1982):16–20.

Huff, D. *How to Lie with Statistics.* New York: Norton, 1954.

Hyatt, D. "M and M's Candy: A Statistical Approach." *The Arithmetic Teacher* 24 (January 1977):34.

Jacobson, M. "Graphing in the Primary Grades: Our Pets." *Arithmetic Teacher* 26 (February 1979):25–26.

Jamski, W. "Introducing Standard Deviation." *The Mathematics Teacher* 74 (March 1981):197–198.

Johnson, E. "Bar Graphs for First Graders." *Arithmetic Teacher* 29 (December 1981):30–31.

Joiner, B., and C. Campbell. "Some Interesting Examples for Teaching Statistics." *The Mathematics Teacher* 68 (May 1975):364–369.

Kimberling, C. "Mean, Standard Deviation, and Stopping the Stars." *The Mathematics Teacher* 77 (November 1984):633–636.

Klitz, R., and J. Hofmeister. "Statistics in the Middle School." *Arithmetic Teacher* 26 (February 1979):35–36.

Landwehr, J., and A. Watkins. "Stem-and-Leaf Plots." *The Mathematics Teacher* 78 (October 1985):528–532, 537–538.

MacDonald, A. "A Stem-Leaf Plot: An Approach to Statistics." *The Mathematics Teacher* 75 (January 1982):25, 27, 28.

Mosteller, F., et al. *Statistics: A Guide to the Unknown.* New York: Holden Day, 1972.

Newman, C., and S. Turkel. "The Class Survey: A Problem-Solving Activity." *Arithmetic Teacher* 32 (May 1985):10–12.

Noether, G. "The Nonparametric Approach in Elementary Statistics." *The Mathematics Teacher* 67 (February 1974):123–126.

Råde, L., ed. *Statistics at the School Level.* New York: Wiley, 1975.

Richbart, L. "Probability and Statistics for Grades 9–11." *The Mathematics Teacher* 74 (May 1981):346–348.

Shulte, A. "A Case for Statistics." *Arithmetic Teacher* 26 (February 1979):24.

Shulte, A., ed. *Teaching Statistics and Probability.* Reston, Va.: National Council of Teachers of Mathematics, 1981.

Smith, R. "Bar Graphs for Five Year Olds." *Arithmetic Teacher* 27 (October 1979):38–41.

Sullivan, D., and M. O'Neil. "THIS IS US! Great Graphs for Kids." *Arithmetic Teacher* 28 (September 1980):14–18.

CHAPTER 10

Introductory Geometry

Preliminary Problem

Jernigan, a stained-glass window maker, was asked by a customer to cut a convex polygonal piece of glass in which the smallest interior angle is 120° and each successive angle is 5° greater than its predecessor. Can he make such a construction, and if so, how many sides will the piece of glass have?

Introduction

Geometry has evolved in many ways since its inception. The word *geometry* comes from two Greek words, *ge* and *metria,* which might literally be translated as "earth measuring." Since the time of Euclid, geometry has developed into the first mathematics course in which students use logic in a deductive way to develop theorems, that is, statements that can be proved. The proofs are based on **undefined terms** such as set, point, line, and plane, and a set of basic assumptions, called **axioms,** that are considered to be true. This format, developed by Euclid in *The Elements,* has been used for over 2000 years. Other types of geometry based on the Euclidean format include transformational geometry, developed in the late 1800s, and coordinate geometry, developed in the 1600s. Coordinate geometry is investigated in Chapter 13. Other types of geometry have also been developed; one branch, called **topology,** is informally called "rubber-sheet geometry." In this chapter, we consider some basic notions of Euclidean geometry and topology. We approach these topics using informal methods and intuition, but at times we use deductive-type methods to consider specific topics in depth.

undefined terms

axioms

topology

Section 10-1   Basic Notions

Points, lines, and planes are basic notions in geometry. However, these words are commonly used in daily life to represent physical objects. The tip of a compass, the sharpened end of a pencil, the pointed end of a safety pin, and the tip of the Washington Monument are all thought of as points. A railroad track (one rail), a highway, and the trail of smoke left by a jet going across the sky are all considered as lines in the everyday world. A tabletop, a floor, and any smooth, level surface are all thought of as planes. All these objects are part of a child's world before the child is ready to understand the mathematical abstraction of point, line, and plane.

point

We represent a **point** on paper as a dot made by a pencil and label it with a capital letter, as in Figure 10-1(a), with which we can refer to the point.

line

Similarly, we represent a **line** by a streak of pencil lead or ink drawn using a pen or pencil and a straightedge, as in Figure 10-1(b). To refer to a line, we use either a single lowercase letter or capital letters representing two dots (points) on the line. Line AB, written as $\overleftrightarrow{AB}$ or ℓ, is pictured in Figure 10-1(b).

plane

A **plane** is usually represented by a parallelogram, as pictured in Figure

HISTORICAL NOTE

Euclid (ca. 300 B.C.) was the author of *The Elements,* a work that was so systematic and encompassing that many earlier mathematical works were discarded and lost for all future generations.

Figure 10-1

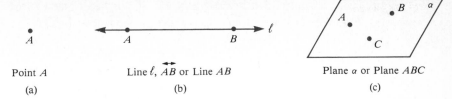

Point A

(a)

Line ℓ, $\overset{\leftrightarrow}{AB}$ or Line AB

(b)

Plane α or Plane ABC

(c)

10-1(c), and is commonly denoted by a lowercase Greek letter, such as alpha (α), beta (β), or gamma (γ), or by capital letters representing three points in the plane, such as ABC, where the points are not all on the same line.

A line is considered to be "straight," to extend indefinitely in the directions of the arrowheads, and to contain infinitely many points. Because a line is a set of points, we say that the points A and B belong to $\overset{\leftrightarrow}{AB}$ or are contained in $\overset{\leftrightarrow}{AB}$, and write $A \in \overset{\leftrightarrow}{AB}$ and $B \in \overset{\leftrightarrow}{AB}$. Points that belong to the same line are called **collinear points.** Thus, points A, B, and C in Figure 10-2 are collinear. Points B, D, and C are noncollinear. If three collinear points A, B, and C are arranged as in Figure 10-2, we say that B is **between** A and C. Point D is not between B and C because B, D, and C are not collinear.

collinear points

between

Figure 10-2

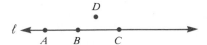

Certain subsets of a line are given separate names and symbols. Several of these are defined and illustrated in Table 10-1, with symbols shown beneath the illustrations.

Table 10-1

Definition	Illustration
line segment segment A **line segment,** or **segment,** is a subset of a line that contains two points of the line and all points between those two points.	$A \quad\quad\quad\quad B$ $\overline{AB}$
half-line A **half-line** is a subset of a line that contains all points on the line on one side of a given point (excluding the point itself).	$A \quad\quad B$ $\overset{\rightarrow}{AB}$
ray A **ray** is a subset of a line that contains a point and all points on the line on one side of the point.	$A \quad\quad B$ $\overset{\rightarrow}{AB}$

A plane is considered to be "flat," to extend indefinitely in all directions with no thickness, and also to contain infinitely many points. Because a plane is a set of points, we say that points A, B, and C belong to plane ABC, or

coplanar points

noncoplanar points

coplanar, noncoplanar lines

are contained in plane *ABC*, or lie in plane *ABC*. Points that belong to the same plane are called **coplanar points.** Figure 10-3(a) shows coplanar points *A*, *B*, and *C*, and Figure 10-3(b) shows noncoplanar points *D*, *E* and *F*, *G*. Points are **noncoplanar** if and only if there can be no one plane that contains them. Points *D*, *E*, and *G* are coplanar because there is a plane that contains them, which is not shown. Similarly, we can define **coplanar** and **noncoplanar lines.**

Figure 10-3

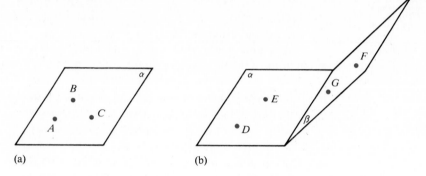

(a)　　　　　　　　(b)

Definitions and illustrations of various types of lines are given in Table 10-2. Exercises using these definitions are given in the problem set.

Table 10-2

	Definition	Illustration
intersecting lines	Two coplanar lines *m* and *n* are called **intersecting lines** if and only if they have exactly one point in common.	*n* *P* *m*
concurrent lines	**Concurrent lines** are lines that contain the same point. Concurrent lines may be either coplanar or noncoplanar.	*o* *q* *n* *P* *m*
parallel lines	Two coplanar lines *m* and *n* that have no points in common are called **parallel lines.**	*m* *n* *m* ‖ *n*
skew lines	Two lines that cannot be contained in the same plane are called **skew lines.** $\overleftrightarrow{AB}$ and $\overleftrightarrow{CD}$ are skew lines.	*A* *B* *C* *D*

Remark Skew lines cannot intersect. However, skew lines are not parallel because there is no single plane that contains them.

ANGLES

angle   An angle is a subset of two intersecting lines. Specifically, an **angle** is the union of two rays with a common endpoint. Figure 10-4(a) illustrates an angle.

Figure 10-4

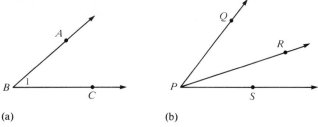

(a)   (b)

sides   The rays of an angle are called the **sides** of the angle, and the common
vertex   endpoint is called the **vertex** of the angle. An angle can be named by three different points: the vertex and a point on each ray, with the vertex always listed between the other two points. Thus, the angle in Figure 10-4(a) can be named as $\angle CBA$ or $\angle ABC$. The latter is read "angle ABC." When there is no confusion, it is also customary to name an angle either by its vertex or by a number. Thus, the angle in Figure 10-4(a) can be named as $\angle B$ or $\angle 1$. However, in Figure 10-4(b), there is more than one angle with vertex P, namely, $\angle QPR$, $\angle RPS$, and $\angle QPS$. Thus, the notation $\angle P$ is inadequate for naming any one of the angles.

Angles are classified according to their measure. The attribute measured is the amount of "opening" between the two rays or the amount of "turning" that occurs as one of the rays moves from a position coinciding with the first ray to the position of the second ray. A unit commonly used for measuring
degree   angles is the **degree.** A complete rotation about a point is an opening of 360°. One degree is then $\frac{1}{360}$ of a complete rotation. Figure 10-5 shows that $\angle BAC$ has a measure of 30 degrees, written $m(\angle BAC) = 30°$. The measuring device
protractor   pictured is called a **protractor.**

Figure 10-5

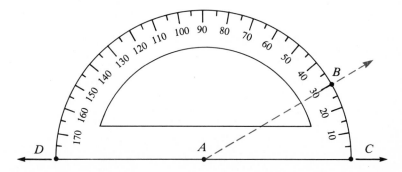

minutes   A degree is subdivided into 60 equal parts called **minutes,** and each minute
seconds   is further subdivided into 60 equal parts called **seconds.** The measurement 29 degrees, 47 minutes, 13 seconds is written 29°47′13″.

Example 10-1   (a) In Figure 10-6, find the measure of $\angle BAC$ if $m(\angle 1) = 27°58′$ and $m(\angle 2) = 19°47′$.
(b) Express 21.8° in degrees and minutes without decimals.

Figure 10-6

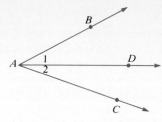

Solution

(a) $m(\angle BAC) = 27°58' + 19°47'$
$\qquad\qquad\quad = (27° + 19°) + (58' + 47')$
$\qquad\qquad\quad = 46° + 105'$
$\qquad\qquad\quad = 46° + 1° + 45'$
$\qquad\qquad\quad = 47°45'$

(b) $21.8° = 21° + 0.8°$. There are 60 minutes in 1 degree. Thus,
$0.8° = 0.8(60') = 48'$ and, therefore, $21.8° = 21°48'$.

Remark In the solution of Example 10-1(a), we used the fact that $m(\angle BAC) = m(\angle 1) + m(\angle 2)$. In general, if D is in the interior of $\angle BAC$, then $m(\angle BAC) = m(\angle BAD) + m(\angle DAC)$. Also, $m(\angle BAC) - m(\angle BAD) = m(\angle DAC)$.

The different types of planar angles follow:

1. If the degree measure of an angle is greater than $0°$ and less than $90°$, *acute angle*   the angle is called an **acute angle.**
2. If the degree measure of an angle is greater than $90°$ but less than $180°$, *obtuse angle*   the angle is called an **obtuse angle.**
right angle 3. If the degree measure of an angle is $90°$, the angle is called a **right angle.**
straight angle 4. If the degree measure of an angle is $180°$, the angle is called a **straight angle.**

Remark Angles with measure greater than $180°$ or with negative measure are important in mathematics but are not discussed in this text.

PERPENDICULARS

When two lines intersect so that the angles formed are right angles, we say *perpendicular lines* that the lines are **perpendicular lines.** In Figure 10-7, lines m and n are

Figure 10-7

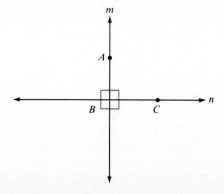

perpendicular and we write $m \perp n$. (The symbol $\neg$ is used to indicate a right angle.) Two intersecting segments, two intersecting rays, or a segment and **perpendicular** a ray that intersect are called **perpendicular** if they lie on perpendicular lines. For example, in Figure 10-7, $\overline{AB} \perp \overline{BC}$, $\overrightarrow{BA} \perp \overrightarrow{BC}$, and $\overrightarrow{AB} \perp \overrightarrow{BC}$.

OTHER RELATIONS AMONG POINTS, LINES, AND PLANES

Many lines can be drawn through a given point as seen in Figure 10-8(a). Similarly, many planes can be drawn through a given point, as in Figure 10-8(b), and many planes can be drawn through two given points, as shown in Figure 10-8(c). However, exactly one plane can be drawn through three noncollinear points, as illustrated by the sheet of glass resting on the three pencil points in Figure 10-8(d).

Figure 10-8

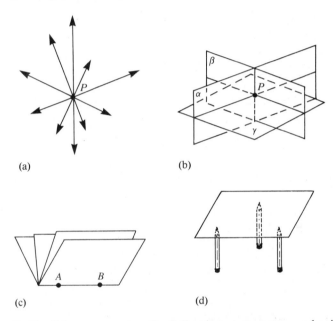

(a) (b)

(c) (d)

In Euclidean geometry, the following statements are basic axioms (or postulates) accepted as true. It is left as an exercise to find physical models for each of these statements.

INCIDENCE AXIOMS

1. There is exactly one line containing any two distinct points.
2. Every line is a set of points containing at least two points.
3. There exist at least three noncollinear points.
4. There exists exactly one plane containing any three distinct noncollinear points.
5. Every plane is a set of points containing at least three noncollinear points.
6. If two points lie in a plane, then the line containing the points lies in the plane.
7. If two planes intersect, then their intersection is a line.
8. There exist at least four noncoplanar points.

Axiom 4 gives one method of determining a plane. Several other ways to determine a plane are as follows:

1. A line and a point not on the line determine a plane.
2. Two parallel lines determine a plane.
3. Two intersecting lines determine a plane.

Axiom 7 discusses intersecting planes. Two distinct planes either intersect parallel planes in a line or are parallel. In Figure 10-9(a), the **planes** are **parallel;** that is, $\alpha \cap \beta = \varnothing$. In Figure 10-9(b), the planes intersect in a line, $\overleftrightarrow{AB}$; that is, $\alpha \cap \beta = \overleftrightarrow{AB}$.

Figure 10-9

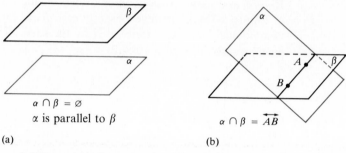

$\alpha \cap \beta = \varnothing$
α is parallel to β

(a)

$\alpha \cap \beta = \overleftrightarrow{AB}$

(b)

A line and a plane can be related in one of three possible ways. If a line parallel to the plane and a plane have no points in common, we say that the line is **parallel to the plane.** If two points of a line are in the plane, then the entire line containing the points is contained in the plane. If a line shares all its points with a plane, we say the line is in the plane. If a line intersects a plane, but is not contained in the plane, it intersects the plane in only one point. The three relative positions between a line ℓ and a plane α are shown in Figure 10-10(a), (b), and (c), respectively.

Figure 10-10

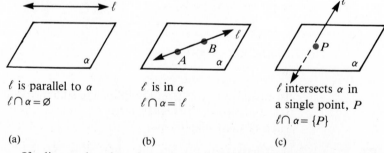

ℓ is parallel to α
$\ell \cap \alpha = \varnothing$

(a)

ℓ is in α
$\ell \cap \alpha = \ell$

(b)

ℓ intersects α in
a single point, P
$\ell \cap \alpha = \{P\}$

(c)

If a line and a plane intersect, as in Figure 10-10(c), it is possible for them to be perpendicular. For example, consider Figure 10-11, where planes β and γ represent two walls intersecting along line AB. The edge $\overleftrightarrow{AB}$ is perpendicular to the floor. Also, every line in the plane of the floor (plane α) passing through point A is perpendicular to $\overleftrightarrow{AB}$. This discussion leads to the following definition.

DEFINITION

> **A line and a plane are perpendicular** if and only if they intersect and the line is perpendicular to every line in the plane that passes through the point of intersection.

Remark   It is possible to prove that a line is perpendicular to a plane if and only if it is perpendicular to and concurrent with two intersecting lines forming the plane.

The plane containing one wall and the plane containing the floor of a typical room, such as α and β in Figure 10-11, are perpendicular planes. Notice that β and γ contain $\overleftrightarrow{AB}$, which is perpendicular to α. In fact, any plane containing $\overleftrightarrow{AB}$ is perpendicular to plane α. Thus, $\beta \perp \alpha$ and $\gamma \perp \alpha$.

Figure 10-11

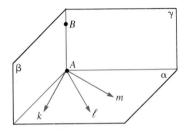

DEFINITION

> **Two planes are perpendicular** if and only if one plane contains a line perpendicular to the other plane.

Example 10-2

Given Figure 10-12, answer each of the following.

Figure 10-12

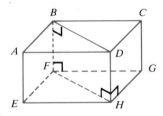

(a) Name two pairs of skew lines.
(b) Are $\overleftrightarrow{BD}$ and $\overleftrightarrow{FH}$ parallel, skew, or intersecting lines?
(c) Are $\overleftrightarrow{BD}$ and $\overleftrightarrow{GH}$ parallel?
(d) Find the intersection of $\overleftrightarrow{BD}$ and plane EFG.
(e) Find the intersection of $\overleftrightarrow{BH}$ and plane DCG.
(f) Name two pairs of perpendicular planes.
(g) Name two lines that are perpendicular to plane EFH.

Solution

(a) $\overleftrightarrow{BC}$ and $\overleftrightarrow{DH}$, and $\overleftrightarrow{AE}$ and $\overleftrightarrow{BD}$. Others are possible.
(b) $\overleftrightarrow{BD}$ and $\overleftrightarrow{FH}$ are parallel.
(c) No, $\overleftrightarrow{BD}$ and $\overleftrightarrow{GH}$ are skew lines.
(d) The intersection is the empty set because $\overleftrightarrow{BD}$ and plane EFG have no points in common.
(e) The intersection of $\overleftrightarrow{BH}$ and plane DCG is $\{H\}$.
(f) Planes BFC and EFG are perpendicular, as are planes BFD and EFG.
(g) $\overleftrightarrow{BF}$ and $\overleftrightarrow{DH}$ are perpendicular to plane EFH.

SPACE

half-plane

A point separates a line into two half-lines and the point itself. Similarly, a line separates a plane into two half-planes and the line itself. In Figure 10-13, ℓ separates the plane α into two **half-planes.** Point A is in one half-plane determined by ℓ and point B is in the other half-plane. The line separating the plane does not belong to either half-plane. A line and the two half-planes determined by the line are three disjoint subsets of a plane. Points, lines, and

space

planes are all subsets of space. **Space** is the set of all points. A plane separates

half-space

space into two **half-spaces.** A plane and the two half-spaces determined by the plane are three disjoint subsets of space.

Figure 10-13

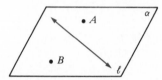

PROBLEM 1

What is the greatest number of points of intersection determined by n distinct lines?

UNDERSTANDING THE PROBLEM Because the greatest number of intersection points for n distinct lines is required, the lines cannot be parallel. As shown in Figure 10-14, the greatest number of points of intersection for two, three, and four lines is one, three, and six, respectively. We are to determine the greatest number of points of intersection for n lines.

Figure 10-14

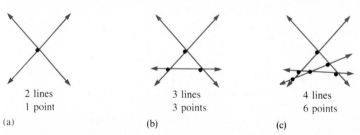

DEVISING A PLAN In order to discover a pattern for the maximum number of intersection points of n distinct lines, we reason as follows. Because no two lines are parallel, when one new line is added to a drawing containing a given number of lines, the new line must intersect each of the existing lines. Thus, when a new line is added to the two lines in Figure 10-14(a), we obtain Figure 10-14(b) with 1 existing point of intersection and 2 new ones, for a total of $1 + 2$ points of intersection. Next, when a new line is added to Figure 10-14(b), we obtain Figure 10-14(c), with $1 + 2$ existing points of intersection and 3 new points of intersection created by the fourth line. Thus, the maximum number of intersection points for four lines is $1 + 2 + 3$. Similarly, for five lines, we have all the existing intersection points for four lines, plus four new ones created by the fifth line, giving a total of $1 + 2 + 3 + 4$. We summarize this in Table 10-3.

Table 10-3

Number of Lines	Greatest Number of Points of Intersection
2	1
3	$3 = 1 + 2$
4	$6 = (1 + 2) + 3$
5	$10 = (1 + 2 + 3) + 4$
$\vdots$	$\vdots$
n	$? = 1 + 2 + 3 + 4 + \cdots + (n - 1)$

CARRYING OUT THE PLAN From the previous discussion, it follows that for n lines, we have all the intersection points created by $n - 1$ lines plus $n - 1$ new points created by the nth line. Thus, the number of intersection points for n distinct lines is given by $1 + 2 + 3 + 4 + \cdots + (n - 1)$. Recalling Gauss' formula from Chapter 1, we can write this sum as follows.

$$1 + 2 + 3 + 4 + \cdots + (n - 1) = \frac{(n - 1)[(n - 1) + 1]}{2} = \frac{(n - 1) \cdot n}{2}$$

LOOKING BACK The solution to this problem can also be approached as follows. No two lines are parallel, so each line intersects all the lines except itself. Thus, using n lines, each line must intersect $n - 1$ lines. Hence, on each line there are $n - 1$ points of intersection. Because there are n lines, we can count a total of $n \cdot (n - 1)$ intersection points. However, in this counting process, each intersection point is counted twice because it is on two lines. Thus, the actual number of intersection points is $\frac{1}{2}$ of $n(n - 1)$, or $\dfrac{n(n - 1)}{2}$.

Other Looking Back activities include determining how many lines are formed by n intersecting planes, how many planar regions are formed by n intersecting lines, and how many spatial regions are formed by n intersecting planes.

PROBLEM SET 10-1

1. A line, a line segment, or a ray can be considered as a set of points. Given the figure, find a more concise name for each of the following.

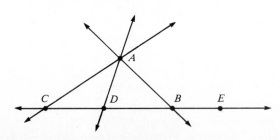

(a) $\overleftrightarrow{AC} \cap \overleftrightarrow{BE}$ (b) $\overline{AC} \cap \overline{BE}$
(c) $\overleftrightarrow{CA} \cap \overrightarrow{EB}$ (d) $\overrightarrow{CA} \cap \overleftrightarrow{BC}$
(e) $\overline{CB} \cup \overrightarrow{BE}$ (f) $\overrightarrow{AB} \cup \overrightarrow{AB}$
(g) $\overrightarrow{AB} \cup \overrightarrow{BA}$ (h) $\overrightarrow{AD} \cup \overrightarrow{DA}$

2. Given the line ℓ, answer the following.

(a) In how many different ways can you name line ℓ using the points labeled on the line?
(b) How many different line segments are determined using the points labeled on the line?

3. Consider the accompanying figure and answer each of the following questions. (Point D is in neither plane α nor plane β; $\alpha \cap \beta = \overleftrightarrow{AB}$.)

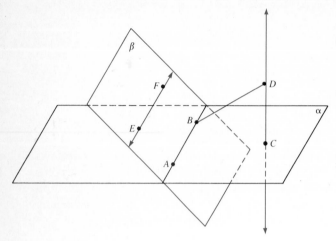

(a) Name a pair of skew lines.
(b) If $\overleftrightarrow{EF}$ and $\overleftrightarrow{AB}$ are parallel, what can be said about $\overleftrightarrow{EF}$ and α?
(c) Find and name the intersections for each of the following pairs of planes.
   (i) α and β
   (ii) BDC and α
   (iii) ABD and BDC
(d) Is there a single plane containing the points E, F, B, and D? Explain your answer.

4. Indicate whether each of the following statements is true or false. If false, explain why.
(a) Two distinct planes either intersect in a line or are parallel.
(b) If there are two points common to a line and a plane, then the entire line is in the plane.
(c) It is always possible to find a plane through four given points in space.
(d) If two distinct lines do not intersect, they are parallel.
(e) The intersection of three planes may be a single point.
(f) If two distinct lines intersect, there is one and only one plane containing the lines.
(g) There are infinitely many planes containing two skew lines.
(h) If each of two parallel lines is parallel to a plane α, then the plane determined by the two parallel lines is parallel to α.
(i) If three points are coplanar, then they must be collinear.
(j) If two distinct lines are parallel to a third line in space, then the two lines are parallel to each other.

(k) If a plane α contains one line ℓ, but not another line m, and ℓ is parallel to m, then α is parallel to m.
(l) A line parallel to each of two intersecting planes is parallel to the line of intersection of these planes.

5. Suppose ℓ is a line and A is a point not on ℓ.
(a) How many lines intersecting ℓ may be drawn through A?
(b) How many planes contain ℓ and A?

6. Suppose ℓ is a line, and two points A and B are not on ℓ. For each of the following, how many planes contain A and B and at least one point on ℓ?
(a) $\overleftrightarrow{AB}$ and ℓ are skew lines.
(b) $\overleftrightarrow{AB}$ and ℓ are not skew lines.

7. (a) If two parallel planes α and β intersect a third plane γ in two lines ℓ and m, are ℓ and m necessarily parallel? Explain your answer.
(b) If two planes α and β intersect a third plane in two parallel lines, are α and β always parallel? Why?
(c) Suppose two intersecting lines are both parallel to a plane α. Is the plane determined by these intersecting lines parallel to α? Why?

8. How many rays are determined by each of the following?
(a) Three collinear points
(b) Four collinear points
(c) Five collinear points
(d) n collinear points

9. (a) How many lines are determined by three non-collinear points?
(b) How many lines are determined by four points, no three of which are collinear?
(c) How many lines are determined by five points, no three of which are collinear?
(d) How many lines are determined by n points, no three of which are collinear?

10. Give a mathematical explanation of why a three-legged stool is always stable and a four-legged stool sometimes rocks.

11. In the given figure, m is a line perpendicular to plane α. This intersection of m with α is C. Points A and B are in plane α. $D \in m$, but $D \notin \alpha$.

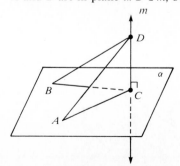

(a) Is $\angle BDC$ a right angle? Explain your answer.

(b) Is it possible to find a point P in plane α so that $\angle DPC$ is obtuse? Justify your answer.

(c) Is the plane determined by the points A, D, and C perpendicular to plane α? Why?

12. (a) Is it possible that a line is perpendicular to one line in a plane but is not perpendicular to the plane?

(b) Is it possible that a line can be perpendicular to two distinct lines in a plane and not be perpendicular to the plane?

(c) If a line not in a given plane is perpendicular to two distinct lines in the plane, is the line necessarily perpendicular to the plane?

13. Use a protractor to find the measures of each of the pictured angles.

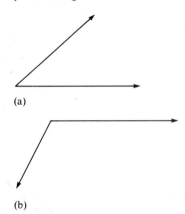

(a)

(b)

14. Perform each of the following operations, leaving your answers in simplest form.
(a) $18°35'29'' + 22°55'41''$
(b) $93°38'14'' - 13°49'27''$

15. Express each of the following in degrees, minutes, and seconds without decimals.
(a) $0.9°$ (b) $15.13°$

16. Trace each of the following drawings. In your tracing, use dashed lines for segments that would not be seen, and use solid lines for segments that would be seen. (Different people may see different perspectives.)

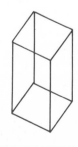

(a)

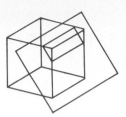

(b)

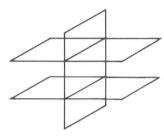

(c)

(d)

17. Describe a physical model for each of the incidence axioms listed on page 435.

★ 18. Use the statement "There is one and only one plane containing three distinct, noncollinear points" to prove each of the following.
(a) A line and a point not on the line determine a plane.
(b) Two intersecting lines determine a plane.

★ 19. Prove that if two parallel planes are intersected by a third plane, the lines of intersection are parallel.

20. Write Logo procedures to draw each of the following.
(a) A procedure called ANGLE with input :SIZE to draw a variable-sized angle
(b) A procedure called SEGMENT with input :LENGTH to draw a variable-sized segment
(c) A procedure called PERPENDICULAR with inputs :LENGTH1 and :LENGTH2 to draw two variable-sized perpendicular segments
(d) A procedure called PARALLEL with inputs :LENGTH1 and :LENGTH2 to draw two variable-sized parallel segments

LABORATORY ACTIVITY

If a sheet of paper is creased and unfolded, then two regions are formed. If the paper is creased again, how many regions are formed? Could there be more than one answer? How should the second crease be made in order to obtain the maximum number of regions? What is the least number of creases needed in order to obtain: (a) 11 regions; (b) 23 regions?

Section 10-2

Curves in a Plane

In mathematics, curves are subsets of a plane. A careful definition of a curve requires advanced mathematical concepts. Therefore, we intuitively describe a plane curve. A **plane curve** is a set of points in a plane that can be traced without lifting a pencil from the paper and without retracing any portion of the drawing other than single points. We use the terms *plane curve* and *curve* interchangeably. Figure 10-15(a), (b), (c), and (d) are examples of curves. Figure 10-15 (e) and (f) are not curves because they cannot be traced without lifting the pencil.

plane curve

Figure 10-15

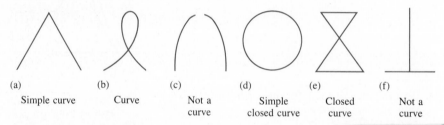

| (a) | (b) | (c) | (d) | (e) | (f) |
| Simple curve | Curve | Not a curve | Simple closed curve | Closed curve | Not a curve |

simple curve

Figure 10-15(a) and (d) are examples of simple curves. A **simple curve** is a curve that can be traced in such a way that no point is traced more than once with the exception that the tracing may stop at the same point where it started. Figure 10-15(d) and (e) are examples of **closed curves.** A closed curve is a curve that can be traced so that the starting and stopping points are the same. Notice that Figure 10-15(d) is a **simple closed curve.**

closed curve

simple closed curve

Example 10-3

Which of the figures in Figure 10-16 represent the following?

Figure 10-16

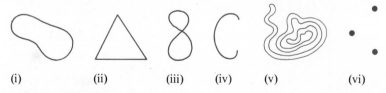

| (i) | (ii) | (iii) | (iv) | (v) | (vi) |

(a) Curves
(b) Simple curves
(c) Closed curves
(d) Simple closed curves

Solution

(a) Figure 10-16(i), (ii), (iii), (iv), and (v) are curves.
(b) Figure 10-16(i), (ii), (iv), and (v) are simple curves.
(c) Figure 10-16(i), (ii), (iii), and (v) are closed curves.
(d) Figure 10-16(i), (ii), and (v) are simple closed curves.

JORDAN CURVE THEOREM

As shown in Figure 10-17, any simple closed curve separates the plane into three mutually disjoint sets of points—the curve itself, the interior, and the exterior of the curve. This property of simple closed curves is known as the **Jordan Curve Theorem.**

Jordan Curve Theorem

Figure 10-17

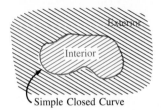

A slightly different version of the theorem is that if a point in the exterior of the curve is joined with a point in the interior of the curve by a continuous path of points, then this path will intersect the curve itself. The Jordan Curve Theorem is not easy to prove, nor is it always easy to use. Deciding whether a point is inside or outside a curve is investigated in Problem 2.

PROBLEM 2

Determine whether point X is inside or outside the simple closed curve of Figure 10-18.

Figure 10-18

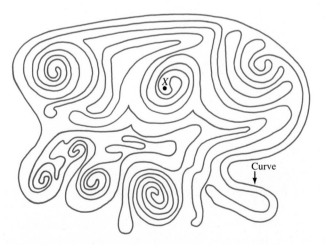

Curve

UNDERSTANDING THE PROBLEM We must determine whether point X is inside the curve in Figure 10-18; that is, does point X belong to the exterior or the interior of the curve?

DEVISING A PLAN One approach to this problem is to start shading the area surrounding point X. If we do this and stay between the lines, then we should be able to decide eventually whether the shaded area is inside or outside the curve.

CARRYING OUT THE PLAN If we shade the area around point X and stay within the boundaries, we obtain a drawing similar to Figure 10-19.

Figure 10-19

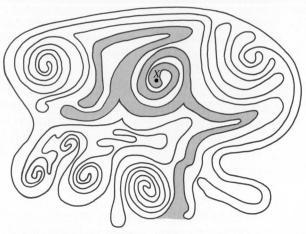

The shaded area of Figure 10-19 indicates that point X is located outside the curve.

LOOKING BACK Another strategy is explored in Figure 10-20(a) and (b), in which point X is connected with any point Y, where point Y is a point that is definitely outside the curve. How many times does the dashed segment cross the curve in each of these cases? Try different locations for point Y outside the curve in Figure 10-20(a) and (b). What is your conjecture?

Figure 10-20

(a)   (b)

A different strategy for solving this problem is to think of X as a person in a maze trying to find a way out (though it may turn out that X is outside the maze). One method for the person to find a way out of a maze is to mark the spot where he currently is and to put a hand on one wall and start walking, always letting the hand touch the wall and not stopping until either the outside is reached, or the original spot is found again. If the original spot is found again, then the person should put his hand on the other wall and try again. This time, the person either finds a way out, the maze has no exit, or the person is on the outside. Would the strategy work if applied in Figure 10-19?

POLYGONS

polygonal curve

Any plane curve that is the union of line segments only is called a **polygonal curve.** All the curves in Figure 10-21 are examples of polygonal curves.

Figure 10-21

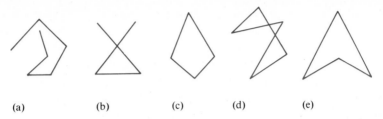

(a)   (b)   (c)   (d)   (e)

polygon

sides

vertex

polygonal region

Polygonal curves that are simple and closed, such as in Figure 10-21(c) and (e), are called polygons. A **polygon** is a simple, closed polygonal curve such that no two segments with a common endpoint are collinear. The line segments forming a polygon are called **sides** of the polygon. A point where two sides meet is called a **vertex.** Together, a polygon and its interior are called a **polygonal region.**

Polygons are classified according to the number of sides or vertices they have. For example, consider Table 10-4.

TABLE 10-4

Polygon	Number of Sides or Vertices
Triangle	3
Quadrilateral	4
Pentagon	5
Hexagon	6
Heptagon	7
Octagon	8
Nonagon	9
Decagon	10
n-gon	n

Polygons could also be named by the number of angles they have because they have the same number of angles as sides. Strictly speaking, a polygon contains no angles because it has no rays, but the sides of the polygon can be used to determine angles.

diagonal

Any line segment connecting nonconsecutive vertices of a polygon is called a **diagonal.** Thus, in Figure 10-22(a), segments $\overline{AC}$, $\overline{AD}$, $\overline{BE}$, $\overline{BD}$, and $\overline{CE}$ are diagonals of the given pentagon. In Figure 10-22(b), segments $\overline{QS}$ and $\overline{PR}$ are the diagonals of the quadrilateral $PQRS$.

Figure 10-22

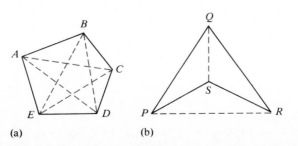

(a)   (b)

Notice that in Figure 10-22(a), the diagonals (except for their endpoints) of the pentagon lie in the interior of the pentagon. The quadrilateral in Figure 10-22(b) has a diagonal that, except for its endpoints, lies in the exterior of the quadrilateral. A polygon having no portion of its diagonals in its exterior is called a **convex polygon,** whereas a polygon having any portion of one of its diagonals in its exterior is called a **concave polygon.** The pentagon in Figure 10-22(a) is convex, and the quadrilateral in Figure 10-22(b) is concave. Because a triangle has no diagonals, it is convex. (A definition of a convex region is given in Problem 13 of Problem Set 10-2.)

convex polygon
concave polygon

Example 10-4

Which of the polygons in Figure 10-23 are convex and which are concave?

Figure 10-23

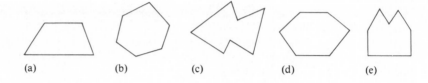

(a)   (b)   (c)   (d)   (e)

Solution

Polygons in (a), (b), and (d) are convex because they have no portions of their diagonals in their exteriors. Polygons in (c) and (e) are concave because in each case, at least a portion of one diagonal can be drawn in the exterior.

In the following problem, we investigate a relationship between the number of sides of a polygon and the number of diagonals it has.

PROBLEM 3

How many diagonals does a convex n-gon have?

UNDERSTANDING THE PROBLEM We are given a polygon with n sides and we are to determine how many different diagonals can be drawn by connecting the n vertices of the polygon in all possible ways.

DEVISING A PLAN We use the strategy of examining related simple cases of the problem in order to develop a pattern for the original problem. Figure 10-24 shows that a triangle has no diagonals, a square has two diagonals, a pentagon has five diagonals, and a hexagon has nine diagonals.

Figure 10-24

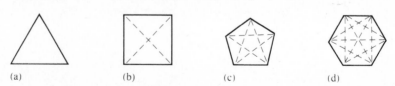

(a)   (b)   (c)   (d)

Examining Figure 10-24(c), we see that if we choose any vertex, then we can draw only two diagonals from that vertex. In general, we cannot draw a diagonal from a chosen vertex to itself or from a chosen vertex to either of its two adjacent vertices. Thus, in Figure 10-24(d), the number of diagonals that can be drawn from any one vertex is three less than the number of vertices, that is, $6 - 3$, or 3. In a polygon with n sides, the number of diagonals that can be drawn from any one vertex is three less than the number of vertices, that is, $n - 3$. From each of the n vertices of an n-gon, $n - 3$ diagonals can be drawn, and it appears that there are $n(n - 3)$ diagonals in the n-gon.

Based on this formula, the number of diagonals for the hexagon in Figure 10-24(d) is 18. This result does not agree with the actual answer of 9. Because each diagonal is determined by two vertices, when the number of diagonals from each vertex was counted, we counted each diagonal twice. In general, to obtain the number of diagonals of a given n-gon, we must divide the number $n(n - 3)$ by 2.

CARRYING OUT THE PLAN From the preceding discussion, we have the following formula for determining the number of diagonals of a convex n-gon:

$$\frac{n(n - 3)}{2}$$

LOOKING BACK The formula developed in Carrying Out the Plan gives results consistent with the number of diagonals pictured in Figure 10-24. An alternate solution to this problem uses the notion of combinations developed in Chapter 8. The number of ways that all the vertices in an n-gon can be connected two at a time is the number of combinations of n vertices chosen two at a time, that is, $_nC_2$, or $\frac{n(n - 1)}{2}$. This number of segments includes both the number of diagonals and the number of sides. If we subtract the number of sides n from $\frac{n(n - 1)}{2}$, we find that the number of diagonals is $\frac{n(n - 3)}{2}$.

POLYGONS WITH CONGRUENT PARTS

congruent figures

Congruent figures are figures with the same size and shape. Figures do not have to be polygons to be congruent. They may be such shapes as snowflakes, as seen in the cartoon. Most frequently, when we discuss congruent figures, we are discussing figures in a plane. For example, two line **segments** are

congruent segments

congruent angles

described as **congruent** if and only if they have the same length. (Length is discussed in Chapter 12.) In the case of line segments, having the same length means that a tracing of one line segment can be fitted exactly on top of the other. If $\overline{AB}$ is congruent to $\overline{CD}$, we write $\overline{AB} \cong \overline{CD}$. The symbol $\cong$ is read "is congruent to." In a similar manner, we say that two **angles** are **congruent** to each other if and only if they have the same measure. Congruent segments and congruent angles are seen in Figure 10-25(a) and (b), respectively.

Figure 10-25

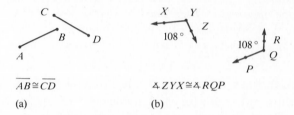

$\overline{AB} \cong \overline{CD}$

(a)

$\angle ZYX \cong \angle RQP$

(b)

regular polygons

Polygons in which all the angles are congruent and all the sides are congruent are called **regular polygons.** We say that a regular polygon is both *equiangular* and *equilateral*. A regular triangle is an equilateral triangle. A regular pentagon and a regular hexagon are illustrated in Figure 10-26. The congruent sides and congruent angles are marked.

Figure 10-26

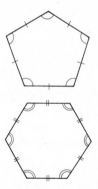

Triangles and quadrilaterals may be classified according to their sides and angles, as seen in Table 10-5.

Remark Some texts define a trapezoid as a quadrilateral with exactly one pair of parallel sides. (Many elementary school texts do this.)

With the definitions in Table 10-5, it is possible to prove many properties of both triangles and quadrilaterals. Among them are the following:

1. An equilateral triangle is isosceles.
2. A square is a regular quadrilateral.
3. A square is a rhombus with a right angle.

Table 10-5

	Definition	Illustration
right triangle	A triangle containing a right angle is a **right triangle.**	
acute triangle	A triangle in which all the angles are acute is an **acute triangle.**	
obtuse triangle	A triangle containing an obtuse angle is an **obtuse triangle.**	
equilateral triangle	A triangle with three sides congruent is an **equilateral triangle.**	
isosceles triangle	A triangle with at least two sides congruent is an **isosceles triangle.**	
scalene triangle	A triangle with no sides congruent is a **scalene triangle.**	
trapezoid	A **trapezoid** is a quadrilateral with at least one pair of parallel sides.	
parallelogram	A **parallelogram** is a quadrilateral in which each pair of opposite sides is parallel	
rectangle	A **rectangle** is a parallelogram with a right angle	
square	A **square** is a rectangle with all sides congruent.	
rhombus	A **rhombus** is a parallelogram with all sides congruent.	

PROBLEM SET 10-2

1. For each of the following, which figures labeled (1)–(12) can be classified by the given term?
   (a) Curves
   (b) Simple curves
   (c) Simple closed curves
   (d) Polygons
   (e) Convex polygons
   (f) Concave polygons

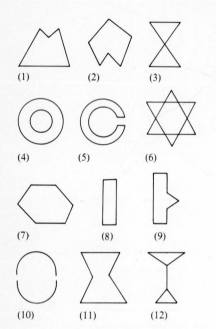

(1) (2) (3)

(4) (5) (6)

(7) (8) (9)

(10) (11) (12)

2. In each of the following diagrams, determine whether point X is inside or outside the curve.

(a)

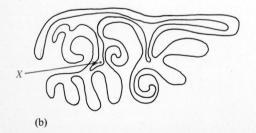

(b)

3. Find a path out of each of the following mazes if you start at point X.

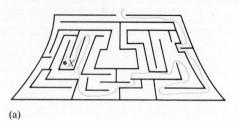

(a)

(b)

4. In the following drawing, is it possible to connect points A and B with a single curve without crossing a boundary? If so, sketch the curve.

5. For each of the following figures, determine if it is possible to connect like numerals by lines that do not cross each other or any other lines in the figure.

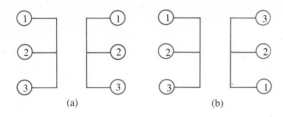

(a)   (b)

6. Which of the printed capital letters of the English alphabet can be classified as follows?
(a) Simple curves   (b) Closed curves
(c) Simple closed curves   (d) Polygons

7. How many diagonals does each of the following have?
(a) Decagon   (b) 20-gon   (c) 100-gon

8. Use the given drawing to find each of the following.
(a) $\ell \cap$ (polygon $ABCD$)
(b) $\ell \cap$ (interior of polygon $ABCD$)
(c) $\ell \cap$ (exterior of polygon $ABCD$)
(d) $\ell \cap \overleftrightarrow{AC}$

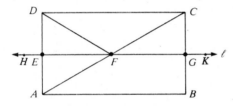

9. Find the number of triangles in each of the following figures.

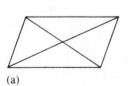 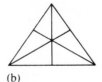

(a)   (b)

10. Identify each of the following triangles as scalene, isosceles, or equilateral.

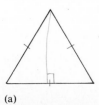 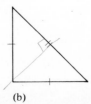

(a)   (b)

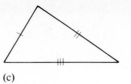

(c)

11. Tell whether each of the following is true or false. If the statement is false, explain why.
(a) Every isosceles triangle is equilateral.
(b) All equilateral triangles are isosceles.
(c) All squares are rectangles.
(d) Some rectangles are rhombi.
(e) All parallelograms are quadrilaterals.
(f) Every rhombus is a regular quadrilateral.
(g) Every parallelogram is a trapezoid.
(h) Every equilateral triangle is an isosceles triangle.
(i) Every isosceles triangle is equilateral.
(j) Some rectangles are squares.
(k) No square is a rectangle.
(l) No trapezoid is a parallelogram.
(m) Some right triangles are isosceles.

12. Use Venn diagrams to describe the relationships among the sets of all quadrilaterals (Q), parallelograms (P), trapezoids (T), rhombi (R), rectangles (F), and squares (S).

13. A region is called convex if, for every two points in the region, a segment joining them lies completely within the region. Otherwise, the region is called concave. Which of the following regions are convex and which are concave?

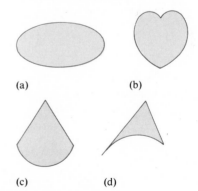

(a)   (b)

(c)   (d)

14. The maximum number of intersection points for a square and a triangle in which no two sides lie on the same straight line is six, as shown in the figure. If we have two polygons with m and n sides, respectively, what is the maximum number of intersection points where no two sides lie on the same straight line?

15. Write Logo procedures to draw each of the following.
    (a) A simple curve
    (b) A closed curve
    (c) A nonsimple nonclosed curve
    (d) A simple closed curve

Review Problems

16. If three distinct rays with the same vertex are drawn as shown, then three different angles are formed: $\angle AOB$, $\angle AOC$, and $\angle BOC$.
    (a) How many different angles are formed using ten distinct noncollinear rays with the same vertex?
    (b) How many different angles are formed using n distinct noncollinear rays with the same vertex?

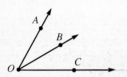

17. Use the accompanying figure to solve each of the following.

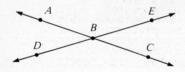

(a) Name at least four different angles.
(b) Find $\angle ABE \cap \angle EBC$.
(c) Find $\angle EBA \cap \angle DBC$.
(d) Find $\angle EBC \cap \angle CBE$.
(e) Is it true that $\angle ABE \cup \angle EBC = \angle ABC$?

18. What are the possible intersection sets of a line and an angle?

19. Find each of the following in the given figure.

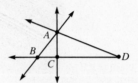

(a) $\overleftrightarrow{AC} \cap \overline{BC}$
(b) $\overline{BD} \cup \overline{CD}$
(c) List three line segments containing point A using the letters in the figure.
(d) $\overrightarrow{DC} \cap \overrightarrow{DA}$

20. Classify the following as true or false. If false, tell why.
    (a) A ray has two endpoints.
    (b) For any points M and N, $\overleftrightarrow{MN} = \overleftrightarrow{NM}$.
    (c) Skew lines are coplanar.
    (d) $\overrightarrow{MN} = \overrightarrow{NM}$
    (e) A line segment contains an infinite number of points.
    (f) If two distinct planes intersect, their intersection is a line segment.

21. Draw two line segments $\overline{AB}$ and $\overline{CD}$ such that $\overline{AB} \cap \overline{CD} = \varnothing$ and $\overline{AB} \cup \overline{CD}$ is a single line.

BRAIN TEASER

Given three buildings A, B, and C, as shown below, and three utility centers for electricity (E), gas (G), and water (W), is it possible to connect each of the three buildings to each of the three utility centers without crossing lines?

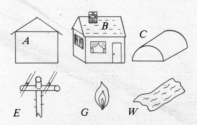

LABORATORY ACTIVITY

A geoboard consists of a square array of nails driven into a board at equally spaced intervals. Students form various geometric shapes by stretching rubber bands around the nails. Geoboard exercises can be simulated by connecting dots on paper.

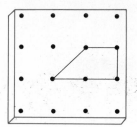

Form each of the following using either geoboards or dotted paper.

(a) Scalene triangle   (b) Isosceles triangle
(c) Square   (d) Parallelogram
(e) Trapezoid   (f) Pentagon
(g) Convex hexagon   (h) Concave hexagon
(i) Simple closed curve   (j) Nonsimple closed curve

Section 10-3   More About Angles

adjacent angles

Two intersecting lines form four nonstraight angles in the plane. In Figure 10-27, the four angles are ∢1, ∢2, ∢3, and ∢4. Angles 1 and 2 are called **adjacent angles.** Adjacent angles are angles that have a common vertex, a common side, and nonoverlapping interiors. Can you name three more pairs of adjacent angles in Figure 10-27?

Figure 10-27

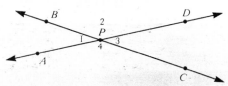

vertical angles

Nonadjacent angles formed by two intersecting lines, such as ∢1 and ∢3 in Figure 10-27, are called **vertical angles.** Another pair of vertical angles in Figure 10-27 is ∢2 and ∢4.

supplementary angles
supplement

Figure 10-27 also illustrates pairs of supplementary angles. Two **angles** are called **supplementary** if the sum of their measures is 180°. Each is said to be a **supplement** of the other. Angles 1 and 2, 1 and 4, 2 and 3, and 3 and 4 are pairs of supplementary angles in Figure 10-27.

complementary angles
complement

Two angles are called **complementary angles** if the sum of their measures is 90°. Each is said to be a **complement** of the other. Figure 10-28 shows examples of supplementary and complementary angles.

Figure 10-28

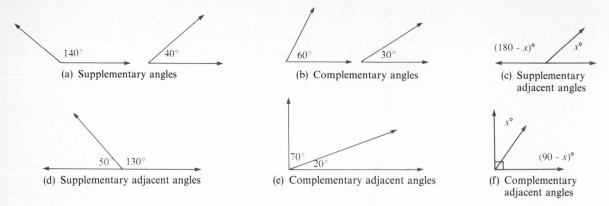

(a) Supplementary angles

(b) Complementary angles

(c) Supplementary adjacent angles

(d) Supplementary adjacent angles

(e) Complementary adjacent angles

(f) Complementary adjacent angles

Using the notion of congruence of angles, we can derive the following theorems involving supplementary and complementary angles.

THEOREM 10-1

(a) Supplements of the same angle, or of congruent angles, are congruent.
(b) Complements of the same angle, or of congruent angles, are congruent.

Using Theorem 10-1(a), it is easy to prove that vertical angles are congruent. Look at Figure 10-29. Because ℓ is a straight line, $\angle 1$ is a supplement of $\angle 4$. Because m is a straight line, $\angle 2$ is a supplement of $\angle 4$. As $\angle 1$ and $\angle 2$ are the supplements of the same angle, $\angle 4$, they are congruent and equal in measure. Similarly, $\angle 3$ and $\angle 4$ are supplements of $\angle 1$ and, therefore, are congruent. Thus, vertical angles are congruent.

Figure 10-29

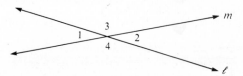

We summarize the preceding result in the following theorem.

THEOREM 10-2

Vertical angles formed by intersecting lines are congruent.

Theorem 10-1(b) can also be used to deduce congruence relationships among certain angles, as shown in Example 10-5.

Example 10-5

In Figure 10-30, suppose that $\angle APC$ and $\angle BPD$ are right angles. Prove that $\angle 1$ and $\angle 3$ are congruent.

Figure 10-30

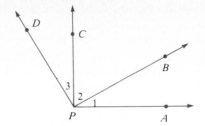

Solution

Because $\measuredangle APC$ is a right angle, $\measuredangle 1$ is a complement of $\measuredangle 2$. Because $\measuredangle BPD$ is a right angle, $\measuredangle 3$ is also a complement of $\measuredangle 2$. Thus, $\measuredangle 1$ and $\measuredangle 3$ are complements of the same angle and hence are congruent.

We have seen vertical angles and adjacent angles formed by two intersecting lines. Angles are also formed when a line intersects two distinct lines. Any line that intersects a pair of lines is called a **transversal** of these lines. In Figure 10-31(a), line p is a transversal of lines m and n. Angles formed by these lines are listed below.

transversal

Figure 10-31

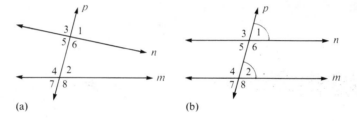

(a)   (b)

interior angles
exterior angles
alternate interior angles
alternate exterior angles
corresponding angles

Interior angles: $\measuredangle 2$, $\measuredangle 4$, $\measuredangle 5$, $\measuredangle 6$
Exterior angles: $\measuredangle 3$, $\measuredangle 1$, $\measuredangle 7$, $\measuredangle 8$
Alternate interior angles: $\measuredangle 5$ and $\measuredangle 2$, $\measuredangle 4$ and $\measuredangle 6$
Alternate exterior angles: $\measuredangle 1$ and $\measuredangle 7$, $\measuredangle 3$ and $\measuredangle 8$
Corresponding angles: $\measuredangle 3$ and $\measuredangle 4$, $\measuredangle 5$ and $\measuredangle 7$, $\measuredangle 1$ and $\measuredangle 2$, $\measuredangle 6$ and $\measuredangle 8$

If corresponding angles, such as $\measuredangle 1$ and $\measuredangle 2$, are congruent, as in Figure 10-31(b), it can be shown that members of each pair of corresponding angles are congruent. We leave it as an exercise to show that if a transversal intersecting two lines forms congruent corresponding angles, then the alternate interior angles formed are congruent, as are the alternate exterior angles.

If we further examine Figure 10-31(b), we see that lines m and n appear to be parallel when $\measuredangle 1$ is congruent to $\measuredangle 2$. Now, consider the statement "If lines m and n [in Figure 10-31(b)] are parallel, then $\measuredangle 1$ and $\measuredangle 2$ are congruent." The fact that this is true depends on the following basic assumption, known as the Euclidean Parallel Postulate.

**EUCLIDEAN
PARALLEL
POSTULATE**

Given a line and a point P not on the line, there exists exactly one line through P parallel to the given line.

The preceding discussion leads to the following theorem.

THEOREM 10-3

> If any two distinct lines are cut by a transversal, then a pair of corresponding angles, alternate interior angles, or alternate exterior angles are congruent if and only if the lines are parallel.

THE SUM OF THE MEASURES OF THE ANGLES OF A TRIANGLE

The sum of the measures of the angles in a triangle can intuitively be shown to be 180° by using a torn triangle as in Figure 10-32.

Figure 10-32

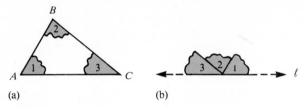

(a)   (b)

Angles 1, 2, and 3 of triangle ABC in Figure 10-32(a) are torn as pictured and placed along line ℓ as shown in Figure 10-32(b). Because the sum of the measures of the angles equals the measure of a straight angle, then the sum of the measures of the angles of triangle ABC is 180°.

To prove that the sum of the measures of the angles of a triangle is 180°, consider triangle ABC in Figure 10-33(a). We want to show that $m(\angle 1) + m(\angle 2) + m(\angle 3) = 180°$. To prove this assertion, we show that the sum of the measures of the three angles of the triangle is the same as the measure of a straight angle. This can be accomplished by drawing line ℓ parallel to $\overleftrightarrow{BC}$ through vertex A, as shown in Figure 10-33(b). Because ℓ and $\overleftrightarrow{BC}$ are parallel with transversals $\overleftrightarrow{AB}$ and $\overleftrightarrow{AC}$, it follows that alternate interior angles are congruent. Consequently, $m(\angle 1) = m(\angle 4)$ and $m(\angle 3) = m(\angle 5)$.

Figure 10-33

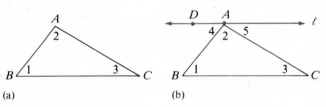

(a)   (b)

HISTORICAL NOTE

The Euclidean Parallel Postulate is so named because it was the fifth postulate assumed to be true by Euclid in *The Elements*. The denial of this postulate led to the development of non-Euclidean geometries by Karl Gauss (1777–1855), Nikolai Lobachevski (1793–1856), János Bolyai (1802–1860), and Bernhard Riemann (1826–1866).

Thus, $m(\angle 1) + m(\angle 2) + m(\angle 3) = m(\angle 4) + m(\angle 2) + m(\angle 5) = 180°$. So, $m(\angle 1) + m(\angle 2) + m(\angle 3) = 180°$.

Based on the preceding proof, we have the following theorem.

THEOREM 10-4

> The sum of the measures of the angles of a triangle is 180°.

Example 10-6

(a) In Figure 10-34(a), $m(\angle D) = 90°$ and $m(\angle E) = 25°$. Find $m(\angle A)$.
(b) In Figure 10-34(b), the measures of $\angle A$ and $\angle B$ are twice the measure of $\angle C$. Find the measures of each of the angles in the triangle.
(c) In Figure 10-34(c), $m(\angle A) = 70°$ and $m(\angle B) = 30°$. Find $m(\angle 1)$.

Figure 10-34

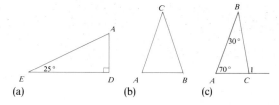

(a)   (b)   (c)

Solution

(a) The sum of the measures of the angles in a triangle is 180°. Thus, $m(\angle A) + 90° + 25° = 180°$, and, consequently, $m(\angle A) = 65°$.
(b) Suppose $m(\angle C) = x$. Then, $m(\angle A) = 2x$, and $m(\angle B) = 2x$. Thus, $x + 2x + 2x = 180°$. Consequently, $5x = 180°$ and $x = 36°$. Because $2x = 72°$, $m(\angle C) = 36°$, $m(\angle A) = 72°$, and $m(\angle B) = 72°$.
(c) The sum of the measures of the angles of a triangle is 180°. Thus, $m(\angle BCA) = 180° - (30° + 70°)$, or 80°. Now, $m(\angle BCA) + m(\angle 1) = 180°$, so $m(\angle 1) = 180° - 80°$, or 100°.

In Figure 10-34(c), $\angle 1$, which is formed by a side of triangle ABC and an-
exterior angle of a triangle   other side extended, is an **exterior angle of the triangle.** Exterior angles of other polygons can be formed similarly.

Example 10-7

In Figure 10-35, assume that m and n are parallel lines cut by a transversal.

Figure 10-35

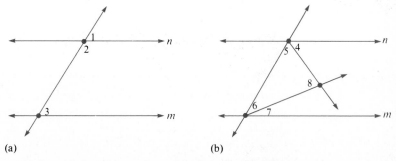

(a)   (b)

(a) In Figure 10-35(a), show that $m(\angle 2) + m(\angle 3) = 180°$.
(b) In Figure 10-35(b), show that if $\angle 4 \cong \angle 5$ and $\angle 6 \cong \angle 7$, then $m(\angle 8) = 90°$.

Solution

(a) $m(\angle 2) + m(\angle 1) = 180°$. Because $\angle 1$ and $\angle 3$ are corresponding angles formed by a transversal cutting parallel lines, $m(\angle 1) = m(\angle 3)$. Consequently, $m(\angle 2) + m(\angle 3) = 180°$.

(b) Let $m(\angle 4) = m(\angle 5) = x$ and $m(\angle 6) = m(\angle 7) = y$. Then, by part (a), it follows that $2x + 2y = 180°$. Dividing both sides of this equation by 2, we obtain $x + y = 90°$. The sum of the measures of angles of a triangle is $180°$, so we have $x + y + m(\angle 8) = 180°$, which implies $m(\angle 8) = 90°$.

PROBLEM 4

Find the sum of the measures of the interior angles in any convex n-gon.

UNDERSTANDING THE PROBLEM Given a polygon with n sides, we are to find a formula that will give the sum of the measures of the angles. We know that the sum of the measures of the angles in any triangle is $180°$. Any formula that we develop for an n-gon must hold for a triangle.

DEVISING A PLAN Consider several simple cases before trying to generalize the result. From any vertex of a polygon, diagonals can be drawn to form adjacent, nonoverlapping triangles. For example, in the quadrilateral in Figure 10-36(a), the diagonal from B partitions the quadrilateral into two triangles.

Figure 10-36

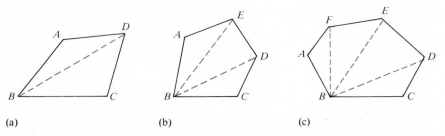

(a)   (b)   (c)

In the pentagon in Figure 10-36(b), the diagonals from B partition the pentagon into three triangles. In the hexagon in Figure 10-36(c), the diagonals from B partition the hexagon into four triangles. In general, the diagonals from a single vertex in any n-gon partition the n-gon into $(n - 2)$ triangles. This fact and the fact that the sum of the measures of the angles of a triangle is $180°$ can be used to solve the problem.

CARRYING OUT THE PLAN Since the sum of the measures of the angles in any triangle is $180°$, the sum of the measures of the angles in $(n - 2)$ triangles is $(n - 2)\,180°$.

LOOKING BACK An interesting exercise is to determine whether the formula developed holds for concave polygons. Another activity is to determine the measure of the exterior angles of an n-gon. Because there are n vertices, there are n straight angles formed by the interior and exterior angles for a total measure of $180n$. Subtracting the sum of the measures of the interior angles from $180n$, we have $180n - (n - 2)180$, or $360°$. Hence, the sum of the measures of the exterior angles of any convex polygon is $360°$.

The two major results in the preceding problem are summarized in the following theorem.

THEOREM 10-5

> (a) The sum of the measures of the interior angles of any convex polygon with n sides is $(n - 2)180°$.
> (b) The sum of the measures of the exterior angles of any convex polygon is $360°$.

Example 10-8

(a) Find the measure of each angle of a regular decagon.
(b) Find the number of sides of a regular polygon, each of whose angles has a measure of $175°$.

Solution

(a) The sum of the measures of the angles in any n-gon is $(n - 2)180°$, and a decagon has ten sides. Thus, the sum of the measures of the angles of a decagon is $(10 - 2)180°$, or $1440°$. A regular decagon has ten angles, all of which are congruent, so each one has a measure of $\dfrac{1440°}{10}$, or $144°$.

(b) Each interior angle of the regular polygon is $175°$. Thus, the measure of each exterior angle of the polygon is $180° - 175°$, or $5°$. Because the sum of the measures of all exterior angles of a convex polygon is $360°$, we have that the number of exterior angles is $\frac{360}{5}$, or 72. Hence, the number of sides is 72.

BRAIN TEASER

Find the sum of the measures of the angles ∡1, ∡2, ∡3, ∡4, and ∡5 in any five-pointed star like the one in the accompanying figure. What is the sum of the measures of the angles in any seven-pointed star?

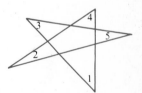

PROBLEM SET 10-3

1. If $m(∡1) = 50°$ in the given figure, find each of the following.
   (a) $m(∡2)$
   (b) $m(∡3)$
   (c) $m(∡4)$

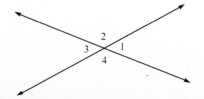

2. In the given figure, m and n are parallel lines and $m(∡4) = 60°$. Find $m(∡1)$, $m(∡2)$, $m(∡3)$, $m(∡5)$, $m(∡6)$, $m(∡7)$, and $m(∡8)$.

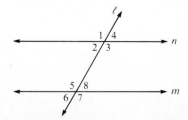

3. For each of the given figures, which pairs of angles marked are adjacent and which are vertical?

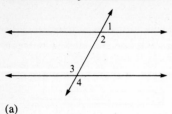

(a)

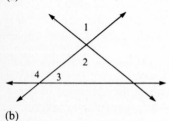

(b)

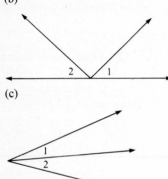

(c)

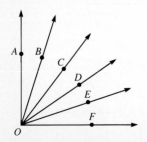

(d)

4. For each of the following, sketch a pair of angles whose intersection is given.
(a) The empty set
(b) Exactly two points
(c) Exactly three points
(d) Exactly four points
(e) More than four points

5. If five lines all meet in a single point, how many pairs of vertical angles are formed?

6. How many pairs of adjacent angles are there in the figure?

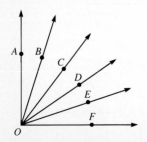

7. In the following figure, $\overleftrightarrow{DE}\|\overleftrightarrow{BC}$, $\overleftrightarrow{EF}\|\overleftrightarrow{AB}$, and $\overleftrightarrow{DF}\|\overleftrightarrow{AC}$. Also, $m(\angle 1) = 45°$ and $m(\angle 2) = 65°$. Find each value.
(a) $m(\angle 3)$ (b) $m(\angle D)$
(c) $m(\angle E)$ (d) $m(\angle F)$

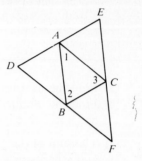

8. In each of the pictured cases, are m and n parallel lines? Justify your answer.

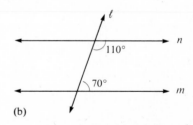

(a)

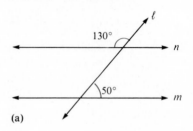

(b)

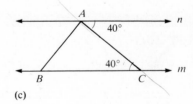

(c)

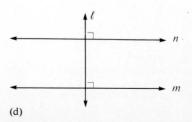

(d)

9. (a) If one of the angles in a triangle is obtuse, can another angle be obtuse? Why?
   (b) If one of the angles in a triangle is acute, can the other two angles be acute? Why?
   (c) Can a triangle have two right angles? Why?
   (d) If a triangle has one acute angle, is the triangle necessarily acute? Why?

10. Find the measure of the third angle in each of the following triangles.

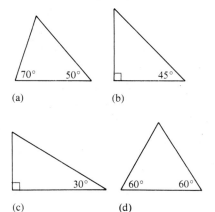

(a)   (b)

(c)   (d)

11. In each figure, find the measures of the angles marked x and y.

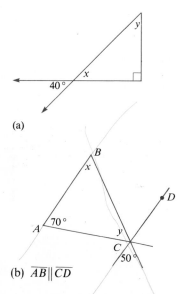

(a)

(b) $\overline{AB} \| \overline{CD}$

12. (a) Find the sum of the measures of the angles of any convex pentagon.
    (b) Find the sum of the measures of the angles of any convex hexagon.
    (c) How many sides does a convex polygon have if the sum of the measures of its angles is 2880°?

13. (a) In a regular polygon, the measure of each angle is 162°. How many sides does the polygon have?
    (b) Find the measure of each of the angles of a regular dodecagon.

14. (a) Show how to find the sum of the measures of the angles of any convex pentagon by choosing any point P in the interior and constructing triangles as shown in the figure.

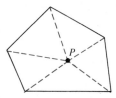

    (b) Using the method suggested by the diagram in (a), find the sum of the measures of the angles of any convex n-gon. Is your answer the same as the one already obtained in this section, that is, $(n - 2)180°$?

15. (a) What is the relationship between $m(\angle 4)$ and $[m(\angle 1) + m(\angle 2)]$?

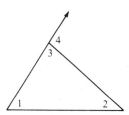

    *(b) Prove your conjecture in (a).

16. Calculate the measure of each angle of a pentagon if the measures of the angles form an arithmetic sequence and the least measure is 60°.

17. What is the measure of an angle whose measure is twice the measure of its complement?

18. If two angles of a triangle are complementary, what is the measure of the third angle?

19. If the measures of the three angles of a triangle are $(3x + 15)°$, $(5x - 15)°$, and $(2x + 30)°$, what is the measure of each angle?

20. In the figure, A is a point not on line ℓ. Why is it impossible to have two distinct perpendicular segments from A to ℓ?

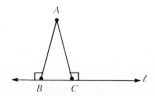

21. Find the sum $a + b + c + d + e + f$ in the figure.

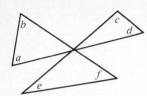

★22. Tiff A. Nee, a noted stained-glass window maker, needed assorted triangular pieces of glass for a project. One rectangular plate of glass that she planned to cut contained ten air bubbles, no three in a line, as shown in the figure. To avoid having an air bubble showing in her finished project, she decided to cut triangular pieces by making the air bubbles and the corners of the plate the vertices of the triangles. How many triangular pieces did she cut?

23. (a) Study the accompanying figure and notice that a parallelogram can be determined by knowing the length of two sides :L and :W and the measure of one angle :A. Write a procedure called PARALLELOGRAM with inputs :L, :A, and :W that draws such a parallelogram.

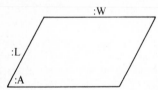

(b) Write a procedure called RECTANGLE that calls the PARALLELOGRAM procedure to draw a rectangle.

(c) Write a procedure called RHOMBUS that calls the PARALLELOGRAM procedure to draw a rhombus.

(d) How could a square of size 50 be generated by the PARALLELOGRAM procedure?

(e) How could a square of size 50 be generated by the RHOMBUS procedure?

★24. Prove Theorem 10-1(a) and (b).

★25. Prove that two distinct coplanar lines perpendicular to the same line are parallel.

★26. Suppose that the polygon $ABCD$ shown is a parallelogram. Prove each of the following.

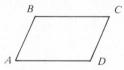

(a) $m(\angle A) + m(\angle B) = 180°$

(b) $m(\angle A) = m(\angle C)$ and $m(\angle B) = m(\angle D)$

★27. Use the definition of a rectangle and properties of parallel lines to show that all the angles in a rectangle are right angles.

★28. Prove that if the opposite angles in a quadrilateral are congruent, then the quadrilateral is a parallelogram.

★29. What is the measure of the angle between the hands of the clock at exactly 4:37?

Review Problems

30. If four distinct lines lie in a plane, what is the maximum number of intersection points of the four lines?

31. Is it possible for the union of two rays to be a line segment? Explain your answer.

32. Draw a polygonal curve that is closed but not simple.

33. Sketch two angles whose intersection is exactly one line segment.

Section 10-4   Geometry in Three Dimensions

SIMPLE CLOSED SURFACES

simple closed surface   A concept analogous to a simple closed curve in a plane is a **simple closed surface** in space. A simple closed surface partitions space into three sets—points outside the surface, points belonging to the surface, and points inside the surface. Simple closed surfaces have no holes and are hollow. (Simple closed surfaces can be thought of as figures that can be distorted into spheres.) For example, in Figure 10-37, parts (a), (b), (c), and (d) are simple closed surfaces; (e) and (f) are not. A **polyhedron** is a simple closed surface formed entirely by polygonal regions. Figures 10-37(a) and (b) are examples of polyhedra, but (c), (d), (e), and (f) are not. The union of the points on a simple closed surface and the interior points is referred to as a **solid.**

polyhedron

solid

Figure 10-37

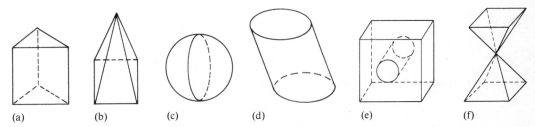

(a)   (b)   (c)   (d)   (e)   (f)

Each of the polygonal regions of a polyhedron is called a **face.** The vertices of the polygonal regions are called the **vertices** of the polyhedron, and the sides of each polygonal region are called the **edges** of the polyhedron.

face
vertices
edges
prism

A **prism** is a polyhedron in which two congruent polygonal faces lie in parallel planes, and the other faces are bounded by parallelograms. Figure 10-38 shows four different prisms. The parallel faces of a prism, like the faces *ABC* and *DEF* on top and bottom of the prism in Figure 10-38(a), are called the **bases** of the prism. A prism usually is named after its bases. Thus, the prism in Figure 10-38(a) is called a triangular prism, the one in Figure 10-38(b) is a quadrilateral prism, and the prisms in Figure 10-38(c) and (d) are hexagonal prisms.

bases

Figure 10-38

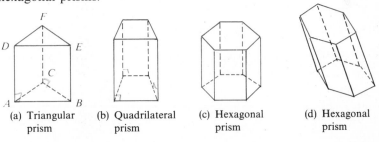

(a) Triangular   (b) Quadrilateral   (c) Hexagonal   (d) Hexagonal
    prism   prism   prism   prism

The **lateral faces** of a prism, the faces other than the bases, are bounded by parallelograms. If the lateral faces of a prism are all bounded by rectangles, the prism is called a **right prism.** The first three prisms in Figure 10-38 are right prisms. Figure 10-38(d) is called an **oblique prism** because its lateral edges are *not* perpendicular to the bases, and, therefore, its faces are *not* bounded by rectangles.

lateral faces

right prism
oblique prism

A **pyramid** is a polyhedron determined by a simple closed polygonal region, a point not in the plane of the region, and triangular regions

pyramid

base

apex / lateral faces

determined by the point and each pair of consecutive vertices of the polygonal region. The polygonal region is called the **base** of the pyramid, and the point is called the **apex**. The faces other than the base are called **lateral faces**. Pyramids are classified according to their bases, as shown in Figure 10-39.

Figure 10-39

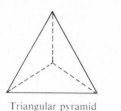 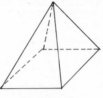 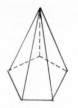

Triangular pyramid   Square pyramid   Pentagonal pyramid

convex polyhedron

A polyhedron is **convex** if and only if a segment connecting any two points in the interior of the polyhedron is itself in the interior. Figure 10-40 shows a polyhedron that is not convex.

Figure 10-40

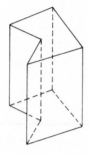

REGULAR POLYHEDRA

regular polyhedron

A **regular polyhedron** is a polyhedron whose faces are congruent regular polygonal regions such that the number of edges that meet at each vertex is the same for all the vertices of the polyhedron.

HISTORICAL NOTE

The regular solid polyhedra are called the **Platonic solids,** after the Greek philosopher Plato (fourth century B.C.). Plato attached a mystical significance to the five regular polyhedra, associating them with what he believed were the four elements—earth, air, fire, water—and the universe. Plato suggested that the smallest particles of earth have the form of a cube, those of air look like an octahedron, those of fire have a tetrahedral shape, those of water are shaped like an icosahedron, and those of the universe have the shape of a dodecahedron.

PROBLEM 5

How many regular polyhedra are there?

UNDERSTANDING THE PROBLEM We are asked to find the number of different types of regular polyhedra. We know that each face on a given regular polyhedron is congruent to each of the other faces on that polyhedron. This means that the measures of all the exterior angles on the faces are the same and the lengths of all the sides are the same.

DEVISING A PLAN We know that the sum of the measures of all the angles at a vertex of a regular polyhedron must be less than 360°. (Do you see intuitively why this is true?) We next examine the measures of the interior angles of regular polygons to determine which of the polygons could be faces of a regular polyhedron and then try to determine how many types of polyhedra there are.

CARRYING OUT THE PLAN From Theorem 10-5(a), we deduce that the measure of an interior angle of a regular n-gon is $[(n-2)180°]/n$. We use this formula to determine the size of an angle of some regular polygons in Table 10-6.

Table 10-6

Polygon	Measure of an Interior Angle
Triangle	60°
Square	90°
Pentagon	108°
Hexagon	120°
Heptagon	$\left(\frac{900}{7}\right)°$

Could a regular heptagon be a face of a regular polyhedron? We must have at least three figures to fit together at a vertex to make a polyhedron. (Why?) If three angles of a regular heptagon were together at one vertex, then the sum of the measures of these angles would be $\dfrac{3 \cdot 900°}{7}$, or $\dfrac{2700°}{7}$, which is greater than 360°. Similarly, more than three angles cannot be used at a vertex. Thus, a heptagon cannot be used to make a regular polyhedron.

Because the measure of an interior angle of a regular polygon increases as the number of sides of the polygon increases (why?), any polygon with more than six sides will have an interior angle greater than 120°. Hence, if three angles were to fit together at a vertex, the sum of the measures of the angles would be greater than 360°. Thus, the only possible polygons that can be used to make regular polyhedra are equilateral triangles, squares, regular pentagons, or regular hexagons. Consider the possibilities in Table 10-7.

Notice that we were not able to use six equilateral triangles to make a polyhedron because 6(60°) = 360° and the triangles would lie in a plane. Similarly, we could not use four squares or any hexagons. We also could not use more than three pentagons because the sum of the angles would have been more than 360°.

Table 10-7

Polygon	Measure of an Interior Angle	Number of Polygons at a Vertex	Sum of the Angles at the vertex	Polyhedron Formed	Model
Triangle	60°	3	180°	**Tetrahedron**	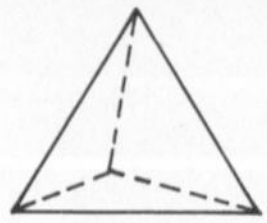
Triangle	60°	4	240°	**Octahedron**	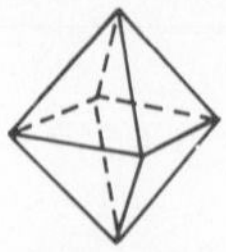
Triangle	60°	5	300°	**Icosahedron**	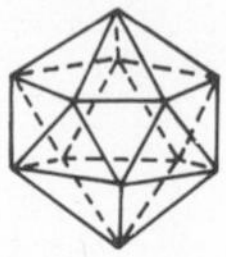
Square	90°	3	270°	**Cube**	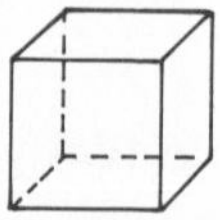
Pentagon	108°	3	324°	**Dodecahedron**	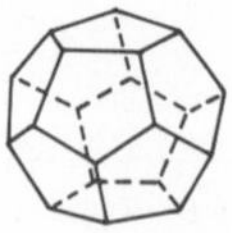

semiregular polyhedra

LOOKING BACK Interested readers may want to investigate **semiregular polyhedra.** These are also formed by using regular polygons as faces, but the regular polygons used need not have the same number of sides. For example, a semiregular polyhedron might have squares and regular octagons as its faces.

EULER'S FORMULA

A simple relationship between the number of faces, edges, and vertices of any polyhedron was discovered by the French mathematician and philosopher René Descartes (1596–1650) and rediscovered by the Swiss mathematician Leonhard Euler (1707–1783). Table 10-8 suggests the relationship for the numbers of vertices (V), edges (E), and faces (F).

Table 10-8

Name	V	F	E	$V + F - E$
Tetrahedron	4	4	6	2
Cube	8	6	12	2
Octahedron	6	8	12	2
Dodecahedron	20	12	30	2
Icosahedron	12	20	30	2

Euler's formula

In each case, $V + F - E = 2$. This result is known as **Euler's formula.** Prisms, pyramids, and Euler's formula are investigated in the problem set.

CYLINDERS AND CONES

cylinder

bases

A cylinder is an example of a simple closed surface that is not a polyhedron. Consider a line segment $\overline{AB}$ and a line ℓ as shown in Figure 10-41. When AB moves so that it is always parallel to a given line ℓ and points A and B trace simple closed curves other than polygons, the surface generated by $\overline{AB}$, along with the simple closed curves and their interiors, form a **cylinder.** The simple closed curves along with their interiors are called the **bases** of the cylinder and the remaining points constitute the *lateral surface of the cylinder.* Three different cylinders are pictured in Figure 10-41.

Figure 10-41

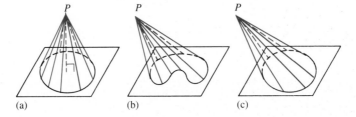

(a)   (b)   (c)

circular cylinder

right cylinder

oblique cylinder

If a base of a cylinder is a circular region, the cylinder is called a **circular cylinder.** If the line segment forming a cylinder is perpendicular to a base, the cylinder is called a **right cylinder.** Cylinders that are not right cylinders are called **oblique cylinders.** The cylinder in Figure 10-41(a) is a right cylinder; those in Figure 10-41(b) and (c) are oblique cylinders.

cone

vertex

Suppose we have a simple closed curve, other than a polygon, in a plane and a point P not in the plane of the curve. The union of the set of line segments connecting point P to each point of a simple closed curve and the simple closed curve and its interior is called a **cone.** Cones are pictured in Figure 10-42. Point P is called the **vertex** of the cone. The points of the cone

Figure 10-42

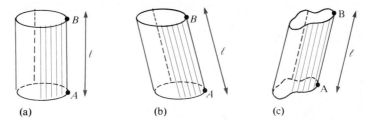

(a)   (b)   (c)

HISTORICAL NOTE

Leonhard Euler went blind in 1766 and for the remaining 17 years of his life continued to do mathematics by dictating to a secretary and by writing formulas in chalk on a slate for his secretary to copy down. He published 530 papers in his lifetime and left enough work to supply the *Proceedings of the St. Petersburg Academy* for the next 47 years.

that are not in the base constitute the *lateral surface of the cone*. A line segment from the vertex P perpendicular to the plane of the base is called the

altitude
right circular cone

altitude. A **right circular cone,** such as the one in Figure 10-42(a), is a cone whose altitude intersects the base (a circular region) at the center of the circle. Figure 10-42(b) illustrates an oblique cone and Figure 10-42(c) illustrates an

oblique circular cone

oblique circular cone.

SPHERES

sphere

A **sphere,** as pictured in Figure 10-43, is sometimes considered the most perfect of all figures. It can be defined as the set of all points in space at a given distance from a given point, its center. A sphere is a simple closed surface.

Figure 10-43

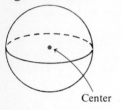

Center

LABORATORY ACTIVITY

1. The following are patterns for constructing the five regular polyhedra. Enlarge these patterns and fold them appropriately to construct the corresponding polyhedra.

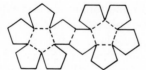 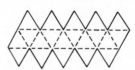

2. (a) Construct a pattern for making a square pyramid.
   (b) Construct a pattern for making a right pentagonal prism. (*Hint:* Imagine a pentagonal prism cut along one of the lateral edges.)
   (c) Construct a pattern for making a right circular cone.

PROBLEM SET 10-4

1. Identify each of the following polyhedra. If a polyhedron can be described in more than one way, give as many names as possible.

(a)

(b)

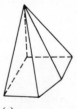

(c)

2. Given the tetrahedron shown on the next page, name the following.
   (a) Vertices (b) Edges (c) Faces
   (d) Intersection of face DRW and edge RA.

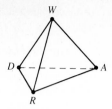

3. What type of polygon is each face of the following polyhedra?
(a) Dodecahedron   (b) Icosahedron

4. For each of the following, what is the minimum number of faces possible?
(a) Prism   (b) Pyramid   (c) Polyhedron

5. Classify each of the following as true or false.
(a) If the lateral faces of a prism are rectangles, it is a right prism.
(b) Every pyramid is a prism.
(c) Every pyramid is a polyhedron.
(d) The bases of a prism lie in perpendicular planes.
(e) The bases of all cones are circles.
(f) A cylinder has only one base.
(g) All lateral faces of an oblique prism are rectangular regions.
(h) All regular polyhedra are convex.

6. Given a rectangular prism, how many possible pairs of bases does it have? Explain.

7. For each of the following, draw a prism and a pyramid having the given region as a base.
(a) Triangle   (b) Pentagon
(c) Regular hexagon

8. Verify Euler's formula for each of the polyhedra in Problem 1.

9. Answer each of the following concerning a pyramid and a prism, each having an n-gon as a base.
(a) How many faces does each have?
(b) How many vertices does each have?
(c) How many edges does each have?
(d) Use your answers to (a), (b), and (c) to verify Euler's formula for all pyramids and all prisms.

10. Complete the table for each of the polyhedra listed in the table.

Polyhedron	Vertices	Faces	Edges
(a)		8	12
(b)	20	30	
(c)	6		15
(d) Prism with an n-gon as base			
(e) Pyramid with an n-gon as base			

11. Check whether Euler's formula holds for each figure.

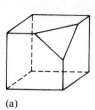
(a)

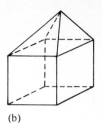
(b)

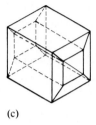
(c)

12. In the cube, $\overline{BF}$ and $\overline{AE}$ are diagonals of the upper and lower faces, respectively.

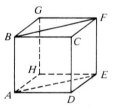

(a) Is quadrilateral $ABFE$ a parallelogram? Is it a rectangle? Explain.
(b) Find six planes perpendicular to the plane containing square $ADEH$.
(c) Is $\overleftrightarrow{CD}$ parallel to the plane containing quadrilateral $ABFE$? Why?

Review Problems

13. Triangles ABC and CDE are equilateral triangles. Find the measure of $\angle BCD$.

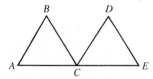

14. What is the measure of each angle in a regular nonagon?

15. Classify the following as true or false. If false, tell why.
(a) Every rhombus is a parallelogram.
(b) Every polygon has at least three sides.
(c) Triangles can have at most two acute angles.

(d) An angle is a polygon.———
(e) Two vertical angles can be supplementary.
(f) If $\angle ABC \cong \angle XYZ$, then $\overline{AB} \cong \overline{XY}$.

16. In a plane, how many of each of the following regular polygons will fit together at a vertex without overlapping and without leaving gaps?
   (a) Equilateral triangles
   (b) Squares
   (c) Hexagons

17. (a) If two angles of a triangle are complementary, what type of triangle is it?
   *(b) Prove your answer.

18. If two lines are intersected by a third line in such a way that the sum of the measures of two interior angles formed by the transversal (the third line) is less than 180°, what can be said about the two original lines?

BRAIN TEASER

A rectangular region can be rolled to form the lateral surface of a right circular cylinder. What shape of paper is needed to make an oblique circular cylinder? (See "Making a Better Beer Glass" by A. Hoffer.)

---

*Section 10-5   Networks and Topological Equivalence

A famous problem introduced by Leonhard Euler in 1735 is known as the *Königsberg bridge problem.* The old German city of Königsberg contained a river, two islands, and seven bridges, as shown in Figure 10-44. The problem is to determine if a person can take a walk around the city in such a way that each bridge is crossed exactly once. A person can start at any land area and end at the same or a different land area. The person may visit any part of the city more than once. We designate the land areas *A, B, C,* and *D* by points and a path between land areas by a curve connecting the appropriate points.

Figure 10-44

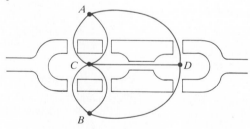

network
vertices / arcs

    The diagram in Figure 10-44 is an example of a **network.** The points are called **vertices,** and the curves are called **arcs.** Using a network diagram, the Königsberg bridge problem can be restated as follows: Is there a path through the network beginning at some vertex and ending at the same or another vertex such that each arc is traversed exactly once? A network having

traversable

such a path is called **traversable;** that is, each arc is passed through exactly once.

    Consider the networks in Figure 10-45. The first three networks, (a), (b), and (c), are traversable; the fourth network, (d), is not. Notice that the number of arcs meeting at each vertex in networks (a) and (c) is even. Any such vertex

Figure 10-45

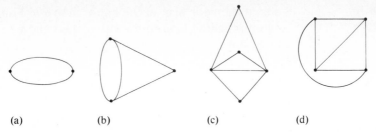

(a) (b) (c) (d)

even vertex
odd vertex

is called an **even vertex.** If the number of arcs meeting at a vertex is odd, it is called an **odd vertex.** In network (b), only the odd vertices are possible starting or stopping points. In network (d), which is not traversable, all the vertices are odd. If a network is traversable, each arrival at a vertex other than a starting or a stopping point requires a departure. Thus, each vertex that is not a starting or stopping point must be even. The starting and stopping vertices in a traversable network may be even or odd, as seen in Figure 10-45(a) and (b), respectively.

In general, networks have the following properties:

1. *If a network has all even vertices, it is traversable. Any vertex can be a starting point, and the same vertex must be the stopping point.*
2. *If a network has two odd vertices, it is traversable. One odd vertex must be the starting point, and the other odd vertex must be the stopping point.*
3. *If a network has more than two odd vertices, it is not traversable.*
4. *There is no network with exactly one odd vertex.*

Example 10-9

Which of the networks in Figure 10-46 are traversable?

Figure 10-46

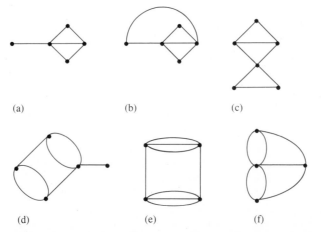

(a) (b) (c)

(d) (e) (f)

Solution

Networks in (b) and (e) have all even vertices and therefore are traversable. Networks in (a) and (c) have exactly two odd vertices and are traversable. Networks in (d) and (f) have four odd vertices and are not traversable.

The network of Figure 10-46(f) represents the Königsberg bridge problem. The network has four odd vertices, and, consequently, the network is not traversable; hence, no walk is possible to complete the problem.

Example 10-10

Look at the floor plan of the house shown in Figure 10-47. Is it possible to go through all the rooms of the house and pass through each door exactly once?

Figure 10-47

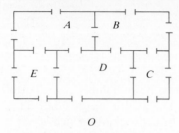

Solution

Represent the floor plan as a network. Designate the rooms and the outside as vertices and the paths through the doors as arcs.

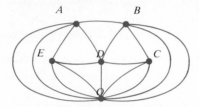

The network has more than two odd vertices, namely, *A*, *B*, *D*, and *O*. Thus, the network is not traversable, and it is impossible to go through all the rooms and pass through each door exactly once.

Network problems are useful in determining the most efficient routes for such tasks as mail delivery and garbage collection where it is desirable to travel along a street only once.

TOPOLOGICAL EQUIVALENCE IN A PLANE

topology
topologically equivalent

Networks are frequently studied in the field of topology. The study of **topology** has been referred to as "rubber-sheet" geometry. In topology, one figure is **topologically equivalent** to another figure as long as one figure can be deformed into the other by simply stretching or shrinking. No cutting or tearing is allowed. As seen in Figure 10-48, a circle may be deformed in many ways into different figures that are topologically equivalent.

Figure 10-48

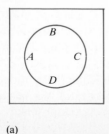

(a)

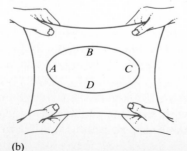

(b)

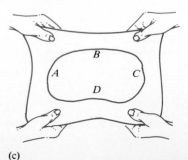

(c)

In general, any simple closed curve is topologically equivalent to a circle.

Example 10-11

Which of the following figures are topologically equivalent?

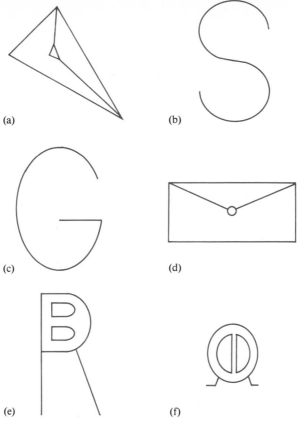

(a)

(b)

(c)

(d)

(e)

(f)

Solution

(a) and (d) are topologically equivalent.
(b) and (c) are topologically equivalent.
(e) and (f) are topologically equivalent.

TOPOLOGICAL EQUIVALENCE IN THREE DIMENSIONS

In a manner similar to that of determining topological equivalence in a plane, objects in three dimensions can be considered topologically equivalent if one object can be deformed into another by stretching or shrinking but without cutting, tearing, or puncturing. For example, in Figure 10-49(a), the beach ball is topologically equivalent to the slightly deflated beach ball; in Figure 10-49(b), the doughnut is topologically equivalent to the coffee cup because the doughnut mass can be reshaped into the coffee cup (the hole becomes the hole for the handle); and in Figure 10-49(c), the sugar bowl is topologically equivalent to the two-handled satchel.

Intuitively speaking, the objects in Figure 10-49(a) are topologically equivalent because they have no holes; the objects in Figure 10-49(b) are topologically equivalent because they have one hole, and the objects in Figure 10-49(c) are topologically equivalent because they have two holes. In each of the equivalences, the number of holes remained unchanged although the shapes were altered.

Figure 10-49

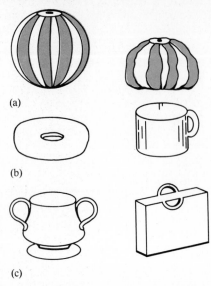

(a)

(b)

(c)

PROBLEM SET 10-5

1. Which of the following networks are traversable? If the network is traversable, draw an appropriate path, labeling the starting and stopping vertices.

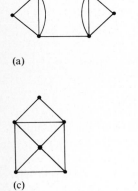

(a)

(b)

(g)

(h)

(c)

(d)

(i)

(j)

(e)

(f)

2. A city contains a river, three islands, and ten bridges, as shown in the accompanying figure. Is it possible to take a walk around the city by starting at any land area and returning after visiting every part of the city and crossing each bridge exactly once? If so, show such a path both on the original figure and on the corresponding network.

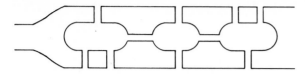

3. Use the accompanying floor plans for each of the following.
   (a) Draw a network that corresponds to each floor plan.
   (b) Determine if it is possible to pass through each room of each house by passing through each door exactly once. If possible, draw such a trip.

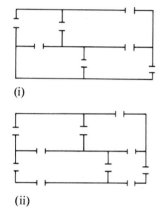

(i)

(ii)

4. Can a person walk through each door once and only once and also go through both of the following houses in a single path? If possible, draw such a path.

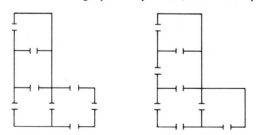

5. At a party, some people shake hands with each other. No person shakes hands more than once with the same person. A person who shakes hands with an odd number of people is called an odd fellow and a person who shakes hands with an even number of people is called an even fellow. Someone makes the statement, "At every party, regardless of how many handshakes take place, the number of odd fellows is even."

(a) Check the validity of the above statement for at least four different cases by drawing appropriate networks.
(b) Is a similar statement regarding even fellows true? Why?

6. Euler's formula for polyhedra can be interpreted for networks by designating F as the number of regions in the plane, V as the number of vertices, and E as the number of arcs. For example, network (a) in the figure separates the plane into three regions and network (b) forms only one region, the outside. For network (a), $V - E + F = 2 - 3 + 3 = 2$, and for network (b), $V - E + F = 6 - 5 + 1 = 2$. Verify Euler's formula for each of the networks in Problem 1.

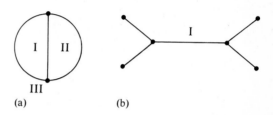

(a)   (b)

7. Molly is making her first trip to the United States and would like to tour the eight states pictured. She would like to plan her trip so that she can cross each border between neighboring states exactly once, that is, the Washington-Oregon border, the Washington-Idaho border, and so on. Is such a trip possible? If so, does it make any difference in which state she starts her trip?

8. Which of the following pairs of figures are topologically equivalent?

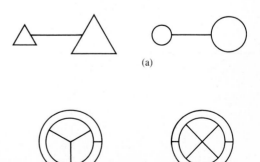

(a)

(b)

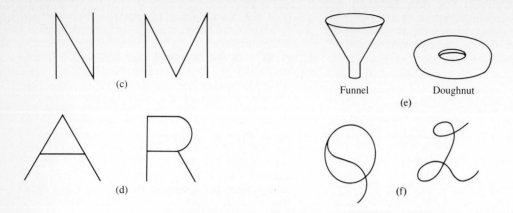

(c)

(d)

Funnel   Doughnut

(e)

(f)

LABORATORY ACTIVITY

1. Take a strip of paper like the one shown in the figure. Give one end a half-twist and join the ends by taping them. The surface obtained is called a Möebius strip.

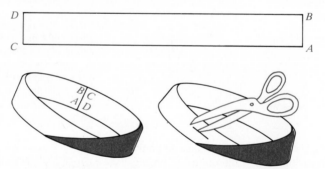

(a) Use a pencil to shade one side of a Möebius strip. What do you discover?

(b) Imagine cutting a Möebius strip all around midway between the edges. What do you predict will happen? Now do the actual cutting. What is the result?

(c) Imagine cutting a Möebius strip one third of the way from an edge and parallel to the edge all the way through until you return to the starting point. Predict the result. Then actually do the cutting. Was your prediction correct?

(d) Imagine cutting around a Möebius strip one fourth of the way from an edge. Predict the result. Then actually do the cutting. How does the result compare with the result of experiment (c)?

2. (a) Take a strip of paper and give it two half-twists (one full twist). Then join the ends together. Answer the questions in (1).

(b) Repeat the experiment in (a), using three half-twists.

(c) Repeat the experiment in (a), using four half-twists. What do you find for odd-numbered twists? Even-numbered twists?

*Section 10-6   Introducing Logo as a Tool in Geometry

This section is optional and can be skipped without affecting the content of remaining chapters or other optional Logo sections. Appendix II on Logo should be completed before this section is begun. In this section, we attempt to show some examples of how Logo might be used as a problem-solving tool in mathematics.

THE TOTAL TURTLE TRIP THEOREM

One of the first figures we learn to draw in Logo is a square. Why is the square an easy figure to draw? A major reason is that in a square, both the internal and external angles have measures of 90°. For figures in which the angles are not apparent, the problem-solving strategy of *guess and check* can be used to determine the angle. We demonstrate this strategy by writing a procedure to draw a five-pointed star of side length 50, as shown in Figure 10-50.

Figure 10-50

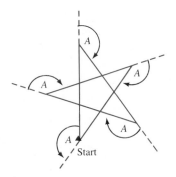

If we begin at the point marked Start in Figure 10-50 and have the turtle trace out the figure, we notice that to draw the star we must go forward 50 units, turn through some angle *A*, and repeat this process four more times. Thus, we should be able to draw the star in Figure 10-50 once we determine the value of :A in the following procedure.

```
TO STAR :A
  REPEAT 5 [FD 50 RT :A]
END
```

When we use the guess and check strategy, our initial guess should be as good as possible. Then, we test our initial guess and if it is wrong, we should learn something to make the next guess better. Continuing this process, we may obtain the exact angle.

From Figure 10-50, we see that the turn angle must be greater than 90° and less than 180°. Suppose 140° is our first guess. Figure 10-51(a) shows the result of executing STAR 140.

Figure 10-51

(a) STAR 140   (b) STAR 150

We see from Figure 10-51(a) that using 140 for :A did not result in sufficient turning to close the figure. We now know that :A is between 140 and 180. If our next guess is 150 and STAR 150 is executed, then Figure 10-51(b) results. We still do not have the desired shape, but we have learned that too much turning takes place when 150 is input for :A. Therefore, the turn angle must be between 140 and 150. If we execute STAR 145, it is not clear whether the correct drawing is obtained. To check whether 145 is the desired value for :A, we may execute REPEAT 20 [STAR 145]. If we have used the desired value for :A, then the same star should be drawn 20 times. The result of executing REPEAT 20 [STAR 145] is given in Figure 10-52.

Figure 10-52

REPEAT 20 [STAR 145]

Figure 10-52 clearly shows that we have a bug and that 145 is not the desired angle. Returning to the STAR procedure, we find that STAR 144 gives the desired result and executing REPEAT 20 [STAR 144] yields a five-pointed star.

The guess and check strategy may not always be effective and, in any case, it is time-consuming. Hence, we develop an alternate way of finding the desired size for :A using the strategy of examining simpler cases. Recall the procedure given in Appendix II for drawing an equilateral triangle. A similar procedure for drawing a variable-sized triangle is given in Figure 10-53, along with a figure it produces.

Figure 10-53

```
TO TRIANGLE :SIZE
  REPEAT 3 [FD :SIZE RT 120]
END
```

TRIANGLE 40

The amount of turning that takes place when walking around the triangle in Figure 10-53 and returning to the original position and heading is equal to the amount of turning in a complete circle. This concept can be generalized into a statement often referred to as the Total Turtle Trip Theorem.

TOTAL TURTLE TRIP THEOREM

Any convex polygon can be drawn with the total turtle turning being 360°.

A more general case of the Total Turtle Trip Theorem is the Closed Path Theorem.

CLOSED PATH THEOREM

The total turtle turning around any closed path is a multiple of 360°

Remark   In the Closed Path Theorem, the curve is allowed to cross itself.

The Total Turtle Trip Theorem can be used to write procedures to draw other regular polygons. For example, to draw a regular pentagon (five sides), each of the five angles must have measure $\frac{1}{5}$ of the total turning involved in walking around the regular pentagon. Thus, each turn angle has measure $360°/5$, or $72°$. A SQUARE procedure could also be developed by using the Total Turtle Trip Theorem. Because there are four turns of equal measure and because the total turning is $360°$, then each angle must be $360°/4$, or $90°$. In general, to draw an *n*-sided polygon, we could write the following procedure, where :N is the number of sides and :SIZE is the length of a side.

```
TO POLYGON :N :SIZE
  REPEAT :N [FD :SIZE RT 360/:N]
END
```

POLYGON 3 50 will draw a triangle with length of side 50, and POLYGON 5 50 will draw a pentagon with length of side 50.

We now use the ideas in the POLYGON procedure to write a procedure to draw the five-pointed star. From the Closed Path Theorem, we know that the total turning must be a multiple of $360°$. Thus, we could write the following STARS procedure, where :N is the number of sides, :SIZE is the length of each side, and :MULT is an integer we multiply times 360 to give multiples of 360.

```
TO STARS :N :SIZE :MULT
  REPEAT :N [FD :SIZE RT 360*:MULT/:N]
END
```

STARS 5 50 1 gives a pentagon; STARS 5 50 2 gives the desired star, and hence the turning angle is $(360° \cdot 2)/5$, or $144°$. This agrees with the result we obtained by using the guess and check strategy.

Could you draw a seven-pointed star using the STARS procedure? Is only one seven-pointed star possible? How about a six-pointed star?

The Total Turtle Trip Theorem can also be used to show other mathematical relationships. For example, consider how we might show that the sum of the measures of the interior angles of any triangle is $180°$. For that purpose, consider the triangle in Figure 10-54 with vertices A, B, and C.

Suppose the turtle is located at vertex A with a heading set toward vertex B. For the turtle to draw triangle ABC and end at the initial position and heading, we must have the turtle move forward the length of segment $\overline{AB}$ and turn right b_2 degrees, then move forward the length of $\overline{BC}$ and turn right c_2 degrees, and then move forward the length of $\overline{CA}$ and turn right a_2 degrees.

Figure 10-54

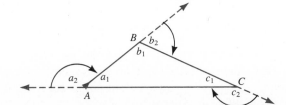

From the Total Turtle Trip Theorem, we know that the total turtle turning around the triangle is $360°$; that is, $a_2 + b_2 + c_2 = 360°$. We also notice that $a_1 + a_2 = b_1 + b_2 = c_1 + c_2 = 180°$. Using these observations, we develop the following.

$$(a_1 + a_2) + (b_1 + b_2) + (c_1 + c_2) = 3 \cdot 180$$

$$(a_1 + b_1 + c_1) + (a_2 + b_2 + c_2) = 3 \cdot 180$$

$$(a_1 + b_1 + c_1) + 360 = 3 \cdot 180$$

$$a_1 + b_1 + c_1 = 3 \cdot 180 - 360 = 180°$$

Thus, we have shown that the sum of the measures of the interior angles of a triangle is $180°$. Using the same ideas of total turtle turning, it can be shown that the sum of the measures of the interior angles of any convex n-gon is $(n - 2)180°$.

PROBLEM SET 10-6

1. How many degrees should the turtle turn at each angle to draw each of the following?
   (a) A regular hexagon (6 sides)
   (b) A regular heptagon (7 sides)
   (c) A regular octagon (8 sides)
   (d) A regular dodecagon (12 sides)
2. Predict the results of executing each of the following and use the computer to check your predictions.
   (a) STARS 5 50 3
   (b) STARS 5 50 4
   (c) STARS 5 50 5
   (d) STARS 5 50 6
   (e) STARS 5 50 7
3. Predict the result of executing the following.

   REPEAT 20 [STAR 143]

4. How many sides does a regular polygon have if the turning angle is each of the following?
   (a) $12°$ (b) $30°$
5. Is it possible to draw a six-pointed star by using the methods developed in this section? Why or why not?
6. Write procedures for drawing each of the following.

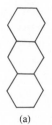

(a)

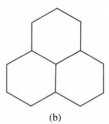

(b)

7. Write a procedure called THIRTY that draws a $30°$ angle.
8. (a) Write a procedure called SEG that draws a segment of length 100 turtle steps with midpoint at home and heading of 45.
   (b) Write a procedure called PAR to draw a segment of length 100 turtle steps that is parallel to the segment drawn in (a).
9. Use the Total Turtle Trip Theorem to show that the sum of the interior angles of any convex polygon is $(n - 2)180°$.

SOLUTION TO THE PRELIMINARY PROBLEM

UNDERSTANDING THE PROBLEM Jernigan was asked to cut a convex polygonal piece of glass in which the smallest interior angle is $120°$ and each successive angle is $5°$ greater than its predecessor. A part of such a piece of glass is pictured in Figure 10-55.

Figure 10-55

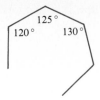

We are to determine whether such a construction is possible and, if so, how many sides the piece of glass will have.

DEVISING A PLAN Because the problem involves the interior angles of a polygon, we might first consider the formula for the sum of the interior angles of a convex n-gon, that is, $(n - 2)180°$. However, because we do not know the number of sides of the n-gon, this approach does not appear fruitful.

A different approach is to consider the sum of the exterior angles of a convex polygon. We know from earlier work in this chapter that in every convex polygon, this sum is 360°. In Figure 10-55, we see that the successive exterior angles of the polygon (if it exists) are $180° - 120°$, $180° - 125°$, $180° - 130°$, and so on, or 60°, 55°, 50°, ... Our goal then is to determine how many terms of this sequence sum to 360°. Because the measure of the greatest exterior angle is 60°, we conclude that we must add at least 360°/60°, or 6, terms of the sequence to obtain the sum of 360°. We also know that there can be no exterior angle with measure less than 5°, so the maximum number of sides is $\frac{360}{5}$, or 72. In fact, we know that the number of sides must be considerably less than 72 because of the size of the first few exterior angles considered.

CARRYING OUT THE PLAN If possible, we are to find the number of terms of the following sequence whose sum is 360.

$$60 + 55 + 50 + \cdots? = 360$$

One way to do this is to use a calculator and subtract the successive terms from 360. If we do that, we start with 360 and see the following display after each successive subtraction.

300, 245, 195, 150, 110, 75, 45, 20, 0

Because it took nine subtractions and the remainder at that time is zero, the piece of glass could be cut into a convex polygon with nine sides.

LOOKING BACK The problem also could have been solved by first considering that the sequence of numbers 60, 55, 50, . . . is an arithmetic sequence, then finding the sum of this sequence in terms of n, setting the sum equal to 360, and solving for n.

QUESTIONS FROM THE CLASSROOM

1. A student claims that if any two planes that do not intersect are parallel, then any two lines that do not intersect should also be parallel. How do you respond?

2. A student says that it is actually impossible to measure an angle, since each angle is the union of two rays that extend infinitely and, therefore, continue forever. What is your response?

3. A student asks, "If every rhombus is a parallelogram, why is a special name for a rhombus necessary?" What is your reply?

4. A student asks whether a polygon whose sides are congruent is necessarily a regular polygon and whether a polygon with all angles congruent is necessarily a regular polygon. How do you answer?

5. A student thinks that a square is the only regular polygon with all right angles. The student asks if this is true and if so, why. How do you answer?

6. A student says that a line is parallel to itself. How do you reply?

7. A student says that a line in the plane of the classroom ceiling cannot be parallel to a line in the plane of the classroom floor because the lines are not in the same plane. Is this student correct? Why?

8. A student says she heard that the shortest distance between any two points is a straight line. Therefore, straight lines should have endpoints. What is your reply?

9. A student asks if you can determine exactly how many semiregular polyhedra exist. How do you respond?

CHAPTER OUTLINE

I. Basic geometric notions
 A. Points, lines, and planes
  1. **Points, lines,** and **planes** are basic, but undefined, terms.
  2. **Collinear points** are points that belong to the same line.
  3. Important subsets of lines are **segments, half-lines,** and **rays.**
  4. **Coplanar points** are points that lie in the same plane. **Coplanar lines** are defined similarly.
  5. Two coplanar lines with exactly one point in common are **intersecting lines.**
  6. **Concurrent lines** are lines that contain a common point.
  7. Two coplanar lines with no points in common are **parallel.**
  8. **Skew lines** are lines that cannot be contained in the same plane
  9. An **angle** is the union of two rays with a common endpoint.
  10. Angles are classified according to size as **acute, obtuse, right,** or **straight.**
  11. Two lines that meet to form a right angle are **perpendicular.**
  12. **Parallel planes** are planes with no points in common.
  13. **Space** is the set of all points.
 B. Plane figures
  1. A **plane curve** is a set of points in a plane that can be traced without lifting a pencil from the paper or retracing any portion of the drawing other than single points.
  2. A **simple closed curve** is a plane curve that can be traced so that the starting and stopping points are the same and no point other than the endpoint is traced more than once. It also separates the plane into three disjoint subsets.
  3. A **polygon** is a simple closed curve that is the union of line segments such that no two segments with a common endpoint are collinear.
   (a) A **diagonal** is any line segment connecting two nonconsecutive vertices of a polygon.
   (b) A **convex polygon** is a polygon with no portion of its diagonals in the exterior.
   (c) A **concave polygon** is a polygon with at least some portion of a diagonal in the exterior.
   (d) A **regular polygon** is a polygon in which all the angles are congruent and all the sides are congruent.
  4. **Congruent figures** are figures with the same size and shape.
  5. Triangles are classified according to the lengths of their sides as being **scalene, isosceles,** or **equilateral,** and according to the measures of their angles as **acute, obtuse,** or **right.**
  6. Quadrilaterals with special properties are **trapezoids, parallelograms, rectangles, rhombi,** and **squares.**
II. Theorems involving angles
 A. **Supplements** of the same angle, or of congruent angles, are congruent.
 B. **Complements** of the same angle, or of congruent angles, are congruent.
 C. **Vertical angles** formed by intersecting lines are congruent.
 D. If any two distinct lines are cut by a transversal, then a pair of corresponding angles, alternate

interior angles, or alternate exterior angles are congruent if and only if the lines are parallel.

E. The sum of the measures of the angles of a triangle is 180°.

F. The sum of the measures of the interior angles of any convex polygon with n sides is $(n - 2)180°$.

G. The sum of the measures of the exterior angles of any convex polygon is 360°.

III. Three-dimensional figures

A. A **polyhedron** is a simple closed surface formed by polygonal regions.

B. Three-dimensional figures with special properties are **prisms, pyramids, regular polyhedra, cylinders, cones** and **spheres.**

C. **Euler's formula,** $V + F - E = 2$, holds for polyhedra, where V, E, and F represent the number of vertices, the number of edges, and the number of faces of a polyhedron, respectively.

*IV. Networks and topology

A. A **network** is a collection of points called **vertices** and a collection of curves called **arcs.**

B. A vertex of a network is called an **even vertex** if the number of arcs meeting at the vertex is even. A vertex is called an **odd vertex** if the number of arcs meeting at a vertex is odd.

C. A network is called **traversable** if there is a path through the network such that each arc is passed through exactly once.

1. If all the vertices of a network are even, then the network is traversable. Any vertex can be a starting point and the same vertex must be the stopping point.

2. If a network has two odd vertices, it is traversable. One odd vertex must be the starting point and the other odd vertex must be the stopping point.

3. If a network has more than two odd vertices, it is not traversable.

4. No network has exactly one odd vertex.

D. A figure is **topologically equivalent** to another when the first can be deformed into the other by simply stretching or shrinking. No cutting or tearing is allowed.

*V. Logo notions

A. **Total Turtle Trip Theorem:** Any convex polygon can be drawn with the total turning being 360°.

B. **Closed Path Theorem:** The total turning around any closed path is a multiple of 360°.

CHAPTER TEST

1. (a) List three different names for line m.

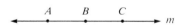

(b) Name two different rays on m with endpoint B.
(c) Find a simpler name for $\overrightarrow{AB} \cap \overrightarrow{BA}$.
(d) Find a simpler name for $\overrightarrow{AB} \cap \overrightarrow{BC}$.
(e) Find a simpler name for $\overrightarrow{BA} \cap \overrightarrow{AC}$.

2. In the figure, $\overrightarrow{PQ}$ is perpendicular to α.

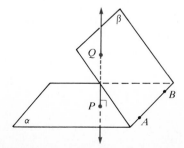

(a) Name a pair of skew lines.
(b) Using only the letters in the figure, name as many planes as possible each perpendicular to α.
(c) What is the intersection of planes APQ and β?
(d) Is there a single plane containing A, B, P, and Q? Explain your answer.

3. List at least three ways to determine a plane.

4. For each of the following, sketch two parallelograms, if possible, that satisfy the given conditions.
(a) Their intersection is a single point.
(b) Their intersection is exactly two points.
(c) Their intersection is exactly three points.
(d) Their intersection is exactly one line segment.

5. Draw each of the following curves.
(a) A simple closed curve
(b) A closed curve that is not simple
(c) A concave hexagon
(d) A convex decagon

6. (a) Can a triangle have two obtuse angles? Justify your answer.

(b) Can a parallelogram have four acute angles? Justify your answer.

7. In a certain triangle, the measure of one angle is twice the measure of the smallest angle. The measure of the third angle is seven times greater than the measure of the smallest angle. Find the measures of each of the angles in the triangle.

8. (a) Explain how to derive an expression for the sum of the measures of the angles in a convex n-gon.
(b) In a certain regular polygon, the measure of each angle is 176°. How many sides does the polygon have?

9. (a) Sketch a convex polyhedron with at least ten vertices.
(b) Count the number of vertices, edges, and faces for the polyhedron in (a) and determine if Euler's formula holds for this polyhedron.

10. If $3x°$ and $(6x - 18)°$ are measures of corresponding angles formed by two parallel lines and a transversal, what is the value of x?

11. Find $6°48'59'' + 28°19'36''$. Write your answer in simplest terms.

12. In the figure, ℓ is parallel to m, and $m(\angle 1) = 60°$. Find each of the following.

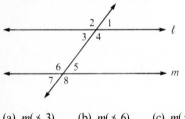

(a) $m(\angle 3)$ (b) $m(\angle 6)$ (c) $m(\angle 8)$

13. If a pyramid has an octagon for a base, how many lateral faces does it have?

14. If ABC is a right triangle and $m(\angle)A = 42°$, what is the measure of the other acute angle?

*15. (a) Which of the following networks are traversable?
(b) Find a corresponding path for those networks that are traversable.

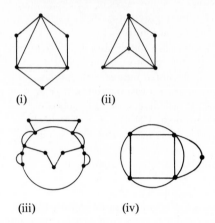

(i)   (ii)

(iii)   (iv)

*16. Write a Logo program to construct two perpendicular segments.

*17. Write a Logo program to draw a variable-sized isosceles triangle.

SELECTED BIBLIOGRAPHY

Alexick, H., and F. Kidder. "Why Is a Rectangle Not a Square?" *Arithmetic Teacher* 27 (December 1979): 26–27.

Barr, S. *Experiments in Topology.* New York: Thomas Y. Crowell, 1964.

Bright, G. "Using Tables to Solve Some Geometry Problems." *Arithmetic Teacher* 25 (May 1978):39–43.

Brydegaard, M., and J. Inskeep, Jr. *Readings in Geometry from the Arithmetic Teacher.* Washington, D.C.: National Council of Teachers of Mathematics, 1970.

Burger, W. "Geometry." *Arithmetic Teacher* 32 (February 1985):52–56.

Campbell, P. "Cardboard, Rubber Bands, and Polyhedron Models." *Arithmetic Teacher* 31 (October 1983):48–52.

Charles, R. "Some Guidelines for Teaching Geometry Concepts." *Arithmetic Teacher* 27 (April 1980): 18–20.

Cox, P. "Informal Geometry—More Is Needed." *The Mathematics Teacher* 78 (September 1985):404, 405, 435.

Damarin, S. "What Makes a Triangle." *Arithmetic Teacher* 29 (September 1981):39–41.

Henderson, G., and C. Collier. "Geometric Activities for Later Childhood Education." *The Arithmetic Teacher* 20 (October 1973):444–453.

Hoffer, A. "Making a Better Beer Glass." *The Mathematics Teacher* 75 (May 1982):378–379.

Immerzeel, G. "Geometric Activities for Early Childhood Education." *The Arithmetic Teacher* 20 (October 1973):438–443.

Maletsky, E. "Generating Solids." *The Mathematics Teacher* 76 (October 1983):499, 500, 504–507.

Morrell, L. "GE-O-ME-TR-Y." *Arithmetic Teacher* 27 (March 1980):52.

O'Daffer, P., and S. Clemens. *Geometry: An Investigative Approach*. Reading, Mass.: Addison-Wesley, 1976.

Ore, O. *Graphs and Their Uses*. New York: Random House, L. W. Singer, 1963.

Phillips, J. "The History of the Dodecahedron." *The Mathematics Teacher* 58 (March 1965):248–250.

Prevost, F. "Geometry in the Junior High School." *The Mathematics Teacher* 78 (September 1985):411–418.

Reynolds, J. "Build a City." *Arithmetic Teacher* 33 (September 1985):12–15.

Ross, J. "How to Make a Möebius Hat." *The Mathematics Teacher* 78 (April 1985):268–269.

Shaughnessy, J., and W. Burger. "Spadework Prior to Deduction in Geometry." *The Mathematics Teacher* 78 (September 1985):419–428.

Steinhaus, H. *Mathematical Snapshots*. 3rd ed. Oxford: Oxford University Press, 1983.

Suydam, M. "The Shape of Instruction in Geometry: Some Highlights from Research." *The Mathematics Teacher* 78 (September 1985):481–486.

Trigg, C. "Collapsible Models of Regular Octahedrons." *The Mathematics Teacher* 65 (October 1972):530–533.

Wahl, M. "Marshmallows, Toothpicks, and Geodesic Domes." *Arithmetic Teacher* 25 (December 1977): 39–42.

Walle, J., and C. Thompson. "Promoting Mathematical Thinking." *Arithmetic Teacher* 32 (February 1985): 7–13.

Walter, M. "Frame Geometry: An Example in Posing and Solving Problems." *Arithmetic Teacher* 28 (October 1980):16–18.

Young, J. "Improving Spatial Abilities with Geometric Activities." *Arithmetic Teacher* 30 (September 1982): 38–43.

Zaslavsky, C. "Networks—New York Subways, A Piece of String, and African Traditions." *Arithmetic Teacher* 29 (October 1981):42–47.

CHAPTER 11

Constructions, Congruence, and Similarity

Preliminary Problem

A hiker, carrying a bucket, sees that his tent is on fire. To what point on the bank of the river should the hiker run to fill his bucket in order to make his trip to the tent as short as possible?

Introduction

In this chapter, we introduce the concepts of congruence and similarity. Properties of congruent triangles are investigated through compass-and-straight-edge constructions. Construction problems have always been a favorite topic in geometry. The restriction to straightedge and compass goes back to antiquity. The straight line and circle were considered the basic geometric figures by the Greeks and the straightedge and compass are their physical analogues. It is also believed that the Greek philosopher PLATO (427–347 B.C.) rejected the use of other mechanical devices for geometric constructions because they emphasized practicality rather than "ideas," which he regarded as more important. In teaching geometry, compass-and-straightedge constructions are important because they reinforce the learning of geometric concepts. The basic constructions, which are introduced and explained in this chapter, are summarized in a step-by-step approach in Appendix III. Constructions are also done in this chapter using paper folding and a plastic device called a Mira.

Throughout the chapter, we use linear metric measurement and the notion of length, although a formal discussion of measurement is postponed until Chapter 12.

Section 11-1

Congruence Through Constructions

In mathematics, the word **congruent** is used to describe objects that have the same size and shape. Tracing is a method for determining congruence in elementary schools. For example, the squares in Figure 11-1 are congruent because a tracing of one square can be made to match the other. Also, we

Figure 11-1

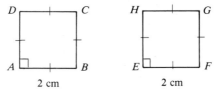

2 cm   2 cm

can say that the two squares in Figure 11-1 are congruent because each has a side of measure 2 cm (centimeters). We say that *ABCD* is congruent to *EFGH* and write *ABCD* ≅ *EFGH*.

Any two line segments have the same shape, so *two line segments are congruent if they have the same size (length). The length of the line segment* $\overline{AB}$ *is denoted by AB. Thus* $\overline{AB} \cong \overline{CD}$ *if and only if AB = CD. Two angles are congruent if their measures are the same.* Also, any segment is congruent to itself and any angle is congruent to itself; that is, congruence is a relation that has the reflexive property.

Ancient Greek mathematicians constructed geometric figures with a straightedge (no markings on it) and a collapsible compass. Figure 11-2(a) shows a modern compass. It is used to mark off and duplicate lengths but not to measure them. The compass is also used to draw arcs or circles, as in Figure 11-2(b). To draw a circle or an arc, open the compass to some width; hold the pointer in place, marking the center of the circle or arc; then, move the pencil. The figure formed is a circle or an arc.

Figure 11-2

Construct a circle or an arc

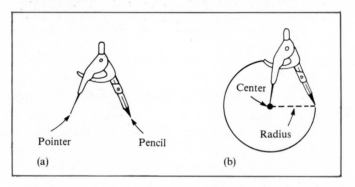

Pointer   Pencil   Center   Radius

(a)   (b)

circle
radius
center

arc

center of an arc

The construction of a circle with a compass shows that a **circle** can be defined as the set of all points in a plane at a given distance, the **radius,** from a given point, the **center.** A circle with center *C* is called circle *C*.

An **arc** of a circle can be thought of as any part of the circle that can be drawn without lifting a pencil. An arc is either a part of a circle or the entire circle. Thus, the **center of an arc** is the center of the circle containing the arc.

Two points on a circle determine two different arcs. To avoid this ambiguity, an arc is normally named by three letters, such as arc *ACB* in Figure 11-3. Arc *ACB* is denoted by $\overparen{ACB}$. In this notation, the first and last letters indicate the endpoints of the arc and the middle letter indicates which of two possible arcs is intended. If there is no danger of ambiguity in a discussion, we use two letters to name the arc formed. For example, in Figure 11-3, the

Figure 11-3

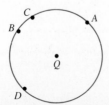

minor arc / major arc
semicircle

smaller arc is named either $\overgroup{ACB}$ or $\overgroup{AB}$. The smaller arc, $\overgroup{ACB}$, is called the **minor arc,** and the larger arc, $\overgroup{ADB}$, is called the **major arc.** If the major arc and the minor arc of a circle are the same size, each is called a **semicircle.**

CONSTRUCTING SEGMENTS AND CIRCLES

There are many ways to construct a segment congruent to a given segment $\overline{AB}$. A natural approach is to use a ruler, measure $\overline{AB}$, and then draw the congruent segment. A different way is to trace $\overline{AB}$ onto another piece of paper. A third method is to use a straightedge and a compass. To copy $\overline{AB}$ on any line ℓ using a compass, first fix the compass so that the pointer is on A and the pencil is on B, as in Figure 11-4(a). The compass opening represents the length of $\overline{AB}$. Then, on ℓ, choose a point C. Next, without changing the compass setting, place the point of the compass at C and strike an arc that intersects the line, as in Figure 11-4(b). Label the point of intersection of the arc and the line as D. Then $\overline{AB} \cong \overline{CD}$. (A summary of each boxed construction in this chapter is given in Appendix III.)

Figure 11-4

Construct a line segment congruent to a given segment

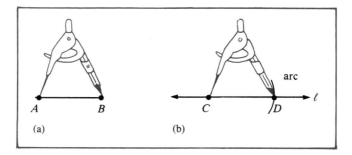

(a)

(b)

In Figure 11-5(a), circle C is given. By opening the compass to a width equal to CR and placing the compass point at an arbitrary point Q, circle Q can be constructed congruent to circle C. Thus, *two circles are congruent if their radii have the same length.*

Figure 11-5

Construct a circle congruent to a given circle

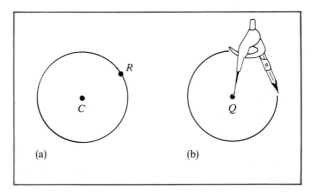

(a)

(b)

We use the concept of congruence for segments and angles as the basis for determining whether polygons, specifically triangles, are congruent. Attempting to construct congruent triangles provides motivation for necessary and sufficient conditions for determining congruent triangles.

TRIANGLE CONGRUENCE

Consider the two triangles shown in Figure 11-6. *If triangle ABC is congruent to triangle A′B′C′, written* $\triangle ABC \cong \triangle A′B′C′$, *then the congruency establishes a one-to-one correspondence between vertices A and A′, B and B′, C and C′ such that* $\overline{AB} \cong \overline{A′B′}$, $\overline{AC} \cong \overline{A′C′}$, $\overline{BC} \cong \overline{B′C′}$, $\angle A \cong \angle A′$, $\angle B \cong \angle B′$, *and* $\angle C \cong \angle C′$.

Figure II-6

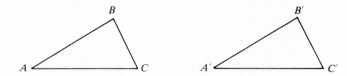

The order of the letters in the symbolic congruence is important. For example, in Figure 11-7, if $\triangle ABC \cong \triangle DEF$, then vertex A corresponds to vertex D, B corresponds to E, and C corresponds to F. This correspondence also identifies the congruent angles and sides of the triangles, as listed.

$\angle A \cong \angle D$, $\angle B \cong \angle E$, and $\angle C \cong \angle F$

$\overline{AB} \cong \overline{DE}$, $\overline{BC} \cong \overline{EF}$, and $\overline{AC} \cong \overline{DF}$

Figure II-7

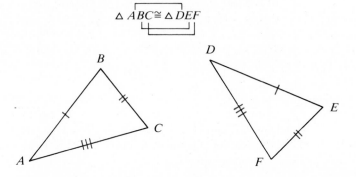

If $\triangle ABC \cong \triangle DEF$, as in Figure 11-7, then any rearrangement of the letters ABC and the corresponding rearrangement of DEF results in another symbolic representation of the same congruence. For example, $\triangle BAC \cong \triangle EDF$. Because there are $3 \cdot 2 \cdot 1$, or 6, ways to rearrange the letters A, B, and C, each pair of congruent triangles can be symbolized in six ways. However, each of the six symbolic representations gives the same information about the triangles.

Example II-I

Assume that each of the pairs of triangles in Figure 11-8 is congruent and write an appropriate symbolic congruence in each case.

Solution

(a) Vertex C corresponds to D because the angles at C and D are right angles. Also, $\overline{CB} \cong \overline{DF}$ and C corresponds to D, so B corresponds to F. Consequently, the remaining vertices must correspond; that is, A corresponds to E. Thus, one possible symbolic congruence is $\triangle ABC \cong \triangle EFD$.

Figure 11-8

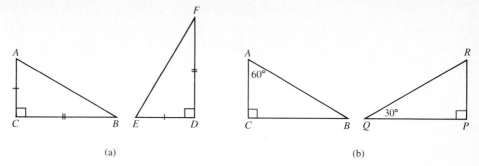

(a)   (b)

(b) Vertex C corresponds to P because the angles at C and P are both right angles. To establish the other correspondences, we first find the missing angles in the triangles. We see that $m(\angle B) = 90° - 60° = 30°$ and $m(\angle R) = 90° - 30° = 60°$. Consequently, A corresponds to R because $m(\angle A) = m(\angle R) = 60°$ and B corresponds to Q because $m(\angle B) = m(\angle Q) = 30°$. Thus, one possible symbolic congruence is $\triangle ABC \cong \triangle RQP$.

SIDE, SIDE, SIDE (SSS)

Is it necessary to use all three sides and all three angles of a triangle ABC to construct another triangle congruent to it? Actually, $\triangle ABC$ can be duplicated by copying fewer parts of the triangle. For example, using only segments of lengths AB, BC, and AC, as shown in Figure 11-9(a), we can construct $\triangle A'B'C'$ congruent to $\triangle ABC$.

Figure 11-9

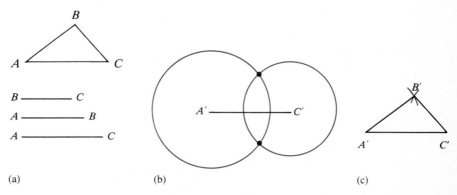

(a)   (b)   (c)

First, we construct a segment congruent to any of the three segments. For example, we may construct $\overline{A'C'}$ so that it is congruent to $\overline{AC}$. To complete the triangle construction, the other vertex, B', must be located. The distance from A' to B' is AB. All points at a distance AB from A' are on a circle with center at A' and radius of length AB. Similarly, B' must be on a circle with center C' and radius of length BC. Figure 11-9(b) shows the two circles. Because B' is on both circles, the only possible locations for B' are at the points where the two circles intersect. Either point is acceptable. Usually, a picture of the construction shows only one possibility, and the construction uses only arcs, as pictured in Figure 11-9(c).

Remark Starting the construction with a segment $\overline{A'B'}$ congruent to $\overline{AB}$ or with $\overline{B'C'}$ congruent to $\overline{BC}$ would also result in triangles congruent to $\triangle ABC$.

From the preceding construction, it may seem that given any three segments, it is possible to construct a triangle whose sides are congruent to the given segments. However, this is not the case. For example, consider the segments in Figure 11-10(a), whose measures are p, q, and r. If we choose the base of the triangle to be a side of length p and attempt to find the third vertex by intersecting arcs, as in Figure 11-10(b), we find that the arcs do not intersect. Because no intersection occurs, a triangle is not determined. Similarly, if we attempt to construct a triangle with the given sides p, q, and r starting with side q or r, we see that the construction would fail as well.

Figure II-10

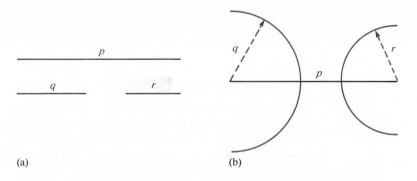

(a)   (b)

Thus, we see that *the sum of the measures of any two sides of a triangle must be greater than the measure of the third side.* This property is called the

Triangle Inequality **Triangle Inequality.** For example, segments of length 3 cm, 5 cm, and 9 cm do not determine a triangle because $3 + 5$ is not greater than 9.

Now, cut three narrow rectangular pieces of cardboard of different lengths. Then, using paper fasteners in the corners, try to assemble the pieces into a triangle, as shown in Figure 11-11. When a triangle can be assembled, you will see that it is rigid; that is, the pieces do not move. The rigidity of a triangle is used in real-life constructions such as bicycle frames and frames of buildings or towers like the Eiffel Tower. The rigidity of the triangle in Figure 11-11 and the construction in Figure 11-9 suggest that the size and shape of a triangle are determined by its three sides. In other words, if three sides of one triangle are congruent, respectively, to three sides of another triangle, then

Side, Side, Side (SSS) the triangles are congruent. This property is called **Side, Side, Side** and is abbreviated **SSS.**

Figure II-II

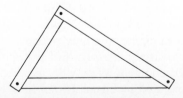

Property Side, Side, Side (SSS) If the three sides of one triangle are congruent, respectively, to the three sides of a second triangle, then the triangles are congruent.

Example 11-2

For each of the parts in Figure 11-12, use SSS to explain why the given pair of triangles is congruent.

Figure 11-12

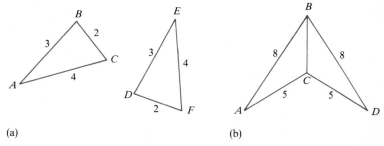

(a)   (b)

Solution

(a) $\triangle ABC \cong \triangle EDF$ by SSS because $\overline{AB} \cong \overline{ED}$, $\overline{BC} \cong \overline{DF}$, and $\overline{AC} \cong \overline{EF}$.
(b) $\triangle ABC \cong \triangle DBC$ by SSS because $\overline{AB} \cong \overline{DB}$, $\overline{AC} \cong \overline{DC}$, and $\overline{BC} \cong \overline{BC}$.

CONSTRUCTING CONGRUENT ANGLES

We use the SSS notion of congruent triangles to construct an angle congruent to a given angle $\angle B$ by making $\angle B$ a part of a triangle and then by reproducing this triangle. For example, given $\angle B$ in Figure 11-13(a), we draw a segment having endpoints A and C on the sides of $\angle B$ to determine $\triangle ABC$. We then construct $\triangle A'B'C'$ congruent to $\triangle ABC$ using SSS, as shown in Figure 11-13(b). Because congruent triangles have corresponding congruent parts, $\angle B \cong \angle B'$.

Figure 11-13

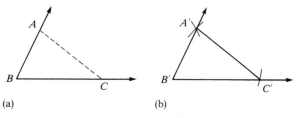

(a)   (b)

A more efficient way to copy $\angle B$ is as follows. First, construct an isosceles triangle, $\triangle ABC$, with $\overline{AB} \cong \overline{BC}$ by marking off any arc $\overparen{AC}$ with center B. Then, duplicate the triangle. Figure 11-14 shows the construction.

Figure 11-14

Copy an angle

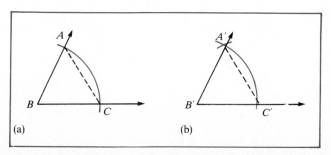

(a)   (b)

We have seen that three sides of a triangle determine the triangle. Are two sides sufficient to determine a triangle; that is, are two sides sufficient to construct a triangle congruent to a given triangle? Consider Figure 11-15(b), which shows three different triangles with sides congruent to the segments given in Figure 11-15(a). The length of the third side depends on the measure of the angle between the other two sides.

Figure 11-15

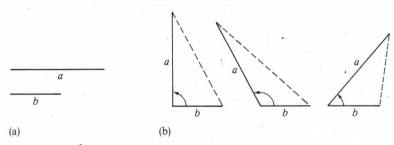

(a)   (b)

SIDE, ANGLE, SIDE (SAS)

Figure 11-16 shows the construction of a triangle congruent to $\triangle ABC$ using two sides $\overline{AB}$ and $\overline{AC}$ and the *included angle,* $\angle A$, formed by these sides. First, a ray with an arbitrary endpoint A' is drawn, and $\overline{A'C'}$ is constructed congruent to $\overline{AC}$. Then, $\angle A'$ is constructed so that $\angle A' \cong \angle A$, and B' is marked on the side of $\angle A'$ not containing C' so that $\overline{A'B'} \cong \overline{AB}$. Connecting B' and C' completes $\triangle A'B'C'$ so that $\triangle A'B'C' \cong \triangle ABC$.

Figure 11-16

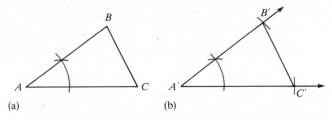

(a)   (b)

Side, Angle, Side (SAS)

Thus, two triangles are congruent if two corresponding sides and the included angle of each triangle are congruent. This property is called **Side, Angle, Side** and is abbreviated **SAS**.

Property   Side, Angle, Side (SAS)   If two sides and the included angle of one triangle are congruent to two sides and the included angle of another triangle, respectively, then the two triangles are congruent.

Remark   When A is written between S and S, as in SAS, it is assumed to be the included angle.

Example 11-3

For each part of Figure 11-17, use SAS to prove that the given pair of triangles is congruent.

Solution

(a) $\triangle ABC \cong \triangle EDF$ by SAS because $\overline{AB} \cong \overline{ED}$, $\angle B \cong \angle D$, and $\overline{BC} \cong \overline{DF}$.
(b) $\triangle ABD \cong \triangle CDB$ by SAS because $\overline{AB} \cong \overline{CD}$, $\angle ABD \cong \angle CDB$, and $\overline{DB} \cong \overline{BD}$.

Figure 11-17

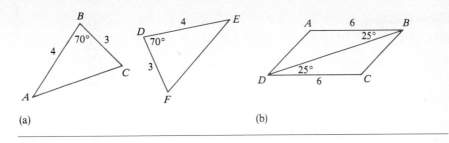

(a)   (b)

Example 11-4

Given isosceles triangle ABC with $\overline{AB} \cong \overline{AC}$ and $\overrightarrow{AD}$ the bisector of $\angle A$, as shown in Figure 11-18, use SAS to prove that $\angle B \cong \angle C$.

Figure 11-18

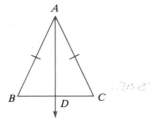

Solution

Because $\overrightarrow{AD}$ is the bisector of $\angle A$, then $\angle BAD \cong \angle CAD$. Also, $\overline{AD} \cong \overline{AD}$ and $\overline{AB} \cong \overline{AC}$, so $\triangle BAD \cong \triangle CAD$ by SAS. Therefore, $\angle B \cong \angle C$ because the angles are corresponding parts of congruent triangles.

Example 11-4 proves the following theorem.

THEOREM 11-1

> If two sides of a triangle are congruent, then the angles opposite these sides are congruent.

If, in two triangles, two sides and an angle not included between these sides are respectively congruent, the information is not sufficient to guarantee congruent triangles. For example, use $\overline{AB}$, $\overline{AC}$, and $\angle C$ of Figure 11-19(a). By making $\overline{A'C'} \cong \overline{AC}$, reproducing $\angle C$ as $\angle C'$, and finding the set of all points at a distance AB from A', it is possible to construct two noncongruent triangles, as shown in Figure 11-19(b) and (c). In certain special cases, if the arc formed by the circle with center A' and radius AB intersects the side of $\angle C'$ in exactly one point, only one triangle can be formed. (For what kind of triangles does this happen? For what cases is no triangle formed?)

Figure 11-19

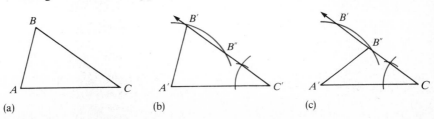

(a)   (b)   (c)

PROBLEM SET 11-1

1. For each of the following, determine whether the given conditions are sufficient to prove that $\triangle PQR \cong \triangle MNO$. Justify your answers.
   (a) $\overline{PQ} \cong \overline{MN}$, $\overline{PR} \cong \overline{MO}$, $\angle P \cong \angle M$
   (b) $\overline{PQ} \cong \overline{MN}$, $\overline{PR} \cong \overline{MO}$, $\overline{QR} \cong \overline{NO}$
   (c) $\overline{PQ} \cong \overline{MN}$, $\overline{PR} \cong \overline{MO}$, $\angle Q \cong \angle N$

2. For each of the following, determine from the given information if it is possible to conclude that triangles (1) and (2) are congruent. Justify your answers.

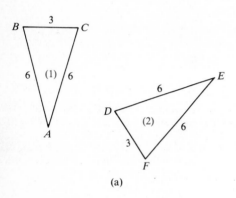

(a)

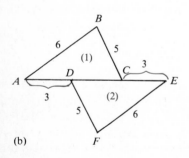

(b)

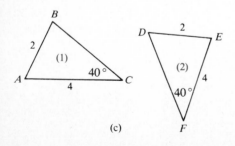

(c)

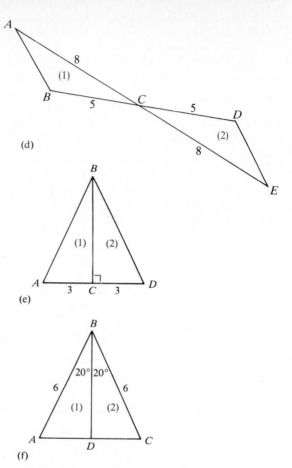

(d)

(e)

(f)

3. Using a ruler, protractor, compass, or tracing paper, construct each of the following, if possible.
   (a) A segment congruent to $\overline{AB}$ and an angle congruent to $\angle CAB$

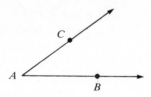

   (b) A triangle with sides of lengths 2 cm, 3 cm, and 4 cm
   (c) A triangle with sides of lengths 4 cm, 3 cm, and 5 cm (What kind of triangle is it?)
   (d) A triangle with sides 4 cm, 5 cm, and 10 cm
   (e) An equilateral triangle with sides 5 cm

(f) A triangle with sides 6 cm and 7 cm and an included angle of measure 75°

(g) A triangle with sides 6 cm and 7 cm and a non-included angle of measure 40°

(h) A triangle with sides 6 cm and 6 cm and a non-included angle of measure 40°

(i) A right triangle with legs 4 cm and 8 cm (The legs include the right angle.)

4. For each of the conditions in Problem 3(b)–(h), does the given information determine a unique triangle? Explain why or why not.

5. Using only a compass and a straightedge, perform each of the following.
   (a) Reproduce ∡A.

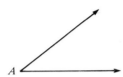

   (b) Construct an equilateral triangle with side $\overline{AB}$.

   A   B

   (c) Construct a 60° angle.
   (d) Construct an isosceles triangle with ∡A as the angle included between the two congruent sides.

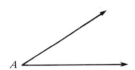

6. Using only a compass and a straightedge, perform each of the following.
   (a) Construct ∡C so that $m(\angle C) = m(\angle A) + m(\angle B)$.

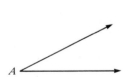

   (b) Using the angles in (a), construct ∡C so that $m(\angle C) = m(\angle B) - m(\angle A)$.

7. In the accompanying drawing, $\overrightarrow{BD}$ bisects ∡ABC of isosceles triangle ABC with $\overline{AB} \cong \overline{CB}$.
   (a) Make a conjecture about a relation between $\overline{AD}$ and $\overline{CD}$.
   *(b) Prove or disprove your conjecture in (a).
   (c) What are the measures of ∡ADB and ∡CDB?
   *(d) Prove your answer in (c).

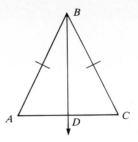

8. Suppose polygon ABCD is any square.
   (a) What is the relationship between point F and the diagonals $\overline{BD}$ and $\overline{AC}$?
   *(b) Prove your answer in (a).
   (c) What are the measures of ∡BFA and ∡AFD?
   *(d) Prove your answer in (c).

9. A group of students on a hiking trip wants to find the distance AB across a pond. One student suggests choosing any point C, connecting it with B, and then finding point D such that ∡DCB ≅ ∡ACB and $\overline{DC} \cong \overline{AC}$. How and why does this help in finding the distance AB?

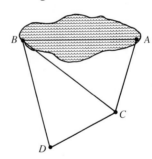

10. In each of the following, find two congruent triangles. State whether the triangles are congruent by SSS or by SAS.

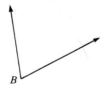

   (a) $\overline{AB} \cong \overline{AC}$

   $\overline{AE} \cong \overline{AD}$

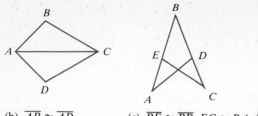

(b) $\overline{AB} \cong \overline{AD}$

$\overline{BC} \cong \overline{DC}$

(c) $\overline{BE} \cong \overline{BD}$, $EC \cong DA$

$\measuredangle BDA \cong \measuredangle BEC$

11. The diagonals of a quadrilateral bisect each other (that is, each diagonal is divided by the point of intersection into two congruent segments).
(a) What kind of quadrilateral must it be?
*(b) Justify your answer in (a).

12. Construct several noncongruent rhombi and noncongruent parallelograms that are not rhombi. In each case, construct the diagonals.
(a) Based on your observations, what is true about the angles formed by the diagonals of a rhombus that is not necessarily true about the angles formed by the diagonals of a parallelogram?
*(b) Prove your conjecture in (a).

*13. (a) What kind of figure is a quadrilateral in which both pairs of opposite sides are congruent?
(b) Prove your answer in (a).

*14. Prove that an equilateral triangle is also equiangular.

*15. The theorem that states that the base angles of an isosceles triangle are congruent followed from Example 11-4, where the angle bisector $\overrightarrow{AD}$ was drawn. It is also possible to prove this theorem without drawing an angle bisector. Prove that $\triangle BAC \cong \triangle CAB$ by using one of the congruence properties, and hence conclude the theorem.

16. Write a Logo procedure to draw a variable-sized equilateral triangle.

17. Logo programs can be used to construct triangles using parts of a triangle. Type the accompanying program into your computer and then run the following. Each time, make sure that the turtle starts at home with heading 0.
(a) SAS 50 75 83
(b) SAS 60 120 60

```
TO SAS :SIDE1 :ANGLE :SIDE2
   FORWARD :SIDE1
   RIGHT 180 — :ANGLE
   FORWARD :SIDE2
   HOME
END
```

18. After seeing the procedure in Problem 17, a student attempted to write a Logo procedure called SSS, with inputs :SIDE1, :SIDE2, and :SIDE3, to construct a triangle given the lengths of its three sides, but did not succeed. What are the difficulties in writing such a program?

Section 11-2   Other Congruence Theorems

ANGLE, SIDE, ANGLE (ASA)

We have seen that triangles can be determined to be congruent by SSS and SAS. Can a triangle be constructed congruent to a given triangle using two angles and a side? There are two possibilities, one with the side included between the angles and one with the side not included between the angles. Figure 11-20 shows the construction of a triangle $A'B'C'$ such that $\overline{A'C'} \cong \overline{AC}$, $\measuredangle A' \cong \measuredangle A$, and $\measuredangle C' \cong \measuredangle C$. It seems that $\triangle A'B'C' \cong \triangle ABC$. This construction illustrates a property of congruence called **Angle, Side, Angle,** abbreviated **ASA**.

Angle, Side, Angle (ASA)

Figure 11-20

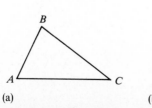

(a)

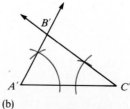

(b)

Property Angle, Side, Angle (ASA) If two angles and the included side of one triangle are congruent to two angles and the included side of another triangle, respectively, then the triangles are congruent.

Angle, Angle, Side (AAS)

Angle, Angle, Side (abbreviated **AAS**) follows directly from ASA. Because the sum of the measures of the angles in any triangle is 180°, if two angles in one triangle are congruent to two angles in another triangle, then the third angle must also be congruent. Consequently, the triangles are congruent by ASA.

Property Angle, Angle, Side (AAS) If two angles and a side of one triangle are congruent to two angles and a side of another triangle, respectively, then the triangles are congruent.

Example 11-5

Use ASA to prove that each of the given pairs of triangles in Figure 11-21 is congruent.

Figure 11-21

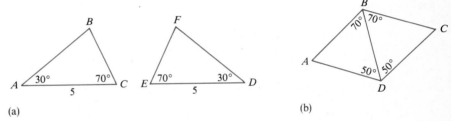

(a)   (b)

Solution

(a) $\angle A \cong \angle D$, $\overline{AC} \cong \overline{DE}$, and $\angle C \cong \angle E$. Consequently, by ASA, $\triangle ABC \cong \triangle DFE$.

(b) $\angle ABD \cong \angle CBD$, $\overline{BD} \cong \overline{BD}$, and $\angle ADB \cong \angle CDB$. Consequently, by ASA, $\triangle ABD \cong \triangle CBD$.

Example 11-6

Use AAS to prove that each of the given pairs of triangles in Figure 11-22 is congruent.

Figure 11-22

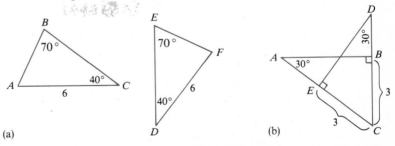

(a)   (b)

Solution

(a) $\angle B \cong \angle E$, $\angle C \cong \angle D$, and $\overline{AC} \cong \overline{FD}$. Consequently, by AAS, $\triangle ABC \cong \triangle FED$.

(b) $\angle A \cong \angle D$, $\angle ABC \cong \angle DEC$, and $\overline{BC} \cong \overline{EC}$. Consequently, by AAS, $\triangle ABC \cong \triangle DEC$.

In Figure 11-23, the angles of one triangle are congruent to corresponding angles in another triangle, and the triangles are not congruent. Thus, an AAA

Figure 11-23

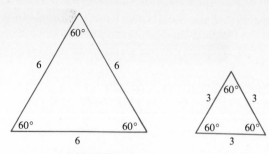

property for congruency does not exist. (The triangles are *similar*, a concept discussed later in this chapter.)

The properties of congruent triangles can be used in a variety of ways. One common use is to show that angles or segments of a given figure are congruent. This is illustrated in the following problem.

PROBLEM 1

Prove that a quadrilateral in which all sides are congruent is a rhombus.

UNDERSTANDING THE PROBLEM We are told that all the sides of the quadrilateral in Figure 11-24 are congruent and we have to show that the figure is a rhombus. Recall that a rhombus is a parallelogram in which all sides are congruent. Thus, we must show that the given quadrilateral is a parallelogram.

Figure 11-24

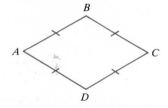

DEVISING A PLAN To show that a quadrilateral is a parallelogram, it is sufficient to show that its opposite sides are parallel. Thus, we need to show that $\overleftrightarrow{AB} \| \overleftrightarrow{DC}$ and $\overleftrightarrow{AD} \| \overleftrightarrow{BC}$. This can be done by showing that a pair of alternate interior angles, alternate exterior angles, or corresponding angles formed by a transversal are congruent.

CARRYING OUT THE PLAN To show that $\overleftrightarrow{BC}$ and $\overleftrightarrow{AD}$ are parallel, a transversal, such as the diagonal $\overline{AC}$ in Figure 11-25, is needed. The diagonal forms ∡1 and ∡2, which are alternate interior angles of the lines $\overleftrightarrow{BC}$ and $\overleftrightarrow{AD}$. Are these angles congruent? Using SSS, we see that △ABC ≅ △CDA; hence, the corresponding parts of the triangles—specifically, the desired angles—are

Figure 11-25

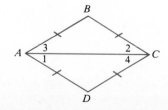

congruent. It follows that $\overleftrightarrow{BC}\,\|\,\overleftrightarrow{AD}$. From the congruence of triangles ABC and CDA, it follows that $\angle 3 \cong \angle 4$ and hence that $\overleftrightarrow{AB}\,\|\,\overleftrightarrow{DC}$. (Why?) Thus, $ABCD$ is a parallelogram and hence a rhombus.

LOOKING BACK One possible Looking Back activity is to investigate whether a quadrilateral in which all angles are congruent must also be a rhombus.

Using properties of congruent triangles, it is possible to deduce various properties of quadrilaterals. Table 11-1 summarizes the definitions and lists some properties of four quadrilaterals. These and other properties of quadrilaterals are further investigated in the problem set.

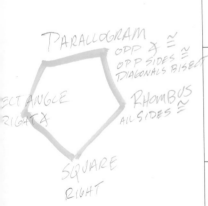

Table 11-1

Quadrilateral and Its Definition	Properties of the Quadrilateral
Parallelogram: A quadrilateral in which each pair of opposite sides is parallel	(a) Opposite sides are congruent. (b) Opposite angles are congruent. (c) Diagonals bisect each other.
Rectangle: A parallelogram with a right angle	(a) A rectangle has all the properties of a parallelogram. (b) All the angles of a rectangle are right angles. (c) A quadrilateral in which all the angles are right angles is a rectangle.
Rhombus: A parallelogram with all sides congruent	(a) A rhombus has all the properties of a parallelogram. (b) A quadrilateral in which all the sides are congruent is a rhombus. (c) The diagonals of a rhombus are perpendicular to each other.
Square: A rectangle with all sides congruent	A square has all the properties of a parallelogram, a rectangle, and a rhombus.

CONGRUENT POLYGONS

Determining congruency conditions for polygons other than triangles is not an easy task. For example, the SSS property for congruent triangles has no analogy for quadrilaterals. The quadrilaterals in Figure 11-26 do not have the same shape. *One way to be sure that two polygons are congruent is to know that all corresponding sides and angles of the polygons are congruent.* This may be done by "moving" one figure to see if it "fits" exactly on top of the other figure. The moving process is discussed in more detail in Sections 11-5 and 11-6.

Figure 11-26

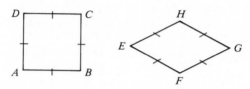

PROBLEM SET 11-2

1. For each of the following, determine whether the given conditions are sufficient to prove that $\triangle PQR \cong \triangle MNO$. Justify your answers.
   (a) $\angle Q \cong \angle N, \angle P \cong \angle M, \overline{PQ} \cong \overline{MN}$
   (b) $\angle R \cong \angle O, \angle P \cong \angle M, \overline{QR} \cong \overline{NO}$
   (c) $\overline{PQ} \cong \overline{MN}, \overline{PR} \cong \overline{MO}, \angle N \cong \angle Q$
   (d) $\angle P \cong \angle M, \angle Q \cong \angle N, \angle R \cong \angle O$

2. Determine whether each of the following pairs of triangles, (1) and (2), is congruent. Justify your answers.

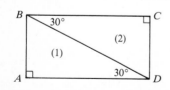

(a)

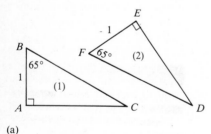

(b)

3. Use a ruler, protractor, or compass to construct each of the following, if possible.

(a) A triangle with angles 60° and 70° and an included side of 8 inches.
(b) A triangle with angles 60° and 70° and a non-included side of 8 cm on a side of the 60° angle.
(c) A right triangle with one acute angle of 75° and a leg of 5 cm on a side of the 75° angle.
(d) A triangle with angles of 30°, 70°, and 80°.

4. For each of the conditions in Problem 3(a)–(d), is it possible to construct two noncongruent triangles? Explain why or why not.

5. What information is needed to determine congruency for each of the following?
   (a) Two squares
   (b) Two rectangles
   (c) Two parallelograms

6. (a) Construct quadrilaterals having exactly one, two, and four right angles.
   (b) Why can a quadrilateral not have exactly three right angles?
   (c) Can a parallelogram have exactly two right angles?

7. In parallelogram $ABCD$, suppose we connect P, a point on $\overline{DC}$, to O and extend $\overline{PO}$ until it intersects $\overline{AB}$ at Q.
   (a) How are $\overline{OP}$ and $\overline{QO}$ related?
   *(b) Prove your answer in (a).

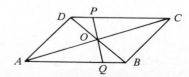

8. Figure *ABCD* is a quadrilateral with two pairs of congruent sides meeting at two opposite vertices; that is, $\overline{AB} \cong \overline{AD}$ and $\overline{BC} \cong \overline{DC}$. Such a quadrilateral is called a **kite.**

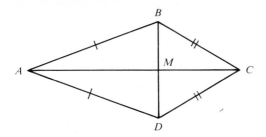

(a) Construct several noncongruent kites in which not all sides are congruent. Label each *ABCD*.
(b) Construct the diagonals of each of the kites in (a) and check that $\overline{AC}$ bisects ∠ *A* and ∠ *C*. Does $\overline{BD}$ bisect ∠ *B* and ∠ *D* in every kite?
(c) In (a), if $\overline{BD}$ bisects ∠ *B* and ∠ *D*, what type of special quadrilateral must *ABCD* be?
(d) Let *M* be the point where the diagonals of kite *ABCD* intersect. Measure ∠ *AMD* in each of the kites in (a) and make a conjecture concerning the angle between the diagonals of a kite.
(e) If two kites have corresponding congruent sides, are they necessarily congruent? Justify your answer.
(f) Is there a kite in which $\overline{AM} \cong \overline{MC}$? If so, what kind of special quadrilateral must the kite be?
(g) Check your answers in (b) and (d) by cutting out several noncongruent kites and folding the kites along their diagonals.
*(h) Prove your conjecture in (d).
*(i) Show that $\overline{BM} \cong \overline{MD}$.

9. In each of the following, if possible, fill in the blank by choosing one of the words *parallelogram, rectangle, rhombus,* or *square* so that the resulting sentence is true. If none of the words makes the sentence true, answer "none" and justify your answer.
(a) A quadrilateral is a _____ if and only if its diagonals bisect each other.
(b) A quadrilateral is a _____ if and only if its diagonals are congruent.
(c) A quadrilateral is a _____ if and only if its diagonals are perpendicular to each other.
(d) A quadrilateral is a _____ if and only if its diagonals are congruent and bisect each other.
(e) A quadrilateral is a _____ if and only if its diagonals are perpendicular to each other and bisect each other.
(f) A quadrilateral is a _____ if and only if its diagonals are congruent, perpendicular to each other, and bisect each other.

(g) A quadrilateral is a _____ if and only if a pair of opposite sides is parallel and congruent.

10. (a) What type of figure is formed by joining the midpoints of a rectangle?

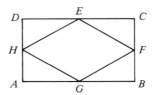

*(b) Prove your answer in (a).
(c) What type of figure is formed by joining the midpoints of the sides of a parallelogram?
*(d) Prove your answer in (c).
(e) Make a conjecture concerning the type of figure formed by joining the midpoints of any quadrilateral.

11. An **isosceles trapezoid** is a trapezoid in which the nonparallel sides are congruent.
(a) Make a conjecture concerning the angles of an isosceles trapezoid.
(b) Make a conjecture concerning the diagonals of an isosceles trapezoid.
*(c) Prove your conjectures in (a) and (b).

12. (a) If *ABCDE* is a regular pentagon, how are $\overline{AC}$, $\overline{CE}$, $\overline{BE}$, $\overline{BD}$, and $\overline{DA}$ related?
*(b) Prove your answer in (a).

*13. Suppose polygon *ABCD* is any parallelogram. Use congruent triangles to prove each of the following.
(a) ∠ *A* ≅ ∠ *C* and ∠ *B* ≅ ∠ *D* (opposite angles are congruent).
(b) $\overline{BC} \cong \overline{AD}$ and $\overline{AB} \cong \overline{CD}$ (opposite sides are congruent).
(c) $\overline{BF} \cong \overline{DF}$ and $\overline{AF} \cong \overline{CF}$ (the diagonals bisect each other).
(d) Prove that ∠ *DAB* and ∠ *ABC* are supplementary.

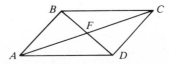

*14. Suppose polygon $ABCD$ is a rectangle. Prove each of the following.

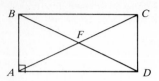

(a) $\overline{AC}$ and $\overline{BD}$ bisect each other (the diagonals bisect each other).
(b) $\overline{AC} \cong \overline{BD}$

*15. If $\overline{AB}$ is perpendicular to plane α, $\measuredangle C \cong \measuredangle D$, and points C, B, and D are in plane α, prove that $\overline{AC} \cong \overline{AD}$.

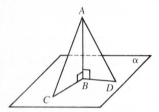

 16. (a) Logo programs can be used to construct triangles using the ASA property. Type the given procedures into your computer and then run the following.
(i)   ASA 60 50 70
(ii)   ASA 80 50 60
(iii) AAS 60 50 70
(iv)   AAS 130 20 50

```
TO ASA :A1 :S :A2
  FORWARD 120
  BACK 120
  LEFT :A1
  FORWARD :S
  RIGHT (180 - :A2)
  FORWARD 120
END
```

```
TO AAS :A1 :A2 :S
  ASA :A1 :S 180 - (:A1 + :A2)
END
```

(b) Predict the outcomes when the following are executed.
(i) AAS 130 50 100   (ii) AAS 90 45 120

 17. (a) Write a Logo procedure called **RHOMBUS** with inputs :SIDE and :ANGLE in which the first variable is the length of the side of the rhombus and the second is the measure of an interior angle of the rhombus.
(b) Execute **RHOMBUS 80 50** and **RHOMBUS 80 130**. What is the relationship between the two figures? Why?
(c) Write a Logo procedure called **SQ.RHOM** with inputs :SIDE and :ANGLE that will draw a square by calling on the **RHOMBUS** procedure.

Review Problems

18. If possible, construct a triangle having the following three segments a, b, and c as its sides.

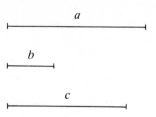

19. Construct an equilateral triangle whose sides are congruent to the following segment.

20. For each pair of triangles shown, determine whether the given conditions are sufficient to show that the triangles are congruent. If the triangles are congruent, tell which property can be used to verify this fact.

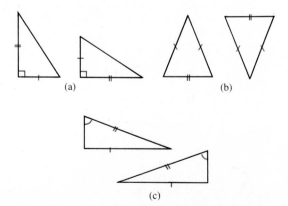

BRAIN TEASER

A treasure map, shown in the accompanying figure, floated ashore in a bottle. It showed Shipwreck Island, where a treasure was buried. According to the directions on the map, the treasure is equidistant from two roads, one joining Bluebeard's Cove with Bottle O'Rum Inn and the other joining Long John's Bay with Bottle O'Rum Inn. Also, the treasure is equidistant from Long John's Bay and Bottle O'Rum Inn. Can you find the treasure?

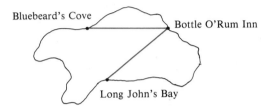

Bluebeard's Cove

Bottle O'Rum Inn

Long John's Bay

Section 11-3

Other Constructions

In the previous section, we proved that a quadrilateral in which all sides are congruent is a rhombus. We use this fact and the following properties of a rhombus to do basic compass-and-straightedge constructions.

Properties
1. The diagonals of a rhombus are perpendicular to each other.
2. The diagonals of a rhombus bisect each other.
3. The diagonals of a rhombus bisect the angles of the rhombus.

CONSTRUCTING PARALLEL LINES

The properties of a rhombus can be used for a variety of constructions. For example, to construct a line parallel to a given line ℓ through a point P not on ℓ, consider the following. In Figure 11-27(a), in constructing a line parallel to ℓ through point P, our strategy is to construct a rhombus with one of its vertices at P and one of its sides on line ℓ. Because the opposite sides of a rhombus are parallel, one of the sides through P will be parallel to ℓ. Through P, we draw any line intersecting ℓ, as shown in Figure 11-27(b). We then construct a rhombus, as shown in Figure 11-27(c); $\overleftrightarrow{PY}$ is the required line parallel to ℓ.

Figure 11-27

Constructing parallel lines (rhombus method)

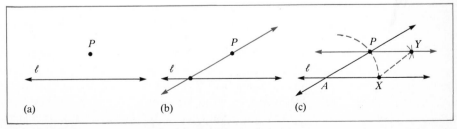

(a)   (b)   (c)

Figure 11-28 shows another way to do the construction. If congruent corresponding angles are formed by a transversal cutting two lines, then the lines are parallel. Thus, the first step is to draw a transversal through P that intersects ℓ. The angle marked α is formed by the transversal and line ℓ. By constructing an angle with a vertex at P congruent to α, as shown in Figure 11-28(b), congruent corresponding angles are formed; therefore, $m \| \ell$. Two more ways to construct parallel lines use congruent alternate interior or alternate exterior angles. (These constructions are left as exercises.)

Figure 11-28

Constructing parallel lines (corresponding angle method)

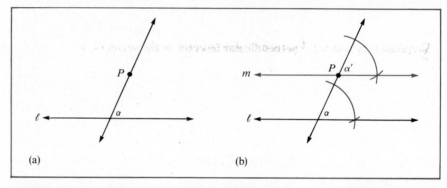

(a)   (b)

CONSTRUCTING ANGLE BISECTORS

angle bisector

Another construction that is based on a property of a rhombus is that of constructing an **angle bisector,** a ray that separates an angle into two congruent angles. In Figure 11-29(a), given $\angle A$, a rhombus having A as a vertex and sides on the rays is constructed. The diagonal of the rhombus through A bisects $\angle A$, as shown in Figure 11-29(b). In other words, $\overline{AC}$ bisects $\angle A$.

Figure 11-29

Bisecting an angle

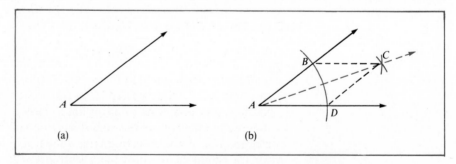

(a)   (b)

CONSTRUCTING PERPENDICULAR LINES

In order to construct a line through P perpendicular to line ℓ, where P is not a point on ℓ, as shown in Figure 11-30(a), again use properties of the diagonals of a rhombus. Recall that the diagonals of a rhombus are perpendicular to each other. By constructing a rhombus with a vertex at P and two vertices A and B on ℓ, as in Figure 11-30(b), the segment connecting the fourth vertex Q to P is perpendicular to ℓ because $\overline{AB}$ and $\overline{PQ}$ are diagonals. To obtain A and B, we choose any length longer than the distance between P and ℓ and draw an arc with center P that intersects ℓ. Then, the rhombus with vertices P, A, and B can be completed and the perpendicular determined.

Figure 11-30

Constructing a
perpendicular to a
line from a point not
on a line

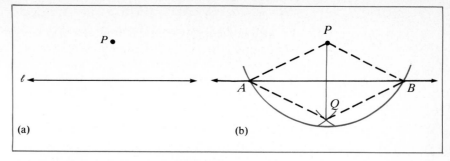

(a)   (b)

The line that is perpendicular to a segment at its midpoint is called the

perpendicular bisector **perpendicular bisector** of the segment. To construct the perpendicular bisector
of a line segment $\overline{AB}$, as shown in Figure 11-31(a), we use the fact that the
diagonals of a rhombus are perpendicular bisectors of each other. The construction yields a rhombus such that $\overline{AB}$ is one of its diagonals. The other
diagonal of the rhombus is the perpendicular bisector. Arcs with the same
radius and with centers at A and B are drawn. The points P and Q where
the arcs intersect are the other vertices of the rhombus because $\overline{AP} \cong \overline{PB} \cong$
$\overline{AQ} \cong \overline{BQ}$. Connecting P and Q gives the perpendicular bisector of $\overline{AB}$ at M.

Figure 11-31

Bisecting a line segment

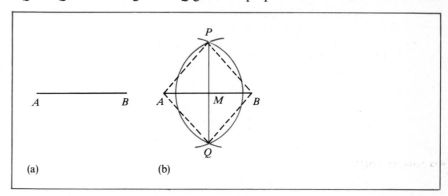

(a)   (b)

Determining a perpendicular to a line ℓ at a point P on ℓ, as shown in
Figure 11-32(a), is also based on a property of a rhombus. We determine
points A and B on ℓ so that P is the midpoint of $\overline{AB}$. Then, we construct any
rhombus with two vertices at A and B. In Figure 11-32(b), $ADBC$ is such a
rhombus, and $\overleftrightarrow{CD}$ is the required perpendicular. Notice that because point P
is given, the required perpendicular could have been determined by con-
necting C with P.

Figure 11-32

Constructing a
perpendicular to a line
from a point on the line

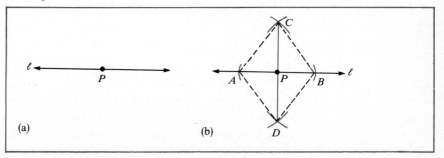

(a)   (b)

MIRA CONSTRUCTIONS

The perpendicularity constructions can also be completed by paper folding or by using a Mira. A Mira is a plastic device that acts as a reflector so that the image of an object can be seen behind the Mira. The drawing edge of the Mira acts as a folding line on paper. In fact, any construction demonstrated in this text that uses paper folding can be done using a Mira.

To construct a perpendicular to a given line ℓ at a point P on the line using paper folding, we fold the line onto itself as in Figure 11-33(a). The fold line is perpendicular to ℓ. To perform the construction with a Mira, we place the Mira with the drawing edge on P, as in Figure 11-33(b), so that ℓ is reflected onto itself. The line along the drawing edge is the required perpendicular.

Figure 11-33

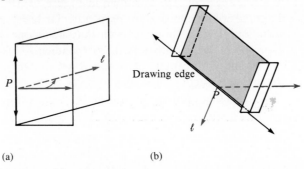

(a)   (b)

Using this same procedure, it is possible to construct any number of lines perpendicular to ℓ. In Figure 11-34, m and n are both perpendicular to ℓ. Because two lines perpendicular to the same line are parallel, $m\|n$. Thus, perpendicularity constructions can be used to construct parallel lines.

Figure 11-34

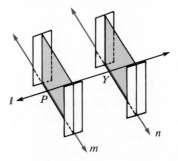

A Mira can also be used to construct the bisector of an angle by placing the Mira on the vertex of the angle and reflecting one side of the angle onto the other.

PROPERTIES OF ANGLE BISECTORS AND PERPENDICULAR BISECTORS

Consider the angle bisector in Figure 11-35. It seems that any point P on the angle bisector is equidistant from the sides of the angle; that is, $\overline{PD} \cong \overline{PE}$. (The distance from a point to a line is the length of the perpendicular from the point to the line.)

Figure 11-35

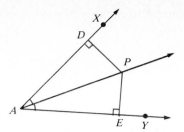

To prove this, find two congruent triangles that have these segments as corresponding sides. The only triangles pictured are $\triangle ADP$ and $\triangle AEP$. What do we know about these triangles? Because $\overrightarrow{AP}$ is the angle bisector, $\angle DAP \cong \angle EAP$. Also, $\angle PDA$ and $\angle PEA$ are right angles and are thus congruent. Because $\overrightarrow{AP}$ is congruent to itself, $\triangle PDA \cong \triangle PEA$ by AAS. Thus, $\overline{PD} \cong \overline{PE}$ because they are corresponding parts of congruent triangles PDA and PEA. Consequently, we have the following theorem.

THEOREM 11-2

> Any point P on an angle bisector is equidistant from the sides of the angle.

Remark   It can also be proved that if a point is equidistant from the sides of an angle, it must be on the angle bisector of that angle.

Next, consider the perpendicular bisector of a segment. In Figure 11-36(a), ℓ is the perpendicular bisector of $\overline{AB}$. Consider some point P on ℓ. It appears that P is equidistant from points A and B; that is, $\overline{PA} \cong \overline{PB}$. To prove this, we find two congruent triangles with sides $\overline{PA}$ and $\overline{PB}$. Triangles PCA and PCB, as shown in Figure 11-36(b), appear to be such triangles.

Figure 11-36

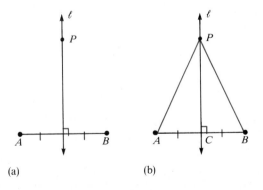

(a)   (b)

To prove that $\triangle PCA \cong \triangle PCB$, we notice that because ℓ is the perpendicular bisector of $\overline{AB}$, $\overline{AC} \cong \overline{BC}$ and $\angle PCA$ and $\angle PCB$ are congruent right angles. Also, $\overline{PC} \cong \overline{PC}$ so that $\triangle PCA \cong \triangle PCB$ by SAS. Hence, $\overline{PA} \cong \overline{PB}$ because the line segments are corresponding sides of congruent triangles. Because P is an arbitrary point, we have the following theorem.

THEOREM 11-3

> Any point on the perpendicular bisector of a line segment is equidistant from the endpoints of the segment.

Remark   It can also be proved that a point equidistant from the endpoints of a segment must be on a perpendicular bisector of the segment.

PROBLEM SET 11-3

1. Use a compass and a straightedge to construct a line *m* through *P* parallel to *ℓ* using each of the following.
   (a) Alternate interior angles
   (b) Alternate exterior angles

   P •

   ◄─────────────► *ℓ*

2. Construct each of the following using (a) a compass and a straightedge; (b) paper folding; and (c) a Mira, if available.
   (i)   Bisector of ∡A

   (ii) Perpendicular bisector of $\overline{AB}$

   (iii) Perpendicular from *P* to *ℓ*

   P •

   ◄─────────────► *ℓ*

3. An **altitude** of a triangle is the perpendicular from a vertex to the opposite side or extended side of the triangle. Construct the three altitudes of each of the following types of triangles using any method.

   (a) Acute triangle

(b) Right triangle   (c) Obtuse triangle

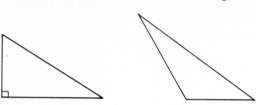

   (d) Make a conjecture about the three altitudes of an acute triangle.
   (e) Make a conjecture about the three altitudes of a right triangle.
   (f) Make a conjecture about the three altitudes of an obtuse triangle.
4. Construct the perpendicular bisectors of each of the sides of the triangles in Problem 3.
5. A **median** of a triangle is a segment from a vertex of the triangle to the midpoint of the opposite side. Construct the three medians of each triangle in Problem 3.
6. Construct a square with $\overline{AB}$ as a side.

   A ─────────────── B

7. Using a compass and a straightedge, construct a parallelogram with *A*, *B*, and *C* as vertices.

   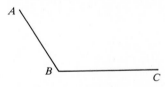

8. Using only a compass and a straightedge, construct angles with each of the following measures.
   (a) 30°   (b) 15°   (c) 45°
   (d) 75°   (e) 105°
9. A planning committee for a new tri-city airport wants to build the airport so that it will be the same distance from each city. A map of the three cities is shown at the top of the following page. How can the location of the airport be found?

City A
•

City C
•

City B
•

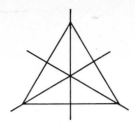

10. A chord of a circle is a segment with endpoints on the circle.
    (a) Construct a circle, several chords, and a perpendicular bisector of each chord. Make a conjecture concerning the perpendicular bisector of a chord and the center of the circle.
    *(b) Prove your conjecture in (a).
    (c) Given a circle with an unmarked center, find the center of the circle.

11. In the concave quadrilateral $APBQ$, $\overline{PQ}$ and $\overline{AB}$ are the diagonals; $\overline{AP} \cong \overline{BP}$, $\overline{AQ} \cong \overline{BQ}$; and $\overline{PQ}$ has been extended until it intersects $\overline{AB}$ at C.
    (a) Make a conjecture concerning $\overline{PQ}$ and $\overline{AB}$.
    *(b) Prove your conjecture in (a).
    (c) Make conjectures concerning the relationships between $\overrightarrow{PQ}$ and $\angle APB$ and between $\overline{QC}$ and $\angle AQB$.
    *(d) Prove your conjectures in (c).

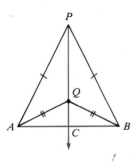

12. Construct each of the following, if possible. If the construction is not possible, explain why.
    (a) A square, given one side.
    (b) A square, given one diagonal.
    (c) A rectangle, given one diagonal.
    (d) A parallelogram, given two of its adjacent sides.
    (e) A rhombus, given two of its diagonals.
    ★(f) An isosceles triangle, given its base and the angle opposite the base.
    ★(g) A trapezoid, given four of its sides.

 13. Write a Logo procedure to draw an equilateral triangle and three segments containing the altitudes of the triangle, as shown in the figure.

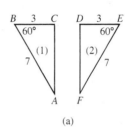

Review Problems

14. For each of the following, determine whether the two triangles (1) and (2) are congruent. Justify your answers.

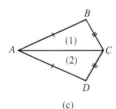

(a)   (b)

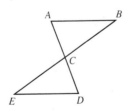   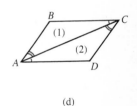

(c)   (d)

15. Given that $\overleftrightarrow{AB} \| \overleftrightarrow{ED}$ and $\overline{BC} \cong \overline{CE}$, why is $\overline{AC} \cong \overline{CD}$?

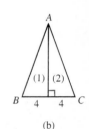

16. Draw $\triangle ABC$; then, construct $\triangle PQR$ congruent to $\triangle ABC$ by each of the following methods.
    (a) Using two sides of $\triangle ABC$ and an angle included between these sides
    (b) Using the three sides of $\triangle ABC$
    (c) Using two angles and a side included between these angles

BRAIN TEASER

Given $\overline{AB}$ in the accompanying figure, use a compass and a straightedge to construct the perpendicular bisector of $\overline{AB}$. You are not allowed to put any marks below $\overline{AB}$.

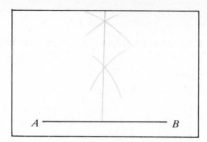

Section 11-4

Circles and Spheres

A circle is a set of points in a plane equidistant from a given point called the center, as shown in Figure 11-37. The radius is the length of any segment connecting the center with a point of the circle. Any segment with both end-

chord   points on the circle is called a **chord.** A line that contains a chord is called
secant   a **secant.** A chord that passes through the center of the circle is called a
diameter   **diameter.** A diameter is the longest chord of the circle, and its length equals twice the length of the radius.

Figure 11-37

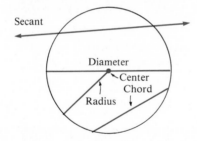

Congruent chords in a circle seem to intersect the circle to form congruent arcs. For example, in Figure 11-38 chords $\overline{AB}$ and $\overline{CD}$ are congruent. The chords or their corresponding arcs determine two angles, $\angle AOB$ and
central angles $\angle COD$. These angles are called **central angles** because their vertices are the center of the circle. By performing a turn about O, one chord can be placed on top of the other. The arrows show which way to turn. One outcome of the turn is that $\overarc{AB}$ matches $\overarc{CD}$. Thus, congruent chords have congruent

Figure 11-38

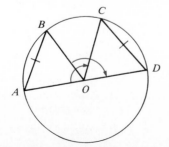

arcs. Also, the turn suggests that $\angle AOB$ is congruent to $\angle COD$. This also follows from the congruence of triangles OAB and OCD. Thus, *congruent chords determine congruent central angles and congruent arcs of the circle.* Conversely, it can be shown that *congruent central angles determine congruent chords and congruent arcs of a circle.*

INSCRIBING POLYGONS IN A CIRCLE

inscribed polygon

When all the vertices of a polygon are points of a given circle, the polygon is called an **inscribed polygon.** A regular hexagon inscribed in a circle is shown in Figure 11-39(a). All sides of a regular hexagon are congruent, so the corresponding arcs are congruent and the six corresponding central angles are congruent. Because the sum of the measures of these angles is 360°, the measure of each central angle is 60°. This fact is sufficient to inscribe a hexagon in a given circle using a protractor. A compass-and-straightedge construction can also be accomplished. Look at $\triangle AOB$. Because $\overline{OA} \cong \overline{OB}$, the triangle is isosceles. Hence, the base angles $\angle BAO$ and $\angle ABO$ are congruent. The central angle is 60°, so $m(\angle BAO) + m(\angle ABO) = 120°$. Consequently, $m(\angle BAO) = m(\angle ABO) = 60°$, and the triangle is equiangular and equilateral. Thus, $\overline{AB}$ is congruent to a radius of the circle. As a result, to inscribe a regular hexagon in a circle, we pick any point P on the circle and mark off chords congruent to the radius. Figure 11-39(b) shows such a construction.

Figure 11-39

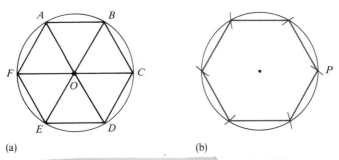

(a)   (b)

To inscribe a square in a circle, we determine four congruent central angles. The central angles must be right angles because the sum of their measures is 360°. Hence, we need only to construct two perpendicular diameters of the circle. Figure 11-40 shows the construction. First, we draw any diameter $\overline{PQ}$. Then, we construct a perpendicular to $\overline{PQ}$ at O and thus determine points R and S. Quadrilateral $PRQS$ is the required square.

Figure 11-40

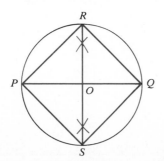

Determining which polygons can and cannot be inscribed in a circle using only a compass and a straightedge has intrigued mathematicians for centuries. In fact, Gauss considered one of his master achievements to be the inscription of a regular 17-gon in a circle, and he wanted a replica of his construction placed on his tombstone.

CIRCUMSCRIBING CIRCLES ABOUT TRIANGLES

circumscribing

A triangle is inscribed in a circle by connecting any three points of the circle with line segments. Conversely, given three vertices of any triangle, a circle that contains the vertices can be drawn. This process is called **circumscribing a circle about a triangle**. For example, in Figure 11-41, circle O is circumscribed about $\triangle ABC$. Such a circle must contain $\overline{AB}$, $\overline{BC}$, and $\overline{AC}$ as chords. Also, it must have $\overline{OA} \cong \overline{OB} \cong \overline{OC}$, since they are all radii. Hence, O must be equidistant from A and B and, consequently, O must be on the perpendicular bisector of $\overline{AB}$. Similarly, O is on the perpendicular bisectors of $\overline{BC}$ and $\overline{AC}$. Hence, to find the center of the circle, construct perpendicular bisectors of any two chords. The point of intersection of the chords is the center of the circle. Segments connecting O with A, B, and C are the radii of the circle.

Figure 11-41

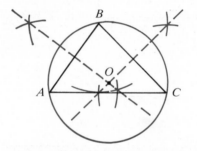

INSCRIBING CIRCLES IN TRIANGLES

tangent

A line that intersects a circle in exactly one point is called a **tangent**. In Figure 11-42, it appears that tangent ℓ and the radius pictured form right angles at their point of intersection or **point of contact**. In fact, this is true in general and can be proved. However, we will assume this property of a

point of contact

HISTORICAL NOTE

At the age of 19, Gauss proved that a regular n-gon can be inscribed in a circle if all the odd prime factors of n are of the form $2^{2^k} + 1$. Thus, a regular heptagon cannot be inscribed in a circle with a compass and a straightedge because 7 is not of the form $2^{2^k} + 1$. However, because the only factors of 17 are 1 and 17, and $2^{2^2} + 1 = 2^4 + 1 = 17$, it follows from Gauss' Theorem that a 17-gon can be inscribed in a circle using only a compass and a straightedge.

Figure 11-42

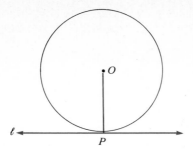

tangent without proof. Thus, to construct a tangent to a given circle at any point on the circle, we construct a perpendicular to the radius at that point.

inscribed   A circle is **inscribed** in a triangle if it is tangent to the three sides of the triangle. For example, in Figure 11-43(a), circle O is inscribed in $\triangle DEF$ and A, B, and C are the points of contact. Because $\overline{OA}$, $\overline{OB}$, and $\overline{OC}$ are radii, they all have the same length, and they are perpendicular to the three sides of the triangle they each intersect. Thus, O is equidistant from the sides, so it lies on the bisectors of $\angle 1$, $\angle 2$, and $\angle 3$ (see Section 11-3).

Figure 11-43

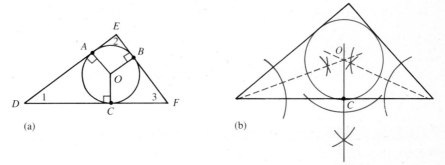

(a)   (b)

To inscribe a circle in a triangle, we first construct the bisectors of two of the angles. Their intersection point O is the center of the inscribed circle. The radius of the circle can be determined by constructing a perpendicular from O to a side of the triangle. Figure 11-43(b) shows the construction. The circle with center O and radius $\overline{OC}$ is the required circle.

SPHERES

sphere   A **sphere** is the three-dimensional analogue of a circle. It is defined as the set of all points in space that are the same distance from a given point (called the center). The definitions of chord, secant, and tangent apply to spheres as well as to circles. A plane is tangent to a sphere if it intersects the sphere in exactly one point.

If a plane intersects a sphere in more than one point, then the intersection is a circle, as shown in Figure 11-44(a).

The largest of all such circles, a circle that contains a diameter of a sphere, great circle   is called a **great circle**. Any plane containing the center of the sphere intersects the sphere in a great circle. On the globe, the equator is a great circle. If the globe is cut by a plane parallel to the equator, the circles obtained circles of latitude   are called **circles of latitude**. They become smaller the farther they are from

Figure 11-44

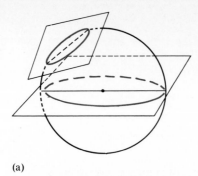

(a)

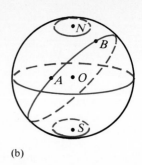

(b)

circles of longitude

the equator and become very small near the North and South Poles, as shown in Figure 11-44(b). Any circle passing through the North and South Poles is called a **circle of longitude.** Each circle of longitude is a great circle. (Why?)

In a plane, the shortest route between two points is the segment connecting the points. What is the shortest distance between two points A and B on a sphere? It is possible to prove that the shortest route between two points on a sphere is the minor arc $\overset{\frown}{AB}$ of the great circle obtained by cutting the sphere with a plane through A, B, and the center of the sphere. For that reason, if you take a nonstop flight between Seattle and London, it is likely that you will pass over Greenland.

Remark   Note that when the two points A and B are relatively close, the distance along the minor arc $\overset{\frown}{AB}$ is close to the length of the segment $\overline{AB}$.

PROBLEM SET 11-4

1. What is the relation between a diameter of a circle and any chord that is not a diameter?
2. If a triangle is drawn in a circle so that one vertex is at the center and the other two vertices are on the circle, what type of triangle must it be? Why?
3. If one side of a triangle is a diameter of a circle and the third vertex is a point on the circle, what type of triangle must it be? Measure the angles of several such triangles to decide.
4. Draw a circle on a piece of paper and use paper folding (or a Mira) to determine the center of the circle.
5. **Concentric circles** are circles with the same center. Can you construct a common tangent to two distinct concentric circles? Why?
6. Inscribe a regular dodecagon (12-gon) in a circle by first inscribing a regular hexagon in the circle and then bisecting the six central angles of the hexagon.
7. Inscribe an equilateral triangle in a circle.
8. Inscribe a regular octagon in a circle.
9. Draw a circle.
   (a) Inscribe several quadrilaterals.

   (b) Measure the angles of the quadrilaterals from (a) and find the sums of the measures of pairs of opposite angles.
   (c) What seems to be true about the relationships among the angles?
10. Inscribe a circle in the given square.

11. Is it possible to inscribe a circle in every quadrilateral? Explain.
12. Construct a circle with center O that is tangent to ℓ.

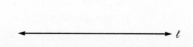

13. Construct a circle that is tangent to lines ℓ, m, and n, where $\ell \| m$.

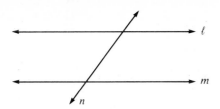

14. In the accompanying figure, $\overline{AC}$ is a diameter of circle O and $\overline{CB}$ is a chord of the circle.
   (a) What type of triangle is $\triangle OCB$?
   (b) Find a relationship between $m(\angle 1) + m(\angle 2)$ and $m(\angle 3)$.
   (c) Find a relationship between $m(\angle 1)$ and $m(\angle 3)$.

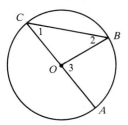

   (d) Use your answer in (c) to find a relationship between angle measures α and β in each of the accompanying figures. (O is the center of the circle in each figure.)

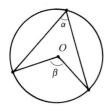

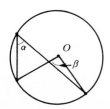

   (e) Find the relationships between the measures of angles 1, 2, and 3, where the points P_1, P_2, and P_3 are arbitrary points on the major arc $\overparen{AB}$.

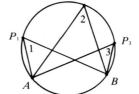

15. (a) In how many points can a line intersect a sphere?
   (b) In how many points can a plane intersect a sphere?

⋆**16.** Use the result of Problem 14 to prove your conjecture in Problem 3.

⋆**17.** Prove that congruent chords in a circle are the same distance from the center.

⋆**18.** Construct a circle that contains point P and that is tangent to the two given parallel lines ℓ and m.

19. Write a Logo procedure called FILL. CIRCLE with variable :RADIUS to shade the interior of a circle of a given radius.

20. Write a Logo procedure to draw a circle and a segment containing one of its diameters.

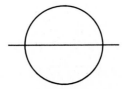

Section 11-5

Transformations: Slides and Flips

Euclid seems to have envisioned moving one geometric figure and placing it on top of another to determine if the two figures were congruent. Felix Klein carried these ideas further by defining geometry as the study of those properties of figures that do not change when a figure is transformed in a certain way into another figure.

Any one-to-one correspondence between the points of a plane and itself such that every point in the plane has exactly one image point and such that each point is the image of some point is called a transformation of the plane. **transformation** **A transformation** of the plane is a function from the plane to itself such that the domain and range are the plane and such that different points have different images. If point P corresponds to P', we say that the image of P is P'.

SLIDES (TRANSLATIONS)

Plane figures can be moved from one position to another by different transformations. One such transformation is described in Figure 11-45.

Figure 11-45

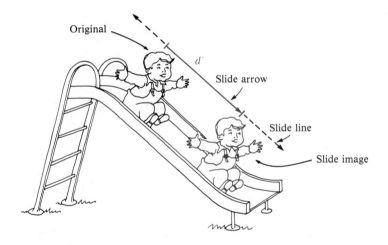

A child gliding down a slide has moved a certain distance d in a certain direction along a line. This type of transformation is called a **slide,** or **translation.**

slide / translation

HISTORICAL NOTE

In 1872, Felix Klein, at age 23, was appointed to a chair at the University of Erlangen. His inaugural address, referred to as the *Erlangen Programm,* has had great impact on the development of modern geometry and of mathematics in general.

DEFINITION

> A slide (or translation) is a transformation of a specified distance and direction along a straight line without any accompanying twisting or turning.

slide arrow

Distance and direction of a slide are both indicated by a **slide arrow.** Figure 11-46 shows a slide of $\triangle ABC$ to $\triangle A'B'C'$. The arrow indicates a slide of d units to the right. The drawing on the piece of paper labeled X is traced on the tracing paper labeled Y. When the tracing paper is slid along the slide line $\overleftrightarrow{MN}$ until M matches N, the slide images of A, B, C, and D are A', B', C', and D'. The physical motion of sliding tracing paper establishes a one-to-one correspondence between the points of plane X and itself such that $AA' = BB' = CC' = DD' = d$ and such that $\overline{AA'} \| \overline{BB'} \| \overline{CC'} \| \overline{DD'}$. Notice that any point of plane X has exactly one image point and, moreover, that each point is the image of some point.

Figure 11-46

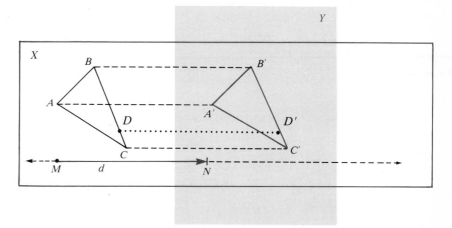

Notice that the slide in Figure 11-46 transformed an arbitrary $\triangle ABC$ to $\triangle A'B'C'$ in such a way that the triangles are congruent. (Why?) Thus, if A' and B' are the images of any two points A and B under a slide, then $\overline{A'B'} \cong \overline{AB}$. Consequently, a slide is a transformation that preserves distance. There are transformations of the plane other than slides that preserve distance. Any transformation that preserves distance (that is, in which the distance between the images of any two points is the same as the distance between the two isometry original points) is called an **isometry** (derived from Greek and meaning "equal measure"). Any isometry also preserves congruence. (Why?) Also, notice that a slide preserves parallelism between lines. This can be seen in Figure 11-46, where $\overline{A'B'} \| \overline{AB}$, $\overline{B'C'} \| \overline{BC}$, and $\overline{A'C'} \| \overline{AC}$. (Why?) In general, if P and Q have images P' and Q' under a slide, then $\overleftrightarrow{P'Q'} \| \overleftrightarrow{PQ}$.

FLIPS (REFLECTIONS)

flip / reflection

Another isometry is called a **flip,** or **reflection.** One example of a flip often encountered in our daily lives is a mirror image. Figure 11-47 shows a figure with its mirror image.

Figure 11-47

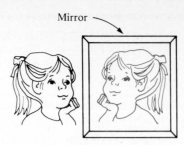

Mirror

In a plane, we can simulate reflections in various ways. Consider the half tree shown in Figure 11-48(a). Folding the paper along the **flip line** ℓ and drawing the image gives the **flip image** of the tree. In Figure 11-48(b), the paper is unfolded. The figure obtained is symmetric about the fold line in much the same way that a mirror gives symmetry in space. Another way to simulate a reflection or flip in a line uses a Mira and is illustrated in Figure 11-48(c).

flip line
flip image

Figure 11-48

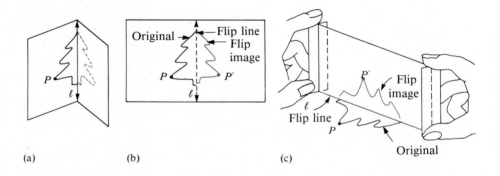

(a)   (b)   (c)

In Figure 11-49(a), the image of P under a flip in line ℓ is P'. In Figure 11-49(b), P is its own image under the flip in line ℓ. By folding the paper along the flip line ℓ or by using a Mira, you will notice that $\overline{PP'}$ in Figure 11-49(a) is perpendicular to ℓ and is bisected by ℓ or, equivalently, that ℓ is the perpendicular bisector of $\overline{PP'}$. Based on this observation, we define a flip in a line as follows.

Figure 11-49

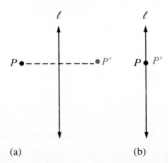

(a)   (b)

DEFINITION

A flip (or reflection) in a line ℓ is a transformation among points in a plane that pairs each point P of the plane with a point P' in such a way that ℓ is the perpendicular bisector of $\overline{PP'}$ as long as $P \notin \ell$. If $P \in \ell$, then $P = P'$.

Given any point A and its flip image A', the flip line ℓ can be found as long as $A \notin \ell$ because ℓ is the perpendicular bisector of $\overline{AA'}$. This can be done by placing a Mira so that A is reflected onto A' and drawing the flip line ℓ along the drawing edge, as shown in Figure 11-50(a). With paper folding, we simply fold A onto A', as shown in Figure 11-50(b). The folding line is the required flip line. With a compass and a straightedge, the flip line can be constructed by finding the perpendicular bisector of $\overline{AA'}$ using the methods of Section 11-3. This is illustrated in Figure 11-50(c).

Figure 11-50

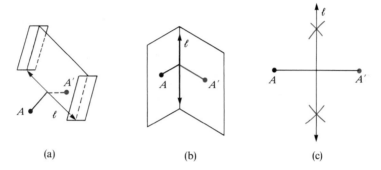

(a)   (b)   (c)

LINE SYMMETRIES

The concept of a flip, or reflection, can be used to identify line symmetries of a figure. Line symmetries are sometimes called reflectional symmetries, or flip symmetries. All the drawings in Figure 11-51 have symmetries about the dashed lines.

Figure 11-51

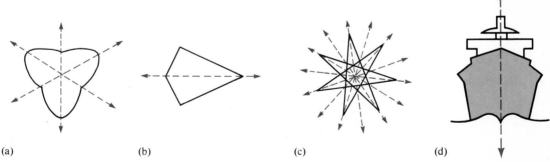

(a)   (b)   (c)   (d)

line of symmetry

Mathematically, we could say that a line ℓ is a **line of symmetry** of a figure if, for every point P of the figure not on the line, there is another point P' on the figure so that line ℓ is the perpendicular bisector of $\overline{PP'}$, as shown in Figure 11-52.

Figure 11-52

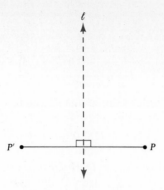

Example 11-7

How many lines of symmetry does each of the drawings in Figure 11-53 have?

Figure 11-53

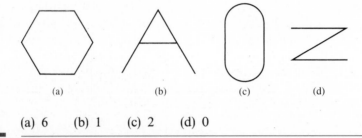

      (a)   (b)   (c)   (d)

Solution

(a) 6   (b) 1   (c) 2   (d) 0

PROBLEM 2

At the site of an ancient settlement, archaeologists found a fragment of a saucer, as shown in Figure 11-54. To restore the saucer, the archaeologists had to determine the radius of the original saucer. How can they find the radius?

Figure 11-54

UNDERSTANDING THE PROBLEM A shard of a fragile pottery saucer was found by archaeologists. The border of the shard (shown in Figure 11-54) was part of a circle. In order to reconstruct the saucer, the archaeologists must determine the radius of the circle.

DEVISING A PLAN A mathematical model can be used to determine the radius. Trace an outline of the three-dimensional shard on a piece of paper.

The result is an arc of a two-dimensional circle, as shown in Figure 11-55. To determine the radius, find the center, O. A circle has infinitely many lines of symmetry, and each line passes through the center of the circle, where all the lines of symmetry intersect.

Figure 11-55

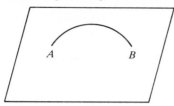

CARRYING OUT THE PLAN To find a line of symmetry, fold the paper containing $\overset{\frown}{AB}$ so that a portion of the arc is folded onto itself. Then, unfold the paper and draw the line of symmetry on the fold mark, as shown in Figure 11-56(a). By refolding the paper in Figure 11-56(a) so that a different portion of the arc $\overset{\frown}{AB}$ is folded onto itself, determine a second line of symmetry as shown in Figure 11-56(b). The two dotted lines of symmetry intersect in O, the center of the circle of which $\overset{\frown}{AB}$ is an arc. To complete the problem, measure the length of either $\overline{OB}$ or $\overline{OA}$. (They should be the same.)

Figure 11-56

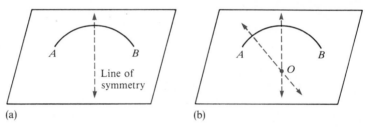

(a)   (b)

LOOKING BACK In the first fold, endpoint B of the arc was folded onto another point of the arc. Label this other point X. The result is shown in Figure 11-57. Because the fold line ℓ is a line of symmetry of the circle containing $\overset{\frown}{AB}$, it must be the perpendicular bisector of $\overline{XB}$ and contain the center of the circle. This is the property proved in Section 11-4 that states that the center of the circle lies on the perpendicular bisector of a chord. This property could have been used to determine the center of the circle by choosing two chords on the arc and finding the point where the perpendicular bisectors of the chords intersect.

A related problem is: What would happen if the piece of pottery had been part of a sphere? Would the same ideas still work?

Figure 11-57

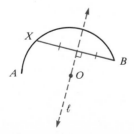

PROBLEM SET II-5

1. What type of motion is involved in each of the following?
   (a) A skier skiing straight down a slope.
   (b) A leaf floating down a stream.
2. For each of the following, find the image of the given quadrilateral.

   (a) A flip in ℓ (b) A slide from A to B

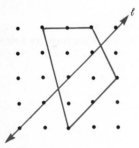

   (c) A flip in ℓ

3. Use (a) tracing paper and (b) compass and straightedge to construct the images for each of the following.

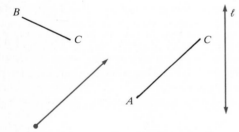

   (i) The slide image   (ii) The flip image of
        of $\overline{BC}$ $\overline{AC}$ about ℓ

4. (a) Find the image of $\triangle ABC$ under a flip in line ℓ.

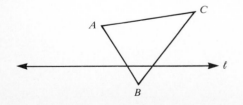

   (b) Is it possible to find the image of $\triangle ABC$ in (a) without first finding the image of B? If so, explain how.
5. Draw a line and a circle whose center is not on the line.
   (a) Find the image of the circle under a flip in the line.
   (b) Is the image a circle? Why?
6. Which of the following figures have a flip line such that the image of the figure under the flip line is the figure itself? In each case, find as many such flip lines as possible, sketching appropriate drawings.
   (a) Circle   (b) Segment
   (c) Ray   (d) Square
   (e) Rectangle   (f) Scalene triangle
   (g) Isosceles triangle (h) Equilateral triangle
   (i) Trapezoid whose base (j) Isosceles trapezoid
       angles are not congruent
   (k) An arc   (l) Kite
   (m) Rhombus   (n) Regular hexagon
   (o) Regular n-gon
7. Justify your answers in Problem 6 by paper folding.
8. Draw a slide arrow and a circle. Find the image of the circle under the slide indicated by the slide arrow.
9. Use any construction method to find the image of $\triangle ABC$ if it is flipped about ℓ to obtain $\triangle A'B'C'$ and then $\triangle A'B'C'$ is flipped about m to obtain $\triangle A''B''C''$. (Lines ℓ and m are parallel.)

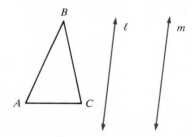

10. Can the result in Problem 9 be accomplished using a single motion? Explain why or why not.
11. What is the result of performing two successive flips about line ℓ in the figure?

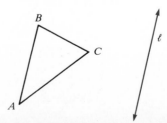

12. Suppose ℓ and m are parallel and $\triangle ABC$ is flipped about ℓ and then m. How does the final image compare with the final image after flipping about m, then ℓ? Are the images ever the same?

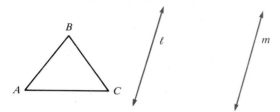

13. In each of the following, complete the sketches so that they have line symmetry about ℓ.

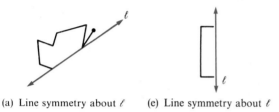

(a) Line symmetry about ℓ (e) Line symmetry about ℓ

14. (a) Determine the number of lines of symmetry of each of the following flags.
(b) Sketch the lines of symmetry for each flag.

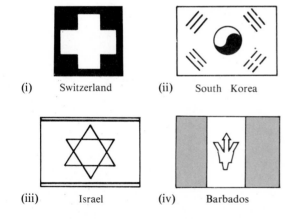

(i) Switzerland   (ii) South Korea

(iii) Israel   (iv) Barbados

15. Find the lines of symmetry, if any, for each of the following trademarks.

(a) The Bell System   (b) The Yellow Pages

(c) Chevrolet   (d) Volkswagen of America

(e)   Chrysler Corporation   (f) International Harvester

16. If possible, sketch a triangle that satisfies each of the following.
(a) It has no lines of symmetry.
(b) It has exactly one line of symmetry.
(c) It has exactly two lines of symmetry.
(d) It has exactly three lines of symmetry.

17. A **glide reflection** is defined as the result of a successive slide and flip when the slide arrow and the flip line are parallel. Find the image of the footprint in the glide reflection that is the result of a slide from M to N followed by a flip about ℓ.

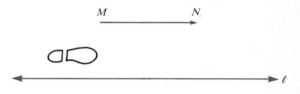

*18. If a Mira is available, use it to investigate Problems 9–12 and 17.

*19. Two cities, represented by points A and B, are located near two perpendicular roads as shown. The cities' mayors found it necessary to build another road connecting A with a point P on road 1, then connecting P with a point Q on road 2, and finally connecting Q with B. How should the road $APQB$ be constructed if it is to be as short as possible? Copy the figure shown and use a straightedge and a compass, a Mira, or paper folding to construct the shortest possible path.

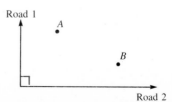

★**20.** When a billiard ball bounces off a side of a pool table, the angle of incidence is usually congruent to the angle of reflection; that is, $\angle 1 \cong \angle 2$. If a cue ball is at point A, show how the player should aim to hit three sides of the table and then the ball at B.

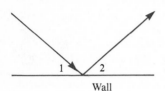

Wall

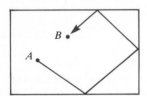

 21. Enter the given procedures into your computer and then describe the transformations illustrated in each of the following.

```
TO SQ
  REPEAT 4 [FD 40 RT 90]
END

TO FSQ
  REPEAT 4 [FD 40 LT 90]
END
```

(a)
```
TO MOVE1
  SQ
  RT 150
  SQ
END
```
(b)
```
TO MOVE2
  SQ
  FSQ
END
```
(c)
```
TO MOVE3
  SQ
  PU RT 45 FD 60 PD
  SQ
END
```

 22. (a) Write a simple Logo procedure called FIG1 using FD, BK, RT, and LT several times. Run your procedure.
(b) Write a new procedure, FIG2, in which you replace every FD in your FIG1 procedure with BK and every BK with FD. How does the drawing made with FIG2 compare with the drawing made with FIG1?
(c) Write a new procedure, FIG3, in which you replace every RT in your FIG1 procedure with LT and every LT with RT. How does the drawing made with FIG3 compare with the drawings made with FIG1 and FIG2?

23. (a) Slides may be explored in Logo using a figure called an EE. Type the given programs into your computer and then run the following, with the turtle starting at home with heading 0.
  (i) SLIDE 40 45
  (ii) SLIDE 200 57
  (iii) SLIDE (-50) (-75)

```
TO SLIDE :DIRECTION :DISTANCE
  EE
  PENUP
  SETHEADING :DIRECTION
  FORWARD :DISTANCE
  PENDOWN
  SETHEADING 0
  EE
END

TO EE
  FORWARD 50
  RIGHT 90
  FORWARD 25
  BACK 25
  LEFT 90
  BACK 25
  RIGHT 90
  FORWARD 10
  BACK 10
  LEFT 90
  BACK 25
  RIGHT 90
  FORWARD 25
  BACK 25
  LEFT 90
END
```

(b) Edit the SLIDE procedure in (a) so that it will slide an equilateral triangle.

Review Problems

24. Use a compass and a straightedge to construct the following.
(a) A parallelogram in which one of the angles is 60°.
(b) A right triangle in which the longest side is twice as long as the shortest side.
(c) A 165° angle.
25. Divide $\overline{AB}$ into four congruent segments.

A B

26. Use a compass and a straightedge to construct the following.
   (a) A quadrilateral in which the diagonals are of different lengths but are perpendicular bisectors of each other.

   (b) A quadrilateral with congruent diagonals that are perpendicular bisectors of each other.
   (c) A quadrilateral that is not a parallelogram and in which the diagonals are congruent and perpendicular.

BRAIN TEASER

Two cities are on opposite sides of a river, as shown. The cities' engineers want to build a bridge across the river that is perpendicular to the banks of the river and access roads to the bridge, so that the total distance between the cities is as short as possible. Where should the bridge and the roads be built?

A •

• B

Section 11-6   Turns

TURNS (ROTATIONS)

turn / rotation   A **turn,** or **rotation,** is another kind of isometry. Figure 11-58 illustrates congruent figures resulting from a turn. The image of point P is P', and the image of P' is P''.

Figure 11-58

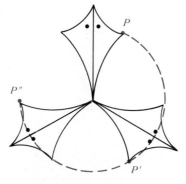

In Figure 11-59(a), $\triangle ABC$ and point O are traced on tracing paper.
turn image   Holding point O fixed, the tracing paper can be turned to obtain a **turn image,**
center of the turn $\triangle A'B'C'$, as shown in Figure 11-59(b). Point O is called the **center of the turn,**
angle of the turn   and $\angle COC'$ is called the **angle of the turn.**

Figure 11-59

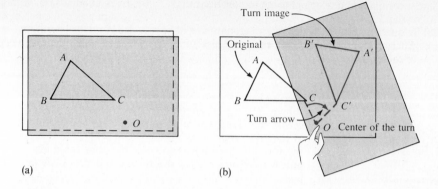

(a)   (b)

In order to determine a turn, three things must be given: (1) the center of the turn; (2) the direction of the turn—either clockwise or counterclockwise; and (3) the amount of the turn. The amount and the direction of the turn can *turn arrow* be illustrated by a **turn arrow**, as shown with $\angle COC'$ in Figure 11-59(b), or specified as a number of degrees.

DEFINITION

> A turn (or rotation) is a transformation of the plane determined by holding one point, the center, fixed and rotating the plane about this point by a certain amount in a certain direction.

Because a rotation is an isometry, the image of any figure under a rotation is congruent to the original figure. As with slides and flips, the image of a line under a rotation is a line, and the image of a circle is a circle. Also, the images of parallel lines remain parallel.

The image of a point under a turn about a given point by a given angle can be accomplished using a compass and a straightedge. Suppose we want to find the images of points P and Q under a turn by $\angle A$ counterclockwise about point O, as shown in Figure 11-60. Notice that P' must be on the circle whose radius is OP so that $\angle P'OP \cong \angle A$. Thus, P' can be found by drawing an arc with center O and radius OP, as shown in Figure 11-60(b), and then constructing an angle congruent to $\angle A$ with vertex O and one of the rays as $\overrightarrow{OP}$. The point counterclockwise to P where the other ray of the angle intersects the arc with center O and radius OP is the required point. The image of point Q can be found in a similar way.

Figure 11-60

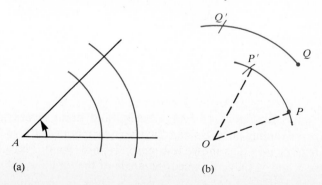

(a)   (b)

Using a compass and a straightedge, it is possible to find the images of many figures under a turn by an arbitrary angle about a given point.

Example 11-8

Find the image of line ℓ in Figure 11-61 under a turn of 45° counterclockwise about point O.

Figure 11-61

Solution

Because a line is determined by two points, it is sufficient to pick any two points on ℓ and find the images of these points under the given turn. In Figure 11-62, we pick two arbitrary points A and B on ℓ and find their images A' and B'. The line ℓ' connecting A' with B' is the image of ℓ under the turn.

Figure 11-62

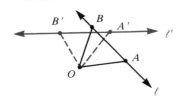

A turn of 360° will transform any figure onto itself. A turn of 180° about a point is also of particular interest. A rotation by 180° about a point is called half-turn a **half-turn.** Because a half-turn is a rotation, it has all the properties that rotations have. However, because a half-turn is a special kind of rotation, it may have properties that other rotations do not have. Figure 11-63 shows some shapes and their images under a half-turn about point O.

Figure 11-63

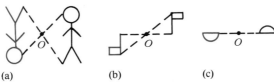

(a)   (b)   (c)

Example 11-9

Use a compass and a straightedge to find the image of a line ℓ under a half-turn about point O in Figure 11-64.

Figure 11-64

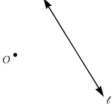

Solution

Because a line is determined by two points, it is sufficient to pick any two points on ℓ and find the images of these points under the half-turn. In Figure 11-65, we pick two arbitrary points A and B on ℓ and find their images A' and B'. The line ℓ' connecting A' with B' is the image of ℓ under the half-turn.

Figure 11-65

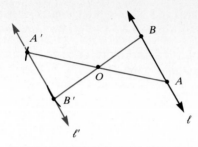

TURN SYMMETRIES

turn symmetry
rotational symmetry

A figure has **turn symmetry,** or **rotational symmetry,** when the traced figure can be turned less than 360° about some point so that it matches the original figure. Note that the condition "less than 360°" is necessary because any figure will coincide with itself after being turned 360°. In Figure 11-66, the equilateral triangle coincides with itself after a turn of 120° about point O. Hence, we say that the triangle has 120° turn symmetry. In addition, in Figure 11-66, if we turned the triangle another 120°, we would find that it again matches the original, so we can say that the triangle also has 240° turn symmetry.

Figure 11-66

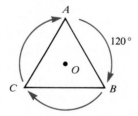

Other examples of figures that have turn symmetry are shown in Figure 11-67. In Figure 11-67, (a), (b), (c), and (d) have 72°, 90°, 180°, and 180° turn symmetries, respectively. [Parts (a) and (b) also have other turn symmetries.]

Figure 11-67

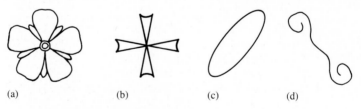

(a)　　　　　(b)　　　　(c)　　　　(d)

In general, we can determine whether a figure has turn symmetry by tracing it and turning the tracing about a point (the center of the figure) to see if it aligns on the figure before the tracing has turned in a complete circle, or 360°. The amount of the turn can be determined by measuring the angle, ∡POP', through which a point P is turned around a point O to match another point P' when the figures align. Such an angle, ∡POP', is labeled using points P, O, and P' of Figure 11-68 and has measure 120°. Point O, the point held fixed when the tracing is turned, is called the center of the turn, or

turn center
the **turn center.**

Figure 11-68

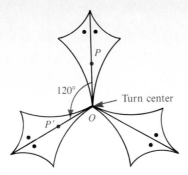

120°   ← Turn center

Example 11-10

Determine the amount of the turn for the turn symmetries of each figure in Figure 11-69.

Figure 11-69

(a)   (b)   (c)

Solution

(a) The amounts of the turns are $\frac{360°}{5}$ or 72°, 144°, 216°, and 288°.
(b) The amount of the turn is 180°.
(c) The amounts of the turns are 60°, 120°, 180°, 240°, and 300°.

The turn in Figure 11-69(b) exemplifies yet another type of symmetry, namely, point symmetry.

POINT SYMMETRY

point symmetry   Any figure that has 180° turn symmetry is said to have **point symmetry** about the center of the turn. Figures with point symmetry are shown in Figure 11-70.

Figure 11-70

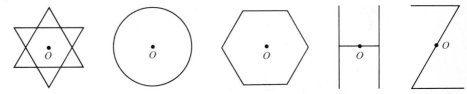

Suppose P is any point of a figure with point symmetry, such as in Figure 11-71(a). If the figure is turned 180° about its center, point O, there is a corresponding point P', as shown in part (b) of the figure. Points P, O, and P' are on the same line, and O divides the segment connecting points P and P' into two parts of equal length; that is, O is the midpoint of $\overline{PP'}$.

Figure 11-71

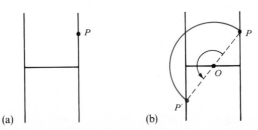

(a)   (b)

APPLICATIONS OF SYMMETRIES IN GEOMETRY

Geometric figures in a plane can be classified in terms of the number of symmetries they have. Consider a triangle described as having exactly one line of symmetry and no turn symmetries at all. What could the triangle look like? The only possibility is a triangle in which two sides are congruent, that is, an isosceles triangle. The line of symmetry passes through a vertex, as shown in Figure 11-72.

Figure 11-72

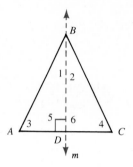

Because $\triangle ABC$ has line symmetry about line m, the following pairs of angles should be congruent: $\angle 1$ and $\angle 2$; $\angle 3$ and $\angle 4$; $\angle 5$ and $\angle 6$. Further, notice that line m divides $\overline{AC}$ to make $\overline{AD}$ and $\overline{CD}$ congruent. Thus, we say
bisect   that line m **bisects** $\overline{AC}$. In addition, because $\angle 5$ and $\angle 6$ are congruent angles whose exterior sides form a straight line, they are right angles. When two lines meet to form right angles, we say that the lines are perpendicular. Hence, in Figure 11-72, line m is the perpendicular bisector of $\overline{AC}$.

Just as we used the number of lines of symmetry to describe an isosceles triangle, we could describe equilateral and scalene triangles in terms of the number of lines of symmetry that they have. This is left as an exercise.

A square as in Figure 11-73 could be defined as a four-sided figure with four lines of symmetry—d_1, d_2, h, and v—and three turn symmetries about point O. In fact, we could use lines of symmetry and turn symmetries to define various types of quadrilaterals normally used in geometry, as seen on the student page from *Heath Mathematics,* 1987, Grade 7 (page 533).

Figure 11-73

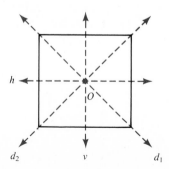

Quadrilaterals

We can use points of symmetry and lines of symmetry to study properties of some special **quadrilaterals** (4-sided figures).

A quadrilateral with a point of symmetry is a **parallelogram.**

A quadrilateral with a point of symmetry and two lines of symmetry through opposite vertices is a **rhombus.**

A quadrilateral with a point of symmetry and two lines of symmetry through opposite sides is a **rectangle.**

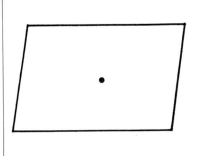

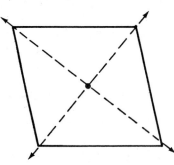

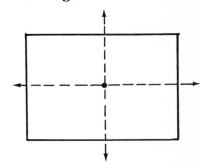

A quadrilateral with a point of symmetry and four lines of symmetry is a **square.**

A quadrilateral with one line of symmetry through opposite sides is an **isosceles trapezoid.**

A quadrilateral with one line of symmetry through opposite vertices is a **kite.**

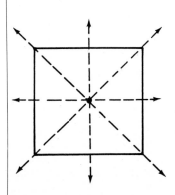

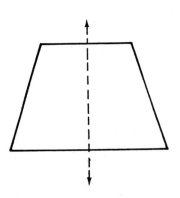

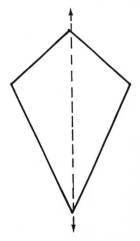

PROBLEM SET 11-6

1. Name three "everyday" examples of turns.
2. Find the image of the given quadrilateral for a 90° counterclockwise turn about *O*.

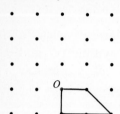

3. Find the turn image of $\overline{AB}$ by the given angle about *O* using: (a) tracing paper; (b) compass and straightedge.

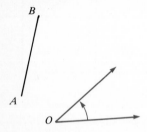

4. Use a compass and a straightedge to find the image of the circle *M* under a half-turn about *O*.

5. In each of the following, find the image of the circle *M* under a 120° counterclockwise turn about *O*.

(a)

(b)

6. In each of the following figures, find the image of the figure under a half-turn about *O*.

(a)

(b)

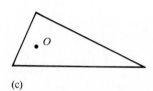

(c)

7. Draw three arbitrary points *P*, *P'*, and *Q*. If *P'* is the image of *P* under a half-turn, construct the image of *Q* under that half-turn.
8. For the following, use any construction methods to find the image of △*ABC* if △*ABC* is flipped about ℓ to obtain △*A'B'C'* and then △*A'B'C'* is flipped about *m* to obtain △*A"B"C"* (ℓ and *m* intersect at *O*).

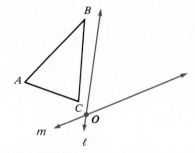

9. Can the result in Problem 8 be accomplished using a single motion? Explain why or why not.
10. Suppose lines ℓ and *m* intersect and triangle *ABC* is flipped first about ℓ and then about *m*. How does the final image compare with the final image after flipping first about *m* and then about ℓ?

11. (a) In succession, perform the two turns, each with center O, in the figure.
(b) What is the result of the two turns?
(c) Is the order of the turns important?
(d) Could the result have been accomplished in one turn?

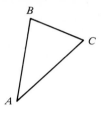

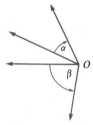

*12. If a Mira is available, use it to investigate Problems 8 and 10.

13. Answer each of the following. If your answer is no, provide a counterexample.
(a) If a figure has point symmetry, must it have turn symmetry? Why?
(b) If a figure has turn symmetry, must it have point symmetry? Why?
(c) Can a figure have point, line, and turn symmetry? If so, sketch a figure with these properties.
(d) If a figure has point symmetry, must it have line symmetry? Is the converse true?
(e) If a figure has both point and line symmetry, must it have turn symmetry? Why?

14. In each of the following, complete the sketches so that they have the indicated symmetry.

(a)   (b)

Point symmetry about O 60° turn symmetry about O

 15. Write a Logo procedure that will draw a square and produce the image of the square when the square is rotated by an arbitrary angle :A about one of its vertices.

 16. Write a Logo procedure that draws a square and produces a figure with turn symmetry of (a) 60°; (b) 120°; (c) 180°; (d) 240°; (e) 300°.

17. Write a Logo procedure that will draw a circle passing through the home of the turtle and produce the image of the circle under the following transformations.
(a) A half-turn about the turtle's home
(b) A 90° counterclockwise turn about the turtle's home

Review Problems

18. Using a compass and a straightedge, construct each of the following.
(a) A rectangle with one side three times as long as the other
(b) An angle whose measure is the sum of the measures of the two angles given in the figure

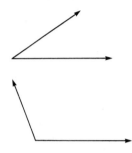

(c) A triangle with angles of 90°, 60°, and 30°

19. For each case, find the image of the given figure.

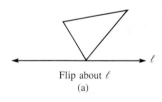

Flip about ℓ
(a)

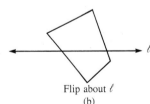

Flip about ℓ
(b)

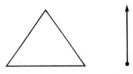

A slide from A to B
(c)

*Section 11-7 Tessellations of the Plane

tessellation

Figure 11-74 shows two ways of tessellating the plane with a square. A **tessellation** of a plane is the filling of the plane by repeating a figure in such a way that no figures overlap and there are no gaps. The tiling of a floor and various mosaics are examples of tessellations. Perhaps the simplest tessellation of the plane can be achieved with squares. Figure 11-74 shows two different tessellations of the plane with squares.

Figure 11-74

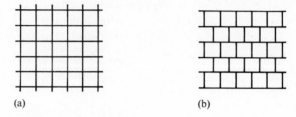

(a)   (b)

REGULAR TESSELLATIONS

Tessellations with regular polygons are appealing and interesting because of their simplicity. Figure 11-75 shows portions of tessellations with equilateral triangles and regular hexagons.

Figure 11-75

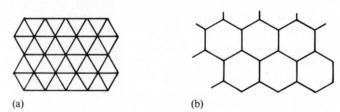

(a)   (b)

What other regular polygons tessellate the plane? To answer this question, we investigate the possible size of the interior angle of a tessellating polygon. If n is the number of sides of a regular polygon, then because the sum of the measures of the exterior angles is 360° [see Theorem 10-5(b)], the measure of an exterior angle is $360°/n$. Hence the measure of an interior angle is $180° - 360°/n$. Table 11-2 gives some values of n, the type of regular polygon related to each, and the angle measure of an interior angle found using the expression $180° - 360°/n$.

Table 11-2

Number of Sides	Regular Polygon	Measure of Interior Angle
3	Triangle	60°
4	Square	90°
5	Pentagon	108°
6	Hexagon	120°
7	Heptagon	900/7°
8	Octagon	135°
9	Nonagon	140°
10	Decagon	144°

If a regular polygon tessellates the plane, the angles around every vertex must be congruent, and the sum of their measures must be 360°. Thus 360 divided by the angle measure gives the number of angles around a vertex and hence must be an integer. If we divide 360 by each of the angle measures in the table, we find that only 60, 90, and 120 divide 360; hence only an equilateral triangle, a square, and a regular hexagon could tessellate the plane. Can other regular polygons tessellate the plane? Notice that $\frac{360}{120} = 3$, and hence 360 divided by a number greater than 120 is smaller than 3; however, the number of sides of a polygon cannot be less than 3. Because a polygon with more than six sides has an interior angle greater than 120°, it is actually not necessary to consider polygons with more than six sides.

You may wonder whether nonregular polygons can tessellate the plane. Cut a scalene triangle out of cardboard, produce several triangles congruent to the one you cut out, and try to tessellate a part of the plane with these triangles.

Next, we consider tessellating the plane with arbitrary convex quadrilaterals. Before reading on, you may wish to investigate the problem yourself with the help of cardboard quadrilaterals. Figure 11-76 shows an arbitrary convex quadrilateral and a way to tessellate the plane with the quadrilateral. Successive 180° turns of the quadrilateral about the midpoints P, Q, R, and S of its sides will produce four congruent quadrilaterals around a common vertex. Notice that the sum of the measures of the angles around vertex A is $a + b + c + d$, which is the sum of the measures of the interior angles of the quadrilateral and hence 360°.

Figure 11-76

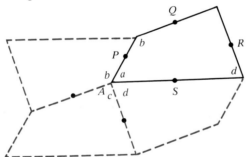

As we have seen earlier, a regular pentagon does not tessellate the plane. However, there is a nonregular pentagon that does tessellate the plane. Such a pentagon, along with a tessellation of the plane by the pentagon, is shown in Figure 11-77.

Figure 11-77

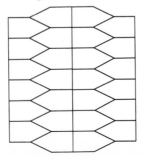

PROBLEM SET II-7

1. On square-dot paper, draw a tessellation of the plane using the given triangle.

2. On square-dot paper, draw a tessellation of the plane using the trapezoid shown.

3. (a) Tessellate the plane with the quadrilateral shown.

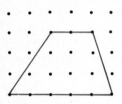

   (b) Is it possible to tessellate the plane with any quadrilateral?

4. On square-dot paper, use each of the following four pentominoes, one at a time, to make a tessellation of the plane, if possible. (A pentomino is a polygon composed of five congruent, nonoverlapping squares.) Which of the pentominoes tessellate the plane?

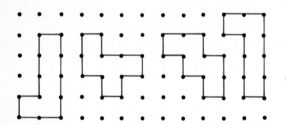

5. The **dual of a tessellation** is the tessellation obtained by connecting the centers of the polygons in the original tessellation that share a common side. The dual of the tessellation of equilateral triangles is the tessellation of regular hexagons (shown in color).

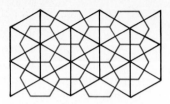

Describe and show the dual of each of the following.
   (a) The regular tessellation of squares shown in Figure 11-74(a) (page 536).
   (b) The tessellation of squares shown in Figure 11-74(b).
   (c) A tessellation of hexagons

6. We have seen that equilateral triangles, squares, and regular hexagons are the only regular polygons that will tessellate the plane by themselves. However, there are many ways to tessellate the plane using combinations of these and other regular polygons, as shown in the figure. Try to come up with other such tessellations using the following.
   (a) Only equilateral triangles, squares, and regular hexagons
   (b) Regular octagons (8-gons) and squares

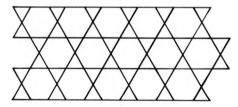

7. Write Logo procedures to draw partial tessellations of the following figures. Have each tessellation appear on the screen in the form of two vertical strips.
   (a) Squares
   (b) Equilateral triangles
   (c) Regular hexagons

8. A sidewalk is made of tiles of the type shown in the figure. Each tile is made of three regular hexagons from which three sides have been removed. Write a Logo procedure to draw a partial tessellation made of four such figures.

Review Problems

9. What type of motion is involved in each of the following?
   (a) A circular radio knob turned from "off" to "on"
   (b) A child swinging
   (c) Two children on a teeter-totter
10. Find the image of △ABC when it is flipped about side $\overline{AC}$.

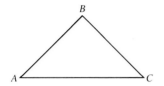

11. Draw any triangle ABC and then find its image when it is turned counterclockwise by ∡A about each of the following.
    (a) Vertex A
    (b) Vertex B
12. Use a straightedge and a compass to construct a right triangle if a is one of the sides and c is the side opposite the right angle.

   a   c

13. Which types of symmetry—point, line, or turn—does each of the following have? In each case, identify the point, line, or turn.
    (a) An equilateral triangle
    (b) A regular polygon
    (c) A rectangle

Section 11-8

Similar Triangles and Similar Figures

If an 8 by 10 inch reprint is made of an 8 by 10 inch picture, then the two pictures are congruent; that is, they have the same size and shape. However, if an 8 by 10 inch picture is blown up to obtain a 16 by 20 inch picture, as shown in Figure 11-78, the resulting photographs are not congruent. They have the same shape, but not the same size. When a germ is examined through a microscope, when a slide is projected on a screen, or when a wet wool sweater shrinks when dried in a clothes dryer, the shapes in each case remain the same, but the sizes are altered. In mathematics we say that *two figures that have the same shape but not necessarily the same size are* **similar.**

similar

Figure 11-78

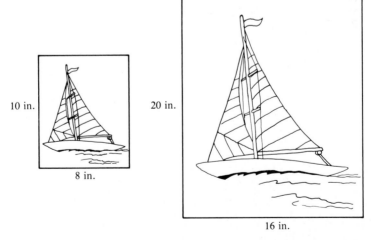

For example, if we project an equilateral triangle onto a screen without distortion (so that the same shape is kept), the image on the screen is an equilateral triangle, as shown in Figure 11-79. In this figure, △ABC is enlarged by a **scale factor** of 2, so the following proportion holds.

scale factor

Figure 11-79

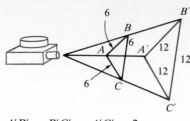

$$\frac{A'B'}{AB} = \frac{B'C'}{BC} = \frac{A'C'}{AC} = \frac{2}{1}$$

The ratio of the length of the sides is 2:1. However, the angle sizes pictured do not change because both triangles are equilateral and hence equiangular. It is reasonable to assume that *any* triangle projected in this manner has an image triangle similar to the original. The angle measures remain the same, and the sides are proportional. In general, we have the following definition of similar triangles.

DEFINITION

$\triangle ABC$ is similar to $\triangle DEF$, written $\triangle ABC \sim \triangle DEF$, if and only if $\angle A \cong \angle D$, $\angle B \cong \angle E$, $\angle C \cong \angle F$, and $\dfrac{AB}{DE} = \dfrac{AC}{DF} = \dfrac{BC}{EF}$.

Remark   Note that the one-to-one correspondence in similar triangles is analogous to that in congruent triangles.

Example 11-11

Given the pairs of similar triangles in Figure 11-80, find a one-to-one correspondence among the vertices of the triangles such that the corresponding angles are congruent. Then, write the proportion for the corresponding sides that follows from the definition.

Figure 11-80

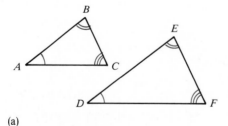

(a)

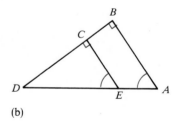

(b)

Solution

(a) $\triangle ABC \sim \triangle DEF$

$$\frac{AB}{DE} = \frac{BC}{EF} = \frac{AC}{DF}$$

(b) $\triangle ABD \sim \triangle ECD$

$$\frac{AB}{EC} = \frac{BD}{CD} = \frac{AD}{ED}$$

ANGLE, ANGLE, ANGLE (AAA)

Angle, Angle, Angle (AAA)

As with congruent triangles, minimal conditions may be used to determine when two triangles are similar. For example, suppose two triangles each have angles with measures of 50°, 30°, and 100°, but the side opposite the 100° angle is 5 units long in one of the triangles and 1 unit long in the other. The triangles appear to have the same shape, as shown in Figure 11-81. The figure suggests that if the angles of the two triangles are congruent, then the sides are proportional and the triangles are similar. There is no easy proof of this statement, but it is true in general. It is called the **Angle, Angle, Angle** property of similarity for triangles, abbreviated **AAA.**

Figure 11-81

(a)   (b)

Property   **Angle, Angle, Angle (AAA)**   If three angles of one triangle are congruent to the three angles of a second triangle, respectively, then the triangles are similar.

Remark   Given the measures of any two angles of a triangle, the measure of the third angle can be found. Hence, if two angles in one triangle are congruent to two angles in another triangle, respectively, then the third angles must also be congruent. Consequently, the AAA condition may be reduced to **Angle, Angle (AA).**

Angle, Angle (AA)

Example 11-12

For each part of Figure 11-82, determine if the pairs of triangles are similar.

Figure 11-82

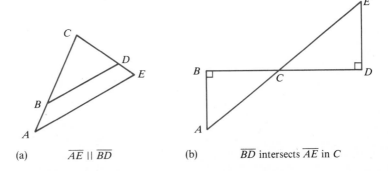

(a) $\overline{AE} \parallel \overline{BD}$ (b) $\overline{BD}$ intersects $\overline{AE}$ in C

Solution

(a) Because $\overline{AE} \parallel \overline{BD}$, congruent corresponding angles are formed by a transversal cutting the parallel segments. Thus, $\angle CBD \cong \angle CAE$, and $\angle CDB \cong \angle CEA$. Also, $\angle C \cong \angle C$, so that $\triangle CBD \sim \triangle CAE$ by AAA.

(b) $\angle B \cong \angle D$ because both are right triangles. Also, $\angle ACB \cong \angle ECD$ because they are vertical angles. Thus, $\triangle ACB \sim \triangle ECD$ by AA.

similar polygons

In general, knowing that the corresponding angles are congruent is not sufficient to determine similarity for any two polygons. For example, in a square of side 4 cm and a rectangle 2 cm by 4 cm, all the angles are congruent, but the two figures are not similar. In fact, *two* **polygons** are **similar** *if and only if the corresponding angles are congruent and the corresponding sides are proportional.*

Example 11-13

In each pair of similar triangles in Figure 11-83, find x.

Figure 11-83

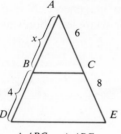

(a)   △$ABC \sim$ △ADE

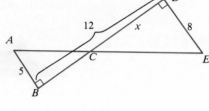

(b)   △$ABC \sim$ △EDC

Solution

(a) △$ABC \sim$ △ADE, so

$$\frac{AB}{AD} = \frac{AC}{AE} = \frac{BC}{DE}$$

Now, $AB = x$, $AD = x + 4$, $AC = 6$, and $AE = 6 + 8 = 14$. Thus,

$$\frac{x}{x + 4} = \frac{6}{14}$$

$$14x = 6(x + 4)$$

$$14x = 6x + 24$$

$$8x = 24$$

$$x = 3$$

(b) △$ABC \sim$ △EDC, so

$$\frac{AB}{ED} = \frac{AC}{EC} = \frac{BC}{DC}$$

Now, $AB = 5$, $ED = 8$, and $CD = x$, so that $BC = 12 - x$. Thus,

$$\frac{5}{8} = \frac{12 - x}{x}$$

$$5x = 8(12 - x)$$

$$5x = 96 - 8x$$

$$13x = 96$$

$$x = \frac{96}{13}$$

PROPERTIES OF PROPORTION

Similar triangles give rise to various properties involving proportions. For example, in Figure 11-84, if $\overline{BC}\|\overline{DE}$, then $\dfrac{AB}{BD} = \dfrac{AC}{CE}$. This can be justified as follows: $\overline{BC}\|\overline{DE}$, so $\triangle ADE \sim \triangle ABC$. (Why?) Consequently, $\dfrac{AD}{AB} = \dfrac{AE}{AC}$, which may be written as follows.

Figure 11-84

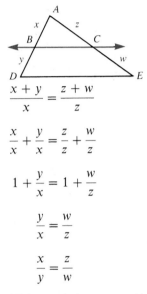

$$\frac{x + y}{x} = \frac{z + w}{z}$$

$$\frac{x}{x} + \frac{y}{x} = \frac{z}{z} + \frac{w}{z}$$

$$1 + \frac{y}{x} = 1 + \frac{w}{z}$$

$$\frac{y}{x} = \frac{w}{z}$$

$$\frac{x}{y} = \frac{z}{w}$$

This result is summarized in the following theorem.

THEOREM 11-4

> If a line parallel to one side of a triangle intersects the other sides, then it divides those sides into proportional segments.

In Figure 11-84, if B is the midpoint of $\overline{AD}$, then $x = y$. Consequently, $\dfrac{x}{y} = 1$. Because $\dfrac{x}{y} = \dfrac{z}{w}$, it follows that $\dfrac{z}{w} = 1$ and, hence, that $z = w$. That is, if B is the midpoint of $\overline{AD}$ and $\overline{BC}\|\overline{DE}$, then C is the midpoint of $\overline{AE}$. Similarly, if parallel lines intersect $\triangle ADE$, as shown in Figure 11-85, so that $a = b = c = d$, it can be shown that $e = f = g = h$. This result is stated in the following theorem.

Figure 11-85

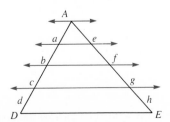

THEOREM 11-5

> If parallel lines cut off congruent segments on one transversal, then they cut off congruent segments on any transversal.

The preceding theorem is the basis for separating a line segment into any number of congruent parts. Consider dividing the segment $\overline{AB}$ in Figure 11-86(a) into three congruent parts. To obtain a figure similar to the one in Figure 11-85, we proceed as follows:

1. Through A, draw any ray $\overrightarrow{AC}$ such that A, B, and C are not collinear.
2. Mark off any three congruent segments on $\overrightarrow{AC}$, as shown in Figure 11-86(b).
3. Connect B with A_3.
4. Construct parallels to $\overline{BA_3}$ through A_1 and A_2, as shown in Figure 11-86(c).
5. The intersection points P and Q of the parallels with $\overline{AB}$ determine the three congruent parts of $\overline{AB}$.

Figure 11-86

Separate a line segment into congruent parts.

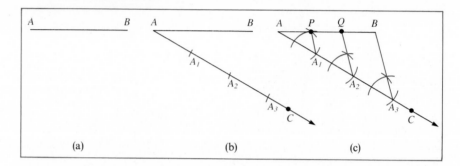

(a) (b) (c)

Similar triangles have also been used to make indirect measurements since the time of Thales of Miletus (ca. 600 B.C.), who is believed to have determined the height of the Great Pyramid of Egypt. Most likely, he used ratios involving shadows, similar to those in Figure 11-87. The sun is so far away that it should make approximately congruent angles at B and B'. Because the angles at C and C' are right angles, $\triangle ABC \sim \triangle A'B'C'$. Hence,

$$\frac{AC}{A'C'} = \frac{BC}{B'C'}$$

and because $AC = AE + EC$, the following proportion is obtained.

$$\frac{AE + EC}{A'C'} = \frac{BC}{B'C'}$$

Figure 11-87

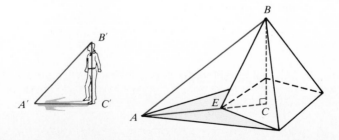

The person's height and shadow can be measured. Also, the length of the shadow of the pyramid AE can be measured, and EC can be found because the base of the pyramid is a square. Each term of the proportion except the height of the pyramid is known. Thus, the height of the pyramid can be found by solving the proportion.

Example 11-14

On a sunny day, a tall tree casts a 40 m (meter) shadow. At the same time, a meter stick held vertically casts a 2.5 m shadow. How tall is the tree?

Solution

Look at Figure 11-88. The pictured triangles are similar by AA because the tree and the stick both meet the ground at right angles, and the angles formed by the sun's rays are congruent (because the shadows are measured at the same time).

$$\frac{x}{40} = \frac{1}{2.5}$$

$$2.5x = 40$$

$$x = 16$$

The tree is 16 m tall.

Figure 11-88

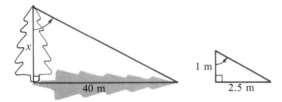

PROBLEM 3

A toy maker wants to cut the plastic rectangle $EFGH$ shown in Figure 11-89 into four right triangles and a rectangle. Given the measurements in Figure 11-89, how long is $\overline{CE}$?

Figure 11-89

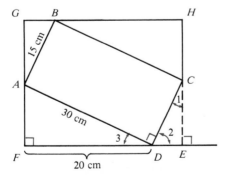

UNDERSTANDING THE PROBLEM Given the data in Figure 11-89, we are to find the length of $\overline{CE}$, which is perpendicular to $\overline{FE}$.

DEVISING A PLAN $\overline{CE}$ is a side in the right triangle EDC. If we could find a triangle with some known sides that is similar to $\triangle EDC$, we could set up a proportion and find CE. Triangle FAD is a right triangle in which two sides are known. Are the two triangles similar? The triangles have right angles at F and E, respectively. Also, $m(\angle 1) = 90° - m(\angle 2)$. Because $\triangle ADC$ is an angle in a rectangle, it is a right angle and $m(\angle 3) + 90° + m(\angle 2) = 180°$ or $m(\angle 3) = 90° - m(\angle 2)$. Thus, $m(\angle 1) = m(\angle 3)$ and $\triangle EDC$ is similar to $\triangle FAD$ by AA.

CARRYING OUT THE PLAN Because $\triangle EDC \sim \triangle FAD$, we have the following proportions.

$$\frac{EC}{FD} = \frac{DC}{AD} = \frac{ED}{FA}$$

Because $AD = 30$ cm, $FD = 20$ cm, and $DC = AB = 15$ cm, it follows that

$$\frac{EC}{20} = \frac{15}{30}$$

$$EC = 10 \text{ cm}$$

LOOKING BACK Given the data in the problem, it seems that we should also be able to find the length of $\overline{AF}$. However, this requires the use of the Pythagorean Theorem, which is introduced in Chapter 12.

PROBLEM 4

Two neighbors, Smith and Wesson, planned to erect flagpoles in their yards. Smith wanted a 10-foot pole, and Wesson wanted a 15-foot pole. In order to keep the poles straight while the concrete bases hardened, they agreed to tie guy wires from the tops of the flagpoles to a fence post on the property lines and to the bases of the flagpoles as shown in Figure 11-90. How high should the fence post be and how far apart should they erect flagpoles for this scheme to work?

Figure 11-90

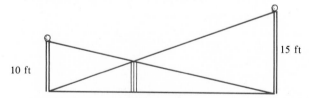

UNDERSTANDING THE PROBLEM In Figure 11-91, $AB = 10$ feet and $DC = 15$ feet; we need to find EF and AC. We know that $\overline{AB}$, $\overline{EF}$, and $\overline{DC}$ are perpendicular to $\overline{AC}$ and are therefore parallel.

Figure 11-91

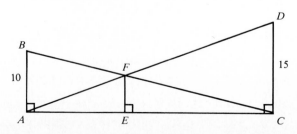

DEVISING A PLAN $\overline{EF}$ is a side in $\triangle EFC$. Because $\triangle EFC$ and $\triangle ABC$ are right triangles and share $\angle BCA$, it follows by AA that $\triangle EFC \sim \triangle ABC$. $\overline{EF}$ is also a side in $\triangle AFE$ and we have $\triangle AFE \sim \triangle ADC$. (Why?) From the two pairs of similar triangles, we will have proportions containing the unknown FE. The distance AC between the poles will appear in those proportions as well. We will then attempt to find FE and AC by solving the equations.

CARRYING OUT THE PLAN Let $FE = x$. Then, from $\triangle EFC \sim \triangle ABC$ and $\triangle AFE \sim \triangle ADC$, we have

$$\frac{x}{10} = \frac{EC}{AC}$$

$$\frac{x}{15} = \frac{AE}{AC}$$

We also know that $EC + AE = AC$. This suggests adding the proportions.

$$\frac{x}{10} + \frac{x}{15} = \frac{EC}{AC} + \frac{AE}{AC}$$

or

$$\frac{x}{10} + \frac{x}{15} = \frac{EC + AE}{AC} = \frac{AC}{AC} = 1$$

Thus, $\dfrac{x}{10} + \dfrac{x}{15} = 1$. We may solve this equation as follows.

$$\left(\frac{1}{10} + \frac{1}{15}\right)x = 1$$

$$\frac{5}{30}x = 1$$

$$\frac{1}{6}x = 1$$

$$x = 6$$

Thus, the fence post should be 6 feet high. Notice that when finding the height of the fence post, we did not have to know how far apart the poles are. This means that if the poles are placed farther apart, we would have the same height for the fence post. Thus, the poles could be any distance apart.

LOOKING BACK We could solve the problem for any length of flagpoles. If $AB = a$ and $CD = b$, then we would have $\dfrac{x}{a} + \dfrac{x}{b} = 1$ (why?) and, hence,

$$\left(\frac{1}{a} + \frac{1}{b}\right)x = 1 \quad \text{or} \quad \frac{a + b}{ab} \cdot x = 1 \quad \text{or} \quad x = \frac{ab}{a + b}$$

PROBLEM SET 11-8

1. Which of the following triangles is not similar to the other three?

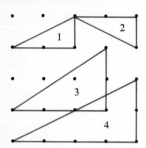

2. Which of the following are always similar? Why?
(a) Any two equilateral triangles
(b) Any two squares
(c) Any two rectangles
(d) Any two rhombi
(e) Any two circles
(f) Any two regular polygons
(g) Any two regular polygons with the same number of sides

3. Use a grid like the following one to draw a figure that has sides three times as large as the given figure.

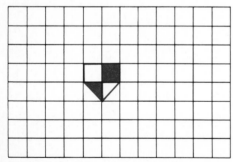

4. (a) Which pairs of the following triangles are similar? If they are similar, explain why.
(b) For each pair of similar triangles, find the ratio of the sides of the triangles.

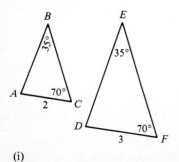

(i)

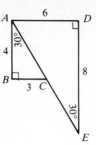

(ii)

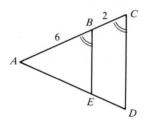

(iii)

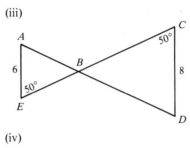

(iv)

5. Assume that the triangles in each part are similar and find the measures of the unknown sides.

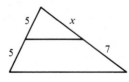

(a)

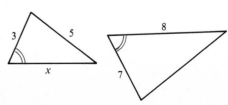

(b)

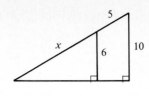

(c)

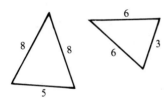

(d)

6. Polly claims that each of the following pairs of triangles is similar. In each part, determine if Polly is right or wrong. Explain why.

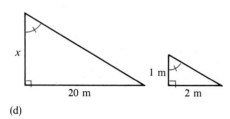

(a)

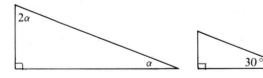

(b)

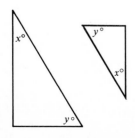

(c)

7. For each of the following, find x.

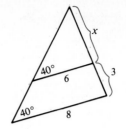

(a)

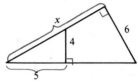

(b)

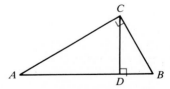

(c)

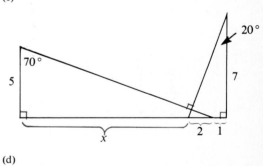

(d)

8. In right triangle ABC, we have $\overline{CD} \perp \overline{AB}$.

(a) Find three pairs of similar triangles. Justify your answers.
(b) Write the corresponding proportions for each set of similar triangles.

9. Are congruent triangles similar? Why?

10. (a) Construct a triangle with lengths of sides 4 cm, 6 cm, and 8 cm.
    (b) Construct another triangle with lengths of sides 2 cm, 3 cm, and 4 cm.
    (c) Make a conjecture about the similarity of triangles having proportional sides only.

11. (a) Construct a triangle with sides of lengths 4 cm and 6 cm and an included angle of 60°.
    (b) Construct a triangle with sides of lengths 2 cm and 3 cm and an included angle of 60°.
    (c) Make a conjecture about the similarity of triangles having two sides proportional and the included angles congruent.

12. (a) Sketch two nonsimilar polygons for which corresponding angles are congruent.
    (b) Sketch two nonsimilar polygons for which corresponding sides are proportional.

13. Examine several examples of similar polygons to make a conjecture concerning the ratio of their perimeters.

14. Use a compass and a straightedge to separate $\overline{AB}$ into five congruent pieces.

    _____
    A B

15. Construct a square and then construct another square with a side two-thirds the length of the first square.

16. Find the distance AB across the pond using the similar triangles shown.

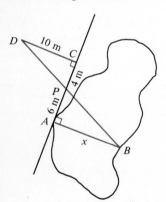

17. In the isosceles triangle ABC, $m(\angle A) = 36°$, $\overrightarrow{BD}$ bisects $\angle ABC$, and $\overline{AB} \cong \overline{AC}$.
    (a) Find two similar triangles in the figure.
    (b) Why are the triangles in (a) similar?

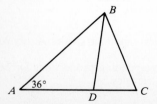

18. If $ABCD$ is a parallelogram, show that $\triangle BFE \sim \triangle CDE$.

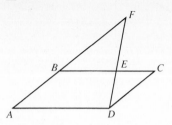

19. In the figure, $DEFG$ is a square and $m(\angle ACB) = 90°$.
    (a) Show that $\triangle ADG \sim \triangle GCF$.
    (b) Is it true that $\triangle ADG \cong \triangle GCF$? Justify your answer.

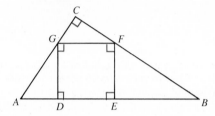

20. To find the height of a tree, a group of Girl Scouts devised the following method. A girl walks away from the tree along its shadow until the shadow of the top of her head coincides with the shadow of the top of the tree. If the girl is 150 cm tall, her distance to the foot of the tree is 1500 cm, and the length of her shadow is 300 cm, how tall is the tree?

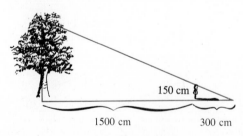

21. If $ABCD$ is a parallelogram, $BF = 6$, $FC = 3$, and $BD = 7.5$, find BE and ED.

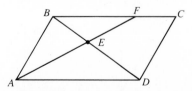

*22. A **dilation** is a transformation of the plane that is defined as follows. Let O be a point and k be a positive number. The dilation with center O and ratio (or scale factor) k is the transformation of the plane such that the image of O is O itself and the image of any point P other than O is point P' on $\overrightarrow{OP}$ such that $OP' = k(OP)$. (In Figure 11-79 on page 540, $\triangle A'B'C'$ is the image of $\triangle ABC$ under the dilation with center at the lens of the projector and the ratio $k = 2$.) Find the images of the following figures under the given dilation determined by k and O. What is the relationship of the images to the original figure?

(a) $k = 3$

(b) $k = 2$

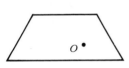

(c) $k = 2$

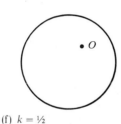

(d) $k = 2.5$

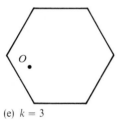

(e) $k = 3$

(f) $k = \frac{1}{2}$

23. (a) Write a procedure called RECTANGLE that draws a rectangle of variable size with inputs :LEN and :WID, and then write a procedure called SIM.RECT that draws a rectangle twice as large as the one drawn by RECTANGLE if the same inputs are used for :LEN and :WID.
   (b) Write a procedure called SIM.RECTANGLE that draws a rectangle similar to the one drawn by RECTANGLE with a scale factor called :SCALE that affects the size of the rectangle.
   (c) Write a procedure called PARALLELOGRAM to draw a parallelogram of variable size with inputs :LEN, :WID, and :ANGLE, and then write a procedure called SIM.PAR to generate similar parallelograms.

24. (a) Write a Logo procedure called TRISECT to draw a line segment of length determined by input :LEN and have the turtle divide it into three congruent parts.
   (b) Write a procedure called PARTITION to draw a line segment of length determined by input :LEN and have the turtle divide it into :NUM parts, where :NUM is also an input.

Review Problems

25. Explain why it is impossible to tessellate the plane with regular octagons.
26. Draw a quadrilateral with no two sides congruent and tessellate the plane with that quadrilateral.
27. Sketch a figure with a 45° turn symmetry about a point.

BRAIN TEASER

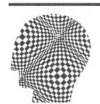

Poles $\overline{AB}$, $\overline{CF}$, and $\overline{DE}$ are constructed perpendicular to the ground in such a way that when B, C, D, and F are connected by wires, $BCDF$ is a rectangle. If $\overline{AB}$ is 9 m long and $\overline{DE}$ is 4 m long, how long is $\overline{CF}$ and how far apart are $\overline{AB}$ and $\overline{DE}$?

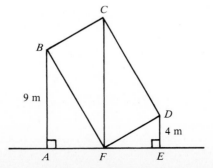

*Section 11-9   Using Logo to Draw Circles

Recall the POLYGON procedure that was developed in Chapter 10 for drawing regular polygons with :N and :SIZE representing the number of sides and the length of a side, respectively. The procedure is as follows.

```
TO POLYGON :N :SIZE
  REPEAT :N [FD :SIZE RT 360/:N]
END
```

The ideas in the POLYGON procedure can be used to demonstrate the mathematical concept that as the number of sides in a regular polygon increases, the figure approaches a circle. When the turtle is at home with heading 0, the procedure called POLYGONS that follows can be used to draw an equilateral triangle, followed by a square, followed by a regular pentagon, followed by a regular hexagon, and so on until a regular 20-gon is drawn. The result of executing POLYGONS 3 is shown in Figure 11-92.

Figure 11-92

```
TO POLYGONS :N
  FULLSCREEN
  POLYGON :N 20
  IF :N > 20 STOP
  POLYGONS :N + 1
END
```

Remark   The command FULLSCREEN gives full graphics capability for drawing.

DRAWING TURTLE-TYPE CIRCLES

To instruct the turtle to draw a figure that looks like a circle (*turtle-type circle*), we must tell the turtle to move forward a little and turn a little and then repeat this sequence of motions until it comes back to its original position. If the turtle is told to go forward 1 unit and then to turn right 1°, then this sequence of motions repeated 360 times yields a turtle-type circle. The CIRCLE1 procedure from Appendix II along with its output is given in Figure 11-93.

Figure 11-93

```
TO CIRCLE1
  REPEAT 360 [FD 1 RT 1]
END
```

CIRCLE1

The turtle-type circle determined by CIRCLE1 is actually a regular 360-gon (a polygon with 360 sides), but it is a close approximation of a circle and is referred to in Logo as a circle. One way to vary the size of the circle is to vary the amount the turtle moves forward. For example, suppose the turtle moves foward 0.5 unit rather than 1 unit, or—in general—any number of units *S*. We define a new procedure called VCIRCLE that accepts a variable input :S. Figure 11-94 shows various circles drawn by the VCIRCLE procedure.

Figure 11-94

VCIRCLE 0.8   VCIRCLE 0.5   VCIRCLE 0.1

```
TO VCIRCLE :S
  REPEAT 360 [FD :S RT 1]
END
```

Sometimes, it is more useful to draw a circle of a given radius. To write a procedure for drawing a circle of radius *R*, we utilize the procedure for VCIRCLE and the formula $2\pi r$ for the circumference of a circle. (This formula is discussed in Chapter 12.) To understand the general case better, we first solve a special case of the problem. Suppose we want to draw a circle with radius 50. What should the side *S* of the approximating polygon be? Because the perimeter of the polygon is $360 \cdot S$, and the circumference of a circle with radius 50 is $2\pi \cdot 50$, then $360 \cdot S \doteq 2\pi \cdot 50$. Now, $S \doteq (2\pi \cdot 50)/360$, or 0.873. Thus, VCIRCLE 0.873 will draw a circle with radius approximately 50 units long.

In general, to find a procedure to draw a circle with radius *R* as an input, we need to find *S* in terms of *R*. This can be done as follows.

$$360 \cdot S \doteq 2\pi R$$

$$S \doteq \frac{2\pi R}{360}$$

Hence, a procedure called CIRCLE for drawing a circle with radius *R* can be written as shown, where π is approximated as 3.1416.

```
TO CIRCLE :R
  VCIRCLE (2 * 3.1416 * :R) / 360
END
```

How can we check that CIRCLE 50 draws a turtle-type circle of radius 50? This can be done by turning the turtle toward the center (after the circle has been completed) and instructing the turtle to go forward 100 units, which is the diameter of a circle with radius 50. If the turtle draws a diameter of the circle, the circle has a radius of 50 units. This check can be accomplished by executing the line

```
RT 90 FD 100 HT
```

Remark It should be noted that this check is not totally accurate because our turtle-type circle is not a true circle.

DRAWING CIRCLES FASTER

One way to draw circles faster by using the CIRCLE procedure is to hide the turtle before executing the procedure so that the turtle does not have to be drawn on the screen for each move. You can also speed up the circle by varying the number of repeats. To close the figure, the turtle must complete a 360° trip. To make sure this happens, the number of times the moves are repeated, multiplied by the number of degrees for each turn, must equal 360. For example, if we decide that the turtle should turn 15° each time, the process should be completed $\frac{360}{15}$, or 24, times because $15° \cdot 24 = 360°$.

In addition, if we wish the size of the faster circle to be approximately the same as that of the original circle, we need to make the perimeter of the polygon approximating the faster circle be the same as the perimeter of the polygon that drew the original approximation by using the CIRCLE procedure. This can be done by adapting the length of each side of the polygon. For example, if the original figure has perimeter 360 units, and the new figure is to have 24 sides and perimeter 360 units, then each side must have length $\frac{360}{24}$, or 15, turtle steps. Consequently, we obtain the following FCIRCLE procedure.

```
TO FCIRCLE
  REPEAT 24 [FD 15 RT 15]
END
```

As an exercise, write a procedure for drawing circles, using variables for both the length of a side and the amount of the turn.

Procedures can also be designed for drawing arcs, that is, continuous parts of a circle. For example, if we wished to draw a semicircle, we could write the following procedure.

```
TO SEMICIRCLE
  REPEAT 180 [FD 1 RT 1]
END
```

As an exercise, develop a procedure called RARC for drawing arcs of variable size.

PROBLEM SET 11-9

1. (a) In the CIRCLE1 procedure in this section, suppose the instruction RT 1 is changed to RT 5. How does the new figure differ from the original one?
   (b) How does the figure differ if RT 1 is changed to LT 1?

2. Generalize the FCIRCLE procedure to include variable-sized sides and a variable number of repeats.

3. In the VCIRCLE procedure, if the turtle repeats the sequence FD :S RT 1 fewer than 360 times, it will draw an arc of a circle.

(a) Write a procedure for drawing an arc when the inputs are the length of a side of an approximating polygon and the number of degrees in the arc.

(b) Write a procedure for drawing an arc, given the radius of the arc and number of degrees in the arc.

4. Create your own designs, using the arc procedure developed in Problem 3(b).

5. Design a procedure to fill in a circle, that is, color in its interior.

6. Write procedures to draw figures similar to each of the following.

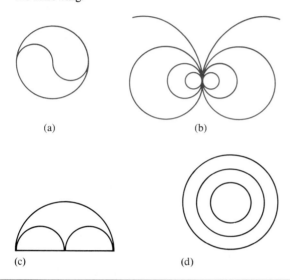

(a)   (b)

(c)   (d)

(e)

7. Write a procedure called **SYMBOL** for drawing the Olympic symbol in variable sizes.

8. Use the procedures developed in Problem 3 to write a procedure to draw variable-sized flowers similar to the one shown.

9. Write a procedure called **DIAMCIRC** with radius :R of a circle as an input and that draws the circle along with its diameter.

SOLUTION TO THE PRELIMINARY PROBLEM

UNDERSTANDING THE PROBLEM To better understand the problem, we first draw a diagram, as seen in Figure 11-95. We label the hiker H, the tent T, and the river r. The hiker needs to find point P on the bank of the river so that the distance $HP + PT$ is as short as possible.

Figure 11-95

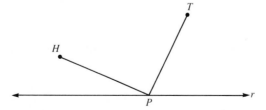

DEVISING A PLAN From the properties of reflections, we know that if T' is the reflection of the tent T in line r, then r is the perpendicular bisector of $\overline{TT'}$, as shown in Figure 11-96(a). Hence, any point on r is equidistant

Figure 11-96

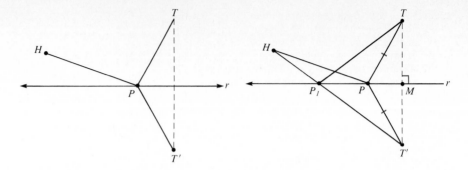

from T and T'. Thus, $PT = PT'$. Therefore, the hiker may solve the problem by finding a point P on r such that the path from H to P and then to T' is as short as possible. The shortest path connecting H and T' is a segment. The intersection of $\overline{HT'}$ and r determines the point on the river toward which the hiker should run.

CARRYING OUT THE PLAN Connect H with T', as shown in Figure 11-96(b). The point of intersection P_1 is the required point. The hiker should run to P_1 and then from P_1 to T.

LOOKING BACK To prove that the path from H to P_1 to T is the shortest possible, we need to prove that $HP_1 + P_1T < HP + PT$, where P is any point on r different from P_1. Because $HP_1 + P_1T = HP_1 + P_1T' = HT'$ (why?), and $HP + PT = HP + PT'$ (why?), the inequality that we needed to prove is equivalent to $HT' < HP + PT'$. This last inequality follows from the Triangle Inequality discussed in Section 11-1.

QUESTIONS FROM THE CLASSROOM

1. On a test, a student wrote $AB \cong CD$ instead of $\overline{AB} \cong \overline{CD}$. Is this answer correct?
2. A student asks if there are any constructions that cannot be done using a compass and a straightedge. How do you answer?
3. A student asks for a mathematical definition of congruence that holds for all figures. How do you respond? Is your response the same for similarity?
4. One student claims that by trisecting $\overline{AB}$ and drawing $\overrightarrow{CD}$ and $\overrightarrow{CE}$ as shown, she has trisected $\angle ACB$.

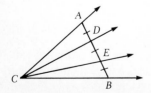

How do you convince her that her construction is wrong?

5. In the following drawing, a student claims that polygon $ABCD$ is a parallelogram if $\angle 1 \cong \angle 2$. Is he correct?

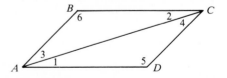

6. A student claims that by connecting the midpoints of the sides of any polygon, a polygon similar to the original results. Is this true?
7. A student asks if the only transformations are flips, slides, turns, or glide reflections. How do you respond?

8. A student asks why $\cong$ rather than $=$ is used to discuss triangles that have the same size and shape. What do you say?

9. A student draws the following figure and claims that because every triangle is congruent to itself, then we can write $\triangle ABC \cong \triangle BCA$. What is your response?

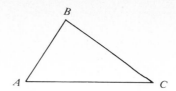

CHAPTER OUTLINE

I. Congruence
   A. Two geometric figures are **congruent** if and only if they have the same size and shape.
   B. Two triangles are congruent if they satisfy any of the following conditions.
      1. **Side, Side, Side (SSS)**
      2. **Side, Angle, Side (SAS)**
      3. **Angle, Side, Angle (ASA)**
      4. **Angle, Angle, Side (AAS)**

II. Circles and spheres
   A. A **circle** is a set of points in a plane that are the same distance (radius) from a given point (center).
   B. A **chord** is a segment with endpoints on a circle.
   C. A **secant** is a line that contains a chord of a circle.
   D. A **tangent** is a line that intersects a circle in exactly one point.
   E. A **sphere** is a set of points in space that are the same distance (radius) from a given point (center).

III. Transformations of the plane
   A. An **isometry** is a transformation of the plane that preserves distance.
   B. The simple isometries of the plane are slides, flips, and turns.
      1. A **slide** (or **translation**) is a motion of a specified distance and direction along a straight line without any accompanying turning or twisting.
      2. A **flip** (or **reflection**) in a line ℓ is a motion that pairs each point P of the plane with a point P' in such a way that ℓ is the perpendicular bisector of $\overline{PP'}$ if $P \notin \ell$, and $P = P'$ if $P \in \ell$.
      3. A **turn** (or **rotation**) is a motion determined by holding one point, the center, fixed and rotating the plane about this point a certain amount in a certain direction.

*IV. Tessellations of a plane
   C. A **tessellation** of a plane is a filling of the plane by repeating a figure in such a way that no figures overlap and there are no gaps.
      1. The only regular polygons that tessellate the plane are an equilateral triangle, a square, and a regular hexagon.
      2. Any convex quadrilateral tessellates the plane.

V. Types of symmetry
   A. A figure has **line symmetry** if it is its own image under a flip.
   B. A figure has **turn symmetry** if it is its own image under a turn of less than 360° about its center.
   C. A figure that has 180° turn symmetry is said to have **point symmetry.**

VI. Similar figures
   A. Two polygons are **similar** if and only if their corresponding angles are congruent and their corresponding sides are proportional.
   B. **AAA** or **AA:** If three (two) angles of one triangle are congruent to three (two) angles of a second triangle, respectively, the triangles are similar.

VII. Proportion
   A. If a line parallel to one side of a triangle intersects the other sides, then it divides those sides into proportional segments.
   B. If parallel lines cut off congruent segments on one transversal, then they cut off congruent segments on any transversal.

VIII. Constructions using compass and straightedge
   A. Copy a line segment.
   B. Copy a circle.
   C. Copy an angle.
   D. Bisect a segment.
   E. Bisect an angle.
   F. Construct a perpendicular from a point to a line.

G. Construct a perpendicular bisector of a segment.

H. Construct a perpendicular through a point on a line.

I. Construct a parallel to a line through a point not on the line.

J. Divide a segment into congruent parts.

K. Inscribe regular polygons in a circle.

L. Circumscribe a circle about a triangle.

M. Inscribe a circle in a triangle.

*IX. Using Logo to draw circles

In Logo, a turtle-type circle is a regular polygon with (usually) 360 sides. Procedures for drawing variable-sized circles include the following.

1. VCIRCLE with an input :S for the length of a side of the approximating polygon

2. CIRCLE with an input :R for the radius of the circle

CHAPTER TEST

1. In each of the following figures, there is at least one pair of congruent triangles. Identify them and tell why they are congruent.

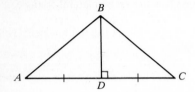

(a)

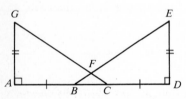

(b)

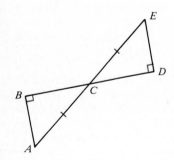

(c)

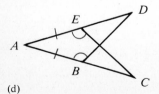

(d)

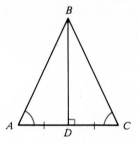

(e)

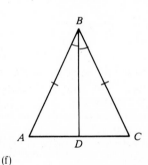

(f)

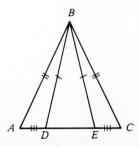

(g)

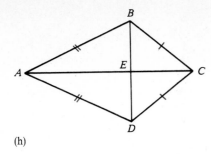

(h)

2. In the figure, $ABCD$ is a square and $\overline{DE} \cong \overline{BF}$. What kind of figure is $AECF$? Justify your answer.

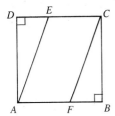

3. Complete each of the following motions.

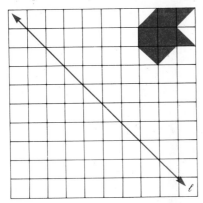

(a) A flip about ℓ

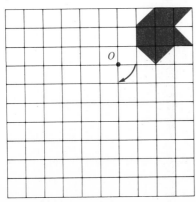

(b) A turn about O through the given arc

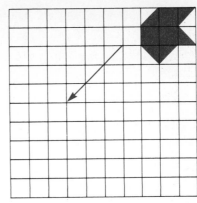

(c) A slide as pictured

4. For each of the following, construct the image of $\triangle ABC$.

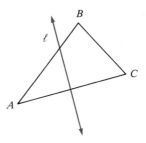

(a) Through a flip about ℓ

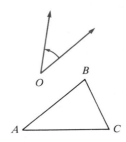

(b) Through the given turn in O

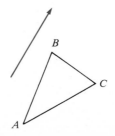

(c) Through the slide pictured

5. Construct each of the following using (a) compass and straightedge; (b) paper folding.

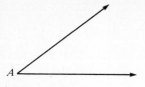

(a) Bisector of ∢ A

(b) Perpendicular to ℓ at B

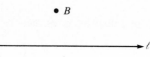

(c) Perpendicular to ℓ from B

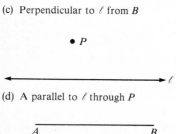

(d) A parallel to ℓ through P

(e) The perpendicular bisector of $\overline{AB}$

6. How many lines of symmetry, if any, does each of the following figures have?

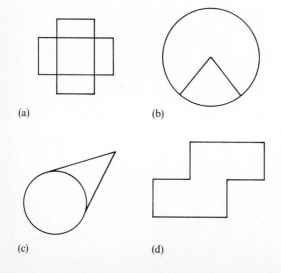

(a)   (b)

(c)   (d)

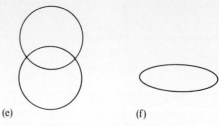

(e)   (f)

7. For each of the following, identify the types of symmetry (line, turn, or point) of the given figure.

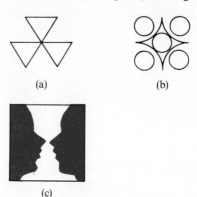

(a)   (b)

(c)

8. For each of the following pairs of similar triangles, find the missing measures.

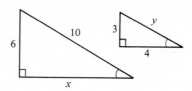

(a)

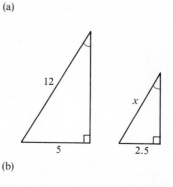

(b)

9. Divide the given segment into five congruent parts.

A   B

10. If *ABCD* is a trapezoid, $\overline{EF} \parallel \overline{AD}$, and $\overline{AC}$ is a diagonal. What is the relationship between $\dfrac{a}{b}$ and $\dfrac{c}{d}$? Why?

11. Construct a circle containing *A* and *B* whose center is on ℓ.

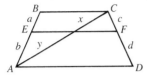

12. For each of the following, show that appropriate triangles are similar and find *x* and *y*.

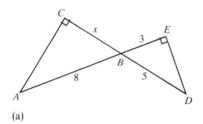

(a)

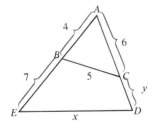

(b) Given: $\triangle ABC \cong \triangle AED$

13. Determine whether each of the following is true or false. If false, explain why.

(a) A radius of a circle is a chord of the circle.

(b) A diameter of a circle may be a tangent of the circle.

(c) If a radius bisects a chord of a circle, then it is perpendicular to the chord.

(d) Two spheres may intersect in exactly one point.

(e) Two spheres may intersect in a circle.

*14. In the figure, $\overline{AC}$ and $\overline{BD}$ are diameters of a circle with center *P*.

(a) Prove that $\overline{AD} \parallel \overline{BC}$.

(b) Prove that polygon *ABCD* is a rectangle.

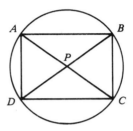

15. A person 2 m tall casts a shadow 1 m long when a building has a 6 m shadow. How high is the building?

16. (a) Which of the following polygons can be inscribed in a circle? Assume that all sides of each polygon are congruent and all the angles of polygons (iii) and (iv) are congruent.

(b) Based on your answer in (a), make a conjecture about what kinds of polygons can be inscribed in a circle.

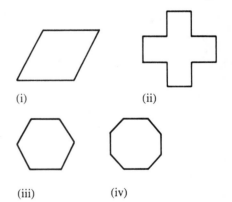

(i)   (ii)

(iii)   (iv)

SELECTED BIBLIOGRAPHY

Billstein, R., S. Libeskind, and J. Lott. *Logo, MIT Logo for the Apple.* Menlo Park, Calif.: Benjamin/Cummings, 1985.

Billstein, R., S. Libeskind, and J. Lott, *Apple Logo, Programming, and Problem Solving.* Menlo Park, Calif.: Benjamin/Cummings, 1986.

Brown, R. "Making Geometry a Personal and Inventive Experience." *The Mathematics Teacher* 75 (September 1982):442–446.

Burger, W. "Geometry." *Arithmetic Teacher* 32 (February 1985):52–56.

Edwards, R. "Discoveries in Geometry by Folding and Cutting." *The Arithmetic Teacher* 24 (March 1977): 196–198.

Hiatt, A. "Problem Solving in Geometry." *The Mathematics Teacher* 65 (November 1972):595–600.

Horak, V., and W. Horak. "Using Geometry Tiles as a Manipulative for Developing Basic Concepts." *Arithmetic Teacher* 30 (April 1983):8–15.

Immerzeel, G. "Geometric Activities for Early Childhood Education." *The Arithmetic Teacher* 20 (October 1973):438–443.

Johnson, M. "Generating Patterns for Transformations." *The Arithmetic Teacher* 24 (March 1977): 191–195.

Juraschek, W., and G. McGlathery. "Funny Letters: A Discrepant Event." *Arithmetic Teacher* 27 (April 1980):43–47.

Kerr, D. "The Study of Space Experiences: A Framework for Geometry for Elementary Teachers." *The Arithmetic Teacher* 23 (March 1976):169–174.

Kidder, R. "Euclidean Transformations: Elementary School Spaceometry." *The Arithmetic Teacher* 24 (March 1977):201–207.

Lindquist, M., and M. Dana. "The Surprising Circle!" *Arithmetic Teacher* 25 (January 1978):4–10.

Lindquist, M., and M. Dana. "Wallpaper Capers." *Arithmetic Teacher* 26 (February 1979):4–9.

Lott, J., and I. Dayoub. "What Can Be Done with a Mira?" *The Mathematics Teacher* 70 (May 1977): 394–399.

Maletsky, E. "Activities: Fun with Flips." *The Mathematics Teacher* 66 (October 1973):531–534.

Mansfield, H. "Projective Geometry in the Elementary School." *Arithmetic Teacher* 32 (March 1985):15–19.

Mathematics Resource Project. *Geometry and Visualization.* Palo Alto, Calif.: Creative Publications, 1985.

Moulton, J. "Some Geometry Experiences for Elementary School Children." *The Arithmetic Teacher* 21 (February 1974): 114–116.

Reid, J. "Cutting Across a Circle." *Arithmetic Teacher* 26 (April 1979):27.

Sanok, G. "Living in a World of Transformations." *Arithmetic Teacher* 25 (April 1978):36–40.

Sawada, D. "Symmetry and Tessellations from Rotational Transformations on Transparencies." *Arithmetic Teacher* 33 (December 1986):12–13.

Silverman, H. "Geometry in the Primary Grades: Exploring Geometric Ideas in the Primary Grades." *Arithmetic Teacher* 26 (February 1979):15–16.

Thompson, C., and J. Van de Walle. "Patterns and Geometry with Logo." *Arithmetic Teacher* 32 (March 1985):6–13.

Troccolo, J. "The Rhombus Construction Company." *The Mathematics Teacher* 76 (January 1983):37–42.

Turner, S. "Windowpane Patterns." *The Mathematics Teacher* 76 (September 1983):411–413.

Thomas, D. "Geometry in the Middle School: Problem Solving with Trapezoids." *Arithmetic Teacher* 26 (February 1979): 20–21.

Van de Walle, J., and C. Thompson. "Concepts, Art, and Fun from Simple Tiling Patterns." *Arithmetic Teacher* 28 (November 1980):4–8.

Van de Walle, J., and C. Thompson. "Cut and Paste for Geometric Thinking." *Arithmetic Teacher* 31 (September 1983):8–13.

Van de Walle, J., and C. Thompson. "A Triangle Treasury." *Arithmetic Teacher* 28 (February 1981):6–11.

Van de Walle, J., and C. Thompson. "Promoting Mathematical Thinking." *Arithmetic Teacher* 32 (February 1985):7–13.

Walter, M. *Boxes, Squares and Other Things.* Reston, Va.: National Council of Teachers of Mathematics, 1970.

Walter, M. "Do We Rob Students of a Chance to Learn?" *For the Learning of Mathematics* 1, 3 (March 1981):16–18.

Walter, M. *The Mirror Puzzle Book.* Stradbroke, England: Tarquin Publications, 1985. (Distributed by Park West Publishers, New York.)

Zurstadt, B. "Tessellations and the Art of M. C. Escher." *Arithmetic Teacher* 31 (January 1984):54–55.

CHAPTER 12

Concepts of Measurement

Preliminary Problem

A manufacturer of metal cans has a large quantity of rectangular metal sheets 20 cm wide by 30 cm long. Without cutting the sheets, the manager wants to make cylindrical pipes with circular cross sections from some of the sheets and box-shaped pipes with square cross sections from the other sheets so that the volume of the box-shaped pipes is greater than the volume of the cylindrical pipes. Is this possible? If so, how should the pipes be made and what are their volumes?

Introduction

In this chapter, we develop the metric system of measurement for length, area, volume, mass, and temperature with the philosophy that students should learn to think within a measurement system. Consequently, conversions among units of measure in the metric and the English systems are not considered.

In addition, we develop formulas for the areas of plane figures and for surface areas and volumes of solids. We also use the concept of area to discuss the Pythagorean Theorem.

Section 12-1

The Metric System: Units of Length

Three fundamental quantities of measure are length, mass, and time, from which the units of measure for area, volume, and other physical quantities are derived. Early attempts at measurement lacked a standard unit object and used hands, arms, and feet as units of measure. These early crude measurements were eventually refined and standardized by the English into a very complicated system, including three types of weights: troy, avoirdupois, and apothecary. The English system of weights and measures has been used in many countries, including the United States.

The metric system was proposed in France in 1670 by Gabriel Mouton. However, not until the French Revolution in 1790 did the French Academy of Sciences bring various groups together to develop the new system. The academy recognized the need for a standard base unit of linear measurement. The members chose $\frac{1}{10,000,000}$ of the distance from the equator to the North Pole, on a meridian through Paris, as the base unit of length and called it the **meter.** Later, the meter was redefined in terms of krypton 86 wavelengths. The name *meter* was derived from the Greek word *metron,* meaning "a measure." Base units of volume and mass were derived from the meter. For ease in computation, larger and smaller units were created by multiplying or dividing the base units by powers of ten. Thus, the metric system is a decimal system.

The krypton 86 definition of meter is important for accuracy but not very meaningful in everyday life. If you turn your head away from your outstretched arm, then the distance from your nose to your fingertip is about 1 meter. Also, 1 meter is about the distance from a doorknob to the floor;

HISTORICAL NOTE

In 1585, Simon Stevin (1548–1620), a Dutch mathematician-inventor, recommended a system of weights and measures based on the decimal system and declared that the universal introduction of decimal measure would be only a question of time. The metric system adopted in France in 1799 was such a system. Three hundred years later, the United States is the only developed country in which the decimal system of measure is not in widespread use.

1 meter is about 39 inches, slightly longer than 1 yard. Most educators strongly recommend that the metric system be taught independently and not taught as conversions to and from the English system.

Different units of length in the metric system are obtained by combining an appropriate prefix with the base unit. The prefixes, the multiplication factors they indicate, and their symbols are given in Table 12-1.

Table 12-1

Prefix	Factor		Symbol
kilo	1000	(one thousand)	k
hecto	100	(one hundred)	h
deka	10	(ten)	da
deci	0.1	(one tenth)	d
centi	0.01	(one hundredth)	c
milli	0.001	(one thousandth)	m

Remark   Hecto, deka, and deci are not common prefixes and have limited use. These should not be stressed when teaching the metric system. Kilo, hecto, and deka are Greek prefixes, whereas deci, centi, and milli are Latin prefixes.

Using the metric prefixes along with meter gives the names for different units of length. Table 12-2 gives these units along with their relationship to the meter and the symbol for each. The symbol m stands for meter. Notice that there is no period after the m; it is a symbol rather than an abbreviation.

Table 12-2

Unit	Symbol	Relationship to Base Unit	
kilometer	km	1000	meters
*hectometer	hm	100	meters
*dekameter	dam	10	meters
meter	**m**	**base unit**	
*decimeter	dm	0.1	meter
centimeter	cm	0.01	meter
millimeter	mm	0.001	meter

* Not commonly used, although some educators recommend the use of decimeter in elementary school (see Lindquist and Dana, "The Neglected Decimeter").

The relationships among metric units of length are based on powers of ten, as reflected by the prefixes in the names of the units. For example, 1 centimeter is 0.01 of a meter, because "centi" means one-hundredth. We write this as 1 cm = 0.01 m. Consequently, when 1 m is divided into 100 congruent parts, each part is 1 cm long. Hence, 1 m = 100 cm. One centimeter is about the width of your little finger, the diameter of the head of a thumbtack, or the width of a white Cuisenaire rod. A unit smaller than a centimeter is found by dividing 1 m into 1000 congruent parts or by dividing 1 cm into 10 congruent parts. Thus, 1 mm = 0.1 cm = 0.001 m, or 1000 mm = 100 cm = 1 m. One millimeter is about the thickness of a paper clip or a dime. Some estimations for a meter, a centimeter, and a millimeter are shown in Figure 12-1.

Figure 12-1

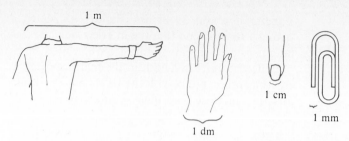

The units decimeter, dekameter, and hectometer represent 0.1 m, 10 m, and 100 m, respectively, but, as indicated in Table 12-2, they are not commonly used. The kilometer is commonly used for measuring long distances. Because "kilo" stands for 1000, 1 km = 1000 m. Nine football fields, including end zones, laid end to end are approximately 1 km long.

Because metric units of length are based on powers of ten, the conversion from one metric unit to another is easy. As with money, we simply move the decimal point to the left or right, depending on the units. For example,

$$0.123 \text{ km} = 1.23 \text{ hm} = 12.3 \text{ dam} = 123 \text{ m} = 1230 \text{ dm} = 12,300 \text{ cm}$$
$$= 123,000 \text{ mm}$$

It is possible to convert units using the chart in Figure 12-2. We count the number of steps from one unit to the other and move the decimal point that many steps in the same direction.

Figure 12-2

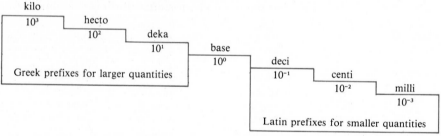

Example 12-1

Convert each of the following.

(a) 1.4 km = _____ m   (b) 285 mm = _____ m

Solution

(a) 1 km = 1000 m, so to change from kilometers to meters, we multiply by 1000. Therefore, we move the decimal point three places to the right. Hence, 1.4 km = 1400 m.

(b) 1 mm = 0.001 m, so to change from millimeters to meters, we multiply by 0.001. In other words, we move the decimal point three places to the left. Thus, 285 mm = 0.285 m.

In geometry, units of length are usually used to measure distances along lines and thus are called linear measure. Recall that in the development of the number line (Chapter 3), we chose a point on the line to represent 0 and a second point to represent 1. If we select the points so that the distance between 0 and 1 is 1 centimeter and develop the number line accordingly, then the number line can be used to measure lengths of segments in terms of

Figure 12-3

centimeters. Similarly, by making the distance between 0 and 1 an inch, a meter, a foot, and so on, we can develop other rulers for measuring lengths. Figure 12-3 shows part of a centimeter ruler.

The following are three basic properties of distance:

1. The distance between any two points A and B is greater than or equal to 0, written $AB \geq 0$.
2. The distance between any two points A and B is the same as the distance between B and A, written $AB = BA$.
3. For any three points A, B, and C, the distance between A and B plus the distance between B and C is greater than or equal to the distance between A and C, written $AB + BC \geq AC$.

Remark   Notice that, as shown in Figure 12-4(a), $AB + BC = AC$ if and only if A, B, and C are collinear and B is between A and C. If A, B, and C are not collinear, as in Figure 12-4(b), then $AB + BC > AC$, which is the Triangle Inequality discussed in Chapter 11.

Figure 12-4

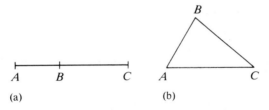

(a)   (b)

DISTANCE AROUND A PLANE FIGURE

perimeter   The **perimeter** of a simple closed curve is the length of the curve, that is, the distance around the figure. If a figure is a polygon, its perimeter is the sum of the lengths of the sides. Perimeter is always expressed using linear measure.

Example 12-2   Find the perimeter of each of the shapes in Figure 12-5.

Figure 12-5

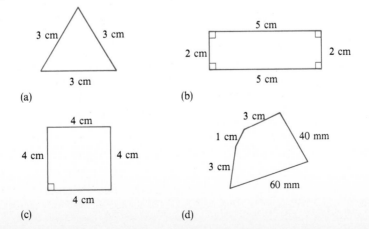

Solution

(a) The perimeter is 3(3) = 9, or 9 cm.
(b) The perimeter is 2(2) + 2(5) = 14, or 14 cm.
(c) The perimeter is 4(4) = 16, or 16 cm.
(d) Because 40 mm = 4 cm and 60 mm = 6 cm, the perimeter is
   1 + 3 + 4 + 6 + 3 = 17, or 17 cm.

---

circumference   The distance around a circle is called its **circumference.** The ancient Greeks discovered that if they divided the circumference of a circle by the length of a diameter, they always obtained approximately the same number, regardless of the size of the circle. The value of the number is approximately 3.14.

pi   Today, the ratio of circumference C to diameter d is symbolized as π **(pi)**. In the late eighteenth century, mathematicians proved that this ratio $\dfrac{C}{d}$, or π, is not a terminating or repeating decimal but an irrational number.

The relationship $\dfrac{C}{d} = \pi$ gives a formula for finding the circumference of a circle. Usually, it is written as $C = \pi d$ or $C = 2\pi r$ because the length of a diameter d is twice the radius of the circle. For most practical purposes, π is approximated by $\frac{22}{7}$, $3\frac{1}{7}$, or 3.14. These values are only approximations and are not exact values of π. If you are asked for the exact circumference of a circle with diameter 6 cm, the answer is 6π cm. Circumference is always expressed in linear measure.

Example 12-3

Find each of the following.

(a) The circumference of a circle if the radius is 2 m.
(b) The radius of a circle if the circumference is 15π m.

Solution

(a) $C = 2\pi(2) = 4\pi$. Thus, the circumference is 4π m.
(b) $C = 2\pi r$ implies $15\pi = 2\pi r$. Hence, $r = \frac{15}{2}$. Thus, the radius is $\frac{15}{2}$ m.

PROBLEM SET 12-1

1. A millimeter is the smallest distance pictured on the metric ruler in the following figure. Starting from the left end of the ruler, the distance from the end to A is 1 mm, and the distance from the end to B is 10 mm, or 1 cm. The distance from the end to J is 100 mm, 10 cm, or 1 dm.

Use the ruler to answer each of the following.
(a) C points to _____ mm   or   _____ cm
(b) D points to _____ mm   or   _____ cm
(c) E points to _____ mm   or   _____ cm
(d) F points to _____ cm   or   _____ mm
(e) G points to _____ cm   or   _____ mm

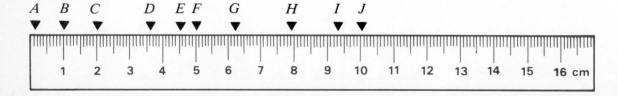

(f) *H* points to _____ cm   or   _____ mm

(g) *I* points to _____ mm   or   _____ cm

2. Draw segments that you estimate to be of the following lengths. Then, using a metric ruler, check the estimates.

(a) 10 mm   (b) 100 mm   (c) 1 cm

(d) 10 cm   (e) 0.01 m   (f) 15 cm

(g) 0.1 m   (h) 27 mm

3. Estimate the length of the following segment and then measure it. Express the measurement in each of the following units.

|⊢———————————————⊣|

(a) Millimeters   (b) Centimeters   (c) Meters

4. Choose an appropriate metric unit and estimate each of the following. Measure, if possible, to check the estimate.

(a) The length of a pencil

(b) The diameter of a nickel

(c) The width of the top of a desk

(d) The thickness of the top of a desk

(e) The length of this sheet of paper

(f) The height of a door

(g) Your height

(h) Your hand span

5. Complete the following table.

Item	m	cm	mm
(a) Length of a piece of paper	3.5	350	3500
(b) Height of a woman	1.63	163	1630
(c) Width of a filmstrip	.035	3.5	35
(d) Length of a cigarette	.1	10	100
(e) Length of two meter sticks laid end to end	2	200	2000

6. For each of the following, place a decimal point in the number to make the sentence reasonable.

(a) A stack of ten dimes is 1000 mm high.

(b) The desk is 770 m high.

(c) It is 100 m across the street.

(d) A dollar bill is 155 cm long.

(e) The basketball player is 1950 cm tall.

(f) A new piece of chalk is about 8100 cm long.

(g) The speed limit in town was 400 km/hour.

7. List the following in decreasing order:

8 cm, 38 dm, 5218 mm, 245 cm, 91 mm, 6 m, 700 mm, 52 dm

8. Complete each of the following.

(a) 17 m + 24 cm = _____ cm

(b) 1 m + 40 mm + 2 cm = _____ cm

(c) 3 m + 130 mm + 3 cm = _____ cm

9. Guess the perimeter of each figure in centimeters and then check the estimates using a ruler.

(a)

(b)
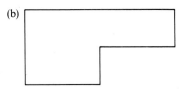

(c)
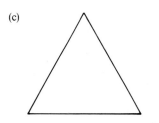

(d)
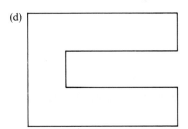

10. Complete each of the following.

(a) 10 mm = _____ cm

(b) 17 cm = _____ m

(c) 262 m = _____ km

(d) 3 km = _____ m

(e) 30 mm = _____ m

(f) 0.17 km = _____ m

(g) 35 m = _____ cm

(h) 26,418 m = _____ km

(i) 359 mm = _____ m

(j) 1 mm = _____ cm

(k) 647 mm = _____ cm

a   b   c   d
6π   6π   4cm   6π cm

(l)   0.1 cm = _____ mm
(m)   5 km = _____ m
(n)   51.3 m = _____ cm

11. (a) Use a dictionary to complete the following using English measures.
    (i) 1 ft = _____ in.   (ii) 1 yd = _____ in.
    (iii) 1 yd = _____ ft   (iv) 1 mi = _____ ft
    (v) 1 rod = _____ ft   (vi) 1 furlong = _____ ft
    (b) Choose an appropriate English unit and estimate each of the following. If possible, measure to check the estimate.
    (i)   The length of a pencil
    (ii) The thickness of a piece of paper
    (iii) The height of a door
    (iv) Your hand span

12. Find the perimeter of each of the following.

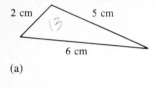

2 cm   13   5 cm

6 cm

(a)

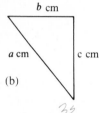

b cm

a cm   c cm

(b)

3s

(c) An equilateral triangle with a side of length s.
(d) A square with a side of length s   4s
(e) A rectangle with one side of length l and another side of length w   2l + 2w
(f) A regular polygon with n sides, each of whose length is s   ns

13. For each of the following circumferences, find the length of the radius of the circle.
    (a) 12π cm   (b) 6 m   (c) 0.67 m   (d) 92π cm

14. For each of the following, if a circle has the dimensions given, what is its circumference?

(a) 6 cm diameter   (b) 3 cm radius
(c) $\dfrac{2}{\pi}$ cm radius   (d) 6π cm diameter

15. What happens to the circumference of a circle if the length of the radius is doubled?

16. The following figure is a circle whose radius is r units. The diameters of the two semicircular regions inside the large circle are both r units as well. Compute the length of the curve that separates the shaded and white regions.

r

r

$= C = \pi r$

17. Draw a triangle ABC. Measure the length of each of its sides in millimeters. For each of the following, tell which is greater and by how much.
    (a) $AB + BC$ or AC (b) $BC + CA$ or AB
    (c) $AB + CA$ or BC

18. (a) If, in two similar triangles, the ratio between the lengths of the corresponding sides is 2:1, what is the ratio between their perimeters?
    (b) Make a conjecture concerning the relationship between the ratio of the perimeters of two similar triangles and the ratio of the corresponding sides.
    ★(c) Justify your conjecture from (b).

BRAIN TEASER

Suppose a wire is stretched tightly around the earth. (The radius of the earth is approximately 6400 km.) If the wire is cut, its circumference increased by 20 m, and the wire is then placed back around the earth so that the wire is the same distance from the earth at every point, could you walk under the wire?

Section 12-2   Areas of Polygons and Circles

area

The term **area** refers to a number assigned to the amount of surface in the interior region determined by a figure. For example, by the area of a rectangle, we mean the number assigned to the rectangular region determined by the rectangle. The unit used for measuring area is the square. Using the square as a unit of area, the area of a region is the number of square units required to cover the region without overlapping the squares and allowing no gaps.

A square measuring 1 inch on each side has area of 1 square inch, denoted by 1 sq in. A square measuring 1 cm on each side has an area of 1 square centimeter, denoted by 1 cm². A square measuring 1 m on each side has an area of 1 square meter, denoted by 1 m². Recall that perimeters and circumferences are measured using linear units. The measure of area is always in square units.

To determine how many square centimeters are in a square meter, look at Figure 12-6(a). There are 100 cm in 1 m, so each side of the square meter has a measure of 100 cm. Thus, it takes 100 rows of 100 square centimeters each to fill a square meter—that is, 100 · 100, or 10,000 cm². In general, the area A of a square that is s units on a side is s^2, as given in Figure 12-6(b).

Figure 12-6

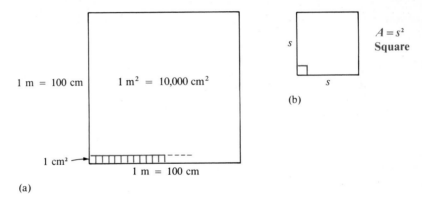

(a)

Other metric conversions of area measure can be developed using the formula for the area of a square. For example, Figure 12-7(a) shows that 1 m² = 10,000 cm² = 1,000,000 mm². Likewise, Figure 12-7(b) shows that 1 m² = 0.000001 km². Similarly, 1 cm² = 100 mm² and 1 km² = 1,000,000 m².

Figure 12-7

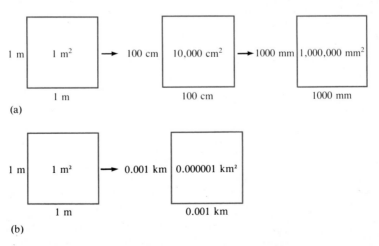

Table 12-3 shows the symbols for metric units of area and their relationship to the square meter.

Table 12-3

Unit	Symbol	Relationship to Square Meter	
square kilometer	km²	1,000,000	m²
*square hectometer	hm²	10,000	m²
*square dekameter	dam²	100	m²
square meter	**m²**	**1**	**m²**
*square decimeter	dm²	0.01	m²
square centimeter	cm²	0.0001	m²
square millimeter	mm²	0.000001	m²

* Not commonly used.

Example 12-4

Convert each of the following.

(a) $5 \text{ cm}^2 =$ _____ mm^2 (b) $124{,}000{,}000 \text{ m}^2 =$ _____ km^2

Solution

(a) $1 \text{ cm}^2 = 100 \text{ mm}^2$ implies $5 \text{ cm}^2 = 5 \cdot 1 \text{ cm}^2 = 5 \cdot 100 \text{ mm}^2 = 500 \text{ mm}^2$.

(b) $1 \text{ m}^2 = 0.000001 \text{ km}^2$ implies $124{,}000{,}000 \text{ m}^2 = 124{,}000{,}000 \cdot 1 \text{ m}^2 =$
$124{,}000{,}000 \cdot (0.001 \text{ km})^2 = 124{,}000{,}000 \cdot 0.000001 \text{ km}^2 = 124 \text{ km}^2$.

LAND MEASURE

One of the most common applications of area today is in land measure. Old
deeds in the United States include land measures in terms of chains, poles,
rods, acres, sections, lots, and townships. In the metric system, small land
areas are measured in terms of a square unit 10 m on a side, called an **are**
(pronounced "air") and denoted by a. Larger land areas, currently measured
in acres, are measured in **hectares.** A hectare is 100 a. A hectare, denoted by
ha, is the amount of land whose area is $10{,}000 \text{ m}^2$, about $2\frac{1}{2}$ acres. One
hectare is the area of a square 100 m on a side. For very large land measures,
the **square kilometer,** denoted by km^2, is used. One square kilometer is the
area of a square with a side 1 km, or 1000 m, long.

are

hectares

square kilometer

Example 12-5

A square field has a side of 400 m. Find the area of the field in hectares.

Solution

$A = (400 \text{ m})^2 = 160{,}000 \text{ m}^2 = 16 \text{ ha}$

AREA OF A RECTANGLE

One way to measure area is to count the number of units of area contained
in any given region. For example, suppose the square in Figure 12-8(a) represents one square unit. Then, the rectangle $ABCD$ in Figure 12-8(b) contains

Figure 12-8

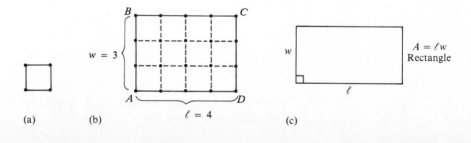

(a)   (b)   (c)

3 · 4, or 12, nonoverlapping square units because there are three rows of squares with four squares in a row.

Hence, the area of rectangle *ABCD* is 12 square units. If the unit is 1 cm², then the area of rectangle *ABCD* is 12 cm². As with rectangle *ABCD*, the area of any rectangle may be found by multiplying the lengths of two adjacent sides. In general, if *A* represents the area of any rectangle whose adjacent sides have lengths ℓ and *w* (each in the same unit length), then $A = \ell w$, as given in Figure 12-8(c).

Example 12-6

Find the area of each rectangle in Figure 12-9.

Figure 12-9

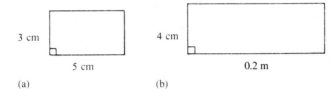

(a)   (b)

Solution

(a) $A = (3 \text{ cm})(5 \text{ cm}) = 15 \text{ cm}^2$

(b) First, write the lengths of the sides in the same unit of length. Because 0.2 m = 20 cm, $A = (4 \text{ cm})(20 \text{ cm}) = 80 \text{ cm}^2$. Alternately, 4 cm = 0.04 m, so $A = (0.04 \text{ m})(0.2 \text{ m}) = 0.008 \text{ m}^2$.

AREA OF A PARALLELOGRAM AND A TRIANGLE

Formulas for areas of various polygons follow from the formula for the area of a rectangle. Consider, for example, the parallelogram *ABCD* in Figure 12-10(a).

Figure 12-10

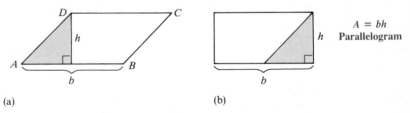

(a)   (b)

The parallelogram can be separated into two parts. The shaded triangle can be moved to the right of the parallelogram, as in Figure 12-10(b), to obtain a rectangle with length *b* and width *h*. This can be achieved by sliding the shaded triangle in the direction from *C* to *D* along $\overleftrightarrow{DC}$ by a distance of *DC*. The parallelogram and the rectangle have the same area. (Why?) Because the area of the rectangle is *bh*, the area of the original parallelogram *ABCD* is also *bh*. In general, any side of a parallelogram can be designated as a **base** with measure *b* . We will use *b* to represent either the base or its measure, depending on the context. The **height** *h* is always the length of a segment from the opposite side to the base and perpendicular to the base. Thus, the area of a parallelogram with base *b* and height *h* to that base is $A = b \cdot h$, as given in Figure 12-10(b).

base

height

A formula for the area of a triangle follows from the formula for the area of a parallelogram. In Figure 12-11(a), $\triangle ABC$ has base b and altitude h. If $\triangle ABD$ is constructed congruent to $\triangle ABC$ and placed as shown in Figure 12-11(b), it can be proved that quadrilateral $BCAD$ is a parallelogram. The area of parallelogram $BCAD$ is bh, so the area of $\triangle ABC$ is $\frac{1}{2}bh$. Similar reasoning applies if the triangle is obtuse, as shown in Figure 12-11(c). Thus, the area of a triangle is equal to one-half the product of the length of a side and the altitude to that side or to the line containing that side.

Figure 12-11

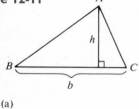

(a)

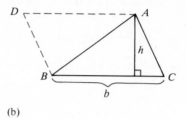

$A = \frac{1}{2}bh$

Triangle

(b)

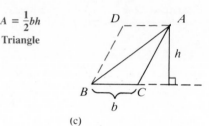

(c)

Example 12-7

Find the area of each drawing in Figure 12-12. Assume that the quadrilaterals in (a) and (b) are parallelograms.

Figure 12-12

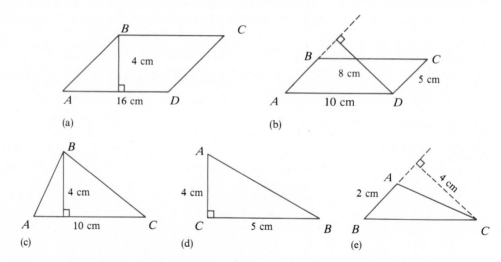

(a)

(b)

(c)

(d)

(e)

Solution

(a) $A = bh = (16 \text{ cm})(4 \text{ cm}) = 64 \text{ cm}^2$
(b) $A = bh = (5 \text{ cm})(8 \text{ cm}) = 40 \text{ cm}^2$
(c) $A = \frac{1}{2}bh = \frac{1}{2}(10 \text{ cm})(4 \text{ cm}) = 20 \text{ cm}^2$
(d) $A = \frac{1}{2}bh = \frac{1}{2}(5 \text{ cm})(4 \text{ cm}) = 10 \text{ cm}^2$
(e) $A = \frac{1}{2}bh = \frac{1}{2}(2 \text{ cm})(4 \text{ cm}) = 4 \text{ cm}^2$

AREA OF A TRAPEZOID

Areas of other polygons can be found by partitioning the polygons into triangles. Trapezoid $ABCD$ in Figure 12-13(a) has bases b_1 and b_2 and height h. By drawing diagonal $\overline{BD}$ (or $\overline{AC}$), as in Figure 12-13(b), two triangles are

Figure 12-13

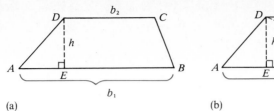 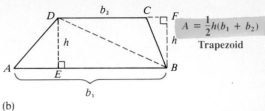

(a)   (b)

formed, one with base $\overline{AB}$ and height $\overline{DE}$ and the other with base $\overline{CD}$ and height $\overline{BF}$. Because $\overline{DE} \cong \overline{BF}$, each has height h. Thus, the areas of triangles ADB and DCB are $\frac{1}{2}(b_1h)$ and $\frac{1}{2}(b_2h)$, respectively. Hence, the area of trapezoid $ABCD$ is $\frac{1}{2}(b_1h) + \frac{1}{2}(b_2h)$, or $\frac{1}{2}h(b_1 + b_2)$. That is, the area of a trapezoid is equal to one-half the length of the height times the sum of the lengths of the bases.

Example 12-8

Find the areas of the trapezoids in Figure 12-14.

Figure 12-14

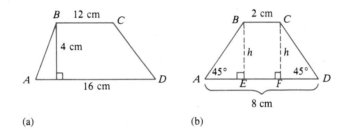

(a)   (b)

Solution

(a) $A = \frac{1}{2}h(b_1 + b_2) = \frac{1}{2}(4 \text{ cm})(12 \text{ cm} + 16 \text{ cm}) = 56 \text{ cm}^2$

(b) To find the area, we need to find h, the height of the trapezoid. In Figure 12-14(b), $BE = CF = h$. Also, $\overline{BE}$ is a side of $\triangle ABE$, which has angles with measures of 45° and 90°. Consequently, the third angle in triangle ABE is $180 - (45 + 90)$, or 45°. Therefore, $\triangle ABE$ is isosceles and $AE = BE = h$. Similarly, it follows that $FD = h$. Because $BCFE$ is a rectangle, $EF = 2 \text{ cm}$ and we have the following equation for h.

$$AD = AE + EF + FD = h + 2 + h = 8$$

Thus, $h = 3 \text{ cm}$ and the area of the trapezoid is $A = \frac{1}{2}(3 \text{ cm})(2 \text{ cm} + 8 \text{ cm})$, or 15 cm^2.

PROBLEM 1

Rancher Larry purchased a plot of land surrounded by a fence. The former owner had marked off nine squares of equal size to subdivide the land, as shown in Figure 12-15. Larry wants to divide the land into two plots of equal area. To divide the property, he wishes to build a single, straight fence beginning at the far left corner (point P on the drawing). Is such a fence possible? If so, where should it be?

Figure 12-15

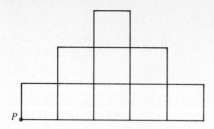

UNDERSTANDING THE PROBLEM We wish to divide the land in Figure 12-15 into two plots of equal area with a straight fence starting at point P. Because the area of the entire plot is 9 square units, the area of each part formed by the fence must be $4\frac{1}{2}$ square units.

DEVISING A PLAN In order to find an approximate location for the fence, consider a fence connecting P with point A shown in Figure 12-16.

Figure 12-16

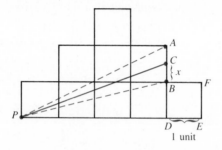

1 unit

If we denote the length of the side of each square by one unit, then the area of the land below the fence $\overline{PA}$ can be found as the sum of the areas of $\triangle APD$ and the square $DBFE$. The area of $\triangle APD$ is $\dfrac{PD \cdot DA}{2}$ and the area of square $DBFE$ is 1. Hence, the desired area below the fence $\overline{PA}$ is

$$\frac{PD \cdot DA}{2} + 1 = \frac{4 \cdot 2}{2} + 1 = 5 \text{ square units}$$

Because the area of each plot is supposed to be $4\frac{1}{2}$ square units, this allows too much area below the fence. Consequently, the other end of the fence should be closer to D.

A similar argument shows that the area below $\overline{PB}$ is 3 square units and the end of the fence should be closer to A. It follows that the other end of the fence should be at a point C between A and B, as shown in Figure 12-16. To find the exact location of the fence, we need to find CB. To do this, we designate CB by x, write an equation for x by finding the area below $\overline{PC}$ in terms of x, make it equal to $\frac{9}{2}$, and solve for x.

CARRYING OUT THE PLAN The area below $\overline{PC}$ equals the area of $\triangle PCD$ plus the area of the square $DBFE$. The area of $\triangle PCD$ is

$$\frac{PD \cdot DC}{2} = \frac{4(1 + x)}{2} = 2(1 + x)$$

Thus, the total area below $\overline{PC}$ is $2(1 + x) + 1$. This area should equal half the area of the plot, that is, $\frac{9}{2}$. Consequently, we have the following.

$$2(1 + x) + 1 = \frac{9}{2}$$

$$2 + 2x + 1 = \frac{9}{2}$$

$$2x = \frac{3}{2}$$

$$x = \frac{3}{4}$$

Therefore, the fence should be built along the line connecting point P to the point C, which is $\frac{3}{4}$ unit directly above point B.

LOOKING BACK The point C can be found by dividing $\overline{AB}$ into four equal parts. We can also check that the solution is correct by finding the area above $\overline{PC}$. To find the area above $\overline{PC}$, we consider the areas of the trapezoids $STAC$ and $PQRS$ and of square $UVWY$ as shown in Figure 12-17(a). The areas of the trapezoids are not easy to find because the length of $\overline{RS}$ is not known. However, if square $UVWY$ is moved to the shaded space shown in Figure 12-17(b), then the desired area above $\overline{PC}$ is the area of trapezoid $PCAO$, that is, $\frac{1}{2}(OP + AC) \cdot OA = \frac{1}{2} \cdot (2 + \frac{1}{4}) \cdot 4$, or $4\frac{1}{2}$.

Figure 12-17

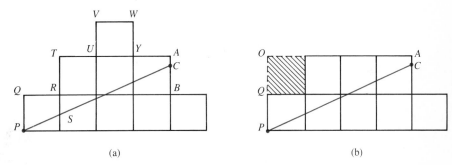

(a)   (b)

An alternate approach for solving the problem utilizes trapezoid $PCAO$ in Figure 12-17(b). Let $AC = y$. We find the area of trapezoid $PCAO$ in terms of y and set that area equal to $\frac{9}{2}$. Then, we have $\frac{1}{2}(2 + y)4 = \frac{9}{2}$, or $y = \frac{1}{4}$. That is, point C is $\frac{1}{4}$ unit below point A.

AREA OF A REGULAR POLYGON

Just as the area of a triangle was used to find the area of a trapezoid, it can be used to find the area of any regular polygon. For example, consider the regular hexagon pictured in Figure 12-18(a). The hexagon can be separated into six congruent triangles, each with a vertex at the center, with side s, and height a. (The height of such a triangle of a regular polygon is called the

apothem   **apothem** and is denoted by a.) The area of each triangle is $\frac{1}{2}as$. Since there

Figure 12-18

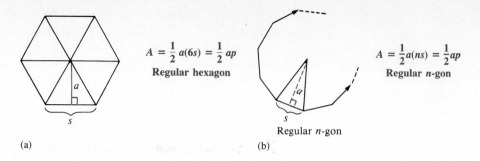

$$A = \frac{1}{2} a(6s) = \frac{1}{2} ap$$
Regular hexagon

$$A = \frac{1}{2} a(ns) = \frac{1}{2} ap$$
Regular n-gon

(a)

(b)

Regular n-gon

are six triangles that make up the hexagon, the area of the hexagon is $6(\frac{1}{2}as)$ or $\frac{1}{2}a(6s)$. However, $6s$ is the perimeter p of the hexagon, so the area of the hexagon is $\frac{1}{2}ap$. The same process can be used to develop the formula for the area of any regular polygon. That is, the area of any regular polygon is $\frac{1}{2}ap$, where a is the height of one of the triangles involved and p is the perimeter of the polygon.

AREA OF A CIRCLE

The formula for the area of a regular polygon can be used to develop the formula for the area of a circle. Consider, for example, the circle in Figure 12-19(a). The area of a regular polygon inscribed in the circle as in Figure 12-19(b) approximates the area of the circle. The area of any inscribed regular n-gon is $\frac{1}{2}ap$, where a is the height of a triangle of the n-gon and p is the perimeter. If the number of sides n is made very large, then the perimeter and the area of the n-gon are close to those of the circle. Also, a is approximately equal to the radius r of the circle and the perimeter approximates the circumference $2\pi r$. Because the area of the circle is approximately equal to the area of the n-gon, then $\frac{1}{2}ap \doteq \frac{1}{2}r \cdot 2\pi r = \pi r^2$, as given in Figure 12-19(b). In fact, the area of the circle is precisely πr^2.

Figure 12-19

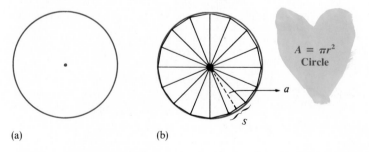

$$A = \pi r^2$$
Circle

(a)

(b)

AREA OF A SECTOR

sector   A **sector** of a circle is a pie-shaped region of the circle determined by a
central angle   **central angle** of the circle, that is, an angle whose vertex is at the center of the circle. The area of a sector depends on the radius of the circle and the central angle determining the sector. If the angle has a measure of 90°, as in Figure 12-20(a), the area of the sector is one-fourth the area of the circle, or $\frac{90}{360}\pi r^2$. In any circle, there are 360 sectors, each of whose central angle has measure

Figure 12-20

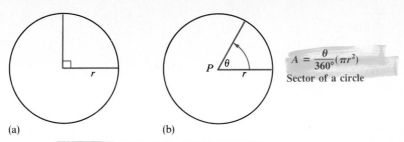

(a)   (b)

$$A = \frac{\theta}{360°}(\pi r^2)$$
Sector of a circle

of 1°, so the area of each such sector is $\frac{1}{360}(\pi r^2)$. A sector whose central angle has measure θ degrees has area

$$\theta\left(\frac{1}{360}\right)(\pi r^2) \quad \text{or} \quad \frac{\theta}{360}(\pi r^2)$$

as shown in Figure 12-20(b).

Example 12-9   Find the area of the sector shown in Figure 12-21.

Figure 12-21

Solution $$A = \frac{80}{360} \cdot \pi(5 \text{ cm})^2 = \frac{50}{9}\pi \text{ cm}^2$$

PROBLEM SET 12-2

1. Choose the most appropriate metric units (cm², m², or km²) for measuring each of the following.
   (a) Area of a sheet of notebook paper
   (b) Area of a quarter
   (c) Area of a desk top
   (d) Area of a classroom floor
   (e) Area of a parallel parking space
   (f) Area of an airport runway
2. Complete the following conversion table.

Item	m²	cm²	mm²
Area of a sheet of paper	5.88	588	5880
Area of a cross section of a crayon	.192	19.2	192
Area of a desk top	1.5	150	1500
Area of a dollar bill	1	100	1000
Area of a postage stamp	.05	5	50

3. Estimate, then measure, each of the following using either cm², m², or km².
   (a) Area of a door   (b) Area of a chair seat
   (c) Area of a desk top   (d) Area of a chalkboard
4. Explain the difference between a 2-m square and 2 m².
5. Find the area of each of the following triangles.

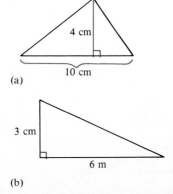

(a)

(b)

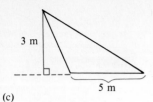

(c)

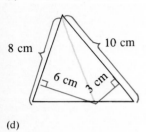

(d)

6. Find the area of each of the following quadrilaterals.

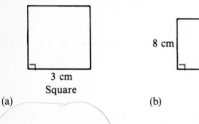

(a) Square

(b) Rectangle

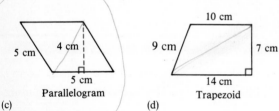

(c) Parallelogram

(d) Trapezoid

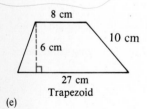

(e) Trapezoid

7. In the figure, $\ell \parallel \overleftrightarrow{AB}$. If the area of $\triangle ABP$ is 10 cm², what are the areas of $\triangle ABQ$, $\triangle ABR$, $\triangle ABS$, $\triangle ABT$, and $\triangle ABU$? Explain your answers.

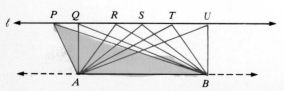

8. Find the area of each regular polygon.

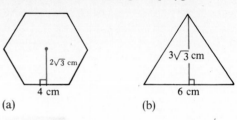

(a)

(b)

9. Find the area of each of the following. Leave your answers in terms of π.

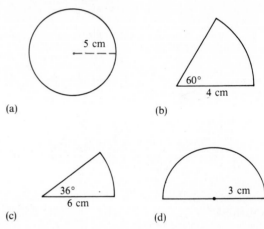

(a)

(b)

(c)

(d)

10. (a) If a circle has a circumference of 8π cm, what is its area?

(b) If a circle with radius r and a square with a side of length s have the same area, express r in terms of s.

11. Find the area of each of the following shaded parts. Assume all arcs are circular.

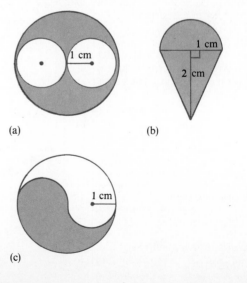

(a)

(b)

(c)

12. Solve for x.

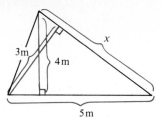

13. Find the area of a rhombus $ABCD$ if $AC = 6$ m and $BD = 8$ m.

14. Complete each of the following:
(a) A football field is about 49 m by 100 m or _____ m².
(b) About _____ ares are in two football fields.
(c) About _____ hectares are in two football fields.

15. A circular flower bed is 6 m in diameter and has a circular sidewalk around it 1 m wide. Find the area of the sidewalk in square meters.

16. (a) A rectangular piece of land is 1300 m by 1500 m. What is the area in square kilometers? What is the area in hectares?
(b) A rectangular piece of land is 1300 yards by 1500 yards. What is the area in square miles? What is the area in acres? Compare this problem with part (a).

17. Joe uses stick-on square carpet tiles to cover his 3-m by 4-m bathroom. If each tile is 10 cm on a side, how many tiles does he need?

18. A rectangular plot of land is to be seeded with grass. If the plot is 22 m by 28 m and if a 1-kg bag of seed is needed for 85 m² of land, how many bags of seed will it take?

19. The area of the shaded quadrilateral shown on the geoboard can be found by constructing the colored rectangle around the quadrilateral as shown and then subtracting the areas of the three nonshaded triangles. Based on this approach, or in a different way, find the areas of each of the following figures if the distance between two adjacent nails in a row or a column is one unit.

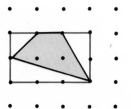

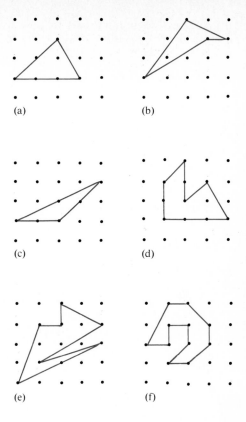

(a)   (b)

(c)   (d)

(e)   (f)

20. (a) Find the area of each polygon in the figure if the area of the figure in the upper right-hand corner is one square unit.

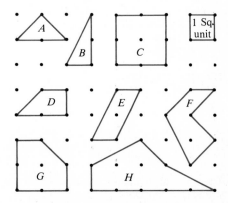

(b) If all vertices of a polygon are points on square-dot paper, the polygon is called a **lattice polygon.** In 1899, G. Pick discovered a surprising theorem involving I, the number of dots *inside* the polygon, and B, the number of dots that lie *on* the polygon. The theorem states that the area of any lattice polygon is $I + \frac{1}{2}B - 1$. Check that this is true for the polygons in (a).

21. (a) Explain how the drawing can be used to determine a formula for the area of $\triangle ABC$.

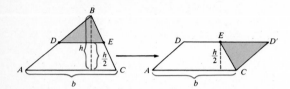

(b) Use paper cutting to reassemble $\triangle ABC$ in (a) into parallelogram $ADD'C$.

22. The area of a parallelogram can be found by using the concept of a half-turn (a turn by 180°). Consider the parallelogram $ABCD$, and let M and N be the midpoints of $\overline{AB}$ and $\overline{CD}$, respectively. Rotate the shaded triangle with vertex M about M by 180° clockwise, and rotate the shaded triangle with vertex N about N by 180° counterclockwise. What kind of figure do you obtain? Now, complete the argument to find the area of the parallelogram.

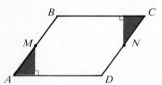

23. The area of a triangle can be found by using a half-turn. Consider the triangle ABC and the midpoint M of $\overline{BC}$. Rotate $\triangle ABC$ about M by 180° clockwise, and explain how the figure obtained from $\triangle ABC$ and its image can be used to derive the formula for the area of a triangle.

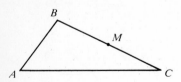

24. Consider the trapezoid $ABCD$. Rotate the trapezoid 180° clockwise about the midpoint M of $\overline{BC}$. Use the figure obtained from the union of the original trapezoid and its image to derive the formula for the area of a trapezoid.

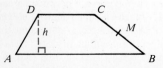

25. The given figure consists of five congruent squares. Find a line through point P that divides the figure into two parts of equal area.

26. Use a dictionary to complete the following.
(a) 1 ft² = _____ in.²
(b) 1 yd² = _____ ft²
(c) 1 mi² = _____ ft²
(d) 1 yd² = _____ in.²
(e) 100 yd² = _____ in.²
(f) 786 in.² = _____ yd²

27. A different method for approximating the area of a circle is to separate the circle into congruent sectors and place them as pictured. Explain how these drawings can be used to approximate the area of the circle.

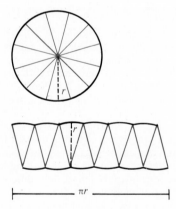

28. Find the area of the shaded region.

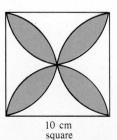

10 cm square

29. (a) If, in two similar triangles, the ratio of the lengths of the corresponding sides is 2:1, what is the ratio of their areas?

(b) Make a conjecture concerning the relationship between the ratio of the areas of two similar triangles and the ratio of the corresponding sides.

*(c) Justify your conjecture in (b).

★**30.** Congruent circles are cut out of a rectangular piece of tin, as shown, to make lids. Find what percent of the tin is wasted.

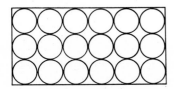

★**31.** In the drawing, quadrilateral $ABCD$ is a parallelogram and P is any point on $\overline{AC}$. Prove that the area of $\triangle BCP$ is equal to the area of $\triangle DPC$.

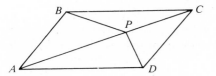

Review Problems

32. Complete each of the following.
  (a) 100 mm = _____ cm
  (b) 10.4 cm = _____ mm
  (c) 350 mm = _____ m
  (d) 0.04 m = _____ mm
  (e) 8 km = _____ m
  (f) 6504 m = _____ km

33. Find the perimeters for each of the following if all arcs shown are semicircles.

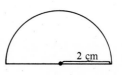

(a)

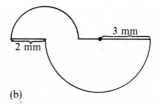

(b)

BRAIN TEASER

The accompanying rectangle was apparently formed by cutting the square shown along the dotted lines and reassembling the pieces as pictured.
1. What is the area of the square?
2. What is the area of the rectangle?
3. How do you explain the discrepancy?

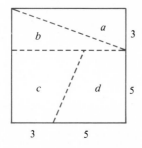

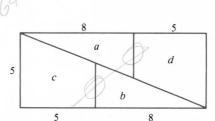

Section 12-3

The Pythagorean Relationship

Pythagoras is one of the two most famous geometers of Greek antiquity. Exactly how much geometry Pythagoras himself either discovered or invented is not known because he was the head of a group known as the Pythagoreans who attributed all their discoveries to him. One of the most famous and useful discoveries is known as the Pythagorean Theorem, which involves a right triangle.

hypotenuse / legs

In Figure 12-22, the side c of the triangle opposite the right angle is called the **hypotenuse** of the triangle. The other two sides are called **legs.** The hypotenuse is always the longest side of a right triangle.

Figure 12-22

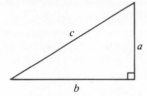

THEOREM 12-1

> **The Pythagorean Theorem**   If a right triangle has legs of lengths a and b and hypotenuse of length c, then $c^2 = a^2 + b^2$.

Interpreted in terms of area, the Pythagorean Theorem says that the area of a square with the hypotenuse of a right triangle as a side is equal to the sum of the areas of the squares with the legs as sides. This relationship was illustrated on a Greek stamp in 1955, as shown in Figure 12-23, to honor the 2500th anniversary of the founding of the Pythagorean School.

Figure 12-23

The Pythagoreans affirmed geometric results on the basis of special cases. As a result, mathematical historians believe that they did not have a proof of the Pythagorean Theorem. It is possible that the Pythagoreans discovered the theorem by looking at a floor tiling consisting of squares like the ones shown in Figure 12-24. Each square can be divided by its diagonal into two

Figure 12-24

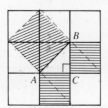

congruent isosceles right triangles, so we see that the shaded square constructed with $\overline{AB}$ as a side consists of four triangles each congruent to $\triangle ABC$. Similarly, each of the shaded squares with legs $\overline{BC}$ and $\overline{AC}$ as sides consists of two triangles congruent to $\triangle ABC$. Thus, the area of the larger square is equal to the sum of the areas of the two smaller squares.

The preceding argument does not constitute a proof of the Pythagorean Theorem because it holds only for a right isosceles triangle, not for a right triangle in general. There are hundreds of known proofs for the Pythagorean Theorem today. The classic book *The Pythagorean Proposition* contains many of these proofs.

Many proofs of the Pythagorean Theorem involve constructing a square with area c^2 from squares of areas a^2 and b^2.

Figure 12-25(a) shows two squares with areas a^2 and b^2 side by side. Dissect Figure 12-25(b) along the dotted lines. Then, rotate triangle I counterclockwise $90°$ about point A to its new position in Figure 12-25(c). Similarly, rotate triangle II $90°$ clockwise about point C to its new position in Figure 12-25(c). As quadrilateral $ABCD$ in Figure 12-25(c) is composed of pieces of the squares in Figure 12-25(a), it must have the same area—that is, $a^2 + b^2$. However, it can be shown that quadrilateral $ABCD$ is a square with side c, and hence it has area c^2. Consequently, $a^2 + b^2 = c^2$.

Figure 12-25

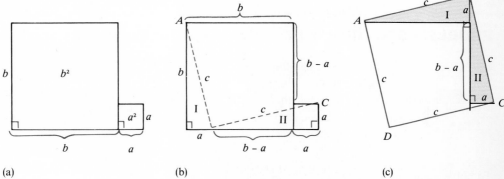

(a)   (b)   (c)

A proof of the Pythagorean Theorem using similar triangles is discussed in Problem 7 of Problem Set 12-3. Other proofs of the Pythagorean Theorem are discussed in Problems 8 and 9 of Problem Set 12-3.

Example 12-10

In Figure 12-26, find x by using the Pythagorean Theorem.

Figure 12-26

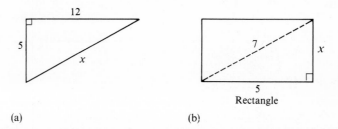

(a)   (b)

Solution

(a) By the Pythagorean Theorem,

$$5^2 + 12^2 = x^2$$

$$25 + 144 = x^2$$

$$169 = x^2$$

$$13 = x$$

(b) In the rectangle, the diagonal partitions the rectangle into two right triangles with length 5 units and width x units. Thus, we have the following.

$$5^2 + x^2 = 7^2$$

$$25 + x^2 = 49$$

$$x^2 = 24$$

$$x = \sqrt{24}, \quad \text{or approximately 4.9}$$

The Pythagorean Theorem is used in solving many real-life problems, as shown on the student page from *Addison-Wesley Mathematics,* 1987, Grade 8, below.

PROBLEM SOLVING: Making Drawings for Problems

QUESTION
DATA
PLAN
ANSWER
CHECK

An A-frame cabin has the shape of an isosceles triangle. The base is 10 m and the two congruent sides are each 9 m. What is the height of the cabin?

To solve some problems, it will help if you make a drawing and label the parts of the drawing with the given data.

The drawing shows that we need to find the length of leg a.

$$a^2 + 5^2 = 9^2$$
$$a^2 + 25 = 81$$
$$\sqrt{a^2} = \sqrt{56}$$
$$a \approx 7.48$$

The height is about 7.48 m.

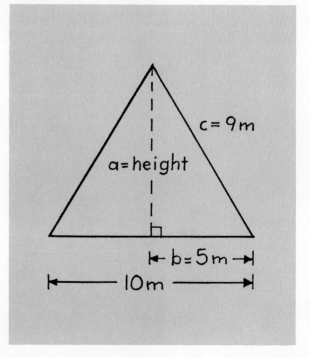

CONVERSE OF THE PYTHAGOREAN THEOREM

Given a triangle with sides of lengths a, b, and c such that $a^2 + b^2 = c^2$, must the triangle be a right triangle? This is the case, and we state the following without proof.

THEOREM 12-2

> **Converse of the Pythagorean Theorem**   If $\triangle ABC$ is a triangle with sides of lengths a, b, and c such that $a^2 + b^2 = c^2$, then $\triangle ABC$ is a right triangle with the right angle opposite the side of length c.

Example 12-11

Determine whether the following can be the lengths of the sides of a right triangle.

(a) 51, 68, 85   (b) 2, 3, $\sqrt{13}$ (c) 3, 4, 7

Solution

(a) $51^2 + 68^2 = 7225 = 85^2$, so 51, 68, and 85 can be the lengths of the sides of a right triangle.

(b) $2^2 + 3^2 = 4 + 9 = 13 = (\sqrt{13})^2$, so 2, 3, and $\sqrt{13}$ can be the lengths of the sides of a right triangle.

(c) $3^2 + 4^2 \neq 7^2$, so the measures cannot be the lengths of the sides of a right triangle.

PROBLEM SET 12-3

1. Use the Pythagorean Theorem to find x in each of the following.

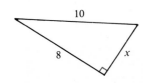

(a)

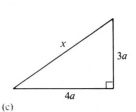

(c)

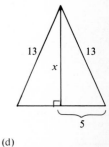

(d)

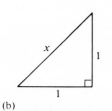

(b)

(e)

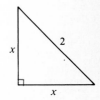

(f)

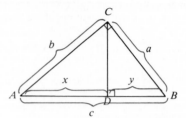

(g)   (h)

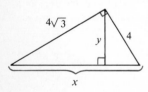

(i) Base is a square   (j)

2. If the hypotenuse of a right triangle is 30 cm long and one of the legs is twice as long as the other, how long are the legs of the triangle?

3. For each of the following, can the given numbers represent lengths of sides of a right triangle?

(a) 10, 24, 16   (b) 2, $\sqrt{3}$, 1
(c) 16, 34, 30   (d) $\sqrt{2}$, $\sqrt{3}$, $\sqrt{5}$
(e) $\sqrt{2}$, $\sqrt{2}$, 2   (f) $\dfrac{3}{2}$, $\dfrac{4}{2}$, $\dfrac{5}{2}$

4. For each of the following, solve for the unknowns.

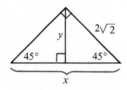

(a)   (b)

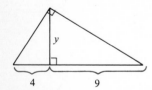

(c)

5. What is the longest line segment that can be drawn in a right rectangular prism that is 12 cm wide, 15 cm long, and 9 cm high?

6. Two cars leave a house at the same time. One car travels 60 km per hour north, while the other car travels 40 km per hour east. After 1 hour, how far apart are the cars?

7. Use the following drawing to prove the Pythagorean Theorem by using corresponding parts of similar triangles $\triangle ACD$, $\triangle CBD$, and $\triangle ABC$. Lengths of sides are indicated by a, b, c, x, and y. (*Hint:* Show that $b^2 = cx$ and $a^2 = cy$.)

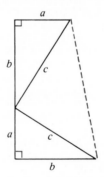

8. Before he was elected president of the United States, James Garfield discovered a proof of the Pythagorean Theorem. He formed a trapezoid like the one that follows and found the area of the trapezoid in two different ways. Can you discover his proof?

9. Use the given figure to prove the Pythagorean Theorem by first proving that the quadrilateral with side c is a square; then, compute the area of the square with side $a + b$ in two different ways: (a) as $(a + b)^2$; and (b) as the sum of the areas of the four triangles and the square with side c.

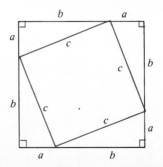

10. Find the area of each of the following.

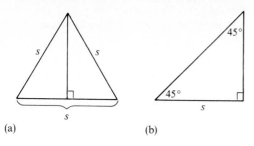

(a)   (b)

11. Construct semicircles on right triangle ABC with $\overline{AB}$, $\overline{BC}$, and $\overline{AC}$ as diameters. Is the area of the semicircle on the hypotenuse equal to the sum of the areas of the semicircles on the legs?

12. If the hypotenuse and a leg of one right triangle are congruent to the hypotenuse and a leg of the other right triangle, respectively, must the triangles be congruent?

13. What is the length of the diagonal of the cube? (*Hint:* Draw a diagonal of a base.)

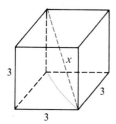

14. A 15-foot ladder is leaning against a wall. The base of the ladder is 3 feet from the wall. How high above the ground is the top of the ladder?

15. (a) Prove that the side opposite the 30° angle in a 30°-60°-90° triangle is half as long as the hypotenuse. (*Hint:* Two such triangles can be placed to make an equilateral triangle.)

   (b) If the hypotenuse in a 30°-60°-90° triangle is c units long, what is the length of the side opposite the 60° angle?

16. If the length of the hypotenuse in a 45°-45°-90° triangle is c, find the length of a leg.

17. Find x in the given figure.

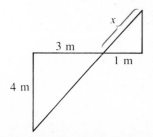

18. Given any four congruent right triangles with legs a and b and hypotenuse c, it is possible to arrange them to form a square with sides $a + b$, as shown in the figure. The shaded figure, a square whose area is c^2, also has area equal to the area of the large square minus the sum of the areas of the four congruent triangles.

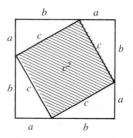

In the next figure, the shaded area also equals the area of the large square minus the areas of the four congruent triangles. Use this discussion and both figures to prove the Pythagorean Theorem.

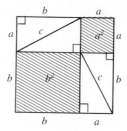

*19. On each side of a right triangle, construct an equilateral triangle. Is the area of the triangle constructed on the hypotenuse always equal to the sum of the areas of the triangles constructed on the legs? Justify your answer.

*20. Point P is in the interior of a rectangle $ABCD$. If $PA = 6$, $PB = 8$, and $PC = 10$, find PD.

Review Problems

21. Arrange the following in decreasing order: 3.2 m, 322 cm, 0.032 km, 3.020 mm.

22. Find the area of each figure.

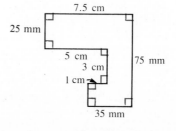

(a)

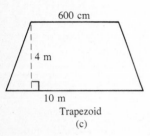

(b)

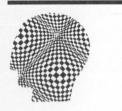

600 cm

4 m

10 m

Trapezoid

(c)

23. A wire 10 m long is wrapped around a circular region. If the wire fits exactly, what is the area of the region?

24. Complete the following table concerning circles.

	Radius	Diameter	Circumference	Area
(a)	5 cm			
(b)		24 cm		
(c)				17π m^2
(d)			20π cm	

BRAIN TEASER

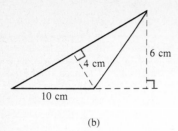

A spider sitting at A, the midpoint of the edge of the ceiling in the room shown, spies a fly on the floor at C, the midpoint of the edge of the floor. If the spider must walk along the wall, ceiling, or floor, what is the length of the shortest path the spider can travel to reach the fly?

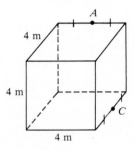

4 m

4 m

4 m

A

C

Section 12-4   Surface Areas of Three-Dimensional Figures

SURFACE AREA OF A PRISM

The surface area of a polyhedron is the sum of the areas of the faces of the polyhedron. Cubes are the simplest polyhedra. The surface area of the cube in Figure 12-27(a) is the sum of the areas of the faces of the cube. Because each of the six faces is a square of area 16 cm^2, the surface area is $6 \cdot (16$ cm$^2)$, or 96 cm^2.

In general, if the edges of a cube are e units, as in Figure 12-27(b), then each face is a square with area e^2 units. Because there are six faces, the surface

Figure 12-27

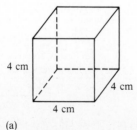

4 cm

4 cm

4 cm

(a)

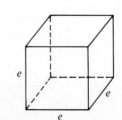

e

e

e

(b)

$S.A. = 6e^2$

Cube

area of the cube is given by $S.A. = 6e^2$, where e is the length of a side and $S.A.$ is the surface area.

To find the surface area of other right prisms, we find the sum of the areas of the rectangles that comprise the lateral faces and the areas of the top and

lateral surface area

surface area

bottom. The sum of the areas of the lateral faces is called the **lateral surface area.** Thus, the **surface area** is the sum of the lateral surface area and the area of the bases.

Figure 12-28

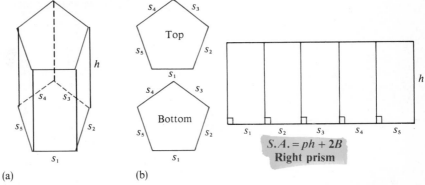

(a)   (b)

Figure 12-28(a) shows a right pentagonal prism and Figure 12-28(b) shows the figure cut into three pieces. The cuts show the top, the bottom, and the lateral faces. The section formed by the lateral faces is stretched out flat. It forms a rectangle whose length is $s_1 + s_2 + s_3 + s_4 + s_5$ and whose width is h. Because $s_1 + s_2 + s_3 + s_4 + s_5$ is the perimeter p of the base of the prism, the lateral surface area is $(s_1 + s_2 + s_3 + s_4 + s_5) \cdot h$, or ph. If B stands for the area of each of the prism's bases, then the surface area $S.A.$ of the right prism is given by the following formula.

$$S.A. = ph + 2B$$

This formula holds for any right prism regardless of the shape of its bases.

Example 12-12

Find the surface area of each of the right prisms in Figure 12-29.

Figure 12-29

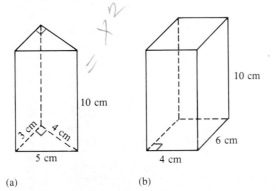

(a)   (b)

Solution

(a) Each base is a right triangle. Hence, the area of the bases is $2(\frac{1}{2} \cdot 3 \text{ cm} \cdot 4 \text{ cm})$, or 12 cm^2. The perimeter of a base is $3 \text{ cm} + 4 \text{ cm} + 5 \text{ cm}$, or 12 cm. Hence, the lateral surface area is $(12 \text{ cm})(10 \text{ cm})$, or 120 cm^2, and the surface area is 132 cm^2.

(b) The area of the bases is 2(4 cm)(6 cm), or 48 cm². The lateral surface area is 2(4 cm + 6 cm) · 10 cm, or 200 cm², so the surface area of the right prism is 248 cm².

SURFACE AREA OF A CYLINDER

To find the surface area of the right circular cylinder shown in Figure 12-30(a), cut it into a top and a bottom and the lateral surface shown in Figure 12-30(b).

Figure 12-30

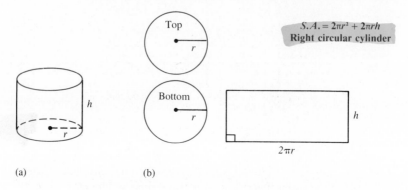

(a)   (b)

The lateral surface stretched out is a rectangle whose length is the circumference of the circular base $2\pi r$ and whose width is the height of the cylinder h. Hence, the surface area is the sum of the areas of the two circular bases and the lateral surface areas.

$$S.A. = 2\pi r^2 + 2\pi r h$$

SURFACE AREA OF A CONE

slant height

Similarly, the surface area of a right circular cone can be determined by cutting the cone along a **slant height** ℓ, removing the base, and flattening the lateral surface, as shown in Figure 12-31.

Figure 12-31

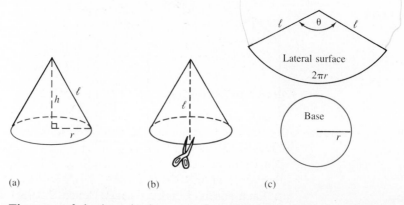

(a)   (b)   (c)

The area of the base is the area of a circle with radius r, namely, πr^2. The lateral surface area is the sector of a circle whose radius is ℓ shown in Figure 12-31(c). Because the area of a sector with radius ℓ and central angle

θ degrees is $\dfrac{\theta}{360} \cdot \pi\ell^2$, the area of the sector can be found if the measure of the central angle θ is known. Thus, we need to find θ in terms of the given quantities r and ℓ. An equation involving θ, r, and ℓ can be obtained by finding the given arc length in two different ways. The length of the arc corresponding to θ is $\dfrac{\theta}{360} \cdot 2\pi\ell$. Also, the length of this arc is $2\pi r$, because it is the circumference of the circular base of the cone. Hence, $\dfrac{\theta}{360} \cdot 2\pi\ell = 2\pi r$.

Therefore, $\dfrac{\theta}{360} = \dfrac{r}{\ell}$. Consequently, the area of the sector is $A = \dfrac{\theta}{360} \cdot \pi\ell^2 = \dfrac{r}{\ell} \cdot \pi\ell^2 = \pi r\ell$. Thus, the surface area of a cone is given by

$$S.A. = \pi r^2 + \pi r\ell$$

Example 12-13

Find the surface area of each of the figures in Figure 12-32.

Figure 12-32

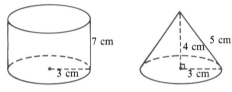

(a) Right circular cylinder   (b) Right circular cone

Solution

(a) $S.A. = 2\pi r^2 + 2\pi rh$
$= 2\pi(3 \text{ cm})^2 + 2\pi(3 \text{ cm})(7 \text{ cm})$
$= 18\pi \text{ cm}^2 + 42\pi \text{ cm}^2$
$= 60\pi \text{ cm}^2$

(b) $S.A. = \pi r^2 + \pi r\ell$
$= \pi(3 \text{ cm})^2 + \pi(3 \text{ cm})(5 \text{ cm})$
$= 9\pi \text{ cm}^2 + 15\pi \text{ cm}^2$
$= 24\pi \text{ cm}^2$

SURFACE AREA OF A PYRAMID

right regular pyramid

The surface area of a pyramid is the sum of the lateral surface area of the pyramid and the area of the base. A **right regular pyramid** is a pyramid such that the segments connecting the apex to each vertex of the base are congruent and the base is a regular polygon. The lateral faces of the right regular pyramid pictured in Figure 12-33 are congruent triangles. Each triangle has an altitude of length ℓ called the slant height. Since the pyramid is right regular, each side of the base has the same length b. Hence, the lateral surface area of the right regular pyramid pictured is $4(\frac{1}{2}b\ell)$. Adding the lateral surface area to the area of the base B gives the surface area.

Figure 12-33

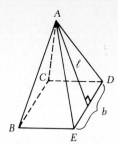

$$S.A. = B + \frac{1}{2}p\ell$$
Right regular pyramid

In general, for any right regular pyramid, the surface area is found by adding the area B of the base and the area of the n congruent triangular faces, each with side b and slant height ℓ. The surface area is given by the following formula.

$$S.A. = B + n\left(\frac{1}{2}b\ell\right)$$

Because nb is the perimeter of the base, the formula reduces to the following.

$$S.A. = B + \frac{1}{2}p\ell$$

Example 12-14

Find the surface area of the right regular pyramid in Figure 12-34.

Figure 12-34

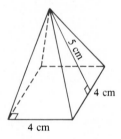

4 cm

4 cm

5 cm

Solution

$$S.A. = B + \frac{1}{2}p\ell$$

$$= (4 \text{ cm})(4 \text{ cm}) + \frac{1}{2}[4(4 \text{ cm})](5 \text{ cm})$$

$$= 16 \text{ cm}^2 + 40 \text{ cm}^2$$

$$= 56 \text{ cm}^2$$

SURFACE AREA OF A SPHERE

Finding a formula for the surface area of a sphere is not a simple task using elementary mathematics. The formula for the surface area of a sphere is $S.A. = 4\pi r^2$. That is, the surface area of a sphere is four times the area of the great circle pictured in Figure 12-35. What happens to the surface area if r is doubled? Tripled?

Figure 12-35

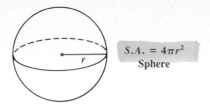

$$S.A. = 4\pi r^2$$
Sphere

PROBLEM 2

A toy maker decides to design a wooden cube with square holes in each of the cube's faces. The holes extend all the way through the cube, as shown in Figure 12-36. The toy maker wants the length of each side of the square holes to be one-third the length of a side of the cube. If the total surface area of the toy is to be 2 m², how long should the sides of the cube be?

Figure 12-36

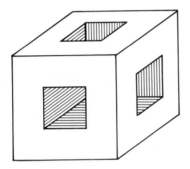

UNDERSTANDING THE PROBLEM We know that the total surface area of the toy in Figure 12-36 is 2 m². The space formed by the cutting may be thought of as seven congruent cubes, six corresponding to the faces and one to the hole in the middle. The hole in the middle has no surface area. The length of a side of each hole is to be one-third the length of a side of the cube. We are asked to find the length of a side of the cube.

DEVISING A PLAN We designate the length of the side of the cube by x so that the length of a side of one of the holes is $\dfrac{x}{3}$. If we can find the total surface area of the toy in terms of x, then by setting this expression equal to 2 and solving for x, we will have the required length of a side of the cube.

CARRYING OUT THE PLAN Because a hole is to be cut through each face of the cube, the area of each face, excluding the area of the hole, is

$$x^2 - \left(\frac{x}{3}\right)^2 \quad \text{or} \quad x^2 - \frac{x^2}{9} \quad \text{or} \quad \frac{8}{9}x^2$$

Because the cube has six faces, the area of these six faces with the areas of the holes excluded is $6 \cdot \frac{8}{9}x^2$, or $\frac{16}{3}x^2$. Due to cutting, there is an "inside cube" (which corresponds to each of the six faces) cut away. Cutting away an inside cube leaves only four faces to be considered for the total surface area. The surface area of the four faces is $4 \cdot \frac{x^2}{9}$. Now, the surface area of these

six inside cubes is

$$6 \cdot 4 \cdot \frac{x^2}{9} \quad \text{or} \quad \frac{8}{3}x^2$$

The space in the center of the original cube is empty and has no surface area. Therefore, the total surface area of the toy is $\frac{16}{3}x^2 + \frac{8}{3}x^2$, or $\frac{24}{3}x^2$, or $8x^2$. Consequently,

$$8x^2 = 2$$

$$x^2 = \frac{1}{4}$$

$$x = \frac{1}{2}$$

Thus, the side of the cube should be $\frac{1}{2}$ m, or 50 cm, long.

LOOKING BACK A related problem is to find the total surface area if cylindrical holes are drilled through each face of a cube.

PROBLEM SET 12-4

1. Find the surface area of each of the following right prisms.

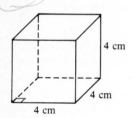

(a) Cube

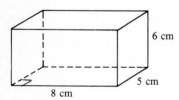

(b) Right rectangular prism

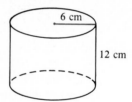

(b) Right circular cylinder

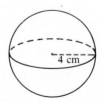

(c) Sphere

2. Find the surface area of each of the following.

(a) Right circular cone

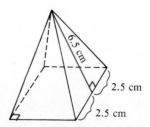

(d) Right square pyramid

3. Find the surface area of each of the following.

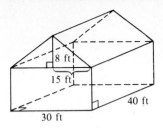

(a)

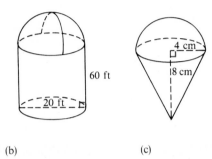

(b)   (c)

4. How many liters of paint are needed to paint the walls of a room 6 m long, 4 m wide, and 2.5 m tall if 1 L (liter) of paint covers 20 m²? (Assume there are no doors or windows.)

5. The napkin ring pictured is to be resilvered. How many square millimeters of surface area must be covered?

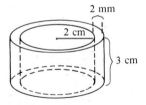

6. Assume that the radius of the earth is 6370 km and the earth is a sphere. What is its surface area?

7. Two cubes have sides of length 4 cm and 6 cm, respectively. What is the ratio of their surface areas?

8. A sphere is inscribed in a right cylinder, as shown in the figure. Compare the surface area of the sphere with the lateral surface area of the cylinder.

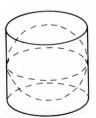

9. Suppose one cylinder has radius 2 m and height 6 m and another has radius 6 m and height 2 m.
   (a) Which cylinder has the greater lateral surface area?
   (b) Which cylinder has the greater total surface area?

10. The base of a right pyramid is a regular hexagon with sides of length 12 m. The altitude of the pyramid is 9 m. Find the total surface area of the pyramid.

11. (a) What happens to the surface area of a cube if the length of each edge is tripled?
   (b) What is the effect on the lateral surface area of a cylinder if the height is doubled?

12. How does the surface area of a box (including top and bottom) change if:
   (a) each dimension is doubled?
   (b) each dimension is tripled?
   (c) each dimension is multiplied by a factor of k?

13. How does the lateral surface area of a cone change if:
   (a) the slant height is tripled but the radius of the base remains the same?
   (b) the radius of the base is tripled but the slant height remains the same?
   (c) the slant height and the radius of the base are tripled?

14. The sector shown in the figure is rolled into a cone so that the dotted edges just touch. Find the following.
   (a) The lateral surface area of the cone
   (b) The total surface area of the cone

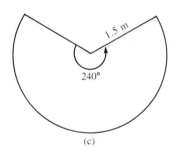

(c)

★15. Find the total surface area of the following stand, which was cut from a right circular cone.

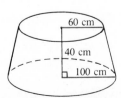

16. The total surface area of a cube is 10,648 cm³. What is the length of each of the following?
(a) One of the sides
(b) A diagonal that is not a diagonal of a face

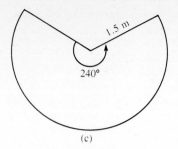

(c)

Review Problems

17. Complete each of the following.
(a) $10 \text{ m}^2 = $ _____ cm^2
(b) $13,680 \text{ cm}^2 = $ _____ m^2
(c) $5 \text{ cm}^2 = $ _____ mm^2
(d) $2 \text{ km}^2 = $ _____ m^2
(e) $10^6 \text{ m}^2 = $ _____ km^2
(f) $10^{12} \text{ mm}^2 = $ _____ m^2

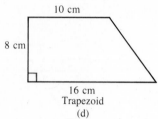

16 cm
Trapezoid
(d)

18. The sides of a rectangle are 10 cm and 20 cm. Find the length of a diagonal of the rectangle.

19. The length of the side of a rhombus is 30 cm. If the length of one of the diagonals is 40 cm, find the length of the other diagonal.

20. Find the perimeters and the areas of the following figures.

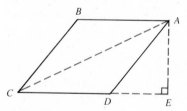

(e)

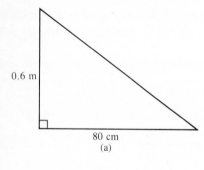

80 cm
(a)

★**21.** The length of the longer diagonal $\overline{AC}$ of rhombus $ABCD$ is 40 cm. $AE = 24$. Find the length of a side of the rhombus and the length of the other diagonal.

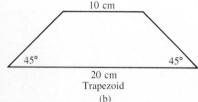

20 cm
Trapezoid
(b)

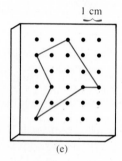

Section 12-5   Volume Measure and Volumes

METRIC MEASURE OF VOLUME

As area measure is used to describe the interior region of a planar geometric figure, volume measure is associated with three-dimensional figures. Volume is concerned with how much space a figure occupies. The unit of measure for volume must be a shape that will "fill space." Cubes can be closely stacked with no gaps and fill space. Standard units of volume are based on cubes and are called cubic units. The volume of a rectangular right prism can be measured, for example, by determining how many cubes are needed to build it. One way is to count how many cubes cover the base and then count how many layers of these cubes are used to reach the height of the prism, as shown in Figure 12-37(a). There are $8 \cdot 4$, or 32, cubes in the base and there are five such layers. Hence, the volume of the rectangular prism is $8 \cdot 4 \cdot 5$ cubic units. For any rectangular right prism with dimensions ℓ, w, and h measured in the same linear units, the volume of the prism is given by $V = \ell wh$, as shown in Figure 12-37(b).

Figure 12-37

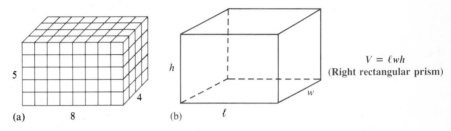

$V = \ell wh$
(Right rectangular prism)

(a)   8   (b) ℓ

cubic centimeter
cubic meter

In the English system of measurement, a commonly used unit of volume is the cubic foot. The most commonly used metric units are the **cubic centimeter** and the **cubic meter.** A cubic centimeter is the volume of a cube whose length, width, and height are each one centimeter. One cubic centimeter is denoted by 1 cm^3. Similarly, a cubic meter is the volume of a cube whose length, width, and height are each 1 m. One cubic meter is denoted by 1 m^3. Other metric units of volume are also symbolized with a raised 3 next to the standard symbol.

Figure 12-38 shows that since $1 \text{ dm} = 10 \text{ cm}$, $1 \text{ dm}^3 = (10 \text{ cm}) \cdot (10 \text{ cm}) \cdot (10 \text{ cm}) = 1000 \text{ cm}^3$.

Figure 12-38

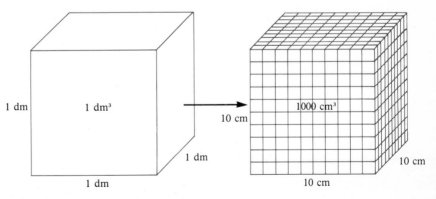

1 dm   1 dm³   1000 cm³
                    10 cm
            1 dm
1 dm   10 cm
                    10 cm

Similarly, Figure 12-39(a) shows that $1 \text{ m}^3 = 1,000,000 \text{ cm}^3$ and Figure 12-39(b) shows that $1 \text{ dm}^3 = 0.001 \text{ m}^3$.

Each metric unit of length is 10 times as great as the next smaller unit. Each metric unit of area is 100 times as great as the next smaller unit. Each metric unit of volume is 1000 times as great as the next smaller unit. Hence, to convert from cubic decimeters to cubic centimeters, multiply by 1000; that

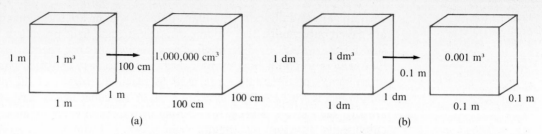

(a)   (b)

Figure 12-39

is, move the decimal point three places to the right. Also, since 1 cm = 0.01 m, then 1 cm³ = (0.01 × 0.01 × 0.01) m³, or 0.000001 m³. Thus, to convert from cubic centimeters to cubic meters, all that is required is to move the decimal point six places to the left.

Example 12-15

Convert each of the following.

(a) 5 m³ = _____ cm³   (b) 12,300 mm³ = _____ cm³

Solution

(a) 1 m = 100 cm, so 1 m³ = (100 cm)(100 cm)(100 cm), or 1,000,000 cm³.
   Thus, 5 m³ = (5)(1,000,000 cm³) = 5,000,000 cm³.

(b) 1 mm = 0.1 cm, so 1 mm³ = (0.1 cm)(0.1 cm)(0.1 cm), or 0.001 cm³.
   Thus, 12,300 mm³ = 12,300(0.001 cm³) = 12.3 cm³.

In the metric system, cubic units may be used for either dry or liquid measure, although units such as liters and milliliters are usually used for capacity measures, that is, for liquids. By definition, one **liter,** symbolized by L, equals, or is the capacity of, one cubic decimeter; that is, 1 L = 1 dm³. Note that L is not a universally accepted symbol for liter. However, since the liter is not a standard international unit but is derived from other units, there is no proper standard international symbol. In the United States, L is preferred to either ℓ or l.

liter

Because 1 L = 1 dm³ and 1 dm³ = 1000 cm³, then 1 L = 1000 cm³ and 1 cm³ = 0.001 L. Prefixes can be used with all base units in the metric system, so 0.001 L = 1 milliliter = 1 mL. Hence, 1 cm³ = 1 mL. These relationships are summarized in Figure 12-40.

Figure 12-40

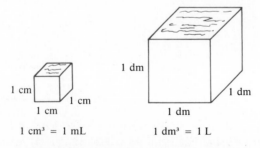

1 cm³ = 1 mL   1 dm³ = 1 L

The metric prefixes used with linear measure can also be used with the liter. Symbols and conversions work the same as they did for length. Table 12-4 shows how metric units involving the liter are related.

Table 12-4

Unit	Symbol	Relation to Liter
kiloliter	kL	1000 liters
*hectoliter	hL	100 liters
*dekaliter	daL	10 liters
liter	**L**	1 **liter**
*deciliter	dL	0.1 liter
centiliter	cL	0.01 liter
milliliter	mL	0.001 liter

* Not commonly used.

Example 12-16

Convert each of the following as indicated.

(a) 27 L = _____ mL   (b) 362 mL = _____ L
(c) 3 mL = _____ cm^3 (d) 3 m^3 = _____ L

Solution

(a) 1 L = 1000 mL, so 27 L = 27 · 1000 mL = 27,000 mL.
(b) 1 mL = 0.001 L, so 362 mL = 362(0.001 L) = 0.362 L.
(c) 1 mL = 1 cm^3, so 3 mL = 3 cm^3.
(d) 1 m^3 = 1000 dm^3 and 1 dm^3 = 1 L, so 1 m^3 = 1000 L and
    3 m^3 = 3000 L.

VOLUME OF RIGHT PRISMS AND RIGHT CYLINDERS

The volume of a right rectangular prism is given by $V = \ell wh$, where ℓ and w are the length and width of a base, respectively, and h is the height of the prism. Notice that ℓw is the area of a base of the prism. Hence, using B for the area of the base, the formula can be written as $V = Bh$. The same formula holds for any three-dimensional figure *if* all cross sections parallel to the base are congruent to the base. The formulas for volumes of right prisms and right circular cylinders are given in Figure 12-41.

Figure 12-41

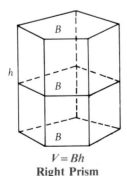

$V = Bh$
Right Prism

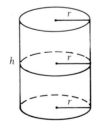

$V = Bh = \pi r^2 h$
Right circular cylinder

The formulas of Figure 12-41 can be intuitively justified by considering three-dimensional figures made of clay. For example, consider the right prism in Figure 12-42(a). Because all the parallel cross sections of the prism are congruent, it seems that we should be able to deform the clay model into the

Figure 12-42

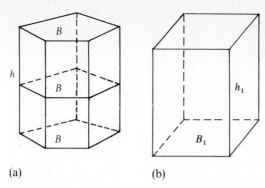

(a)   (b)

right rectangular prism shown in Figure 12-42(b) without changing its altitude or the area of the base. Because the amount of material does not change, the volume of the rectangular prism should be the same as the volume of the original prism. The volume of the rectangular prism is $B_1 h_1$, where B_1 is the area of the rectangular base and h_1 is the height of the rectangular prism. Because $B_1 = B$ and $h_1 = h$, where B and h are the area of the base and the height of the original prism, respectively, it follows that the volume of the original prism is Bh.

Example 12-17

Find the volume of each of the figures in Figure 12-43.

Figure 12-43

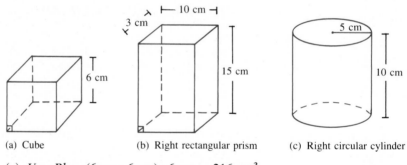

(a) Cube   (b) Right rectangular prism   (c) Right circular cylinder

Solution

(a) $V = Bh = (6 \text{ cm} \cdot 6 \text{ cm}) \cdot 6 \text{ cm} = 216 \text{ cm}^3$
(b) $V = Bh = (10 \text{ cm} \cdot 3 \text{ cm}) \cdot 15 \text{ cm} = 450 \text{ cm}^3$
(c) $V = \pi r^2 h = \pi (5 \text{ cm})^2 \cdot 10 \text{ cm} = 250 \, \pi \text{ cm}^3$

HISTORICAL NOTE

Bonaventura Cavalieri (1598–1647), a disciple of Galileo, became a professor of mathematics at the University of Bologna in 1629. He made many contributions to geometry, trigonometry, and algebra. Cavalieri is best known for his principle concerning the volumes of solids.

Figure 12-44 shows a right triangular prism with an equilateral triangle as a base. This prism can be separated into three pyramids that have bases with the same area and height the same as that of the prism. In this special case, the volume of the right triangular pyramid is one-third the volume of the triangular prism; that is, $V = \frac{1}{3}Bh$. This can also be demonstrated by building three paper models of the pyramids and fitting them together into a prism.

Figure 12-44

Formulas for many other three-dimensional figures can be derived using a principle based on a phenomenon described in Figure 12-45. In Figure 12-45(a), a rectangular box has been sliced into thin layers. If the layers are shifted to form the solids in Figure 12-45(b) and (c), the volume of each of the three solids is the same as the volume of the original rectangular box. The principle based on the phenomenon described in Figure 12-45 is referred to as *Cavalieri's Principle.*

Figure 12-45

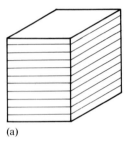
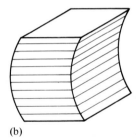
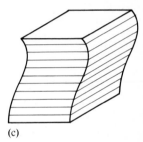

(a)   (b)   (c)

CAVALIERI'S PRINCIPLE

Two solids with bases in the same plane have equal volumes if every plane parallel to the bases intersects the solids in cross sections of equal area.

Using Cavalieri's Principle, it can be shown that two pyramids that have the same altitude and the same base also have the same volume. Consequently, it can be shown that the volume of any pyramid is $\frac{1}{3}Bh$, where B is the area of the base and h is the height.

VOLUME OF A RIGHT CIRCULAR CONE

To find the volume of a right cone with a circular base, as shown in Figure 12-46, consider the polygonal base of a pyramid with many sides. The base approximates a circle and the volume of the pyramid is approximately the volume of the cone with the circle as a base and the same height as the pyramid. The area of the base is approximately πr^2, where r is the apothem of the polygon. Hence, the formula for the volume of a right circular cone with a circular base is $V = \frac{1}{3}\pi r^2 h$ or $V = \frac{1}{3}Bh$.

Figure 12-46

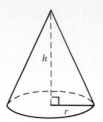

$$V = \frac{1}{3}\pi r^2 h$$
Right circular cone

Example 12-18

Find the volume of each of the figures in Figure 12-47.

Figure 12-47

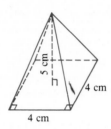

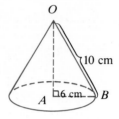

(a) Right square pyramid   (b) Right circular cone

Solution

(a) The figure is a pyramid with a square base whose area is (4 cm · 4 cm) and whose height is 5 cm. Hence, $V = \frac{1}{3}Bh = \frac{1}{3}(4 \text{ cm} \cdot 4 \text{ cm})(5 \text{ cm}) = \frac{80}{3}$ cm^3.

(b) The base of the cone is a circle of radius 6 cm. Because the volume of the cone is given by $V = \frac{1}{3}\pi r^2 h$, we need to know the height. In the right triangle OAB, $OA = h$ and, by the Pythagorean Theorem, $h^2 + 6^2 = 10^2$. Hence, $h^2 = 100 - 36$, or 64, and $h = 8$ cm. Thus, $V = \frac{1}{3}\pi r^2 h = \frac{1}{3}(6 \text{ cm})^2(8 \text{ cm}) = 96\pi$ cm^3.

VOLUME OF A SPHERE

To find the volume of a sphere, imagine that a sphere is composed of a great number of congruent pyramids with apexes at the center of the sphere and that the vertices of the base touch the sphere, as shown in Figure 12-48.

Figure 12-48

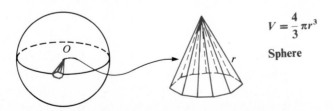

$$V = \frac{4}{3}\pi r^3$$
Sphere

If the pyramids have very small bases, then the height of each pyramid is nearly the radius r. Hence, the volume of each pyramid is $\frac{1}{3}Bh$ or $\frac{1}{3}Br$, where

B is the area of the base. If there are n pyramids each with base area B, then the total volume of the pyramids is $V = \frac{1}{3}nBr$. Because nB is the total surface area of all the bases of the pyramids and the sum of the areas of all the bases of the pyramids is very close to the surface area of the sphere, $4\pi r^2$, the volume of the sphere is given by $V = \frac{1}{3}(4\pi r^2)r = \frac{4}{3}\pi r^3$.

Example 12-19

Find the volume of a sphere whose radius is 6 cm.

Solution

$$V = \frac{4}{3}\pi(6 \text{ cm})^3 = \frac{4}{3}\pi(216 \text{ cm}^3) = 288\pi \text{ cm}^3$$

PROBLEM 3

Half the air is let out of a spherical balloon. If the balloon remains in the shape of a sphere, how does the radius of the smaller balloon compare with the original radius?

UNDERSTANDING THE PROBLEM In Figure 12-49(b), the volume of the smaller balloon is half the volume of the original balloon in Figure 12-49(a). We are to find a relationship between the radii R and r of the two balloons.

Figure 12-49

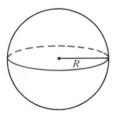

DEVISING A PLAN We can express the volume of each balloon in Figure 12-49 in terms of its radius. Because the volume of the smaller balloon is half the volume of the original balloon, we know that the ratio of their volumes is $1:2$, or $\frac{1}{2}$. From that ratio, we should be able to find the ratio between the radii.

CARRYING OUT THE PLAN Let V be the volume of the original balloon and v be the volume of the smaller balloon. Using the formula for the volume of a sphere, we obtain the following ratio: $\frac{v}{V} = \frac{\frac{4}{3}\pi r^3}{\frac{4}{3}\pi R^3} = \frac{r^3}{R^3}$. Because $\frac{v}{V} = \frac{1}{2}$, we have $\frac{1}{2} = \frac{r^3}{R^3}$, or $\left(\frac{r}{R}\right)^3 = \frac{1}{2}$. Hence, $\frac{r}{R} = \sqrt[3]{\frac{1}{2}}$, or $\sqrt[3]{.5}$. Using a calculator with a cube-root function, we find that $r/R \doteq 0.8$, or $r \doteq 0.8R$.

LOOKING BACK Similar questions could also be asked concerning other solids. For example, we could ask how the sides of two square boxes compare if the volume of one of the boxes is half the volume of the other. We could also generalize the original question by assuming that an arbitrary fraction (or percent) of the air is let out of the balloon.

PROBLEM SET 12-5

1. Complete each of the following.
   (a) $8 \text{ m}^3 = $ _____ dm^3
   (b) $500 \text{ cm}^3 = $ _____ m^3
   (c) $675,000 \text{ m}^3 = $ _____ km^3
   (d) $3 \text{ m}^3 = $ _____ cm^3
   (e) $7000 \text{ mm}^3 = $ _____ cm^3
   (f) $0.002 \text{ m}^3 = $ _____ cm^3
2. Why is a unit sphere, a sphere with radius 1 cm, not a "good" unit of volume measure, even for measuring the volume of another sphere?
3. Find the volume of each of the following.

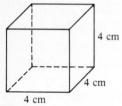

4 cm
4 cm
4 cm

(a) Right rectangular prism

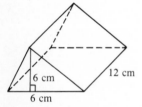

3 cm
5 cm
8 cm

(b) Right rectangular prism

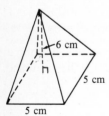

6 cm
6 cm
12 cm

(c) Right triangular prism

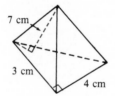

7 cm
3 cm
4 cm

(d) Pyramid with a right triangle as base

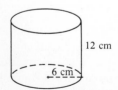

6 cm
5 cm
5 cm

(e) Square pyramid

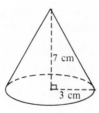

7 cm
3 cm

(f) Right circular cone

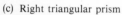

12 cm
6 cm

(g) Right circular cylinder

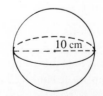

10 cm

(h) Sphere

4. Find the volume of each of the following.

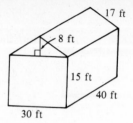

17 ft
8 ft
15 ft
40 ft
30 ft

(a)

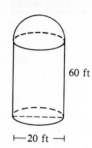

60 ft
—20 ft—

(b)

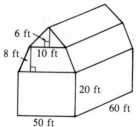

6 ft
8 ft   10 ft
20 ft
50 ft
60 ft

(c)

4 cm
8 cm

(d)

5. What volume of silver is needed to make the napkin ring out of solid silver? Give your answer in cubic millimeters.

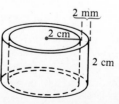

2 mm
2 cm
2 cm

6. Two cubes have sides of lengths 4 cm and 6 cm, respectively. What is the ratio of their volumes?
7. What happens to the volume of a sphere if the radius is doubled?
8. Complete the following.

	(a)	(b)	(c)	(d)	(e)	(f)
cm³		500			750	4800
dm³	2					
L			1.5			
mL				5000		

9. Complete the chart for right rectangular prisms with the given dimensions.

	(a)	(b)	(c)	(d)
Length	20 cm	10 cm	2 dm	15 cm
Width	10 cm	2 dm	1 dm	2 dm
Height	10 cm	3 dm		
Volume in cm³				
Volume in dm³				7.5 dm³
Volume in L			4 L	

10. Place a decimal point in each of the following to make it an accurate sentence.
    (a) A paper cup holds about 2000 mL.
    (b) A regular soft drink bottle holds about 320 L.
    (c) A quart milk container holds about 10 L.
    (d) A teaspoonful of cough syrup would be about 500 mL.
11. A right cylindrical tank holds how many liters if it is 6 m long and 13 m in diameter?
12. If the length of the diameter of the earth is approximately four times the length of the diameter of the moon and both are spheres, what is the ratio of their volumes?
13. A bread pan is 18 cm × 18 cm × 5 cm. How many liters does it hold?
14. An Olympic pool in the shape of a right rectangular prism is 50 m long and 25 m wide. If it is 2 m deep throughout, how many liters of water does it hold?
15. If a faucet is dripping at the rate of 15 drops per minute and there are 20 drops per milliliter, how many liters of water are wasted in a 30-day month?

16. A standard straw is 25 cm long and 4 mm in diameter. How much liquid can be held in the straw at one time?
17. A theater decides to change the shape of its popcorn container from their regular box to a right regular pyramid and charge only half as much. If the containers are the same height and the tops are the same size, is this a bargain for the customer?

18. Which is the better buy, a grapefruit 5 cm in radius that costs 22¢ or a grapefruit 6 cm in radius that costs 31¢?
19. A regular square pyramid is 3 m high and the perimeter of its base is 16 m. Find the volume of the pyramid.
20. A right rectangular prism with base *ABCD* as the bottom is shown in the figure. Suppose *X* is drawn so that $AX = 3 \cdot AP$, where *AP* is the height of the prism, and *X* is connected to *A*, *B*, *C*, and *D*, forming a pyramid. How do the volumes of the pyramid and the prism compare?

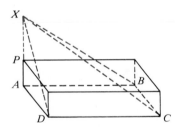

21. A right cylindrical can is to hold exactly 1 L of water. What should the height of the can be if the radius is 12 cm?
22. A box is packed with six pop cans as shown in the figure. What percent of the volume of the interior of the box is not occupied by the pop cans?

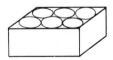

23. Use a dictionary to complete the following.
    (a) 1 ft³ = _____ in.³
    (b) 45830 in.³ = _____ ft³
    (c) 1 yd³ = _____ ft³
    (d) 3000 ft³ = _____ yd³

Review Problems

24. Find the surface areas of the following.

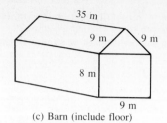

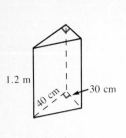

(a) Right prism

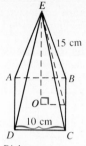

(b) Right square pyramid
(*EB* = 15 cm)

(c) Barn (include floor)

25. The diagonal of a rectangle has measure 1.3 m and a side has measure 120 cm. Find each of the following.
(a) Perimeter of the rectangle
(b) Area of the rectangle

26. Find the area of a triangle with sides 3 m, 3 m, and 2 m.

---

*Section 12-6   Mass and Temperature

Three centuries ago, Isaac Newton pointed out that in everyday life, the term "weight" is used for what is really mass. He called *mass* a quantity of matter as opposed to *weight*, which is a force exerted by gravitational pull. When an astronaut is in orbit above the earth, his weight has changed even though his mass remains the same. For common use on the earth, weight and mass are still used interchangeably.

gram

In the metric system, the base unit for mass is the **gram,** denoted by g. A gram is the mass of 1 cm³ of water. An ordinary paper clip or a thumbtack each has a mass of about 1 g.

As with other base metric units, prefixes are added to gram to obtain other units. For example, a kilogram (kg) is 1000 g. Since 1 cm³ of water has a mass of 1 g, the mass of 1 L of water is 1 kg. A person's mass is measured in kilograms. Two standard loaves of bread have a mass of about 1 kg. A newborn baby has a mass of about 4 kg. Another unit of mass in the metric

metric ton

system is the **metric ton** (t), which is equal to 1000 kg. The metric ton is used to record the masses of objects such as cars and trucks. A small foreign car has a mass of about 1 t.

Table 12-5 lists metric units of mass. Conversions involving metric units of mass are handled in the same way as units of length.

Table 12-5

Unit	Symbol	Relationship to Gram	
ton (metric)	t	1,000,000	grams
kilogram	kg	1000	grams
*hectogram	hg	100	grams
*dekagram	dag	10	grams
gram	**g**	**1**	**gram**
*decigram	dg	0.1	gram
*centigram	cg	0.01	gram
milligram	mg	0.001	gram

* Not commonly used.

Example 12-20

Complete each of the following.

(a) 34 g = _____ kg   (b) 6836 kg = _____ t

Solution

(a) 34 g = 34(0.001 kg) = 0.034 kg
(b) 6836 kg = 6836(0.001 t) = 6.836 t

The relationship among the units of volume and mass in the metric system is illustrated in Figure 12-50.

Figure 12-50

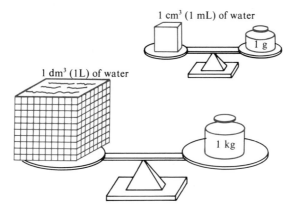

1 cm³ (1 mL) of water

1 g

1 dm³ (1L) of water

1 kg

Example 12-21

A water bed is 180 cm wide, 210 cm long, and 20 cm thick.

(a) How many liters of water can it hold?
(b) What is its mass in kilograms when it is full of water?

Solution

(a) The volume of the water bed is found by multiplying the length times the width times the height.

$$V = \ell wh$$

$$= 180 \text{ cm} \cdot 210 \text{ cm} \cdot 20 \text{ cm}$$

$$= 756,000 \text{ cm}^3 \text{ or } 756,000 \text{ mL}$$

Because 1 mL = 0.001 L, the volume is 756 L.
(b) Because 1 L of water has a mass of 1 kg, 756 L of water has a mass of 756 kg.

Remark   To see one advantage of the metric system, suppose the bed is 6 feet by 7 feet by 9 inches. Try to find the volume in gallons and the weight of the water in pounds.

TEMPERATURE

degree Kelvin

The base unit of temperature for the metric system is the **degree Kelvin.** However, it is used only for scientific measurements and not for everyday measurements of temperature. For normal temperature measurements in the metric system, the base unit is the **degree Celsius,** named for Anders Celsius, the Swedish scientist who invented the system. The Celsius scale has 100

degree Celsius

equal divisions between 0 degrees Celsius (0°C), the freezing point of water, and 100 degrees Celsius (100°C), the boiling point of water. In the English system, the Fahrenheit scale has 180 equal divisions between 32°F, the freezing point of water, and 212°F, the boiling point of water. Because the Celsius scale has 100 divisions between the freezing point and boiling point of water, whereas the Fahrenheit scale has 180 divisions, the relationship between the two scales is 100 to 180 or 5 to 9. Hence, for every 5 degrees on the Celsius scale, there are 9 degrees on the Fahrenheit scale, and for each degree on the Fahrenheit scale, there is $\frac{5}{9}$ degree on the Celsius scale. Figure 12-51 gives some temperature comparisons on the two scales and further illustrates the relationship between them.

Figure 12-51

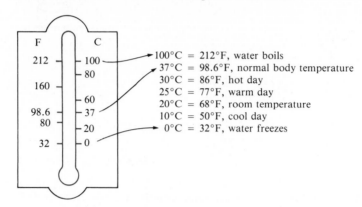

The fact that the ratio between the number of degrees above freezing on the Celsius scale and the number of degrees above freezing on the Fahrenheit scale remains the same and equals $\frac{5}{9}$ enables us to convert the temperature from one system to the other. For example, suppose we want to convert 50° on the Fahrenheit scale to the corresponding number on the Celsius scale. On the Fahrenheit scale, 50° is 50 − 32, or 18°, above freezing, but on the Celsius scale, it is $\frac{5}{9} \cdot 18$, or 10°, above freezing. Because the freezing temperature on the Celsius scale is 0°, 10° above freezing is 10° Celsius. Thus, 50°F = 10°C. In general, F degrees is $F − 32$ above freezing on the Fahrenheit scale, but only $\frac{5}{9}(F − 32)$ above freezing on the Celsius scale. Thus, we have the relation $C = \frac{5}{9}(F − 32)$. If we solve the equation for F, we obtain $F = \frac{9}{5}C + 32$. Rather than memorize these formulas, we encourage you to reason as shown to convert from one scale to the other.

Example 12-22

Convert 20°C to degrees Fahrenheit.

Solution

For 100 divisions on the Celsius scale, we have 212 − 32, or 180, divisions on the Fahrenheit scale. Hence, for every 1 degree on the Celsius scale, there are $\frac{180}{100}$, or $\frac{9}{5}$, degrees on the Fahrenheit scale. Because 20°C is 20° above freezing, on the Fahrenheit scale it would be $\frac{9}{5} \cdot 20$, or 36, degrees above freezing, or 32 + 36, or 68 degrees. Thus, 20°C = 68°F.

Remark The Celsius scale is also known as the centigrade scale because it is divided into 100 degrees.

PROBLEM SET 12-6

1. For each of the following, select the appropriate metric unit of measure (gram, kilogram, or metric ton).
   (a) Car
   (b) Woman
   (c) Can of frozen orange juice
   (d) Elephant
   (e) Jar of mustard
   (f) Bag of peanuts
   (g) Army tank
   (h) Cat
   (i) Dictionary
2. For each of the following, choose the correct unit (milligram, gram, or kilogram) to make each sentence reasonable.
   (a) A staple has a mass of about 340 _____.
   (b) A professional football player has a mass of about 110 _____.
   (c) A vitamin tablet has a mass of 1100 _____.
   (d) A dime has a mass of 2 _____.
   (e) The recipe said to add 4 _____ of salt.
   (f) One strand of hair has a mass of 2 _____.
3. Complete each of the following.
   (a) 15,000 g = _____ kg
   (b) 8000 kg = _____ t
   (c) 0.036 kg = _____ g
   (d) 72 g = _____ kg
   (e) 4230 mg = _____ g
   (f) 3 g 7 mg = _____ g
   (g) 5 kg 750 g = _____ g
   (h) 5 kg 750 g = _____ kg
   (i) 0.03 t = _____ kg
   (j) 0.03 t = _____ g
4. If a paper dollar has a mass of approximately 1 g, is it possible to lift $1,000,000 in the following denominations?
   (a) $1 bills   (b) $10 bills   (c) $100 bills
   (d) $1000 bills   (e) $10,000 bills
5. A fish tank, which is a right rectangular prism, is 40 cm by 20 cm by 20 cm. If it is filled with water, what is the mass of the water?
6. In a grocery store, one kind of meat costs $5.80 per kilogram. How much does 400 g of this meat cost?
7. If a certain spice costs $20 per kilogram, how much does 1 g cost?
8. Abel bought a kilogram of Moxwill coffee for $9 and Babel bought 400 g of the same brand of coffee for $4.60. Who made the better buy?
9. Answer each of the following.
   (a) The thermometer reads 20°C. Can you go snow skiing?
   (b) The thermometer reads 26°C. Will the outdoor ice rink be open?
   (c) Your temperature is 37°C. Do you have a fever?
   (d) If your body temperature is 39°C, are you ill?
   (e) It is 40°C. Will you need a sweater at the outdoor concert?
   (f) The temperature reads 35°C. Should you go water skiing?
   (g) The temperature reads ⁻10°C. Is it appropriate to go ice fishing?
   (h) Your bath water is 16°C. Will you have a hot, warm, or chilly bath?
   (i) It's 30°C in the room. Are you uncomfortably hot or cold?
10. Convert each of the following from degrees Fahrenheit to the nearest integer degree Celsius.
    (a) 10°F   (b) 0°F   (c) 30°F
    (d) 100°F   (e) 212°F   (f) ⁻40°F
11. Convert each of the following from degrees Celsius to the nearest integer degree Fahrenheit.
    (a) 10°C   (b) 0°C   (c) 30°C
    (d) 100°C   (e) 212°C   (f) ⁻40°C

Review Problems

12. Find the perimeter and the area of the following.

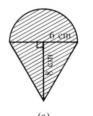

(a)

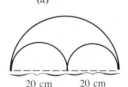

20 cm   20 cm

(b)

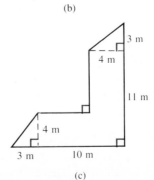

(c)

13. Complete the following.
   (a) 350 mm = _____ cm
   (b) 1600 cm^2 = _____ m^2
   (c) 0.4 m^2 = _____ mm^2
   (d) 5.2 m^3 = _____ cm^3
   (e) 5.2 m^3 = _____ L
   (f) 3500 cm^3 = _____ m^3

14. Determine whether each of the following is a right triangle.

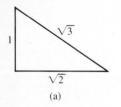

(a)

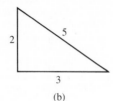

(b)

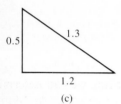

(c)

15. A person walks 5 km north, 3 km east, 1 km north, and then 2 km east. How far is the person from the starting point?

16. Find the volume and the surface area of each of the solids.

(a) Right circular cone

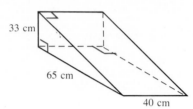

(b)   Right prism in which the faces are either rectangles or right triangles

---

LABORATORY ACTIVITY

1. Record the mass of each U.S. coin. Which coin has the greatest mass? Which of the following sets have the same mass?
   (a) A half-dollar vs. two quarters
   (b) A quarter vs. two dimes and a nickel
   (c) A dime vs. two nickels
   (d) A dime vs. ten pennies
   (e) A nickel vs. five pennies
2. Record the temperature of the room on a Celsius thermometer. Pour 200 mL of water into a liter container. Record the temperature of the water. Add 100 mL of ice to the water. Wait one minute and record the temperature of the ice water.

SOLUTION TO THE PRELIMINARY PROBLEM

UNDERSTANDING THE PROBLEM A manufacturer wants to use 20-cm by 30-cm rectangular sheets of metal to make some cylindrical pipes and some box-shaped pipes with square cross sections that have a greater volume than the cylindrical pipes. Is this possible, and if so, how should the pipes be designed and what are their volumes?

Figure 12-52 shows a sheet of metal and two sections of pipe made from it, one cylindrical and the other box-shaped. A model for such pipes can be designed from a piece of paper by bending it into a cylinder or by folding it into a right rectangular prism as shown.

Figure 12-52

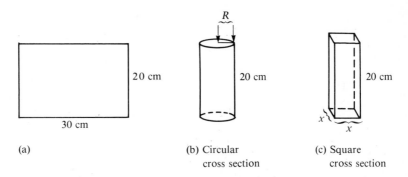

(a)

30 cm

20 cm

(b) Circular
cross section

R

20 cm

(c) Square
cross section

20 cm

x x

DEVISING A PLAN If we can compute the volume of the cylinder in Figure 12-52(b) and the volume of the prism in Figure 12-52(c), we can determine which has a greater volume. If the prism has a greater volume, the solution of the problem will be complete. If not, we will need to look for other ways to design the cans before concluding that a solution is impossible.

To compute the volume of the cylinder, we need to find the area of the base. The area of the circular base is πR^2. To find R, we note that the circumference, $2\pi R$, of the circle is 30 cm because the base of the rectangular sheet of metal was bent into a circle. The equation $2\pi R = 30$ determines the value of R. With the given information, we can also find the area of the base of the rectangular box.

CARRYING OUT THE PLAN Denoting the volume of the cylindrical pipe by V_1 and the volume of the box-shaped pipe by V_2, we have $V_1 = \pi R^2(20)$. Because $2\pi R = 30$, we have $R = 30/2\pi$ or $15/\pi$ cm. Substituting this value for R in the preceding formula for the volume, we obtain $V_1 = \pi(15/\pi)^2 \cdot 20$, or $(15^2 \cdot 20)/\pi$, or approximately 1432.4 cm³. If we denote the length of the side of the box-shaped pipe in Figure 12-52(c) by x, we have $V_2 = x \cdot x \cdot 20$, or $20x^2$. Because the perimeter of the square is 30 cm, we have $4x = 30$ or $x = 7.5$. Consequently, $V_2 = 20(7.5)^2$ or 1125 cm². We see that in our first design for the pipes, the volume of the cylindrical pipe is greater than the volume of the box-shaped pipe.

Are there other ways to design the pipes? Rather than bending the rectangular sheet of metal along the 30-cm side, we could bend it along the 20-cm side to obtain either pipe, as shown in Figure 12-53. Denoting the radius of the cylindrical pipe by r, the side of the box-shaped pipe by y, and their volumes by V_3 and V_4, respectively, we have $V_3 = \pi r^2 \cdot 30 = \pi(20/2\pi)^2 \cdot 30 = (10^2 \cdot 30)/\pi$, or approximately 954.9 cm³. Also, $V_4 = y^2 \cdot 30 = (\frac{20}{4})^2 \cdot 30 = 25 \cdot 30$ or 750 cm³. Because $V_2 = 1125$ cm³ and $V_3 = 945.9$ cm³, we see that the volume of the box-shaped pipe with an altitude of 20 cm [see Figure

Figure 12-53

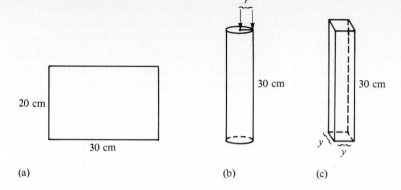

(a)   (b)   (c)

12-52(c)] is greater than the volume of the cylindrical pipe with an altitude of 30 cm [see Figure 12-53(b)].

LOOKING BACK We could ask for the volumes of other three-dimensional objects that can be obtained by bending the rectangular sheets of metal. Also, because the lateral surface areas of the four types of pipes were the same but their volumes were different, we might want to investigate whether there are other cylinders and prisms that have the same lateral surface area and the same volume. Also, is it possible to find a circular cylinder with lateral surface area of 600 cm² and smallest possible volume? Similarly, is there a circular cylinder with the given surface area and largest possible volume?

QUESTIONS FROM THE CLASSROOM

1. A student asks if the units of measure must be the same for each term to use the formulas for volumes. How do you respond?
2. In the discussion of the Pythagorean Theorem, squares were constructed on each side of a right triangle. A student asks, "If different similar figures are constructed on each side of the triangle, does the same type of relationship still hold?" How do you reply?
3. A student asks, "Can I find the area of an angle?" How do you respond?
4. A student argues that a square has no area because its interior can be thought of as the union of infinitely many line segments, each of which has no area. How do you react?
5. A student asks whether the volume of a prism is always a lesser number than its surface area. How do you answer?
6. A students asks, "Why should the United States switch to the metric system?" How do you reply?

7. A student claims that in a triangle with 20° and 40° angles, the side opposite the 40° angle is twice as long as the side opposite the 20° angle. How do you reply?
8. A student interpreted 5 cm³ using the drawing below. What is wrong with this interpretation?

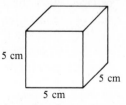

9. A student has a can containing three tennis balls. To the student's surprise, the perimeter of the top of the can is longer than the height of the can. The student wants to know if this fact can be explained without performing any measurements. Can you help?

CHAPTER OUTLINE

I. The metric system
   A. A summary of relationships among prefixes and the base unit of linear measure follows.

Prefix	Unit	Relationship to Base Unit		Symbol
kilo	kilometer	1000	meters	km
*hecto	hectometer	100	meters	hm
*deka	dekameter	10	meters	dam
meter		**1**	**meter**	**m**
*deci	decimeter	0.1	meter	dm
centi	centimeter	0.01	meter	cm
milli	millimeter	0.001	meter	mm

   * Not commonly used.

   B. Area measure
      1. Units commonly used are the square kilometer (km^2), square meter (m^2), square centimeter (cm^2), and square millimeter (mm^2).
      2. Land can be measured using the **are** (100 m^2) and the **hectare** (10,000 m^2).
   C. Volume measure
      1. Units commonly used are the **cubic meter** (m^3), **cubic decimeter** (dm^3), and **cubic centimeter** (cm^3).
      2. 1 dm^3 = 1 L and 1 cm^3 = 1 mL.
   *D. Mass
      1. Units of mass commonly used are the **milligram** (mg), **gram** (g), **kilogram** (kg), and **metric ton** (t).
      2. 1 L and 1 mL of water have masses of approximately 1 kg and 1 g, respectively.
   *E. Temperature
      1. The official unit of metric temperature is the **degree Kelvin,** but the unit commonly used is the **degree Celsius.**
      2. Basic temperature reference points are the following:

   100°C—boiling point of water
   37°C—normal body temperature
   20°C—comfortable room temperature
   0°C—freezing point of water

      3. $C = \frac{5}{9}(F - 32)$ and $F = \frac{9}{5}C + 32$

II. Distance
   A. **Distance,** or length, has the following properties. Given points A, B, and C:
      1. $AB \geq 0$
      2. $AB = BA$
      3. Triangle Inequality: $AB + BC \geq AC$
   B. The distance around a two-dimensional figure is called the **perimeter.** The distance C around a circle is called the **circumference.** $C = 2\pi r = \pi d$, where r is the radius of the circle and d is the diameter.

III. Areas
   A. Formulas for areas
      1. **Square:** $A = s^2$, where s is a side.
      2. **Rectangle:** $A = \ell w$, where ℓ is the length and w is the width.
      3. **Parallelogram:** $A = bh$, where b is the base and h is the height.
      4. **Triangle:** $A = \frac{1}{2}bh$, where b is the base and h is the altitude to that base.
      5. **Trapezoid:** $A = \frac{1}{2}h(b_1 + b_2)$, where b_1 and b_2 are the bases and h is the height.
      6. **Regular polygon:** $A = \frac{1}{2}ap$, where a is the apothem and p is the perimeter.
      7. **Circle:** $A = \pi r^2$, where r is the radius.
      8. **Sector:** $A = \theta \pi r^2 / 360$, where θ is the measure of the central angle forming the sector and r is the radius of the circle containing the sector.
   B. **The Pythagorean Theorem:** In any right triangle, the square of the length of the hypotenuse is equal to the sum of the squares of the lengths of the legs.
   C. **Converse of the Pythagorean Theorem:** In any triangle ABC with sides of lengths a, b, and c such that $a^2 + b^2 = c^2$, $\triangle ABC$ is a right triangle with the right angle opposite the side of length c.

IV. Surface areas and volumes
   A. Formulas for areas
      1. **Right prism:** $S.A. = 2B + ph$, where B is the area of a base, p is the perimeter of the base, and h is the height of the prism.
      2. **Right circular cylinder:** $S.A. = 2\pi r^2 + 2\pi rh$,

where r is the radius of the circular base and h is the height of the cylinder.

3. **Right circular cone:** $S.A. = \pi r^2 + \pi r \ell$, where r is the radius of the circular base and ℓ is the slant height.

4. **Right regular pyramid:** $S.A. = B + \frac{1}{2}p\ell$, where B is the area of the base, p is the perimeter of the base, and ℓ is the slant height.

5. **Sphere:** $S.A. = 4\pi r^2$, where r is the radius of the sphere.

B. Formulas for volumes
1. **Right prism:** $V = Bh$, where B is the area of the base and h is the height.

(a) **Right rectangular prism:** $V = \ell w h$, where ℓ is the length, w is the width, and h is the height.

(b) **Cube:** $V = e^3$, where e is an edge.

2. **Right circular cylinder:** $V = \pi r^2 h$, where r is the radius of the base and h is the height of the cylinder.

3. **Pyramid:** $V = \frac{1}{3}Bh$, where B is the area of the base and h is the height of the pyramid.

4. **Circular cone:** $V = \frac{1}{3}\pi r^2 h$, where r is the radius of the circular base and h is the height.

5. **Sphere:** $V = \frac{4}{3}\pi r^3$, where r is the radius of the sphere.

CHAPTER TEST

1. Complete the following chart converting metric measures.

	mm	cm	m	km
(a)				0.05
(b)		320		
(c)	260,000,000			
(d)			190	

2. For each of the following, choose an appropriate metric unit—millimeter, centimeter, meter, or kilometer.
   (a) The thickness of a penny
   (b) The length of a new lead pencil
   (c) The diameter of a dime
   (d) The distance the winner travels in the Indianapolis 500
   (e) The height of a doorknob
   (f) The length of a soccer field

3. For each of the following, describe how you can find the area of the parallelogram.
   (a) Using DE (b) Using BF

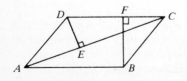

4. What is the area of the shaded region in the figure?

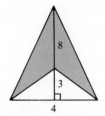

5. What is the area of the shaded region on the geoboard if the unit of measure is 1 cm²?

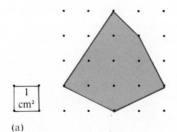

(a)

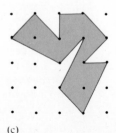

(b)   (c)

6. Find the area of the kite.

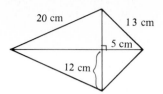

7. Explain how the formula for the area of a trapezoid can be found using the given pictures.

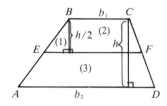

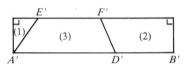

8. Use the figure to find each of the following.
(a) The area of the hexagon
(b) The area of the circle

9. Find the area of each shaded region.

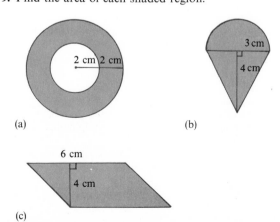

(a)

(b)

(c)

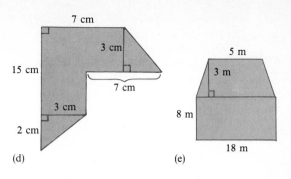

(d)

(e)

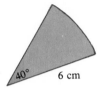

(f)

10. For each of the following, can the measures represent sides of a right triangle? Explain your answers.
(a) 5 cm, 12 cm, 13 cm
(b) 40 cm, 60 cm, 104 cm

11. Find the surface area and volume of each of the following.

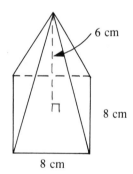

(a) Right square pyramid

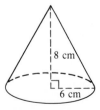

(b) Right circular cone

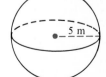

(c) Sphere

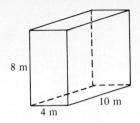

(d) Right circular cylinder   (e) Right rectangular prism

12. Complete each of the following.
   (a) Very heavy objects have mass that is measured in _____.
   (b) A cube whose length, width, and height are each 1 cm has a volume of _____.
   (c) If the cube in (b) is filled with water, the mass of the water is _____.
   (d) Which has a larger volume, 1 L or 1 dm³?
   (e) If a car uses 1 L of gas to go 12 km, the amount of gas needed to go 300 km is _____ L.
   (f) 20 ha = _____ a
   (g) 51.8 L = _____ cm³
   (h) 10 km² = _____ m²
   (i) 50 L = _____ mL
   (j) 5830 mL = _____ L
   (k) 25 m³ = _____ dm³
   (l) 75 dm³ = _____ mL

*(m) 52,813 g = _____ kg
*(n) 4800 kg = _____ t
*13. For each of the following, fill in the correct unit to make the sentence reasonable.
   (a) Anna filled the gas tank with 80 _____.
   (b) A man has a mass of about 82 _____.
   (c) The textbook has a mass of 978 _____.
   (d) A nickel has a mass of 5 _____.
   (e) A typical adult cat has a mass of about 4 _____.
   (f) A compact car has a mass of about 1.5 _____.
   (g) The amount of coffee in the cup is 180 _____.
*14. For each of the following, decide if the situation is likely or unlikely.
   (a) Carrie's bath water has a temperature of 15°C.
   (b) She found 26°C too warm and lowered the thermostat to 21°C.
   (c) Jim was drinking water with a temperature of ⁻5°C.
   (d) The water in the teakettle has a temperature of 120°C.
   (e) The outside temperature dropped to 5°C, and ice appeared on the lake.
*15. Complete each of the following.
   (a) 2 dm³ of water has a mass of _____ g.
   (b) 1 L of water has a mass of _____ g.
   (c) 3 cm³ of water has a mass of _____ g.
   (d) 4.2 mL of water has a mass of _____ kg.
   (e) 0.2 L of water has a volume of _____ m³.

SELECTED BIBLIOGRAPHY

Barnett, D. "A 'Metric Review Show.'" *The Mathematics Teacher* 77 (February 1984):106–107.

Brougher, J. "Discovery Activities with Area and Perimeter." *The Arithmetic Teacher* 20 (May 1973):382–385.

Bruni, J. "Geometry for the Intermediate Grades." *Arithmetic Teacher* 26 (February 1979):17–19.

Donegan, J., and J. Pricken. "Putting an Old Puzzle to Work." *Arithmetic Teacher* 28 (May 1981):15–16.

Ewbank, W. "If Pythagoras Had a Geoboard . . ." *The Mathematics Teacher* 66 (March 1973):215–221.

Harrison, W. "How to Make a Million." *Arithmetic Teacher* 33 (September 1985):46–47.

Hart, K. "Which Comes First—Length, Area, or Volume?" *Arithmetic Teacher* 31 (May 1984):16–18, 26–27.

Hawkins, V. "The Pythagorean Theorem Revisited: Weighing the Results." *Arithmetic Teacher* 32 (December 1984):36–37.

Hiebert, J. "Why Do Some Children Have Trouble Learning Measurements?" *Arithmetic Teacher* 31 (March 1984):19–24.

Hildreth, D. "The Use of Strategies in Estimating Measurements." *Arithmetic Teacher* 30 (January 1983):50–54.

Hirstein, J., C. Lamb, and A. Osborne. "Student Misconceptions About Area Measure." *Arithmetic Teacher* 25 (March 1978):10–16.

Hunt, J. "How High Is a Flagpole?" *Arithmetic Teacher* 25 (February 1978):42–43.

Jamski, W. "So Your Students Know About Area?" *Arithmetic Teacher* 26 (December 1978):37.

Jensen, R. "Multilevel Metric Games." *Arithmetic Teacher* 32 (October 1984):36–39.

Jensen, R., and D. O'Neil. "Informal Geometry Through Geometric Blocks." *Arithmetic Teacher* 29 (May 1982):4–8.

Jensen, R., and D. O'Neil. "Meaningful Linear Measurement." *Arithmetic Teacher* 29 (September 1981):6–12.

Leutzinger, L., and G. Nelson. "Let's Do It: Meaningful Measurements." *Arithmetic Teacher* 27 (March 1980):6–11.

Lindquist, M., and M. Dana. "Let's Do It: Measurement for the Times." *Arithmetic Teacher* 26 (April 1979):4–9.

Lindquist, M., and M. Dana. "The Neglected Decimeter." *Arithmetic Teacher* 24 (October 1977):10–17.

Litwiller, B., and D. Duncan. "Areas of Polygons on Isometric Dot Paper: Pick's Formula Revised." *Arithmetic Teacher* 30 (April 1983):38–40.

Loomis, E. *The Pythagorean Propositions.* Washington, D.C.: National Council of Teachers of Mathematics, 1972.

Nelson, R., and D. Whitaker. "Another Use for Geoboards." *Arithmetic Teacher* 30 (April 1983):34–37.

Ott, J., D. Sommers, and K. Creamer. "But Why Does $C = \pi d$?" *Arithmetic Teacher* 31 (November 1983): 38–40.

Shaw, J. "Exploring Perimeter and Area Using Centimeter Squared Paper." *Arithmetic Teacher* 31 (December 1983):4–11.

Shaw, J. "Student-Made Measuring Tools." *Arithmetic Teacher* 31 (November 1983):12–15.

Sherman, H. "Take the Metric System Personally—Play 'Merrily Metric.'" *Arithmetic Teacher* 29 (October 1981):19–20.

Thomas, D. "Geometry in the Middle School: Problem Solving with Trapezoids." *Arithmetic Teacher* 26 (February 1979):20–21.

Thompson, C., and J. Van de Walle. "Learning About Rulers and Measuring." *Arithmetic Teacher* 32 (April 1985):8–12.

Tolman, M. "The 'Steps' of Metric Conversion." *Arithmetic Teacher* 30 (November 1982):32–33.

Urion, D. "Using the Cuisenaire Rods to Discover Approximations of Pi." *Arithmetic Teacher* 27 (December 1979):17.

Walter, M. "A Common Misconception About Area," *The Arithmetic Teacher* 17 (April 1970):286–289.

Walter, M. "Frame Geometry: An Example in Posing and Solving Problems." *Arithmetic Teacher* 28 (October 1980):16–18.

CHAPTER 13

Coordinate Geometry

Preliminary Problem

Surveyors found the coordinates of three landmarks *A*, *B*, and *C*. They had to determine the coordinates of point *D* northeast of *A* so that *A*, *B*, *C*, and *D* are vertices of a parallelogram. Because point *D* was not easily accessible, the surveyors calculated the coordinates of *D* without further measurements. If *B* is at (7, 19.3), *C* is at (17.8, 5.9), and *A* is at (2.5, 4.7), find the coordinates of point *D*.

Introduction

In this chapter, we introduce the Cartesian coordinate system, which will enable us to study geometry using algebra and to interpret algebraic phenomena geometrically. This is the basis for graphing quantitative information and characterizing geometric figures with algebraic equations.

Section 13-1

Coordinate System in a Plane

origin

x-axis / *y*-axis

To set up a Cartesian coordinate system (named for Descartes), two number lines are placed perpendicular to each other at the point where both have coordinate 0. The intersection point of the two lines is called the **origin.** The two lines are usually drawn as shown in Figure 13-1, with the horizontal line called the **x-axis** and the vertical line called the **y-axis.**

Figure 13-1

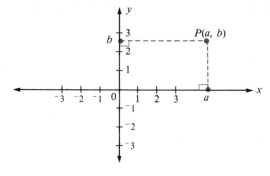

The location of any point P can be described by an ordered pair of numbers, as shown in Figure 13-1. If a perpendicular from P to the x-axis intersects the x-axis at a and a perpendicular from P to the y-axis intersects the y-axis at b, then we say that point P has coordinates (a, b). The first component in the ordered pair (a, b) is called the **abscissa,** or **x-coordinate,** of P.

abscissa / x-coordinate
ordinate / y-coordinate

The second component is called the **ordinate,** or **y-coordinate,** of P.

In Figure 13-2, the x-coordinate of P is $^-3$ and the y-coordinate of P is 2, so P has coordinates $(^-3, 2)$. Similarly, R has an x-coordinate of $^-4$ and a y-coordinate of $^-3$, which can be written as $R(^-4, ^-3)$.

To each point in the plane, there corresponds an ordered pair (a, b). Conversely, to every ordered pair of real numbers, there corresponds a point in the plane. Hence, there is a one-to-one correspondence between all the points

---

HISTORICAL NOTE

Coordinate geometry was invented by the French philosopher René Descartes (1596–1650) and the French lawyer and mathematician Pierre de Fermat (1601–1665). The need for quantitative methods in science motivated both Descartes and Fermat to find an association between algebraic equations and geometric curves and figures.

Figure 13-2

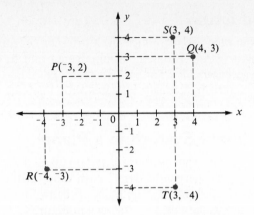

in the plane and all the ordered pairs of real numbers. Such a one-to-one

coordinate system   correspondence is called a **coordinate system** for the plane.

Together, the x-axis and y-axis separate the plane into four parts called

quadrants   **quadrants.** Figure 13-3 shows the four quadrants.

Figure 13-3

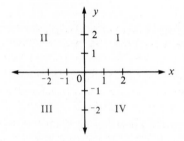

The quadrants do not include points on the axes. Every point on the x-axis has a y-coordinate of zero. Thus, the x-axis can be described as the set of all points (x, y) such that $y = 0$. The set of points on the x-axis is usually denoted by the equation $y = 0$, and we say that the equation of the x-axis is $y = 0$. Similarly, the y-axis can be described as a set of points in the plane, (x, y), for which $x = 0$ and y is an arbitrary real number. Thus, $x = 0$ is the equation of the y-axis. If we plot the set of all points that satisfy a given condition,

graph   the resulting picture on the Cartesian coordinate system is called the **graph** of the set.

Example 13-1

Sketch the graph for each of the following.

(a) $x = 2$ (b) $y = 3$
(c) $x < 2$ and $y = 3$ (d) $x < 2$

Solution

(a) The equation $x = 2$ represents the set of all points (x, y) for which $x = 2$ and y is any real number. This set represents a line perpendicular to the x-axis at $(2, 0)$ (Figure 13-4). Note that the set does not consist of a single point only.

(b) The equation $y = 3$ represents the set of all points (x, y) for which $y = 3$ and x is any real number. This set represents a line perpendicular to the y-axis at $(0, 3)$ (Figure 13-5).

Figure 13-4

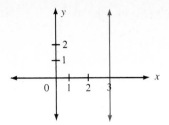

Figure 13-5

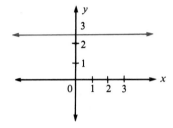

(c) Together, the statements represent the set of all points (x, y) for which $x < 2$ but y is always 3. The set describes a half-line, as shown in Figure 13-6. Note that the circle at $(2, 3)$ indicates that this point is not included in the solution.

Figure 13-6

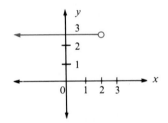

(d) The statement $x < 2$ indicates all points (x, y) for which $x < 2$ and y is any real number, that is, $\{(x, y) | x < 2 \text{ and } y \in R\}$. Because there are no restrictions on the y-coordinates, the coordinates of any point to the left of the line with equation $x = 2$, but not on the line, satisfy the condition. The half-plane in Figure 13-7 is the graph.

Figure 13-7

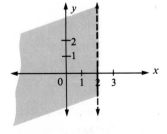

Remark   Had the inequality in the graph of Example 13-1(d) been $x \leq 2$, then the line $x = 2$ would have been a part of the set and would have been shown as a solid line. The fact that the line is not included is indicated by using the dashed line.

PROBLEM SET 13-1

1. (a) Give the coordinates of each of the points A, B, C, D, E, F, G, and H of the accompanying figure.

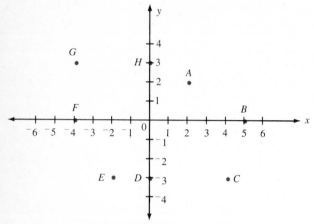

   (b) Find the coordinates of another point (not drawn) that is collinear with E, D, and C.

2. Name the quadrant in which each ordered pair is located.
   (a) $(3, 7)$
   (b) $(^-5, ^-8)$
   (c) $(^-10, 32)$
   (d) $(10, ^-40)$
   (e) $(0, 7)$

3. The first quadrant can be described as a set of ordered pairs (x, y) as follows.

   Quadrant I $= \{(x, y) \mid x > 0 \text{ and } y > 0\}$

   Describe the other quadrants in a similar way.

4. Find the coordinates of two other points collinear with each pair of given points.
   (a) $P(2, 2), Q(4, 2)$
   (b) $P(^-1, 0), Q(^-1, 2)$
   (c) $P(^-3, 0), Q(3, 0)$
   (d) $P(0, ^-2), Q(0, 3)$
   (e) $P(0, 0), Q(0, 1)$
   (f) $P(0, 0), Q(1, 1)$

5. For each of the following, give as much information as possible about x and y.
   (a) The ordered pairs $(^-2, 0), (^-2, 1)$, and (x, y) represent collinear points.
   (b) The ordered pairs $(^-2, 1), (0, 1)$, and (x, y) represent collinear points.

   (c) The ordered pair (x, y) is in the fourth quadrant.

6. Consider the lines through $P(2, 4)$ and perpendicular to the x- and y-axes, respectively. Find both the area and the perimeter of the rectangle formed by these lines and the axes.

7. Plot each of the points $A(^-3, ^-2)$, $B(^-3, 6)$, and $C(4, 6)$ and then find the coordinates of a point D such that quadrilateral $ABCD$ is a rectangle.

8. Plot at least six points, each having the sum of its coordinates equal to 4.

9. Sketch the graphs for each of the following.
   (a) $x = ^-3$
   (b) $y = ^-1$
   (c) $x > ^-3$
   (d) $y > ^-1$
   (e) $x > ^-3$ and $y = 2$
   (f) $y \geq ^-1$ and $x = 0$

10. Find the equations for each of the following.
   (a) The line containing $P(3, 0)$ and perpendicular to the x-axis
   (b) The line containing $P(0, ^-2)$ and parallel to the x-axis
   (c) The line containing $P(^-4, 5)$ and parallel to the x-axis
   (d) The line containing $P(^-4, 5)$ and parallel to the y-axis

11. Use the figure to answer the following questions.

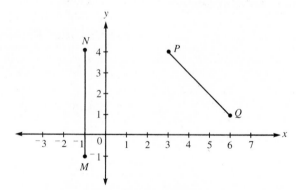

   (a) Give the coordinates of the endpoints of $\overline{PQ}$.
   (b) Give the coordinates of the endpoints of $\overline{MN}$.
   (c) Write the equation of the line parallel to $\overline{MN}$ and containing point P.
   (d) Write the equation of the line perpendicular to $\overline{MN}$ and containing point Q.

12. Use the graph to answer the following questions.

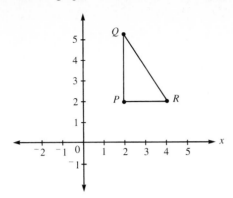

(a) Give the coordinates of the images of points P, Q, and R if $\triangle PQR$ is reflected in the x-axis.
(b) Give the coordinates of the images of points P, Q, and R if $\triangle PQR$ is rotated $90°$ counterclockwise with the origin as the center of the rotation.

13. Find the coordinates of the images of each of the points $(0, 1), (1, 0), (2, 4), (^-2, 4), (^-2, ^-4)$, and $(2, ^-4)$ under the given transformations.
(a) A flip in the x-axis
(b) A flip in the y-axis
(c) A turn by $90°$ counterclockwise about $(0, 0)$
(d) A half-turn whose center is $(0, 0)$
(e) A slide along the segment $\overline{OA}$ from $O(0, 0)$ to $A(0, ^-4)$.

14. Consider $\triangle ABC$ whose vertices are at $A(^-2, 5)$, $B(2, 6)$, and $C(5, 1)$. Find the coordinates of the vertices of the image of the triangle if $\triangle ABC$ is transformed by the following.
(a) A flip in the x-axis
(b) A flip in the y-axis
(c) A flip in the y-axis followed by a flip in the x-axis

15. (a) Flip the point $P(2, 4)$ in the y-axis and then flip its image in the x-axis. What are the coordinates of the final point?
(b) If the point $P(a, b)$ is in the first quadrant and is flipped in the y-axis, and then its image is flipped in the x-axis, what are the coordinates of the final image point?
(c) Can the final image points in (a) and (b) be obtained by a single transformation?

16. Find the equation of the image of the line $x = 3$ in the following circumstances.
(a) The line is flipped in the x-axis.
(b) The line is flipped in the y-axis.
(c) The line is rotated $90°$ counterclockwise about the origin.

17. Find the images of each point $A(1, 0), B(2, 2), C(3, 1)$, $D(3, ^-1)$, and $E(a, b)$ when it is reflected in the line $\overline{OP}$ where P has the coordinates $(5, 5)$ and O is the origin.

18. Find the coordinates of the image of point $P(a, b)$ when it is rotated $90°$ counterclockwise about the following points.
(a) $(a, 0)$ (b) The origin

Section 13-2   Equations of Lines

EQUATIONS OF HORIZONTAL LINES

The graph of the equation $x = a$, where a is some real number, is a line perpendicular to the x-axis through the point with coordinates $(a, 0)$, as shown in Figure 13-8. Similarly, the graph of the equation $y = b$ is a line perpendicular to the y-axis through the point with coordinates $(0, b)$.

Figure 13-8

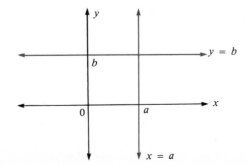

GRAPHING LINES

To graph the equation $y = x$, we plot all points whose x- and y-coordinates are equal. For example, $(0, 0)$, $(1, 1)$, $(1.3, 1.3)$, $(4, 4)$, $(4.5, 4.5)$, $(10, 10)$, and $(^-3, ^-3)$ all belong to the graph. However, $(1, ^-1)$ and $(2, 4)$ do not belong to the graph. Plotting some of the points shows that the points lie on a line ℓ, as shown in Figure 13-9. In fact, all points represented by the equation $y = x$ lie on line ℓ.

Figure 13-9

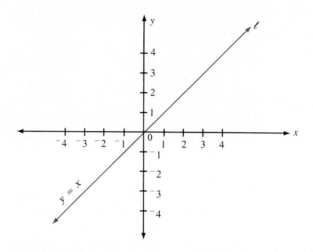

Next, consider the equation $y = 2x$. For any value of x, there is a corresponding value of y. Table 13-1 shows several values of x with corresponding values of y.

Table 13-1

x	$y = 2x$
0	0
1	2
2	4
$^-1$	$^-2$
$^-2$	$^-4$

These five coordinate pairs are plotted in Figure 13-10, along with the graph of $y = x$. The five points appear to be on a straight line. In fact, it is possible to prove that all points whose coordinates satisfy the equation $y = 2x$ lie on the same straight line.

As Figure 13-10 shows, the graph of $y = 2x$ is *steeper* than the graph of $y = x$. We further explore the notion of steepness by examining the graphs in Figure 13-11.

All six lines in Figure 13-11 have equations of the form $y = mx$, where m takes the values 2, 1, $\frac{1}{2}$, $^-\frac{1}{2}$, $^-1$, and $^-2$. The number m is a measure of

slope   steepness and is called the **slope** of the line whose equation is $y = mx$. The graph goes up from left to right (increases) if m is positive and goes down from left to right (decreases) if m is negative.

Figure 13-10

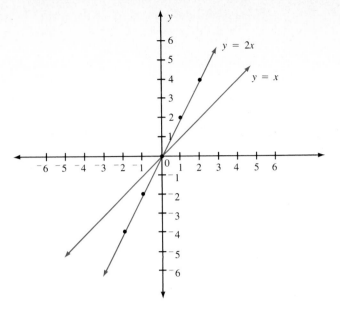

Figure 13-11

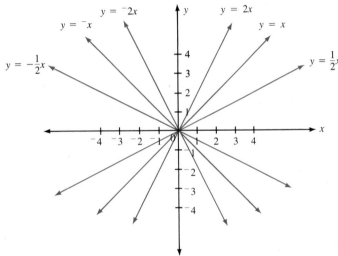

Observe that all six lines in Figure 13-11 pass through the origin. This is true for any line whose equation is $y = mx$. If $x = 0$, then $y = m \cdot 0 = 0$, and $(0, 0)$ is a point on the graph of $y = mx$. Conversely, it is possible to show that any nonvertical line passing through the origin has an equation of the form $y = mx$, for some value of m.

Example 13-2

Find the equation of the line that contains $(0, 0)$ and $(2, 3)$.

Solution

The line goes through the origin; therefore, its equation has the form $y = mx$. To find the equation of the line, we must find the value of m. The line contains $(2, 3)$, so substitute 2 for x and 3 for y into the equation $y = mx$ to obtain $3 = m \cdot 2$, and thus $m = \frac{3}{2}$. Hence, the required equation is $y = \frac{3}{2}x$.

Next, we consider equations of the form $y = mx + b$, where b is a real number. To do this, we examine the graphs of $y = x + 2$ and $y = x$. Given the graph of $y = x$, the graph of $y = x + 2$ can be obtained by "raising" each point on the first graph by two units because, for a certain value of x, the corresponding y value is two units greater. This is shown in Figure 13-12(a). Similarly, to sketch the graph of $y = x - 2$, we first draw the graph of $y = x$ and then lower each point vertically by two units, as shown in Figure 13-12(b).

The graphs of $y = x + 2$ and $y = x - 2$ are straight lines. Moreover, the lines whose equations are $y = x$, $y = x + 2$, and $y = x - 2$ are parallel. In general, for a given value of m, the graph of $y = mx + b$ is a straight line through $(0, b)$ and parallel to the line whose equation is $y = mx$. Hence, *two nonvertical lines are parallel if their slopes are equal.*

Figure 13-12

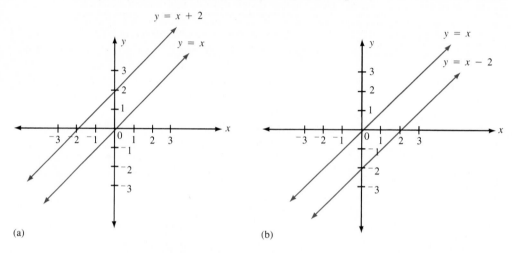

(a)   (b)

The graph of the line $y = mx + b$, where $b > 0$, can be obtained from the graph of $y = mx$ by sliding $y = mx$ up b units, as shown in Figure 13-13. If $b < 0$, $y = mx$ must be slid down $|b|$ units.

Figure 13-13

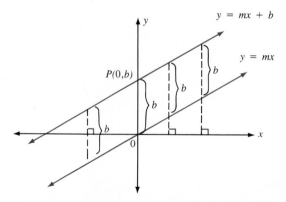

The graph of $y = mx + b$ in Figure 13-13 crosses the y-axis at the point $P(0, b)$. The value of y at the point of intersection of any line with the y-axis
y-intercept   is called the **y-intercept.** Thus, b is the y-intercept of $y = mx + b$, and this
slope-intercept form   form of the equation of a straight line is called the **slope-intercept form.** Sim-

ilarly, the value of x at the point of intersection of a line with the x-axis is
x-intercept   called the **x-intercept.**

Example 13-3

Given the equation $y - 3x = {}^-6$, find each of the following.

(a) The slope of the line
(b) The y-intercept
(c) The x-intercept
(d) Sketch the graph of the equation.

Solution

(a) To write the equation in the form $y = mx + b$, we add $3x$ to both sides
of the given equation to obtain $y = 3x + ({}^-6)$. Hence, the slope is 3.
(b) The form $y = 3x + ({}^-6)$ shows that $b = {}^-6$, which is the y-intercept.
(The y-intercept can also be found directly by substituting $x = 0$ in the
equation and finding the corresponding value of y.)
(c) The x-intercept is the x-coordinate of the point where the graph
intersects the x-axis. At that point, $y = 0$. Substituting 0 for y in
$y = 3x - 6$ gives 2 as the x-intercept.
(d) The y-intercept and x-intercept are located at $(0, {}^-6)$ and $(2, 0)$ on the
line. Plot these points and draw the line through them to obtain the
desired graph, as shown in Figure 13-14. Note that any two points
of the line can be used to sketch the graph because any two points
determine a line.

Figure 13-14

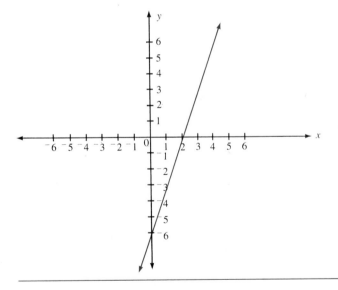

The equation $y = b$ can be written in slope-intercept form as $y = 0 \cdot x + b$.
Consequently, its slope is 0 and its y-intercept is b. This should not be surprising because the line is parallel to the x-axis; consequently, its steepness,
or slope, should be 0. Any vertical line parallel to the y-axis has equation
$x = a$ for some real number a. This equation cannot be written in slope-intercept form. The slope of a vertical line is undefined and will be discussed
later in the chapter. In general, *every straight line has an equation of either*

linear equation

the form $y = mx + b$ *or* $x = a$. Any equation that can be put in one of these forms is called a **linear equation.**

EQUATION OF A LINE

> Every straight line has an equation of either the form $y = mx + b$ or $x = a$.

WRITING LINEAR EQUATIONS

Because a line is determined by any two of its points, then given the coordinates of two points on a line, it is possible to find the equation of the line. For example, given $A(4, 2)$ and $B(1, 6)$, we can find the equation of $\overrightarrow{AB}$. Because the line is not perpendicular to the x-axis (why?), it must be of the form $y = mx + b$. Substituting the coordinates of A and B in $y = mx + b$ results in the following equations.

$$2 = m \cdot 4 + b \quad \text{or} \quad 2 = 4m + b$$

$$6 = m \cdot 1 + b \quad \text{or} \quad 6 = m + b$$

To find the equation of the line, we must find the values of m and b. If we solve for b in each of these equations, we obtain $b = 2 - 4m$ and $b = 6 - m$, respectively. Consequently, $2 - 4m = 6 - m$, so $m = {}^-\frac{4}{3}$. Substituting this value of m in either of the equations gives $b = \frac{22}{3}$. Consequently, the equation of the line through A and B is $y = {}^-\frac{4}{3}x + \frac{22}{3}$. The correctness of this equation can be checked by substituting the coordinates of the two given points, $A(4, 2)$ and $B(1, 6)$, in the equation.

Using an analogous approach, it is possible to find a general formula for the slope of a line given two points on the line, $A(x_1, y_1)$ and $B(x_2, y_2)$. If the line is not a vertical line, its equation is given by $y = mx + b$. Substituting the coordinates of A and B into this equation gives the following.

$$y_1 = mx_1 + b \quad \text{and, therefore,} \quad y_1 - mx_1 = b$$

$$y_2 = mx_2 + b \quad \text{and, therefore,} \quad y_2 - mx_2 = b$$

By equating these two values for b and solving for m, the formula for slope results.

$$y_1 - mx_1 = y_2 - mx_2$$

$$mx_2 - mx_1 = y_2 - y_1$$

$$m(x_2 - x_1) = y_2 - y_1$$

$$m = \frac{y_2 - y_1}{x_2 - x_1}$$

SLOPE FORMULA

> Given two points $A(x_1, y_1)$ and $B(x_2, y_2)$ with $x_1 \neq x_2$, the slope m of the line $\overleftrightarrow{AB}$ is given by $m = \dfrac{y_2 - y_1}{x_2 - x_1}$.

By multiplying both the numerator and denominator on the right side of the slope formula by $^-1$, we obtain

$$m = \frac{y_2 - y_1}{x_2 - x_1} = \frac{(y_2 - y_1)(^-1)}{(x_2 - x_1)(^-1)} = \frac{y_1 - y_2}{x_1 - x_2}$$

This shows that it is irrelevant which point is named (x_1, y_1) and which is named (x_2, y_2) but *the order of the coordinates in the subtraction must be consistent.* The slope of the line $\overleftrightarrow{AB}$ is the change in y-coordinates divided by the corresponding change in x-coordinates of any two points on $\overleftrightarrow{AB}$. The difference $x_2 - x_1$ is often called the **run,** and the difference $y_2 - y_1$ is called the **rise.** Thus, the slope is often defined as "rise over run," or $\dfrac{\text{rise}}{\text{run}}$. The slope formula can be interpreted geometrically as shown in Figure 13-15.

run

rise

Figure 13-15

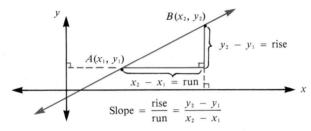

$$\text{Slope} = \frac{\text{rise}}{\text{run}} = \frac{y_2 - y_1}{x_2 - x_1}$$

Example 13-4

Find the slope of $\overleftrightarrow{AB}$ given $A(3, 1)$ and $B(5, 4)$.

Solution

$$m = \frac{4 - 1}{5 - 3} = \frac{3}{2} \quad \text{or} \quad \frac{1 - 4}{3 - 5} = \frac{^-3}{^-2} = \frac{3}{2}$$

Example 13-5

Find the slope and the equation of the line passing through the points $A(^-3, 4)$ and $B(^-1, 0)$.

Solution

First method.

$$m = \frac{4 - 0}{^-3 - (^-1)} = \frac{4}{^-2} = {}^-2$$

The equation of the line must be of the form $y = mx + b$. Because $m = {}^-2$, $y = {}^-2x + b$ and now the value of b must be found. The required line contains each of the given points, so the coordinates of each point must satisfy the equation. We substitute the coordinates of $B(^-1, 0)$ into $y = {}^-2x + b$ and proceed as follows.

$$y = {}^-2x + b$$
$$0 = {}^-2(^-1) + b$$
$$0 = 2 + b$$
$${}^-2 = b$$

The required equation is $y = {}^-2x + {}^-2$, or $y = {}^-2x - 2$. To check that $y = {}^-2x - 2$ is the required equation, we must verify that the coordinates of both A and B satisfy the equation. The verification is left for you.

Second method. This approach uses the fact that $\dfrac{\text{rise}}{\text{run}}$ is the same for any two points on a line. We found that $m = {}^-2$. Point $P(x, y)$ represents a point on the line shown in Figure 13-16 if and only if the slope determined by P and B (or P and A) equals the slope of the line, which was found to be ${}^-2$. Using the slope formula, the slope determined by P and B is

$$\frac{y - 0}{x - ({}^-1)} \quad \text{or} \quad \frac{y}{x + 1}$$

Figure 13-16

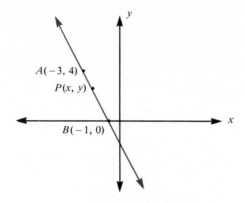

Hence, $P(x, y)$ is on $\overrightarrow{AB}$ if and only if

$$\frac{y}{x + 1} = {}^-2$$

$$y = {}^-2(x + 1), \text{ or}$$

$$y = {}^-2x - 2$$

Following the second method of solution in the preceding example, we can use the slope formula to find the equation of a line given any point on the line and the slope of the line. In Figure 13-17, line ℓ has slope m and contains a given point (x_1, y_1). Point (x, y) represents any other point on line ℓ if and only if the slope determined by points (x_1, y_1) and (x, y) is m. We use the slope formula and proceed as follows.

Figure 13-17

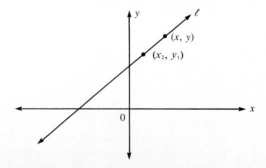

$$\frac{y - y_1}{x - x_1} = m$$

$$y - y_1 = m(x - x_1)$$

point-slope form   The result is called the **point-slope form** of a line.

POINT-SLOPE
FORM OF A LINE

> The equation of a line with slope m through a given point (x_1, y_1) is $y - y_1 = m(x - x_1)$.

To examine the slope of a vertical line, pick any two points on the line, (x_1, y_1) and (x_2, y_2). Since the line is vertical, $x_1 = x_2$. Consequently,

$$m = \frac{y_2 - y_1}{x_2 - x_1} = \frac{y_2 - y_1}{0}$$

which is not meaningful. Thus, *the slope of a vertical line is undefined.* Consequently, we can also state that *any two lines are parallel if they both have the same slope or both lines have undefined slope.*

GRAPHING INEQUALITIES

In applications of mathematics, we often need to graph inequalities as well as equations. Consider, for example, the inequality $y - 3x > {}^-6$. This inequality is equivalent to $y > 3x + ({}^-6)$. A point whose coordinates satisfy $y > 3x + ({}^-6)$ is above the line represented by $y = 3x + ({}^-6)$. Consequently, the graph of the inequality is the half-plane above the line given by $y = 3x + ({}^-6)$. The graph is sketched in Figure 13-18. To indicate that the line itself is not included in the graph, the line is dashed.

Figure 13-18

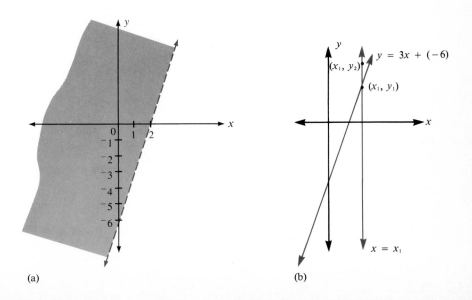

(a)

(b)

Remark   The fact that the graph of $y > 3x + (^-6)$ is the region above the line can be explained using Figure 13-18(b) as follows. For every point (x_1, y_1) on the line $y = 3x + (^-6)$, we have $y_1 = 3x_1 + (^-6)$. If $y_2 > y_1$, then (x_1, y_2) is on the line $x = x_1$ above the point (x_1, y_1).

The graph of any inequality in one of the forms $y > mx + b$ or $y < mx + b$ is a half-plane either above or below the line $y = mx + b$. Thus, in order to graph an inequality like $y - 3x > ^-6$, we first graph the corresponding straight line. Then, we check some point not on the line to see if it satisfies the inequality. If it does, the half-plane containing the point is the graph, and if not, the half-plane not including the point is the graph. For example, checking $(0, 0)$ in $y - 3x > ^-6$ gives $0 - 3 \cdot 0 > ^-6$, which is a true statement. Thus, the half-plane determined by $y - 3x = ^-6$ and containing the origin is the graph of the inequality, as pictured in Figure 13-18(a).

Example 13-6

Graph the following inequalities on the same coordinate system to determine all points that satisfy both inequalities.

(1) $2x + 3y > 6$

(2) $x - y \leq 0$

Solution

First, we graph the lines represented by the equations $2x + 3y = 6$ and $x - y = 0$. Next, we must determine the half-planes to be shaded. Substituting $x = 0$ and $y = 0$ in inequality (1) gives $0 > 6$, a false statement, so the required half-plane determined by the first inequality does not contain the point $(0, 0)$. In Figure 13-19, the graph of this inequality is marked with vertical colored lines. Substituting $x = 0$ and $y = 0$ in inequality (2) gives $0 \leq 0$, a true statement. Thus, $(0, 0)$ is part of the required solution. However, $(0, 0)$ is on the line $x - y = 0$, so it is in neither of the half-planes determined by this line. Another point must be checked. Consider, for example, $(1, 2)$. Substituting $x = 1$ and $y = 2$ in inequality (2) gives $^-1 \leq 0$, a true statement; hence, $(1, 2)$ is in the half-plane determined by equation

Figure 13-19

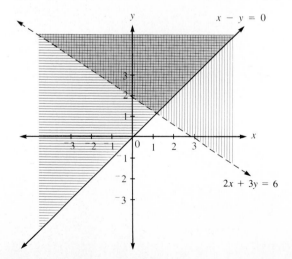

(2). In Figure 13-19, the graph of this inequality is marked with horizontal black lines. Hence, the set of common points is the crosshatched, shaded portion of Figure 13-19.

PROBLEM SET 13-2

1. Sketch the graphs of the equations $y = {}^-x$ and $y = {}^-x + 3$ on the same coordinate system.
2. The graph of $y = mx$ is given in the accompanying figure. Sketch the graphs for each of the following on the same figure.
   (a) $y = mx + 3$ (b) $y = mx - 3$

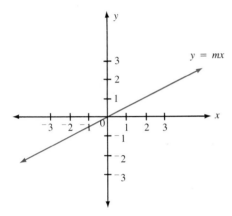

3. Sketch the graphs for each of the following equations or inequalities.

   (a) $y = \dfrac{{}^-3}{4}x + 3$ (b) $y = 3x - 1$

   (c) $y = {}^-3$ (d) $x = {}^-2$

   (e) $y \geq 15x - 30$ (f) $y \leq \dfrac{1}{20}x$

4. Find the x-intercept and y-intercept for the equations in Problem 3, if they exist.
5. In Section 12-6, a relationship between the Fahrenheit and Celsius scales for measuring temperature was discussed. Sketch the graphs of the following.
   (a) The temperature y in degrees Fahrenheit as a function of the temperature x in degrees Celsius using the formula $y = \frac{9}{5}x + 32$
   (b) The temperature y in degrees Celsius as a function of the temperature x in degrees Fahrenheit using the formula $y = \frac{5}{9}(x - 32)$
   (c) If the graphs in (a) and (b) are drawn in the same coordinate system, describe their relationship to each other.
6. Write each of the equations in slope-intercept form.
   (a) $3y - x = 0$ (b) $x + y = 3$

   (c) $3x - 4y + 7 = 0$ (d) $x = 3y$
   (e) $x - y = 4(x - y)$
7. For each of the following, find the slope, if it exists, of the line determined by the given pair of points.
   (a) $(4, 3)$ and $({}^-5, 0)$
   (b) $({}^-4, 1)$ and $(5, 2)$
   (c) $(\sqrt{5}, 2)$ and $(1, 2)$
   (d) $({}^-3, 81)$ and $({}^-3, 198)$
   (e) $(1.0001, 12)$ and $(1, 10)$
   (f) (a, a) and (b, b)
8. For each of the following, write the equation of the line determined by the given pair of points in slope-intercept form or in the form $x = a$.
   (a) $({}^-4, 3)$ and $(1, {}^-2)$
   (b) $(0, 0)$ and $(2, 1)$
   (c) $(0, 1)$ and $(2, 1)$
   (d) $(2, 1)$ and $(2, {}^-1)$

   (e) $\left(0, \dfrac{{}^-1}{2}\right)$ and $\left(\dfrac{1}{2}, 0\right)$

   (f) $({}^-a, 0)$ and $(a, 0)$, $a \neq 0$
9. Use slopes to determine which of the following pairs of lines are parallel.
   (a) $y = 2x - 1$ and $y = 2x + 7$
   (b) $4y - 3x + 4 = 0$ and $8y - 6x + 1 = 0$
   (c) $y - 2x = 0$ and $4x - 2y = 3$

   (d) $\dfrac{x}{3} + \dfrac{y}{4} = 1$ and $y = \dfrac{4}{3}x$

10. For each of the following, find the equation of a line through $P({}^-2, 3)$ and parallel to the line represented by the given equation.
    (a) $y = {}^-2x$ (b) $3y + 2x + 1 = 0$
    (c) $x = 3$ (d) $y = {}^-4$
11. Determine the slopes of each of the following lines.

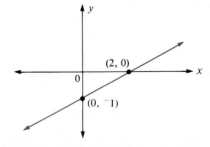

(a)

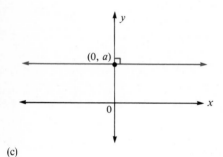

(b)

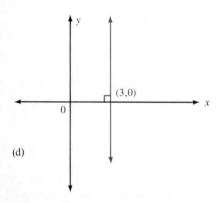

(c)

(d)

12. The door on a house was 4 feet above ground level. To allow handicap access, a ramp with a slope of $\frac{1}{10}$ was placed from the ground to the door. How long was the ramp?

13. (a) Let ℓ be a nonvertical line through the origin. Let n be a vertical line through $(1, 0)$. Show that P, the point of intersection of ℓ and n, has coordinates $(1, m)$, where m is the slope of ℓ.
    (b) Let b be a real number and ℓ be a nonvertical line through $(0, b)$. Let P be the point where ℓ intersects the vertical line n through $(1, 0)$. Show that the y-coordinate of P is the sum of b and the slope of ℓ.

14. Use slopes to show that the vertices $A(2, 1)$, $B(3, 5)$, $C(^-5, 1)$, and $D(^-6, ^-3)$ form a parallelogram.

15. Use slopes to show that the points represented by $(0, ^-1)$, $(1, 2)$, and $(^-1, ^-4)$ are collinear.

16. For each of the following, find the equation of the line that passes through the given point and has the given slope.

    (a) $(^-3, 0)$ with slope $\dfrac{^-1}{2}$

    (b) $(1, ^-3)$ with slope $\dfrac{2}{3}$

    (c) $(^-1, ^-5)$ with slope $\dfrac{^-5}{7}$

17. Find the x-intercept and y-intercept of the line whose equation is $\dfrac{x}{a} + \dfrac{y}{b} = 1$, where $a \neq 0$ and $b \neq 0$.

18. Find the equation of the flip image of the line $y = 3x + 1$ in each of the following.
    (a) The x-axis
    (b) The y-axis
    (c) The line $y = x$

19. Graph each of the following inequalities.
    (a) $x - y + 3 > 0$ (b) $2x > 3y$
    (c) $x - 2y + 1 \leq 0$ (d) $x - 2y + 1 \geq 0$

20. Graph all the points that satisfy the following.
    (a) $x - y + 3 > 0$ and $y - 2x - 1 < 0$
    (b) $x > 3$, $y < ^-4$, and $x - y - 3 > 0$
    (c) $x + y + 3 = 0$ and $x - y > 3$

21. Find the equation of the image of the line $y = x$ under the following transformations.
    (a) Flip in the x-axis
    (b) Flip in the y-axis
    (c) Turn of $45°$ counterclockwise about the origin
    (d) Turn of $90°$ counterclockwise about the origin
    (e) Half-turn with the center at the origin
    (f) A slide in the direction of the x-axis, three units to the right
    (g) A slide in the direction of the y-axis, three units up

22. (a) Sketch the graphs of $y = 2x + 3$ and $y = ^-2x - 3$ on the same coordinate system. How are the graphs related?
    ★(b) How are the graphs $y = mx + b$ and $y = ^-mx - b$ related?

23. Find the equation of the image of the line $x - y = 1$ under the following transformations.
    (a) Flip in the x-axis
    (b) Flip in the y-axis
    (c) Flip in the line $y = x$
    (d) Half-turn with the center at the origin

24. (a) The number of chirps made by a cricket is linearly related to the temperature. If a cricket chirped 40 times a minute when it was $10°C$ and 112 times a minute when it was $20°C$, find an equation to describe this relationship.
    (b) At what temperature would you expect the cricket not to chirp?

25. (a) Sketch the graphs of $y = \frac{2}{3}x + 1$ and $y = ^{-}\frac{3}{2}x + 1$ on the same coordinate system.
(b) Use a protractor to measure the angle between the lines in (a).
(c) Repeat (a) and (b) for $y = \frac{4}{5}x + 2$ and $y = ^{-}\frac{5}{4}x + 2$.
(d) Make a conjecture that generalizes your findings in (b) and (c).

★ 26. (a) Use the given drawing and properties of similar triangles to prove that the slopes m_1 and m_2 of two perpendicular lines ℓ_1 and ℓ_2 satisfy the relationship $m_1 m_2 = ^{-}1$.
(b) Prove that if $CD = 1$, then $m_1 = AD$ and $m_2 = ^{-}DB$.

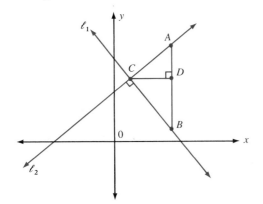

★ 27. Graph each of the following equations.
(a) $y = |x|$ (b) $|y| = x$
(c) $|y| = |x|$ (d) $|x + y| = 1$
(e) $|x| + |y| = 1$ (f) $|x| \leq |y|$

Review Problems

28. Find the equations for each of the following.
(a) The line containing $(^{-}7, ^{-}8)$ and parallel to the x-axis
(b) The line containing $(^{-}7, ^{-}8)$ and perpendicular to the x-axis

29. Find the coordinates of two other points collinear with the given points.
(a) $P(^{-}2, ^{-}2), Q(^{-}4, ^{-}2)$
(b) $P(^{-}7, ^{-}8), Q(3, 4)$

30. Plot each of the points $A(2, 2)$, $B(6, 6)$, and $C(8, ^{-}4)$ and then find the coordinates of a point D such that quadrilateral $ABCD$ is a parallelogram.

31. Find the area of the triangle whose vertices are the following.
(a) $(0, 0), (3, 0), (1, 1)$
(b) $(0, 0), (6, 3), (10, 0)$
(c) $(0, 0), (0, ^{-}5), (3, 3)$
(d) $(1, 2), (5, 2), (^{-}8, 8)$
(e) $(0, 0), (1, 1), (7, 1)$

Section 13-3

Systems of Linear Equations

The mathematical descriptions of many problems involve more than one equation, each involving more than one unknown. To solve such problems, a common solution to the equations must be found, if it exists. For example, finding the solution to a problem may involve finding all x and y values that satisfy both $y = x + 3$ and $y = 2x - 1$. Together, $y = x + 3$ and $y = 2x - 1$ are an example of a **system of linear equations.** Any solution to the system is an ordered pair (x, y) that satisfies both equations. Systems of linear equations arise in many story problems. Consider the following.

system of linear equations

Example 13-7

May Chin ordered lunch for herself and several friends by phone without checking prices. Once, she paid $7.00 for 5 soyburgers and 4 orders of fries, and another time she paid $6.00 for 4 of each. Set up a system of equations with two unknowns representing the prices of a soyburger and an order of fries, respectively.

Solution

Let x be the price in dollars of a soyburger and let y be the price of an order of fries. Five soyburgers cost $5x$ dollars and 4 orders of fries cost $4y$ dollars. Because May paid $7.00 for the order, we have $5x + 4y = 7$. Similarly, $4x + 4y = 6$, or $2x + 2y = 3$.

SYSTEMS WITH ONE SOLUTION

Geometrically, an ordered pair satisfying both equations is a point that belongs to each of the lines. Figure 13-20 shows the graphs of $5x + 4y = 7$ and $2x + 2y = 3$. The two lines appear to intersect at $(1, \frac{1}{2})$. Thus, $(1, \frac{1}{2})$ appears to be the solution of the given system of equations. This solution can be checked by substituting 1 for x and $\frac{1}{2}$ for y in each equation. Because $5 \cdot 1 + 4 \cdot \frac{1}{2} = 7$ and $2 \cdot 1 + 2 \cdot \frac{1}{2} = 3$, the ordered pair $(1, \frac{1}{2})$ is a solution. The lines intersect in one point. Thus, $(1, \frac{1}{2})$ is the only solution to the system.

Figure 13-20

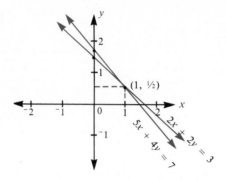

In the upper elementary grades, students learn to graph linear equations. Often, they also learn the relationship between a pair of linear equations and the intersection of two lines, as the excerpt on page 639 from *Addison-Wesley Mathematics*, 1987, Grade 8 shows.

There are certain drawbacks to graphically estimating a solution to a system of equations. The sketch of a graph is often inaccurate, especially if noninteger real numbers are involved in the solution. Moreover, the graphic approach is impractical in solving linear equations with three variables and impossible when more than three variables are involved. There are various algebraic methods for solving systems of linear equations. Consider, for example, the system $y = x + 3$ and $y = 2x - 1$. Because the solution (x, y) must satisfy each equation, we want x and y in each equation to be the same. Consequently, the expressions $x + 3$ and $2x - 1$ can be equated. The equation $x + 3 = 2x - 1$ has one unknown, x. Solving for x gives $3 + 1 = 2x - x$, and, hence, $4 = x$. Substituting 4 for x in either equation gives $y = 7$. Thus, $(4, 7)$ is the solution to the given system. As before, this solution can be checked by substituting the obtained values for x and y in the original equation. This method for solving a system of linear equations is called the

substitution method

substitution method.

Example 13-8

Solve the following system.

$3x - 4y = 5$

$2x + 5y = 1$

Solution

First, rewrite each equation, expressing y in terms of x.

$$y = \frac{3x - 5}{4} \quad \text{and} \quad y = \frac{1 - 2x}{5}$$

Graphing Pairs of Equations

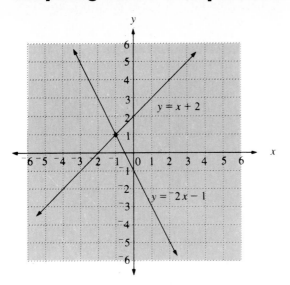

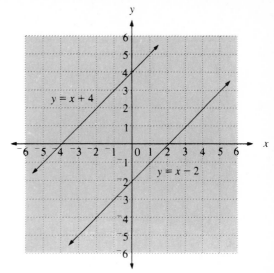

The two lines appear to intersect at Point P with coordinates $(-1, 1)$. To check, substitute $(-1, 1)$ in each equation.

$y = x + 2$ $y = {}^-2x - 1$

$1 = {}^-1 + 2$ $1 = {}^-2 \cdot {}^-1 - 1$

True   True

The graphs of the equations $y = x + 4$ and $y = x - 2$ do not intersect. The two lines are **parallel.**

Then, equate the expressions for y and solve the resulting equation for x.

$$\frac{3x - 5}{4} = \frac{1 - 2x}{5}$$

$$5(3x - 5) = 4(1 - 2x)$$

$$15x - 25 = 4 - 8x$$

$$23x = 29$$

$$x = \frac{29}{23}$$

Substituting $\dfrac{29}{23}$ for x in $y = \dfrac{3x - 5}{4}$ gives $y = \dfrac{{}^-7}{23}$. Hence, $x = \dfrac{29}{23}$ and $y = \dfrac{{}^-7}{23}$. This can be checked by substituting the values for x and y in the original equations.

Remark   Sometimes, it is more convenient to solve a system of equations by expressing x in terms of y in one of the equations and substituting the obtained expression for x in the other equation.

elimination method

   The **elimination method** for solving two equations with two unknowns is based on eliminating one of the variables by adding or subtracting the original or equivalent equations. For example, consider the system

$$x - y = {}^-3$$

$$x + y = 7$$

By adding the two equations, the variable y is eliminated. The resulting equation can be solved for x.

$$
\begin{array}{rl}
x - y = & {}^-3 \\
x + y = & 7 \\
\hline
2x \quad\;\; = & 4 \\
x \quad\;\; = & 2
\end{array}
$$

Substituting 2 for x in the first equation (either equation may be used) gives $2 - y = {}^-3$ and, hence, $y = 5$. Checking this result shows that $x = 2$ and $y = 5$, or $(2, 5)$, is the solution to the system.

   Often, another operation is required before equations are added so that an unknown can be eliminated. For example, consider the following system.

$$3x + 2y = 5$$

$$5x - 4y = 3$$

Adding the equations does not eliminate either unknown. If the first equation contained $4y$ rather than $2y$, the variable y could be eliminated by adding. To obtain $4y$ in the first equation, multiply both sides of the equation by 2 to obtain the equivalent equation $6x + 4y = 10$. Adding the equations in the equivalent system gives the following.

$$
\begin{array}{rl}
6x + 4y = & 10 \\
5x - 4y = & 3 \\
\hline
11x \quad\;\; = & 13 \\
x \quad\;\; = & \dfrac{13}{11}
\end{array}
$$

To find the corresponding value of y, substitute $\frac{13}{11}$ for x in either of the original equations and solve for y, or use the elimination method again and solve for y.

   To eliminate the x-values from the original system, multiply the first equation by 5 and the second by $^-3$ (or the first by $^-5$ and the second by 3). Then, add and solve for y.

$$
\begin{array}{rl}
15x + 10y = & 25 \\
{}^-15x + 12y = & {}^-9 \\
\hline
22y = & 16 \\
y = \dfrac{16}{22} & \text{or} \quad \dfrac{8}{11}
\end{array}
$$

Consequently, $(\frac{13}{11}, \frac{8}{11})$ is the solution of the original system. This solution, as always, should be checked by substitution in the *original* equations.

SOLUTIONS TO OTHER SYSTEMS

All examples thus far have had unique solutions. However, other situations may arise. Geometrically, a system of two linear equations can be characterized as follows:

1. The system has a unique solution if and only if the graphs of the equations intersect in a single point.
2. The system has no solution if and only if the equations represent parallel lines.
3. The system has infinitely many solutions if and only if the equations represent the same line.

Consider the following system.

$$2x - 3y = 1$$

$$^-4x + 6y = 5$$

In an attempt to solve for x, we multiply the first equation by 2 and then add as follows.

$$\begin{array}{r} 4x - 6y = 2 \\ ^-4x + 6y = 5 \\ \hline 0 = 7 \end{array}$$

A false statement results. Logically, a false result can occur only on the basis of a false assumption or an incorrect procedure. Because our procedure is correct in this case, there must be a false assumption. We assumed that the system has a solution. That assumption caused a false statement; therefore, the assumption itself must be false. Hence, the system has no solution. In other words, the solution set is $\varnothing$. This situation arises if and only if the corresponding lines are parallel.

Next, consider the following system.

$$2x - 3y = 1$$

$$^-4x + 6y = {}^-2$$

To solve this system, we multiply the first equation by 2 and add as follows.

$$\begin{array}{r} 4x - 6y = 2 \\ ^-4x + 6y = {}^-2 \\ \hline 0 = 0 \end{array}$$

The resulting statement, $0 = 0$, is always true. Rewriting the equation as $0 \cdot x + 0 \cdot y = 0$ shows that all values of x and y satisfy this equation. The values of x and y that satisfy both $0 \cdot x + 0 \cdot y = 0$ and $2x - 3y = 1$ are those that satisfy $2x - 3y = 1$. There are infinitely many such pairs x and y that correspond to points on the line $2x - 3y = 1$ and hence to $^-4x + 6y = {}^-2$.

One way to check that a system has infinitely many solutions is by observing whether each of the original equations represents the same line. In the preceding system, both equations may be written as $y = \frac{2}{3}x - \frac{1}{3}$. Another way to check that a system has infinitely many solutions is to observe whether one equation can be multiplied by some number to obtain the second equation. For example, multiplying the equation $2x - 3y = 1$ by $^-2$ yields the second equation, $^-4x + 6y = ^-2$.

Example 13-9

Identify each of the following systems as having a unique solution, no solution, or infinitely many solutions.

(a) $2x - 3y = 5$ (b) $\dfrac{x}{3} - \dfrac{y}{4} = 1$ (c) $6x - 9y = 5$

$\dfrac{1}{2}x - y = 1$ $3y - 4x + 12 = 0$ $^-8x + 12y = 7$

Solution

One approach is to attempt to solve each system. Another approach is to write each equation in the slope-intercept form and interpret the system geometrically.

(a) *First method.*   To eliminate x, multiply the second equation by $^-4$ and add the equations.

$$
\begin{array}{r}
2x - 3y = 5 \\
^-2x + 4y = ^-4 \\
\hline
y = 1
\end{array}
$$

Substituting 1 for y in either equation gives $x = 4$. Thus, $(4, 1)$ is the unique solution of the system.

Second method.   In slope-intercept form, the first equation is $y = \frac{2}{3}x - \frac{5}{3}$. The second equation is $y = \frac{1}{2}x - 1$. The slopes of the corresponding lines are $\frac{2}{3}$ and $\frac{1}{2}$, respectively. Consequently, the lines are distinct and are not parallel and, therefore, intersect in a single point whose coordinates are the unique solution to the original system.

(b) *First method.*   Multiply the first equation by 12 and rewrite the second equation as $^-4x + 3y = ^-12$. Then, adding the resulting equations gives the following.

$$
\begin{array}{r}
4x - 3y = 12 \\
^-4x + 3y = ^-12 \\
\hline
0 = 0
\end{array}
$$

Because every pair (x, y) satisfies $0 \cdot x + 0 \cdot y = 0$, the original system has infinitely many solutions.

Second method.   In slope-intercept form, both equations have the form

$$y = \frac{4}{3}x - 4$$

Thus, the two lines are identical, so the system has infinitely many solutions.

(c) *First method.*   To eliminate y, multiply the first equation by 4 and the second by 3; then, add the resulting equations.

$$24x - 36y = 20$$
$$^-24x + 36y = 21$$
$$\overline{ 0 = 41}$$

No pair of numbers satisfies $0 \cdot x + 0 \cdot y = 41$, so this equation has no solutions, and, consequently, the original system has no solutions.

Second method.   In slope-intercept form, the first equation is $y = \frac{2}{3}x - \frac{5}{9}$. The second equation is $y = \frac{2}{3}x + \frac{7}{12}$. The corresponding lines have the same slope, $\frac{2}{3}$, but different y-intercepts. Consequently, the lines are parallel and the original system has no solution.

Example 13-10

At the Park Street Restaurant, one can get two eggs with sausage for $1.80, or one egg with sausage for $1.35. If there is no break in price for quantity, what is the cost of one egg?

Solution

Let x be the cost of one egg and y be the cost of the sausage. The cost of two eggs and sausage is $2x + y$, or $1.80. The cost of one egg and sausage is $x + y$, or $1.35. Thus, the following system is obtained.

$$2x + y = 1.80$$
$$x + y = 1.35$$

Subtracting the equations gives $x = 0.45$. Thus, the cost of one egg is $0.45.

PROBLEM SET 13-3

1. Use the equation $2x - 3y = 5$ for each of the following.
   (a) Find four solutions of the equation.
   (b) Graph all the solutions for which $^-2 \le x \le 2$.
   (c) Graph all the solutions for which $0 \le y \le 2$.
2. Solve each of the following systems, if possible. Indicate whether the system has a unique solution, infinitely many solutions, or no solution.
   (a) $y = 3x - 1$
       $y = \ x + 3$
   (b) $2x + 3y = 1$
       $3x - \ y = 1$
   (c) $3x + 4y = \ ^-17$
       $2x + 3y = \ ^-13$
   (d) $5x - 18y = 0$
       $x - 24y = 0$
   (e) $2x - 6y = \ 7$
       $3x - 9y = 10$
   (f) $8y - \ 6x = 78$
       $9x - 12y = 12$
3. Solve each of the following systems, if possible. If a solution is not possible, explain why not.
   (a) $y = x + 3$
       $3x - 4y + 1 = 0$
   (b) $\dfrac{x}{3} - \dfrac{y}{4} = 1$
       $\dfrac{x}{5} - \dfrac{y}{3} = 2$

(c) $3x - 4y = \ ^-x + 3$
    $x - 2\ \ = 4(y - 3)$
(d) $x - y = \dfrac{x}{3}$

    $y - x = \dfrac{3}{4}y + 1$

(e) $x - y = \dfrac{2}{3}(x + y)$
    $x + y = \dfrac{2}{3}(x - y)$
(f) $\sqrt{2}x - y = 3$
    $x - \sqrt{2}y = 1$

4. Using the concept of slope, identify whether each of the following systems has a unique solution, infinitely many solutions, or no solution.
   (a) $3x - 4y = 5$
       $\dfrac{x}{3} - \dfrac{y}{5} = 1$
   (b) $4y - 3x + \ 4 = 0$
       $8y - 6x + 40 = 0$
   (c) $3y - 2x = 15$
       $\dfrac{2}{3}x - y + 5 = 0$

5. The vertices of a triangle are given by (0, 0), (10, 0), and (6, 8). Show that the segments connecting (5, 0) and (6, 8), (10, 0) and (3, 4), and (0, 0) and (8, 4) intersect at a common point.
6. Two adjacent sides of a parallelogram are on lines with equations $x - 3y + 3 = 0$ and $x + 2y - 2 = 0$. One vertex is at (0, ⁻4). Write the equations of the lines containing the other two sides.
7. Find the area of the triangle bounded by the lines $y = 2x + 3$, $x + y = 5$, and $x = 3$.
8. Find the area of $\triangle ABC$ in the figure if the equations of lines ℓ and m are $y = 4x + 2$ and $\dfrac{x}{3} + \dfrac{y}{5} = 1$, respectively, $\overline{AB}$ is parallel to the x-axis, and A is on the y-axis.

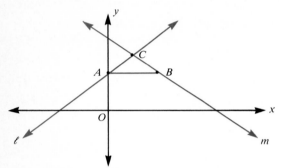

9. The sum of two numbers is $\frac{3}{4}$ and their difference is $\frac{7}{9}$. Find the numbers.
10. The owner of a 5000-gallon oil truck loads the truck with gasoline and kerosene. The profit on each gallon of gasoline is 13¢ and on each gallon of kerosene is 12¢. Find how many gallons of each fuel the owner loaded if the profit was $640.
11. A health-food store has two different kinds of granola—cashew nut granola selling at $1.80 a pound and golden granola selling at $1.20 a pound. How much of each kind should be mixed to produce a 200-pound mixture selling at $1.60 a pound?
12. A laboratory carries two different solutions of the same acid, a 60% solution and a 90% solution. How many liters of each solution should be mixed in order to produce 150 L of 80% solution?
13. A physician invests $80,000 in two stocks. At the end of the year, the physician sells the stocks, the

first at a 15% profit and the second at a 20% profit. How much did the physician invest in each stock if the total profit was $15,000?
14. At the end of 10 months, the balance of an account earning simple interest is $2100.
 (a) If, at the end of 18 months, the balance is $2180, how much money was originally in the account?
 (b) What is the rate of interest?
15. If five times the width of a water bed equals four times its length and its perimeter is 270 inches, what are the length and width of the bed?
16. Josephine's bank contains 27 coins. If all the coins are either dimes or quarters and the value of the coins is $5.25, how many of each kind of coin are there?
★17. (a) Solve each of the following systems of equations. What do you notice about the answers?
 (i) $x + 2y = 3$ (ii) $2x + 3y = 4$
   $4x + 5y = 6$ $5x + 6y = 7$
 (iii) $31x + 32y = 33$
   $34x + 35y = 36$
 (b) Write another system similar to those in (a). What solution did you expect? Check your guess.
 (c) Write a general system similar to those in (a). What solution does this system have? Why?

Review Problems

18. Which of the following are not equations of lines?
 (a) $x + y = 3$ (b) $xy = 7$
 (c) $2x + 3y \le 4$ (d) $y = 5$
19. Find the slope and y-intercept of each of the following.
 (a) $6y + 5x = 7$ (b) $\dfrac{2}{3}x + \dfrac{1}{2}y = \dfrac{1}{5}$
 (c) $0.2y - 0.75x - 0.37 = 0$ (d) $y = 4$
20. Write the equations of each of the following.
 (a) A line through (4, 7) and (⁻6, ⁻2)
 (b) A line through (4, 7) parallel to the line $y = \frac{5}{3}x + 6$
 (c) A line through (⁻6, ⁻8) perpendicular to the y-axis
21. Graph each of the following.
 (a) $3x + 2y = 14$ (b) $⁻x - y = ⁻8$
 (c) $2x + 3y \le 4$ (d) $x - 16 \ge ⁻8y$

BRAIN TEASER

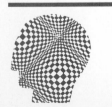

A school committee meeting began between 3:00 and 4:00 P.M. and ended between 6:00 and 7:00 P.M. The positions of the minute hand and the hour hand of the clock were reversed at the end of the meeting from what they were at the beginning of the meeting. When did the meeting start and end?

Section 13-4   The Distance and Midpoint Formulas

THE DISTANCE FORMULA

One way to *approximate* the distance between two points in a coordinate plane is to measure it with a ruler that has the same scale as the coordinate axes. Using algebraic techniques, we can calculate the *exact distance* between two points in the plane. First, suppose that the two points are on one of the axes. For example, in Figure 13-21(a), $A(2, 0)$ and $B(5, 0)$ are on the x-axis. The distance between these two points is three units.

$$AB = OB - OA = 5 - 2 = 3$$

Figure 13-21

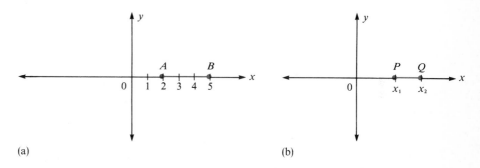

(a)   (b)

In general, if two points P and Q are on the x-axis, as in Figure 13-21(b), with x-coordinates x_1 and x_2, respectively, and $x_2 > x_1$, then $PQ = x_2 - x_1$. In fact, the distance between two points on the x-axis is the absolute value of the difference between the x coordinates of the points. (Why?)

DEFINITION

> Given two points $P(x_1, 0)$ and $Q(x_2, 0)$, the distance between them is given by $PQ = |x_2 - x_1| = |x_1 - x_2|$.

A similar definition is given for any two points on the y-axis.

DEFINITION

> Given two points $P(0, y_1)$ and $Q(0, y_2)$, the distance between them is given by $PQ = |y_2 - y_1| = |y_1 - y_2|$.

Figure 13-22 shows two points in the plane, $C(2, 5)$ and $D(6, 8)$. The distance between C and D can be found by drawing perpendiculars from the points to the x-axis and y-axis, respectively, which determines right triangle CDE. The lengths of the legs are found using horizontal and vertical distances and properties of rectangles.

$$CE = |6 - 2| = 4$$
$$DE = |5 - 8| = 3$$

Figure 13-22

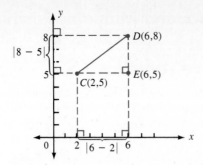

The distance between C and D can be found by applying the Pythagorean Theorem.

$$CD^2 = DE^2 + CE^2$$
$$= 3^2 + 4^2$$
$$= 25$$
$$CD = \sqrt{25}, \text{ or } 5$$

The method just described can be used to find a formula for the distance between any two points $A(x_1, y_1)$ and $B(x_2, y_2)$. Construct a right triangle with $\overline{AB}$ as one of its sides by drawing a line through A parallel to the x-axis and a line through B parallel to the y-axis, as shown in Figure 13-23. These lines intersect in point C, forming right triangle ABC. Now, apply the Pythagorean Theorem.

Figure 13-23

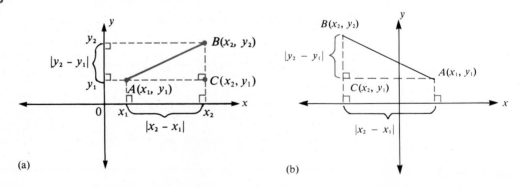

(a)   (b)

Figure 13-23 shows that $AC = |x_2 - x_1|$ and $BC = |y_2 - y_1|$. By the Pythagorean Theorem, $(AB)^2 = |x_2 - x_1|^2 + |y_2 - y_1|^2$, and, consequently, $AB = \sqrt{|x_2 - x_1|^2 + |y_2 - y_1|^2}$. Because $|x_2 - x_1|^2 = (x_2 - x_1)^2$ and $|y_2 - y_1|^2 = (y_2 - y_1)^2$, $AB = \sqrt{(x_2 - x_1)^2 + (y_2 - y_1)^2}$. As shown in Figure 13-23(b), a similar derivation applies to the length of a segment $\overline{AB}$ whose slope is distance formula   negative. This result is known as the **distance formula.**

DISTANCE FORMULA

> The distance between the points $A(x_1, y_1)$ and $B(x_2, y_2)$ is given by
>
> $$AB = \sqrt{(x_2 - x_1)^2 + (y_2 - y_1)^2}$$

Remark   In using the distance formula, it is important to remember that it makes no difference whether $x_2 - x_1$ or $x_1 - x_2$ is used, because $(x_2 - x_1)^2 = (x_1 - x_2)^2$. The same is true for the y-values.

Example 13-11

For each of the following, find the distance between P and Q.

(a) $P(2, 7)$, $Q(3, 5)$
(b) $P(0, 0)$, $Q(3, \,^-4)$

Solution

(a) $PQ = \sqrt{(3 - 2)^2 + (5 - 7)^2} = \sqrt{1 + 4} = \sqrt{5}$

(b) $PQ = \sqrt{(0 - 3)^2 + [0 - (^-4)]^2} = \sqrt{9 + 16} = \sqrt{25} = 5$

Example 13-12

(a) Show that $A(7, 4)$, $B(^-2, 1)$, and $C(10, \,^-5)$ are the vertices of an isosceles triangle.
(b) Show that $\triangle ABC$ in (a) is a right triangle.

Solution

(a) Using the distance formula, find the lengths of the sides.

$$AB = \sqrt{(^-2 - 7)^2 + (1 - 4)^2} = \sqrt{(^-9)^2 + (^-3)^2} = \sqrt{90}$$

$$BC = \sqrt{[10 - (^-2)]^2 + (^-5 - 1)^2} = \sqrt{12^2 + (^-6)^2} = \sqrt{180}$$

$$AC = \sqrt{(10 - 7)^2 + (^-5 - 4)^2} = \sqrt{3^2 + (^-9)^2} = \sqrt{90}$$

$AB = AC$, so the triangle is isosceles.

(b) Because $(\sqrt{90})^2 + (\sqrt{90})^2 = (\sqrt{180})^2$, $\triangle ABC$ is a right triangle with $\overline{BC}$ as hypotenuse and $\overline{AB}$ and $\overline{AC}$ as legs.

EQUATION OF A CIRCLE

Using the distance formula, we can find the equation of a circle. A circle can be described by knowing the location of the center and the length of the radius. Figure 13-24 shows the circle with center $C(5, 4)$ and radius 3 units long. To find the equation of this circle, consider a point $P(x, y)$ on the circle. The distance from P to the center of the circle is 3 units—that is, $CP = 3$. By the distance formula, $\sqrt{(x - 5)^2 + (y - 4)^2} = 3$. Squaring both sides of the equation, we obtain $(x - 5)^2 + (y - 4)^2 = 9$. Thus, the coordinates of any point on the circle satisfy the equation $(x - 5)^2 + (y - 4)^2 = 9$.

Figure 13-24

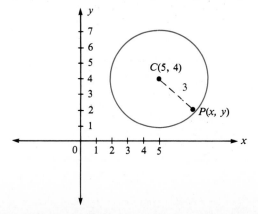

To find the equation of any circle with center $C(a, b)$ and radius r, proceed in a similar way. Figure 13-25 shows that any point $P(x, y)$ is on the circle if and only if $PC = r$, that is, if and only if $\sqrt{(x - a)^2 + (y - b)^2} = r$. Squaring both sides results in the *equation of a circle*.

Figure 13-25

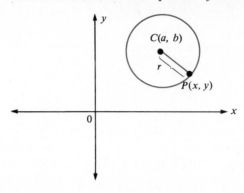

EQUATION OF A CIRCLE

The equation of a circle with center (a, b) and radius r is

$$(x - a)^2 + (y - b)^2 = r^2$$

Example 13-13

(a) Find the equation of the circle with the center at the origin and radius 4.
(b) Find the equation of the circle with center at $C(^-4, 3)$ and radius 5.
(c) Sketch the graph of $(x + 2)^2 + (y - 3)^2 = 9$.
(d) Write a condition for the set of points in the interior of the circle given in (c).

Solution

(a) The center is at $(0, 0)$ and $r = 4$, so the equation $(x - a)^2 + (y - b)^2 = r^2$ becomes $(x - 0)^2 + (y - 0)^2 = 4^2$, or $x^2 + y^2 = 16$.
(b) The equation is $[x - (^-4)]^2 + (y - 3)^2 = 5^2$, or $(x + 4)^2 + (y - 3)^2 = 25$.
(c) The equation $(x + 2)^2 + (y - 3)^2 = 9$ is in the form $(x - a)^2 + (y - b)^2 = r^2$ if and only if $x - a = x + 2$, $y - b = y - 3$, and $r^2 = 9$. Thus, $a = {}^-2$, $b = 3$, and $r = 3$. Hence, the equation is that of a circle with center at $(^-2, 3)$ and $r = 3$. Figure 13-26 shows the graph of the circle.

Figure 13-26

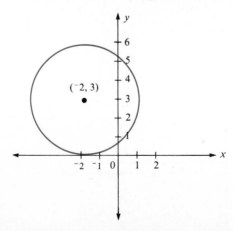

(d) A point (x, y) is in the interior of the circle if and only if the distance between the point and the center of the circle is less than the radius. In this case, $\sqrt{[x - (^-2)]^2 + (y - 3)^2} < 3$, or $(x + 2)^2 + (y - 3)^2 < 9$.

Example 13-14

Find all points on the y-axis that are 10 units away from $C(8, 3)$.

Solution

Suppose P is a point on the y-axis satisfying the given requirements. Then, P has 0 as its x-coordinate. Thus, the coordinates of P are $(0, y)$. Find y so that $PC = 10$.

$$\sqrt{(0 - 8)^2 + (y - 3)^2} = 10$$

Square both sides of the equation and solve for y.

$$(0 - 8)^2 + (y - 3)^2 = 100$$

$$64 + (y - 3)^2 = 100$$

$$(y - 3)^2 = 36$$

Thus, $y - 3 = 6$ or $y - 3 = {}^-6$, so $y = 9$ or $y = {}^-3$. Hence, two points, $P_1(0, 9)$ and $P_2(0, {}^-3)$, satisfy the condition.

THE MIDPOINT FORMULA

Using the distance formula, it is possible to find the length of a segment if the coordinates of its endpoints are known. In addition, the notion of distance can be used to find the coordinates of the midpoint of a segment. Given two points $A(x_1, y_1)$ and $B(x_2, y_2)$, the coordinates of the midpoint M of the segment $\overline{AB}$ can be found as follows. First, consider a simpler problem. Let $y_1 = y_2 = 0$. Then, the two points $A(x_1, 0)$ and $B(x_2, 0)$ lie on the x-axis, as shown in Figure 13-27 with $x_1 < x_2$. To find the x-coordinate of the midpoint M, use the given information to write an equation for x in terms of x_1 and x_2 and then solve for x. Because M is the midpoint of $\overline{AB}$, $AM = MB$, which implies that $x - x_1 = x_2 - x$; therefore,

$$2x - x_1 = x_2$$

$$2x = x_1 + x_2$$

$$x = \frac{x_1 + x_2}{2}$$

Figure 13-27

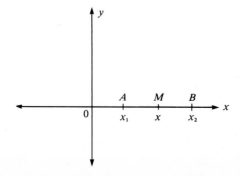

Similarly, for the case in which two points lie on the y-axis, the two points are $A(0, y_1)$ and $B(0, y_2)$ and the y-coordinate of the midpoint is $\dfrac{y_1 + y_2}{2}$.

Now, consider the general case. Let $A(x_1, y_1)$ and $B(x_2, y_2)$ be the endpoints of segment $\overline{AB}$ whose midpoint $M(x, y)$ is shown in Figure 13-28. Because $\overline{AA_1}$, $\overline{MM_1}$, and $\overline{BB_1}$ are parallel, and M is the midpoint of $\overline{AB}$, M_1 is the midpoint of $\overline{A_1B_1}$. (Why?) Hence, $x = \dfrac{x_1 + x_2}{2}$. By an analogous argument, $y = \dfrac{y_1 + y_2}{2}$.

Figure 13-28

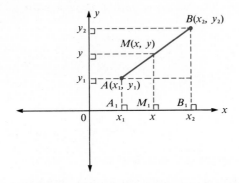

MIDPOINT FORMULA

Given $A(x_1, y_1)$ and $B(x_2, y_2)$, the midpoint M of $\overline{AB}$ is

$$M\left(\frac{x_1 + x_2}{2}, \frac{y_1 + y_2}{2}\right)$$

Remark To find the midpoint of a line segment, simply find the arithmetic mean of the respective coordinates of the two endpoints.

Example 13-15

(a) Find the coordinates of the midpoint of $\overline{AB}$ if A has coordinates $(^-3, 2)$ and B has coordinates $(3, \,^-5)$.

(b) Suppose M is the midpoint of $\overline{AB}$, A has coordinates $(2, \,^-3)$, and M has coordinates $(^-2, 1)$. Find the coordinates of B.

Solution

(a) Let (x, y) be the coordinates of the midpoint of $\overline{AB}$. Then, use the midpoint formula.

$$x = \frac{x_1 + x_2}{2} = \frac{^-3 + 3}{2} = 0$$

$$y = \frac{y_1 + y_2}{2} = \frac{2 + (^-5)}{2} = \frac{^-3}{2}$$

Hence, the midpoint has coordinates $(0, \frac{^-3}{2})$.

(b) Let the coordinates of B be (x, y), as shown in Figure 13-29. The coordinates of the midpoint M are the arithmetic means of the respective coordinates of the endpoints of $\overline{AB}$.

Figure 13-29

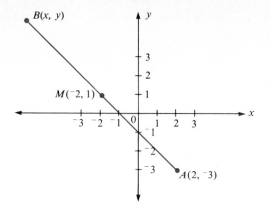

$$-2 = \frac{x + 2}{2} \qquad 1 = \frac{y + (^-3)}{2}$$

$$-4 = x + 2 \qquad 2 = y + (^-3)$$

$$x = {}^-6 \qquad y = 5$$

Consequently, $B(^-6, 5)$ is the required point.

PROBLEM 1

One day, Linda left home H for school S. Rather than stopping at school, she went on to the corner A, which is twice as far from home as the school and on the same street as her home and the school. Then she headed for the ice cream parlor I. Passing the ice cream parlor, she headed straight for the next corner B, which is on the same street as A and I and twice as far from A as I. Walking toward the park P, she continued beyond it to the next corner C, so that C, P, and B are on the same street and C is twice as far from B as P. At this point, she again headed for the school but continued walking in a straight line twice as far, reaching point D. Then, she headed for the ice cream parlor, but continued in a straight line twice as far to point E. From E, Linda headed for the park but continued in a straight line twice as far to F, where she stopped. Figure 13-30 shows the first part of Linda's walk. What is the location of Linda's final stop?

Figure 13-30

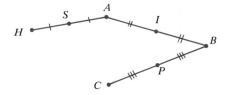

UNDERSTANDING THE PROBLEM Linda went for a walk, as shown in Figure 13-31. She started at H and walked to A, then to B, from B to C, and from C to D in such a way that S, I, P, and S were the midpoints of $\overline{HA}$, $\overline{AB}$, $\overline{BC}$, and $\overline{CD}$, respectively. From D, Linda continued her walk to E and then to F so that I and P were the midpoints of $\overline{DE}$ and $\overline{EF}$, respectively. We are to find the exact location of Linda's final stop F.

Figure 13-31

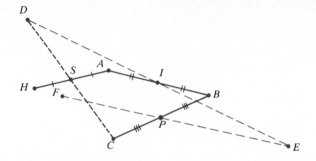

DEVISING A PLAN Because the entire problem is based on midpoints, one strategy is to use the midpoint formula. For convenience, we consider a coordinate system with H at the origin; that is, H has coordinates $(0, 0)$. We let the coordinates of the points S, I, and P be (x_1, y_1), (x_2, y_2), and (x_3, y_3), respectively. Applying the midpoint formula to the midpoint S of $\overline{HA}$, we can find the coordinates of A. Then, applying the midpoint formula to the midpoint I of $\overline{AB}$, we can express the coordinates of B using the coordinates of S and I. Continuing in this way, we can express the coordinates of F in terms of the coordinates of S, I, and P.

CARRYING OUT THE PLAN We have to apply the midpoint formula six times and then each time solve the corresponding equation for the coordinates of an endpoint. To reduce the amount of work, we develop a formula to find the coordinates of an endpoint of a segment if we are given its midpoint and the other endpoint. Let M be the midpoint of some segment $\overline{RQ}$ with (x_R, y_R), (x_M, y_M), and (x, y) the coordinates of R, M, and Q, as shown in Figure 13-32.

Figure 13-32

Using the midpoint formula, we have $x_M = \dfrac{x_R + x}{2}$, which implies $x =$

endpoint formula $2x_M - x_R$. Similarly, $y = 2y_M - y_R$. We refer to this result as the **endpoint formula**. We now apply the endpoint formula to the six segments $\overline{HA}$, $\overline{AB}$, $\overline{BC}$, $\overline{CD}$, $\overline{DE}$, and $\overline{EF}$, where $x_A, x_B, x_C, x_D, x_E,$ and x_F are the x-coordinates of A, B, C, D, E, and F, respectively.

$$x_A = 2x_1 - 0 = 2x_1$$

$$x_B = 2x_2 - x_A = 2x_2 - 2x_1$$

$$x_C = 2x_3 - x_B = 2x_3 - (2x_2 - 2x_1) = 2x_1 - 2x_2 + 2x_3$$

$$x_D = 2x_1 - x_C = 2x_1 - (2x_1 - 2x_2 + 2x_3) = 2x_2 - 2x_3$$

$$x_E = 2x_2 - x_D = 2x_2 - (2x_2 - 2x_3) = 2x_3$$

$$x_F = 2x_3 - x_E = 2x_3 - 2x_3 = 0$$

Thus, $x_F = 0$; similarly, $y_F = 0$, where y_F is the y-coordinate of F. Consequently, F has coordinates $(0, 0)$ and thus Linda stops where she started, at home.

LOOKING BACK Regardless of the values of (x_1, y_1), (x_2, y_2), and (x_3, y_3), the coordinates of F are always $(0, 0)$. Consequently, no matter where S, I, and P are located, Linda's final stop will be at home.

   The problem can be extended in different ways. For example, would Linda's final stop be at home if four locations were used rather than three (S, I, and P)? If not, how many other locations can be used if Linda's final stop is at home?

PROBLEM SET 13-4

1. For each of the following, find the length of $\overline{AB}$.
   (a) $A(0, 3)$, $B(0, 7)$ (b) $A(0, {}^-3)$, $B(0, {}^-7)$
   (c) $A(0, 3)$, $B(4, 0)$ (d) $A(0, {}^-3)$, $B({}^-4, 0)$
   (e) $A({}^-1, 2)$, $B(3, {}^-4)$
   (f) $A(4, 0)$, $B(5.2, {}^-3.7)$
   (g) $A(5, 3)$, $B(5, {}^-2)$ (h) $A(0, 0)$, $B({}^-4, 3)$
   (i) $A(5, 2)$, $B({}^-3, 4)$ (j) $A(4, {}^-5)$, $B\left(\dfrac{1}{2}, \dfrac{{}^-7}{4}\right)$

2. Find the perimeter of the triangle with vertices at $A(0, 0)$, $B({}^-4, {}^-3)$, and $C({}^-5, 0)$.
3. Show that $(0, 6)$, $({}^-3, 0)$, and $(9, {}^-6)$ are the vertices of a right triangle.
4. Show that the triangle whose vertices are $A({}^-2, {}^-5)$, $B(1, {}^-1)$, and $C(5, 2)$ is isosceles.
5. Find x if the distance between $P(1, 3)$ and $Q(x, 9)$ is 10 units.
6. For each of the following, find the midpoint of the line segment whose endpoints have the given coordinates.
   (a) $({}^-3, 1)$ and $(3, 9)$
   (b) $(4, {}^-3)$ and $(5, {}^-1)$
   (c) $(1.8, {}^-3.7)$ and $(2.2, 1.3)$
   (d) $(1 + a, a - b)$ and $(1 - a, b - a)$
7. One endpoint of a diameter of a circle with center $C({}^-2, 5)$ is given by $(3, {}^-1)$. Find the coordinates of the other endpoint.
8. (a) Find the midpoints of the sides of a triangle whose vertices have the coordinates $(0, 0)$, $({}^-4, 6)$, and $(4, 2)$.
   (b) Find the lengths of the medians of the triangle in (a). (A *median* is a segment connecting the vertex of a triangle to the midpoint of the opposite side.)
9. For each of the following, write the equations of the circle with center C and radius r.
   (a) $C(3, {}^-2)$ and $r = 2$
   (b) $C({}^-3, {}^-4)$ and $r = 5$
   (c) $C({}^-1, 0)$ and $r = 2$
   (d) $C(0, 0)$ and $r = 3$

10. Given the circle whose equation is $x^2 + y^2 = 9$, which of the following points are in its interior, which are in its exterior, and which are on the circle?
   (a) $(3, {}^-3)$ (b) $(2, {}^-2)$
   (c) $(1, 8)$ (d) $(3, 1982)$
   (e) $(5.1234, {}^-3.7894)$ (f) $\left(\dfrac{1}{387}, \dfrac{1}{1983}\right)$
   (g) $\left(\dfrac{{}^-1}{2}, \dfrac{35}{2}\right)$

11. Find the equation of the circle whose center is at the origin and that contains the point with coordinates $({}^-3, 5)$.
12. For each of the following, find the equation of the circle whose center is at $C(4, {}^-3)$ and that passes through the point indicated.
   (a) The origin   (b) $(5, {}^-2)$
13. Find the equation of the circle with a diameter having endpoints at $({}^-8, 2)$ and $(4, {}^-6)$.
14. Graph each of the following equations, if possible.
   (a) $x^2 + y^2 > 4$ (b) $x^2 + y^2 \le 4$
   (c) $x^2 + y^2 - 4 = 0$ (d) $x^2 + y^2 + 4 = 0$
15. Find the equation of the circle that passes through the origin and the point $(5, 2)$ and has its center on the x-axis.
16. Is $2x^2 + 2y^2 = 1$ an equation of a circle? If it is, find its center and radius; if not, explain why not.
★17. Graph the region enclosed between the curves $x^2 + y^2 = 1$ and $|x| + |y| = 1$.
★18. Three vertices of a parallelogram are given by $({}^-1, 4)$, $(3, 8)$, and $(5, 0)$. For each of the following, find the coordinates of the fourth vertex if it is in the specified quadrant.
   (a) Quadrant I   (b) Quadrant II
   (c) Quadrant IV
★19. Use the distance formula to show that the points with coordinates $({}^-1, 5)$, $(0, 2)$, and $(1, {}^-1)$ are collinear.

*20. Use coordinates to prove that the midpoint M of the hypotenuse of a right triangle is equidistant from the vertices. (*Hint:* Use the coordinate system shown in the accompanying figure.)

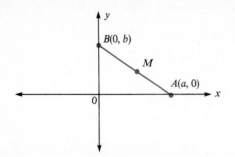

21. The vertices of $\triangle ABC$ are $A(0, 0)$, $B(1, 0)$, and $C(a, b)$. Answer the following.
(a) Write the equations of the three medians of $\triangle ABC$.
*(b) Show that the three medians intersect in one point.

*(c) Show that the point of intersection of the medians divides each median in the ratio 1:2.

*22. Use coordinates to prove that the diagonals of a parallelogram bisect each other.

Review Problems

23. Find the equation of the line parallel to the x-axis which contains the point of intersection of the lines with equations $3x + 5y = 7$ and $2x - y = {}^{-}4$.

24. Solve each of the following systems if possible. If a solution is not possible, explain why not.
(a) $x + y = 2x - y + 1$ (b) $2x - 3y = 5$
$3(x + y) = \dfrac{2}{3}(x + y)$ $6y - 4x = 0$

25. Find the inequality or inequalities representing each of the following:
(a) The half-plane determined by $y = \dfrac{3}{4}x + 5$.
(b) The triangular region determined by the line $x + y = {}^{-}5$, the x-axis, and the y-axis.

BRAIN TEASER

Among his great-grandfather's papers, José found a parchment describing the location of a hidden treasure. The treasure was buried by a band of pirates on a deserted island that contained an oak tree, a pine tree, and a gallows where the pirates hanged traitors. The map looked like the accompanying figure and gave the following directions.

"Count the steps from the gallows to the oak tree. At the oak, turn 90° to the right. Take the same number of steps and then put a spike in the ground. Next, return to the gallows and walk to the pine tree, counting the number of steps. At the pine tree, turn 90° to the left, take the same number of steps, and then put another spike in the ground. The treasure is buried halfway between the spikes."

José found the island and the two trees but could not find the gallows or the spikes, which had long since rotted. José dug all over the island, but because the island was large, he gave up. Devise a plan to help José find the treasure.

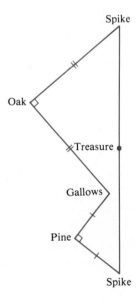

---

*Section 13-5   Coordinate Geometry and Logo

In Logo, the screen is treated as a Cartesian coordinate system in which each point of the screen is associated with an ordered pair of numbers (x, y). The origin, $(0, 0)$, is at the turtle's home. Figure 13-33 pictures the point $({}^{-}30, 20)$.

Figure 13-33

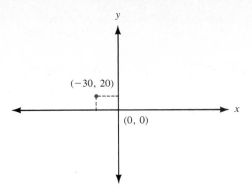

SETX   The primitive **SETX** is used with a number input to move the turtle in a horizontal direction to the position whose x-coordinate is the given input. This command changes neither the turtle's heading nor its y-coordinate.

SETY   **SETY** works the same way with the y-coordinate. For example, if the turtle is at home and we type SETY 50, the turtle moves vertically up to the point where it has 50 as its y-coordinate. If we now type SETY ⁻50, the turtle moves down to the point where the y-coordinate is ⁻50. SETY does not affect the turtle's heading. Explore at which inputs to SETX and SETY the turtle begins to wrap around the screen. As an example of SETX and SETY, suppose we start the turtle at home and type the following.

```
SETX 50 SETY 70 SETX −30 SETY −50
```

The turtle's final position has coordinates (⁻30, ⁻50), and the path that is drawn is shown in Figure 13-34.

Figure 13-34

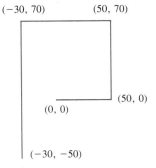

To place the turtle at the point with coordinates (⁻30, ⁻50), we could type SETX ⁻30 and then SETY ⁻50. With the SETXY command, the opera-

SETXY   tion can be done in one step. **SETXY** (*SETPOS in Apple Logo*) takes two inputs; the first is the x-coordinate and the second is the y-coordinate. (*In Apple Logo, the inputs to SETPOS must be in the form of a list; that is, they must be enclosed in brackets.*) For example, typing SETXY 30 50 (*SETPOS [30 50] in Apple Logo*) moves the turtle from its present position to the point with coordinates (30, 50) without changing the heading. Do you think that typing SETXY ⁻30 ⁻50 (*SETPOS [⁻30 ⁻50] in Apple Logo*) will move the turtle to the point with coordinates (⁻30, ⁻50)? Try it. If the experiment did not work, Logo probably treated ⁻30 ⁻50 as a subtraction and thought that there was only one input, namely, ⁻80. Parentheses can be used to overcome this, as in SETXY ⁻30 (⁻50). (*The parentheses are not necessary in Apple Logo.*)

Example 13-16

Write a procedure, using coordinate commands, to draw the parallelogram in Figure 13-35.

Figure 13-35

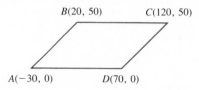

B(20, 50) C(120, 50)

A(−30, 0) D(70, 0)

Solution

The solution is given in the following P.GRAM procedure.

```
TO P.GRAM
 PENUP
 SETXY -30 0
 PENDOWN
 SETXY 20 50
 SETXY 120 50
 SETXY 70 0
 SETXY -30 0
END
```

(*In Apple Logo, SETXY is replaced with SETPOS and the inputs are enclosed in brackets.*)

Remark Note that in P.GRAM, we could have used SETX 120 in place of SETXY 120 50 and SETX ⁻30 in place of SETXY ⁻30 0 (*or in place of SETPOS [120 50] and SETPOS [⁻30 0] in Apple Logo.*)

Logo coordinate commands can be used for drawing geometric figures. Compare the following two procedures.

```
TO RECTANGLE :WIDTH :LENGTH
 REPEAT 2 [FD :WIDTH RT 90 FD :LENGTH RT 90]
END

TO RECTANGLE1 :WIDTH :LENGTH
 SETXY :WIDTH 0
 SETXY :WIDTH :LENGTH
 SETXY 0 :LENGTH
 SETXY 0 0
END
```

(*In Apple Logo, when variables are used as inputs, SETXY is replaced with SETPOS LIST; for example, SETPOS LIST :WIDTH :LENGTH.*)

If the turtle starts at home with heading 0, the RECTANGLE and RECTANGLE1 procedures produce identical figures. If the turtle is not at home, then the figures drawn by the two procedures are different. Experiment with these procedures to see that this is true.

We use the coordinate system to investigate several other geometric concepts. Consider how we might write a procedure to draw a line segment connecting two points, given their coordinates (:X1, :Y1) and (:X2, :Y2). To draw the segment, we must pick the pen up, move the turtle to the coordinates of the first point, put the pen down, and have the turtle move to the second point. The procedure called SEGMENT is given in Figure 13-36 along with a figure produced by SEGMENT.

Figure 13-36

```
TO SEGMENT :X1 :Y1 :X2 :Y2
  PENUP
  SETXY :X1 :Y1
  PENDOWN
  SETXY :X2 :Y2
END
```

(50, 50)

(0, 0)

SEGMENT 0 0 50 50

(*In Apple Logo, replace SETXY with SETPOS LIST.*)

Now, consider how to write a procedure called COOR.TRI to draw a triangle, given the coordinates of its three vertices. The SEGMENT procedure can be used to draw the three sides. The procedure is given in Figure 13-37 along with an execution of it.

Figure 13-37

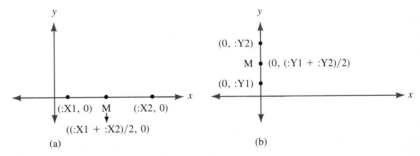

```
TO COOR.TRI :X1 :Y1 :X2 :Y2 :X3 :Y3
  SEGMENT :X1 :Y1 :X2 :Y2
  SEGMENT :X2 :Y2 :X3 :Y3
  SEGMENT :X3 :Y3 :X1 :Y1
END
```

COOR.TRI 0 0 80 50 110 0

Next, we consider how to construct the three medians of the triangles generated by COOR.TRI. Recall that medians are line segments drawn from a vertex of a triangle to the midpoint of the opposite side. If a given segment is horizontal with coordinates (:X1, 0) and (:X2, 0), as shown in Figure 13-38(a), then the midpoint is determined by using the midpoint formula. Thus, the coordinates of the midpoint are obtained by computing (:X1 + :X2)/2 and retaining 0 as the y-coordinate. Similarly, the midpoint of a vertical line with coordinates (0, :Y1) and (0, :Y2), as in Figure 13-38(b), is (0, (:Y1 + :Y2)/2).

Figure 13-38

y

(0, :Y2) ●

M ● (0, (:Y1 + :Y2)/2)

(0, :Y1) ●

x

x

(:X1, 0) M   (:X2, 0)

((:X1 + :X2)/2, 0)

(a)

(b)

If the line is neither horizontal nor vertical, as shown in Figure 13-39, then the midpoint is the arithmetic mean of the x- and y-coordinates.

Figure 13-39

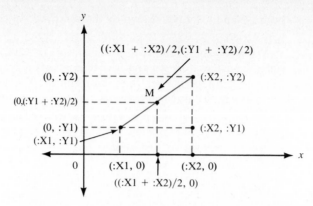

A procedure called **MIDPOINT**, which moves the turtle to the midpoint of a segment determined by the coordinates of two points, follows.

```
TO MIDPOINT :X1 :Y1 :X2 :Y2
  SETXY (:X1 + :X2)/2 (:Y1 + :Y2)/2
END
```

(*In Apple Logo, replace SETXY with SETPOS LIST.*)
Once the sides of the triangle are drawn and the midpoints determined, the medians can be drawn by using the TRI.MEDIANS procedure given in Figure 13-40.

Figure 13-40

```
TRI.MEDIANS 0 0 80 50 110 0
```

```
TO TRI.MEDIANS :X1 :Y1 :X2 :Y2 :X3 :Y3
  COOR.TRI :X1 :Y1 :X2 :Y2 :X3 :Y3
  SEGMENT :X1 :Y1 (:X2 + :X3)/2 (:Y2 + :Y3)/2
  SEGMENT :X2 :Y2 (:X1 + :X3)/2 (:Y1 + :Y3)/2
  SEGMENT :X3 :Y3 (:X1 + :X2)/2 (:Y1 + :Y2)/2
END
```

medial triangle

A **medial triangle** is a triangle formed by connecting the midpoints of its three sides. A procedure called MEDIAL.TRI for drawing a medial triangle is given in Figure 13-41.

Figure 13-41

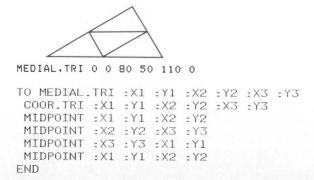

```
MEDIAL.TRI 0 0 80 50 110 0
```

```
TO MEDIAL.TRI :X1 :Y1 :X2 :Y2 :X3 :Y3
  COOR.TRI :X1 :Y1 :X2 :Y2 :X3 :Y3
  MIDPOINT :X1 :Y1 :X2 :Y2
  MIDPOINT :X2 :Y2 :X3 :Y3
  MIDPOINT :X3 :Y3 :X1 :Y1
  MIDPOINT :X1 :Y1 :X2 :Y2
END
```

FINDING LENGTHS OF LINE SEGMENTS

It is possible to find the lengths of line segments by using coordinate commands. Recall that we can find the length of a segment with the distance formula, which follows.

$$d = \sqrt{(x_2 - x_1)^2 + (y_2 - y_1)^2}$$

For example, to find the distance between points ($^{-}$10, 5) and (20, 30), we compute the following.

$$d = \sqrt{(^{-}10 - 20)^2 + (5 - 30)^2} \text{ or } \sqrt{1525}, \text{ or approximately } 39.0512.$$

SQRT We can write a Logo procedure for computing the distance between any two points by using the SQRT primitive. **SQRT** takes one numerical input and outputs the square root of the number. The PRINT (PR) command can be used with SQRT to display the result. For example, PRINT SQRT 2 gives 1.41421. A DISTANCE procedure that prints out the distance between any two points follows.

```
TO DISTANCE :X1 :Y1 :X2 :Y2
  PRINT SQRT (:X2 - :X1) * (:X2 - :X1) + (:Y2 - :Y1) * (:Y2 - :Y1)
END
```

If we execute DISTANCE $^{-}$10 20 20 40, where ($^{-}$10, 20) and (20, 40) are the coordinates of the two points, then 36.0555 is displayed on the screen.

The DISTANCE procedure can also be used to compute the distance from a point with given coordinates even if we do not know the exact coordinates of the turtle. Logo has two primitives, XCOR and YCOR, that can be used
XCOR to determine the coordinates of the turtle. If we type PRINT **XCOR** and press RETURN, the *x*-coordinate of the turtle is displayed. Similarly, PRINT
YCOR **YCOR** yields the *y*-coordinate of the turtle. With this in mind, the distance from any point where the turtle is located to the point (5, 10) can be determined by executing DISTANCE 5 10 XCOR YCOR.

The DISTANCE procedure has its limitations. For example, consider writing a procedure to draw a square, given two consecutive vertices of the square. To draw square *ABCD*, where we know the vertices *A*($^{-}$10, 20) and *B*(0, 40), we need to know the length of segment $\overline{AB}$ and then make each of the other sides the same length. Because the figure is a square, each angle is a right angle. Such a square is pictured in Figure 13-42.

Figure 13-42

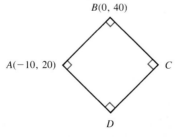

$B(0, 40)$

$A(-10, 20)$ C

D

A procedure called CSQUARE might first lift the pen up and move the turtle to vertex *A*. Now, we want the procedure to draw the square with sides the same length as segment $\overline{AB}$. We can find the length of segment $\overline{AB}$ by using the DISTANCE procedure. However, if we do not know the turtle's initial heading, we do not know how to make the turtle go to vertex *B* and turn 90°. Thus, we need to know the heading when the turtle draws segment $\overline{AB}$. Two Logo primitives can be used to determine the heading that will ensure that the turtle passes through vertex *B*. The primitive **TOWARDS** takes two numerical inputs that are interpreted as the *x*- and *y*-coordinates of a point and outputs the heading the turtle would have in going from its present location to the point with the coordinates given as inputs. (*In Apple Logo, the two numerical inputs are enclosed in brackets.*) The PRINT (PR) command can be used with TOWARDS to display the heading. For example, if the turtle is at home, then PR TOWARDS ⁻10 0 (*in Apple Logo, PR TOWARDS [10 0]*) yields 270. TOWARDS gives the heading toward some point from the turtle's current position, but it does not actually set the heading. The SETHEADING (SETH) primitive does this. **SETHEADING (SETH)** requires one input and turns the turtle to the heading indicated by the input. SETHEADING does not change the position of the turtle, only its heading. For example, SETHEADING 50 turns the turtle so it has heading 50.

SETHEADING and TOWARDS can be used to complete the CSQUARE procedure. If the turtle is at (⁻10, 20), we can determine the heading that would be needed for the turtle to pass through (0, 40) by using TOWARDS 0 40 (*in Apple Logo, TOWARDS [0 40]*). To actually turn the turtle toward (0, 40) to draw the line segment, we use the output from TOWARDS as input to SETHEADING, as in SETHEADING TOWARDS 0 40 (*in Apple Logo, SETHEADING TOWARDS [0 40]*). Now that the proper heading for drawing the square can be determined and because all sides of the square are the same length and all angles are 90°, we can write the following CSQUARE procedure.

TOWARDS

SETHEADING (SETH)

```
TO CSQUARE
 PU SETXY -10 20 PD
 SETHEADING TOWARDS 0 40
 REPEAT 4 [FD DISTANCE -10 20 0 40 RT 90]
END
```

(*In Apple Logo, replace SETXY ⁻10 20 with SETPOS [⁻10 20] and TOWARDS 0 40 with TOWARDS [0 40].*)

If CSQUARE is executed, a bug occurs. This is because the value of DISTANCE ⁻10 20 0 40 is printed by DISTANCE and is not kept in the computer's memory to be passed as input to another procedure or another primitive. The primitive OUTPUT (OP) is useful here. **OUTPUT (OP)** takes one input and causes the current procedure to stop and output the result to a calling procedure.

OUTPUT (OP)

To debug the CSQUARE procedure, we change the DISTANCE procedure to include an OUTPUT statement instead of a PRINT statement. The edited DISTANCE procedure follows.

```
TO DISTANCE :X1 :Y1 :X2 :Y2
 OUTPUT SQRT((:X2 - :X1) * (:X2 - :X1) + (:Y2 - :Y1) * (:Y2 - :Y1))
END
```

Now, the distance from ($^-$10, 20) to (0, 40) is given by PR DISTANCE $^-$10 20 0 40.

The CSQUARE procedure can be generalized to start with the coordinates of any two points. The generalized procedure, called TWO.POINTS, follows.

```
TO TWO.POINTS :X1 :Y1 :X2 :Y2
  PU SETXY :X1 :Y1 PD
  SETHEADING TOWARDS :X2 :Y2
  REPEAT 4 [FD DISTANCE :X1 :Y1 :X2 :Y2 RT 90]
END
```

(*In Apple Logo, use SETPOS LIST :X1 :Y1 and TOWARDS LIST :X2 :Y2.*)

CONSTRUCTING TRIANGLES WITH SAS

MAKE   The **MAKE** command can be used to assign a value to a variable. For example, if we execute MAKE "X 5 and then type PRINT :X, which means "Print the value associated with X," then the computer will print 5. The MAKE command can be used inside or outside a procedure. In general, the MAKE command accepts two inputs; the first, preceded by a quotation mark, is the name of the variable, and the second is the value of the variable we are defining. The MAKE command can be used with the other commands introduced in this chapter. For example, we could write a procedure called SAS.TRI to draw a triangle given that two sides have length 80 and 50 and an included angle of 30°. To write a SAS.TRI procedure to accomplish this, we could tell the turtle to go forward 80 units, the length of the first side, and learn the *x*- and *y*-coordinates of its position. We could then back the turtle up 80 units, turn it right 30°, and move it forward 50 units, the length of the second side. To complete the triangle, we could then send the turtle to the coordinates it learned when it drew the first side. The SAS.TRI procedure follows, and the result is shown in Figure 13-43.

Figure 13-43

SAS.TRI

```
TO SAS.TRI
  FD 80
  MAKE "X XCOR
  MAKE "Y YCOR
  BK 80
  RT 30
  FD 50
  SETXY :X :Y
END
```

(*In Apple Logo, replace SETXY with SETPOS LIST.*)
It is left as an exercise to write a variable procedure called SAS with inputs :S1, :A, :S2 for drawing a triangle given two sides and the included angle.

SUMMARY OF COMMANDS

SETX	Takes one number input and moves the turtle horizontally to the point with that x-coordinate. Draws a trail if the pen is down.
SETY	Takes one number input and moves the turtle vertically to the point with that y-coordinate. Draws a trail if the pen is down.
SETXY*	Takes two number inputs A and B and moves the turtle to the point with the given coordinates (A, B). Draws a trail if the pen is down.
SQRT	Takes one nonnegative number input and yields the square root of that input.
XCOR	Takes no inputs; outputs the turtle's current x-coordinate.
YCOR	Takes no inputs; outputs the turtle's current y-coordinate.
TOWARDS†	Takes two number inputs, which are interpreted as x- and y-coordinates of a point, and outputs the heading from the turtle to that point.
SETHEADING (SETH)	Takes one number input and rotates the turtle to point in the direction specified.
OUTPUT (OP)	Takes one input and causes the current procedure to stop and output the result to the calling procedure.
MAKE	Takes two inputs. The first, preceded by a quotation mark, is the name of a variable. The second is the value of the variable.

* In Apple Logo, SETPOS is used with the list of coordinates as input, for example, SETPOS [20, 30].

† In Apple Logo, TOWARDS is used with the list of coordinates as input, for example, TOWARDS [20, 30].

PROBLEM SET 13-5

1. Use SETX, SETY, and SETXY (*in Apple Logo, SETPOS*) to draw the largest rectangle possible on the monitor screen.
2. How are the triangles generated by the MEDIAL.TRI procedure related?
3. Write a procedure called AXES that uses the SETXY (*in Apple Logo, SETPOS*) primitive to draw the x- and y-axes with the origin placed at home.
4. If given two vertices of a square, how many different squares can be drawn?
5. Write a procedure called FILL.RECT that uses the SETXY (*in Apple Logo, SETPOS*) command to fill (color in) a rectangle that has length 50 and width 30. Assume the turtle starts at home with heading 0.
6. Write a procedure called CCIRCLE to draw a circle in which the coordinates of the center of the circle and the radius are inputs. For example, CCIRCLE 10 20 30 should draw a circle that has center (10, 20) and radius 30.
7. Write a procedure called QUAD to draw a quadrilateral if the coordinates of the vertices are input.
8. (a) Write a procedure called MEDIAL.QUAD to draw a medial figure for a quadrilateral if the coordinates of the vertices are inputs.
   (b) Execute your procedure in (a) for several cases and make a conjecture concerning the quadrilateral formed by the midpoints.
9. Write a procedure called MEDIAL.QUADS with inputs :X1, :Y1, :X2, :Y2, :X3, :Y3, :X4, and :Y4, which are the coordinates of the vertices, and :NUM, which gives the number of medial figures drawn.

10. Write a variable procedure called SAS to draw a triangle given two sides :S1 and :S2 and the included angle :A.
11. Write a procedure called R.ISOS.TRI to draw a right isosceles triangle of side leg given by the input :LEN.
★12. Write a procedure called MEDIAL.TRIS that uses

recursion such that :NUM, the number of medial triangles that are to be drawn, is included as input.
13. Write a procedure to draw a circle that has radius 50 and passes through the point ($^-$20, $^-$40).
14. Write a procedure to draw a circle in which the coordinates of the center of the circle and the radius are inputs.

SOLUTION TO THE PRELIMINARY PROBLEM

UNDERSTANDING THE PROBLEM Knowing the points $A(2.5, 4.7)$, $B(7, 19.3)$, and $C(17.8, 5.9)$, we are asked to find the coordinates of point D northeast of A such that A, B, C, and D are vertices of a parallelogram. The approximate location of point D is shown in Figure 13-44.

Figure 13-44

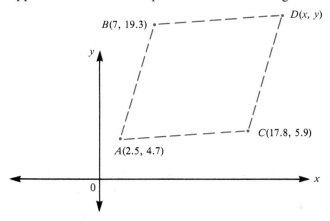

DEVISING A PLAN We denote the coordinates of D by x and y and look for properties of parallelograms that may help to determine the values of x and y. We know that in a parallelogram, the diagonals bisect each other. The point of intersection of the diagonals, denoted by M, is shown in Figure 13-45. The coordinates of M can be found as a midpoint of the diagonal $\overline{BC}$ using the

Figure 13-45

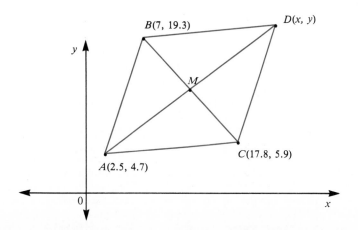

midpoint formula. $\Big[$ Recall that the midpoint of a segment with endpoints (x_1, y_1) and (x_2, y_2) is $\left(\dfrac{x_1 + x_2}{2}, \dfrac{y_1 + y_2}{2}\right).\Big]$ However, because M is also the midpoint of the diagonal $\overline{AD}$, we can use the midpoint formula again to obtain equations for x and y. Solving each of the equations will give us the values of x and y.

CARRYING OUT THE PLAN Because $M(x_M, y_M)$ is the midpoint of $\overline{BC}$, we have $x_M = \dfrac{7 + 17.8}{2} = 12.4$. Similarly, $y_M = \dfrac{19.3 + 5.9}{2} = 12.6$. Using the fact that M is the midpoint of $\overline{AD}$, we have $12.4 = \dfrac{2.5 + x}{2}$. Thus, $24.8 = 2.5 + x$, or $x = 22.3$. Similarly, $12.6 = \dfrac{4.7 + y}{2}$, or $25.2 = 4.7 + y$, or $y = 20.5$. Consequently, the point D is determined by the ordered pair (22.3, 20.5).

LOOKING BACK The problem can be extended by not restricting the point D to be northeast of A. How many different locations for D are possible if A, B, C, and D are the vertices (not necessarily consecutive) of a parallelogram?

QUESTIONS FROM THE CLASSROOM

1. A student asks, "If slope is such an important concept, why is slope of a vertical line undefined?" What is your response?
2. A student argues, "Since 0 is nothing and a horizontal line has slope 0, a horizontal line also has no slope." How do you reply?
3. Trying to find the midpoint M of $\overline{AB}$, where A and B have coordinates $(x_1, 0)$ and $(x_2, 0)$ and $x_2 > x_1$, a student argues as follows. "Since $AB = x_2 - x_1$, half that distance is $\dfrac{x_2 - x_1}{2}$ and, since the midpoint M is halfway between A and B, the x-coordinate of M is $\dfrac{x_2 - x_1}{2}$." How do you respond?
4. A student does not understand why, when solving a system of linear equations, it is necessary to check the solution in the original equations rather than in some simpler equivalent equations. How do you respond?
5. A student claims that the graph of every inequality of the form $ax + by + c > 0$ is the half-plane above the line $ax + by + c = 0$, while the graph of $ax + by + c < 0$ is always below the line. How do you respond?
6. A student claims that the distance formula can be further simplified as follows.
$$d = \sqrt{(x_1 - x_2)^2 + (y_1 - y_2)^2}$$
$$= \sqrt{(x_1 - x_2)^2} + \sqrt{(y_1 - y_2)^2}$$
$$= |x_1 - x_2| + |y_1 - y_2|$$
How do you respond?
7. A student wishes to know how to check the solution of a system of inequalities. How do you respond?

CHAPTER OUTLINE

I. Coordinate system in a plane
  A. Any point in the plane can be described by an ordered pair of real numbers, the first of which is the **x-coordinate** and the second the **y-coordinate.**

  B. Together, the x-axis and y-axis divide the plane into four **quadrants.**
II. Equations of sets of points and notions of slope
  A. The **slope** of a line is a measure of its steepness.

1. Given (x_1, y_1) and (x_2, y_2) with $x_2 \neq x_1$, the slope m of the line through the two points is given by $m = \dfrac{y_2 - y_1}{x_2 - x_1}$.

   2. The slope of a vertical line is not defined.
   B. The equation of any nonvertical line can be written in the form $y = mx + b$, where m is the slope and b is the y-intercept.
   C. The equation of any vertical line can be written in the form $x = a$.
III. Systems of linear equations
   A. A system of linear equations can be solved graphically by drawing the graphs of the equations.
      1. If the equations represent two intersecting lines, the system has a unique solution, that is, the ordered pair corresponding to the point of intersection.
      2. If the equations represent two different parallel lines, the system has no solutions.
      3. If the two equations represent the same line, the system has infinitely many solutions.
   B. A system of linear equations can be solved algebraically by either the **substitution method** or the **elimination method.**

IV. Distance concepts
   A. The **distance** between the points (x_1, y_1) and (x_2, y_2) is given by $d = \sqrt{(x_2 - x_1)^2 + (y_2 - y_1)^2}$.
   B. Given $A(x_1, y_1)$ and $B(x_2, y_2)$, the coordinates of the **midpoint** M of $\overline{AB}$ are
   $$\left(\frac{x_1 + x_2}{2}, \frac{y_1 + y_2}{2} \right)$$
   C. The equation of the circle with center at (a, b) and radius r is $(x - a)^2 + (y - b)^2 = r^2$.
*V. Coordinate geometry and Logo
   The following primitives are used:
   SETX
   SETY
   SETXY
   SQRT
   XCOR
   YCOR
   TOWARDS
   SETHEADING
   OUTPUT
   MAKE

CHAPTER TEST

1. Find the perimeter of the triangle with vertices at $A(0, 0)$, $B(^-4, 3)$, and $C(0, 6)$.
2. Show algebraically in at least two different ways that $(4, 2)$, $(0, ^-1)$, and $(^-4, ^-4)$ are collinear points.
3. Sketch the graphs for each of the following.
   (a) $3x - y = 1$ (b) $3x - y \leq 1$
   (c) $2x + 3y + 1 = 0$
4. For each of the following, write the equation of the line determined by the given pair of points.
   (a) $(2, ^-3)$ and $(^-1, 1)$ (b) $(^-3, 0)$ and $(^-3, 2)$
   (c) $(^-2, 3)$ and $(2, 3)$
5. The vertices of $\triangle ABC$ are $A(^-3, 0)$, $B(0, 4)$, and $C(2, 5)$. Find each of the following.
   (a) The equation of the line through C and parallel to $\overleftrightarrow{AB}$.
   (b) The equation of the line through C and parallel to the x-axis.
   (c) The point where the line found in (b) intersects $\overleftrightarrow{AB}$.
6. Solve each of the following systems, if possible. Indicate whether the system has a unique solution, infinitely many solutions, or no solution.

   (a) $x + 2y = 3$ (b) $\dfrac{x}{2} + \dfrac{y}{3} = 1$
        $2x - y = 9$ $4y - 3x = 2$
   (c) $x - 2y = 1$
        $4y - 2x = 0$
7. A store sells nuts in two types of containers, regular and deluxe. Each regular container contains 1 pound of cashews and 2 pounds of peanuts. Each deluxe container contains 3 pounds of cashews and 1.5 pounds of peanuts. The store used 170 pounds of cashews and 205 pounds of peanuts. How many containers of each kind were used?
8. (a) Find the midpoint of the line segment whose endpoints are given by $(^-4, 2)$ and $(6, ^-3)$.
   (b) The midpoint of a segment is given by $(^-5, 4)$ and one of its endpoints is given by $(^-3, 5)$. Find the coordinates of the other endpoint.
9. Graph each of the following.
   (a) $x^2 + y^2 = 16$
   (b) $(x + 1)^2 + (y - 2)^2 = 9$
   (c) $x^2 + y^2 \leq 16$

10. Find the equation of the circle whose center is at $C(^-3, 4)$ and that passes through the origin.
11. Graph each of the following systems.
    (a) $x \geq {}^-7$ (b) $y \leq 2x + 3$
         $y \leq 4$ $y \geq x + {}^-7$
12. The sum of the numbers of red and black jelly beans on Ronnie's desk is 12. Also, the sum is twice the difference of the numbers of the two colors. How many jelly beans of each color does he have if there are more red than black jelly beans?
13. The freshman class at the university has 225 fewer enrolled than the sophomore class. The number in the sophomore class is only 50 students short of being twice as great as the number in the freshman class. How many students are in each class?
14. In the presidential election of 1932, Franklin D. Roosevelt received 6,563,988 more votes than Herbert Hoover. If one fifth of Roosevelt's votes had been won by Herbert Hoover, then Hoover would have won the election by 2,444,622 votes. How many votes did each receive?

SELECTED BIBLIOGRAPHY

Arnsdorf, E. "Orienteering, New Ideas for Outdoor Mathematics." *Arithmetic Teacher* 25 (April 1978): 14–17.

Avery, J. "The Cartesian Classroom." *The Mathematics Teacher* 76 (September 1983):407–408.

Battista, M. "Distortions: An Activity for Practice and Exploration." *Arithmetic Teacher* 29 (January 1982): 34–36.

Bell, W. "Cartesian Coordinates and Battleship." *The Arithmetic Teacher* 21 (May 1974):421–422.

Bergen, S. "A Discovery Approach for the *y*-Intercept." *The Mathematics Teacher* 70 (November 1977): 675–676.

Bruni, J., and H. Silverman. "Using a Pegboard to Develop Mathematical Concepts." *The Arithmetic Teacher* 22 (October 1975):452–458.

Burns, M. "Ideas." *The Arithmetic Teacher* 22 (April 1975):296–304.

Dossey, J. "Do All Graphs Have Points with Integral Coordinates?" *The Mathematics Teacher* 74 (September 1981):455–457.

Dugdale, S. "Green Globs: A Micro-computer Application for Graphing of Equations." *The Mathematics Teacher* 75 (March 1982):208–214.

Freidland, H. "Chalkboard Coordinates." *Arithmetic Teacher* 31 (November 1983):10.

Giles, D. "Graphing Inequalities Directly." *The Arithmetic Teacher* 18 (March 1971):185–186.

Kalman, D. "Up *n/m*!" *Arithmetic Teacher* 32 (April 1985):42–43.

Lappan, G., and M. Winter. "A Unit on Slope Functions—Using a Computer in Mathematics Class." *The Mathematics Teacher* 75 (February 1982):118–122.

Miller, W. "Graphs Alive." *The Mathematics Teacher* 71 (December 1978):756–758.

Nicolai, M. "A Discovery in Linear Algebra." *The Mathematics Teacher* 67 (May 1974):403–404.

Pereira-Mendoza, L. "Graphing and Prediction in Elementary School." *The Arithmetic Teacher* 24 (February 1977):112–113.

Rainsbury, R. "Where is Droopy?" *The Arithmetic Teacher* 19 (April 1972):271–272.

Ruppel, E. "Business Formulas As Cartesian Curves." *The Mathematics Teacher* 75 (May 1982):398–403.

Smith, R. "Coordinate Geometry for Third Graders." *Arithmetic Teacher* (April 1986):10.

Terc, M. "Coordinate Geometry—Art and Mathematics." *Arithmetic Teacher* 33 (October 1985):22–24.

Wallace, E. "Unifying Slopes, Proportions, and Graphing." *The Mathematics Teacher* 73 (November 1980): 597–600.

CHAPTER 14

Problem Solving Revisited

Introduction

In this chapter, a knowledge of the material in the text is assumed, and we introduce problems that require skills from various chapters. This provides an opportunity of looking at problem solving from a broader point of view, one in which the problem solver does not know to which specific topics the problem is related.

In the following examples, problem-solving strategies and the motives for various steps in a solution are discussed. Although not specifically indicated, the examples are solved by following the approach of *Understanding the Problem, Devising a Plan, Carrying Out the Plan,* and *Looking Back.* Following these examples is a collection of problems, some of which are nontrivial. Do not expect to solve these problems without some hard work.

Example 14-1

In the circle in Figure 14-1, two perpendicular diameters are shown. From a point C on the circle, two segments $\overline{AC}$ and $\overline{CB}$ are drawn so that quadrilateral $ACBO$ is a rectangle. If the diameter of the circle is 10 cm, find the length of $\overline{AB}$.

Figure 14-1

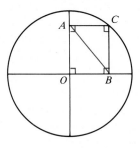

Solution

$\overline{AB}$ is the hypotenuse of right triangle AOB. One possible way to find AB is to use the Pythagorean Theorem, from which it follows that $(AB)^2 = (AO)^2 + (OB)^2$. Thus, to find AB, we need to know the lengths of both $\overline{AO}$ and $\overline{OB}$. The lengths of these sides are not given. Moreover, it seems that knowing only the diameter of the circle is not sufficient to determine AO and OB. Thus, using the Pythagorean Theorem does not appear to be a productive strategy.

Our new strategy is to find parts of a triangle using congruent or similar triangles. Triangle BCA is congruent to $\triangle AOB$. However, there is no more information about $\triangle BCA$ than about $\triangle AOB$. Because Figure 14-1 shows no other triangles, we need to draw an additional segment to define a new triangle. The newly constructed triangle should have sides of

Figure 14-2

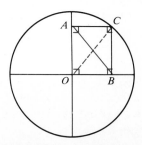

known lengths. Because the length of the diameter is 10 cm and the radius is 5 cm, the most natural choice is $\overline{OC}$, as shown in Figure 14-2. The diagonals of a rectangle are congruent. (In Chapter 11, this was shown by proving $\triangle ABO \cong \triangle COB$.) Thus, $\overline{OC} \cong \overline{AB}$ and $AB = 5$ cm.

The solution to Example 14-1 focused on the goal of finding AB and relied on previous experiences in solving such problems by trying the Pythagorean Theorem and using congruent triangles. The Pythagorean Theorem approach was abandoned because of insufficient information. Next, a search for appropriate congruent triangles became the focus. This search became the new goal. In the congruent-triangle approach, we used all possible information from the problem along with previous definitions and related theorems. The related theorems gave new information that resulted in a solution.

Example 14-2

The king of Ilusia lost a war and was forced to divide his kingdom into a number of smaller countries, no two the same size. The king also had to distribute all 1000 bars of his gold in such a way that each country received 1 bar more than the next smaller country. No bars could be broken. If the king divided his kingdom into the least number of countries possible and divided his gold as described, how many countries were formed and how many bars of gold did each country receive?

Solution

Each country received one bar more than the next smaller country. Suppose the smallest country received n bars of gold. Then, the next larger country received 1 bar more, and the next larger country 2 bars more, and so on. That is, the countries in order of size received n bars, $(n + 1)$ bars, $(n + 2)$ bars, and so on. The number of countries is unknown, so we designate that number by k.

Ordering countries according to size from smallest to largest and making Table 14-1 reveals a pattern. The kth country receives $n + (k - 1)$ bars of gold.

Table 14-1

Order of Country	Number of Bars Received
1	n
2	$n + 1$
3	$n + 2$
4	$n + 3$
5	$n + 4$
$\vdots$	$\vdots$
k	$n + (k - 1)$

The total number of gold bars is 1000. Because the total number of bars received by all countries is 1000, we have

$$n + (n + 1) + (n + 2) + (n + 3) + \cdots + (n + k - 1) = 1000$$

Thus, the problem involves finding a sum of consecutive natural numbers.

Recall that in Chapter 1 the similar problem of finding the sum of the first 100 natural numbers was solved by listing the numbers in the following way and computing the sum.

$$
\begin{array}{c}
1 +\quad 2 +\quad 3 +\quad 4 + \cdots + 100 \\
100 + 99 + 98 + 97 + \cdots + \quad 1 \\
\hline
101 + 101 + 101 + 101 + \cdots + 101
\end{array}
$$

There are 100 sums of 101 in twice the desired sum, so we divide by 2 to obtain $\dfrac{100(101)}{2} = 5050$.

A similar approach can be used to find the sum $n + (n + 1) + (n + 2) + (n + 3) + \cdots + (n + k - 1)$.

$$
\begin{array}{c}
n \quad +\quad (n + 1) \quad +\quad (n + 2) \quad + \cdots + (n + k - 1) \\
(n + k - 1) + (n + k - 2) + (n + k - 3) + \cdots + \quad n \\
\hline
(2n + k - 1) + (2n + k - 1) + (2n + k - 1) + \cdots + (2n + k - 1)
\end{array}
$$

There are k sums of $2n + k - 1$ shown above and this is twice the desired sum. Hence, we divide by 2 to obtain $\dfrac{k(2n + k - 1)}{2}$. This result can be used as follows.

$$n + (n + 1) + (n + 2) + \cdots + (n + k - 1) = 1000$$

$$\frac{k}{2}(2n + k - 1) = 1000$$

$$k(2n + k - 1) = 2000$$

The last equation has two unknowns, k and n. To find k and n, we need another equation involving k and n. Unfortunately, no other condition that yields an additional equation is given in the problem.

A useful strategy in solving any problem is to make sure that no important information is neglected. One condition of the problem states that the number of countries k is the least number possible and $k \neq 1$. Also, because no bar can be broken, n and k must be natural numbers. Keeping these conditions in mind, we focus on $k(2n + k - 1) = 2000$. Because k and $2n + k - 1$ are natural numbers, they are factors of 2000. Also, k is the least number possible, so we start with $k = 2$. If $k = 2$, then $2 \cdot (2n + 2 - 1) = 2000$ and $n = 499\frac{1}{2}$, which is not a natural number. Hence, $k \neq 2$. Similarly, if $k = 4$, the next factor of 2000, then $n = 248\frac{1}{2}$, and hence, $k \neq 4$. However, if $k = 5$, then $n = 198$. Thus, the smallest country receives 198 bars of gold, and, consequently, the five countries receive 198, 199, 200, 201, and 202 bars, respectively.

It is easy to check the solution because $198 + 199 + 200 + 201 + 202 = 1000$. Can the problem be solved if there is a different number of bars? What solutions does the problem have if the number of countries is not minimized?

Example 14-3

In a portion of a large city, the streets divide the city into square blocks of equal size, as shown in Figure 14-3. A taxi driver drives daily from point A to P. One day she drove from A to B along $\overline{AB}$ and then from B to P along $\overline{BP}$. If she does not want to cover any distance longer than $AB + BP$, how many possible routes are there from A to P?

Figure 14-3

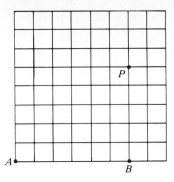

Solution

In order to travel the minimum distance, the taxi driver should only go north (upward) and east (to the right). Two routes are shown in Figure 14-4. For each of the routes, the total length of the horizontal segments is *AB*. Similarly, the total length of the vertical segments is *BP*. Thus, the length of each of the taxi driver's routes from *A* to *P* equals *AB* + *BP*.

Figure 14-4

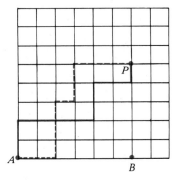

One way to solve the problem is by drawing all possible routes from *A* to *P* and counting them. Since that is an enormous task, we try looking for simpler versions of the problem. In Figure 14-5, there is only one possible route from *A* to *C* and only one route from *A* to *F*. In fact, each of the points on $\overleftrightarrow{AC}$ and $\overleftrightarrow{AF}$ can be reached via only one route.

Figure 14-5

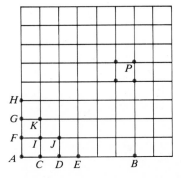

Next, we examine the routes from *A* to *I*. Only two are possible, *A—F—I* and *A—C—I*. From *A* to *J* there are three routes, namely, *A—C—D—J*, *A—C—I—J*, and *A—F—I—J*. Similarly, the number of routes to various other points from *A* can be counted. Figure 14-6 shows the number of possible routes to various points, starting from *A*.

Figure 14-6

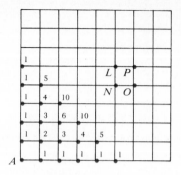

It appears that the number of routes to any given point from *A* is the sum of the number of routes to each of its two neighboring points, one immediately to the left and the other immediately below. If this pattern continues, it would be easy to work from point to point until we reach point *P*. The pattern can be justified because each of the routes from *N* to *P* in Figure 14-6 can be obtained from the two neighboring points *L* and *O*. Any route from *A* to *P* must pass through either *L* or *O*. The number of routes from *A* to *P* that pass through *L* is the same as the number of routes from *A* to *L* because, for each route from *A* to *L*, there is one single route to *P* that passes through *L*. Similarly, the number of routes from *A* to *P* that pass through *O* is the same as the number of routes from *A* to *O*. Thus, the number of routes from *A* to *P* is the sum of the routes from *A* to *L* and from *A* to *O*. Because the pattern in Figure 14-6 continues, there are 462 routes from *A* to *P*, as shown in Figure 14-7.

Figure 14-7

1	6	21	56	126	252	462		
1	5	15	35	70	*P* 126	210		
1	4	10	20	35	56	84		
1	3	6	10	15	21	28		
1	2	3	4	5	6	7		
	1	1	1	1	1	1		

A

You may wish to investigate this example further using the concept of combinations discussed in Chapter 8.

Example 14-4

Howie, Frank, and Dandy each tried to predict the winners of Sunday's professional football games. The only team not picked that is playing Sunday was the Giants. The choices for each person were as follows.

Howie: Cowboys, Steelers, Vikings, Bills

Frank: Steelers, Packers, Cowboys, Redskins

Dandy: Redskins, Vikings, Jets, Cowboys

    If the only teams playing Sunday are those just mentioned, which teams will play which other teams?

Solution

At first glance, it may appear that there is not enough information to solve this problem, but recording the information in a Venn diagram may provide the insight we need. A Venn diagram with circles *H*, *F*, and *D* for each of the sportscasters is shown in Figure 14-8. The three circles divide the universal set into eight disjoint regions: (*a*), (*b*), (*c*), (*d*), (*e*), (*f*), (*g*), and (*h*).

Figure 14-8

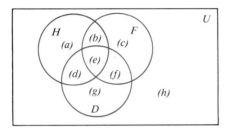

Each sportscaster picked the Cowboys to win. Because this was the only team that all three picked to win, region (*e*) consists only of the Cowboys. We can place the Giants in region (*h*) because none of the three picked the Giants. Howie and Frank both picked the Steelers, so now the Steelers belong in region (*b*). Howie and Dandy both picked the Vikings, so the Vikings belong in region (*d*). Frank and Dandy both picked the Redskins, so they belong in region (*f*). This leaves region (*a*) for the Bills, region (*c*) for the Packers, and region (*g*) for the Jets. This information is given in Figure 14-9. To complete the problem, we must now determine which teams will play each other.

Figure 14-9

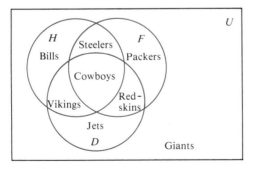

From Figure 14-9, we know the Cowboys will not play the Steelers, Bills, or Vikings because Howie picked all these teams as winners. Likewise, the Cowboys will not play the Packers or the Redskins because Frank picked all these teams as winners. Similarly, the Cowboys will not play the Jets because Dandy picked both the Cowboys and Jets as winners.

This leaves the Cowboys with only one possible opponent, namely, the Giants.

Next, we can determine which team the Vikings will play. Because the Vikings are picked by both Howie and Dandy, their opponent must be outside circles *H* and *D*. This means that the Vikings will play the Packers. In a similar manner, we can deduce that the Steelers will play the Jets, and the Redskins will play the Bills. The four games on Sunday will be

Cowboys vs. Giants

Vikings vs. Packers

Steelers vs. Jets

Redskins vs. Bills

Each team has an opponent and there are no contradictions in the given information. Problems of this type can also be generated from other events, such as baseball, basketball, or even dating, in which some type of pairing is used.

PROBLEM SET 14-1

Problems, 19, 20, 21, 24, 25, 32, and 33 are modifications of the following problems from the Mathematical Association of America's Annual High School Mathematics Examination: 9 (1972); 31 (1970); 15 (1971); 23 (1971); 34 (1970); 32 (1970); and 34 (1968). Also, Problems 17 and 18 are modifications of Problems 190 and 153, respectively, taken from the *Comprehensive School Mathematics Program, Elements of Mathematics, Book B, EM Problem Book,* by CEMREL Inc. (1975).

1. A ball bounces 0.8 of the distance from which it is dropped each time it is dropped. If it is dropped from a height of 6 feet, what is the least number of bounces the ball makes before it rises to a height of less than 1 foot?

2. Jim has saved some silver dollars. He wants to divide them among Tom, Dick, Mary, and Sue so that Tom gets $\frac{1}{2}$ of the total amount, Dick gets $\frac{1}{4}$, Mary gets $\frac{1}{5}$, and Sue gets 9 of the dollars. How many dollars has Jim saved?

3. During the baseball season thus far, Reggie has been at bat 381 times and has a batting average of approximately 0.291—that is, his number of hits divided by 381 is 0.291. If he has 60 more official times at bat this season, how many hits must he get in order to end the season with a batting average of 0.300 or better?

4. A race track is 400 feet along the straight section and has a semicircle of radius 50 feet at each end. If one horse runs 10 feet from the inside railing at all times and a second horse runs 20 feet from the railing at all times, what is the difference in distance covered by the two horses in one lap of the track?

5. A circular object $\frac{1}{2}$ inch in diameter is dropped on a large grid consisting of squares that measure 3 inches on a side. If the circular object falls within the grid, what is the probability that it will not touch a grid line?

6. Willie can row 4 miles per hour in still water. If it takes him 2 hours to cover a certain distance rowing upstream and only 1 hour to row the same distance downstream, how fast is the current moving?

7. What is the least number of weights that can be used in order to be able to weigh any amount from 1 ounce to 680 ounces on a balance scale?

8. A computer is programmed to scan digits of successive integers. For example, if it scans the integers 1, 2, 3, 4, 5, 6, 7, 8, 9, 10, 11, 12, it has scanned 15 digits. How many digits has the computer scanned if it scans the consecutive integers from 1 through 10,000,000?

9. Find the remainder when $5^{999,999}$ is divided by 7.

10. A box contains ten red balls and five white balls. One ball is drawn at random from the box and is replaced by a ball of the opposite color. Now, if a ball is drawn from the box, what is the probability that it is red?

11. If Tom can beat Dick by 100 m in a 2-km race and Dick can beat Harry by 200 m in a 2-km race, then by how many meters can Tom beat Harry in a 2-km race?

12. Suppose you have one 5-L container and one 3-L container. How can you take out exactly 7 L of water from a well?

13. A single-elimination handball tournament was organized. There were 98 entrants, so in the first round there were 49 matches. In the second round, the 49 players were paired in 24 matches and one player received a bye. In the third round, the 25 players were then paired in 12 matches with one bye. The play and the pairing continued until a champion was determined.
   (a) How many matches were played?
   (b) If *n* players were entered in the tournament, how many matches would be required?

14. A circular race track for two runners has a 40-m radius for the inside running lane and a 41-m radius for the outside running lane.
   (a) How much of a head start should the outside runner be given?
   (b) How much of a head start should the outside runner be given if the radius of the inside running lane is 80 m and the radius of the outside lane is 81 m?

15. Without using a calculator, find the number of digits in the number $2^{12} \cdot 5^8$.

16. (a) Discover a pattern for the following sequence.
$$\frac{3}{5}, \frac{7}{9}, \frac{11}{13}, \frac{15}{17}, \frac{19}{21}, \cdots$$
   (b) Find the 1000th fraction in the sequence.
   ★(c) Prove that all the fractions (there are infinitely many) in the sequence are in simplest form.

17. Start with a piece of paper. Cut it into five pieces. Take any one of the pieces and again cut it into five pieces. Then, pick one of these pieces and cut it into five pieces, and so on.
   (a) What numbers of pieces can be obtained in this way?
   (b) What is the number of pieces after the *n*th experiment?

18. In the figure, $\overline{BC}$ and $\overline{BE}$ represent two positions of a ladder. How wide is $\overline{AD}$ and how long is the ladder if $AC = 12$ m, $ED = 9$ m, $\overline{CB} \cong \overline{BE}$, and $\overline{CB} \perp \overline{BE}$?

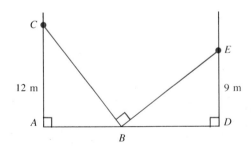

19. Ann and Sue bought identical boxes of stationery. Ann used hers to write 1-sheet letters and Sue used hers to write 3-sheet letters. Ann used all the envelopes and had 50 sheets of paper left, and Sue used all the sheets of paper and had 50 envelopes left. Find the number of sheets of paper in each box.

20. If a number is selected at random from the set of all five-digit numbers in which the sum of the digits equals 43, what is the probability that the number is divisible by 11?

21. An aquarium is in the shape of a right rectangular prism. It has a rectangular face that is 10 inches wide and 8 inches high. When the aquarium is tilted, the water in it just covers an 8 by 10 inch end, but only three-fourths of the rectangular bottom. Find the depth of the water when the aquarium is level on the table.

22. From a wire 10 units long, different shapes are constructed: a square, a rectangle with one side 2 units long, an equilateral triangle, a right isosceles triangle, and a circle.
   (a) Find the area of each shape. Which shape has the greatest area?
   (b) Make a conjecture concerning which figure has the greatest area among all figures with a given perimeter.

23. Susan's executive salary increased each of the past 2 years by 50% over the preceding year. Her present salary is $100,000 per year. To the nearest dollar, how much did she make 2 years ago?

24. Teams A and B play a series of games. The odds of either team winning any game are even. Team A must win two games and Team B must win three games to win the series. Find the odds in favor of Team A winning the series.

25. Find the greatest integer such that when each of the numbers 13,511, 13,903, and 14,589 is divided by this integer, the remainders are the same.

26. Take a two- or three-digit number and create a new number by reversing the digits of the original number. Then, subtract the lesser number from the greater. Observe that the difference is divisible by 9. For example, $561 - 165$ is 396, which is divisible by 9. Is this always true? Justify your answer.

27. What is the angle between the clock hands at 2:15?

28. Given a regular hexagon and a point in its plane, and using only a straightedge and a compass, construct a straight line through the given point that separates the given hexagon into two parts of equal area.

29. Find the sum of all the digits in the integers 1 through 1,000,000,000.

30. Two adjacent sides of a parallelogram are on the lines given by $3x - 2y = 6$ and $5x + 4y = 21$. One vertex is at $(2, ^-1)$. Without graphing, find the equations of the lines containing the other two sides and the coordinates of the point where the diagonals intersect.

31. Without graphing, find the center and radius of the circle passing through the points with coordinates $(0, 0)$, $(1, ^-3)$, and $(4, 0)$.

★**32.** Starting at the same time from diametrically opposite points, Linda and David travel around a circular track at uniform speeds in opposite directions.

They meet after David has traveled 100 m and a second time 60 m before Linda completes one lap. Find the circumference of the track.

★33. With 400 members voting, the House of Representatives defeated a bill. A revote, with the same members voting, resulted in passage of the bill by twice the margin with which it was originally defeated. The number voting for the bill on the revote was $\frac{12}{11}$ of the number voting against it originally. How many more members voted for the bill the second time than voted for it the first time?

★34. Lines from the vertices of square $ABCD$ to the midpoints of the sides M, N, O, and P are shown in the following figure.
(a) Prove that quadrilateral $HGFE$ is a square.
(b) What is the area of square $HGFE$ if the area of quadrilateral $ABCD$ is 100 cm²? Justify your answer.

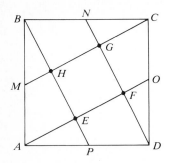

35. The "triangle" pictured below is called **Pascal's triangle,** after the French mathematician Blaise Pascal. Each number in the triangle, except the ones on the "boundary," equals the sum of two immediate neighboring numbers in the preceding row. (Note how the numbers in the triangle compare with those in Figure 14-6.)

```
                                        Row
                                        ───
              1                         (0)
           1     1                      (1)
        1     2     1                   (2)
      1     3     3     1               (3)
    1     4     6     4     1           (4)
  1     5    10    10     5     1       (5)
1     6    15    20    15     6     1   (6)
1   7   21   35   35   21   7   1       (7)
```

(a) Continue the triangle by finding two more rows.
(b) Find the sums of the numbers in the first row, the second row, the third row, and the fourth row. Do you notice a pattern? Can you predict the sum of the numbers in the tenth row? Make a general conjecture for the sum of the numbers in the nth row.
(c) Find the "alternate" sum of numbers in each row after row 1; that is,

$$1 - 1$$
$$1 - 2 + 1$$
$$1 - 3 + 3 - 1$$
$$1 - 4 + 6 - 4 + 1$$

(d) Find other patterns among the numbers in Pascal's triangle.

★36. Justify your conjecture in Problem 35(b).

SELECTED BIBLIOGRAPHY

Averbach, B., and O. Chein. *Mathematics, Problem Solving Through Recreational Mathematics.* San Francisco, Calif.: Freeman, 1980.

Brousseau, A. *Mathematics Contest Problems.* Palo Alto, Calif.: Creative Publications, 1972.

Charosh, M. *Mathematical Challenges.* Reston, Va.: National Council of Teachers of Mathematics, 1965.

Greenes, C., J. Gregory, and D. Seymour. *Successful Problem Solving Techniques.* Palo Alto, Calif.: Creative Publications, 1977.

Greenes, C., R. Spungin, and J. Dombrowski. *Problem-Mathics.* Palo Alto, Calif.: Creative Publications, 1977.

Hill, T. *Mathematical Challenges 11 Plus Six.* Reston, Va.: National Council of Teachers of Mathematics, 1974.

Honsberger, R. *Mathematical Morsels.* Washington, D.C.: The Mathematical Association of America, 1978.

Hughes, B. *Thinking Through Problems.* Palo Alto, Calif.: Creative Publications, 1976.

Kordemsky, B. *The Moscow Puzzles.* New York: Scribner, 1972.

Krulik, S., and J. Rudnick. *Problem Solving: A Handbook for Teachers.* Boston, Mass.: Allyn and Bacon, 1980.

Krulik, S., and R. Reys. *Problem Solving in School Mathematics, 1980 Yearbook.* Reston, Va.: National Council of Teachers of Mathematics, 1980.

Libeskind, S. "A Problem Solving Approach to Teaching Mathematics." *Educational Studies in Mathematics* 8 (1977):167–179.

Mira, J. *Mathematical Teasers*. New York: Barnes, 1970.

Pederson, J., and F. Armbruster. *A New Twist*. Reading, Mass.: Addison-Wesley, 1979.

Polya, G. *How To Solve It*. Princeton, N.J.: Princeton University Press, 1957.

Polya, G. *Mathematical Discovery*. 2 vols. New York: Wiley, 1962–1965.

Polya, G. *Mathematics and Plausible Reasoning*. 2 vols. Princeton, N.J.: Princeton University Press, 1954.

Porter, R. *Project a Puzzle*. Reston, Va.: National Council of Teachers of Mathematics, 1978.

Salkind, C., and J. Earl. *The Contest Problem Book III*. Washington, D.C.: The Mathematical Association of America, 1973.

An Introduction to Computers and the BASIC Language

Introduction

The computer is a machine capable of doing a large number of arithmetic calculations in a very short time, but its primary usefulness is in the sequential processing, storage, and retrieval of large quantities of information. Our primary goal in this appendix is to familiarize you with the rudiments of the BASIC language and to provide practice in using some of the commands of BASIC. We believe that one way to become more computer literate is to realize that a computer must be told in precise detail how to perform a given task. To communicate with a computer and to tell it how to perform tasks, we write a set of instructions called a **program,** or use programs that other people have written. Computer programs are generally referred to as **software.** Before considering computer commands and programs, we first discuss the parts of a computer.

program
software

THE PARTS OF A COMPUTER

Many people are overwhelmed by computer vocabulary when they are first introduced to it. Some computer terminology is useful in reading journal articles and understanding the basics of computer literacy. A minimum of terminology is introduced here. A computer system, known as **hardware,** consists of three major groups of components: the *input/output* group, the *computing* group, and the *auxiliary storage* group. A schematic picture of such a computer system is shown in Figure AI-1.

hardware

Figure AI-1

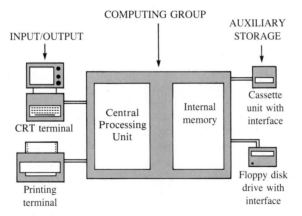

COMPUTING GROUP

INPUT/OUTPUT

AUXILIARY STORAGE

CRT terminal

Central Processing Unit

Internal memory

Cassette unit with interface

Floppy disk drive with interface

Printing terminal

input unit
output unit
central processing unit (CPU)   *internal memory*

The **input unit** is used to get information into the computer. The **output unit** sends obtained information to the user.

The computing group consists of a **central processing unit (CPU)** and an **internal memory.** The central processing unit contains an arithmetic/logic unit consisting of electronic circuits that perform arithmetic and logical operations, and a control unit that coordinates all the computer's activities. The internal memory unit is used for temporary storage of programs, input data, intermediate results, and output results. It also can hold permanent software to run the system.

auxiliary storage group

The **auxiliary storage group** provides a method of storing written programs so that they are not lost when the computer is turned off. Minicomputers commonly use either floppy disks or cassette tapes for storage.

HISTORY OF COMPUTING

Next, we consider how we got to the place that is sometimes called the "Second Industrial Revolution."

One of the earliest computing devices was the abacus, as pictured in Figure AI-2.

Figure AI-2

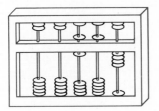

Another forerunner of the modern computer was Napier's "bones." John Napier, in 1617, published a work describing methods of performing computations on rods, or "bones" (made of ivory), on which multiples of numbers were printed.

In 1642, Blaise Pascal, a French scientist-philosopher, built a digital calculating machine that resembled a modern desk calculator and used gears to carry out computations. Pascal's machine could be used for addition and subtraction.

In 1671, Gottfried Wilhelm von Leibnitz, one of the fathers of calculus, invented the "Stepped Reckoner." This machine could add, subtract, multiply, divide, and extract square roots through the use of repeated additions in the binary system. The machine was unreliable, but its historical significance is in the use of the binary system instead of the decimal system in computing machinery.

In the 1830s, Charles Babbage, of England, developed plans for an "analytical engine," now referred to commonly as Babbage's Machine. This machine was to be essentially self-controlled; that is, computed answers could be used in further calculations. Although the machine was not built, the plans had a significant impact on computing because the proposed device could compare quantities and, depending on the comparison, move to another instruction. Also, because the device could use a result in subsequent calculations, it was possible for the machine to modify its own programs.

Babbage envisioned a machine that used punched cards similar to those used by Joseph-Marie Jacquard, a turn-of-the-nineteenth-century French weaver, for both input and output. In addition, he formulated plans for his machine to have sequential control, that is, program control that allowed branching, looping, and storage units.

Lady Ada Lovelace (1815–1852) was a close friend of Babbage's who helped clarify the efforts of Babbage and who is generally credited with being the "first programmer." The programming language Ada is named for her.

George Boole, an English logician and mathematician, developed binary logic operators in 1859 in his *Treatise on Differential Equations* and set the stage for the use of binary switching in computers.

In 1886, a U.S. statistician named Herman Hollerith furthered Jacquard's notion of punched cards and combined them with electromagnetic inventions to aid in counting the data in the Census of 1890. The cards developed by Hollerith won him fame and are essentially the same type used today. In 1911, Hollerith helped form the Computing-Tabulating-Recording Company, which later became International Business Machines Corporation (IBM).

In the late 1930s and early 1940s, Howard Aiken of Harvard University, in cooperation with IBM, developed the Mark I calculator, an electromechanical machine about 50 feet long and 8 feet high. The Mark I was a fully automatic calculator. In 1946, the ENIAC (**E**lectronic **N**umerical **I**ntegrator **a**nd **C**omputer) was developed by J. Prosper Eckert and John W. Mauchly. ENIAC was the first all-purpose, all-electronic digital computer. Its developers later helped complete the UNIVAC I, the first computer to handle both numerical and alphanumeric information.

One of the people who developed programs for both the Mark I and early UNIVAC computers was Grace Hopper (b. 1906), who later became a pioneer in the field of computer languages. She developed the first practical compiler and helped in the development of COBOL (**CO**mmon **B**usiness **O**riented **L**anguage). In addition, she gave us the word "**bug**" for problems in computer programs. The use of this word was the result of her finding a moth in an early computer that caused it to malfunction.

bug

In 1947, John von Neumann, a pure mathematician who studied the mathematical logic of the computer, devised a method for developing the stored-program computer, the EDVAC (**E**lectronic **D**iscrete **V**ariable **A**utomatic **C**omputer), which became operational in 1951. Possibly, only von Neumann could have envisioned today's high-speed multipurpose computers.

The microcomputer was developed when advances in computer chips were made in the mid-seventies. It is impossible to predict with any degree of accuracy what the next two decades will bring in the computer industry.

machine language

As computers have developed rapidly, so have different computer languages. A computer understands instructions coded in **machine language,** that is, the fundamental language understood by a particular computer. Machine language consists of numerical codes in the form of binary numbers, which are sequences of 0s and 1s (base two) that instruct the computer to perform its basic functions. Because machine language is hard for people to use, computer scientists have developed easier languages to use with computers that the computer in turn converts to its particular machine language.

One of the most widespread and easiest-to-learn languages is BASIC (Beginner's All-purpose Symbolic Instruction Code). BASIC was originally developed in the mid-sixties at Dartmouth College by two mathematics professors, John Kemeny and Thomas Kurtz.

WRITING COMPUTER PROGRAMS

To communicate with a computer, we write a program. The four-step, Polya-type approach introduced in Chapter 1 is very useful in writing computer programs to solve problems. In the first step—Understanding the Problem—we should be sure of what the program is to accomplish, that is, what the output is to be. We must identify what information is input data. We must determine if we have enough input data to obtain the desired output. In the second step—Devising a Plan—we must decide how to organize the sequence to produce the desired output. The strategy used in this step will depend on the programmer's experience and the difficulty of the problem. In the third step—Carrying Out the Plan—we run the program and make any necessary corrections; that is, we debug the program. In the fourth step—Looking Back—we analyze the program to see if it accomplished the goal. In this step, we can revise the program to become more efficient, to improve the format, or to perform different tasks. All four steps are helpful when writing computer programs.

Section AI-1

BASIC: Variables and Operations

system commands
programming commands

BASIC is a language consisting of words, punctuation, and syntax used in combination to form statements. Some BASIC key words are **system commands,** such as RUN and LIST; other BASIC key words are **programming commands,** such as PRINT, LET, INPUT, REM, END, GOTO, IF-THEN, and FOR-NEXT. Statements are put together, using programming commands, to form a program. Figure AI-3 illustrates two examples of very simple BASIC programs: the first for printing a message and the second for calculating the value of Y for a given value of X, where

$$Y = 5X^4 + \frac{4}{X} - 3$$

Figure AI-3

(a)
```
10 PRINT "HERE WE GO"
20 PRINT "LET'S LEARN TO PROGRAM"
30 END
```

(b)
```
10 INPUT X
20 LET Y = 5 * X ∧ 4 + 4 / X - 3
30 PRINT Y
40 END
```

numeric variables

In BASIC, **numeric variables** may be denoted by single letters, by two letters placed next to each other with no spaces between them, by a letter followed by a single digit, or by a letter followed by a number in parentheses. In Figure AI-3(b), the variables X and Y are used. A different type of variable, called a **string variable,** is denoted by a letter followed by a dollar sign, for example, A\$. A string variable may be used for nonnumeric values such as words or strings of symbols.

string variables

Some of the symbols in Figure AI-3(b) that are used in BASIC to represent arithmetic operations are different from usual symbols. Multiplication is indicated by an asterisk (∗); raising a quantity to a power is indicated by a caret (∧) or two asterisks (∗∗) or by a vertical arrow (↑); addition is represented by a plus sign (+); subtraction by a minus sign (−); and division by a slash (/). Examples are given in Table AI-1.

Table AI-1

Operation	Math Symbol	Math Example	BASIC Symbol	BASIC Example
Addition	$+$	$2 + 3$	$+$	$2 + 3$
Subtraction	$-$	$5 - 2$	$-$	$5 - 2$
Multiplication	$\times$ or $\cdot$	5×3 or $5 \cdot 3$	$*$	$5 * 3$
Division	$\div$	$16 \div 4$	$/$	$16 / 4$
Exponentiation		2^3	$\wedge$ or $\uparrow$ or $**$	$2 \wedge 3$ or $2 \uparrow 3$ or $2 ** 3$

Remark Most computers that use BASIC are not fussy about spacing around arithmetic operation symbols. Thus, $2+3$, $2+\ 3$, $2\ +3$, and $2\ +\ 3$ would be equally recognized. Some programmers prefer not to space in division, multiplication, and exponentiation but like to space in addition and subtraction. Try different styles on your computer to see how it responds.

SYSTEM COMMANDS

line number

RUN

LIST

NEW

Each line in the programs in Figure AI-3 is a statement that gives the computer an instruction. Notice that each statement begins with a **line number.** A system command such as RUN does not require a line number. When **RUN** is entered with a program in the internal memory, the computer executes the instructions in the program in the order of the line numbers. In most cases, the numbers 10, 20, 30, . . . or 100, 200, 300, . . . are used for line numbers to leave room for forgotten statements, which may be added later. For example, suppose that after typing line 30 in Figure AI-3(b) (PRINT Y), you realize that you should have had a statement between lines 10 and 20. All that is necessary is to type the new statement preceded by a line number between 10 and 20, such as 15. The new line can be typed at any time when the program is still active. The computer will rearrange all the lines in the correct order and will execute the program in the correct order. To delete errors in a given line, you may retype the line correctly. It should be noted that some computers allow full-screen editing, in which parts of a line may be changed without retyping an entire line. When the system command **LIST** is entered, the program will be displayed with all the line numbers in proper numerical order and all corrections included. LIST can be used at any time to see the complete program that is currently in the computer's memory.

Another system command that is useful if more than one program is being written is **NEW.** If we type NEW and press the $\boxed{\text{RETURN}}$ key, the computer's memory is cleared, and a new program can be written without the danger of having the lines of the new program merged with a program that is already in the computer's memory. For this reason, it is a good idea to type NEW before writing each new program. (Other commands may serve the same purpose as NEW on various machines.) However, remember that when NEW is typed and the $\boxed{\text{RETURN}}$ key is pressed, the old program in the internal memory is lost. If we want the old program saved, it must be stored in the auxiliary memory.

There are many other system commands, including SAVE, DEL, LOAD, and SCR. Readers should consult their microcomputer BASIC manuals to see how these and other commands work.

PROGRAMMING COMMANDS

The four BASIC key words that were used in Figure AI-3(b) are INPUT, LET, PRINT, and END. These are called programming commands. In line

INPUT   10, the key word **INPUT** is followed by the variable X. The INPUT statement causes the computer to stop during the run and print "?". The user must assign a specific numerical value to X in this particular program by typing in that value and pressing the | RETURN | key. After the value is entered, the program will continue. An INPUT statement always consists of the word INPUT and a variable or list of variables separated by commas.

LET   In line 20, we see a statement that contains the key word **LET**. A LET statement is used to assign a value to a variable. The LET statement places data in a memory location. In Figure AI-3(b), the variable Y is assigned the value

$$5 * X \wedge 4 + 4 / X - 3$$

and this value is stored in the memory location labeled Y. The statement is composed of a line number, followed by the word LET, followed by a variable that equals a mathematical expression. The command LET is frequently optional. For example, LET $X = 17$ is simply written as $X = 17$ on many machines.

PRINT   In line 30, we see the key word **PRINT.** PRINT Y is a direction to the computer to print the value of the variable Y when the program is run. (Other uses of the key word PRINT will be discussed later.)

END   The **END** statement indicates the end of a program. Some systems do not require an END statement, but it is good programming style to use it.

When the program in Figure AI-3(b) is run, the computer acts as the function machine shown in Figure AI-4. When the value of the variable X is input, the machine assigns a value for Y according to the rule $Y = 5X^4 + \dfrac{4}{X} - 3$.

Thus, if the input is 2 (that is, $X = 2$), the output will be $Y = 5 \cdot 2^4 + \dfrac{4}{2} - 3 = 79$.

Figure AI-4

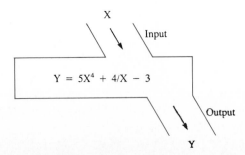

To use the program in Figure AI-3(b) to find the value of Y for a given X, such as X = 2, type RUN and then press the ⎡RETURN⎤ key. (*For the remainder of the chapter, it is assumed that the* ⎡RETURN⎤ *key is pressed as needed.*) The computer will print a question mark, which indicates that the user should input a value, in our case, 2. The computer then prints the corresponding value of Y, which is 79. The interaction with the computer will look like this (*the boldface characters are typed by the computer*):

RUN

? 2

79

On many computers, the word READY is printed when the run is completed. Other machines may indicate this by the word OK or a flashing cursor or some other device. These are the computer's ways of saying that it is ready for your next instruction. If you wish to input a new number for X into the program, type RUN again and press the ⎡RETURN⎤ key. Another question mark will appear, and the new number may be input. If we input 180 for X and run the program, the printout appears as follows.

RUN

? 180

5.2488E + 09

E-notation   The answer, 5.2488E + 09, is represented using **E-notation.** This notation is like scientific notation in that the letter E means "exponent" and indicates the power or exponent on the base ten. The number of places before a machine reports E-notation may vary from one brand of computer to another.

1.876E + 07 means $1.876 \cdot 10^7$, or 18,760,000

7.9325E − 04 means $7.9325 \cdot 10^{-4}$, or 0.00079325

The order of operations that a computer uses is the same as those discussed in previous chapters; that is, exponentiations (if any) are done first; multiplications and divisions are done next, in order from left to right; and additions and subtractions are done last, also in order from left to right unless parentheses indicate otherwise. *When you are in doubt as to how the computer will execute the operations, use parentheses.*

Example AI-I

Write (a) through (c) in BASIC notation, and (d) and (e) in base-ten notation.

(a) $b^2 - 4ac$ (b) $\dfrac{3(4 + b)}{c}$

(c) $3 + 4c^3$ (d) 3.4798E + 08

(e) 4.5935E − 05

Solution

(a) $B \wedge 2 - 4 * A * C$ (b) $3 * (4 + B) / C$
(c) $3 + 4 * C \wedge 3$ (d) $3.4798 \cdot 10^8 = 347,980,000$
(e) $4.5935 \cdot 10^{-5} = 0.000045935$

Several BASIC programming commands are used in the solution to the following problem.

PROBLEM I

In 1626, Peter Minuit, a Dutch settler, bought Manhattan Island for $24 worth of trinkets. (a) If this money had been invested in 1626 in a bank at 5% interest compounded annually, what would it be worth 364 years later, in 1990? (b) What would the investment have been worth if the money had been invested at 5% annual interest compounded monthly?

UNDERSTANDING THE PROBLEM The problem is to determine the amount of interest earned on $24 if it was invested from 1626 until 1990, 364 years later, at 5% interest compounded annually. The second question is to determine the amount of interest if the compounding was monthly for the same time period.

DEVISING A PLAN We can find the amount A if P dollars are invested at I% interest rate per time period for N time periods by using the following formula.

$$A = P(1 + I)^N$$

We can write a program for calculating the balance A by entering the values of P, I, and N, defining A, and asking the computer to print the value of A, as shown.

```
10 LET P = 24
20 LET I = 5
30 LET N = 364
40 LET A = P * (1 + I / 100) ^ N
50 PRINT A
60 END
```

CARRYING OUT THE PLAN

(a) If we execute the program, we find that A is approximately equal to $1,239,127,790.
(b) We can find the amount that the investment would be worth if the interest had been compounded monthly by changing the values of I and N. Because 5% is an annual interest rate, the monthly rate would be $\frac{5}{12}$%. Also, because there are 12 months in a year, the new value of N should be $364 \cdot 12$. If we run the program with these values, we find that the interest would be approximately $1,853,322,550.

LOOKING BACK This problem shows in a very vivid way that over a long period of time, interest compounded monthly will earn much more than interest compounded annually. Investigate what would happen if the interest were compounded daily.

So that other people may use a program, it is always wise to tell what a program does. To accomplish this, appropriate PRINT statements may be used. For example, the preceding program may be changed to the following.

```
 7 PRINT "THIS PROGRAM FINDS THE BALANCE ON $24 AT"
 8 PRINT "AN ANNUAL INTEREST RATE OF 5% COMPOUNDED"
 9 PRINT "MONTHLY FOR 364 YEARS."
10 LET P = 24
20 LET I = 5 / 12
30 LET N = 364 * 12
40 LET A = P * (1 + I / 100) ^ N
50 PRINT "THE BALANCE IS $";A
60 END
```

In lines 7, 8, and 9, we have used the programming command PRINT. When the program is run, the computer prints everything inside the quotation marks. When a semicolon is placed at the end of a PRINT statement, the computer continues the next PRINT statement on the same line, one space to the right of the last printed character. (This placement may vary on different machines.) In line 50, PRINT is used with a phrase in quotation marks followed by a semicolon and the letter A. When the semicolon is used, the value of A is printed immediately following the phrase. (You should investigate what happens when a comma is used in place of a semicolon.) When the program is run, the printout will appear as follows.

**THIS PROGRAM FINDS THE BALANCE ON $24 AT
AN ANNUAL INTEREST RATE OF 5% COMPOUNDED
MONTHLY FOR 364 YEARS.
THE BALANCE IS $1.85332255E+09**

Because the computer prints exactly what is inside the quotation marks, if A were inside the quotation marks in line 30, the last line of the executed program would appear as follows.

THE BALANCE IS $A

Other uses of the key word PRINT will be investigated in the exercises.

A programmer may wish to make a remark or title the program on the very first line. This can be done by using the programming command PRINT or a new programming command, **REM** (for REMARK). If a REM statement is used, the computer will save the line as an explanation of the program for anybody who desires to list the program. The REM statement is ignored during execution and is not printed during a run. To title the preceding program, the following REM statement may be added.

REM

```
 6 REM THE MANHATTAN ISLAND PROBLEM
```

Example AI-2

Fair State University is increasing the salaries of its faculty based on performance. A department secretary needs a computer program to check the controller's figures. The program must calculate the next year's salary for each faculty member, given the present salary and the percent of increase of the salary of that faculty member. Write a program for the secretary to calculate each new salary. Try your program for an old salary of $38,479 and a percent of increase of 17%.

Solution

If the old salary and the percent of increase are denoted by S and P, respectively, then the new salary N is given by $N = S + S \cdot \frac{P}{100}$, or

$N = S \cdot \left(1 + \frac{P}{100}\right)$. A program for this computation follows.

```
10 REM UNIVERSITY SALARY INCREASE
20 PRINT "ENTER THE OLD SALARY AND THE PERCENT"
30 PRINT "OF INCREASE SEPARATED BY A COMMA."
40 INPUT S, P
50 LET N = S * (1 + P / 100)
60 PRINT "THE NEW SALARY IS $"; N
70 END
```

When the program is run for the given salary and percent of increase, the printout will be as follows.

**ENTER THE OLD SALARY AND THE PERCENT
OF INCREASE SEPARATED BY A COMMA.**
?38479,17
THE NEW SALARY IS $45020.43

SUMMARY OF COMMANDS

RUN	Causes the computer to execute a program.
LIST	Causes the computer to print a listing of a program.
NEW	Clears the computer's memory.
INPUT	Takes one input and causes the computer to pause during execution and output "?" as a prompt for data.
LET	Assigns a value to a variable.
PRINT	Causes the computer to print an input.
END	Indicates the end of a program.
REM	Used to include a remark or reminder.

PROBLEM SET AI-I

1. Which of the following are valid variables in BASIC?

(a) P (b) M4 (c) 3Z (d) M
(e) AB (f) BA(3) (g) A 4

2. Write each of the following using BASIC notation.

(a) $X^2 + Y^2 - 3Z$ (b) $\left(\dfrac{24 \cdot 34}{2}\right)^3$

(c) $a + b - \dfrac{c^2}{d}$ (d) $\dfrac{a + b}{c + d}$

(e) $\dfrac{15}{a(2b^2 + 5)}$

3. Perform the following calculations in the same order a computer would.

(a) 3 * 5 - 2 * 6 + 4
(b) 7 * (6 - 2) / 4
(c) 3 * (5 + 7) / (3 + 3)
(d) 3 ∧ 3 / 9
(e) (2 * (3 - 5)) ∧ 2
(f) 9 ∧ 2 - 5 ∧ 3

4. Write each of the following as a base-ten number in standard form.
(a) 3.52E+07   (b) 1.93E−05
(c) −1.233E−06   (d) −7.402E+03

5. Predict the output, if any, for each of the following programs. If possible, check your answers on a computer.

(a)
```
10 A = 5
20 B = 10
30 PRINT A,B
40 END
```

(b)
```
10 A = 5
20 B = 10
30 PRINT "A,B"
40 END
```

(c)
```
10 A = 5
20 B = 10
30 PRINT A,,B
40 END
```

(d)
```
10 A = 5
20 B = 10
30 PRINT A;B
40 END
```
```
10 A = 5
20 B = 10
   PRINT A,B
40 END
```

(f)
```
10 A = 5
20 B = 10
30 PRINT A
40 PRINT B
50 END
```

(g)
```
10 A = 5
20 B = 10
30 PRINT A;
40 PRINT B
50 END
```

(h)
```
10 A = 5
20 B = 10
30 PRINT "THE VALUE OF A"
35 PRINT "IS ";A;".";
40 PRINT " THE VALUE OF B"
45 PRINT "IS ";B;"."
50 END
```

(i)
```
10 A = 5
20 B = 10
30 PRINT "THE VALUE OF A"
35 PRINT "IS ",A,".";
40 PRINT " THE VALUE OF B"
45 PRINT "IS ";B;"."
50 END
```

6. (a) Write a computer program for calculating the value of Y for a given X, where

$$Y = 13X^5 - \frac{27}{X} + 3.$$

(b) Use the program in (a) to find the value of Y for: (i) $X = 1.873$; (ii) $X = 7$.

7. Most computers can be used as calculators by using a PRINT statement with no line number. For example, typing PRINT 5 + 3 [RETURN] causes the computer to print **8**. Write a single PRINT statement to compute $25 \cdot (0.97)^{365}$.

8. (a) Write a program (including a title and directions) for converting degrees Fahrenheit into degrees Celsius, using the formula $C = \frac{5}{9}(F - 32)$.
   (b) Use the program from (a) to convert the following Fahrenheit temperatures to Celsius.
   (i) 212°F   (ii) 98.6°F   (iii) 68°F
   (iv) 32°F   (v) ⁻40°F   (vi) ⁻273°F

9. Write a program for computing the perimeter P of a rectangle given its length L and width W, where $P = 2L + 2W$. Try your program for L = 16 cm and W = 5 cm.

10. Write a program for computing the volume of a right rectangular prism given its three dimensions L, W, and H, where V = LWH. Try your program for L = 8, W = 5, and H = 3.

In Problems 11–13, use the formula for compound interest.

*11. $100 is invested in a bank for 25 years at 18% interest compounded annually. (a) Find the balance by using a single PRINT statement. (b) Find the balance by writing a program with an input N, where N is the number of years the money is invested.

*12. (a) A certain bank pays 7% interest compounded annually. Write a program to calculate the balance after a given number of years for a given initial investment. Make the program give directions to the user, and utilize an INPUT statement.
   (b) Use the program in (a) to find the balance if $800 is invested in the bank for 8 years.

*13. (a) A $30,000 property depreciates after 1 year by 3% of its value. Write a program for finding the value of the property after N years, assuming this rate of depreciation stays constant.
   (b) Find the value of the property after 30 years.

Section AI-2   Branching

IF-THEN STATEMENTS

One possible use of the computer in education is in computer-assisted instruction—for example, in designing programs to create drill problems. Suppose we want to design a program that can be used repeatedly to allow students to practice adding two numbers. We want the students to keep

branching

IF-THEN

working on a problem until they get it correct; then, they will receive a new problem. This can be accomplished through **branching.** One way that branching occurs is when decisions are made in a program through the use of the programming statement **IF-THEN.** (This type of branching is called *conditional branching.*) The general form of an IF-THEN statement is IF (condition) THEN (line number or command). For example,

```
30 IF X < 2 THEN 60
```

When the computer executes line 30, it evaluates the condition $X < 2$. If the value of X is less than 2, then the computer branches to the line number following the word THEN, in this case, line 60. If the value of X is not less than 2, the computer executes the next statement listed in numerical order. The condition following the IF part always includes an equality or inequality symbol. However, in BASIC, some of these symbols differ from their mathematical counterparts. The symbols are compared in Table AI-2.

Table AI-2

Mathematical Symbol	BASIC Symbol	Meaning
$=$	$=$	Equals
$<$	$<$	Is less than
$\leq$	$<=$	Is less than or equal to
$>$	$>$	Is greater than
$\geq$	$>=$	Is greater than or equal to
$\neq$	$<>$	Is not equal to

We now attempt to write the two-number drill program mentioned previously. In order for a program to be meaningful to another user, it should be "user friendly"; that is, it should contain instructions telling the user exactly what to do. These instructions can be given by using PRINT statements. The numbers to be added must either be input by the user or generated by the computer's random-number generator. For this program, we choose the second option. However, before doing this, we investigate the computer's random-number generator.

RND

The general form of the function is **RND**(X), where RND is the name of the function and X is the argument of the function. On some computers, the value of the argument is important; on others, it is not. (On some computers, the argument is not needed at all.) The reader should consult the user's manual for specifics. For this text, we use RND(1).

The RND function causes some computers to select a random (unpredictable) six-digit number between 0 and .999999, such as .893352, .158723, or .931562. Because many programs require the use of random numbers in ranges other than from 0 to 1, we must find a way to select numbers in other ranges. For example, suppose we want the computer to select a nonnegative integer less than 100. If we multiply the RND function by 100, it will generate values between 0 and 99.9999. If we want random-integer values between 0 and 99.9999, we use the INT function, as follows.

```
10 LET N = INT(100 * RND(1))
```

Now, N takes on nonnegative integer values less than 100.

INT   **INT,** called the greatest-integer function, is a BASIC command used in the form of INT(X), where X is the argument. When used in a program, INT(X) will produce the greatest integer less than or equal to X. For example, executing PRINT INT(3.5) produces the computer output **3**.

If we want our two-number addition program to give us addition facts involving numbers between 1 and 10, we use the expression INT(10 ∗ RND(1)) + 1 in our program.

Once the numbers are chosen and added, we must inform the user whether the sum is correct. We must also determine whether the user wishes to continue the practice. IF-THEN and GOTO statements are used to accomplish

GOTO   this. **GOTO** statements allow the program to branch to another statement instead of following the statements in the order given by the line numbers. (Observe that the GOTO command allows unconditional branching to another line of the program.) These ideas are incorporated in the following program.

```
10 PRINT "THIS PROGRAM PROVIDES ADDITION PRACTICE."
20 LET A = INT (10 * RND(1)) + 1
30 LET B = INT (10 * RND(1)) + 1
40 PRINT "AFTER THE QUESTION MARK, TYPE THE SUM."
50 PRINT A;"+";B;"=";
60 INPUT C
70 IF A + B = C THEN 100
80 PRINT "SORRY, TRY AGAIN."
90 GOTO 40
100 PRINT "VERY GOOD. DO YOU WANT TO ADD"
110 PRINT "OTHER NUMBERS?  IF YES, TYPE 1."
120 INPUT D$
130 IF D$ = "YES" THEN 20
140 END
```

Note that there are two IF-THEN statements in the preceding program. When the program is run and line 70 is reached, and if A + B = C is true, then the computer branches to line 100 and continues the run. In line 70, if A + B = C is not true, the computer automatically goes to the next line, line 80, and continues the run.

When the program is run and the computer reaches line 90, the program automatically loops back to line 40, and the run continues. It should be noted that if a student continually misses the addition, the run will never get past line 90. (The program could have been written to ask the student if another try is desired.) On different machines, the procedure to get out of such a loop varies. On many machines, the keys $\boxed{\text{STOP}}$ or $\boxed{\text{BREAK}}$ are used. On

CONTROL-C   some other machines, the user should press the $\boxed{\text{CONTROL}}$ key and the $\boxed{\text{C}}$ key at the same time (called a **CONTROL-C**), or press the $\boxed{\text{RESET}}$ key or $\boxed{\text{CONTROL}}$ $\boxed{\text{RESET}}$. This may have to be done several times to stop the run, at which time the computer will indicate that it is ready for you to proceed.

COUNTERS

Suppose we want to keep a record of how many drill exercises an individual attempts. This can be done by using a *counter*, which uses either an IF-THEN or a GOTO statement along with a LET statement. A LET statement allows us to set the value of a variable, for example, LET X = 10. BASIC also allows a variable to be defined in terms of itself, for example, LET X = X + 1. The computer does not interpret X = X + 1 as an equation, but rather as "replace X with X + 1." This is useful in a program that counts how many exercises were correctly answered or, in general, how many times a certain section of a program has been executed. Consider the following program.

```
10 LET X = 0
20 LET X = X + 1
30 PRINT X
40 IF X < 10 THEN 20
50 END
```

initialized   In line 10, X is **initialized,** or set to 0. Line 20 is the counter. When the program is run, the output appears as follows.

1

2

3

⋮

10

To understand this output, notice that in line 10, X equals 0. In line 20, the new value of X becomes 0 + 1, or 1. Hence, at line 30, the value 1 is printed. Next, the computer executes the instruction in line 40. Because 1 < 10, it branches to line 20. As X now has value 1, the new value of X in line 20 becomes 1 + 1, or 2. Thus, 2 is printed, and so on. After 9 is printed, we are again at line 40. Because 9 < 10, the computer again branches to line 20, and the new value of X becomes 9 + 1, or 10. This value is printed; because 10 < 10 is false, the program continues to line 50 and ends.

We now return to our original addition-drill program. To keep a record of the number of drill exercises attempted, a counter is inserted between lines 30 and 40. A PRINT statement in line 140 outputs the desired record. The revised program is as follows.

```
10 PRINT "THIS PROGRAM PROVIDES ADDITION PRACTICE."
15 LET X = 0
20 LET A = INT (10 * RND(1)) + 1
30 LET B = INT (10 * RND(1)) + 1
35 LET X = X + 1
40 PRINT "AFTER THE QUESTION MARK, TYPE THE SUM."
50 PRINT A;"+";B;"=";
60 INPUT C
70 IF A + B = C THEN 100
80 PRINT "SORRY, TRY AGAIN."
90 GOTO 40
100 PRINT "VERY GOOD. DO YOU WANT TO ADD"
110 PRINT "ANOTHER PAIR OF NUMBERS?"
120 INPUT D$
130 IF D$ = "YES" THEN 20
140 PRINT "THE NUMBER OF EXERCISES WAS " ;X
150 END
```

The program could be edited to allow the computer to tell not only the number of exercises attempted but also the number done correctly.

FOR-NEXT STATEMENTS

FOR-NEXT

Another method for having the computer count is through the use of the key words **FOR-NEXT.** In a BASIC program, FOR-NEXT statements always occur in pairs, with the FOR statement preceding the associated NEXT statement. For example, we could utilize FOR-NEXT statements as shown.

```
20 FOR X = 1 TO 10
.
.
.
120 NEXT X
```

If a program containing the preceding lines is run and line 20 is reached, the computer initializes a counter by assigning the value of 1 to X. At line 120, the computer loops back to line 20, assigns the value 2 to X, again continues to line 120, loops back, and so on, until X = 10. When X is 10 and line 120 is reached, the computer continues on to the next line of the program following line 120. With no other directions in line 20, the computer automatically increments X by 1 each time the loop is passed through. X

STEP

can be incremented for other values by using the word **STEP** and the desired value. For example, replace line 20 with the following.

```
20 FOR X = 1 TO 10 STEP 0.5
```

This line will initialize X with a value of 1 and increase this value by 0.5 each time line 20 is reached. The values of X will be 1, 1.5, 2, 2.5, 3, . . . , 9, 9.5, 10.

STEP can also be used to decrement, rather than increment, the FOR-NEXT loop. For example, consider the following line.

```
20 FOR X = 10 TO 1 STEP -0.5
```

Here, the value of X will be initialized at 10 and will decrease in steps of 0.5 until it reaches X = 1. Thus, the values of X will be 10, 9.5, 9, 8.5, 8, . . . , 1.

FOR-NEXT commands are very useful when you know how many times to go through the loop. The counter and the IF-THEN loop are useful when you are not sure of the number of iterations. A further use of the FOR-NEXT command is given in the following problem.

Example AI-3

Maria Alvarez was asked to create a table of squares of the integers from 1 to 100 for her math class. Help her by writing a program to generate such a table.

Solution

A loop using FOR-NEXT commands can easily generate all the integers from 1 through 100, as follows.

```
10 FOR X = 1 TO 100
20 PRINT X,
30 NEXT X
40 END
```

When the program is run, a list of all the integers from 1 to 100 is printed in preset columns. This is the result of using a comma after the PRINT command.

Now, we must write a program to print the squares of those numbers. To do this, we modify line 20 to include both X and X^2. The entire program is as shown.

```
5 REM MARIA ALVAREZ TABLE OF SQUARES
6 PRINT "NUMBER","SQUARE"
10 FOR X = 1 TO 100
20 PRINT X, X ^ 2
30 NEXT X
40 END
```

When the program is run, the printout appears as follows.

NUMBER	SQUARE
1	1
2	4
3	9
4	16
⋮	⋮
100	10000

PROBLEM 2

Professor Anna Litik was asked by the university athletic director to devise a chart for converting the heights of visiting basketball players from inches to centimeters. Help Dr. Litik by writing a program that will print a table giving the conversions incremented by half inches from 65 inches to 84 inches.

UNDERSTANDING THE PROBLEM The problem is to write a program that will output the number of centimeters that corresponds to a certain number of inches. Furthermore, the numbers of inches are from 65 to 84, inclusive, and the conversions made must be for each half inch. To solve this problem, the conversion factor 1 inch = 2.54 cm is needed. Thus, 2 inches = 2(2.54) cm, or 5.08 cm, and, in general, N inches = N(2.54) cm.

DEVISING A PLAN We can write a program using FOR-NEXT statements to produce a table for converting heights from inches to centimeters. We let X represent the number of inches starting at 65, increment by 0.5, and end at 84. Between the FOR and NEXT statements, we must print the value of X to represent the equivalent number of centimeters. Because it would be inappropriate to report that a player's height is 196.62 cm, we need to report the heights as integers. We do this by using INT. In our program, we can use INT(X * 2.54) to assign an integer number of centimeters to X inches. However, INT does not round numbers. If we would like to build in a rounding factor, we might consider using INT(X * 2.54 + 0.5). (Why?)

To write the program, we set the first value of X equal to 65 inches. Next, we convert 65 inches to centimeters by multiplying by 2.54 and then choose the greatest integer less than or equal to $65 \cdot 2.54 + 0.5$. We then print X and the obtained integer and loop back for the next value of X, which is 0.5 greater than the last value converted. This procedure continues until all

SECTION AI-2 BRANCHING **695**

values have been converted. The complete program follows. In line 50, the PRINT statement is used to provide the desired output in a more readable format. When a PRINT statement is typed with no inputs, a blank line is left between the outputs.

```
10 REM THIS PROGRAM WILL PRINT A
20 REM TABLE FOR CONVERTING INCHES
30 REM TO CENTIMETERS
40 PRINT "INCHES", "CENTIMETERS"
50 PRINT
60 FOR X = 65 TO 84 STEP 0.5
70 LET Y = INT(X * 2.54 + 0.5)
80 PRINT X,Y
90 NEXT X
100 END
```

CARRYING OUT THE PLAN A shortened version of the printout obtained when the program is run follows. Notice that the space between the headings and the data was obtained from line 50 in the program.

INCHES	CENTIMETERS
65	165
65.5	166
66	168
66.5	169
67	170
67.5	171
68	173
68.5	174
69	175
69.5	177
⋮	⋮
83.5	212
84	213

LOOKING BACK This program could be revised to generate other conversion charts. All that would be necessary would be to find the required conversion factors and edit the program accordingly.

nested loop

Another use of FOR-NEXT programming commands involves a loop within a loop, which is called a **nested loop.** The following program contains a nested loop. The program has the computer print a multiple-choice answer sheet for a ten-question test. Each item has choices (1), (2), (3), and (4), and students are to circle the correct choice. The answer sheet is printed by having the computer type "1.", followed by "(1)", "(2)", "(3)", "(4)". Then, the computer types "2.", followed by "(1)", "(2)", "(3)", "(4)", and continues until the ten-question answer sheet is completed.

The order in which the nested loops are used is important. One loop is placed in the range of another loop. The only restriction is that the loops cannot cross. For example, the loops in the program in Figure AI-5(a) are acceptable, and the ones in Figure AI-5(b) are not, as shown in the following printouts.

Figure AI-5

```
(a) 10 REM THIS PROGRAM PRINTS A MULTIPLE-CHOICE
    20 REM ANSWER SHEET FOR 10 QUESTIONS
    30 FOR N = 1 TO 10
    40 PRINT N;". ";
    50 FOR P = 1 TO 4
    60 PRINT "(";P;")   ";
    70 NEXT P
    80 PRINT
    90 NEXT N
    100 END
```

1.	(1)	(2)	(3)	(4)
2.	(1)	(2)	(3)	(4)
3.	(1)	(2)	(3)	(4)

⋮

| 10. | (1) | (2) | (3) | (4) |

```
(b) 10 REM THIS PROGRAM PRINTS A MULTIPLE-CHOICE
    20 REM ANSWER SHEET FOR 10 QUESTIONS
    30 FOR N = 1 TO 10
    40 PRINT N;". ";
    50 FOR P = 1 TO 4
    60 PRINT "(";P;")   ";
    70 NEXT N
    80 PRINT
    90 NEXT P
    100 END
```

1.	(1)	2.	(1)	3.	(1)	4.	(1)	5.
(1)	6.	(1)	7.	(1)	8.	(1)	9.	(1)
10.	(1)

?NEXT WITHOUT FOR ERROR IN 90

READ AND DATA STATEMENTS

READ / DATA   When large blocks of data are used, the key words **READ** and **DATA** are very useful. The formats for the READ and DATA statements are as follows.

READ Variable(s)

DATA Constant(s)

The variables in a READ statement are separated by commas. Similarly, the constants in a DATA statement are separated by commas. A comma should not be used at the end of the data. An example of statements containing the commands READ and DATA follows.

```
10 READ A1, B, B2, Z
50 DATA 9, 6, 2, .5
```

When a program containing READ-DATA statements is run, the computer assigns the constants in the DATA statement to the variables in the READ statement in the order they are listed. A branching command, such as GOTO, is normally used to have the computer loop back to the READ statement so that it will use all the DATA when the program is run. It should be noted that several READ statements can be used with one DATA statement as long as there are sufficient data for each of the variables in the READ statement; or, one READ statement may be used with several DATA statements. An example of the use of the READ-DATA commands to solve a problem is given in Problem 3.

PROBLEM 3

Dr. Jubal, an English professor, had five test scores for each of his five graduate students in English. The grades for the students are as follows.

Student # (S)	Grammar (G)	Writing (W)	Drama (D)	Poetry (P)	Novel (N)
1	72	93	86	82	96
2	83	86	95	74	80
3	91	82	76	60	89
4	88	94	72	76	84
5	75	84	98	92	79

Determine averages for Dr. Jubal by writing a program to find the mean for each student.

UNDERSTANDING THE PROBLEM In this problem, we are given a list of scores for Dr. Jubal's students on various tests. We are to write a program to calculate the mean for each student, that is, the arithmetic average of the scores for each student. Thus, we need to find the sum of the five scores for each student and divide by 5.

DEVISING A PLAN We can write a progam to find the mean for each student by using READ-DATA statements. To find the mean for each student, we use a READ statement with the variable S for student number and variables G, W, D, P, and N for grammar, writing, drama, poetry, and novel scores, respectively. For example, for student 1, we want the computer to calculate $M = (G + W + D + P + N)/5$, or $(72 + 93 + 86 + 82 + 96)/5$. After the mean is computed for each student, we need a printout that lists student numbers and corresponding means. A sample program to compute the means is as follows.

```
10 REM THIS PROGRAM PRINTS MEANS FOR DR. JUBAL.
20 PRINT "STUDENT #, "MEAN"
30 READ S, G, W, D, P, N
40 LET M = (G + W + D + P + N) / 5
50 PRINT
60 PRINT S, M
70 GOTO 30
80 DATA 1,72,93,86,82,96,2,83,86,95,74,80,3,91,82,76,60,89
90 DATA 4,88,94,72,76,84,5,75,84,98,92,79
100 END
```

Remark Note that not all the data could be listed in one DATA line. The computer will accept data from as many DATA lines as you wish, but the number of DATA items should be a multiple of the number of variables in a READ statement. The DATA statements may be anywhere in the program, but they are usually at the end.

CARRYING OUT THE PLAN A run for the program would appear as follows.

STUDENT #	MEAN
1	85.8
2	83.6
3	79.6
4	82.8
5	85.6

?OUT OF DATA ERROR IN 30

Now, we have the averages of each of Dr. Jubal's students. Note the message at the end of the output. This message tells us that all the data have been used.

LOOKING BACK Various computers may print different messages or no message at all when all the data are used. To eliminate the message at the end of the printout, a method called **flagging** can be used. See a BASIC computer manual for more information about this method.

flagging

A FOR-NEXT loop could also be used to signal that all the data for Dr. Jubal's class have been used, as seen in the following modified program.

```
10 REM THIS PROGRAM PRINTS MEANS FOR DR. JUBAL.
20 PRINT "STUDENT #", "MEAN"
30 FOR S = 1 TO 5
40 READ S, G, W, D, P, N
50 LET M = (G + W + D + P + N) / 5
60 PRINT
70 PRINT S,M
80 NEXT S
90 DATA 1,72,93,86,82,96,2,83,86,95,74,80,3,91,82,76,60,89
100 DATA 4,88,94,72,76,84,5,75,84,98,92,79
110 END
```

We now have three methods of getting data into the computer: LET statements, INPUT statements, and READ-DATA statements. One of the primary advantages of READ-DATA statements over INPUT statements is the speed with which the computer is able to accept and use the information. Another advantage is not having to enter information every time the program is run. There is no lag time while the computer waits for the user to input information during the run of the program. However, when using READ-DATA statements, the program itself must be changed to input new data; the use of INPUT allows the user to input new data without altering the program.

PROBLEM 4

In 1980, the number of cars using the Chicago Loop and Inter-Mountain Bypass highways were 220,819,000 and 66,944,000, respectively. If the annual usage growth rates for these two highways were 1.5% and 2.9%, respectively, and if these usage rates were to remain constant, in what year would the number of cars using the Inter-Mountain Bypass equal or surpass the number of cars using the Chicago Loop? How many cars would use each highway in that year?

UNDERSTANDING THE PROBLEM A useful strategy in problem solving is to compare the given problem to any related problems that have previously been solved. Problem 1 of Section AI-1 was a similar problem that concerned the computation of compound interest in the Manhattan Island problem. Each number of cars in the current problem plays the role of the principal in the compound-interest problem. Thus, the number of cars using the Chicago Loop is growing according to the formula $220{,}819{,}000(1 + .015)^N$, where N is the number of years involved. Similarly, the number of cars using the Inter-Mountain Bypass is growing according to the formula

$$66{,}944{,}000(1 + .029)^N$$

DEVISING A PLAN The program must be written so that the number of cars on each road is computed for different years; in addition, the first time the number of Inter-Mountain cars is greater than or equal to the number of Chicago Loop cars, the computer should print the value of N added to 1980, giving the desired year. The total number of cars for both highways should also be output at this time. The program must have a counter, and it must contain a loop to compute values for different Ns. A program based on this discussion follows.

```
10 REM A TRAFFIC PROBLEM INVOLVING THE CHICAGO LOOP AND IM BYPASS
15 LET N = 0
20 LET N = N + 1
30 LET C = 220819000 * 1.015 ^ N
40 LET I = 66944000 * 1.029 ^ N
50 IF I >= C THEN 70
60 GOTO 20
70 PRINT "IN ";N + 1980;", THE NUMBER OF CHICAGO"
80 PRINT "LOOP CARS WILL BE ";C
90 PRINT "IN ";N + 1980;", THE NUMBER OF IM BYPASS"
100 PRINT "CARS WILL BE ";I
110 END
```

CARRYING OUT THE PLAN A run of the preceding program produces the following.

**IN 2068, THE NUMBER OF CHICAGO
LOOP CARS WILL BE 818555517
IN 2068, THE NUMBER OF IM BYPASS
CARS WILL BE 828446826**

LOOKING BACK An alternative activity might be to modify the program to find the number of cars of both the Chicago Loop and the Inter-Mountain

Bypass in the year 2000, assuming the usage rates in the problem remain constant. In what year will the number of cars on the Chicago Loop exceed one-half billion?

PROBLEM 5

Suppose candy sells for 15¢ a bar in a certain machine. Suppose also that the machine will accept nickels, dimes, quarters, half-dollars, and dollars, and that it will give nickels, dimes, and quarters as change. Write a program that will calculate the number of quarters, dimes, and nickels returned for any amount placed in the machine. Assume that the change is given with the least number of coins.

UNDERSTANDING THE PROBLEM The problem is to write a program that will calculate the number of quarters, dimes, and nickels returned for any amount of money placed in the machine when a 15¢ candy bar is purchased. The machine accepts nickels, dimes, quarters, half-dollars, and dollars.

DEVISING A PLAN Let A be the amount in cents put into the machine. Then, the value C, in cents, of the change is $A - 15$. Let Q, D, and N be the number of quarters, dimes, and nickels that are returned. The value A must be input, and then the value of the change must be calculated. To determine the number of quarters to be returned, the amount of change C must be divided by 25. Because only whole numbers of quarters can be returned, the greatest-integer function is used on this result. If any quarters are returned, the value of the quarters must be subtracted from C to obtain a new value of C. The process is repeated, using the new value of C for dimes. A similar procedure is then used for nickels. The computed information must then be output in a form that can be interpreted. A program using these ideas follows.

```
10 REM PROGRAM TO COMPUTE CHANGE
20 INPUT A
30 LET C = A - 15
40 LET Q = INT(C / 25)
50 LET C = C - 25 * Q
60 LET D = INT(C / 10)
70 LET C = C - 10 * D
80 LET N = INT(C / 5)
90 PRINT "QUARTERS", "DIMES", "NICKELS"
100 PRINT
110 PRINT Q,D,N
120 END
```

CARRYING OUT THE PLAN If we execute the preceding program with input 50¢, we obtain the following output.

? 50

QUARTERS	DIMES	NICKELS
1	1	0

LOOKING BACK This problem may easily be varied by changing the cost of the candy, the denominations of money that will be accepted by the machine, and the form of the change returned.

SUMMARY OF COMMANDS

IF-THEN	Used in the form IF (condition) THEN (line number of condition).
RND(X)	Causes the computer to select a random six-digit number between 0 and .999999.
INT(X)	Outputs the greatest integer less than or equal to X.
GOTO	Used in the form GOTO (line number) for branching.
CONTROL-C	Stops execution of a program.
FOR-NEXT	FOR-NEXT statements occur in pairs in a program, with the FOR statement preceding the NEXT statement.
STEP	Increments values of a variable.
READ-DATA	Used to enter large blocks of data in a program.

PROBLEM SET AI-2

1. Determine the output for the following programs and then run the programs on the computer to check your answers.

   (a)
   ```
   10 FOR I = 1 TO 15
   20 PRINT I,
   30 NEXT I
   40 END
   ```

   (b)
   ```
   10 FOR I = 1 TO 15
   20 PRINT I * 10,
   30 NEXT I
   40 END
   ```

   (c)
   ```
   10 FOR X = 1 TO 4 STEP 0.2
   20 PRINT X,
   30 NEXT X
   40 END
   ```

   (d)
   ```
   10 FOR X = 15 TO 1 STEP -1
   20 PRINT X,
   30 NEXT X
   40 END
   ```

   (e)
   ```
   10 LET X = 100
   20 PRINT X,
   30 LET X = X - 1
   40 IF X < 0 THEN 60
   50 GOTO 20
   60 END
   ```

   (f)
   ```
   10 LET X = 10
   20 LET X = X + 1
   30 PRINT X
   40 IF X <= 10 THEN 20
   50 END
   ```

   (g)
   ```
   10 READ X, Y
   20 DATA 3,2
   30 IF X > Y THEN 50
   40 GOTO 60
   ```

   ```
   50 PRINT X; " IS GREATER THAN ";Y
   60 END
   ```

   (h)
   ```
   10 READ X, Y
   20 DATA 2, 3
   30 IF X > Y THEN 50
   40 PRINT X; " IS LESS THAN ";Y
   50 END
   ```

   (i)
   ```
   10 FOR I = 2 TO 5
   20 FOR J = 1 TO 3
   30 PRINT I; J
   40 NEXT J
   50 NEXT Y
   60 END
   ```

   (j)
   ```
   10 FOR X = 5 TO 1
   20 IF X < 6 GOTO 40
   30 PRINT X
   40 PRINT "FOOLED YOU"
   50 END
   ```

2. Write a program to print all whole numbers from 1 to 500.

3. Determine the outputs of each of the following programs. Why are the outputs different?

   (a)
   ```
   10 PRINT "HEY YOU OUT THERE"
   15 LET K = 0
   20 LET K = K + 1
   30 IF K > 5 THEN 50
   40 GOTO 20
   50 END
   ```

   (b)
   ```
   10 LET K = K + 1
   20 PRINT "HEY YOU OUT THERE"
   30 IF K > 5 THEN 50
   40 GOTO 10
   50 END
   ```

4. Rewrite the following program using a FOR-NEXT loop so that the outputs in (a) and (b) are obtained.

```
10 LET N = 1
20 IF N > 20 THEN 60
30 PRINT 2 * N
40 LET N = N + 1
50 GOTO 20
60 END
```

(a) 2
    4
    6
    ·
    ·
    ·

(b) 2 4 6 8 . . .

5. Write a program to find the sum of the squares of the first 100 positive integers.

6. Modify the two-number addition program of this section to do two-number multiplications.

7. **SQR** is the BASIC square-root function. It is used in the form SQR(X), where X is the argument. X must be nonnegative. For example, PRINT SQR(16) produces the output **4**. Write and run a program to print a list of numbers from 1 to 10, their square roots, and their squares.

8. Write a program to determine if any positive integer N is a prime number.

9. Write a program to convert degrees Fahrenheit to degrees Celsius, using the formula $C = \dfrac{(F - 32)5}{9}$.

Make the program print Fahrenheit temperatures and corresponding Celsius temperatures from $^-40°F$ to $220°F$, in intervals of $10°F$.

10. Write a program to calculate the area A and the circumference C of a circle for any radius R that is input. Use $A = \pi R^2$ and $C = 2\pi R$, with $\pi = 3.14159$.

11. Write a program to compute N! where N is any natural number. $(N! = 1 \cdot 2 \cdot 3 \cdot 4 \cdot \ldots \cdot (N - 1) \cdot N.)$

12. Laura won a lottery prize of $50,000. She put the money into a Certificate of Deposit at 15% per year paid annually. Suppose that, just after the interest is paid at the end of the first year, she withdraws $10,000 for a trip. The remainder is reinvested with the same terms. If she repeats this act year after year, write a program to find out how long her money will last.

13. Write a program to verify that

$$1^3 + 2^3 + 3^3 + \cdots + N^3 = (1 + 2 + 3 + \cdots + N)^2$$

is true for the first 10 natural numbers.

14. Write a program to compute the sum of the first 1000 odd natural numbers.

15. Write a program to find the sum

$$1 + \frac{1}{2} + \frac{1}{3} + \frac{1}{4} + \frac{1}{5} + \frac{1}{6} + \cdots + \frac{1}{N}$$

Run the program for N = 100.

16. Plastic Card Company computes its bills on the last day of the month. If a customer pays the bill within the first 10 days of the next month, a 5% discount is given. If the bill is paid within the next 10 days, the face value of the bill is paid. If the bill is paid after the 20th day, a penalty of 2% is added to the original bill computed at the end of the previous month. Write a program to take the customer I.D. number and the amount of the bill and print the amounts to be paid for each of the three options.

17. Write a program to compute and print out the value of the cube and the cube root of the first 20 natural numbers.

18. If you have $1000 invested in a bank at 5% annual interest compounded daily, how long would you have to leave it in the bank to have a balance of $5000?

19. Write a program to generate the first N Fibonacci numbers where N is any natural number. The Fibonacci sequence 1, 1, 2, 3, 5, 8, 13, 21, . . . is obtained by starting with 1, 1 and generating each successive term by summing the two previous terms. Check your program by finding the first ten Fibonacci numbers.

20. In baseball, the number of hits H a player gets divided by the number of times at bat B is called the "batting average." Write a program to have the computer print a player's number and batting average. (The decimal need not be rounded.)

21. Imagine that you are paid 1¢ on the first day, 2¢ on the second day, 4¢ on the third day, 8¢ on the fourth day, and, in general, 2^{n-1} cents on the nth day. Each day's salary is double that of the previous day. Compare the salary on the 15th day with the sum of the salaries for the first 14 days.

22. Write and run a program to find all numbers less than 40 than can be written as a sum of two square numbers.

An Introduction to Logo Turtle Graphics

Introduction

Turtle graphics, implemented using the computer language Logo, are especially suited for studying geometry. Students learn geometry by giving instructions to a creature known as a **turtle,** a triangular figure on the display screen. The following discussion refers to MIT Logo run on an Apple or Commodore 64 computer. Most commands also work in Apple Logo, a slightly different version of the language. In this text, if commands differ, the Apple Logo version is shown in parentheses. If an abbreviation can be used in place of a Logo command, then it will be given in parentheses immediately following the command.

turtle

Section AII-I   Introducing the Turtle

In Logo, the computer accepts instructions in the nodraw, draw, and edit modes. After Logo is loaded into the computer, the first mode that appears on the screen is the **nodraw mode.** A question mark, called a *prompt,* and a flashing *cursor* appear on the screen as the computer awaits instructions. To execute turtle graphics commands, we enter the **draw mode** by typing

nodraw mode

draw mode

DRAW

NODRAW (ND)

primitives

Figure AII-I

DRAW [*in Apple Logo, CLEARSCREEN (CS)*] and pressing the RETURN key. After the DRAW command is executed, we can return to the nodraw mode by executing **NODRAW (ND)** (*in Apple Logo, TEXTSCREEN*). In the draw mode, the turtle appears in the center of the screen, as shown in Figure AII-1. The turtle's position in the center of the screen is called "home." These built-in words that the computer understands, such as DRAW and NODRAW, are called **primitives.**

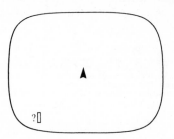

In Figure AII-1, the prompt at the bottom left of the screen indicates that the computer is ready to accept instructions, and the rectangular cursor shows where the next character that is typed will appear. Logo reserves the lines at the bottom of the screen for the user's input and the computer's responses. The remainder of the screen is used for drawing. This division of the screen into a drawing portion and a text portion is referred to as the *split-screen mode.*

MOVING THE TURTLE

FORWARD (FD)

BACK (BK)

To make the turtle change position, we use the primitives **FORWARD (FD)** and **BACK (BK),** followed by a space and a numerical input. The numerical input tells the turtle how far to move. For example, after the DRAW command is executed, typing FORWARD 100 and pressing RETURN causes the turtle to move 100 "turtle units" in the direction it is pointing, as shown in Figure AII-2(a). Similarly, the BACK command with a numerical input causes

Figure AII-2

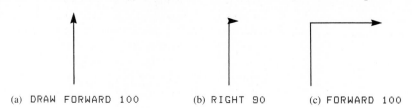

(a) DRAW FORWARD 100   (b) RIGHT 90   (c) FORWARD 100

(d) LEFT 45   (e) BACK 75

the turtle to move backwards the specified number of units. For example, BACK 75 causes the turtle to move backwards 75 units. Giving the turtle too great an input causes the turtle to "wrap around" the screen. To explore how the turtle wraps, try FD 250 and observe what happens.

TURNING THE TURTLE

RIGHT (RT)
LEFT (LT)

To make the turtle change direction, we use the commands **RIGHT (RT)** and **LEFT (LT).** The RIGHT and LEFT commands, along with numerical inputs, cause the turtle to turn in place the specified number of degrees. For example, typing RIGHT 90 and pressing RETURN causes the turtle to turn 90° to the right of the direction it previously pointed. A sequence of moves illustrating these commands is given in Figure AII-2.

Logo accepts a sequence of commands written on one line. For example, Figure AII-2(e) could be drawn by typing the following and pressing RETURN . (*In Apple Logo, replace DRAW with CS.*)

```
DRAW FD 100 RT 90 FD 100 LT 45 BK 75
```

PENUP (PU)

PENDOWN (PD)
HIDETURTLE (HT)
SHOWTURTLE (ST)

HOME

To make the turtle move without leaving a trail, the command **PENUP (PU)** may be used. To make the turtle leave a trail again, the command **PENDOWN (PD)** may be used. It is possible to hide the turtle by typing **HIDETURTLE (HT).** To make the turtle reappear, type **SHOWTURTLE (ST).**

To return the turtle to the center of the screen with heading 0, the command **HOME** may be used. However, a trail to the center of the screen will be drawn from the position the turtle occupied before HOME was typed unless the command PENUP is used before HOME.

To start a new drawing with a clear screen, we type DRAW [*in Apple Logo, CLEARSCREEN (CS)*]. This returns the turtle to its initial position and direction in the center of the screen and clears the screen. Any time the turtle points straight north (up), we say it has heading 0. A heading of 90 is directly east, 180 is directly south, and 270 is directly west. The screen could be marked as shown in Figure AII-3.

Figure AII-3

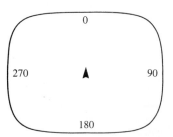

HEADING

PRINT (PR)

To learn the turtle's heading, we use the primitive HEADING. **HEADING** needs no inputs, and in the draw mode, it outputs the turtle's heading. To have the computer print only the value of the heading, we use the primitive **PRINT (PR)** along with HEADING, as in PRINT HEADING. For example, if the turtle is at home with heading 0, and we type RT 45 PR HEADING, then 45 will be displayed. Now, predict the results of executing LT −45.

Execute PR HEADING to check your prediction. Explore what happens when HEADING is used without the PRINT command.

Remark PRINT (PR) normally takes one input, causes the input to be printed on the screen, and moves the cursor to the next line. PRINT (PR) may take a word or a list of words as input. For example, PR "TURTLE and PR [TURTLE POWER] are both acceptable.

A summary of commands introduced thus far is shown in Table AII-1.

Table AII-I

Command	Abbreviation	Example
DRAW*		DRAW
NODRAW†	ND	ND
FORWARD	FD	FD 50
BACK	BK	BK 60
RIGHT	RT	RT 90
LEFT	LT	LT 45
PENUP	PU	PU
PENDOWN	PD	PD
HIDETURTLE	HT	HT
SHOWTURTLE	ST	ST
HEADING		PR HEADING
PRINT	PR	PR "LOGO
HOME		HOME

* *The command in Apple Logo is CLEARSCREEN (CS).*
† *The command in Apple Logo is TEXTSCREEN (CTRL-T)*

Remark CTRL-T means press the T key while holding down the CONTROL key.

People studying Logo are encouraged to "play turtle" and act out their commands. For example, to act out drawing a square, we may walk around the square by moving forward 50 units, turning right 90°, moving forward

HISTORICAL NOTE

The computer language Logo was developed by the Logo Group of the Massachusetts Institute of Technology (MIT) under the direction of Seymour Papert. The name "Logo" is derived from the Greek word for "thought." The developers of Logo were influenced by the field of artificial intelligence, the computer language LISP, and the theories of Jean Piaget. The tradition of calling the display creature a turtle can be traced to early experiments involving robot-like creatures referred to as "tortoises." When computer graphics were implemented, the screen creature inherited the turtle terminology.

50 units, turning right 90°, moving forward 50 units, turning right 90°, and finally moving forward 50 units. The sequence of commands for these moves is summarized in Figure AII-4(a), with the resulting square and final position of the turtle shown in Figure AII-4(b).

Figure AII-4

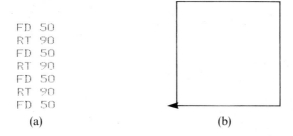

```
FD 50
RT 90
FD 50
RT 90
FD 50
RT 90
FD 50
```
(a)   (b)

Notice that the turtle's position in Figure AII-4(b) is the same as its initial position, but its heading is different. When drawing a figure, it is often convenient to have the turtle's final state be the same as its initial state. When a set of commands returns the turtle to its initial position and heading, we say that

state transparent

the set of commands is **state transparent.**

To return the turtle to its initial state in Figure AII-4(b), we turn it right 90° by adding the line RT 90 at the end of the sequence of commands in Figure AII-4(a). The new sequence of commands is given in Figure AII-5(a), with the resulting square and turtle shown in Figure AII-5(b).

Figure AII-5

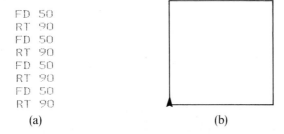

```
FD 50
RT 90
FD 50
RT 90
FD 50
RT 90
FD 50
RT 90
```
(a)   (b)

The sequence of commands in Figure AII-5(a) contains the instructions FD 50 and RT 90 repeated four times. Logo allows us to use the REPEAT command to repeat a list of instructions. For example, to draw the square in Figure AII-5(b), we could type the following.

```
REPEAT 4 [FD 50 RT 90]
```

REPEAT

In general, **REPEAT** takes two inputs: a number and a list of commands. The commands in the brackets are repeated the designated number of times. The space before the left bracket is optional. (To obtain brackets on the Apple II Plus computer, the SHIFT M and SHIFT N keys must be used.)

Example AII-I

Predict the results of each of the following, indicating the initial and final turtle states. Then, check your answers with a computer. In each case, assume the turtle starts at home with heading 0.

(a) FD 100
    RT 135
    FD 100
    RT 45
    FD 100
    RT 135
    FD 100
    RT 45
(b) REPEAT 2 [FD 100 RT 135 FD 100 RT 45]
(c) REPEAT 8 [FD 50 RT 45]

Solution

Results are depicted in Figure AII-6.

Figure AII-6

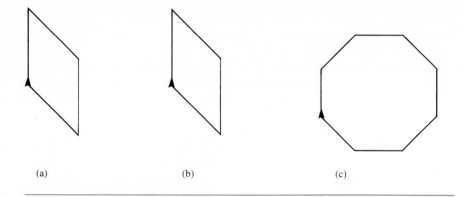

(a)   (b)   (c)

DEFINING PROCEDURES

The sequence of commands in Figure AII-5(a) instructed the turtle to draw a square. If the screen is cleared, the figure is lost. To redraw the square, the entire sequence of commands must be retyped. Fortunately, with Logo, it is possible to store instructions in the computer's memory by creating a

procedure

procedure. A **procedure** is a group of one or more instructions to the computer that the computer can store to be used at a later time.

To create a procedure in MIT Logo (Terrapin/Krell or Commodore 64),

TO

we type **TO** followed by the name we wish to call the procedure, and press RETURN . (In Apple Logo, we type EDIT (ED), followed by a set of double quotation marks and the procedure name—for example, ED "TRIANGLE.)

edit mode

When RETURN is pressed, the computer enters the **edit mode,** or the teaching mode. In this mode, the lines that follow are not executed, but may be stored in memory under the given name. The name must be a sequence of symbols with no spaces, and it may not be the name of a primitive. For example, to create a procedure to draw a square, the following is entered. (To signify the end of a procedure, it is good practice to type END as the last line of the procedure.)

```
TO SQUARE1
  REPEAT 4 [FD 50 RT 90]
END
```

To define and store a procedure and exit the edit mode, the C key must be pressed while holding down the CONTROL key. This is called a CONTROL-C

CTRL-C **(CTRL-C).** After the procedure has been defined, typing the name of the procedure and pressing RETURN causes the computer to immediately execute the instructions in the procedure. In the remainder of this section, we assume that the SQUARE1 procedure just given and all subsequent procedures are stored in the computer's memory and can be reused.

In Logo, it is possible for one procedure to call on another procedure, as shown in Example AII-2. If the SQUARE1 procedure has not been defined on your computer, please define it before working the example.

Example AII-2

Predict what figures will be drawn by defining and executing each of the following procedures. Assume the turtle starts at home with heading 0.

(a)
```
TO SQUARE2
   RT 90
   SQUARE1
END
```

(b)
```
TO SQUARESTACK
   SQUARE1
   RT 90
   SQUARE1
END
```

(c)
```
TO STAIR
   SQUARE1
   RT 180
   SQUARE1
END
```

(d)
```
TO TURNSQUARE
   SQUARE1
   RT 45
   SQUARE1
END
```

Solution

Results are depicted in Figure AII-7.

Figure AII-7

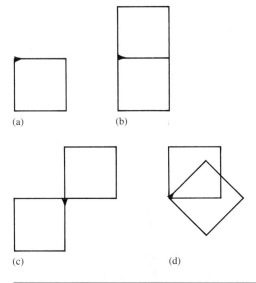

(a)   (b)

(c)   (d)

PROBLEM I

Write a procedure for drawing a triangle whose sides each have length of 50 turtle steps and whose angles each have measure of 60°.

UNDERSTANDING THE PROBLEM We are to write a procedure to draw a triangle with all sides of length 50 turtle units and all angles of measure 60°.

DEVISING A PLAN To write this procedure, it is helpful to sketch a triangle to determine what angle the turtle needs to turn at each vertex of the triangle. Suppose the turtle starts at point *A* with heading 0 and moves 50 turtle steps to point *B*, as in Figure AII-8. This can be done by telling the turtle to move FD 50.

Figure AII-8

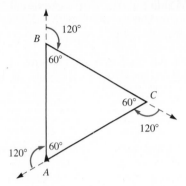

At point *B*, the turtle still has heading 0. To walk on $\overline{BC}$, the turtle may turn 120° to the right. Thus, the next command should be RT 120. The triangle has three sides of equal length, so three turns are necessary to achieve the turtle's initial heading. If we repeat the sequence FD 50 RT 120 three times, this should cause the turtle to walk around the triangle and finish in its original position with its original heading.

CARRYING OUT THE PLAN A procedure called TRIANGLE1 based on the preceding discussion follows.

```
TO TRIANGLE1
  REPEAT 3 [FD 50 RT 120]
END
```

LOOKING BACK Executing the TRIANGLE1 procedure yields the desired figure. Additional investigations include writing a procedure to draw the same type of triangle by turning left instead of right or writing a procedure to draw a triangle with one horizontal side. Procedures for drawing other polygons could also be explored.

One of the great advantages of Logo is its ability to use procedures to define new procedures. Consider the following problem.

PROBLEM 2

Write a procedure to draw the "house" in Figure AII-9.

Figure AII-9

UNDERSTANDING THE PROBLEM We are to write a procedure to draw the "house" pictured in Figure AII-9. The top of the house appears to be a triangle similar to the one in Problem 1, and the bottom appears to be a square.

DEVISING A PLAN One way to solve the problem is to break down the problem of drawing a house into smaller problems, that of drawing the bottom of the house (the square) and that of drawing the roof (the triangle). The type of programming that starts with a general idea and breaks down the problem into smaller parts is called **top-down programming.** We have a procedure SQUARE1 for drawing a square of length 50 units, and a procedure TRIANGLE1 for drawing a triangle of length 50 units. If we use these two procedures, then we should be able to draw the house.

top-down programming

CARRYING OUT THE PLAN If the turtle has heading 0, it may seem that typing SQUARE1 followed by TRIANGLE1 would draw the desired house. The result of this effort is shown in Figure AII-10(a). Why did this not produce the desired figure? The turtle first drew the square in Figure AII-10(a) and returned to its initial position at point *A* with heading 0. Then, typing TRIANGLE1 caused the turtle to draw triangle *ABC* as in Figure AII-8. To draw the roof in proper position, we need the turtle to be at the upper left vertex of the square. This can be achieved by typing FD 50. But, if TRIANGLE1 is typed now, we obtain the shape in Figure AII-10(b), which is still not the desired house.

Figure AII-10

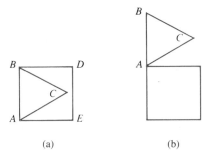

(a)   (b)

Trial and error is an important activity in Logo; it helps the user to get acquainted with the problem and eventually to find the correct solution. This process of rewriting a program that does not do what we want it to do is called **debugging.** To debug the program, we examine how the turtle should walk from the top left vertex of the square in order to draw the roof in Figure AII-11(a). After typing SQUARE1 and FD 50, the turtle is at point *A* with heading 0. Thus, to walk on $\overline{AB}$, the turtle needs to turn right by $90° - 60°$, or $30°$. With this heading, typing TRIANGLE1 should cause the turtle to draw the desired roof. The complete procedure, called HOUSE, is shown in Figure AII-11(b).

debugging

Figure AII-11

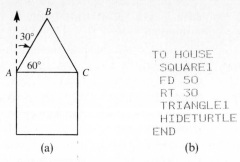

```
TO HOUSE
    SQUARE1
    FD 50
    RT 30
    TRIANGLE1
    HIDETURTLE
END
```

(a)   (b)

LOOKING BACK If the HOUSE procedure is executed, the desired figure is obtained. Alternate techniques for drawing the figure could also be explored. Houses of other sizes could be drawn and windows and doors could be added.

It is important to understand how Logo works when a procedure calls another procedure. A telescoping model of the HOUSE procedure in Problem 2 is given in Figure AII-12.

Figure AII-12

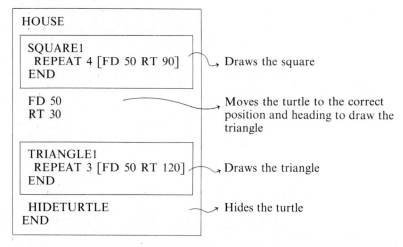

When HOUSE is run, it encounters the call for SQUARE1. At this point, all the lines of SQUARE1 are inserted. After SQUARE1 has been completed, control is returned to the procedure that called it, namely, HOUSE. Now, HOUSE continues where it left off and executes FD 50 RT 30, then calls on the TRIANGLE1 procedure. After TRIANGLE1 has been executed, it returns control to HOUSE, which hides the turtle and encounters its own END statement.

In working through the HOUSE procedure, we went through several steps. A summary of these steps is as follows. These steps might be useful in a variety of problems presented in this text.

1. Sketch your drawing on paper, preferably graph paper, to get an idea of the scale to be used and of how the final picture should look.
2. Divide the drawing into parts that are repeated, that you already know how to draw, or that are smaller parts of the whole. Separate procedures

for drawing each individual part are easier to check than a single procedure for the whole drawing.

3. Decide how your individual procedures are going to fit together to form the complete picture. Some procedures may be necessary just to move the turtle to the right position for drawing the individual parts.

4. Write your procedures. One approach is to write individual procedures, make sure they work, and then try to put them all together to form the complete picture. Another approach is to fit the procedures together as they are completed. Either approach is an acceptable problem-solving strategy, and each has advantages in different situations.

We demonstrate how these steps can be used in a problem-solving format in Problem 3.

PROBLEM 3

Write a procedure to draw the figure sketched on the graph paper in Figure AII-13.

Figure AII-13

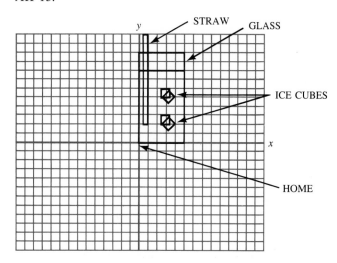

UNDERSTANDING THE PROBLEM We are to write a procedure to draw a figure similar to the one shown in Figure AII-13. The graph paper gives a scale to draw the various parts.

DEVISING A PLAN The figure can be broken into three separate parts: the glass, the straw, and the ice cubes. Thus, a procedure called DRINK to draw this figure might appear as follows.

```
TO DRINK
  GLASS
   ICE.CUBES
   ICE.CUBES
  STRAW
  HT
END
```

We must write procedures for each portion of the DRINK procedure.

CARRYING OUT THE PLAN First, we design a procedure called GLASS for drawing the glass. If the turtle starts at home with heading 0, one possible procedure and its output are given in Figure AII-14.

Figure AII-14

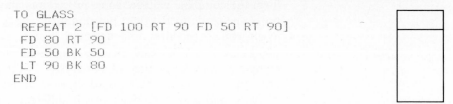

```
TO GLASS
  REPEAT 2 [FD 100 RT 90 FD 50 RT 90]
  FD 80 RT 90
  FD 50 BK 50
  LT 90 BK 80
END
```

Likewise, procedures called STRAW and ICE.CUBES can be designed to draw the other two parts, as shown in Figure AII-15(a) and (b).

Figure AII-15

```
TO STRAW
  REPEAT 2 [FD 100 RT 90 FD 5 RT 90]
END

TO ICE.CUBES
  SQUARE3
  RT 45
  SQUARE3
  LT 45
END

TO SQUARE3
  REPEAT 4 [FD 10 RT 90]
END
```

(a)

(b)

If we now attempt to execute the DRINK procedure as defined, the result is as shown in Figure AII-16.

Figure AII-16

Here, we encounter a bug. To correct the DRINK procedure to draw the desired figure, we must keep track of the turtle's position and heading. Sometimes, it is convenient to move the turtle to the required positions and headings by using a set of procedures. The following procedures—called SETUP.CUBES1, SETUP.CUBES2, and SETUP.STRAW—move the turtle to the correct position and heading to draw each part.

```
TO SETUP.CUBES1
  PU FD 50 RT 90 FD 25 LT 90 PD
END

TO SETUP.CUBES2
  PU BK 30 PD
END
```

```
TO SETUP.STRAW
  PU LT 90 FD 20 RT 90 PD
END
```

If we edit DRINK and add these new procedures, we obtain the procedures and figure shown in Figure AII-17.

Figure AII-17

```
TO DRINK
  GLASS
  SETUP.CUBES1
  ICE.CUBES
  SETUP.CUBES2
  ICE.CUBES
  SETUP.STRAW
  STRAW
  HT
END
```

LOOKING BACK When the DRINK procedure is executed, it yields the desired figure. The procedure could have been written in many different ways. Although various strategies could be used to develop the procedure, we see that the top-down strategy can be very useful. One advantage of the top-down strategy is that it is easier to work with and debug smaller portions of the figure than to try to do the complete figure all at one time.

WRITING PROCEDURES WITH VARIABLES

The SQUARE1 procedure in this section allowed us to draw only squares of side 50. If we want to draw smaller or larger squares, we need to write a new procedure. It would be more convenient if we could write one procedure that would work for a square of any size. This can be accomplished with Logo by using a variable as input, rather than a fixed number such as 50 in FD 50. We can use variable input in Logo as long as we warn the computer that the "thing" we are going to type is a variable. This is done by using a colon. The computer understands that anything that follows a colon is a variable. For example, a variable input to the SQUARE procedure might be called :SIDE, where :SIDE stands for the length of a side of the square. We define a new SQUARE procedure with variable input :SIDE, and we place the name of the variable in the title line.

```
TO SQUARE :SIDE
  REPEAT 4 [FD :SIDE RT 90]
END
```

If we want the turtle to draw a square of size 40, we type SQUARE 40. Notice that we do not type SQUARE :40 because 40 is not a variable. (In fact, the computer will not understand the instruction SQUARE :40.) Investigate what happens if SQUARE is typed with no inputs.

Remark   We call the new variable square procedure SQUARE instead of SQUARE1. If we attempt to enter the edit mode to define a new SQUARE1 procedure and the old procedure has not been erased the computer will display the old SQUARE1 procedure on the screen for us to edit. You should consult your Logo manual for directions on how to edit procedures.

A procedure may have more than one input. For example, consider the following equivalent procedures for drawing a rectangle. Two variables are used so that two inputs can be accepted.

```
TO RECTANGLE :HEIGHT :WIDTH
  FD :HEIGHT RT 90
  FD :WIDTH RT 90
  FD :HEIGHT RT 90
  FD :WIDTH RT 90
END

TO RECTANGLE :HEIGHT :WIDTH
  REPEAT 2 [FD :HEIGHT RT 90 FD :WIDTH RT 90]
END
```

Figure AII-18 shows rectangles drawn by either of the RECTANGLE procedures with different inputs for the sides.

Figure AII-18

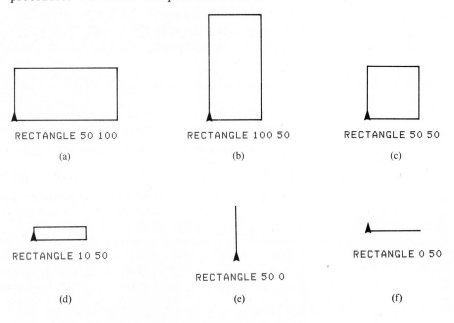

RECTANGLE 50 100

(a)

RECTANGLE 100 50

(b)

RECTANGLE 50 50

(c)

RECTANGLE 10 50

(d)

RECTANGLE 50 0

(e)

RECTANGLE 0 50

(f)

BRAIN TEASER

Write a procedure for drawing the following figure, using a continuous path and without retracing any segment. (Single points may be retraced.)

SUMMARY OF COMMANDS

DRAW*	Needs no input. It sends the turtle home and clears the graphics screen.
NODRAW (ND)†	Needs no input. It exits the graphics mode, clears the screen, and places the cursor in the upper left corner.
FORWARD (FD)	Takes one input. If the input is positive, it moves the turtle forward (in the direction the turtle is facing) the number of turtle units that are input. For example, FD 20 moves the turtle forward 20 units.
BACK (BK)	Takes one input. If the input is positive, it moves the turtle backwards the number of turtle units that are input. For example, BK 40 moves the turtle backwards 40 units.
RIGHT (RT)	Takes one input. If the input is positive, it turns the turtle right from its present heading the number of degrees that are input. For example, RT 90 turns the turtle right 90°.
LEFT (LT)	Takes one input. If the input is positive, it turns the turtle left from its present heading the number of degrees that are input. For example, LT 90 turns the turtle left 90°.
PENUP (PU)	Needs no input. In the graphics mode, it enables the turtle to move without leaving a track.
PENDOWN (PD)	Needs no input. In the graphics mode, it causes the turtle to leave a track.
HIDETURTLE (HT)	Needs no input. It causes the turtle to disappear.
SHOWTURTLE (ST)	Needs no input. It causes the turtle to reappear.
PRINT (PR)	Takes one input. It causes the input to be printed on the screen and moves the cursor to the next line.
HEADING	Needs no input. In the draw mode, it outputs the turtle's heading.
HOME	Needs no input. It returns the turtle to the center of the screen and sets its heading to 0. If the pen is down, it leaves a track from the turtle's present location to the home position.
REPEAT	Takes a number and a list as input. It executes the instructions in the list the designated number of times.
TO‡	Takes the name of a procedure as input and causes Logo to enter the edit mode.

* In Apple Logo, this command is CLEARSCREEN (CS).
† In Apple Logo, this command is TEXTSCREEN (CTRL-T).
‡ In Apple Logo, this command is EDIT (ED).

PROBLEM SET AII-I

1. Sketch figures drawn by the turtle, using each of the following sets of instructions. Check your sketches by executing the instructions on a computer. Type DRAW (*CS in Apple Logo*) after each lettered part.

   (a) FD 50
   RT 90
   FD 50
   RT 45
   FD 50
   RT 135
   FD 50

   (b) FD 50
   RT 90
   BK 50
   RT 60
   FD 50

   (c) FD -50 FD 50
   (d) LT -90 BK -50 PR HEADING
   (e) RT 360 PR HEADING

2. Experiment with the turtle to find the dimensions of the screen from the home position.

3. Tell what the turtle will do with the following sets of instructions. Check your answers by executing the instructions on the computer.

   (a) REPEAT 8 [SQUARE1 RT 45]
   (b) REPEAT 6 [TRIANGLE1 RT 60]
   (c) REPEAT 36 [SQUARE1 RT 10]

4. Write procedures to draw figures similar to each of the following.

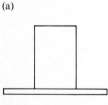

Rectangle that
is not a square

(a)

Flag

(b)

A hat

(c)

The letter *T*

(d)

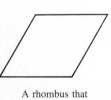

A rhombus that
is not a square

(e)

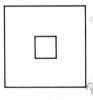

A square with
a smaller square
inside

(f)

5. Write a procedure to draw the following.

6. Use any procedures in this section to write new procedures that will draw each of the following figures.

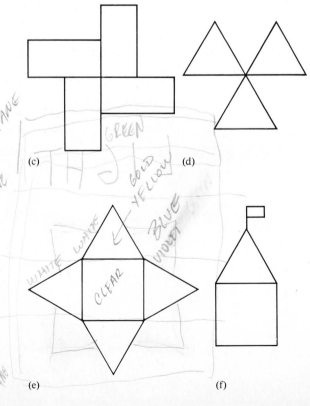

(a)

(b)

(c)

(d)

(e)

(f)

7. Write procedures to draw figures similar to each of the following.

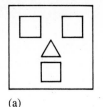

(a)

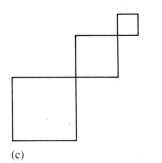

(b)

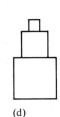

(c)   (d)

8. Write a procedure called DOG to draw a figure similar to the following.

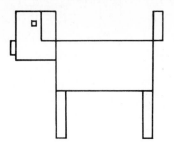

9. Write a procedure called KITE to draw a figure similar to the following.

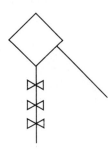

10. Write procedures to draw figures similar to those in Problem 4, but of variable size.

Section AII-2   Using Recursion as a Problem-Solving Tool

recursion

In Section AII-1, we considered procedures that called on other procedures. **Recursion** is the process of a procedure calling on a copy of itself. As a first example of recursion, we write a procedure for drawing a "turtle-type" circle. This could be done by having the turtle move forward "a little," then turn right "a little," and continuing this process until a closed figure is obtained. Thus, we could start the procedure with FD 1 RT 1 and then have the turtle start the procedure anew each time the instruction is executed. Such a procedure, called CIRC, follows.

```
TO CIRC
  FD 1 RT 1
  CIRC
END
```

To understand how CIRC works and, in general, what happens when a procedure calls itself, we introduce the telescoping model in Figure AII-19, which shows how CIRC works when it is executed.

Figure AII-19

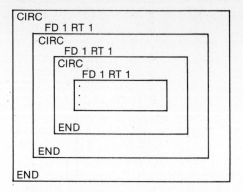

When CIRC is executed, the computer reads FD 1 RT 1 and causes the turtle to move forward 1 unit and then turn right 1°. CIRC then calls a copy of the CIRC procedure, which again executes FD 1 RT 1 and in turn calls another copy of CIRC, and so on. The process goes on and on because we have made CIRC one of the instructions in the CIRC procedure. The END statement is never reached, and the instruction FD 1 RT 1 is executed indefinitely. You may stop the execution of the procedure at any time by CTRL-G pressing **CTRL-G** (the [CONTROL] key in combination with the [G] key).

The infinitely repetitive process shown in the CIRC procedure occurs in tail-end recursion the type of recursion called **tail-end recursion.** In tail-end recursion, only one recursive call is made within the body of the procedure, and it is the final step before the END statement. Later, we introduce another type of recursion that is sometimes called *non–tail-end,* or *embedded,* recursion.

When drawing a circle with right turns of 1°, the turtle only has to turn through 360° to complete the circle. A CIRCLE1 procedure could be written using the REPEAT command as follows.

```
TO CIRCLE1
  REPEAT 360 [FD 1 RT 1]
END
```

The CIRCLE1 procedure stops, whereas the CIRC procedure does not.

Recursion is particularly valuable when we do not know how many times to repeat a set of instructions to accomplish some goal. For example, consider the shapes that can be drawn by repeating the instruction "Go forward some fixed distance and turn right some fixed angle." A recursive procedure called POLY that does this is as follows.

```
TO POLY :SIDE :ANGLE
  FD :SIDE RT :ANGLE
  POLY :SIDE :ANGLE
END
```

To execute the POLY procedure, we need two numerical inputs, one for :SIDE and the other for :ANGLE. Figure AII-20 shows shapes drawn by POLY with eight different inputs. The drawings were stopped using CTRL-G.

The POLY procedure draws regular polygons (polygons that have congruent sides and congruent angles), as in Figure AII-20(a), (b), and (c), and also star shapes, as in Figure AII-20(d), (e), and (f).

Figure AII-20

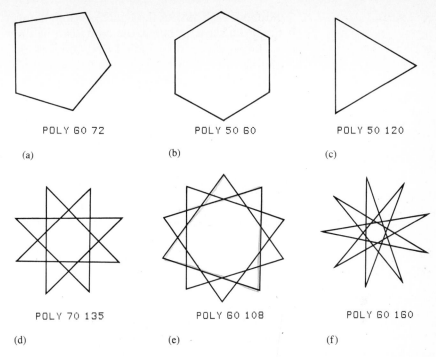

POLY 60 72   POLY 50 60   POLY 50 120

(a)   (b)   (c)

POLY 70 135   POLY 60 108   POLY 60 160

(d)   (e)   (f)

Try other executions of POLY, such as POLY 50 180, POLY 50 181, POLY 60 288, POLY 6000 300, and POLY 7000 135. As an experiment, try to predict which inputs produce regular polygons and which produce star shapes.

Notice that all the figures drawn by the POLY procedure in Figure AII-20 are closed; that is, they can be drawn by starting and stopping at the same point. Will all figures drawn by POLY be closed? We can also ask the following questions:

1. Given the value of :ANGLE in the POLY procedure, is it possible to predict (before the figure is drawn) how many vertices the figure will have?
2. If we wish the POLY procedure to draw a figure with a given number of vertices, can we determine what the correct angle input should be?

With the help of recursion, we can accomplish tasks that cannot be easily done with just the REPEAT command, especially if we do not know how many times to repeat a sequence of instructions. Consider drawing a square-type spiral as shown in Figure AII-21.

Figure AII-21

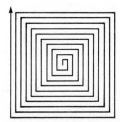

Suppose each side of the figure is 5 units longer than the preceding side. If the turtle starts at home, the figure can be drawn by telling the turtle to move forward a certain length :LEN, turn right 90°, move forward a distance 5 units greater than the previous value of :LEN, and so on. A recursive procedure called SQSPI shows how this can be done.

```
TO SQSPI :LEN
  FD :LEN RT 90
  SQSPI :LEN + 5
END
```

IF

Notice that each time SQSPI calls itself, the length of :LEN is increased by 5 units. When SQSPI is run, the sides grow too large to fit on the screen. Rather than stopping SQSPI with CTRL-G, it is possible to write a "stop" instruction in the procedure. This can be done with the IF and STOP primitives. **IF** is a primitive that tests one of three conditions: equal ($=$), less than ($<$), or greater than ($>$). An action occurs if the result of the test is true. The IF primitive is used in the following form.

IF (*Condition*)   (*Action to be taken if condition is true*)

The parentheses should not be typed. (*In Apple Logo, the format is IF* (*Condition*) [*Action to be taken if condition is true*], *where the square brackets must be typed.*)

For example, if we do not want the turtle to draw any segment longer than 100 units, we insert the following instruction.

```
IF :LEN > 100 STOP
```

STOP

(*In Apple Logo, IF :LEN > 100* [*STOP*].) When this line is inserted into a procedure, the IF statement causes the computer to check whether the value of :LEN is greater than 100. If it is, the procedure stops; if not, the next line is executed. The **STOP** primitive causes the current procedure to stop and returns control to the calling procedure, if there is one. An edited form of the SQSPI procedure is as follows.

```
TO SQSPI    :LEN
  IF :LEN > 100 STOP
  FD :LEN RT 90
  SQSPI :LEN + 5
END
```

(*In Apple Logo, replace STOP with* [*STOP*].) The SQSPI procedure can be generalized to draw other spiral-type figures. Investigate the following POLYSPI procedure for various inputs.

```
TO POLYSPI :SIDE :ANGLE
  IF :SIDE > 100 STOP
  FD :SIDE RT :ANGLE
  POLYSPI :SIDE + 5 :ANGLE
END
```

(*In Apple Logo, replace STOP with* [*STOP*].)

What inputs should be given to POLYSPI in order to achieve the same effect as SQSPI? Also, investigate what happens when :ANGLE, rather than :SIDE, is incremented each time the recursive call is made.

EMBEDDED RECURSION

embedded recursion

Tail-end recursion involves only one recursive call within the body of the procedure, and it is the final step before the END statement. Recursive calls also can be **embedded;** that is, the recursive call is not the last line before the END statement. For example, consider the tail-end recursion in the T.SQUARE procedure and the embedded recursion in the E.SQUARE procedure that follow. Predict the results of executing each of these procedures with input 30; then, execute them to see if you were correct.

```
TO T.SQUARE :SIDE              TO E.SQUARE :SIDE
  IF :SIDE < 5 STOP              IF :SIDE < 5 STOP
  REPEAT 4 [FD :SIDE RT 90]      REPEAT 4 [FD :SIDE RT 90]
  T.SQUARE :SIDE - 10            E.SQUARE :SIDE - 10
END                              LT 45 FD :SIDE
                               END
```

(*In Apple Logo, remember to replace STOP with* [*STOP*].) The T.SQUARE procedure probably did exactly what you expected; however, the E.SQUARE procedure may have surprised you. To see why E.SQUARE behaved the way it did, we use the telescoping model in Figure AII-22.

Figure AII-22

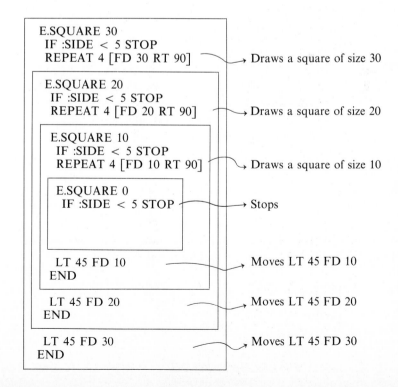

Notice that when :SIDE < 5 in E.SQUARE 0, the STOP command is finally reached. However, STOP stops only the procedure it is in, not the calling procedure. Control is then returned to the previous procedure, and so on.

From our model, we see that recursion works according to the following rules:

1. Executions in Logo programs proceed line by line. When a procedure calls itself, it puts on hold any instructions that are written after the call and inserts a copy of itself at the point where the call occurs. If the called procedure stops, control is returned to the calling procedure at the point where the call occurred. The remainder of the lines in the calling procedure are then executed.
2. The process in (1) applies to any successive calls.

SUMMARY OF COMMANDS

IF*	Takes two inputs. The first input must be either true or false. The second input contains instructions that are carried out if and only if the first input is true.
STOP	Takes no inputs. Causes the current procedure to stop and returns control to the calling procedure.

* In Apple Logo, the second input must be enclosed in brackets, for example,
IF :SIDE > 100 [STOP].

PROBLEM SET AII-2

1. Predict the shapes that will be drawn by the following procedures and then check your predictions on the computer. The SQUARE and TRIANGLE procedures are defined as follows, (*In Apple Logo, replace STOP with [STOP] in each of the procedures.*)

```
TO TRIANGLE :SIDE
  REPEAT 3 [FD :SIDE RT 120]
END
TO SQUARE :SIDE
  REPEAT 4 [FD :SIDE RT 90]
END
```

(a)
```
TO FIGURE :SIDE
   TRIANGLE :SIDE
   RT 10
   FIGURE :SIDE
END
```

(b)
```
TO FIGURE1 :SIDE
   IF :SIDE < 5 STOP
   TRIANGLE :SIDE
   RT 10
   FIGURE1 :SIDE - 5
END
```

(c)
```
TO TOWER :SIDE
   SQUARE :SIDE
   FD  SIDE
   TOWER :SIDE * 0.5
END
```

(d)
```
TO TOWER1 :SIDE
   IF :SIDE < 2 STOP
   SQUARE :SIDE
   FD :SIDE
   TOWER :SIDE * 0.5
END
```

(e)
```
TO SQ :SIDE
   IF :SIDE < 2 STOP
   SQUARE :SIDE
   SQ :SIDE - 5
END
```

(f)
```
TO SPIRAL :SIDE
   IF :SIDE > 50 STOP
   FD :SIDE
   RT 30
   SPIRAL :SIDE + 3
END
```

2. Given the following NEWPOLY, POLYSPIRAL, and INSPI procedures, predict the shapes that will be drawn by each and then check your predictions on the computer.

```
TO NEWPOLY :SIDE :ANGLE
   FD :SIDE RT :ANGLE
   FD :SIDE RT :ANGLE * 2
   NEWPOLY :SIDE :ANGLE
END
```

```
TO POLYSPIRAL :SIDE :ANGLE :INC
 FD :SIDE RT :ANGLE
 POLYSPIRAL (:SIDE + :INC) :ANGLE :INC
END
TO INSPI :SIDE :ANGLE :INC
 FD :SIDE RT :ANGLE
 INSPI :SIDE (:ANGLE + :INC) :INC
END
```

(a) NEWPOLY 50 30
(b) NEWPOLY 50 144
(c) NEWPOLY 50 125
(d) POLYSPIRAL 2 85 3
(e) POLYSPIRAL 1 119 2
(f) POLYSPIRAL 1 100 5
(g) INSPI 10 2 20
(h) INSPI 2 0 10
(i) INSPI 10 5 10

3. Write recursive procedures to draw figures similar to the following. Use the STOP command in your procedures.

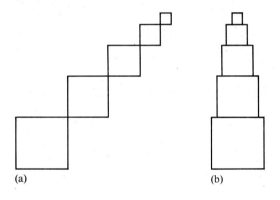

(a)   (b)

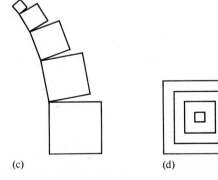

        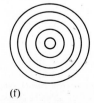

(c)   (d)

(e)   (f)

4. Write a recursive procedure with a STOP command to draw a figure similar to the following.

5. (a) Execute each of the following to see how embedded recursion can be used to "unwind" the turtle. (*Use* [*STOP*] *in Apple Logo.*)

```
TO WOW :X
 IF :X < 5 STOP
 FD :X RT 87
 WOW :X - 2
 LT 87 BK :X
END
TO WOW1 :X
 IF :X < 5 STOP
 FD :X RT 118
 WOW1 :X - 2
 LT 118 BK :X
END
```

(b) Write a procedure, using embedded recursion, that "unwinds" like those in (a).

6. (a) Predict what happens when REFLECT 6 is executed. Check your predictions by executing the procedure. (*Use* [*STOP*] *in Apple Logo.*)

```
TO REFLECT :N
 IF :N < 3 STOP
 REPEAT :N [FD 30 RT 360/:N]
 REFLECT :N - 1
 REPEAT :N [FD 30 RT 360/:N]
END
```

(b) Try REFLECT with various other values of :N.

7. Write a procedure called SPIN.SQ that uses recursion and a STOP command to spin a variable-sized square while "shrinking" its size, as shown.

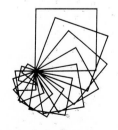

Basic Compass Constructions

The following diagrams show how to perform the basic compass-and-straightedge constructions that were discussed in detail in Chapter 11.

1. Construct a segment congruent to a given segment.

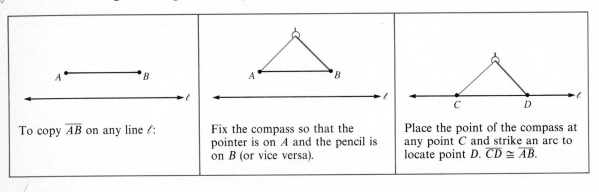

To copy $\overline{AB}$ on any line ℓ:	Fix the compass so that the pointer is on A and the pencil is on B (or vice versa).	Place the point of the compass at any point C and strike an arc to locate point D. $\overline{CD} \cong \overline{AB}$.

2. Construct a circle, given its center and radius.

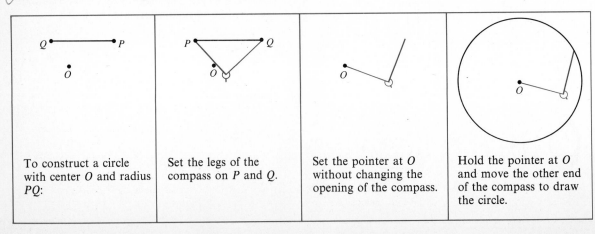

To construct a circle with center O and radius PQ:	Set the legs of the compass on P and Q.	Set the pointer at O without changing the opening of the compass.	Hold the pointer at O and move the other end of the compass to draw the circle.

3. Copy an angle.

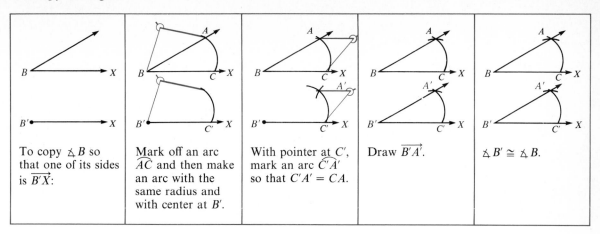

To copy ∡ B so that one of its sides is $\overrightarrow{B'X}$:	Mark off an arc $\overset{\frown}{AC}$ and then make an arc with the same radius and with center at B'.	With pointer at C', mark an arc $\overset{\frown}{C'A'}$ so that C'A' = CA.	Draw $\overrightarrow{B'A'}$.	∡ B' ≅ ∡ B.

4. Through a given point P, construct a line parallel to a given line ℓ.

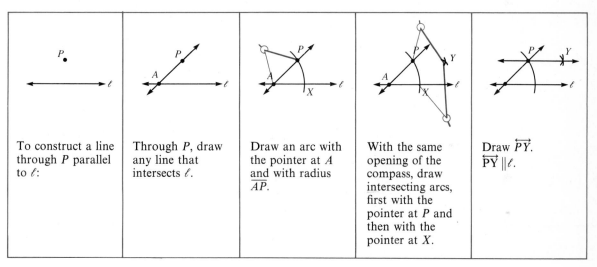

To construct a line through P parallel to ℓ:	Through P, draw any line that intersects ℓ.	Draw an arc with the pointer at A and with radius $\overline{AP}$.	With the same opening of the compass, draw intersecting arcs, first with the pointer at P and then with the pointer at X.
			Draw $\overleftrightarrow{PY}$. $\overleftrightarrow{PY} \parallel ℓ$.

5. Through a given point P, construct a line parallel to a given line ℓ, using properties of corresponding angles.

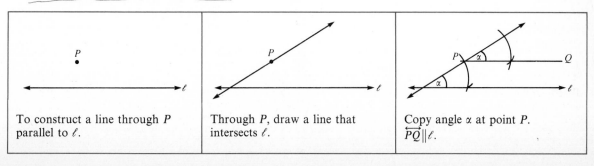

To construct a line through P parallel to ℓ.	Through P, draw a line that intersects ℓ.	Copy angle α at point P. $\overleftrightarrow{PQ} \parallel ℓ$.

6. Bisect a given angle.

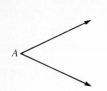		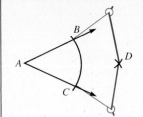	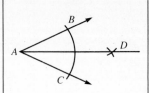
To bisect a given angle:	With the pointer at A, draw any arc intersecting the angle at B and C.	Draw an arc with center at B and radius AB. Then, draw an arc with center at C and radius AB. The arcs intersect at D.	Connect A with D. $\overrightarrow{AD}$ is the angle bisector.

7. Construct a perpendicular to a line ℓ through a point P not on line ℓ.

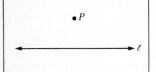	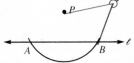	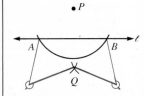	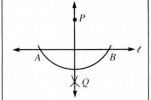
To construct a perpendicular to ℓ through P:	Draw an arc with center at P that intersects the line in two points.	With the same compass opening, make two intersecting arcs, one with center at A and the other with center at B. The arcs intersect at Q.	Connect P with Q. $\overleftrightarrow{PQ}$ is the required line.

8. Construct a perpendicular to a line ℓ at a point P on line ℓ.

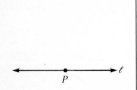	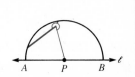	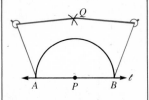	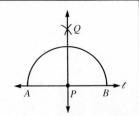
To construct a perpendicular to ℓ at P:	Draw any arc with center at P that intersects ℓ in two points A and B.	Use a larger opening for the compass and draw two intersecting arcs with centers at A and B.	Connect P with Q, the point where the arcs intersect. $\overleftrightarrow{PQ}$ is the required line.

9. Construct the perpendicular bisector of a segment.

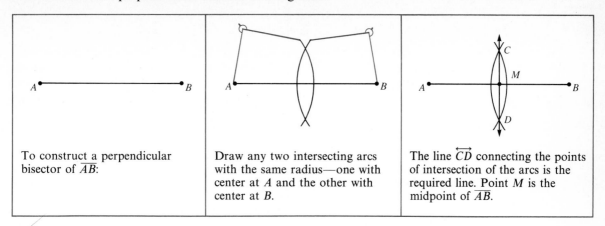

To construct a perpendicular bisector of $\overline{AB}$:	Draw any two intersecting arcs with the same radius—one with center at A and the other with center at B.	The line $\overleftrightarrow{CD}$ connecting the points of intersection of the arcs is the required line. Point M is the midpoint of $\overline{AB}$.

10. Separate a line segment into any number of congruent parts. The following construction illustrates the procedure for three congruent parts.

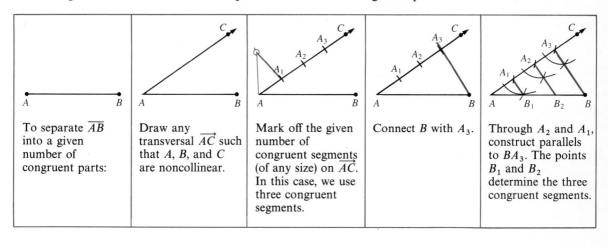

To separate $\overline{AB}$ into a given number of congruent parts:	Draw any transversal $\overrightarrow{AC}$ such that A, B, and C are noncollinear.	Mark off the given number of congruent segments (of any size) on $\overrightarrow{AC}$. In this case, we use three congruent segments.	Connect B with A_3.	Through A_2 and A_1, construct parallels to BA_3. The points B_1 and B_2 determine the three congruent segments.

Answers to Odd-Numbered Problems

CHAPTER 1

Problem Set 1-1 **1. (a)** 5×6, 6×7, 7×8
(b) 000000, □□□□□□□, 00000000 **(c)** 45, 41, 37
(d) 15, 20, 26 **(e)** 26, 37, 50 **(f)** X, Y, X (answers
vary). **(g)** 1, 18, 1 **(h)** 34, 55, 89 **(i)** 111111,
1111111, 11111111 **(j)** 123456, 1234567, 12345678
(k) $6 \cdot 2^6$, $7 \cdot 2^7$, $8 \cdot 2^8$ **(l)** 2^{32}, 2^{64}, 2^{128}
(m)

3. (a) 30, 42, 56 **(b)** $100 \cdot 101 = 10{,}100$
(c) $n(n + 1) = n^2 + n$ **5. (a)** 3, 5, 9, 15, 23, 33
(b) 4, 6, 10, 16, 24, 34 **(c)** 15, 17, 21, 27, 35, 45
7. (a) 100 **(b)** 101 **(c)** 100 **(d)** 61 **(e)** 200
9. (a) 3, 6, 11, 18, 27 **(b)** 4, 9, 14, 19, 24
(c) 9, 99, 999, 9999, 99999 **11. (a)** 1, 1, 2, 3, 5, 8,
13, 21, 34, 55, 89, 144 **(b)** Yes **(c)** 143
(d) The sum of the first n terms equals the
$(n + 2)$th term minus 1.
13. 15 L **15. (a)** $1660 **(b)** $7500 **(c)** 103 months
17. (a) Yes. The difference between terms in the new
sequence is the same as in the old sequence. **(b)** Yes.
If the fixed number is k, the difference between terms
of the second sequence is k times the difference
between terms of the first sequence.
19. Yes. The common ratio is the same as the ratio
of the original sequence.

Problem Set 1-2 **1.** Yes; it works with an even or
an odd number of numbers. **3.** $1.19 **5.** 325 **7.** 12
9. 5 inches **11.** $2.45
13. Answers vary.

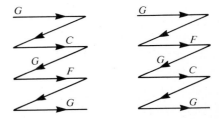

15. (a) Weigh four against four, pick the heavier side,
weigh two against two, and, finally, weigh one against
one. **(b)** Divide them into groups of three, three,
and two and weigh three against three. If they
balance, only one more weighing is necessary. If
they do not balance, select any two from the heavier
side and weigh one against one. Either they balance
or they do not. Thus, only one more weighing is
necessary.
17. 310 and 230 **19. (a)** 1001 **(b)** 300 **(c)** 150
21. 170 **23.** 2, 4, 6, 8, 10, 12, or 14
25. JC   QD   KH   AS
    KS   AH   JD   QC
    AD   KC   QS   JH
    QH   JS   AC   KD

where J represents jack, Q represents queen, K represents king, A represents ace, C represents club, D represents diamond, H represents heart, and S represents spade

27. 35 moves   **29.** $10(n + 1) + 2$ **31.** 903

Problem Set 1-3

1. (a) (i) 541   (ii) $12\overline{\smash{\big)}754}$
$\times\,72$

(b) (i) 257   (ii) $75\overline{\smash{\big)}124}$
$\times\,14$

3. $3.99, $5.87, $6.47   **5.** 17
7. Depends on the calculator   **9.** Answers may vary.
11. Answers may vary.   **13.** 3,628,800   **15.** $2 \div 6$
17. Play second and make sure that the sum showing when you hand the calculator to your opponent is a multiple of 3.
19. Play first and press 3. After that, make sure that each time you hand your opponent the calculator, it displays 3 more than a multiple of 10.
21. Play second; use a strategy similar to that of Problem 20, but use a multiple of 4.   **23. (a)** 35, 42, 49
(b) 1, 16, 1   **25.** 21   **27.** 160 pounds

Chapter Test   1. (a) 15, 21, 28   **(b)** 32, 27, 22
(c) 400, 200, 100   **(d)** 21, 34, 55   **(e)** 17, 20, 23
(f) 256, 1024, 4096   **(g)** 5, 25   **(h)** 16, 20, 24
(i) 125, 216, 343   **3. (a)** $3n + 2$ **(b)** n^3 **(c)** 3^n
5. (a) 10,100   **(b)** 10,201
7. 89 years, because there is no year 0   **9.** 26
11. 21   **13.** $3 \cdot 5 \cdot 9 \cdot 11 \cdot 13$

CHAPTER 2

Problem Set 2-1   1. (c) is well defined; **(a)** and **(b)** are not.   **3. (a)** $B = \{x, y, z, w\}$ **(b)** $3 \notin B$
(c) $\{1, 2\} \subset \{1, 2, 3, 4\}$ **(d)** $D \nsubseteq E$ **(e)** $A \nsubseteq B$
5. $\bar{A} = \{x \mid x$ is a college student who does not have a straight-A average$\}$
7. $\{\varnothing, \{x\}, \{y\}, \{z\}, \{x, y\}, \{x, z\}, \{y, z\}, \{x, y, z\}\}$
9. $A = C = D; E = H$ **11.** Sets C and D are equal.
13. (a) $\in$ **(b)** $\in$ **(c)** $\notin$ **(d)** $\notin$ **(e)** $\notin$ **(f)** $\notin$ **(g)** $\notin$
(h) $\notin$ **(i)** $\in$ **(j)** $\notin$
15. No; suppose $A = \{1, 2\}$ and $B = \{3\}$. Then, $A \nsubseteq B$ and $B \nsubseteq A$.
17. (a) Yes   **(b)** No   **(c)** Yes   **(d)** No   **(e)** No
19. (a) $4 \cdot 3 \cdot 2 \cdot 1 = 24$ **(b)** $5 \cdot 4 \cdot 3 \cdot 2 \cdot 1 = 120$
(c) $n \cdot (n - 1) \cdot (n - 2) \cdot \ldots \cdot 3 \cdot 2 \cdot 1$ **21.** 35

Problem Set 2-2   1. (a) Yes   **(b)** Yes   **(c)** Yes
(d) Yes   **(e)** No   **(f)** Yes   **3. (a)** B **(b)** A

5. (a) $B - A$, or $B \cap \bar{A}$ **(b)** $\overline{A \cup B}$, or $\bar{A} \cap \bar{B}$
(c) $A \cap B \cap C$ **(d)** $A \cap B$
(e) $(A \cap C) - B$, or $(A \cap C) \cap \bar{B}$
(f) $[(A \cup C) - B] \cup (A \cap C \cap B)$
7. (a) U **(b)** U **(c)** S **(d)** $\varnothing$ **(e)** S **(f)** U
(g) $\varnothing$ **(h)** S **(i)** $\bar{S}$ **(j)** S
9. (a) A **(b)** $\varnothing$ **(c)** $\varnothing$ **(d)** $\varnothing$
11. (a)   **(b)**

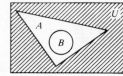

(c)   **(d)**

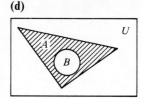

13. (a) F   **(b)** F   **15. (a)** No   **(b)** No   **(c)** No
17. $A = B$ **19.** 18   **21.** 93
23. (a) False; let $A = \{a\}$ and $B = \{b\}$.
(b) False; let $A = B$.   **(c)** False; let $A \subseteq B$.
(d) True   **(e)** False; let $A = \{2, 4, 6, 8, \ldots\}$ and $B = \{1, 2, 3, 4, \ldots\}$.   **(f)** False; let $A = \{1, 2\}$ and $B = \{4, 5, 6\}$.
25. (a) $\{(x, a), (x, b), (x, c), (y, a), (y, b), (y, c)\}$
(b) $\{(0, a), (0, b), (0, c)\}$
(c) $\{(a, x), (a, y), (b, x), (b, y), (c, x), (c, y)\}$ **(d)** $\varnothing$
(e) $\{(0, 0)\}$ **(f)** $\varnothing$ **(g)** $\{(x, 0), (y, 0), (a, 0), (b, 0), (c, 0)\}$
(h) $\{(x, 0), (y, 0), (a, 0), (b, 0), (c, 0)\}$ **(i)** $\varnothing$ **(j)** $\varnothing$
27. (a) 3   **(b)** 6   **(c)** 9   **(d)** 20   **(e)** $m \cdot n$
(f) $m \cdot n \cdot p$ **29.** 5   **31.** 12   **33.** 60
35. (a) 8   **(b)** 31   **37.** Answers may vary.   **39.** Yes
41. (a) {Massachusetts, Maryland, Mississippi, Minnesota, Missouri, Michigan, Maine, Montana}
(b) $\{x \mid x$ is a state in the United States starting with the letter M$\}$

Problem Set 2-3   1. Answers may vary.   **(a)** The second component is the square of the first component.   **(b)** The second component is the husband of the first component.   **(c)** The second component is the capital of the first component.
(d) The second component is the cost of the first component.   **3.** Answers may vary.
5. (a) No properties; not an equivalence relation
(b) Reflexive, symmetric, transitive; an equivalence relation   **(c)** Reflexive, symmetric, transitive; an equivalence relation   **(d)** Symmetric; not an

equivalence relation   **(e)** Reflexive, symmetric, transitive; an equivalence relation   **(f)** Symmetric; not an equivalence relation
7. (a) Reflexive, transitive   **(b)** Symmetric
(c) Reflexive, symmetric, transitive
9. (a) {Abe, Aza}, {George}, {Laura}, {Ben, Betty}, {Sue}, {Dax, Doug}, {Zachary}, {Mike, Mary}, {Carolyn}   **(b)** {Abe, George, Sue, Mike}, {Laura, Aza}, {Ben, Carolyn}, {Betty, Zachary, Mary}, {Dax}, {Doug}   **(c)** {Abe, Ben, Sue, Dax, Aza}, {George}, {Laura, Betty}, {Zachary, Carolyn}, {Doug, Mike, Mary}
11. Answers may vary.   **(a)** $f(x) = 2x$
(b) $f(x) = x - 2$ **(c)** $f(x) = x + 6$
(d) $f(x) = x^2 + 1$
13. Yes. Each element in the first set is used and each is associated with only one element in the second set.
15. Answers may vary.
17. (a)

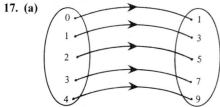

(b) {(0, 1), (1, 3), (2, 5), (3, 7), (4, 9)}
(c)

x	$f(x)$
0	1
1	3
2	5
3	7
4	9

(d)

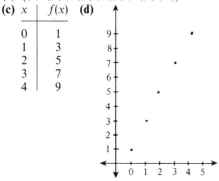

19. (a) $f(x) = \frac{1}{7}x$ **(b)** $f(x) = x + 5$
21. (a) 30 chirps in 15 seconds, or 2 chirps per second
(b) 50°F   **23. (a)** $5n - 2$ **(b)** 3^n **(c)** $2n$ **25.** No
27. No; rich is not well defined.
29. (a) {a, b, c, d} or U   **(b)** {a, d}   **(c)** ∅   **(d)** ∅
(e) ∅   **31.** Answers may vary.
33. $(A \cup B) \cup C = \{h, e, l, p, m\} \cup \{n, o, w\}$
       $= \{h, e, l, p, m, n, o, w\}$
$A \cup (B \cup C) = \{h, e, l, p\} \cup \{m, e, n, o, w\}$
       $= \{h, e, l, p, m, n, o, w\}$

Problem Set 2-4   1. (a) False statement   **(b)** Not a statement   **(c)** False statement   **(d)** Not a

statement   **(e)** Not a statement   **(f)** Not a statement
(g) True statement   **(h)** Not a statement
3. (a) For all natural numbers x, $x + 8 = 11$.
(b) For no natural number x, $x + 0 = x$.   **(c)** For no natural number x, $x^2 = 4$.   **(d)** For all natural numbers x, $x + 1 = x + 2$, or there exists a natural number x such that $x + 1 \neq x + 2$.
5. (a)

p	$\sim p$	$\sim(\sim p)$
T	F	T
F	T	F

(b)

p	$\sim p$	$p \vee \sim p$	$p \wedge \sim p$
T	F	T	F
F	T	T	F

(c) Yes   **(d)** No
7. (a) F   **(b)** T   **(c)** T   **(d)** F   **(e)** F   **(f)** T
(g) F   **(h)** F   **(i)** F   **(j)** F
9. (a) No   **(b)** Yes   **(c)** No   **(d)** Yes
11. (a) Today is not Wednesday or the month is not June.   **(b)** Yesterday I did not eat breakfast or I did not watch television.   **(c)** It is not true that both it is raining and it is July.
13. (a) {2, 3}   **(b)** {2, 3, 5}   **(c)** {1, 2, 3, 4, 5, 6, 7, 8} or U **(d)** {4, 5, 6, 7, 8}   **(e)** {1}
15. $A \cap B = \{b, c, d\} = B \cap A$
17.

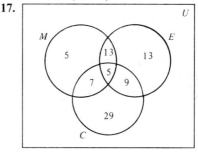

Problem Set 2-5   1. (a) $p \to q$ **(b)** $\sim p \to q$
(c) $p \to \sim q$ **(d)** $p \to q$ **(e)** $\sim q \to \sim p$ **(f)** $q \leftrightarrow p$

3. (a)

p	q	$p \vee q$	$p \to (p \vee q)$
T	T	T	T
T	F	T	T
F	T	T	T
F	F	F	T

(b)

p	q	$p \wedge q$	$(p \wedge q) \to q$
T	T	T	T
T	F	F	T
F	T	F	T
F	F	F	T

(c)

p	$\sim p$	$\sim(\sim p)$	$p \to \sim(\sim p)$	$\sim(\sim p) \to p$	$p \leftrightarrow \sim(\sim p)$
T	F	T	T	T	T
F	T	F	T	T	T

(d)

p	q	$p \to q$	$\sim(p \to q)$
T	T	T	F
T	F	F	T
F	T	T	F
F	F	T	F

5. (a) T **(b)** F **(c)** T **(d)** T **(e)** F **(f)** T
7. No. Tom can go to the movies or not and the implication is still true.
9. Answers may vary. For example, "If a number is not a multiple of 4, then it is not a multiple of 8."
11. (a) p: Mary's little lamb follows her to school.
$\qquad q$: The lamb breaks the rules.
$\qquad r$: Mary is sent home.
$\qquad p \to (q \wedge r)$
(b) p: Jack is nimble.
$\qquad q$: Jack is quick.
$\qquad r$: Jack makes it over the candlestick.
$\qquad \sim(p \wedge q) \to \sim r$
(c) p: The apple hit Isaac Newton on the head.
$\qquad q$: The laws of gravity were discovered.
$\qquad \sim p \to \sim q$
13. (a) Helen is poor. **(b)** Some freshmen are intelligent. **(c)** If I study for the final, then I will look for a teaching job. **(d)** Some pigs are not eagles. **(e)** There may exist triangles that are not equilateral.
15. (a) If an animal is my poultry, then the animal is not an officer. **(b)** If a person can manage a crocodile, then the person is not a baby. **(c)** If a kitten is teachable, then it has green eyes and will play with a gorilla. **(d)** If you are my son, you are not fit to serve on a jury.

17. 11

Chapter Test **1.** $\{x \mid x$ is a letter of the English alphabet$\}$
3. (a) $\overline{A}$ is the set of people living in Montana who are less than 30 years old. **(b)** $A \cap C$ is the set of people living in Montana who are 30 or older and own a gun. **(c)** $A \cup B$ is the set of people living in Montana. **(d)** $\overline{C}$ is the set of people living in Montana who do not own a gun. **(e)** $\overline{A \cap C}$ is the set of people living in Montana who are younger than 30 or do not own a gun. **(f)** $A - C$ is the set of people living in Montana who are 30 or older and do not own a gun.

5. (a) 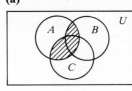 **(b)**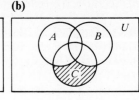

$A \cap (B \cup C)$ $\qquad\qquad$ $\overline{A \cup B} \cap C$

7. $2^6 - 1 = 63$
9.

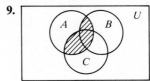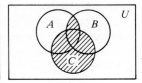

$A \cap (B \cup C) \neq (A \cap B) \cup C$

11. $(A \cap B) \cap C = \{3\} = A \cap (B \cap C)$;
$A \cup B = \{1, 2, 3, 4, 5\} = B \cup A$
13.

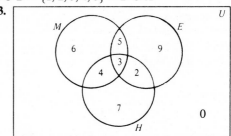

(a) 36 **(b)** 6 **(c)** 5
15. (a) 7 **(b)** 31 **(c)** 37 **17. (a)** Reflexive, symmetric, transitive **(b)** Transitive **(c)** Symmetric **(d)** None **19. (a)** No women smoke. **(b)** $3 + 5 \neq 8$ **(c)** Some acid rock is not loud. **(d)** Beethoven wrote some nonclassical music. **21. (a)** Equivalent **(b)** Not equivalent **23. (a)** Joe Czernyu loves Mom and apple pie. **(b)** The Statue of Liberty will eventually rust. **(c)** Albertina will pass Math 100.
25. (a) Valid **(b)** Not valid **(c)** Valid **(d)** Valid

CHAPTER 3

Problem Set 3-1 **1. (a)** $\overline{\overline{MCDXXIV}}$ **(b)** 46,032
(c) < ▼▼ **(d)** ⌐ ∩ ∣
3. (a) Use place value in columns, as done in the Hindu-Arabic system. Group the numerals in each column; trade symbols and shift columns if possible.

(b) Group all the same symbols for each number; trade if possible to make the sum using as few symbols as possible. **(c)** Add values of symbols and trade to make the sum as simple as possible.

5. (a) ∩∩∩∩∩ || **(b)** 𝓕||| **(c)** ⟋|||

(d) ∩∩∩ ||||||| **7. (a)** ▼ ⟨▼▼:∩∩∩∩∩∩∩||:

LXXII **(b)** 602; 𝟫𝟫𝟫 / 𝟫𝟫𝟫 ||: DCII

(c) 1223; ⟨⟨   ⟨⟨ ▼▼▼ : MCCXXIII

(d) 667; ⟨▼ ▼▼▼▼▼▼▼ :𝟫𝟫𝟫𝟫𝟫𝟫∩∩∩∩∩∩||||||

9. (a) Hundreds **(b)** Tens **(c)** Thousands
(d) Hundred thousands **11.** 4,782,969

Problem Set 3-2   1. (a) $k = 2$ **(b)** $k = 3$
3. For example, let $A = \{1, 2\}$ and $B = \{2, 3\}$; then, $A \cup B = \{1, 2, 3\}$. Thus, $n(A) = 2$, $n(B) = 2$, and $n(A \cup B) = 3$, but $n(A) + n(B) = 2 + 2 = 4 \neq n(A \cup B)$.
5. (a) 5 **(b)** 2 **(c)** 0, 1, 2 **(d)** 3, 4, 5, 6, . . .
7. (a) Commutative property for addition
(b) Associative property for addition
(c) Commutative property for addition
(d) Closure property for addition
(e) Associative property for addition
9. (a) 3 **(b)** 3 **(c)** 13 **(d)** a **(e)** 0
(f) 3, 4, 5, 6, 7, 8, 9 **(g)** 10, 11, 12, . . .
11. 9 pages

13. (a)

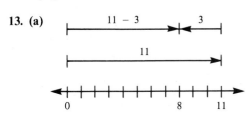

(b)

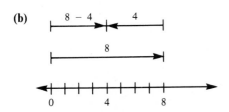

15. Answers may vary; for example, let $A = \{a, b\}$ and $B = \{a, b, c, d\}$. Then,
$4 - 2 = n(B - A) = n(\{c, d\}) = 2$.
17. (a) $a = b$
　(b) If $c = 0$, then it is true for all whole-number values for which $(a - b)$ is defined.
　(c) $a = 0$

(d) All whole-number values of a, b, and c for which $(b - c)$ is meaningful

19. (a)

8	1	6
3	5	7
4	9	2

(b)

17	10	15
12	14	16
13	18	11

21. Depends on the individual calculator **23.** 26
25. There are fewer symbols to remember, and place value is used.

Problem Set 3-3
1.

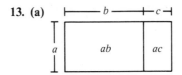

3. \$35.00 **5.** $8 \cdot 3 = (6 + 2) \cdot 3$
$$= 6 \cdot 3 + 2 \cdot 3$$
$$= 18 + 6 = 24$$
7. (a) $ac + ad + bc + bd$ **(b)** $3x + 3y + 15$
(c) $\square \cdot \triangle + \square \cdot \bigcirc$
(d) $x^2 + xy + xz + yx + y^2 + yz$, or
　$x^2 + 2xy + xz + y^2 + yz$
9. (a) $5x$ **(b)** $14x$ **(c)** $5(x + 1)$, or $5x + 5$
(d) $(2 + x)(x + 3)$
11. $a(b + c + d) = a[(b + c) + d]$
$$= a(b + c) + ad$$
$$= (ab + ac) + ad$$
$$= ab + ac + ad$$

13. (a)

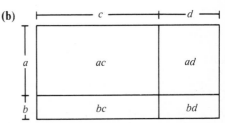

(b)

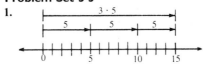

15. (a) $40 = 8 \cdot 5$ **(b)** $326 = 2 \cdot x$ **(c)** $48 = x \cdot 16$
(d) $x = 5 \cdot 17$ **(e)** $a = b \cdot c$ **(f)** $(48 - 36) = 6x$
17. $(a \cdot b) \div b = a$ if and only if $a \cdot b = b \cdot a$. By the commutative property for multiplication, $a \cdot b = b \cdot a$, for all whole numbers.
19. 2; 3 left

21. **(a)**

□	△
0	34
1	26
2	18
3	10
4	2

(b) △ = 66

(c)

□	△
25	1
1	25

Also, □ = 5 and △ = 5 if □ = △.

23. 12 **25. (a)** 3 **(b)** 2 **(c)** 2 **(d)** 6 **(e)** 4

27. (i) ∩∩∩∩∩∩ |||||
(ii) LXXV
(iii) ▼ <▼▼▼▼▼

29. For example, {0, 1}

31.

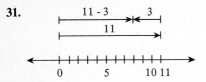

Problem Set 3-4

1. (a)   ¹3 ²7 ¹8 9
  9 ₃2 ₁9 ₈6 ₅
 +6 8 4₂ 3
 ――――――――
 1 9 9 2 8

(b) 3 0 ¹0 4   **(c)** ¹5 ²2 4
 + 9 8 7   3 2 8₂
 ―――――――   5₄ 6₂ 7
 3 9 9 1   +1 3 5₄
               ――――――――
               1 5 5 4

3. The columns separate place value and show that
7 + 8 = 15 and 20 + 60 = 80. Finally, 15 + 80 = 95.

5. (a) 357; 357 + 79 = 436   **(b)** 902; 902 + 99 = 1001
(c) 2874; 2874 + 129 = 3003

7. (a) One possibility: 863
                 +752
                ――――
                1615

(b) One possibility: 368
                +257
               ――――
                625

9. 433   **11. (a)** 34, 39, 44   **(b)** 82, 79, 76
13. No, not all at dinner. He can have either the steak
or the salad.

15. Answers may vary; one possibility is

      000
      770
      000
      330
    +011
    ――――
    1111

17. (a)

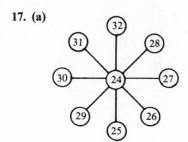

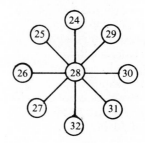

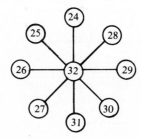

(b) 3
19. $5280 = 5 \cdot 10^3 + 2 \cdot 10^2 + 8 \cdot 10 + 0 \cdot 1$
21.

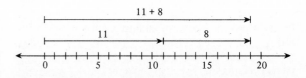

23. (a) $a \cdot (x + 1)$ **(b)** $(3 + a) \cdot (x + y)$

Problem Set 3-5

1. (a)

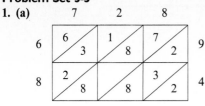

(b)

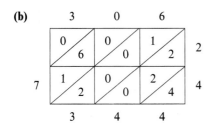

3. $386 \cdot 10,000 = (3 \cdot 10^2 + 8 \cdot 10 + 6) \cdot 10^4$
$= (3 \cdot 10^2) \cdot 10^4 + (8 \cdot 10) \cdot 10^4 + 6 \cdot 10^4$
$= 3 \cdot 10^6 + 8 \cdot 10^5 + 6 \cdot 10^4$
$= 3,860,000$

5. (a) 5^{19} **(b)** 6^{15} **(c)** 10^{313} **(d)** 10^{12}
7. 86,400; 604,800; 31,536,000 (365 days)
9. (a) $293 \cdot 476 = 139,468$
(b) Placement still indicates place value.
(c)
$$363$$
$$\times\, 84$$
$$\overline{2904}$$
$$1452$$
$$\overline{30492}$$

11. (a) Let xy be the number. Then, we want $(10x + y) + (10y + x)$ or $11(x + y)$ to be close to 50. Therefore, the sum we want must be a multiple of 11. 55 is the multiple of 11 closest to 50. Therefore, the number could be 14, 23, 32, or 41. **(b)** By similar reasoning, the number could be 18, 27, 36, 45, 54, 63, 72, or 81. **13. (a)** 22 **(b)** 190 **(c)** 7 **(d)** 39
15. (a) 77 remainder 7 **(b)** 8 remainder 10
(c) 10 remainder 91 **17.** 12 km/sec
19. She will finish on the eleventh day **21.** 3
23. (a)
$$763$$
$$\times\, 8$$
$$\overline{6104}$$
(b)
$$678$$
$$\times\, 3$$
$$\overline{2034}$$
25. 7,500,000 cows
27. (a) 9 **(b)** 5 **(c)** 143; 11; 13
(d) 333; 111; 37; 9; 3 **29.** There are fourteen 7s in 98.
31. $60; $3600; $86,400; $604,800; $2,592,000 (30 days); $31,536,000 (365 days); $630,720,000 (approximately)
33. 19 **35.** 300,260 **37. (a)** $x \cdot (a + b + 2)$
(b) $(3 + x)(a + b)$ **39.** 724

Problem Set 3-6 1. (a) $(1, 10, 11, 100, 101, 110, 111, 1000, 1001, 1010, 1011, 1100, 1101, 1110, 1111)_{two}$
(b) $(1, 2, 10, 11, 12, 20, 21, 22, 100, 101, 102, 110, 111, 112, 120)_{three}$ **(c)** $(1, 2, 3, 10, 11, 12, 13, 20, 21, 22, 23, 30, 31, 32, 33)_{four}$ **(d)** $(1, 2, 3, 4, 5, 6, 7, 10, 11, 12, 13, 14, 15, 16, 17)_{eight}$
3. $2032_{four} = (2 \cdot 10^3 + 0 \cdot 10^2 + 3 \cdot 10 + 2)_{four}$
$= 2 \cdot 4^3 + 0 \cdot 4^2 + 3 \cdot 4 + 2$
5. (a) There is no numeral 4 in base four.
(b) There are no numerals 6 or 7 in base five.
(c) There is no numeral T in base three.
7. (a) 3212_{five} **(b)** 1177_{twelve} **(c)** 12110_{four}
(d) 100101_{two} **(e)** 1431304_{five} **(f)** $1E3T4_{twelve}$
(g) $9000E0_{twelve}$ **9.** 100010_{two} **11.** One prize of $625, two prizes of $125, and one of $25
13. (a) 8 weeks, 2 days **(b)** 4 years, 6 months
(c) 1 day, 5 hours **(d)** 5 feet, 8 inches
15. $E66_{twelve}$; 1662 **17.** 4; 1, 2, 4, 8; 5; 1, 2, 4, 8, 16
19. (a) 121_{five} **(b)** 20_{five} **(c)** 1010_{five} **(d)** 14_{five}
(e) 1001_{two} **(f)** 1010_{two}
21. (a) 9 hours, 33 minutes, 25 seconds
(b) 1 hour, 39 minutes, 40 seconds
23.
$$
\begin{array}{r}
{}^{3}3\,2 \\
{}_{1} \\
1\,3 \\
{}^{0} \\
2\,2 \\
4\,3 \\
{}^{3\ 0} \\
2\,3 \\
{}^{0} \\
1\,2 \\
{}_{0} \\
\hline
3\,1\,0_{five}
\end{array}
$$
25. There is no numeral 5 in base five; $2_{five} + 3_{five} = 10_{five}$.
27. (a) 233_{five} **(b)** 4_{five} remainder 1_{five}
(c) 2144_{five} **(d)** 31_{five} **(e)** 67_{eight}
(f) 15_{eight} remainder 3_{eight}
(g) 110_{two} **(h)** 1101110_{two} **29.** 30221_{five}

Chapter Test 1. (a) 400,044 **(b)** 117 **(c)** 1704
(d) 11 **(e)** 1448 **3. (a)** 3^{17} **(b)** 2^{21} **(c)** 3^5
5. (a) $3 < 13$, because $3 + 10 = 13$ **(b)** $12 > 9$, because $12 = 9 + 3$ **7. (a)** 1119 **(b)** $173E_{twelve}$
9. (a) 5 remainder 243 **(b)** 91 remainder 10
(c) 120_{five} remainder 2_{five} **11. (a)** Tens
(b) Thousands **(c)** Hundreds
13. (a)

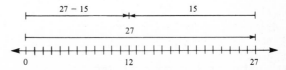

(b)

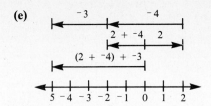

(c)

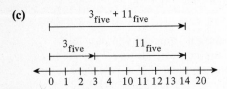

(d)

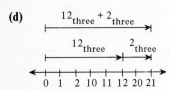

15. (a) Addition; 25 **(b)** Division; 8
(c) Multiplication; 72 **(d)** Subtraction; $26
17. $4380 **19.** $3842 **21.** 69 miles **23.** 12 outfits
25. $900E000T_{twelve}$

CHAPTER 4

Problem Set 4-1 1. (a) $^-2$ **(b)** 5 **(c)** ^-m **(d)** 0
(e) m **(f)** $^-(a + b)$, or $^-a + ^-b$, or $^-a - b$
3. (a) 5 **(b)** 10 **(c)** 3 **(d)** 7 **(e)** $^-5$ **(f)** $^-5$
5. (a)

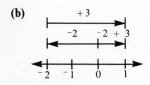

(b)

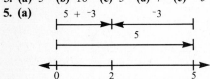

(c)

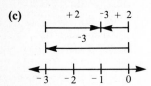

(d)

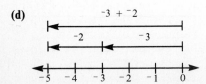

(e)

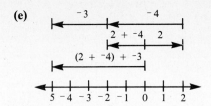

7. (a) $300 + ^-45 + ^-55 + ^-165 + ^-35 + ^-100 + 75 + 25 + 400$ **(b)** $400
9. (a) $^-9$ **(b)** 3 **(c)** 1 **(d)** $^-19$ **(e)** $^-13$ **(f)** $^-6$
11. (a) Yes **(b)** Yes
13. One possibility is the following.

2	5	$^-10$
$^-13$	$^-1$	11
8	$^-7$	$^-4$

15. 33 points **17.**

1	3
2	5
4	6
8	7

19. (a) $^-18$ **(b)** $^-106$ **(c)** $^-6$ **(d)** 22 **(e)** $^-11$
(f) 2 **(g)** $^-18$ **(h)** 23
21. (a) True **(b)** True **(c)** True **(d)** True
(e) False; $|(^-2)^3| \neq (^-2)^3$ **(f)** True

Problem Set 4-2 1. (a) 12 **(b)** $^-15$ **(c)** $^-15$
(d) 0 **(e)** 30 **(f)** $^-30$ **(g)** 0 **(h)** 16 **3. (a)** $^-10$
(b) $^-40$ **(c)** a, if $b \neq 0$ **(d)** $^-10$ **(e)** a, if $b \neq 0$
(f) $^-32$ **(g)** $^-5$ **(h)** 0 **(i)** Impossible **(j)** $^-4$
(k) Impossible **(l)** 13 **(m)** $^-1$ **(n)** $^-2$
5. (a) $^-1(^-5 + ^-2) = ^-1(^-5) + ^-1(^-2)$
(b) $^-3(^-3 + 2) = ^-3(^-3) + ^-3(2)$
(c) $^-5(2 + ^-6) = ^-5(2) + ^-5(^-6)$
7. (a) Yes **(b)** Yes **(c)** Yes **(d)** Yes **9.** $^-15°C$
11. (a) $^-13, ^-17, ^-21$ **(b)** $^-12, ^-14, ^-16$
(c) $^-9, 3, ^-1$ **(d)** $^-5, ^-2, 1$
13. $3(^-1) = ^-1 + ^-1 + ^-1 = ^-3$
$2(^-1) = ^-1 + ^-1 = ^-2$
$1(^-1) = ^-1$
$0(^-1) = 0$
$^-1(^-1) = 1$ (By continuing the pattern)
15. (a) and **(f)** are always negative; **(b), (c), (g)**, and **(h)**
are always positive. **17. (a)** xy **(b)** $2xy$ **(c)** 0
(d) ^-x **(e)** $x + 2y$ **(f)** b **(g)** x **(h)** y
19. (a) $(50 + 2)(50 - 2) = 50^2 - 2^2 = 2496$
(b) $5^2 - 100^2 = ^-9975$ **(c)** $x^2 - y^2$ **(d)** $4 - 9x^2$
(e) $x^2 - 1$ **(f)** 45,200 **21. (a)** $(3 + 5)x = 8x$
(b) $(a + 2)x$ **(c)** $x(y + 1)$ **(d)** $(a - 2)x$
(e) $x(x + y)$ **(f)** $(3 - 4 + 7)x = 6x$

(g) $x(3y + 2 - z)$ **(h)** $x(3x + y - 1)$
(i) $a(bc + b - 1)$ **(j)** $(a + b)(c + 1 - 1) = (a + b)c$
(k) $(4 - a)(4 + a)$ **(l)** $(x - 3y)(x + 3y)$
(m) $(2x - 5y)(2x + 5y)$ **(n)** $(x + y)(x - y + 1)$
23. 28th day
25. (a) The additive inverse of $^-(a \cdot b)$ is $a \cdot b$. Also, $(^-a) \cdot b + a \cdot b = [(^-a) + a] \cdot b = 0 \cdot b = 0$. Thus, the additive inverse of $(^-a) \cdot b$ is also $a \cdot b$. Hence, by uniqueness of additive inverses, $(^-a) \cdot b = {}^-(a \cdot b)$.
(b) The additive inverse of $a \cdot b$ is $^-(a \cdot b)$, or $(^-a) \cdot b$ by part (a). Also, $(^-a) \cdot b + (^-a) \cdot (^-b) = (^-a)(b + {}^-b) = (^-a) \cdot 0 = 0$. Thus, the additive inverse of $(^-a) \cdot (^-b)$ is also $(^-a) \cdot b$. Hence, by uniqueness of additive inverses, $a \cdot b = (^-a)(^-b)$.   **(c)** The additive inverse of $^-(a + b)$ is $a + b$. Also,

$$(^-a + {}^-b) + (a + b) = {}^-a + (^-b + a) + b$$
$$= {}^-a + (a + {}^-b) + b$$
$$= (^-a + a) + (^-b + b)$$
$$= 0 + 0$$
$$= 0$$

Thus, the additive inverse of $(^-a + {}^-b)$ is also $a + b$. Hence, by the uniqueness of additive inverses, $^-(a + b) = {}^-a + {}^-b$.
27. (a) $^-3$ **(b)** 1   **(c)** 13   **(d)** 3   **(e)** $^-3$ **(f)** $^-13$
29. (a) 5   **(b)** $^-7$ **(c)** 0

Problem Set 4-3   **1. (a)** $^-20, {}^-13, {}^-5, {}^-3, 0, 4$
(b) $^-6, {}^-5, 0, 5, 6$ **(c)** $^-100, {}^-20, {}^-15, {}^-13, 0$
(d) $^-3, {}^-2, 5, 13$ **3. (a)** $^-18$ **(b)** $x > {}^-18, x \in I$
(c) 18   **(d)** $x < 18, x \in I$ **(e)** $^-18$ **(f)** $x < {}^-18$,
$x \in I$ **(g)** $^-7$ **(h)** $x < {}^-7, x \in I$ **(i)** $^-2$
(j) $x \geq {}^-2, x \in I$ **(k)** $^-1$ **(l)** $x < {}^-1, x \in I$ **(m)** $^-2$
(n) $x < {}^-3, x \in I$ **5. (a)** Yes   **(b)** No   **(c)** Yes
(d) Yes   **(e)** Yes   **(f)** No   **7. (a)** $^-3$;
$^-2(^-3) + {}^-11 = 3(^-3) + 4$ **(b)** 0; $5(0 + 1) = 5$
(c) 1; $^-3(1) + 4 = 1$ **(d)** 0; $^-3(0 - 1) = 8 \cdot 0 + 3$
9. $^-5$ **11.** Nureet is 10; Ran is 14.   **13.** 40 pounds of 60¢-per-pound tea and 60 pounds of 45¢-per-pound tea   **15.** 78, 79, 80   **17.** 7, 14   **19. (a)** Yes.
$x^2 + y^2 \geq 2xy$ if and only if $x^2 - 2xy + y^2 \geq 0$ and $x^2 - 2xy + y^2 = (x - y)^2 \geq 0$.   **(b)** $x = y$ **21.** No; $^-5 < 2$, but $(^-5)^2 \not< 2^2$.   **23. (a)** $^-3, {}^-2, {}^-1, 0, 1$
(b) $^-2, {}^-3, {}^-4, {}^-5, \ldots$ **25. (a)** $^-10$ **(b)** 4   **(c)** $^-4$
(d) 10   **(e)** $^-21$ **(f)** 21   **(g)** $^-4$ **(h)** $^-3$ **(i)** 3
(j) $^-4$ **(k)** 7   **(l)** $^-21$ **(m)** 21   **(n)** 56   **(o)** 15
(p) $^-1$

Chapter Test   **1. (a)** $^-3$ **(b)** a **(c)** 0
(d) $^-(x + y)$, or $^-x + {}^-y$, or $^-x - y$ **(e)** $^-(^-x + y)$, or $x + {}^-y$, or $x - y$ **3. (a)** 3   **(b)** $^-5$ **(c)** $x \in I$; $x \neq 0$ **(d)** $\varnothing$ **(e)** $^-41$ **(f)** $x \in I$

5. (a) $(x - y)(x + y) = (x - y)x + (x - y)y$
$$= (x^2 - yx) + (xy - y^2)$$
$$= (x^2 + {}^-yx) + (xy - y^2)$$
$$= x^2 + (^-yx + xy) - y^2$$
$$= x^2 + (^-xy + xy) - y^2$$
$$= x^2 + 0 - y^2$$
$$= x^2 - y^2$$
(b) $(^-2 - x)(^-2 + x) = (^-2)^2 - x^2 = 4 - x^2$
7. (a) $(1 - 3)x = {}^-2x$ **(b)** $x(x + 1)$ **(c)** $5(1 + x)$
(d) $(x - y)(x + 1 - 1) = (x - y)x$ **9.** 1010 seniors, 895 juniors, 2020 sophomores, 1790 freshmen
11. $^-7°C$ **13.** 14 pounds   **15.** 7 nickels and 17 dimes

CHAPTER 5

Problem Set 5-1   **1. (a)** T   **(b)** T   **(c)** T   **(d)** T
(e) T   **(f)** F   **3.** Yes; $9 \nmid 1379$.
5. (a) Theorem 5-3   **(b)** Theorem 5-1(b)   **(c)** None
(d) Theorem 5-1(b)   **(e)** Theorem 5-3
(7) (a) 5   **(b)** 0
9. (a) A number N is divisible by 16 if and only if the number formed by the last four digits is divisible by 16.
(b) A number N is divisible by 25 if and only if the number formed by the last two digits is divisible by 25.
11. Yes   **13.** 85,041
15. (a) No. Suppose the number is divisible by 10; then, it must be divisible by 5, a contradiction.   **(b)** Yes. For example, $5 \mid 5$, but $10 \nmid 5$.
17. Because each digit, except 0, appears three times, 3 divides the sums of all like digits. Also, $3 \mid 0$, so 3 divides the sum of all digits.
19. (a) Yes   **(b)** No   **(c)** Yes   **(d)** No
21. (a) The difference is always equal to 9.   **(b)** The difference is always equal to $2 \cdot 9$, or 18.   **(c)** Let ab be a two-digit number. Then,

$$ab - ba = (10a + b) - (10b - a)$$
$$= 9a - 9b = 9(a - b)$$

Because $a, b \in I$, then $9 \mid ab - ba$.   **(d)** The difference is always a multiple of 9.
23. Let $N = a_4 \cdot 10^4 + a_3 \cdot 10^3 + a_2 \cdot 10^2 + a_1 \cdot 10^1 + a_0$.
$9 \mid 9$ implies $9 \mid 9a_1$
$9 \mid 99$ implies $9 \mid 99a_2$
$9 \mid 999$ implies $9 \mid 999a_3$
$9 \mid 9999$ implies $9 \mid 9999a_4$
Thus, $9 \mid (9999a_4 + 999a_3 + 99a_2 + 9a_1)$. Because $N = (9999a_4 + a_4) + (999a_3 + a_3) + (99a_2 + a_2) + (9a_1 + a_1) + a_0$, then $9 \mid [(9999a_4 + 999a_3 + 99a_2 + 9a_1) + (a_4 + a_3 + a_2 + a_1 + a_0)]$ if and only if $9 \mid (a_4 + a_3 + a_2 + a_1 + a_0)$
25. 243; yes; $7 \cdot 11 \cdot 13 = 1001$, and any number of the form $abcabc$ is divisible by 1001.

Problem Set 5-2 **1. (a)** $504 = 2^3 \cdot 3^2 \cdot 7$
(b) $2475 = 3^2 \cdot 5^2 \cdot 11$ **(c)** $11{,}250 = 2 \cdot 3^2 \cdot 5^4$
3. 73 **5.** 53, 59, 61, 67, 71, 73, 79, 83, 89, 97, 101,
103, 107, 109, 113, 127, 131, 137, 139, 149, 151, 157, 163,
167, 173, 179, 181, 191, 193, 197, 199
7. (a) 1×48; 2×24; 3×16; 4×12 **(b)** Only one;
1×47 **9. (a)** 3, 5, 15, or 29 members **(b)** 145
committees of 3; 87 committees of 5; 29 committees of
15; or 15 committees of 29 **11.** 2^6, or 64 **13.** 27,720
15. 3 and 5; 11 and 13; 17 and 19; 29 and 31; 41 and
43; 59 and 61; 71 and 73; 101 and 103; 107 and 109;
137 and 139; 149 and 151; 179 and 181; 191 and 193;
197 and 199
17. No. The student who checked for divisibility by 12
using 2 and 6 is incorrect because $2 | n$ and $6 | n$ do not
imply that $12 | n$. They imply only that $6 | n$.
19. For example, $6 = 2 \cdot 3$ or $6 = 1 \cdot 2 \cdot 3$. Therefore,
6 would have at least two prime factorizations.
21. (a) 49, 121, 169. These numbers are the squares of
prime numbers. **(b)** 81, 625, 2401. These numbers are
the primes raised to the fourth power. **(c)** 38, 39, 46.
These numbers are the products of two primes or the
cubes of primes.
23. If any prime q in the set $\{2, 3, 5, \ldots, p\}$ divides N,
then $q | 2 \cdot 3 \cdot 5 \cdot \ldots \cdot p$. Because $q \nmid 1$ by Theorem 5-1(b),
$q \nmid (2 \cdot 3 \cdot 5 \cdot \ldots \cdot p + 1)$; that is, $q \nmid N$.
25. (a) F **(b)** T **(c)** T **(d)** T
27. Let N be a number such that $12 | N$. $12 | N$
implies $12m = N$, where $m \in I$.

$$3 \cdot 4 \cdot m = N$$
$$3(4 \cdot m) = N$$

Therefore, $3 | N$.

Problem Set 5-3 **1. (a)** 2; 90 **(b)** 12; 72
(c) 4; 312 **3. (a)** 4 **(b)** 1 **(c)** 16 **5. (a)** 160,280
(b) 158,433,320 **(c)** 941,866,496 **7.** 24 **9.** 15
11. (a) ab **(b)** a; a **(c)** a; a^2 **(d)** a; b **(e)** 1; ab
(f) $a | b$ **(g)** $b | a$ **13.** 15 **15.** 36 minutes
17. 1, 2, 3, 4, 6, 7, 8, 9, 11, 12, 13, 14, 16, 17, 18, 19,
21, 22, 23, 24 **19. (a)** $\frac{7}{12}$ **(b)** $\frac{7}{11}$ **(c)** $\frac{13}{32}$ **(d)** $\frac{1}{4}$
21. Yes. $d | \text{GCD}(a, b)$, and $\text{GCD}(a, b) | a$, so $d | a$.
Similarly, $d | b$. **23.** No; $3 | 3111$.
25. $2^3 \cdot 3^2 \cdot 5 \cdot 7 \cdot 11 = 27{,}720$

Problem Set 5-4 **1. (a)** 3 **(b)** 2 **(c)** 6 **(d)** 8
(e) 3 **(f)** 4 **(g)** Impossible **(h)** 10
3. (a)

$\oplus$	1	2	3	4	5	6	7
1	2	3	4	5	6	7	1
2	3	4	5	6	7	1	2
3	4	5	6	7	1	2	3
4	5	6	7	1	2	3	4
5	6	7	1	2	3	4	5
6	7	1	2	3	4	5	6
7	1	2	3	4	5	6	7

(b) 6; 4
(c) Each subtraction problem $a - b = x$ can be
rewritten as $a = b + x$. If every number x shows up
exactly once in every row and column, then no matter
what a and b are, x can be found.
5. (a)

$\otimes$	1	2	3
1	1	2	3
2	2	1	3
3	3	3	3

$\otimes$	1	2	3	4
1	1	2	3	4
2	2	4	2	4
3	3	2	1	4
4	4	4	4	4

$\otimes$	1	2	3	4	5	6
1	1	2	3	4	5	6
2	2	4	6	2	4	6
3	3	6	3	6	3	6
4	4	2	6	4	2	6
5	5	4	3	2	1	6
6	6	6	6	6	6	6

$\otimes$	1	2	3	4	5	6	7	8	9	10	11
1	1	2	3	4	5	6	7	8	9	10	11
2	2	4	6	8	10	1	3	5	7	9	11
3	3	6	9	1	4	7	10	2	5	8	11
4	4	8	1	5	9	3	6	10	3	7	11
5	5	10	4	9	3	8	2	7	1	6	11
6	6	1	7	2	8	3	9	4	10	5	11
7	7	3	10	6	2	9	5	1	8	4	11
8	8	5	2	10	7	4	1	9	6	3	11
9	9	7	5	3	1	10	8	6	4	2	11
10	10	9	8	7	6	5	4	3	2	1	11
11	11	11	11	11	11	11	11	11	11	11	11

(b) 3 and 11
(c) On the n-hour clocks on which divisions can be
performed, n is prime.
7. Wednesday **9. (a)** 4 **(b)** 0 **(c)** 0 **(d)** 7
11. (a) $24 \equiv 0 \pmod 8$ **(b)** $^{-}90 \equiv 0 \pmod 3$
(c) $n \equiv 0 \pmod n$
13. (a) 1 **(b)** 5 **(c)** 10
15. Let $N = a_k \cdot 10^k + a_{k-1} \cdot 10^{k-1} + \cdots +$
$a_2 \cdot 10^2 + a_1 \cdot 10^1 + a_0$. $4 | N$ if and only if
$4 | (a_1 \cdot 10 + a_0)$. Proof: $100 \equiv 0 \pmod 4$. Hence,
$N = 100(a_k 10^{k-2} + a_{k-1} 10^{k-3} + \cdots + a_2) +$
$a_1 10 + a_0 \equiv a_1 10 + a_0 \pmod 4$. Consequently, $4 | N$
if and only if $4 | (a_1 \cdot 10 + a_0)$.
17. (1) $a \equiv a \pmod m$ because $m | (a - a)$.
(2) If $a \equiv b \pmod m$, then $b \equiv a \pmod m$. Proof:
$a \equiv b \pmod m$ means $m | (a - b)$, which implies
$m | (^{-}1)(a - b)$, or $m | (b - a)$. Hence, $b \equiv a \pmod m$.
(3) If $a \equiv b \pmod m$, and $b \equiv c \pmod m$, then
$a \equiv c \pmod m$. Proof: Because $a - b = k_1 m$ and
$b - c = k_2 m$ for some integers k_1 and k_2, it follows
that $(a - b) + (b - c) = k_1 m + k_2 m$, or $a - c =$
$(k_1 + k_2)m$. Hence, $a \equiv c \pmod m$.

(4) If $a \equiv b \pmod{m}$, then $a + c \equiv b + c \pmod{m}$.
Proof: Because $a - b = km$ for some integer k, it follows that $a + c - (b + c) = a - b = km$, and hence that $a + c \equiv b + c \pmod{m}$.
(5) If $a \equiv b \pmod{m}$, then $ac \equiv bc \pmod{m}$. Proof: Because $a - b = km$ for some integer k,
$ac - bc = (a - b)c = (km)c = (kc)m$. Because kc is an integer, it follows that $ac \equiv bc \pmod{m}$.
(6) If $a \equiv b \pmod{m}$ and $c \equiv d \pmod{m}$, then $ac \equiv bd \pmod{m}$. Proof: By (5), $a \equiv b \pmod{m}$ implies $ac \equiv bc \pmod{m}$, and $c \equiv d \pmod{m}$ implies $bc \equiv bd \pmod{m}$. Now, applying (3) to $ac \equiv bc \pmod{m}$ and $bc \equiv bd \pmod{m}$, we obtain $ac \equiv bd \pmod{m}$.
(7) Applying (6) with $c = a$ and $d = b$, we obtain $a^2 \equiv b^2 \pmod{m}$. Again by (6), $a^2 \equiv b^2 \pmod{m}$ with $a \equiv b \pmod{m}$ imply $a^3 \equiv b^3 \pmod{m}$. In this way, it can be shown that $a^4 \equiv b^4 \pmod{m}$, $a^5 \equiv b^5 \pmod{m}$, and so on. In general, $a^k \equiv b^k \pmod{m}$. The formal proof is by mathematical induction, which is beyond the scope of this text.

Chapter Test   1. (a) F   **(b)** F   **(c)** T
(d) F   **(e)** F
3. (a) 83,160 is divisible by 2, 3, 4, 5, 6, 7, 8, 9, and 11.
(b) 83,193 is divisible by 3 and 11.
5. $N = a \cdot 10^2 + b \cdot 10 + c = (99a + 9b) + (a + b + c)$. Because $9 | 9 \, (11a + b)$, then, using Theorem 5-1, $9 | N$ if and only if $9 | (a + b + c)$.
7. The number must be divisible by both 8 and 3. Because $3 | 4152$ and $8 | 4152$, then $24 | 4152$.
9. (a) $2^4 \cdot 5^3 \cdot 7^4 \cdot 13 \cdot 29$ **(b)** $278 \cdot 279$, or 77,562
11. 1, 2, 3, 4, 6, 8, 9, 12, 16, 18, 24, 36, 48, 72, 144
13. 15 minutes   **15.** 9:30 A.M.

CHAPTER 6

Problem Set 6-1   1. (a) The solution to $8x = 7$ is $\frac{7}{8}$.
(b) Jane ate seven eighths of Jill's candy.
(c) The ratio of boys to girls is seven to eight.
3. (a) $\frac{2}{3}$ **(b)** $\frac{4}{6}$ **(c)** $\frac{6}{9}$ **(d)** $\frac{8}{12}$; the diagram illustrates the Fundamental Law of Fractions.
5. (a) $\frac{52}{31}$ **(b)** $\frac{3}{5}$ **(c)** $\frac{-5}{7}$ **(d)** $\frac{0}{1}$ **(e)** $\frac{144}{169}$
(f) Reduced
7. Only the fractions in (c), (e), and (f) are equal.
9. (a) $\frac{32}{3}$ **(b)** $^-36$
(c) x is any rational number except 0.
11. Impossible to determine. Because $\frac{20}{25} = \frac{24}{30} = \frac{4}{5}$, the same fraction of students passed in each class.
13. (a) 1 **(b)** $\frac{2x}{9y}$ **(c)** a **(d)** $\frac{a^3 + 1}{a^3 b}$ **(e)** $\frac{1}{3 + b}$
(f) $\frac{a}{3a + b}$ **15.** Only the fractions in (c) are equal.

Problem Set 6-2
1.
$$\frac{1}{5} + \frac{2}{3} = \frac{13}{15}$$

3. (a) $\frac{^-31}{20}$ **(b)** $\frac{58}{35}$ **(c)** $\frac{^-19}{40}$ **(d)** $\frac{5y - 3x}{xy}$
5. (a) $18\frac{2}{3}$ **(b)** $2\frac{4}{5}$ **(c)** $^-(2\frac{93}{100})$ **(d)** $^-(5\frac{7}{8})$
7. (a) $\frac{7}{12}$ **(b)** $\frac{49}{12}$ **(c)** $\frac{41}{24}$ **(d)** $\frac{71}{24}$ **(e)** $\frac{^-23}{3}$ **(f)** $\frac{^-23}{12}$
(g) $\frac{43}{2^4 \cdot 3^4}$ **(h)** $\frac{36,037}{168,070,000}$ **(i)** $\frac{472}{45}$ **(j)** $\frac{^-1}{2}$
(k) $3\frac{9}{16}$ **9. (a)** $\frac{3 + 3}{3} \neq \frac{3}{3} + 3$ **(b)** $\frac{4}{2 + 2} \neq \frac{4}{2} + \frac{4}{2}$
(c) $\frac{ab + c}{a} \neq \frac{\cancel{a}b + c}{\cancel{a}}$ **(d)** $\frac{a \cdot a - b \cdot b}{a - b} \neq \frac{a \cdot \cancel{a} - b \cdot b}{\cancel{a} - \cancel{b}}$
(e) $\frac{a + c}{b + c} \neq \frac{a + \cancel{c}}{b + \cancel{c}}$ **11.** $6\frac{7}{12}$ yards **13.** $1\frac{7}{8}$ cups
15. $2\frac{1}{6}$ hours   **17.** $22\frac{1}{8}$ inches
19. (a) $\frac{1}{2} + \frac{3}{4} = \frac{5}{4} \in Q$ **(b)** $\frac{1}{2} + \frac{3}{4} = \frac{3}{4} + \frac{1}{2} = \frac{5}{4}$
(c) $\frac{1}{2} = \frac{2}{4}$, $\frac{1}{2} + \frac{1}{4} = \frac{3}{4}$, and $\frac{2}{4} + \frac{1}{4} = \frac{3}{4}$
(d) $(\frac{1}{2} + \frac{1}{3}) + \frac{1}{4} = \frac{13}{12}$ and $\frac{1}{2} + (\frac{1}{3} + \frac{1}{4}) = \frac{13}{12}$
21. (a) $1\frac{1}{2}$, $1\frac{3}{4}$, 2; arithmetic; $\frac{1}{2} - \frac{1}{4} = \frac{3}{4} - \frac{1}{2}$
(b) $\frac{6}{7}, \frac{7}{8}, \frac{8}{9}$; not arithmetic; $\frac{2}{3} - \frac{1}{2} \neq \frac{3}{4} - \frac{2}{3}$
(c) $\frac{17}{3}, \frac{20}{3}, \frac{23}{3}$; arithmetic;
$\frac{5}{3} - \frac{2}{3} = \frac{8}{3} - \frac{5}{3} = \frac{11}{3} - \frac{8}{3} = \frac{14}{3} - \frac{11}{3}$
(d) $\frac{1}{7}, \frac{1}{8}, \frac{1}{9}$; not arithmetic; $\frac{1}{3} - \frac{1}{2} \neq \frac{1}{4} - \frac{1}{3}$
(e) $\frac{^-5}{4}, \frac{^-7}{4}, \frac{^-9}{4}$; arithmetic;
$\frac{3}{4} - \frac{5}{4} = \frac{1}{4} - \frac{3}{4} = \frac{^-1}{4} - \frac{1}{4} = \frac{^-3}{4} - (\frac{^-1}{4})$
23. 1, $\frac{7}{6}, \frac{8}{6}, \frac{9}{6}, \frac{10}{6}, \frac{11}{6}$, 2 **25. (a)** $f(0) = ^-2$
(b) $f(^-2) = 0$ **(c)** $f(^-5) = \frac{1}{2}$ **(d)** $f(5) = \frac{7}{4}$
27. (a) They are all in simplest form (all numerators and denominators are relatively prime).
(b) Answers vary.   **(c)** Each fraction has the form $\frac{n + 1}{2n + 1}$, where n is a positive integer. If $d | n + 1$ and $d | 2n + 1$, then $d | 2(n + 1) - (2n + 1)$ or $d | 1$. Hence $d = 1$.
29. (a), (c), (d), and (e) are equal.

Problem Set 6-3   1. (a) $\frac{1}{4} \cdot \frac{1}{3} = \frac{1}{12}$ **(b)** $\frac{2}{5} \cdot \frac{3}{5} = \frac{6}{25}$
3. (a) $\frac{3}{4}$ **(b)** $\frac{3}{8}$ **(c)** $\frac{1}{5}$ **(d)** $\frac{b}{a}$ **(e)** $\frac{^-5a}{3b}$ **(f)** $\frac{za}{x^2 y}$
(g) $8\frac{3}{4}$ **(h)** $^-23\frac{1}{4}$ **(i)** $14\frac{2}{3}$ **(j)** $^-6\frac{1}{4}$
5. (a) $^-3$ **(b)** $\frac{5}{3}$ **(c)** $\frac{1}{2}$ **(d)** $\frac{3}{10}$ **(e)** $\frac{y}{x}$ **(f)** $\frac{^-1}{7}$

7. (a) $\frac{11}{5}$ **(b)** $\frac{77}{12}$ **(c)** $\frac{22}{3}$ **(d)** $\frac{5}{2}$ **(e)** 5 **(f)** $^-42$

(g) 2 **(h)** $\dfrac{z}{y}$ **(i)** z **(j)** $\dfrac{5}{x}$ **(k)** $\dfrac{xy}{z}$

9. Answers vary. **(a)** $\frac{3}{4}$ **(b)** $\frac{5}{12}$ **(c)** $\frac{9}{16}$ **(d)** $2\frac{1}{2}$
(e) $\frac{7}{10}$ **(f)** 24 **(g)** 300,000 **11.** 400 **13.** $\frac{1}{6}$

15. (a) $2 \div 1 \neq 1 \div 2$ **(b)** $(1 \div 2) \div 3 \neq 1 \div (2 \div 3)$
   (c) There is no rational number a such that
   $2 \div a = a \div 2 = 2$.
   (d) Because there is no identity, there can be
   no inverse.

17. (a) $\frac{1}{32}, \frac{1}{64}$; geometric; ratio $= \frac{1}{2}$
(b) $\frac{-1}{32}, \frac{1}{64}$; geometric; ratio $= \frac{-1}{2}$
(c) $\frac{81}{256}, \frac{243}{1024}$; geometric; ratio $= \frac{3}{4}$
(d) $\frac{5}{3^4}; \frac{6}{3^5}$; not geometric; $\frac{2}{3^2} \div \frac{1}{3} \neq \frac{3}{3^3} \div \frac{2}{3^2}$

19. (a) (i) $\frac{-4}{5}$ **(ii)** $\frac{-26}{17}$ **(iii)** $\frac{-14}{33}$
(b) (i) $\frac{-4}{3}$ **(ii)** $\frac{-30}{7}$ **(iii)** $\frac{-3}{10}$ **(c)** $\frac{5}{4}$

21. $13\frac{1}{3}$ hours **23.** $c = 0$ or $a = b$, where $b \neq 0$.

25. (a) $2S = 2\left(\dfrac{1}{2} + \dfrac{1}{2^2} + \cdots + \dfrac{1}{2^{64}}\right) =$

$1 + \dfrac{1}{2} + \dfrac{1}{2^2} + \cdots + \dfrac{1}{2^{63}}$

(b) Note that $2S = 1 + S - \dfrac{1}{2^{64}}$. Hence,

$2S - S = 1 + S - \dfrac{1}{2^{64}} - S = 1 - \dfrac{1}{2^{64}}.$

(c) $1 - \dfrac{1}{2^n}$

27. (a) $1\frac{49}{99}$ **(b)** $25 \cdot (2\frac{49}{99})$ **29.** 120 students

Problem Set 6-4 **1. (a)** > **(b)** > **(c)** <
(d) < **(e)** = **(f)** =
3. (a) $x \leq \frac{27}{16}$ **(b)** $x \geq \frac{115}{3}$ **(c)** $x < \frac{17}{5}$ **(d)** $x \geq \frac{141}{22}$
5. (a) $399\frac{80}{81}$ **(b)** $180\frac{89}{90}$ **(c)** $3\frac{699}{820}$
7. Every 3 pounds of birdseed yields about 4 packages.
Thus, there are about 28 packages.

9. $\dfrac{a}{b} < 1$ and $\dfrac{c}{d} > 0$ imply $\dfrac{a}{b} \cdot \dfrac{c}{d} < 1 \cdot \dfrac{c}{d}$ or $\dfrac{a}{b} \cdot \dfrac{c}{d} < \dfrac{c}{d}$

11. We need to show that $\dfrac{n}{n+1} < \dfrac{n+1}{n+2}$. This
inequality is equivalent to $n^2 + 2n < n^2 + 2n + 1$,
or $0 < 1$.

13. (a) $\frac{0}{1}, \frac{1}{5}, \frac{1}{4}, \frac{1}{3}, \frac{2}{5}, \frac{1}{2}, \frac{3}{5}, \frac{2}{3}, \frac{3}{4}, \frac{4}{5}, \frac{1}{1}$ (order 5)
$\frac{0}{1}, \frac{1}{6}, \frac{1}{5}, \frac{1}{4}, \frac{1}{3}, \frac{2}{5}, \frac{1}{2}, \frac{3}{5}, \frac{2}{3}, \frac{3}{4}, \frac{4}{5}, \frac{5}{6}, \frac{1}{1}$ (order 6)

(b) The numerator is 1, and the denominator is equal
to the product of the denominators of the consecutive
fractions.

(c) Yes. If a/b is a term in a Farey sequence, then a
and b are relatively prime. This implies that $a - b$
and b are relatively prime and, consequently,
$(a - b)/b$ is a term in the Farey sequence.

15. Answers may vary. The following are possible
answers. **(a)** $\frac{10}{21}, \frac{11}{21}$ **(b)** $\frac{-22}{27}, \frac{-23}{27}$ **(c)** $\frac{997}{1200}, \frac{998}{1200}$
(d) $0, \frac{1}{2}$

17. We are considering $\dfrac{a}{b}$ and $\dfrac{a+x}{b+x}$ when $a < b$.

$\dfrac{a}{b} < \dfrac{a+x}{b+x}$ because $ab + ax < ab + bx$.

19. $6\frac{7}{18}$ hours

Problem Set 6-5 **1.** $\frac{3}{2}$ **3.** $\frac{16}{9}$ **5.** 2469 **7.** 270 miles
9. 72 minutes for 30 inches

11. $\dfrac{a}{b} = \dfrac{c}{d}$ implies $ad = bc$, which is equivalent to

$d = \dfrac{bc}{a}$; then, $\dfrac{d}{c} = \dfrac{b}{a}$.

13. (a) $\frac{1}{2}$ **(b)** Let $\dfrac{a}{b} = r$; thus, $a = br$. Similarly,

$c = dr$ and $e = fr$. We now have $\dfrac{a + c + e}{b + d + f} =$

$\dfrac{r(b + d + f)}{b + d + f} = r = \dfrac{a}{b} = \dfrac{c}{d} = \dfrac{e}{f}.$

15. (a) $\frac{-3}{5}, \frac{-2}{5}, 0, \frac{1}{5}, \frac{2}{5}$ **(b)** $\frac{13}{24}, \frac{7}{12}, \frac{13}{18}$
17. Answers vary. Examples are: **(a)** $\frac{11}{30}, \frac{12}{30}, \frac{13}{30}$
(b) $\frac{-1}{12}, \frac{-1}{9}, \frac{-5}{36}$

Problem Set 6-6 **1. (a)** $\dfrac{1}{3^{13}}$ **(b)** 3^{13} **(c)** 5^{11}

(d) 5^{19} **(e)** $\dfrac{1}{(^-5)^2}$, or $\dfrac{1}{5^2}$ **(f)** a^5 **(g)** a^2

3. (a) F. $2^3 \cdot 2^4 \neq (2 \cdot 2)^{3+4}$
(b) F. $2^3 \cdot 2^4 \neq (2 \cdot 2)^{3 \cdot 4}$
(c) F. $2^3 \cdot 2^3 \neq (2 \cdot 2)^{2 \cdot 3}$
(d) F. $a^0 = 1$ if $a \neq 0$
(e) F. $(2 + 3)^2 \neq 2^2 + 3^2$

(f) F. $(2 + 3)^{-2} \neq \dfrac{1}{2^2} + \dfrac{1}{3^2}$

(g) F. $a^{mn} = (a^m)^n \neq a^m \cdot a^n$

(h) $\left(\dfrac{a}{b}\right)^{-1} = \dfrac{1}{a/b} = \dfrac{b}{a}$ **5.** $2 \cdot 10^{11}; 2 \cdot 10^5$

7. (a) $\dfrac{1 - x^2}{x}$ **(b)** $\dfrac{x^2 y^2 - 1}{y^2}$ **(c)** $\dfrac{1 + y^6}{y^3}$

(d) $6x^2 + 4x$ **(e)** $(3a - b)^2$ **(f)** $8x^2 + 67a^3$

(g) $\dfrac{x^2 y}{y + 3x^2}$

9. 216   **11. (a)** $\frac{2}{7}$ **(b)** $\frac{40}{3}$ **(c)** $\frac{1}{3^4}$ **(d)** $\frac{1}{100}$ **(e)** $\frac{9}{4}$
(f) $\frac{49}{100}$ **(g)** $\frac{9}{16}$ **(h)** $\frac{x}{x+y}$ **13.** $1\frac{1}{5}$ days

15. $\frac{-6}{7}, \frac{-3}{4}, \frac{-2}{3}, \frac{-1}{2}, 0, \frac{7}{9}, \frac{4}{5}, \frac{6}{7}, \frac{9}{7}$

Chapter Test

1. (a)

(b)

3. (a) $\frac{6}{7}$ **(b)** $\frac{ax}{b}$ **(c)** $\frac{0}{1}$ **(d)** $\frac{5}{9}$ **(e)** b **(f)** $\frac{2}{27}$

5. (a) $\frac{11}{10}$ **(b)** $\frac{13}{175}$ **(c)** $\frac{10}{13}$ **(d)** $\frac{25}{24}$ **(e)** $\frac{50}{9}$ **(f)** $\frac{-26}{27}$

7. (a) 6   **(b)** $\frac{5}{4}$ **(c)** $\frac{-1}{4}$

9. $\frac{a}{b} \div \frac{c}{d} = x$ if and only if $\frac{a}{b} = \frac{c}{d} \cdot x$. $x = \frac{d}{c} \cdot \frac{a}{b}$ is the

solution of the equation because $\frac{c}{d} \cdot \left(\frac{d}{c} \cdot \frac{a}{b}\right) = \frac{a}{b}$.

11. (a) $\frac{1}{2^{11}}$ **(b)** $\frac{1}{5^{20}}$ **(c)** $\left(\frac{3}{2}\right)^{28}$, or $\frac{3^{28}}{2^{28}}$ **(d)** 3^{18}

13. (a) 15   **(b)** 15   **(c)** 4

CHAPTER 7

Problem Set 7-1
1. (a) $0 \cdot 10^{-1} + 2 \cdot 10^{-2} + 3 \cdot 10^{-3}$
(b) $2 \cdot 10^2 + 0 \cdot 10^1 + 6 \cdot 10^0 + 0 \cdot 10^{-1} + 6 \cdot 10^{-2}$
(c) $3 \cdot 10^2 + 1 \cdot 10^1 + 2 \cdot 10^0 + 0 \cdot 10^{-1} +$
$1 \cdot 10^{-2} + 0 \cdot 10^{-3} + 3 \cdot 10^{-4}$
(d) $0 \cdot 10^{-1} + 0 \cdot 10^{-2} + 0 \cdot 10^{-3} + 1 \cdot 10^{-4} +$
$3 \cdot 10^{-5} + 2 \cdot 10^{-6}$
3. (a) 536.0076   **(b)** 3.008   **(c)** 0.000436
(d) 5,000,000.2   **5. (a)** Yes   **(b)** Yes   **(c)** Yes
(d) Yes   **(e)** Yes   **(f)** Yes   **(g)** No   **(h)** No
(i) No   **7. (a)** 39.202   **(b)** 168.003   **(c)** ⁻390.6313
(d) 1.49093   **(e)** ⁻10.4   **(f)** 4.681
9. (a) 463,000,000   **(b)** 4,000,000   **(c)** 4,630,000,000
(d) 46,300,000,000   **(e)** 463,000   **(f)** 4.63
11. (a) 5.4, 6.3, 7.2   **(b)** 0.13, 0.15, 0.17
(c) 0.0625, 0.03125, 0.015625   **(d)** 6.7, 8, 9.3
13. Because lining up decimals acts as using place
value   **15.** 1.679   **17.** 0.8 inch

19.

8.2	1.9	6.4
3.7	5.5	7.3
4.6	9.1	2.8

21. (a) 0.077   **(b)** 406   **23.** No
25. The number of digits in the terminating decimal
is the greater of m or n.

Problem Set 7-2   **1. (a)** $0.\overline{4}$ **(b)** $0.\overline{285714}$ **(c)** $0.\overline{27}$
(d) $0.0\overline{6}$ **(e)** $0.02\overline{6}$ **(f)** $0.\overline{01}$ **(g)** $0.8\overline{3}$ **(h)** $0.\overline{076923}$
3. (a) $3.2\overline{3}$, $3.\overline{23}$, 3.23, $3.\overline{22}$, 3.2   **(b)** ⁻1.45, ⁻1.454,
⁻$1.45\overline{4}$, ⁻$1.\overline{454}$, ⁻$1.4\overline{54}$ **5. (a)** $\frac{1}{1}$
(b) No positive number k can be found such that
$0.\overline{9} + k = 1$ or $1 + k = 0.\overline{9}$.   **(c)** $\frac{1}{3} = 0.\overline{3}$ implies
$3 \cdot \frac{1}{3} = 3 \cdot 0.\overline{3}$, or $1 = 0.\overline{9}$.   **7. (a)** 3.25   **(b)** 462.245
(c) 0.01515   **(d)** $462.2\overline{43}$ **9. (a)** $3.325 \cdot 10^3$
(b) $4.632 \cdot 10^1$ **(c)** $1.3 \cdot 10^{-4}$ **(d)** $9.30146 \cdot 10^5$
11. (a) $1.27 \cdot 10^7$ **(b)** $5.797 \cdot 10^6$ **(c)** $5 \cdot 10^7$
13. \$37   **15. (a)** $1.\overline{6}$, 2, $2.\overline{3}$ **(b)** $\frac{6}{7} = 0.\overline{857142}$,
$\frac{7}{8} = 0.875$, $\frac{8}{9} = 0.\overline{8}$ **17. (a)** $4.8 \cdot 10^{28}$,   **(b)** $4 \cdot 10^7$,
(c) $2 \cdot 10^2$ **19.** 10^{200} **21.** 28,000 years
23. Let $S = a + ar + ar^2 + ar^3 + \cdots + ar^{n-1}$. Then
$rS = ar + ar^2 + ar^3 + ar^4 + \cdots + ar^n$.
Therefore $rS - S = ar^n - a$
$$S(r - 1) = a(r^n - 1)$$
$$S = \frac{a(r^n - 1)}{r - 1}$$
25. (a) (i) $0.\overline{142857}$ (ii) $0.\overline{285714}$ (iii) $0.\overline{428571}$
(iv) $0.\overline{571428}$ (v) $0.\overline{714285}$ (vi) $0.\overline{857142}$ **(b)** 6
(c) The answers all contain the same digits: 1, 2, 4, 5,
7, and 8. The digits in each answer repeat in the
same sequence—that is, in each case a 1 is always
followed by a 4, which is always followed by a 2,
which is always followed by an 8, and so on. In each
of the answers in 1–6, the starting digit is different,
but the sequence of numbers is the same.
27. (a) 21.6 pounds   **(b)** 48 pounds

29. A fraction in simplest form, $\frac{a}{b}$, can be written

as a terminating decimal if and only if the prime
factorization of the denominator contains no primes
other than 2 or 5.

Problem Set 7-3   **1. (a)** 789%   **(b)** 3.2%
(c) 19,310%   **(d)** 20%   **(e)** $83.\overline{3}\%$, or $83\frac{1}{3}\%$ **(f)** 15%
(g) $1.\overline{3}\%$, or $1\frac{1}{3}\%$ **(h)** Approximately 571.43%, or
$571\frac{3}{7}\%$ **3. (a)** 2.04   **(b)** 50%   **(c)** 60   **5.** \$16,960
7. (a) Bill, 221   **(b)** Joe, 90%   **(c)** Ron, 265
9. Approximately 89.7%   **11.** \$5.10
13. Approximately 18.4%   **15. (a)** 4   **(b)** 2   **(c)** 25
(d) 200   **(e)** 12.5   **17.** \$336   **19.** \$3200
21. $16.\overline{6}\%$, or $16\frac{2}{3}\%$ **23.** \$10.37
25. (a) \$3.30   **(b)** \$24   **(c)** \$1.90   **(d)** \$24.50
27. \$440   **29. (a)** 4%   **(b)** 32%   **(c)** 64%
31. \$187.50   **33.** Approximately \$9207.58
35. $\frac{3321}{100}$ **37.** $\frac{2795}{90} = \frac{559}{18}$ **39. (a)** 32.0   **(b)** 30

Problem Set 7-4

1.

	Period	Principal	Annual Rate	Time (years)	Interest per Period	Number of Periods	Interest (rounded)
(a)	Semiannual	$1000	6%	2	3%	4	$125.51
(b)	Quarterly	$1000	8%	3	2%	12	$268.24
(c)	Monthly	$1000	10%	5	0.8$\overline{3}$%	60	$645.31
(d)	Daily	$1000	12%	4	$\frac{12}{365}$%	1460	$615.95

3. Approximately $24.45
5. Approximately $32,040.82
7. Approximately $4416.35
9. Approximately $81,628.70
11. Approximately $1231.90
13. (c) 13.2%
15. Approximately $5918.41
17. $10,935

Problem Set 7-5 **1.** Answers may vary; one possibility is 0.232233222333.... **3. (a)** Yes **(b)** No **(c)** No **(d)** Yes **(e)** Yes **(f)** Yes
5. (a) 4.12 **(b)** 2.65 **(c)** 4.58 **(d)** 0.11 **(e)** 4.51
(f) 1.28 **7.** No. $\sqrt{9+16} \neq \sqrt{9}+\sqrt{16}$
9. Answers may vary; for example, $\sqrt{2}, \sqrt{3}, \sqrt{5}, \sqrt{6}, \sqrt{7}, \sqrt{8}, 1+\sqrt{2}$.
11. Because $\frac{22}{7}$ is rational, π is irrational, and the set of rationals and the set of irrationals are disjoint, these two numbers cannot equal each other.
13. (a) 64 **(b)** $\varnothing$ **(c)** $^-64$ **(d)** $\varnothing$ **(e)** $x > 0$
(f) $\varnothing$ **15.**

	N	I	Q	R
(a)	√	√	√	√
(b)			√	√
(c)				√
(d)	√	√	√	√
(e)				
(f)			√	√

17. (a) 8.98 seconds **(b)** 20.07 seconds
19. Suppose $\sqrt{p}$ is rational, where p is a prime. Then,
$\sqrt{p} = \dfrac{a}{b}$, where a and b are integers.

$$p = \frac{a^2}{b^2}$$

$$pb^2 = a^2$$

Because b^2 has an even number of ps in its prime factorization, pb^2 has an odd number of ps in its prime factorization. Thus, a^2 has an odd number of ps in its prime factorization, and this is impossible. Thus, $\sqrt{p}$ is irrational.

21. (a) $0.5 + \dfrac{1}{0.5} = 0.5 + 2 = 2.5 \geq 2$

(b) Suppose $x + \dfrac{1}{x} < 2$. Then, $\dfrac{x^2+1}{x} < 2$. Because $x > 0$, then

$$x^2 + 1 < 2x$$
$$x^2 - 2x + 1 < 0$$
$$(x-1)^2 < 0$$

which is false. Thus, $x + \dfrac{1}{x} \geq 2$.

23. $4.09, 4.09\overline{1}, 4.099, 4.0\overline{9}$
25. (a) 203,000 **(b)** 0.00038 **27.** 60%

Problem Set 7-6 **1. (a)** $6\sqrt{5}$ **(b)** 23 **(c)** $11\sqrt{3}$
(d) $6\sqrt{7}$ **(e)** $\frac{13}{14}$ **(f)** $\frac{7}{14}$, or $\frac{1}{2}$
3. (a) $2\sqrt{3} + 3\sqrt{2} + 6\sqrt{5}$ **(b)** $2\sqrt[3]{5}$ **(c)** $30 + 12\sqrt{6}$
(d) $\dfrac{1}{\sqrt{2}}$, or $\dfrac{\sqrt{2}}{2}$ **(e)** $17\sqrt{2}$ **(f)** $\sqrt{6}$
5. No; $\sqrt{3^2 + 4^2} \neq 3 + 4$. **7. (a)** 4 **(b)** $\frac{3}{2}$ **(c)** $\frac{^-4}{7}$
(d) $\dfrac{5}{6}$ **9. (a)** $\dfrac{2\sqrt{3}}{3}$ **(b)** $\dfrac{7\sqrt{10}}{5}$ **(c)** $\dfrac{5\sqrt{10}}{6}$ **(d)** $\dfrac{\sqrt{3}}{3}$
(e) $\sqrt{2}$ **(f)** $\dfrac{3\sqrt{2}}{4}$

Chapter Test **1. (a)** $^-0.693$ **(b)** 31.564
(c) 0.2284 **(d)** 0.032 **(e)** $^-0.097$ **(f)** 0.00000016
3. A fraction in simplest form a/b can be written as a terminating decimal if and only if the prime factorization of the denominator contains no primes other than 2 or 5.
5. (a) $0.\overline{571428}$ **(b)** 0.125 **(c)** $0.\overline{6}$ **(d)** 0.625
7. (a) 307.63 **(b)** 307.6 **(c)** 308 **(d)** 300

9. (a) 25% **(b)** 192 **(c)** $56.\overline{6}$ **(d)** 20%
11. (a) 0.6 or 0.60 **(b)** $0.00\overline{6}$ **(c)** 1
13. $4.7958 \doteq 4.796$
15. (a), (b), and (e) are irrational; (c) and (d) are rational.
17. $3.\overline{3}\%$ **19.** $5750 **21.** $80
23. Approximately $15,110.69
25. (a) $\dfrac{1}{2^{11}}$ **(b)** $\dfrac{1}{5^{20}}$ **(c)** $\left(\dfrac{3}{2}\right)^{28}$, or $\dfrac{3^{28}}{2^{28}}$ **(d)** 3^{18}

CHAPTER 8

Problem Set 8-1 **1. (a)** {1, 2, 3, 4} **(b)** {Red, Blue}
(c) $S = \{(1,\text{Red}), (1,\text{Blue}), (2,\text{Red}), (2,\text{Blue}), (3,\text{Red}),$
 $(3,\text{Blue}), (4,\text{Red}), (4,\text{Blue})\}$
(d) $S = \{(\text{Red}, 1), (\text{Red}, 2), (\text{Red}, 3), (\text{Red}, 4), (\text{Red}, 5),$
 $(\text{Red}, 6), (\text{Blue}, 1), (\text{Blue}, 2), (\text{Blue}, 3),$
 $(\text{Blue}, 4), (\text{Blue}, 5), (\text{Blue}, 6)\}$
(e) $S = \{(1, 1), (1, 2), (1, 3), (1, 4), (2, 1), (2, 2),$
 $(2, 3), (2, 4), (3, 1), (3, 2), (3, 3), (3, 4), (4, 1),$
 $(4, 2), (4, 3), (4, 4)\}$
(f) $S = \{(\text{Red}, \text{Red}), (\text{Red}, \text{Blue}), (\text{Blue}, \text{Red}),$
 $(\text{Blue}, \text{Blue})\}$
3. (b) $P(A) = \frac{5}{10}$, or $\frac{1}{2}$ **(c)** $P(B) = \frac{5}{10}$, or $\frac{1}{2}$
(d) $P(C) = \frac{9}{10}$
5. (a) $P(\text{Brown}) = \frac{4}{12}$, or $\frac{1}{3}$
(b) $P(\text{Either black or green}) = \frac{8}{12}$, or $\frac{2}{3}$
(c) $P(\text{Red}) = \frac{0}{12} = 0$
(d) $P(\text{Not black}) = \frac{6}{12}$, or $\frac{1}{2}$
7. $P(\text{Vowel}) = \frac{5}{26}$; $P(\text{Consonant}) = 1 - \frac{5}{26} = \frac{21}{26}$
9. (a) $P(\text{Black}) = \frac{18}{38}$, or $\frac{9}{19}$
 (b) $P(\bigcirc \text{ or } \bigcirc\bigcirc) = \frac{2}{38}$, or $\frac{1}{19}$
(c) $P(\text{not } 1\text{--}12) = \frac{26}{38}$, or $\frac{13}{19}$
(d) $P(\text{Odd or green}) = \frac{20}{38}$, or $\frac{10}{19}$ **11.** 70%

Problem Set 8-2 **1. (a)** $\frac{1}{216}$ **(b)** $\frac{1}{120}$ **3.** $\frac{1}{30}$
5. (a) $\frac{64}{75}$ **(b)** $\frac{11}{75}$
7. (a) $P(\bigcirc\bigcirc) = \frac{1}{5}$ **(b)** $P(\text{at least one black}) = \frac{4}{5}$
(c) $P(\text{at most one black}) = \frac{11}{15}$ **(d)** $P(\bullet\bigcirc, \bigcirc\bullet) = \frac{8}{15}$
9. $\frac{1}{16}$ **11.** $\frac{1}{32}$ **13. (a)** $\frac{16}{81}$ **(b)** $\frac{8}{27}$
15. $\dfrac{1152}{39,916,800}$, or $\dfrac{1}{34,650}$
17. (a) A is the best choice, followed by B and then C.
(b) No. C is now the best choice.
 $P(C \text{ winning}) = \frac{35}{99}$; $P(B \text{ winning}) = \frac{34}{99}$;
 $P(A \text{ winning}) = \frac{30}{99}$.
19. (a) $\frac{1}{30}$ **(b)** 0 **(c)** $\frac{19}{30}$

Problem Set 8-3 **1. (a)** $\frac{6}{18}$, or $\frac{1}{3}$ **(b)** $\frac{2}{11}$ **3.** $\frac{1}{4}$
5. $\frac{4}{12}$ or $\frac{1}{3}$ **7.** $\frac{1}{4}$ **9. (a)** $\frac{1}{12}$ **(b)** $\frac{27}{132}$, or $\frac{9}{44}$
(c) $\dfrac{216}{1320}$, or $\dfrac{9}{55}$ **(d)** $\dfrac{1512}{11,800}$, or $\dfrac{7}{55}$
11. (a) $\frac{38}{100}$, or $\frac{19}{50}$ **(b)** $\frac{10}{100}$, or $\frac{1}{10}$ **(c)** $\frac{25}{36}$
13. 1200 fish
15. Pick a starting spot in the table and count the number of digits it takes before all the numbers 1 through 9 are obtained. Repeat this experiment many times and find the average number of coupons.
17. For example, let the digits 0, 1, 2, 3, 4, 5, 6, 7 represent rain on Monday and the digits 8, 9 represent dry weather on Monday. Based on this result, continue to simulate the rest of the week.

Problem Set 8-4 **1.** 12 to 40, or 3 to 10; 40 to 12, or 10 to 3 **3.** 15 to 1 **5.** $\frac{5}{8}$
7. $0.25 **9.** $3.00 **11.** Approximately 8¢
13. (a) Al gets $75; Betsy gets $25.
(b) 3 to 1
(c) Al gets approximately $89; Betsy gets approximately $11.
(d) 57 to 7

Problem Set 8-5 **1.** 224 **3.** 32 **5.** 1352; 35,152
7. (a) T **(b)** F **(c)** F **(d)** F **(e)** T **(f)** T
(g) T **9.** 15 **11. (a)** 24,360 **(b)** 4060
13. $9! = 362,880$ **15.** 45 **17. (a)** 10 **(b)** 1 **(c)** 1
(d) 3 **19. (a)** 12 **(b)** 210 **(c)** 3360 **(d)** 34,650
(e) 3780 **21.** 1260 **23.** 720
25. (a) $\frac{15}{19}$ **(b)** $\frac{56}{361}$ **(c)** $\frac{28}{171}$

Chapter Test **1. (a)** $S = \{$Sunday, Monday, Tuesday, Wednesday, Thursday, Friday, Saturday$\}$
(b) $E = \{$Tuesday, Thursday$\}$ **(c)** $P(T) = \frac{2}{7}$
3. (a) $P(\text{Black}) = \frac{5}{12}$ **(b)** $P(\text{Black or white}) = \frac{9}{12}$, or $\frac{3}{4}$
(c) $P(\text{Neither red nor white}) = \frac{5}{12}$ **(d)** $P(\text{Not red}) = \frac{9}{12}$, or $\frac{3}{4}$ **(e)** $P(\text{Black and white}) = 0$
(f) $P(\text{Black or white or red}) = 1$ **5. (a)** $P(3W) = \frac{64}{729}$
(b) $P(3W) = \frac{24}{504}$, or $\frac{1}{21}$ **7.** $P(L) = \frac{6}{25}$ **9.** $\frac{7}{45}$
11. $\frac{3}{3}$, or $\frac{1}{1}$ **13.** 30¢ **15.** 900 **17.** 24 **19.** 5040
21. (a) 60 **(b)** $\frac{1}{20}$ **(c)** $\frac{1}{60}$ **23.** $\frac{2}{5}$
25. (a) $n!$ **(b)** n **27.** $\frac{6}{27}$ or $\frac{2}{9}$

CHAPTER 9

Problem Set 9-1 **1. (a)** November, 30 cm
(b) October, 15 cm; December, 25 cm; January, 10 cm

3.

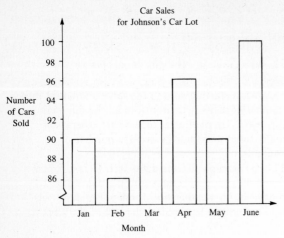

Car Sales
for Johnson's Car Lot

(b)

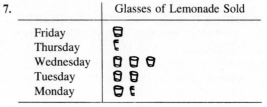

Course Grades

A – 24°
B – 60°
C – 222°
D – 48°
F – 6°

Percentages are approximate

7.

Glasses of Lemonade Sold	
Friday	🥤
Thursday	🥤
Wednesday	🥤 🥤 🥤
Tuesday	🥤 🥤
Monday	🥤 🥤

🥤 represents 10 glasses

5. (a)

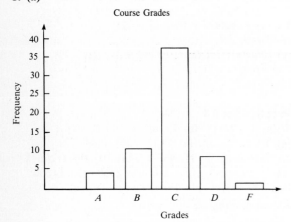

Course Grades

9. Answers may vary.   **11.** Answers may vary.

Problem Set 9-2   1. (a) Mean $= 6.625$;
median $= 7.5$; mode $= 8$ **(b)** Mean $= 13.\overline{4}$; median $=$
12; mode $= 12$ **(c)** Mean $\doteq 19.9$; median $= 18$;
modes $= 18$ and 22 **(d)** Mean $= 81.4$; median $= 80$;
mode $= 80$ **(e)** Mean $= 5.8\overline{3}$; median $= 5$; mode $= 5$
3. 1500 **5.** $78.\overline{3}$ **7.** Mean $= \$22{,}700$; median $=$
$\$20{,}000$; mode $= \$20{,}000$ **9.** 2.59 **11.** $\$320$
13. (a) $\$41{,}275$ **(b)** Approximately $\$21{,}756$
15. $s \doteq 7.3$ cm   **17. (a)** $s = 0$ **(b)** Yes

19. $v = \dfrac{(x_1 - \bar{x})^2 + (x_2 - \bar{x})^2 + \cdots + (x_n - \bar{x})^2}{n}$

$= \dfrac{(x_1^2 - 2\bar{x}x_1 + \bar{x}^2) + (x_2^2 - 2\bar{x}x_2 + \bar{x}^2) + \cdots + (x_n^2 - 2\bar{x}x_n + \bar{x}^2)}{n}$

$= \dfrac{(x_1^2 + x_2^2 + \cdots + x_n^2) - 2\bar{x}(x_1 + x_2 + \cdots + x_n) + n\bar{x}^2}{n}$

$= \dfrac{x_1^2 + x_2^2 + \cdots + x_n^2}{n} - \dfrac{2\bar{x}(x_1 + x_2 + \cdots + x_n)}{n} + \dfrac{n\bar{x}^2}{n}$

$= \dfrac{x_1^2 + x_2^2 + \cdots + x_n^2}{n} - 2\bar{x}^2 + \bar{x}^2$

$= \dfrac{x_1^2 + x_2^2 + \cdots + x_n^2}{n} - \bar{x}^2$

Problem Set 9-3   **1. (a)** 1020   **(b)** 1425   **(c)** 15
(d) 7.5, so approximately 8
3. 0.68   **5. (a)** $Q_2 = P_{50} = 65$ **(b)** $P_{16} = 53$
(c) $P_{84} = 72$
7. (a) Cum/n
   0
   2.5
   2.5
   10.3
   15.4
   30.8
   43.6
   61.5
   74.4
   94.9
   100

(b)

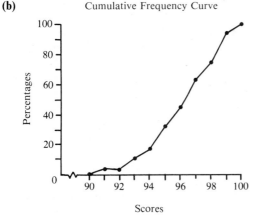

Cumulative Frequency Curve

(c) Yes; the curves should always slope up to 100%.
9. 0.91%   **11.** 27.74

Problem Set 9-4   **1.** Answers vary.
3. Answers may vary. One possibility is that the
temperature is always 25°C.
5. When the radius of a circle is doubled, the area
is quadrupled, which is misleading because the
population has only doubled.
7. Answers vary.
9. It could very well be that most of the pickups sold
in the past 10 years were actually sold during the
last 2 years. In such a case, most of the pickups have
been on the road for only 2 years, and therefore the
given information would not imply that the average
life of a pickup is around 10 years.
11. The three-dimensional drawing distorts the
graph and makes it hard to discern whether the
proportionate amounts for each sector are correct.
13. Bimodal: 74 and 83   **15.** 61.2°

Chapter Test   **1.** If it said that the average is 2.41
children, then the mean average is being used. If it
said 2.5, then the mean or the median might have
been used.
3. (a) Mean = 30; median = 30; mode = 10
(b) Mean = 5; median = 5; modes = 3, 5, 6
5. (a)

3	99
4	00
4	11
4	2222
4	33
4	4
4	5
4	6
4	7
4	8
4	999

(b)

Weight	Tally	Frequency
39	||	2
40	||	2
41	||	2
42	||||	4
43	||	2
44	|	1
45	|	1
46	|	1
47	|	1
48	|	1
49	|||	3
		20

(c)

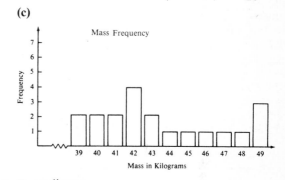

Mass Frequency

7. Expenditures

Bribes – 108°
Legal fees – 72°
Bail – 54°
Contracts – 54°
P.R. – 72°

9. $2840   **11. (a)** 525   **(b)** 600
(c) 675   **13.** Approximately 50th   **15.** Answers vary.

CHAPTER 10

Problem Set 10-1   **1. (a)** C **(b)** $\varnothing$ **(c)** C
(d) C **(e)** $\overline{CE}$ **(f)** $\overrightarrow{AB}$ **(g)** $\overrightarrow{BA}$ **(h)** $\overleftrightarrow{AD}$

3. (a) Answers may vary; one possibility is $\overleftrightarrow{EF}$ and $\overleftrightarrow{DC}$. **(b)** $\overleftrightarrow{EF}$ and α are parallel. **(c)** (i) $\overrightarrow{AB}$ (ii) $\overrightarrow{BC}$ (iii) $\overrightarrow{BD}$ **(d)** No. E, F, and B determine β, and D is not in β. **5. (a)** An infinite number **(b)** One **7. (a)** Yes; if ℓ and m were not parallel, they would intersect in a point common to planes α and β, which contradicts the fact that α and β are parallel. **(b)** No; see the figure.

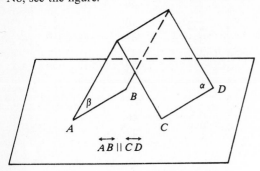

$$\overleftrightarrow{AB} \parallel \overleftrightarrow{CD}$$

(c) Yes; if the planes were not parallel, they would intersect in a line ℓ and at least one of the given lines would intersect ℓ and hence would intersect plane α, which contradicts the fact that the given lines are parallel to α. **9. (a)** 3 **(b)** 6 **(c)** 10

(d) $1 + 2 + 3 + \cdots + (n-1) = \dfrac{n(n-1)}{2}$

11. (a) No. If $\angle BDC$ were a right angle, then both $\overleftrightarrow{BD}$ and $\overleftrightarrow{BC}$ would be perpendicular to $\overleftrightarrow{DC}$ and thus be parallel. **(b)** No. The angle formed by $\overrightarrow{PD}$ and $\overrightarrow{PC}$ must have measure less than a right angle. Otherwise, $\overrightarrow{DP}$ would be parallel to either $\overleftrightarrow{DC}$ or $\overleftrightarrow{PC}$. This is impossible. **(c)** Yes. Use the definition of perpendicular planes. **13. (a)** $42°$ **(b)** $117°$ **15. (a)** $54'$ **(b)** $15°7'48''$ **17.** Answers may vary. **19.** Suppose that $\alpha \parallel \beta$, γ intersects α in $\overleftrightarrow{AB}$, and γ intersects β in $\overleftrightarrow{CD}$. If $\overleftrightarrow{AB}$ intersects $\overleftrightarrow{CD}$ in point Q, then Q is a point of both plane α and plane β. This cannot happen, so $\overleftrightarrow{AB} \parallel \overleftrightarrow{CD}$.

Problem Set 10-2   1. (a) 1, 2, 3, 5, 6, 7, 8, 9, 11, 12 **(b)** 1, 2, 5, 7, 8, 9, 11 **(c)** 1, 2, 5, 7, 8, 9, 11 **(d)** 1, 2, 7, 8, 9, 11 **(e)** 7, 8 **(f)** 1, 2, 9, 11 **3. (a)**

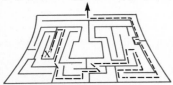

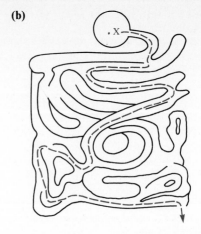

5. (a) Yes **(b)** No **7. (a)** 35 **(b)** 170 **(c)** 4850 **9. (a)** 8 **(b)** 16 **11. (a)** F. The triangle in 10(b) is isosceles but not equilateral. **(b)** T **(c)** T **(d)** T **(e)** T **(f)** F. In a rhombus, the angles do not have to be congruent. **(g)** T **(h)** T **(i)** F. An isosceles triangle needs only one pair of congruent sides, and an equilateral triangle must have all three sides congruent. **(j)** T **(k)** F. All squares are rectangles. **(l)** F. Some trapezoids are parallelograms. **(m)** T **13. (a)** and **(c)** are convex; **(b)** and **(d)** are concave. **15.** Answers may vary. **17. (a)** $\angle ABD$, $\angle DBC$, $\angle EBC$, $\angle EBA$ **(b)** $\overrightarrow{BE}$ **(c)** $\{B\}$ **(d)** $\angle EBC$ **(e)** No **19. (a)** $\{C\}$ **(b)** $\overline{BD}$ **(c)** $\overline{AB}$, $\overline{AC}$, and $\overline{AD}$ **(d)** D

Problem Set 10-3   1. (a) $130°$ **(b)** $50°$ **(c)** $130°$ **3. (a)** $\angle 1$ and $\angle 2$ are adjacent; $\angle 3$ and $\angle 4$ are vertical. **(b)** $\angle 1$ and $\angle 2$ are vertical; $\angle 3$ and $\angle 4$ are adjacent. **(c)** No vertical or adjacent angles are marked. **(d)** $\angle 1$ and $\angle 2$ are adjacent. **5.** 20 **7. (a)** $70°$ **(b)** $70°$ **(c)** $65°$ **(d)** $45°$ **9. (a)** No. Two or more obtuse angles will produce a sum of more than $180°$. **(b)** Yes. For example, each angle may be $60°$. **(c)** No. The sum of the measures of the three angles would then be more than $180°$. **(d)** No. It may have an obtuse or a right angle as well. **11. (a)** $x = 40$; $y = 50$ **(b)** $x = 50$; $y = 60$ **13. (a)** 20 **(b)** $150°$ **15. (a)** Equal

(b) $m(\angle 4) = 180° - m(\angle 3)$ (straight angle)
$= 180° - [180° - m(\angle 1) - m(\angle 2)]$
$= m(\angle 1) + m(\angle 2)$

17. $60°$ **19.** $60°$ **21.** $360°$ **23.** Answers may vary.

(a) TO PARALLELOGRAM :L :W :A
    REPEAT 2 [FD :L RT 180 — :A FD :W RT :A]
    END

(b) TO RECTANGLE :L :W
    PARALLELOGRAM :L :W 90
  END

(c) TO RHOMBUS :L :A
    PARALLELOGRAM :L :L :A
  END

(d) Execute **PARALLELOGRAM** 50 50 90.
(e) Execute **RHOMBUS** 50 90.
25. If two lines are perpendicular to the same line, then congruent corresponding angles of 90° each are formed, and hence the lines are parallel.
27. This follows directly from Problem 26.
29. 83.5°, or 83°30′
31. No; the union of two rays will always extend infinitely in at least one direction.
33. $\angle DBA \cap \angle BAC = \overline{AB}$

Problem Set 10-4   1. (a) Quadrilateral pyramid
(b) Quadrilateral prism   **(c)** Pentagonal pyramid
3. (a) A regular pentagon   **(b)** An equilateral triangle
5. (a) T   **(b)** F   **(c)** T   **(d)** F   **(e)** F   **(f)** F
(g) F   **(h)** T   **7.** Drawings may vary.

9.

	Pyramid	Prism
(a)	$n+1$	$n+2$
(b)	$n+1$	$2n$
(c)	$2n$	$3n$

11. (a) $V + F - E = 10 + 7 - 15 = 2$
(b) $V + F - E = 9 + 9 - 16 = 2$
(c) $V + F - E = 16 + 16 - 32 = 0$, so Euler's formula does not hold.
13. 60°   **15. (a)** T   **(b)** T
(c) F. A triangle can have three acute angles.
(d) F. An angle is not closed.   **(e)** T
(f) F. See the figure.

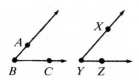

17. (a) Right triangle
(b) Suppose the complementary angles of the triangle are $\angle 1$ and $\angle 2$; suppose $\angle 3$ is the third angle.

$$m(\angle 1) + m(\angle 2) = 90$$
$$m(\angle 1) + m(\angle 2) + m(\angle 3) = 180$$
$$90 + m(\angle 3) = 180$$
$$m(\angle 3) = 90$$

Therefore, a triangle with angles $\angle 1$, $\angle 2$, and $\angle 3$ as specified contains a right angle and is a right triangle.

Problem Set 10-5   1. (a), (b), (c), (e), (g), (h), and (j) are traversable.
(a) Path: *ABCACDEFDFA*; any point can be a starting point.

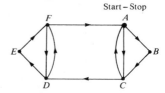

(b) Path: *ABACBCDCDA*; any point can be a starting point.

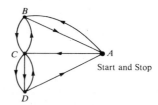

(c) Path: *ABCFAEDCEFB*; only points *A* and *B* can be starting points.

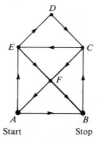

(e) Path: *ABCBDCAD*; only points *A* and *D* can be starting points.

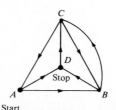

(g) Path: *FADABCBGFEDCHEHG*; only points *F* and *G* can be starting points.

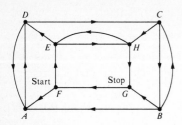

(h) Path: *ACBCDCDAB*; only points *A* and *B* can be starting points.

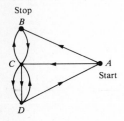

(j) Path: *EFHKLNABDFGHLMNBCDE*; any point can be a starting point.

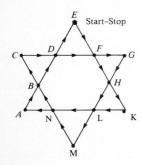

3. (a)

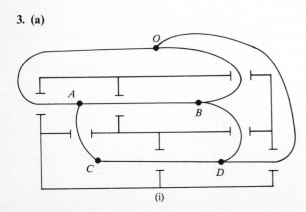

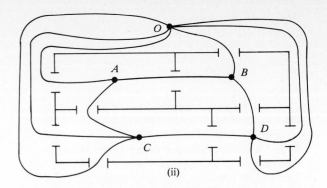

(b) Network (i) is not traversable because it has four odd vertices. Network (ii) has two odd vertices, so it is traversable, as shown.

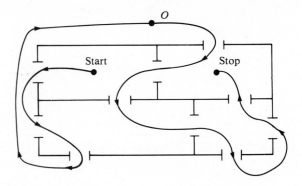

5. (a) (i) The number of odd fellows is 0.

(ii) The number of odd fellows is 2.

(iii) The number of odd fellows is 4.

(iv) The number of odd fellows is 4.

(b) The number of even fellows may be either even or odd.

7. Because all vertices are even, the trip is possible. It makes no difference where she starts.

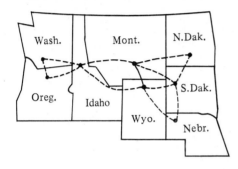

Problem Set 10-6 1. (a) 60° (b) $(\frac{360}{7})°$ (c) 45°
(d) 30° 3. Execute it on the computer.
5. No; the methods of this section yield an equilateral triangle if a six-pointed star is attempted.
7. Answers may vary.

(a)
```
TO THIRTY
   FD 100
   BK 100
   RT 30
   FD 100
   BK 100
   LT 30
END
```

9. By the Total Turtle Trip Theorem, the amount of turning around any convex polygon is 360°. Each exterior angle of the n-gon is the supplement to an interior angle. Thus, the sum of the measures of the interior angles and the exterior angles is $180n°$. Because the sum of the measures of the exterior angles is 360°, the sum of the measures of the interior angles is $180n° - 360°$, or $(n - 2)180°$.

Chapter Test 1. (a) $\overleftrightarrow{AB}, \overleftrightarrow{BC}, \overleftrightarrow{AC}$ (b) $\overrightarrow{BA}, \overrightarrow{BC}$
(c) $\overline{AB}$ (d) $\overrightarrow{AB}$ (e) $\overline{AB}$ 3. (a) Three noncollinear points (b) Two distinct intersecting lines (c) Two distinct parallel lines (d) A line and a point not on the line 5. Answers may vary. 7. 18°, 36°, 126°
9. (a) Answers may vary. (b) Euler's formula holds.
11. 35°8′35″ 13. 8

15. (a) (i), (ii), and (iv) are traversable.
   (b) (i) Path: $ABCDEFACEA$; any point can be used as a starting point.

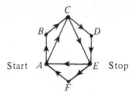

   (ii) Path: $ABCDAEDBE$; points A and E are possible starting points.

   (iv) Path: $ACDEACDEABC$; points A or C are possible starting points.

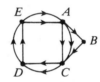

17. Answers may vary.

```
TO ISOS :LEG :ANGLE
   DRAW
   FD :LEG
   RT 180 - :ANGLE
   FD :LEG
   RT 90 + :A / 2
   HOME
   RT 90 + :A / 2
END
```

(In Apple Logo, replace DRAW with CLEARSCREEN.)

CHAPTER 11

Problem Set 11-1 1. (a) Yes; SAS (b) Yes; SSS
(c) No 3. (c) Right triangle (d) Impossible
7. (a) $\overline{AD} \cong \overline{CD}$ (b) $\angle ABD \cong \angle CBD$; definition of angle bisector. $\overline{AB} \cong \overline{BC}$; given. $\overline{BD} \cong \overline{BD}$; $\triangle ABD \cong \triangle CBD$; SAS. $\overline{AD} \cong \overline{CD}$; corresponding parts of congruent triangles are congruent (CPCTC).
(c) $m(\angle ADB) = m(\angle CDB) = 90°$

(d) $\triangle ADB \cong \triangle CDB$, by CPCTC [using (a) above]; $\triangle ADB$ and $\triangle CDB$ are adjacent, by definition of adjacent angles; $m(\triangle ADB) + m(\triangle CDB) = 180°$ because $\triangle ADC$ is a straight angle; $m(\triangle ADB) \cong m(\triangle CDB)$, by definition of congruent angles; $m(\triangle ADB) = m(\triangle CDB) = 90°$.
9. $\triangle BCD \cong \triangle BCA$ by SAS, so that $\overline{AB} \cong \overline{DB}$, and DB can be measured.
11. (a) A parallelogram **(b)** Let $ABCD$ be the quadrilateral, with E the intersection point of its diagonals. Show that $\triangle AED \cong \triangle CEB$ and that $\triangle BEA \cong \triangle DEC$. Use congruent alternate interior angles to show $\overline{BC} \| \overline{AD}$ and $\overline{AB} \| \overline{CD}$.

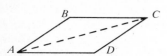

13. (a) A parallelogram **(b)** Let $\overline{AB} = \overline{CD}$ and $\overline{BC} \cong \overline{AD}$. Prove that $\triangle ABC \cong \triangle ADC$ and conclude that $\overline{BC} \| \overline{AD}$ and $\overline{AB} \| \overline{DC}$. **15.** $\triangle BAC \cong \triangle CAB$; SAS. $\triangle ABC \cong \triangle ACB$ by CPCTC.

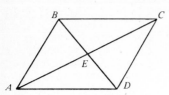

Problem Set 11-2 **1. (a)** Yes; ASA **(b)** Yes; AAS
(c) No **(d)** No **3. (d)** Infinitely many such triangles are possible. **5. (a)** One side of the square
(b) Two perpendicular sides of the rectangle
(c) Answers vary. One solution is: two adjacent sides of the parallelogram and the angle between them.
7. (a) $\overline{OP} \cong \overline{QO}$.
(b) $\triangle PDO \cong \triangle QBO$; alternate interior angles formed by the transversal $\overline{DB}$ and parallel lines $\overleftrightarrow{DC}$ and $\overleftrightarrow{AB}$. $\triangle DPO \cong \triangle BQO$ because $\overline{PQ}$ is a transversal of $\overleftrightarrow{DC}$ and $\overleftrightarrow{AB}$. $\overline{DO} \cong \overline{BO}$; diagonals of a parallelogram bisect each other. $\triangle POD \cong \triangle QOB$; AAS. $\overline{OP} \cong \overline{QO}$; CPCTC.
9. (a) Parallelogram **(b)** None **(c)** None
(d) Rectangle **(e)** Rhombus **(f)** Square
(g) Parallelogram **11. (a)** The base angles are congruent. **(b)** The diagonals are congruent.
(c) To prove (a), construct $\overline{CE} \| \overline{BA}$ and prove that

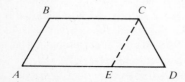

$\triangle ECD$ is isosceles. To prove (b), show that $\triangle ABD \cong \triangle DCA$.
13. (a) Prove that $\triangle ABD \cong \triangle CDB$ and $\triangle ADC \cong \triangle CBA$.
(b) Use a pair of triangles from (a). **(c)** Prove that $\triangle ABF \cong \triangle CDF$. **(d)** Extend AB and look for corresponding angles.
15. Show that $\triangle ABC \cong \triangle ABD$.
17. (a)
```
TO RHOMBUS :SIDE :ANGLE
  REPEAT 2 [FD :SIDE RT (180 - :ANGLE)
            FD :SIDE RT :ANGLE]
END
```
(b) They are congruent because 50° and 130° are measures of supplementary angles.
(c)
```
TO SQ.RHOM :SIDE
   RHOMBUS :SIDE 90
   END
```

Problem Set 11-3 **3. (d)** All three intersect at a point inside the triangle. **(e)** All three intersect at the vertex of the right angle. **(f)** All three intersect at a point outside the triangle. **9.** Find the intersection point of the perpendicular bisectors of $\overline{AB}$ and $\overline{AC}$.
11. (a) $\overleftrightarrow{PQ}$ is on the perpendicular bisector of $\overline{AB}$.
(b) Q is on the perpendicular bisector of $\overline{AB}$ because $\overline{AQ} \cong \overline{QB}$. Similarly, P is on the perpendicular bisector of $\overline{AB}$. Because a unique line contains two points, the perpendicular bisector contains $\overleftrightarrow{PQ}$. **(c)** $\overrightarrow{PQ}$ is the angle bisector of $\triangle APB$; $\overrightarrow{QC}$ is the angle bisector of $\triangle AQB$. **(d)** Show that $\triangle APQ \cong \triangle BPQ$ by SSS; then, $\triangle APQ \cong \triangle BQP$ by CPCTC. Show that $\triangle AQC \cong \triangle BQC$ and conclude that $\triangle AQC \cong \triangle BQC$.
13.
```
TO ALTITUDES
   REPEAT 3[RT 30 FD 60 RT 90 FD 110
   BK 130 FD 20 LT 90 FD 60 RT 90]
END
```
15. $\triangle ABC \cong \triangle DEC$ by ASA ($\overline{BC} \cong \overline{CE}$, $\triangle ACB \cong \triangle ECD$ as vertical angles, and $\triangle B \cong \triangle E$ as alternate interior angles formed by the parallels $\overleftrightarrow{AB}$ and $\overleftrightarrow{ED}$ and the transversal $\overleftrightarrow{EB}$). $\overline{AC} \cong \overline{DC}$ by CPCTC.

Problem Set 11-4 **1.** The diameter is the longest chord of a circle. **3.** Right triangle
5. No. The tangent line will intersect one circle in two points.
7. *Hint:* First inscribe a regular hexagon in the given circle.
9. (c) Opposite angles are supplementary.
11. No, only if sides are equidistant from some point. A circle cannot be inscribed in a general rectangle that is not a square.

13. *Hint:* Bisect the interior angles on the same side of the transversal. The center of the circle is the point of intersection of the angle bisectors.
15. (a) 0, 1, or 2, depending on how the line is chosen. **(b)** 0, 1 (if tangent to the sphere), infinitely many (if the intersection is a circle).
17. Given that $\overline{AB} \cong \overline{CD}$ (see the figure), prove that $\overline{OM} \cong \overline{ON}$. First, prove that $\overline{AM} \cong \overline{MB}$ and $\overline{CN} \cong \overline{ND}$. Then, show that $\triangle ABO \cong \triangle COD$. Hence, conclude that $\angle A \cong \angle C$. Now, prove that $\triangle AMO \cong \triangle CNO$ (by SAS). Consequently, $\overline{OM} \cong \overline{ON}$. See the following figure.

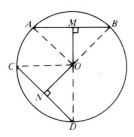

19. TO FILL.CIRCLE :R
    REPEAT 360 [FD :R BK :R RT 1]
    END

Problem Set 11-5 1. (a) Slide **(b)** Slide
5. (b) Yes, because a flip is an isometry, the distance between all points of the circle and its center is preserved, and thus the image is also a circle.
11. The last image is the original image.
13. (a)

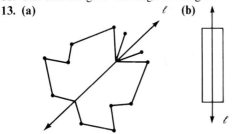

15. (a) One vertical **(b)** One vertical **(c)** None
(d) One vertical **(e)** Five lines **(f)** One vertical
17.

19. Reflect A in road 1 and B in road 2. Connect the reflections by a straight line. The intersection points

with road 1 and road 2 are the desired locations for P and Q. **21. (a)** 150° rotation about the turtle's starting point **(b)** Flip in a vertical line containing the turtle's starting point **(c)** 45° rotation and slide
23. (b)

TO TRIANGLE :SIDE
  REPEAT 3 [FD :SIDE RT 120]
END

TO SLIDE :DIRECTION :DISTANCE :SIDE
  TRIANGLE :SIDE
  PU
  SETHEADING :DIRECTION
  FD :DISTANCE
  PD
  SETHEADING 0
  TRIANGLE :SIDE
END

Problem Set 11-6 1. A circular radio knob is turned from "off" to "on," a child is swinging, a record is turning.
9. Yes. The net result is a rotation about point O; the angle of rotation equals twice the measure of the angle between lines m and ℓ.
11. (b) One turn of $\alpha + \beta$ about point O **(c)** No **(d)** Yes **13. (a)** Yes. It must have turn symmetry of 180° about the point of symmetry. **(b)** No. Counter-examples vary. **(c)** Yes. Figures vary. **(d)** No to both questions. Counterexamples vary.
15. TO RSQUARE :A
      REPEAT 4 [FD 40 RT 90]
      LEFT :A
      REPEAT 4 [FD 40 RT 90]
      END
17. TO CIRCLE
      REPEAT 360 [FD 1 RT 1]
      END
(a) TO HTCIRCLE **(b)** TO CCCIRCLE
      CIRCLE   CIRCLE
      LT 180   LT 90
      CIRCLE   CIRCLE
      END   END

Problem Set 11-7 1. Rotate the triangle 180° about the midpoint of each leg. Repeat the process for each triangle constructed in this way.
3. (a) Rotate the quadrilateral 180° about the midpoint of each side. Repeat the process for each quadrilateral constructed in this way. **(b)** Yes
5. (a) The dual is also a tessellation of squares.
(b) The dual is a tessellation of triangles.
(c) The dual is a tessellation of equilateral triangles.

7. (a)
```
TO TESSELSQUARE
    PU
    BK 70
    PD
    REPEAT 9 [SQUARE 20 FD 20]
    PU
    BK 180
    RT 90
    FD 20
    LT 90
    PD
    REPEAT 9 [SQUARE 20 FD 20]
END

TO SQUARE :SIDE
    REPEAT 4 [FD :SIDE RT 90]
END
```

(b)
```
TO TESSELTRI
    PU
    BK 70
    PD
    REPEAT 9 [TRIANGLE 20 FD 20]
    PU
    BK 180
    RT 60
    FD 20
    LT 60
    PD
    REPEAT 9 [TRIANGLE 20 FD 20]
END

TO TRIANGLE :SIDE
    REPEAT 3 [FD :SIDE RT 120]
END
```

(c)
```
TO TESSELHEX
    PU
    BK 70
    LT 90
    PD
    REPEAT 4 [HEXAGON 20 RT 120 FD 20
    LT 60 HEXAGON 20 FD 20 LT 60]
END

TO HEXAGON :SIDE
    REPEAT 6 [FD :SIDE RT 60]
END
```

9. (a) Turn **(b)** Turn **(c)** Turn
13. (a) Turn (the center) and line (each of the altitudes) **(b)** Turn (the center), line (perpendicular bisector of each side, and diagonals if the polygon has an even number of sides), and point (if the polygon has an even number of sides) **(c)** Line; each of the altitudes

Problem Set 11-8   1. Triangle 3
3. This illustration is one possibility.

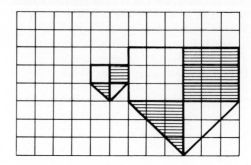

5. (a) $x = 7$ **(b)** $x = \frac{24}{7}$ **(c)** $x = \frac{15}{2}$ **(d)** $x = 10$ m
7. (a) 9 **(b)** $\frac{14}{3}$ **(c)** $7\frac{1}{2}$ **(d)** $\frac{29}{3}$
9. Yes. Corresponding angles are congruent.

11. (c) If, in $\triangle ABC$ and $\triangle DEF$, we have $\dfrac{AB}{DE} = \dfrac{AC}{DF}$ and $\angle A \cong \angle D$, then $\triangle ABC \sim \triangle DEF$.
13. The ratio of the perimeters is the same as the ratio of the sides.
17. (a) $\triangle ABC \sim \triangle BDC$.
(b) $m(\angle ABC) = m(\angle ACB)$. (Base angles of an isosceles triangle are congruent and have the same measure.)

$$m(\angle ABC) + m(\angle ACB) + 36° = 180°$$
$$2m(\angle ABC) = 144°$$
$$m(\angle ABC) = 72°$$
$$\tfrac{1}{2}m(\angle ABC) = m(\angle DBC) = 36°$$

19. (a) $\angle C \cong \angle ADG$ because both are right angles. $\angle CGF$ and $\angle AGD$ are complementary, as are $\angle AGD$ and $\angle GAD$. Thus, $\angle CGF \cong \angle GAD$ and $\triangle GCF \sim \triangle ADG$ by **AA**.
(b) No. $\overline{GF}$ is the hypotenuse of $\triangle GCF$ and congruent to a leg of $\triangle ADG$. They are not corresponding sides, and the hypotenuse $\overline{AG}$ of $\triangle ADG$ must be longer than $\overline{GF}$.
21. $BE = 3$; $ED = 4.5$

23. (a)
```
TO RECTANGLE :LEN :WID
    REPEAT 2 [FD :LEN RT 90 FD :WID RT 90]
END


TO SIM.RECT :LEN :WID
    RECTANGLE (:LEN * 2) (:WID * 2)
END
```

(b)
```
TO SIM.RECTANGLE :LEN :WID :SCALE
  RECTANGLE (:LEN * :SCALE) (:WID * :SCALE).
END
```

(c)
```
TO PARALLELOGRAM :LEN :WID :ANGLE
  REPEAT 2 [FD :LEN RT 180 - :ANGLE FD :WID RT :ANGLE]
END

TO SIM.PAR :LEN :WID :ANGLE :SCALE
  PARALLELOGRAM (:LEN * :SCALE) (:WID * :SCALE) :ANGLE
END
```

Problem Set 11-9   1. (a) A circle with $\frac{1}{5}$ the radius is drawn.   **(b)** The new circle is a reflection of the old circle with respect to the tangent of the circle at the turtle's starting position.

3. (a)
```
TO ARC :D :S
  REPEAT :D [FD :S RT 1]
END
```

(b)
```
TO ARCRAD :R :D
  REPEAT :D [FD :R * .017 RT 1]
END
```

5. Answers vary. For example,
```
TO FILL.CIRCLE :S
  REPEAT 360 [FD :S BK :S RT 1]
END
```

7.
```
TO OLYMPIC :R
  RCIRCLE :R
  REPEAT 2 [PU RT 90 FD (2 * :R) + 10 LT 90 PD RCIRCLE :R]
  PU
  LT 90
  FD 5
  LT 90
  FD :R
  RT 90
  FD :R
  RT 90
  PD
  RCIRCLE :R
  PU
  LT 90
  FD (2 * :R) + 10
  RT 90
  PD
  RCIRCLE :R
END

TO RCIRCLE :R
  REPEAT 360 [FD 2 * 3.1416 * :R / 360 RT 1]
END
```

9.
```
TO DIAMCIRC :R
  RCIRCLE :R
  RT 90
  FD 2 * :R
END

TO RCIRCLE :R
  REPEAT 360 [FD 2 * 3.1416 * :R / 360 RT 1]
END
```

Chapter Test **1. (a)** $\triangle ABD \cong \triangle CBD$ by SAS
(b) $\triangle AGC \cong \triangle DEB$ by SAS
(c) $\triangle CBA \cong \triangle CDE$ by AAS
(d) $\triangle ABD \cong \triangle AEC$ by ASA
(e) $\triangle ABD \cong \triangle CBD$ by ASA or by SAS
(f) $\triangle ABD \cong \triangle CBD$ by SAS
(g) $\triangle ABD \cong \triangle CBE$ by SSS
(h) $\triangle ABC \cong \triangle ADC$ by SSS
3. (a)

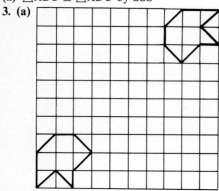

(b)

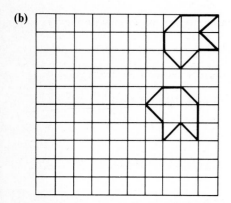

(c)

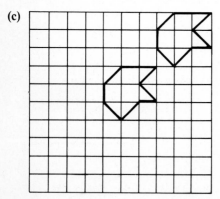

7. (a) Line and turn **(b)** Line, turn, and point
(c) Line **11.** Intersect the perpendicular bisector of
$\overline{AB}$ with ℓ

13. (a) F. A chord has its endpoints on the circle.
(b) F. A diameter intersects a circle in two points,
and a tangent intersects it in only one point.
(c) T **(d)** T **(e)** T
15. 12 m

CHAPTER 12

Problem Set 12-1 **1. (a)** 20; 2 **(b)** 36; 3.6
(c) 45; 4.5 **(d)** 5; 50 **(e)** 6.2; 62 **(f)** 7.9; 79
(g) 93; 9.3 **3. (a)** 98 **(b)** 9.8 **(c)** 0.098
5. (a) 3.5; 3500 **(b)** 163; 1630 **(c)** 0.035; 3.5
(d) 0.1; 10 **(e)** 200; 2000 **7.** 6 m, 5218 mm,
52 dm, 38 dm, 245 cm, 700 mm, 91 mm, 8 cm
9. (a) 8 cm **(b)** 12 cm **(c)** 9 cm **(d)** 20 cm
11. (a) (i) 12; (ii) 36; (iii) 3; (iv) 5280; (v) 16.5;
(vi) 660 **(b)** (i) inches; (ii) inches; (iii) feet; (iv) inches
13. (a) 6 cm **(b)** $\dfrac{3}{\pi}$ m **(c)** $\dfrac{0.335}{\pi}$ m **(d)** 46 cm
15. The circumference is doubled.
17. (a) $AB + BC > AC$; answers vary.
(b) $BC + CA > AB$; answers vary.
(c) $AB + CA > BC$; answers vary.

Problem Set 12-2 **1. (a)** cm^2 **(b)** cm^2 **(c)** cm^2
(d) m^2 **(e)** m^2 **(f)** km^2 **3.** Answers vary.
5. (a) 20 cm^2 **(b)** 900 cm^2, or 0.09 m^2
(c) 7.5 m^2 **(d)** 39 cm^2
7. The area of each triangle is 10 cm^2 because they
all have the same base $\overline{AB}$ and the same height.
9. (a) 25π cm^2 **(b)** $\frac{8}{3}\pi$ cm^2 **(c)** 3.6π cm^2
(d) 4.5π cm^2 **11. (a)** 2π cm^2 **(b)** $\left(2 + \dfrac{\pi}{2}\right)$ cm^2
(c) 2π cm^2 **13.** 24 m^2 **15.** 7π m^2 **17.** 1200
19. (a) 3 units **(b)** 3 units **(c)** 2 units **(d)** 5 units
(e) 6 units **(f)** $4\frac{1}{2}$ units
21. (a) Rotate the shaded region 180° clockwise
about point E. The area of the triangle is the same
as the area of the parallelogram. Thus, $A = \dfrac{h}{2} \cdot b$
23. The figure obtained from $\triangle ABC$ and its image is
a parallelogram whose area is twice that of $\triangle ABC$.
Therefore, the area of the triangle is one-half that of
the parallelogram, which is $(\frac{1}{2})(\text{base})(\text{height})$.
25. P should be connected to the point that is 2 units
above P and $1\frac{1}{2}$ units to the right of P.
27. The sectors of the circle approximate a
parallelogram with base πr and height r, and hence
an area of πr^2.
29. (a) 4:1 **(b)** If r is the ratio of corresponding
sides, then r^2 is the ratio of their areas.

(c) Given: $\triangle ABC \sim \triangle A'B'C'$, with $\dfrac{AB}{A'B'} = r$. From

$\triangle ABD \sim \triangle A'B'D'$ (AA), we have $\dfrac{BD}{B'D'} = r$. Hence, the

ratio of their areas is

$$\frac{\frac{1}{2}AC \cdot BD}{\frac{1}{2}A'C' \cdot B'D'} = \frac{AC}{A'C'} \cdot \frac{BD}{B'D'} = r \cdot r = r^2$$

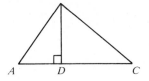

31. Draw altitudes $\overline{BE}$ and $\overline{DF}$ of triangles BCP and DCP, respectively. $\triangle ABE \cong \triangle CDP$ by AAS. Thus, $\overline{BE} \cong \overline{DF}$. Because $\overline{CP}$ is a base of $\triangle BCP$ and $\triangle DCP$, and because the heights are the same, the area must be the same.

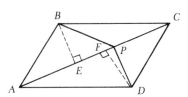

33. (a) $(2\pi + 4)$ cm **(b)** $(6 + 5\pi)$ mm

Problem Set 12-3 **1. (a)** 6 **(b)** $\sqrt{2}$ **(c)** $5a$
(d) 12 **(e)** $\sqrt{3}s$ **(f)** $\sqrt{2}$ **(g)** 9 **(h)** 13
(i) $\dfrac{\sqrt{32}}{2}$, or $2\sqrt{2}$ **(j)** $\sqrt{45}$, or $3\sqrt{5}$ **3. (a)** No
(b) Yes **(c)** Yes **(d)** Yes **(e)** Yes **(f)** Yes
5. $\sqrt{450}$, or $15\sqrt{2}$

7. $\triangle ACD \sim \triangle ABC$. Thus, $\dfrac{b}{x} = \dfrac{c}{b}$ implies $b^2 = cx$.

$\triangle BCD \sim \triangle BAC$. Thus, $\dfrac{a}{y} = \dfrac{c}{a}$ implies $a^2 = cy$.
Consequently, $a^2 + b^2 = cx + cy = c(x + y) = c^2$.
9. The area of the large square is equal to the sum of the areas of the smaller square and the four triangles. Thus,

$$(a + b)^2 = c^2 + 4\left(\frac{ab}{2}\right)$$

$$a^2 + 2ab + b^2 = c^2 + 2ab$$

$$a^2 + b^2 = c^2$$

You should also verify that the smaller quadrilateral is a square.

11. Yes **13.** $\sqrt{27}$, or $3\sqrt{3}$
15. (a)

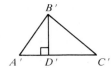

(b) $\dfrac{\sqrt{3}c}{2}$

Draw $\triangle DCB$ congruent to $\triangle ABC$. Because all the interior angles in $\triangle ABD$ are $60°$, the triangle is equilateral. Hence, $AB = BD = AD$. Because $AC = CD$, it follows that $AC = \frac{1}{2}AD$, and hence $AC = \frac{1}{2}AB$. **17.** $\frac{5}{3}$ m
19. Yes. Let a right triangle have legs of lengths a and b and hypotenuse of length c. Because an equilateral triangle with base of length x has height $\dfrac{\sqrt{3}}{2}x$, its area is $\dfrac{\sqrt{3}}{4}x^2$. Thus, the sum of the areas of the equilateral triangles constructed on the legs is $\dfrac{\sqrt{3}}{4}a^2 + \dfrac{\sqrt{3}}{4}b^2$, or $\dfrac{\sqrt{3}}{4}(a^2 + b^2)$. The area of the equilateral triangle constructed on the hypotenuse is $\dfrac{\sqrt{3}}{4}c^2$. By the Pythagorean Theorem, $c^2 = a^2 + b^2$, and hence $\dfrac{\sqrt{3}}{4}(a^2 + b^2) = \dfrac{\sqrt{3}}{4}c^2$.

21. 0.032 km, 322 cm, 3.2 m, 3.020 mm **23.** $\dfrac{25}{\pi}$ m²

Problem Set 12-4 **1. (a)** 96 cm² **(b)** 236 cm²
3. (a) 4900 square feet **(b)** 1500π square feet
(c) $32\pi + 16\sqrt{5}\pi$ cm², or $(32 + 16\sqrt{5})\pi$ cm²
5. 2688π mm² **7.** $\frac{16}{36}$, or $\frac{4}{9}$
9. (a) They are the same. **(b)** The one with radius 6 m **11. (a)** The area is nine times the original.
(b) It is doubled. **13. (a)** It is tripled.
(b) It is tripled. **(c)** It is nine times the original area.
15. $(6400\sqrt{2}\pi + 13{,}600\pi)$ cm²
17. (a) 100,000 **(b)** 1.368 **(c)** 500 **(d)** 2,000,000
(e) 1 **(f)** 1,000,000
19. $20\sqrt{5}$
21. The length of the side is 25 cm. The length of the diagonal is 30 cm.

Problem Set 12-5 **1. (a)** 8000 **(b)** 0.0005
(c) 0.000675 **(d)** 3,000,000 **(e)** 7 **(f)** 2000

3. (a) 64 cm³ **(b)** 120 cm³ **(c)** 216 cm³
(d) 14 cm³ **(e)** 50 cm³ **(f)** 21π cm³ **(g)** 432π cm³
(h) $\frac{4000}{3}$ π cm³ **5.** 1680π mm³ **7.** It is multiplied by 8.

9.

	(a)	(b)	(c)	(d)
Height	10 cm	3 dm	20 cm	25 cm
cm³	2000	6000	4000	7500
dm³	2	6	4	7.5
L	2	6	4	7.5

11. 253,500π L **13.** 1.62 L **15.** 32.4 L
17. No; the customer pays $\frac{1}{2}$ as much for $\frac{1}{3}$ of the
popcorn. **19.** 16 m³ **21.** Approximately 2.2 cm
23. (a) 1728 **(b)** 26.52 **(c)** 27 **(d)** 111.11
25. (a) 340 cm **(b)** 6000 cm²

Problem Set 12-6 **1. (a)** Tons or kilograms
(b) Kilograms **(c)** Grams **(d)** Tons **(e)** Grams
(f) Grams **(g)** Tons **(h)** Kilograms or grams
(i) Kilograms or grams **3. (a)** 15 **(b)** 8 **(c)** 36
(d) 0.072 **(e)** 4.230 **(f)** 3.007 **(g)** 5750 **(h)** 5.750
(i) 30 **(j)** 30,000 **5.** 16,000 g, or 16 kg **7.** $0.02
9. (a) No **(b)** No **(c)** No **(d)** Yes **(e)** No
(f) Yes **(g)** Yes **(h)** Chilly **(i)** Hot
11. (a) 50°F **(b)** 32°F **(c)** 86°F **(d)** 212°F
(e) 414°F **(f)** ⁻40°F **13. (a)** 35 **(b)** 0.16
(c) 400,000 **(d)** 5,200,000 **(e)** 5,200 **(f)** 0.0035
15. $\sqrt{61}$ km

Chapter Test **1. (a)** 50,000; 5000; 50 **(b)** 3200; 3.2;
0.0032 **(c)** 26,000,000; 260,000; 260 **(d)** 190,000;
19,000; 0.19 **3. (a)** Find the area of △ADC and
double it; $A = 2(\frac{1}{2} \cdot DE \cdot AC)$.
(b) $A = b \cdot h = DC \cdot FB$ **5. (a)** 8$\frac{1}{2}$ **(b)** 5$\frac{1}{2}$ **(c)** 7
7. The area of the trapezoid is equal to the area of
the rectangle constructed from its component parts.
The area of the rectangle is $\frac{h}{2}(b_1 + b_2)$, which is the
formula for the area of a trapezoid.
9. (a) 12π cm² **(b)** (12 + 4.5π) cm² **(c)** 24 cm²
(d) 64.5 cm² **(e)** 178.5 m² **(f)** 4π cm²
11. (a) S.A. = 32(2 + $\sqrt{13}$) cm²; V = 128 cm³
(b) S.A. = 96π cm²; V = 96π cm³
(c) S.A. = 100π m²; V = $\frac{500}{3}$π m³
(d) S.A. = 54π cm²; V = 54π cm³
(e) S.A. = 304 m²; V = 320 m³
13. (a) L **(b)** kg **(c)** g **(d)** g **(e)** kg **(f)** t
(g) mL **15. (a)** 2000 **(b)** 1000 **(c)** 3 **(d)** 0.0042
(e) 0.0002

CHAPTER 13

Problem Set 13-1 **1. (a)** A(2, 2); B(5, 0); C(4,⁻3);
D(0, ⁻3); E(⁻2, ⁻3); F(⁻4, 0); G(⁻4, 3); H(0, 3)
(b) (⁻2, ⁻3); answers may vary.
3. Quadrant II = {(x, y)|x < 0 and y > 0}
Quadrant III = {(x, y)|x < 0 and y < 0}
Quadrant IV = {(x, y)|x > 0 and y < 0}
5. (a) x = ⁻2; y is any real number.
(b) x is any real number; y = 1.
(c) x > 0 and y < 0; x and y are real numbers.
7. D has coordinates (4, ⁻2).
9. (a)

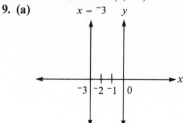

(b)

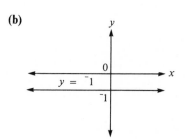

(c)

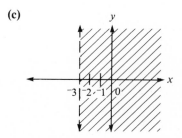

(d)

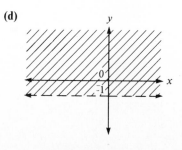

(e)

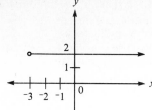

(f)

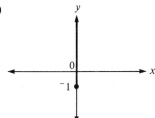

(b)

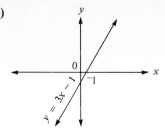

(c)

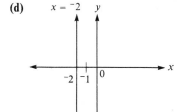

11. (a) $P(3, 4)$; $Q(6, 1)$ **(b)** $N(^-1, 4)$; $M(^-1, ^-1)$
(c) $x = 3$ **(d)** $y = 1$
13. (a) $(0, ^-1)$, $(1, 0)$, $(2, ^-4)$, $(^-2, ^-4)$ $(^-2, 4)$, $(2, 4)$
(b) $(0, 1)$, $(^-1, 0)$, $(^-2, 4)$, $(2, 4)$, $(2, ^-4)$, $(^-2, ^-4)$
(c) $(^-1, 0)$, $(0, 1)$, $(^-4, 2)$, $(^-4, ^-2)$, $(4, ^-2)$, $(4, 2)$
(d) $(0, ^-1)$, $(^-1, 0)$, $(^-2, ^-4)$, $(2, ^-4)$, $(2, 4)$, $(^-2, 4)$
(e) $(0, ^-3)$, $(1, ^-4)$, $(2, 0)$, $(^-2, 0)$, $(^-2, ^-8)$, $(2, ^-8)$
15. (a) $(^-2, ^-4)$ **(b)** $(^-a, ^-b)$
(c) Yes; a half-turn about $(0, 0)$ **17. (a)** $A'(0, 1)$,
$B'(2, 2)$, $C'(1, 3)$, $D'(^-1, 3)$, $E'(b, a)$

(d)

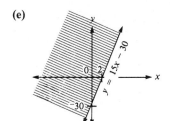

Problem Set 13-2
1.

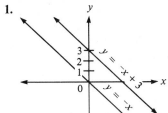

(e)

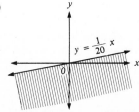

3. (a)

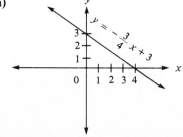

(f)

5. (a)

Degrees Fahrenheit
Degrees Celsius

(b)

Degrees Celsius
Degrees Fahrenheit

(c) Each line is the reflection of the other in the line $y = x$. **7. (a)** $\frac{1}{3}$ **(b)** $\frac{1}{9}$ **(c)** 0 **(d)** No slope
(e) 20,000 **(f)** 1 if $a \neq b$ **9. (a)** Parallel
(b) Parallel **(c)** Parallel **(d)** Not parallel
11. (a) $\frac{1}{2}$ **(b)** $\frac{-1}{2}$ **(c)** 0 **(d)** Undefined—no slope
13. (a) The equation of ℓ is $y = mx$; the equation of n is $x = 1$. The point of intersection can be found by substituting 1 for x in $y = mx$. Thus, $y = m \cdot 1$, or m, so the point of intersection of ℓ and m is $(1, m)$.
(b) The equation for ℓ is $y = mx + b$; the equation for n is $x = 1$. Substituting 1 for x in $y = mx + b$ yields

$y = m \cdot 1 + b$, or $y = m + b$. Thus, the y-coordinate of P is $m + b$.
15. Let A, B, and C have coordinates $(0, \ ^-1)$, $(1, 2)$, and $(^-1, \ ^-4)$, respectively. The slope of $\overline{AB}$ is 3; the slope of $\overline{BC}$ is 3; the slope of $\overline{AC}$ is 3. Hence, A, B, and C are collinear.
17. The x-intercept is a; the y-intercept is b.
19. (a)

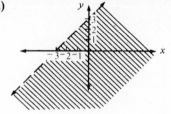

(b)

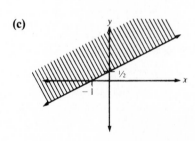

(c)

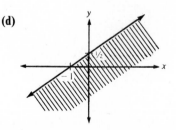

(d)

21. (a) $y = \ ^-x$ **(b)** $y = \ ^-x$ **(c)** $x = 0$ **(d)** $y = \ ^-x$
(e) $y = x$ **(f)** $y = x - 3$ **(g)** $y = x + 3$
23. (a) $y = \ ^-x + 1$ **(b)** $y = \ ^-x - 1$ **(c)** $y = x + 1$
(d) $y = x + 1$

25. (a), (b)

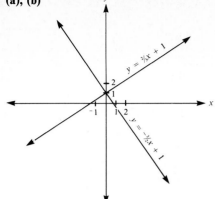

(c)

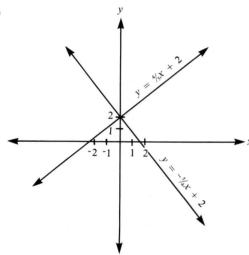

(d) If the product of the slopes of two lines is ⁻1, the lines are perpendicular.

27. (a)

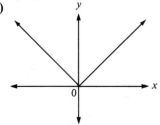

(b)

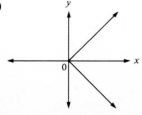

(c)

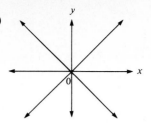

(d)

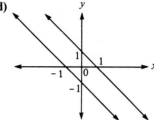

(e)

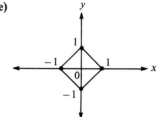

(f)

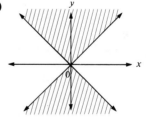

29. (a) Answers may vary: (3, ⁻2) and (7, ⁻2)
(b) Answers may vary: (⁻2, ⁻2) and (8, 10)
31. (a) $1\frac{1}{2}$ square units   **(b)** 15 square units
(c) $7\frac{1}{2}$ square units   **(d)** 12 square units
(e) 3 square units

Problem Set 13-3   1. (a) $(0, \frac{-5}{3})$; $(\frac{5}{2}, 0)$; $(1, \,^-1)$; $(2, \frac{-1}{3})$. Answers may vary.
(b)

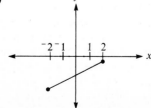

(c)

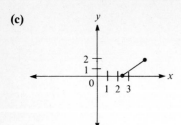

3. (a) $(^-11, ^-8)$ **(b)** $(\frac{-30}{11}, \frac{-84}{11})$ **(c)** $(\frac{13}{3}, \frac{43}{12})$
(d) $(\frac{-6}{5}, \frac{-4}{5})$ **(e)** $(0, 0)$ **(f)** $(^-1 + 3\sqrt{2}, 3 - \sqrt{2})$
5. The equations of the medians are $y = \frac{1}{2}x$,
$y = 8x - 40$, and $y = \frac{-4}{7}x + \frac{40}{7}$. They intersect at
$(\frac{16}{3}, \frac{8}{3})$.
7. $8\frac{1}{6}$ square units **9.** $\frac{55}{72}$ and $\frac{-1}{72}$
11. $133\frac{1}{3}$ pounds of cashew-nut granola and $66\frac{2}{3}$
pounds of golden granola
13. $20,000 and $60,000, respectively
15. Width 60 inches; length 75 inches
17. (a) The answers are all $(^-1, 2)$.
(b) $13x + 14y = 15$
$16x + 17y = 18$ The solution is $(^-1, 2)$.
(c) $ax + (a + 1)y = a + 2$
$(a + 3)x + (a + 4)y = a + 5$
The solution is $(^-1, 2)$ because $x = ^-1, y = 2$ satisfy
each equation.

	Slope	y-intercept
19. (a)	$\frac{-5}{6}$	$\frac{7}{6}$
(b)	$\frac{-4}{3}$	$\frac{2}{5}$
(c)	3.75	1.85
(d)	0	4

21. (a)

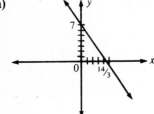

(b)

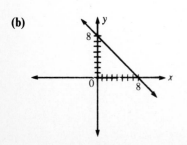

(c)

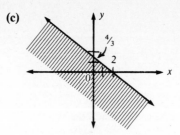

(d)

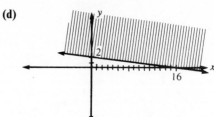

Problem Set 13-4 1. (a) 4 **(b)** 4 **(c)** 5 **(d)** 5
(e) $\sqrt{52}$, or $2\sqrt{13}$ **(f)** Approximately 3.89
(g) 5 **(h)** 5 **(i)** $\sqrt{68}$, or $2\sqrt{17}$
(j) $\frac{\sqrt{365}}{4}$, or approximately 4.78

3. The sides have lengths $\sqrt{45}$, $\sqrt{180}$, and $\sqrt{225}$.
Because $(\sqrt{45})^2 + (\sqrt{180})^2 = (\sqrt{225})^2$, the triangle
is a right triangle.
5. $x = 9$, or $x = ^-7$ **7.** $(^-7, 11)$
9. (a) $(x - 3)^2 + (y + 2)^2 = 4$
(b) $(x + 3)^2 + (y + 4)^2 = 25$ **(c)** $(x + 1)^2 + y^2 = 4$
(d) $x^2 + y^2 = 9$ **11.** $x^2 + y^2 = 34$
13. $(x + 2)^2 + (y + 2)^2 = 52$
15. $(x - \frac{29}{10})^2 + y^2 = (\frac{29}{10})^2$
17.

19. Let A, B, and C have coordinates $(^-1, 5)$, $(0, 2)$, and
$(1, ^-1)$. $AB = \sqrt{10}$, $BC = \sqrt{10}$, and $AC = \sqrt{40} = 2\sqrt{10}$,
so $AB + BC = AC$ because $\sqrt{10} + \sqrt{10} = 2\sqrt{10}$.
Consequently, A, B, and C are collinear.

21. (a) The median from C: $y = \dfrac{2b}{2a-1}\left(x - \dfrac{1}{2}\right)$

The median from B: $y = \dfrac{b}{a-2}(x-1)$

The median from A: $y = \dfrac{b}{a+1}x$

(b) Solve any two equations and check that the solution satisfies the third equation. The medians intersect at $\left(\dfrac{a+1}{3b}, \dfrac{b}{3}\right)$.   **(c)** Use the distance formula to find the ratios.   **23.** $y = 2$

25. (a) $y < \frac{3}{4}x + 5$ **(b)** $x + y \geq {}^-5$ and $x \leq 0$ and $y \leq 0$

Problem Set 13-5   1. This answer will vary, depending on the version of Logo used.

3.
```
TO AXES
   SETXY 0 120
   SETXY 0 (-120)
   SETXY 0 0
   SETXY 130 0
   SETXY -130 0
   SETXY 0 0
END
```

In Apple Logo, use SETPOS instead of SETXY.

5.
```
TO FILLRECT
   REPEAT 50 [SETY 30 SETY 0 RT 90 FD 1 LT 90]
END
```

7.
```
TO QUAD :X1 :Y1 :X2 :Y2 :X3 :Y3 :X4 :Y4
   PU SETXY :X1 :Y1 PD
   SETXY :X2 :Y2
   SETXY :X3 :Y3
   SETXY :X4 :Y4
   SETXY :X1 :Y1
END
```

9. Use the QUAD procedure from Problem 7 and the following.
```
TO MEDIAL.QUADS :NUM :X1 :Y1 :X2 :Y2 :X3 :Y3 :X4 :Y4
   IF :NUM = 0 STOP
   QUAD :X1 :Y1 :X2 :Y2 :X3 :Y3 :X4 :Y4
   MIDPOINT :X1 :Y1 :X2 :Y2
   MIDPOINT :X2 :Y2 :X3 :Y3
   MIDPOINT :X3 :Y3 :X4 :Y4
   MIDPOINT :X4 :Y4 :X1 :Y1
   MIDPOINT :X1 :Y1 :X2 :Y2
   MEDIAL.QUADS :NUM - 1(:X1 + :X2) / 2 (:Y1 + :Y2) / 2 (:X2 + :X3) / 2
   (:Y2 + :Y3) / 2 (:X3 + :X4) / 2 (:Y3 + :Y4) / 2 (:X4 + :X1) / 2
   (:Y4 + :Y1) / 2
END

TO MIDPOINT :X1 :Y1 :X2 :Y2
   SETXY (:X1 + :X2) / 2 (:Y1 + :Y2) / 2
END
```

11.
```
TO R.ISOS.TRI :LEN
   FD :LEN
   RT 90
   FD :LEN
   RT 135
   FD (SQRT2) * :LEN
END
```

13.
```
TO CIRC50
   PU
   SETXY (-20) (-40)
   PD
   REPEAT 360 [FD 3.141 * 50/180 RT 1]
END
```

Chapter Test   1. 16

3. (a)

(b)

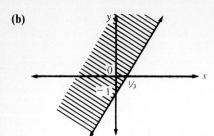

(c)

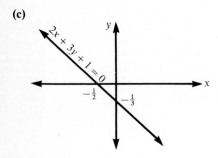

5. (a) $y = \frac{4}{3}x + \frac{7}{3}$ **(b)** $y = 5$ **(c)** $(\frac{3}{4}, 5)$

7. 80 regular and 30 deluxe

9. (a)

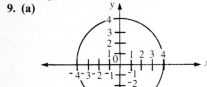

(b)

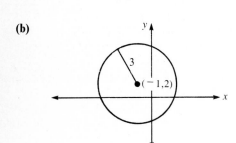

(c)

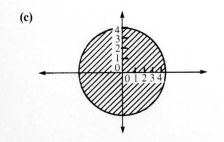

11. (a)

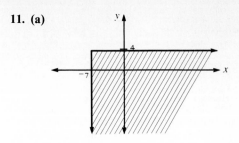

(b)

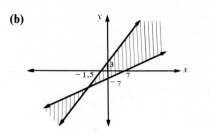

13. 275 freshmen and 500 sophomores

CHAPTER 14

Problem Set 14-1   1. 9 bounces

3. Because $H/381 \doteq 0.291$, then $H \doteq 110.871$. If x is the number of hits he must get by the end of the year, then we must solve the following.

$$\frac{110.871 + x}{441} > .300$$

$$x > 21.43$$

Thus, he must get 22 hits.

5. If the distance between the center of the coin and the grid line is less than or equal to $\frac{1}{4}$ inch, the coin will touch a grid line. If the coin lands within the boundaries of a square $2\frac{1}{2}$ inches on a side that is located inside each 3-inch square, the coin will not touch. Thus, the probability of the coin not touching a grid line is given by the ratio of the areas of the squares that measure $2\frac{1}{2}$ inches and 3 inches, respectively. Hence, the probability is $\frac{6.25}{9}$, or $69.\overline{4}\%$.

7. The minimum number of weights is 10. The weights are 1, 2, 4, 8, 16, 32, 64, 128, 256, and 512. Notice that these are just the powers of 2 contained in 680.

9. We reduce the problem to simpler cases, look for a pattern, and generalize. A table for various exponents and remainders is as follows.

Exponent	Remainder	
1	5 ⎫	
2	4 ⎪	
3	6 ⎬ Repeating	
4	2 ⎪ block	
5	3 ⎪	
6	1 ⎭	
7	5	
8	4	
9	6	

To see how many times this block repeats in our problem, we divide 999,999 by 6 to obtain 166,666 with a remainder of 3. Thus, the block repeats 166,666 times and then goes three steps further. Because the third number in the repeating block is 6, this is the desired answer.

11. The distances run by each of the runners when Tom and Dick finish the 2-km race are given in the table.

	Tom	Dick	Harry
(1)	2000 m	1900 m	x m
(2)		2000 m	1800 m

To find x, we solve the proportion $\dfrac{1900}{2000} = \dfrac{x}{1800}$.

Thus, $x = 290$ m.

13. (a) The short way to solve this problem is to realize that if there are 98 players and only 1 winner, there must be 97 losers. To obtain 97 losers, 97 matches must be played.   **(b)** By similar reasoning, there must be $(n-1)$ matches.

15. $2^{12} \cdot 5^8 = 2^4 \cdot (2^8 \cdot 5^8) = 2^4 \cdot (2 \cdot 5)^8 = 16 \cdot 10^8$. Hence, the number of digits is 10.

17. (a) $1, 5, 4+5, 4+4+5, 4+4+4+5,$ $4+4+4+4+5, \ldots$, that is, $1, 5, 9, 13, 17, 21, \ldots$
(b) $4(n-2)+5$, or $4n-3$

19. Let x be the number of sheets of paper and y be the number of envelopes. Then, for Ann, we have $x - 50 = y$, or $x = y + 50$. For Sue, we have $3(y - 50) = x$. Thus, $y + 50 = 3(y - 50)$ and $y = 100$, $x = 150$. There were 150 sheets of paper in each box.

21. Let x be the length of the bottom and y be the depth of the water when the bottom is level. The volume of the water is $10xy$. When the aquarium is tilted, the water forms a right triangular prism with an altitude of 10 inches. The volume of this triangular prism is $\frac{1}{2} \cdot 10 \cdot 8(\frac{3}{4} \cdot x)$, which is $30x$. Setting the volumes equal, we obtain $10xy = 30x$, and therefore $y = 3$. Thus, the water depth is 3 inches.

23. Let x be the amount Susan made 2 years ago. Because her salary increased 50% each year, her salary after the first year was $1.5x$ and after the second year was $(1.5)(1.5)x$. Thus, $(1.5)^2 \cdot x = \$100,000$ and $x = \$44,444.44$, or $\$44,444$.

25. Let d be the integer. Because the remainders are the same, then $d \,|\, (13,903 - 13,511)$ and $d \,|\, (14,589 - 13,903)$. That is, $d \,|\, 392$ and $d \,|\, 686$. Because GCD(392, 686) = 98, then $d = 98$.

27. In 1 hour, the hour hand covers $\dfrac{360°}{12} = 30°$.

Thus, in 15 minutes it covers $\dfrac{30°}{4} = 7°30'$.

Consequently, the angle between the hands at 2:15 is $30° - 7°30' \cong 22°30'$.

29. Pair the numbers as follows:

999,999,998   and   1
999,999,997   and   2
999,999,996   and   3
999,999,995   and   4
999,999,994   and   5
⋮   ⋮
500,000,000   and   499,999,999

There are 499,999,999 pairs, and the sum of the digits in each pair is $9 \cdot 9$, or 81. The unpaired numbers are 999,999,999 and 1,000,000,000. The sums of the digits in these numbers are 81 and 1, respectively. Hence, the total sum of the digits is $499,999,999(81) + 1(81) + 1 = 500,000,000(81) + 1 = 40,500,000,001$.

31. Let (x, y) be the center of the circle; then, using the distance formula, we have $x^2 + y^2 = (x - 4)^2 + y^2$ and $x^2 + y^2 = (x - 1)^2 + (y + 3)^2$. These two equations reduce to $16 - 8x = 0$ and $3y - x + 5 = 0$. Solving these equations, we find $x = 2$ and $y = {}^-1$. Hence, the center is at $(2, {}^-1)$. The radius is the distance from any point—for example, $(0, 0)$—to the center $(2, {}^-1)$. Thus, $r = \sqrt{2^2 + 1^2} = \sqrt{5}$.

33. Let x be the number that voted against the bill the first time. Then, we have the following:

	Against	For
First vote	x	$400 - x$
Second vote	$400 - \frac{12}{11}x$	$\frac{12}{11}x$

In the second vote, the bill passed by twice the margin, so

$$2[x - (400 - x)] = \tfrac{12}{11}x - (400 - \tfrac{12}{11}x)$$

$$2(2x - 400) = \tfrac{12}{11}x - 400 + \tfrac{12}{11}x$$

$$20x = 4400$$

$$x = 220$$

The difference between the "for" votes the first and second time is $\frac{12}{11}x - (400 - x) = \frac{12}{11}(220) - (400 - 220) = 60$, or 60 votes.

35. (a) 1, 8, 28, 56, 70, 56, 28, 8, 1; 1, 9, 36, 84, 126, 126, 84, 36, 9, 1 **(b)** $s_1 = 1$, $s_2 = 2$, $s_3 = 4$, $s_4 = 8$, $s_{10} = 512$, $s_n = 2^{n-1}$ **(c)** The alternate sum in each row after row 1 is zero. **(d)** Answers may vary.

APPENDIX AI

Problem Set AI-I **1. (a), (b)**, and **(f)** **3. (a)** 7
(b) 7 **(c)** 6 **(d)** 3 **(e)** 16 **(f)** ⁻44
5. Answers may vary, depending on the computer used.
7. PRINT 25 * 0.97 ^ 365

9.
```
10 REM THIS PROGRAM COMPUTES THE PERIMETER OF A RECTANGLE
20 PRINT "WHAT IS THE LENGTH ";
30 INPUT L
40 PRINT "WHAT IS THE WIDTH ";
50 INPUT W
55 REM P IS THE PERIMETER OF THE RECTANGLE
60 LET P = 2 * L + 2 * W
70 PRINT "THE PERIMETER OF A RECTANGLE WITH LENGTH ";L;" CM AND ";
80 PRINT "WIDTH ";W;" CM IS ";P;" CM"
90 END


RUN
WHAT IS THE LENGTH? 16
WHAT IS THE WIDTH? 5
THE PERIMETER OF A RECTANGLE WITH LENGTH 16 CM AND WIDTH 5 CM IS 42 CM
```

11. (a)
```
PRINT 100 * 1.18 ^ 25
6266.8628
```

(b)
```
5  REM N IS THE NUMBER OF YEARS THE MONEY IS INVESTED
10 INPUT N
15 REM B IS THE BALANCE
20 LET B = 100 * 1.18 ^ N
30 PRINT "AFTER ";N;" YEARS, THE BALANCE IS $";B
40 END
```

[The balance in (b) is the same as in (a).]

13. (a)
```
10 REM PROPERTY DEPRECIATION
20 PRINT "TYPE THE NUMBER OF YEARS OF DEPRECIATION ";
30 INPUT N
35 REM V IS THE VALUE AFTER DEPRECIATION
40 LET V = 30000 * (1 - 3 / 100) ^ N
50 PRINT "AFTER ";N;" YEARS, THE VALUE OF A $30000 PROPERTY ";
60 PRINT "WHICH DEPRECIATES AT A 3% RATE IS $";V
70 END
```

(b)
```
RUN
TYPE THE NUMBER OF YEARS OF DEPRECIATION? 30
AFTER 30 YEARS, THE VALUE OF A $30000 PROPERTY
WHICH DEPRECIATES AT A 3% RATE IS $12030.2122
```

Problem Set AI-2 **1.** Answers may vary, depending on the computer used.

3. (a) HEY YOU OUT THERE

(b) HEY YOU OUT THERE
HEY YOU OUT THERE
HEY YOU OUT THERE
HEY YOU OUT THERE
HEY YOU OUT THERE
HEY YOU OUT THERE
HEY YOU OUT THERE

Outputs differ because the PRINT statement is placed outside the loop in (a) and inside the loop in (b).

(continued on page 767)

5.
```
5  REM THIS PROGRAM COMPUTES THE SUM OF THE SQUARES OF THE
6  REM FIRST 100 POSITIVE INTEGERS
7  REM N IS A POSITIVE INTEGER
10 FOR N = 1 TO 100
15 REM Y IS USED TO ACCUMULATE
20 LET Y = Y + N * N
30 NEXT N
40 PRINT Y
50 END

RUN
```
5050

7.
```
5  REM THIS PROGRAM COMPUTES SQUARES AND SQUARE ROOTS
8  REM N REPRESENTS A NATURAL NUMBER
10 PRINT "NUMBER","SQUARE ROOT","SQUARE"
20 FOR N = 1 TO 10
30 PRINT N,SQR(N),N ∧ 2
40 NEXT N
50 END
```

9.
```
10 REM THIS PROGRAM CONVERTS DEGREES FAHRENHEIT
20 REM TO DEGREES CELSIUS
25 REM F REPRESENTS A NUMBER OF DEGREES FAHRENHEIT
26 REM C REPRESENTS A NUMBER OF DEGREES CELSIUS
30 PRINT "DEGREE FAHRENHEIT", "DEGREE CELSIUS"
40 FOR F = -40 TO 220 STEP 10
50 LET C = 5/9 * (F - 32)
60 PRINT F,,C
70 NEXT F
80 END
```

11.
```
10 REM THIS PROGRAM CALCULATES N!
15 REM N IS A NATURAL NUMBER
16 REM T IS USED TO ACCUMULATE PRODUCTS
17 REM A IS USED AS A COUNTER
20 PRINT "WHAT IS THE VALUE OF N";
30 INPUT N
40 LET T = 1
50 FOR A = 1 TO N
60 LET T = T * A
70 NEXT A
80 PRINT "N","N!"
90 PRINT N, T
100 END
```

13.
```
10 REM SUM OF CUBES EQUALS SQUARES OF SUM OF INTEGERS
15 REM N IS AN INTEGER
16 REM Y IS THE CUBE OF N
17 REM K IS TO ACCUMULATE THE SUM OF THE CUBES
18 REM Z IS TO ACCUMULATE THE SUM OF THE NUMBERS
19 REM S IS TO SQUARE Z
20 PRINT "1 ∧ 3 + 2 ∧ 3 + ... + N ∧ 3","(1 + 2 + 3 + ... + N) ∧ 2"
25 LET K = 0
26 LET Z = 0
30 FOR N = 1 TO 10
40 LET Y = N ∧ 3
50 LET K = K + Y
60 LET Z = Z + N
70 LET S = Z ∧ 2
80 PRINT K,,S
90 NEXT N
100 END
```

15.
```
10 REM HARMONIC SERIES
11 REM K IS A COUNTER
12 LET K = O
13 REM Y ACCUMULATES THE SUM
14 LET Y = O
20 PRINT "HOW MANY TERMS DO YOU WANT";
30 INPUT N
40 LET K = K + 1
50 LET Y = Y + 1 / K
60 IF K >= N THEN 80
70 GOTO 40
80 PRINT "THE VALUE OF THE FIRST ";N;" TERMS OF THE ";
90 PRINT "HARMONIC SERIES IS ";Y
100 END


RUN
HOW MANY TERMS DO YOU WANT? 100
THE VALUE OF THE FIRST 100 TERMS OF THE HARMONIC SERIES IS 5.187377
```

17.
```
10 REM TABLE OF CUBES AND CUBE ROOTS
11 REM N IS A NATURAL NUMBER
20 PRINT "NUMBER","CUBE","CUBE ROOT"
30 FOR N = 1 TO 20
40 PRINT N,N ^ 3,N ^ (1 / 3)
60 NEXT N
70 END
```

19.
```
5   REM THIS PROGRAM PRINTS FIBONACCI NUMBERS
10 REM X IS THE FIRST TERM
11 REM Y IS THE SECOND TERM
12 REM A COUNTS THE TERMS AFTER THE THIRD
13 REM Z FINDS SUCCESSIVE TERMS
14 PRINT "HOW MANY TERMS OF THE SEQUENCE DO YOU WANT";
15 INPUT N
20 LET X = 1
30 PRINT X;" ";
40 IF N = 1 THEN 140
50 LET Y = 1
60 PRINT Y;" ";
70 IF N = 2 THEN 140
80 FOR A = 3 TO N
90 LET Z = X + Y
100 LET X = Y
110 LET Y = Z
120 PRINT Z;" ";
130 NEXT A
140 END


RUN
HOW MANY TERMS OF THE SEQUENCE DO YOU WANT? 10
1 1 2 3 5 8 13 21 34 55
```

21.
```
10 REM THIS PROGRAM DOUBLES SALARY
11 REM D COUNTS DAYS
12 REM S COMPUTES SALARY FOR DAY
13 REM T ACCUMULATES SALARY
14 LET T = 0
20 FOR D = 1 TO 15
30 LET S = 2 ^ (D - 1)
35 IF D = 15 THEN 60
40 LET T = T + S
50 NEXT D
60 PRINT "THE DIFFERENCE OF THE 15TH DAY'S SALARY AND"
70 PRINT "THE TOTAL FOR 14 DAYS IS ";S - T
80 END


RUN
```
**THE DIFFERENCE OF THE 15TH DAY'S SALARY AND
THE TOTAL FOR 14 DAYS IS 1**

APPENDIX AII

Problem Set AII-I

1. (a)
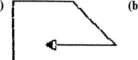

(b)

(c)

(d) The heading is 90.

(e) The turtle stays in place and a heading of 360 is displayed.

3. (a)
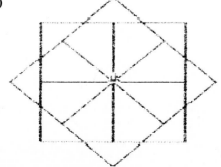

3. (b)
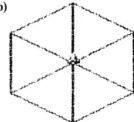

(c)
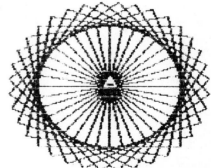

(d)

5. Answers may vary. For example,

```
TO L
  FD 40 BK 40
  RT 90 FD 20
  BK 20 LT 90
END

TO O
  REPEAT 2 [FD 40 RT 90 FD 25 RT 90]
END

TO G
  FD 40
  RT 90 FD 25
  PU RT 90 FD 20 PD
  RT 90 FD 10 BK 10
  LT 90
  FD 20 RT 90 FD 25 RT 90
END

TO SPACE
  PU RT 90 FD 35 LT 90 PD
END

TO LOGO
  PU LT 90 FD 50 RT 90
  PD L
  SPACE
  O
  SPACE
  G
  SPACE
  O
  SPACE
END
```

7. Answers may vary. For example,

(a)

```
TO SQUARE.FACE
  SQUARE 60
  FD 5 PU RT 90 FD 25 LT 90 PD
  SQUARE 10
  PU FD 18 PD RT 30
  TRIANGLE 10
  PU LT 30 FD 15 LT 90 FD 10 RT 90 PD
  SQUARE 10
  PU RT 90 FD 20 LT 90 PD
  SQUARE 10
END

TO SQUARE :S
  REPEAT 4 [FD :S RT 90]
END

TO TRIANGLE :S
  REPEAT 3 [FD :S RT 120]
END
```

(b)
```
TO BUILD.SQR :S
  SQUARE :S
  SQUARE :S + 10
  SQUARE :S + 20
  SQUARE :S + 30
  SQUARE :S + 40
END
```

(c)
```
TO TAIL :S
  SQUARE :S
  FD :S RT 90 FD :S LT 90
  SQUARE :S / 2
  FD :S / 2 RT 90 FD :S / 2 LT 90
  SQUARE :S / 4
END
```

(d)
```
TO TOWER :SIZE
  SQUARE :SIZE
  FD :SIZE RT 90 FD :SIZE / 4 LT 90
  SQUARE :SIZE / 2
  FD :SIZE / 2 RT 90 FD :SIZE / 8 LT 90
  SQUARE :SIZE / 4
END
```

9.
```
TO KITE
  LT 45
  REPEAT 4 [FD 40 RT 90]
  RT 45
  REPEAT 3 [BK 20 K.TAIL RT 60]
  BK 20
  FD 80 RT 45 FD 30
  RT 90 FD 80
END

TO K.TAIL
  RT 60
  REPEAT 3 [FD 10 RT 120]
  LT 120
  REPEAT 3 [FD 10 LT 120]
END
```

Problem Set AII-2   1. Type the procedures on the computer.

3. (a)
```
TO STRETCH :SIDE
  IF :SIDE < 5 STOP
  SQUARE :SIDE
  FD :SIDE RT 90
  FD :SIDE LT 90
  STRETCH :SIDE - 10
END
```

(b)
```
TO TOWER :S
  IF :S < 5 STOP
  SQUARE :S
  FD :S RT 90 FD :S / 4
  LT 90
  TOWER :S / 2
END
```

(c)
```
TO PIZA :SIDE :ANGLE
  IF :SIDE < 5 STOP
  SQUARE :SIDE
  FD :SIDE LT :ANGLE
  PIZA :SIDE * .75 :ANGLE
END
```

(d)
```
TO CONSQRS :S
  IF :S < 5 STOP
  SQUARE :S
  PU FD :S
  CONSQRS :S / 2
END
```

(e)
```
TO EYE :R
  IF :R < 5 STOP
  CIRCLE :R
  EYE :R * .8
END
```

(f)
```
TO CONCIRC :R
  IF :R < 10 STOP
  CIRCLE :R
  PU RT 90 FD :R / 2 LT 90 PD
  CONCIRC :R / 2
END
```

```
TO SQUARE :SIDE
  REPEAT 4 [FD :SIDE RT 90]
END
```

```
TO CIRCLE :R
  VCIRCLE :R * 0.01745
END
```

```
TO VCIRCLE :S
  REPEAT 360 [FD :S RT 1]
END
```

5. Answers vary.

7.
```
TO SPIN.SQ :S
  IF :S < 5 STOP
  SQUARE :S
  RT 20
  SPIN.SQ :S - 5
END
```

```
TO SQUARE :S
  REPEAT 4 [FD :S RT 90]
END
```

Index

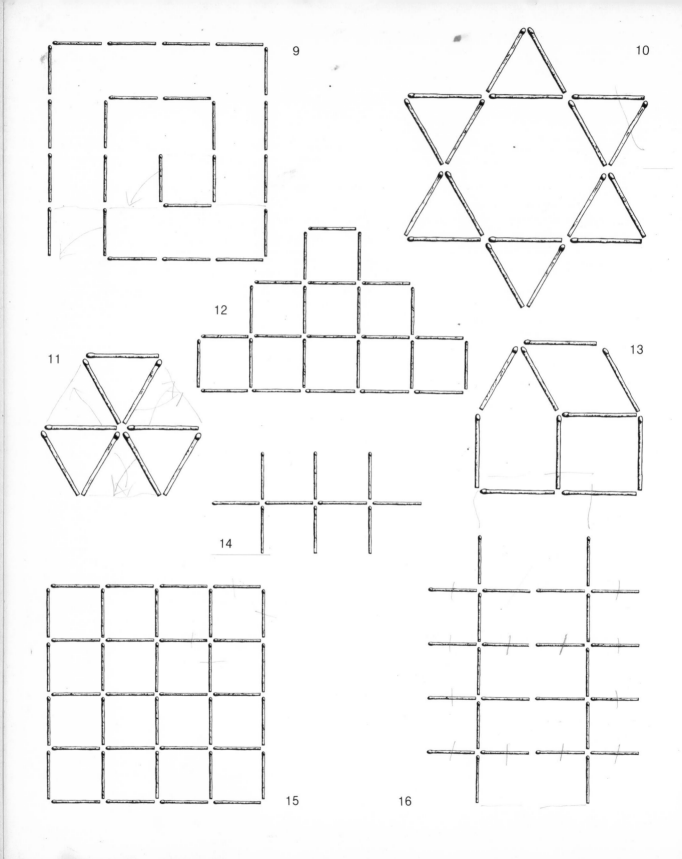

9

10

12

11

13

14

15

16